NEITHER JEW NOR GREEK

CHRISTIANITY IN THE MAKING

Volume 3

NEITHER JEW NOR GREEK

A Contested Identity

James D. G. Dunn

WILLIAM B. EERDMANS PUBLISHING COMPANY
GRAND RAPIDS, MICHIGAN

© 2015 James D. G. Dunn
All rights reserved

Hardcover edition 2015
Paperback edition 2021

Wm. B. Eerdmans Publishing Co.
4035 Park East Court SE, Grand Rapids, MI 49546

Library of Congress Cataloging-in-Publication Data

Dunn, James D. G., 1939-
Neither Jew nor Greek : a contested identity / James D.G. Dunn.
pages   cm. — (Christianity in the making ; Volume 3)
Includes bibliographical references.
ISBN 978-0-8028-7801-4 (pbk. : alk. paper)
1. Church history — Primitive and early church, ca. 30-600. 2. Identification (Religion)
3. Judaism — Relations — Christianity. 4. Christianity and other religions — Judaism.
5. Judaism (Christian theology) I. Title.
BR165.D863   2015
270.1 — dc23
2015029835

www.eerdmans.com

For
Hannah, Tijs, Julia and Sam,
Barney and Megan,
and Alfie
with whom lies the future

Contents

Preface		xi

PART TEN: A NEW BEGINNING

38.	**Christianity in the Making**	**3**
	38.1 Introduction	3
	38.2 The Emergence of the Great Church	7
	38.3 Christianity and Judaism	12
	38.4 The Hellenization of Christianity	26
	38.5 A Contested Identity	40
39.	**The Sources — First Century**	
	(the New Testament)	**43**
	39.1 The Diversity and Character of the Source Material	43
	39.2 The Canonical Gospels	46
	39.3 The Rest of the New Testament	80
40.	**The Sources — Second Century**	**111**
	40.1 The Apostolic Fathers	111
	40.2 The Apologists	130
	40.3 Eusebius and the Heresiologists	140
	40.4 The Other Gospels	143
	40.5 Other Letters	159
	40.6 The Other Acts	162
	40.7 Other Apocalypses	176
	40.8 Summary	182

CONTENTS

PART ELEVEN: JESUS STILL REMEMBERED

41.	From gospel to Gospel	187
	41.1 The gospel before the Gospel	188
	41.2 The Gospel of Mark	192
	41.3 The Gospels of Matthew and Luke	199
	41.4 The Gospel of John	202
	41.5 The Gospel	206
42.	Retelling the Story of Jesus: Mark, Matthew and Luke	**209**
	42.1 From Oral Tradition to Written Gospel	210
	42.2 The Gospel according to Mark	221
	42.3 The Gospel according to Matthew	246
	42.4 The Gospel according to Luke — and Acts	276
	42.5 Jesus Remembered Becomes the Gospel of Jesus Christ	309
43.	Reshaping the Gospel of Jesus: John and Thomas	**312**
	43.1 The Gospel according to John	313
	43.2 The *Gospel of Thomas*	371
	43.3 Comparing John and *Thomas*	397
	43.4 Is *Thomas* a 'Gospel'?	399
	43.5 Two Different Gospels, Two Different Hermeneutical Strategies	402
44.	The Jesus Tradition in the Second Century	**405**
	44.1 Introduction	405
	44.2 The Oral Jesus Tradition into the Second Century — The Apostolic Fathers	408
	44.3 The Oral Jesus Tradition into the Second Century — The Apologists	451
	44.4 Other Streams of Jesus Tradition	462
	44.5 Gnostic Gospels 1 — The Issue of Early Source Material	472
	44.6 Gnostic Gospels 2	479
	44.7 Narrative Gospels	488
	44.8 The Recognition of the Four (Canonical) Gospels	493
	44.9 Conclusions	503

Contents

PART TWELVE: JEWISH CHRISTIANITY AND THE PARTING OF THE WAYS

45. **Jewish Christianity** — 509
    - 45.1 Introduction — 509
    - 45.2 The Enigma of James — 512
    - 45.3 What Happened to the Jerusalem Church? — 524
    - 45.4 The Jewish Christian Writings of the New Testament — 528
    - 45.5 The Jewish Character of Second-Century Christian Writings — 550
    - 45.6 The Heritage of Second Temple Judaism — 569
    - 45.7 The *Minim* — 574
    - 45.8 Jews Who Also Followed Jesus — 577
    - 45.9 Conclusions — 595

46. **The Parting of the Ways** — 598
    - 46.1 The Imagery to Be Used — 598
    - 46.2 Early Strains and Stresses — 602
    - 46.3 Rome Changes Everything — 610
    - 46.4 Development of and Developments within Judaism — 621
    - 46.5 The New Testament Writings — 631
    - 46.6 Second-Century Christian Literature — 650
    - 46.7 Conclusion — 671

PART THIRTEEN: THE CONTINUING INFLUENCE OF PAUL AND PETER

47. **Paul** — 675
    - 47.1 Introduction — 675
    - 47.2 Paul as Depicted in Second-Generation NT Documents — 677
    - 47.3 The Reception of Paul in the Second Century — 686
    - 47.4 The Legendary Paul — 704
    - 47.5 'The Apostle of the Heretics'? — 710
    - 47.6 Paul and Irenaeus — 720
    - 47.7 In Sum — 723

48.	**Peter**	**724**
	48.1 Introduction	724
	48.2 The Epistles of Peter	726
	48.3 Peter in the Rest of the New Testament	731
	48.4 Peter in the Apostolic Fathers and Apologists	739
	48.5 The Jewish-Christian Peter	745
	48.6 The Apocryphal Peter	747
	48.7 Conclusion	754

PART FOURTEEN: BEYOND THE FIRST GENERATION

49.	**John**	**757**
	49.1 Introduction	757
	49.2 Recap	759
	49.3 Let John Be John	764
	49.4 1-3 John	774
	49.5 The Apocalypse of John	782
	49.6 The *Odes of Solomon*	791
	49.7 The Gnostic John	792
	49.8 The Montanists	796
	49.9 Conclusion	799
50.	**A Contested Identity**	**801**
	50.1 The Continuing Impact of Jesus and of the First-Generation Leaders	802
	50.2 Christianity in Process of Being Defined	811
	50.3 Conclusion	823

Abbreviations	**825**
Bibliography	**830**
Index of Authors	**873**
Index of Subjects	**890**
Index of Scripture and Other Ancient Writings	**896**

Preface

With this volume (volume 3) I come to the end of my attempt to sketch out *Christianity in the Making*. 70 CE was an appropriate place to stop volume 2, since the first generation of Christianity (30-70) was so crucial to determining how the impact of Jesus had spread beyond the immediate disciples of Jesus and the borders of ancient Israel. The destruction of Jerusalem by the Roman legions certainly marked a transition point of the greatest significance — both for the founding community of Christianity (Jerusalem) and for Christianity's mother religion, Judaism. But the majority of the New Testament writings probably emerged in the period following that epochal event. And 70 in effect marked the transition from the first-generation leaders, James, Peter and Paul, into a second generation of still significant leaders, like Clement and Ignatius, but where the issues and influences were beginning to shift towards the more diverse and more developed questions and challenges which shaped the early churches. Here the last of the first-generation apostles (John) comes into play in unexpected ways. But with Justin Martyr, the challenges posed by Valentinus and Marcion, and the consolidation provided by Irenaeus in particular, it becomes evident what Christianity was becoming, and what the principal features were which would be consolidated and shaped in the decades ahead. Much as it would have been attractive to go further into Tertullian and Origen, or still further into Cyprian and beyond, the die had been cast in the first 150 years, and what followed was, in an important sense, only a further working out of what had been established in that initial or initiating period.

    I wrestled long in deciding what title to give to this volume. Initially I wanted it to be 'tertium genus', a phrase drawn from Tertullian, *ad Nationes* 1.8, though more widely used.[1] It well represents the sense, shared by both

---

1. See particularly A. von Harnack, *The Mission and Expansion of Christianity in the*

Christians and their opponents at the beginning of the third century, that in the course of the hundred or so years covered by this volume Christianity had emerged as a force with its own distinctive character, indeed a 'third race', distinct not only from the principal Graeco-Roman religious polity of the time but also from the Judaism which had given it birth. But in the event I settled for the less obscure 'neither Jew nor Greek', drawn from Paul (Gal. 3.28) and well representing both the transcending of old distinctions and boundaries and the 'new creation' which Paul had already sensed in the first generation of the new movement (2 Cor. 5.17) and which became more of a reality through the second century. The cover art, the second-century paleo-Christian fresco of the eucharist from the catacomb of Priscilla, Rome, catches at least something of the atmosphere in which Christianity came of age.

Volumes 1 (*Jesus Remembered*) and 2 (*Beginning from Jerusalem*) had been published at a stately six-year interval (2003 and 2009). Completing the trilogy has been the principal writing concern of the second phase of my retirement, when in the wake of a significant health crisis on my part, it became evident that my wife (Meta) and I should leave Durham to be closer to two of our children in the south of England — hence our home now in Chichester, on England's south coast — quite a hard thing for Scots to be so far furth of bonnie Scotland! In having to downsize my personal library, from 7,000 to 3,000 volumes, I was at least able to keep to hand the volumes I needed for this final lap. Unfortunately, when I had run through my own library, it was to find that library resources on the south coast were much less adequate for my needs. Fortunately King's College, London, came to my aid and kindly granted me a Visiting Professorship, thanks to Richard Burridge. This allowed me much valued access to the Maughan Library, as well as good relations with the King's faculty; the support of Eddie Adams was particularly appreciated (not least when the London underground went on strike!), as also the chairing and critique of Joan Taylor. Also much appreciated were links with Oxford (Cambridge was just too far away), with the support particularly of Markus Bockmuehl and David Lincicum, the splendid hospitality of Bishop John Pritchard and his wife Wendy, and the benefit of the great Bodleian Library. Volunteers at both Keble College (Oxford) and King's kindly participated in a series of seminars where my draft chapters provided the principal topic of debate — to the immense benefit of the second draft. Matthew Thomas was particularly helpful in a series of comments, as also Anna Grojinowski, Piotr Ashwin-Siejkowski and Graham Stevenson.

First Three Centuries (ET 1908; New York: Harper Torchbook, 1962) Book II ch. 7, with Excursus, 'Christians as a third race, in the judgment of their opponents' (266-78). See further A. McGowan, '"A Third Race" or Not: The Rhetoric of Self-Definition in Tertullian', *Patristica Bostoniensa* (2001-02) available on-line.

Preface

As usual, a round of lectures and commissions gave me opportunity to try out my developing ideas, and to gain from responses and critiques. I should mention particularly

- 'John's Gospel and the Oral Gospel Tradition'
- 'How Did Matthew Go About Composing His Gospel?'
- 'The Earliest Interpreters of the Jesus Tradition: A Study in Early Hermeneutics'
- 'The Rise and Expansion of Christianity in the First Three Centuries C.E.: Why and How Did Embryonic Christianity Expand beyond the Jewish People?'
- 'Tertullian and Paul on the Spirit of Prophecy'

Full details are in the bibliography at the end of this volume.

The first draft of the present volume also benefited hugely from the comments and critique of various friends and colleagues who responded to my request for a critical read of initial draft chapters. Chris Tuckett, Simon Gathercole, Helen Bond, Bruce Longenecker and Graham Stevenson all contributed much encouragement. Several chapters were critiqued by Bob Morgan and William Baird. Several more by Karl-Wilhelm Niebuhr, Jens Schröter and Michael Wolter. Uli Luz sent several lengthy letters full of sharp comments, and Paul Trebilco read and critiqued every chapter — a real work of supererogation on his part. They all engaged helpfully with what they read, asking probing questions, pointing out weaknesses (and some strengths!) in the draft material, and recommending further reading. The resulting volume is stronger than I could have achieved with my own resources and I am grateful to all who have contributed to it.

The sense that I had more or less completed the task that I had set myself, and the realization that I could go on searching out relevant articles and books for many more months, pushed me to the conclusion that I should run the risk of leaving out of account some really important items that would sway my conclusions one way or another. So, with an eye to having the manuscript off my desk in time for a good summer holiday, and a sigh at having at least brought this fifteen-year project to (what I hope is) a successful conclusion, I will bid farewell to the large undertakings of my writing career — and devote myself more to husbandly, fatherly and grandfatherly responsibilities and pleasures, not forgetting the joys of friendship and the opportunities/ challenges of some preaching, lecturing, Festschriften contributions — oh yes, and housework and gardening. And there's all these novels which we've been collecting for some years, which I have still to read!

I am most grateful to those who assisted in the final phase of the process, when time was pressing. Ellen Steinke and Ronald "Charlie" Hurlocker, graduates of the School of Theology and Ministry at Indiana Wesleyan University, did the main work in creating the Author and Ancient Sources indexes, spurred on by Ken Schenk, one of my own postgrads from past years. And thank you to John Simpson and all at Eerdmans who saw the book through the process toward publication.

But I cannot end without expressing my gratitude to the good Lord for the grace which has sustained me throughout my career, and to my beloved wife Meta, whose encouragement and critique have been such a wonderful counterpoise for more than 50 years (we celebrated our golden wedding in a golden way in 2013). Since volume 1 was dedicated to Meta and volume 2 to our much loved children (Catrina, David and Fiona), volume 3 is naturally dedicated to our wonderful grandchildren — Hannah, Tijs, Julia, Barney, Sam, Megan and Alfie. So there really was no need or occasion for a fourth volume!

JAMES D. G. DUNN
July 2014

P. S. Of the publications which have come out since I completed the manuscript for volume 3, I am particularly sorry that I have been unable to take account of Tobias Nicklas's *Jews and Christians?* (Mohr Siebeck, 2014) and Judith Lieu's *Marcion and the Making of a Heretic* (Cambridge University, 2015).

PART TEN

A NEW BEGINNING

CHAPTER 38

Christianity in the Making

38.1 Introduction

The executions of the three great leaders of first-generation Christianity in the early 60s (James, Paul and Peter), and the destruction of the mother church in Jerusalem, as of Jerusalem itself, in 70, were almost as disastrous for emerging Christianity as had been the execution of Jesus himself. Certainly the initial form of the movement, the messianic renewal sect of Second Temple Judaism, represented by James and the Judaean believers, suffered a devastating blow from which it never fully recovered. But the developing movement, already well established in Syria and spreading through the northeast quadrant of the Mediterranean cities of the Roman empire, was sufficiently well rooted and sufficiently remote from the catastrophe in Israel/Palestine to maintain its appeal for seekers after spiritual truth and salvation and to continue its expansion. Moreover, the Jesus tradition and the gospel of Jesus' death and resurrection were still sufficiently fresh, and there were still a goodly number of the first-generation disciples active in the churches, for the character stamped on the movement by Jesus, by the events commemorated today as the first Good Friday, Easter and Pentecost, and by the first-generation disciples (Paul especially), to remain firm at the heart of the movement and to provide a continuing motivating force of considerable effect.

In fact, however, this was the period, following the disaster of 70, and running well through the second century, when the new Jesus movement firmed up its distinctive identity markers and the structures on which it would establish its distinctive and growing appeal in the following decades and centuries. Prior to 70, and despite its expansion among non-Jews within the Roman empire, the Jesus movement had still remained within the matrix of Second Temple Judaism. During the forty years from Jesus to the temple's destruction, the movement focusing on Messiah/Christ Jesus was still essentially, legally and in the self-understanding of its leaders a sect of the national religion of the Jews. It was not yet 'Christianity'. As already noted, 'Christianity' as a distinctive entity was not so named until the second decade of the second century.[1] So the period between the two Jewish revolts (66-73 and 132-135) and beyond was critical both for the redefinition of Judaism which these calamities made necessary and for the first attempts to define 'Christianity', particularly because the redefinition of Judaism also made necessary the definition of 'Christianity' in relation to the Judaism which had been its birth mother. Other religious developments, in part stimulated by emerging Christianity itself, notably all that falls traditionally under the heading of 'Gnosticism', also required a careful charting of Christianity's distinctives. Nor should we assume that emerging Christianity itself was a single, uniformly coherent movement. Consequently, the questions, What is Christianity? and What are the distinctive and defining features of Christianity?, were forced upon the theologians and leaders of this still adolescent religion both from without and from within.

The task confronting us in this volume is much more difficult to manage than in the previous two volumes. It is not simply that the time periods are so different — only some three years for *Jesus Remembered* and about forty years for *Beginning from Jerusalem*, but now more than one hundred years for this crucial phase for Christianity in the making. More challenging is the fact that we have no clear guideline or template to follow through that hundred years. With *Jesus Remembered*, the Gospels, particularly the Synoptic Gospels, provided a coherent and relatively limited body of material to work with, and offered a structure and a sequence for ordering the analysis and discussion of the material. With *Beginning from Jerusalem*, the narrative history provided by Luke in the Acts of the Apostles and the collection of letters preserved from Paul served in the same way, however awkward it was at times to fit the two testimonies into a single story or picture.[2] But now we have no Luke to guide us, no Acts at least to start from. The account provided by the fourth-century Eusebius, valuable as it is, is too remote and (as we shall see) too patchy and anachronistic to provide a role equivalent to that of Luke's Acts. The other NT writings are usually hard to pin down as to both their origin and the testimony they provide for a rounded picture of the Christianity to which they testify, and

---

1. See *Beginning from Jerusalem* (Grand Rapids: Eerdmans, 2009) 5-6.
2. The use of Acts as a historical source for the first decades of what became known as Christianity remains controversial. I dealt with the issue in *Beginnings* §§21.2 and 21.3; and see now C. S. Keener, *Acts: An Exegetical Commentary* (Grand Rapids: Baker Academic; vol. 1, 2012) 90-382.

hard to relate each to the other, quite unlike the different NT Gospels in their testimony to Jesus or the relation of Acts to the Pauline letters. The Christian writings which have been preserved give us only episodic pictures of the period, and the contribution of rabbinic tradition, other Jewish and Jewish-Christian writings, and Gnostic documents is at best contested at almost every point of relevance.

So how to go about the task? In some ways it is fortunate that there have been far fewer attempts to write a detailed history of Christianity in the making through this period (less secondary literature to confuse and to debate with!). NT specialists have usually been content to confine themselves to the NT itself and its immediate context. Similarly specialists in 'the early church' have usually in effect begun at the end of the NT period and focused on the second century and thereafter. One problem with such an approach is that some of the early church writings may be earlier than some of the NT writings.[3] The period of overlap should be examined more closely. But in addition, a NT specialist can hardly be uninterested in the effect the NT writings had, and in the influence they exercised which resulted in due course in their being recognized as 'canonical', that is, in a word now much used, in their 'reception'. Similarly, the reasons why they and not others became designated as the NT canon tell us much both about the documents themselves and about the way they were read in these early decades. It is, assuredly, no longer acceptable to assume that 'the apostolic age' was an ideal and a pure period, from which the subsequent period fell away (the 'sub-apostolic' age, in its *double entendre* sense).[4] But how did the successors of the first disciples shape Christianity, not least in the way they handled the traditions stemming from the first generation and the writings of the first disciples?

A similar line of reflection points to the most logical end-point for this analysis. For, as we shall see, Irenaeus marks a decisive watershed in early Christianity. It was with Irenaeus that the four-Gospel canon was effectively established. It was Irenaeus who ensured that the two most influential contributors to the NT, Paul and John, were not commandeered by Gnostic sects but were recognized to be determinative for the mainstream of Christianity which Irenaeus represented. With Irenaeus the internal and external conflicts with the Gnostic and Judaeo-Christian sects reached a decisive point, and it was Irenaeus who re-secured the character of Christianity that endured

---

3. Notably *1 Clement*; see below §40.1a.

4. See particularly R. L. Wilken, *The Myth of Christian Beginnings* (London: SCM, 1979).

beyond these conflicts. As the first genuinely 'biblical theologian', Irenaeus[5] provides a natural stopping place. So our story will reach its conclusion or climax with Irenaeus.

But how to get from the end of the first generation to Irenaeus, from 70 to, say, 180?[6] Previous attempts to trace the path, or diversity of paths, have usually found that one or more of the following perspectives have provided the way to be pursued, characterized by:

- the emergence of the Christian distinctives, that is, of NT canon, creed, ritual and episcopacy; alternatively expressed, the emergence of the old Catholic Church,[7] the phenomenon of 'early Catholicism' (*Frühkatholizismus*);[8]
- the growing separation of Christianity from Judaism and the divergence or apostasy of Judaeo-Christian sects;[9]
- the Hellenisation of Christianity and the divergence or apostasy of Gnostic Christianity;[10]
- a focus on the great centres of Christianity in turn — Antioch, Ephesus, Rome, etc.[11]

A brief review of these different perspectives will help clarify the conflicted character of the material we have to deal with, may give some pointers on how the material is best handled, and should provide plenty of items for our agenda in what follows.

---

5. See e.g. M. A. Donovan, 'Irenaeus', *ABD* 3.457-61, who cites (458) J. Lawson, *The Biblical Theology of St. Irenaeus* (London, 1948), and G. Wingren, *Man and the Incarnation: A Study of the Biblical Theology of Irenaeus* (Philadelphia, 1959); also E. Osborn, *Irenaeus of Lyons* (Cambridge University, 2001) 14, 23, 162, 172.

6. Irenaeus's *Adversus Haereses* is dated to about 180 (Donovan, 'Irenaeus' 457).

7. Notably A. Ritschl, *Die Entstehung der altkatholischen Kirche* (Bonn, 1850, ²1857).

8. E. Troeltsch, *The Social Teaching of the Christian Church* (ET London: Allen & Unwin, 1931), passes from ch. 1, 'The Foundations in the Early Church', and ch. 2, 'Paul' (69-89), to ch. 3, 'Early Catholicism' (89-164). *Frühkatholizismus* has proved to be a less interesting topic in the last two or three decades, but see my *Unity and Diversity in the New Testament: An Inquiry into the Character of Earliest Christianity* (London: SCM, 1977, ²1990, ³2006) ch. 14, 'Early Catholicism', with bibliography 484-85.

9. This was the principal inheritance from F. C. Baur; see below at n.35.

10. The principal inheritance from Adolf von Harnack; see below at n.103.

11. This was sparked off by Walter Bauer's focus on different centres of Christianity's development; see below at n.26. The procedure has been followed through most consistently by H. Koester, *Introduction to the New Testament* vol. 2: *History and Literature of Early Christianity* (Berlin: de Gruyter/Philadelphia: Fortress, 1982).

38.2 The Emergence of the Great Church[12]

The publication of the *Ecclesiastical History* of Eusebius (roughly 311-325)[13] coincided more or less with the development of the Constantinian settlement which established Christianity as the favoured religion of the empire.[14] As such it effectively established the pattern for telling the story of Christianity's establishment; that is, a story told from the perspective of the winners after several generations of conflict and persecution. Its account is of a church whose structures, according to Eusebius, were already clear from the first, structures which had enabled it to endure and succeed. Eusebius's main aim, indeed, was to establish the principle of apostolic succession, the successors of the apostles and the succession of bishops in the principal sees. It was this succession which had been the key to the church's success.

Eusebius thus inaugurated the triumphalist view of Christianity's beginnings, where the historian saw his task as to tell the story of what became the principal features of the victorious church, and by implication, the reasons for its success. The early mists are dispersed and the clear outlines of the subsequent established church are traced to the very beginnings of Christianity. So, for example, James, the brother of Jesus, had been 'the first elected to the throne of the bishopric of the church in Jerusalem' (*HE* 2.1.2). The apostolic succession was established from the beginning in the bishopric of the church in Rome, with Linus (of 2 Tim. 4.21) as the first successor to Peter, and Clement the third bishop of Rome. And the first bishop of the church in Athens could simply be identified as the Dionysius of Acts 17.34 (*HE* 3.4.8-10). Whether the title 'bishop' had already emerged in these church plantings of the first century and whether the title was appropriate for the first generation Christian groups and for the way church leadership was initially conceived and practised are questions not even considered.[15] And as for the competitors for the

---

12. To avoid what could properly be regarded as anachronistic references to early Christianity, to the mainstream of Christianity, or to what became 'orthodox' Christianity as 'the Church', I prefer to use the referent provided by Celsus — 'the great Church' (Origen, *Contra Celsum* 5.59). In the *Martyrdom of Polycarp*, Polycarp is referred to as 'bishop of the catholic/universal church in Smyrna' (16.2); the *Epistula Apostolorum* (150-175) is addressed 'to the Catholics'.

13. See §40 n.172 below.

14. The key dates were Constantine's victory at the Milvian Bridge, north of Rome, in 312, and the subsequent victory at Chrysopolis which made him sole emperor, in 324. He at once implemented his religious policy in favour of Christianity in the Edict of Milan (313), which decreed that Christians should be allowed to follow their faith without oppression and returned church property which had been confiscated, and in summoning the Council of Nicaea, in 325.

15. Interesting is the fact that Paul is never designated 'bishop' by Eusebius — per-

heritage from Jesus and of the first generation Christians, these are only to be dismissed as never really part of the emerging great church; he who disagrees with us was never one of us.

This has proved to be the dominant view of Christianity's beginnings for most of Christianity's history. The assumption has been: What is (now) has always been. In particular, following the lead given by Eusebius, it was assumed that there has always been the threefold ministry of deacon, priest and bishop. At the heart of Christian ministry has always been the concept and practice of priesthood. The eucharist has always been as it is. Such historical concern as there has been is a concern to trace the emergence of the monarchical bishop. The evidence that the first generation of Christians recognized no special order of priests among their number, and that the letter to the Hebrews regarded such an order as passé, belonging to the old covenant now superseded (Heb. 9-10), was somewhat embarrassing but could be largely ignored.[16] The likelihood that the re-emergence of sacrificing priests within Christianity was an instinctive or social conformity to what everyone took for granted to be characteristic and defining of religion and religious practice could likewise be ignored. Notably, and surprisingly, the views of J. B. Lightfoot, that when an order of priesthood was reintroduced in the second century, the priests initially were seen to represent the priesthood of the believing congregation rather than the priesthood of Christ, seem to have been lightly passed over, despite the towering reputation of Lightfoot.[17] So too the possibilities both that the beginnings of the eucharist had more to do with the shared meals of Jesus and the first Christians,[18] and that the narrowing of the subsequent ritual

---

haps he was too controversial a character to be thus easily embraced within such a structured account of Christianity's beginnings. But K.-W. Niebuhr points out (in private correspondence) that for Eusebius, far from being too controversial a character, Paul would have been much more than a bishop, because he was able to instruct and to command the bishops in the church (cf. 1 Tim. 3.2; Tit. 1.7; see also Acts 20.28).

16. I still find it surprising that a document like the Second Vatican Council's 'Dogmatic Constitution on the Church (Lumen Gentium)' could simply take its model of priesthood from the letter to Hebrews (§28), while totally ignoring the teaching of Hebrews to the effect that the ministry of Christ had brought an end to the need for such an order of priesthood. In lecturing on Hebrews in the Gregorian Pontifical University in 1990 I had to abandon the lecture to engage in vigorous discussion on the subject; see my *The Partings of the Ways between Christianity and Judaism* (London: SCM, 1991, ²2006) 117-19, 127-28.

17. J. B. Lightfoot, 'The Christian Ministry', in *Saint Paul's Epistle to the Philippians* (London: Macmillan, 1868, 1885) 181-269. Christ qualified for priesthood (the order of Melchizedek) in that he resembled Melchizedek, 'without father, without mother, without genealogy, having neither beginning of days nor end of life' (Heb. 7.3). Who else could be appointed to such an order?

18. Paul's name is 'the Lord's supper', that is, a dinner (*deipnon*) whose host is the Lord; note 1 Cor. 11.25 — the cup is circulated 'after dining'. The meal continued to be the

to the reception of a wafer and a sipping of wine has lost something integral to the Lord's Supper/evening meal, are hardly even worthy of consideration. What is has always been.

Similar assumptions have been characteristic of the traditional inquiries into Christianity's beginnings. Apostolicity became the determinative factor in according canonical authority to certain writings and not to others.[19] That is, the authorship of the apostles or their near companions (Mark and Luke) was what settled the issue of canonical status. And if a case could be made even for writings like Hebrews or 2 Peter, that they had been written by an apostle (Paul or Peter), that proved in the event to be decisive. Whereas a Clement and an Ignatius failed the test. The apostolic age had a hagiography all to itself.[20] So even if the scope and contents of the canon were not definitively resolved for three centuries, it was the link back to the sacred time of beginnings, the initial voice still sounding, still determinative, which really mattered. All this despite the evidence within these documents themselves that their writers had not seen eye to eye on quite a number of controverted issues. All this despite the fact that an undeclared hermeneutical reading of these texts (a canonical perspective) ensured that they could be heard to speak with a common voice and in accord with the presuppositions and priorities of third- and fourth-century ecclesiastics. Still today, Orthodox Christianity lives in the world of the (Greek) Fathers and knows no other way to read the NT scriptures than through and in tune with the Fathers.

The same point could be made with regard to the creedal confessions. Of course it is fully recognized that these were formulated by the ecumenical councils, from Nicaea (325) onwards. But the implicit claim in them all is that they only spell out 'the rule of faith' which had been accepted and lived by more or less from the first.[21] Here again there is little or no concern to confront the possibility that the first Christians had functioned with differing rules

---

focal point in our period — Jude 12; 2 Pet. 2.13; Ignatius, *Smyrn.* 8.2; Pliny, *Ep.* 10.96 (cited in *Beginning* 61); Tertullian, *Apol.* 39.

19. The classic studies are T. Zahn, *Geschichte des Neutestamentlichen Kanons* (2 vols.; Erlangen: Deichert, 1888, 1890); and H. von Campenhausen, *The Formation of the Christian Bible* (London: Black, 1972). However, as becomes clearer in what follows, 'apostolicity was not a matter of name so much as content' (§50.2c).

20. Niebuhr (n. 15 above) notes the more surprising omission of the *Epistle of Barnabas*, given Barnabas's relative prominence in the NT, and wonders whether the letter was not well known in influential circles or his critical position in regard to Paul counted against him.

21. Tertullian is first to speak of 'the rule of faith', tracing it back to the apostles (*Praescript.* 13, 21-22, 27; *adv. Marc.* 3.1; 4.2, 5); but Irenaeus also assumes a unity of the faith, 'received from the apostles and their disciples', and universally shared by the church (*adv. haer.* 1.10.1). See e.g. J. N. D. Kelly, *Early Christian Creeds* (London: Longmans, 1960), index 'rule of faith'.

of faith, a shared faith in (most of) its key beliefs about Jesus, but understood and lived out differently. Here again the fact that various biblical texts could be taken most naturally to support divergent views, for example, regarding the creation of Sophia and the Logos, or the resurrection of the flesh, was too uncomfortable to be taken seriously, and the texts could be simply explained away or ignored apart from occasional liturgical mention.[22]

In Western Christianity the Reformation posed some sharp questions to a mediaeval church which in effect had simply read its key tradition back into the canonical texts. But by and large the Reformers were in fact concerned to do the same with the history of Christianity's beginnings, that is, to read them from their own perspective, to find in them the support they needed for their reforms. It was not until the Enlightenment brought a more critical approach to historical sources that the questions long suppressed or ignored could come into play. Even so, as represented by Albrecht Ritschl, the goal was to trace 'the origin of the ancient Catholic Church',[23] and the search for the beginnings of the great church continued to be the dominant concern, determinative of the mode of inquiry for more popular presentations of Christianity in the making.[24]

The Reformation and the Enlightenment, however, had begun the process by which was steadily loosened the firm hand of tradition that had controlled how the beginnings of Christianity were perceived. The early History of Religions pioneers carried forward the process by loosening the controlling focus on doctrine and dogma, and William Wrede by loosening the controlling hand of the NT canon.[25] The historian should give as much attention to other documents outside the NT as to the NT writings, if indeed not more attention, since the NT itself had hitherto exercised a monopolistic role in determining the data and facts to be considered in talking about the beginnings of Christianity.

In fact, as noted in the opening pages of *Jesus Remembered*, it was not until well into the twentieth century, until Walter Bauer's inquiry into *Orthodoxy and Heresy in Earliest Christianity*,[26] that the traditional way of looking at the data

---

22. I reflected on these issues in *Unity and Diversity in the New Testament*.
23. See n.7 above.
24. For a lively treatment covering the ground of my three volumes, see L. M. White, *From Jesus to Christianity* (HarperSanFrancisco, 2004).
25. W. Wrede, *Über Aufgabe und Methode der sogenannten neutestamentichen Theologie* (Göttingen: Vandenhoeck & Ruprecht, 1897; ET 'The Task and Methods of "New Testament Theology"', in R. Morgan, *The Nature of New Testament Theology* (London: SCM, 1973) 68-116 (here 70-71). See also H. Räisänen, *The Rise of Christian Beliefs: The Thought-World of Early Christians* (Philadelphia: Fortress, 2009).
26. *Rechtgläubigkeit und Ketzerei im ältesten Christentum* (1934, ²1964); ET *Orthodoxy and Heresy in Earliest Christianity* (Philadelphia: Fortress, 1971).

was decisively challenged and the presuppositions from Eusebius onwards called into question. For it was precisely the assumption that 'orthodoxy' had always been first and that 'heresy' had always entered later that Bauer questioned, the assumption that false teaching was a corruption of and a falling away from the original purity of faith which, of course, had originally characterized the churches established in the apostolic age. But Bauer asked, What were the original forms of Christianity, particularly in the centres on which the Acts of the Apostles had not focused attention — in Edessa (eastern Syria) and in Alexandria, for example? Were the earliest forms of Christianity much more a 'mixed bag' than had previously been thought? Was there ever a 'pure' form of Christianity?! Was the victory of the great church which emerged not so much a victory over *outside* pressures (persecuting authorities, competing religious systems) as a victory of one faction over other rivals *within* the early churches? Is that why the voices still to be heard speaking for themselves are only the Ignatiuses, the Justins and the Irenaeuses? The rest had been silenced. The victors had destroyed the writings of the losers. However, the discovery of the Nag Hammadi writings in the mid 1940s[27] jerked historians of Christianity's beginnings into a fresh awareness of the voices from the second and third centuries which had long been silenced, into a fresh recognition that so many writings of the first few centuries of the Christian era had been lost, and into the startling thought that with a more representative body of writings to draw on, the historians' reconstructions of the beginnings of Christianity might have been very different.

Bauer's thesis focused on the second century and so falls directly on to the agenda for the present volume. The questions which we will have to bear in mind are the ones Bauer posed and those which follow from the Nag Hammadi codices. Were the beginnings of Christianity in various Mediterranean centres a good deal more 'mixed' than the traditional accounts have allowed? Was there a straight line from Paul, or Peter, into the great church, or did the line follow a much more twisting course, or were there several lines pushing in different directions, even pushing against each other? Were the Clements and the Ignatiuses and Justins as representative of the second to fourth generations of Christians as those who maintain the more traditional reconstruction of Christianity's earliest history would like to think? What was the 'Christianity' which emerged into the second century, how diverse, how different from the Christianity which Constantine elevated into the established religion of the empire?[28]

27. See below n.125.
28. The issue has been posed more and more sharply since J. M. Robinson and H. Koester, *Trajectories through Early Christianity* (Philadelphia: Fortress, 1971). See particularly J. D. Crossan, *The Birth of Christianity* (HarperSanFrancisco, 1998); B. D. Ehrman, *Lost Christianities: The Battle for Scripture and the Faiths We Never Knew* (Oxford University, 2003), particularly 176-80 and chs. 9-12; R. Cameron and M. P. Miller, *Redescribing*

38.3 Christianity and Judaism

The relation of Christianity to Judaism is at the heart of Christianity. Both terms, of course, need to be carefully defined; otherwise the assertion becomes unhelpfully controversial. If by 'Christianity' we mean the movement that began in Jerusalem in 30 CE, then all that has been said in the first two volumes of *Christianity in the Making* underlines and reinforces the fact that the movement began within first-century Judaism and drew heavily on the heritage of Judaism, as illustrated not least by the fact that the scriptures of the new movement were the scriptures of Israel and of first-century Judaism.[29] And if by 'Judaism' we mean Second Temple Judaism, then it is sufficiently clear that Second Temple Judaism embraced a diverse set of sects and emphases,[30] which included the sect of the Nazarenes. If, however, by 'Christianity' we mean the Christianity that gained its distinctive shape in the patristic period, and if by 'Judaism' we mean the rabbinic Judaism which began to gain its distinctive shape in the post-70 period, then the opening assertion becomes much more problematic. One of the key questions which will lie behind what follows is the extent to which the post-70 situation and context differ from the pre-70 situation and context for both Judaism and Christianity.

For a start, we need to recall what was previously noted, that 'Christianity' only emerged, linguistically speaking, early in the second century. That is, the term 'Christianity' was first coined (so far as we can now tell), or at least first used in writing that has endured, by Ignatius in the 110s.[31] More significant here is the fact that in its first usage 'Christianity' was understood as defined in contrast to 'Judaism'.[32] Ironically, the pattern set by the first formu-

---

Christian Origins (Atlanta: SBL, 2004); in German scholarship note also G. Lüdemann, *Heretics: The Other Side of Early Christianity* (London: SCM, 1996). Ehrman's earlier *The Orthodox Corruption of Scripture: The Effect of Early Christological Controversies on the Text of the New Testament* (New York: Oxford University, 1993), with its important thesis — that 'proto-orthodox scribes of the second and third centuries occasionally modified their text of Scripture in order to make them coincide more closely with the christological views embraced by the party that would seal its victory at Nicea and Chalcedon' (275) — could not be adequately discussed without venturing well beyond the second century.

29. William Horbury, *Jews and Christians in Contact and Controversy* (Edinburgh: T & T Clark, 1998), observes that 'the Christians, recognizing their biblical inheritance as Jewish, wanted to share the Jewish Bible in the canonical form recognized by Jews. . . . recognition of a biblical canon was a fundamental common presupposition, and both communities shared a biblical culture focused on what can properly be called a common Bible' (25-26, and further 26-35 and ch. 8).

30. See *Jesus Remembered* (Grand Rapids: Eerdmans, 2003) §9.

31. Ign. *Magn.* 10.1-3; *Rom.* 3.3; *Phil.* 6.1; *Mart. Pol.* 10.1.

32. 'It is out of place to talk of Jesus Christ and to judaize. For Christianity did not

lation of the term 'Judaism' was followed in the earliest talk of 'Christianity'. For as 'Judaism' was defined as other than and as opposed to 'Hellenism',[33] so 'Christianity' was already being defined as other than 'Judaism'. If 'Judaism' was defined by the Maccabean rebellion as in effect 'not-Hellenism', so 'Christianity' was defined by Ignatius as in effect 'not-Judaism'.[34] As we shall see, this attempt to distance Christianity grew steadily stronger through the patristic period and readers will not need reminding that it became entrenched in the anti-Jewish and anti-semitic traditions of Christianity.

Our starting point here, however, is the impact made by F. C. Baur on the modern study of Christianity's origins.[35] Baur focused attention once again on the fact that Christianity emerged from a Jewish matrix, or perhaps better, from its matrix within Second Temple Judaism. And Baur's focus on this fact ensured that the question of how Christianity did in fact so emerge had to be of primary interest to historians. The reasons are obvious. The fact that Jesus was hailed as Messiah, that is, the Messiah expected by the Jews, the fact that all the first believers in Messiah Jesus were Jews, and the fact that their scriptures were the scriptures of Second Temple Judaism, in any case made inevitable and unavoidable the task of defining emerging Christianity as distinct from and in its distinctiveness from Judaism. Baur's own characterization of Christianity's distinctiveness from Judaism was rather crass.[36] The whole issue was for a long time skewed by the traditional Christian distaste for Judaism. And the fascination with the issue of pre-Christian Gnosticism for a long time diverted attention from the challenge which Baur had left to his successors.[37] But since the Second World War and the catastrophe of the Holocaust/Shoah, Christian scholarship and leadership have resolutely decried the previous anti-Judaism and lamented its gross outworkings.[38] As a consequence the question of Christianity's emergence from its Second Temple Jewish matrix can be reopened.

---

believe in Judaism, but Judaism in Christianity . . .' (Ign. *Magn.* 10.3). 'But if anyone interprets Judaism to you, do not listen to him; for it is better to hear Christianity from a man who is circumcised, than Judaism from one uncircumcised' (*Phil.* 6.1).

33. See *Jesus Remembered* §9.2a.

34. See further K.-W. Niebuhr, '"Judentum" und "Christentum" bei Paulus und Ignatius von Antiochien', *ZNW* 85 (1994) 218-33, especially 224-33.

35. F. C. Baur, *Paul: The Apostle of Jesus Christ* (1845; ET 2 vols., London: Williams & Norgate, 1873, 1875); *The Church History of the First Three Centuries* (1854; ET 2 vols., London: Williams & Norgate 1878-79). See also *Jesus Remembered* §1 and *Beginning from Jerusalem* §20.3a.

36. See Baur's formulation of the historical process cited in *Beginning from Jerusalem* §20.3a.

37. See again *Beginning from Jerusalem* §20.3b, c.

38. The Roman Catholic Church's repudiation and denunciation of anti-Semitism in 'Nostra Aetate' 4 (1965) was a tipping point.

The question has re-emerged in different ways and for our inquiry has three aspects:

- when did the ways finally part between emerging Christianity and (rabbinic) Judaism?
- the status of Judaeo-Christianity within the spectrum of Christianity;
- the issue of anti-semitism in the NT documents.

a. The Partings of the Ways between Christianity and Judaism[39]

If it is hardly to be denied that Christianity and rabbinic Judaism emerged from the same matrix of Second Temple Judaism,[40] it is even more obvious that Christianity and Judaism are now two distinct religions, and that they have been so for many centuries. So an important issue is, How soon and under what circumstances did they become so distinct? If the two movements emerging from the catastrophe of 70 had the same broad starting place, when did the ways they followed separate? When did their ways part?

In the first edition of *Partings*, I used the plural form (*Partings* not *Parting*) in order to make the point that the separation of Christianity from rabbinic Judaism cannot neatly be identified as taking place at a particular point in time or place, as though there was only one 'parting of the ways'.[41] The separation from each other of what are now two quite independent religions was much more of a process, and took much longer to become clear-cut and final than most people realise.[42] To be sure, there were various points at which the

---

39. In what follows I draw on the 'Preface' to the second edition of *The Partings of the Ways between Christianity and Judaism and Their Significance for the Character of Christianity* (London: SCM, 1991, ²2006) xi-xxx.

40. Alan Segal nicely characterized the relation by his title *Rebecca's Children: Judaism and Christianity in the Roman World* (Harvard University, 1986). More strongly D. Boyarin, *Border Lines: The Partition of Judaeo-Christianity* (Philadelphia: University of Pennsylvania, 2004): 'Judaism is not the "mother" of Christianity; they are twins, joined at the hip' (5).

41. B. Wander's title makes the same point — *Trennungsprozesse zwischen frühen Christentum und Judentum im 1. Jahrhundert n. Chr.* (Tübingen: Mohr Siebeck, 1994); see particularly 2 and 289. The main thesis of A. H. Becker and A. Y. Reed, eds., *The Ways That Never Parted* (TSAJ 95; Tübingen: Mohr Siebeck, 2003), is obvious from the title, but unfortunately the editors see their task as dispelling 'the notion of a single and simple "Parting of the Ways" in the first or second century CE' (22); but 'single and simple' is too much of a straw man. Becker himself concludes that 'There were, in fact, many "partings", and they happened in different places at different times in different ways' (392).

42. The first conclusion to the 1989 Durham/Tübingen Research Symposium on 'The Parting of the Ways, AD 70-135', pointed to a less clear-cut process: '"The parting of

tear(s), or pulling apart, was more evident than at others; there were various events and confrontations in particular locations which markedly accelerated the process. But how decisive, how final, how universal were they?[43]

In the first edition of *Partings* I made bold to draw the conclusion that a final 'parting' can be discerned in the second century — with the second Jewish revolt against Rome (132-135), and certainly by the end of the second century.[44] The opinion is shared by several scholars.[45] However, the imagery of two ways may itself be far too simple; it can too easily imply two embryonic religions as two homogeneous (or even monolithic) entities each pursuing a single path, with developments in each case marching forward uniformly across the diverse contexts of the Mediterranean and Middle East;[46] whereas

---

the ways", properly speaking, was very "bitty", long drawn out and influenced by a range of social, geographical, and political, as well as theological factors' — J. D. G. Dunn, ed., *Jews and Christians: The Parting of the Ways AD 70 to 135* (Tübingen: Mohr Siebeck, 1992/Grand Rapids: Eerdmans, 1999) 367.

43. To argue that 'the ways *never* parted' (Becker and Reed, eds., *The Ways That Never Parted*) is surely an over-reaction. As one of the essayists, R. A. Kraft, 'The Weighing of the Parts' (87-94), observes, 'It is quite obvious that the "ways" that led to classical Christianity and rabbinic Judaism did indeed "part" by the fourth century CE' (87). Becker and Reed also press the case for 'convergences' subsequent to partings (22-23), but I question whether resort to the Hebrew Bible by Origen and Jerome is well described as a 'convergence' of the ways, as A. Salvesen argues in a subsequent essay — 'A Convergence of the Ways?', 233-58 — or that such use is well described as 'the judaizing of Christian Scripture' (the article's sub-title; the title of the final diagram, 'The "Hebraization" of Greek and Latin Scripture', 258, is more appropriate).

44. *Partings* 243 (= ²317-18).

45. Qualified support, and on the basis of a much fuller treatment of second-century texts, is given by S. G. Wilson, *Related Strangers: Jews and Christians 70-170 CE* (Minneapolis: Fortress, 1995), particularly 285-88; also 306 n.37. R. Bauckham, 'The Parting of the Ways: What Happened and Why', *Studia Theologica* 47 (1993) 135-51, also thinks the non-participation of Christians in the Bar Kokhba revolt 'probably sealed their exclusion from common Judaism and removed the rabbis' main rivals for dominance in Palestinian Judaism' (145-46). And similarly the essays by P. J. Tomson and S. Schoon, in P. J. Tomson and D. Lambers-Petry, eds., *The Image of the Judaeo-Christians in Ancient Jewish and Christian Literature* (WUNT 158; Tübingen: Mohr Siebeck, 2003), consider the decisive factors to be the political and social upheavals caused by the two Jewish revolts (here 22-27 and 309-11). This in fact has been the consensus view (Becker and Reed, *The Ways That Never Parted* 1; with a good statement of the 'master narrative', 4-5).

46. See particularly J. Lieu, '"The Parting of the Ways": Theological Construct or Historic Reality?', *JSNT* 56 (1994) 101-19, reprinted in *Neither Jew nor Greek? Constructing Christian Identity* (Edinburgh: T & T Clark, 2003) 11-29; 'The problem with the model of the "parting of the ways" is that . . . it operates essentially with the abstract or universal conception of each religion, Judaism and Christianity, when what we know about is the specific and local' ('Parting' 108/18). Other weaknesses of the 'parting of the ways' imagery in Becker and Reed, *The Ways That Never Parted* 19-22; but also strengths (15-16, 18-19). M. Zetterholm,

the sociological reality might be better depicted as 'a criss-crossing of muddy tracks'.[47] 'The partings of the *ways*' should certainly not be taken to imply that there were only two ways in view, as though both rabbinic Judaism and Christianity each travelled a single well-defined path which diverged into two similarly single and well-defined paths.[48] To change the metaphor, there were various currents within the broader streams which became rabbinic Judaism and Christianity. But I still prefer the imagery of 'ways' or 'paths'. The alternative of 'trajectories' which became popular in the 1970s[49] implies predetermined 'flight-paths' for the entities in view. And 'stream' suffers somewhat from the same defect, as implying an irresistable force carving out its own channel. Whereas the imagery of 'ways' or 'paths' need not imply directness and can include a landscape of moor or hillside criss-crossed by several or many paths, whose directions are not always clear and which ramblers or fell-walkers may follow without a clear sense of where they are headed; the path actually travelled is always clearer looking back![50]

More important, however, are three further factors which have been given inadequate emphasis in discussion of 'the parting of the ways'. One is that rabbinic Judaism cannot be assumed to be the only form of Judaism with

---

The Formation of Christianity in Antioch: A Special-Scientific Approach to the Separation Between Judaism and Christianity (London: Routledge, 2003), also criticizes me for focusing on ideological aspects of the 'partings'; he emphasizes the importance of taking 'into consideration the role of social mechanisms as well' and focuses rather on 'the sociological aspects of the separation process' (4-5).

47. Lieu, 'Parting' 119/29. Lieu returns to the theme in *Christian Identity in the Jewish and Graeco-Roman World* (Oxford University, 2004). Observing that debate on the relationship between Christianity and Judaism has largely failed to achieve a consensus as to how, when and why the two parted, she continues: 'There are two key reasons for this failure: first, because it is never clear whether the objects of that question are ideas, or people, or systems; and secondly, because much depends on whether the respondent is a hypothetical Jew, Christian, or pagan of the time, or is the contemporary scholar, or even the believer, both the latter having the benefits . . . of hindsight and of subsequent history' (305, and further 305-10). In correspondence Lieu adds the further complicating factor of 'the filter of literary genre'.

48. This is also the weakness of the various models diagrammed by M. Goodman, 'Modeling the "Parting of the Ways"', in Becker and Reed, eds., *The Ways That Never Parted* 119-29, which mostly have to rely on single, one-dimensional lines, when at least two-dimensional breadth is surely necessary to model complex social phenomena such as diverse religious movements.

49. Robinson and Koester, *Trajectories through Earliest Christianity*.

50. For other models see D. Boyarin, 'Semantic Differences; or, "Judaism"/"Christianity"', in Becker and Reed, eds., *The Ways That Never Parted* 74-77: the familiar family tree, or, adapted to languages, the emergence of families of languages or dialects which continue to interact even when they have become largely distinct, or Boyarin's own 'wave-theory' ('innovations disseminate and interact like waves caused by stones thrown in a pond').

which or against which emerging Christianity interacted. In contrast to the older, simplistic and anachronistic view that Judaism became rabbinic Judaism when it was reconstituted at Yavneh following the destruction of Jerusalem in 70, the growing consensus today is that the rabbis did not succeed in winning over or imposing their interpretation of Israel's heritage until much later[51]—probably, indeed, at about the same period, in the latter half of the fourth century, when Christianity's state recognition presumably hastened the final parting. The corollary to this is that the great mass of Jews in the western diaspora during the first two or three centuries of the common era should not in the strict sense be regarded as part of rabbinic Judaism.[52] In other words, the lack of clear boundaries between Jew, Messiah-Jesus-believing Jew and Christian in these early centuries becomes still more evident, and we gain a further reminder that the partings of the ways took a lot longer to become clear and effective than has usually been thought.[53] This will require fuller attention in the pages that follow.

A second important aspect of post-70 interaction between Christianity and Judaism which should be noted is that it was Christians, and not the rabbis, who preserved much of the Jewish literature of the late Second Temple period and beyond.[54] Christians obviously valued and worked with documents like the *Ascension of Isaiah* and the *Testaments of the Twelve Patriarchs*. But should they be regarded as 'Christian' redactions of originally 'Jewish' documents? Or should they be seen more appropriately as Jewish-Christian writings, manifesting a Jesus-devotion within a Jewish self-definition?[55] That is, do they attest a period when the ways certainly had not yet parted, at least for those who valued these documents, a period when the definitions of 'Judaism' and 'Christianity' were still taking shape and firm boundary lines separating

---

51. See e.g. the essays by P. S. Alexander, '"The Parting of the Ways" from the Perspective of Rabbinic Judaism', and M. Goodman, 'Diaspora Reactions to the Destruction of the Temple', in Dunn, ed., *Jews and Christians* 1-25 and 27-38 respectively.

52. Justin's dialogue partner, Trypho, is a fascinating figure at this point.

53. Niebuhr (n.15 above), however, refers to possible hostility from emerging early 'Christian' groups to emerging (rabbinic) 'Judaism', citing M. Goodman, *Mission and Conversion* (Oxford University, 1994), and P. Schäfer, *Die Geburt des Judentums aus dem Geist des Christentum* (Tübingen: Mohr Siebeck, 2010).

54. J. H. Charlesworth, 'Christian and Jewish Self-Definition in Light of the Christian Additions to the Apocryphal Writings', in E. P. Sanders, ed., *Jewish and Christian Self-Definition* vol. 2: *Aspects of Judaism in the Graeco-Roman Period* (London: SCM, 1981) 27-55.

55. So argued by D. Frankfurter, 'Beyond "Jewish Christianity"', in Becker and Reed, eds., *The Ways That Never Parted* 131-43, who warns more generally about the tendency 'to retroject modern anxieties about religious clarity and orthodoxy onto a period of blur and flux in religious boundaries' (131).

the one from the other, as though they were already clearly distinctive entities, had still to be drawn for those who used these documents? The evidence and issues here will require closer attention.

The third striking fact to be noted is one which has been well documented by James Parkes and Marcel Simon,[56] but which has been too little taken into account in discussions of early Christianity's relations with Judaism. This is the fact that Christian leaders, as late as the fourth century, had to continually rebuke and warn their congregations against attending synagogues and observing Jewish feasts and customs. For example, Ignatius found it necessary to warn his Christian Jewish readers against living 'according to Judaism' and keeping the Sabbath (*Magn.* 8-10). Origen in his homilies frequently attacked Christians who observed the Jewish fasts and feasts, and warned Christians listening to him on a Sunday not to refer back to what they had learnt the day before in the synagogue.[57] Aphrahat in his first homily (about 345) likewise warned his readers against observing Sabbaths, new moons and festivals of the Jews. And the Council of Antioch (341) had to pass legislation (Canon 1) prohibiting Christians from dining at Passover with Jews.[58] Similarly the Council of Laodicea (c. 363) prohibited Christians from practising their religion with Jews, in particular, 'celebrating festivals with them', 'keeping the sabbath', and 'eating unleavened bread' during the Passover; Christians should work on the Sabbath and read the Gospels as well as the Jewish scriptures on Saturday (Canons 16, 29, 37, 38).[59] From about the same time the *Apostolic*

---

56. J. Parkes, *The Conflict of the Church and the Synagogue* (Jewish Publication Society, 1934; reprinted New York: Macmillan); M. Simon, *Verus Israel: A Study of the Relations between Christians and Jews in the Roman Empire (AD 135-425)* (1964; Oxford: Oxford University, 1986). In what follows I draw on my essay 'Two Covenants or One? The Interdependence of Jewish and Christian Identity', in H. Lichtenberger, ed., *Geschichte-Tradition-Reflexion: III. Frühes Christentum*; M. Hengel FS (Tübingen: Mohr Siebeck, 1996) 97-122; reprinted with some additional material in the second edition of *The Partings of the Ways* 339-65.

57. Origen, *Homilies on Leviticus* 5.8; *Selecta on Exodus* 12.46. See N. de Lange, *Origen and the Jews: Studies in Jewish-Christian Relations in Third-Century Palestine* (Cambridge: Cambridge University, 1976) 36, 86; 'What he does not make clear is whether the offenders were Jews who had embraced Christianity or Christians who were attracted to the outward forms of Judaism' (36).

58. L. H. Feldman, *Jew and Gentile in the Ancient World* (Princeton: Princeton University, 1993) 376.

59. Parkes, *Conflict* 175-76; but the correlation of Canon 16 ('The Gospels are to be read on the Sabbath with the other Scriptures') with Canon 29 ('Christians must not judaize by resting on the Sabbath, but must work on that day, rather honouring the Lord's Day') is unclear. See further Parkes, *Conflict* 174-77 and 381-82, for a summary of the canons of other councils prior to the Theodosian Code. 'The interest of the councils is only in Jewish Christian relationships, and they thereby reveal how close those relationships were' (174).

Constitutions found it necessary to prohibit Christians (including bishops and clergy?) from entering Jewish synagogues, keeping feasts with the Jews, and following Jewish customs, though it still sanctioned observance of the Passover and keeping Saturday as well as Sunday as days of rest.[60] A few decades later, correspondence between Augustine and Jerome instances the converted Jew who circumcises his son, observes the Sabbath, abstains from (unclean) foods and keeps the Passover.[61] And it is equally clear from Chrysostom's polemic that many members of his congregation observed the Sabbath, joined in the Jewish feasts and fully respected the synagogue.[62] Such Christians were evidently commonly described as *nostri judaizantes*,[63] the 'our' (*nostri*) indicating continuing willingness to 'own' such 'judaizers'.[64] As Simon notes, 'What we are faced with is an uninterrupted tradition of Judaizing, reaching down from the time when the epistles to the Galatians and the Colossians were written'.[65]

This clearly indicates that throughout the first three to four centuries what we might call 'ordinary Christians' did *not* see Christianity and Judaism as two separate far less opposed religions.[66] Rather the position was more like what is common in the days of denominational Christianity; that

---

60. *Apostolic Constitutions* 2.61; 5.17; 6.27, 30; 7.23; 8.33, 47.

61. Jerome, *Ep.* 67.4; 112.15. Chrysostom likewise instances a Christian who has been circumcised, not as a convert to Judaism, but as a Christian (*Hom.* 2.2, PG 48.858B-860A; W. A. Meeks and R. L. Wilken, *Jews and Christians in Antioch in the First Four Centuries of the Common Era* [Missoula: Scholars, 1978] 32). See now also D. S. Ben Ezra, '"Christians" observing "Jewish" Festivals of Autumn', in Tomson and Lambers-Petry, eds., *The Image of the Judaeo-Christians* 53-73; also 'Whose Fast Is It? The Ember Day of September and Yom Kippur', in Becker and Reed, eds., *The Ways that Never Parted* 259-82.

62. Chrysostom, *Hom. ad Jud.* 1, PG 48.844-45. Chrysostom's homilies 'show that the Judaizers' enthusiasm was not for any one rite in particular, but for the entire religious life of the Jews' (Simon, *Verus Israel* 326). Meeks and Wilken speak of 'a widespread Christian infatuation with Judaism' (*Jews and Christians* 31).

63. Simon, *Verus Israel* 322, 328.

64. It should be noted that 'judaizers' is being used here in its original sense — non-Jews attracted to Jewish customs and living as Jews.

65. Simon, *Verus Israel* 330.

66. Speaking of Christian leaders' attempts to end contacts with Jews, Parkes justifiably notes: 'So far as the common people are concerned, it is indeed questionable whether any of these prohibitions succeeded in securing their objects. Their frequent repetition in the next century suggests their ineffectiveness' (*Conflict* 193; see further 268-69, 320, 324). 'The active influence of Judaism upon Christianity in Antioch was perennial until Christian leaders succeeded at last in driving the Jews from the city in the seventh century' (Meeks and Wilken, *Jews and Christians* 18). On the situation in Alexandria see e.g. B. A. Pearson, 'Christians and Jews in First-Century Alexandria', in G. W. E. Nickelsburg and G. W. MacRae, eds., *Christians Among Jews and Gentiles*; K. Stendahl FS (Philadelphia: Fortress, 1986) 206-16. And for Spain see Feldman's references (*Jew and Gentile* 373, 380, 398) to the Council of Elvira (c. 300).

is, where 'ordinary Christians' feel free to attend the services of different denominations without thinking that they are being untrue to their more specific Christian heritage. The two ways were evidently seen by very many as (still) overlapping, so that participation in the synagogue could be seen as entirely consistent with their ecclesial commitment. The fact that such rebukes and warnings are to be found so frequently through this period tells us two things. One is that such a perception of the continuing overlap of Judaism and Christianity was widespread among Christians of the period. The other is that it was the Christian leadership which considered it necessary to press for a much clearer and sharper divide between the ways of Christianity and Judaism.[67] An appropriate question, however, is whether it was the Christian leadership or the 'ordinary Christians' who were being truer to the heritage of first-century Christianity.

At this point special mention should be made of the most recent contribution of Daniel Boyarin, one of the most stimulating of contributors to the debate on the partings of the ways.[68] His basic thesis elaborates the above perception that 'Judaism and Christianity were not separate entities until very late in late antiquity'.[69] His particular argument is that both Christian writers and the rabbis developed the model of orthodoxy/heresy precisely as a means of establishing their respective self-identities, that in both cases there was a major transition from a sectarian structure to one of orthodoxy and heresy which began to take place in the first half of the second century, 'the transformation of both nascent Christianity and nascent Judaism from groups of sects . . . into orthodox churches with their heretical others'.[70] The observation is sal-

---

67. Becker and Reed put forward the proposition 'that Jews and Christians (or at least the elites among them) may have been engaged in the task of "parting" throughout Late Antiquity and the early Middle Ages, *precisely because* the two never really "parted" during that period with the degree of decisiveness or finality needed to render either tradition irrelevant to the self-definition of the other, or even to make participation in both an unattractive or inconceivable option' (*The Ways That Never Parted* 23).

68. Boyarin, *Border Lines*; see also his earlier *Dying for God: Martyrdom and the Making of Judaism and Christianity* (Stanford: Stanford University, 1999), and his more recent *The Jewish Gospels: The Story of the Jewish Christ* (New York: New Press, 2012); cf. also M. S. Taylor, *Anti-Judaism and Early Christian Identity: A Critique of the Scholarly Consensus* (Leiden: Brill, 1995).

69. In almost the same breath Boyarin observes that 'There is no reason to imagine . . . that "rabbinic Judaism" ever became the popular hegemonic form of Jewish religiosity among the "People of the Land", and there is good reason to believe the opposite'; and that 'In the earliest stages of their development — indeed I suggest until the end of the fourth century, if we consider all of their varieties and not just the nascent "orthodox" ones — Judaism and Christianity were phenomenologically indistinguishable as entities . . .' (*Border Lines* 89).

70. Boyarin, *Border Lines* 21, 28, 30; see particularly his ch. 2, with the telling quota-

utary, partly because the categories of 'orthodoxy' and 'heresy' have usually been reckoned as Christian terms. More important, however, is the fact that since Walter Bauer's epochal study they have been somewhat controversial and contested terms of Christian self-definition — Bauer's claim being that 'orthodoxy' was the creed of the winners of a contested identity, and 'heresy' the creed of the losers, the categorisation, of course, being the language of the 'winners'. The point being made by Boyarin, however, is that very similar processes were taking place within emergent Judaism as well as within emergent Christianity. In terms of the imagery used here, both Christianity and Judaism defined themselves as narrower paths within the broader ways which emerged from the first century, a process which included the 'orthodox' designation of the overlap areas between the two ways as 'heresy'.[71] There are crucially important issues here as we attempt to trace out the course(s) of Christianity's emerging christology.

The issues raised by Boyarin's argument are considerable for our inquiry. For the challenge he poses is whether a properly historical study of the period can be satisfied with the straightforward tracing back (or reading back) of the distinctives of Christianity (or of Judaism) into the second century (or earlier). Was the Christianity of the period much less clearly defined, its boundaries less clearly drawn, its identity less clearly perceived and expressed, than the Christianity of the later centuries would recognize, or indeed than the voices which have been preserved from that period would suggest? In my earlier *Unity and Diversity in the New Testament* I tentatively posed a question which still stands: given that other responses to Jesus and the gospel were recognized to produce too extreme expressions, would it not be wise to recognize that orthodoxy too could have its too extreme aspects?[72] Is the failure of overscrupulous restrictiveness any worse than the failure of overgenerous hospitality to diverging ideas and practices?

In short, then, in response to the question, When did the ways part?, the answer has to be, Over a lengthy period, at different times and places, and

---

tion from J. Lieu, '"I am a Christian": Martyrdom and the Beginning of "Christian Identity"', in *Neither Jew nor Greek?*: 'It is in opposition that Christianity gains its true identity, so all identity becomes articulated, perhaps for the first time, in the face of "the other", as well as in face of attempts by the "other" to deny its existence' (72). See further Lieu, *Christian Identity* ch. 4 ('Boundaries') and ch. 9 ('The Other'); also several essays in G. N. Stanton and G. G. Stroumsa, eds., *Tolerance and Intolerance in Early Judaism and Christianity* (Cambridge University, 1998).

71. The issue finds focus in the *Birkat-ha-minim*, the Jewish malediction against heretics; see below §46.4b.

72. I develop the reflections on 'scripture and tradition' (*Partings* §12.5) in the Foreword to the third edition of *Unity and Diversity* (xvii-xxx).

as judged by different people differently, depending on what was regarded as a non-negotiable boundary marker and by whom. So, early for some, or demanded by a leadership seeking clarity of self-definition, but for many ordinary believers and practitioners there was a long lingering embrace which was broken finally(?) only after the Constantinian settlement.[73]

The issues raised by such factors for our study of *Christianity in the Making* are obviously immense and will dominate much of what follows. Without forgetting about christology, two in particular deserve special notice.

b. Judaeo-Christianity

'Jewish Christianity' has had a 'bad press' in both Christianity and Judaism, as a heresy unacceptable to both sides.[74] That is unfortunate, since it could well be argued that Judaeo-Christianity is an appropriate fuller way of characterizing Christianity itself.[75] If such an argument simply obscures the issue, however, it is at least as important to recognize that Jewish Christianity largely filled the middle-ground which was opening up between the two diverging ways.[76] And if what has already been observed and argued above is valid, then the two emerging religions themselves overlapped for several centuries, so that the 'middle-ground' is best seen as the area of overlap rather than as disjoint segments cut off from the two main movements. In other words, Jewish Christians, as defined by Origen, 'Christians (who) still want to live according to the law of the Jews like the multitude of the Jews' (*contra Celsum* 5.61), may constitute a very large and significant overlapping body which deserves close attention in the following pages.

I have already drawn attention to the substantial literature which can be fittingly described as 'Jewish Christian', writings which cannot be described simply as either Jewish or Christian, as though the two categories were clearly

---

73. A. D. Crown, 'Judaism and Christianity: The Parting of the Ways', in A. J. Avery-Peck et al., eds., *When Judaism and Christianity Began* (Leiden: Brill, 2004) 2.545-62, concludes that 'the work of the Council of Nicaea must be seen as the parting of the ways for Judaism and Christianity' (561).

74. Often quoted are the comments of Jerome on the Nazarenes: 'While they want to be both Jews and Christians, they are neither Jews nor Christians' (*Ep.* 112.13). A valuable overview is provided by J. Carleton Paget, 'Jewish Christianity', in W. Horbury et al., *The Cambridge History of Judaism* Vol. 3: *The Early Roman Period* (Cambridge University, 1999) 731-75.

75. Cf. J. Daniélou, *A History of Early Christian Doctrine before the Council of Nicaea* Vol. 1: *The Theology of Jewish Christianity* (London: Darton, Longman & Todd, 1964).

76. See again Wilson, *Related Strangers* 143-59; and further the essays in Tomson and Lambers-Petry, eds., *The Image of the Judaeo-Christians*.

distinct. This literature needs to be borne in mind when we consider the descriptions and references to the 'heretical' Jewish-Christian sects, and the pseudo-Clementines.[77] In addition, as we shall see, just as early Christian leaders had enduring problems with church members who regarded the synagogue as also a natural reference point or even as a second spiritual home, so the rabbis seem to have had a rather similar problem with Jews who believed in Jesus as Messiah but who wished nevertheless to continue practising as Jews.[78] Furthermore, the parting of the ways discussion has tended to focus too narrowly on the west (up to the Constantinian settlement) and has failed to examine the relationship between Jews and Christians not living under a Roman empire which became Christian. Indeed, in Arabia, Mesopotamia and Syria the Christians initially encountered by burgeoning Islam may fairly (and most accurately) be described as Jewish-Christians.[79] The agenda here becomes much larger than is usually allowed for in tracing the beginnings of Christianity.

It is no surprise, then, that the disappearance of 'Jewish Christianity' more or less coincides with a final 'parting' between Christianity and Judaism in the latter half of the fourth century,[80] as, presumably, the remnants of Jewish-Christian groups were absorbed into the now two quite distinct religions.[81] A salutary reminder of the poignancy of that disappearance and of the possibilities which 'Jewish Christianity' represented is the reappearance of Messianic Jews ('Jews for Jesus') in the last thirty or so years. It should occasion no surprise, either, that such Messianic Jews seem to be disowned equally by Christian and Jewish leadership today.[82] Evidently the challenge posed by such a movement to identities which were formed by contrast (or antithesis) is as sensitive today as it was in the early centuries of the common era. Such sensitivities and the reasons for them will have to be kept in mind in the following chapters.

---

77. See below §40.6g.

78. See also Wilson, *Related Strangers* ch. 6; Horbury, *Jews and Christians* ch. 5.

79. A. H. Becker, 'Beyond the Spatial and Temporal *Limes*', in Becker and Reed, eds., *The Ways That Never Parted* 373-92. See further in the same volume, J. G. Gager, 'Did Jewish Christians See the Rise of Islam?' 361-65.

80. Cf. especially A. Y. Reed, '"Jewish Christianity" after the "Parting of the Ways"', in Becker and Reed, eds., *The Ways That Never Parted* 189-231.

81. That may be the case, for example, with Nabatean Christians, though Chaldean Christians, a Syriac Church historically centered in Assyria, northern Mesopotamia, continued to flourish in Iraq until the beginning of the twenty-first century; and Samaritans and Mandaeans have also survived in relatively small groups.

82. Observed by D. Cohn-Sherbok, 'Modern Hebrew Christianity and Messianic Judaism', in Tomson and Lambers-Petry, eds., *The Image of the Judaeo-Christians* 287-98.

c. Anti-Judaism in the New Testament?

As already implied, the partings of the ways between Christianity and rabbinic Judaism, and the irritation occasioned by the substantial overlap of Judaeo-Christianity, resulted in a good deal of mutual hostility and vituperation born not least of exasperation. The point has already been alluded to in reference to the *Birkat-ha-minim*, and we shall soon enough see the same dismissive antagonism in the pseudo-Clementines. But where the issue bites most deeply for Christianity-in-the-making is on the question whether the anti-Judaism (and anti-semitism) which is certainly to be acknowledged at least in some influential Christian voices from the second century onwards, was already evident in the NT writings themselves.

Some NT specialists are convinced that the only clear answer that can be given is Yes: there is anti-Judaism in the NT; anti-semitism is rooted in the NT.[83] Several (or all) of the Gospels and Acts are cited as clear-cut examples. In Matthew we need only give two obvious examples. First, the sustained polemic against the Pharisees in Matthew 23. This has been the principal basis for the traditional Christian denigration of the Pharisees which has given the word 'Pharisee' such negative connotations in English usage.[84] Second, the words of the Jerusalem crowd in Jesus' trial scene in Matt. 27.25: 'All the people answered, "His blood be on us and on our children!"' This in turn has provided one of the most virulent roots of (or excuses for) the centuries of the anti-Judaism and anti-semitism which have so besmirched Christianity's history, providing as it has a scriptural warrant for countless denunciations of Jews of later centuries as 'Christ killers'.[85] In such Christian hatred of the Jews, it was perhaps inevitable that the hate figure of Judas (*Ioudas*), the betrayer of Jesus in the Gospel story, was taken as typically characteristic of the Jew (*Ioudaios*), that is, of all Jews.[86]

In John's Gospel 'the Jews' are represented as typically hostile to Jesus and to all that he stands for.[87] Most striking of all is John 8.44 and the depth

---

83. We should distinguish the two. Anti-Judaism was/is a hostility to religion and not race as such; Jews who converted to Christianity escaped from anti-Jewish persecution. Anti-semitism was/is racial and emerged as such only in the nineteenth century; conversion to Christianity would not necessarily save a Jew from anti-semitism, as the Nazi period all too well illustrated.

84. E.g. *The Concise Oxford Dictionary of Current English* gives as the second meaning of 'Pharisee', 'self-righteous person, formalist, hypocrite'.

85. S. Sandmel, *Anti-Semitism in the New Testament* (Philadelphia: Fortress, 1978), gives examples from his childhood (155).

86. H. Maccoby, *Judas Iscariot and the Myth of Jewish Evil* (London: Peter Halban, 1992).

87. See below §46.5c.

of hostility expressed there: 'Jesus said to them [the Jews] . . . "You are of your father the devil, and your will is to do your father's desires"'. Here we find another tap-root of Christian anti-semitism, giving scriptural ground for later identification of Jews with all that is evil.[88] Not surprisingly, then, John is regarded by some as 'either the most anti-Semitic or at least the most overtly anti-Semitic of the Gospels'.[89]

Somewhat more unexpected is the fact that in the latter half of the twentieth century Luke-Acts, particularly Luke's second volume, has been held out as anti-Jewish. At the beginning of the century Adolf Harnack had called Acts 'the first stage of developing early Christian anti-semitism'.[90] But at the latter end of the century J. T. Sanders had no hesitation in describing Acts as itself 'antisemitic' without qualification.[91] And Norman Beck has described Acts as the most anti-Jewish document in the NT.[92] Somewhat as in John's Gospel, 'the Jews' regularly appear, dogging Paul's footsteps, causing nothing but trouble and implacably opposed to the gospel.[93] Paul's turn from the Jews to the Gentiles is emphasized, repeated three times.[94] And the final note of Acts (28.26-28) seems to be dismissive of all Jews; salvation is (only) for the Gentiles. According to Ernst Haenchen, 'Luke has written the Jews off'.[95]

Of other NT writings, frequently cited would be Paul's angry language in 1 Thess. 2.14-16,[96] the seer of Revelation's reference to a 'synagogue of Satan' (Rev. 2.9), and particularly Hebrews' dismissal of the old covenant as incapable of meeting the needs of penitent worshippers (Heb. 10.1-4), and as 'obsolete' and soon to disappear (8.13).

What are we to make of such material? Does it signify that anti-Judaism, or even anti-semitism, is integral to and endemic in Christianity? Rosemary Ruether posed the issue starkly: 'Is it possible to say "Jesus is Messiah", without, implicitly or explicitly, saying at the same time "and the Jews be damned"?'[97] The question is shocking, but it brings home the seriousness of

---

88. R. R. Ruether, *Faith and Fratricide: The Theological Roots of Anti-Semitism* (New York: Seabury, 1974) 116.

89. Sandmel, *Anti-Semitism* 101.

90. Cited by J. T. Sanders, *The Jews in Luke-Acts* (London: SCM, 1987) xvi.

91. Sanders, *Jews* xvi-xvii.

92. N. A. Beck, *Mature Christianity: The Recognition and Repudiation of the Anti-Jewish Polemic of the New Testament* (London/Toronto: Associated University Presses, 1985) 270.

93. Sanders, *Jews* 77, 80. Details below (§46.5a).

94. Acts 13.46-47; 18.6; 28.28.

95. E. Haenchen, 'The Book of Acts as Source Material for the History of Early Christianity', in L. E. Keck and J. L. Martyn, eds., *Studies in Luke-Acts* (Philadelphia: Fortress, 1966) 258-78 (here 278); regularly quoted by Sanders, *Jews* — here 80-83, 297-99.

96. But see *Beginning from Jerusalem* 713 n.269.

97. Ruether, *Faith and Fratricide* 246.

the issue. And it reflects on the other questions raised in this section (§38.3). How can we correlate such attitudes and material within the NT writings with the evidence of a long overlap between Christianity and Judaism? How were such passages read and heard in the second century? Does a setting of these passages within a historical context (a historical critical reading) or within the NT canon (a canonical reading) reduce the sharpness and severity of the issue? Nor should we forget the broader question for continuing Christian usage of such passages. Should they be effectively expunged from the NT by never being included in Christian liturgy?[98] Should sermons on such texts ignore or skirt round the problem? Or should translations soften the offensiveness of such passages by, for example, translating references to *hoi Ioudaioi* not as 'the Jews', but as 'the Jewish authorities' or some similar euphemistic rendering?[99] Even to pose these as potentially desirable, or at least as possibly acceptable options, simply underlines the need to take such material seriously and the imperative necessity of clarifying its role within the historical, sociological and theological process which we describe as Christianity in the making.

38.4 The Hellenization of Christianity

A natural, perhaps inevitable counter to the interest in Christianity's disentanglement from Judaism was the interest in the why and how of Christianity's expansion into the larger Greco-Roman world. What Christianity became proved to be the more enduring question than what Christianity had been or began as.

a. Gnosticism

As already indicated,[100] the Hellenization of early Christianity became a subject of great fascination towards the end of the nineteenth century. It had al-

---

98. Much as imprecatory Psalms like Ps. 137.8-9 are rarely if ever used in Christian worship.

99. BDAG's translation of *Ioudaios* as 'Judean' (but see *Jesus Remembered* §9 n.28) raises the possibility of diminishing the negative implications of rendering the hostile references to *hoi Ioudaioi* in John as 'the Judeans', as in D. H. Stern, *Jewish New Testament: A Translation of the New Testament That Expresses Its Jewishness* (Jerusalem: Jewish New Testament Publications, 1989). See further the notes by A. Reinhartz and J. D. Garroway in A.-J. Levine and M. Z. Brettler, eds., *The Jewish Annotated New Testament* (Oxford University, 2011) 154-56 and 524-26; also §46.5c below.

100. *Beginning from Jerusalem* §20.3.

ways been recognized that during the patristic period Christian thought drew progressively on the language and ideas of Greek philosophy to express what were emerging as its distinctive theological claims, particularly in reference to Christ. In this, of course, they were following a course already opened up by the Jewish philosopher, Philo of Alexandria, an older contemporary of Paul's. In his expositions of the Torah, Philo of Alexandria had adapted Platonic and Stoic ideas and language and had demonstrated that by penetrating below the surface of the biblical text, including its problem passages, and by use of allegorical interpretation, more profound claims about God and insights into divine revelation could be sustained.[101] Not surprisingly, perhaps, the Alexandrian school of Christian theology, as represented particularly by Clement of Alexandria and Origen, was greatly influenced by Philo. And Philo's Logos theology provided such an effective precedent for Christianity's Logos christology that he could be regarded as an honorary Church Father.[102]

The Liberal Protestantism of the late nineteenth century, in focusing on the moralistic message of Jesus and posing a sharp contrast between the historical Jesus and the Christ of faith, had regarded the drift into dogma as a somewhat unfortunate inevitability. Harnack regarded 'the influx of Hellenism, of the Greek spirit, and the union of the Gospel with it, (as forming) the greatest fact in the history of the Church in the second century',[103] but also as a grave corruption of Jesus' own gospel.[104] The rise of Gnosticism he saw as marking a still steeper decline — the acute Hellenization (or secularization) of Christianity.[105]

Gnosticism was well known as the greatest competitor with and threat to Christianity in the second and third centuries. From the Christian heresiol-

---

101. See e.g. E. R. Goodenough, *An Introduction to Philo Judaeus* (Oxford: Blackwell, 1940, ²1962); P. Borgen, 'Philo of Alexandria', *ABD* 5.333-42.

102. D. T. Runia, *Philo in Early Christian Literature: A Survey* (Assen: Van Gorcum, 1993) ch. 1.

103. A. von Harnack, *What Is Christianity?* (1900; ET London: Williams & Norgate, 1901; 5th edition, London: Ernest Benn, 1958) 145; Harnack felt able to date the 'real influx of definitely Greek thought and Greek life', the entrance of 'the religious philosophy of Greece' to Christianity, to about the year 130 (148).

104. 'Dogma in its conception and development is a work of the Greek spirit on the soil of the Gospel' (*History of Dogma* [³1900; ET London: Constable/New York: Dover, 1961] Vol. 1.17.

105. *History of Dogma* Book I ch. 4. See further K. L. King, *What Is Gnosticism?* (Cambridge: Harvard University Press, 2003) ch. 3.

ogists it is fairly easy to draw a clear picture of Gnosticism as they perceived it.[106] W. Foerster summarizes 'the main points of Gnosis' thus:[107]

1. Between this world and the God incomprehensible to our thought, the 'primal cause', there is an irreconcilable antagonism.
2. The 'self', the 'I' of the Gnostic, his 'spirit' or soul, is unalterably divine.
3. This 'I', however, has fallen into this world, has been imprisoned and anaesthetized by it, and cannot free itself from it.
4. Only the divine 'call' from the world of light looses the bonds of captivity.
5. But only at the end of the world does the divine element in man return again to its home.

We also know from the Christian heresiologists that there were several leading teachers associated with the Gnostic phenomenon. A brief survey of the most prominent fills out the picture of second-century Gnosticism through the eyes of the heresiologists, including the diversity of the different systems attributed to the teachers. I draw chiefly from the principal Christian spokesman writing within our period, Irenaeus, although the Nag Hammadi findings (n.125 below) have called in question some of Irenaeus's descriptions.[108]

Simon Magus is the same Simon of Samaria referred to in Acts 8. Justin Martyr, himself from Samaria, reports that Simon was a native of a Samaritan village named Gitto and came to Rome during the reign of Claudius (41-54) (*1 Apol.* 26.2). He is regarded in patristic texts as the originator of the Gnostic heresy,[109] no doubt in part at least influenced by the story in Acts 8, where Simon is said to have been hailed by the Samaritans as 'the power of God that is called Great' (Acts 8.10).[110] According to Irenaeus, Simon went about with

---

106. In what follows I draw on the texts conveniently collected by W. Foerster, *Gnosis: A Selection of Gnostic Texts; 1. Patristic Evidence* (Oxford: Clarendon, 1972). See also the earlier collection by R. M. Grant, *Gnosticism: An Anthology* (London: Collins, 1961).

107. Foerster, *Gnosis* 1.9. For Harnack's summary of Gnosticism's 'rule of faith', and W. Bousset's summary of Gnostic thought, see King, *Gnosticism* 62-63, 97-98.

108. See particularly A. Marjanen and P. Luomanen, eds., *A Companion to Second-Century Christian 'Heretics'* (Supp.VC 76; Leiden: Brill, 2005) — chapters with excellent bibliographies; also C. B. Smith, *No Longer Jews: The Search for Gnostic Origins* (Peabody: Hendrickson, 2004) 126-49, with tabulation summary of the various teachings (147-49).

109. E.g. Irenaeus, *adv. haer.* 1.23.2; 1.27.4; Eusebius, *HE* 2.13.5-6. To avoid the suggestion that Gnosticism was a single and early system I attempt to distinguish gnostic ideas from the more fully blown subsequent Gnostic systems.

110. Justin says he was considered to be a god (*1 Apol.* 26.2), but his report that a statue was erected to him at the Tiber with the inscription 'Simoni Deo Sancto' is probably a mistaken reading of a statue to the Sabine god Semo Sancus — H. J. Klauck, *The Apocryphal Acts of the Apostles: An Introduction* (2005; ET Waco: Baylor University, 2008) 90; Ehrman

a woman called Helena, and between them they represented an early Gnostic formulation: she, representing the first emanation (*Ennoia*, Thought) from the divine mind which was Simon, had descended to the lower regions, where she was detained by the powers and angels which she had generated and by which the world was formed, and was shut up in a human body, at last becoming a common prostitute; he as the redeemer who came to free her from slavery, and thus also, when the world was dissolved, to free those who followed him from the rule of them that made the world; the 'mystery priests [of this cult] live licentiously and perform sorceries' (*adv. haer.* 1.23.2-4).

Menander, also from Samaria, is remembered as a disciple and successor of Simon, who, like Simon, claimed to have been sent as a saviour for the salvation of men, and to have conquered the angels who created the world. 'His disciples received resurrection through baptism into him, and can no longer die' (*adv. haer.* 1.23.5). If Simon was indeed a contemporary of Peter, then he must have flourished in the middle of the first century, and Menander somewhat later.

Cerinthus, probably late first century, likewise taught that the world was not created by the first God, but by a power remote and separated from the supreme power, which did not know the God who is over all. He is forever remembered as teaching that Jesus was the ordinary son of Joseph and Mary, upon whom, after his baptism, Christ descended in the form of a dove; 'but at the end Christ separated again from Jesus, and Jesus suffered and was raised again, but Christ remained impassible' (*adv. haer.* 1.26.1).[111]

Carpocrates, said to have lived under Hadrian (117-38),[112] claimed that the world had been made by angels, much inferior to the unbegotten Father. An intriguing facet of Carpocratian teaching was their interpretation of Matt. 5.25-26: the prison, from which no deliverance is possible until the last farthing has been paid, is the body (Irenaeus, *adv. haer.* 1.25.4). According to Clement of Alexandria (some of) the Carpocratians' 'love-feasts' were dissolute and licentious (*Strom.* 3.2).

Basilides was active in Alexandria before 150, and was thought by some to be the first of the Gnostics.[113] He gives the first elaborate sequence of aeons,

---

reproduces a photo of the inscription (*Lost Christianities* 166). On the legends of further conflict between Peter and Simon see below §48.6c.

111. See also *ODCC* 313-14; and further M. Myllykoski, 'Cerinthus', in Marjanen and Luomanen, *Companion* 213-46, who argues that Cerinthus was not an early Gnostic but a spokesman for a traditional possession or separation christology.

112. Foerster, *Gnosis* 1.34, citing Theodoret, *Haer. Fab.* 1.5.

113. B. A. Pearson, 'Basilides the Gnostic', in Marjanen and Luomanen, *Companion* 1-31 (here 1). 'Basilidian gnosis seems not to have taken hold outside of Egypt, but in Egypt it spread throughout the country and persisted into the late fourth century.' 'Basilides was

powers and angels which descend from the unoriginate Father, from which 365 heavens are created. The last angels created the world and apportioned the nations; their chief, the Jewish God, wanted his nation to subjugate the others. Into this situation the Most High God sent his first-born Nous, that is Christ, 'to liberate those who believe in him from the power of those who made the world'. He could not suffer, but made Simon of Cyrene assume his appearance, while he, in the form of Simon, stood laughing at them.[114] Belief, then, should not be in the crucified, but in him who came in the form of a man and was only supposed to have been crucified. 'If anyone confesses the crucified, he is still a slave, and under the power of those who made the bodies; he who denies [the crucified] has been set free from them, and he knows the [saving] dispensation made by the unoriginate Father. Salvation is for their soul alone; the body is by nature corruptible' (Irenaeus, *adv. haer.* 1.24.3-5).[115]

Valentinus was the most prominent and probably most influential of the Gnostic teachers.[116] He came from Egypt to Rome about 136 and was active as a teacher there, having several pupils who themselves became very influential, including Ptolemy/Ptolemaeus, Heracleon and Marcus. Although a plausible candidate to become bishop of Rome, he was passed over and withdrew from the church, went to the East, but later returned to Rome where he died about 165.[117] The different schools of Valentinianism also promulgated an elaborate process of decline from the heavenly Pleroma (Irenaeus, *adv. haer.* 1.1-5), the fundamental disjointedness beginning when Sophia misbegets a formless substance without her consort.[118] But a distinctive feature was the introduc-

---

a Gnostic. But, more importantly, he was a Christian.... Indeed, he can truly be said to be the very first Christian philosopher known to us' (28).

114. See further Pearson, 'Basilides the Gnostic' 21-24.

115. According to Hippolytus's rather different account, Basilides had an entirely monistic system, with 'no need of any evil matter, or of an evil or even a merely mediating creator' (Foerster, *Gnosis* 1.62; see further 62-83; *ODCC* 168-69).

116. Irenaeus begins his *adversus haereses* with a lengthy description and critique of the ideas of the disciples of Valentinus (*adv. haer.* 1.1-8). See particularly C. Markschies, *Valentinus Gnosticus? Untersuchungen zur valentinianischen Gnosis mit einem Kommentar zu den Fragmenten Valentin* (WUNT 65; Tübingen: Mohr Siebeck, 1992); also I. Dunderberg, 'The School of Valentinus', in Marjanen and Luomanen, *Companion* 64-99.

117. 'There is no evidence that Valentinus or any other Valentinian teacher was excommunicated in Rome in the second century.... Victor, Bishop of Rome (189-199), still had a Valentinian presbyter called Florinus as his assistant.... It was only later, at the turn of the third century, that Marcosians clearly formed a church of their own' (Dunderberg, 'School of Valentinus' 95-97).

118. See e.g. K. Rudolph, *Gnosis: The Nature and History of an Ancient Religion* (Edinburgh: T & T Clark, 1983) 78-81. Markschies and Dunderberg note that 'the surviving fragments from Valentinus' own teaching betray no close contact to the Valentinian body of thought described by Irenaeus' (Dunderberg, 'School of Valentinus' 70, also 66, 85), but

tion of an intermediate class of people, the psychics, between the spiritual people (pneumatics) and the earthly people (choics). According to Irenaeus on the system of Ptolemaeus, the Gnostics regarded those 'of the Church' as psychics who could be saved by good conduct, whereas they saw themselves as pneumatics, who would be saved 'not by means of conduct, but because they are spiritual by nature'; but it was impossible for the choics to be saved.[119] A further variation is that the world is a product of error or ignorance and not to be identified with evil.[120] But characteristic is Irenaeus's description of the Valentinianism of Marcus: 'They claim that they have more knowledge than all others, and that they alone have attained the greatness of the knowledge of the ineffable power'; 'The inner, spiritual man is redeemed through knowledge: sufficient for them is the knowledge of all things, and this is the true redemption' (*adv. haer.* 1.13.6; 21.4).

From a Eusebian perspective on the history of Christianity it was then simply a matter of describing how Christianity fended off these 'savage wolves' which Paul had warned would come among the church founded by the apostles, 'not sparing the flock' (Acts 20.29), a warning often echoed in the following century,[121] reinforcing the idea of 'false teaching' as a later corruption of the teaching of the apostles, of 'heresy' as 'orthodoxy' corrupted.[122]

b. The Question of Pre-Christian Gnosticism

In the late nineteenth century the History of Religions School, however, turned the assumption of a gradual Hellenization of Christianity upside down by arguing that Hellenistic elements were integrated into Christianity from the earliest days, in terms particularly of cultic ritual and Christ mysticism.[123] Still more challenging was the great push in the early twentieth century for a reassessment of Gnosticism: that Gnostic ideas were not later corruptions

---

Dunderberg also confirms that 'there is multiple attestation for the existence of the basic Valentinian myth, though there is considerable variation in details' (71), and that 'Theodotus was closer than any other Valentinian teachers . . . to the Valentinian body of thought described by Irenaeus' (81).

119. Irenaeus, *adv. haer.* 1.6.2, 4; 1.7.5. 'The spiritual is saved by nature; the psychic, being possessed of free will, has an inclination towards faith and towards incorruptibility, but also towards unbelief and destruction, according to its own choice; but the material perishes by nature' (Clem. Alex., *Excerpta ex Theodoto* 55.3).

120. Foerster, *Gnosis* 1.121-22.

121. *Did.* 16.3; Ignatius, *Philad.* 2.2; *2 Clem.* 5.2-4; Justin, *Dial.* 35.3.

122. It was this view of Christianity's beginnings, original purity corrupted by later error, which Bauer undermined (see Bauer, *Orthodoxy* xxiii).

123. See again *Beginning from Jerusalem* 36-40.

of or intrusions into Christianity, but were integral to the gospel proclaimed by Paul and expressed in John's Gospel. The quest for pre-Christian Gnosticism was a dominant feature of NT studies in the middle decades of the twentieth century.[124]

Since then there have been two major developments. The first, and still the more important, has been the discovery of a library of fourth-century papyrus manuscripts at Nag Hammadi in Egypt in 1945, written in Coptic.[125] These (or most of them) are generally regarded as Gnostic in character, and may indeed be described as Gnostic documents, expressive of a Gnostic religious world-view or ideology. Their importance is immeasurable for historians of religion in particular, since prior to that time our knowledge of Gnostic systems was more or less confined to the references to them in patristic Christianity. And since the references are uniformly disparaging (Gnosticism being treated as a Christian 'heresy'), it had been difficult for modern historians to gain an unbiased view of the philosophies and ideologies involved.[126] But now the Nag Hammadi library has provided us with Gnostic documents in their own terms,[127] so that a clearer perspective can be gained on what can or should be described as 'Gnostic', and on how Gnostic ideas interacted with what emerged into the second century as 'Christianity'.

The Nag Hammadi documents both shattered the idea that there was a distinctive historical phenomenon which could be described as 'Gnosticism',[128] and at the same time gave a clearer and more diverse perspective on themes and issues which the heresiologists had treated in a very tendentious way. For example, many Nag Hammadi texts have no evil Demiurge, and for Ptolemy

---

124. I summarize *Beginning from Jerusalem* 40-42. The push is particularly identified with R. Reitzenstein, W. Bousset and R. Bultmann (40-41). For Bultmann's outline of the pre-Christian Gnostic redeemer myth, see King, *Gnosticism* 102-3; and Bultmann's *Theology of the New Testament* (vol. 1; ET London: SCM, 1952) 165-67; he saw *The Gospel of John* (1941; ET Oxford: Blackwell, 1971) as presupposing (and correcting) Gnosticism. See further King, *Gnosticism* 83-107 and below §43 n.161.

125. For an account of the discovery of the codices and a brief introduction, see particularly Rudolph, *Gnosis* 34-52; J. M. Robinson, ed., *The Nag Hammadi Library* (Leiden: Brill, ³1988) 1-26: 'the library of fourth-century papyrus manuscripts consists of twelve codices plus eight leaves from a thirteenth and contains fifty-two separate tractates, . . . forty-five separate titles' (ix). See also W. Foerster, *Gnosis 2. Coptic and Mandaic Sources* (Oxford: Clarendon, 1974). N. D. Lewis and J. A. Blunt, 'Rethinking the Origins of the Nag Hammadi Codices', *JBL* 133 (2014) 399-419, question the deductions made by Robinson and argue that the codices may have derived from private Greco-Egyptian citizens in late antiquity.

126. See the critique of the early heresiologists by Rudolph, *Gnosis* 10-25.

127. Several of them are clearly representative of Valentinianism — notably the *Gospel of Truth*, the *Gospel of Philip*, and *The Treatise on the Resurrection* (King, *Gnosticism* 154).

128. See below n.143.

the creator God is neither good nor evil, but merely just.[129] In *The Tripartite Tractate* the primary emanations from the Father, the Son and the Church, together with the Father form an initial triad or trinity (57.8–59.38).[130] In *The Book of Thomas the Contender* 'the Gnostic myth of the creation of the world by a divine accident or evil power is neither mentioned nor apparently presupposed, and the dualism of the treatise is much more anthropological (body/soul) than cosmic (the above/below)'.[131] In the (albeit Valentinian) *Gospel of Truth* Sophia is absent. Again, the resolution of the tension between body and spirit, as resolved in docetic christology, is more nuanced than had previously been appreciated,[132] and the *Gospel of Truth* shows no qualms in describing Jesus as 'nailed to the tree' without qualification (*NHL* I.20.25). And 'while most of the Nag Hammadi texts tend toward asceticism, there is no evidence in the corpus for libertine views or practices'.[133] The Nag Hammadi texts also made scholars more alert to the distinctive character of the Sethians (Irenaeus, *adv. haer.* 1.30; Hippolytus, *Ref.* 5.14-17).[134]

At the same time, however, the Nag Hammadi texts confirmed and elaborated many of the key features attributed to Gnostic teaching by the heresiologists. For example, as might have been expected from the heresiologists' accounts, the list of emanations from the Monad, the great invisible Spirit, is extensive (as in the *Apocryphon of John* and the *Gospel of the Egyptians*), and the cosmic myth of the fall of Sophia is found in many of the texts.[135] In the *Exegesis of the Soul* unusually the soul is female and she follows a path similar to that of Helena in Irenaeus's account of Simon Magus. And *The Tripartite Tractate* provides the clearest expression of the Valentinian tripartition of mankind into the spiritual, the psychic and the material (118.14–122.12). Somewhat striking, then, is the fact that the 1966 Messina Colloquium on Gnosticism could still summarize second-century 'Gnosticism' as 'the idea of

---

129. King, *Gnosticism* 46, 187-88.

130. Cf. the *Trimorphic Protennoia* which develops the ancient distinction between the unexpressed thought (*logos endiathetos*) and the thought expressed in speech (*logos prophorikos*) into a triadic expression.

131. J. D. Turner, *NHL* 200.

132. King, *Gnosticism* 208-13. On 'Docetism' see Rudolph, *Gnosis* 157-71.

133. King, *Gnosticism* 203; see 201-8.

134. King, *Gnosticism* 156-62. Clement of Alexandria explains why Seth was given special prominence: 'From Adam three natures are derived: first, the irrational, from which Cain comes; secondly, the rational and just, from which Abel springs; and thirdly, the spiritual, from which Seth comes' (*Exc. Theod.* 54.1-2). See also M. A. Williams, 'Sethianism', in Marjanen and Luomanen, *Companion* 32-63.

135. E.g., the *Gospel of Truth*, the *Apocryphon of John*, the *Hypostasis of the Archons* and *On the Origins of the World*; Hippolytus's account of Valentinianism (*Ref.* 6.30.6–6.34.1). See also Rudolph, *Gnosis* 320-22. On the *Apocryphon of John* see further below §49.7a.

a divine spark in man, deriving from the divine realm, fallen into this world of fate, birth and death, and needing to be awakened by the divine counterpart of the self in order to be finally reintegrated'.[136]

Ironically, the discovery of the Nag Hammadi library more or less coincided with the beginning of a broad retreat from the quest for pre-Christian Gnosticism — a growing recognition that 'pre-Christian Gnosticism' was more a twentieth-century construct than a first-century phenomenon. The conclusion steadily became more persuasive that language and motifs evident in the first century which were/(became) part of later systems should not be taken as evidence that the systems already existed.[137] A classic case was the Jewish Wisdom myth, as in *1 Enoch* 42, which indicates the sort of speculation which may have contributed to subsequent Gnostic speculation,[138] but which provides no evidence of a pre-Christian Gnostic redeemer myth. It was necessary to learn once again that parallel does not denote dependence, that analogy is not the same as genealogy.[139]

At the same time, the Nag Hammadi documents provided opportunity to argue that although themselves late (fourth century), perhaps they reflected or drew on earlier documents and oral traditions. So the question of Gnostic influence on or within earliest Christianity has not gone away. But the terms of the debate were changed. It is no longer a question whether 'the Gnostic Redeemer myth', so prominent in Bultmann's reconstruction of Christianity's emergence, was in fact pre-Christian. The observation that Christian claims for Jesus seem to have provided the precedent for Gnostic redeemer figures, like Simon Magus and Menander, rather than the reverse, is much the more persuasive.[140]

---

136. U. Bianchi, *Le origini dello Gnosticismo* (Leiden: Brill, 1967) xxvi-xxvii. See Rudolph's analysis of 'the essential basic features of Gnosis': gnosis — 'the basic insight into the divine nature of man, his origin and destiny'; a dualistic view of the world; the creation of the world as 'an explanation for the present condition of man, remote from God'; soteriology — including 'the idea of the heavenly journey of the soul' and 'the doctrine of the redeemer'; eschatology — 'the deliverance of the heavenly soul'; and cult and community (*Gnosis* 55-59; fully analysed, 59-272).

137. See particularly C. Colpe, *Die religionsgeschichtliche Schule: Darstellung und Kritik ihres Bildes vom gnostischen Erlösermythus* (Göttingen: Vandenhoeck & Ruprecht, 1961); also King, *Gnosticism* 109, 137-47: 'The pre-Christian Gnostic redeemer myth was the invention of modern scholarship' (138).

138. G. W. MacRae, 'The Jewish Background of the Gnostic Sophia Myth', *NovT* 12 (1970) 86-101.

139. See also Rudolph, *Gnosis* 307-8.

140. As R. M. Grant, ed., *Gnosticism: An Anthology* (London: Collins, 1961), put it: 'The most obvious explanation of the origin of the Gnostic redeemer is that he was modelled after the Christian conception of Jesus. It seems significant that we know no redeemer before Jesus, while we encounter other redeemers (Simon Magus, Menander) immediately after his time' (18).

The issue, then, is no longer in terms of influence on the gospel as it spread into the wider Greco-Roman world (baptism, ritual meals, Christ mysticism, redeemer myth). The question now is whether some of the Nag Hammadi texts provide evidence that Gnostic influence reaches back into the teaching of Jesus himself (the Jesus tradition). More precisely, the issue is whether some Nag Hammadi texts show that Jesus was heard and perceived by some early or earliest followers in different terms from those encapsulated in the NT Gospels. The most prominent case has been made for the *Gospel of Thomas*, the most famous of the Nag Hammadi texts.[141] Does it go back to the first century? Was its earliest form as early as or earlier than the NT Gospels? Does it provide evidence of how Jesus was heard and understood already in the first century or early in the second? Does it demonstrate that there was teaching available to the NT Gospel writers, which they took on board only partially, and which others preserved and developed? Is there evidence in the NT Gospels that one or more of the NT Evangelists were reacting against views still preserved in some of the Nag Hammadi codices?[142] There are crucial questions here which we will have to deal with, particularly in relation to the issue of the continuing impact of the Jesus tradition into the second century (§44).

c. The Question of Gnosticism

The second major development cuts across but also interacts with the first. It is the rise of the question whether it is justified to speak of 'Gnosticism' at all. Like 'the pre-Christian Gnostic Redeemer myth', and the 'divine man' — important reference points in twentieth-century NT study — 'Gnosticism' itself has also come to be regarded as more a modern construct than a historical phenomenon.[143]

---

141. The first edition of the *Gospel of Thomas* is dated to 30-60 CE by J. D. Crossan, *The Historical Jesus: The Life of a Mediterranean Jewish Peasant* (San Francisco: Harper, 1991). And note the title of R. W. Funk and R. W. Hoover, *The Five Gospels: The Search for the Authentic Words of Jesus* (New York: Macmillan, 1993), the fifth, of course, being the *Gospel of Thomas*. I offered a provisional treatment of the *Gospel of Thomas* in *Jesus Remembered* §7.6.

142. The issues here have been posed most sharply by H. Koester, *Ancient Christian Gospels: Their History and Development* (London: SCM, 1990).

143. See particularly M. A. Williams, *Rethinking "Gnosticism": An Argument for Dismantling a Dubious Category* (Princeton University, 1996); and King, *Gnosticism*: 'There was and is no such thing as Gnosticism, if we mean by that some kind of ancient religious entity with a single origin and a distinct set of characteristics. Gnosticism is, rather, a term invented in the early modern period to aid in defining the boundaries of normative Christ-

The debate at the beginning of the twenty-first century, then, is not so much whether these views should be labeled as 'Gnostic'. It is rather whether there was a single recognizable phenomenon which may be entitled 'Gnosticism'. Or are we actually talking about a series of religious ideas which may not have cohered into a single recognizable system, but some or all of which influenced a diverse range of individuals and groups/schools of thought? And the debate for us in particular would be whether some or any of these ideas were much more integral to early forms of Christianity than has traditionally been recognized.[144] Did the later Gnostic systems or groups actually draw more closely on Jesus and Paul than the great church cared to recognize or admit? Should any of the Gnostic systems be regarded as sub-sets of a very diverse phenomenon (Christianity), or should we return to the patristic view of 'Gnosticism' as a Christian heresy?[145]

Without becoming caught up in the ongoing debate as to whether we can speak of Gnosticism (or Gnosticisms), or the debate on origins of 'Gnosticism',[146] we can at least agree that there were ideas about the human condition, about the reasons for it and about its resolution which were widespread in the Near East and Greco-Roman world and which provided an alternative or counterpoint or complementary (differently perceived by different people) explanation and solution to the gospel as articulated by Paul and his successors.[147] We can readily sketch in what seem to have been its chief elements, as indicated not just from the Christian heresiologists but from various of the Nag Hammadi documents.

- A sense that the real person, the 'I', is distinct from the physical body in which the 'I' lives or which embodies the 'I', and a dissatisfaction with

---

ianity' (King, *Gnosticism* 1-2; see also 108); 'In the end, I think the term "Gnosticism" will most likely be abandoned, at least in its present usage' (218).

144. The issues posed by Bauer, as noted at the beginning of this study (*Jesus Remembered* 5).

145. S. Pétrement, *A Separate God: The Christian Origins of Gnosticism* (San Francisco: HarperCollins, 1994), has revived the view that Gnosticism was originally a second-century Christian heresy.

146. See King, *Gnosticism* 169-98; Smith, *No Longer Jews,* who argues that Gnosticism arose in a Jewish Egyptian context following the revolt under Trajan; 'Primary among the candidates for the genesis of Gnosticism are alienated Jewish intellectuals, Jewish Christians, and Platonic converts to Judaism or Jewish Christianity' (244).

147. See particularly the Messina colloquium definition at n.136 above; also B. A. Pearson, 'Gnosticism as a Religion', *Gnosticism and Christianity in Roman and Coptic Egypt* (New York: Continuum, 2004) 201-23. It is important not to limit the referent 'Gnostic' to the full-blown systems involving multiple aeons and an evil or ignorant demiurge. See also C. Markschies, *Gnosis: An Introduction* (London: T & T Clark, 2003).

the body's limitations, some degree of discomfort, disjointedness, even alienation from the material context and constraints of this life.[148] This I suspect was the common root of the various more elaborate systems which evolved ultimately to explain and resolve this existential Angst.

- This readily chimed in with a basically Platonic dualism between mind/spirit and matter. An obvious outworking of any feeling of alienation would have been to regard the physical and material as inferior, negative or evil in character, the human being as imprisoned within this physical body and material world;[149] but the true person (the 'I', or the soul) as spiritual and belonging to a different realm (the spiritual world, heaven).[150]

- A similarly natural elaboration is to regard creation (of the material world) as not the work of God, or of the ultimate God, but of a lesser divine being, the Demiurge of Plato's *Timaeus*, 'the god of this world'. In the developed systems the analysis of the falling away from the supreme being until the being emerges who created the material world is marked by a lengthy sequence of decline in quality and character of aeons or emanations.[151]

- The true spiritual person (the soul) is usually blind to its true nature and its imprisoned condition (the parallel of drunkenness is often drawn). Salvation for the imprisoned soul, then, is achieved by knowledge (*gnosis*) being brought to it/him, knowledge of its/his true nature.[152] In the

---

148. This emphasis was brought out particularly by H. Jonas, *The Gnostic Religion: The Message of the Alien God and the Beginning of Christianity* (Boston: Beacon, ²1958). It is not surprising that the interest in Gnosticism arose when Existentialism was a dominant force in European philosophy since the existentialist sense of *Geworfenheit* ('thrownness') matched the Gnostic's sense of 'alienation' so closely (cf. Rudolph, *Gnosis* 33-34).

149. The Orphic belief that 'the body (*sōma*) is the tomb (*sēma*) of the soul' was referred to by Plato more than once (*Gorgias* 493a; *Phaedr.* 250c); see E. Schweizer, *TDNT* 7.1026, 1028.

150. 'The totality of Gnosis can be comprehended in a single image. This is the image of "gold in the mud"'; 'The mud is that of the world: it is first of all the body, which with its sensual desires drags man down and holds the "I" in thrall'. All the Gnostic systems 'have the one aim, to explain how the opposition of the divine world and the world in which man now lives came about, how it happens that a divine part lies imprisoned in this world in the Gnostic' (Foerster, *Gnosis* 1.2-3, 9). Of the Nag Hammadi texts, the *Gospel of Truth* and the *Gospel of Thomas* express this perspective clearly; see below §43.2c(ii).

151. One of the most elaborate Gnostic systems on this point was Barbelognosis, as represented by Irenaeus, *adv. haer.* 1.29.1-4; but also the Valentinians as reported e.g. by Hippolytus, *Ref.* 6.25, and represented by the Nag Hammadi *Apocryphon of John* (Foerster, *Gnosis* 1 ch. 7; F. Wisse, 'The Apocryphon of John', *NHL* 104-24). Rudolph illustrates the world-view diagrammatically (*Gnosis* 68-69).

152. A classic example is the *Gospel of Truth* (*NHL* I.22.13-20): 'He who is to have

developed systems this knowledge is provided by a divine redeemer figure who imparts the *gnosis* to the imprisoned spiritual beings,[153] so that when the material corrupts into death the soul can escape, by means of passwords given by the divine redeemer, through the ranks of lesser divine beings back to its celestial home.
- Given such antagonism to the material body, the true Gnostic would normally regard it as his responsibility to live an ascetic life. Some may have concluded that it was equally appropriate to live a self-indulgent and licentious life, since, after all, the body does not count in the process of salvation,[154] but, as already noted,[155] that may be the result of the same sort of black propaganda which accused the Christian love-feasts of serving as excuses and covers for debauchery.

As the last century has vividly demonstrated, there was an almost unquenchable instinct on the part of scholars of the period to construct out of these elements a system ('Gnosticism'), with the chief argument being whether this system or systems predated Christianity, or were indeed, as the Christian heresiologists maintained, later corruptions which grew on and round Christianity. In fact, however, it is unnecessary to go down this track or to debate the issue of origins.[156] What is clear is that there were such ideas, held individually or variously grouped, and that those who held to these ideas were regarded as a threat by the principal Christian thinkers of the late second and into the third century who have come down to us. Whether we call them 'Gnostic' or

---

knowledge in this manner knows where he comes from and where he is going. He knows as one who having been drunk has turned away from his drunkenness, (and) having returned to himself, has set right what are his own' (*NHL* 42). Clement of Alexandria provides a summation of Gnostic self-understanding: 'It is not the bath (washing) alone which makes us free, but also the knowledge: who were we? what have we become? where were we? into what place have we been cast? whither are we hastening? from what are we delivered? what is birth? what is rebirth?' (*Exc. Theod.* 78.2; Foerster, *Gnosis* 1.230). Williams notes that 'most of the Sethian sources reflect a preoccupation with the question of human nature and human origins.... Recovery of an awareness of one's membership in this divine family belongs to the essence of salvation in Sethian traditions' ('Sethianism' 58).

153. 'Many Gnostic systems have a "Redeemer", a figure from the world of light who awakens the divine element in man from its stupor and breaks through the spell of oblivion' (Foerster, *Gnosis* 1.14); the variation of the 'redeemed Redeemer' is not so frequent as was earlier assumed (1.16-17; Rudolph, *Gnosis* 121-31). This, of course, was where Jesus was slotted in (or contributed to) the Gnostic redemption myth (Rudolph, *Gnosis* 148-56).

154. 'From the basic theme of hostility to the body Gnosis derived not only asceticism but also its converse, libertinism, in which man shows his contempt for the body and satisfies its desires because fundamentally they are no concern of his' (Foerster, *Gnosis* 1.3).

155. Above n.122.

156. A principal concern of the debate on 'Gnosticism', as King shows (n.143 above).

infer a system of 'Gnosticism' does not count for anything. What matters is that there were abroad such influential ideas, as referred to by the heresiologists and as documented by the Nag Hammadi texts. The real question for us, then, is whether these ideas influenced the early Christians, or were taken up by them, or even sprang from Paul, or John, or Jesus.

d. Marcion

And then there is Marcion, who is sometimes regarded as a Gnostic, and whose theology certainly can be described as having a Gnostic tint, but who was an independent thinker.[157] The little that we know about his history can be told briefly.[158] He was born in Sinope in Pontus in the late first century. Pseudo-Tertullian's report that he was the son of a bishop of Sinope, but was excommunicated by his father for seducing a virgin (*adv. haer.* 6), may have to be set aside as another case of black propaganda. But Tertullian's reference to Marcion as 'that shipmaster of Pontus, the zealous student of Stoicism' (*de praescr. haer.* 30) may be ranked as good information. He came to Rome in the 130s, was active there and in western Asia Minor, and was excommunicated from Rome in 144 ('the "one secure date" of Marcion's career')[159] for maintaining that the church had been mistaken in retaining the OT and in claiming that Jesus was the Messiah foretold by the prophets.

His most famous writing, *Antitheses* (Tertullian, *adv. Marc.* 5.1), was built on a sharp antithesis between the creator God and the God revealed by Jesus, and between the Old Testament and a Christianity constructed round a dismembered Paul and a mutilated Gospel of Luke.[160] It evidently proved to be

---

157. See Rudolph, *Gnosis* 313-16; S. Moll, *The Arch-Heretic Marcion* (WUNT 250; Tübingen: Mohr Siebeck, 2010) 72-74 — 'Although Marcion certainly believes in Christ as a redeemer figure who "descends from a higher sphere and ascends to it again", he would never emphasise *knowledge* as being crucial in any way. For Marcion, it is faith in Christ which leads to salvation' (74). H. Räisänen, 'Marcion', in Marjanen and Luomanen, *Companion* 100-124: 'Marcion acknowledges no divine spark in man. . . . Even his docetism is incomplete: Christ suffers and dies' (107). See also §47 n.177 below.

158. Moll, *Marcion* ch. 2. See further R. J. Hoffmann, *Marcion: On the Restitution of Christianity* (AARAS 46; Chico: Scholars, 1984) chs. 1-2.

159. J. J. Clabeaux, 'Marcion', *ABD* 4.514.

160. The classic study remains that of A. Harnack, *Marcion: Das Evangelium vom fremden Gott* (Leipzig: Hinrichs, 1924), but Moll disputes Harnack's influential view that Marcion simply rejected the Old Testament and argues as one of his key theses: 'Marcion did not understand the Old Testament in the light of the New, he interpreted the New Testament in the light of the Old' (*Marcion* 82, 106). Räisänen notes that Marcion read the OT in a literal way, in protest against the more 'orthodox' treatment of the OT's difficult

a major attraction for many who presumably liked their faith and world-view to be drawn in clear black and white colours. At all events Marcion set out to organize his own church, 'the True Church' in his mind. 'Marcion's church taught from its own scriptures and required sexual abstinence (procreation being a command of the Creator God), but otherwise looked very much like the church which had rejected him.... Scholars conjecture that in numbers alone the Marcionites may have nearly surpassed non-Marcionites in the decades of the 160s and 170s'.[161] Marcion's church had faded in the West before the time of Constantine but remained strong in the East for several centuries.[162]

However, since he was heavily influenced by Paul and can be regarded as a radical Paulinist, we will leave further consideration of Marcion till we deal with the continuing influence of Paul into the second century (§47).

38.5 A Contested Identity

The history of Christianity between 70 and 180 is much more complex, then, than has traditionally been thought. Or perhaps the point should be made more sharply: the history of Christianity (the actual sequel and succession of events) is much more complex than the history of Christianity (the account given by ecclesiastical historians) has usually allowed for. The historical reality was evidently much more of a tension and struggle between competing ideas/faiths/practices than the disputed but apparently irresistible emergence of the great church with a clearly defined rule of faith and clearly defined structures. There were those who promoted and fought for a clear-cut identity, especially in episcopal structure, an identity over against Jew, Jewish-Christian and Gnostic; but the everyday reality was different groups defining themselves variously by reference to Jesus. The identity of what was and what should

---

passages by allegorizing them. 'To Marcion goes the credit for not explaining away the moral problems raised by the Old Testament.... Marcion read the Old Testament with common sense' ('Marcion' 108-9).

161. Clabeaux, *ABD* 4.515; 'For many in the second century, whether Christian believers or outside observers, the word "Christianity" would have meant "Marcionite Christianity"' (Wilson, *Related Strangers* 208; see Justin, *1 Apol.* 26.5 and 58.1-2; Tertullian, *adv. Marc.* 5.19; Harnack, *Marcion* 153-60). Moll maintains that the members of Marcion's church were not converts from paganism or Judaism but were exclusively poached from the orthodox church — Justin likened Marcion to a wolf that snatches away lambs from the flock (*1 Apol.* 58.2) — which also explains why 'the great church' saw Marcion as such a dangerous threat (*Marcion* 128-29).

162. 'In the East, traces of Marcionite groups are found in Arabic sources as late as the 10th century' (Räisänen, 'Marcion' 101).

count as 'Christianity' was still in process of definition, and contested on all the main factors which make for identity.

How to trace this process of definition? Not, I think, by looking forward and taking our lead from what eventuated. That is certainly a possible way to proceed, as we have seen. The problem is, however, that it allows the eventual outcome to determine the evaluation of the various conflicts and tensions. In crude terms, it assumes the model of history-writing as the account given by the winners. It assumes that what was left behind or disowned was of no value or worth to be taken seriously. It assumes that self-definition by opposition and antithesis was not only the way Christian identity was formed but the only way. It assumes that 'Gnosticism' was a well-defined entity which by definition could have no place in Christianity. It assumes that all that was not 'orthodoxy' was irretrievably 'heresy', and not just the loser in some game of imperial power politics.

My preference is to look at the period from the opposite direction. Not from the future, from what was to eventuate or be achieved, to evaluate all the historical data from the perspective of how it came to be regarded by Eusebius and his fellows. But from the past, that is, from the character of the first generation we have so far sketched out, from the perspective of those who gave the beginnings of Christianity its strength and opened up its potentiality and possibilities for the future. I want to ask the unrealistic, but nevertheless fascinating question: would Peter, James and Paul have been as satisfied with what happened in the second century, and thereafter, as Eusebius was? Would they have affirmed that the emergence of the great church, the antithesis with Judaism, the disowning of Jewish-Christianity and denunciation of the Gnostic variation, was the best or most desirable outcome of the influences they experienced and the convictions they held dear? And were there other formative influences which were operative during the first generation but which have so far been hidden from our sight (above all, the influence of John)? As these influences begin to come into view, how do they affect evaluation of the other formative figures of the first generation and of their influence? As embryonic Christianity comes to birth, are we actually confronted with a single child or twins or triplets, or . . . ?

Consequently I structure this third volume by asking how the major factors which shaped first-generation Christianity were received into the second, third and fourth generations. In each case the answer is that their influence was still prized and laid claim to, but also that their heritage was contested and the definition which they gave to Christianity was in effect the subject of intense controversy. As we saw in *Beginning from Jerusalem*, the defining factors in first-generation Christianity were fourfold, to which must be added the contribution of John (John's Gospel and letters), and it is on these that we focus in what follows:

- the Jesus tradition, as the principal means by which the mission of Jesus continued to exert its impact on subsequent generations — embodied and slowly constricted within the written Gospels, diverse as between even the canonical Gospels, but contested in content and character by other claimants to embody and carry forward the impact of Jesus; in short, the emergence of the Gospel format (§§41-44);
- the impact of James in offering a different model of Jewish and Gentile church — his heritage largely lost to sight for those who defined Christianity over against Judaism and largely yielded to the diverging 'Jewish-Christian' sects with only a modest struggle; the relationships between emerging Christianity and rabbinic Judaism, with the 'Jewish-Christian' overlap challenging both (§§45-46);
- the impact of Paul in shaping a Jewish messianic sect into a religion open to non-Jews and attracting increasing numbers of Gentiles — his heritage claimed by the Pastoral Epistles (and Acts), but also by Marcion, and in between a contest between the Clements and the Valentinians; the reception of Paul between 70 and 180 (§47);
- the impact of Peter, at times surprisingly hidden in the first generation, but exerting increasing force in the subsequent generations — his heritage increasingly claimed as first bishop of Rome, but as part of an institutionalizing and centralizing trend which was more controversial and controverted than the history of catholic Christianity has allowed (§48);
- the impact of John, hardly evident in the survey of the first generation, but a major voice at the turn of the first and second century — his impact raising fresh questions about the way the Jesus tradition was received, about the influences shaping Christianity, and his heritage being still more controversial and disputed in the period of our concern, not only by Gnostics but also by Montanists (§49);
- the findings of these chapters will inevitably call for some reassessment or refinement of the traditional account of the emergence of the 'notes of the church' — the rule of faith, christology, NT canon, and monarchical episcopacy — with Irenaeus marking the fulcrum or tipping point (§50).

This provides the outline structure for volume 3, but as in volumes 1 and 2 we have to begin by giving some account of the sources on which we draw.

CHAPTER 39

The Sources — First Century (the New Testament)

39.1 The Diversity and Character of the Source Material

In the Preface to the second volume of his *Introduction*, Helmut Koester notes that in order to reconstruct the historical development of early Christianity, the student 'must learn from the outset to understand the writings of the earliest period within their proper historical context'.[1] The history of early Christianity is a history of the early literature which the movement both spawned and provoked. So, as in the previous volumes of *Christianity in the Making*, we must begin by listing and assessing the value of our sources. Here, as already noted, we are in a very different situation from the one which confronted us in volumes 1 and 2. In *Jesus Remembered* the NT Gospels, or at least the Synoptic Gospels, provided the obvious lead sources round which other more secondary sources could be conveniently grouped. Likewise in *Beginning from Jerusalem* the Acts of the Apostles and the letters of Paul played a similar lead role. But now we have no equivalent. The most obvious candidate for such a role, Eusebius's *Ecclesiastical History*, is late (fourth century) and far from adequate for our purposes.

At the same time, however, there are actually far more documents available to us from the period under review than we had for the two periods already covered. Apart from the Pauline letters, more or less all the NT documents probably come from the thirty or so years following the destruction of Jerusalem. Although Second Temple Judaism in effect ended with the destruction of the Jerusalem temple, some of the most distinctive Jewish writings, notably the classic apocalypses of *4 Ezra* and *2 Baruch*, came from the same period, as did, of course, the writings of the Jewish historian Josephus. The Apostolic Fathers

---

1. Koester, *Introduction* 2.xvii.

follow closely on their heels. In terms of date, some of the classic Roman historians (notably Tacitus and Suetonius), as well as some of the sources drawn on by Eusebius (Papias and Hegesippus in particular), fall in the same period. There is debate as to the dating of Jewish-Christian, early Gnostic and various syncretistic writings, but a second century date for many at least of their traditions and sources is a very strong likelihood. And then there are the big figures of the middle and second half of the second century, notably Justin and Irenaeus, not to mention Valentinus and Marcion, to be considered. Finally there are the steadily increasing papyrological and epigraphical materials being uncovered for various centres. So materials we lack not.

The problem is how to correlate these materials and to draw on them for our inquiry. One option would be to use a chronological taxonomy: decide the dating of each document and piece of information and then review the documents in sequence.[2] Another would be to use a geographical taxonomy: decide where each item originated from and group them accordingly.[3] The problem in both cases is that many/most of both the dates and the locations of origin of the relevant literature are unclear and disputed. The consequence is that a mass of uncertainties and speculative hypotheses have to be lumped together with the limited number whose dates or locations are at least relatively more certain (the letters of Ignatius, for example),[4] which may skew the total picture or point towards conclusions which are then more confidently drawn than the evidence allows.

A third option, towards which I incline, is to look for broader trends and developments without trying to tie them too closely to particular places and times or to make their significance too dependent on such findings. This strategy, of course, does not exempt us from enquiring about authorship, dates and locations of the sources to be drawn on. What it does mean, and this is less satisfactory, is that it will make less sense to assign each of the most relevant documents to some particular chapter of the present volume to be dealt with completely there, as we were able to do with Paul's letters, precisely because dates and locations could be so much more precise. Instead, as each document contributes something towards the particular development being scrutinized, so we will draw on it. In some cases that will allow us to give a fairly comprehensive account of the document (as we did with the Pauline letters). In others an overall grasp of the document will be possible only by pulling together the discussions of the relevant sections of two or three chapters.

2. This can be done more effectively when a limited number of documents are in view, such as the Apostolic Fathers.
3. Notably Koester's *Introduction* vol. 2, as noted above §38 n.11.
4. But see §40 n.24 below.

An important preliminary point to be noted is that our use of the documents to be examined most closely depends on the extent to which we can be confident that the texts available to us are sufficiently close to what was originally written, for us to use them as evidence for the views and policies of that time. The actual sources we have are (a) the full text, but in a copy usually several centuries after it was written; (b) earlier but more fragmentary texts, sometimes much closer to the time when the text was written; (c) translations of the text from the language of original authorship to other Mediterranean languages; and (d) quotations (often at some length) from the documents or references to them by later writers.[5] In all this, as will become apparent, we are many times better off with the texts which became part of the NT than with the other documents to be drawn on. Whereas we have many texts, fragmentary, partial or complete for the NT writings, in regard to the others (e.g. apocryphal documents and Roman historians) we often have to depend on very few and much later copies. This will give more confidence regarding the early Christian writings, the main focus of our interest, that we have texts which are indeed close to what was written. The greater uncertainties regarding the other source material need cause us less concern since the material less directly bears upon our task. This is not to ignore the fact that the textual criticism of the NT writings does throw up important questions about the forms or versions of these writings known to different churches, but the issues raised thereby were only beginning to emerge in the late second century and can be referred to only briefly in §50.2a below.

The task of this chapter, then, is the fairly modest one of covering the traditional introductory questions, of author, place of writing (or place to which the writing bears testimony, implicitly or explicitly) and date of writing. In this task we may proceed, or at least start most sensibly by grouping the documents in what is likely to have been their chronological sequence — NT Gospels, the rest of the NT writings (§39), the Apostolic Fathers and Apologists (§40). It is more difficult to follow the same procedure when dealing with documents whose dating (or earlier form) is a matter of controversy. So the sequence of the rest of §40 is somewhat arbitrary — including the apocryphal Gospels, the apocryphal Acts, and the other Apocalypses. As will be appreciated, the procedure to be followed is more for convenience than anything else. Questions as to where some items are grouped and whether there are clear boundaries between the groups are not answered by this procedure.

---

5. This has been the range of information traditionally covered in attempts to recover the original text of the NT documents; see e.g. B. M. Metzger, *The Text of the New Testament: Its Transmission, Corruption, and Restoration* (Oxford University, 1964, [4]2005 with B. D. Ehrman); C. E. Hill and M. J. Kruger, eds., *The Early Text of the New Testament* (Oxford University, 2012).

At the end of §40 we will summarize our findings by indicating in a table the range of possible datings covered by the documents reviewed and the range of possible geographical areas from which they sprang and/or to which they were addressed.

39.2 The Canonical Gospels

I divide review of the early Christian Gospel material into two categories — the canonical Gospels (Matthew, Mark, Luke, John), and the other documents also usually known as Gospels. This is primarily a matter of compositional preference. A single chapter covering all the documents known as Gospels would be inordinately long. And though the procedure may be regarded as privileging the canonical Gospels over the rest, it actually reflects the most likely historical reality that the canonical Gospels appeared before the others and were more highly and more universally regarded as of authority and value than the others. There is an idealistic historicism which, understandably, wants not to be bound by early decisions made by churches and councils and to treat all relevant documentation 'on a level playing field'. But part of the historian's integrity is to recognize that some material *was* privileged in these early decades and centuries and to ask why. The consequent critique may well include criticism of the attempts to de-privilege or condemn several of the materials. But it is hardly distortive of history to acknowledge that some of the many first- and second-century documents were valued more highly and more widely than others, and to treat them first.

With the NT Gospels the amount of textual data drawn upon by textual critics is enormous. The four categories of sources listed above give us more than enough by which to grasp a clear form of each Gospel text and of its early history. We have (a) the great fourth-century uncials, Sinaiticus and Vaticanus, and subsequent copies; (b) papyrological fragments, in some cases from the second century; (c) translations of the Gospels, particularly Old Latin and Syriac, again in some cases reaching back to the fourth century; and (d) many quotations and references in the early Christian Fathers, again in several cases from the second century.[6]

---

6. Here we can draw on A. Gregory and C. Tuckett, eds., *The Reception of the New Testament in the Apostolic Fathers*, and *Trajectories through the New Testament and the Apostolic Fathers* (Oxford: Clarendon, 2005); previously the most useful reference work was the Oxford Society of Historical Theology's *The New Testament in the Apostolic Fathers* (Oxford: Clarendon, 1905).

a. The Gospel of Mark

I start with Mark[7] since I follow the strong consensus view that Mark was the earliest of the Gospels which became part of and foundational for the NT. This conclusion does not depend on secure dating having been established for each of these Gospels. It is purely a matter of their literary inter-relationships. I have already indicated the reasons why most scholars conclude from the character of these inter-relationships that Matthew and Luke were able to make use of the written Gospel of Mark when they came to write their own Gospels, and I need not cover the same ground again.[8] As to the usual introductory questions regarding author, date and place of writing, each influences the others and there is so little to go on, that it makes little difference in which order we take them. In this case, however, discussion of the place of writing depends so much on the issues of author and date that we leave the question of location, from which or for which, to the end.[9]

i. Author

The author is not named within the Gospel itself. This could imply a document written for a group familiar to and with the author. On the other hand, we should avoid the equivalent of the 'one document fallacy' referred to several times already in these volumes: that each community used only one document which can therefore be taken as a definitive expression of that community's theology.[10] The equivalent fallacy here is the assumption that each Gospel was written for a single or inter-related group of churches within a small area and therefore can be read as expressive of their theology as distinct from the theologies of other churches, nearby or more distant. However, each of the Gospels may have been written with a wider possible or likely circulation in view.[11]

---

7. For the text-critical data see A. Y. Collins, *Mark* (Hermeneia; Minneapolis: Fortress, 2007) 120-25.

8. See *Jesus Remembered* §7.3.

9. So far as the integrity of the text of Mark is concerned, the only substantial issue is its conclusion. However, there is little or no disagreement that Mark 16.9-20 is a later addition and a less strong consensus that the Gospel originally ended at 16.8 (see e.g. W. G. Kümmel, *Introduction to the New Testament* [Nashville: Abingdon, 1975] 99-101; B. M. Metzger, *A Textual Commentary on the Greek New Testament* [London: United Bible Societies, 1971, 1975] 122-28). U. Schnelle, *The History and Theology of the New Testament Writings* (1994; ET London: SCM, 1998) 207, and C. A. Evans, *Mark 8:27-16:20* (WBC 34B; Nashville: Nelson, 2001) 538-39, favour a lost ending.

10. See particularly *Jesus Remembered* 150-52.

11. See particularly R. Bauckham, 'For Whom Were the Gospels Written?', in R. Bauckham, ed., *The Gospels for All Christians: Rethinking the Gospel Audiences* (Grand Rapids: Eerdmans, 1998) ch. 1; Bauckham's argument is treated sympathetically by M. E.

We know that Paul expected his letters to be circulated to other churches in the vicinity (particularly Col. 4.16), and it is likely that they achieved steadily widening circulation quite quickly, as emissaries and travelers took copies of particular letters to churches they visited.[12] Written Gospels would probably be more attractive materials to pass on and share, especially when the growing number of churches made it less possible for regular visits to be made to each church by the earliest disciples/apostles. And as the first generation of disciples began to die off, the stimulus to preserve their witness in writing more widely for the growing number of churches would no doubt be strong.

If we follow this logic, the likelihood is that such writings would be known by a title and author. As soon as we think of churches or individuals beginning to make small collections or libraries of Christian documents, letters and then Gospels, each of the documents would need to have some distinguishing label before being popped into its 'pigeon-hole'. That may not have been the responsibility of the author himself. But, as soon as the book began to be circulated, such an identifying title would almost certainly have been provided by the one who circulated it or the ones who received it. That is to say, the bestowing of an identifying title may not have been the responsibility of the author so much as that of the recipient.[13]

Here we come to the title which was actually given to the Gospel, sooner or later — *EUANGELION KATA MARKON*, '(The) Gospel accord-

---

Boring, *Mark* (NTL; Louisville: WJK, 2006) 15-16. *Pace* J. Marcus, *Mark 1-8* (AB 27; New York: Doubleday, 1999) 25-28, it is entirely possible that Mark wrote primarily or in the first instance for his own community, while also mindful of the likelihood that his Gospel would be passed on to other churches; it evidently reached and was well known to Matthew and Luke within ten to twenty years. See also Collins's discussion (*Mark* 97-98). M. Hengel, *The Four Gospels and the One Gospel of Jesus Christ* (London: SCM, 2000), likewise infers from the commission to 'all nations' (Matt. 28.19-20) that 'contrary to a widespread view, the self-confident evangelist [Matthew] wrote his work not only for his communities in Southern Syria and Palestine . . . but for the whole church' (77-78), and makes a similar claim for Mark (94), as indeed for all four Gospels: 'we should stop talking automatically about *"the community of Mark", "of Luke", "of Matthew", "of John"* as the one really responsible for the composition of the Gospel writing and its theology. . . . Even more nonsensical is the term "Q community"' (107, and further 106-15).

12. *Beginning from Jerusalem* §29.8d, §30.8.

13. 'It is fair to say that in antiquity the giving and use of titles belonged somewhat more to the reception of works than to their production' (Collins, *Mark* 2), citing particularly M. Hengel, *Studies in the Gospel of Mark* (London: SCM, 1985) 74-75. 'Anonymous works were relatively rare and *must have* been given a title in the libraries' (Hengel, *Four Gospels* 48; see further 48-50, 54-55, 59-60, 247-48 n.247). The comment of Marcus is more qualified: 'Unlike most Hellenistic biographers, but like most biblical authors, the evangelist does not consider his own authorial personality to be important' (*Mark 1-8* 17); on that point Hengel agrees: 'The real "author" of the one Gospel was Jesus Christ himself' (*Four Gospels* 49).

ing to Mark'. Two of the most famous manuscripts, the fourth-century uncials Sinaiticus and Vaticanus, read simply *KATA MARKON*. But that is probably an abbreviation of the fuller *Euangelion kata Markon*, which suggests that the fuller title was well enough known for it to be thus abbreviated. And though we do not have earlier examples of the fuller title of Mark's Gospel, we do have second and very early third century examples of the other canonical Gospels known by the equivalent titles — *EUANGELION KATA MATHTHAION, EUANGELION KATA LOUKAN, EUANGELION KATA IŌANNĒN*.[14]

An important corollary consideration is relevant here: that the Gospels were not known by a variety of titles. Such an outcome was likely if titles depended on recipients rather than the author; each recipient of an anonymous writing was likely to choose an identifying label most convenient to him.[15] The fact, then, that the Gospels are almost universally known by the fuller title, 'The Gospel according to . . .', or simply 'According to . . .', strongly suggests that the title was given to each Gospel as soon as they began to be circulated,[16] to be more widely known and used beyond their places of origin.

The upshot of these considerations is that although the author of the Gospel of Mark did not identify himself, it is very likely that its title, 'The Gospel according to Mark', was very soon attached to his book, and attached so firmly that it stuck to the Gospel thereafter. Here it is significant that in his testimony cited below, Papias refers to the Gospels of Mark and Matthew *by name*, and attributes such reference to what 'the Elder used to say', presumably years earlier (c. 100?); in other words, 'Mark' was the name by which the Gospel of Mark was identified. This suggests in turn that there was no real problem of anonymity associated with the Gospel of Mark, and that it was well known that a person named Mark was its author, that is, already before the end of the first century (see §39.2a(ii) below). Apart from anything else, the natural tendency would be to attribute an anonymous writing of this character

---

14. Hengel, *Studies in Mark* 66; Collins, *Mark* 3 — referring to p^{64} and p^{67} (Matthew), p^{75} (Luke and John) and p^{66} (John).

15. Hengel cites the example of Galen, who notes that he did not give titles to his own works, and that when they began to be circulated the same work was given different titles in varying circumstances (*Studies in Mark* 74, 82).

16. Hengel thinks it could have been as early as the first copyist making copies of Mark to be sent to other communities, describing it to the recipients as *euangelion kata Markon* (*Studies in Mark* 83). In §41 I develop the argument that it was Mark's introduction of his writing as 'The beginning of the gospel of Jesus Christ' (Mark 1.1) which established the term 'gospel' as the title of his book, which was in effect followed by the subsequent Evangelists or by those similarly responsible for circulating their books. Hengel is followed by P. Pokorny, *From the Gospel to the Gospels: History, Theology and Impact of the Biblical Term 'Euangelion'* (BZNW 195; Berlin: de Gruyter, 2013) 186-90.

to one of the apostles;[17] the fact that it was *not* so attributed probably indicates that the authorship by Mark was never substantially questioned.[18]

Who then was this 'Mark'? The obvious contender is the Mark well known from the early history of emerging Christianity — John Mark,

- the well-known Jerusalemite (Acts 12.12),
- who accompanied Paul and Barnabas on their mission from Antioch (12.25; 13.5),
- who then became the reason why Paul and Barnabas split from each other (13.13; 15.37-39),
- but who subsequently was reconciled to Paul (Col. 4.10; Phlm. 24; also 2 Tim. 4.11),
- and who is hailed in 1 Peter as 'my son Mark' (1 Pet. 5.13).

None of these references, it should be noted, gives any hint of Mark as an author; for example, he is never named as a co-author of Paul's letters (unlike the other member of Paul's mission team named in 1 Pet. 5.12 — Silvanus — though Mark is given the more honorary title of 'co-worker').[19]

However, the last named reference (1 Pet. 5.13) provides an intriguing tie-in to the tradition narrated by Papias, bishop of the church in Hierapolis in the early second century:

> And the Elder used to say this, "Mark became Peter's interpreter (*hermēneutēs*) and wrote accurately all that he remembered, not, indeed, in order, of the things said or done by the Lord. For he had not heard the Lord, nor had he followed him, but later on, as I said, followed Peter, who used to give teaching as necessity demanded but not making, as it were, an arrangement of the Lord's oracles, so that Mark did nothing wrong in thus writing down single points as he remembered them. For to one thing he gave attention, to leave out nothing of what he had heard and to make no false statements in them." This is related by Papias about Mark, and about Matthew this was said, "Matthew collected the oracles in the Hebrew language, and each interpreted them as best he could" (Eusebius, *HE* 3.39.15-16).[20]

---

17. 'What would have prevented the copyists or the communities in a secondary attribution in the second century from transferring the Gospel of Mark to Peter and the Gospel of Luke to Paul? In the second century they would certainly no longer have come up with the relatively remote names of Mark and Luke' (Hengel, *Four Gospels* 45).

18. R. A. Guelich, *Mark 1-8:26* (WBC 34A; Dallas: Word, 1989) xxviii; Schnelle, *History* 199; Marcus, *Mark 1-8* 17-18.

19. Details of Paul's co-workers are given in *Beginning from Jerusalem* §29.6.

20. Text in K. Aland, *Synopsis quattuor Evangeliorum* (Stuttgart: Württembergische

Papias does not call Mark's writing a Gospel, but the fact that he immediately goes on to speak of Matthew (also 1 John, 1 Peter and 'the Gospel according to the Hebrews') makes it more than likely that he was referring to the Gospel of Mark. Justin Martyr, writing a few decades later, refers somewhat similarly to the 'memoirs/reminiscences (*apomnēmoneumata*) of the apostles, which are called Gospels' (*I Apol.* 66.3), and similarly regards Mark's Gospel as the 'memoirs/reminiscences (*apomnēmoneumata*)' of Peter (*Dial.* 106.3).[21]

While Papias, as quoted by Eusebius, should not be followed blindly,[22] his testimony links well with the inferences which may be drawn from the title of the Gospel itself ('according to Mark').[23] One could well infer from the NT references to Mark that knowledge of him was well established within the early churches, so that the general assumption would be that the 'Gospel according to Mark' attributed it to the well-known Mark, rather than to some otherwise unknown Mark. Objections that the Gospel shows too much ignorance of Palestinian geography and too little familiarity with Jewish customs to be linked with the NT John Mark are greatly exaggerated.[24] Moreover, the fact that Mark seems to draw on pre-Markan formed tradition[25] does not necessarily imply a lack of immediate dependence on a single figure like Peter. And Papias's description of Mark as Peter's 'interpreter' (*hermēneutēs*) need not imply that Mark had to translate Peter speaking in Aramaic, though it could imply Mark's assistance for one who was not very proficient in Greek.[26] After all, there is no reason why

---

Bibelanstalt, [13]1984) 531; ET in J. Stevenson, ed., *A New Eusebius* (London: SPCK, 1960) 52. Papias (c. 60-135) attributes this tradition to the presbyter John, whom he describes as, together with Aristion, 'the Lord's disciples' (*HE* 3.39.4). See also Eusebius's other references to the same effect (2.15.1; 5.8.3; 6.14.6-7; 6.25.5).

21. Justin refers in the same sentence to the sons of Zebedee as *Boanerges* (Mark 3.17), a name for the sons of Zebedee not recorded by Matthew and Luke (text in Aland, *Synopsis* 532).

22. See e.g. Marcus's hesitation on the subject (*Mark 1-8* 21-24).

23. A strong body of opinion thinks that a special connection of Mark with Peter is unlikely; see e.g. Kümmel, *Introduction* 94-96, with further bibliography in n.48. But Kümmel also shows himself ready to accept the testimony of the Muratonian Canon (text in Aland, *Synopsis* 538) that Mark was present at some of the events he records (96), and the testimony of 1 Pet. 5.13 of a close relation between Peter and Mark ('my son') is no later than late first century and cannot be so lightly disregarded as Kümmel suggests (97).

24. Guelich, *Mark* xxviii, and Marcus, *Mark 1-8* 19-21, respond effectively to K. Niederwimmer, 'Johannes Markus und die Frage nach dem Verfasser des zweiten Evangeliums', *ZNW* 58 (1967) 173-88. See also Collins, *Mark* 6, 8-10.

25. See *Beginning from Jerusalem* §21.5d and below §41.2a.

26. It is quite possible that Peter himself could have functioned effectively enough in Greek (see *Beginning from Jerusalem* 1148-49), though M. Casey, *Aramaic Sources of Mark's Gospel* (SNTSMS 102; Cambridge: Cambridge University, 1998), is confident of his ability to reconstruct such sources and to date them as early as 40 CE. The view that Mark drew on

Mark's grouping of Jesus tradition (for example, controversy stories, teaching on parables, sequence of miracle stories) could not reflect Peter's own teaching style or repertoire of Jesus tradition. Moreover, there are several passages in Mark's Gospel which invite the explanation that Mark had Peter as a special source for at least some of the detail which his Gospel provides — notably, perhaps, those details most embarrassing to Peter, recalled by him with some shame for the stronger portrayal they gave of Jesus.[27] Richard Bauckham perceives a 'Petrine perspective in the Gospel of Mark',[28] and though the case is not very substantial,[29] it strengthens the impression of remembrances (*apomnēmoneumata*) of Jesus which were personal and not merely handed down through tradition. However, such considerations are more relevant to the earlier volumes of *Christianity in the Making* and need not be pursued further here. What matters for us in volume 3 is that the authorship of the Gospel of Mark was probably well enough known as soon as the Gospel began to be more widely circulated, and that already in the early second century the Gospel of Mark was valued as a particular record of Peter's own reminiscences.

ii. Date

A regularly used means of determining the date of a document is to check when it is first quoted or referred to by later writers. In Mark's case this is little help, since Mark's Gospel is not referred to in the second century prior to Justin Martyr in the middle of the century. Thereafter we have to await Irenaeus and Clement of Alexandria.[30] The use of Mark by Matthew and Luke,

---

Aramaic sources was more common at the beginning of the twentieth century (N. Turner, *A Grammar of New Testament Greek* vol. IV: *Style* [Edinburgh: T & T Clark, 1976] 11-15). Hengel also notes 'the remarkable thing about the Gospel of Mark' 'that it contains . . . more Aramaic formulae than any other original Greek literary text' (*Studies in Mark* 29, 46), citing H. P. Rüger, 'Die lexikalischen Aramaismen im Markusevangelium', in H. Cancik ed., *Markus-Philologie* (WUNT 33; Tübingen: Mohr Siebeck, 1984) 73-84.

27. Mark 8.29-33; 9.5-6; 14.29-31, 37 and 66-72; also 16.7.

28. R. Bauckham, *Jesus and the Eyewitnesses: The Gospels as Eyewitness Testimony* (Grand Rapids: Eerdmans, 2006) ch. 7; see also Hengel, *Studies in Mark* 50-51; and further *Four Gospels* 78-89, though he later acknowledges that Mark 'grew out of a living oral presentation' (96). Cf. Koester: 'the role of Peter in that gospel [Mark] shows that Mark indeed used materials in which the authority of this apostle was expressed' (*Introduction* 2.167). *Pace* Kümmel, *Introduction* 95-96 (and n.23 above), Bauckham's protest against the assumption that all Jesus tradition was 'anonymous' should be given more weight.

29. See my response to Bauckham, 'Eyewitnessses and the Oral Jesus Tradition', *JSHJ* 6 (2008) 85-105; and cf. R. E. Brown, *Introduction to the New Testament* (New York: Doubleday, 1997) 160-61. Kümmel quotes Jülicher-Fascher appropriately: 'Without the stimulus from Papias, we should scarcely have advertised Peter as the guarantor for the material in the Markan narrative' (*Introduction* 94).

30. H. Koester, 'Gospels and Gospel Traditions in the Second Century', in Gregory

of course, points to a date for Mark prior to their writing; but again, since we cannot be very precise about their datings, which in part depend on the date given to Mark, we are only a little way forward.

So we are forced to rely principally on the internal evidence of the Gospel itself. Here there is a widespread agreement that the most significant information comes in Mark 13, 'the little apocalypse' which grows out of Jesus' reported prediction of the temple's destruction.[31] Do Jesus' words that 'not one stone will be left upon another; all will be thrown down' (Mark 13.2) reflect knowledge of the destruction of the temple in 70? Or are they remembered as a prediction which would soon be fulfilled? The fact that some of the massive stones which supported the temple platform did indeed remain in place (notably the well-known western wall sacred to modern Judaism) could suggest a prophecy not completely fulfilled — although given the devastation which actually did occur,[32] that may be pressing the case for a pre-70 date too far.

Potentially more promising is Mark 13.14: 'When you see the desolating sacrilege set up where it ought not to be (let the reader understand), then those in Judea must flee to the mountains . . .'. There is a strong possibility that the wording reflects the earlier crisis caused by the Emperor Gaius Caligula's insistence that his statue be erected within the temple.[33] But the note to the reader looks like a Markan insertion, an instruction to the one who would be responsible for reading the Gospel to an assembled congregation. In which case, it is certainly plausible that the Gospel was written some time after the start of the Jewish revolt against Rome, presumably after the murderous factions within the revolt had seized the temple and in effect desecrated it by their bloodthirsty tactics.[34] This would fit with the Petra tradition, that is, the tradition that the believers in Jerusalem fled from the city before the Roman legions made that impossible.[35] That could suggest a date for the writing of the Gospel in 68 or 69, perhaps during the 'wars and rumours of wars' (13.7)

---

and Tuckett, eds., *Trajectories* 27-44 (here 33). Koester goes on to note that 'the *Secret Gospel of Mark*, however, could indicate that Mark's Gospel was popular in Egypt earlier in the second century' (33); but on 'secret Mark' see §40.4d below.

31. J. G. Crossley, *The Date of Mark's Gospel: Insights from the Law in Earliest Christianity* (JSNTS 266; London: T & T Clark, 2004), argues that Mark 13 could point to a date anywhere from the 30s (the Caligula crisis began in 39; see n.33), and that Mark's treatment of the law points to a date between the mid to late 30s and mid-40s; but it is highly implausible to read Mark's note in 7.19 as indicating anything other than an abrogation of the laws of clean and unclean, and therefore as reflecting the later disputes, illustrated in Romans 14 (Crossley 50 recognizes the link between Rom. 14.14 and Mark 7.19).

32. See *Beginning from Jerusalem* §36.4.

33. See again *Beginning from Jerusalem* 403.

34. Cf. particularly Marcus, *Mark 1-8* 37-39.

35. See again *Beginning from Jerusalem* §36.3.

following the death of Emperor Nero and before Vespasian was able to establish his authority.[36] To be fully credible, however, this possibility depends on where the Gospel was written and whether it was capable of being read in Jerusalem or Judaean churches at this period.[37]

Alternatively, it is hardly implausible to envisage the Gospel being written in the wake of the revolt, and while Jewish (and Christian?) communities within the Roman Empire were still reeling from the outcome.[38] The Gospel's stress on the suffering which disciples of Jesus could expect to endure (8.34-35;[39] 10.29-30; 13.9-20) could equally reflect that situation. And in those circumstances, 13.14 would serve as a comfort and reassurance that Jesus had predicted the destruction of the temple so clearly.

Most find the link between Mark 13 and the destruction of the temple sufficiently close to date the Gospel to the period 65-75.[40] Earlier than 65 would probably not give enough weight to the foreboding and the expectation of suffering in the Gospel. And later than 75 begins to narrow uncomfortably the time-frame for the Gospels (Matthew and Luke); these clearly were familiar with the written Mark which possibly took some time after its publication to reach them. With that we will have to be content, and just ensure that we do not put too much weight on a more precise dating.

iii. Place of Writing — From or For

The principal options canvassed here are Rome and Syria.[41]

Rome is an obvious deduction which may be drawn from the combined testimony of 1 Pet. 5.13 and Papias quoted above.[42] If indeed 1 Peter was

---

36. See Hengel, *Studies in Mark* ch. 1 (particularly 26-28); Guelich, *Mark* xxxi-xxxii; Collins, *Mark* 13-14.

37. The Roman legions conquered most of Israel's territory in the period 67-68.

38. 'After the fall of Masada [74], further Jewish disturbances occurred in Alexandria and Cyrene' — E. Schürer, *The History of the Jewish People in the Age of Jesus Christ*, revised and edited by G. Vermes and F. Millar (4 vols., Edinburgh: T & T Clark, 1973-87) 1.512; see also below §46 at n.62.

39. The daily crucifixions carried out by the Romans during the siege (Josephus, *War* 4.450-451) would have brought home the force of Jesus' words.

40. E.g. Kümmel, *Introduction* 98; D. Lührmann, *Das Markusevangelium* (HNT 3; Tübingen: Mohr Siebeck, 1987) 6; M. D. Hooker, *The Gospel according to St Mark* (BNTC; London: A & C Black, 1991) 8; Brown, *Introduction* 163-64; Boring, *Mark* 14-15; D. A. Hagner, *The New Testament* (Grand Rapids: Baker Academic, 2012) 184.

41. Schnelle thinks that Asia Minor also deserves consideration (*History* 201). Chrysostom's comment that Mark was written in Egypt was perhaps an inference falsely drawn from Eusebius's report that Mark was the first to preach in Egypt, using the Gospel he had written (*HE* 2.16.1); it lacks any supportive evidence (Hooker, *Mark* 7); see also n.30 above.

42. Hengel, *Four Gospels* 67; Hagner, *New Testament* 183, 185.

written from Rome (in code 'Babylon'), when Mark was present (1 Pet. 5.13) some time after Peter's martyrdom there,[43] and if it does consist of Peter's record of 'the things said or done by the Lord' (Papias), then it is natural to infer that the Gospel was written by Mark from Rome.[44] The argument is rendered less certain by the likelihood that Peter's death was the result of Nero's persecution (64?), so that if Mark was a close aide to Peter, his own continued residence and survival in Rome become more questionable.

The presence of Latinisms in Mark could indeed point to a document written in Italy or the Western empire or for recipients located in these regions, since Latin was not much used outside Roman administration in the Eastern empire.[45] In particular, in Mark 12.42 and 15.16, Mark clarifies a Greek term by providing the Latin equivalent: the two smallest Greek coins (*lepta*) Mark explains as equivalent to the smallest Roman coin (*quadrans*) (12.42); the courtyard (of the palace) (*aulē*) likewise is explained as the *praetorium*, the headquarters of the Roman governor (15.16). However, the fact that Mark also saw the need to explain Jewish customs (notably 7.3-4) may simply suggest that he wrote his Gospel for a wide range of communities well beyond Israel-Palestine, conscious that such audiences would not all be well versed in such descriptive detail and would need some translation or explanation.[46] Familiarity with Latin usage may only confirm that the author of Mark had spent some time in Italy, without necessarily implying that the Gospel was written either in Rome itself or exclusively for Roman recipients.[47] The lack of any correlation between Mark and other writings which can be firmly asso-

---

43. See *Beginning from Jerusalem* 1156-57; but dismissed by O. Zwierlein, *Petrus in Rom: die literarische Zeugnisse* (UALG 96; Berlin: de Gruyter, 2009) 7-13.

44. This deduction may have been made by Irenaeus, who infers that Mark wrote what Peter proclaimed after Peter's 'departure' (= death) (*adv. haer.* 3.1.1), though Clement of Alexandria inferred (from the Papias tradition) that Mark was written in Rome during Peter's lifetime (Eusebius, *HE* 6.14.5-7; text in Aland, *Synopsis* 539); fuller detail in Collins, *Mark* 7. The anti-Marcionite prologue (160/180) says that Mark wrote his Gospel 'in the regions of Italy'.

45. Hengel, *Studies in Mark* 28-30 and 137 n.161, referring to the full listing (for the NT as a whole) in Blass Debrunner, *Grammar* 4-6; listing of Markan Latinisms also in Kümmel, *Introduction* 97-98; Schnelle, *History* 201. The fact that the Latinisms are from the military and economic world weakens the case for a link specifically to Rome (Schnelle 201; similarly Collins, *Mark* 100).

46. To suggestions that Mark's knowledge of such Jewish customs was inaccurate, Collins justifiably responds: 'Our knowledge of such customs in this period, both for Palestine and the Diaspora, is quite limited. On what grounds, therefore, can we say that Mark, one of our primary sources for Palestinian Jewish practices in the first century, is inaccurate?' (*Mark* 6).

47. See further Marcus, *Mark 1-8* 31-33.

ciated with Rome (Paul's Romans, 1 Peter, *1 Clement,* Hermas) also weakens the case for linking Mark specifically with Rome.[48]

Syria or *Transjordan* as the place of origin is more favoured by those who see the suffering reflected or anticipated in Mark as referring more to the Jewish revolt than to the Neronian persecution.[49] Joel Marcus, for example, observes that the prediction of 'false messiahs and false prophets' who 'produce signs and omens' and lead astray others (13.22) well reflected the circumstances recorded by Josephus in the build-up to the Jewish revolt and during the revolt itself.[50] And he refers to the use of the word 'brigands' in Jesus' 'cleaning of the temple' — 'you have made it a den of brigands (*lēstōn*)' (11.17) — noting that 'brigands' was 'Josephus' term of opprobrium for the revolutionaries who in his view hijacked the Jewish people into the disastrous conflict with the Romans'.[51] This suggests a close knowledge of the Jewish revolt and its antecedents. Our knowledge of Christian communities in Israel-Palestine during and immediately after the war is virtually non-existent. But it is certainly plausible to allow the possibility that someone who had endured some of the early hardships of the revolt wrote his Gospel for the benefit of Jesus-Messianists who were still in Judaea and when his note to the reader in 13.14 would still have relevance; or, alternatively, in the wider region of Syria when there would be many readers or auditors who had experienced the war and who resonated with the Gospel's warnings and encouragement.

In the end, however, no firm conclusion can be drawn with any confidence.[52] It is quite conceivable that Mark had returned to Jerusalem following Peter's death and had experienced something of the Jewish revolt. That he wrote his Gospel, both to consolidate his own reminiscences of Peter's preaching and teaching, and well aware of how badly things were going or had gone in Israel and Judaea, is about as much as we can say. Where and for whom eludes further clarification and we would do well not to make any further theories about its purpose overly dependent on firmer answers to these introductory questions.

---

48. Boring, *Mark* 18-19. Pace B. Incigneri, *The Gospel to the Romans: The Setting and Rhetoric of Mark's Gospel* (Leiden: Brill, 2003), the threat of crucifixion (Mark 8.34) need hardly imply a setting for Mark in Rome. J. G. Cook, *Roman Attitudes Towards Christians: From Claudius to Hadrian* (WUNT 261; Tübingen: Mohr Siebeck, 2010), comments, somewhat enigmatically, 'If Mark was written elsewhere, could an author have been unaware how Nero treated the Christians in Rome?' (110).

49. E.g. H. C. Kee, *Community of the New Age* (London: SCM, 1977) 176.

50. J. Marcus, 'The Jewish War and the Sitz im Leben of Mark', *JBL* 111(1992) 441-62 (here 457-59), with reference to Josephus, *War* 2.433-34, 444, 652; 6.313; 7.29-31.

51. Marcus, *Mark 1-8* 35.

52. See the review in Brown, *Introduction* 161-62.

b. The Gospel of Luke

We turn, secondly, to Luke's Gospel. This is not because we can ascertain with any confidence the relative dates of Matthew or Luke. In fact Matthew is usually treated before Luke in Introductions, perhaps with the implicit implication that Matthew was written before Luke.[53] Similarly, the minority who question the existence of Q and the need to hypothesize a Q source usually assume that Luke derived the non-Mark material shared with Matthew (the Q material) from Matthew.[54] In fact, however, if it was simply a choice between Luke deriving the Q material from Matthew, or Matthew deriving the Q material from Luke, the latter would be the more probable,[55] since Luke's omissions and reordering of the Q material from the settings provided by Matthew are harder to explain than the opposite.[56] The greater likelihood, then, is that Luke was written earlier than Matthew.[57] To be sure, this consideration cannot bear much weight. The fact, which I presuppose, that the variations of the written Gospels reflect and continue the variation of the oral renderings of the Jesus tradition prior to their being transcribed, has the unavoidable corollary that more extensive variation is no proof that a version is later. Any particular tradent or Evangelist could have imposed his own variations on his

---

53. I suspect this *de facto* assumption is a carry-over from the traditional dominance of Matthew, in the second century, and maintained in the ordering of the four canonical Gospels (see below n.84).

54. Particularly M. D. Goulder, *Luke: A New Paradigm* (JSNTS 20; Sheffield: Sheffield Academic, 1989); E. Franklin, *Luke: Interpreter of Paul, Critic of Matthew* (JSNTS 92; Sheffield: Sheffield Academic, 1994); M. Goodacre, *The Case Against Q* (Harrisburg: TPI, 2002).

55. Hengel argues strongly that Matthew used the earlier Luke (*Four Gospels* 169-207). See also D. Catchpole, *The Quest for Q* (Edinburgh: Clark, 1993) 1-59, referred to in *Jesus Remembered* 147 n.28.

56. As G. N. Stanton, 'The Origin and Purpose of Matthew's Gospel: Matthean Scholarship from 1945 to 1980', *ANRW* II.25.3 (1985) 1889-1951, observed: 'If Luke has used Matthew, why is it so difficult to find traces in Luke of Matthew's expansions, abbreviations or modifications of Mark's content and order?' (1902); see also his brief critique of Goulder in *A Gospel for a New People: Studies in Matthew* (Edinburgh: T & T Clark, 1992) 32-34. See also J. A. Fitzmyer, *The Gospel according to Luke* (AB 28; 2 vols.; New York: Doubleday, 1981, 1985) 1.73-75; and below §42 n.180 for some indication of how Luke would have had to tear apart, e.g., Matthew's Sermon on the Mount to achieve his ordering of the parallel material; on any reckoning, Luke's 'Sermon on the Plain' (Luke 6.17-49) is a formulation independent of Matthew's 'Sermon on the Mount' (Matt. 5-7). It is no accident that Q material is usually referred to by the Lukan verse numbers: e.g. Q 12.8 = Luke 12.8 (J. M. Robinson, P. Hoffmann and J. S. Kloppenborg, *The Critical Edition of Q: Synopsis* [Leuven: Peeters, 2000] lxvii); see again Fitzmyer, *Luke* 1.77-79.

57. Hengel, *Four Gospels* 68-70, 72, and further 186-205.

rendition of the tradition, early or late. There is no law of the transmission of oral tradition which dictates that more elaborate or complex versions of a tradition are, by virtue of that very fact, to be dated later.[58] So the resolution of the question (which of Matthew and Luke was written earlier) remains obscure (although I do regard Luke as written earlier than Matthew), and the decision to treat Luke first is somewhat arbitrary.[59]

i. Author

The Gospel of Luke is generally regarded as the first of a two-volume work — Luke-Acts.[60] So what has already been said in *Beginning from Jerusalem* §21.2a about the authorship of Acts can be taken over here. This is important, since were we to depend solely on the internal evidence of the Gospel we would literally have no idea as to the identity of its author.[61] But when we include Acts, as written by the same author as the Gospel, the probability becomes strong that the author of the Gospel was the same person as the one who told parts of the story of Acts in first-person terms. As noted in §21.2a, there has been a strong and rather strange unwillingness to recognize that the first person in the 'we/us' sections of Acts could be the narrator himself. In some cases it almost appears to be regarded as a test of critical integrity, a proof of critical virility, to find an explanation for these passages which can provide a believable alternative to the most obvious solution (that the narrator was personally involved in the episodes related).[62] In fact, however, none of the alternatives has proved so credible as the most obvious solution. And the most probable solution remains that the author of Acts was indeed personally involved in the 'we/us' episodes, and so provides an eye-witness and near third-hand authority for most of at least the second half of Acts.[63] In this connection

---

58. This, we may recall, was Bultmann's mistaken assumption which E. P. Sanders demonstrated to be false (*Jesus Remembered* 194 and nn.112-14).

59. In fact, as we shall see, it makes better sense to treat Matthew immediately after Mark in §42 below.

60. See *Beginning from Jerusalem* 65 and nn.44, 45.

61. All that we can learn from the Gospel itself regarding its author is such information as the fact that he did not belong to Jesus' own immediate circle of disciples (Luke 1.2), and that he was well educated and very familiar with the LXX (e.g. Fitzmyer, *Luke* 1.35; H. Klein, *Das Lukasevangelium* [KEK; Göttingen: Vandenhoeck, 2006] 65-66).

62. *Beginning from Jerusalem* 66 n.50; and further Keener, *Acts*, referred to in §38 n.2 above.

63. *Beginning from Jerusalem* 66-67 n.51. The fact that Acts does not give a portrayal of Paul that Paul would have wholly accepted should not be given the weight that it often receives (Kümmel, *Introduction* 149; Koester, *Introduction* 2.310; Schnelle, *History* 241-42; Klein, *Lukasevangelium* 64). The issue really belongs to discussion of Acts and has been dealt with at some length in *Beginning from Jerusalem*. Suffice here to say that a 'personal

it may be significant that the author of Luke refers to himself in first-person terms — 'I too decided . . .' (1.3).[64]

Who this companion of Paul was is never identified in Acts. But the traditional identification has been Luke, the one described as 'the beloved physician' in Col. 4.14 (cf. 2 Tim. 4.11; Phlm. 24), affirmed as the author of the joint work, Luke-Acts.[65] This tradition was already well established by late second century, as p[75], Irenaeus, the Muratonian fragment and the anti-Marcionite prologue to Luke attest,[66] although there is no evidence for it prior to Irenaeus.[67] But as with Mark, the title *EUANGELION KATA LOUKAN* presumably indicates that as soon as the Gospel began to be circulated and known more widely, it was identified as the work of Luke.[68] Here the fact that the Gospel was written for and sent to 'most excellent Theophilus' (Luke 1.3) comes into play. For if Theophilus was an actual person (as most conclude),[69] then it can probably be assumed that he would not have regarded the document as written solely for his own personal use. More likely, it was sent to him

---

associate' (Schnelle) of Paul could have had a view of Paul's work and an intention in his presentation of Paul's work which varied in several degrees from Paul's own (see also Fitzmyer, *Luke* 1.47-51; and further below §47.2b).

64. 'The I of the author is a novum in the early Christian Gospel tradition' (F. Bovon, *Das Evangelium nach Lukas* [EKK 3; 4 vols.; Zürich: Benziger, 1989, 1996, 2001, 2009] 1.37).

65. The traditional view is that Luke was a Gentile Christian — the fact that Col. 4.14 distinguishes Luke from Paul's 'fellow-workers of the circumcision' (4.11) is often cited (Kümmel, *Introduction* 147; Fitzmyer, *Luke* 1.41-42, 44) — though as noted in *Beginning from Jerusalem* 66 n.49, there is a recent tendency to argue that Luke was a Jewish Christian, or at least a God-fearer with roots in Hellenistic-Jewish Christianity (cf. Bovon, *Lukas* 1.22; Brown, *Introduction* 268; full discussion in Fitzmyer, *Luke* 1.41-47, who concludes that Luke was a non-Jewish Semite).

66. *Beginning from Jerusalem* 65-66 n.48; and further Fitzmyer, *Luke* 1.37-40. Koester is prepared to date the part of the Lukan Prologue containing this information to the last decades of the second century (*Ancient Christian Gospels* 335); see also n.67 below. Unlike Mark and Matthew, Eusebius has preserved no accounts of the origins of Luke's Gospel.

67. A. Gregory, *The Reception of Luke and Acts in the Period before Irenaeus* (WUNT 2.169; Tübingen: Mohr Siebeck, 2003) 53.

68. See above at nn.14 and 15; cf. J. Nolland, *Luke* (WBC 35, 2 vols.; Dallas: Word, 1989, 1993) xxxv-xxxvi. Contrast the implausible argument of Bovon, that the original title of the Lukan double-work (and so the name of the author) was lost with the canonization of the Gospel (*Lukas* 1.24). Gregory thinks the evidence too weak to support Hengel's case (*Reception of Luke* 50-53).

69. E.g. Fitzmyer, *Luke* 1.299-300; Bovon, *Lukas* 1.39; Klein, *Lukasevangelium* 75. L. Alexander, *The Preface to Luke's Gospel* (SNTSMS 78; Cambridge: Cambridge University, 1993), notes that 'Theophilus' was a favourite name among Hellenistic Jews, and that there is very little evidence, if any, for dedications to imaginary people (73-75, 133, 188). 'Perhaps "Theophilus", the "friend of God", was a prominent Roman whose real name had to be kept secret' (Hengel, *Four Gospels* 40, 102).

with a view to his making copies of it for wider use.[70] And if 'Theophilus' was a way of inviting each and every 'friend/lover of God' to read the document,[71] then again the corollary is that the Gospel was written for wide dispersion. In which case the logic is once again that it would have been given its title at the beginning of that process. Which also means that the tradition of Lukan authorship can be dated back to early second century or late first century.

It could of course be argued that the tradition of Lukan authorship was the product of a desire to give the document authority by attributing it to a companion of Paul.[72] But the literature itself hardly gives a person called Luke such an important status as one of Paul's mission team; he is mentioned only three times in the Pauline corpus, no more than Demas. And even as a close (or 'last') companion of Paul, an account of Jesus' life and mission written by a companion of Paul would carry much less weight than such a document written by one of Jesus' own disciples; the Luke referred to in the Pauline passages was already two removes from Jesus' own circle.[73] Here once more the most obvious solution takes some beating: that the Gospel became known as 'the gospel according to Luke' simply because it was well enough known by those who promoted the document round a widening circle of Christian groups that the Gospel was the composition of Luke, that is, the former companion of Paul.[74]

ii. Date

The issue of date falls within tighter constraints than the other canonical Gospels. For on the one hand, the consensus view of the 'Synoptic problem' is still that Luke was able to use Mark as one of his sources. The *a quo* date for Luke is therefore almost certainly post-70. In addition, Luke 21.24 probably implies that the author was able to look back on the destruction of Jerusalem (cf. 19.43-44).[75] On the other hand, the Gospel of Luke was certainly written

---

70. Hengel, *Four Gospels* 103; Bovon, *Lukas* 1.23; Luke's 'opus is not a private writing; Theophilus stands for the Christian readers of Luke's own day and thereafter' (Fitzmyer, *Luke* 1.300).

71. Cf. Kümmel, *Introduction* 129-30. Nolland argued that Luke wrote his Gospel particularly for God-fearers (*Luke* 1.xxxii-xxxiii).

72. Bovon, *Lukas* 1.24; Schnelle suggests that 2 Tim. 4.11's testimony about Luke as 'the last of Paul's faithful coworkers' 'predestines him to be named as the author of the two volume work "To Theophilus"' (*History* 241).

73. See also Fitzmyer, *Luke* 1.41.

74. Eusebius quotes the tradition, which he seems to accept: 'They say that Paul was actually accustomed to quote from Luke's Gospel since when writing of some Gospel as his own he used to say, "According to my Gospel"' (*HE* 3.4.7).

75. Kümmel, *Introduction* 150; and further Fitzmyer, *Luke* 1.54-57; G. Theissen, *The Gospels in Context: Social and Political History in the Synoptic Tradition* (1989; ET Minneapolis: Fortress, 1991) 278-79.

before the Acts of the Apostles, that is, (by common consensus) before a date in the 80s or early 90s.[76] If we deduce that Luke, as the companion of Paul, had used the two years of Paul's imprisonment in Caesarea to gather information about the beginnings of Christianity,[77] then we can equally infer that he used such opportunities to garner as much Jesus tradition as he could. My own presupposition is that all newly founded churches would have been given a store of Jesus tradition for catechetical purposes, for worship and witness. So, as Luke moved around different churches he would have had considerable access to such tradition. We need not infer from the prologue to Luke's Gospel (Luke 1.1-3) that it was only recently that he had become interested in collecting traditions of Jesus and of the Jesus-sect's beginnings. It is equally possible that Jesus' mission and Christianity's beginnings had been a long-term interest of his. How much time he was able to give during the 60s and 70s to indulging that interest we have no way of knowing. But it is likely that the investigations he carried out (1.3) involved time and travel, so that a date in the late 70s or early 80s for the Gospel is entirely plausible and viable.[78] As a companion of Paul during the 50s, it is quite possible to envisage Luke doing his research and composing his writings when he was still in his fifties and sixties.[79]

iii. Place of Writing — From or For

The evidence, such as it is, is of Luke as a traveller. The 'we/us' passages in Acts are all records/(memories?) of travel.[80] The implication of the three NT references to Luke is that he remained faithful to Paul during his imprisonment(s), in Rome(?). The curiosity of Acts 16.10-17 and 20.5-6 suggests that Luke may have been resident in Philippi for some time, or perhaps even came from there.[81] Eusebius refers to Luke as 'from Antioch' (*HE* 3.4.6), and the anti-Marcionite prologue to Luke describes him as 'a Syrian from Antioch'.[82]

---

76. *Beginning from Jerusalem* 67 and n.54. Koester thinks that Luke may have been composed as late as 125 (*Introduction* 2.310). In contrast, Hagner thinks early 70s the most plausible (*New Testament* 246-48).

77. *Beginning from Jerusalem* 76.

78. Kümmel — between 70 and 90 (*Introduction* 151); Fitzmyer — 80-85 (*Luke* 1.57); Bovon — 80-90 (*Lukas* 1.23); Brown — 85, give or take five to ten years (*Introduction* 274).

79. The anti-Marcionite prologue claims that Luke died at the age of 84 in Boeotia (Aland, *Synopsis* 533), though the Latin version reads 'LXXIIII annorum obiit in Bithynia' (539). If the author had been a companion of Paul, a date around 90 — Acts between 90 and 100 (as Schnelle, *History* 243, 260) — would be harder to maintain.

80. Acts 16.10-17; 20.5-15; 21.8-18; 27.1–28.16.

81. *Beginning from Jerusalem* 676 n.82; Bovon, *Lukas* 1.23; Klein, *Lukasevangelium* 68-69.

82. Aland, *Synopsis* 533, 539; Fitzmyer, *Luke* 1.45-47. As Schnelle notes (*History* 241 n.305), P. Stuhlmacher, *Biblische Theologie des Neuen Testaments* (2 vols.; Göttingen:

In an important sense, therefore, it does not much matter where Luke actually wrote his Gospel, for he may well have been what we today would describe as more 'internationally minded' than other early Christians, although the term would be relative, given the actual area in view — from Jerusalem to Rome, and many points between.[83] The composition of the Gospel would have been a major enterprise depending on a stable setting and adequate facilities. But again the implication of Luke 1.1-4 is that Luke took time to inquire and investigate. So here certainly we should avoid the quite standard inference today that as a Gospel it was written for a particular community and reflected the beliefs, priorities and practices of a particular community. More than with any other NT Gospel we can confidently deduce that Luke's Gospel was written from a wider perspective and probably reflects the concerns of an individual with cosmopolitan interests and experience.

We should bear this in mind when we look at how Luke's Gospel has handled the Jesus tradition (§42.4a). It is likely that we will find little to instruct us on the life-settings of particular Christian communities, and more on the character of a movement as it appealed to more and more, and more widely through the late first century and early second century Mediterranean world.

c. The Gospel of Matthew

We turn, thirdly, to Matthew's Gospel. As already indicated, Matthew is regularly regarded (or treated) as written prior to Luke, and possibly as the source for much of Luke. This is certainly a well-rooted opinion, since the tradition that Matthew was the first of the four Gospels was firmly established in the early Church.[84] That Matthew was the earliest Gospel to be written is clearly the opinion of Clement of Alexandria, Origen and Eusebius.[85] The view is wholly understandable, given that what were almost certainly the

---

Vandenhoeck, 1992, 1999), takes up an ancient suggestion that the Lucius (*Loukios*) of Acts 13.1 and Rom. 16.21 was identical with Luke (*Loukas*) (1.227-28), but the disposition of the 'we/us' narratives in Acts, and the total disappearance of Lucius in the narrative subsequent to Acts 13.1 would be hard to explain if Lucius = Luke (see also Fitzmyer, *Luke* 1.43).

83. The diversity of locations suggested as the place of the Gospel's composition — Schnelle lists Aegea, Antioch, Ephesus, Macedonia, Achaia, Caesarea and Asia Minor, before settling on Rome (*History* 243; cf. Kümmel, *Introduction* 151) — may in itself suggest a well-travelled author (cf. Brown, *Introduction* 271). Klein describes Luke as having a Mediterranean perspective (*Lukasevangelium* 67-68).

84. Conveniently tabulated in J. Moffatt, *Introduction to the Literature of the New Testament* (Edinburgh: T & T Clark, ³1918) 14.

85. W. D. Davies and D. C. Allison, *The Gospel according to Saint Matthew* (ICC; 3 vols.; Edinburgh: T & T Clark, 1988, 1991, 1997) 1.129.

earlier Gospels (Mark and Luke) were attributed to what were essentially secondary sources — Mark, dependent on Peter, and Luke, dependent on Paul (Eusebius, *HE* 5.8.3). Matthew, however, was one of Jesus' own twelve disciples. For those who wanted first-hand accounts and eyewitness testimony, Matthew was bound to have a credibility and to carry an authority which Mark and Luke could claim only at second-hand. In the case of Matthew, then, the issue of authorship is a good deal more sensitive than with Luke, or even Mark.

i. Author

Unhelpfully, the authorship of Matthew is as problematic as that of Mark. Here too, as with Mark and Luke, the title *EUANGELION KATA MATHTHAION* presumably indicates that as soon as the Gospel began to be circulated and known more widely, it was identified as the work of Matthew.[86] Papias, writing in the early second century, refers to Matthew's Gospel, it would appear, in close conjunction with Mark's.[87] So it would appear that by the early second century the Gospel of Matthew was known as the version of the gospel provided by Matthew.

However, Papias's description of Matthew's work as an author is even more problematical than his description of Mark's. There are two possible ways of understanding Papias's testimony. One is to infer that Papias was referring to the Gospel as such, Papias assuming that Matthew gathered the tradition of Jesus' sayings ('the oracles') in the Aramaic which Jesus had used in his teaching. That is, Matthew's Gospel was composed entirely from the Aramaic oral Jesus tradition.[88] Or does Papias's added

---

86. See above §39.2a(i). Hengel points out that 'apart from the First Gospel, Matthew plays no role in primitive Christianity. . . . That makes it utterly improbable that the name of the apostle was attached to the Gospel only at a secondary stage' (*Four Gospels* 71 and n.295, 98).

87. '. . . This is related by Papias about Mark, and about Matthew this was said, "Matthew collected the oracles in the Hebrew language (*Ebraidi dialektō*), and each interpreted them as best he could"' (Eusebius, *HE* 3.39.15-16) — full quotation above at n.20.

88. The belief that Matthew wrote a Gospel in Hebrew is also affirmed by Eusebius, Irenaeus, Pantanaeus, the teacher of Clement of Alexandria, and Origen (Eusebius, *HE* 3.24.6; 5.8.2; 5.10.3; 6.25.4). But it is generally agreed that Papias is the source for this opinion (J. Gnilka, *Das Matthäusevangelium* [HTKNT; 2 vols.; Freiburg: Herder, 1986, 1988] 2.517-18; Davies and Allison, *Matthew* 1.12). The argument of J. Kürzinger, 'Irenäus und sein Zeugnis zur Sprache des Matthäusevangeliums', *NTS* 10 (1963-64) 108-15, that by *Ebraidi dialektō* Papias meant 'in Jewish forms of expression' has gained little support. On the possibility that the reference is to the Hebrew/Aramaic Gospel of the Nazaraeans or Gospel according to the Hebrews, see Hengel, *Four Gospels* 73-76; Brown, *Introduction* 209-10; and below §40.4a.

note, that 'each interpreted them as best he could', imply that someone else translated Matthew's Hebrew Gospel into the Greek with which Papias was presumably familiar?[89] The problem with an argument along this line is that, by general consent, Matthew drew much of his material from Mark, that is, from Mark's *Greek*,[90] including, as we shall see (§41), Mark's 'Gospel' structure.

The other way of interpreting Papias is that Papias was actually referring to the Q material, consisting as it does almost exclusively of sayings ('oracles').[91] The value of Papias's testimony would be, then, that he attests a tradition that it was Matthew who actually transcribed some or much of the tradition known to us now as shared by Matthew and Luke and set it out in writing — the Q document. The difficulty here is that Papias is clear that Matthew gathered together the material in Hebrew (Aramaic), and if he speaks also of the Hebrew/Aramaic[92] being translated (into Greek), he attributes the translation to others. And though we can be confident that the Jesus tradition was being put about in Greek from a much earlier stage in the life of earliest Christianity,[93] that would certainly not exclude the possibility that the transcription of the Q material into Greek was done in a more systematic way at a later stage. The logic would then be that because the Q material made up such a significant proportion of the Gospel of Matthew, it was judged appropriate to attribute the Gospel as a whole to the one who provided the Q material which gives the Gospel of Matthew so much of its distinctive character. The problem would remain, however, that the one who actually wrote the Gos-

---

89. What Papias meant by 'each interpreted (*hermēneusen*) them as best he could' remains unclear, but *hermēneusen* could quite feasibly be rendered as 'each translated them . . .' (Gnilka, *Matthäusevangelium* 2.517-18).

90. See *Jesus Remembered* §§4.4b, 7.3. For those who assume that the relation between Matthew and Mark (and Q) is to be explained exclusively in terms of literary dependence, it could be said that Matthew incorporated 90% of Mark (*Jesus Remembered* 144 n.15). But even if my point is taken, that Matthew almost certainly knew other versions of many of the Mark (and Q) traditions (see below §42.3a), it is still the case that Matthew knew and drew heavily upon Greek Mark.

91. A popular suggestion; see e.g. Kümmel, *Introduction* 120 n.69, though Kümmel himself dismisses it as 'a completely groundless assumption' (120); history of the debate in Robinson et al., *Critical Edition of Q* xx-xxxiii. Koester seems to be more sympathetic (*Introduction* 2.172). Brown caustically describes the suggestion as an attempt to 'explain the unknown through the more unknown' (*Introduction* 210). See also D. A. Hagner, *Matthew* (WBC 33; 2 vols.; Dallas: Word, 1993, 1995) xliii-xlvi.

92. It should be recalled that Acts 6.1 describes one of the two main segments of the earliest Jerusalem church as 'Hebrews', where the implication is that they were so called because they communicated in Aramaic; see *Beginning from Jerusalem* 248-51.

93. *Beginning from Jerusalem* §24.9a.

pel itself, on this thesis, is now two removes from Matthew.[94] Moreover, the author of the Gospel has not simply copied the Markan and Q material but has clearly put his own stamp upon the Gospel as a whole. So much so, that if the author of the Gospel itself was not Matthew, then the attribution of the Gospel as such to Matthew is at best misleading.

In short, if we take Papias's testimony seriously, we have to say that he was either mistaken (at least in part) or attributed the Gospel to Matthew unfairly.

The internal clues to authorship are equally problematic. As we will see in §42.3, we can certainly identify the author as a Jewish Christian, or Hellenistic Jewish Christian.[95] However, three verses in particular invite interpretation as personal references.[96] In Matt. 13.52 Jesus is quoted as saying, 'Therefore every scribe who has been trained for the kingdom of heaven is like the master of a household who brings out of his treasure what is new and what is old'. It is possible to see this as a description of what the author saw himself as doing.[97] In Matt. 9.9, in a passage in which Matthew seems to follow Mark closely, Matthew alters the name of the toll-collector called by Jesus from 'Levi' (Mark 2.14) to 'Matthew'. And in Matt. 10.3 Matthew alone adds to the names of Jesus' twelve disciples the brief description of Matthew as 'the toll-collector', confirming the identity of the toll-collector earlier called by Jesus as 'Matthew' (9.9). Quite why the author of the first canonical Gospel changed Mark's 'Levi' to 'Matthew' is unclear and disputed.[98] But it is certainly possible that 'Matthew' was the name by which the toll-collector disciple came to be known, and that the insertion of the name here was an attempt to identify the 'scribe' regarded as responsible for the Gospel itself — in principle, possibly even by the author himself.[99] This would certainly help explain why the Gospel itself so quickly became known as 'the Gospel according to Matthew'.

The basic problem with attributing the Gospel to the disciple Matthew, however, is the *date* of the Gospel's composition. If, as we shall see in the next

---

94. 1. Matthew — Aramaic Q; 2. translator of Q into Greek; 3. author of Matthew's Gospel.

95. E.g. Brown, *Introduction* 211.

96. Much as does Mark 14.51-52 in the case of Mark's Gospel (see below §42 n.155).

97. See e.g. Davies and Allison, *Matthew* 2.445; U. Luz, *Das Evangelium nach Matthäus* (EKK 1; 4 vols.; Düsseldorf: Benziger, ⁵2002, 1990, 1997, 2002) 2.364 n.21, though Luz himself is dubious (2.364).

98. See e.g. Gnilka, *Matthäusevangelium* 1.330-31; Davies and Allison, *Matthew* 2.98-99.

99. Luz thinks the attribution to Matthew is secondary, though early (*Matthäus* 1.104-105); but I fail to see why it is 'impossible' that the apostle Matthew, in writing the Gospel, would have used Mark 2.14 as his source (2.42-43); similarly Kümmel — 'completely impossible' (*Introduction* 121). Hagner is much more open: 'it is not at all inconceivable that Matthew might depend upon a Petrine account represented by Mark' (*Matthew* lxxvi-lxxvii); also *New Testament* 215-17.

section, a date no earlier than the early 80s is most likely, then we would have to conceive the disciple Matthew writing the Gospel when he was already in his 80s or older. That possibility must be judged at best very unlikely. The attribution of the Gospel to Matthew, then, given that the attribution itself must have been very early, probably implies that it was the work of a close assistant or disciple of Matthew, who after Matthew's death gathered Jesus tradition which Matthew had used, and composed the Gospel to honour his teacher and in the spirit of his teacher.[100] Such an act of pious devotion to a notable teacher would have been well known and well understood in the religious and philosophical groups of the time.[101] The most obvious alternative — that an influential individual or group wanted to claim apostolic authorship for the Gospel and lighted on the distinctive Matthean references in the Gospel (but, then, why not Peter, who features much more prominently in the Gospel than Matthew?)[102]— does not provide such a compelling explanation for the title so quickly ascribed to the Gospel. The question, however, remains obscure and a definitive answer is probably well beyond our ability to provide.

ii. Date

Given that Matthew almost certainly knew and drew on Mark, the date of Mark becomes the *terminus a quo* for the date of Matthew. That is, Matthew must have been written some time after 70.[103]

This accords also with Matthew's version of the parable of the royal wedding feast (Matt. 22.1-14). In a story form which Jesus may have been remembered as using more than once (cf. Luke 14.15-24),[104] Matthew alone includes the sub-plot that when the king summoned his guests to the feast, the guests maltreated and killed his slaves, and the king in response 'sent his troops, destroyed those murderers and burned their city' (Matt. 22.7). The addition rather ruins the main plot, since it seems to envisage a military expedition mounted and executed even while the feast was ready to be eaten. The most obvious deduction to draw is that Matthew (or his tradition) saw the rejection of the summons to the wedding, and maltreatment of the king's slaves, as predicting the rejection of the summons of the gospel of Jesus by the bulk of the people of Israel. The king's violent response almost certainly

---

100. Or should we be prepared to envisage a group product? Cf. K. Stendahl, *The School of St. Matthew and Its Use of the Old Testament* (Philadelphia: Fortress, ²1968).

101. See further below §39.3a and at n.179.

102. Gnilka, *Matthäusevangelium* 2.519.

103. Despite Irenaeus's assertion that Matthew 'issued a written Gospel among the Hebrews in their own dialect while Peter and Paul were preaching at Rome' (*adv. haer.* 3.1.1).

104. See *Jesus Remembered* 235-36.

reflects the destruction of Jerusalem in 70 by the army of Titus,[105] understood by the author (or his tradition) as God's (the king's) judgment on Israel for its refusal to accept the gospel, that Jesus was indeed God's Messiah (the king's son).[106] The parallel with Matt. 8.12 is striking: Jesus' prediction that the heirs of the kingdom would have no place at the heavenly banquet with Abraham, Isaac and Jacob. This reflection on the events of 70 clearly indicates a date for the writing of the Gospel of Matthew subsequent to 70.[107]

Can we be more specific? The dating of Mark, it may be recalled, was largely dependent on what Mark 13 (or specifically 13.14) reveals. The Matthean equivalent (Matt. 24) provides an equivalent puzzle. For if it envisaged 'the end of the age' (24.3) to be the 'final cosmic catastrophe'[108] and linked it to the destruction of the temple (24.2-3), then it would become difficult to conceive of Matthew writing at a date many years after 70 (since no 'final cosmic catastrophe' had happened). However, it is possible either to read Matthew 24 as distinguishing the recent destruction of the temple (24.2) from the still/soon to come 'end of the age'[109] or as referring entirely to the fall of Jerusalem using apocalyptic imagery.[110] So Matthew 24 is actually little help in resolving the question of Matthew's date.

But still we must ask, if later than 70, how much later? A *terminus ad quem* is probably given by Ignatius, who shows knowledge of Matthew's Gospel.[111] Particularly striking is his reference to Jesus' baptism by John 'in order that all righteousness might be fulfilled' (*Smyrn.* 1.1), where it is hard to doubt

---

105. The majority view; see e.g. Davies and Allison, *Matthew* 1.131-32; Luz, *Matthäus* 3.242-43.

106. Similarly Matt. 23.37-38.

107. A small minority argue for a date prior to 70 CE: J. A. T. Robinson, *Redating the New Testament* (London: SCM, 1976) 116 — late 50s or early 60s; R. H. Gundry, *Matthew: A Commentary on His Literary and Theological Art* (Grand Rapids: Eerdmans, 1982) 599-609 — before 63; Hagner, *Matthew* lxxiv-lxxv 'inclines' toward a pre-70 date; also *New Testament* 212-14); but see Stanton, *ANRW* II.25.3 1942-43. It is unclear to me how R. T. France, *Matthew — Evangelist and Teacher* (Exeter: Paternoster, 1989) can argue for a date before the mid-60s, even though he agrees that Mark may be dated as late as the early 60s (*The Gospel of Mark* [NIGTC; Grand Rapids: Eerdmans, 2002] 38). Davies and Allison list the range of dates advocated (*Matthew* 1.127-28).

108. A. Schweitzer, *The Mystery of the Kingdom of God: The Secret of Jesus' Messiahship and Passion* (New York: Schocken, 1925) 114.

109. Cf. Davies and Allison, *Matthew* 3.328-31, and Luz, *Matthäus* 3.436-37.

110. M. Theophilos, *The Abomination of Desolation in Matthew 25.15* (LNTS 437; London: T & T Clark, 2012).

111. The testimony of Papias (if his reference is to the Gospel of Matthew) may be dated to c. 100 or even earlier, but his magnum opus, *Expositions of the Sayings of the Lord*, is traditionally dated later (c. 130-140); see e.g. Davies and Allison, *Matthew* 1.128-29, and below §40.1i.

that he has drawn the phrase from Matthew's distinctive telling of the story of Jesus' baptism.[112] Since Ignatius's letters can be confidently dated somewhere between 100 and his death in about 118,[113] it can be safely inferred that Matthew's Gospel had begun to be circulated at least some years earlier. The possibility of detecting influence of Matthew's Gospel in the still earlier Christian writings of *1 Clement* (mid-90s) and the *Didache* (100-120?)[114] is much less clear, and so far as possible echoes are concerned, it is as likely that *1 Clement* and *Didache* reflect oral rather than written tradition.[115] So, can we be more precise?

As we shall see (§46.5b), Matthew's Gospel seems to reflect a period of tension and antagonism with the post-70 successors of the Pharisees (Matt. 23, especially vv. 7-8). If so, that immediately narrows down options for both date and place of origin for the Gospel. The question is, then, how soon after 70 CE would it be possible to envisage the life-setting of Matthew's Gospel? On the one hand we can dismiss the likelihood that the rabbis who set about reconstituting Judaism at Yavneh could have resolved all the halakhic issues straightaway and could have exerted their influence immediately over the whole of Israel and Judaism. The other factions of Second Temple Judaism had been either effectively destroyed (Essenes, Zealots) or sharply diminished in power (Sadducees and wealthy families). Even so, however, it must be judged highly unlikely that the heirs of the Pharisees would have gained immediate and universal authority over their fellow Jews.[116] On the other hand, the possibility of widespread support for the one remaining Jewish authority (apparently recognized by the Romans) and also a growing (if still limited) acceptance of their rulings should not be dismissed out of hand either.[117] There

---

112. See below §44 n.38.

113. E.g. W. R. Schoedel, *Ignatius of Antioch* (Hermeneia; Philadelphia: Fortress, 1985) 5; *ODCC* 817 (c. 107); Schnelle, *History* 222 (c.110); further §40.1b below.

114. See §40.1a, e below.

115. Christopher Tuckett and Andrew Gregory in Gregory and Tuckett, eds., *Reception* 95-127, 131-39. E. Massaux, *The Influence of the Gospel of Matthew on Christian Literature before Saint Irenaeus* (2 vols.; Macon: Mercer University, 1990), concludes that *1 Clem.* 15.2, 27.5 and 46.7-8 demonstrate literary dependence on Matthew (1.7-32). W.-D. Köhler, *Die Rezeption des Matthäusevangeliums in der Zeit vor Irenäus* (WUNT 2.24; Tübingen: Mohr Sieback, 1987), thinks that *Did.* 8.1-2 probably shows dependency on Matthew (30-36). Gnilka thinks it possible that 1 Peter knew Matthew's Gospel — cf. 1 Pet. 2.12 with Matt. 5.16, and 1 Pet. 3.14 with Matt. 5.10 (*Matthäusevangelium* 2.519). Detailed discussion in §44 below. That 2 Pet. 1.17f. obviously draws on Matthew's version (Matt. 17.5) of the transfiguration story does not much help since 2 Peter was later than Matthew on any reckoning (see §39.3f below).

116. See n.122 below.

117. Davies and Allison, *Matthew* 3.700-701; see also §42 n.196 below.

is more to be discussed on the question of whether Matthew reflects a breach with Judaism (§46.5), but the discussion is unlikely to provide a firmer date. So we will have to be content with the large consensual view that the Gospel of Matthew was probably written in the 80s, probably in the mid- to late 80s.[118]

iii. Place of Writing — From or For

The above discussion of the likely protagonists targeted in Matt. 23 has an immediate corollary for the detection of the place where Matthew's Gospel was written. For as we have seen, there is a considerable question as to how quickly the Yavnean sages established their authority and how widely and quickly they were able to extend their influence over Jewish communities. It is likely, for example, that as a phenomenon, rabbinic Judaism initially commanded respect only within Judaea itself, a respect which grew only gradually. Apart from the transformation of the half-shekel temple tax into the *fiscus Iudaicus* (now to be paid to the temple of Jupiter Capitolinus in Rome), most of diaspora Judaism probably was substantially unaffected by the disaster of the Jewish war.[119] They would not feel such necessity for the sages' rulings at Yavneh as the sages themselves no doubt hoped to inculcate. This makes it very unlikely that the life-setting for Matthew's Gospel can be located far beyond the borders of the land of Israel.

Even with Galilee[120] it may be significant that rabbinic tradition includes indications that Yohanan ben Zakkai, the founding father of the Yavneh 'academy', was not much appreciated in Galilee. The accounts are of his time in Galilee, in the village of 'Arav, well before the Jewish revolt itself: that during that time only two cases of halakhah were brought to him, and that he parted from Galilee with the bitter condemnation, 'O Galilee, Galilee! You hate

---

118. Of recent commentators, Gnilka suggests around 80 (*Matthäusevangelium* 2.520); Luz, not long after 80 (*Matthew* 1.104); Davies and Allison, 80-95 (*Matthew* 1.127-38); Schnelle, around 90 (*History* 222); Brown, 80-90 (*Introduction* 216-17); D. C. Sim, *The Gospel of Matthew and Christian Judaism: The History and Social Setting of the Matthean Community* (Edinburgh: T & T Clark, 1998) 31-40 — between 85 and 95; 'the First Gospel cannot have been composed before AD 90, and it can have been composed even later (between 90 and 100), because it presupposes the powerful consolidation of Judaism in Jewish Palestine after the catastrophe of AD 70' (Hengel, *Four Gospels* 72). J. D. Kingsbury, concluding the conference papers published as D. L. Balch, ed., *Social History of the Matthean Community: Cross-disciplinary Approaches* (Minneapolis: Fortress, 1991), reaffirms the common assumption of between 85 and 100 (263).

119. See again below §46.3b.

120. J. A. Overman, *Matthew's Gospel and Formative Judaism. The Social World of the Matthean Community* (Minneapolis: Fortress, 1990), argues in favour of a Galilean provenance (155-59). See also L. M. White, 'Crisis Management and Boundary Maintenance: The Social Location of the Matthean Community', in Balch, ed., *Social History* ch. 10.

the Torah!'.[121] Did the preservation of this tradition reflect an ongoing resistance in Galilee to the developing halakhoth under Yohanan's leadership in Yavneh? And if the influence of Yavneh took well into the 80s to establish itself in Galilee, then presumably the further extension into the diaspora communities of Syria took even longer.

The characterization of an ever widening ripple of influence from Yavneh extending steadily and uninterruptedly beyond Judaea to the diaspora communities outside the holy land, and extending evenly as it spread, is almost certainly unrealistic.[122] Diaspora Judaism was variously affected by the Jewish revolt.[123] And there may well have been pockets of Jewish loyalists within the (probably) near diaspora who thought the Yavnean sages were heading in the right direction and sought to follow their lead or to emulate them. It is not simply a matter of assuming that a later date for Matthew's Gospel allows a place of origin further beyond the borders of the land of Israel/Palestine. Nevertheless, the strongest probability (relatively speaking) is that Matthew's Gospel reflects a situation in the near-abroad — that is, within Syria.[124] Of all the diaspora, Jews were most numerous in Syria and particularly in Antioch (Josephus, *War* 7.43); and though they had attracted many (God-fearing) Gentiles in the years before the Jewish revolt (7.45),[125] the savage persecution they experienced during the revolt (7.46-62) may have made the more conservative Judaism emerging from Yavneh more attractive to many of the survivors as they too sought to reaffirm their Jewish identity in the aftermath of the catastrophe of 70. Syria, then, and perhaps specifically Antioch, is the most plausible location of the Matthean community and for the composition of the Gospel.[126] Since our knowledge of the place of origin

---

121. J. Neusner, *First Century Judaism in Crisis* (Nashville: Abingdon, 1975) 58-64.

122. That the influence of the rabbis extended only gradually over several centuries is now the consensus view; see §38 n.51 above, §46.6g below, and A. J. Saldarini, *Matthew's Christian-Jewish Community* (University of Chicago, 1994) 13-18.

123. There were several Jewish revolts in the diaspora (Egypt, Cyrene, Cyprus, Mesopotamia) during Trajan's reign (115-117 CE); see Schürer, *History* 1.529-32, and further below §46.3c.

124. G. D. Kilpatrick, *The Origins of the Gospel according to Saint Matthew* (Oxford: Clarendon, 1946), argued for a Phoenician port, perhaps Tyre or Sidon (ch. 7).

125. This helps explain why it was in Antioch that the early Christian mission made the decisive opening to the Gentiles (Acts 11.19-26); see further *Beginning from Jerusalem* §24.8.

126. So most — e.g. Kümmel, *Introduction* 119; J. P. Meier in R. E. Brown and J. P. Meier, *Antioch and Rome: New Testament Cradles of Catholic Christianity* (London: Geoffrey Chapman, 1983) 18-27 — emphasizing Ignatius's knowledge and use of Matthew (24-25; see also §44.2d); Gnilka, *Matthäusevangelium* 2.514-15; Kingsbury in Balch, ed., *Social History* 264; Brown, *Introduction* 212-14; Sim, *Gospel of Matthew* 40-62, 104-7; Luz, *Matthäus* 1.100-103; Hagner, *New Testament* 214-15; Davies and Allison are less confident (*Matthew*

of all four canonical Gospels is so limited, the location of Matthew in Syria may be the firmest of a number of disputed conclusions!

d. The Gospel of John

Of the four NT Gospels, John is the one which might most justifiably be treated with the non-NT Gospels. For, as we shall see, it is very different from the three other NT Gospels, the Synoptic Gospels. And, at least superficially, it seems closer in its presentation of Jesus, its character and emphases, to some of the other Gospels, *The Dialogue of the Saviour*, for example.[127] So, one of the principal tasks to be undertaken will be the demonstration that this superficial reading of John *is* superficial, and that John is closer to the Synoptic Gospels than to the non-NT Gospels — that John is a 'Gospel' as that category has been determined by Mark and the other Synoptics (§41).[128] First, however, we must ask the usual introductory questions, to locate John's Gospel as best we can in history, before pursuing our first main thematic question — how the Gospels (canonical and other) handle the Jesus tradition (Part Eleven).

i. Author

From the title of the Gospel, *EUANGELION KATA IŌANNĒN*, the same reasoning works as with the other NT Gospels.[129] The fact that the Gospel of John is never attributed to other than 'John' must mean that this label was attached to it from the beginning, and that this ascription to 'John' was more or less universally understood.[130] But as with the other canonical Gospels

---

1.143-47). The fact that Ignatius, from Syrian Antioch, provides the earliest testimony to familiarity with the Gospel of Matthew (§39.2c(ii)) is probably significant here. Some find support in the reference to Syria in Matt. 4.24 ('his fame spread throughout all Syria' (e.g. Schnelle, *History* 222). Stanton briefly reviews other suggestions (*ANRW* II.25.3 1941-42). E.-J. Vledder, *Conflict in the Miracle Stories: A Socio-Exegetical Study of Matthew 8 and 9* (JSNTS 152; Sheffield: Sheffield Academic, 1997), gathers together such indications as there are of the social stratification of the Matthean community (118-39); see also W. Carter, *Matthew and the Margins: A Socio-Political and Religious Reading* (JSNTS 204; Sheffield: Sheffield Academic, 2000) 17-29, 43-49.

127. See below §43 n.98 and §44.4d.
128. See further §43.1 below.
129. The earliest text attributing the Gospel to John (*KATA IŌANNĒN*) is p[66], but that is usually dated to about 200 CE, though perhaps earlier. As with the other inscriptions, the *KATA IŌANNĒN* is presumably an abbreviation of the fuller, already established and taken for granted title, *EUANGELION KATA IŌANNĒN*.
130. Some anti-Montanists attributed the Gospel of John to the Gnostic Cerinthus (Kümmel, *Introduction* 196-97); see also below §49.3d.

the question was naturally asked, and asked quite early, 'Which John?' The question has an unusual sharpness and relevance, since we know from church tradition of several Johns: notably John, son of Zebedee, brother of James, one of the apostles; but also John the seer, the author of Revelation (the Apocalypse of John — Rev. 1.1, 4, 9; 22.8); and 'the elder (*presbyteros*) John', so designated by Papias;[131] not to mention John Mark.[132] The issue is made more complicated by the question of 'the beloved disciple' (who was he?), and the probability that John 21 (at least) is an appendix added to the Gospel to complete its composition as 'the Gospel according to John'.[133]

The first and potentially most revealing evidence is John 21.24, where a wider community attest the source of their authority, and, it would appear, the author of the Gospel: 'This is the disciple who testifies to these things and has written them; and we know that his testimony is true'.[134] The intriguing feature is that the disciple so referred to is 'the disciple whom Jesus loved' (21.20). The implication of 21.23 (Jesus had *not* said that this disciple would not die) is that the disciple in fact *had* died.[135] So his community, or disciples, or circle, take the opportunity, by adding the conclusion (21.24-25) to what presumably had already been known as an established tradition (21.1-23), to attribute both the witness and the written account of it to him.

The reasoning can take another obvious step. For 'the beloved disciple' appears on several occasions in the main body of the Gospel;[136] so it would be unwise to limit 'these things' to the account only of John 21. This reasoning is confirmed by 19.35 — a passage very similar to 21.24: 'he who saw this

---

131. Eusebius, *HE* 3.39.4. The fact that Eusebius goes on immediately to discuss the tradition that there were two Johns, both linked with Ephesus (3.39.5-7), indicates that the name 'John' itself was not a sufficiently explicit identification.

132. Some suggest an otherwise unknown John — see e.g. those cited by Schnelle, *History* 474 n.109; Brown — 'a minor figure during the ministry of Jesus' who 'became important in Johannine community history' (*Introduction* 369).

133. See e.g. Hagner, *New Testament* 273-75 and further below §43.1b.

134. Somewhat surprisingly Bauckham argues that 21.24 is the author's personal testimony ('the disciple' = 'we' = 'I') (*Jesus and the Eyewitnesses* 369-70, 379-80). But see R. A. Culpepper, 'John 21:24-25: The Johannine *Sphragis*', in P. N. Anderson et al., eds., *John, Jesus and History* vol. 2: *Aspects of Historicity in the Fourth Gospel* (Atlanta: SBL, 2009) 349-64: 'The Johannine *sphragis* implies a set of relationships. The writer is a member of a group ("we") who were sufficiently close to the Beloved Disciple to certify the truth of his Gospel' (363). In his earlier treatment (1993), reprinted in *The Testimony of the Beloved Disciple* (Grand Rapids: Baker, 2007) ch. 3, Bauckham takes the more obvious line: the 'editor distinguishes both himself and the school from the author of the Gospel (v. 24), who is identified as the beloved disciple to whom the preceding three verses refer' (79, 82).

135. Kümmel, *Introduction* 236.

136. John 13.23-25; 19.26-27; 20.2-8; as well as 21.7, 20. Is he the same as the unnamed 'other disciple' of 18.15-16? But why does he not appear before ch. 13?

[the blood and water from the side of the crucified Jesus] has testified, and his testimony is true; and he knows that he speaks the truth, in order that you might believe'.[137] Since the Gospel has just reported that 'the disciple whom Jesus loved' was one of the small band who stood near the cross (the others being women), the obvious implication is that 'he who saw [and attested] this' was the beloved disciple.[138] Striking also is 19.35's parallel with 20.31, which reads like the conclusion to the Gospel (before the addition of ch. 21): 'these things are written in order that you might believe that Jesus is the Christ, the Son of God, and that believing you might have life in his name'.

The point is obvious, though sometimes overshadowed by discussion of the patristic testimony regarding John's Gospel. Here, already within the Gospel in its final form, is explicit testimony regarding the Gospel's authorship. This is exceptional. None of the other canonical Gospels contain such affirmations regarding their authorship. Long before second-century Christians discussed or mentioned the authorship of John's Gospel, the puzzle of authorship was given a resolution. To be noted is the fact that the attestation is twofold. (1) It is an attestation that the personal *source*, and therefore *authority* ('his testimony is true'), of such details, as of the whole story, was personally involved, was actually a participant eye- and ear-witness. (2) The attestation is also that this first-hand witness also *wrote* 'these things'; John's Gospel was authored by one who had been a close disciple of Jesus.

Unfortunately we cannot move much further beyond these conclusions. For the identity of 'the beloved disciple' remains one of the great mysteries — a mystery perhaps intended to avoid too much attention being paid to him or too much prestige being attributed to him. The possibility that he was a literary invention, symbolic of discipleship close to Jesus (cf. 13.23), has been frequently mooted.[139] But the passages already noted, which refer back to him as a figure of authority whose testimony can be trusted, point

---

137. For some, the parallel carries the implication that 19.35 was added by the author of ch. 21 (Kümmel, *Introduction* 208 and n.52).

138. C. K. Barrett, *The Gospel according to St John* (London: SPCK, 1955, ²1978) 118-19, 557-58.

139. Kümmel, *Introduction* 238 n.187; Schnelle, *History* 482; A. T. Lincoln, *The Gospel according to Saint John* (BNTC; London: Continuum, 2005) 22-24; H. Thyen, *Das Johannesevangelium* (HNT 6; Tübingen: Mohr Siebeck, 2005) 2; I. Dunderberg, *The Beloved Disciple in Conflict? Revisiting the Gospels of John and Thomas* (Oxford: Oxford University, 2006) 147-48; M. Theobald, 'Der Jünger, den Jesus liebte', *Studien zum Corpus Iohanneum* (WUNT 267; Tübingen: Mohr Siebeck, 2010) ch. 21. R. A. Culpepper, *John: The Son of Zebedee; The Life of a Legend* (Edinburgh: T & T Clark, 2000), comments: 'Solutions that interpret the Beloved Disciple solely as a symbolic figure do not satisfactorily explain the concern in John 21:20-23 over the death of the Beloved Disciple. As has often been remarked, symbolic figures do not die' (84).

rather to one who was genuinely believed to be and so presented as a reliable eyewitness. The earlier references to the beloved disciple also imply that he was one of Jesus' close disciples, one of the twelve (13.23; 19.26-27). And if we take the early attribution of the Gospel to John seriously (*EUANGELION KATA IŌANNĒN*), then the most obvious candidate for 'the beloved disciple' is John, the son of Zebedee. This John is never so named in the Gospel, though 21.2 refers to 'the sons of Zebedee'.[140] Is that because John was 'the beloved disciple'? The close association of 'the beloved disciple' with Peter (20.2-10; 21.20-23) also parallels the close association between Peter and John attested in Acts.[141] More to the point, these two passages also seem to boost the role of 'the beloved disciple' as an equal or alternative authority to the more widely recognized Peter[142]— perhaps even as a counter-authority, or even more reliable authority than Peter.[143] To this issue we will have to return (§49).

Nothing here is certain. The Gospel itself seems almost deliberately to tantalize the reader as to the identity of 'the beloved disciple'. Thus tantalized, several alternative identifications have been mooted as scholarship wrestles with the enigma.[144] And the testimony of the second-century Christian writers

---

140. I am unclear why 21.2-3 make it unlikely ('completely without foundation') that 'the beloved disciple' was one of those named, one of the sons of Zebedee, as Kümmel seems to think (*Introduction* 236).

141. Acts 3.1, 3, 4, 11; 4.13, 19; 8.14.

142. See particularly Bauckham, *Jesus and the Eyewitnesses* 358-411 (though see n.132 above); idem, 'The Fourth Gospel as the Testimony of the Beloved Disciple', in R. Bauckham and C. Mosser, eds., *The Gospel of John and Christian Theology* (Grand Rapids: Eerdmans, 2008) 120-39; idem, *Testimony* 82-87. M. Hengel, *The Johannine Question* (ET London: SCM, 1989), argues that the Fourth Evangelist had been a resident in Jerusalem, possibly belonging to the priestly aristocracy in Jerusalem, that he was an eyewitness of Jesus' death and a member of the earliest community, and that he emigrated to Asia Minor in the early 60s and founded a school; he there wrote his Gospel in his old age, 'in which typical "Jewish Palestinian" reminiscences are combined with more "Hellenistic", "enthusiastic" and indeed even Pauline approaches into a great synthesis [in which] the christological doctrinal development of primitive Christianity reached its climax' (134); the German version is much expanded — *Die johanneische Frage* (WUNT 67; Tübingen: Mohr Siebeck, 1993) (here 324-25). See also Culpepper, *John* ch. 3; T. Thatcher, 'The Legend of the Beloved Disciple', in R. T. Fortna and T. Thatcher, eds., *Jesus in the Johannine Tradition* (Louisville: Westminster John Knox, 2001) 91-99; A. T. Lincoln, '"We Know That His Testimony Is True": Johannine Truth Claims and Historicity', in P. N. Anderson et al., eds., *John, Jesus and History* vol. 1: *Critical Appraisals of Critical Views* (Symposium Series 44; Atlanta: SBL, 2007) 179-97 (here 180-83).

143. John 21 'was written in the interests of adjusting competing claims of ecclesiastical authorities' (Koester, *Introduction* 2.186-87).

144. E.g. Lazarus: Kümmel, *Introduction* 237-38; B. Witherington, 'What's in a Name? Rethinking the Historical Figure of the Beloved Disciple in the Fourth Gospel', in

does little to resolve it. True, Irenaeus, towards the end of the second century, clearly attests that the author of the Gospel was John — 'John, the disciple of the Lord, who also reclined on his breast, himself also gave out the gospel'.[145] Irenaeus thus affirms the identity of the beloved disciple as John. It is entirely possible that this tradition reaches well back into the early years of the second century. For Irenaeus traces his knowledge of 'John, the disciple of the Lord', back to 'all the elders, who in Asia conferred with John, the disciple of the Lord, and bear witness to what John had handed down'.[146] Above all Irenaeus would have had in mind Papias and Polycarp, for elsewhere he speaks glowingly of his own boyhood memory of Polycarp speaking about John.[147] And he also describes Papias, a companion (*hetairos*) of Polycarp, as 'the hearer (*akoustēs*) of John' (*HE* 3.39.1).[148] Polycarp, bishop of Smyrna, and probably the leading Christian in Asia Minor in the middle of the second century, was executed in about 155 when he was well into his 80s; and Papias, bishop of Hierapolis, is usually dated to about 60-130.[149] So an overlap with John, 'the disciple of the Lord', is entirely probable. In other words, the testimony of Irenaeus, even though about 80 years after the likely publication of John's Gospel, is linked almost directly to the person (through Polycarp) to whom he attributed the Gospel of John.[150]

It is somewhat of a puzzle, however, that in the quotations from Papias provided by Eusebius there is no reference to John as the author of the fourth Gospel. It is equally puzzling that Ignatius, in writing to Ephesus, where the

---

Anderson et al., eds., *John, Jesus and History* 2.203-12. Thomas: J. H. Charlesworth, *The Beloved Disciple* (Valley Forge, Pa.: TPI, 1995); critique in I. Dunderberg, 'Thomas and the Beloved Disciple', in R. Uro, ed., Thomas *at the Crossroads: Essays on the* Gospel of Thomas (Edinburgh: T & T Clark, 1998) 65-88 (here 73-80); Lincoln, *Saint John* 20-22.

145. Irenaeus, *Against Heresies* 3.1.1 = Eusebius, *HE* 5.8.4 — using the wording of John 13.25.

146. Irenaeus, *Against Heresies* 2.22.5 = Eusebius, *HE* 3.23.3.

147. 'I remember the events of those days more clearly than those which happened recently . . . so that I can speak even of the place in which the blessed Polycarp sat and discoursed, . . . the discourses which he made to the crowd, and how he reported his intercourse with John and with the others who had seen the Lord, how he remembered their words and some of the things concerning the Lord which he had heard from them, his miracles and his teaching . . .' (Eusebius, *HE* 5.20.5-6). Eusebius quotes Irenaeus's recollections of Polycarp, including his stories about John, on several occasions (*HE* 3.28.6; 3.36.12; 3.39.1; 4.14.1-9 — cited by Schnelle, *History* 472; 5.24.16-17); Irenaeus (and Eusebius) clearly regarded Polycarp as a primary link with the apostles.

148. Kümmel, however, notes that to describe Papias as a 'hearer of John' does not square well with what Papias himself claimed, in *HE* 3.39.3-4 (*Introduction* 241-42).

149. Polycarp — S. C. Wilson, *ABD* 5.389-90; Papias — W. R. Schoedel, *ABD* 5.140-42.

150. The tradition of John as the author of the fourth Gospel was wider (probably general) in Asia Minor, but also in Rome; see Kümmel, *Introduction* 239-40.

memory of John was particularly treasured, also makes no mention of John. And Polycarp himself makes no reference to his relationship with the apostle John in his letter to the Philippians. The puzzle is that, if there was such a strong line of tradition, as Irenaeus maintains, it was never picked up or referred to prior to Irenaeus.[151] Nevertheless, the internal testimony of the Gospel itself, the implication of the inscription, and the claim of Irenaeus to a reliable chain of witness, together make a strong case for the tradition that the Gospel of John should be attributed to John, son of Zebedee, who is probably referred to in the Gospel itself as the beloved disciple.[152]

However, there are also indications, which we shall explore more fully in §43, that the Gospel as it has come down to us was the final product of a lengthy process of developing tradition and possibly earlier drafts or versions. So the possibility has to be allowed that the attribution of the Gospel to John began as or was even primarily an attribution to John as the *source* and *authority* for the tradition and materials which make up the Gospel of John.[153] One plausible suggestion, though it only adds to (or reflects?) the confusion on the subject, is that an earlier draft or version of the Gospel was edited and expanded by another John, 'John the Elder', who conveniently can be linked to 'the Elder' who wrote 2 and 3 John.[154] The confusion is not helped by the fact that Papias refers to 'the elder John', along with Aristion, as 'disciples of

---

151. A negative argument built on such silence assumes that there is no good reason (not necessarily a reason still discernible) which might explain such failure to make a specific reference.

152. Hagner, *New Testament* 266-73. Cf. the careful evaluations of R. Schnackenburg, *The Gospel according to St John* vol.1 (1965; ET New York: Herder & Herder, 1968) 75-104; R. E. Brown, *The Gospel according to John* (AB 29; 2 vols.; New York: Doubleday, 1966) 1.lxxxviii-xcviii; Barrett, *John* 100-105, 132. However, Schnackenburg, *Das Johannesevangelium*, part 3 (HKNT; Freiburg: Herder, ³1979) 449-64, and Brown, *The Community of the Beloved Disciple* (London: Chapman, 1979) 31-34, both changed their minds on the identification of the beloved disciple with John, son of Zebedee. For Schnackenburg, the beloved disciple was most probably a Jerusalem disciple of Jesus, but not one of the twelve (461). According to Brown the beloved disciple remains anonymous, but is still to be identified with the disciple of the Baptist in 1.35-40; but I question Brown's conclusion 'that the external and internal evidence are probably not to be harmonized' (33-34 and n.46). Contrast J. A. T. Robinson, *The Priority of John* (London: SCM, 1985), who argues strenuously 'that the ancient testimony of the church is correct that John wrote it [the Gospel] "while still in the body"', though not 'smoothly or finally edited' (xiii), with Bauckham, who, somewhat surprisingly, maintains that 'John the son of Zebedee is a phantom that needs to be finally and completely exorcised' (*Testimony* 75).

153. Brown, *John* 1.xcviii-cii.

154. E.g. Kümmel, *Introduction* 244; Hengel, *Johannine Question* chs. 2, 4; *johanneische Frage* chs. 2, 4; G. Strecker, *Theology of the New Testament* (1996; Berlin: de Gruyter, 2000) 463-66. But see also Barrett, *John* 105-109, and cf. his own hypothesis (132-34).

the Lord' (*HE* 3.39.4) — the same formula used to describe 'John, the disciple of the Lord'. It is difficult to see how the confusion between the two Johns might arise: would a John who had been so close to Jesus himself be described simply as 'the elder (*prebyteros*)'? Even so, it is quite plausible to argue that Papias himself thought the beloved disciple and author of John's Gospel was John the Elder.[155]

Perhaps we simply have to be content with the basic claim expressed in 19.35 and 21.24, and by implication in 20.2-10 and 21.20-23, that John's Gospel was rooted and sourced in the eyewitness testimony of one who was close to Jesus. If we also take the *KATA IŌANNĒN* with the seriousness it seems to call for, we can fairly conclude further that this inscription was attached because it was firmly believed by those who first received the Gospel, that John (apostle or Elder) was that source and authority.[156] And we may further infer, though with greater hesitancy, that this version of the gospel of Jesus Christ was put forth somewhat deliberately as an alternative or even counter to the version(s) whose source and authority were traced back primarily to Peter. This may not be much, but it is much more than we could have expected after asking the author question of the other NT Gospels.

ii. Place of Writing

There is a firm patristic tradition which links John to Asia Minor, and specifically to Ephesus. Eusebius quotes Irenaeus twice as attesting John's presence in Asia 'until the times of Trajan' (*HE* 3.23.3), and that 'the church at Ephesus was founded by Paul, but John stayed there until the times of Trajan' (*HE* 3.23.4). Also already noted is Irenaeus's testimony that John, the disciple of the Lord, 'gave out the gospel, while he was still living at Ephesus in Asia' (*HE* 5.8.4). To his earlier account, Eusebius adds a lengthy passage from Clement of Alexandria attesting John's missionary work from a base in Ephesus (*HE* 3.23.5-19). Later he cites Polycrates, bishop of Ephesus, attesting John's

---

155. See also R. J. Bauckham, 'Papias and Polycrates on the Origin of the Fourth Gospel', *JTS* 44 (1993) 24-69, slightly revised in *Testimony* ch. 2; P. Trebilco, *The Early Christians in Ephesus from Paul to Ignatius* (WUNT 166; Tübingen: Mohr Siebeck, 2004) 242-52.

156. See again Hagner, *New Testament* 266-73. The hesitancy shown by so many to attribute the original source and authority to John, son of Zebedee, is understandable, but when such evidence as there is points to a disciple of Jesus and eyewitness, or to a close disciple of John, as the source and author, it is not clear what purpose is served by denying that John himself was the original or primary source. Bauckham points out that it is a long way from authorship (as attested by 21.24, including 'written by a secretary') 'to the idea of the beloved disciple as merely the source or guarantor of the tradition that the Gospel incorporates' (*Testimony* 79). But I question his judgment that if the beloved disciple was one of the Twelve, 'it would be incomprehensible that the story [his testimony] tells is so different from the Synoptics' (27; similarly Hengel, *Johannine Question* 130; *johanneische Frage* 319).

death in Ephesus (*HE* 3.31.3), and the report that there were 'two tombs at Ephesus both still called John's' (*HE* 3.39.6). Eusebius also cites what was evidently a famous and much retold story which tells of John, the disciple of the Lord, who goes to bathe in Ephesus, but on seeing Cerinthus therein exited forthwith from the baths (*HE* 4.14.6).[157]

In view of such unanimous, and uncontested tradition, the most probable conclusion is that John, the beloved disciple, whether John the apostle or John the Elder, spent the latter years of his ministry in Ephesus and Asia. However, since there is no reason to doubt that the material which makes up John's Gospel was the outcome of a lengthy traditioning process, it is quite possible to nuance that main conclusion. For example, as we shall see (§43.1a(ii)), roots of the tradition in Galilee and Palestine are quite evident.[158] And before or after the destruction of the temple it is entirely plausible to see John, no doubt with (many) others moving out of Palestine, say into Syria, before moving more decisively into the western diaspora.[159] Asia Minor, and Ephesus in particular, with its strong Jewish minority or immigrant community, and its Pauline church foundation, would be an obvious location. We can say little more, and need say no more.

iii. Date

Intrinsically there are a few features in the Gospel of John itself which suggest a date later than the Synoptics. References to expulsion from the synagogue (John 9.22; 12.42; 16.2) are not much help, since it is not clear when believers in Messiah Jesus were first so expelled; and the events reflected in these passages may be very local.[160] John 11.48 seems to presuppose the destruction of Jerusalem and the temple.[161] John 19-21 seems to assume both that 'the

---

157. See also *HE* 3.1.1 and 5.24.3; and the full discussion of external evidence in Trebilco, *Early Christians in Ephesus* 241-63.

158. K. Wengst, *Bedrängte Gemeinde und verherrlichter Christus: Der historische Ort des Johannesevangeliums als Schlüssel zu seiner Interpretation* (Neukirchener-Vluyn: Neukirchener, 1981), concluded that the community for which John's Gospel was written lived in the southern part of the kingdom of Agrippa II — Gaulanitis and Batanea (97).

159. See e.g. those cited by Kümmel, *Introduction* 247 n.222; also Brown, *John* 1.ciii-civ. Kümmel himself argues that John's Gospel evinces 'substantive contacts with the Odes of Solomon . . . and Ignatius of Antioch', and that John arose somewhere in Syria is probably the best hypothesis (247). Similarly Koester, *Introduction* 178; *Ancient Christian Gospels* 244-46. There had been strong Jewish communities in Asia Minor since the third century BCE; see P. Trebilco, *Jewish Communities in Asia Minor* (SNTSMS 69; Cambridge University, 1991).

160. See further below §46.5c. U. C. von Wahlde, *The Gospel and Letters of John* (3 vols.; Grand Rapids: Eerdmans, 2010), thinks it possible to distinguish three editions of the Gospel: 1. 55-65?; 2. 60-65?; 3. 90-95? (1.50-54).

161. Schnelle, *History* 476.

beloved disciple' had already died (21.23), and that he was an alternative authority for Jesus tradition to the already well-established authority of Peter (21.24). And as we shall see, John's christology seems more developed than that of the Synoptics.[162] That is not to assume that early christology developed in a straight chronological line. But when the controversies over healing on the Sabbath are overwhelmed by christological implications (as in chs. 5 and 9), the historical context implied in the Synoptics seems to have become largely passé.

External testimony may provide some help. There is no clear evidence that the Apostolic Fathers knew John.[163] The earliest clear evidence of knowledge of John in Christian circles is Justin Martyr (*1 Apology* 1.61.4-5 — John 3.3-5), though Justin's first *Apology* cannot be dated earlier than about 150.[164] But the *Odes of Solomon* were either influenced by John's Gospel, or share a very similar spirituality,[165] and a strong case can be made for their composition in the first quarter of the second century.[166] This may relieve pressure on the textual fragment of John known as p^{52} which, until recently, was thought to provide decisive evidence that the Gospel of John must have been written no later than the first decade of the second century, since the fragment was generally dated to about 125 CE.[167] This dating, however, has come under question in recent years and a date around 150 argued for instead.[168] Even so, the fragment found in Egypt implies a Gospel already well circulated beyond its most likely place of origin and initial circulation.[169] So the most popular date for the Gospel of John in recent scholarship, in the last decade of the first

---

162. See below §43.1 and §49.3.

163. Barrett, *John* 110-11 (and further 111-15); Gregory and Tuckett, eds., *Reception* 93-94, 139-40, 197-99, 237-39, 252-53, 322. The most plausible suggestions are two passages written by Ignatius, *Rom.* 7.2 (John 4.10b, 14) and *Phld.* 7.1 (John 3.8); but see Paul Foster's evaluation in *Reception* 183-85.

164. See below §40.2e.

165. See below §49.6.

166. See particularly J. H. Charlesworth, 'The *Odes of Solomon*: Their Relation to Scripture and the Canon in Early Christianity', in J. H. Charlesworth et al., eds., *Sacra Scriptura: How "Non-Canonical Texts Functioned in Early Judaism and Early Christianity* (London: Bloomsbury, 2013) 89-107 (here n.5).

167. K. Aland and B. Aland, *The Text of the New Testament* (ET Grand Rapids: Eerdmans, ²1989) 84-87. Kümmel, *Introduction* 246, and Koester, *Introduction* 2.185, were confident on the point; and Thyen remains confident that p^{52} is from the first quarter of the second century (*Johannesevangelium* 1). p^{52} is one of the treasures of the John Rylands Library in Manchester; the fragment contains only John 18.31-33, 37-38.

168. Details in Schnelle, *History* 477 and nn.117-19; Strecker, *Theology* 461-62 and n.17.

169. That the Gospel of John originated in Egypt is generally regarded as very unlikely.

century or around the turn of the century, may well still be the most likely.[170] Here again, however, there can be little confidence and no certainty and it would be wise not to make any thesis regarding the development of early Christianity depend on a clear and firm date for John's Gospel.

39.3 The Rest of the New Testament

On a chronological scheme, it makes best sense to consider the other writings which have been preserved as part of the New Testament, since the NT writings constitute almost all of the Christian material which was written in the first century and therefore are the earliest (extant) Christian writings.[171]

a. The Issue of Pseudepigraphy

Several of the NT writings still to be considered are regarded by most scholars as pseudepigraphical or pseudonymous. So it makes good sense to clarify and discuss the issue before looking at the documents individually. The issue posed by the possibility or probability of pseudepigraphy is indicated by the term itself. The words 'pseudepigraphical' and 'pseudonymous' denote literary works *falsely* (*pseudo-*) attributed (*epigraphē* = 'inscription'), or falsely named (*onoma* = 'name'), although only the former term goes back to antiquity.[172] In both cases what is in view are writings which explicitly claim to have been written by a certain person, but which by common consent were written by someone else.

It is on the issue of falseness that the significance of pseudepigraphy within the NT hangs. The issue should not be confused with that of anonymity. Many NT writings are anonymous (notably the Gospels and Hebrews). But that fact raises no point of principle about such writings being included in the NT.[173] Nor should pseudepigrapha be confused with apocrypha. Both terms were used in the early church regarding those books which today are almost

---

170. The discussion of Brown, *John* 1.lxxx-lxxxvi, is exemplary.

171. We have already dealt in *Beginning from Jerusalem* with the main bulk of the Pauline corpus, including Ephesians, with James and 1 Peter, as also in effect Acts, even though all those specified most probably were written during the last three decades of the first century. Not all the NT can be confidently dated to the first century (notably 2 Peter), and of the Apostolic Fathers *1 Clement* was almost certainly written before 100. On the *Gospel of Thomas*, see §43.2 below.

172. It is attested in a second century BCE inscription from Priene.

173. We will return to the issue of 'apostolicity' in §50.2c.

§39.3 *The Sources — First Century*

universally known as the OT Pseudepigrapha,[174] but in this case 'apocryphal' has the sense of unsuitable for public reading, as opposed to the public reading of apostolic and hence canonical works.[175]

By putting the emphasis on false attribution, however, the term 'pseudepigraphy' implies a negative judgment as to a document's integrity and acceptability. This is clear from its earliest attested use in Christian circles, when Serapion applies it to the *Gospel of Peter*: 'the writings which falsely bear their names [Peter and the other apostles] we reject . . . knowing that such were not handed down to us' (Eusebius, *HE* 6.12.3). It is this judgment of falseness, of an intent to deceive and mislead, particularly by passing off as apostolic what should not be so regarded, which makes the issue of pseudepigraphy in the NT so sensitive.[176]

In the light of the negative judgment implicit in the term itself, the presence of pseudepigraphy in the NT would seem to pose a moral and theological problem for the notion of an authoritative canon of scripture. The uncomfortable fact is, however, that a large consensus of NT scholarship does indeed maintain that certain NT writings, particularly Ephesians, the Pastorals, and 2 Peter, are pseudepigraphic, the first two falsely attributed to Paul, the last falsely attributed to Peter. How then to handle the seeming contradiction within the very term 'NT pseudepigraphy'?

In the modern period there have been various attempts to hold together the conflicting ideas of pseudepigraphy within the canon.

(1) An early attempt was to argue that writers in antiquity did not share the modern idea of 'copyright'. If indeed writings had no 'author ownership' as such and were in effect common property, then use of another's name need not be understood as an attempt to deceive by claiming the named person's authority for the writing. The strength of this argument is that there is a difference between modern copyright mentality and the lack of inhibition among ancient writers in the way they freely incorporated material written by others within their own works. Nevertheless, W. Speyer has shown that the sense of 'intellectual ownership' was already well developed in Greek culture long before the first century BCE.[177] And though the Israelite literary tradition was characterized by anonymity, and it was the influence of Hellenism which brought the practice of pseudonymity into Judaism,[178] the same influence

---

174. See Charlesworth, *OTP*.

175. *Synopsis Scripturae Sacrae* 75, attributed to Athanasius.

176. J. I. Packer, *'Fundamentalism' and the Word of God* (London: IVF, 1958), put the point tersely: 'Pseudonymity and canonicity are mutually exclusive' (184).

177. W. Speyer, 'Religiöse Pseudepigraphie und Literarische Fälschung im Altertum', *Jahrbuch für Antike und Christentum* 8/9 (1965-66) 88-125.

178. M. Hengel, *Judaism and Hellenism* (ET 2 vols.; London: SCM, 1974) 1.129-30.

also brought the sense of 'intellectual ownership' into Jewish culture. This is evident, for example, in the ready acknowledgment which the writer of 2 Maccabees makes to the five volumes of Jason of Cyrene (2 Macc. 2.23), and in the sensitivities regarding false attribution in 2 Thess. 2.2 and Rev. 22.18.

(2) A second suggestion is that pseudepigraphy was widely recognized as an acceptable literary device in the ancient world. This argument works well with documents which first appeared centuries after the claimed author had died. As B. M. Metzger observes,[179] the Neo-Pythagoreans attributed their writings to Pythagoras himself, even though he had lived many centuries earlier. According to Iamblichus (c. 300 CE), indeed, it was an honourable act to publish one's treatises in the name of so venerable a teacher. It is hard to believe that such a convention was not recognized, at least by most thoughtful readers, in the case of, say, the *Enoch* corpus, the various *Testaments of the Twelve Patriarchs*, or the *Apocalypse of Adam*, all written probably between the second century BCE and second century CE. Similarly in the Christian period with the sixth-century works claiming Dionysius (or Denys) the Areopagite (Acts 17.34) as their author, but clearly drawing on Neo-Platonic philosophy.[180] But does the argument work so well in the case of, say, Ephesians, which must have appeared within a decade or two of Paul's death? There is a major difference between a writer adopting the pseudonym of an ancient or symbolic figure from an earlier epoch, not hitherto known as an author, and someone purporting to continue a particular literary tradition within a few years of its author's demise. The former may count as an acceptable device which was not seriously intended to deceive. The issue of deception is more delicate in the latter, and there is sufficient evidence that the ancients were alive to the issue.[181]

(3) A more popular view has been that pseudepigraphy was acceptable when it embodied the writer's claim to some sort of mystical or spiritual identity with the one whose name was used.[182] This is certainly possible to conceive within cultures where inspired individuals could speak in 'I' terms, that is, assuming the persona of the one in whose name they spoke or acting as the mouthpiece for the divine being who inspired/possessed them. The OT prophets

---

179. B. M. Metzger, 'Literary Forgeries and Canonical Pseudepigrapha', *JBL* 91 (1972) 3-24 (here 7).

180. To describe such writing simply as *pseud*epigraphic is misleading and betrays a lack of appreciation of and sympathy with ancient convention.

181. Metzger, 'Literary Forgeries' 12-16.

182. Cf. Brown, who speaks in relation to the late Pauline letters of 'treating Paul as the author in the sense of the authority behind a letter that was intended as an extension of his thought — an assumption of the great apostle's mantle to continue his work' (*Introduction* 586).

so spoke, and in the second century CE Celsus claimed that there were many such.[183] K. Aland in particular saw a solution here to the problem of pseudepigraphy in the first century and a half of Christianity: the attribution of authorship in effect to the Holy Spirit by the Spirit-inspired author threw 'a bridge across the generations'; the Spirit being the real author, the identity of the human author did not matter.[184] But in so arguing he ignores the widespread recognition in earliest Christianity of the danger of false prophecy.[185] The argument does have greater plausibility when applied to writings which themselves purport to describe visions and heavenly journeys on the part of the author.[186] But even there the sense of a mystical or ecstatic identification of the actual author with his pseudonym is lacking in the writing itself. And whether the argument works at all with, say, a letter genre must be regarded as highly questionable.

(4) The weighty contribution of N. Brox draws attention to three features in particular which at least help us understand the 'why' of the phenomenon of pseudepigraphy.[187] One is the characteristic 'love of antiquity' which is such a feature of the epoch. So, for example, since what was ancient called for respect, it was evidently important for the Jewish apologist Aristobulus (2nd century BCE) to argue that famous Greek thinkers like Pythagoras and Plato had been imitators of Moses. Pseudepigraphy then was a way of expressing the value of the past and of enabling readers to participate in it. Another relevant point is the similarly widespread idea of the 'noble falsehood', the idea that falsehood in support of a noble cause like religion was acceptable and did not attract the stigma of deceit. Brox notes that the Fathers too seem to have accepted the principle of what we might call the white lie, the good objective legitimating the questionable means. The third feature is the related principle, again evident in the Fathers, that the content of the writing was deemed more important than its authorship. An illustration would be Serapion's evaluation of the *Gospel of Peter* already quoted, where Serapion goes on to note 'that the most part [of the *Gospel*] was in accordance with the true teaching of the Saviour, but that some things were added' (Eusebius, *HE* 6.12.6).[188] However,

---

183. Origen, *contra Celsum* 7.9.

184. K. Aland, 'The Problem of Anonymity and Pseudonymity in Christian Literature of the First Two Centuries', in *The Authorship and Integrity of the New Testament* (SPCK Theological Collections 4; London: SPCK, 1965) 1-13.

185. E.g. 1 Cor. 12.3; 1 John 4.1-3; Hermas, *Mand.* 11.

186. Hence, presumably, its appeal to D. S. Russell in his treatment of apocalyptic writings — *The Method and Message of Jewish Apocalyptic* (London: SCM, 1964); similarly Speyer's category of 'echt religiöse Pseudepigraphie'.

187. N. Brox, *Falsche Verfasserangaben: Zur Erklärung der frühchristlichen Pseudepigraphie* (SB 79; Stuttgart: KBW, 1975).

188. On the *Gospel of Peter* see further below §40.4d.

valuable as these observations are in catching something of the relevant attitudes of the times, it is questionable how much they contribute to the specific issue of NT pseudepigraphy.[189]

(5) The most promising contribution to the discussion of NT pseudepigraphy in recent decades has been the thesis of D. G. Meade.[190] He argues that the most obvious context within which to examine the issue of NT pseudepigraphy is not Greco-Roman literary genres and practices,[191] and not simply particular Jewish apocrypha and pseudepigrapha, but the process in Jewish religious writing whereby tradition has accrued to a prominent historical figure, and particularly the process whereby an original oral or literary deposit has been expanded by the attribution of further material to the originating figure. He instances the Pentateuch, Isaiah, the Solomonic corpus, and the Daniel and Enoch traditions.[192] In each case he finds that 'attribution is primarily a claim to authoritative tradition, not a statement of literary origins',[193] a consistent pattern of living tradition with the same three features: (1) a revered figure in the past to whom a particular character of authoritative tradition could properly be attributed; (2) an elaboration of that tradition from within or at least in a manner whose continuity with and contemporizing of the original tradition were widely acknowledged; and (3) a recognition that the vitality of the tradition could not be maintained in that way when the connection and continuity with the authoritative originator became too distant, tenuous or wooden. When Meade turns to the NT he observes similar features in the letters usually regarded as pseudepigraphical, 'a consistent relationship between the development of the Petrine and Pauline traditions and the literary forms which they take'.[194] In other words, the relation of Ephesians and the Pastorals to the undisputed Paulines could be regarded as equivalent to the relation of Second and Third Isaiah to First Isaiah. In each case the motivation was to 'make present, contemporize' *(Vergegenwärtigung)* or renewedly actualize the authoritative Petrine and Pauline traditions for the following generation.[195]

---

189. See also J. Frey, ed., *Pseudepigraphie und Verfasserfiktion in frühchristlichen Briefen* (WUNT 246; Tübingen: Mohr Siebeck, 2009).

190. D. G. Meade, *Pseudonymity and Canon* (WUNT 39; Tübingen: Mohr Siebeck, 1986).

191. As still L. R. Donelson, *Pseudepigraphy and Ethical Argument in the Pastoral Epistles* (Tübingen: J. C. B. Mohr, 1986) 14-15.

192. See further my 'Pseudepigraphy', *DLNT* 977-84, on which I draw in this section (here 979-81).

193. Meade, *Pseudonymity* 102.

194. Meade, *Pseudonymity* 192-93.

195. Similarly on 2 Peter, R. J. Bauckham, *Jude, 2 Peter* (WBC 50; Waco: Word, 1983): The writer's 'authority lies in the faithfulness with which he transmits, and interprets for a new situation, the normative teaching of the apostles. . . . The pseudepigraphal device is

Of all the approaches to the issue of NT pseudepigraphy, Meade's seems to have the greatest potential to explain the conundrum of pseudepigraphy within the canon, that is, how it could be that the earliest Christians seem to have accepted documents claiming as author someone who was already dead. There was what might be called a biblical practice of continuing and developing a literary tradition, begun by an authoritative figure, after his death.[196] In each case, if Meade is correct, the developed tradition would have been recognized as sharing in the authority of the tradition's originator and would have been accepted as also authoritative under his name.[197]

b. The Pastoral Epistles

As with the other source material reviewed in this chapter, we limit our discussion to the same three questions, of authorship, recipients and dates.

i. Author

On the face of it the question, Who wrote the Pastoral Epistles?, has a straightforward answer. The three letters present themselves as written by Paul to Timothy (two letters) and Titus, whom he greets as his 'true' (and 'beloved') children. And their Pauline authorship was not really questioned in the second century, even though there are some questions difficult to answer.[198] But for

---

therefore not a fraudulent means of claiming apostolic authority, but embodies a claim to be a faithful mediator of the apostolic message' (161-62). See also J. D. Quinn, *The Letter to Titus* (AB 35; New York: Doubleday, 1990) 6-8; Hagner, *New Testament* 428-32.

196. To the extent that the Gospels can be seen as developing as well as transmitting the Jesus tradition, they too can be regarded as illustrating this attitude and practice.

197. For a robust rejection of such arguments, see W. D. Mounce, *Pastoral Epistles* (WBC 46; Nashville: Nelson, 2000) cxxiii-cxxvii. I. H. Marshall, *The Pastoral Epistles* (ICC; Edinburgh: T & T Clark, 1999), is more open on the issue (82-84, 92, 97-98). K.-W. Niebuhr refers to A. Baum, *Pseudepigraphie und literarische Fälschung im frühen Christentum* (Tübingen: Mohr Siebeck, 2001), who denies that there was an ancient convention to use pseudepigraphical names without any aim of fraud. Niebuhr tries to understand the exceptional phenomenon of using personal names of individual contemporaries, well known to their own circle and passed away only recently, as a mask for one's own statements as a sort of experiment in early Christianity caused by a change of situation (the passing away of earlier authorities) which in the end was not really successful and therefore was given up rather soon (evidence for this phenomenon runs for only a very short period of time) (personal correspondence).

198. Marcion's rejection of the Pastorals and the absence of the Pastorals and Philemon from p[46] are open to various explanations; and the probable echoes of the Pastorals, particularly Polycarp (cf. Polycarp, *Phil.* 4.1 with 1 Tim. 6.7, 10), Athenagoras (*Plea* echoes 1 Tim. 2.2) and Theophilus (*Autolycus* 3.14 quotes 1 Tim. 2.2), may only provide evidence

the past two hundred years the majority of NT specialists have concluded that they were not written by Paul himself and should be regarded as pseudonymous.[199] Their judgment is based on several features of the letters.[200]

- Language and style. The vocabulary is highly distinctive, with a much larger number of *hapax legomena* in each of the three letters than any of the other ten letters in the Pauline corpus.[201] Probably equally significant, there are a number of characteristically Pauline words which do not appear in the Pastorals, including various particles which serve as fingerprints of style.[202]
- Historical circumstances. It is difficult to square the details of Paul's movements implied in the Pastorals with what we know of them from elsewhere, since they imply Paul's release from house-arrest in Rome,[203]

---

for the existence of the letters rather than an assessment of their authorship. Discussion in Marshall, *Pastoral Epistles* 2-8; Mounce, *Pastoral Epistles* lxiv-lxix; L. T. Johnson, *The First and Second Letters to Timothy* (AB 35A; New York: Doubleday, 2001) 20-22.

199. The alternative suggestion that the letters were written by an amanuensis or secretary has been quite popular (see e.g. those referred to by Schnelle, *History* 332), but unlike Colossians, for example, for whom the amanuensis hypothesis makes good sense (*Beginning from Jerusalem* §34.6), there is no indication of composite authorship (cf. Col. 1.1) and no attempt by Paul to add his own handwritten note at the end (cf. Col. 4.18). Romans, transcribed by a secretary (Rom. 16.22), has typical characteristics of Paul's style. For the episodically popular suggestion that Luke wrote the Pastorals, see S. G. Wilson, *Luke and the Pastoral Epistles* (London: SPCK, 1979). For a more differentiated view with regard to 1 Timothy on the one hand and 2 Timothy and Titus on the other, cf. particularly J. Herzer, 'Fiktion oder Täuschung? Zur Diskussion über die Pseudepigraphie der Pastoralbriefe', in Frey, ed., *Pseudepigraphie und Verfasserfiktion* 489-536.

200. The following is almost the standard way of reviewing the evidence; see e.g. L. Oberlinner, *Die Pastoralbriefe: Erste Timotheusbrief* (HTKNT XI/2/1; Freiburg: Herder, 1994) xxxiii-xlv.

201. See particularly P. N. Harrison, *The Problem of the Pastoral Epistles* (Oxford University, 1921) 20-24 — e.g. 1 Timothy has 15.2 *hapax legomena* per page, whereas the nearest parallel in the earlier Paulines is Philippians (6.2 per page). Schnelle, *History* 330, drawing on K. Aland, ed., *Vollständige Konkordanz zum griechischen Neuen Testament* (vol. II; Berlin: de Gruyter, 1978) 456-57, provides different statistics, but to the same effect.

202. E.g. 'die', 'give thanks', 'boast', 'Spirit', 'wisdom', 'body', 'son'; see again Harrison, *Problem* 31-38. See also Kümmel, *Introduction* 371-74. C. K. Barrett, *The Pastoral Epistles* (Oxford: Clarendon, 1963), provides a clear summary of Harrison's statistics (5-7). Having reviewed the same data, Marshall concludes: 'there should be no room for doubt that the P[astoral] E[pistles] are distinctive in the Pauline corpus in that the three letters share a common shape of vocabulary, style and method of argument which is somehow different from that of the other ten letters in it' (*Pastoral Epistles* 63, 79). See also Johnson's warning not to overemphasize the significance of the differences in style (*1 and 2 Timothy* 68-72).

203. Eusebius, *HE* 2.22.2; 2 Tim. 4.9-18 speaks of Paul's 'first defence' and implies his release.

and his further travel in the Aegean area,[204] whereas the earlier Paul had been determined to go from Rome to Spain (Rom. 15.23-28).[205] Had Paul engaged in further mission, it would be surprising that Luke did not continue his story, whereas the implication of the closing scene of Acts (28.30-31), in the light of Paul's farewell speech in Acts 20, is that Paul's proclamation in Rome was the climax and 'finish' of his course (20.22-24) and that the Aegean believers would not see him again (20.38).[206]

- The opposition. If we can assume that all three letters reflect similar threats to the individuals or communities addressed, then we have to conclude that the alternative systems were Jewish[207] veering off in a Gnostic direction,[208] or a syncretistic mix of Jewish and proto-Gnostic elements. There is nothing parallel to this in the pre-70 NT literature,[209] but oddly we find a similar suggestion in Hegesippus that classic Gnostic heresies sprang from the Jewish believers-in-Jesus who survived the destruction of Jerusalem.[210]

- Increasing institutionalization. The Pastorals seem to reflect a degree of ecclesiastical organization which is closer to what we find in Ignatius than in the pre-70 Paul: 'elders' appear for the first and only time in the Pauline corpus;[211] 'overseers' (bishops) and 'deacons' appear as established offices;[212] Timothy and Titus are envisaged as ranking above both, exercising authority to ordain (1 Tim. 5.22), to appoint (Tit. 1.5),[213]

---

204. 1 Tim. 1.3; 2 Tim. 1.18; 4.20; Tit. 1.5; 3.12.

205. As Kümmel observes (*Introduction* 377-78), *1 Clem.* 5.7 could imply a trip to Spain — explicit in the Muratonian fragment (Luke omitted 'the departure of Paul from the city [of Rome] when he journeyed to Spain') — but neither refers or alludes to a further Aegean mission.

206. 1 Timothy implies further contact with the church in Ephesus (1.3; 3.14; 4.13), to whose 'elders', according to Acts 20.17, Paul's 'farewell speech' was delivered. See further *Beginning from Jerusalem* 953-54, 1052-57; also Schnelle, *History* 328-29. Marshall concludes that the considerations here are too indeterminate to contribute decisively to the issue of authorship (*Pastoral Epistles* 70-72). Johnson's reflections on possibilities do not help to resolve particular questions (*1 and 2 Timothy* 65-68).

207. Particularly 1 Tim. 1.7; Tit. 1.10; 3.9; see further below §45.4b.

208. 'Occupy themselves with myths and endless genealogies' (1 Tim. 1.4; 4.7; Tit. 3.9); 'Jewish myths' (Tit. 1.14); high value placed on 'knowledge' (1 Tim. 6.20); 'the resurrection has already taken place' (2 Tim. 2.18); a strong asceticism (1 Tim. 4.3; Tit. 1.15).

209. The attempts to explain the oppositions in Corinth and Colossae in terms of the later Gnostic systems are now generally regarded as failures; see above *Beginning from Jerusalem* §32.5b and §34.6c, d.

210. See below §45.3.

211. 1 Tim. 5.(1), 17, 19; Tit. 1.5.

212. 1 Tim. 3.1-7, 8-13; Tit. 1.7-9; 'office of overseer/(bishop)' (1 Tim. 3.1).

213. According to Acts 14.23, Paul (and Barnabas) appointed elders in the churches

to enroll (1 Tim. 5.9, 11) and to act as a court of appeal (1 Tim. 5.19); whereas in the earlier Paulines *charisma* was understood as engracing given to all members of the body of Christ (Rom. 12.4-8; 1 Cor. 12.4-11), now it seems to be understood as a formal empowering for office (1 Tim. 4.14; 2 Tim. 1.6).[214]

- Crystallization of the faith into set forms.[215] A coherent body of teaching seems to have been formed as a touchstone of what might already be described as 'orthodoxy': 'the teaching',[216] 'sound teaching',[217] 'the good teaching' (1 Tim. 4.6), 'the teaching which accords with godliness' (1 Tim. 6.3), 'the faith',[218] 'sound words',[219] or 'that which has been entrusted';[220] of which the 'faithful sayings'[221] are presumably typical. The role of the church hierarchy is to preserve, cling to, protect this tradition, and to pass it on faithfully to the next generation.[222]

In the light of all this data it is very difficult to avoid the conclusion that the Pastorals were not written by Paul and reflect situations which are most probably to be dated to a post-70 context. One can certainly hypothesize that Paul's tribulations changed his style significantly (even though only an extra two years are assigned to him by taking the Pastorals at face value). And the historical circumstances do not exclude the possibility of a further Aegean mission.[223] But the other factors point firmly to developments which take

---

founded during the(ir) first missionary journey, but Paul himself never refers to his having or exercising such authority; see also *Beginning from Jerusalem* 434-35.

214. See also my *Unity and Diversity* §30.1, §72.1. The structure envisaged for the churches in view seems to demonstrate the sort of institutionalizing tendencies which are characteristic of the second and third generations of charismatic movements. Cf. Marshall, *Pastoral Epistles* 95-97; and see further M. Y. MacDonald, *The Pauline Churches: A Socio-Historical Study of Institutionalization in the Pauline and Deutero-Pauline Writings* (SNTSMS 60; Cambridge University, 1988) Part 3. Johnson ignores some of these differences from the earlier Paulines and plays down the rest (*1 and 2 Timothy* 74-76).

215. Johnson regards the differences from the teaching of the earlier Paulines as 'one of the most effective of the arguments against authenticity' (*1 and 2 Timothy* 77-78).

216. 1 Tim. 4.16; 6.1; 2 Tim. 3.10; Tit. 2.7.

217. 1 Tim. 1.10; 2 Tim. 4.3; Tit. 1.9; 2.1.

218. 1 Tim. 1.19; 3.9; 4.1, 6; 5.8; 6.10, 12, 21; 2 Tim. 3.8; 4.7; Tit. 1.13; 2.2. 'While in Paul "faith" is the means by which salvation is appropriated, in 1 Timothy the dominant meaning is the content of faith as doctrine to be believed' (Schnelle, *History* 331).

219. 1 Tim. 6.3; 2 Tim. 1.13.

220. 1 Tim 6.20; 2 Tim. 1.12, 14.

221. 1 Tim. 1.15; 3.1; 4.9; 2 Tim. 2.11; Tit. 1.9; 3.8.

222. 1 Tim. 6.1, 14, 20; 2 Tim. 1.13-14; 2.2; 4.7; Tit. 1.9. See also *Unity and Diversity* §17.4 and §73b; Hagner, *New Testament* 626-32.

223. Mounce envisages a brief visit to Spain, a 'somewhat extensive' ministry in Crete,

us beyond the Paul of the earlier letters. It would not be surprising if one or more zealous disciples attempted to preserve what they regarded as the Pauline heritage in churches, which he or members of his mission team had established, by presenting him in a more conservative way, despite it being a portrayal which ill-fitted the more radical Paul who pioneered the Gentile mission. This being so, it is most probable that we should regard the Pastorals as pseudonymous, in the terms of pseudepigraphy as outlined in §39.3a above, and attribute them to an unknown (conservative) disciple who thought he was doing what Paul would have approved of and whose further 'letters of Paul' were accepted in the same spirit.[224]

There is one further intriguing possibility: that the author(s) built the letters round and as what he/they regarded as appropriate expansions of one or more brief letters which Paul had managed to dispatch after his imprisonment in Rome took a turn for the worse, perhaps following an initial hearing before Nero.[225] The key passage here is 2 Tim. 4.6-18, which has a very personal character and whose composition by someone else would make the charge of deliberate deceit hard to avoid.[226] It could

---

and 'years of Roman imprisonment' (presumably including the two years of Acts 28.30) (*Pastoral Epistles* liv-lxiv), which fits awkwardly with the tradition of Paul being martyred under Nero, that is, 64 (Eusebius, *HE* 2.22.2). This is presumably why Johnson stretches the date of Paul's death to ca. 64-68 (*1 and 2 Timothy* 84).

224. Marshall's hypothesis is that the Pastorals 'belong to the period shortly after the death of Paul. They, especially 2 Tim, are based on authentic Pauline materials whose extent cannot now be traced precisely, and they may well have been produced in a group which included Timothy and Titus themselves' (*Pastoral Epistles* 92). Johnson gives too little thought to the psychology and theology of 'pseudonymity' so conceived (*1 and 2 Timothy* 83-85). On Paul being presented as the source and architect of the tradition being passed on see especially M. Wolter, *Die Pastoralbriefe als Paulustradition* (FRLANT 146; Göttingen: Vandenhoeck, 1988), particularly 114-30. M. M. Yarbrough, *Paul's Utilization of Preformed Traditions in 1 Timothy* (LNTS 417; London: T & T Clark, 2009), notes that recognition of such preformed material does not resolve the question of authorship. See also A. Merz, *Die fictive Selbstauslegung des Paulus: Intertextuelle Studien zur Intention und Rezeption der Pastoralbriefe* (NTOA 52; Göttingen: Vandenhoeck, 2004).

225. Cf. J. D. Miller, *The Pastoral Letters as Composite Documents* (SNTSMS 93; Cambridge University, 1997). Miller's thesis of the incoherence of the Pastorals is countered by Marshall, *Pastoral Epistles* particularly 16-18. Mounce reviews the 'fragment hypothesis' negatively in *Pastoral Epistles* cxx-cxxiii; Marshall is more open on the possibility (*Pastoral Epistles* 73).

226. As noted in *Beginning from Jerusalem* 1054 n.411, the most plausible case for authenticity can be made for 2 Timothy; see e.g. J. Murphy-O'Connor, *Paul: A Critical Life* (Oxford University, 1996) 357-59. Marshall suggests that the stimulus for the composition of the Pastorals 'came from the existence of the authentic letter behind 2 Tim' (*Pastoral Epistles* 92). It has become customary to speak of 2 Timothy as a 'testament' of Paul — Koester, *Introduction* 2.300-301; 'testamentary exhortation' (Wolter, *Pastoralbriefe* 222-41);

suggest that following a first hearing, in which he had escaped condemnation (4.16-17), Paul was faced with the prospect of a second hearing which looked as though it might have a fatal outcome (4.6-7). In much harsher prison conditions, it is possible that Paul could have both lamented his situation, asked for help from friends and reaffirmed his faith in one or two brief letters. The plausibility of this suggestion is in itself no greater than the plausibility of a further Aegean mission carried out by Paul himself, but it fits better with the (post-Pauline) character of the letters themselves. As with other late Pauline letters, Colossians and Ephesians, there is too much uncertainty as to actual authorship for confident conclusions to be drawn, but the unlikelihood that Paul himself was the author of the Pastorals as they have come down to us is the strongest of the conclusions which can be drawn.[227]

ii. Why and to Whom?

To whom were the letters written? Or, if pseudonymous, for what reason were they written? In the latter case the answer must be based on the content of the letters. And given the character of the letters, all three, the most obvious answer is that they were written to consolidate the riches of the first generation, as perceived by the writers, and to ensure that the most enduring structure of the Pauline churches was passed on to the next and future generations.[228] Possibly also to ensure that Paul was remembered as demonstrating such concern for the future well-being of the churches he had founded or been responsible for founding.[229] There may even have been the motivation to pull Paul back firmly into the mainstream of Christianity as it was developing, so that his ecclesiastical legacy could not be interpreted primarily in terms of 1 Corinthians. Such a line of thought again suggests that the author(s) were more conservative disciples of Paul, or that they thought that in order to conserve the influence of Paul, he/they had to depict a Paul concerned to be thus conservative.[230] It also invites the thought that the Pastorals were written to

---

L. Oberlinner, *Die Pastoralbriefe: Zweiter Timotheusbrief* (HTKNT XI/2/2; Freiburg: Herder, 1995) 1-5.

227. See also Hagner's careful discussion (*New Testament* 614-26). In Meade's terms, their attribution to Paul was 'primarily an assertion of authoritative tradition, not of literary origins' (*Pseudonymity* 139).

228. 'The envisaged readers of the letters are people who can model themselves on Timothy and Titus, and this must include persons like them who were in a supervisory capacity over congregations' (Marshall, *Pastoral Epistles* 76); though Marshall believes that the key reason for the writing of the Pastorals was to combat 'false teachers' (41).

229. Cf. Wolter, *Pastoralbriefe* 243-56.

230. Contrast the *Acts of Paul* (§47.4a below).

be included in what we may infer was already in the latter decades of the first century a collection or collections of Paul's letters.

It is not impossible that the Pastorals were written to Timothy and Titus, or to mark some anniversary of their leadership, or to ensure that the values shown in their leadership were set down and preserved in writing. Eusebius records that Timothy was the first bishop of Ephesus and Titus the first bishop of the churches in Crete (*HE* 3.4.5). No doubt such an inference was drawn from the Pastorals themselves. But there is no reason why we should not infer from the Pauline correspondence that Timothy and Titus[231] exercised significant leadership roles in the Aegean churches of the Pauline mission following Paul's death.[232] At any rate, the Pastorals do indicate that Timothy and Titus were among the closest of Paul's co-workers and were regarded as appropriate figures to carry forward the Pauline inheritance, as they may well have done in any case.

iii. Date

The date too depends primarily on how soon the developed ecclesiology of the letters can be dated. On a rough estimate the date seems to fall somewhere between the ecclesiology of Ephesians and that of Ignatius,[233] and to match that of Acts.[234] This suggests a date in the last two decades of the first century.[235]

c. Hebrews

Hebrews is one of the great puzzles of the NT. Its quality as a writing (a tractate, or teaching sermon with exhortation blended in — a 'word of exhortation' [13.22] — and rounded off as a letter) is substantial; it is generally reckoned to be the finest Greek composition within the NT.[236] But the usual questions, particularly as to author and recipients, make it a far more unknown quantity than almost all of the other NT writings.

---

231. It remains an unresolved puzzle why Titus is nowhere mentioned in Acts.
232. Heb. 13.23 has the intriguing note that 'our brother Timothy has been set free'.
233. See below §40.1b.
234. Note the *episkopoi* (overseers/bishops) of Acts 20.28 and the *presbyteroi* (elders) of Acts 14.23 and 20.17.
235. E.g. Kümmel advocates 'the very beginning of the second century' (*Introduction* 387); Quinn favours 80-85 (*Titus* 19); Schnelle argues for c. 100 and cites others who share this view (*History* 333); Koester favours the older view of a date between 120 and 160 (*Introduction* 2.305), which hardly squares with the clear use of 1 Tim. 6.7, 10 in Polycarp, *Phil.* 4.1 (dated, probably, in the 110s — §40.1c).
236. Turner, *Grammar of New Testament Greek* 106-8.

i. Author

The biggest unknown is the document's author. The subsequent attribution to Paul, though not generally affirmed in the West till the fourth century, is given some credibility by the reference to 'our brother Timothy' in 13.23, and by the document's inclusion with the Pauline corpus in p^{46}.[237] But its style and outlook are very different from that of Paul,[238] and Pauline authorship has been almost universally discounted in the modern period.[239]

The most helpful, though still inadequate, clue is what can best be described as Hebrews' distinctively Hellenistic Jewish thought world.[240] For there are strong parallels to its thought world in Alexandrian Judaism, as illustrated by the Wisdom of Solomon and Philo. The initial impression given in the rhetorically powerful opening paragraph[241] is reinforced by the way in which the writer is able to use Exod. 25.40 ('See that you make them [the furnishings of the tabernacle] according to the pattern [*typos*] for them, which is being shown you on the mountain') to tie his line of thought into the Platonic-like cosmology of earthly entities as only copies or shadows of the heavenly ideals.[242] This

---

237. Kümmel, *Introduction* 392-93.

238. See e.g. Brown, *Introduction* 694.

239. See further H. W. Attridge, *Hebrews* (Hermeneia; Philadelphia: Fortress, 1989) 1-3, who observes, *inter alia*, that 'It is quite inconceivable that Paul, who so emphatically affirms his status as an apostle and eyewitness of the risen Christ, could have put himself in the subordinate position of a secondhand recipient of tradition as does our author at 2:3' (2).

240. Schnelle, *History* 378, 381. The Gnostic background presupposed by E. Käsemann, *The Wandering People of God: An Investigation of the Letter to the Hebrews* (ET Minneapolis: Augsburg, 1984), a thesis so characteristic of the middle decades of the 20th century, and still maintained in Koester, *Introduction* 2.274-76, is now generally discounted; see e.g. W. L. Lane, *Hebrews* (WBC 47; 2 vols; Dallas: Word Books, 1991) 1.cix; Schnelle, *History* 376-77.

241. The description of the Son as 'the radiance (*apaugasma*) of [God's] glory and exact representation (*charactēr*) of his real being' (Heb. 1.3) echoes both Wisd. 7.26 where *apaugasma* appears for the only time in the LXX, as a description of Wisdom, and Philo's reference to the eternal Logos as the *charactēr* of the divine and invisible Spirit (*Plant.* 18).

242. Heb. 8.5; 9.23-24; 10.1. Note the series of antithetical contrasts:

	the earthly copy	the heavenly reality
8.5	*hypodeigma kai skia* (sketch and shadow)	the heavenlies
9.24	sanctuary made with human hands	heaven itself
9.24/8.5	*antitypos* (copy) of the heavenlies	*typos* (archetype)
10.1	the law as shadow	of the good things to come
	and not	the very image of the realities

But note also the qualifications mentioned e.g. by E. Adams, 'The Cosmology of Hebrews', in R. Bauckham et al., eds., *The Epistle to the Hebrews and Christian Theology* (Grand Rapids: Eerdmans, 2009) 122-39 (here 132-33): 'While he uses Platonic-sounding language in his comparison and contrast of the earthly and heavenly shrines, there is no hard evidence

latter was a worldview characteristic of Philo, notably in *de Opificio Mundi* (e.g. 36), who also drew on Exod. 25.40 similarly to describe the furnishings of the tabernacle as copies of what Moses saw.[243] This is not to say that Hebrews knew or was dependent on Philo's writings.[244] But it is clear enough that Hebrews' evaluation of the wilderness tabernacle drew on the same or similar philosophical cosmology in order to make its point regarding the imperfections or inadequacies of the tabernacle and its sacrificial rituals. More distinctively, Hebrews blends this Platonic cosmological imagery with more typically Jewish apocalyptic tradition of the heavenly journey in which the patriarch enters heaven and views the divine thrones.[245] This enables the writer to portray the Aaronic cult not only as a shadow of the heavenly cult, but as also foreshadowing the fulfilling reality which Jesus had brought into effect, the old age giving way to the new, the old covenant to the new covenant.[246] The two emphases, foreshadowing and imperfect copy, do not detract from each other, but rather reinforce both the critique of the old sacrificial ritual and the claim that Christ had brought into effect the heavenly reality as seen also in apocalyptic vision.[247]

This line of thought does not bring us nearer to identifying a particular author, though of the relatively few names known to us from the first century, Apollos, from Alexandria, makes an attractive speculation and guess.[248] But

---

to suggest that Platonic dualism influences his understanding of the structure of cosmic reality' (138).

243. *Leg. All.* 3.102-3; *Mos.* 2.74; *Qu.Ex.* 2.52.

244. The overstatement of C. Spicq, *Hébreux* (EB Vol. 1, 1952) 39-91, was properly called in question by R. Williamson, *Philo and the Epistle to the Hebrews* (Leiden: Brill, 1970). The similarities and differences are neatly summed up by K. Schenck, *Understanding the Book of Hebrews* (Louisville: Westminster John Knox, 2003) 30.

245. E.g. Isa. 6.3; Ezek. 1; *1 Enoch* 14.10-20; *T. Levi* 3.2-4; see also Attridge, *Hebrews* 222.

246. Heb. 8.6-13; 9.8-12, 15, 26; 10.1, 9, 16. Further discussion and bibliography in my *Christology in the Making* (London: SCM, ²1989/Grand Rapids: Eerdmans, 1996) 52-54 and nn.210, 211.

247. H. F. Weiss, *Der Brief an die Hebräer* (KEK; Göttingen: Vandenhoeck, 1991), sees in Hebrews' thought a synthesis between 'apocalyptic' and 'Hellenism', not untypical of the syncretistic character of late antique religious thought (114). C. R. Koester, *Hebrews* (AB 36; New York: Doubleday, 2001) 59-63, 97-104 (with extensive bibliography): 'The problem is that Hebrews operates with both categories [Platonic philosophy and Jewish apocalyptic], yet it fits neatly into neither category' (98). See also the discussions in Attridge, *Hebrews* 29-30, 222-24; L. D. Hurst, *The Epistle to the Hebrews: Its Background of Thought* (SNTSMS 65; Cambridge University, 1990) ch. 1; W. Eisele, *Ein unerschütterliches Reich: Die mittelplatonische Umformung des Parusiegedankens im Hebräerbrief* (BZNW 116; Berlin: de Gruyter, 2003); K. L. Schenck, *Cosmology and Eschatology in Hebrews: The Settings of the Sacrifice* (SNTSMS 143; Cambridge University, 2007).

248. First suggested by Luther (details in Koester, *Hebrews* 35). For other suggestions see Kümmel, *Introduction* 401-3; Attridge, *Hebrews* 3-6; Koester, *Hebrews* 44-46.

given the uncertainty regarding the author already in the early centuries, the more relevant fact is that the quality and forcefulness of the writing were sufficient (just) for it to be accorded canonical status (by most). It is on this latter fact, rather than identifying some specific author, on which the value of the witness of Hebrews to the late first century of Christianity's beginnings depends, and with that we must be content.

ii. Recipients

'To the Hebrews' is almost certainly a title which was added, when the writing began to be more widely circulated, as an appropriate deduction from the intensely Jewish character of the writing, focusing as it does on Israel's sacerdotal and sacrificial ritual.[249] It was natural to infer that the recipients would be particularly interested in and informed about Israel's cult, able to appreciate the finer points of an argument that this cult and its sacrificial ritual had been overtaken and superseded by a higher (heavenly) reality which it had prefigured. So a popular answer to the question about recipients would be Jewish believers in Jesus who were hankering after the tangibility and splendour of the traditional temple worship.[250] It would also be natural to deduce that such a readership were diaspora Jews who were or had been frustrated by their distance from Jerusalem and inability to participate regularly in the temple cult, or who were devastated by the destruction of the Jerusalem temple in 70. At the same time, however, it could equally be argued that the recipients were God-fearing Gentile believers, whose attraction to Judaism had focused particularly on the Jerusalem temple and its rituals.[251] So the later title, 'To the Hebrews', hardly settles the question.[252]

Perhaps the most important clue is given in chapter 10, where the climax to the argument of the document is that sacrifices for sin which have to be repeated are ineffective (10.1-4, 11), whereas a once-for-all sacrifice which brings forgiveness has made repeated sin-offerings unnecessary (10.12-18). The repeated reference to 'conscience' in chs. 9 and 10[253] suggests that the

249. But the title is attested already in Clement of Alexandria (Eusebius, *HE* 6.14.2-4) and appears in codex Sinaiticus.

250. Spicq suggested that the 'great crowd of priests' who 'became obedient to the faith' (Acts 6.7) were the addressees (*Hébreux* 1.226-31), though there is no hint in Hebrews that the recipients had actually participated in Israel's sacrificial cult.

251. Kümmel, *Introduction* 399-400; at any rate the author was able to assume knowledge and respect for the LXX and the traditional Jewish cult (see further below §45.4c).

252. Koester, *Hebrews* 46-48; Hagner, *New Testament* 646-49.

253. 9.9 — '... the present time, during which gifts and sacrifices are offered that cannot perfect the conscience of the worshipper'; 9.14 — 'how much more will the blood of Christ . . . purify our conscience from dead works'; 10.1-2 — repeated sacrifices can never 'make perfect those who approach. Otherwise, would they not have ceased being offered,

pastoral concern was to address those who were troubled in conscience and harked back to the tangibility of the sacrificial cult, in that the ritual actions calmed the unquiet conscience.[254]

Where were they? The greetings from 'those from Italy' (13.24) could suggest a letter written to Rome, though the phrase is ambiguous.[255] The clear indication that Clement of Rome knew the letter[256] also points in that direction. And the reference to Timothy having been set free (from prison) might suggest a letter written from Ephesus (cf. 1 Tim. 1.3; 2 Tim. 1.18) to Rome. But little more can be usefully said.

iii. Date

The fact that no reference, explicit or otherwise, is made to the destruction of the Jerusalem temple would appear to favour a date before 70, and there is nothing in terms of the letter's christology or ecclesiology which would provide a clear objection to that.[257] On the other hand, it is noticeable that other post-70 Jewish writings continued to speak of the temple and its ritual in present terms — notably Josephus and the Mishnah.[258]

Probably more significant is the fact that the argument of the letter is all in terms of the wilderness tabernacle and its ritual as laid down in the Torah, and not with any reference to the Second Temple cult as such. This suggests that it was the scriptural principles, the foundational Torah legislation, whose continuing necessity and legitimacy were what the author wished to call into question. If his case could be made with respect to the Aaronic priesthood and the wilderness tabernacle, then the critique undermined Herod's Second Temple just as effectively. Indeed, such a strategy may well

---

since the worshippers, cleansed once for all, would no longer have any consciousness of sin?'; 10.22 — 'let us approach with a true heart in full assurance of faith, with our hearts sprinkled clean from an evil conscience . . .'; also 13.18.

254. B. Lindars, *The Theology of the Letter to the Hebrews* (Cambridge University, 1991) particularly 12-15. 'The focal problem Hebrews addresses is a waning confidence in the Christian confession' (Schenck, *Understanding the Book of Hebrews* 107).

255. See e.g. Weiss, *Hebräer* 76; Lane, *Hebrews* 1.lxviii-lx; Brown, *Introduction* 699-701; Koester, *Hebrews* 48-50. Schnelle favours a Roman origin (*History* 367-68).

256. See *1 Clem.* 17.1, 5 (cf. Heb. 11.37; 3.2); *1 Clem.* 36.1 (cf. Heb. 2.18; 3.1); *1 Clem.* 36.2, 3, 4, 5 (cf. Heb. 1.3-4, 5, 7, 13); *1 Clem.* 43.1 (cf. Heb. 3.5); *1 Clem.* 56.4 (cf. Heb. 12.6). 'At least in the case of [*1 Clem.*] 36.2-6 it is impossible to assume anything but literary dependence' (on Heb. 1.3-13) (Attridge, *Hebrews* 6-7).

257. Robinson, between 62 and 68 (*Redating* ch. 7); Lindars, between 65 and 70 (*Theology* 21); Lane, between 64 and 68 (*Hebrews* 1.lxvi); Hagner, early 60s (*New Testament* 651-52).

258. E.g. Josephus, *Ant.* 3.224-57; *Ap.* 2.77, 193-98; also *1 Clem.* 40-41; *Diog.* 3. See also Brown in Brown and Meier, *Antioch and Rome* 149-51; and below §46 nn.113, 114.

reflect a post-70 situation, in that any negative case made with reference to the now destroyed Jerusalem temple could be undermined by a response that the validity of the Torah-determined cult nevertheless remained, no doubt in hope that the temple would be restored again, as was Solomon's temple after the Babylonian exile.[259] By focusing on the Torah foreshadowings, and by showing their irrelevance now that the foreshadows had been fulfilled, *not* by the Jerusalem temple and its cult but by Jesus' death and entry into heaven, Hebrews could effectively undermine both any hankering after what had been destroyed, and any hope reliant on a future rebuilding of the temple. This line of reflection undermines the plausibility of a pre-70 date based on the lack of reference to the destruction of the Jerusalem temple by Titus's legions and strengthens the case for a post-70 date — while Timothy was still alive (13.23), and a decade or so before *1 Clement*, which is usually dated to about 96.[260]

d. James and 1 Peter

For James and 1 Peter I may simply refer to *Beginning from Jerusalem* §§37.2 and 37.3.[261] The two letters of Jude and 2 Peter can be considered in close company, since the general view is that the two letters are literally interdependent, most deducing that 2 Peter has drawn on Jude. So we turn to Jude first.

e. The Letter of Jude

i. Author

The letter claims to be written by Jude (*Ioudas*), 'brother of James'. Although there was more than one James associated with the beginnings of Christianity, the reference to 'James' without further identifying feature (even 'brother of our Lord') indicates the most prominent and most widely known 'James', which can only be James, the brother of Jesus and well known in earliest Christianity as the leader of the mother church in Jerusalem in the middle of the first century. We also know from Mark 6.3 that Jesus had brothers named

---

259. See §40 nn.65, 67 and §46 nn.87 and 110.
260. So most — e.g. E. Grässer, *An die Hebräer* (EKK; Zürich: Benziger, 1990, 1993, 1997) 1.25; Weiss, *Hebräer* 77; Brown, *Introduction* 696-97. See also §40.1f(iii) and §46.3a below.
261. On the whole question of early Christian letter writing see L. Doering, *Ancient Jewish Letters and the Beginning of Christian Epistolography* (WUNT 298; Tübingen: Mohr Siebeck, 2012), especially 429-81.

'James and Joses and Judas and Simon'.[262] Hegesippus also refers to a Judas 'who was said to have been his brother according to the flesh', whose grandsons, though simple folk, were leaders of the churches (in Judaea) during the reign of Domitian (Eusebius, *HE* 3.19.1–3.20.6).[263] So, there can be little doubt that the intention was to identify the writer of the letter as Jude, the brother of James and Jesus.[264]

Could this have been written by Jude himself? — presumably in the late 50s or 60s: after all, he may have been involved in missionary work (1 Cor. 9.5),[265] and, as just noted, his grandsons were church leaders in the 90s, according to Eusebius.[266] But as we shall see, such indications as there are point to a later date. So the letter Jude is probably pseudonymous, though the fact that it is Jude, brother of James, to whom the letter was attributed, probably indicates that he had a stature and significant role in the early (Judaean) churches which has been lost to us. It might even be the case that, as with the letter of James, the letter of Jude represents teaching which was known to have come from Jude or could be plausibly attributed to one of Jesus' brothers. Its very strongly Jewish character (§45.4c(ii)) certainly indicates a Jewish author, but also one deeply into Jewish apocalyptic reflection on present evil and its future judgment.

ii. To Whom Was It Written?

No one in particular, it would appear. Rather it reads more like a sermon topped with a letter introduction and tailed with a doxology, and circulated for wider distribution. The fact that several of the allusions to the OT[267] reflect a knowledge of the Hebrew text rather than the LXX[268] suggests that the

---

262. Matthew reads 'James and Joseph and Simon and Judas' (Matt. 13.55).

263. See further below §45.3.

264. So e.g. K. H. Schelkle, *Die Petrusbriefe; Der Judabrief* (HTKNT XIII.2; Freiburg: Herder, 1976) 140-43. On the implausibility of identifying Jude/Judas with Judas Thomas, identified as Jesus' twin brother in the *Acts of Thomas* and the *Book of Thomas the Contender* (*NTA* 2.324-25), see R. Bauckham, *Jude and the Relatives of Jesus in the Early Church* (Edinburgh: T & T Clark, 1990) 32-36.

265. Intriguingly, the *Acts of Paul* attributes Paul's acceptance by the Damascus church to 'the blessed Judas, the brother of the Lord, who from the beginning gave me the exalted love of faith' (*NTA* 2.264); and a Coptic legend speaks of Judas 'the brother of the Lord, who preached in Syria and Mesopotamia' (*NTA* 2.480).

266. Bauckham regards Jude, the Lord's brother, as 'entirely plausibly the author of this letter' (*Jude and the Relatives of Jesus* 178); earlier, Bauckham, *Jude, 2 Peter* 14-16.

267. See again §45.4c(ii) below.

268. Bauckham, *Jude and the Relatives of Jesus* 136-37. C. D. Osborn, 'The Christological Use of 1 Enoch 1.9 in Jude 14', *NTS* 23 (1976-77) 334-41, argues that Jude's citation of *1 Enoch* 1.9 (Jude 14-15) is closer to the Aramaic fragment of *1 Enoch* found at Qumran than to either the Ethiopic or fragmentary Greek text; see also Bauckham 138-39.

document was initially distributed in Palestine.[269] Possible reaction to Pauline themes[270] may also suggest a Jewish-Christian (Judaean) grappling with Pauline heritage.[271]

iii. Date

Our ability to determine a date for Jude is dependent on what we make of its character and various temporal hints:

- the apocalyptic character could reflect the surge of apocalypticism which was one of the principal reactions within emerging Judaism and Christianity to the catastrophe of 70;[272]
- 'the faith once for all delivered to the saints' (3) is very similar to the Pastorals' crystallization of faith into 'the faith' (§39.3b(i));[273]
- the reference to the apostles in verse 17 ('you must remember the predictions of the apostles of our Lord Jesus Christ') reads like the exhortation of a second generation looking back to the time of the apostles (cf. Eph. 2.20);
- the warnings against false teachers as a sign of the last days (4, 11, 18-19) is characteristically second generation;[274]
- the warnings of vv. 7, 11-12, 15 are more similar to those of Rev. 2.14-15, 20-22 than to those of the first-generation writers, though identification of those attacked as 'libertine Gnostics'[275] is probably more specific than the evidence allows;[276]
- that the letter is all warning with no teaching, and exhortation principally to hold to the faith and to avoid those causing division gives it a very second (or third) generation feeling.

---

269. J. H. Neyrey, *2 Peter, Jude* (AB 37C; New York: Doubleday, 1993), thinks Alexandria more probable (29-30).

270. Schnelle, *History* 422-23.

271. For socio-rhetorical studies of both Jude and 2 Peter see Neyrey, *2 Peter, Jude* 32-41, 113-18, 128-41; R. L. Webb and P. H. Davids, eds., *Reading Jude with New Eyes* (LNTS 383; London: T & T Clark, 2008); R. L. Webb and D. F. Watson, eds., *Reading Second Peter with New Eyes* (LNTS 382; London: T & T Clark, 2010).

272. See also below §39.3h and §40.7.

273. To list this as a feature of 'early Catholicism' skews the discussion too much; cf. Bauckham, *Jude, 2 Peter* 8-10; also *Jude and the Relatives of Jesus* 155-62; Hagner, *New Testament* 710.

274. Cf. 1 Tim. 4.1-3; 2 Tim. 4.3-4; 1 John 2.18; 4.1-3; *Did.* 16.3 (Schnelle, *History* 417).

275. Kümmel, *Introduction* 426; Koester, *Introduction* 2.246-47.

276. See e.g. Brown, *Introduction* 758-59; fuller discussion in Bauckham, *Jude and the Relatives of Jesus* 162-66, and Schnelle, *History* 421-22. Bauckham hypothesizes 'itinerant charismatics' who were 'libertines by principle' (167-68).

In short, a date late in the first century seems as early as Jude can be comfortably dated.[277] The *terminus ad quem* depends on how late 2 Peter is to be dated.

f. 2 Peter

One of the most striking features of 2 Peter is the degree of overlap with Jude, in themes, illustrations and wording. Particularly striking are the agreements between Jude 6-8, 12-16, 17-18 and 2 Pet. 2.4-10, 17-18, 3.1-3:[278]

Jude	2 Peter
6 The angels who did not keep their own position, but left their proper dwelling, he has kept in eternal chains in the nether darkness until the judgment of the great day.	2.4 For if God did not spare the angels when they sinned, but cast them into hell and committed them to chains of nether darkness to be kept there until the judgment. . . .
7 Likewise Sodom and Gomorrah and the surrounding cities, which practised immorality in the same way (as the angels) and went after strange flesh, serve as an example by undergoing the punishment of eternal fire.	2.6 and if by reducing the cities of Sodom and Gomorrah to ashes he condemned them to extinction, making them an example of what is coming to the ungodly. . . .
8 Yet in the same way these dreamers defile the flesh, reject the authority of the Lord, . . .	2.10 especially those who indulge their flesh in depraved lust, and flout the authority of the Lord.
12 These people are . . . waterless clouds blown by the winds; . . . 13 . . . wandering stars for whom the nether gloom of darkness has been reserved forever. . . .	2.17 These people are waterless wells, mists driven by a fierce wind; for whom the nether gloom of darkness has been reserved.
16 These are grumblers and malcontents; they indulge their own lusts and their mouths speak bombastic words. . . .	2.18 For uttering bombastic but empty words they entice with licentious lusts of the flesh people who are only just escaping from those who live in error.

---

277. This is the strongest consensus among recent commentators; see table in Bauckham, *Jude and the Relatives of Jesus* 169.

278. Following particularly Bauckham, *Jude, 2 Peter* 245-46, 272, 283; see the fuller synopsis in J. B. Mayor, *The Epistle of St. Jude and the Second Epistle of St. Peter* (London: Macmillan, 1907) 2-15; also T. Fornberg, *An Early Church in a Pluralistic Society* (Lund: Gleerup, 1977).

Jude	2 Peter
17 But you, <u>beloved</u>, <u>must remember the predictions of the apostles of</u> our <u>Lord</u> Jesus Christ, 18 that they said to you, '<u>In the last</u> time there will be <u>scoffers, who will follow</u> their ungodly <u>lusts</u>'.	3.1 ... <u>beloved</u> ... 2 you <u>must remember the predictions of</u> the holy prophets and the commandment <u>of the Lord</u> and Saviour through your <u>apostles</u>. 3 First of all you must understand this, that <u>in the last</u> days <u>scoffers</u> will come, scoffing, <u>following</u> their own <u>lusts</u>.

The warnings against licentiousness (*aselgeia* Jude 4; 2 Pet. 2.2) and denying the Master (Jude 4; 2 Pet. 2.1), the repeated warnings against slander/blasphemy (Jude 8, 9, 10; 2 Pet. 2.2, 10, 11, 12), and of coming judgment/condemnation (Jude 4, 6, 9, 15; 2 Pet. 2.4, 9, 11; 3.7), the same sequence of parallel illustrations — rebellious angels (Jude 6; 2 Pet. 2.4),[279] Sodom and Gomorrah (Jude 7; 2 Pet. 2.6) and Balaam (Jude 11; 2 Pet. 2:15-16) — the dismissal of opponents as 'like irrational animals' (Jude 10; 2 Pet. 2.12), and the similar reference to 'feasting together' (Jude 12; 2 Pet. 2.13), plus the uncommon terms common to both,[280] all add to the very strong impression of a close degree of literary interdependence. The impression is equally strong that 2 Peter has used the briefer, more tightly argued Jude as a stimulus and resource for its more loosely presented exhortation. Consequently the great majority of commentators conclude that 2 Peter was written after Jude and drew on Jude.[281]

i. Author

There are several factors which point firmly to the conclusion that Peter was not the author of 2 Peter:[282]

---

279. Jude 5 adds the wilderness generation, and 2 Pet. 2.5 adds Noah and the flood.
280. 'Mocker' (*empaiktēs* — Jude 18; 2 Pet. 3.3); 'discolouring spots' (*spilas/spilos* — Jude 12; 2 Pet. 2.13); 'feast together' (*syneuōchomai* — Jude 12; 2 Pet. 2.13); 'nether darkness' (*zophos* — Jude 6, 13; 2 Pet. 2.4, 17); 'bombastic' (*hyperonkos* — Jude 16; 2 Pet. 2.18).
281. See e.g. Mayor, *St. Jude* i-xxv; Kümmel, *Introduction* 430-31; Schelkle, *Petrusbriefe* 138-39; Bauckham, *Jude, 2 Peter* 141-43; though Schnelle's conclusion 'that the Letter of Jude has been almost entirely incorporated in 2 Peter' is an overstatement (*History* 429). G. L. Green, 'Second Peter's Use of Jude: *Imitatio* and the Sociology of Early Christianity', in Webb and Watson, eds., *Reading Second Peter* 1-25, notes that the practice of *imitatio* was common in ancient literature: 'According to the ancient canons of *imitatio*, if the author of 2 Peter used a letter composed by the half-brother of Jesus, the borrowing would point to the special honor the Christian community ascribed to the relatives of Jesus. Indeed, this honor would supersede that ascribed to the apostles, including Peter' (2).
282. The consensus view of NT scholars.

§39.3 *The Sources — First Century*

- as just noted, 2 Peter almost certainly draws on Jude;
- the differences in terminology and ideas are too striking for 1 Peter and 2 Peter to be attributed to the same author;[283]
- the indications of a second- or third-generation perspective are too clear, as we shall see — (iii. below).

There is very little alternative to the conclusion that 2 Peter is pseudonymous.[284] Indeed, 2 Peter is the most obvious candidate for that description, since it not only claims to be written by 'Simeon Peter, a servant and apostle of Jesus Christ' (2 Pet. 1.1), but goes on to make autobiographical reminiscences. The writer's claim to know that his death will come soon, 'as indeed our Lord Jesus Christ has made clear to me' (1.14), most obviously draws on the distinctively Petrine tradition found only in John's Gospel (John 21.18-19). The claim to have been an eyewitness of Jesus' majesty in that he had heard the heavenly voice proclaiming 'This is my Son, my Beloved, with whom I am well pleased', while with Jesus 'on the holy mountain' (2 Pet. 1.16-18; Matt 17.1-9 pars.)[285] could hardly give the author a higher status. And the assertion that 2 Peter was the second letter which the author had written (3.1) is clearly an allusion to what was already accepted and well known as a letter of Peter (1 Peter).[286] Notable also is the reference to Paul as 'our beloved brother' (3.15).[287]

In this case the other options — a close disciple or group gathering up Peter's teachings (as with James and possibly with 1 Peter), or summing up the scope and significance of Peter's work (as in Ephesians), or building round more fragmentary writings of Peter (as possibly in the case of 2 Timothy), or of different amanuenses (as likely in Colossians) — do not seem to provide an adequate explanation. And yet, the letter (slowly) gained acceptance[288]

---

283. See particularly Bauckham, *Jude, 2 Peter* 143-47.

284. 'The pseudonymity of II Pet is more certain than that of any other NT work' (Brown, *Introduction* 767); see also Hagner, *New Testament* 713-17.

285. The fact that the quotation is closest to Matthew's version of the transfiguration story is consistent with the considerable evidence that Matthew was the best known and used of the four NT Gospels in the second century; see below §44.8b.

286. Less plausible is the argument of F. Lapham, *Peter: The Myth, the Man and the Writings* (JSNTS 239; London: Sheffield Academic, 2003) ch. 6, that 2 Peter is a conflation of two letters (chs. 1-2 and ch. 3), so that 3.1 refers back to the first letter (chs. 1 and 2).

287. Niebuhr (in private correspondence) notes that there seems to be some sort of intertextuality between 2 Peter and Paul also with regard to the prescript (the combination of *doulos* and *apostolos* in NT letters occurs only in 2 Peter, Romans and Titus) and to the letter opening (cf. 2 Pet. 1.3f. with Gal. 1.15, Phil. 3.10 and 2 Cor. 4.6).

288. Kümmel notes that 2 Peter was nowhere mentioned in the second century; Origen regarded it as contested, p[72] (3rd century) including it with 1 Peter and Jude along with other non-NT writings, and Eusebius listed it among the antilegomena. 'Even down

and presumably was regarded as a fitting expression of what Peter would have wanted to say at the time it was written.[289] It is always uneasy-making when we have to confront the likely fact that early Christianity was more gullible or less questioning or more disingenuous in the acceptance of 2 Peter than should be acceptable in a matter like the canon of the NT. But that seems to be the position in this case.

ii. Place of Writing and Recipients

Where and to whom 2 Peter was written are virtually impossible to determine.[290] By the time the status of the letter was being discussed, the questions of where it first emerged and how widely it was known had been lost to sight. The assumption that those denounced were Gnostics[291] is hardly borne out by the references to their false teaching (1.16; 2.1-2; 3.3-5), and a libertine life-style (2.10, 13, 18-20) is hardly exclusive to Gnostic groups.[292] But other specific labels are equally questionable.[293]

iii. Date

The lateness of 2 Peter is most clearly indicated by two features:

- The delay of the parousia, for the first time in the NT, has become a serious problem — 'Where is the promise of his coming?' (3.4).[294] The

---

to the fourth century II Pet was largely unknown or not recognized as canonical. . . . The Peshitta does not have II Pet, and it never achieved full canonical authority among the Syrians' (*Introduction* 433-34). Eusebius notes that 'the so-called second Epistle we have not received as canonical, but nevertheless it has appeared useful to many, and has been studied with other Scriptures' (*HE* 3.3.1).

289. 'The pseudepigraphical device is therefore not a fraudulent means of claiming apostolic authority, but embodies a claim to be a faithful mediator of the apostolic message' (Bauckham, *Jude, 2 Peter* 161-62).

290. 'Rome is . . . at least a plausible candidate for the composition of II Pet within a Petrine "school"'; and Brown notes, as do many, that 2 Pet. 3.1 supposes the same audience as 1 Peter (Brown, *Introduction* 768). Rome is more strongly supported by Bauckham, *Jude, 2 Peter* 159-60.

291. Kümmel, *Introduction* 432; Koester, *Introduction* 2.296.

292. Bauckham is as dubious on the Gnostic identification of 2 Peter's 'opponents' (*Jude, 2 Peter* 154-57) as he was in the case of Jude (n.276 above).

293. See also T. Fornberg, *An Early Church in a Pluralistic Society: A Study of 2 Peter* (Lund: Gleerup, 1977) 130-42. Neyrey finds it probable 'that the opponents of 2 Peter voice a doctrine usually associated with "atheists" such as Epicureans' (*2 Peter, Jude* 122-27).

294. In discussions of the NT writings, the 'delay of the parousia' has regularly featured as an indicative factor of date; see particularly H. Conzelmann, *The Theology of Saint Luke* (1953, ²1957; ET London: Faber & Faber, 1960, ²1961). In fact, however, there are very few indications that other NT writings express such a concern (probably most noticeably

problem is dealt with at some length, by the somewhat unsatisfactory reflection that 'with the Lord one day is like a thousand years, and a thousand years are like one day' (3.8), and by the pastoral thought of God's patience giving further time for repentance (3.9), before a firm reassertion that 'the day of the Lord will come like a thief' and the heavens will be dissolved with fire (3.10-12).

- Paul's letters are regarded as scripture (3.15-16), a status not otherwise expressly attributed to NT writings till *2 Clement* and Justin (§44). It is noticeable that despite the support which Paul's letters evidently gave to the 'false teachers' (2 Pet. 2.1) attacked in the letter, 2 Peter has no doubt as to the scriptural status and authority of Paul's letters (3.15-16).[295]

Most likely, then, 2 Peter first emerged in the second century, very likely the only NT writing to be firmly dated after 100. When it first appeared is as difficult to resolve as its place of origin and intended recipients. Some time in the first half of the second century is probably as good as we can now guess.

g. 1-3 John

Two important issues for specialists in the Johannine literature have been the relation (authorship, chronology, thought) of the three letters of John to the Gospel of John, and the chronological sequence of the three letters. Only some of these issues need concern us here, since it is clear enough, and there is general agreement, (1) that the three letters share the distinctively Johannine characteristics of the Gospel,[296] and (2) that the three letters be-

---

Luke 19.11), and no real indications that 'the delay of the parousia' was a serious *problem*. See also D. E. Aune, 'The Significance of the Delay of the Parousia for Early Christianity', in G. E. Hawthorne, ed., *Current Issues in Biblical and Patristic Interpretation* (Grand Rapids: Eerdmans, 1975) 87-109. The problem as such first appears in *1 Clem.* 23 (cf. *2 Clem.* 11), but is not dealt with as thoroughly as in 2 Peter. The appropriateness of the once popular description of 2 Peter as 'early Catholic' is also rightly to be questioned (Bauckham, *Jude, 2 Peter* 151-54; cf. Hagner, *New Testament* 719-21).

295. 'The author of 2 Peter belonged to those orthodox Christians who named Paul as an authority of the church, but secretly wished that the great apostle had not written any letters' (Koester, *Introduction* 2.297).

296. The agreement of vocabulary, style and theology is documented by Schnelle, *History* 434-35. The differences, illustrated by Kümmel, *Introduction* 443-44, and Brown, *Introduction* 389, may lose significance since 2 and 3 John are too brief to provide 'characteristic' features, and since the differing situations confronted in the Gospel and the letters may well be sufficient to explain most of the differences (*pace* Schnelle 455-56; or they may point to a Johannine School rather than a common personal author (R. A. Culpepper,

long together, whatever the sequence of their composition.[297] Beyond noting these wider issues, it is sufficient at this stage, the stage of identifying the bit-players in the drama of earliest Christianity's emergence, to focus on the usual three questions.

i. Author

Given the degree of closeness between the Gospel of John and 1-3 John, the question of the letters' authorship is inevitably caught up in the uncertainties on the same question regarding the Gospel. Since 'John the Elder' is one of the strongest candidates for the authorship of the Gospel (§39.2d), the fact that 2 John and 3 John both present themselves as written by 'the Elder' constitutes an important consideration in favour of the view that the final author of the Gospel and the author of 2-3 John were the same person. The fact that 'the Elder' (2 John 1; 3 John 1) does not identify himself as 'John' may weaken the argument, though since the author of the Gospel is not even identified either as 'John', or as 'the Elder', it hardly weakens the argument much.[298] On the other hand, the identification of the author of 2-3 John as 'the Elder' did not carry the same weight in the patristic evaluation of the letters — for

---

The Johannine School [SBLDS 26; Missoula: Scholars, 1975; Schnelle 436). 'Many statements in 1 John could be placed on the lips of the Johannine Jesus, and there would be no way to distinguish between them and the words actually assigned to him in John' (Brown, *Introduction* 389).

297. Note the following parallels, indicative of shared style and emphases:

1 John	2 John	3 John
(1.4)	12	13-14
2.4	2	
	4	3-4
2.7, 5.3	5-6	
2.18	7	
2.23	7, 9	
2.24	9	
3.6, 10		11
3.7	7	
3.18	1	1
4.2	7	

See further particularly R. E. Brown, *The Epistles of John* (AB; New York: Doubleday, 1982) 14-19; for parallels between 2 and 3 John see J. Lieu, *The Second and Third Epistles of John* (Edinburgh: T & T Clark, 1986) 224-29.

298. For a careful discussion of the question of possibly common authorship, see Brown, *Epistles* 19-30; H.-J. Klauck, *Der erste Johannesbrief* (KEK 23/1; Zürich: Benziger, 1991) 42-47, and *Der zweite und dritte Johannesbriefe* (KEK 23/2; Zürich: Benziger, 1992) 19-22; von Wahlde, *Gospel and Letters of John* 3.409-34; also Culpepper, *Johannine School* 90-95; J. Beutler, 'Johannesevangelium, Johannesbriefe', *Neue Studien zu den johanneischen Schriften* (BBB 167; Bonn University, 2012) 25-51.

the author to designate himself as 'the Elder' could well imply that he made no apostolic claim for himself, a consideration which probably played a part in the lateness of the letters' acceptance in the NT canon.[299] Today we can hardly move beyond the confusion and uncertainties of the patristic evidence on the authorship both of the Gospel and of the letters.[300]

Unlike 2-3 John, 1 John does not present itself as a letter and offers no hint as to its author. But the similarities between the three letters and the Gospel are sufficient to indicate the probability that they came from the same stable.[301] In these circumstances our inability to identify a specific author is of little consequence.

ii. Place of Writing

Since the letters seem to reflect the same milieu as the Gospel, it is most natural to infer the same origin — that is, most likely Ephesus.[302] 1 John addresses 'my little children',[303] and the letter recipients as 'beloved',[304] so presumably it had a wider range of congregations in view, perhaps even deserving the title 'Catholic Epistle'. 2 John is addressed to 'the elect lady', probably not an individual but a local congregation, and is sent from a sister congregation ('the children of your elect sister' — 2 John 13). And though 3 John is addressed to an individual, Gaius, it was presumably intended for public reading. What the letters tell us about the churches reflected in the letters will be more appropriately considered later (§49.4), but churches in Asia Minor are probably in view.

iii. Date

The dates of the letters are equally hard to tie down. The fact that 2-3 John are so brief and imply that their initial acceptance, preservation and circulation were secured presumably because they were written by a well-known and respected author (he did not need to identify himself more than as 'the

---

299. Eusebius notes that Clement of Alexandria gave 'concise explanations of . . . even the disputed writings . . . the Epistle of Jude and the remaining Catholic Epistles' (*HE* 6.14.1), but also that Origen was uncertain about the authorship of two of the epistles (6.25.10), an uncertainty which he himself shared (3.25.3). See further Lieu, *Epistles* particularly 10-30.

300. Brown observes that we may have to allow for 'at least *four figures in the Johannine School* of writers: the Beloved Disciple (who was the source of the tradition), the evangelist who wrote the body of the Gospel, the presbyter who wrote the Epistles, and the redactor of the Gospel' (*Introduction* 389).

301. See also §49.4 below. Barrett suggests that the different Johannine writings were produced by different disciples of the apostle John (*John* 133).

302. Brown, *Epistles* 101-3; Klauck, *erste Johannesbrief* 48-49.

303. 1 John 2.1, 12, 28; 3.7, 18; 4.4; 5.21.

304. 1 John 2.7; 3.2, 21; 4.1, 7, 11.

Elder'), is one of the main arguments in favour of their having been written before 1 John.[305] But there is no real reason why the sermon or tract which is 1 John could not have emerged at the same time or earlier.[306]

More important is the question whether the letters appeared before or after the Gospel. The principal difference is that the Gospel mostly reflects a confrontation between the Johannine believers in Jesus and 'the Jews', without much hint of internal dispute, whereas the letters reflect a different confrontation,[307] which seems to have caused or been caused by internal dispute (1 John 2.19). The likelihood, as we shall see (§49.4), is that the letters reflect a different and later phase in the development of the early assertions about Christ which emerged within the Johannine congregations in their disputes with 'the Jews'. If we are right to envisage the Johannine distinctives as the fruit of a lengthy process, which included a post-70 transition to Syria and then Ephesus, it would make best sense to read the letters as attempts to deal with the subsequent challenges which the transition and the new contexts provoked.[308] This suggests a date later than the Gospel, but not necessarily by much — the Gospel reflecting the earlier development of the Johannine churches, the letters reflecting the most recent phase.[309] So a date around the end of the first century or very early second century is entirely possible and plausible.[310] But again the issues and probabilities will become clearer as the role of the Gospel and the letters is explored in more detail in the subsequent chapters.

h. Revelation/The Apocalypse of John

Revelation is the only apocalypse as such within the NT. As a document which presents itself as the unveiling of heavenly secrets to one privileged to see what is happening in heaven, it makes the most explicit claim of all the NT writings to be inspired and to convey divine revelation (Rev. 1.1; 22.8).

---

305. Schnelle, *History* 439, 441-42 (if 3 John 9 refers to 2 John, then 2 John was written before 3 John); but Koester argues that 2 John is 'a rather superficial compilation of Johannine sentences' drawing on both 1 John and 3 John (*Introduction* 2.196).

306. Brown, *Epistles* 30-32, 100-101.

307. The letters contain no references to 'the Jews'.

308. Brown, *Epistles* 32-35, 69-71; also *Introduction* 390-91; cf. Koester, *Introduction* 2.194-95.

309. Hagner, *New Testament* 732-33. Contrast Schnelle who argues strongly for the sequence 2 John, 3 John, 1 John, Gospel of John (*History* 458-59, 468).

310. Brown (*Epistles* 8-9) notes that the clearest of the possible echoes of 1-3 John in the Apostolic Fathers is in Polycarp, *Philippians* 7.1 (cf. 1 John 4.2-3 and 2 John 7); also Eusebius's report that Papias 'used quotations from the first Epistle of John' (*HE* 3.39.17). Klauck settles for 100/110 (*erste Johannesbrief* 49; *zweite und dritte Johannesbriefe* 22-23).

i. Author

Unusually in the NT, apart from most of the letters, the writing is quite open about its author — John, who can be distinguished most simply from the other Johns of the NT as 'John the seer' (1.1, 4; 22.8).[311] He writes letters too (Rev. 2-3), but he is not presented as their author; he is merely the amanuensis — 'To the angel of the church in Ephesus write' (2.1).[312] Although the letters indicate awareness of the conditions of the seven churches, the principal focus of John's Apocalypse is on his report of the heavenly mysteries unveiled to him, delivered throughout in first-person terms.[313] John describes himself as a prophet (22.9), one of a favoured band of prophets,[314] and his writing as a 'prophecy'.[315]

Who was John the prophet and seer? All we learn from the text itself is that John was a Christian ('brother') who shared with his fellow believers 'in the tribulation (*thlipsis*) and kingdom and patient endurance in Jesus' (1.9). He further reports that the revelation came to him when he was 'on the island called Patmos because of the word of God and the testimony of Jesus' (1.9). Since the same or very similar phrases are used in 6.9 and 20.4 in reference to those killed 'for the word of God and the testimony they bore', the most obvious implication is that John had been suffering some form of persecution, in the form of banishment, penal or voluntary, to the island of Patmos, off the coast of Asia Minor.[316] John's use of the apocalyptic genre, his familiarity with the Hebrew Bible, and the Semitic character of his speech suggest that he was a Palestinian Jew, probably part of the Jewish diaspora consequential upon the first Jewish revolt.[317]

It was generally assumed in the patristic period that John the seer was

---

311. The identification of the author marks out John's Apocalypse from its predecessors and contemporary apocalypses, which pseudonymously attributed their revelations to a heroic figure of the past — Enoch, Daniel, Ezra, Baruch. His unveiling of present heavenly realities, rather than history that had already unfolded, but presented as prophecy from the claimed author's perspective, also marks out John's Apocalypse. 'In distinction from Jewish apocalyptic there is lacking here any look back into the past and any forward view out of that fictional past into the present' (Kümmel, *Introduction* 461).

312. But Niebuhr (in personal correspondence) notes that the whole book of Revelation starts, after the heading in 1.1-3, like a letter (1.4-5); see for this M. Karrer, *Die Johannesoffenbarung als Brief* (FRLANT 140; Göttingen: Vandenhoeck, 1986).

313. 'I saw' (*eidon*) introduces John's visions in every chapter, chs. 4-10 and chs. 13-21.

314. Rev. 10.7; 11.18; 16.6; 18.20, 24; 22.6.

315. Rev. 1.3; 10.11; 19.10; 22.7, 10, 18, 19.

316. See the full discussion of D. E. Aune, *Revelation* (WBC 52; 3 vols.; Dallas: Word, 1997-98), who points out that despite the tradition already in Clement of Alexandria and Origen that John had been condemned or banished to Patmos, there is no evidence that Patmos was ever a Roman penal colony, and who reviews the historical options (1.76-82, 116).

317. Aune, *Revelation* 1.l.

in fact the apostle John.[318] But the language and style of the Apocalypse is so different from both the Gospel and 1-3 John that few today would follow that line, even allowing for the usual possibility of secretarial freedom in detailed composition.[319] Moreover, the style of the Apocalypse is so intensely personal that its composition can hardly be other than the verbal reports of John the seer. And so different is the Apocalypse's style from that of the other Johannine writings in the NT that they can hardly be attributed to John the seer.[320] At best we are back into the patristic confusion on the different Johns. And if there is a legitimate concern to relate John the seer to John the apostle (or John the Elder)[321]— but why the different designations ('the disciple whom Jesus loved', 'the Elder', prophet?) — then at best we could envisage John the seer as another disciple of the apostle John, whose style differed from the other disciples of John who most probably played (a) major role(s) in the production of the other Johannine NT literature.[322] On the other hand, there is no reason to exclude the possibility that John the seer was quite independent of the Johannine school, his composition gaining its acceptance and authority because its explicit claims to be a 'revelation' were accepted, and because it provided inspiration, challenge and support to the churches of Asia Minor.

318. Justin Martyr, *Dial.* 81.4, is the earliest identification of John the seer with the apostle John. Of recent commentators, S. S. Smalley, *The Revelation to John* (London: SPCK, 2005), belongs to a minority in inferring that 'John' is John the Apostle (2-3).

319. The differences in style were fully appreciated by Bishop Dionysus of Alexandria (mid-third century) whom Eusebius quotes at length on the subject (*HE* 7.25; note particularly 7-8, 22-26). See the analysis of R. H. Charles, *Revelation* (ICC; 2 vols.; Edinburgh: T & T Clark, 1920) 1.xxix-xxxii, xxxiv-xxxvii; even though some of the differences of content (as noted by Schnelle, *History* 522-23) could be described as complementary — the inward-looking Gospel and letters (love the brothers) and the outward-looking Apocalypse (confronting a hostile imperial power).

320. Only of Revelation could it be said that 'the author thought in Hebrew but wrote in Greek' (Charles, *Revelation* 1.cxliii; quoted by Kümmel, *Introduction* 465); see also G. K. Beale, *The Book of Revelation* (NIGTC; Grand Rapids: Eerdmans, 1999) 100-105.

321. For points of similarity see Charles, *Revelation* 1.xxxii-xxxiii; Schnelle, *History* 521; A. Satake, *Die Offenbarung des Johannes* (KEK; Göttingen: Vandenhoeck, 2008) 39-44 — e.g. the strong emphasis on 'witness, testimony':

	Gospel	1-3 John	Apocalypse
martyrein	33	10	4
martyria	14	7	9

322. 'It is therefore possible to assume that the reputation of this "John of Ephesus" led to the establishment of an Ephesian Johannine tradition which was later understood as originating from "John the son of Zebedee", and which in turn attracted the tradition of the Gospel of John and of the Johannine Epistles to this city' (Koester, *Introduction* 2.250); cf. E. S. Fiorenza, *The Book of Revelation: Justice and Judgment* (Philadelphia: Fortress, 1985) ch. 3.

ii. Place of Writing

Since John uses a past tense in 1.9, we should not assume that the document was written from Patmos. But since Patmos was less than forty miles from Miletus and only fifty miles from Ephesus, and since the letters in chs. 2-3 are written to seven churches which are all located in Asia Minor, it is most natural to infer that the document was composed in Asia Minor, and possibly in Ephesus itself — the first letter is addressed to Ephesus (2.1-7).[323] That, of course, does strengthen the likelihood that John the seer had at least some association with the Johannine school located most probably in Ephesus.

iii. Date

There is a broad consensus on the date of Revelation, which most specify as the early 90s.[324] The main consideration is that under the reign of Emperor Domitian, social and political pressure probably intensified on the Asian believers to accede to or take part in the imperial cult, probably explicitly or implicitly as a loyalty test (to Rome) for citizens and residents.[325] In particular, in Ephesus the double Temple of Divus Julius and Dea Roma had been recently overshadowed by a huge Temple of the Flavian Sebastoi,[326] probably built during Domitian's reign (89/90?), with a massive statue of either Titus or Domitian.[327] Such pressure to conform is probably indicated in John's

---

323. C. J. Hemer, *The Letters to the Churches of Asia in Their Local Setting* (JSNTS 11; Sheffield: JSOT, 1986), notes that 'the Ephesian letter, like the others, has a strongly Asian background which indicates that the writer must have known the city intimately' (55).

324. '... towards the end of Domitian's reign' (Irenaeus, *adv. haer.* 5.30.3); Domitian reigned from 81 to 96. But Niebuhr (in personal correspondence) notes that there is a lively debate now on proposals for a rather late date for Revelation, in the time of Hadrian; see T. Witulski, *Die Johannesoffenbarung und Kaiser Hadrian: Studien zur Datierung der neutestamentlichen Apokalypse* (FRLANT 221; Göttingen: Vandenhoeck, 2007). Others argue for a longer time of literary development starting under the Flavians and coming to its end only under Trajan; see F. Tóth, 'Von der Vision zur Redaktion', in J. Frey et al., eds., *Die Johannesapokalypse* (WUNT 287; Tübingen: Mohr Siebeck, 2012) 319-411.

325. There is no evidence that the earlier persecution of Nero extended beyond Rome. For the legend of Nero's return, probably reflected in the number of the beast in 13.18 as 666, see R. Bauckham, 'Nero and the Beast', *The Climax of Prophecy: Studies on the Book of Revelation* (Edinburgh: T & T Clark, 1993) 384-452. Full discussion of the date with bibliography in Aune, *Revelation* 1.lxvi-lxx; Beale, *Revelation* 4-27.

326. *Sebastos* = 'August' and so 'Augustus', used of emperors (Acts 25.21, 25) and entirely appropriate in reference to the imperial cult — *theos Sebastos* (W. Foerster, *TDNT* 7.174-75; LSJ 1587).

327. C. M. Thomas, 'At Home in the City of Artemis', in H. Koester, ed., *Ephesos: Metropolis of Asia* (HTS 41; Harvard University, 2004) 81-117 (here 108). For the widespread influence of the imperial cult throughout Asia during the second half of the first century see *Beginning from Jerusalem* 550 n.124.

banishment to Patmos, in the threat of imminent imprisonment (2.9-10), in an instance of martyrdom already suffered (2.13), and in the churches of Pergamum and Thyatira being beguiled to eat idol-food, that is, most likely, to take part in festival celebrations of the Caesar cult (2.14, 20). Roman imperial power is almost certainly referred to in the frightening imagery of the beast, 'with ten horns and seven heads'[328] and its blasphemous claims summoning all to worship it (13.1-8),[329] and in Babylon denounced in ch. 18.[330] It is true that there is little evidence that Christians suffered state persecution under Domitian,[331] but the dominant mood of John's Apocalypse is one of foreboding at the prospect of imminent and fearful tribulation.[332] So the dating of the Apocalypse to the final years of Domitian's reign is not dependent on the disputed traditions of Domitian's slide into a reign of terror.[333] The likelihood remains, however, that the Apocalypse reflects the pressures building up from the local provincial elite for citizens and residents to express their loyalty to Rome by participating in the imperial cult during the reign of Domitian.[334]

This completes the introductory notes on the writings which became part of the New Testament.

---

328. The phrase was omitted for some reason in early printings of the NRSV.

329. The second beast (13.11-18) is usually identified as the imperial priesthood in the provinces responsible for ratcheting up the social and political pressure to support the imperial cult (so, e.g. Kümmel, *Introduction* 460). The pressure on the Christ-believers to conform is indicated in 12.17 and 13.7.

330. With which of the kings (emperors) the seven heads are to be identified remains disputed; see e.g. Kümmel, *Introduction* 468-69; Aune, *Revelation* 3.945-47.

331. Note particularly L. L. Thompson, *The Book of Revelation: Apocalypse and Empire* (New York: Oxford University, 1990) 103-9; on Domitian see ch. 6.

332. '... the hour of trial that is coming on the whole world to test the inhabitants of the earth' (Rev. 3.10).

333. See e.g. B. W. Jones, 'Domitian', *ABD* 2.221-22; Brown, *Introduction* 805-9. Kümmel also points out that the church of Smyrna had evidently been established for some time, although Polycarp (of Smyrna) implies that the church there was not established in Paul's time (*Phil.* 11.3); and that Laodicea was evidently flourishing, even though almost completely destroyed by an earthquake in 60/61 (*Introduction* 469).

334. See further S. Friesen, 'The Cult of the Roman Emperors in Ephesos', in Koester, ed., *Ephesos* 228-50 (particularly 245-50); Satake, *Offenbarung* 51-58.

CHAPTER 40

The Sources — Second Century[1]

40.1 The Apostolic Fathers

'The Apostolic Fathers' is the name given to the Christian writings which have been preserved from the early decades of the second century and whose authors are regarded and revered as associates or disciples of the apostles to whom the NT writings themselves were attributed.[2] That some of them were sometimes bound up with the NT writings themselves[3] attests the esteem in which they were held. Initially only the letters of Clement, Ignatius, Polycarp and Barnabas with the *Shepherd* of Hermas were included, with Diognetus and Papias later added, as also *Didache*, following its discovery in 1873. As with the NT writings, I will limit discussion here to the basic questions of author, place of writing and recipients, and date.[4]

---

1. A much valued introduction to the literature, with extensive bibliography, is J. Quasten, *Patrology* vol. 1: *The Beginnings of Patristic Literature* (Westminster, MD: Newman, 1962). See also B. Altaner, *Patrology* (ET Freiburg: Herder, 1960) chs. 1-4.

2. J. B. Lightfoot, *Apostolic Fathers* Part I: *S. Clement of Rome* (London: Macmillan, ²1890) 1.3-6. The collection was first made in 1672 by J. B. Cotelier; details in Lightfoot, *Clement* 1.3; also M. W. Holmes, *The Apostolic Fathers* (Grand Rapids: Baker, 1989) 3. Lightfoot also notes the early use of the term 'apostolic' (2-3). See also S. Tugwell, *The Apostolic Fathers* (London: Geoffrey Chapman, 1989).

3. The most famous and striking examples are the fourth-century Codex Sinaiticus, which contains the *Epistle of Barnabas* and part of the *Shepherd* of Hermas, and the somewhat later Codex Alexandrinus, which contains large sections of *1* and *2 Clement*.

4. They will be examined in what I regard as the most probable chronological sequence, leaving the *Epistle to Diognetus* to the next section since it has more the character of an apology and probably belongs in timing to the period when the Apologists mainly flourished (second half of second century). For a survey of literature on the Apostolic Fathers up

a. *1 Clement*

The premier member of the Apostolic Fathers is undoubtedly *1 Clement*, primarily because it/he was almost certainly the earliest of the Apostolic Fathers, and because it was attributed to Clement, subsequently designated as bishop of Rome, more or less from the beginning. This and the opening of the letter itself provide almost all that is needed in terms of author, origin, occasion and recipients, and date.

The clearest information comes in the letter's introduction: it was written from 'the church of God that temporarily resides in Rome to the church of God that temporarily resides in Corinth'. The reason is clear also: the writer was concerned to have learned that there was factionalism in the Corinthian church; evidently younger members were rebelling against the leadership of the senior members (presbyters) (3.3), failing to give them the respect due to their seniority (1.3; 21.6), and causing strife and schism (2.6; 46.5, 9; 54.2).[5] Clement writes to ensure and exhort due respect to the established leadership. It is somewhat ironic that the first-century church into which we have most insight (Corinth) occasioned the letters which provide that information (1 Cor., 2 Cor., *1 Clem.*) because of its factiousness.[6]

The letter was obviously written by a leading member of the church of Rome, who could write with the authority of the church in the Empire's capital, making in effect a claim to some authority over a provincial church.[7] The references to bishops in 42.4-5 and 44.1, 4 and the authority exercised in the letter itself could suggest that the writer was someone who claimed episcopal authority, echoing the exhortation and authority of 'the epistle of that blessed apostle, Paul' (47.1; 58.2; 63.2-4; 65.1).[8] There never seems to have been any

---

to the 1980s see W. R. Schoedel, 'The Apostolic Fathers', in E. J. Epp and G. W. MacRae, eds., *The New Testament and Its Modern Interpreters* (Atlanta: Scholars, 1989) 457-98.

5. See L. L. Welborn, 'Clement, First Epistle of', *ABD* 1.1058-59; and further D. G. Horrell, *The Social Ethos of the Corinthian Correspondence* (Edinburgh: T & T Clark, 1996) 244-50.

6. Paul Trebilco reminds me that we have as much or more evidence regarding Ephesus — a little in Paul, Acts, 1-2 Timothy, John's Gospel, 1-3 John, and Rev. 2.1-7; see, of course, his *Early Christians in Ephesus*.

7. But C. N. Jefford, *The Apostolic Fathers and the New Testament* (Peabody, MA: Hendrickson, 2006), points out that 'the advice given throughout is pastoral and pleading, never authoritative' (16-18).

8. See further C. C. Richardson, *Early Christian Fathers* (London: SCM, 1953) 36-37, and B. D. Ehrman, *The Apostolic Fathers* (LCL; 2 vols.; Cambridge, MA: Harvard University, 2003) 1.21-23, 27-28, who justifiably question whether a monarchical episcopacy was established in Rome quite so early, noting that the terms 'bishop' and 'presbyter' were not clearly distinguished and were interchangeable in Clement's time (*1 Clem.* 44.4-5), and that

doubt in the patristic period that the author was Clement, venerated as the third (or second) bishop of the church of Rome.[9] The earliest supporting evidence may be provided by the *Shepherd* of Hermas, who was instructed to write two little books and to send one to Clement who had the responsibility (and authority) to forward it to other centres (*Vis.* 8.3).[10] And later in the second century (before 170) Dionysius of Corinth refers to a letter 'sent to us through Clement', which was still being read in the Corinthian church for its admonition (*HE* 4.23.11). Hegesippus similarly refers to the epistle of Clement to the Corinthians (*HE* 4.22.1).[11] The subscription added later at the end of the letter, 'The First Epistle of Clement to the Corinthians', simply reflects the unanimous opinion of the early church.

As to date, the most striking indication is the reference in ch. 5 to Peter and Paul as 'noble examples of our own generation', and the clear implication of ch. 44 is that those appointed by the apostles should not be removed from their ministry, and therefore were still in post. So the traditional view, that *1 Clement* was written at the end of Domitian's reign, that is, 95 or 96, appears to be well founded.[12] It should not escape notice that *1 Clement* was almost

---

Ignatius writing to the church in Rome some years later gives no indication that the Roman church had a single bishop. Similarly, Brown in Brown and Meier, *Antioch and Rome* 159-64; Koester, *Introduction* 2.287-88. Earlier discussion in Lightfoot, *Clement of Rome* 1.67-69.

9. Irenaeus, *adv. haer.* 3.3.1; Eusebius, *HE* 3.4.21; 4.23.11 (cited below on *2 Clement*). Eusebius's identification of bishop Clement with the Clement commended by Paul in Phil. 4.3 (*HE* 3.15) is usually discounted. Lightfoot suggested that Clement was a freedman of the household of the consul Flavius Clemens (*Clement of Rome* 1.61). Lightfoot's examination of the records of the early Roman succession (1.201-345) is unsurpassed.

10. But should this 'Clement' be identified with the author of *1 Clement*? We should not simply assume that there was only one significant person named Clement in Rome during the first half of the second century. See below §40.1h; also K. Lake, *The Apostolic Fathers* (LCL; 2 vols.; London: Heinemann, 1912, 1913) 1.3-4; Horrell, *Social Ethos* 241-44.

11. Lightfoot provides a thorough examination of all possible references to or echoes of *1 Clement*, from Barnabas onwards (*Clement of Rome* 1.148-200); see also R. M. Grant and H. H. Graham, *First and Second Clement* (R. M. Grant, ed., *The Apostolic Fathers* vol. 2; London: Nelson, 1965) 5-8; H. E. Lona, *Der erste Clemensbrief* (KAV 2; Göttingen: Vandenhoeck, 1998) 89-110.

12. Similarly Lightfoot, *Clement of Rome* 1.346-58; Horrell, *Social Ethos* 239-42; Lona, *erste Clemensbrief* 75-78; and Ehrman, *Apostolic Fathers* 1.23-25. T. J. Herron, *Clement and the Early Church of Rome: On the Dating of Clement's First Epistle to the Corinthians* (Steubenville, OH: Emmaus Road Publishing, 2008), argues for a 65-70 date; and Jefford prefers a date before 70. But we have already noted that reference to the Jerusalem temple as though still active does not necessarily imply that the temple was still active (§39 n.258). On the other hand, Welborn is too skeptical in concluding that there can be no greater confidence than between AD 80 and 140 (*ABD* 1.1060), though Clement's allusion to 'sudden and repeated misfortunes and setbacks we have experienced' (1.1) hardly sounds like a reference to a persecution by Domitian; *pace* L. W. Barnard, 'St. Clement of Rome and the

certainly earlier than some of the writings which were (finally) included within the NT. Had it not been for the fact that Clement so clearly distinguished himself from the apostles (5.3; 42.1-2; 4.1; 47.1-4), *1 Clement* might well have been a strong candidate to be included in the NT canon.

b. Ignatius

The letters of Ignatius provide one of the most vivid and moving depictions of Christianity in Asia Minor in the early decades of the second century. Ignatius had evidently been arrested during some persecution or unrest in Antioch (perhaps factional division within his church itself),[13] and was being led under military escort, 'night and day, bound to ten leopards, which is a company of soldiers' (*Rom.* 5.1), on his way to face the wild beasts in the arena in Rome (*Eph.* 1.2).[14] It was a martyrdom which he gladly anticipated, and in the only letter he wrote to churches ahead of him, to Rome where he was destined for execution, he urged them not to intervene on his behalf (*Rom.* 1–2, 4–7).

There is no need for any discussion as to the author of the Ignatian epistles, since he introduces himself in the opening of each of the letters as 'Ignatius, who is also called God-bearer'. In *Rom.* 2.2 he refers to himself as 'the bishop of Syria', and he closes each letter with a request that the letter recipients pray for the church in Syria,[15] or expresses gratitude for their prayer for the church at Antioch in Syria.[16] He was evidently feted by the Asia Minor believers, and his letters were written probably to churches in cities his escort did not pass through. His principal aim in writing seems to have been primarily political, in that he used the opportunity to enhance the importance of each community's bishop: as, for example, in *Eph.* 6.1 — 'We are clearly obliged to look upon the bishop as the Lord himself'.[17]

The only real issue is whether Ignatius wrote more letters and whether

---

Persecution of Domitian', *Studies in the Apostolic Fathers and Their Background* (Oxford: Blackwell, 1966) 5-15.

13. The issue was provocatively posed by Bauer, *Orthodoxy* 61-70. The reasons for Ignatius's arrest and why he was being sent to Rome are never indicated. W. R. Schoedel, *Ignatius of Antioch* (Hermeneia; Philadelphia: Fortress, 1985), argues that there had been a dispute over Ignatius's authority, or the authority he claimed (10-11); see also the brief discussion in Ehrman, *Apostolic Fathers* 1.208-9.

14. His story is told at some length by Eusebius, drawing on his letters (*HE* 3.36).

15. *Eph.* 21.2; *Magn.* 14.1; *Trall.* 13.1; *Rom.* 9.1.

16. *Philad.* 10.1; *Smyrn.* 11.1; *Polyc.* 7.1; the subject of his earlier concern seems to have been resolved.

17. See further *Eph.* 1, 2, 3, 4, 5-6; *Magn.* 2-4, 6-7, 13; *Trall.* 2-3, 7, 13.2; *Philad.* Inscrip., 1, 3-4, 7-8; *Smyrn.* 8-9; *Polyc.* 5-6; (*Romans* is an exception).

§40.1   *The Sources — Second Century*

the seven are as he wrote them; a longer recension, with five more letters attributed to Ignatius and another purportedly written to him, circulated in the mediaeval period. The main issues were more or less settled by the detailed studies of Theodor Zahn and J. B. Lightfoot,[18] and today there is a strong consensus that only seven can and should be classified as genuine.[19]

Likewise there is no need for dispute as to the place of writing or the recipients, since the letters themselves make both matters clear. The first four (*Ephesians, Magnesians, Trallians* and *Romans*) were all written from Smyrna,[20] where, presumably, the detachment assigned to deliver Ignatius to Rome rested for some days, allowing friends of Ignatius the opportunity to visit him.[21] The last three (*Philadelphians, Smyrneans* and *Polycarp*) were written from Troas,[22] the next rest-place, presumably while awaiting a ship to transport them to Europe. This allowed further opportunity for visits,[23] though it seems to have been cut short by the unexpected opportunity to sail from Troas to Neapolis (*Polyc.* 8.1), which prevented him writing more letters as he had hoped to do; so he commissioned Polycarp, whom he had come to know well during the pause in Smyrna, 'to write to the churches before me' (*Polyc.* 8.1).[24]

Unclear, however, is the date of Ignatius's journey to martyrdom through Asia Minor, during which the letters were written. All we learn from patristic sources is that Ignatius was bishop of Antioch during the reign of Trajan (98-117) (Eusebius, *HE* 3.22, 36.2). A date in the late 100s or early 110s seems early (surprisingly early for some), but there is nothing in the letters, in terms of their antagonism to Judaism (§46.6a), or their opposition to docetic views

---

18. T. Zahn, *Ignatius von Antiochien* (Gotha: Perthes, 1873); J. B. Lightfoot, *The Apostolic Fathers* Part II: *S. Ignatius, S. Polycarp* (3 vols.; London: Macmillan, 1885).

19. See the brief reviews of Schoedel, *Ignatius* 3-7; Ehrman, *Apostolic Fathers* 209-15. The initial collection of Ignatius's letters seems to have been made by Polycarp — 'We have forwarded to you the letters of Ignatius that he sent to us, along with all the others we had with us, just as you directed us to do' (*Phil.* 13.2) — clear evidence that letters from such iconic figures were gathered together and copies circulated to churches who requested them.

20. *Eph.* 21.1; *Magn.* 15; *Trall.* 12.1; *Rom.* 10.1.

21. *Eph.* 1.3–2.1; *Magn.* 2; *Trall.* 1; *Rom.* 9.3; 10.1. Schoedel notes how carefully Ignatius's several contacts were organized (*Ignatius* 11-12).

22. *Philad.* 11.2; *Smyrn.* 12.1; *Polyc.* 8.1.

23. *Philad.* 11.1-2; *Smyrn.* 12.1.

24. We may deduce that the terms of Ignatius's custody deteriorated and made it impossible for him to write other letters (since the ones written in province Asia were so valued, it is likely that any others would have been collected and passed on too). Possibly we should also deduce that the churches in the places through which he subsequently passed were less sympathetic to him, though Polycarp gives no such hint in reminding the Philippians that they had seen Ignatius with their own eyes (Polycarp, *Phil.* 9.1).

(§49 n.88), or their christology,[25] or promotion of monoepiscopacy, or emphasis on the eucharist (§50.2b) which rules out such an early date.[26] It is equally as probable, or more so, that Ignatius provides evidence of how early were the issues, and the attitudes expressed on these issues, within second-century Christianity. The more important question, in fact, is how representative was Ignatius in the views he expressed, and how typical were the developments within Christian thought and organization to which he attests. Or is he more to be regarded as the most effective spokesman for a particular faction within developing Christianity?[27]

c. Polycarp

We have already met Polycarp as bishop of Smyrna, where Ignatius lodged for some days during his traverse across Asia province, where they communed together, and to whom Ignatius wrote what was probably his last letter. Polycarp is still better known as a martyr, the account of whose martyrdom is an early Christian classic (see below — §40.1d). And according to Irenaeus, Polycarp himself provided a first-hand link back to the apostle John, and a bridge between the apostles and Irenaeus, enabling Irenaeus to depict himself as only two generations distant from the disciples of the Lord (Eusebius, *HE* 5.20.5-8).[28] If his martyrdom can be dated to 155, and he was 86 when he died (*Mart. Polyc.* 9.3 — or 86 years since his conversion?), then he must have been born about 70, and have met and supported Ignatius when he was about 40, and already a bishop.[29]

Polycarp's letter to the *Philippians* has more the character of a general

---

25. Ignatius regularly refers to Jesus as God, 'our God', 'God come in the flesh', etc. (*Eph.* inscr.; 1.1; 7.2; 15.3; 18.2; 19.3; *Trall.* 7.1; *Rom.* inscr.; 3.3; 6.3; *Smyrn.* 1.1; 10.1; *Polyc.* 8.3).

26. 'Within a few years of A.D. 110, before or after' (Lightfoot, *Ignatius* 1.30); 'the traditional view ... sometime during the years 107-109' (Jefford, *Apostolic Fathers* 12). But see also R. M. Hübner, 'Thesen zur Echtheit und Datierung der sieben Briefe des Ignatius', *ZAC* 1 (1997) 44-72, with several critical reactions in the same issue.

27. See further below §50.2b.

28. Discussion in W. R. Schoedel, 'Polycarp, Epistle of', *ABD* 5.390-91; P. Hartog, *Polycarp's* Epistle to the Philippians *and the* Martyrdom of Polycarp (Oxford University, 2013) 11-16, with review of the debate about Polycarp's theology (68-72). In the epilogue added to the *Martyrdom of Polycarp* Irenaeus is also referred to as a disciple of Polycarp (*Mart. Polyc.* 22.2); on the epilogue as a later addition, see W. R. Schoedel, *The Apostolic Fathers* vol. V: *Polycarp, Martyrdom of Polycarp, Fragments of Papias* (London: Nelson, 1967) 77.

29. Ehrman, *Apostolic Fathers* 1.362; Jefford, *Apostolic Fathers* 13-14 (further bibliography in n.12).

exhortation, not so political or polemical as Ignatius's letters, but fitting naturally with them as a kind of addendum. For Polycarp makes it clear that he wrote in response to Ignatius's request, perhaps as already referred to in Ignatius, *Polyc.* 8.1 above. *Phil.* 9.1-2 is usually taken to imply that Ignatius had already been martyred, though it is quite possible that what the Philippians saw was someone doomed to death and already being savagely treated. But if 9.1-2 does imply Ignatius's martyrdom, then, taken with 13.2,[30] we would have to envisage some months elapsing between Ignatius passing through Philippi and his death — time for him to reach Rome, for his sentence to be executed, and for the news to reach back to Polycarp. Even so, Polycarp's letter to the *Philippians* quite likely followed Ignatius's letters only a few months later — that is, still in the 110s.[31]

d. The *Martyrdom of Polycarp*

The account of Polycarp's martyrdom has the form of a letter written by someone called Marcion (20.1), from the church in Smyrna to the church in Philomelium (in Phrygia) and for wider distribution (prescript).[32] It is a vivid and moving account of Polycarp's execution, which became the model for subsequent acts of Christian martyrs.[33] The *Martyrdom* recounts how Polycarp was caught up in a persecution of Christians by local Roman authorities, in which several were persuaded to 'take the oath and offer a sacrifice' (4). When arrested, Polycarp was urged several times to 'swear by the Fortune of Caesar', make a sacrifice and revile Christ (8-10), but responded in unforgettable words, 'For eighty-six years I have served him, and he has done me no wrong. How can I blaspheme my king who has saved me? . . . I am a Christian' (9.3-10.1). The execution is recorded in some detail, including legendary elements (the fire having no effect, he was stabbed, a dove came forth, and his blood pouring out extinguished the fire — 15-16).

The date of Polycarp's martyrdom is usually taken to be 155, on the basis

---

30. On the likelihood that the letter was a combination of two letters (chs. 1-12, and chs. 13-14) see Schoedel, 'Apostolic Fathers' 466.

31. Schoedel, *Polycarp, Martyrdom of Polycarp* 37-38; Holmes, *Apostolic Fathers* 120-21; Hartog, *Polycarp* 40-45. Hartog concludes: 'Generally speaking, questions and reservations have failed to shake the claim of Polycarp, *Philippians* genuineness' (27-32; here 32). See also his *Polycarp and the New Testament* (WUNT 2.134; Tübingen: Mohr Siebeck, 2002) 69-72, 148-69.

32. On the textual tradition see Ehrman, *Apostolic Fathers* 1.361-63; Hartog, *Polycarp* 167-86.

33. J. C. Wilson, 'Polycarp', *ABD* 5.389-90. The text of *Martyrdom* is reproduced in extenso by Eusebius, *HE* 4.15.

of *Mart. Polyc.* 21 ('the second day of the new month of Xanthikos, seven days before the kalends of March [February 23], a great Sabbath, at the eighth hour ... when Statius Quadratus was proconsul').[34] The account claims to have been written by an eyewitness (15.1), so a date for the *Martyrdom* of 156,[35] perhaps in anticipation of its first anniversary (18.3), is entirely plausible.

e. The *Didache*

The *Teaching of the Twelve Apostles* is one of the most fascinating members of the Apostolic Fathers.[36] Although mentioned by Eusebius,[37] it was not known till a complete text was discovered by Philotheos Bryennios in Constantinople in 1873 — Codex Hierosolymitanus, dated 1056[38]— though that text itself may not be complete.[39] Some earlier fragments are also known, and, following Bryennios's discovery, it became apparent that the fourth-century *Apostolic Constitutions* 7.1-32 drew heavily on the *Didache* or on the materials of which the *Didache* is composed.[40] But it was the discovery of the *Didache* itself which revolutionized the study of early Christianity.

This was because each of the main sections of the *Didache* seems to provide highly valuable insights into early Christianity's development: the section on 'the two ways' (chs. 1-6) confirmed the importance of this Jewish paraenetic tradition in Christian catechesis;[41] the treatment of baptism and eucharist (chs. 7-10) sheds fascinating light on the liturgical developments of the early second century;[42] particularly intriguing is the prominence given to the ministry of

---

34. The proconsulship of Quadratus is usually dated to 154/155. Eusebius dates Polycarp's martyrdom to the period following the death of Antoninus Pius, that is, after 161 (*HE* 4.14), but that is generally regarded as mistaken. See discussion in Schoedel, *Polycarp, Martyrdom of Polycarp* 78-79; also 'Polycarp, Martyrdom of', *ABD* 5.392-93; Hartog, *Polycarp* 215-21.

35. Cf. Schoedel, 'Apostolic Fathers' 467.

36. For a survey of research and discussion see J. A. Draper, 'The Didache in Modern Research: An Overview', in J. A. Draper, ed., *The Didache in Modern Research* (Leiden: Brill, 1996) 1-42.

37. 'Among the books which are not genuine must be reckoned the Acts of Paul, the work entitled the Shepherd, ... and the so-called Teachings of the Apostles' (*HE* 3.25.4). See further K. Niederwimmer, *Die Didache* (KAV; Göttingen: Vandenhoeck, ²1993) 15-33.

38. Full details in Niederwimmer, *Didache* 33-36.

39. Ehrman, *Apostolic Fathers* 1.410.

40. Details in Niederwimmer, *Didache* 45-47; Ehrman, *Apostolic Fathers* 1.412-13.

41. The fact that 7.1 begins, 'But with respect to baptism, baptize as follows. Having said all these things in advance, baptize ...', suggests that chs. 1-6 were understood as baptismal catechesis. See further §45.5b below.

42. As Draper notes, Hans Lietzmann saw the *Didache* as containing the 'oldest ex-

itinerant apostles (missionaries), prophets and teachers (chs. 11-13), alongside that of the locally appointed bishops (plural) and deacons (ch. 15),[43] which indicated that the early modes of church ministry and governance were more diverse than what could be deduced from the Pastoral and Ignatian Epistles;[44] and ch. 16 indicated the continuing of apocalyptic expectation.

i. Author

The document is not attributed to any single author and the main body of it has more the character of catechetical instruction and guidance on church discipline drawn up by a church committee (a manual of church tradition and order)![45] It would be quite in accord with the structure and content of the document if the document as it now stands had been produced by putting together three or four sections of teaching which had previously been known and used in oral form.[46] At any rate, we can take the opening words seriously ('The teaching of the Lord through the twelve apostles to the nations') as indicating a conviction that the 'teaching' represented a true heritage which had come down to the subsequent generations from the founding apostles of Christianity. It is not necessary to put the material to the test of oldness and originality, though the dependence on Matthew's Gospel in particular is noticeable (§44.2f), for such a conviction to be deserving of respect.

ii. Provenance

As to where the *Didache* arose in its present form, opinion is divided between Egypt and Syria. If *Barnabas* is to be assigned to Egypt (§40.1f), then the strong similarity between *Did.* 1-6 and *Barn.* 18-20 would support an Egyptian provenance.[47] But the *Didache* does not reflect the Hellenistic Jewish character which is usually associated with Alexandria; and the interaction which *Didache* expresses between Jew(ish tradition) and Christian (tradition), more typical of Syria, together with the influence of Matthew, probably gives Syria the edge.[48]

---

tant formulary' of the Christian Eucharist and argued that the *Didache* envisaged a eucharist followed by an agape meal (*Didache in Modern Research* 27).

43. 15.1 — 'Elect for yourselves bishops and deacons . . .'.

44. So particularly A. Harnack, *The Mission and Expansion of Christianity in the First Three Centuries* (ET 1908; New York: Harper Torchbook, 1962) 334-54.

45. R. A. Kraft, *Barnabas and the Didache* (R. M. Grant, ed., *The Apostolic Fathers* vol. 3; London: Nelson, 1965), calls it a '"school" or "community" product' (2-3); also 59-65.

46. See e.g. Niederwimmer's discussion (*Didache* 64-70); and further below §44.2f.

47. Richardson, *Early Christian Fathers* 163, though he locates the source of 6.3-15 in Syria (166).

48. Jefford, *Apostolic Fathers* 21-22, argues strongly for Antioch. Cf. Niederwimmer, *Didache* 79-80; R. A. Kraft, 'Didache', *ABD* 2.197; Ehrman, *Apostolic Fathers* 1.411-12. See

iii. Date

The influence of distinctively Matthean features suggests a *terminus a quo* for the *Didache* of the mid 80s.[49] But the partial development of the final ascription of the Lord's Prayer ('For the power and the glory are yours forever' — 8.2), the fact that the eucharist is still a meal (10.1), and the prominence given to itinerant missionaries and prophets (11-13), suggest an early stage in liturgical and ecclesiastical development, and an *ad quem* not far into the second century. A date in the period 100-120 seems as good a fit with that sequence of data as any other.[50]

f. The *Epistle of Barnabas*

A complete text of *Barnabas* was unknown till the discovery of Codex Sinaiticus (1859) and Codex Hierosolymitanus (1873).[51] The *Epistle* poses more or less unanswerable questions on each of the issues to which we confine these introductory sections.

i. Author

The text itself is anonymous. Attribution to Barnabas is already taken for granted by Clement of Alexandria,[52] but is now almost universally doubted, not least because of the likely date of the letter. However, the letter is written in first-person terms, as a personal address, and despite the author's disclaim-

---

also J. K. Zangenberg, 'Reconstructing the Social and Religious Milieu of the Didache: Observations and Possible Results', in H. van de Sandt and J. K. Zangenberg, eds., *Matthew, James and Didache: Three Related Documents in Their Jewish and Christian Settings* (Atlanta: SBL, 2008) 43-69.

49. Some who dispute Matthean influence as such but affirm the Jewish character of *Didache* argue for an earlier, even pre-70 date — so particularly J.-P. Audet, *La Didache* (EB: Paris: Gabalda, 1958) 192, 210; J. A. Draper, 'Didache', *NIDB* 2.122 — 'perhaps even as early as the mid-1st cent.'.

50. Niederwimmer, *Didache* 79; Ehrman, *Apostolic Fathers* 1.411. C. N. Jefford, 'Did Ignatius of Antioch Know the Didache?' in C. N. Jefford, ed., *The Didache in Context: Essays on Its Text, History and Transmission* (NovTSupp 77; Leiden: Brill, 1995) 330-51, answers: remotely possible, but unlikely (351).

51. See the brief treatment in Ehrman, *Apostolic Fathers* 2.9-10.

52. *Strom.* 2.6.31 (quoting 'the Apostle Barnabas' [*Barn.* 1.5]); 2.7.35 ('Barnabas the apostle having said [quoting *Barn.* 4.11]'); 2.20.116 ('Barnabas, and he was one of the seventy, and a fellow-worker of Paul', quoting *Barn.* 16.7). Eusebius numbers *Barnabas* among the *nothoi* ('spurious, not genuine'), along with the *Acts of Paul*, the *Shepherd* (of Hermas), the *Apocalypse of Peter* and the *Didache* — possibly also the Revelation of John (*HE* 3.25.4). See further Kraft, *Barnabas and the Didache* 40-41; J. C. Paget, *The Epistle of Barnabas* (WUNT 2.64; Tübingen: Mohr Siebeck, 1994) 248-58.

ers in 1.8 and 4.9 (writing 'not as a teacher'), it is more than likely that he regarded himself as a teacher (1.5-6), as his command of scripture (§45.5c) also suggests.[53] Why then was the letter attributed to Barnabas? Possibly because it displays so much interest in and knowledge of Levitical regulations (chs. 7 and 10), and Barnabas is the only first-generation Christian leader who is explicitly identified as a Levite (Acts 4.36).[54] But the letter's perspective on the Jewish law is more that of an outsider: he talks of the 'us' who are to 'their law' as 'latecomers' (3.6),[55] of 'their covenant' and 'the circumcision in which they trusted' (9.4, 6); and he speaks as representative of converted Gentiles (16.7 — 'before we believed in God'; cf. 14.5).[56] It is not impossible, of course, that a Jew who became Christian felt so disaffected from his Jewish past[57] that he could be justifiably described as an apostate, though that was hardly true of Barnabas (Gal. 2.12-13). On the other hand, it is entirely envisageable that a Gentile Christian became fascinated about Christianity's Jewish heritage, knowledgeable about Jewish law and tradition, and saw it as his task to make that heritage as meaningful as possible to Gentile believers.

ii. Provenance

Barnabas has traditionally been thought to have originated in Alexandria. And there are some traditions which locate Barnabas in Alexandria — notably Ps.-Clem. *Hom.* 1.9, though *Hom.* 1.14 has Barnabas leaving Alexandria for 'home', and Ps.-Clem. *Recog.* 1.7, 11 similarly shows Barnabas arriving at and departing from Rome to his dwelling in Judaea. More weighty is the fact that Clement of Alexandria not only knew *Barnabas*, but evidently found its thought conducive,[58] implying his appreciation of a similar cast of mind. This is

---

53. Kraft, *Barnabas and the Didache* 44; R. Hvalvik, *The Struggle for Scripture and Covenant: The Purpose of the Epistle of Barnabas and Jewish-Christian Competition in the Second Century* (WUNT 2.82; Tübingen: Mohr Siebeck, 1996) 46-52; F. R. Prostmeier, *Der Barnabasbrief* (KAV 8; Göttingen: Vandenhoeck, 1999) 131.

54. Paget, *Barnabas* 7, who also notes that both *Barnabas* and Barnabas were associated with Alexandria.

55. *Epēlytoi* ('latecomers, newcomers') is the reading of Sinaiticus; but Hierosolymitanus (11th cent.) and the Latin version read *prosēlytoi* ('proselytes').

56. Wilson, *Related Strangers* 128-29; Hvalvik, *Struggle* 43-44; Prostmeier, *Barnabasbrief* 132; see also the brief discussion in Paget, *Barnabas* 7-9.

57. But there is no real parallel with Matthew (Matt. 23) or Paul (Phil. 3); see further below §46.6b.

58. See n.52 above. 'There is a real sense in which Clement is still the best commentary on Barnabas. . . . earlier and later products of the same Christian environment/ school. . . . The epistle is best known in Alexandria and its approach can be called Alexandrian in such matters as exegetical gnosis and ethical parenesis. . . . Barnabas is the work of a Christian teacher whose thought, in general, is oriented towards Alexandria, and whose

strengthened by the fact that the closest parallels to *Barnabas*'s interpretation of various Torah passages and rituals are to be found in Alexandrian literature: Philo of Alexandria, with his similarly 'allegorizing' exposition of Torah;[59] and the *Letter of Aristeas* (145-48, 166)[60] similarly reading the regulations against unclean animals and birds as warnings against people who behave like pigs, or weasels, etc. (*Barn.* 10). The fact that *Barnabas* seems also to be familiar with rabbinic tradition (especially chs. 7-8) may weaken an argument based on parallels, but insofar as much weight can be placed on such parallels, the case for recognizing an Alexandrian origin seems to be a little weightier.[61]

iii. Date

There is broad agreement that the letter has to be dated after the destruction of the Jerusalem temple: 'because of their war, it [the temple] was destroyed by their enemies' (16.4). But how long after? In 4.3-5, the 'little horn' of Dan. 7.7-8, said to have 'drawn near', may be identified with one or the other of the emperors Vespasian or Nerva, but the issue is at best obscure.[62] More intriguing is the prospect held out in 16.3-4 that associates of the Romans would rebuild the temple.[63] That the temple would be rebuilt, as it had been following the Babylonian exile, must have been the hope of all Jews. But there is no indication that such a hope had any realistic prospect of success in the time of Vespasian or Nerva. The best that could be argued is that Nerva's more tolerant attitude to Jews (following Diocletian)[64] stirred up the hope to some degree.[65]

---

area of ministry is in northeast Egypt' (Kraft, *Barnabas and the Didache* 45, 46, 48, 55; see the whole discussion, 45-56).

59. Thematic parallels are listed in Prostmeier, *Barnabasbrief* 121-22 n.69.

60. *Aristeas* is usually linked with Alexandria, where the second half of its story is located.

61. See further the careful discussion of Paget, *Barnabas* 30-42, and Prostmeier, *Barnabasbrief* 119-30. Hvalvik regards the issue as still an open question (*Struggle* 35-42).

62. Hvalvik concludes that 4.3-6 has no bearing on the dating of *Barnabas* (*Struggle* 25-26); on the ten kings see *Struggle* 27-34, set out in a table (29).

63. Hvalvik thinks a reference to the Jupiter-temple is 'quite probable (*Struggle* 19-22, also 23-25); discussion in Prostmeier, *Barnabasbrief* 114-18.

64. See below §46.3b.

65. See particularly M. B. Shukster and P. Richardson, 'Barnabas, Nerva and the Yavnean Rabbis', *JTS* 33 (1983) 31-55; W. Horbury, 'Jewish-Christian Relations in Barnabas and Justin Martyr', in Dunn, ed., *Jews and Christians* 315-45 (here 319-21). Paget again provides a thorough study of the whole dating issue, concluding that the hope of a rebuilt temple during the reign of Nerva is 'believable', so that the suggestion that the epistle was written during Nerva's reign 'becomes almost *probable*' (*Barnabas* 9-28, 66-68). See also Wilson, *Related Strangers* 132-36. Jefford notes that the majority(?) of scholarship tends to favour 96-100, and agrees (*Apostolic Fathers* 33-34).

Probably more attractive is the hypothesis that Hadrian had laid plans to build a temple to Zeus during his visit to Jerusalem in 130, a prospect which did much to provoke the Bar Kokhba revolt and encouraged a fresh wave of enthusiasm for the Jewish temple to be rebuilt,[66] even though the rebels' hold on Jerusalem was almost certainly not secure or long enough for any such hope to be realistic of fulfillment.[67] A late Jewish legend and late Christian accounts do speak of an attempt to rebuild the temple thwarted by Hadrian;[68] and the fact that after crushing the revolt Hadrian both founded a new city, Aelia Capitolina, on the site of the destroyed Jerusalem, and erected a temple to Zeus on the site of the Temple, may well indicate that Hadrian was resolved to crush any (further) hope of the Jewish temple being restored. If a Hadrianic date is most probable, then the fact that Barnabas makes no reference or allusion to the Bar Kokhba revolt or its failure (which would have been grist for his mill) pushes us to an *ad quem* date of 131/132 so that a date of 130/131 seems the most plausible[69] (though 'plausible' is a relative term).

g. The *Shepherd* of Hermas

The *Shepherd* of Hermas contains a lengthy series of five *Visions*, twelve *Commandments/Mandates* and ten *Parables/Similitudes*, most of them explained to Hermas by an angel, particularly with reference to the problem of postbaptismal sin.[70] It is one of the most intriguing Christian writings to have emerged from the early second century — intriguing because it operates at a rather naive level, and yet proved to be very popular, included even with *Barnabas* in the Codex Sinaiticus together with the NT writings.[71] It presumably, therefore,

---

66. R. S. MacLennan, *Early Christian Texts on Jews and Judaism* (BJS 194; Atlanta: Scholars, 1990), argues that *Barnabas* was written as 'a moderating voice' against a particular form of Judaism caught up in enthusiastic hope for the rebuilding of the Temple, but seems to date the Bar Kokhba rebellion to 115-117 (21-24, 44-48).

67. Cassius Dio 69.12.1-2 seems to think that the foundation of Aelia Capitolina and the building of the temple to Zeus was the cause of the Bar Kokhba revolt; but Eusebius, *HE* 4.6.4, is clear that the establishment of Aelia followed the crushing of the revolt. Mary Smallwood observes that 'the two authorities can be combined without difficulty by supposing that Dio records the inception of the plan and Eusebius its fulfilment' (*Jews* 433; see further Schürer, *History* 1.536-37, 540-42; *GLAJJ* 2.395-96).

68. Schürer, *History* 1.535-36.

69. Schoedel, 'Apostolic Fathers' 468; Hvalvik, *Struggle* 23; Prostmeier, *Barnabasbrief* 118-19, in agreement with Harnack.

70. Hermas's answer: forgiveness is possible to those who repent, but once only.

71. 'Judging from the manuscript remains, it was copied and read more widely in the second and third centuries than any other noncanonical book, even more than many of the

indicates the level of intellectual engagement and ethical discipleship which typified the main body of Christians during these decades.

Although the book's three sections suggest the possibility of multiple authors, most believe it to have a single authorship, though perhaps composed at different times.[72] The only indication of the author's identity is his opening self-identification — 'The one who raised me sold me to a certain woman named Rhoda, in Rome' (*Vis.* 1.1.1) — presumably able now to write as a freedman.[73] And he identifies himself as 'Hermas' a few sentences later (*Vis.* 1.1.4), and regularly thereafter.[74] He makes no claim to have any leadership position in the church of Rome, nor does he identify himself as a prophet or teacher.[75] From the fifth vision onwards Hermas is instructed by the 'Shepherd', identified in *Vis.* 5.7 as 'the angel of repentance'.[76] But there is no indication of why he was chosen to be the recipient of such visions. We may envisage a not very learned member of one of the Roman congregations who came to prominence as one who had been so favoured.[77]

The origin of the book in Rome is rarely questioned:[78] the author claims to be local, as just noted (*Vis.* 1.1.1), and refers to his passing the river Tiber

---

books that later came to be included in the New Testament' (Ehrman, *Apostolic Fathers* 2.162). Details in C. Osiek, *The Shepherd of Hermas* (Hermeneia; Minneapolis: Fortress, 1999) 4-7.

72. G. F. Snyder, *The Shepherd of Hermas* (R. M. Grant, ed., *The Apostolic Fathers* vol. 6; London: Nelson, 1968) 23-24; Osiek, *Hermas* 8-10; Ehrman, *Apostolic Fathers* 2.165-66; Jefford, *Apostolic Fathers* 25-28.

73. P. Lampe, *From Paul to Valentinus: Christians in Rome in the First Two Centuries* (Minneapolis: Fortress, 2003) 218-20, and further 220-24.

74. *Vis.* 1.2.2-4; 1.4.3; 2.2.2; 2.3.1; 3.1.6, 9; 3.8.11; 4.1.4, 7. The identification (initially by Origen) of Hermas with the Hermas of Rom. 16.14 (Eusebius, *HE* 3.3.6) is at best fanciful.

75. Hermas was rather suspicious about those who claimed to be prophets (*Mand.* 11), or teachers (*Sim.* 9.22.2-3). His venture into christology (*Sim.* 5.5-6) is unsophisticated.

76. Also explicitly in *Sim.* 9.1.1 and 9.33.1. Although the shepherd is never identified as such in the *Mandates*, it is explicitly 'the angel of repentance' to whom the instruction on the commandments is attributed (*Mand.* 12.4.7; 12.6.1), and the title is used several times in the *Similitudes*.

77. His early attempts to write, to copy 'a little book' for the instruction of 'the ones chosen by God', suggest that his degree of literacy was not high — 'I copied the whole thing, letter by letter, for I could not distinguish between the syllables [it was written in continuous script with no division between words] . . . I completed the letters of the book' (*Vis.* 2.1.4). Lampe instances cases of his carelessness and ineptness, and the book's 'often clumsy' style; he concludes that 'Hermas possessed a rudimentary literary ability', notwithstanding his book's 'colorful absurdities' (*Paul to Valentinus* 231-34, and further 234-36). Eusebius notes that the *Shepherd* was judged to be valuable by some 'especially to those who need elementary instruction' (*HE* 3.3.6).

78. 'Hermas's Roman provenance is above dispute' (Schoedel, 'Apostolic Fathers' 471).

years later (*Vis.* 1.1.2) and to walking along the Via Campana (*Vis.* 4.1.2). The date, however, is more disputed. The most obvious dating is suggested by the Muratorian fragment, which notes that 'Hermas wrote the *Shepherd* very recently, in our times, in the city of Rome, while bishop Pius, his brother,[79] was occupying the [episcopal] chair' (73-76). Since Pius I was bishop of Rome in 142-157, this would suggest a date about 145-155. The problem is that the date of the Muratorian fragment is itself disputed, though the references to Pius, also to Valentinus, Marcion and Basilides as also, by implication, currently or recently active (81-85), support the most commonly argued date of late second century.[80] In which case, a date for the *Shepherd* c. 150 would seem to be most plausible. If, however, the testimony of the Muratorian fragment is discounted, or the historical association with Pius regarded as questionable, or the result of some confusion, then the only remaining clue is probably the mention of 'elders' (*Vis.* 2.4.2-3; 3.1.8) and 'bishops' (*Vis.* 3.5.1; *Sim.* 9.27.2), which implies a stage of ecclesiology prior to the establishment of a single bishop, the focus of unity as Ignatius maintained — and this in a book written in Rome.[81] How much weight can be placed on this, and the other clues, is still debated, but perhaps we should think of a date earlier than the one indicated by the Muratorian fragment — say 130-150.[82]

h. *2 Clement*

2 Clement is a homily which was probably written to be read out in a Christian gathering for worship (as implied in *2 Clem.* 19.1). Its author and place of

---

79. That Hermas could have been brother of bishop Pius is dismissed by Snyder, *Shepherd of Hermas* 22-23.

80. See the brief review, with substantial bibliography, in H. Y. Gamble, 'The New Testament Canon: Recent Research and the Status Quaestionis', in L. M. McDonald and J. A. Sanders, eds., *The Canon Debate* (Peabody: Hendrickson, 2002) 267-94 (here 269-70).

81. Here we should recall that his letter to Rome is the only one in which Ignatius does not mention the local church(es)' 'bishop' — raising the question as to how soon monoepiscopacy became established, not least in Rome itself.

82. 'There is now a tendency to date at least the original materials early in the second century' (Schoedel, 'Apostolic Fathers' 470). Osiek, *Hermas* 18-20, and Ehrman, *Apostolic Fathers* 2.167-69, suggest a dating range of 95-140 (Osiek) or 110-140 (Ehrman) (similarly Koester, *Introduction* 2.258), but they probably give too much weight to the reference to 'Clement' in *Vis.* 2.4.3, who cannot easily be identified with Clement of Rome (*pace* also Holmes, *Apostolic Fathers* 191), though the possibility should not be entirely excluded that the Clement referred to by Hermas was the Clement to whom *2 Clement* was attributed (cf. Lightfoot, *Clement of Rome* 1.359-60), since the *Shepherd* and *2 Clement* may have emerged at about the same time.

composition are unknown, and there are no real clues on either point within the document itself.[83] The best clue is probably to be found in Eusebius's reference to a letter of Dionysius (bishop of Corinth, c. 170) written 'to the Romans and addressed to Soter who was then bishop (c. 165-174)' (*HE* 4.23.9). In that letter, continues Eusebius, Dionysius

> also quotes the letter of Clement to the Corinthians, showing that from the beginning it had been the custom to read it in the church. "Today we observed the Lord's holy day, in which we read (out) your letter, which we will always have for our admonition whenever we read it, as also the former (letter) written to us through Clement" (4.23.11).

The 'former (letter)' is most obviously *1 Clement*, so Dionysius was referring to another letter attributed to Clement, which was read regularly in the Corinthian church's gatherings.[84] The obvious inference is that this second letter is what we know as *2 Clement*. If so, it means that *2 Clement* was known and designated as such (to have been written by Clement), round about 170, and understood to have been written also from Rome to Corinth,[85] like *1 Clement*. A further implication is probably that it was the church in Corinth which preserved both *1 Clement* and *2 Clement*, together with copies of the several letters written by Dionysius, to which Eusebius refers (*HE* 4.23.9-13); also that it would have been the church of Corinth which was responsible for giving them the wider circulation which made them known to Eusebius.[86] The chief problem with this is Eusebius's own clear testimony that only one letter was recognized as written by Clement (*HE* 3.16; 3.39.1) and that 'a second letter ascribed to Clement' was neither widely recognized nor widely used (3.38.4).[87] So perhaps we should simply infer that *2 Clement*

---

83. See also Ehrman, *Apostolic Fathers* 1.157-58.

84. Or was the letter read out in the Corinthian church a letter from Soter, to which Dionysius was replying (as Harnack suggested), and *2 Clement* actually a letter from Soter (see further Richardson, *Early Christian Fathers* 185-86)? The fact that Dionysius does not indicate that 'the former (letter)' had *also* been written by/through Clement leaves it open that 'the letter of Clement to the Corinthians' read out in Corinth was an identification made by Eusebius and not by Dionysius.

85. Lightfoot noted that 'the allusion to the athletic games [*2 Clem.* 7], and presumably to the Isthmian festival, is couched in language which is quite natural if addressed to Corinthians, but not so if spoken elsewhere' (*Clement* 2.197). But he also thinks that *2 Clement* was written in Corinth (2.199). Richardson argues for Alexandria (*Early Christian Fathers* 186-87), and Koester favours an Egyptian origin (*Introduction* 2.234-36), as also W. Pratscher, *Der zweite Clemensbrief* (KAV; Göttingen: Vandenhoeck, 2007) 659-61.

86. As Polycarp had passed on Ignatius's letters (Polyc., *Phil.* 13.2; see n.19 above).

87. Documentation in Lightfoot, *Clement of Rome* 2.192-94. When Western writers

became associated with *1 Clement* either because both were read every so often in the Corinthian church assemblies, and/or were stored together in the archive of the church in Corinth, with the result that when *2 Clement* began to become better known (as *1 Clement* always had been), it was assumed to be a second letter of Clement to Corinth.[88] In the end, the issue remains at best confused.

The question regarding the date of *2 Clement* is equally obscure. The fact that only 'elders' are mentioned (17.3, 5) is more or less all that we have to go on, the implication being, as probably with the *Shepherd*, that, with no bishop(s) being mentioned, the document was composed before the more widespread establishment of monoepiscopacy.[89] A date about 140 is probably the best that we can guess.[90]

i. Papias

Papias is included here since, although his five-volume work entitled *Expositions of the Sayings of the Lord* is not extant, the quotations from it, particularly in Eusebius but also in various others, provide fascinating information especially about transmission of the Jesus tradition and the composition of some of the NT Gospels.[91] According to church tradition (Eusebius, *HE* 2.15.2; 3.36.2) Papias was the bishop of Hierapolis (one of the Lycus valley cities, not far from Colossae and Laodicea). Irenaeus knew him as 'the hearer of John[92] and a companion of Polycarp'.[93] If this information is trustworthy, these two

---

referred to a 'second epistle' of Clement it was to the pseudepigraphic letter of Clement to James in the pseudo-Clementines (see below §45.2b).

88. Thus, Lightfoot, *Clement of Rome* 2.197-98; Harnack, cited by Lake, *Apostolic Fathers* 1.126. As noted above (n.3), *1 Clement* and *2 Clement* are included with all the NT writings in Codex Alexandrinus.

89. The fact that *2 Clem.* 12.2 quotes a saying of Jesus, which was almost certainly part of the elaboration of the early Jesus tradition, as evidenced by the *Gospel of Thomas* 12.1-5 and Clem. Alex., *Strom.* 3.13 (see §43 n.285 and §44.4a below), also suggests a date some way into the second century.

90. Harnack suggested 130-150, Lightfoot 120-140 (*Clement of Rome* 2.202); Lake plus or minus 150 (*Apostolic Fathers* 1.127); Ehrman 140s (*Apostolic Fathers* 1.159-60); Jefford 120-150 (*Apostolic Fathers* 30); see also Holmes, *Apostolic Fathers* 65-67, and Pratscher, *zweite Clemensbrief* 62-64.

91. See further below §44.2j. On the range of fragments of Papias which have been variously drawn on, see Holmes, *Apostolic Fathers* 308, 312.

92. The reference to 'John', of course, revives the discussion as to whether the apostle or the elder John was in view.

93. Irenaeus, *adv. haer.* 5.33.4; Eusebius, *HE* 3.39.1 — though Eusebius adds that Papias himself in the preface of his writings 'makes plain that he had in no way been a hearer

figures (John and Polycarp) provide a frame within which Papias must have flourished, that is, between c. 90 and 135. And if we assume that it was when he was bishop that he wrote his magnum opus, that would push us to about 130 for the date when he wrote,[94] and presumably in Hierapolis.

j. The *Odes of Solomon*

It is not at all clear under what heading the *Odes of Solomon*[95] should be included, but if the *Didache* might be classified as the first book of Church Order, the *Odes* could be classified as 'the first Christian Hymnbook',[96] and so inclusion among the early second century Christian writings is appropriate. Notwithstanding their title and very 'Psalms of David character',[97] they are undoubtedly Christian. They never use the name 'Jesus', but they speak often of the Messiah (9.3; 17.17; 29.6; 41.15), where other titles, 'Lord' (e.g. 24.1; 39.11), 'the Beloved' (7.1; 8.21), 'Son' (19.2; 23.18; 41.13), 'Son of Man', 'Son of God' (36.3; 42.15) and 'Saviour' (42.18), make it clear that it is Jesus Christ who is in view.[98] There are also allusions to his incarnation (7.6; 12.12), his birth from a virgin (19.6-9), his baptism (7.15; 24.1), and his death and resurrection (8.5; 27.1-3; 31.9; 41.12; 42.1-2). Several of the *Odes* could be described as hymns in praise of Christ, the Beloved, the Word, the Son (8, 12, 21, 32, 36, 41). The echoes of John's Gospel (§49.6) suggest that they emerged from a Johannine community, and the parallels with the Dead Sea Scrolls, particularly the light/dark dualism,[99] may even suggest that the *Odes* were written by an Essene who had become a believer in Jesus.[100]

The *Odes* were known only in extracts before all 42 *Odes* were discovered in Syriac in 1909 by Rendel Harris,[101] and were most probably composed in

---

and eyewitness of the holy apostles' (3.39.2). Discussion in Schoedel, *Polycarp, Martyrdom of Polycarp, Fragments of Papias* 89-90.

94. Schoedel is willing to date Papias's writing as early as 110 (*Polycarp, Martyrdom of Polycarp, Fragments of Papias* 92).

95. See particularly J. H. Charlesworth, 'Solomon, Odes of', *ABD* 6.114-15; *OTP* 2.725-34 (text 735-71); also J. A. Emerton, 'The Odes of Solomon', *AOT* 683-90 (text 691-731).

96. J. H. Charlesworth, *The First Christian Hymnbook: The Odes of Solomon* (Eugene, OR.: Wipf & Stock, 2009).

97. See e.g. Charlesworth, *OTP* 731.

98. Note also the triadic statements in *Odes* 19.2 and 23.22.

99. *Odes* 5.5-6; 11.19; 15.2; 16.15-16; 18.6; 21.3.

100. J. H. Charlesworth, *Critical Reflections on the Odes of Solomon* vol. 1: *Literary Setting, Textual Studies, Gnosticism, the Dead Sea Scrolls and the Gospel of John* (JSPSupp 22; Sheffield Academic, 1998) 192-231; briefly *OTP* 728.

101. J. R. Harris, 'An Early Christian Hymn-Book', *Contemporary Review* 95 (1909) 4414-28.

§40.1 *The Sources — Second Century*

that language,[102] so providing valuable insight into early Syrian Christianity.[103] They were caught up in the quest for pre-Christian Gnosticism and traces were found of Gnostic influence in the *Odes*,[104] but there is nothing distinctively Gnostic in them,[105] though they probably can be accounted as evidence of the mixture of ingredients in the melting pot of early second century religiosity in the Mediterranean basin.[106] The strongly Jewish character, the frequent use of the early self-reference of disciples of Jesus as following 'the Way',[107] the vivid spirituality,[108] the undeveloped theology, and the Johannine echoes suggest an early date, quite possibly as early as the first quarter of the second century.[109]

---

102. Charlesworth, *OTP* 2.726 — most probably in or near Antioch (727); Emerton, *AOT* 686-87.

103. Parallels with Ignatius may also suggest a Syrian or Antiochene provenance; see V. Corwin, *St. Ignatius and Christianity in Antioch* (New Haven: Yale University, 1960) 71-80; 'a number of rather striking similarities between the Odes and Ignatius of Antioch . . . leave no doubt that both the author of the Odes and Ignatius were products of the same environment' (Emerton, *AOT* 686).

104. Kümmel, *Introduction* 223; Rudolph, *Gnosis* 29, 221-22; for Bultmann the *Odes* exemplified 'the basic Gnostic view-point' which he thought lay behind John's Gospel (*Gospel of John*, index 'Odes of Solomon').

105. 'Ode xvi witnesses to a doctrine of Creation which would have been impossible for any thoroughgoing Gnostic' (Emerton, *AOT* 684).

106. Cf. Koester, *Introduction* 2.217-18. Passages like *Odes* 17.14-15 (Christ speaking — 'And I sowed my fruits in hearts, and transformed them through myself. Then they received my blessing and lived, and they were gathered to me and were saved'), 21.3 ('I stripped off darkness, and put on light'), 26.8 ('And I was covered with the covering of your spirit, and I removed from me the garments of skin') and 32.2 ('And the Word from the truth who is self-originate') would resonate well with those influenced by a characteristically Gnostic narrative.

107. About 13 times; see particularly 11.3; 22.7 and 39.7, 13; cf. Acts 9.2, and see *Beginning from Jerusalem* 13-14.

108. Most strikingly *Odes* 19.1-4:

'A cup of milk was offered to me,
and I drank it in the sweetness of the Lord's kindness.
The Son is the cup, and the Father is he who was milked;
and the Holy Spirit is she who milked him;
Because his breasts were full,
and it was undesirable that his milk should be released without purpose,
The Holy Spirit opened her bosom,
and mixed the milk of the two breasts of the Father'.

109. See D. Aune, 'The Odes of Solomon and Early Christian Prophecy', *NTS* 28 (1982) 435-60; Charlesworth thinks that *Barn.* 5.5-7 echoes *Odes* 31.8-13 ('*Odes of Solomon*' 100-102 at nn.42-47), and above §39 n.166. See also L. M. McDonald, 'The *Odes of Solomon* in Ancient Christianity: Reflections on Scripture and Canon', in Charlesworth et al., eds., *Sacra Scriptura* 108-36 §1 (108-15).

40.2 The Apologists

'Apologists' is a convenient name to denote the Christian writers whose contribution was to make reasoned defence and recommendation of their faith to others. Christian apologies were by no means the first of their type. For example, Plato and Xenophon had both written an *Apology* on behalf of Socrates. Most of Philo's writings could be regarded as apologetic, particularly his *De Legatione ad Gaium*; and Josephus describes his *contra Apionem* as an 'apology' (*Ap.* 2.147). In the NT, Paul's letter to the Romans, 1 Peter and the book of Acts have an apologetic character. But Christian apologies as such only became a Christian genre in the second century, when writing such apologies became something of an industry, as the Christians tried to clarify and defend who they were (or who the authors thought they were).[110] We could carry forward our introductions as far as Irenaeus, our cut-off point, but Irenaeus is more appropriately to be regarded as probably the most influential of the heresiologists.

a. Quadratus

Quadratus 'is traditionally understood to have been the first to write an apology — that is, a reasoned defense — of the Christian faith'.[111] He is referred to by Eusebius (*HE* 4.3.1) as having addressed his treatise to the Emperor Hadrian, which would place it at about 125. The writing was still extant at the time of Eusebius, who had his own copy, but his brief quotation from it (4.3.2) is the only part of the document known to us. Its only real interest is its reference to Jesus' healings and raisings from the dead, some of the beneficiaries of which had 'survived to our own time'. 'Our own time' would presumably refer to Quadratus's time, rather than narrowly to the time when he wrote his apology;[112] but if it was a reliable testimony it would certainly confirm an early date for Quadratus's writing. Otherwise the brevity of the fragment prevents Quadratus from contributing anything more to our inquiry.

---

110. See R. M. Grant, *Greek Apologists of the Second Century* (London: SCM, 1988).
111. Ehrman, *Apostolic Fathers* 2.89; text in 2.119, also in Holmes, *Apostolic Fathers* 293; C. N. Jefford, ed., *The Epistle to Diognetus (with the Fragment of Quadratus)* (Oxford University, 2013) 190-91.
112. See R. M. Grant, 'Quadratus', *ABD* 5.582-83.

b. Aristides

According to Eusebius, the *Apology* of Aristides of Athens was also addressed to Hadrian (*HE* 4.3.3). But in the Syriac translation, only discovered in 1889, the *Apology* is addressed to Caesar Titus Hadrianus Antoninus, that is, to Antoninus Pius (emperor from 138 to 161), which would imply a date no earlier than the 140s, though the Syriac version may itself be a revised version for a later emperor.[113] It is a more ambitious attempt to mount a philosophical defence of the Christian (and Jewish) perception of God over against the idolatry and naturalism of the Chaldeans, the all too human folly and weakness of the gods of the classic Greek myths, and the animal gods of the Egyptians.[114] Most striking are the clear distinctions between Chaldeans/Barbarians, Greeks, Jews and Christians, with the evident implication that Aristides was speaking for a body of Christians who regarded themselves as a distinct species or genus of the Mediterranean and Middle Eastern world.[115]

c. The *Kerygma Petrou*[116]

The *Kerygma Petrou* is preserved only in a few fragments quoted by Clement of Alexandria,[117] in which, as in Aristides, the oneness of God is asserted and the worship of the Greeks dismissed as idolatry. There may well be a link between the *Kerygma* and Aristides, but which way the influence ran is unclear. At any rate the *Kerygma* can most plausibly be dated to the first three decades of the second century. Clement evidently regarded it as authentic teaching of Peter, but Origen was more dubious (*On John* 13.17).[118]

---

113. R. M. Grant, *Greek Apologists* 45; also 'Aristides', *ABD* 1.382. 'The shorter Greek version . . . as well as the Armenian fragments, could well come from the reign of Hadrian, and the relatively favorable picture of Judaism suggests a date well before 132' (Grant, *Greek Apologists* 39).

114. 'The Syriac version emphasizes Christian and Jewish dislike of homosexuality, perhaps more appropriately mentioned to Antoninus than to Hadrian' (Grant, 'Aristides' 382).

115. See also Koester, *Introduction* 2.341.

116. Not to be confused with the *Kerygmata Petrou*; see below at nn.339 and 340.

117. *Strom.* particularly 6.5, but also 1.29, 6.6 and 6.15.

118. Grant, *Greek Apologists* 39-40; W. Schneemelcher, *NTA* 2.34-41; J. K. Elliott, *ANT* 20-24 (both Schneemelcher and Elliott including the text of the *Kerygma*).

d. The *Epistle to Diognetus*[119]

The *Epistle to Diognetus* is usually included with the Apostolic Fathers but is more naturally ranked with the Apologists in date and character. It is one of the most polished pieces of early Christian writing, of a markedly higher rhetorical quality than its predecessors. It is most famous for its characterization of Christians as in the world what the soul is in the body, a theme beautifully elaborated in ch. 6. Equally impressive is the rhetorical elaboration of the Pauline understanding of the gospel in terms of the righteous one given for the unrighteous (ch. 9).

The author of chs. 11-12 describes himself as 'a disciple of the apostles' (11.1),[120] but otherwise is unknown, as also the author of chs. 1-10, though that has not stopped guesses being made — including Apollos, Clement of Rome, Justin Martyr, Hippolytus of Rome and Melito of Sardis — but none carrying conviction.[121] Who Diognetus was is equally unknown, though he is addressed with a characteristic title of respect ('most excellent'); but he remains as much a puzzle as the similarly addressed Theophilus in Luke 1.3.[122]

The date is likewise a puzzle, with few threads of theology and sentiment to connect it with other writings which can be more readily dated. Some would date it in the third century, but a date in the second half of the second century is entirely plausible, perhaps even early in that period.[123]

e. Justin Martyr

Justin, the most significant of the mid-second-century apologists, does not require much time spent on him and his writings in this introductory section (§40). He tells us that he was son of Priscus, a native of Flavia Neapolis (Shechem) in Syrian Palestine (*1 Apol.* 1.1). He refers to his nation as the Samaritans, referring also to 'Simon the Magician' (*Dial.* 120.6),[124] but he was presumably thinking of his place of origin, since he elsewhere refers to

---

119. Jefford, *Epistle to Diognetus*, provides an extensive Introduction and Commentary.

120. This would be why *Diognetus* was included in the Apostolic Fathers; on the high probability that chs. 11-12 are the fragment of a different apology see §45 n.190 below.

121. Richardson, *Early Christian Fathers* 206-10; Ehrman, *Apostolic Fathers* 2.124-26.

122. Ehrman, *Apostolic Fathers* 2.126.

123. See Holmes, *Apostolic Fathers* 293; R. M. Grant, 'Diognetus, Epistle to', *ABD* 2.201 — 'late second century'. Jefford concludes an extensive discussion (*Diognetus* 15-29) by assuming a mid to late 2nd-century date and a likely final setting in Alexandria (28-29).

124. Also *1 Apol.* 26.2-4; 56.1.

himself as a Gentile (29.1; 64.1; 121.1). At the beginning of his *Dialogue with Trypho* he gives his testimony of how in his search for truth he had found most satisfaction in Plato's philosophy (2) before he met 'a venerable and elderly person' (3.1) who persuaded him to find the truth that he was seeking in the prophets and in the Christ whom they proclaimed (7).[125] This was the philosophy to which he committed himself (8.1-2), and it was as still a philosopher that the Jew Trypho was drawn into conversation with him (1.1-2).

Justin evidently settled in Rome where he founded his own school (Tatian was one of his pupils). His written work was substantial. He refers to 'a treatise against all the heresies' which he had composed (*1 Apol.* 26.8), and Eusebius ascribes eight works to him (*HE* 4.18). The circumstances of his death are unclear and disputed, though Tatian blames the Cynic Crescens against whom Justin polemicized in *2 Apol.* 8.[126] But *The Martyrdom of the Holy Martyrs* narrates his execution by decapitation on the orders of Rusticus the prefect, in 165, along with six companions, for their refusal to sacrifice to the gods.

Of his undisputed works only three have come down to us complete, his two *Apologies*[127] and his *Dialogue with Trypho*.[128] The *First Apology* was addressed to the emperor Antoninus Pius (138-161), usually dated to about 155.[129] It begins as a plea against the injustice of finding against Christians solely on the basis of their name (4, 7) and attempts to present Christianity as analogous but superior to the classic Greco-Roman beliefs about the gods and superior in ethical ideals and practice (20-29). Its main thrust is to demonstrate that Christ and Christianity are the fulfilment of (OT) prophecy (32-53), again superior to the pale parallels of classical Greco-Roman religion and the false teachings of such as Simon (Magus) and Marcion (54-58, 62, 64); Moses

---

125. Grant, *Greek Apologists* 50-52.

126. 'This man [Crescens], who professed to despise death, was so afraid of death, that he endeavoured to inflict on Justin, and indeed on me, the punishment of death, as being an evil, because by proclaiming the truth he convicted the philosophers of being gluttons and cheats' (Tatian, *Address* 19). Eusebius quotes Tatian and explicitly attributes Justin's martyrdom to Crescens (*HE* 4.16.7-9).

127. See particularly D. Minns and P. Jarvis, *Justin, Philosopher and Martyr: Apologies* (Oxford University, 2009); on the number of *Apologies* see 21-31; 'The Man and His Work' (ch. 2); Justin the 'philosopher' 59-60; text and translation 79-323; 'It is likely that it is to Justin that we owe the very category of "heresiology". If this is so, it might be said that no other Christian writer after the New Testament had so large and enduring an impact on the shaping of Christian discourse' (70).

128. See particularly T. J. Horner, *Listening to Trypho: Justin Martyr's Dialogue Reconsidered* (Leuven: Peeters, 2001).

129. R. M. Grant, *Greek Apologists* 52-53; also 'Justin Martyr', *ABD* 3.1133, relates it to the martyrdom of Polycarp, which Grant dates in 156 (though see above n.34).

was the teacher of Plato (59-60).¹³⁰ Among its most fascinating features are the descriptions of Christian worship gatherings (65-67); and it concludes (68) by attaching three epistles favourable to the Christians, two of them from Antoninus Pius and Marcus Aurelius regarded as spurious.

The *Second Apology* is more like an appendix to the *First*, and presumably was written soon after, though it may have been as late as 161, after the accession of Marcus Aurelius.¹³¹ Its most famous feature is Justin's concept of the implanted word or seminal reason (*logos spermatikos*) present in earlier philosophies but only complete in the incarnate Christ (*2 Apol.* 8.1-3; 13.3-4).

Justin probably refers to his *First Apology* in *Dial.* 120.6, so the *Dialogue with Trypho* must be dated later, that is, no earlier than about 160,¹³² even though Justin sets the scene for the dialogue shortly after the outbreak of the second Jewish revolt (so about 132 or 133). And though the *Dialogue* was probably written also in Rome, Justin probably sets it in Ephesus; he met Trypho while walking 'in the cloisters of the Colonnade' (*Dial.* 1.1), presumably equivalent to the stoa in Athens where philosophers discoursed.¹³³ The *Dialogue* is obviously a fictional composition (set twenty to thirty years earlier), but there is no reason to regard it as drawn solely from Justin's imagination.¹³⁴ And even if it was, the fact that Justin could set up what was, in the last analysis, as we shall see (§45.5h), such a positive interaction between a Jew and a Christian in mid-second century in Asia Minor (and Rome) gives us a most valuable window into the relationship between early Christianity and the Judaism of the western (Roman) diaspora.¹³⁵ There is an evident la-

---

130. 'It may be difficult to accept Justin's assurance that Plato learned from Moses; but it was exactly that view which made it possible to include the entire Greek tradition ... into the dimension of God's saving history' (Koester, *Introduction* 2.344; see further 343-45).

131. *ODCC* 915. Justin begins with reference to what had 'recently happened' in the city under Urbicus (*2 Apol.* 1-2), that is, Quintus Lollius Urbicus, who held office as Prefect of Rome probably from 144 until his death in 160.

132. *Dial.* 120.6 could imply that the Caesar to whom Justin addressed his *Apology* was still in power; Antoninus Pius reigned till 161.

133. A. L. Williams, *Justin Martyr: The Dialogue with Trypho* (London: SPCK, 1930) x.

134. Horner tries to demonstrate that 'within the *Dialogue* there exists an independent text which is less than half the size of the larger *Dialogue*'; his hypothesis is that 'the core text was at one time an independent document which was written by Justin shortly after the supposed dialogue took place at the beginning of his career (circa 135 C.E.). Then toward the end of his life (155-160 C.E.) he published the *Dialogue* in a greatly expanded form' (*Listening to Trypho* 32). He concludes with the hope 'that the Trypho Text can be read as an authentic debate which took place with a second-century Jew from the Diaspora' (196-98).

135. 'Justin's *Dialogue* is . . . the sole surviving example of a type of conversation between Jews and Christians that, in tone as well as content, may have been as rare then as it has been in subsequent Christian centuries. . . . we need not dismiss Trypho and his arguments as implausible fictions'. That it was a real dialogue is suggested by the fact that

cuna at the end of 74.3; and though the division into two days is not explicit, 66.16 indicates that 'the day is advancing', and 78.6 and 85.4 assume that it is the second day of dialogue. The second day also includes references back to previous discussion which is no longer in the text. So the lacuna may have been quite extensive.[136]

f. Tatian

Tatian tells us that he 'was born in the land of the Assyrians' (*Address* 42), and came to Rome where he was converted by reading the (Jewish) Bible (29).[137] There he became a pupil of Justin, 'the most admirable Justin' as he calls him (*Address* 18). But Irenaeus refers to him as a false teacher:

> A certain man named Tatian first introduced the blasphemy. He was a hearer of Justin's, and as long as he continued with him he expressed no such views; but after his martyrdom he separated from the Church, and, excited and puffed up by the thought of being a teacher, as if he were superior to others,[138] he composed his own peculiar type of doctrine. He invented a system of certain invisible Aeons, like the followers of Valentinus; while, like Marcion and Saturninus, he declared that marriage was nothing else than corruption and fornication. But his denial of Adam's salvation was an opinion due entirely to himself (*adv. haer.* 1.28.1).

The influence of Justin is most evident in Tatian's *Address to the Greeks*, usually dated between 155 and 165, in which he goes beyond Justin in ridiculing the common beliefs about the gods and other philosophies (2-3, 8-10, 21-28, 34),[139] and in his argument that Moses preceded Homer, other philos-

---

'Trypho and his friends are not persuaded — surely an odd way to end an argument designed to convert Jews' (Wilson, *Related Strangers* 258, 261, 264). Wilson concludes his discussion: 'Is Trypho a plausible figure? On the whole, he is. . . . in terms of both his peculiar blend of Jewishness and his attitude towards Christianity, there may have been rather more Jews like Trypho than we have been inclined to think' (282-83). See also Horner, *Listening to Trypho* chs. 4 and 5.

136. See further Williams, *Justin Martyr* xviii-xix.

137. See further O. C. Edwards, 'Tatian', *ABD* 6.335; W. L. Petersen, 'Tatian the Assyrian', in Marjanen and Luomanen, *Companion* 125-58; on Tatian's biography, 129-34.

138. See Petersen, 'Tatian', on Tatian's personality (134-38): 'a high opinion of himself . . . an unpleasant, rigid, uncompromising personality' (135).

139. See also Grant, *Greek Apologists* 113-23. 'His onslaught against Greek culture is actually our only source for some information about details of Greek culture' (Edwards, 'Tatian' 335).

ophers and ancient heroes (36-41). Most striking, however, is the fact that he never mentions 'Jesus', 'Christ', or 'Christians' in so many words,[140] even though his exposition of the Logos in creation (5, 7, 13) is sharper than Justin's.[141] So, compared with Justin's, it is a surprisingly undeclaratively Christian apologetic. And Irenaeus's dismissal of him as an Encratite (earlier in the same passage),[142] as abstaining from animal food and preaching against marriage, may be foreshadowed in his *Address* 33-34 with its denunciation of the sexual practices lauded in his day.[143]

After Justin's execution Irenaeus reports that Tatian 'separated himself from the church' and evidently returned to Syria,[144] where he probably composed his *Diatessaron*, the first (preserved) harmony of the four (canonical) Gospels, dated probably in the period 170-175. It is known in the West, but its earliest and extensive circulation in the East, particularly in Syria, strongly suggests that it was written there and in Syriac.[145] It became the standard Gospel text in the Syriac-speaking churches till the fifth century, when it was replaced by the Peshitta version of the four separate Gospels, because its author had been dismissed as a heretic.[146]

---

140. The closest he comes is his assertion that 'we announce that God was born in the form of a man' (21.1), which makes Eusebius's reference to Tatian as one in whose works 'Christ is treated as God' (*HE* 5.28.4) somewhat puzzling. On the suggestion that Tatian denied the real humanity of Jesus, see P. M. Head, 'Tatian's Christology and Its Influence on the Composition of the Diatessaron', *TynB* 43 (1992) 121-37. Petersen draws attention to the 'clear signs of Gnosticism in Tatian's *Oratio*, particularly his placing of an intermediary, a demiurge, between God "the Father" and the created orders of men and angels' ('Tatian' 146-49); 'one would certainly label him a Gnostic; too many Gnostic ideas percolate through the *Oratio* to deny such tendencies' (152).

141. See also Grant, *Greek Apologists* 129-30.

142. 'Encratite' was 'a title applied to several groups of early Christians who carried their ascetic practice and doctrine to extremes'; referred to by Irenaeus, Clement of Alexandria and Hippolytus, but without precision, and including Gnostic, Ebionite and Docetic sects (*ODCC* 545). See further Petersen, 'Tatian' 139-46 and 125 n.2, who points out that 'Christianity, from the very beginning, had certain ascetic — and, therefore, Encratitic — tendencies', including Matt. 19.12 and Paul's advocacy of celibacy (1 Cor. 7) ('Tatian' 140).

143. Irenaeus repeats the charge that Tatian denied the salvation of Adam (*adv. haer.* 3.23.8; Eusebius, *HE* 4.28.2-3).

144. See again Edwards, 'Tatian' 335. Clement of Alexandria's reference to 'an Assyrian' among his teachers (*Strom.* 1.1; 11.2) suggests that he had Tatian in mind.

145. See W. L. Peterson, in Koester, *Ancient Christian Gospels* 403-30 (here 405-13, 428-29).

146. For a concise summary of the textual tradition and bibliography see *ODCC* 477-78. For convenience I have drawn on J. H. Hill, *The Earliest Life of Christ ever compiled from the four Gospels being The Diatessaron of Tatian* (translated from the Arabic) (Edinburgh: T & T Clark, 1894).

g. Apollinarius

Apollinarius, bishop of Hierapolis, was much lauded by Eusebius (*HE* 4.26.1), referring to several books written by him, including a treatise addressed to the Emperor Marcus Aurelius (161-180) (*HE* 4.27.1). Presumably it was in this apology, written about 176, that Apollinarius referred to the naming of a legion as the 'Thundering Legion', to commemorate its delivery in battle with the Germans and Sarmatians and from thirst by a thunderstorm in 172 or 174, a deliverance which Apollinarius attributed to the prayers of Christian legionaries (*HE* 5.5.1-4).[147] Eusebius also describes him as a powerful and invincible champion of truth against the so-called Cataphrygian heresy (that is, Montanism) (5.16.1; 5.19.1-2).[148] But none of his writings have been preserved, in whole or part.

h. Athenagoras

Athenagoras the Athenian is remembered primarily for his *Plea for the Christians*, addressed to the Emperor Marcus Aurelius and his son Commodus in 176 or 177, providing further evidence that Christians were subject to persecution solely for bearing the name 'Christian'. With the other apologists, Athenagoras denies that Christians are atheists, and claims support in the philosophers for the belief that God is one (*Plea* 5-9), going on to mount the first clear expression of God as Trinity (10, 12, 24), in contrast with the wider but far less impressive beliefs in the gods as expressed in the philosophers and poets (17-30), and contrasting also the higher degree of morality among Christians with that of their accusers (31-35).[149] His treatise *On the Resurrection of the Dead*, written probably later but in the same period (175-180), demonstrates both how difficult the Greek mind-set found it to cope with the idea, and how it could nevertheless be argued for in terms which they could appreciate. For some reason he seems to have made little impact on continuing Christian thought; Eusebius makes no mention of him.

i. Theophilus of Antioch

Theophilus is remembered by Eusebius as 'the famous Theophilus [who] was the sixth [bishop of Antioch] from the apostles', successor to Eros (*HE* 4.20),

---

147. See further Grant, *Greek Apologists* 83-85.
148. See again Grant, *Greek Apologists* 87-90.
149. See further Grant, *Greek Apologists* ch. 12.

that is, probably, from c. 170 to the early 180s. Eusebius refers to several of his writings, including 'a noble treatise which he made against Marcion' (4.24), but the only one still extant is his apology to *Autolycus*, a sequence of three books written in Antioch probably shortly after 180.[150] Like other apologists he distinguishes the Christian idea of God sharply from the more common ideas of the gods, with their various absurdities and immoralities (e.g. *Autolycus* 1.9-10; 2.2-4; 3.8). His understanding of creation and the history of the human race is drawn entirely from the Jewish scriptures (2.10-32), as are the high ethical qualities which the Christians display (3.9-14). He transcribes a mind-numbing chronology from Adam to display the antiquity of the Hebrews (3.24-25), and thus also of Christian teaching (3.29).[151] Somewhat surprisingly, Theophilus makes no mention of 'Jesus', or 'Christ';[152] but he does call the Word of God 'his Son' (2.22), and a feature of particular interest is that in his Logos-theology he is the first to take up the Stoic distinction between the unexpressed thought and the expressed thought, that is, between the *logos endiathetos* ('the word in the mind') and the *logos prophorikos* ('the uttered word') (2.10, 22).[153] He is also first to use the word 'trinity' of God: the first three days of creation 'are types of the Trinity (*triados*), of God and his Word (*logos*) and his Wisdom (*sophia*)' (2.15).[154]

j. Melito of Sardis

Melito is little known to us, but according to Eusebius he was 'the well-known bishop of Sardis' (*HE* 4.13.8) and famous for his apologies addressed to Emperor Marcus Aurelius (c. 161)[155] and several other writings (4.26.2). Eusebius

---

150. Theophilus's Roman chronology (*Autolycus* 3.27) ends with the death of Emperor Verus (co-emperor with Marcus Aurelius), who died in 169; but since he gives the length of Verus's reign as 19 years, he was presumably thinking of the death of Marcus Aurelius in 180, having reigned from 161 to 180.

151. See also Grant, *Greek Apologists* 155-56, who gives more attention to Theophilus than to the other Apologists (chs. 16-19).

152. 'The most surprising feature of Theophilus's theology is his remarkable silence in regard to Jesus, Christ, the incarnation, and the atonement' (Grant, *Greek Apologists* 165); and further 169-71.

153. Also used by Philo as a way of expressing the allegorical distinction between Moses and Aaron, on the basis of Exod. 4.16 and 7.1, where Moses represents the *logos endiathetos* and Aaron the *logos prophorikos* (*Det.* 39-40, 126-32; *Migr.* 76-84; *Mut.* 208); see further H. Kleinknecht, *TDNT* 3.85; Dunn, *Christology* 223-24.

154. But he adds: 'And the fourth (day) is the type of man, who needs light, that so there may be God, the Word, Wisdom, man'.

155. See further Grant, *Greek Apologists* 93-95, 96-99. Although we have only a full

§40.2   *The Sources — Second Century*

also quotes Polycrates (c. 194) referring to 'Melito the eunuch, who lived entirely in the Holy Spirit, who lies in Sardis' (5.24.5). None of Melito's writings had survived until papyri were discovered (1940, 1960) which contained a text recognized to be Melito's *Peri Pascha* (*On the Passover*), probably to be dated to about the third quarter of the second century.[156]

The fact that Melito was located in Sardis enables us to gain a unique insight into the context for his writing. For since 1958 archaeological expeditions to Sardis have uncovered what is probably to be regarded as the most impressive synagogue in the western diaspora.[157] It was evidently a prominent and important building in a central position, indicating that the Jewish community was well established, prosperous and influential. Although the synagogue is usually dated to the third century, Jewish communities had been in Asia Minor for four centuries, so it is most natural to infer that their high status in the third century was the natural outworking of several decades of respect. Since a natural inclination among Christian historians is to assume that the later ghetto-status of Jews in mediaeval Europe would have already prevailed in the early days of Christianity, it is, to say the least, salutary to appreciate that in late second century Sardis it would have been the Jewish community which was highly regarded and influential, and that the Christian community was more likely to be confined to back streets.[158] Christian churches were not yet appearing, whereas synagogues were a feature of many cities' architecture. It was centuries before Christian bishops would live in palaces.

Melito's *Peri Pascha* is of considerable value for several reasons:

- it provides a clear explanation of the theology of the 'type' (§46.6h);
- given the high civic status of the Jewish synagogue community, Melito's writing provides an intriguing insight into relations between Jews and Christians, and may help explain its pleading rather than hectoring or intimidatory tone (§46.6h);
- its christology is very distinctive: Christ 'is by nature both God and man' (*Peri Pascha* 8); Melito has no hesitation in attributing to Christ the

---

copy of the *Peri Pascha*, it was as an apologist that Melito was remembered; hence his inclusion here.

156. See further S. G. Hall, *Melito of Sardis: On Pascha and Fragments* (Oxford: Clarendon, 1979) xi-xxii.

157. Full details in G. M. A. Hanfmann, ed., *Sardis from Prehistoric to Roman Times: Results of the Archaeological Exploration of Sardis 1958-1975* (Harvard University, 1983), particularly A. T. Kraabel, 'Impact of the Discovery of the Sardis Synagogue' (173-90).

158. See also MacLennan, *Early Christian Texts* 94-109; 'Jews were not ghettoized or hiding somewhere outside of the city. They were "at home" in Sardis.... the Jews of Sardis were integrated into the Sardian culture' (150).

creation and the divine care for Israel in Egypt, in the wilderness, etc.[159] He makes no use of logos-christology as such, but Christ's role as God's agent, responsible for what had traditionally been attributed to God without qualification, has its most obvious antecedents in Second Temple Judaism's reflection on divine Wisdom.

40.3 Eusebius and the Heresiologists

The principal sources for the history of the great church and of its major competitors in the contest for the identity of Christianity must include Eusebius and the heresiologists — Hegesippus, Irenaeus, Tertullian, Hippolytus, Epiphanius — even though the list runs well beyond our cut-off point of the late second century. They are not particularly noted for their reliability, but they often include information from the second century or information about the second century which would otherwise be unknown to us. They all mark a stage in the history of early Christianity which is also beyond the scope of this volume, when what Celsus called the 'great church' had begun to emerge, a body of Christians with sufficient self-confidence to regard their form of Christianity as 'orthodox' and all other variant forms as 'heresy'. That is, with Irenaeus we begin to move beyond the era where essential identity was contested in terms of relationship with Judaism and of the redeemability of creation. The sharpening refinement of identity continued to be contested, of course, but what we might describe as the transition from apologist to heresiologist is a decisive tipping point in Christianity's history and the point at which this study concludes.

We will treat the six authors, briefly, in chronological order.

---

159. '. . . the firstborn of God, the one who was begotten before the morning star, the one who caused the light to shine forth, the one who made bright the day, the one who parted the darkness . . . the one who set in motion the stars of heaven, the one who caused those luminaries to shine, the one who made the angels in heaven . . . the one who by himself fashioned man upon the earth. This was the one who chose you, the one who guided you from Adam to Noah, from Noah to Abraham, from Abraham to Isaac and Jacob and the Twelve Patriarchs. This was the one who guided you into Egypt, and guarded you, and himself kept you well supplied there. This was the one who lighted your route with a column of fire, and provided shade for you by means of a cloud, the one who divided the Red Sea, and led you across it, and scattered your enemy abroad. This is the one who provided you with manna from heaven, the one who gave you water to drink from a rock, the one who established your laws in Horeb, the one who gave you an inheritance in the land, the one who sent out his prophets to you, the one who raised up your kings' (82-85). Unsurprisingly, Melito's christology has been characterized as 'naïve docetism' (Hall, *Melito* xliii-xliv).

a. Hegesippus

Hegesippus should be given first place, since, according to Eusebius, he 'belongs to the generation after the apostles' (*HE* 2.23.3).[160] It is to Eusebius that we owe our knowledge of Hegesippus. He refers to Hegesippus as a Jewish convert (*HE* 4.22.8) and records that he wrote five treatises of 'Memoirs' (4.22.1), which included a list of succession of the bishops of Rome and an account of the beginnings of an impressive range of heresies, attributed, ironically, to disputes over succession in the mother church of Jerusalem (4.22.3-6). Eusebius draws on him extensively for his account of the Jerusalem church following the death of James.[161]

b. Irenaeus

Irenaeus could be regarded as the last of the apologists, but since his principal writing was his five books *Against Heresies*, he is more appropriately included among the heresiologists.[162] He is the only other one of those noted in this section who lived entirely in the second century (c. 130–c. 200).[163] He is particularly important since he provides a bridge between east and west: he is thought to have been a native of Smyrna, since he heard Polycarp as a boy;[164] he was made bishop of Lyons in 178; and he had good relations with the bishop of Rome and wrote to Pope Victor on behalf of the Quartodecimans of Asia Minor in 190.[165] His major contribution was his magnum opus, *Adversus omnes Haereses*, a detailed polemic against the various forms of Gnosticism, particularly that of Valentinus. It is preserved in part in Greek, but there is a complete Latin version. As the first great Catholic and genuinely biblical theologian,

---

160. See further G. F. Chesnut, 'Hegesippus', *ABD* 3.110-11; 'Hegesippus was the first Christian historiographer to introduce the (usually pernicious) notion of the fall of the church from its apostolic purity at a particular point in its history. In this case, he chose the death of the last blood relatives of Jesus during the reign of Trajan. Until then, he said, "they called the church virgin, for it had not been corrupted"' (111, quoting Eusebius, *HE* 4.22.4; 3.32.7).

161. See below §45.3.

162. See further M. A. Donovan, 'Irenaeus', *ABD* 3.457-61.

163. Though some think he may have lived till about 202.

164. See above at n.28.

165. The Quartodeciman controversy arose because Christians in the Roman province of Asia observed the 14th day (*quartadecima*) of the first month (Lev. 23.5 Vulgate), the date of the Jewish passover, as the date of Jesus' crucifixion, whereas most Christians celebrated Jesus' resurrection on the Sunday, and thus remembered Jesus' crucifixion as having taken place on the preceding Friday (Eusebius, *HE* 5.23, 24.11-18).

Irenaeus marks something of a watershed between the sub-apostolic age and what can properly be described as Catholic Christianity.[166] Not least, his insistence that only the four NT Gospels should be regarded as authentic, and his effective meshing of Pauline and Johannine influence in his own theology mark him as a decisive actor in the drama of defining Christianity's identity and a fitting climax to the developments of the second century.[167]

c. Tertullian

Tertullian was born about 160, brought up in Carthage, may well have trained as a lawyer, and became a Christian some time before 197. He wrote extensively, but for us his most important writings were his polemics against heresy.

> In the early *De praescriptione haereticorum* he disposes of all heresy in principle: the one true Church, visible in history through the episcopal succession (here he follows Irenaeus), alone possesses the authentic tradition from Christ and the apostles, and alone has authority to interpret Scripture.[168]
>
> His most extensive writing was his five books against Marcion (*Adversus Marcionem*), in which he resolutely maintained the identity of the one God of the Old and New Testaments and of Jesus as the Messiah of Old Testament prophecy.[169] His reputation has suffered from his attraction to Montanism, whose asceticism and emphasis on the Spirit and ecstatic prophecy appealed to him.[170]

d. Hippolytus

Hardly anything is known of the early life of Hippolytus (c. 170–c. 236), but he was already active in teaching in Rome in the early third century, where he gained a controversial reputation.[171] His main writing was his *Refutatio Omnium Haeresium* (*Refutation of All Heresies*), some of which has been lost.

---

166. *ODCC* 846-47.
167. See particularly Osborn, *Irenaeus* ch. 1; cf. Koester, *Introduction* 2.10-11.
168. *ODCC* 1591.
169. For more detail see D. E. Groh, 'Tertullian', *ABD* 6.389-91.
170. See further below §49.8.
171. *ODCC* 773-74.

e. Eusebius

Eusebius, bishop of Caesarea (c. 260-c. 340), had a somewhat similarly controversial history, backing Arius and probably giving an unwilling assent to the Nicene Creed. He is generally regarded as the 'Father of Church History', and his ten books of *Ecclesiastical History* (*Historia Ecclesiastica*),[172] though heavily slanted by the perspective of the winners in the Constantinian settlement, nevertheless includes lengthy extracts from earlier writings, some of which would otherwise have been lost to us. So, though he has not the closeness to the events and characters which he describes, as did Luke (Acts of the Apostles), his *History* is nevertheless an invaluable resource, and not just for the perspective of the winners.

f. Epiphanius

This bishop of Salamis (c. 315-403) was a native of Palestine and an enthusiastic, though uncritical upholder of the Nicene faith, 'intolerant of all suspicion of heresy'.[173] His most important writing in defence of orthodoxy was his *Panarion* ('Medicine Chest' — to ward off the poisons of heresy), subsequently known simply as *Adversus Haereses*. It describes and rebuts eighty religious sects, from Adam to his own time (including Hellenism, Samaritanism and Judaism!), and, as with Eusebius and Hegesippus, the *Panarion* provides much information which otherwise would have been unknown to us. It is particularly valuable as a source of information on the Jewish Gospels, the Gospel of the Ebionites and the Gospel according to the Hebrews.

40.4 The Other Gospels[174]

The division of the study of Gospel sources into the two categories (§§39.2 and 40.4) is partly a matter of convenience and partly a reflection of the greater,

---

172. Most conveniently available in two volumes, translated by Kirsopp Lake and J. E. L. Oulton, in LCL (London: Heinemann, 1926, 1932). It appeared probably in several editions; see e.g. discussion in the editions by H. J. Lawlor and J. E. L. Oulton, *Eusebius: The Ecclesiastical History and the Martyrs of Palestine* (2 vols.; London: SPCK, 1954) 2.2-11, and the Introduction to the LCL edition by Kirsopp Lake. See also G. F. Chesnut, 'Eusebius of Caesarea', *ABD* 2.673-76.

173. *ODCC* 553.

174. The fullest collection is B. D. Ehrman and Z. Plese, *The Apocryphal Gospels: Texts and Translations* (Oxford University, 2011).

more widespread and lasting influence of the canonical Gospels. Quite how the two categories relate to one another, however, is part of the agenda for subsequent chapters. Since issues of authorship, date and place of origin (the limited scope of this chapter) are mostly beyond resolution, given the little data we have, the objective here will be simply to provide an overview of the range of documents which seem to have been factors of some significance in the contested character of second-century Christianity.[175]

a. The Jewish-Christian Gospels[176]

Several mainstream church leaders — notably Clement of Alexandria, Origen, Eusebius, Epiphanius and Jerome[177]— refer to or quote from one or another of the Gospels usually referred to as Jewish-Christian Gospels. The commonest interpretation of these references is that there were three such Gospels — the *Gospel according to the Hebrews*, the *Gospel of the Nazareans* and the *Gospel of the Ebionites*.[178] However, the references are sufficiently inconsistent as to pose several questions for which it is almost impossible to produce firm answers:

- Were these different names for the same Gospel or two Gospels?[179]

---

175. Issues raised by the apocryphal Gospels for our understanding of second-century Christianity are well summarized by the Introduction to J. Frey and J. Schröter, eds., *Jesus in apokryphen Evangelienüberlieferungen* (WUNT 1.254; Tübingen: Mohr Siebeck, 2010) 12-23. See also Ehrman and Plese, *Apocryphal Gospels*.

176. See P. Vielhauer and G. Strecker, *NTA* 1.134-78; Elliott, *ANT* 3-25; A. F. J. Klijn, *Jewish-Christian Gospel Tradition* (Leiden: Brill, 1992); D. Lührmann, *Die apokryph gewordenen Evangelien* (NovTSupp 112; Leiden: Brill, 2004) 229-58; C. A. Evans, 'The Jewish Christian Gospel Tradition', in O. Skarsaune and R. Hvalvik, eds., *Jewish Believers in Jesus* (Peabody: Hendrickson, 2007) 241-77 (here 245-58); A. Gregory, 'Jewish-Christian Gospels', in P. Foster, ed., *The Non-Canonical Gospels* (London: T & T Clark, 2008) 54-67; E. K. Broadhead, *Jewish Ways of Following Jesus* (WUNT 266; Tübingen: Mohr Siebeck, 2010) 255-67.

177. Details fully provided by Vielhauer and Strecker, *NTA* 1.135-52; Klijn, *Jewish-Christian Gospel Tradition*, Part Two, provides a complete listing of patristic fragments including original text, translation and commentary.

178. 'Origen (*Hom. 1 on Luke*), Ambrose, and Jerome (*on Matt.* Prol. and *Dialogi contra Pelagianos* 3.2) refer to a "Gospel of the Twelve" or a Gospel "according to the Apostles", and it has been convincingly argued (by Zahn) that this is to be identified with the Gospel of the Ebionites, on the ground that in the fragments located in Epiphanius it is the apostles who are the narrators' (Elliott, *ANT* 5; questioned by Vielhauer and Strecker, *NTA* 1.166).

179. Discussion in Gregory, 'Jewish-Christian Gospels' 56-59.

- Was one or another of the Gospels written in (or translated into) Hebrew?
- How, if at all, were one or another of these Gospels related to the Gospel of Matthew? Indeed, might Papias have been referring to this Gospel when he wrote that 'Matthew collected the oracles in the Hebrew language' (Eusebius, *HE* 3.39.15-16)?[180]

A few quotations should suffice to make clear the problems. Irenaeus refers to those known as Ebionites who used only the Gospel of Matthew (*adv. haer.* 1.26.2; 3.11.7). In discussing the writings which count as the New Testament, Eusebius observes that 'some have also counted [among the recognized books] the Gospel according to the Hebrews, in which especially those Hebrews who have accepted Christ take a special pleasure' (*HE* 3.25.5). Later he notes that the Ebionites 'used only the Gospel called according to the Hebrews and made little account of the rest' (3.27.4). And in *Theophania* 4.12, Eusebius refers to 'the Gospel which is (in circulation) among the Jews in the Hebrew language'. Epiphanius writes at length on the Jewish-Christian sects of the Nazareans who 'have the Gospel according to Matthew complete and in Hebrew ... as it was originally written, in Hebrew script' (*Pan.* 29.9.4); and he later quotes the Gospel of the Ebionites (*Pan.* 30.16.5).[181] And Jerome variously quotes from 'the Hebrew Gospel' (*on Eph.* 5.4), 'the Gospel also entitled according to the Hebrews' (*de Vir. Ill.* 2), 'the Gospel of the Hebrews which the Nazarenes are in the habit of reading' (*on Ezek.* 18.7), and 'the Gospel which is written in Hebrew' (*on Isa.* 11.2).

Unfortunately, the references and quotations from the 'Church Fathers' are the only information we have about these Gospels. Unlike most of the other non-canonical Gospels to be reviewed in this section, no manuscripts or even portions or papyri fragments of the Jewish-Christian Gospels have been found. So it is virtually impossible to build a clear picture of their structure and character, beyond the snippets of information given in the references and quotations. This is entirely frustrating, since it means that we have to view these Gospels almost entirely through the eyes of those who disowned and disparaged them. Again unlike the other non-canonical Gospels, where manuscript and papyri discoveries have provided copies of several of the major Gnostic writings, our view of the Jewish-Christian Gospels is heavily restricted. Whereas the character of 'Gnosticism' is now much clearer, we remain much more in the dark concerning 'Jewish-Christianity'. If Epiphanius and the others are right, such Gospels would presumably have told us much about the

---

180. See §39 n.87 above.
181. See further the quotations in §§44.4a and 44.4d.

branches of second-century Christianity which maintained and developed the form of Christianity which had flourished in Jerusalem under James. These forms of Christianity, too readily set on one side as left behind by the developing mainstream, or dismissed as heretical Jewish-Christian sects, are particularly important for a clear assessment of Syrian Christianity and for Christianity's relationship with emerging Judaism, so our inability to say much about these Gospels is frustrating in the extreme.[182]

All we can say about the dates of the Jewish-Christian Gospels is that they must have appeared some time in the first half or middle of the second century. Authorship is a huge unknown, always bearing in mind the open issue of their relationship to Matthew; as we shall see, the references to them add little to our knowledge of how the Jesus tradition was interpreted and used.

As to their geographical origin a little more can be said. Since the most important witnesses for the *Gospel according to the Hebrews* are Clement of Alexandria and Origen, it could have originated in or had its main circulation in Egypt.[183] According to Epiphanius, 'this sect [the Nazareans] dwells in Beroea in Coelesyria' (*Pan.* 29.7.7), so perhaps the *Gospel of the Nazareans* should be located there. The fact that it could be regarded as Matthew's Gospel written originally in Hebrew/Aramaic (Epiphanius, Jerome)[184] is confusing, but at least attests the influence of Matthew in Syria.[185] And since the Ebionites were rooted in Transjordan, presumably that is where the *Gospel of the Ebionites* should be located and where Epiphanius will have been able to consult it.

In each case, however, we are probing the dark.

b. The *Gospel of Thomas*[186]

The *Gospel of Thomas* deserves special attention. For though it was known about from a handful of early references by Church Fathers,[187] and was often

---

182. See further J. Frey, 'Zur Vielgestaltigkit judenchristlicher Evangelienüberlieferungen', in Frey and Schröter, eds., *Jesus in apokryphen Evangelienüberlieferungen* 93-137; and on 'Jewish Christianity' (§45 below).

183. See further Vielhauer and Strecker, *NTA* 1.176. 'The Gospel according to the Hebrews is an authentic product of Egyptian Christianity' (Klijn, *Jewish-Christian Gospel Tradition* 42).

184. Discussion in Vielhauer and Strecker, *NTA* 1.142-43, 145-48, 154-57.

185. Vielhauer and Strecker have no doubt that *the Gospel of the Nazareans* 'was clearly an Aramaic version of the Greek Mt.' (*NTA* 1.157).

186. For English translations of the *Gospel of Thomas* see *Jesus Remembered* 161 n.104.

187. Hippolytus refers a version of *Thomas* 4.1 to 'the Gospel entitled "according to Thomas"' (*Haer.* 5.7.20; in Foerster, *Gnosis* 1.267); see also e.g. Cyril of Jerusalem, who

confused with what is now known as the *Infancy Gospel of Thomas*,[188] its discovery as part of the Gnostic library at Nag Hammadi, in 1945-46, provided a slow-burning explosion which has rocked the study of early Christianity, of Gnosticism and particularly of the Jesus tradition, its origin, character and development.[189] Above all, although it is only one of several Gospels contained in the Nag Hammadi library, the *Gospel of Thomas* has been regarded by some as having a status, significance and influence equal to, perhaps even surpassing, the value and importance of the NT Gospels.[190]

The Nag Hammadi codices are written in Coptic, but in many cases are demonstrably translated from Greek.[191] The *Gospel of Thomas*, part of the second Nag Hammadi codex (*NHL* II.2), consists of a collection of 114 sayings/logia, without narrative framework. Two features in particular indicate the *Gospel of Thomas*'s potential value for any history of Christianity's beginnings. One is the substantial overlap between the *Gospel of Thomas* logia and the Synoptic tradition, especially the Q material. This raises numerous questions about the content and character of the Jesus tradition, and its transmission and development. Such questions are of prime importance for this present study, and will require close attention in due course (§43.2). The other is the realization that several of the Oxyrhynchus papyri, discovered forty to fifty years earlier, also in Egypt, contain some of the sayings, and may come from or at least provide evidence of earlier (or different) versions of the *Gospel of Thomas*.[192] The possibility of tracing the history of sayings through three

---

regarded the *Gospel of Thomas* as a Manichaean product (*Catech.* 4.36), and Eusebius, who dismissed the Gospels of Peter, Thomas and Matthias as 'put forward by heretics' (*HE* 3.25.6). See further B. Blatz, *NTA* 1.110-11.

188. Cf. M. R. James, *The Apocryphal New Testament* (Oxford: Clarendon, 1924) 14-16; R. Cameron, 'Thomas, Gospel of', *ABD* 6.535.

189. For an account of the discovery of the Nag Hammadi codices see above §38 n.125; also J. M. Robinson, in S. J. Patterson et al., *The Fifth Gospel: The Gospel of Thomas Comes of Age* (London: T & T Clark, 2011) 67-96.

190. 'The basis of the *Gospel of Thomas* is a sayings collection which is more primitive than the canonical gospels' (Koester, in Robinson and Koester, *Trajectories* 186) — a thesis taken to its logical conclusion in Funk and Hoover, *The Five Gospels* (see §38 n.141 above).

191. This was helpfully demonstrated in the translation of the *Gospel of Thomas* by B. M. Metzger, in Aland, *Synopsis* 517-30; see further S. Gathercole, *The Composition of the Gospel of Thomas: Original Language and Influences* (SNTSMS 151; Cambridge University, 2012) ch. 4.

192. POxy 654 = *Thomas* Incipit, 1-7; POxy 1 = *Thomas* 26-30, 77.2, 31-33.1; POxy 655 = *Thomas* 24.3(?), 36-39. The parallels are conveniently set out in English by Blatz, *NTA* 1.117-18, 121-23, and Elliott, *ANT* 135-36, 139-41; see also Lührmann, *apokryph gewordenen Evangelien* ch. 5. A. D. DeConick, *The Original Gospel of Thomas in Translation* (LNTS 287; London: T & T Clark, 2006), sets out the parallels in detail (though surprisingly she leaves *Thomas* 77.2 out of sequence). For the Greek texts of the Oxyrhynchus papyri

phases (the Synoptic tradition, the different Oxyrhynchus papyri and the *Gospel of Thomas*) is an unexpected bonus of the two-fold Egyptian discoveries.[193]

i. Author

The *Gospel of Thomas* does not describe itself as a 'Gospel', but introduces itself as 'the secret words which the living Jesus spoke and Judas who is also called Thomas wrote down'. The Coptic text describes the author more fully as "Didymus Judas Thomas', that is 'Judas the twin'.[194] In the Syrian church Judas Thomas was known as the twin brother of Jesus,[195] and to him was attributed the founding of the east Syrian churches, particularly Edessa[196] (and subsequently India — the Mar Thoma Church).[197] Other writings were attributed to Thomas, particularly the *Acts of Thomas* and probably another Nag Hammadi text, the *Book of Thomas the Contender* (*NHL* II.7). The attribution to Thomas suggests the desire for an apostolic authority: *Gosp. Thom.* 13 does seem to set Thomas over against both Peter and Matthew as granted a special intimate revelation which transcended their insights.[198] And Thomas

---

see A. E. Bernhard, *Other Early Christian Gospels: A Critical Edition of the Surviving Greek Manuscripts* (LNTS 315; London: T & T Clark, 2006) 16-48; and further W. Eisele, *Welcher Thomas? Studien zur Text- und Überlieferungsgeschichte des Thomasevangeliums* (WUNT 259; Tübingen: Mohr Siebeck, 2010). For a brief treatment see S. K. Brown, 'Sayings of Jesus, Oxyrhynchus', *ABD* 5.999-1001. Koester infers that 'the *Gospel of Thomas* is well attested as a Greek gospel writing that circulated widely during the 2d century', and asserts that 'the attestation is just as strong as that for the canonical gospels' (*Ancient Christian Gospels* 77); but see below §43.2.

193. Cf.

Matt. 7.3-5/Luke 6.41-42	POxy 1.1-4	*Thomas* 26
Mark 6.4 pars.	POxy 1.30-35	*Thomas* 31
Matt. 5.14	POxy 1.36-41	*Thomas* 32
Matt. 6.25-30/Luke 12.27-28	POxy 655 1.1-17	*Thomas* 36

194. Although *t'ôma'* in Aramaic means 'twin', it was naturally understood in reference to a person named *Thōmas* in Greek-speaking regions (BDAG 463). It was equally natural for the original sense to be rendered by *Didymos*, the Greek for 'twin'.

195. In *ActsThom.* Jesus is confused with Thomas ('he had the appearance of Judas Thomas') and has to explain, 'I am not Judas Thomas, I am his brother' (11); and Thomas is hailed as 'twin brother of Christ' (39). Similarly to the *Gospel of Thomas, ActsThom.* 1 introduces Thomas as 'Judas Thomas, also called Didymus'.

196. Eusebius, *HE* 1.13.4, 11; 2.1.6; in *HE* 3.1.1, when the world is divided for mission between the apostles, Thomas is allotted Parthia, on the eastern border of Syria; see further below §45.8f.

197. *ActsThom.* 1-3, 17; Parthia bordered Syria to the west and India to the south. See further Klauck, *Apocryphal Acts* 144-46; also 'Malabar Christians', *ODCC* 1022-23; and below §40.6e.

198. *Gosp. Thom.* 13 — 'Jesus said to his disciples, "Speculate about me. Tell me, who am I like?" Simon Peter said to him, "You are like a righteous angel". Matthew said to him,

does seem to have a special status in Syrian Christianity whose historic roots are unknown and can only be guessed at. So some historical link back to the 'historical Thomas' cannot be entirely excluded. But neither can such a link be assumed, for it is also entirely possible that his very name ('the twin') was sufficient to spark off a reflection on Thomas as the twin brother of Jesus, and therefore as privileged with revelation kept from others.[199] Any attempt, however, to see in the Thomas of John 14.5-7, (22-23), and 20.24-29 either a link to the Thomas of *Gosp. Thom.* Incipit and 13 or a response to the *Gospel of Thomas*[200] is extremely tenuous.[201]

ii. Place of Writing

As already indicated, the link between the *Gospel of Thomas* and eastern Syria, particularly Edessa, is strong. The *Acts of Thomas*, attributed to the same Judas Thomas Didymus, is certainly to be closely associated with Edessa,[202] and the tradition of Thomas's grave in Edessa is old.[203] Most scholars agree that the *Acts of Thomas* was originally composed in Syriac and then translated into Greek, though Edessa would almost certainly have been bilingual in culture, and the Greek versions seem to preserve a more primitive form of the text.[204] Given the Thomasine character of early Syrian Christianity, the most obvious

---

"You are like a sage, a temperate person". Thomas said to him, "Master, my mouth cannot attempt to say whom you are like". Jesus said, "I am not your master. After you drank, you became intoxicated from the bubbling fount which I had measured out". And he took him and retreated. He told him three words. Then when Thomas returned to his friends, they asked him, "What did Jesus say to you?" Thomas said to them, "If I tell you one of the words which he told me, you will pick up stones and throw them at me. Then fire will come out of the stones and burn you up"'.

199. See particularly M. Jansen, '"Evangelium des Zwillings?" Das *Thomasevangelium* als Thomas-Schrift', in J. Frey et al., eds., *Das Thomasevangelium: Entstehung — Rezeption — Theologie* (BZNW 157; Berlin: de Gruyter, 2008) 222-48 — 'the etymological potential of his name' (248).

200. See particularly G. J. Riley, *Resurrection Reconsidered: Thomas and John in Controversy* (Minneapolis: Fortress, 1995) 100-126; A. D. DeConick, *Voices of the Mystics: Early Christian Discourse in the Gospels of John and Thomas and Other Ancient Christian Literature* (JSNTS 157; Sheffield Academic, 2001) ch. 3.

201. See further Dunderberg, '*Thomas* and the Beloved Disciple'; and below §43.3.

202. 'The peculiar redundant name Didymus Judas Thomas seems to be attested only in the East' (Cameron, *ABD* 6.536). On Edessa see *ABD* 2.284-87 and below §45.8f.

203. See below n.326.

204. Elliott, *ANT* 439-40; Klauck, *Apocryphal Acts* 142. Gathercole, *Composition of the Gospel of Thomas*, argues convincingly for a Greek original; if Edessa was the place of origin, 'then one must reckon with the fact that she "was culturally a Greek city"' (34, citing H. J. W. Drijvers and J. F. Healey, *The Old Syriac Inscriptions of Edessa and Osrhoene* [Leiden: Brill, 1999] 32).

deduction is that the *Gospel of Thomas* as such also originated there.[205] It can be further argued that *Thomas* was originally written in Syriac,[206] although the only portions of the text of *Thomas* have come down to us in Greek (the Oxyrhynchus papyri) and Coptic (the Nag Hammadi *Gospel of Thomas*). However, the fact that both the latter were discovered in Egypt does not diminish the likelihood that the *Gospel of Thomas* reflects a distinctively Syrian setting.[207]

iii. Date

The Nag Hammadi library was buried around 400 CE,[208] with c. 350 as a likely date for the Coptic *Gospel of Thomas*.[209] But at least one of the Greek (POxy) fragments comes from a manuscript which was written before 200 CE.[210] As already noted, the Coptic *Gospel of Thomas* is a translation from Greek. This does not necessarily imply that there is a direct line from the Greek version to the Coptic, for at several points it would be difficult to read the Coptic as a translation of the Greek. A more likely explanation is that both the Greek and the Coptic are transcriptions of a tradition which was almost completely oral in character and transmission. The Greek and the Coptic texts were transcribed at different phases of what is the same stream of tradition, and their variety in both wording and order reflects the variations typical of oral use and transmission.[211]

That said, the stream of tradition shared by both the Greek and the Coptic versions is certainly the same stream, which must have been flowing vigorously during at least the second half of the second century. If the *Gospel*

---

205. Koester, *Ancient Christian Gospels* 79-80. A. D. DeConick, 'Mysticism and the *Gospel of Thomas*', in Frey, ed., *Das Thomasevangelium* 206-21, notes how resonant the *Gospel of Thomas* is with old Syrian religiosity. 'Now it looks to me to be an old form of Orthodoxy, a kind of "proto-Orthodoxy"' (218-21). Similarly also DeConick, 'The *Gospel of Thomas*', in Foster, ed., *Non-Canonical Gospels* 13-29 (here 27-29).

206. See especially N. Perrin, *Thomas and Tatian: The Relationship between the* Gospel of Thomas *and the* Diatessaron (Atlanta: SBL, 2002); also *Thomas, the Other Gospel* (London: SPCK, 2007); Perrin argues that *Thomas* was dependent on Tatian's *Diatessaron*, which was almost certainly written in Syriac about 170 CE (W. L. Petersen, 'Diatessaron', *ABD* 2.189-90).

207. 'The Syrian "native soil" is just as clear in imagery and parables' (Blatz, *NTA* 1.112).

208. Robinson, *Nag Hammadi Library* 2.

209. Cameron, *ABD* 6.535.

210. H. Koester, in Robinson, *Nag Hammadi Library* 124; Cameron, *ABD* 6.535, 536. Typical of the intriguing possibilities opened up by *Thomas* is the conclusion of S. L. Davies, *The Gospel of Thomas and Christian Wisdom* (New York: Seabury, 1983): 'The Gospel of Thomas is a mid-first-century text' (146); 'Thomas may be as old as, or even older than, Q' (16-17).

211. But see further below §43.2a n.246.

of *Thomas* tradition as such originated in Syria, then the Oxyrhynchus papyri demonstrate that it had spread more widely, certainly into Egypt, to be transcribed there in Greek.

Even more to the point, the degree of overlap between the *Gospel of Thomas* tradition and the Synoptic tradition, not least the Q tradition,[212] indicates that the sources, or at least some of the sources of the *Thomas* tradition, can be traced back into the first century, and to the oral Jesus tradition contained in Q and transcribed by the Synoptic evangelists. This poses a question[213] to which we will have to return for detailed discussion: is the Jesus tradition transmitted in the Synoptic tradition only one tributary which flowed into the *Gospel of Thomas* tradition; or is the Jesus tradition, or the impact made by Jesus, the only source of the *Gospel of Thomas*? Could, for example, the Q tradition be regarded in effect as an early edition of the *Gospel of Thomas*,[214] or is *Thomas* simply an example of early (first century) tradition drawn into a later (mid-second century) composition?[215] The answer to this question, and its corollaries, are obviously crucial for our understanding of the diverse character of early Christianity, and of the history of the Jesus tradition. To find and clarify that answer will be an important goal in the agenda of subsequent chapters (§43.2-4).

c. The Other Nag Hammadi Gospels

Apart from the *Gospel of Thomas*, the Nag Hammadi codices contain three other manuscripts designated as 'Gospels' — the *Gospel of Truth*, the *Gospel of Philip*, and the *Gospel of the Egyptians*. Since papyrus Berolinensis 8502 contains the *Gospel of Mary*, along with the *Apocryphon of John* and the *Sophia of Jesus Christ*, both of which appear also in the Nag Hammadi codices, the *Gospel of Mary* is included in the published *Nag Hammadi Library*. In addition other of the Nag Hammadi documents claim to be providing Jesus

---

212. See again below §43.2a.
213. Cf. E. E. Popkes, 'Das Thomasevangelium als *crux interpretum*. Die methodischen Ursachen einer diffusen Diskussionslage', in Frey and Schröter, eds., *Jesus in apokryphen Evangelienüberlieferungen* 271-92.
214. As Koester (*NHL* 125) and Cameron (*ABD* 6.536) imply; see also Koester's earlier contributions, '*GNOMAI DIAPHOROI*: The Origin and Nature of Diversification in the History of Early Christianity' and 'One Jesus and Four Primitive Gospels', in Robinson and Koester, *Trajectories* 114-57 and 158-204 (here 129-43, 168-87).
215. It is important not to fall into the assumption that the Synoptic or specifically Q material in *Thomas* is to be simply identified as an early version of *Thomas*; *pace* S. J. Patterson, *The Gospel of Thomas and Jesus* (Sonoma, CA: Polebridge, 1993).

tradition, or teaching attributed to Jesus. And there are other documents, like the recently discovered *Gospel of Judas,* which can be included under the broad heading of Gnostic treatments of or claims to provide Jesus tradition.

The title of the *Gospel of Truth* (*NHL* I.3) is taken from its opening words ('the gospel of truth is joy'). It has a clearly Valentinian character, and some think that Valentinus was himself the author, or his immediate disciples. If it can also be identified with the 'Gospel of Truth' referred to by Irenaeus (*adv. haer.* 3.11.9), then it can confidently be dated to the period 150-180, and may have originated in Rome.[216]

The *Gospel of Philip* (*NHL* II.3) 'is a compilation of statements pertaining primarily to the meaning and value of sacraments within the context of a Valentinian conception of the human predicament and life after death. . . . likely a collection of excerpts mainly from a Christian Gnostic sacramental catechesis'.[217] The title given to the document at its end is *The Gospel according to Philip*, but the attribution to Philip may be due to the fact that Philip is the only apostle to appear in the document (73.8). The reference to Syriac (19, 53) suggests a Syrian origin. Date is impossible to compute (3rd century?); as usual, more interesting is the question whether it draws on earlier sources.

Clement of Alexandria refers twice to a *Gospel of the Egyptians*, in which Salome features prominently (at least according to the references in Clement).[218] Clement's knowledge of this Gospel suggests its circulation in Egypt in the late second century. But the lack of other (specific) references probably indicates a document of minor significance and limited circulation. It should not be confused with the Nag Hammadi *Gospel of the Egyptians* (*NHL* III.2 and IV.2 — two versions), otherwise entitled 'The Holy Book of the Great Invisible Spirit', 'a Sethian baptismal handbook that features a baptismal ceremony introduced by an account of the origin of the universe, in Sethian cosmological terms'.[219]

The *Gospel of Mary* (that is, by general consent, Mary Magdalene) is a document never mentioned by the Church Fathers, so far as we are aware. A Coptic text was only discovered in 1896 (P. Berolinensis 8502), and two other fragments were subsequently discovered, both written in Greek (P. Oxy. 3525 and P. Rylands 463).[220] Since these latter two can be dated to the early

---

216. See also Dunderberg, 'School of Valentinus' 84-86.
217. W. W. Isenberg, 'The Gospel of Philip', *NHL* 139-60 (here 139, 141); Dunderberg, 'School of Valentinus' 88-90. See further below §44.6a.
218. See B. D. Ehrman, *Lost Scriptures: Books That Did Not Make It into the New Testament* (Oxford University, 2003) 17-18. The two references specifically to the *Gospel of the Egyptians* are cited below in §44.4a.
219. M. Meyer, *The Gnostic Gospels of Jesus* (New York: HarperCollins, 2005) 115.
220. Text and further details in *NHL* 523-27; H.-C. Puech and B. Blatz, *NTA* 1.391-

third century, it is probable that the *Gospel of Mary* was written in Greek, some time in the second century.[221] The short text is not particularly Gnostic in character, though it may have appealed to Gnostics,[222] and is most interesting as indicating that Mary was regarded in some Christian circles as an authoritative teacher.[223]

Not all discussions of Gnostic or non-canonical Gospels agree on what should be included, and since the dating of the original versions of most of the Nag Hammadi texts is at best obscure, with even a second century date usually disputed, it is hardly necessary to go into further detail. We will see later that the *Apocryphon of James* (*NHL* I.2) and the *Dialogue of the Saviour* (*NHL* III.5) raise interesting questions about the history of the Jesus tradition (§44.5), but others sometimes included in lists of Gospels[224] are too far from the NT Gospels to be considered: *The Apocryphon (or Secret Book) of John* (*NHL* II.1, III.1, IV.1), although attributed to John, the brother of James, sons of Zebedee, is a classic and well developed (Sethian) Gnostic account of the origin, fall and salvation of the world and humanity;[225] and *The Second Treatise of the Great Seth* (*NHL* VII.2), although delivered by Christ (65), is a classically Gnostic interpretation of Christian tradition — with Simon of Cyrene crucified and not Jesus, while he (Jesus) 'was rejoicing in the height ... and laughing at their ignorance' (56).[226]

The Letter of Peter to Philip (*NHL* VIII.2)[227] could be included as a 'revelation dialogue' typical of early Gnostic use and well illustrates the varied ways in which a Gnostic narrative could blend into Christian tradition. There

---

95; Lührmann, *Die apokryph gewordenen Evangelien* 105-24; C. Tuckett, *The Gospel of Mary* (Oxford University, 2007) 3-10.

221. Tuckett, *Gospel of Mary* 10-12; and 'The *Gospel of Mary*', in Foster, ed., *Non-Canonical Gospels* 43-53 (here 43-44); also K. L. King, in Robinson, ed., *NHL* 523-24; Meyer, *Gnostic Gospels of Jesus* 33-35.

222. See the discussion in Tuckett, *Gospel of Mary* ch. 5; also 'The *Gospel of Mary*' 43-53, with bibliography.

223. See particularly E. A. de Boer, *The Gospel of Mary: Beyond a Gnostic and a Biblical Mary Magdalene* (JSNTS 260; London: T & T Clark, 2004); also 'Followers of Mary Magdalene and Contemporary Philosophy', in Frey and Schröter, eds., *Jesus in apokryphen Evangelienüberlieferungen* 315-38.

224. Meyer, *Gnostic Gospels of Jesus*.

225. For more detail see F. Wisse, 'John, Apocryphon of', *ABD* 3.899-900.

226. On Sethian Gnosticism, see J. D. Turner, *Sethian Gnosticism and the Platonic Tradition* (Quebec: University of Laval, 2001). Several of the Nag Hammadi codices are made up of Sethian literature; see e.g. the 'Synopsis of Sethian Gnostic Literature' in A. D. DeConick, *The Thirteenth Apostle: What the Gospel of Judas Really Says* (London: Continuum, 2007) 167-73; DeConick also provides a helpful 'Gnostic Catechism' in ch. 2.

227. M. W. Meyer and F. Wisse, *NHL* 431-37 — Meyer suggests it was written around the end of the second century CE or into the third (433); H.-G. Bethge, *NTA* 1.342-53.

are echoes of the commission of the risen Christ to preach salvation to the whole world. The great light and voice which speaks to them identifies itself, 'I am Jesus Christ who am with you forever' (134.17-18; cf. Matt. 28.19-20). But the echoes of early Christian tradition introduce a more characteristically Gnostic message.[228] The first request put to the risen Christ by the apostles is, 'Lord, we would like to know the deficiency of the aeons and their pleroma', and 'How are we detained in this dwelling place?' (134.20-24). The condition of humanity in its fallen state is explained by reference to the Gnostic myth of 'the disobedience and the foolishness of the mother [Sophia]' wanting 'to raise up aeons' 'without the commandment of the majesty of the Father' (135.10-15).[229] The appeal to the incarnation fits with the Gnostic gospel: 'I am the one who was sent down in the body because of the seed which had fallen away' (136.16-18), and the familiar encouragement is given that 'when you strip off from yourselves what is corrupted, then you will become illuminators' (137.6-8). The tension caused by present suffering is reflected in the recognition that 'our Illuminator, Jesus, [came] down and was crucified', followed by the assertion that 'Jesus is a stranger to this suffering. But we are the ones who have suffered through the transgression of the mother' (139.15-23).

Two other recently discovered Gospels should be mentioned. The *Gospel of the Savior* (P. Beroliniensis 22220) is one of a number of fragmentary Coptic manuscripts acquired from Egypt by the Berlin Museum in 1967. It was discovered in 1991 and first published in 1999.[230] The fragmentary nature of the manuscript leaves much of the text untranslatable. The original language was Greek, and it may derive from the second century, though the Coptic manuscript is much later. The surviving manuscript treats of Jesus' final hours, beginning after the last supper. The lack of any reference to it in the patristic period suggests that it was of modest circulation and minimal significance.

The *Gospel of Judas* should also be mentioned, again not part of the Nag Hammadi corpus, if only because it is the most recently discovered text to be included under the heading of Gnostic Gospels. Although reference is

---

228. In continuing her legitimate questioning of the category 'Gnosticism', K. L. King, 'Toward a Discussion of the Category "Gnosis"/"Gnosticism": The Case of the Epistle of Peter to Philip', in Frey and Schröter, eds., *Jesus in apokryphen Evangelienüberlieferungen* 445-65, plays down too much the features of the text which evidence characteristic narrative of Valentinianism.

229. As in the *Apocryphon of John*: the vital break comes when Sophia 'wanted to bring forth a likeness out of herself without the consent of the Spirit — he had not approved — and without her consort' (II.9.28-31 — *NHL* 110).

230. C. W. Hedrick and P. A. Mirecki, *Gospel of the Savior: A New Ancient Gospel* (Santa Rosa, CA: Polebridge, 1999); C. Markschies, 'Was wissen wir über den Sitz im Leben der apokryphen Evangelien?', in Frey and Schröter, eds., *Jesus in apokryphen Evangelienüberlieferungen* 61-90 (here 81-84).

made to a Gospel of Judas by Irenaeus (*adv. haer.* 1.31.1) and Epiphanius (*Pan.* 38.1.2-5, 38.3.1-5),[231] a copy of the text to which they presumably refer[232] was only discovered in the 1970s (the Codex Tchacos) and published in 2006 to a fanfare of publicity.[233]

d. Other Gospels

To complete our introductory review of early Gospels, several others cannot be ignored.[234]

One of the most interesting of the fragmentary papyri is Papyrus Egerton 2, first published in 1935,[235] from a papyrus codex (rather than a roll) which may be dated as early as 150.[236] It contains two leaves and the remains of a third.[237] Its most striking feature is knowledge of what in the NT is distinctively Johannine material (§44.4b).

A Gospel attributed to Peter (the *Gospel of Peter*) is mentioned in early church literature. Most important is the account given by Eusebius of how Serapion, bishop of Antioch (late second century), had learned that the community at Rhossus (on the coast, 30 miles north-west of Antioch) were using the 'Gospel of Peter'. Serapion initially had seen no reason to disallow its

---

231. Full citation in DeConick, *The Thirteenth Apostle* 174-77. In what follows I draw on DeConick's translation.

232. For discussion whether it is the same Gospel, see S. Gathercole, *The Gospel of Judas: Rewriting Early Christianity* (Oxford University, 2007) ch. 5.

233. See particularly the account given by H. Krosney, *The Lost Gospel: The Quest for the Gospel of Judas Iscariot* (Washington: National Geographic, 2006). For a briefer account see Gathercole, *Judas* ch. 1. DeConick critiques the initial (National Geographic) translation of *Gosp.Judas*, presenting Judas as a heroic figure (*The Thirteenth Apostle* ch. 3 — 'A Mistaken Gospel'); see also DeConick, 'The Mystery of Betrayal: What Does the *Gospel of Judas* Really Say?', in M. Scopello, ed., *The Gospel of Judas in Context* (Nag Hammadi and Manichaean Studies 62; Leiden: Brill, 2008) 239-64.

234. Whether Basilides ever wrote a Gospel is disputed; see J. A. Kelhoffer, '"Gospel" as a Literary Title in Early Christianity and the Question of What is (and is Not) a "Gospel" in Canons of Scholarly Literature', in Frey and Schröter, eds., *Jesus in apokryphen Evangelienüberlieferungen* 399-422 (here 418-22).

235. H. I. Bell and T. C. Skeat, *Fragments of an Unknown Gospel* (London: British Museum, 1935) 1-26.

236. Elliott, *ANT* 37-38; but Schneemelcher notes that it should perhaps be dated later, to about 200 (*NTA* 96).

237. P.Köln 255, first published in 1987, consists of five lines from the bottom of each side of fragment 1. The full text is most conveniently available in Bernhard, *Other Early Christian Gospels* 84-97. See further T. Nicklas, 'Papyrus Egerton 2', in Foster, ed., *Non-Canonical Gospels* 138-49; Lührmann, *Die apokryph gewordenen Evangelien* 125-43.

use, but on learning more, he realized that the said Gospel contained heretical teaching associated with Docetists (*HE* 6.12.2-6). An eighth- or ninth-century fragment of the *Gospel of Peter* was found in upper Egypt in 1886-87 (the Akhmim Fragment),[238] in which Peter is presented as the one giving the account (*Gosp.Pet.* 7.26; 14.60). It begins with Pilate washing his hands and climaxes in a description of Jesus' resurrection.[239] The writing was previously unknown to Serapion, himself a man of some literary standing (*HE* 6.12); it was also being 'put forward' by a group within the church of Rhossus, and was evidently fairly new to the Rhossus church itself.[240] This suggests a recent publication which originated in Syria, perhaps quite locally.[241] At any rate, it is unlikely to be dated before the middle of the second century,[242] though, as we

---

238. For fuller details see P. van Minnen, 'The Akhmim *Gospel of Peter*', in T. J. Kraus and T. Nicklas, eds., *Das Evangelium nach Petrus: Text, Kontexte, Intertexte* (Berlin: de Gruyter, 2007) 53-60; Markschies, 'Was wissen wir?' 71-74; and for the early discussion see P. Foster, 'The Discovery and Initial Reaction to the So-called Gospel of Peter', *Evangelium nach Petrus* 9-30; and further, *The Gospel of Peter: Introduction, Critical Edition and Commentary* (Leiden: Brill, 2010).

239. The text (P.Cair. 10759) can be found in Bernhard, *Other Early Christian Gospels* 49-83, together with two other small fragments: P.Oxy. 4009, part of a discussion between Jesus and Peter, also attested in *2 Clem.* 5.2-4; and P.Oxy. 2949, which overlaps with the Akhmim fragment 3-5. See further Lührmann, *Die apokryph gewordenen Evangelien* 55-104.

240. Hill, *Who Chose the Gospels?* 81-82, 88.

241. In the earliest scholarly assessment of the Akhmim fragment, H. B. Swete, *The Akhmim Fragment of the Apocryphal Gospel of St. Peter* (London: Macmillan, 1893), noted that there was no evidence of the *Gospel of Peter* being used before the end of the second century; he concluded, 'The facts are consistent with a very moderate circulation within the limits of Syria and Palestine' (xxxv). Ehrman is unjustified and very misleading when he claims that 'the Gospel of Peter was widely popular in the early church' (*Lost Christianities* 22), 'was known and used as Scripture in some parts of the Christian church in the second century' (*Lost Scriptures* 31); see Hill's thorough debunking of the arguments used by Ehrman (*Who Chose the Gospels?* particularly ch. 1 and pp. 88-89). As Markschies notes caustically, 'Unfortunately Ehrman finds it "rather hard to say" why the *Gosp.Pet.* was more popular than Mark's Gospel which became canonical' ('Was wissen wir?' 88 n.102).

242. P. M. Head, 'On the Christology of the Gospel of Peter', *VC* 46 (1992) 209-24, shows that the *Gospel of Peter*'s account of Jesus' sufferings reflects martyrological motifs characteristic of second-century Christian writings. 'The bishop of the Syrian metropolis of Antioch shows an amazing ignorance about this makeshift work, a sign that it was not disseminated widely and — contrary to some modern assertions — must have been composed at a relatively late date' (Hengel, *Four Gospels* 13). J. J. Johnston, 'The Resurrection of Jesus in the Gospel of Peter: A Tradition-Historical Study of the Akhmîm Gospel Fragment' (Middlesex University, PhD 2012), argues that 'the Akhmîm fragment exemplifies an apologetic that addresses second-century Jewish and pagan criticisms of the resurrection narratives of the older New Testament gospels, . . . (an apologetic) intended to assure second-century Christians that the proclamation of the resurrection of Jesus rested upon actual eyewitness

shall see (§44.7a), there is some controversy as to whether any of the tradition in it can be dated as early as or earlier than the NT Gospels.[243]

Not unrelated are other Gospels which focus on or elaborate the theme of Jesus' sufferings. They are all late, outside our scope of reference, but the *Gospel of Nicodemus* is of particular interest. It is known as such only in the mediaeval period, but it is made up of an earlier *Acts of Pilate*, to which *Christ's Descent into Hell* had been appended.[244] The *Acts of Pilate* may have been known to Justin (*1 Apol.* 35.9; 48.3), Tertullian knew a tradition about Pilate communicating with Emperor Tiberius which probably derives from the *Acts* (*Apol.* 5, 21),[245] and Epiphanius, writing about 375, refers to a detail of the timing of Jesus' passion, which was probably derived from the *Acts*.[246] As part of what may be termed 'the Pilate Cycle',[247] it contributed to the transformation of Pilate from a cruel and very unsympathetic historical character responsible for Jesus' crucifixion, to one who recognized Jesus' divinity and became a Christian, to be counted among the saints in the Ethiopic and Coptic churches.[248]

Another document named as Gospel hardly calls for attention. The *Gospel of Gamaliel* is not known from patristic reference, but Coptic fragments include a personal testimony of Gamaliel. Like the *Acts of Pilate*, it also seems to focus and elaborate on Jesus' passion, and similarly indicates the rehabilitation of Pilate, presented as a witness to the empty tomb with its grave clothes.[249] Although a *Gospel of Bartholomew* is referred to by Jerome and others, the document sometimes referred to in the modern period as the *Gospel of Bartholomew* is better known as *The Questions of Bartholomew*. Although in touch with Gospel tradition, it is quite remote from the character of Gospel as thus far reviewed, and though it attests that Bartholomew became

---

testimony of the resurrection event itself, not merely the discovery of the empty tomb and later reports of resurrection appearances'.

243. See further Koester, *Ancient Christian Gospels* 216-40 (see also §44 n.302 below); C. Maurer and W. Schneemelcher, 'The Gospel of Peter', *NTA* 1.216-27; Elliott, *ANT* 150-58; R. E. Brown, *The Death of the Messiah* (2 vols.; New York: Doubleday, 1994) 1317-49; Wilson, *Related Strangers* 87-89; P. Foster, 'The *Gospel of Peter*', in Foster, ed., *Non-Canonical Gospels* 30-42 (each with bibliography). Foster urges some caution on too hasty assumption that all the fragments are from the Gospel of Peter referred to by Serapion (40).

244. C. N. Jefford, 'Pilate, Acts of', *ABD* 5.371-72; Elliott, *ANT* 164-66.

245. Jefford, *ABD* 5.371.

246. F. Scheidweiler, *NTA* 1.503.

247. Elliott, *ANT* 164-225.

248. D. R. Schwartz, 'Pontius Pilate', *ABD* 5.400-401; see also Wilson, *Related Strangers* 85-87.

249. M.-A. van den Oudenrijn, *NTA* 1.558-60; Elliott, *ANT* 159-60.

a focus for subsequent speculation most likely in Egypt, there is no indication that it was known or had any influence in the second century.[250]

However, attention should certainly be given to Gospels which focused their attention on the beginnings of Jesus' life rather than his passion. One of the earliest and most famous was *The Protevangelium of James*, which was already very popular by the end of the second century.[251] The main motivation for the *Protevangelium* seems to have been to glorify Mary, her own miraculous birth (4-5), and her virginity, preserved despite the birth of her son (19-20). It therefore provides an early attestation that the cult of Mary, sanctioned by the Council of Ephesus in 431, was already well advanced in the second half of the second century.[252]

The other best known of these Gospels is *The Infancy Gospel of Thomas*, which came to prominence in scholarly circles four centuries ago, and which probably also originated before the end of the second century.[253] Almost certainly the impulse to tell stories about the childhood of great men/heroes which foreshadow their greatness, an impulse which is evident not only in ancient Mediterranean culture but throughout the world, was the motivating factor here too.[254]

A review of first- and second-century documents referred to as 'Gospel' cannot exclude the most controversial — the so-called *Secret Gospel of Mark*. According to Morton Smith, it came to light in the Mar Saba monastery near Jerusalem in 1958.[255] Copied on to the end-pages of a seventeenth-century

---

250. F. Scheidweiler and W. Schneemelcher, *NTA* 1.537-38; Elliott, *ANT* 652-53 (who includes *The Questions of Bartholomew* in his section on 'Apocryphal Apocalypses').

251. O. Cullmann, 'Infancy Gospels', *NTA* 1.421-25; Elliott, *ANT* 48-52; R. Cameron, ed., *The Other Gospels: Non-Canonical Gospel Texts* (Guildford: Lutterworth, 1983) 107-9.

252. Cullmann, *NTA* 1.425; Elliott, *ANT* 50-51; Wilson, *Related Strangers* 83-84; P. Foster, 'The *Protevangelium of James*', in Foster, ed., *Non-Canonical Gospels* 122-25. The later *Gospel of Pseudo-Matthew* carries the same trend to venerate Mary still further, insisting, inter alia, that 'A virgin has conceived, a virgin has brought forth, and a virgin she remains' (13). As Elliott notes, 'Much mediaeval art is indecipherable without reference to books such as Pseudo-Matthew' (*ANT* 84; and further 84-99).

253. T. Chartrand-Burke, 'The *Infancy Gospel of Thomas*', in Foster, ed., *Non-Canonical Gospels* 126-38 (here 126, 132-34). 'The earliest form of Infancy Thomas seems to be the Syriac, but the tradition seems to go back to a Greek model; the Greek alphabet figures in one story' (Elliott, *ANT* 69).

254. Cameron, *Other Gospels* 122-24; Chartrand-Burke, '*Infancy Gospel*' 134; U. U. Kaiser, 'Jesus als Kind', in Frey and Schröter, eds., *Jesus in apokryphen Evangelienüberlieferungen* 253-69 (here 264-69). C. B. Horn and R. R. Phenix, 'Apocryphal Gospels in Syriac and Related Texts Offering Traditions about Jesus', also in Frey and Schröter, eds., *Jesus in apokryphen Evangelienüberlieferungen* 527-55, reviews the reception of the two Infancy Gospels in Syriac (531-44).

255. M. Smith, *Clement of Alexandria and a Secret Gospel of Mark* (Cambridge, MA:

edition of the letters of Ignatius, Smith found a previously unknown letter from Clement of Alexandria, which referred to 'a more spiritual Gospel' which Mark composed in Alexandria subsequent to the more restrained Gospel which he had written in Rome. This latter 'secret Gospel' he wrote 'for the use of those who were being perfected'. Clement's letter goes on to include two citations from this longer text of the Gospel of Mark, following Mark 10.32-34 (a lengthier citation) and 10.46a (one sentence); somewhat oddly the location of the two extracts is indicated with almost pedantic precision. The value of this testimony and of the extracts from a longer Mark is at best dubious, and doubts remain as to whether the letter is authentic or a forgery[256]— a sad note to end this review of relevant Gospel literature of the first two centuries, but not uncharacteristic of the uncertainties, not to say confusion and disputes, which are a feature of the evaluation of second-century data.

40.5 Other Letters

The letters of Paul, so influential within the first generation of emerging Christianity and beyond, provided a precedent followed by John, the seer of Revelation (Rev. 2-3), and the Apostolic Fathers. Somewhat disappointingly, however, most of those literarily active in early Christianity did not find the letter format to be the most suitable format in which to express their views. Consequently, the apocryphal epistles are the least interesting in the full range

---

Harvard University, 1973); and more popularly, *The Secret Gospel: The Discovery and Interpretation of the Secret Gospel according to Mark* (Clearlake, CA: Dawn Horse, 1972, 1980).

256. See particularly S. C. Carlson, *The Gospel Hoax: Morton Smith's Invention of Secret Mark* (Waco: Baylor University, 2005); also Lührmann, *Die apokryph gewordenen Evangelien* 27-29; Ehrman, *Lost Christianities* ch. 4 ('The Forgery of an Ancient Discovery?'). Foster provides a sober summary of the debate (*Non-Canonical Gospels* ch. 14); see also E. Rau, 'Weder gefälscht noch authentisch?' and 'Das Geheimnis des Reiches Gottes', in Frey and Schröter, eds., *Jesus in apokryphen Evangelienüberlieferungen* 139-86, 186-221; and see now T. Burke, ed., *Ancient Gospel or Modern Forgery? The Secret Gospel of Mark in Debate* (Eugene, OR: Cascade Books, 2013). The letter of Clement reflects Clement's well-known attraction to mystery initiations and high evaluation of gnosis. So it is quite likely that 'secret Mark' was indeed a revision of Mark, to imply that Mark also knew of the sort of secret teaching which Gnostic-leaning groups liked to attribute to Jesus, in this case an elaboration of 'the mystery of the kingdom of God' (Mark 4.11), the sort of teaching, indeed, which Clement himself found attractive; see further §44.6f below. The total absence of any manuscript support for an original Mark incorporating secret Mark must make it very doubtful if such an original ever existed. The fact that the letter of Clement, which had been seen by others, has gone missing, so that vital tests which could have been applied to the paper and ink are no longer possible, only intensifies the frustration of the debate about the authenticity of 'secret Mark'.

of apocryphal literature. But a few examples should at least be noted, even though any light they might shed on the second century is at best obscure.[257]

a. *3 Corinthians*

We will refer to *3 Corinthians* below, since it is included in *The Acts of Paul* (§40.6a).

b. The *Epistle to the Laodiceans*

Laodiceans is a brief letter purportedly written by Paul.[258] But it was obviously composed to provide a referent for the letter mentioned in Col. 4.16, as strongly suggested by the letter's conclusion: 'See that [this epistle] is read to the Colossians and that of the Colossians to you' (*Ep.Laod.* 20). The Epistle is generally agreed to have been composed by drawing together phrases from Paul's letters, principally Galatians and Philippians.[259] It is unlikely that the reference in the Muratorian Fragment/Canon to a letter to the Laodiceans (63-65) is to this Epistle, since it describes the letter as 'forged in Paul's name to [further] the heresy of Marcion' (lines 64-65).[260] As to origin, a date somewhere in the period of second to fourth century is as about as precise as can be achieved.

c. The Correspondence of Paul and Seneca[261]

Fourteen letters make up the correspondence between Paul and Seneca, the famous Roman philosopher influential during Nero's reign, eight by Seneca

---

257. For listings of apocryphal epistles see D. A. Thomason, 'Epistles, Apocryphal', *ABD* 2.568-69; Elliott, *ANT* 537-88; Ehrman, *Lost Christianities* xiii-xiv.

258. See Schneemelcher, *NTA* 2.42-46; Elliott, *ANT* 543-46. The article by C. P. Anderson, 'Laodiceans, Epistle to the', *ABD* 4.231-32, is particularly useful.

259. Schneemelcher identifies the phrases in Philippians and Galatians and describes it as a 'paltry and carelessly compiled concoction' (*NTA* 2.45-46).

260. 'The Muratorian Canon' is available, e.g., in B. M. Metzger, *The Canon of the New Testament* (Oxford: Clarendon, 1987) 305-7. Hoffmann, however, argues that Ephesians is an orthodox revision of an original letter to the Laodiceans written by Marcion (*Marcion* 252-80). The same passage in the Muratorian fragment mentions 'another (epistle) to the Alexandrians, also forged in Paul's name' (lines 64-65), but sometimes identified with Hebrews. This is the only reference to such a letter.

261. C. Römer, *NTA* 2.46-53; Elliott, *ANT* 547-53.

and six by Paul. Their style makes it clear that they cannot have been written by either. Since they were probably known to Jerome (*de Vir. Ill.* 12) and Augustine (*ep.* 153.14), most agree that they can be dated to the fourth century, but whether they were written together or some were added later (letters 13 and 14?) is disputed.

d. The *Epistle of Titus*[262]

Pseudo-Titus is a fanatical tirade against all forms of sexual relationship and activity. Probably not composed before the fifth century, it is only of interest for us as confirming that a strong dualistic antipathy to the flesh, and thus a glorifying of virginity and celibacy, became a characteristic feature of much Christian spirituality from the third century onwards.[263] As we will see, the tendency was already well established in the apocryphal Acts, references to which *Ep. Tit.* includes in its extensive quotations from OT, NT and unknown apocryphal works.[264]

e. The *Epistula Apostolorum*

The *Epistula Apostolorum*, although probably composed in Greek, was unknown until large portions of it were discovered in Coptic translation in 1895, and some years later in a complete Ethiopic translation.[265] It is presented as a letter but is primarily an admonitory exhortation. Although it imitates the form of a Gnostic revelation discourse, it seems to be in part at least directed against early Gnostic views: Simon (Magus) and Cerinthus are explicitly targeted (*Ep.Apost.* 1); reference to the incarnation is explicit;[266] and there is repeated insistence that the flesh is resurrected (11, 18, 20, 24, 26). This is probably sufficient indication that it can be dated to about the mid-second

---

262. A. de Santos Otero, *NTA* 2.53-74.

263. Otero sees the environment of the epistle in the ascetic Priscillianist movement in the fifth-century Spanish church (*NTA* 2.54); Priscillianism itself is usually regarded as a development from Manichaeism (see e.g. *ODCC* 1329-30).

264. See nn.58, 78, 84, 110 in Otero's *NTA* translation.

265. Koester, *Introduction* 2.236-38; Cameron, *Other Gospels* 131-33 (text 133-62); Elliott, *ANT* 555-58 (text 558-88). Koester and Cameron favour Egypt as the place of origin; C. E. Hill, 'The *Epistula Apostolorum*: An Asian Tract from the Time of Polycarp', *Journal of Early Christian Studies* 7 (1999) 1-53, argues for a provenance in Asia Minor (perhaps Smyrna), sometime in the 140s.

266. See §44.4c below.

century, or even earlier. In which case, the familiarity it displays with a broad range of NT writings, and some OT apocrypha and earlier second century Christian literature,[267] provides important witness to the wider dispersion and knowledge of these writings.

40.6 The Other Acts

Just as the collections of Jesus-tradition (Q) and the earliest Gospels (beginning with Mark) encouraged an extensive range of other Gospels, so the Acts of the Apostles seems to have provided a precedent and inspiration for a range of other *Acts*.[268] This can be well understood given the circumstances and the attitudes of the time — a desire for stories which engaged, encouraged and informed. There were plenty of such novels in the Greco-Roman world, and the writers of the apocryphal *Acts* probably knew the genre and were influenced by it.[269] In Jewish tradition, stories of Daniel, of Tobit and of Judith must have served as part of the educational programme of parents and teachers. These had already established themselves within Greek-speaking Jewish communities. And the romance of *Joseph and Asenath*, set in Egypt and quite possibly as early as the late first century BCE,[270] provided a still more striking precedent for the beautiful and religiously ardent young woman. Understandably also, in Christian circles the prestige of the apostles naturally encouraged telling stories about them, no doubt stimulated by a curiosity all the stronger in cases where so little was known about them and where very little had been handed down about them. We will focus on the major *Acts* which probably originated before the third century,[271] and which speak most directly to our interest in the continuing influence of the leading figures of the first century.[272] They are interesting because they indicate the character of the religiosity which such stories fed.

---

267. See the footnotes in Elliott's text.
268. The best introduction to this genre is Klauck, *The Apocryphal Acts of the Apostles*.
269. See e.g. R. Pervo, *Profit with Delight: The Literary Genre of the Acts of the Apostles* (Philadelphia: Fortress, 1987; examples of Greco-Roman prose fiction listed on p. 114); Klauck, *Apocryphal Acts* 7-14.
270. C. Burchard, 'Joseph and Asenath', *OTP* 2.177-247; R. D. Chesnutt, 'Joseph and Asenath', *ABD* 3.969-71.
271. For later *Acts*, of which the *Acts of Philip* (*Acta Philippi*) is the most interesting, see A. de Santos Otero, 'Later Acts of Apostles', *NTA* 2.426-82; *Acta Philippi* (468-76).
272. Since the dates and interrelationships are disputed I treat them in the order most suited to this study, and since they are less well known I give some detail.

a. The *Acts of Paul*[273]

Probably the best known and most influential were the stories about Paul and Thecla. These may have circulated independently (the *Acts of Thecla* or the *Acts of Paul and Thecla*) but are best known as part of a much more extensive account of the *Acts of Paul*. The *Acts of Paul* is known only in a very disjointed and often fragmentary state,[274] but can be dated with some confidence to the second half or the late decades of the second century,[275] since Tertullian almost certainly refers to such a writing at the turn of the second/third centuries.[276] The plot line is an account of Paul's travel round various cities — Antioch, Iconium, Myra, Sidon, Tyre, Ephesus, Philippi, Corinth and Italy — where he encounters various believers, occasions opposition by his preaching, and performs miracles.[277] Interestingly no opposition is attributed to Jews, in contrast to the NT Acts, and Jews are only mentioned once in a fragmentary *ActsPaul* 6. More striking are the several references to baptism as 'the seal' (3.25; 4; 11.7), and the attack on beliefs that the resurrection was

---

273. P. Sellew, 'Paul, Acts of', *ABD* 5.202-3; W. Schneemelcher, *NTA* 2.213-70 (translated text 238-65); Elliott, *ANT* 350-89 (text 364-88); Klauck, *Apocryphal Acts* ch. 2; A. Gregory, 'The *Acts of Paul* and the Legacy of Paul', in M. F. Bird and J. R. Dodson, eds., *Paul and the Second Century* (LNTS 412; London: T & T Clark, 2011) 169-89. As in the other *Acts* also, quotations are drawn from Elliott.

274. Schneemelcher, *NTA* 2.216-18; Elliott, *ANT* 356-57; Klauck, *Apocryphal Acts* 49-50.

275. 170-180 CE (Klauck, *Apocryphal Acts* 3).

276. Tertullian, *de Bapt.* 1.17; cited by D. R. MacDonald, 'Thecla, Acts of', *ABD* 6.443-44; and discussed by Schneemelcher, *NTA* 2.214-15, 235. Tertullian bridles at the fact that the *Acts* supported 'women's freedom to teach and baptize' (cf. *ActsPaul* 3.34, 41) and attributes the writing to a presbyter in Asia who confessed that he had made it up ('heaping up a narrative as it were from his own materials under Paul's name'), 'had done it from love of Paul, and resigned his position'. See also A. Hilhorst, 'Tertullian on the Acts of Paul', in J. N. Bremmer, ed., *The Apocryphal Acts of Paul* (Kampen: Kok Pharos, 1996) 150-63. Origen also quotes the *Acts of Paul* with some approval (*de Principiis* 1.2.3).

277. R. Bauckham, 'The *Acts of Paul* as a Sequel to Acts', in B. W. Winter and A. D. Clarke, eds., *The Book of Acts in Its Ancient Literary Setting* (Grand Rapids: Eerdmans, 1993) 105-52, argues that *ActsPaul* was written to supplement Acts, considered to be incomplete, drawing information on what was inferred from Paul's letters to be a later period of his mission and adding an account of his martyrdom. See also D. Marguerat, 'The *Acts of Paul* and the Canonical Acts: A Phenomenon of Rereading', in R. F. Stoops, ed., *Semeia* 80: *The Apocryphal Acts of the Apostles in Intertextual Perspective* (1997) 169-83. Klauck notes that 'there is not even a hint of a journey to Spain'; and he adds, 'The communities that Paul visits as an itinerant missionary were not founded by him, but already exist' (*Apocryphal Acts* 73). 'Paul is no longer primarily a church-planter establishing new communities but rather a pastor who encourages communities that are already established' (Gregory, '*Acts of Paul*' 188).

already past (3.14) or that resurrection is only of the spirit (8). But probably most striking are the actual description of Paul[278]— 'a man small in size, bald-headed, bandy-legged, of noble mien, with eyebrows meeting, rather hook-nosed, full of grace' (3.3)[279]— and the account of Paul's martyrdom by beheading (11.3, 5). The *Acts* seems to have been well known, but never accorded a status above 'apocryphal'.[280]

The most charming of the extant stories is that of *Paul and Thecla*. Thecla, a beautiful young woman, is converted by Paul's preaching when he comes to Iconium. Since it is his preaching of asceticism and virginity which attracts her,[281] Thecla renounces her betrothal to Thamyris, an influential citizen of Iconium. Paul is denounced,[282] scourged and cast out of the city, and Thecla is condemned to be burned. But the fire is miraculously extinguished (3.21-22) and she pursues Paul. He takes her with him and they come to Antioch, where another influential man falls in love with her. She again rejects the suit, is again condemned (this time to fight wild beasts), and again is miraculously preserved (3.26-36). In the course of this, Thecla, naked, throws herself into a

---

278. Interestingly, the description is attributed to Titus (*ActsPaul* 3.2-3); the degree of prominence given to Titus (3.2-3; 11.1, 5, 7) makes up for the lack of reference to Titus in Luke's Acts (the last two *ActsPaul* references have Titus and Luke as Paul's most faithful disciples).

279. A. J. Malherbe, 'A Physical Description of Paul', *Paul and the Popular Philosophers* (Minneapolis: Fortress, 1989) 165-70, points out 'that Paul's hooked nose, bowed legs, and meeting eyebrows were not unflattering features in the context in which the *Acts* was written', citing in particular descriptions of Augustus (Suetonius, *Augustus* 79.2) and Heracles (Philostratus, *Lives of the Sophists* 2.552) by way of comparison. He suggests that the author of the *Acts* derived his description of Paul from these sources (168-69). In contrast, J. Bollok, 'The Description of Paul in the Acta Pauli', in Bremmer, ed., *Apocryphal Acts of Paul* 1-15, notes that the description was perhaps drawn from 2 Corinthians, and that in physiognomic terms 'the first six elements of the description indicate only negative characteristics' (the third translated as 'in good condition, plump'). As J. N. Bremmer, 'Magic, Martyrdom and Women's Liberation in the Acts of Paul and Thecla', in the same volume (36-59), points out, such a negative description would be a way of stressing that the fascination which Paul exerted would have been the result of his message not of his appearance (39).

280. Schneemelcher, *NTA* 2.215-16. D. R. MacDonald, *The Legend and the Apostle: The Battle for Paul in Story and Canon* (Philadelphia: Westminster, 1983): 'the story is laden with folkloric commonplace. Beautiful, nubile women, frustrated lovers, journeys, perils, and miraculous rescues are the storyteller's stock-in-trade' (19).

281. Paul preaches, 'Blessed are those who have kept the flesh chaste, . . . ; blessed are those who have kept aloof from the world, . . . ; blessed are those who have wives as not having them, . . .' (3.5-7); and is reported as saying, 'There is for you no resurrection unless you remain chaste and do not pollute the flesh' (3.12).

282. Thamyris is advised to 'Say that he is a Christian and he will die at once' (*ActsPaul* 3.16), the name 'Christian' being regarded as sufficient grounds for punishment.

large pit filled with water, saying, 'In the name of Jesus Christ I baptize myself on my last day' (3.34). She confesses 'I am a servant of the living God' and is acknowledged as such by the governor (3.37-38), and instructs her patroness in the word of God, bringing many of the maidservants to faith (3.39). When she finds Paul again he commissions her to 'Go and teach the word of God' (3.41). In further elaboration of the story[283] Thecla is described as a hermit, living in a cave upon herbs and water, continuing her preaching for a further seventy-two years (3.43-45).

The notable features are the strong affirmation of virginity, a repeated feature of the apocryphal Acts,[284] the acceptability of Thecla's self-baptism, and the fact that a woman is so honoured as a teacher of the word of God. She belongs to the tradition of strong, devout women, in Jewish tradition beginning with Miriam, and, subsequently, particularly Esther and Judith. And in Christianity she was celebrated as the first of the holy virgins, after, of course, Mary.[285]

Incorporated into the *Acts of Paul* are brief letters from the Corinthians to Paul, and a third letter of Paul to the Corinthians.[286] The most striking features of the former are the Corinthians' report that two false teachers, Simon and Cleobius, have arrived in Corinth, teaching *inter alia* that 'there is no resurrection of the body, man has not been made by God, Christ has neither come in the flesh, nor was he born of Mary, and the world is not the work of God but of angels' (8.1.12-15). This could be deduced partly from Paul's treatment of the resurrection in 1 Cor. 15, but presumably reflects knowledge of and reaction to different elements of Gnostic teaching. The response in *3 Corinthians* describes the false teaching as 'the accursed belief of the serpent' (8.3.20), which suggests the false teaching in view is that of Ophites,[287] and affirms emphatically that the resurrection will be of the flesh (8.3.6, 27): 'those who say that there is no resurrection of the flesh shall have no resurrection' (8.3.24).

283. Elliott, *ANT* 372-74.
284. See particularly V. Burrus, *Chastity as Autonomy: Women in the Stories of Apocryphal Acts* (Lewiston/Queenston: Edwin Mellen, 1987).
285. M. Pesthy, 'Thecla among the Fathers of the Church', in Bremmer, ed., *Apocryphal Acts of Paul* 164-78, notes that 'Ambrose drew a parallel between the virgin Thecla and the virgin Church' (177).
286. On the manuscript tradition see G. Luttikhuizen, 'The Apocryphal Correspondence with the Corinthians and the Acts of Paul', in Bremmer, ed., *Apocryphal Acts of Paul* 75-91.
287. Ophites 'magnify the serpent to such a degree that they prefer him even to Christ himself; for it was he, they say, who gave us the origin of the knowledge of good and of evil. Perceiving his power and majesty (they say), Moses set up the brazen serpent; and whoever gazed upon him obtained health' (Pseudo-Tertullian, *Adversus Omnes Haereses* 2).

Also incorporated into the *Acts of Paul*, as a natural conclusion, is the *Martyrdom of the Holy Apostle Paul*, which came to be valued as a separate text in mediaeval Christianity in the cult of Paul, apostle and martyr. It includes an imaginative account of how Paul's execution came about: Nero's cupbearer, Patroclus, had been restored to life and converted by Paul; Nero, taken aback by Patroclus's restoration, turns against him because Patroclus has transferred his allegiance to 'Christ Jesus, the king of the ages'. Nero condemns to death several of his servants who have also been converted to Christ, and extends the condemnation to 'all Christians and soldiers of Christ' (11.3.2). Paul is brought in with the rest of the prisoners and testifies boldly before Nero, who commands all the prisoners to be burned with fire, but Paul to be beheaded (11.3.3). Paul asserts that if he is executed he will rise again and appear to Nero, and wins his captors to faith, to be subsequently baptized (11.3.4-5, 7). His execution is recorded starkly ('When the executioner cut off his head milk splashed on the tunic of the soldier' — 11.3.5),[288] and true to his word, Paul appears to Nero after his death, warning him of the many evils and great punishment which will follow because of his unjust persecution of the Christians. When Nero hears this he commands the prisoners, including Patroclus, to be released (11.3.6).

This account of Paul's martyrdom helped to establish the tradition of hagiographical martyrdoms already well developed in the account of the *Martyrdom of Polycarp*, and reinforced by the accounts of Justin's martyrdom (*Martyrium S. Justini et sociorum*), of the Scillitan (N. Africa) martyrs (180), and of the *Passion of St Perpetua and St Felicity* (203).[289]

b. The *Acts of Peter*[290]

The *Acts of Peter* has a confused history. The earliest clear reference to a written document is in Eusebius: 'Of the Acts bearing his [Peter's] name, and the Gospel according to him and Preaching (*Kērygma*) called his and the so-called Revelation (*Apokalypsis*), we have no knowledge at all in Catholic tradition, for no orthodox (*ekklēsiastikos*) writer of the ancient time or of our own has

---

288. The milk presumably has a symbolic meaning — Paul whose preaching was milk, the basic elements of the Christian message (1 Cor. 3.2); thus, J. Bolyki, 'Events after the Martyrdom: Missionary Transformation of an Apocalyptical Metaphor in Martyrium Pauli', in Bremmer, ed., *Apocryphal Acts of Paul* 92-106 (here 101-2).

289. H. Musurillo, ed., *The Acts of the Christian Martyrs* (Oxford University, 1972).

290. W. Schneemelcher, 'The Acts of Peter', *NTA* 2.271-321 (translated text 285-317); R. F. Stoops, 'Peter, Acts of', *ABD* 5.267-68; Elliott, *ANT* 390-426 (text 397-426); J. N. Bremmer, ed., *The Apocryphal Acts of Peter* (Leuven: Peeters, 1998); Klauck, *Apocryphal Acts* 81-112.

used their testimonies' (*HE* 3.3.2). There are earlier references to some of the traditions contained in the *Acts of Peter*, though not clearly to the writing itself (Origen, *Didascalia*). But at least they indicate that such traditions were circulating at least as early as the early third century.[291] The relations of the *Acts of Peter* to the *Acts of John* and to the *Acts of Paul* are also disputed. That the *Acts of Peter* is dependent on the *Acts of John* has a fair degree of probability.[292] And the reappearance of the 'Quo vadis?' scene in the Hamburg Papyrus of the *ActsPaul* 10, where it hardly fits (according to tradition Paul was beheaded, not crucified), could imply dependence on *ActsPeter* 35,[293] though the tradition may have been independent of the *Acts of Peter* or a later addition to the *Acts of Paul*.[294]

The principal text for the *Acts of Peter* is the Latin codex Vercellensis (*Actus Vercellensis*).[295] It is a third- to fifth-century translation of an earlier Greek text, of which a fragment (from the final, Martyrdom section) was found among the Oxyrynchus papyri (P. Oxy. 849).[296] A Coptic codex (Berolinensis 8502.4) contains an account of Peter healing his daughter, and the *Epistle of Pseudo-Titus* includes a brief account of Peter raising a gardener's daughter from the dead, both of which probably come from the *Acts of Peter*.[297] In view of the many uncertainties, a date for the *Acts of Peter* is difficult to arrive at, but a date in the final decades of the second century is very plausible.[298] Where it

---

291. Schneemelcher, *NTA* 2.271-73.

292. P. J. Lallemann, 'The Relation between the Acts of John and the Acts of Peter', in J. N. Bremmer, ed., *The Apocryphal Acts of Peter: Magic, Miracles and Gnosticism* (Leuven: Peeters, 1998) 161-77; though Schneemelcher, *NTA* 2.274-75, is dubious; and see the debate between D. R. MacDonald and R. J. Pervo, in Stoops, ed., *Apocryphal Acts* 11-41, 43-56.

293. Koester, *Introduction* 2.325; Schneemelcher, *NTA* 2.275, 280. See also R. F. Stoops, 'The *Acts of Peter* in Intertextual Context', in Stoops, ed., *Apocryphal Acts* 57-86; W. Rordorf, 'The Relation between the Acts of Peter and the Acts of Paul: State of the Question', in Bremmer, ed., *Apocryphal Acts of Peter* 178-91.

294. Elliott thinks that the relationship of the two *Acts* has not yet been satisfactorily resolved (*ANT* 390).

295. A. Hilhorst, 'The Text of the *Actus Vercellensis*', in Bremmer, ed., *Apocryphal Acts of Peter* 148-60.

296. See further Schneemelcher, *NTA* 2.277-78.

297. Augustine refers to the two episodes as belonging to an apocryphal work, presumably the *Acts of Peter* (Schneemelcher, *NTA* 2.276, 278-79; Elliott, *ANT* 391). Both Schneemelcher and Elliott begin their translations of the *Acts of Peter* with the two miracles (Schneemelcher 285-87; Elliott 397-99). Since papyrus Berolinensis 8502 contains the two episodes as '*the Act of Peter*', the *Act of Peter*, like the *Gospel of Mary* (see above §40.4c), is also included in the translation of the Nag Hammadi codices (J. Brashler and D. M. Parrott, *NHL* 528-31); but the *Act of Peter* is hardly Gnostic in character. See also Klauck, *Apocryphal Acts* 105-7.

298. Schneemelcher, *NTA* 2.283; Elliott, *ANT* 392; Bremmer, *Apocryphal Acts of Peter* 18; Klauck, *Apocryphal Acts* 84.

originated is also far from clear; Rome, or (a large city in) Asia Minor or Syria have all been suggested.[299] The earlier view that it was a Gnostic work is now generally abandoned, though occasional Gnostic-type influence is evident.[300]

The Vercelli codex begins, somewhat oddly, with Paul, preparing for his mission to Spain,[301] and sent on his way by a great multitude of women and a number of the social elite (*ActsPet.* 1-3).[302] Simon Magus then appears, introduced in the terms provided by Acts 8: 'He claims to be the great power of God, doing nothing without God' (cf. Acts 8.10). He makes a miraculous, or rather magical, appearance in Rome and is worshipped by the people, who turn against the now absent Paul, accusing him of being a sorcerer and deceiver (4). Peter, in Jerusalem, is commissioned by the Lord to go to Rome to deal with the situation, and in the course of his journey converts the ship's steersman, Theon (5). He is welcomed at Puteoli by Ariston, who had fled from Rome and from the perverting influence of Simon, as counseled by a vision of Paul, who had also commended Peter as the one who would meet the challenge posed by Simon (7). A lengthy tale follows of how Peter restored Marcellus to the faith (8-15).[303] Marcellus, a wealthy Christian, a senator of a noble family, with a wonderful reputation for philanthropy, had been won over by Simon, swayed by the latter's claim to be 'the power of God', and had become Simon's host. Peter goes to Marcellus's house and by miraculous means (including a talking dog and a talking baby) denounces Simon and renders him speechless. Simon leaves Rome.

In the buildup to the climactic confrontation of Peter with Simon, Peter recalls his earlier exposure of a fraudulent robbery in Judaea instigated by Simon (16-18), and further healing ministry by Peter at the house of Marcellus is recorded (19-21). The climax takes place in public in the presence of senators,

---

299. Schneemelcher, *NTA* 2.283; Elliott, *ANT* 392; Klauck, *Apocryphal Acts* 84.

300. *ActsPet.* 20 — "He (Jesus) ate and drank on our account though he was neither hungry nor thirsty'; 38 — Peter, crucified head down, quotes the Lord speaking in a mystery: 'Unless you make the right as the left and the left as the right, and the top as the bottom and the front as the back, you shall not know the Kingdom' (cf. *Gosp.Thom.* 22; *ActsPhil.* 140). Klauck concludes: 'the whole question of gnosis seems not to interest the author' (*Apocryphal Acts* 111).

301. During which he celebrates a eucharist of bread and water 'for the sacrifice' (2); only bread is mentioned in 5.

302. G. Poupon, 'Les "Acts de Pierre" et leur remaniement', *ANRW* II.25.26 (1988) 463-83, thinks that the references to Paul were later interpolations. See also W. Rordorf, 'The Relation between the *Acts of Peter* and the *Acts of Paul*: State of the Question', in Bremmer, *Apocryphal Acts of Peter* 178-91; also §47.4b below.

303. Klauck regards the *Acts of Peter*'s emphasis on forgiveness possible even after apostasy and failure (as also in Peter's own case) as one of its fundamental affirmations — an encouragement to those who lapsed under persecution (*Apocryphal Acts* 112).

prefects and officers (23). To Simon's dismissal of the idea that a God could be born and crucified, Peter responds with a sequence of OT prophecies (24). The deciding contest depends on whether Simon can cause a slave to die and Peter to revive him. Simon whispers in the slave's ear and he dies (25). Peter responds by raising from the dead both the slave and a widow's son (26-27). In a further challenge to restore a dead man to life Simon tries to trick the onlookers that he has done so, but the trick is exposed and Peter succeeds beyond dispute and to universal acclaim (28-29). The encounter with Simon is not ended, since Simon continues to perform many tricks and promises to ascend ('I ascend to the Father' — cf. John 20.17) and to fly over Rome (31). This he does, but Peter cries to the Lord Jesus Christ to cause Simon to fall and break his leg. This is what happens, and Simon is carried out of Rome on a stretcher to Aricia, where 'Following an operation Simon, the messenger of the devil, ended his life' (32).[304]

The martyrdom of Peter soon follows.[305] Enraged by the effect of his preaching concerning chastity on their wives and concubines, who refuse to sleep with them, the prefect Agrippa and Albinus, a friend of the emperor, plan to have Peter killed (33-34).[306] Peter, alerted to his danger, makes to leave Rome, but at the city gate he encounters the Lord coming into Rome. Peter asks the famous question, 'Quo vadis?', 'Where are you going?' To which the Lord replies, 'I go to Rome to be crucified'. Peter returns to Rome, is arrested and asks to be crucified with his head downwards, apostrophizing the cross and explaining the manner of his suspension (36-39). He dies and Marcellus takes his body down, anoints it and buries it in his own tomb — in a scene reminiscent of Jesus' deposition and burial (40). The account ends with Nero angry at being deprived of the chance to deal with Peter more severely, since Peter had converted some of his servants and alienated them from him. But a dream warned him not to persecute his servants, and they were left alone 'from the time in which Peter had died' (41).

There is little of any great historical value in this document, though it does illuminate the social world of the writing.[307] The central section on the confrontation between Peter and Simon Magus may have been drawn from

---

304. See further G. P. Luttikhuizen, 'Simon Magus as a Narrative Figure in the Acts of Peter', in Bremmer, ed., *Apocryphal Acts of Peter* 39-51.

305. The Martyrdom was circulated separately.

306. The emphasis on virginity and chastity is not so pronounced as in the *Acts of Paul* since Peter is married and remains married.

307. R. F. Stoops, 'Patronage in the Acts of Peter', in D. R. MacDonald, ed., *The Apocryphal Acts of the Apostles* 91-100. Although Justin lived for a considerable time in Rome and knew well enough the reputation of Simon in Rome (*1 Apol.* 26, 56), his silence regarding a conflict between Peter and Simon Magus is notable.

Justin's report that a statue had been erected to Simon beside the Tiber, with the inscription 'Simoni Deo Sancto' (*1 Apol.* 26.2).[308] The belief that Simon Magus, the founding father of Gnosis, had visited Rome and spread his teaching there, could have given rise to the belief or inspired the novelistic corollary that Peter, the founding apostle who had already devastatingly confronted Simon in Samaria, would have been the obvious hero to free the Roman Christians from this false teaching.[309] But there is no real attempt to refute the Gnostic teaching attributed to Simon: Simon's attempt to dismiss Jesus the Nazarene as merely 'the son of a carpenter, himself a carpenter', and to undermine standard Christian teaching, 'Is a God born? Is he crucified?' (*ActsPet.* 23), is hardly Gnostic in character.[310] And Peter's response by referring to OT prophecies (24) was no doubt meat and drink within Christian congregations but would hardly cut much ice with skeptical Romans.[311] In fact, there is hardly any theology in the *Acts of Peter*, even in Peter's final speech before and after his suspension from the cross (37-38). The central narrative is content to linger at the rather childish level of the contest between miracle and magic, content to show miracle as (of course) superior in every case. This is popular (ooh-aah!) Christianity, which assumes and builds up the reputation of Peter as a miracle-worker and develops the reverence for Peter as one of the first and most noble martyrs; but it says more about the credulity of the second-century Christians than about the developments which were shaping Christian identity and theology.[312]

c. The *Acts of John*[313]

Knowledge of the *Acts of John* is not certain before the fourth century (particularly Eusebius, *HE* 3.25.6), though their use in the Manichean Psalm Book probably takes us back into the third century. There are various hints and possible allusions to it, or to traditions on which it drew, and it may well have

---

308. See above §38 n.110. In *ActsPet.* 10 it is Marcellus who confesses that he 'erected a statue to him (Simon) with the following inscription: "To Simon, the young god"'.

309. O. Zwierlein, *Petrus in Rom: Die literarischen Zeugnisse* (UALG 96; Berlin: de Gruyter, 2009) 133.

310. The polymorphic images of Christ seen by the blind widows in *ActsPet.* 21 — an old man, a young man, a boy commended by Peter ('the Lord in different forms') — have a more Gnostic flavour than Simon's questions. See also above n.300.

311. Jesus is referred to as 'our God' (*ActsPet.* 6; also 5).

312. 'The *Acts of Peter* reflects the piety of popular Christianity rather than the thoughts of the theologians' (Stoops, *ABD* 5.268).

313. K. Schäferdiek, 'The Acts of John', *NTA* 2.152-212 (translated text 172-205); Elliott, *ANT* 303-47 (text 311-38); Klauck, *Apocryphal Acts* 15-45.

derived from the second half of or late second century.³¹⁴ Since its narrative tale focuses so much on Ephesus, an origin in the Asia province is likely.³¹⁵ As with other *Acts*, restoration of the text is difficult and uncertain. Probably two-thirds of the text has survived, but the relation of different sections (attested by different manuscripts)³¹⁶ to one another is unclear.

The imaginative narrative of the apostle John's ministry in Asia, mainly Ephesus, consists mostly of some quite elaborate accounts of John's healing powers, particularly raising the dead, with narrative twists which retain attention, and which result in conversions. The fullest of these (*ActsJohn* 62-86) lauds the chastity and purity of Drusiana, who had 'separated from her husband out of piety . . . and preferred to die rather than to commit the repugnant act' (63).³¹⁷ She dies pure, but a would-be lover, Callimachus, contrives the possibility of raping the dead Drusiana in her tomb, only to be divinely prevented, and converted. Drusiana is then raised from the dead, but the servant who had given Callimachus access to the tomb dies. Included also is an account of the miraculous collapse of the famous temple of Artemis in Ephesus, resulting in the Ephesus crowd confessing that 'the God of John is the only one' (37-44), and the amusing story of a night spent at an inn where John commands the irritating bed bugs to leave him in peace for the night, but allows them to return in the morning (60-61). The theological and ethical lessons drawn out in each case are rather ponderous.³¹⁸

d. The *Acts of Andrew*

The *Acts of Andrew* is of little value for our purposes, except insofar as the choice of 'the blessed Andrew' as the hero is probably best explained by the assumption that the brother of Peter should be given greater prominence than he had received in the earlier tradition. The *Acts of Andrew* is very typical of the apocryphal Acts in that it depicts the hero as an amazingly suc-

---

314. See further particularly Schäferdiek, *NTA* 2.152-56. P. J. Lalleman, 'The Relation between the *Acts of John* and the *Acts of Peter*', in Bremmer, ed., *Acts of Peter* 161-68, concludes tentatively that 'the author of the *APt* knew the *AJ* in roughly the same form in which we have that text' (168).

315. Schäferdiek, however, argues strongly for a Syrian provenance (*NTA* 2.166-67).

316. Summarized in Elliott, *ANT* 304; and on other stories which may have been part of an original *Acts of John* (304-5), also Klauck, *Apocryphal Acts* 39-40. See also Culpepper, *John* 187-205.

317. John also, preparing for his death, praises God that he had been preserved pure, 'free from intercourse with a woman', and separated from 'the foul madness of the flesh' — 'the repugnance of gazing upon a woman' (113).

318. On the christology see below §49.7c.

cessful exorcist, miracle-worker and rigorous advocate of sexual continence. The story revolves entirely round the effect of the conversion of Maximilla, the wife of the proconsul Aegeates: she becomes 'repulsed by sexual intercourse with him as a heinous and despicable act' (*ActsAndr.* 21) — her love is directed rather heavenward (23) — and in consequence Aegeates contrives Andrew's execution. The theology is more Platonic than Christian, indeed more Platonic than Gnostic, and though Christ is mentioned frequently, there is little which is distinctively Christian and no contact with earlier tradition to speak of. Nevertheless, the Christian clothing ensured that the *Acts of Andrew* (probably early third century in composition) was popular in Christian circles for several centuries and encouraged several sequels or additions.[319]

e. The *Acts of Thomas*

Next to John, Thomas is the figure from the first generation who does not appear much in the pre-70 period, but who features to a surprising extent in the second century, particularly the *Gospel of Thomas*, already referred to (§40.4b). So although the *Acts of Thomas* is usually dated to the (early) third century, and so falls outside the remit of this volume,[320] it adds significantly to our knowledge of the Thomas traditions, particularly in Syria.[321] It is of considerable interest for several features.

- It plays on the thought that Thomas, the twin brother of Jesus, looked very like Jesus (*ActsThom.* 11), which, as already noted,[322] suggests that perhaps the whole focus on Thomas in the Syrian tradition grew out of

---

319. They 'have left so many traces in hagiography, piety, and art . . . that we must conclude that they were very well known and widely diffused. They seem to have been for a time the most popular representative of the genre "apocryphal Acts of Apostles", especially in dualistic and ascetically-minded circles' (Klauck, *Apocryphal Acts* 114; cf. J.-M. Prieur, *NTA* 2.113-14). For the early references to *ActsAndr.* and the complex textual issues see Prieur, *NTA* 2.101-10 (text 118-51); Elliott, *ANT* 231-35, 240 (text 244-302). See also P. M. Peterson, *Andrew, Brother of Simon Peter* (NovTSupp 1; Leiden: Brill, 1963).

320. H. J. W. Drijvers, *NTA* 2.323 (text 339-405); Elliott, *ANT* 442 (text 447-511); Klauck, *Apocryphal Acts* 146.

321. J. K. Henry, 'The Acts of Thomas as Sacred Text', in Charlesworth et al., eds., *Sacra Scriptura* 152-170, argues that *ActsThom.* was highly regarded as a sacred book written to embody Christian truths, with Thomas as an authority for the gospel of Jesus as weighty as any other apostle.

322. See above nn.194, 195 and 199.

the intriguing suggestion that Judas Thomas had indeed been a twin brother of Jesus (31); the apostle was 'a man having two forms' (34).[323]
- As in the *Gospel of Thomas* Incipit and 13, Thomas is the recipient of special and secret teaching (*ActsThom.* 39; cf. 10, 47, 78).
- It was probably written in Syriac, very likely in Edessa,[324] and gives a clearer impression of early Syriac Christianity than most other early Christian writings which can be associated with Syria.
- In particular, it gives clear testimony to the Syriac baptismal ritual — first anointing with oil, then baptism in the triune name, and then eucharist (*ActsThom.* 25-27, 121, 132-33, 157-58), certainly in bread, but perhaps also in water (29, 49, 121).[325]
- It describes Thomas as commissioned to evangelize India (*ActsThom.* 1-2) and recounts his ministry entirely in India. This is the root of the tradition that Thomas was founder of the Mar Thoma Church in south India; the thin root of the tradition is strengthened by the fact that King Gundaphorus, who features in the Second Act (*ActsThom.* 17-38), is historically attested in the first century, BCE or CE.[326]
- The *Acts of Thomas* reinforces the strong impression given by the other apocryphal *Acts* that refraining from sexual relations was integral to a prevalent understanding of spirituality (Encratite) in the late second and early third century — 'filthy intercourse' (*ActsThom.* 12-15, 31, 43, 51, 88, 96-103, 117, 131, 150).[327]
- 'The Hymn of the Pearl', famous in early twentieth-century attempts to find evidence of a pre-Christian Gnostic Redeemer myth,[328] is found in only two manuscripts of *ActsThom.*, and was probably an insertion into an earlier version (*ActsThom.* 108-13).[329] But its message can hardly be

---

323. A. F. J. Klijn, *The Acts of Thomas* (NovTSupp 108; Leiden: Brill, ²2003): 'We are dealing with the idea that Jesus is able to appear in whatever body he likes' (7). *ActsThom.* 45 — the demon crying, 'What have we to do with you, apostle of the Most High?' — is no doubt intended to parallel Mark 5.7.

324. See above n.204; Koester, '*Gnomai Diaphoroi*' 128.

325. See further Klijn, *Acts of Thomas* 12-14.

326. See above nn.196-97, and further Drijvers, *NTA* 2.324-25; Klauck, *Apocryphal Acts* 144-46 — 'Thomas's grave is localized in the East Syrian city of Edessa no later than the fourth century, by Ephrem the Syrian and the pilgrim Egeria; this is reflected in the passage in ActThom 170 about the clandestine translation of the apostle's bones to the west' (145).

327. 'Epiphanius mentions the use of the ATh by encratite sects (*Haer.* [= *Pan.*] 47.1; 61.1). Yet the ATh also enjoyed great popularity in orthodox circles, as is shown by the later revisions in Latin' (Drijvers, *NTA* 2.324).

328. Cf. Rudolph, *Gnosis* 29, 122.

329. Drijvers, *NTA* 2.330-31; Elliott, *ANT* 441.

identified with any of the forms of developed Gnosticism known to us,[330] and may reflect only the disquiet of the religious individual (soul) who, having forgotten his heavenly origin as in a sleep, has been awakened by divine revelation and anticipates his restoration to heaven.[331]

f. The *Acts of Peter and the Twelve Apostles*

The *Acts of Peter and the Twelve Apostles* is a document hardly worth spending much time discussing for our purposes.[332] It is an imaginative fable or allegory[333] of Peter and the other apostles on a mysterious journey in which they encounter an oddly garbed stranger who is selling pearls, who then identifies himself as Lithargoel and subsequently as Jesus. The connecting theme, in what appears to be an amalgam of different stories,[334] is that of mission, with concern for the poor in particular. Apart from Lithargoel, Peter is the principal character, though John also features briefly. It shows little contact with NT tradition, apart from the recollection that Peter's name was given to him by Jesus Christ, and that besides Peter there were eleven original disciples. It is included in the Nag Hammadi codices, but is not distinctively Gnostic in character, though it could certainly fit comfortably into a Gnostic narrative or world view. When and where it originated is a matter of guesswork, but it is unlikely to have emerged before the middle of the third century.[335]

---

330. It reads more as a development of the parable of the prodigal son (Luke 15.11-32) than as a version of the Gnostic Redeemer myth (cf. Drijvers, *NTA* 2.330-33). 'The main theme ... is the pre-existent soul on its way from the Father to this world and its return. All this has been rendered in the form of a fairy-tale and with help of generally known Eastern and especially Parthian motives' (Klijn, *Acts of Thomas* 195).

331. 'I no longer recognized that I was a king's son ... and I fell into a deep sleep' (33-35); but receipt of a letter from the king called him to 'Awake, and rise from your sleep.... Remember you are the son of kings, You have fallen beneath the yoke of slavery' (43-44). 'I rose from sleep when I recognized its voice [the letter] ... and I immediately remembered that I was a son of kings' (53-56; cf. *ActsThom.* 39, 80). 'When I had put it [my royal robe] on I ascended to the land of peace and homage' (98). The negative attitude to this life in the rest of the *Acts* is more Encratite than Gnostic (cf. Drijvers, *NTA* 2.327-29); 'all the characteristic marks of the classic Gnostic systems are completely lacking' (33); Klauck, *Apocryphal Acts* 177-78. The christology is traditional (*ActsThom.* 47, 60, 72, 80, 143, 158).

332. D. M. Parrott and R. McL. Wilson, *NHL* 287-94; H.-M. Schenke, *NTA* 2.412-25; Klauck, *Apocryphal Acts* 181-92.

333. 'What is related appears to be half reality and half a dream, half history and half fable, half apostolic legend and half portrayal of a vision, or allegory' (Schenke, *NTA* 2.414).

334. Parrott, *NHL* 287-88.

335. The presentation of the ideal of poverty 'makes one instinctively think of the Ebionites'; and the asceticism 'recalls the Syrian itinerant ascetics' (Schenke, *NTA* 2.414). But

g. The Pseudo-Clementine Literature

The pseudo-Clementine literature is of much greater interest, despite its still later date. It consists of two documents probably originally independent of each other: the *Homilies*, which together with two letters to James, the first from Peter and the second from Clement, are known from two Greek manuscripts; and the *Recognitions*, which have survived only in the Latin translation of Rufinus; early translations of both in Syriac are also available.[336] Following an already familiar pattern (*Bildungsroman*),[337] they are novelistic accounts of Clement's conversion to Christianity, of his travels with Peter in his preaching along the Mediterranean coast, and of his success in reuniting the scattered members of his family. The writings probably originated in fourth-century Syria, but they seem to reflect or express a form of Jewish Christianity, and the possibility that they draw on earlier sources makes them more relevant to our period than would at first appear.[338]

For more than a hundred years there was a widespread agreement that a writing which could be entitled the *Kerygmata Petrou* was a (determinative) source or *Grundschrift* for the pseudo-Clementines.[339] But the hypothesis has come under increasing pressure in more recent decades and has lost its earlier support.[340] The more likely *Grundschrift*, indicated by passages in *Homilies*

Klauck appositely notes that 'one can also very well envisage the use of ActPaul12 in a Coptic monastery of monks as an introduction to the contemplative life, which brings healing for body and soul' (*Apocryphal Acts* 184).

336. Introductions in *NTA* 2.483-93 (G. Strecker); Klauck, *Apocryphal Acts* 193-229. The full texts are available in ANF 8.77-346; *NTA* 2.504-30 includes the introductory letters and extracts of the main documents.

337. Strecker, *NTA* 2.484; Klauck, *Apocryphal Acts* 198-99.

338. They played a significant role in Baur's reconstruction of early Christianity and have remained a subject of considerable debate for the last century. See F. S. Jones, 'The Pseudo-Clementines: A History of Research', *Second Century* 2 (1982) 1-33, 63-96; also *An Ancient Jewish Christian Source on the History of Christianity: Pseudo-Clementine Recognitions 1.27-71* (Atlanta: Scholars, 1995) 4-38; and summary article in *ABD* 1.1061-62.

339. See particularly G. Strecker, *Das Judenchristentum in den Pseudoklementinen* (Berlin: Akademie, 1981); also 'On the Problem of Jewish Christianity', in ET of Bauer, *Orthodoxy and Heresy* 241-85 (here 257-71). For the reconstructed *Kerygmata*, see J. Irmscher and G. Strecker, *NTA* 2.488-92, 531-41. Wilson takes Strecker's thesis as his working assumption (*Related Strangers* 150-52).

340. G. Lüdemann, *Opposition to Paul in Jewish Christianity* (ET Minneapolis: Fortress, 1989), observes that 'Strecker's pioneering attempt is burdened with the difficulty that he reconstructs a source used by a document that itself must be reconstructed as a source of our existing documents' (he notes that 'In NT scholarship, this would be analogous to reconstructing a source of Q'). He adds that 'Strecker himself emphasizes that no definite stylistic features of the *Kerygmata Petrou* are identifiable', and draws the conclusion

and *Recognitions* in close verbal agreement, has been identified with Origen's references to a work entitled *Periodoi Petrou, Circuits of Peter*, which can be dated to the early third century.[341] In some ways more interesting is the source used by *Recognitions*, probably *Recognitions* 1.27-71, preserved in Latin and Syriac, and partially in Armenian.[342] Possibly it should be identified with the *Anabathmoi Jacobou* which Epiphanius regarded as an Ebionite work (*Pan.* 30.16.6),[343] but even if that link is by no means certain, *Recog.* 1.27-71 certainly seems to put forward views which can be readily identified as distinctive of Jewish believers in Jesus.

40.7 Other Apocalypses

As we have seen, collections of NT apocrypha mirror to a substantial effect the pattern of the NT writings — Gospels, Epistles, Acts.[344] Indeed, since most of the writings considered in §40.4-6 were first composed before the idea of a NT canon was established, and before its content was resolved, the fact that the range of early apocrypha does mirror the content of the NT is itself an attestation of how influential, and in effect already esteemed as authoritative, were the writings which came to make up the NT.

Even more compelling as a precedent, however, was the format of apocalypse. Although the NT ended up containing only one apocalypse (Revelation), the eschatological character of earliest Christianity, with its conviction that the end-time resurrection of the dead and outpouring of the Spirit had

---

that 'the *Kerygmata Petrou* has lost its claim to the designation "source"' (169-70). Jones similarly concludes that the hypothesis of the *Kerygmata Petrou* as a source for the pseudo-Clementines should now be abandoned (*Ancient Jewish Christian Source* xii). In the view of G. N. Stanton, 'Jewish Christian Elements in the Pseudo-Clementine Writings', in Skarsaune and Hvalvik, eds., *Jewish Believers in Jesus* 305-24, 'The alleged *Kerygmata Petrou* as an early Jewish Christian source of the *Grundschrift* seems to be disappearing into thin air' (312).

341. See F. S. Jones, 'Jewish Christianity of the *Pseudo-Clementines*', in Marjanen and Luomanen, eds., *Companion* 315-34.

342. As argued by Jones, who dates it to about 200 CE (*Ancient Jewish Christian Source* 163), composed in the name of Matthew (155).

343. The *Anabathmoi Jacobou* was the other source (the Ebionite Acts of the Apostles), identified by H.-J. Schoeps, *Theologie und Geschichte des Judenchristentums* (Tübingen, 1949) (Luedemann, *Opposition to Paul* 21). See now particularly R. E. Van Voorst, *The Ascents of James: History and Theology of a Jewish-Christian Community* (SBLDS 112; Atlanta: Scholars, 1989). The identification is disputed by Jones, *Ancient Jewish Christian Source* 146-48.

344. If we included a category of prophecy we would have to refer to Montanism, but will return to the Montanists in §49.8 below.

already begun, and its strong belief in the future (imminent) coming (again) of Christ from heaven in judgment, ensured that apocalyptic would be an appropriate genre in which the tensions of these eschatological hopes could be worked out. All the more so since apocalypses had become such an established genre within Second Temple Judaism, especially in the context of the crises caused by Antiochus Epiphanes (Daniel) and Roman conquest (*4 Ezra*, *2 Baruch*).[345]

A particular feature of the second-century eschatological reflections and hopes for the future was chiliasm or millennialism, the belief that Christ on his return would reign for a thousand years with the saints raised from the dead (Rev. 20.4-6). Those who believed and hoped for a literal thousand years reign on earth included a notable array of second-century protagonists. Papias was evidently well known for his millenarian beliefs, as attested explicitly by Eusebius (*HE* 3.39.12); Irenaeus attributes to him, as teaching of the Lord himself, that the days to come would be a period of miraculous fruitfulness (*adv. haer.* 5.33.3), quite possibly influenced by the similar hopes which would follow from the revelation of the Anointed One (*2 Bar.* 29.5-8). According to Eusebius also, it was believed by Gaius, a presbyter of Rome, and by Dionysius, bishop of Corinth, that Cerinthus had shared chiliastic views, based on Rev. 20, and that the kingdom of Christ on earth would be characterized by carnal pleasure (*HE* 3.28.2-5; 7.25.3), which made Eusebius dubious about the Apocalypse of John. Justin also believed that Christ would spend a thousand years in Jerusalem (*Dial.* 81.4), and Tertullian had a similar conviction which he shared with or drew from the new prophecy (Montanism) (*adv. Marc.* 3.25).

Here I will note only the most relevant examples of the second-century Christian apocalypses.[346]

a. The *First Apocalypse of James*

The *First Apocalypse of James* was found among the Nag Hammadi manuscripts, in Codex *NHL* V.3.[347] Since then another copy has been found in the Codex Tchacos, along with the *Gospel of Judas* and the *Letter of Peter to Philip*. It is an example of a 'revelation dialogue', James in dialogue with the Lord,[348] though the subject matter is remote from earliest Christian and

---

345. Wilson also considers *3 Baruch*, though its status as Jewish or Christian is far from clear (*Related Strangers* 98-99).

346. For the Christian interpolated *Ascension of Isaiah*, whose beginnings may be dated to the end of the first century, see below §45.6.

347. W. R. Schoedel, *NHL* 260-68.

348. Is this the tradition which Clement of Alexandria drew on in his *Hypotyposes*:

Jewish Christian subjects and is fairly typically Gnostic in character. Indeed, James addresses Jesus as the Gnostic redeemer:

> You have come with knowledge, that you might rebuke their forgetfulness. . . . For you descended into a great ignorance, but you have not been defiled by anything in it. . . . You walked in mud, and your garments were not soiled, and you have not been buried in their filth (28.7-19).

In Gnostic fashion, James is provided with the answers he should give to the alien powers which will attempt to block his return to the pre-existent Father (32.28–36.1).

b. The *Second Apocalypse of James*

The *Second Apocalypse of James,* in Codex *NHL* V.4,[349] introduces itself as a 'discourse that James the Just spoke in Jerusalem', in effect a revelation received by James from the risen Christ. It contains a curious blend of earliest Christian motifs and Gnostic themes: Jesus identifies himself as 'the first [son] who was begotten' (49.5-6); and the encouragement is given, 'Just as you are first having clothed yourself, you are also the first who will strip himself, and you shall become as you were before you were stripped' (56.7-13; cf. *Gosp. Thom.* 21, 37).

c. The *Apocalypse of Paul*

The *Apocalypse of Paul*[350] was inspired by one of the lacunae in the history of Paul — his account of his being taken up to the third heaven and hearing 'unspeakable words' (2 Cor. 12.1-5). The *Apocalypse* purports to fill the gap. The visions describe the heaven of the just (20-30) and the hell reserved for sinners, including ecclesiastics (34-36) and those 'who in church disparage the Word of God' (37); also, for example, those 'who broke their fast before the appointed hour' (39) and those who did not confess that Christ came in the flesh or that the Eucharistic bread and wine are the body and blood of Christ (41). Together with the *Apocalypse of Peter,* the *Apocalypse of Paul* was

---

'After the resurrection the Lord gave the tradition of knowledge to James the Just and John and Peter' (Eusebius, *HE* 2.1.4; see more fully §45.2b below)?
349. C. W. Hedrick and D. M. Parrott, *NHL* 269-76.
350. H. Duensing and A. de Santos Otero, *NTA* 2.712-48; Elliott, *ANT* 616-44.

responsible for the fascination which popular ideas of heaven and especially hell exercised on mediaeval Christianity, particularly in the West.[351]

d. The Coptic *Apocalypse of Paul*

The Coptic *Apocalypse of Paul* (NHL V.2)[352] also offers an account of Paul's heavenly journey (to the ninth heaven), and as such is a more traditional apocalypse since the heavenly journey reveals the mysteries of the heavens. The echo of Gal. 1.15 (18.15-16) marks the esteem in which Paul was held, but it also portrays 'the old man' (of Dan. 7.13) as trying to block Paul's access to the seventh heaven and to the Ogdoad. Again there is no link between the two *Apocalypses*, but it should not escape notice that representatives both of the great church and of Gnostic Christianity saw it as necessary to present both Peter and Paul as spokesmen of their views.

e. The *Apocalypse of Peter*

The *Apocalypse of Peter*[353] was the best known of the apocryphal apocalypses in the early centuries of Christianity. The Muratorian fragment/ canon includes the *Apocalypse of Peter*, but notes that 'some of us will not allow [it] to be read in church'; and Eusebius dismisses it as unknown in Catholic tradition and not genuine (*HE* 3.3.2; 3.25.4). However, inserted in Codex Claromontanus (fifth or sixth century) there is a stichometric[354] catalogue of OT and NT canons, of uncertain date, the latter of which includes the *Epistle of Barnabas*, the *Shepherd* of Hermas, the *Acts of Paul* and the *Apocalypse of Peter*. So it was evidently of quite widespread use and popularity.[355]

---

351. Cf. Elliott, *ANT* 616.

352. See W.-P. Funk, *NTA* 2.695-700; G. W. MacRae and W. R. Murdock, *NHL* 256-59; N. Perrin, 'Paul and Valentinian Interpretation', in Bird and Dodson, eds., *Paul and the Second Century* 126-39 (here 137-39).

353. D. G. Müller, *NTA* 2.620-38; Elliott, *ANT* 593-612; J. N. Bremmer and I. Czachesz, eds., *The Apocalypse of Peter* (Leuven: Peeters, 2003). See particularly R. Bauckham, 'The Apocalypse of Peter: A Jewish Christian Apocalypse from the Time of Bar Kokhba', *The Fate of the Dead: Studies on the Jewish and Christian Apocalypses* (Leiden: Brill, 1998) 160-258.

354. 'Stichometry' is the measurement (*metron*) of ancient texts by the number of *stichoi* ('rows') or verses of a fixed standard length.

355. The *Apocalypse of Peter* is quoted by several patristic writings, including Clement of Alexandria; see Elliott, *ANT* 598-600; Bauckham, 'Apocalypse of Peter' 256. But A. Jakab, 'The Reception of the *Apocalypse of Peter* in Ancient Christianity', in Bremmer and

Portions of the *Apocalypse of Peter* are known in Greek, particularly as part of the Akhmim manuscript[356] which also contained a fragment of the *Gospel of Peter*.[357] But there is an Ethiopic version of the complete text in an Ethiopic version of the pseudo-Clementine literature.[358] The possibility that the *Apocalypse* is older than the *Gospel* and the fact that Clement of Alexandria knew the *Apocalypse* suggest a date before 150 CE.[359]

The *Apocalypse of Peter* establishes the sense which the term 'apocalyptic' came to assume. Initially it denoted only revelation of heavenly mysteries, including the workings of the cosmos. But with the *Apocalypse of Peter* 'apocalyptic' becomes a term for the horrors and blessings of the final judgment. This *Apocalypse*, in particular, with its detailed description of the different types of sinner (twenty-one in all) and their different punishments (3-13), seems to relish, in its sequence of vivid sketches, the (usually) fiery anguish to which sinners will be condemned. In contrast, the destiny of the elect is mentioned only briefly (6.4; 13.1; 14.1-3). Dante's *Inferno* almost certainly was influenced by this *Apocalypse*, in its sequencing of punishments matching sins, though not in his description of heaven (cf. *ActsThom.* 55-57).

f. The Coptic *Apocalypse of Peter*

The Coptic *Apocalypse of Peter*[360] has nothing to do with the *Apocalypse of Peter* above (§40.7e). It is part of codex 7 of the Nag Hammadi documents (*NHL* VII.3). As a 'revelation' given to Peter 'in secret/in a mystery' it has more the character of visions which unveil the mystery of the human condition than of an eschatological apocalypse like its namesake. It is of interest for two main reasons. One is its polemical character, warning against those who 'are blind and have no leader' (72.10-13; 73.12-14), represented by the priests of the traditional Jesus story. This includes a swipe at the great church, since 'those outside our/your number . . . are called "bishop" and "deacon"'

Czachesz, eds., *Apocalypse of Peter* 174-86, concludes that it was not 'a very popular work', and was only known in some parts of ancient Christianity (184).

356. See P. van Minnen, 'The Greek Apocalypse of Peter', in Bremmer and Czachesz, eds., *Apocalypse of Peter* 15-39.

357. See above n.238.

358. For the relation of the two versions see Müller, *NTA* 2.623-25.

359. Müller, *NTA* 2.622; Elliott, *ANT* 595. Bauckham argues strongly that the warnings against false Messiahs in *Apoc. Pet.* 1-2 had Bar Kokhba in view ('Apocalypse of Peter' 176-94).

360. J. Brashler and R. A. Bullard, *NHL* 372-78; A. Werner, *NTA* 2.700-712.

(79.22-26); and 'a wicked deceiver' (74.19) could conceivably be an echo of the condemnation of Paul in the pseudo-Clementine literature.[361] But the polemic could also be directed against other Gnostic groups.[362] The other noteworthy feature is the classic Gnostic interpretation of the crucifixion of Jesus where 'the living Jesus' watches his fleshly likeness nailed to the tree, laughing at the blindness of those around (81.15-23; 82.21–83.6).[363] Otherwise it is a modest expression of Gnostic anthropology.

g. The *Apocalypse of Thomas*

Other apocalypses confirm that the apocalyptic genre continued to fascinate both Jewish and Christian attention during the first centuries of the Christian era,[364] as indeed thereafter.[365] Of these the only one of interest for us is the *Apocalypse of Thomas* (before the 5th century?).[366] The interest lies partly in the degree to which it is modeled on the Apocalypse of John (Revelation), in that it apportions the End events into seven days, presumably following the pattern of sevens (seven seals, seven trumpets, seven bowls) in Rev. 5-8, 16, thus making the End form an inclusio with the Beginning (seven-day creation). Why it was attributed to Thomas is not at all clear, though the fact that it is suggests that, like the other early leaders and apostles (James, Paul, Peter, John), Thomas was known as a source or medium of secret teaching from Jesus (the early version begins with the Son of God addressing Thomas). That the *Apocalypse* seems to have been valued in Manichean and Priscillianist circles, both evolving in the late fourth century from the earlier broader streams of Gnostic thought, provides some confirmation for the view that Thomas was particularly revered within these broader streams, as indicated also by the *Gospel of Thomas*, the *Acts of Thomas* and the *Book of Thomas the Contender*.

---

361. See below §45 at n.31, and §47 at n.154.
362. Brashler, *NHL* 372; Werner, *NTA* 2.703, who notes that 74.27-34 may have Simon Magus in view.
363. See also G. P. Luttikhuizen, 'The Suffering Jesus and the Invulnerable Christ in the Gnostic *Apocalypse of Peter*', in Bremmer and Czachesz, *Apocalypse of Peter* 187-99.
364. See e.g. Elliott, *ANT* 682-87.
365. See e.g. N. Cohn, *The Pursuit of the Millennium* (Secker & Warburg, 1957); Hagner, *New Testament* 752-55.
366. A. de Santos Otero, *NTA* 2.748-52; Elliott, *ANT* 645-51.

40.8 Summary

In sum, the literary data from the second century illustrate two features of early Christianity.

In the first place, the fact that Gospels, letters, Acts and apocalypses became such dominant and widespread expressions of Christianity surely provides some and substantial confirmation that they were modeled on primary or exemplary versions of these genres. The fact that all four genres are included in the New Testament presumably indicates that these were the documents which provided the model for the further examples which followed. And the fact that just these primary documents made it into the New Testament, the fact that they were or came to be especially prized, presumably indicates, inter alia, that these were the documents which came to be widely esteemed as the models which inspired the subsequent literature.

Second, as a whole, the spin-off literature is much poorer in quality than what became acknowledged as the canonical literature — the poorer, properly second-rate quality of most of the literature reviewed above providing an interesting confirmation that the early church was right to acknowledge the canonical status and value of (almost all) the documents which make up the New Testament. The specific exception of the *Gospel of Thomas* will require closer examination (§43), but for the most part what we might call the sub-canonical value of the literature reviewed above (§§40.4-7) simply confirms that the canonizing *Tendenz* of early Christianity was well founded. The very fact that several of the Apostolic Fathers and Apologists can easily be ranked in value above almost all of the literature reviewed in §§40.4-7 is probably proof enough that those who agreed on the contents of the New Testament canon agreed wisely and well.

So, having now provided a basic introduction to more or less all the material with which we will have to deal in the rest of this volume, we proceed, as indicated in §38.5, by considering particularly how the four principal features of Christianity's founding generation shaped up and provided focal motifs and influences in the post-70 period and second century. The objective is not to write a history of Christianity's beginnings, but simply to examine the factors and primary influences which gave early Christianity its distinctive character.

For most of the writings, provenance is a matter of some guesswork; for almost all of those known only from the Nag Hammadi cache, places of origin are unknown. But even if the guesswork is flawed, the likely spread of the sources of the literature probably overall gives a fair idea of what were the major centres of influence in the first three centuries of Christianity's development.

	Rome	Asia	Syria	Palestine	Alexandria
65-75	Mark				
75-85			Luke	James	
85-90			Matthew		
90	Hebrews 1 Peter	Pastorals Revelation		Jude	
95-100	*1 Clement*	John			
100-110		1-3 John			
110		Ignatius	*Didache*		
110-120	2 Peter	Polycarp	*Odes Sol.*		
130		Papias			*Barnabas*
130-150	Hermas *2 Clement*				
150-160		*Mart.Polyc.*	Tatian *Gosp. Thom.*		*Ep.Apost?*
160	Justin		*Gosp. Peter*		
170-180		*Acts Paul* *Acts Peter* *Acts John*	Theophilus		
180		Melito			
190	(Irenaeus)				
200					*Secret Mark?*

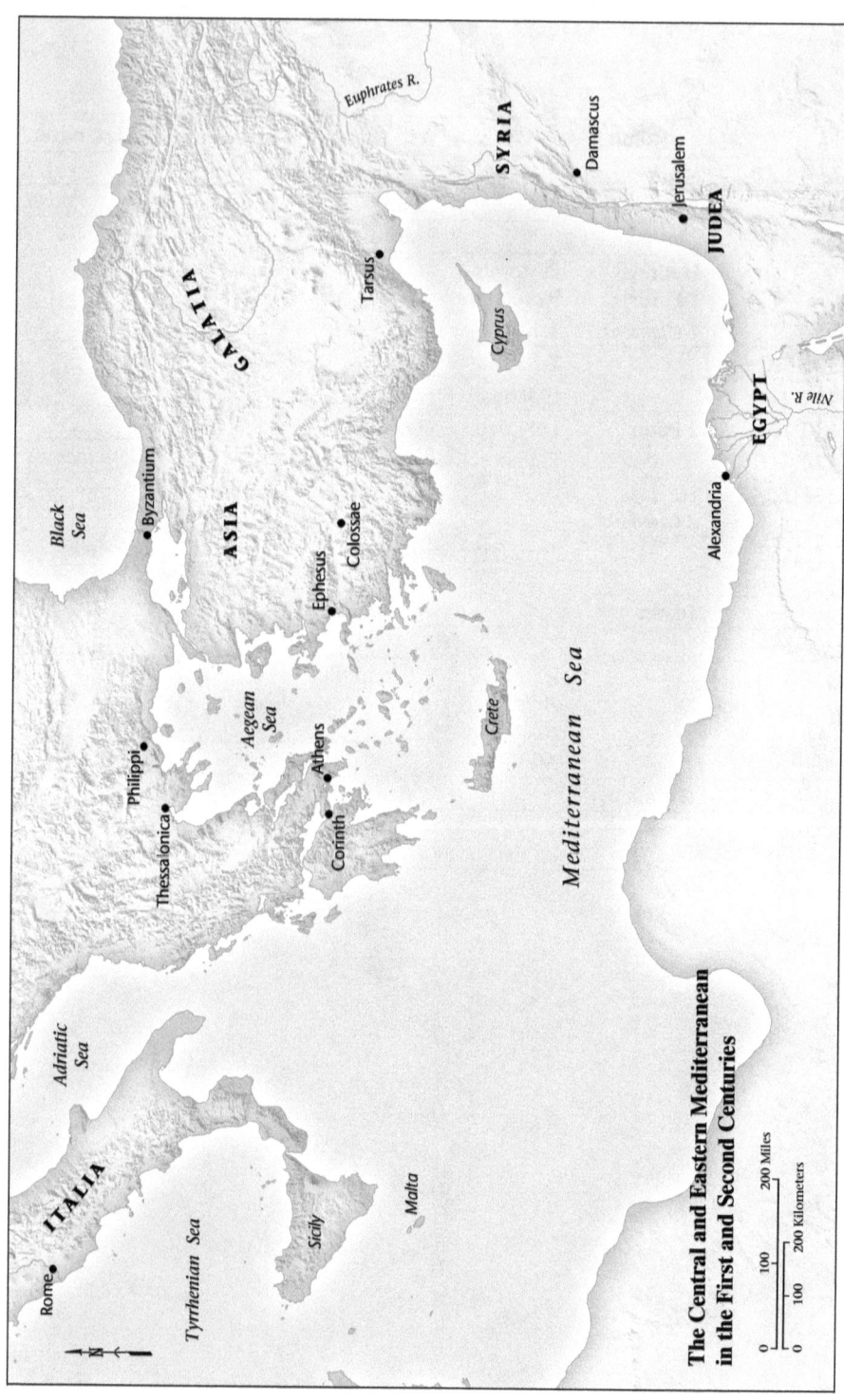

The Central and Eastern Mediterranean in the First and Second Centuries

PART ELEVEN

JESUS STILL REMEMBERED

Following the programme outlined in §38.5, we begin to look at the major factors which emerged from our study of first-generation Christianity. The developments in regard to each do not tell the whole story of late first-century and second-century Christianity, but they help bring out the distinctives of the still new movement. And since they were the principal features of the 'apostolic age' of the movement which became known as 'Christianity', their outworking and development in the second century tell us much as to whether these developments were true to the original impulses or were diversions from 'first (defining?) principles', or indeed were intrusions of alternative, perhaps even alien, analyses of and answers to the human condition.

The first distinctive feature which shaped first-generation Christianity was the Jesus tradition. An initially fascinating feature is the way in which it became integral to the good news which was so much at the heart of first-generation Christianity (§41). The fact that this 'good news' was formulated not just in one format but in three Gospels, the same yet different in content and emphases, is one of the most fascinating features of the final decades of the first century (§42). Even more fascinating is the fact that the two most prominent Gospels to emerge thereafter were so different in character (John and *Thomas*), raising serious questions as to whether the 'gospel' as defined by Paul and Mark was so definitive of Christianity, and whether 'gospel' was a cistern pouring out what had been the original impact made by Jesus or (at the same time) absorbing distinctively new elements and other (contrasting) features (§43). The story through the second century displays similar tensions: particularly the questions, When was the oral Jesus tradition in effect replaced by reliance on written Gospels? How serious contenders were the other Gospels and quasi-Gospels which emerged in this period? How soon did the four-Gospel canon in effect emerge? The picture at the end of our period may be clear (Irenaeus), but was he simply confirming and consolidating a trend which had run through the second century, or did he mark a new, defining development which effectively shaped Christianity's evaluation of its sacred writings thereafter (§44)?

CHAPTER 41

From gospel to Gospel

The impact made by Jesus was the primary formative influence in the making of Christianity. That impact is reflected in the traditions about Jesus which were used to compose the Gospels. And particularly from the impression which Jesus left in the Synoptic tradition, Jesus as he was remembered in the first three Gospels of the New Testament, we can discern the character of the man and the mission which left that impression. That was the main thrust of *Jesus Remembered*. In *Beginning from Jerusalem* the focus was not at all so tightly on the Jesus tradition, but the working assumption continued to be, and was briefly elaborated, that celebration and circulation of the Jesus tradition was an ongoing concern of the first Christians (§21.5). The impact made by Jesus, conveyed through the Jesus tradition, continued to shape the messianic Jesus movement as it expanded beyond Israel/Palestine. Now we have to ask what happened to that Jesus tradition beyond the first generation of the new movement which soon came to be referred to as 'Christianity'. Did it continue to make an impact? How did it continue to shape or at least to contribute to Christianity-in-the-making into and through the second century?

One of the major developments which spanned from the first generation into the subsequent generations of emerging Christianity was the transition from the gospel as preached by Peter, James and Paul, to the Gospels themselves. This indeed could be said to be the most important of the developments — the establishment of the Gospel, the written document, its content and character. There are two aspects to be examined here — the transition from gospel to Gospel and the transition from oral Jesus tradition to written form. Since the transition (both aspects) took place either at the close of the first generation (just before 70) or close to the beginning of the second generation (just after 70),[1] this development commands first attention as we begin to trace these various developments which took Christianity from embryonic status to full birth.

41.1 The gospel before the Gospel

The noun 'gospel, good news' (*euangelion*) is one of several terms which Christianity owes to Paul; 60 of its 76 occurrences in the NT appear in the Pauline corpus.[2] We have already noted that Paul's introduction of this term into Christian vocabulary was unlikely to be the result of his primarily opposing his 'good news' to the *euangelion* (or more likely *euangelia*) of Caesar, even though Paul was probably aware that such an inference could be drawn.[3] More likely he was influenced by the OT use of *bsr* to speak of the bringing of good news,[4] especially of God's saving deeds,[5] and especially as used by Isaiah.[6] Two of these Isaiah passages were evidently influential in the Jewish theological reflection in Second Temple Judaism prior to Jesus and Paul. *Pss. Sol.* 11.1 clearly echoes Isa. 52.7;[7] and 11QMelch 2.15-24 makes explicit exposition of Isa. 52.7, applying it to the

---

1. See above §39.2.

2. 'Most frequently he uses the term without a genitive as a technical term for both the action of the proclamation and for the content of the message. He presupposes that the content is understood and requires no further definition or explication. This use of the word in the absolute sense reflects a distinctively Christian development' (Koester, *Ancient Christian Gospels* 5).

3. See *Beginning from Jerusalem* §29.4d, and particularly P. Stuhlmacher, *Das paulinische Evangelium* (Göttingen: Vandenhoeck, 1968). 'In profane Greek usage . . . the plural is by far the more dominant' (Hengel, *Four Gospels* 3).

4. The substantive *bᵉsôrâ* is used in the sense of 'good tidings' (2 Kgs. 7.9), but also less specifically as 'tidings, news' (2 Sam. 18.20, 25; with the adjective 'good' in 18.27), and in the sense 'reward for good tidings' (2 Sam. 4.10; 18.22) (BDB 142-43); see further Stuhlmacher, *Evangelium* 112-13, 124-35 (Targums and rabbinic tradition). In LXX only the plural of *euangelion* is used (2 Kgdms. [= 2 Sam.] 4.10; 18.22, 25), but also the feminine form *euangelia*, 'good news' (2 Kgdms. [= 2 Sam.] 18.20, 27; 4 Kgdms. [= 2 Kgs.] 7.9). See further Stuhlmacher, *Evangelium* 154-64; W. Horbury, '"Gospel" in Herodian Judaea', in M. Bockmuehl and D. A. Hagner, eds., *The Written Gospel*; G. N. Stanton FS (Cambridge University, 2005) 7-30.

5. Pss. 40.9; 68.11; 96.2; also 2 Sam. 18.31.

6. Isa. 40.9; 41.27; 52.7; 60.6; 61.1; similarly Nah. 1.15. See further O. Schilling, *TDOT* 2.313-16.

7. Isa. 52.7 — 'How beautiful upon the mountains are the feet of the messenger who announces (*euangelizomenou*) peace, who brings good news (*euangelizomenos agatha*), who announces salvation, who says to Zion, "Your God reigns"'.

Pss. Sol. 11.1 — 'Sound in Zion the signal trumpet of the sanctuary; announce in Jerusalem the voice of one bringing good news (*euangelizomenou*)'.

sect's own situation. Of the various allusions to Isa. 61.1 in the Qumran scrolls, the same 11QMelch passage also draws on Isa. 61.1-3; and in a remarkable parallel to Matt. 11.5/Luke 7.22, 4Q521 draws similarly on Isa. 61.1, in expectation of God's messiah who will preach good news to the poor.[8] It is no surprise, then, that Jesus was remembered as similarly seeing in Isa. 61.1-2 ('to bring good news [*euangelisasthai*] to the poor') a foreshadowing of his own ministry.[9] Nor should it cause any surprise that Paul quoted Isa. 52.7 in a passage explaining his understanding of the gospel commission (Rom. 10.15).[10] But it does greatly increase the probability that Paul made a deliberate choice to use the term *euangelion* to characterize his message, precisely because he believed the hope of one who would preach good news (*euangelizomenos*) to the poor had been realized in Jesus, a claim which was recalled as having been made by Jesus himself (Luke 4.16-21). In short, our evidence strongly suggests that it was Paul himself who introduced into Christian vocabulary the noun form of the term familiar to him both from Isaiah[11] and from the Jesus tradition.[12]

The issue, however, is whether this early use of 'gospel' included the Jesus tradition itself. When did *the Jesus tradition* become 'gospel'? The issue is posed since, as we shall see, it seems to have been Mark who introduced the noun *euangelion* into the Jesus tradition. Apart from the possible exception of Mark 14.9, there are no indications that Jesus himself used an equivalent Aramaic form.[13] The term *euangelion* as such never appears in the Q material within the Jesus tradition.

Paul himself usually speaks of the 'gospel' without specifying its content. It is 'the gospel of God',[14] and, more commonly, 'the gospel of Christ'.[15] This

---

8. See further my *Theology of Paul* 168 n.22.

9. See *Jesus Remembered* 448-49, 516-17, 662. Pokorny notes that the message of Isa. 52.7, 'Your God reigns', 'is an analogy to Jesus' proclamation of the coming kingdom of God' (*Gospel* 51-56).

10. See further *Theology of Paul* 164-69.

11. That Paul was himself heavily influenced by Isaiah is well known; see e.g. J. R. Wagner, *Heralds of the Good News: Isaiah and Paul in Concert in the Letter to the Romans* (Leiden: Brill, 2002).

12. Pokorny thinks that the term was probably used before Paul (*Gospel* ch. 2), but the term itself is not part of pre-Pauline formulae which he examines (Rom. 1.3-4; 1 Cor. 15.3-5; 1 Thess. 1.9-10), though Paul certainly used the term to refer to the formulae (Rom. 1.1; 1 Cor. 15.1; 1 Thess. 1.5).

13. The studies of Stuhlmacher and Horbury (n.4 above) make it probable that the substantive 'good news' was already used in Herodian Judaea, but there is no evidence that Jesus himself used the noun, and the evidence from Mark (§41.2 below) strongly suggests that *euangelion* was a Markan insertion into the Jesus tradition.

14. Rom. 1.1; 15.16; 2 Cor. 11.7; 1 Thess. 2.2, 8, 9; also 1 Pet. 4.17.

15. Rom. 1.9; 15.19; 1 Cor. 9.12; 2 Cor. 2.12; 9.13; 10.14; Gal. 1.7; Phil. 1.27; 1 Thess. 3.2; 2 Thess. 1.8.

latter phrase probably means 'the good news about Christ', including his Davidic descent (Rom. 1.1-3; 2 Tim. 2.8), his glory (2 Cor. 4.4), and particularly his death and resurrection.[16] And especially in Galatians Paul vigorously defended his gospel as good news also for Gentiles.[17] Does this imply that Paul did *not* think of the Jesus tradition as 'gospel' but limited the use of the term to the acts of Jesus decisive for salvation, particularly his death and resurrection? Such was a much favoured conclusion at the end of the nineteenth century: that Paul had turned the message *of* Jesus into a message *about* Jesus; that the good tidings of Jesus' proclamation of the kingdom had been transformed into a message of redemption from sin.

However, even if Paul did focus his gospel on the good news of Jesus' death and resurrection, that should not mislead us into thinking that he excluded the tradition of Jesus' life and mission from 'the good news about Christ'.

- As already suggested, Paul's use of *euangelion* probably implies his awareness of *Jesus'* use of Isa. 61.1-2 in self-reference to refer to his own mission. It is hardly likely, then, that it would even have occurred to Paul to bracket out the tradition of Jesus' own mission from the gospel he (Paul) preached.
- The good news about Jesus must have included some narrative explaining of who Jesus was and recounting something at least of the character of what he had said and done during his mission. The gospel which converted so many Gentiles could hardly have been simply that an unidentified X had died and been raised from the dead. As pointed out earlier, since new believers in Paul's gospel were coming to be called 'Christians', baptized 'in the name of Christ', that would inevitably have prompted them to ask more about this 'Christ',[18] not least so that they could give an answer to any questions as to why they had changed their lives and now based them on this 'Christ'.
- We also have already seen that Paul must have conveyed a good deal of Jesus tradition to the churches he founded — his allusions to the Jesus tradition in his exhortations presuppose a web of knowledge of Jesus' teaching, no doubt set reverberating for many or most of his audiences by such allusions.[19]

16. Rom. 1.4; 1 Cor. 1.23; 15.1-5; Gal. 3.1.
17. Gal. 1.6, 7, 11; 2.2, 5, 7, 14; also Rom. 1.16; 15.16; Eph. 3.6.
18. *Beginning from Jerusalem* 574-75, 649-51.
19. What J. M. Foley, *The Singer of Tales in Performance* (Bloomington: Indiana University Press, 1995), chs. 1–3, calls the "metonymic reference" of a performance which enables the performer to use a whole sequence of allusions to the community's store of tradition and enables the community thus to recognize the consistency of the performance

§41.1   *From gospel to Gospel*

- Apart from anything else, various tracts of the Jesus tradition must have been known round the earliest churches. We can hardly assume that the tradition known as Q or the traditions on which Mark drew[20] were submerged for forty years, or remembered and cherished only by a very small band of original disciples (apostles). As we will see in §42, it is entirely probable that the various groups of teaching materials which make up Q included or formed the repertoires for many church teachers, and that Mark was evidently able to draw on blocks of stories told about Jesus and blocks of Jesus' teaching. It is not credible that these materials were regarded as sharply distinct from the gospel that Paul and others preached. To make such a case is to argue *e silentio* and to ignore basic historical probabilities. Subsequent early references to the 'gospel' as a teaching tool strengthen this probability.[21]
- Worth recalling is the fact that the earliest memories of Jesus seem to have included an element of narrative structure,[22] beginning with John the Baptist, taking in Jesus' mission and message, and climaxing in his death and resurrection. In Acts 10.36-40 this whole narrative seems to be summed up as 'the word (*logos*) which God sent to the sons of Israel preaching the good news (*euangelizomenos*) of peace through Jesus Christ' (10.36).[23] It is hardly likely that such usage was strange to Paul. Indeed, since Paul's formulation of the Christian message as 'gospel' took place during the period while the Jesus tradition was still predominantly in oral form, and since the Acts 10 tradition also harks back to the period of oral tradition, we may infer that *the shaping of the Jesus tradition as 'gospel',* and in the shape that Mark was to provide (or consolidate) (§41.2), *was already taking place during that period when the Jesus tradition was still being told in oral form.* So long as we avoid the unjustified and misleading impression that the Jesus tradition existed orally only in fragmentary aphoristic forms or small collections of teaching material or of stories about Jesus,[24] then it becomes entirely plausible that

---

with the whole. Good examples would include Rom. 6.17; 15.3; and Col. 2.6; see further my *Theology of Paul* §8.3. Cf. Pokorny, *Gospel* 60-65; but, *pace* Pokorny 67, there is no evidence that Paul did not quote sayings of Jesus because he was afraid of their misinterpretation.

20. See again *Beginning from Jerusalem* §21.5d.

21. Cf. *Did.* 8.2; Ignatius, *Philad.* 8.2; *Mart. Poly.* 4. We could perhaps compare (and question) the distinction between 'preaching' and 'teaching' in mid-twentieth-century discussion; see further J. I. H. McDonald, *Kerygma and Didache* (SNTSMS 37; Cambridge University, 1980).

22. See also my *A New Perspective on Jesus* 124 and n.93.

23. See further my *Beginning in Jerusalem* §21.3c.

24. One of the key mistakes made by the Jesus Seminar; see *Jesus Remembered* 245-48.

the earliest tradents regularly retold the Jesus tradition conscious of the gospel shape of the material as a whole and often providing mini-Gospel presentations, as are still evident in the Acts 10 tradition, perhaps also in Mark 2.1–3.6, as well as in the passion narrative.[25]

In short, if, as seems most probable, a body of Jesus tradition was part of the message which Paul delivered to his converts, part of the foundation on which he sought to build his churches, it most naturally follows that Paul and his converts would have seen such material as at least complementary to the gospel, if not itself integral to the gospel.[26] We need not argue over terms used, but it is most likely that Paul thought of the information about Jesus and the passing on of the teaching of Jesus as integral to the process by which he became father of many new children 'through the gospel' (1 Cor. 4.15).

The importance of what Paul did and of the influence which he exercised in summarizing his message as 'gospel' was not that he excluded the traditions of Jesus' mission and teaching from the gospel, but that he centred the decisive gospel significance of Jesus' mission on his death and resurrection. It was Mark's Gospel which took the next logical step of giving the title 'Gospel' to his account of Jesus' mission, Gospel as an account which climaxed in Jesus' death and resurrection.

41.2 The Gospel of Mark

I have already indicated the broad consensus in NT and earliest Christianity scholarship that Mark's Gospel is the earliest of the canonical Gospels to have been written. The consensus includes a large measure of agreement that it was most probably written either in the late 60s or early 70s, possibly from Rome, or perhaps more likely in Syria, and in either case reflecting something of the crisis which marked the end of Christianity's beginnings.[27] Given this likelihood, three features of Mark call for attention here.

---

25. C. H. Dodd, *Historical Tradition in the Fourth Gospel* (Cambridge: Cambridge University, 1963), suggested that the transitional passages and topographical notices in John were 'traditional data summarizing periods in the ministry of Jesus, with indications of the places where they were spent' (243).

26. 'We should probably already presuppose this Christological connection of a narrative about Jesus and proclamation with the term *euangelion* in a large number of communities even before the composition of Mark's work' (Hengel, *Studies in Mark* 54); Hengel draws attention to the fact that both Ignatius (*Philad.* particularly 9.2) and *Didache* (particularly 8.2) clearly think of 'the gospel' as including Jesus' life and teaching (159 n.86), and he attempts to detect a particular Petrine link informing Mark's use of *euangelion* (54-56).

27. See again §39.2a above.

a. Mark's Use of *Euangelion*

It is an immediately intriguing consideration that Mark seems to have introduced the term *euangelion* into the Jesus tradition. He uses it seven times;[28] in contrast, Matthew uses it only four times,[29] and Luke and John do not use it at all.[30] What is notable is that Mark's use seems to be consistently his own — either his own use in narrative (1.1, 14), or as an addition to the forms of Jesus tradition passed down to him.

- So, only Mark summarizes Jesus' preaching as a call to 'repent and *believe in the gospel*' (Mark 1.15); whereas Matt. 4.17 has only the call to 'Repent'.
- Again, in a saying which all three Synoptics share, that 'he who loses his life for my sake shall save it', only Mark inserts 'he who loses his life for my sake *and the gospel's* shall save it' (Mark 8.35 pars.).
- Likewise in the promise to those who have left home and family 'for my sake', that they will receive a hundredfold, only Mark adds '*and for the sake of the gospel*' (Mark 10.29 pars.).

In all these cases, the fact is clear that Matthew and Luke, as they drew on Mark, nevertheless omitted Mark's reference to the 'gospel', even when staying close to what Mark otherwise wrote. That fact is probably best explained by the hypothesis that Matthew and Luke were aware that the references to the 'gospel' had been added to the tradition, that is, were a peculiarity of Mark's version of the tradition.[31]

Only in two cases does Matthew follow Mark in attributing the term 'gospel' to Jesus himself. One is Mark 13.10 ('The gospel must first be proclaimed to all the nations'), followed by Matt. 24.14. However, it is generally agreed that the verse (13.10) is a Markan interpretative addition to the 'little apocalypse' (Mark 13) in the light of the much more extensive Gentile mission already well under way.[32] The second is the story of the woman anointing

---

28. Mark 1.1, 14, 15; 8.35; 10.29; 13.10; 14.9; also 16.15.
29. Matt. 4.23; 9.35; 24.14; 26.13.
30. Fitzmyer suggests that 'in avoiding *euangelion* in his first volume, Luke seems to be reacting against the Marcan usage of it', though he also wonders whether too much is made of Luke's omission of *euangelion* (*Luke* 1.173-74). And Luke does use the verb, *euangelizesthai*, fairly frequently (10 times). Somewhat surprisingly, John uses neither verb nor noun.
31. See further my 'Matthew's Awareness of Markan Redaction', in F. Van Segbroeck, ed., *The Four Gospels. Festschrift for Frans Neirynck* (Leuven University, 1992) 1349-59.
32. See further *Jesus Remembered* 435-36.

Jesus in Mark 14. Both Mark and Matthew have Jesus affirming, 'Truly, I say to you, wherever the gospel is proclaimed in the whole world, what she has done will be told in remembrance of her' (Mark 14.9/Matt. 26.13). However, given Mark's predilection for the term 'gospel', it is more than likely that the usage here too betrays Mark's hand. In this case we may envisage Mark's own rendering of tradition which came to him (again reflecting the more universal character of the gospel already apparent in Mark's time). And Matthew this time simply followed suit.[33]

Notwithstanding the ambiguity of Mark 13.10 and 14.9, then, it is clear enough that *euangelion* is Mark's term which he has introduced into the Jesus tradition at several points.[34] In so doing, of course, and particularly in the case of Mark 14.9, Mark shows that in the circles where the Jesus tradition was known and cherished *stories about Jesus and accounts of his preaching were thought of as part of the 'gospel'*.[35]

b. *Euangelion* as Gospel

The second point which demands attention is the fact that Mark begins his Gospel with the words, 'The beginning of the gospel of Jesus Christ (*archē tou euangeliou Iēsou Christou*)' (Mark 1.1). Here again the implication is clear: that it was entirely appropriate for Mark to use the term *euangelion* to refer not only to the preaching of the cross, but to the account of Jesus' mission and record of *his* preaching. It is not just that recollection of the Jesus tradition was complementary to the gospel as preached by Paul. The Jesus tradition here is itself *euangelion*.

But the significance of Mark 1.1 goes still further. For in this use of *euangelion* we probably see the transition from 'gospel' as Jesus tradition, 'details recounting the life and mission of Jesus', to 'Gospel' as 'a book dealing with the life and mission of Jesus'.[36] Here *euangelion* begins to move from *'content'*

---

33. Casey, *Aramaic Sources of Mark's Gospel*, makes no effort to render Mark 13.10 and 14.9 back into Aramaic.

34. This was one of the major conclusions of the first redactional study of Mark — W. Marxsen, *Mark the Evangelist* (1956, 1959; ET Nashville: Abingdon, 1969) 117-50.

35. Hengel, *Studies in Mark* 72; also *Four Gospels* 92-94.

36. So in effect BDAG 403; Hengel, *Studies in Mark* 81-83; *Four Gospels* 90-92; see further L. E. Keck, 'The Introduction to Mark's Gospel', *NTS* 12 (1966) 352-70 (358-60), and particularly R. Guelich, 'The Gospel Genre', in P. Stuhlmacher, ed., *The Gospel and the Gospels* (Grand Rapids: Eerdmans, 1991) 173-208 (here 194-205). See also R. A. Burridge, *What Are the Gospels? A Comparison with Graeco-Roman Biography* (Grand Rapids: Eerdmans, ²2004) 186-89; Pokorny, *Gospel* 108-12; earlier discussion in Koester, *Ancient Christian Gospels* 24-29.

of a message, to the *book* which conveys the message.³⁷ As the Jesus tradition is no longer conceived (if it ever was) as supplementary to the gospel, but as gospel itself, so the writing which contains the Jesus tradition is not to be regarded as merely a container of the gospel, but is here itself becoming the Gospel.³⁸ Almost consciously, Mark in effect was introducing a new genre to the literature of the ancient world, or if not deliberately then certainly in retrospect.³⁹ At all events, Mark's writing soon came to be seen no longer simply as a biography (*bios*) of a great man, but as a *Gospel*, the account of a particular man's mission which made salvation possible, a book which itself is a means to salvation, 'the Gospel according to Mark'. It is Mark who, whether knowingly and intentionally or not, made the transition from 'gospel' to 'Gospel'.⁴⁰ We

---

37. Luz (private correspondence) is not entirely persuaded and suggests that there are three possible interpretations of the phrase: (a) 'the Jesus history (recounted by Mark) as "beginning" of the Christian "proclamation" (which is then instituted after Easter); (b) the (biblically attested) emergence of the Baptist as "beginning" of the book of Mark (= Evangelium); (c) the (whole) book of Mark as "foundation" of the Christian "proclamation"'.

38. 'The Gospel of Mark thus intends to make clear that the Easter Gospel is (should be) inseparably linked with Jesus in his earthly life' (Pokorny, *Gospel* 122-24, commenting on Mark 1.1; also *Gospel* 179-80).

39. Koester expresses the most common view, that Mark does not designate his work as a 'gospel' (*Ancient Christian Gospels* 12-14). In some contrast, Luz maintains that *euangelion* is identified as a book already in *Did*. 8.2; 11.3; 15.3-4 (*Matthäus* 1.249). However, these references (as in n.21 above) could be, as is more likely, to the well-known (oral) gospel, though the repeated references to 'the gospel' have a transitional feel much as Mark 1.1 (as also Ignatius, *Philad*. 8.2; 9.2; *Smyrn*. 7.2; *2 Clem*. 8.5 — to which Luz also refers). Koester thinks that *2 Clement* may use *euangelion* of a written 'gospel', referring particularly to *2 Clem*. 8.5, but dates *2 Clement* after 150 (17-18), and notes that Marcion referred to his version of Luke as 'the gospel' (35-36). The earliest explicit references to *euangelion* as a book are in Justin's *Dialogue with Trypho*, in which Trypho refers to 'the commands given in what is called the (or, the so-called) Gospel', which he had carefully read (10.2); and later on Justin refers to what had been recorded 'in the Gospel' (100.1). Note also his reference to the 'memoirs (*apomnēmoneumata*)' of the apostles 'which are called Gospels (*euangelia*)' (§39 at n.21; also *Dial*. 100.4; 102.5; 103.6-7; 106.1; 107.1); '"are called" (implies) a tradition going back several years if not decades' (Pokorny, *Gospel* 182). See further W. A. Shotwell, *The Biblical Exegesis of Justin Martyr* (London: SPCK, 1965) 23-28; Koester 37-43; Hengel, *Studies in Mark* ch. 3; 'The roots of the title of the Gospel are to be sought solely in Mark' (Hengel, *Four Gospels* 242, see also 63). Collins agrees: 'It is likely that the practice of referring to the four works as "Gospels" ultimately derives from Mark' (*Mark* 3); see also her full discussion of Mark's genre (15-43). 'We consider it very probable that Mark 1:1 served as the title of the whole book' (Pokorny, *Gospel* 128).

40. Stanton argues that it was not Mark who took this step but Matthew, referring particularly to Matt. 24.14 and 26.13 (*A Gospel for a New People* 15-18). But these two verses are drawn from Mark, and where Stanton is 'unable to see a major difference between Matthew and the Didache in the usage of *euangelion*' (18 n.3, with reference to n.33 above), I can see no major difference between Mark 13.10 and Matt. 24.14 or Mark 14.9 and Matt.

shall look more closely in §42.2 at how Mark shaped the Jesus tradition to express the Gospel character of the story he was telling.

c. A Passion Narrative with an Extended Introduction

It was Martin Kähler who, in a famous note, described the Gospels as 'passion narratives with extended introductions'.[41] This description was particularly apposite for Mark, the earliest written Gospel.

- The basic fact is that the passion narrative, covering the last week of Jesus' life and the discovery of his empty tomb (Mark 11.1-16.8), takes up more than one third of the Gospel of Mark.[42]
- Mark's Gospel is structured so that Peter's confession of Jesus as Messiah near Caesarea Philippi (Mark 8.27-30) is the centre and turning point of the Gospel. It is both the geographical turning point (the region is the most northerly point of Jesus' mission in the Galilee) and the dramatic turning point in the Gospel (thereafter Jesus heads south towards Jerusalem and his destiny there).
- The point is marked by the first of Jesus' explicit teaching on the necessity of his suffering (Mark 8.31), a passion prediction which is repeated starkly two more times in the following chapters (9.31; 10.33-34).
- Whether Mark was thus correcting a too triumphalist proclamation of Jesus as one who spoke with divine authority and executed extraordinary miracles, a 'divine man' (*theios anēr*) Christ, as several have argued, is by no means clear.[43] But we can say that Mark's account of Jesus' response to the Caesarea Philippi confession of Peter was a way of shifting the focus from Jesus as Messiah to Jesus as the suffering Son of Man. This strategy presumably included a shift from any claim that the significance of Jesus was to be assessed in terms of the extent to which Jesus had fulfilled the popular hope for a military Messiah who would liberate

---

26.13. I agree with Collins on Mark 14.9: 'It seems likely ... that here the author of Mark refers to his own work as a "gospel".... The usage ... shows that no great distinction was made by this author, and probably his audiences, between an oral summary of the gospel and a written Gospel' (*Mark* 644).

41. M. Kähler, *The So-Called Historical Jesus and the Historic Biblical Christ* (1896; Philadelphia: Fortress, 1964) 80 n.11.

42. R. Pesch, *Das Markusevangelium* (HTKNT II, 2 vols.; Freiburg: Herder, 1977), argues that the passion narrative extends from Peter's confession of Jesus as Messiah (Mark 8.27) (2.1).

43. See below §42.2 at n.93.

Israel from Roman domination. Jesus' significance as Messiah and Son of Man could not be appreciated without reference to his death and resurrection.

- In Mark's narrative an important motif is the failure of Jesus' disciples to understand him. This is part of 'the Messianic secret' which fascinated scholars of the Gospels for most of the twentieth century.[44] Whether Mark introduced the motif, or simply highlighted a facet of the Jesus tradition as it came to him, the point of the motif is clear. It is that Jesus' disciples were unable to understand Jesus when still in the midst of his mission. They could not understand him until they had witnessed the completion of his mission, that is, until he had been killed and had been raised again from the dead.[45]
- The thrust of Mark's strategy is clear from the allusions to and foreshadowings of Jesus' death from early on in his Gospel.
    - The qualification of Jesus' likening his mission to the bridegroom's presence at the wedding feast. 'The days will come when the bridegroom is taken away from them . . .' (2.20).
    - The conclusion to his sequence of adversity stories (2.1-3.5): 'The Pharisees went out and immediately conspired with the Herodians against him, how to destroy him' (3.6) — a decision to do away with Jesus which comes surprisingly early in Mark's narrative.
    - The lengthy and ominous account of the fate of John the Baptist, Jesus' precursor (6.17-29).
    - In the buildup to the passion narrative itself we should note also Jesus' talk of his having to drink the cup (of suffering) and to be baptized with a baptism of death (the image of being drowned) (10.38-39).
    - The parable of the tenants of the vineyard, with its climax in the tenants killing the son and heir of the vineyard owner (12.1-9), with the addition of the rejected stone testimony (12.10-11; Ps. 118.22-23), an addition probably earlier than Mark himself;[46] and the conclusion that the parable incited more virulent opposition to Jesus (12.12).
    - The ominous predictions of suffering, persecution and death for Jesus' followers (13.9-12) imply a fate consequent upon similar rejection of Jesus himself.

---

44. W. Wrede, *The Messianic Secret* (1901; ET Cambridge: Clarke, 1971). See *Jesus Remembered* 624-27, 644-45, 647-49.

45. See further below §42.2b.

46. *Jesus Remembered* 721-22 n.67.

- The anointing of Jesus' body by the woman in Bethany, 'beforehand for its burial' (14.8), Jesus' prediction of his betrayal (14.18-20), and the institution of the Lord's Supper, betokening broken body and spilled blood (14.22-24).
- On the Mount of Olives Jesus warns of the imminent striking of the shepherd (14.27), and in the garden of Gethsemane, the anguish of anticipation of an agonizing death is briefly sketched in stark terms (14.33-36).
- Nor should we ignore the fact that the various scriptural allusions leading into the climax[47] echo Paul's emphasis that Jesus' death and resurrection was 'in accordance with the scriptures' (1 Cor. 15.3-4).[48]

In calling his life of Jesus a 'Gospel', Mark, then, was not leaving behind Paul's understanding of why the message about Jesus counted as 'gospel'. On the contrary, by climaxing his account of Jesus' mission with the passion narrative he reinforced Paul's point. The good news of Jesus was primarily the good news of his death and resurrection. The message about Jesus was good news, not simply because of his teaching, and not because he was a great healer and miracle-worker, but because his death and resurrection brought forgiveness of sins and life from the dead.[49]

At the same time, however, by naming the account of the whole of Jesus' mission, and not just his death and resurrection, as 'Gospel', Mark ensured that the two could not be sundered. The point of Jesus' mission could not be grasped apart from his death and resurrection; but neither could the full significance of Jesus' death and resurrection be grasped outside the context of his mission as a whole. To treasure Jesus' mission apart from his death and resurrection would be to misappropriate it. But to treasure the account of Jesus' death and resurrection apart from his mission as a whole would be equally to misappreciate it. The gospel of Jesus' passion was the central but not the only part of the Gospel of the mission of the Galilean who proclaimed and lived out his message of the kingdom of God.

---

47. Especially

Mark 9.31 and 10.33-34	Isa. 53.12
Mark 10.45	Dan. 7.13
Mark 12.10-11	Ps. 118.22-23
Mark 14.27	Zech. 13.7
Mark 15.24, 29, 34	Ps. 22.1, 8, 18

48. Cf. Collins, *Mark* 80-84.

49. Mark's emphasis here was not necessarily polemical; it could be supplementary or corrective (see discussion in Marcus, *Mark 1-8* 74-79; and further below §42.2b(ii)).

Scholars of the twentieth century often found it difficult to come to terms with this balance which Mark achieves between, as we might say, gospel as biographical history and gospel as kerygma — almost as though it was not possible for Mark to maintain an interest both in Jesus' pre-Easter mission as such and in its kerygmatic significance in the light of Jesus' death and resurrection.[50] But this is precisely what Mark has achieved. He has not allowed the kerygmatic significance of the climax of Jesus' mission to drown the historical rememberings. As we saw in *Jesus Remembered*, it is entirely possible to gain a clear, though not a full historical perspective on Jesus from the Markan account. The point is that Mark did not need to greatly elaborate and enhance the Jesus tradition in order to give it a kerygmatic significance it would not otherwise have had. What he saw and pushed at us by calling his account 'Gospel' was that Jesus' pre-passion mission was already good news, and that Jesus' death and resurrection simply brought out the gospel significance of his whole mission.[51]

41.3 The Gospels of Matthew and Luke

One of the most striking features of the Gospels of Matthew and Luke, as has been well appreciated for more than a century, is that they are heavily dependent on Mark's Gospel. Although I strongly caution against seeing the interdependence of the Synoptic Gospels in exclusively literary terms, the near identical wording of much of the tradition which Matthew and Luke share with Mark is most obviously to be explained by the very strong probability that Matthew and Luke had the written Gospel of Mark to hand when they composed their Gospels.[52] They evidently composed their own Gospels by interweaving other Jesus tradition with Mark, and by using Mark as a framework for their own Gospels. This includes, pre-eminently, the fact that in doing so *they took over the character of Gospel which Mark's structure established* — a passion narrative with an extended introduction.

This is what we find to be the case when we look at Matthew and Luke. They not only take over Mark's structure; they also take over the turning point of Peter's confession (Matt. 16.13-20; Luke 9.18-21), the passion predictions,[53] the correction of any inferences drawn too easily from Jesus' miracles, and the

---

50. Cf. particularly J. Gnilka, *Das Evangelium nach Markus* (EKK II; 2 vols.; Zürich: Benziger, 1978, 1979) 1.22-24.

51. I say 'of his whole mission', not 'of his whole life'; a theology of incarnation has yet to emerge.

52. *Jesus Remembered* §§4.4, 7.3. See also §39.2 and e.g. n.90 there.

53. Matt. 16.21; 17.22-23; 20.18; Luke 9.22, 44; 18.32-33.

various foreshadowings of Jesus' final sufferings and death.[54] These are not simply cases of 'copy and paste'; but the very fact that Matthew and Luke follow Mark's pattern so closely, even when using the Jesus tradition in their own way or also using other versions of Jesus tradition known to them, underlines the commitment which Matthew and Luke in effect took upon themselves, to present the teaching and mission of Jesus as integral to the gospel,[55] *to use Mark's Gospel genre for their own retelling of the story of Jesus* and to follow the pattern of Mark's buildup of his Gospel to the climax of Jesus' death and resurrection.[56]

Integral to this compositional plan was the incorporation of the Q material into the framework provided by Mark. The non-Markan material shared by Matthew and Luke, we recall, is commonly designated as Q, on the hypothesis that Matthew and Luke were both able to draw on a second source, that is, on the same second source. The argument, we may also recall, is on whether the Q material was drawn from a written document. I have pointed out that the similar feature of nearly identical Q passages in Matthew and Luke points to a similar conclusion as regards the passages nearly identical to parallels in Mark. In other words, the likelihood is that some of the Q material was already in Greek and already in writing when Matthew and Luke drew on it. But I have also pointed out that the equally common feature of shared material which is quite diverse, and far from being nearly identical, points away from the likelihood that Matthew and Luke were dependent on a written Q source in these cases. The more likely solution to the conundrum of shared but very diversely worded tradition is that there were various oral versions of Jesus tradition circulating among the early churches and that in such passages Matthew and Luke knew and used diverse versions of the same tradition.[57]

The point here, however, is that the Q material, when disentangled from Matthew and Luke, can *not* be described as 'a passion narrative with an extended introduction'. It does not have a passion narrative. The closeness of Matthew in following Mark's passion narrative, as was most probably the case, makes it virtually impossible to talk of or to identify Q material, since the

---

54. Mark 2.20 pars.; 3.6 pars.; 6.17-29 par. (not Luke); 10.38-39 pars.; 12.6-12 pars.; 13.9-13 pars.; 14.8 par. (Luke has a different version); 14.18-20, 22-24 pars.; 14.27 par. (not Luke); 14.33-36 pars.

55. 'For Matthew it is theologically decisive that all church preaching (*euangelion*) orients itself to the earthly Jesus and has no other content than his words and actions' (Luz, *Matthäus* 1.249).

56. I thus simply disagree with Koester when he claims 'the passion narrative, i.e., the central piece of the "kerygma", is no longer a fundamental structural element of Matthew's Gospel'; and similarly with regard to Luke's Gospel (*Ancient Christian Gospels* 45).

57. I will develop the point in detail in §42.1.

starting point for any definition of Q is the non-Markan material common to Matthew and Luke. And even if it may be hypothesized that Luke was able to draw on a different passion narrative,[58] no one thinks to see such a narrative as part of Q.

Moreover, the Q material lacks almost all of the various structural features and foreshadowings of the passion narrative which are such a feature of Mark. Some indeed argue that the hypothesized Q document expressed a christology different from and antithetical to Mark's passion Gospel. I remain unconvinced.[59] The Q material is better seen as varied collections of Jesus tradition serving as the repertoire for teachers responsible for preserving the Jesus tradition and instructing gatherings of believers in it. And the different allusions in Q to Jesus' death[60] and vindication[61] fit well with material which served a different function from proclamation of the gospel, but which was complementary to proclamation focused on Jesus' death and resurrection.

The key fact, however, is that *in Matthew and Luke the Q material is encased within the structure provided by Mark*. The Q material becomes part of a fuller version of the account of Jesus' mission climaxing in his passion.[62] Moreover, the Q material was evidently not retained independently, as a single, coherent block, or substantive document by the churches which Matthew and Luke represent and for whom they wrote their Gospels.[63] In the church life which picks up from one or more of the canonical Gospels, there is subsequently no hint that a Q document, distinct from the Gospels, was valued. Knowledge of oral Jesus tradition is still clear, but there is no evidence of a document consisting solely of Jesus' teaching being cherished in such churches.[64]

---

58. V. Taylor, *The Passion Narrative of St Luke. A Critical and Historical Investigation* (SNTSMS 19; Cambridge University, 1972).

59. *Jesus Remembered* 150-52.

60. Notably Matt. 10.38/Luke 14.27 ('whoever does not take up his cross and follow me cannot be my disciple'); Matt. 23.37-39/Luke 13.34-35 and Matt. 23.34-36/Luke 11.49-51 (the implication that Jesus is included among the 'prophets and messengers' killed); Matt. 5.11-12/Luke 6.22-23 (similarly, suffering as the lot of disciples as of prophets). See further J. S. Kloppenborg, *Excavating Q* (Minneapolis: Fortress, 2000) 369-74.

61. Matt. 10.32/Luke 12.8; Matt. 23.37-39/Luke 13.34-35. See further Kloppenborg, *Excavating Q* 374-79.

62. Matthew 'in literary terms is a new version of Mark's Gospel, and not a new version of Q' (Luz, *Matthäus* 1.80).

63. 'Q is imbedded in the Marcan outline by Matthew and Luke and continues to be acceptable in the orthodox church only in the context of this other gattung, that of "gospel"' (J. M. Robinson, '*LOGOI SOPHON:* On the Gattung of Q', Robinson and Koester, *Trajectories* 113).

64. The contrast between the fate of Q and the fate of Mark at this point is worth noting already. For it could be said that Mark was absorbed as fully by Matthew as was

We have still to consider the *Gospel of Thomas*, of course.[65] But already important conclusions are beginning to emerge.

- First, that it was only as held within the framework of a story of Jesus' mission climaxing in his death and resurrection that the tradition of Jesus' teaching was preserved in the mainstream churches.
- Second, in these churches it was only as held within Mark's passion framework that Jesus' teaching was retained and valued as itself 'gospel', as part of the Gospel.
- Third, that if the Markan framework, taken over by Matthew and Luke, determines and defines what is a Gospel, then it is inappropriate and misleading to speak of Q, the hypothesized Q document, as a Gospel. As will become apparent, the same rule of thumb applies to those other documents in early Christianity which have become too casually labeled as 'Gospel'.

41.4 The Gospel of John

John's Gospel is usually dated as the latest of the four canonical Gospels. As already noted (§39.2d), John's Gospel differs from the other three in that while the Synoptics are obviously closely inter-related by the fact that they share so much common material, John is not at all closely related in that it shares very little material with the Synoptics. And while both Matthew and Luke most likely show knowledge of and make use of Mark, it is almost as likely that John either did not know or did not use any of the Synoptic Gospels.[66] Where the Johannine material comes closest to that of the Synoptics, the closeness is better explained in terms of John's knowledge and use of variant oral tradition of similar or of the same episodes or teaching from Jesus' mission.[67] The argument here is parallel to that concerning the diverse vari-

---

Q. Yet Mark was preserved and continued to function as a much valued testimony to Jesus in churches which also knew and used Matthew and Luke; whereas Q, as a distinct document, was not retained, and disappeared. The same point can be made with regard to any other postulated written sources of the four canonical Gospels.

65. See below §43.2. The *Gospel of Thomas* made modern scholarship aware of documents consisting only of sayings of Jesus. But it should be noted that *Thomas* introduces itself as 'the secret words which the living Jesus spoke and which Didymus Judas Thomas wrote'; the title 'The Gospel according to Thomas' is attached as a colophon at the end, and may be a later addition.

66. But Luz (in private correspondence) legitimately asks, from where did John derive the 'Gospel' Gattung?

67. I go into this in more detail in §43 below; see particularly n.78. P. N. Anderson, *The*

ations of the shared Q material in Matthew and Luke. If such diversity (lack of nearly identical tradition) points away from Matthew and Luke's *literary* dependence on a *written* Q document (or on each other) and to the flexibility of *oral* Jesus tradition, then the same conclusion follows from the fact that there is a fairly minimal amount of near identical material shared between John and the Synoptics. As argued in some detail below in §43.1b, John's Gospel constitutes further evidence that the Jesus tradition continued to be circulated and used in a variety of oral forms, traditions of the *same* mission of Jesus, regularly of the *same* actions and teachings of Jesus during his mission, but *diverse* in wording, detail, and in the conclusions drawn from them.

Given the differences between John and the Synoptic Gospels,[68] and the lack of evidence of any direct dependence on the Synoptics, it is all the more striking that John nevertheless has used *the same Gospel format* given to the Jesus tradition by Mark and taken over by Matthew and Luke. John has set his Gospel within the same framework — a passion narrative with an extended introduction — even though his 'extended introduction' is so very different in content and character from the 'extended introductions' of the Synoptics. If we reckon the 'passion narrative' as extending from Jesus' entry into Jerusalem, covering Jesus' final week there and climaxing in his trial, execution and resurrection, then John's passion narrative extends from John 12 to the end of the Gospel; that is, it takes up about 40 percent of the Gospel as a whole.

What may we infer from this? Not that John did after all know Mark's Gospel as such; the absence of the sort of closely identical passages, which point to the literary interdependence of a good proportion of the Synoptic Gospels, still remains the decisive consideration at this point. What it probably does mean is that the Markan step of labeling the story of Jesus' whole mission as itself *euangelion*, 'Gospel', quickly became the established way of thinking about the story of Jesus' mission, even when the term *euangelion* itself was not used. Matthew's and Luke's following Mark's example attests the same probability, and they will themselves have strengthened and circulated more widely the conviction that the way to use and reflect on the Jesus tradition was in the narrative form of Mark's 'Gospel'.

This is all the more significant, since the different account John gives

---

Fourth Gospel and the Quest for Jesus (London: T & T Clark, 2006), argues that Luke and Q were able to draw on Johannine oral tradition (102, 113-14, 117-19, 134-35). I would prefer to speak of a widespread shared oral Jesus tradition, before it gained its distinctive Markan, Matthean, Lukan and Johannine characteristics. See further R. Kysar, 'The Dehistoricizing of the Gospel of John', in Anderson et al., eds., *John, Jesus and History* vol. 1, 75-101 (here 89-92), who refers also to Barnabas Lindars and Raymond Brown, and who criticizes Anderson's thesis as entailing 'an enormous amount of speculation and conjecture' (92).

68. See again §43.1a below.

of the Jesus tradition could so easily have pushed in a different direction. A Jesus who came as (primarily) a revealer,[69] and whose teaching was characterized by lengthy discourses, could have focused John's presentation of Jesus precisely in these features or narrowed it to such features, as the Gnostic presentations of Jesus show.[70] Nevertheless, John follows what had been the pattern set by the earlier 'Gospels', by setting his own version of Jesus' mission and revelation within the same framework, beginning with John the Baptist and climaxing in Jesus' passion and resurrection. For all the freedom John's Gospel displays in its presentation of Jesus, and despite all its differences from the Synoptics, it is far closer to them than to the apocryphal Gospels.

What is all the more striking in John's Gospel is the way he makes the imminent passion of Jesus suffuse the whole of his account. Even more than Mark, the 'extended introduction' foreshadows and prepares for the climax of Jesus' death and resurrection.

- Uniquely in the Gospel tradition, John the Baptist hails the one to come as 'the lamb of God who takes away the sin of the world' (John 1.29, 36). Given that John also dates Jesus' execution as happening at the time when the Passover lambs would have been slaughtered in the Temple (18.28), and explicitly identifies Jesus' death with that of the Passover lamb (19.36; Exod. 12.46),[71] that must mean that John saw Jesus' death in terms of the Passover sacrifice, now seen also as a sin-offering.[72]
- John relocates the account of Jesus' 'cleansing of the Temple' to a much earlier phase of Jesus' mission (2.13-22), presumably to serve as a headline for Jesus' whole mission.[73] In it he includes the memory of Jesus speaking about the destruction of the Temple (cf. Mark 13.2; 14.58): 'Destroy this temple, and in three days I will raise it up' (John 2.19). But then he adds the explanatory note: Jesus 'was speaking about the temple of his body', that is, of his death and resurrection (2.22-23).
- Other early signals of the passion climax include the talk of resurrection and of Jesus as the source of life in 5.21-29, the powerful interpretation of the feeding of the five thousand in terms of Jesus himself as the bread

---

69. See below §43.1c, d and §49.3c.
70. See §40.4 above.
71. The fact that the soldiers did not (have to) break the crucified Jesus' legs (19.33) fulfilled the scripture, 'None of his bones shall be broken' (19.36), one of the regulations for the Passover lamb — 'you shall not break any of its bones' (Exod. 12.46).
72. The Passover was not originally thought of as a sin offering, but it was natural, probably inevitable, that the two became merged in later thought. See also §42 at n.349 below.
73. See further below §43.1b.

of life, his flesh to be eaten and his blood to be drunk as the source of life (6.32-58), and the increasing attempts to do away with Jesus, heightening the sense of ever more imminent crisis,[74] matched by Jesus' increasing reference to his imminent departure.[75] Not surprising as the passion narrative draws closer, Jesus talks of the good shepherd who lays down his life for the sheep (10.11, 15, 17-18), of his imminent burial (12.7), and of the wheat grain that must die if it is to bring forth fruit (12.24).

- Particularly notable is the drum beat of references to Jesus' 'hour'.[76] Initially it sounds as a still distant or yet to happen event: certain eventualities could not happen because Jesus' hour 'had not yet come'.[77] There have been hints as to what the 'hour' will bring forth, but it is only when the passion narrative proper has begun that it becomes clear that the 'hour' is the hour of Jesus' death (12.23-24, 27; 13.1; 17.1). The drama of the steadily mounting climax should not be missed.

- Equally notable is John's adaptation of the concept of Jesus' 'glorification' (*doxasthēnai*), where it again becomes steadily clearer that what is in view is not, or not simply, Jesus' exaltation following his death. What is in view is Jesus' being 'glorified' in his death *and* resurrection[78] — particularly, again, 12.23-24. Since the 'glory' (and 'glorifying') of Christ is such an important feature of John's Gospel,[79] it is also to be noted that it is the 'signs' of water transformed into wine, and of life from death (2.11; 11.4), which most clearly reveal that glory — that is, actions which foreshadow the glory of his death and resurrection and what they achieve. This factor, it should be noted, affects all references to Jesus' glory, from the first mention of 'the glory as of the Father's only son', which the Johannine witness attested (1.14). The 'glory' of the only Son which the disciples had witnessed was not in terms of the Synoptic Gospels' scene of Jesus' transfiguration (Mark 9.2-8 pars.). For John that glory was most clearly attested in Jesus' death and resurrection. His Gospel was never simply a Gospel of incarnation but of incarnation-death-resurrection.

- The same point is made in John's talk of Jesus being 'lifted up' (*hypsōthēnai*). As is now generally recognized, John uses this word not only for Jesus' lifting up on the cross, but also for his lifting up to heaven, that is, his ascension.[80] For John, Jesus' decisive saving act was a unitary

---

74. John 5.18; 7.1, 19-20, 25, 30, 32, 44; 8.37, 40; 10.31-33, 39; 11.8, 52-54, 57.
75. John 7.33; 8.14, 21; 13.3, 33, 36; 14.4, 28; 16.5, 10, 17.
76. John 2.4; 7.30; 8.20; 12.23, 27; 13.1; 17.1.
77. John 2.4; 7.30; 8.20; alternatively as Jesus' *kairos* ('critical or right time') (7.6, 8).
78. John 7.39; 12.16, 23; 13.31-32; 17.1.
79. John 1.14; 2.11; 8.50, 54; 12.41; 14.13; 16.14; 17.1, 5, 10, 22, 24.
80. John 3.14; 8.28; 12.32-34. See e.g. Brown, *John* 1.145-46.

conceptual whole, Jesus' dying, rising and ascending in a single upward sweep. To be correlated with this is also John's adaptation of the Son of Man tradition to include talk of the Son of Man ascending as well as descending.[81] Jesus evidently could not be adequately understood except when both were held together, within that Gospel framework.

Wherever John derived his Gospel format from, then, it is clear that he was firmly wedded to that format as the structure within which his more distinctive portrayal should be held. He could have presented Jesus as the great revealer of God and of the mysteries of heaven. He could have developed his mode of presenting the teaching of Jesus even more extensively than he did — Jesus, the divine agent from on high who brought the secret meaning of human existence to those born of the flesh and imprisoned in darkness. Others took that option. But for John it was integral to the message he sought to promote that Jesus had been executed and had been raised from the dead — and not simply as an episode in his life or incidental to his revelation, but central to it, a fundamental element in his message, without which the message could not be adequately grasped and would be misappropriated.[82] In terms of our present discussion, and although John never uses either noun (*euangelion*) or verb (*euangelizesthai*), we can justifiably say that John affirmed and strongly stressed the *sine qua non* of his message about Jesus, incarnation-death-resurrection, as Gospel.

41.5 The Gospel

Quite when we can begin to speak of the 'Gospel' as a book remains obscure. Almost all of the *euangelion* references in the early second century are to the preached gospel.[83] Equally obscure is the question when the definition of 'Gospel' as a written account of Jesus' mission, climaxing in his death, resurrection and ascension, became established. What is clear is that Justin Martyr knew the Gospel in written form (*Dial.* 10.2; 100.1) and of more than one

---

81. John 3.13; 6.62; also 20.17; and cf. 1.51.
82. I thus again disagree with Koester when he claims that John's Gospel 'hardly fits the definition of the genre of the gospel developed on the basis of the Gospel of Mark' (*Ancient Christian Gospels* 45).
83. *1 Clem.* 42.1; 47.2; Ignatius, *Philad.* 5.1-2; 8.2; *Smyrn.* 5.1; Polycarp, *Phil.* 6.3; *Barn.* 5.9; 8.3; Aristides, *Apol.* 2. That the gospel focused on Jesus' death and resurrection is particularly clear in Ignatius, *Philad.* 9.2; *Smyrn.* 7.2; and *M. Polyc.* 1.1; 19.1. But, as already noted, in other cases *euangelion* included reference to Jesus' teaching (*M. Polyc.* 4; 22.1; *Did.* 8.2; 11.3; 15.3, 4; *2 Clem.* 8.5).

'Gospel' (*1 Apol.* 66.3). Moreover, it is evident that the documents known by Justin as 'Gospels' followed the same structure, so that even when references to 'the g/Gospel(s)' do not evoke the 'passion narrative' structure,[84] it can be safely inferred that the only written Gospels they would be referring to were the canonical Gospels which shared that 'passion narrative' structure, and that the essential passion character of 'the gospel' would have been assumed.[85]

Whether there are earlier references to *euangelion* as an authoritative written document is disputed. Several have argued that Marcion was the first to make such a reference, that is, prior to Justin, and probably as early as the 130s or 140s, the reference being to the Gospel of Luke.[86] But a strong case can be made that the *Didache* contains several references to *euangelion* as a written Gospel,[87] which would make the transition from (oral) gospel to (written) Gospel much earlier,[88] and support the suggestion that the reading of *euangelion* in Mark 1.1 as the title of the writing which it introduced had already become established in usage of Mark and its immediate successors.

Not least of significance is a point easily ignored: that what became the title of the genre initiated by Mark was 'The Gospel *according to* Mark', 'The Gospel *according to* Matthew', etc.[89] It was not 'The Gospel *of* Mark', 'the Gospel *of* Matthew', etc. What was thus recognized by the designation was that there was the Gospel, *one* Gospel, but known in different versions.[90] This is reflected in what are the first known references to the written Gospel, by Justin Martyr, referred to above. For though Justin in his first *Apology* refers to the 'Gospels' (plural) (*1 Apol.* 66.3), his earlier references to 'the [written] Gospel', in his *Dialogue with Trypho* (10.2; 100.2), show that these different Gospels were understood by him as versions of the (same) Gospel.

Here becomes more explicit what was deduced from the structure given

---

84. Koester, *Ancient Christian Gospels* 29.

85. In the context of both *Dial.* 10.2 and 100.2 reference is made to Jesus' crucifixion; and *1 Apol.* 66 focuses on the flesh and blood of the eucharist. See further below §44.3b.

86. von Campenhausen, *Formation* 147-63; Koester, *Ancient Christian Gospels* 35-36; R. H. Gundry, '*EUANGELION*: How Soon a Book?', *JBL* 115 (1996) 321-25.

87. *Did.* 8.2; 11.3; 15.3-4; see also *2 Clem.* 8.5. See further below §44 at nn.87, 88, 121.

88. J. A. Kelhoffer, '"How Soon a Book" Revisited: *EUANGELION* as a Reference to "Gospel" Materials in the First Half of the Second Century', *ZNW* 95 (2004) 1-34; also '"Gospel" as a Literary Title in Early Christianity' 402-6, 410-12, who also notes that Marcion was not effecting a novelty but 'assumes that *euangelion* is already intelligible as a designation for a written gospel (that is, Luke's) among his constituency' (405).

89. See above §39.2a(i).

90. Lührmann, *Markusevangelium* 4. It is worth noting that Irenaeus, who first defines the four-Gospel canon, speaks not of the four Gospels but of 'the four-formed Gospel' (*tetramorphon to euangelion*) (*adv. haer.* 3.11.8). See further A. Y. Reed, '*Euangelion:* Orality, Textuality, and the Christian Truth in Irenaeus' *Adversus Haereses*', *VC* 56 (2002) 11-46.

to the genre 'Gospel' by Mark: that the genre 'Gospel' was in effect closely determined and restricted to what came from the apostles and what climaxed in the good news of Jesus' death and resurrection. It was this conviction, we might better say instinct, that the Gospel was expressed in just this written form which must have made those like Justin very suspicious of all claims to the title 'Gospel' which did not accord with this one gospel and did not accord with the genre created by Mark. In the light of other Gospels, it can certainly be argued that the strict definition of 'Gospel' should be broadened to include 'all those writings which are constituted by the transmission, use, and interpretation of materials and traditions from and about Jesus of Nazareth'.[91] Yet Paul's definition of 'gospel', given genre status by Mark, in the event ensured that their definition of 'Gospel' had normative and canon-shaping effect. Should that imply, or be allowed to imply, that since the later (apocryphal) Gospels do not measure up to the Paul- and Mark-given definition of 'gospel',[92] they were justifiably rejected by the great church in subsequent decades? This is an ongoing issue in this volume and we will have to return to it very soon, in §43.

---

91. Koester, *Ancient Christian Gospels* 46; but Koester goes on to list 'writings which are not to be counted as Gospels' — the *Gospel of Philip*, the *Gospel of Truth*, the *Gospel of the Egyptians*, the *Sophia of Jesus Christ*, the *Apocryphon of John*, the *Pistis Sophia* and the *Two Books of Jeu* (47).

92. Cf. and contrast N. T. Wright, 'When Is a Gospel Not a Gospel?', *Judas and the Gospel of Jesus* (Grand Rapids: Baker, 2006) 63-83; critiqued by Kelhoffer, '"Gospel" as a Literary Title in Early Christianity' 399-402.

CHAPTER 42

Retelling the Story of Jesus: Mark, Matthew and Luke

The second aspect of the transition from gospel to Gospel was the transition from oral gospel to written Gospel, the scribalization of the memories of Jesus as the tradition which now forms the Synoptic tradition came to be written down as Gospels. Not least of the fascination of the canonical Gospels is the different ways in which this was done, the different ways the oral Jesus tradition was used to retell the story of Jesus. In each case it is still a matter of 'The Gospel according to . . .', not 'The gospel of . . .'. But what is so interesting is how flexible the 'according to' was in the event. Whether the diversity is such that we should in fact change the 'according to' to 'of' is a question to which we will have to return.

In this chapter we will focus on the three Gospels which are most clearly dependent on the shared tradition which makes up the bulk of the first three New Testament Gospels, the Synoptic Gospels. The inference drawn from this shared tradition, an inference which was the principal working assumption of *Jesus Remembered*, is that this shared tradition most clearly represents how Jesus was remembered by the leading disciples of Jesus and by the main body of churches founded during the first generation of Christianity. So it makes best sense to focus the initial inquiry upon those three Gospels, the Gospels which provide the synopsis which makes clear the character of the Jesus tradition during the period prior to the appearance of the written Gospels.[1] This includes leaving aside the fourth canonical Gospel for this stage of the inquiry. As we shall see, the differences between John's Gospel and the Synoptic Gospels are so substantial that a separate treatment of John's

---

1. I should perhaps stress that this is the primary task of this chapter, not to provide full introductions to each Gospel, but to analyse how they each used and (re)presented the Jesus tradition available to them.

Gospel is appropriate.[2] The same is even more true of the other documents called 'Gospels'. But since of all these other Gospels, the *Gospel of Thomas* has the closest links to the Synoptic tradition, in some degrees closer than John's Gospel, it will be appropriate to treat *Thomas* immediately after, and in comparison with, John in §43.[3]

42.1 From Oral Tradition to Written Gospel

a. The Oral Tradition

It may be helpful to start by briefly recalling the path followed by Christianity's beginnings. In *Jesus Remembered* I emphasized the need to recognize the *oral* character of the early Jesus tradition. Hitherto, and throughout more than two centuries of questing for the historical Jesus, with the accompanying analysis of the Gospels, the dominant working assumption has been that 'the Synoptic problem' can be satisfactorily resolved in purely literary terms. The inter-relationship of the first three (Synoptic) Gospels could (and need only) be explained in terms of the copying and editing of written sources. The likelihood that the great majority (90 percent?) of the typical early Christian congregation were illiterate[4] did not trouble such literary critics. In contrast, however, the probability has to be that the bulk of the Jesus tradition was communicated in *oral* terms for the first two or three decades. So if the inter-relationships of the Synoptic Gospels can only be explained in terms of *literary* dependence, then the inevitable corollary, on that assumption, is that we can say virtually nothing about the Jesus tradition, about how Jesus was remembered, for the first twenty or thirty years of Christianity.[5]

In contrast, again, it seems to me that the character of the Synoptic

---

2. Besides which, to include John's Gospel in this chapter (as was the original intention) would make the chapter far too long.

3. It is not irrelevant that the *Gospel of Thomas* is given by some a status equal to, and in some cases superior to, the four canonical Gospels, as by Funk and Hoover, *The Five Gospels* (see above §38 n.141). As Risto Uro notes in his Introduction to Thomas *at the Crossroads*: 'There is no *a priori* reason to assume that early Christian texts that were canonized at a certain time in the history of Christianity have more historical value than others that were lost or fell out of favour' (2).

4. See above *Jesus Remembered* 313-14 n.277. See also S. E. Young, *Jesus Tradition in the Apostolic Fathers: Their Explicit Appeals to the Words of Jesus in Light of Orality Studies* (WUNT 2.311; Tübingen: Mohr Siebeck, 2011) 74-81.

5. B. W. Henaut, *Oral Tradition and the Gospels: The Problem of Mark 4* (JSNTS 82; Sheffield: Sheffield Academic, 1993), does not hesitate to conclude that 'the oral phase of the Jesus tradition is now forever lost' (295).

tradition is well explained by what we can infer to have been the oral use and process of transmission of the Jesus tradition before it was written down. For the Synoptic tradition consistently displays the character of the same yet different. The same stories are told, but with details different. The same teachings are presented, but differently worded and grouped. And in about half the cases the differences seem to be inconsequential. This feature, 'same-yet-inconsequentially-different', is pre-eminently the character of oral tradition. It could be explained in literary terms, but the literary paradigm presupposes that there was an *original* edition which was then copied and edited, that stories and sayings of Jesus were initially recorded in an *original* version. For such a mind-set it followed that the subsequent editions or versions are not original. And when 'original' is replaced by 'authentic', then the quest of the historical Jesus becomes captivated by the goal of uncovering the 'original', with all the secondary versions regarded as for all intents and purposes 'inauthentic'.[6]

The value, then, of looking at the Synoptic tradition in its 'same-yet-different' character as oral tradition is that it frees the quester and the critic from the will-o'-the-wisp search for the sole original, the exclusively authentic. Instead, quester and critic can look at the Synoptic tradition as enduring evidence of how Jesus was actually remembered, his activities and sayings remembered differently by different disciples, the stories about and teachings of Jesus celebrated and transmitted differently from the beginning. The twenty- to thirty-year gap between Jesus and the earliest written Gospels *can* be bridged — by recognizing that the impact made by Jesus stretches out over the gulf from one side, and the Synoptic tradition seen as the expression of an orally transmitted tradition stretches out from the other side. The consistent character of the central figure of this tradition well indicates and reflects the impact that he made — Jesus as he was remembered.[7]

In *Beginning from Jerusalem* I did not give so much attention to the processes by which the Jesus tradition circulated, was used and developed during

---

6. See again S. E. Young, *Jesus Tradition in the Apostolic Fathers*, on 'Markers of Orality' (81-97).

7. I have elaborated my basic thesis on several occasions — *A New Perspective on Jesus: What the Quest for the Historical Jesus Missed* (Grand Rapids: Baker Academic/London: SPCK, 2005); 'Social Memory and the Oral Jesus Tradition', in S. C. Barton, L. T. Stuckenbruck, and B. G. Wold, eds., *Memory in the Bible and Antiquity: The Fifth Durham-Tübingen Research Symposium* (WUNT 2.212; Tübingen: Mohr Siebeck, 2007) 179-94; 'Eyewitnessses and the Oral Jesus Tradition', *JSHJ* 6 (2008) 85-105; 'Reappreciating the Oral Jesus Tradition', *Svensk Exegetisk* Årsbok 74 (2009) 1-17; and further *The Oral Gospel Tradition* (Grand Rapids: Eerdmans, 2013) — including the note that, despite the title, *Jesus Remembered*, I did not work from a theory of memory but from the probability that the character of the Synoptic tradition is itself evidence of how the impact of Jesus was conveyed to successive circles of believers in Messiah Jesus.

the first generation of Christianity. But I hope it was clear enough that we should *not* envisage the period between Jesus and the Gospels as a great empty space, with Jesus at one end, and stories about Jesus and teaching attributed to Jesus suddenly recalled by ancient apostles or created more or less out of nothing to meet some (previously unforeseen) need at the other end.[8] If Jesus proved to be an influential figure, as I assume, then the space was filled by people influenced by him. Their memories would be shared, they would be circulated, they would be interpreted, they would be elaborated, but initially almost entirely in oral forms.[9] The first disciples, apostles and teachers, would tell stories about Jesus in the gatherings of the first believers in Jesus. They would introduce the stories in their own individual styles and from the stories draw conclusions of relevance to their own situations. They would recall and repeat his teachings, grouping them in different combinations, drawing out different lessons for different circumstances, for the benefit of followers whose only access to that tradition was through those responsible for maintaining and preserving the oral tradition. It was not like the rote-learning or memorization of sacred texts — that is not the character of the Synoptic tradition. Rather it was living tradition, narratives which made the disciples' own life story meaningful, teachings by which they lived their own lives. Elsewhere in the New Testament there is little or no effort made to remember it as Jesus tradition as such. Rather in letters of Paul and James, for example, it has been absorbed into the life-blood of their own ethical teaching.[10]

There are those who draw on theories of social memory to insist that memory is creative, selecting, adapting and creating what is 'remembered' to support and give authority to the particular values and priorities of the remembering community.[11] And there is a sharp observation here which cannot be ignored; the typical museum in its selection of areas covered and material selected for display illustrates how pertinent the observation is. The key point for me, however, has always been the character of the Synoptic tradition, as evidence of *how* Jesus was remembered. The fact that the Synoptic tradition

---

8. Worth quoting again is the observation of Vincent Taylor, *The Formation of the Gospel Tradition* (London: Macmillan, ²1935): 'If the Form-Critics are right, the disciples must have been translated to heaven immediately after the Resurrection' (41).

9. *Beginning from Jerusalem* 193-96, 308-11.

10. *Jesus Remembered* 181-88; *Beginning from Jerusalem* 584-87, 1132-36.

11. M. Halbwachs, *On Collective Memory* (Chicago: University of Chicago, 1992); J. Fentress and C. Wickham, *Social Memory* (Oxford: Blackwell, 1992); M. Bal, J. Crewe and L. Spitzer, eds., *Acts of Memory: Cultural Recall in the Present* (Hanover, NH: Dartmouth College, 1999). See also A. Kirk and T. Thatcher, eds., *Memory, Tradition, and Text: Uses of the Past in Early Christianity* (Semeia Studies 52; Atlanta: Scholars, 2005); A. D. DeConick, *Recovering the Original* Gospel of Thomas: *A History of the Gospel and Its Growth* (LNTS 286; London: T & T Clark, 2005) ch. 1 ('The "New" *Traditionsgeschichtliche* Approach').

evidences the strength and the consistency of the impression made by Jesus, across three different Gospels, is itself proof sufficient that Jesus was remembered characteristically by and for the impression he made. Of course, as we shall see, each Evangelist has selected, adapted and created for his own purposes, or reflecting the emphases of his own community. But the more important factor is that the Synoptic Gospels provide a remarkably consistent portrayal of the one whose story they tell, and one almost certainly indicative of shared memories which attest the impact made by Jesus.[12]

b. The Written Tradition

But now we come to the third stage or phase of the Jesus tradition — the *transition* from *oral* Jesus tradition to *written* Jesus tradition. This development should not be seen as some sort of radical departure from the oral gospel tradition. Such a thesis was argued by Werner Kelber when he drew fresh attention to the oral gospel. He argued, in effect, that the oral tradition was itself the only authentic tradition and that the transcription of the oral tradition into writing was a kind of 'fall' from grace, the death of the living (oral) word.[13] The thesis was unfortunate since it obscured the importance of what he was saying about the oral phase of the Jesus tradition and its character as oral. But there is no reason to press for such a sharp transition between oral and written. On the contrary, there is much to be said for regarding Mark's Gospel as a natural development of the oral phase. Almost certainly it was written not for an individual to read privately, but for an audience to hear being read aloud.[14] It uses the same tricks and techniques of the oral perfor-

---

12. The mature assessment of C. H. Dodd in his last great work, *The Founder of Christianity* (London: Collins, 1971), deserves repetition: 'The first three gospels offer a body of sayings on the whole so consistent, so coherent, and withal so distinctive in manner, style and content, that no reasonable critic should doubt, whatever reservations he may have about individual sayings, that we find here reflected the thought of a single, unique teacher' (21-22). See further my 'Social Memory and the Oral Jesus Tradition', reprinted in *The Oral Gospel Tradition* 230-47.

13. W. H. Kelber, *The Oral and the Written Gospel* (Philadelphia: Fortress, 1983): for example, 'the gospel signals a disruption of the oral synthesis' (92); it constituted an 'indictment of oral process and authorities', an 'alienation from the oral apparatus', 'emancipation from oral identity'; Mark 'repudiates oral representatives' (98); see further ch. 5, and his earlier 'Mark and Oral Tradition', in N. R. Petersen, ed., *Perspectives on Mark's Gospel* 7-55.

14. As Hengel pointed out in the same year: 'The Second Gospel probably developed out of living oral teaching and was composed for solemn reading in worship. The short cola, often with a rhythmic shape, point to oral recitation in the assembled community. The

mance of tradition.¹⁵ It was in effect *a written version of an oral recitation of Jesus tradition*. An important corollary should again not be missed: that what a whole generation of scholars has regarded as (literary) redaction was in the first instance little more than the variation which different oral teachers would give to the tradition they were teaching, to bring out its relevance to the situation of the particular audience addressed. In the case of Mark's Gospel, of course, the variation and application were no doubt more sustained through what was in effect a very full performance of the tradition. But at least it is important to be aware that any redactional adaptation of earlier tradition was not part of some fundamental transition from oral to written, but something most congregations would be familiar with from long experience of the Jesus tradition being celebrated and expounded. We will see how Mark handled the tradition in the next section (§42.2), but some more general comments are appropriate here.

First, the contrast between oral and written as between flexible and fixed runs the risk of repeating the mistake of understanding the quest as a quest for the 'original' version of a story or a saying. The point has already been made that if Jesus taught the same message many times, and in varied terms, then the idea of a single 'original' version of his teachings is a misleading and dangerous delusion. To that has to be added the further observation that if, say, Mark's Gospel is some sort of record of Peter's preaching (Papias),¹⁶ then presumably Peter did not tell any story about Jesus or repeat any teaching of Jesus only once. And presumably in these many preaching occasions Peter did not always use the same words or repeat the same selection of Jesus tradition parrot-like.¹⁷ So it would be equally fatuous to assume that Mark, if he was drawing on Peter's preaching, was restricted to only one version of each story about Jesus and each saying of Jesus. And Mark's version of such

---

Gospel was written for the audience to listen to . . .' (*Studies in Mark* 52); though Hengel also speaks of 'the revolutionary innovation of writing a gospel' (52).

15. T. P. Haverly, *Oral Traditional Narrative and the Composition of Mark's Gospel* (Edinburgh PhD diss., 1983); J. Dewey, 'Oral Methods of Structuring Narrative in Mark', *Interpretation* 43 (1989) 32-44; also 'The Gospel of Mark as an Oral-Aural Event: Implications for Interpretation', in E. S. Malbon and E. V. McKnight, eds., *The New Literary Criticism and the New Testament* (JSNTSup 109; Sheffield: Sheffield Academic Press, 1994) 145-63; C. Bryan, *A Preface to Mark: Notes on the Gospel in Its Literary and Cultural Settings* (Oxford: Oxford University, 1993) Part II; W. Shiner, *Proclaiming the Gospel: First-Century Performance of Mark* (Harrisburg: TPI, 2003). Other bibliography in Young, *Jesus Tradition in the Apostolic Fathers* 7 n.17.

16. See above §39 at n.20.

17. Papias indeed says that Peter 'adjusted his instructions to the needs' of his hearers (Eusebius, *HE* 3.39.15). We may compare even the modern politician's 'stump' campaign speech which would not simply be repeated word-for-word at each rally.

tradition (Petrine recollections?) should be seen less as fixed and final, and more as exemplary of how the Jesus tradition was used and could be used. Mark, then, should not be seen as bringing to an end the flexibility of the oral period, but as providing a more lasting example of how it could be used in extended and Gospel form — an example, of course, which Matthew and Luke followed and thus demonstrated the point that the gospel of/about Jesus could be told variously.

Second, although I have emphasized that the great bulk of the Jesus tradition would have been used and transmitted orally, it is entirely possible that some at least of the Jesus tradition was transcribed at an early stage.[18] It is not that written material would be regarded as more reliable than oral. Such a view is once again an expression of the literary mindset; denizens of twenty-first-century Europe and North America have become so reliant on written records that the ability to absorb quickly into the memory and to retain even information of first importance to them is much less efficient than in oral societies. In contrast, prior to the reliability of the printing press, written texts were generally regarded as *less* reliable than what the memory retained for itself.[19] Writing, of course, would have become a factor when distance was involved; in the same way that letters could serve as a substitute for personal presence.[20] Such writing, however, evidently did not rigidify or imprison the Jesus tradition. Here again we should learn from the Synoptic tradition. The diversity between the Synoptic Gospels again shows that the Evangelists did not regard it as essential that they should convey forms made fixed and rigid by writing. Even though Matthew and Luke evidently knew and used at least one written source (Mark), they did not merely copy what Mark had written, but gave their own version even of the traditions which Mark conveyed. In other words, *the flexibility of the oral transmission period carried over into the written forms of the tradition.*

One of the major failings of the attempts to resolve the Synoptic problem in exclusively literary terms was the inference (not usually consciously formulated) that when Matthew or Luke received their copies of Mark's Gospel, that was the first time that each had encountered the stories and teaching contained in Mark. But such a scenario is scarcely credible. Much or most of the Jesus tradition enscribed by Mark must have been widely circulating and

---

18. We can be confident that at least one of Jesus' twelve close disciples was literate — Matthew — since he would need scribal skills for his post as a toll-collector.

19. L. C. A. Alexander, "The Living Voice: Scepticism towards the Written Word in Early Christianity and in Graeco-Roman Texts," in D. J. A. Clines et al., eds., *The Bible in Three Dimensions: Essays in Celebration of Forty Years of Biblical Studies in the University of Sheffield* (Sheffield: Sheffield Academic Press, 1990) 221-47.

20. *Beginning from Jerusalem* 588-89.

been well known in the Christian communities in Syria and beyond.[21] In at least many cases where Matthew and Mark significantly diverge on the same tradition, the most obvious explanation is that Matthew knew an (oral) version of that tradition different from the Markan version, and that Matthew preferred in these cases to transcribe the other version, which perhaps he knew better.[22] In other words, we probably see in such data evidence of Jesus tradition both oral and written circulating at the same time and among the same churches. Initially the written was essentially a transcription of one version of the oral, or was itself a scribal presentation of Jesus tradition sharing the same characteristics (the same but different) as typical oral presentations. Nor should we forget that most Christians' knowledge of the written Gospels would have been by hearing, and any further reference to the Jesus tradition thus heard would be in oral form ('second orality').

Third, all this means that the understanding of Q has to be revised.[23] The non-Markan material common to Matthew and Luke should not simply be grouped together on the assumption that it all comes from a single document. As I noted earlier, there is certainly evidence that some of the Q material had been put into writing. But beyond that the evidence will not support the hypothesis of a single written document. Beyond the passages of near-identical wording, the diversity is such that another explanation is much more likely: namely, that such diversity exemplifies the varied sequence or sequences of oral tradition, as used by apostles and teachers in the various Christian assemblies, the varied sequences representative of the typical repertoires such as many Christian teachers drew from the community store of tradition for which they were particularly responsible. The fact that the Q hypothesis finds it necessary to envisage different versions or different editions of Q[24] simply underlines the myopic character of the literary mindset at this point. That Matthew and Luke had access to much more material than Mark is clear. That some of it was already in writing is highly probable. But that they also knew the Jesus tradition as living oral tradition, with the sort of diversity which we still find in the Synoptic tradition, is equally probable. The attempt to recover

---

21. Cf. Brown, *Introduction* 206-7. See further below at n.41.

22. See e.g. my 'Matthew's Awareness of Markan Redaction', in *The Four Gospels. Festschrift for Frans Neirynck*, ed. F. Van Segbroeck (Leuven University Press, 1992) 1349-59; reprinted in *The Oral Gospel Tradition* ch. 4.

23. I have made this point before — e.g. *Jesus Remembered* §7.4; and 'Q¹ as Oral Tradition', in M. Bockmuehl and D. A. Hagner, eds., *The Written Gospel*, G. N. Stanton FS (Cambridge: Cambridge University, 2005) 45-69, reprinted in *The Oral Gospel Tradition* ch. 3 — but it bears repeating here.

24. So, e.g., Schnelle, *History* 187.

a Q document is in many ways admirable.[25] But it has prevented us from recognizing that well into the second half of the first century (and beyond)[26] the Jesus tradition was still well known in oral mode. And by assuming the fixity of written sources the attempt to recover a written Q has lost sight of the living character of the Jesus tradition.

Fourth, we should not make the mistake of thinking that there was a single transition from oral to written, as though the writing down of the Jesus tradition made an end to the oral tradition, or brought the flexible character of the Jesus tradition to an end. On the contrary, it is evident from the echoes and uses made of the Jesus tradition, for example in James, 1 Peter,[27] and, as we shall see, in the Apostolic Fathers,[28] that they knew versions of the Jesus tradition alluded to which were different from the versions used by the Gospels. To use such echoes and allusions of Jesus tradition only as evidence in the debates as to whether there was a Q document or whether the canonical Evangelists were already known[29] is once again to lose sight of how widely the Jesus tradition was known in oral form and of its degree of variability. In other words, the oral forms of Jesus tradition continued alongside the written versions into the second century. And here again, as Richard Bauckham has demonstrated with regard to James, the way they drew on the Jesus tradition again evidences the flexibility of the tradition, as they adapted it to the needs which they were addressing.[30]

Here we may simply add, though it takes us beyond the present stage of the investigation, the argument of recent textual critics that the transition to written forms did not kill the flexibility of the tradition.[31] For just as we have seen the inadequacy of thinking in terms of a single original version of items of the Jesus tradition, so these textual critics have moved away from assuming that there must have been a single original text, alone authentic, with all the variations being the result of textual corruption, of scribal error and mistake. On the contrary, what we have in the textual tradition is evidence of different versions of these texts, the different versions which were in fact the NT writings for different churches, often reflecting the differing concerns and needs

---

25. I refer, of course, to Robinson et al., *The Critical Edition of Q*.
26. See below §§44.2-3.
27. See *Beginning from Jerusalem* 1134-36, 1154.
28. See particularly Koester in §44 n.14 below, and further in §44.
29. The issue is fully discussed in §44 below.
30. R. Bauckham, *James: Wisdom of James, Disciple of Jesus the Sage* (London: Routledge, 1999), whom I largely follow (*Beginning from Jerusalem* 1132-36).
31. D. C. Parker, *The Living Text of the Gospels* (Cambridge: Cambridge University, 1997); E. J. Epp, 'The Multivalence of the Term "Original Text" in New Testament Textual Criticism', *HTR* 92 (1999) 245-81.

of their differing communities.[32] In other words, the textual tradition itself attests the continuing flexibility of (in this case) the Jesus tradition. This is a topic to which we will have to return.

c. Evangelists' Awareness of Other Strands of Tradition

One other issue demands some reflection before we turn to the written Gospels as such. This is the question whether those responsible for the different strands or collections of the Jesus tradition were aware of the other strands/collections. When the issue was posed in terms of literary sources, the question would have been, for example, whether Mark knew Q, or the special Matthean material (M), or the special Lukan material (L). And if we follow B. H. Streeter's suggestion, the question could be translated into whether the churches of Rome, Jerusalem, Caesarea and Antioch knew the Jesus tradition possessed by the others.[33] Even if we describe that Jesus tradition as collections of tradition in oral forms rather than (completely) in written sources, the question remains the same. The fact that the Markan material is largely different from the Q material, and the M and L material different again, certainly raises a question which cannot be ignored.

I have thus far resisted the working hypothesis of many studying the Gospels and the Sitze-im-Leben ('life-settings') of the Gospels: that each strand or collection of Jesus tradition was effectively the exclusive possession of one group or church and can therefore serve as a source for that group's/church's theology or christology.[34] I think it hardly methodologically wise or credible to assume that each group/church had a single collection of only one kind of Jesus tradition — wisdom teaching, or miracle stories, or controversy stories, etc. Part of the value of seeing the pre-written Gospel material as very largely consisting of collections of stories and teaching is that it becomes easier to conceive of apostles and teachers as possessing and maintaining varied collections of the diverse material that made up the Jesus tradition. The same apostle, the same teacher, would sometimes tell stories of Jesus' miracle working, at other times of his controversies, at other times his parables, and so

---

32. The point was forcefully made by Ehrman in his *The Orthodox Corruption of Scripture*.

33. B. H. Streeter, *The Four Gospels: A Study of Origins* (London: Macmillan, 1924) ch. 9.

34. This was the trajectory followed by form-criticism, encouraged by Koester's 'One Jesus and Four Primitive Gospels', and reinforced by the burgeoning sociological interpretation of the Gospels.

on. Worship and teaching sessions could draw on different strands as occasion permitted or demanded.[35]

On the other hand, we equally cannot assume that the Jesus tradition *in toto* formed as it were a huge cistern, to which each community had full access, and on which the community's apostle(s) and teachers could freely draw. Are we to assume, for example, that Mark knew the Q material and simply chose to ignore it?[36] Alternatively, are we to assume that what Mark wrote down was the totality of the Jesus tradition that he knew, and that he would (no doubt) have been pleasantly surprised to hear the Q material being drawn on when he (subsequently) visited other congregations? It is impossible to answer such questions with clarity and full conviction. But two observations do emerge from the data themselves.

One is that Mark's emphasis on Jesus as a teacher[37] suggests that he knew more of Jesus' teaching than he has recorded. In which case, why, then, for example, did he not record more of Jesus' parables? An obvious answer would be that he chose his material selectively in order to develop the plot of the story he was telling in his own way. So long as we do not make the unjustified assumption that Mark must have wanted to use all the Jesus tradition he knew in narrating his Gospel, then there is little or no difficulty in recognizing that he might well have selected and trimmed the tradition he actually did use, and that he passed over other material which he might well have used, had he so chosen.[38] There are few if any biographers and historians, ancient or modern, who have used all the material available to them. The probability, then, is that Mark too drew from the material available to him the episodes and the teachings which could be used to tell his story with the emphases he wanted to make.[39]

To give two examples. It is quite possible that Mark knew a fuller version of John the Baptist's teaching (Mark 1.7-8); he was at least well aware that John had a reputation for being outspoken (6.18). But Mark could have chosen to omit the judgmental note which is so strong in the Q material used by Matthew and Luke (Matt. 3.11-12/Luke 3.15-18), perhaps because early

---

35. I refer again to my warning against the 'one document per community' fallacy (*Jesus Remembered* 150).

36. A firmly negative answer is given by Lührmann, *Markusevangelium* 12; C. Tuckett, 'Mark and Q', in *The Synoptic Gospels: Source Criticism and the New Literary Criticism* (BETL 110; Leuven: Leuven University, 1993) 149-75; Marcus, *Mark 1-8* 51-53.

37. See below §42.2c.

38. Cf. the final verse of John's Gospel: 'there are many other things that Jesus did; if every one of them were written down, I suppose that the world itself could not contain the books that would be written' (John 21.25 NRSV).

39. See further below §42.2b.

Christians who knew the Baptist's prediction of another baptism to come, knew too that being baptized in the Spirit as they had experienced it (1 Cor. 12.13) was much less judgmental than John had indicated.[40] Again, it is very unlikely that Mark knew what is now universally known as 'the Sermon on the Mount' (Matt. 5-7). But Luke's briefer 'Sermon on the Plain' (Luke 6.17-49) shows that the teachings collected by Matthew into his Sermon were known in briefer collections; and other Lukan parallels show that the sayings were known and used individually.[41] So we should not ignore the fact that much of Matthew's and Luke's Sermons was known to Mark, but in scattered individual forms,[42] and it becomes entirely plausible that Mark knew a good deal more but chose not to use it since it did not fit so well with the shape and thrust of his Gospel.

The other observation is the number of doublets easily visible and recognized between Mark and Q.[43] In *Jesus Remembered* I noted that Mark and Q seem to have different but overlapping collections of Jesus' teaching about his exorcisms.[44] This indicates: (i) that the interest in what Jesus taught about his exorcistic ministry was such that several (all?) of his sayings on the subject were put together to form a unit; (ii) that there were different groupings of these sayings as used, presumably, by different churches. We could conclude that the one had abbreviated a larger common pool of tradition, or that the other (or both) had elaborated a smaller common pool of tradition. But more likely the differences simply illustrate how the shared memory was actually retained and circulated by different groups. Again Mark 4.21-25 and 8.34-38 are examples of various teachings of Jesus having been grouped by Mark or the tradition on which he drew (and followed by Matt. 16.24-27 and Luke 9.23-26), but recalled by Q in a variety of scattered settings.[45] Here too the obvious deduction to be made is that this was typical of the diverse ways the Jesus tradition was retained, used and transmitted — some being grouped in

---

40. See *Jesus Remembered* 366-69.

41. Matt. 5.13 — Luke 14.34-35; Matt. 5.15-16 — Luke 8.16; Matt. 5.17-18 — Luke 16.16-17; Matt. 5.24-26 — Luke 12.57-59; Matt. 5.31 — Luke 16.18; Matt. 6.9-13 — Luke 11.2-4; etc.

42. Matt. 5.13 — Mark 9.49-50; Matt. 5.15 — Mark 4.21; Matt. 5.30 — Mark 9.43; Matt. 6.14-15 — Mark 11.25[-26]; Matt. 7.2 — Mark 4.24.

43. Still valuable is the listing provided by J. C. Hawkins, *Horae Synopticae: Contributions to the Study of the Synoptic Problem* (Oxford: Clarendon, 1898, ²1909) 80-107. See also Schnelle, *History* 181; Fitzmyer, *Luke* 1.81-82; Marcus, *Mark 1-8* 42-44.

44. Mark 3.22-29; Matt. 12.24-32, 43-45/Luke 11.15-26; 12.10); see *Jesus Remembered* 456.

45. Mark 4.21-25 = Matt. 5.15/Luke 8.16 + Matt. 10.26/Luke 8.17 + Matt. 7.2/Luke 8.18 and 6.38 + Matt. 13.12/Luke 8.18; Mark 8.34-38 = Matt. 10.38/Luke 14.27 + Matt. 10.39/Luke 17.33 + Matt. 10.33/Luke 12.9.

more lasting combinations, others, or the same at other times, being drawn on individually as occasion allowed or need demanded. We should assume neither that Mark was confronted by a ragbag of diverse materials and that he was the first to impose order upon them, nor that all his material had already been set in firm and enduring units and that he might have had qualms about breaking up or selecting from groups which as a group did not serve his purpose.

As for the other two Synoptic Gospels, I will simply say again what I have said before. We should not assume that it was only when Matthew or Luke received the written Gospel of Mark that they became aware of all the Jesus tradition on which Mark had drawn in composing his Gospel. It is much the more likely that they were aware of large portions of the Markan material in varying oral forms, and that they often preferred the version with which they were more familiar rather than Mark's. The point can only be documented explicitly by reference to the same phenomena of doublets (Matthew and Luke both following Mark's version and including other versions as well).[46] But it is entirely plausible that their familiarity with other versions of the Markan materials extended further than the evidence of the doublets. Perhaps above all we need to allow for the fluidity of the Jesus tradition in its pre-written forms, and the diversity in the wording with which the Jesus tradition was remembered and used across the sweep of earliest Christianity.

42.2 The Gospel according to Mark

As with the transition from gospel to Gospel, so with the transition from oral Jesus tradition to written Gospel we have to pay first attention to Mark. For, by general consent, it was Mark who first transcribed the oral Jesus tradition into an extensive written form, into a full-blown narrative, into a Gospel.[47] The procedure by which he enacted this almost revolutionary act — certainly a creative act of inestimable consequences — can best be described by focusing on two questions. The questions are inter-related, but for clarity of discussion can be treated sequentially. (a) How did Mark contrive his Gospel from the Jesus tradition? (b) Why did Mark write his Gospel? What did he hope to achieve?

---

46. See again n.44 above.

47. For the usual introductory questions (author, date, intended recipients) see §39.2a, also §41.2 above. Mark's writing a complete 'Gospel' can be appropriately seen as the outcome of a process in which individual Jesus traditions were grouped and performed in thematic groups. W. R. Telford, *Writing on the Gospel of Mark* (Blandford Forum: Deo, 2009), provides a comprehensive bibliography.

a. How Did Mark Set About Writing His Gospel?[48]

Here once more we need to remind ourselves that we are not talking about Mark's editing of (a) written source(s). It is more a matter of Mark putting into writing what he might otherwise have presented orally in a Christian gathering in morning, afternoon or early evening.[49] We have already noted that the Gospel itself evinces various oral features,[50] which suggests that Mark was accustomed to hearing Jesus tradition being performed in Christian assemblies, and may even himself have been responsible for such use of Jesus tradition catechetically or in other teaching or apologetic situations.[51] The Papias tradition already referred to[52] has in view only Mark's familiarity with the tradition as used by Peter in teaching. But it is not difficult, and wholly plausible historically, to conceive of Mark's familiarity also with the Jesus tradition as drawn upon by other Christian teachers and celebrated in the various churches in whose assemblies he participated. Moreover, the fact that Petrine influences in Mark's Gospel are as allusive and as incidental as they are,[53] suggests that even if Mark was particularly beholden to Peter, he evidently did not think it necessary to underline that his writing down of the Gospel was at Peter's behest or with Peter's authority as such.[54] The gospel whose content formed the Gospel was well enough known as the gospel of Jesus Christ.

The history of the critical study of the Synoptic Gospels began to draw attention to the particularities of the individual Gospels at the beginning of the twentieth century and brought to light several features which help bring out Mark's technique. I have referred to them in earlier volumes,[55] but will repeat the salient points here.

---

48. I refer to 'Mark' here simply to denote the author of the Gospel of Mark; for the question of authorship see above §39.2a. Similarly with the equivalent headings below (§§42.3a and 42.4a).

49. It would take about two hours to read the whole Gospel in a single gathering (Marcus, *Mark 1-8* 68). As Alec McCowen showed in his 1978 solo performance of the complete text of St Mark's Gospel, the Gospel of Mark can be performed in a single evening. France treats Mark as 'A Drama in Three Acts' (*Gospel of Mark* 11-15).

50. See above n.14.

51. The earlier literary mind-set thought almost entirely in terms of written sources; see e.g. those cited by Kümmel, *Introduction* 84-85.

52. See above §39.2a.

53. See again Bauckham (above §39 n.28).

54. This is consistent with the practice of the earliest Christians as evidenced by Paul's use of Jesus tradition and Q material; see *Jesus Remembered* 181-88, and earlier my 'Jesus Tradition in Paul', in B. Chilton and C. A. Evans, eds., *Studying the Historical Jesus: Evaluations of the State of Current Research* (Leiden: Brill, 1994) 155-78.

55. *Jesus Remembered* 50, 74, 247; *Beginning from Jerusalem* 120-27.

First, Julius Wellhausen demonstrated that in each of the Synoptic Gospels one can distinguish between old tradition and the editorial contribution of the Evangelist. It is the editorial work and concerns of the Evangelist which have given each Gospel its present form, whereas Wellhausen thought the earlier tradition to have consisted chiefly of single brief units.[56] K. L. Schmidt went on to examine the connecting links which join together the separate episodes in Mark's Gospel. He concluded that almost all the references to time and place are to be found in the verses which connect the single narratives into the larger whole; that is, they are part of the editorial work of the Evangelist. Schmidt followed Wellhausen in concluding that the original tradition was made up almost entirely of brief, single units which lack note of time or indication of place; that is, which lack historical reference. According to Schmidt, the impression that Mark gives of being a continuous historical narrative is given entirely by the editorial links.[57] These findings provided the basis for the still influential view that the oral tradition on which Mark drew consisted for the most part of brief single units — an assumption which I have already questioned.[58] But the point for us now is the corollary to be drawn directly from the findings of both Wellhausen and Schmidt, that it is by focusing on this editorial material that the intention and the authorial art of the Evangelist can most clearly be discerned.[59]

Wellhausen and Schmidt provided the launch pad for form criticism, the study of the individual units making up the oral tradition before they were put together by the Evangelists. Some decades later, however, H. W. Kuhn drew attention to the fact that it made more sense of the actual evidence of Mark's Gospel to infer that Mark had been able to draw upon not just individual units, but also collections of pre-Markan traditions.[60] Good examples are the group of controversy stories (Mark 2.1-3.6), the block of parables (4.2-33) and the sequence of miracles round the lake (4.35–5.43, 6.32-52). In the sort

---

56. Wellhausen summed up his argument in his *Einleitung in die drei ersten Evangelien* (Berlin: Georg Reimer, 1905): 'The ultimate source of the Gospels is oral tradition, but this contains only scattered material. The units, more or less extensive, circulate in it separately. Their combination into a whole is always the work of an author and as a rule the work of a literary artist (*Schriftsteller*)' (43).

57. K. L. Schmidt, *Der Rahmen der Geschichte Jesus: Literarkritische Untersuchungen zur ältesten Jesusüberlieferung* (Berlin: Trowitzsch & Sohn, 1919): the thesis already spelled out clearly on the first page of the Foreword (v).

58. See *Jesus Remembered* 127-28, 193-95, 241-42, 245-48.

59. See particularly P. Dschulnigg, *Sprache, Redaktion und Intention des Markus-Evangeliums* (SBB 11; Stuttgart: KBW, 1986).

60. H. W. Kuhn, *Ältere Sammlungen im Markusevangelium* (Göttingen: Vandenhoeck, 1971). Note also the quotation from A. B. Lord in *Jesus Remembered* 247 n.300. See also the brief reviews of Brown, *Introduction* 150-51, and Marcus, *Mark 1-8* 57-59.

of oral society which we must envisage for the middle of the first century, it is entirely plausible that such groupings of similar material and bunching of similar stories were typical of the resources treasured by church teachers or elders as to the techniques by which they remembered, taught and transmitted the Jesus tradition for which they had responsibility.

In the second half of the twentieth century form criticism came to be regarded as focusing too much on the pre-Gospels tradition. In consequence, partly by way of reaction, more attention was given to the Evangelists' editing of the preformed material which they had inherited (redaction criticism)[61] and to the Evangelists' overall structuring of their material (narrative or composition criticism).[62] The predecessor here was William Wrede, who, at about the same time as Wellhausen's work on the Gospels, looked at the structure of the Gospels as a whole and discerned a major structural element in their composition, particularly Mark's Gospel. This was 'the messianic secret' motif which he found to be prominent in Mark; that is, the secrecy motif which Mark or his tradition used to explain why Jesus' messiahship had not been recognized by his own people.[63] I have also suggested that by putting the logic of redaction criticism into reverse, the editorial work of Mark may also be recognized. For if Matthew's and Luke's *redaction* of Mark tells us something about the theologies of Matthew and Luke, then perhaps what Matthew and Luke have *omitted* in their reworking of Mark tells us that they were aware of the distinctive features of Mark's retelling of Jesus tradition and that, in several cases at least, chose to omit the Markan distinctives in their own retelling.[64]

The editorial work of Mark, then, can be determined by looking at a

---

61. See e.g. N. Perrin, *What Is Redaction Criticism?* (Philadelphia: Fortress Press, 1969).

62. See particularly D. Rhoads, J. Dewey and D. Michie, *Mark as Story: An Introduction to the Narrative of a Gospel* (Minneapolis: Fortress, ²1999); and more generally M. A. Powell, *What Is Narrative Criticism?* (Minneapolis: Fortress, 1990).

63. W. Wrede, *Das Messiasgeheimnis in den Evangelien: Zugleich ein Beitrag zum Verstandnis des Markusevangeliums* (Göttingen, 1901); ET *The Messianic Secret* (Cambridge: James Clarke, not till 1971). As Schnelle notes, Wrede himself had not attributed the 'secret' to Mark's creation, but subsequently it became a more common view that the messianic secret and its theology should be attributed to Mark himself (*History* 214-15). See also the collection of articles in C. Tuckett, ed., *The Messianic Secret* (London: SPCK, 1983).

64. See my 'Matthew's Awareness of Markan Redaction' (n.22 above); also 'Matthew as Wirkungsgeschichte', in P. Lampe et al., eds., *Neutestamentiche Exegesis im Dialog: Hermeneutik — Wirkungsgeschichte — Matthäusevangelium*; U. Luz FS (Neukirchen-Vluyn: Neukirchener, 2008) 149-66 (here 153-55); both reprinted in *The Oral Gospel Tradition*. See already J. Schreiber, 'Die Christologie des Markusevangeliums', *ZTK* 58 (1961) 154; R. H. Stein, 'The Proper Methodology for Ascertaining Markan Redaction', *NovT* 13 (1971) 181-98, reprinted in D. E. Orton, ed., *The Composition of Mark's Gospel* (Leiden: Brill, 1999) 4-51 (here 40-41).

number of features: (i) the editorial links between passages, often indicated by the distinctive way in which Mark introduces the unit or sequence;[65] (ii) summary statements in which Mark covers ground rapidly between episodes;[66] (iii) consistent thematic emphases which he has given to several of the episodes he relates.[67] I am less persuaded of the value of a fourth criterion which gained some appeal — the distinctiveness of Mark's vocabulary. That worked well enough where terminology was distinctive or unique to Mark.[68] And it worked well enough with terms like *euangelion*, as Willi Marxsen showed.[69] But what about terms which are only *predominantly* Markan, but occur also, less frequently, in what can be regarded as Markan source material? Should we say that a favourite Markan term was therefore introduced by Mark to his version of the tradition? But how then do we allow for the possibility that Mark seized upon a term or motif which occurred only occasionally in the Jesus tradition he knew and that he then inquired whether there were more examples of that term or motif known to other tradents? How, in a word, to distinguish source from redaction?[70]

If we approach Mark looking for his editorial emphases and thumbprints in the ways indicated, then we should gain a clear answer to our second question.

b. The Good News of Jesus Christ

Our second range of questions was, Why did Mark write his Gospel? What did he hope to achieve? The first part of the answer has already been given in §41: that Mark set out to provide the content of 'the gospel of Jesus Christ' (Mark 1.1) and in so doing crafted the first Gospel. Here we need to elaborate

---

65. A good example is the introduction and conclusion which provides the frame for what appears to have been a pre-Markan collection of parables (Mark 4.1, 33-34).

66. I refer to the obvious summary passages in Mark 1.21-22, 32-34; 3.7-12; 6.53-56.

67. I have already drawn attention to Mark's Gospel as a 'passion narrative with extended introduction' (§41.2c).

68. Mark drives his narrative along at a great pace, by frequent use of *euthus* ('immediately') and *palin* ('again'), the historic present tense, and parataxis (clauses linked by 'and'), features which Matthew and Luke regularly fail to reproduce. See e.g. Turner, *Grammar* 19-20, 34; also France, *Mark* 16-18.

69. See above §41.2a.

70. The problem is evident in E. J. Pryke, *Redactional Style in the Markan Gospel* (SNTSMS 33; Cambridge: Cambridge University, 1978). See further Stein, 'Proper Methodology for Ascertaining Markan Redaction'; C. C. Black, *The Disciples according to Mark: Markan Redaction in Current Debate* (JSNTS 27; Sheffield: Sheffield Academic, 1989) 23-38; also Brown's cautionary comments (*Introduction* 150-51).

that answer, first of all by indicating how Mark presented the central figure of his Gospel, Jesus himself, looking at the three most prominent features of Mark's christology. Since our task is to investigate how Mark shaped the Jesus tradition in presenting it as Gospel, we can proceed by giving special attention to Mark's editorial work, insofar as that can be discerned.

i. Jesus as 'the Son of God'

Mark clearly wanted to present Jesus as God's Son and to persuade his audiences accordingly.[71]

- This is the voice which Jesus hears when he is baptized by John: 'You are my beloved Son, with you I am well pleased' (Mark 1.11).[72]
- In the editorial summary, the unclean spirits also hail Jesus, 'You are the Son of God' (3.11);[73] as does the Gerasene demoniac, 'Jesus, Son of the Most High God' (5.7); cf. 1.24, 'the holy one of God'.
- On the Mount of Transfiguration, the heavenly voice announces, 'This is my Son, the beloved, listen to him' (9.7).
- In the parable of the dishonest tenants, the vineyard owner finally sends his 'beloved son' (12.6).[74]
- 'No one knows' when the kingdom will come, 'neither the angels in heaven, nor the Son, but only the Father' (13.32). If reference to 'the Son' was added (by Mark?) to the tradition,[75] it could count as an enhancing of the status of Jesus by denying that his status was even higher — Jesus as (only) 'the Son' of 'the Father'.
- The *abba* prayer ('Abba, Father') of 14.36 is not enhanced by Mark, but

---

71. E. K. Broadhead, *Naming Jesus: Titular Christology in the Gospel of Mark* (JSNTS 175; Sheffield Academic, 1999), examines 16 'titles' used by Mark for Jesus, without giving 'Son of God' particular prominence. Collins highlights Mark's 'interpretation of Jesus' by giving first place to 'Jesus as Prophet' (*Mark* 44-52), though the motif is hardly as important for Mark as 'Son of God' (cf. only Mark 6.4; 6.15; 8.28; 14.65). J. D. Kingsbury, *The Christology of Mark's Gospel* (Philadelphia: Fortress, 1983), justifiably focused on the 'two major aspects' of Mark's portrayal of Jesus: Messiah, and correlated titles (including Son of God), and Son of Man, as complementing each other (173-76).

72. The heavenly voice is usually taken to be a combination of Isa. 42.1 (the Servant of the Lord) and Ps. 2.7 (Messiah); see e.g. Guelich, *Mark 1–8:26* 33-34; Collins, *Mark* 150-51. Mark presumably saw the descent of the Spirit as Jesus' anointing for his messianic role, though it does not follow that Mark thought of the event as Jesus' becoming or adoption as God's Son (see Marcus, *Mark 1–8* 160).

73. This is one of the Markan summaries which Matthew does not follow.

74. Matthew omits the 'beloved' (Matt. 21.37). Evans thinks an allusion to Gen. 22.2 is likely (the offering of Isaac) (*Mark 8:27–16:20* 234-35).

75. *Jesus Remembered* 723.

it reinforces the motif that Jesus' sonship is expressed in suffering, in accordance with God's will.
- In the hearing before the Council, Jesus' fate is sealed by his affirmative reply to the high priest's question, 'Are you the Messiah, the Son of the Blessed?' (14.61-62).[76]
- Most strikingly of all, Mark's Gospel climaxes with the confession of the Roman centurion who has just seen the crucified Jesus breathe his last: 'Truly this man was God's Son' (15.39),[77] the truth that the high priest could not accept.[78]

We should also draw attention to the fact that Mark headlined his whole Gospel as 'the Gospel of Jesus Christ' (Mark 1.1). And he may have added, 'the Son of God'. That last phrase ('the Son of God'), however, is not present in some of the earliest manuscripts of Mark. So it was probably added by later scribes.[79] However, if that was the case, it must be because the scribes in view recognized how central was the theme of Jesus as 'the Son of God' to Mark's Gospel. In other words, those who added the phrase may simply have brought out more clearly and explicitly what was already quite clear for those who read Mark's Gospel carefully. In any case, the bracketing or inclusio character of 1.1 or 1.11 and 15.39 underlines the importance which Mark placed on the claim that his Gospel was 'the gospel of Jesus Christ, Son of God'.

Here, of course, we have to join this emphasis both with Mark's underlining of the *gospel* character of his story (§41.2b) and with the passion theme which dominates the Gospel (§41.2c). The point is that for Mark the good news is not that Jesus is to be understood as God's Son as one might speak of a king or a great philosopher as a son of God.[80] Jesus' sonship is attested by heaven as a special sonship — 'my Son, the beloved'. Nor is Jesus' sonship to be understood as one might understand the sonship of Hanina ben Dosa or Honi the Circle-Drawer — as one whose prayers had special effect.[81] Jesus' sonship for Mark includes suffering and climaxes in his being condemned to death. That is the good news! The superb irony for Mark is that it is the Ro-

---

76. See further below at nn.157, 158.

77. Matt. 27.54 follows Mark, but Luke reads, 'This man was just' (Luke 23.47).

78. 'A kind of christological summation', 'a kind of resume of the gospel' (Gnilka, *Markus* 1.26, 63). Collins has a full discussion of the verse (*Mark* 764-71).

79. See e.g. Collins, *Mark* 130. C. R. Kazmierski, *Jesus, the Son of God: A Study of the Markan Tradition and Its Redaction by the Evangelist* (Würzburg: Echter, 1979) ch. 1, and Guelich, *Mark 1–8:26* 6, defend the longer reading.

80. A customary usage then; see *Christology in the Making* §3.2.

81. G. Vermes, *Jesus the Jew* (London: Collins, 1973), drew particular attention to the parallels to Jesus which these charismatic rabbis provided.

man centurion who is the only human being who confesses Jesus as God's Son. And the one he confesses as God's Son has just died on a cross (Mark 15.39).

ii. Jesus as Healer and Exorcist

Any reading of Mark's Gospel cannot help but notice how consistently Mark portrays Jesus as a very successful healer and exorcist in the first half of his Gospel.

- 1.23-28 — healing of a demoniac[82] in the synagogue;[83]
- 1.29-31 — healing of Peter's mother-in-law;
- 1.32-34 — summary of healings and exorcisms;
- 1.39 — summary of preaching and exorcising;[84]
- 1.40-45 — cleansing of a leper;
- 2.1-12 — healing of a paralyzed man;
- 3.1-5 — healing of a man with a withered hand;
- 3.10-12 — summary of healings and exorcisms;[85]
- 3.22-27 — dispute with Pharisees about his powers of exorcism;
- 4.35-41 — stilling of a storm on the sea of Galilee;[86]
- 5.1-20 — exorcism of a Gerasene demoniac;[87]
- 5.21-43 — healing of a woman with a haemorrhage and of Jairus's daughter;[88]
- 6.3, 5 — Jesus' inability to heal more than a few in Nazareth;[89]
- 6.12-13 — disciples sent out to preach, exorcize and heal;
- 6.32-44 — feeding of 5,000;

---

82. Mark prefers to use the term 'unclean spirit' (Mark 11x, Matt. 2x, Luke 6x); 'demon' is a more common term (Mark 13x; Matt. 11x; Luke 23x); 'possessed by a demon' (Mark 4x; Matt. 7x; Luke 1x).

83. Only Luke (4.33-37) follows Mark here.

84. The equivalent summaries in Matt. 4.23 and Luke 4.44 do not mention exorcisms.

85. Matthew and Luke omit the summary and reference to 'unclean spirits'.

86. By depicting Jesus as commanding the sea similarly to 'Be silent' (*pephimōso* — 4.39), the same term as in 1.25, Mark depicts the storm as demonic in character. Matthew omits all these commands to silence.

87. Both here (Matt. 8.28-34) and in the next episode (Matt. 9.18-26) Matthew greatly abbreviates what he may have regarded as Mark's less well-told account.

88. Mark 5.21-43 is a good example of 'the Markan sandwich', where a second story (here 5.25-34) is inserted between two halves of the first story (here 5.21-24, 35-43). Other striking examples are 3.22-30 inserted between 3.20-21, 31-35; and 11.15-19 between 11.12-14 and 20-24; also 6.14-29 between 6.7-13 and 30-32. See further J. R. Edwards, 'The Markan Sandwich: The Significance of Interpolations in Markan Narratives', *NovT* 31 (1989) 193-216.

89. Matt. 13.58 softens Mark's bluntness and Luke omits it.

- 6.45-52 — walking on water;[90]
- 6.53-56 — summary of healings;
- 7.24-30 — distance healing of a Syrophoenician's daughter;[91]
- 7.31-37 — healing of a deaf and dumb man;
- 8.1-10 — feeding of 4,000;
- 8.22-26 — two-stage healing of a blind man.[92]

This weighty emphasis on Jesus' healing and exorcistic ministry in the first half of Mark's Gospel is very striking. All the more so since Jesus performs only one more exorcism in the second half (the exorcism of the epileptic boy — 9.14-29) and one more healing (the restoration of the sight of blind Bartimaeus — 10.46-52). Mark clearly intended a switch of focus. That the switch comes at the central point of Mark's account points to the reason. For it is in 8.27-33 that Peter's confession of Jesus as Messiah (8.29) is put to one side (8.30) or corrected (8.32-33) by Jesus' prediction that (he as) the Son of Man must suffer, be rejected by the Jerusalem leadership, be killed and after three days rise again (8.31). In other words, the account of Jesus the great healer and exorcist gives way to the passion narrative (§41.2c).

We can infer from this that Mark intended the theme of Jesus as healer or exorcist to dovetail with Mark's christology and with the character of his Gospel as a passion narrative with extended introduction. In the middle decades of the twentieth century this encouraged several scholars to argue that Mark so organized his Gospel in order to correct what he regarded as a lopsided and misleading presentation of Jesus simply or primarily as one who spoke with divine authority and executed extraordinary miracles, what is sometimes described as a 'divine man' (*theios anēr*) Christ.[93] So, when he

---

90. Luke omits the second of what seems to have been a traditional linkage of these miracles, as indicated also by John 6.1-21.

91. Luke again omits both this and the next healing.

92. This episode is unique to Mark.

93. See Koester, 'One Jesus and Four Primitive Gospels' 187-93, and particularly T. J. Weeden, *Mark: Traditions in Conflict* (Philadelphia: Fortress, 1971), who does not hesitate to argue that Jesus' own disciples (*theios-anēr* discipleship) were Mark's target: 'the disciples are reprobates . . . no more than heretics' (52-69, 164). But France justifiably notes that the concept of the *theios anēr* is more like a twentieth-century construct than a category recognized in the first century (*Mark* 21). The thesis also suffers from the same weakness to which I have already pointed several times: the assumption that some collection of Jesus' miracles would be the only information about Jesus known to the group which used the collection and could therefore be read as the sole or exclusive christology of the group (Jesus as the miracle-working 'divine man'). See again *Jesus Remembered* 150-52. See also Brown, *Introduction* 155, with more bibliography in nn.72-73; Evans, *Mark 8:27–16:20* lxxii (with bibliography).

presents Peter as confessing Jesus to be the Messiah, Mark immediately goes on to depict Jesus speaking of his imminent suffering (Mark 8.31). And when Peter protested, Jesus even denounces Peter as the mouthpiece of Satan (8.32-33). In other words, the implication may be that Peter was confessing Jesus as a triumphalist Messiah, the one who, according to popular hope, would soon liberate Israel from Roman domination (as in *Pss. Sol.* 17.21-24).[94] On this thesis, then, the function of the intense focus on Jesus as the Son of Man who must suffer and be rejected, was precisely to correct such views of Jesus which may have still been circulating, on the basis of the miracles which he wrought and the authority with which he taught.

I am less convinced by this argument. For Mark to portray Jesus' healing and exorcistic ministry as so dominant in the first half of his Gospel must mean that he had no embarrassment with this dimension of Jesus' ministry.[95] Perhaps Mark wanted this aspect of Jesus' ministry primarily to be understood as an expression of Jesus' compassion and sometimes emotional responsiveness to trustful need.[96] His record of Jesus' blunt refusal of a Pharisaic demand for a sign (8.11-12) suggests that he did not want Jesus to be seen as a sign prophet.[97] However, what we can say with more confidence is that Mark's account of Jesus' response to the Caesarea Philippi confession of Peter was a way of shifting the focus from Jesus as Messiah to Jesus as the suffering Son of Man. This strategy presumably included a shift from any claim that the significance of Jesus was to be assessed in terms of the extent to which Jesus had fulfilled the popular hope for a military leader who would liberate Israel from Roman domination. Jesus' significance as Messiah and Son of Man could not be appreciated without reference to his death and resurrection.

iii. Jesus as Messiah, That Is, Son of Man

There is no doubt that Mark understood Jesus to be the Messiah, (the) Christ (Mark 1.1; 8.29; 14.61-62).[98] But the more striking feature of Mark's presenta-

---

94. See *Jesus Remembered* §15.2a.

95. 'It is in no way shown as probable that the understanding of Jesus as wonder-worker is presented as a view to be abandoned' (Kümmel, *Introduction* 93); similarly Marcus, *Mark 1–8* 77. See also E. K. Broadhead, *Teaching with Authority: Miracles and Christology in the Gospel of Mark* (JSNTS 74; Sheffield Academic, 1992).

96. 'Compassion' — 1.41 (omitted by Matt. and Luke); 6.34 (omitted by Luke); 8.2-3; 9.22-23 (omitted by Matt. and Luke); 'faith'/'believe' — 2.5; 4.38-40; 5.28-34, 36; 9.23-24; 10.49-52; see also 1.43; 3.5; 5.6-13, 22-24, 40-41; 6.49-50, 56; 7.26-29, 32-33; 8.22-23; 9.19.

97. See again *Jesus Remembered* 658-60. It is significant that Mark includes the Pharisees' demand for a sign and Jesus' refusal (8.11-12) in his buildup to Peter's confession and its clarification (8.27-33). Note also the mocking in the crucifixion scene (15.29-32).

98. See also 'Son of David' (Mark 10.47-48; cf. 12.35. Collins notes that Mark's other

tion is the secrecy motif in which Mark veils the theme, the 'messianic secret' as it has come to be known. Following Wrede, we can draw together several characteristic traits of the Markan narrative.[99]

- The commands with which Jesus silenced the confessions of Jesus' messianic status made by demoniacs/demons — 1.23-25, 34 (a summary); 3.11-12 (a summary);[100] cf. 5.6-7.
- The commands of silence to those healed miraculously (1.43-45; 5.43; 7.36; 8.26; cf. 10.47-48).[101]
- Other commands to silence, after Peter's confession (8.30) and the Transfiguration (9.9).
- Jesus' intention to remain hidden (1.35, 45; 3.7, 9; 6.46; 7.24; 9.30, 33; 10.10) and to perform his healings away from public gaze (5.37, 40; 7.33; 8.23).[102]
- The secrecy/privacy (*kat' idian*) of Jesus' instructions of his disciples (4.34; 6.31-32; 7.17; 9.2, 28-29; 13.3); implicit also in the three passion predictions (8.31; 9.31; 10.32-34).[103]

Whether 'messianic secret' is the best description of this group of narrative traits is something of a question. It is difficult to relate all the above material to the single issue of Jesus' messiahship.[104] And the 'secret' is not kept — those healed or those who witness the healing regularly spread the account of the healing widely abroad.[105] So, if it were the case that Mark introduced the motif in order to explain why Jesus had not been recognized as Messiah,[106] he had undermined his strategy by showing that the secret had not been kept. A

---

characterizations of Jesus (exorcist, healer ['Son of David' — 10.47-48] and teacher) can be put under the heading of Messiah as well (*Mark* 66-69, 73).

99. Wrede, *Messianic Secret* 34-36; Schnelle provides a nicely concise treatment (*History* 211-13).

100. Matthew and Luke do not draw on the Markan summaries with any consistency.

101. Matthew retains only the first of these four commands; Luke only the first two.

102. All omitted by Matthew and Luke.

103. Of Mark's secrecy notes, Matthew omits 4.34 and 7.17 but adds Matt. 20.17. Matthew and Luke also omit Mark's note that Jesus was 'alone' when asked about his parables (Mark 4.10). F. Kermode, *The Genesis of Secrecy* (Cambridge, MA: Harvard University, 1979), made a meal of this motif; but see J. Marcus, 'Mark 4:10-12 and Marcan Epistemology', *JBL* 103 (1984) 557-74.

104. H. Räisänen, *The 'Messianic Secret' in Mark's Gospel* (Edinburgh: T & T Clark, 1990) 17-23.

105. Mark 1.28, 45; 2.12; 3.20; 5.19-20; 6.2-3, 31; 7.24, 36-37; 10.46-52; see further my 'The Messianic Secret in Mark', *TynB* 21 (1970) 92-117, reprinted in Tuckett, ed., *The Messianic Secret* 116-31 (here 120-22); Kümmel, *Introduction* 90-92.

106. Wrede's thesis (*Messianic Secret* 227-30); though see also n.63 above.

more obvious explanation for the source of the 'messianic secret' is that Jesus was remembered as himself discouraging too much publicity.[107] Nevertheless, the features drawn attention to above are, as we saw, fairly distinctive of Mark's narrative. So it is hard to avoid the conclusion that Wrede was basically correct in identifying this motif as a feature of Mark's retelling of the story of Jesus, and expressive of the way he wanted his good news to be received.

The most obvious inference to draw is that Mark took up a trait already present in some degree in the Jesus tradition as he knew it,[108] or in Peter's rehearsing of the story and teaching of Jesus, and elaborated that trait to become a prominent link motif in his own retelling. The fact that it appears so regularly in the first half of the Gospel and is so much linked to Jesus' exorcistic and healing ministry strongly suggests that it was an integral part of Mark's grand strategy — that is, the strategy to swing his story round midway through the telling, and to transform it from a story predominantly of miracle working into a passion narrative proper, from what is bound to appear as Peter's inadequate understanding of Jesus' Messiahship (8.29, 32-33) to Jesus' own understanding of his mission as the Son of Man (8.31). The transition is reflected not least in the increasing prominence of reference to Jesus as the Son of Man: initially as a figure of authority (2.10, 28), but from 8.31 predominantly a figure of suffering and cause of shame,[109] though with promise of vindication beyond.[110]

Here the danger which Jesus himself probably was concerned about, that his mission would be misunderstood in terms of more traditional hopes of one sent by God to redeem Israel, was taken up and highlighted by Mark's expanded secrecy and privacy motifs and his Son of Man christology. Mark was no doubt all too conscious that a Messiah or redeemer figure such as he portrayed was altogether too unexpected and unusual for his audiences readily to accept. So, into his retelling Mark injects mention of commands to silence and notes Jesus' secret instruction at regular intervals from early on, while also accompanying them with regular supernatural revelations of Jesus' divine sonship. Likewise, as an integral part of the narrative strategy of the gradual foreshadowings of the cross, Mark shifts the focus of his Gospel from a supernaturally-empowered Messiah to the rejected Son of Man, while not failing to signal the Son of Man's forthcoming glory. In this way, Mark presumably hoped to alert his audiences to the heart of his message: that this Messiah, God's Son, the Son of Man, was not what most would have expected.[111]

107. *Jesus Remembered* §§15.3-4 and my earlier 'The Messianic Secret in Mark'.
108. See further n.107.
109. Mark 8.31, 38; 9.12, 31; 10.33, 45; 14.21, 41.
110. Mark 9.9; 13.26; 14.62.
111. Mark's use of scripture in pursuing this strategy is well brought out by J. Marcus, *The Way of the Lord: Christological Exegesis of the Old Testament in the Gospel of Mark* (Lou-

Closely related to the messianic secret motif are Mark's regular references to the failure of Jesus' disciples to understand him.[112] For not only was there the implied concern on Jesus' part that the character of his mission might well be misunderstood, but even Jesus' disciples were unable to understand Jesus when still in the midst of his mission. The two-stage healing of the blind man (8.22-26)[113] evidently was intended by Mark to symbolically forewarn audiences that Peter's immediately following confession of Jesus as Messiah was only partial and incomplete (8.27-30).[114] Peter (and the others) could not understand him until they had witnessed the completion of his mission, that is, until he had been killed and had been raised again from the dead (8.31-33). Recognition of this is what points to Mark 9.9 as a key to the whole secrecy motif: during the descent from the mount of transfiguration Jesus ordered his disciples 'to tell no one about what they had seen, until after the Son of Man had risen from the dead' (9.9).[115] Once again, the key to understanding Jesus' mission, including his messianic status, was to be found only in his death and resurrection.

c. A Manual of Discipleship

For Mark, the Jesus tradition was gospel not simply as proclaiming Jesus and the significance of his death and resurrection. It was also gospel as giving instruction for those who responded to this Jesus and became his disciples; Mark did not think of gospel (*kerygma*) and teaching (*didachē*) as two quite separate and distinct categories. 'The Christians' understanding of their discipleship and their ability to follow as disciples emerge out of their understanding of the passion and resurrection of Jesus'.[116]

---

isville: Westminster John Knox, 1992). T. R. Hatina, *In Search of a Context: The Function of Scripture in Mark's Narrative* (JSNTS 232; London: Sheffield Academic, 2002), insists that the narrative framework governs the function of scripture in Mark.

112. Mark 4.13, 40-41; 6.37, 52; 7.18; 8.4, 17, 21, 32-33; 9.5-6, 10, 32; 10.24-26, 35-37.
113. Omitted by Matthew and Luke.
114. See e.g. Gnilka, *Markus* 1.314-15; Guelich, *Mark 1–8:26* 430-31: 'the connection between the prophetic reference to blindness in 8:18 and the beloured healing of the blind man in 8:22-26 has to be more than coincidental' (430).
115. Wrede, *Messianic Secret* 67-70.
116. E. Best, *Following Jesus: Discipleship in the Gospel of Mark* (JSNTS 4; Sheffield: JSOT, 1981) 13.

i. Jesus as a Teacher of Extraordinary Authority

An easily overlooked emphasis in Mark's retelling of the story of Jesus is his presentation of Jesus as a teacher. The fact that he records much less of Jesus' teaching than do Matthew and Luke[117] obscures the fact that Mark refers to Jesus' activity in 'teaching', and to his 'teaching', as much as or more than the two much longer Synoptic Gospels.[118] Somewhat curiously Matthew and Luke consistently either change the reference to Jesus from Mark's 'teacher' to 'Lord' (*kyrios* — Matt.), or 'Master' (*epistatēs* — Luke),[119] or omit the reference altogether.[120] Even more striking is the fact that Matthew and Luke omit the majority of Mark's references to Jesus as 'teaching' (*didaskein*) and to his teaching (*didachē*). Significantly, the same is true in the case of most Markan summaries or links or introductions to an episode, where Mark seems to have more or less taken it for granted that Jesus had been teaching as the occasion for the episode referred to.[121] Clearly, then, it was of considerable importance for Mark to present Jesus as a teacher and to emphasize that he taught both the people and his disciples.[122]

His emphasis, however, is on the disciples. Mark would no doubt be aware that a 'disciple' (*mathētēs*) was a 'learner' (from *manthanein*, 'to learn'). So it will have been no accident that the very first episode of Jesus' mission which Mark records (following his baptism and period of temptation) is the calling of the first four disciples (Mark 1.16-20). Nor that to follow Jesus as a disciple was to be trained to make more disciples ('fishers of people' — 1.17).[123] The call of Levi (2.14) initiates a sequence which epitomizes the character of Jesus' mission and its radical challenge to old attitudes and traditions (2.15-22). Jesus' choice of twelve is also given early prominence (3.13-19). The twelve were chosen 'to be with him and that he might send them out (*apostellē*) to preach' (3.14), and their responsibility to take part in Jesus' mission as 'apostles' is a major feature following the next section of teaching and miracle

---

117. Matthew and Luke absorb the Q material which consists almost entirely of sayings of Jesus.

118. Teacher (*didaskalos*) — Mark 12x; Matt 12x; Luke 17x. Teach (*didaskein*) — Mark 17x; Matt. 14x; Luke 17x. Teaching (*didachē*) — Mark 5x; Matt. 3x; Luke 1x. As Guelich notes, in Mark it is only Jesus who is referred to as 'teacher' (*Mark 1–8:26* 55).

119. Mark 4.38/Matt. 8.25/Luke 8.24; Mark 9.17/Matt. 17.15; Mark 9.38/Luke 9.49.

120. Mark 9.38 (Matt.); 10.20, 35 (Matt.); 12.32; 13.1.

121. Mark 1.21 (Matt.); 1.27; 2.13; 4.1; 4.2 (Matt.); 6.2, 6 (Luke); 6.30, 34; 8.31; 9.31; 10.1; 11.17, 18; 12.14 (Matt.); 12.35, 38; 14.49 (Luke).

122. See also V. K. Robbins, *Jesus the Teacher: A Socio-Rhetorical Interpretation of Mark* (Philadelphia: Fortress, 1984).

123. See further W. T. Shiner, *Follow Me!: Disciples in Markan Rhetoric* (SBLDS 145; Atlanta: Scholars Press, 1995) 175-76.

working (6.7-13, 30).[124] Indeed, Mark refers to Jesus' disciples regularly, in every chapter after the first, and mostly with the phrase 'his disciples'.[125] The story that Mark tells is of 'Jesus and his disciples'. Not least, it is a book about discipleship.[126]

Here we should add that Mark often makes a point of noting the amazement or astonishment which Jesus' teaching evoked,[127] about half of which Matthew or Luke omits. Mark's fondness for the *ek*- verbs reinforces the point — they were *'utterly* astonished' at his teaching.[128] His own fellow-villagers ask in wonderment, 'What is the wisdom that has been given to him?' (6.2). Early on Mark explains the astonishment: it was because Jesus was teaching as one who had 'authority' and not as the scribes (1.22);[129] 'new teaching, with authority' (1.27).[130] This would be of first importance for Mark, not, to be sure, because he wanted to portray Jesus as simply or only a teacher. His concern would much more be that as Jesus' disciples had required to be taught, so those who had subsequently committed themselves to believing in this Christ, likewise needed to be taught.[131] Mark's emphasis on Jesus' teaching makes his Gospel also a teaching manual.

Mark's sense of the privilege of such teaching, a privilege he wanted his audiences (or catechists) to appreciate, is evident in his parable chapter (Mark 4). To Jesus' disciples 'has been given the mystery of the kingdom of God; but for those outside, everything comes in parables' (4.11). So there was an inner teaching, reflected in the privacy of Jesus' teaching of his disciples.

---

124. Mark clearly regarded the twelve as 'apostles' (6.30), though it is disputed whether he so referred to them in 3.14; the textual support is strong, but it is difficult to avoid the suspicion that the phrase 'whom he also named as apostles' was introduced to harmonize with Luke (Metzger, *Textual Commentary* 80; Guelich, *Mark 1–8:26* 154; France, *Mark* 157).

125. Mark uses *mathētēs* 46 times.

126. See also e.g. France, *Mark* 27-29, who refers particularly to C. C. Black, *The Disciples according to Mark* (Grand Rapids: Eerdmans, now 2nd edition, 2012); F. J. Moloney, *Mark: Storyteller, Interpreter, Evangelist* (Peabody: Hendrickson, 2004), especially ch. 7.

127. *Thambein* — 1.27 ('new teaching'); 10.24; (cf. 9.15; 10.32; 16.5-6); *ekplēssein* — 1.22; 6.2; 10.26; 11.18; (cf. 7.37); *(ek)thaumazein* — 5.20; 12.17. *Existēmi* is used by Mark only of the response to Jesus' miracles (2.12; 5.42; 6.51).

128. *Ekthambein, ekthaumazein, ekplēssein*; also *existēmi*.

129. The contrast with the scribes is a feature of Mark's narrative (cf. 2.6, 16; 3.15, 22; 7.1, 5; 11.18, 27; 12.38; 14.1, 43, 53; 15.1, 31) (Marcus, *Mark 1–8* 192). Mark has also retained from the tradition Jesus' unprecedented use of 'Amen' to introduce his own teachings (3.28; 8.12; 9.1, 41; 10.15, 29; 11.23; 12.43; 13.30; 14.9, 18, 25), whereas Luke retains only six examples; see *Jesus Remembered* 700-701.

130. Probably Markan redaction (Guelich, *Mark 1–8:26* 58). See also 2.10; 3.15; 6.7; 11.28-33.

131. 'The disciples are the connecting link between the time of Jesus and the contemporary Markan community' (Schnelle, *History* 210).

And the parables, so typical of Jesus' teaching, were his way of conveying the kingdom's mystery while it still remained a mystery to those who could neither perceive nor understand (4.12).[132] The tension implied here between the *failure* of the disciples to understand Jesus' messiahship and the *privilege* of being given the mystery of the kingdom of God is best explained as the first referring to Jesus' own disciples during his mission, and the second referring to the disciples for whom Mark wrote his Gospel.[133] It was precisely his Gospel which gave the disciples of Mark's time the key to the mystery, the key of a right understanding of Jesus and of the life of discipleship which was its necessary corollary.[134]

ii. The Content of the Teaching

Mark's 'manual of discipleship' contains a sequence of episodes with obvious implications for the Christian audiences listening to his Gospel being read to them, and particular episodes reflected on or elaborated.

The inference of a new teaching which opens up a whole new epoch in God's dealings with his people is vividly portrayed in the parables of old cloak and new cloth, old wineskins and new wine (2.21-22), and of the light which lightens what was otherwise hidden (4.21-22). The eschatological significance of Jesus' exorcisms (the binding of Satan) is likewise clear (3.23-27) and its far-reaching implications even for family relationships not ignored (3.20-21, 31-35).[135] Likewise the implications for reprioritizing the function of the Sabbath (2.23–3.5), for questioning the relation of 'the tradition of the elders' to the word of God (7.1-13), and for re-appreciating the fundamental causes of human impurity (7.14-23), are clearly drawn out for the attention of the Christian audiences.[136] The way in which this new teaching removes barriers which had prevented Gentiles from responding to the word of God is similarly spelt out ('Thus he declares all foods clean' — 7.19).[137] And the

---

132. It was this secrecy motif in Mark which the *Secret Gospel* evidently enhanced in its adaptation of Mark (see above §40 n.255).

133. Cf. particularly Räisänen, *The 'Messianic Secret'* ch. 3.

134. So, e.g., R. C. Tannehill, 'The Gospel of Mark as Narrative Christology', in Petersen, ed., *Perspectives* 57-95 (here 70); Best, *Following Jesus* 136-37.

135. See further S. C. Barton, *Discipleship and Family Ties in Mark and Matthew* (SNTSMS 80; Cambridge: Cambridge University, 1994), here especially 82-86.

136. See also Kee, *Community of the New Age* ch. 6.

137. It is regularly assumed that Mark has retained the original words of Jesus, which thus become the principal evidence in support of the argument that Jesus taught the end of the law, and that Matthew has softened Mark's version (and Jesus' teaching); Albrecht Ritschl set the tone for most of the following century when he pronounced that Jesus' 'renunciation of Judaism and its law ... became a sharp dividing line between his teaching and those of the Jews' (S. Heschel, *Abraham Geiger and the Jewish Jesus* [University of Chicago,

clear implication is pressed home by Mark immediately going on to tell the story of Jesus' ministering to the Syrophoenician woman (7.24-30) and of his ministering round the edges of Galilee (7.31–8.10).[138]

Even when the attention begins to focus more intensively on the redefinition of what Jesus' mission (messiahship) entails, Mark depicts Jesus as pressing home the clear corollaries for discipleship — taking up one's own cross to follow the crucified, losing one's life in order to gain it, confessing Jesus in face of temptations to deny him (8.34-38). To follow Jesus is to follow him into the passion narrative, the way of the cross.[139] A sequence of particular instructions follows:

- the need of prayer for successful ministry (9.28-29);
- the need to revise any estimate of greatness and to follow the example of the servant Son of Man (9.33-37; 10.13-16, 41-45);
- the importance of being open to and of readiness to recognize the good done by those who do not follow with them (9.38-41);
- the dangers of causing other believers to stumble and of false priorities (9.42-48; 10.17-31);
- the ideal of marriage (10.2-9);[140]
- the unavoidability of suffering in the life of discipleship (10.29-30, 38-39);
- and not least, faith/believing/trust as the key to discipleship (11.22-24), driving home the lessons of earlier miracles (4.40; 5.36; 9.23-24),[141] and the importance of forgiving one another if prayer is to be real (and community sustained) (11.25).

1998] 123). U. Schnelle, *Theology of the New Testament* (ET Grand Rapids: Baker Academic, 2009) 140 n.246, cites a 1978 article of Hengel, writing on Mark 7.15: 'Here we meet a fundamental break between Jesus and the Palestinian Judaism of his time'. However, 'the hard-fought struggles over kosher food attested in Acts and Paul would be difficult to explain if Jesus had settled the issue from the beginning' (Brown, *Introduction* 137). So it is equally if not more likely that Jesus' teaching on the subject was more ambiguous, allowing both Mark and Matthew to interpret it differently so far as the continuing validity of the laws of clean and unclean were concerned for Gentile Christians (Mark) and for Jewish Christians (Matthew). The issue is discussed fully, with bibliography, in *Jesus Remembered* 573-77.

138. 'If the feeding of the 5000 forms the conclusion of Jesus' work among the Jews, then the feeding of the 4000 [Mark 8.1-10] represents the conclusion of his work among the Gentiles' (Schnelle, *History* 203). See further K. R. Iverson, *Gentiles in the Gospel of Mark* (LNTS 339; London: T & T Clark, 2007).

139. Best, *Following Jesus* Part I.

140. Only Mark includes mention of the possibility of the wife initiating divorce proceedings (Mark 10.12), probably again reflecting a situation outside Israel/Palestine, since such a possibility is not envisaged in the Torah.

141. See also T. Söding, *Glaube bei Markus* (SBB 12; Stuttgart: KBW, ²1987); C. D. Marshall, *Faith as a Theme in Mark's Narrative* (SNTSMS 64; Cambridge: Cambridge University, 1989).

More instruction is given on Jesus' evaluation of the temple cult, or authorities, and the future of the temple (11.11-21; 12.7-9), and further examples of how Jesus handled tricky political and theological questions (12.13-27) — all salutary guidance for believers' attitude to the Jerusalem temple and response to the various authority figures with whom they had to deal. A climax is reached in Jesus' identification of the two greatest commandments — to love God with all one's being and one's neighbour as oneself (12.28-34),[142] which also counted as the Gentile Christian solution to the debate about the continuing validity of the Jewish law — with further contrast between superficial and true spirituality (12.38-44).[143]

The lengthy eschatological discourse, coming as it does as the final part of the tradition prior to the passion narrative proper, indicates the discourse's importance for Mark and in his view for his audiences (13.1-37).[144] Two striking Markan fingerprints are, first, what appears to be a Markan addition (omitted by Matthew and Luke), that 'the gospel (*euangelion*) must first be preached to all the Gentiles' (13.10).[145] Thus Mark both highlights the crucial importance of the Gentile mission and does not shirk from the implication that there may be a significant interval before the onset of the disasters predicted; 'the end is not yet' (13.7). But second, Mark also reminds the reader of his responsibility here, to read with understanding, that is, presumably, so that his audiences will not fail to recognize the importance of Jesus' message (13.14).[146] Whether Mark had in view the catastrophe of Jerusalem's fall and the destruction of the temple as imminent or recent, he clearly wanted his audiences to appreciate not only Jesus' prophetic powers but also the implications for them of trial, imprisonment and death (13.9-20), of false expectations (13.5-6, 21-22) and of the need to remain alert (13.23, 32-37).[147] The warning that false messiahs and false prophets might lead astray even the elect (13.22) would be particu-

---

142. Mark alone presents Jesus' saying as a reply to a sensitive and sympathetic scribe (Mark 12.28, 32-34), implying that there was still an openness among many of the Jewish scribal elite even to the more radical Jesus presented by Mark.

143. Of the four canonical Evangelists, Mark is the least caught up in the issue, posed by such passages as Mark 7.19 and 12.9: What then of Israel? Contrast, e.g., Matt. 8.11-12; 21.43; Luke 24.21 and Acts 1.6.

144. For discussion of Mark's sources and the tradition history behind 'the little apocalypse' (Mark 13), and bibliographical review, see G. R. Beasley-Murray, *Jesus and the Last Days: The Interpretation of the Olivet Discourse* (Peabody: Hendrickson, 1993); Collins, *Mark* 594-600.

145. See *Jesus Remembered* 435-36.

146. Collins cites E. Best for the view that the phrase 'let the reader understand' was a private note to the public reader, not meant to be read aloud (*Mark* 597).

147. Jesus' regular urging, *blepete* ('watch out, take care, beware'), is one of Mark's most distinctive features (4.24; 8.15; 12.38; 13.5, 9, 23, 33).

larly riveting for Mark's audiences. If indeed Mark was writing as the Jewish revolt neared its climactic denouement,[148] this apocalyptic urgency would be the central emphasis not only of Mark 13 but of the Gospel as a whole.[149]

At the same time it should be noted that, despite Mark 1.15 and 9.1, the imminent coming of the kingdom of God is not part of the eschatological discourse. And Mark evidently qualifies the imminent expectation indicated by the call to remain alert with the 'not yet' of 13.7 and the implications of 13.10. In fact most of the discipleship demands of the Gospel do not fit neatly under the heading of 'interim ethic' (the ethic necessary for the interval before the coming of the kingdom). Indeed, more characteristic of the Markan Jesus' teaching on the kingdom are 'the mystery of the kingdom' (4.11), the kingdom to be received 'as a little child' (10.14-15) and the warning that reliance on riches is liable to exclude from the kingdom (10.23-25). Mark presumably felt himself tugged two ways on the subject and did not attempt a clear resolution of the tension.[150]

d. The Passion Climax

The final chapters of Mark's narrative would be familiar to most of Mark's audiences. Here the fingerprints of Mark's organization and editing are much fewer, the implication being that the structure and most of its infilling had been already well established before Mark. There was no need for him to craft it as for the first time. The story was so fundamental to the earliest Christians' *raison d'être* and probably so central to their worship Easter by Easter, that Mark's task was presumably primarily to tell well the story which would be already well known to the majority of those who heard his Gospel being read. The fact that there is little agreement on the detail of a pre-Markan passion narrative[151] need not lessen the probability that the story of Jesus' last week and its basic structure were well known, since in any case it would almost certainly be impossible to reduce the variety of the oral retellings of the story to a single or uniform version.[152]

---

148. See above §39.2a(ii).
149. Cf. Marcus, *Mark 1–8* 71-73.
150. For further discussion see e.g. Marxsen, *Mark the Evangelist* ch. 4; C. Breytenbach, *Nachfolge und Zukunftserwartung nach Markus* (Zürich: Theologischer, 1984); S. R. Garrett, *The Temptations of Jesus in Mark's Gospel* (Grand Rapids: Eerdmans, 1998) — 'Mark constructs his readership as a community of faithful persons on trial' (158), and further ch. 4 ('Disciples on Trial').
151. See M. L. Soards, 'The Question of a PreMarcan Passion Narrative', in R. E. Brown, *The Death of the Messiah* (2 vols.; New York: Doubleday, 1994) 1492-1524.
152. 'The likelihood that there was a preMarcan passion account does not remove a

Was it Mark's inspiration to begin the story of the climactic week of Jesus' mission with the account of the unnamed woman anointing Jesus' head during the meal in Bethany (14.3-9)? Bracketed by the introductory note of the chief priests' and scribes' intention to arrest and kill him (14.1-2) and by the brief account of Judas's betrayal (14.10-11), the account of her uninhibited outpouring of love certainly makes a striking contrast. We can probably attribute the mention of the story being proclaimed as part of the gospel (14.9) to Mark's retelling of a familiar story (*euangelion* probably being one of Mark's thumbprints).[153] With its own intimation of imminent and shameful (unanointed) death (14.8), in some contrast with the obligation to care for the poor (14.7), the story also calls Christian audiences to recognize the overriding importance of Jesus' death in regard to their continuing obligations.

Was it Mark who gave the account of the last supper its Passover significance (14.1, 12, 14, 16-17)? Probably not, since the thought of Jesus as the paschal lamb was already current (1 Cor. 5.7), though the last supper tradition itself does not speak of the meal as a Passover (Mark 14.22-25). And Mark no doubt consciously uses the same language ('took, blessed, broke and gave') as he used in his earlier descriptions of the meals presided over by Jesus (6.41; 8.6-7). On the other hand, although the timing of Jesus' last meal with his disciples is obscure,[154] its proximity to the Passover meal probably made the connection inevitable. At any rate, the way Mark presses home the point suggests that he was aware of the lack of allusion to the Passover in the last meal tradition itself and thought it necessary to underline its Passover character.

The mounting sense of approaching crisis is well contrived in the sequence of Mark's narrative:

- the plotting to eliminate Jesus (14.1-2, 10-11);
- the preparation for the Passover in secret (14.12-16);
- the last supper framed by the warning of imminent betrayal and the prediction of disaster (14.18-21) and of Peter's denial (14.26-31);
- the stark description of Jesus' lonely agony in Gethsemane (too stark for Matthew and particularly Luke), contrasted with the weakness of Peter, James and John (14.32-42);
- and Judas's treachery in Jesus' arrest (14.43-50).

---

real doubt whether we have the methodology to reconstruct it exactly or at length' (Brown, *Introduction* 150).

153. See above §41.2a.
154. See *Jesus Remembered* 772-73.

The one clear Markan fingerprint is the intriguing mention of the young man following the arrest party and fleeing naked (14.51-52). It inevitably stirs up speculation as to the identity of the young man: if not Mark himself(?), then why the reference?[155]

Characteristic of Mark's style is his using one story to frame another — here the account of Peter's following at a distance and subsequent denial (14.53-54, 66-72) framing the central scene of the hearing before the high priest (14.55-65). The Markan hand is clearest at two points, both missing in the Synoptic parallels. One is the probable addition of the contrast *cheiropoiētos/acheiropoiētos* in the formulation of the charge against Jesus: 'We heard him say, "I will destroy this temple that is made with hands (*cheiropoiēton*), and in three days I will build another not made with hands (*acheiropoiēton*)' (14.58). The formulation probably reflects the degree of hostility towards the Jerusalem temple which is evident among those who led the mission beyond the bounds of Israel/Palestine.[156] The other is the answer which Jesus gives to the high priest's question: 'Are you the Messiah, the Son of the Blessed?' (14.61). The striking feature here is that in all the accounts of Jesus' reply to this question, or to its equivalent from Pilate, Jesus' answer is at best ambivalent: 'You say'.[157] Only Mark 14.62 reads Jesus' reply as 'I am'.[158] The most obvious deduction to be drawn from this is that Mark wanted to present Jesus' reply as an unequivocal declaration that he was God's Son. The declaration sets in bright light Jesus' majesty and unbrokenness, in face of the oppression of false witness testimony, high priestly malice, and soldierly physical abuse (14.56-59, 61-64, 65) — and in contrast with Peter's weakness (14.66-72).

In the following account of Jesus' trial before the Roman prefect, Mark seems to refrain from much adaptation. After the response to the high priest's question, an unequivocal 'I am', Mark reverts to the usual version of Jesus' reply to Pilate's question, 'Are you king of the Jews?' with an ambivalent 'You say' (15.2). Mark may have added the explanatory note about Barabbas, that he was in prison 'with the rebels who had committed murder in the course of

---

155. The debate on the identity of the 'young man' and the significance of the episode has been long-running; see Collins, *Mark* 688-93.

156. The echo of the charge against Jesus in the charge against Stephen in Acts 6.14, and the description of the temple in the speech attributed to Stephen as *cheiropoiētos* (see *Beginning from Jerusalem* 262, 270), suggest the source and reason for the addition of the contrast, which Mark may have inherited from the version of the hearing before the high priest that he knew best.

157. Matt. 26.64; 27.11; Mark 15.2; Luke 22.70 ('You say that I am'); 23.3. See *Jesus Remembered* 651-52.

158. A weakly attested variation reads, 'You say that I am', probably a scribal attempt to harmonize the different Synoptic readings; discussion in Evans, *Mark 8:27–16:20* 450.

the insurrection' (15.7). He may also have begun or extended the tendency of early Christian apologetics to shift the responsibility for Jesus' death from Pilate to the high priests (15.9-15). To the account of the grim procession to crucifixion Mark adds that the one compelled to carry Jesus' cross, Simon the Cyrenian, was the father of Alexander and Rufus, presumably well known to many believers (15.21).

It has been long recognized that the account of Jesus' death (15.22-38) has been shaped to bring out a sequence of scriptural echoes, particularly of the psalms, and especially of Psalm 22.[159] In *Jesus Remembered* I deduced the likelihood that this was how the story of Jesus' crucifixion was told more or less from the first.[160] Here we need only note that whereas the other Synoptic Evangelists seem to have elaborated the tendency to fill out detail, not least by drawing more heavily upon the psalms,[161] Mark seems to have been content to retell the story in the barer, probably traditional form, climaxing in the dramatic symbolism of the curtain of the temple torn in two, from top to bottom (15.38). But he does not miss the chance to achieve the real climax for him, by relating the Roman centurion's confession on witnessing Jesus' death: 'Truly the man was God's Son' (15.39).

Was it Mark who determined that the account of Jesus' burial and resurrection should highlight the women disciples' role (15.40-41; 16.1-8)?[162] At least he probably intruded the note of explanation about the support they had rendered to Jesus during his mission in Galilee (15.41). In addition, the fact that the identity of the women is confused[163] may suggest that different versions circulated and that Mark simply chose the one with which he was most familiar. In any event, Mark did not try to gloss over or diminish the role of the women (15.40-41, 47; 16.1), and in so doing he provided a model which the other Evangelists followed.

The story of the women finding the empty tomb is an example of how a story which presumably had a common origin could take quite varied forms in the different tellings which grew from that common origin. The distinctiveness

---

159. Mark 15.24 — Ps. 22.18; Mark 15.29 — Ps. 22.7; Mark 15.34 — Ps. 22.1; Mark 15.36 — Ps. 69.21. See further Marcus, *The Way of the Lord* 172-86. H. J. Carey, *Jesus' Cry from the Cross* (LNTS 398; London: T & T Clark, 2009), presses the case still more strongly that Mark's citation of Ps. 22.1 was contextual and that he expected his readers (*sic*) to interpret 15.34 in the light of the larger context of Ps. 22.

160. See *Jesus Remembered* 777-81.

161. Matt. 27.43 adds Ps. 22.8; Luke 23.46 adds Ps. 31.5.

162. See also S. Miller, *Women in Mark's Gospel* (JSNTS 259; London: T & T Clark, 2004).

163. Mary Magdalene — Mark 15.40, 47; 16.1; Matt. 27.56, 61 (v.l.); 28.1 (v.l.); Luke 24.10. Mary, mother of James and Joses — Mark 15.40, 47; 16.1; Matt. 27.56, 61; 28.1; Luke 24.10. Salome — Mark 15.40; 16.1. The mother of James and John — Matt. 27.56.

of Mark's version (16.1-8) is threefold. First the reference to the interpreting agent as a 'young man' sitting within the empty tomb (16.5) — presumably an angel,[164] though the 'white robe' is hardly decisive evidence on the point, and perhaps inevitably audiences' thoughts would slip back to the 'young man' who escaped naked from the garden of Gethsemane (14.51-52),[165] though with what authorial intention is hardly clear. Second, in the reference to the young man's instruction that the women should go and tell Jesus' disciples what they had seen and heard, Mark adds 'and Peter' — a nicely sensitive note bearing in mind Peter's last appearance (14.72), and possibly a hint that Mark derived his version from Peter himself.

The third and certainly most striking feature of Mark's version is that he does not narrate any appearance of the resurrected Jesus, but simply refers the women forward to appearances in Galilee (16.7). With that Mark seems to have decided that his story, the gospel, had been fully told, and, somewhat surprisingly, he rounds off his Gospel on a note of pathos: 'they fled from the tomb, for trembling and astonishment had seized them; and they said nothing to anyone, for they were afraid' (16.8). The ending is so astonishing that it is tempting to conclude that the original version of the Gospel was mutilated, with the (fuller) end torn off and lost.[166] But a more attractive explanation is that Mark ended with 16.8 as he intended. To end a writing with the preposition 'for' (*gar*) is exceptional, but need not have appeared to be totally unacceptable to Mark.[167] Moreover, the description of the women's state is carefully chosen: 'trembling' (*tromos*) can describe a consciousness of human inability which rests all the more on God's enabling, as in the other NT occurrences of the term;[168] and 'astonishment' (*ekstasis*) elsewhere denotes amazement among onlookers of a signal miracle as well as a trance in which divine revelation is received.[169] And apart from anything else, Mark would have been well aware that he was writing for audiences who had responded to the gospel of the crucified and risen Christ and who knew the basics of the story, even if only in confessional form (1 Cor. 15.3-5). The hints that Mark himself gave in Mark 14.28 and 16.7 were clear enough; 16.8 was not the end of the story.[170] So

---

164. See e.g. Evans, *Mark 8:27–16:20* 535-36; Collins, *Mark* 795-96.

165. Mark uses the terms *neaniskos* ('young man') and *peribeblēmenos* ('wearing') only in these two passages (14.51 and 16.5). Such detail could have provided a further incitement to the elaboration of *Secret Mark* (see again §40 n.255).

166. See above §39 n.9.

167. See Collins, *Mark* 797-99 (with bibliography).

168. 1 Cor. 2.3; 2 Cor. 7.15; Eph. 6.5; Phil. 2.12.

169. Mark 5.42, Luke 5.26 and Acts 3.10; Acts 10.10, 11.5 and 22.17. See also T. Dwyer, *The Motif of Wonder in the Gospel of Mark* (JSNTS 128; Sheffield: Sheffield Academic, 1996) 188-93.

170. P. G. Bolt, *Jesus' Defeat of Death: Persuading Mark's Early Readers* (SNTSMS 125;

we probably do most justice to Mark by recognizing that he intended to finish as he did, precisely because he and his audiences knew well that the pathos was by no means the end of the story; it had more the character of the numinous pointing forward to the further revelations to come. In other words, Mark may deliberately have wanted to end as he did because he saw the story as continuing in the spread of Christianity, and wanted his audiences to experience the continuation of the story in their own lives.

e. The Reception of Mark's Gospel

Here, then, in Mark we have a very good example of how the Jesus tradition was passed on to the second generation of Christianity. The data reviewed shows clearly how it was used and handled. There was no attempt, and we may infer, no desire, to pass on the tradition in rote learning form. Mark evidently felt free not only to order and to organize the tradition he knew, from Peter and/or other teachers, and/or from his own church or circle of churches, but also to shape and mould it to his own ends. But not, so far as we can tell, to create whole motifs (like 'the messianic secret') *de novo*. Rather he worked with and from the (principally oral) tradition he received. The impact made by Jesus himself is still clearly marked; the character of the man and the mission which created that impression is still clearly reflected. What Mark did, was to take what he (or Peter?) regarded as the key features in the tradition and to use his own narrative and summary links to reinforce these features:

- the gospel character of Jesus' whole mission, climaxing in the passion narrative;
- Jesus as God's beloved Son;
- Jesus as eschatological exorcist and healer;
- Jesus as Messiah reinterpreted as the suffering Son of Man;
- Jesus as the authoritative teacher whose teaching on discipleship new disciples still needed to hear and heed.

This was the living Jesus tradition à la Mark; this was the gospel according to Mark.

Once again we should not allow ourselves to fall into the trap of thinking that Mark's putting the Jesus tradition into written form either ended the period of the oral tradition or fixed the tradition in a way that made it much

---

Cambridge: Cambridge University, 2003), argues that Jesus' defeat of death is foreshadowed in a sequence of earlier episodes (most obviously 5.1-43).

less flexible than Mark's usage had shown it to be. On the contrary, for many years there would be churches which did not yet know Mark's Gospel, and knew only their own variations of Jesus tradition. Not only so, but in the predominantly oral societies of the time, familiarity with Mark's Gospel would be mostly aural knowledge, passed on and talked about orally.[171] So the reception of Mark's Gospel would probably be warm, but we have no way of knowing how quickly and how widely it was circulated. Most who ask who the Gospel was written for answer by inferring from the Gospel's content that it was written for a community threatened by or already suffering from persecution.[172] But how successful it was in speaking to such crises we cannot tell, except by way of inference from the fact that it was preserved, obviously welcomed and made use of by some/many of the early churches.

Our first real evidence of Mark's reception is the fact that it was obviously known to and used by Matthew and Luke. So depending where each of the three Synoptic Gospels originated, it is almost impossible to avoid the conclusion that Mark's Gospel was being passed on to other churches, scribes making fresh copies for wider circulation more or less from the beginning. Whether Mark was passed on to Matthew and Luke as a special favour, or simply became known to them as a presumably steadily widening circulation reached them, we cannot say.[173] But the fact that Matthew and Luke were able to make use of Mark as they evidently did must mean:

(a) Mark had been quite widely circulated within ten to twenty years;

(b) it was highly regarded as an authentic and authoritative source regarding Jesus' mission;

(c) its structure of 'Gospel' (passion narrative with extended introduction) provided the norm or precedent for their own accounts of Jesus;

(d) though they probably regarded Mark as *primus inter pares* among their varied source material, they evidently did not regard their other oral tradition as any less valuable; and

(e) they did not treat either Mark or the other tradition as scripture from which they could not depart, but rather drew on it and adapted it with the same flexibility as the teachers and tradents of the oral Jesus tradition had done before them.

---

171. See also Koester, *Ancient Christian Gospels* 273-75; Collins, *Mark* 103-5. It is difficult to discern evidence of knowledge and use of Mark as such, since so much of Mark was in effect taken over by Matthew; and, as we shall see, Matthew dominates the early references, echoes and allusions to written tradition. See further below §44.8.

172. E.g. Marcus, *Mark 1–8* 28-29.

173. On the early circulation of Christian writings see also A. M. O'Leary, *Matthew's Judaization of Mark: Examined in the Context of the Use of Sources in Graeco-Roman Antiquity* (LNTS 323; London: T & T Clark, 2006) 108-10.

42.3 The Gospel according to Matthew

Although I believe Luke was written before Matthew, Matthew is much closer to Mark than is Luke. Matthew indeed can be fairly regarded as a supplement to Mark, or even a second, expanded edition of Mark.[174] So it makes good sense to turn from Mark directly to Matthew, making the comparisons easier. In contrast, there are no persuasive indications either that Matthew knew Luke's Gospel or that Luke knew Matthew's Gospel;[175] consequently, there is no obvious logic, other than relative chronology, to determine the order in which they are treated here.

As with Mark we proceed by asking two questions: (a) How did Matthew contrive his Gospel from the Jesus tradition available to him? And (b) what did he hope to achieve by writing this 'second edition' of Mark? The second question could be particularly valuable, since it may tell us a great deal about the relation of emerging Christianity to emerging rabbinic Judaism in the aftermath of the disastrous end to the second temple and so in effect to Second Temple Judaism.[176] The way in which Matthew handled the Jesus tradition and the way it informed and served Matthew's purpose are equally fascinating.

a. How Did Matthew Go About Composing His Gospel?

The solution to 'the Synoptic problem', which still commands consensus support, provides the clearest answer. Matthew was in the happy position of having two written sources on which to draw — Mark and Q.[177] Despite a small minority attempting to promote what became known as 'the Griesbach hypothesis', that the traditional view of Matthew's priority should not be abandoned, the two-source solution has retained much the strongest support of specialists in the Synoptic Gospels.[178] However, the assump-

---

174. Stanton thinks that 'F. C. Burkitt's seventy year old formulation can hardly be bettered: "Matthew is a *fresh edition* of Mark, revised, rearranged, and enriched with new material"' (*A Gospel for a New People* 51-52, citing F. C. Burkitt, *The Earliest Sources for the Life of Jesus* [London: Constable, 1922] 97). On introductory questions see again §39.2c above.

175. Though, see the beginning of §39.2b above.

176. See above §39.2c(ii) and below §46.5b.

177. See *Jesus Remembered* §4.4b. Full analysis in Davies and Allison, *Matthew* 1.97-127.

178. See particularly C. M. Tuckett, *The Revival of the Griesbach Hypothesis* (SNTSMS 44; Cambridge: Cambridge University, 1983).

tion on which most research since then has operated is that an exclusively *literary* hypothesis (that Matthew drew the Jesus tradition which it shared with Mark and Luke entirely from the written documents, Mark and Q) is all that is needed to explain Matthew's source of that tradition, and therefore all that need be envisaged for Matthew's main sources. But, as I have repeatedly noted, such an assumption both ignores the oral culture of the earliest Christian communities and the inevitably oral character of the earliest transmission of the Jesus tradition. The issue is posed particularly by the almost ridiculous confidence which many invest in the assumption that all the non-Markan material shared by Matthew and Luke must have been derived from a written document (Q), a document which can be almost fully retrieved from that shared material, even when so much that is shared is strikingly divergent in detail.[179]

A historically more plausible hypothesis is that Matthew was able to draw on five collections (or categories) of Jesus tradition.[180]

1. Mark's Gospel. In *Jesus Remembered* I noted a series of passages in Matthew where the closeness of wording between Mark and Matthew is best explained in terms of Matthew's literary dependence on Mark.[181]
2. Tradition which Mark has transcribed but which Matthew seems to have known in an independent and somewhat different oral form.[182]
3. Written Q tradition. I have never disputed that much of the Q material

---

179. See again e.g. *Jesus Remembered* 147-60, 231-38; and further *The Oral Gospel Tradition*. Hengel writes dismissively of such confidence (*Four Gospels* 68-70).

180. Ulrich Luz (in private correspondence) points out that talk of 'five collections' is open to misunderstanding, since it is not distinct collections which are in view but overlapping categories, and since the distinction between oral and (already) written down is often a venture into the unknown. I continue to press that there are five categories on which Matthew drew, but am open as to what items of Jesus tradition should be put where; the content is clear only in the case of Mark.

181. *Jesus Remembered* 144 n.15.

182. I instance:

Matt.	Mark	Matt.	Mark	Matt.	Mark
5.30	9.43	10.42	9.41	17.14-21	9.14-29
8.23-27	4.35-41	15.21-28	7.24-30	18.1-5	9.33-37
9.27-31	10.46-52	16.1-4	8.11-13	28.1-8	16.1-8

Many of these are set out in *Jesus Remembered* 217-20; *New Perspective on Jesus* 106-10; 'Matthew as Wirkungsgeschichte' 157-59; and 'Reappreciating the Oral Jesus Tradition' 6-8. Recognition that Matthew was probably dependent on oral versions of Markan tradition as well as on Mark removes the need to hypothesize either an Ur-Markus or a Deutero-Mark (cf. Gnilka, *Matthäusevangelium* 2.526).

common to Matthew and Luke is again so closely parallel in form and wording that a shared literary source (Q) provides the best solution.[183]

4. Q material[184] which was in oral form, hence the divergences between the Matthean and Lukan versions.[185]

5. Tradition which is unique to Matthew (M), again suggesting that Matthew's stock of oral Jesus tradition was still wider.[186]

---

183. See again *Jesus Remembered* 147 n.29. Cf. U. Luz, 'Matthew and Q', *Studies in Matthew* (Grand Rapids: Eerdmans, 2005) ch. 3.

184. Cf. Hengel, *Four Gospels* 205. I would still prefer to distinguish the non-Markan Jesus tradition actually shared by Matthew and Luke from the hypothesized document containing some or much of that material by designating the former as 'q' and only the latter as 'Q' (*Jesus Remembered* 148-49). But since the suggestion has gained little or no traction I here use 'Q' for both.

185. I instance the following, though here too in some cases the variations could be explained as Matthew's variations on written Q tradition in oral manner:

Matt.	Luke	Matt.	Luke	Matt.	Luke
5.3-12	6.20-23	7.16	6.44	16.1	11.16
5.13	14.34-35	7.21	6.46	18.10-14	15.3-7
5.15	8.16	7.23	13.27	18.15	17.3
5.18	16.17	7.24-27	6.47-49	18.21-22	17.4
5.25-26	12.58-59	8.5-13	7.1-10	19.28	22.30
5.32	16.18	10.7-16	9.2-5/10.3-12	22.1-14	14.15-24
5.39-42	6.29-30	10.24-25	6.40	23.23	11.42
5.38-48	6.27-28, 32-36	10.26-33	12.2-9	23.25	11.39
		10.34-36	12.51-53	23.29	11.47
6.9-13	11.2-4	10.37-38	14.26-27	23.34-36	11.49-51
6.20-21	12.33-34	10.39	17.33	24.27	17.24
7.12	6.31	10.40	10.16	24.37-41	17.26-36
7.13-14	13.23-24	11.12-13	16.16	25.14-30	19.11-27

Several of the above are also set out in full in *Jesus Remembered* 221, 226, 232-35; *A New Perspective on Jesus: What the Quest for the Historical Jesus Missed* (Grand Rapids: Baker Academic/London: SPCK, 2005) 110-13, 116-17; 'Q¹ as Oral Tradition' 45-69; 'Matthew as Wirkungsgeschichte' 160-62; and 'Reappreciating the Oral Jesus Tradition' 8-10. Stanton regards Matt. 5.13a, 14a, 16; 6.9-13; 7.12, 15-20, 21; 10.8, 24-25, 41; 18.10a, 14; 23.28, 32-34 as Matthew's additions of 'new' words to his Q traditions, 'but his intention is to elucidate, apply and summarize his traditions rather than to supplement them with sayings which he has created *de novo*' (*A Gospel for a New People* 133-39).

186. Notably the complete units unique to Matthew chs. 1–2; 5.33-37; 6.1-6, 16-18; 7.6; 11.28-30; 13.24-30, 36-52; 17.24-27; 18.15-20, 23-35; 20.1-16; 21.28-32; 23.1-36; 25.1-13, 31-46; 27.3-10; 27.52-53; 28.9-20; but also 7.18-20; 10.5-6, 23; 12.5-6, 11-12, 34-37; 14.28-31; 16.17-19; 21.14-17; 24.28; 27.17, 24-25. Kilpatrick assumed that M was a written document, 'more primitive in type if not in date than Mark or Q' (*Origins* ch. 2, here 36). But Kümmel notes the unlikelihood of the above material being drawn from a common written source and concludes that Matthew used only oral tradition in addition to Mark and Q (*Introduc-*

To discern Matthew's composition technique is somewhat easier than in the case of Mark. Most obviously, if Matthew was drawing on written source material, then comparison of Matthew's text with Mark, and with what appears to have been the written Q tradition (best preserved by Luke), should provide fairly straightforward evidence of Matthew's editing. This was the main feature in the initial development of redaction criticism in the early 1960s,[187] though it soon became obvious that over-concentration on editorial changes to sources could give an unbalanced perspective on the subject.[188] Redaction criticism and narrative (or composition) criticism had to go hand in hand. Thus, in addition to evidence of redaction, the indications of editorial links, elaboration and consistent themes and motifs naturally call for attention.[189]

Good examples of Matthew's stylistic editing of Mark are the slower and more measured tone achieved by dropping so many of the devices which gave Mark's storytelling such pace — *euthys* ('immediately') and *palin* ('again'), the historic present tense and parataxis.[190] He drops or modifies some of Mark's more negative comments about Jesus' disciples or responses to Jesus.[191] Other good examples are Matthew's severe abbreviation of some of Mark's miracle stories,[192] all of which he successfully halves in length — no doubt in Matthew's view improving the story-telling.[193]

As noted above (§41.3), Matthew has followed Mark's Gospel model (passion narrative with extended introduction) very closely, but he has not hesitated to adapt or mould the tradition that came to him for his own purposes.[194] Examples of Matthew's probable theological editing include:

- 3.14-15 — to explain why Jesus came to be baptized by the Baptist;

---

tion 109-10); similarly S. H. Brooks, *Matthew's Community: The Evidence of His Special Sayings Material* (JSNTS 16; Sheffield: JSOT, 1987) 111-15; Brown, *Introduction* 206; Luz, *Matthäus* 1.50-52.

187. In the case of Matthew, most notably G. Bornkamm, G. Barth, and H. J. Held, *Tradition and Interpretation in Matthew* (1960; ET London: SCM, 1963).

188. See also Stanton, 'The Origin and Purpose of Matthew's Gospel', 1896-99.

189. See further Stanton, *A Gospel for a New People* chs. 2-3.

190. See above n.68.

191. E.g. Mark 3.21; 4.38; 5.31; 6.5; 8.17b; 9.10, 32; 10.35.

192. Mark 5.1-20/Matt. 8.28-34, Mark 5.21-43/Matt. 9.18-26, and Mark 9.14-29/Matt. 17.14-21. See also Hawkins, *Horae Synopticae* 158-60.

193. For other examples of Matthew's editorial and compositional style see Kümmel, *Introduction* 106-7; Luz, *Matthäus* 1.27-32. Gnilka notes that Matthew favours an antithetic structure (*Matthäusevangelium* 2.525); Davies and Allison draw particular attention to Matthew's tendency to arrange his material in threes (*Matthew* 1.62-71, 86-87).

194. See also O'Leary, *Matthew's Judaization of Mark* 111-17; she finds further evidence that Matthew 'judaizes Mark' (136-51) and 'torahizes' Mark in Matt. 10 and 18 (ch. 6).

- 5.17, 19-20 — elaborating a Q (oral) tradition (Luke 16.17) to give a positive slant to Jesus' attitude on the law;
- 5.32 — qualifying Jesus' apparent denial of the legitimacy of divorce (Luke 16.18);
- 9.13 and 12.7 — the addition of Hos. 6.6, 'I desire mercy, not sacrifice', to two stories drawn from Mark (Mark 2.13-17, 23-28);[195]
- 10.5-6 — the mission commission as attested in both Mark and Luke is prefaced by Jesus restricting the mission to 'the lost sheep of the house of Israel';
- 13.58 — Mark's assertion that Jesus was unable to work miracles apart from just a few (Mark 6.5) becomes the report that Jesus did not perform many miracles there;
- 14.28-31 — Matthew adds to Mark's story of Jesus walking on the water (Mark 6.45-52) the episode of Peter failing in an attempt to do the same;
- 14.33 — Mark's anti-climactic conclusion to the same story (Mark 6.52) becomes an occasion for worship and confession;
- 15.17 — in Mark 7.18-19 Jesus denies that what enters into a person can render him unclean, and Mark adds that thereby Jesus cleansed all foods; in Matthew the denial is removed and Mark's note omitted;
- 15.24 — Matthew inserts into the story of the Syrophoenician woman Jesus' assertion that he was sent only to 'the lost sheep of the house of Israel';
- 16.17-19 — Matthew adds to the story of Peter's confession of Jesus as Messiah (Mark 8.27-30) Jesus' very strong affirmation of Peter's status;
- 17.13 — the implication of Mark 9.11-13 that John the Baptist was the promised Elijah is spelled out;
- 19.3, 9 — Matthew subtly changes the issue of divorce into the issue of possible cause for divorce and adds the exception clause ('except for unchastity') to the more rigid view in Mark (10.2-12);
- 21.43-45 — Matthew adds fierce condemnation of the Jerusalem leadership to Mark's parable of the tenant farmers (Mark 12.1-12);
- 22.40 — to Mark 12.28-31 is added the Christian view (cf. Rom. 13.9; Gal. 5.14) that Jesus' designation of the two great commandments sums up the whole law.

In many of these cases, of course, Matthew may have been able to draw on alternative versions of the Jesus tradition. But in that case we would have to say

---

195. Stanton regards Matt. 9.13a and 12.7, 10.5-6 and 15.24, 21.41c and 43, 24.10-12 and 26, 26.52-54 as Matthean expansions of Mark; 'Matthew has creatively added "new" sayings of Jesus into Marcan traditions' (*A Gospel for a New People* 328-33, here 333).

that his choice of version was theologically motivated — which is not so very different. We will examine the significance of such redaction or selection in §42.3b-e. Less open to dispute is the fact that Matthew has regularly firmed up or identified Jesus' opponents as Pharisees[196]— the significance of which bears directly on the issue of the Gospel's life-setting and objectives.[197] As for the Q material, as often noted, Matthew mostly inserts the Q material in blocks into the Markan framework,[198] though a good example of his interweaving of Mark and Q tradition is Matthew's version of Jesus' commissioning of the twelve for mission (Matt. 10.7-16).

As with Mark, Matthew's composition style includes the provision of linking passages.[199] Furthermore, Matthew has obviously gathered most of Jesus' teaching into five great discourses — including, notably, the Sermon on the Mount (Matt. 5–7)[200] and a fresh collection of parables, several of

---

196. Pharisees in Matthew:

Matthew	Mark	Luke	Matthew	Mark	Luke
3.7		3.7	19.3	10.2	
5.20			21.45		
9.11	2.16	5.30	22.15	12.13	
9.14	2.18	5.33	22.34	12.28	
9.34			22.41	12.35	
12.2	2.24	6.2	23.2		
12.14	3.6		23.13		11.52
12.24	3.22	11.15	23.15		
12.38		11.29	23.23		11.42
15.1	7.1		23.25		11.39
15.12			23.26		11.40
16.1	8.11		23.27		11.44
16.6	8.15	12.1	23.29		11.47
16.11			27.62		
16.12					

197. As R. Hummel, *Die Auseinandersetzung zwischen Kirche und Judentum im Matthäusevangelium* (Munich: Kaiser, 1966), notes: the fact that Matthew had to deal with a uniformly Pharisaic-led Judaism points clearly to a time after the destruction of the temple (17).

198. Well illustrated by the chart provided by A. Barr, *A Diagram of Synoptic Relationships* (Edinburgh, 1976), familiar from student days.

199. Matt. 4.23–5.2; 6.7-8; 7.28-29; 9.32; 11.1, 20; 12.22-23; 13.1; 15.29-31; 19.1; 26.1.

200. H. D. Betz, *The Sermon on the Mount* (Hermeneia; Minneapolis: Fortress, 1995), argues that the Sermon on the Mount was a pre-synoptic Jewish Christian composition (44-45); but though he recognizes the oral character of both the Sermon on the Mount and the Sermon on the Plain (Luke 6.20-49) (83), he assumes too readily that the latter was a pre-synoptic written document, whereas the overlap with Luke's Sermon on the Plain suggests that it was Matthew himself who drew other oral tradition together with the Q material

which were not recorded elsewhere (Matt. 13.1-53).[201] As explanation of why Jesus used parables so intensely (Mark 4.34/Matt. 13.34), Matthew adds to Mark's somewhat depressing 'parable theory' (Mark 4.10-12, but lightened by 4.34b) the further explanations of Matt. 13.35 and 51-52. Not least, there are several verbal motifs which are distinctive of Matthew — for example, 'the kingdom of heaven',[202] 'your/my Father who is in heaven',[203] 'weeping and gnashing of teeth',[204] and particular terms which, as we shall see, express important aspects of Matthew's theology: *anomia* ('lawlessness'),[205] *dikaiosynē* ('righteousness'),[206] *proskynein* ('worship'),[207] and 'dissembler, play-actor' (*hypocritēs*).[208]

From such data it will not be too difficult to find an answer or answers to our second question: What did Matthew hope to achieve by writing his Gospel? Since his Gospel followed the model provided by Mark, the answers, initially, are similar to those of Mark.

b. The Significance of Jesus for Israel

(1) Somewhat surprisingly for a Gospel of Jesus, *Son of God*, Matthew breaks Mark's inclusio formed by Mark 1.1 and 15.39. He retains the confession of the centurion (Matt. 27.54/Mark 15.39), but his opening verse designates Jesus Christ as 'son of David, son of Abraham' (Matt. 1.1). Matthew also omits one of Mark's summary accounts of unclean spirits hailing Jesus as 'the Son of God' (Mark 3.11). On the other hand, Matthew significantly heightens the Son of God motif.[209]

(oral and written) to form the Sermon on the Mount. See further the critique of Stanton, *A Gospel for a New People* ch. 13.

201. See also below nn.226 and 227.

202. 32 times in Matthew (and only in Matthew), in place of Mark's and Luke's regular 'kingdom of God' (used by Matthew only 5 times).

203. Matt. 5.16, 45, 48; 6.1, 9, 26; 7.11, 21; 10.32, 33; 12.50; 15.13; 16.17; 18.10, 14, 19, 35; 23.9.

204. Matt. 8.12; 13.42, 50; 22.13; 24.51; 25.30.

205. Of the Gospels, only in Matthew — 7.23; 13.41; 23.28; 24.12.

206. Matt. 3.15; 5.6, 10, 20; 6.1, 33; 21.32. Elsewhere in the Gospels only Luke 1.75 and John 16.8, 10. We might add *dikaios* ('just'): Matt. 17x, Mark 2x; Luke 11x; John 3x.

207. Matt. 13x, Mark 2x, Luke 2x, John 11x.

208. Matt. 13x; Mark 1x; Luke 3x. For full lists of words and phrases characteristic of Matthew's Gospel or favoured by Matthew see Hawkins, *Horae Synopticae* 3-10; Davies and Allison, *Matthew* 1.74-80; Luz, *Matthäus* 1.57-78.

209. J. D. Kingsbury, *Matthew: Structure, Christology, Kingdom* (Philadelphia: Fortress, 1975), summarized his discussion at this point: 'while Jesus Messiah is to be sure the Son of David and the Son of Abraham, he is preeminently the Son of God' (78). Luz is

- He begins his Gospel with his version of the birth narratives whose core assertion is that Jesus was both Son of God and son of David,[210] though Matthew delays the explicit reference to Jesus' divine sonship till the quotation from Hos. 11.1 in Matt. 2.15 ('Out of Egypt I called my son').
- The temptations following Jesus' baptism are presented as tests of Jesus' sonship — 'If you are God's son . . .' (4.3, 6) — a double temptation echoed in the mocking of the crucified Jesus (27.40, 43).
- Matthew draws from the Q material the powerful saying, 'All things have been handed over to me by my Father [cf. 28.18], and no one knows the Son except the Father, and no one knows the Father except the Son, and anyone to whom the Son chooses to reveal him' (11.27).
- His revised account of Jesus walking on the water ends with the disciples confessing, 'Truly you are God's son' (14.33).
- Peter's confession is elaborated — 'You are the Christ, the son of the living God' (16.16).
- Not to be ignored is the considerable expansion of references to God as 'Father' in sayings of Jesus.[211]

(2) Matthew refers to Jesus as the *Messiah* (Christ) about as often as Mark, slightly emphasizing the titular significance of 'Christ' (1.16; 27.17, 22), but he has weakened the messianic secret motif so prominent in Mark.[212] As for the 'son of man' motif, its more frequent usage in Matthew (principally due to Matthew's incorporation of Q material) somewhat diminishes the effectiveness of Mark's abrupt juxtaposition of Peter's confession of Jesus' as Messiah with the first of the suffering Son of Man predictions (Mark 8.29-31).[213]

---

critical of Kingsbury but agrees that '"Son of God" is the most fundamental title for Christ' (*Studies in Matthew* 96).

210. *Jesus Remembered* 342-43.

211. J. Jeremias, *The Prayers of Jesus* (1966; ET London: SCM, 1967) 30, 38, 44, drew attention to the following statistics:
God as 'Father' in the sayings of Jesus: Mark 3, Q 4, special Luke 4, special Matthew 31;
Jesus referring to God as 'my Father': Mark 1(?), Q 1, special Luke 3, special Matthew 13;
Jesus referring to 'your Father': Mark 1, Q 2, special Luke 1, special Matthew 12.

212. See above at nn.99-103.

213. Mark has only the Mark 2.10 and 28 references to 'the son of man' prior to the first of the passion predictions (8.31); but Matthew adds another eight references prior to Peter's confession, and the first passion prediction in Matthew is not a 'son of man' saying (Matt. 16.21). The Markan 'messianic secret' is dissolved (Gnilka, *Matthäusevangelium* 2.541), and there is no distinctively Matthean Son of Man christology, except that he strengthens the apocalyptic emphasis: he gives more prominence to the Son of Man's role as judge (25.31-46; also 13.41-42; 19.28), and to the Son of Man's future 'coming' (10.23;

(3) In contrast to Mark, Matthew highlights the messianic theme of Jesus as *'son of David'*.[214] The few references in Mark[215] are all taken over.[216] But the theme is significantly strengthened.

- The genealogy in Matt. 1 emphasises the line of descent from David (1.1, 6, 17, 20).
- Seeing Jesus' healing power the crowds ask, 'Can this be the son of David?', a distinctive element in Matthew's version (12.23).
- Even the Syrophoenician woman appeals to Jesus as 'son of David', again distinctive of Matthew's version (15.22), along with the insertion of Jesus' affirmation that he had been sent only for the lost sheep of the house of Israel (15.24).
- In the triumphal entry, the crowd's acclamation ('Hosanna! Blessed is he who comes in the name of the Lord; blessed is the coming kingdom of our father David' — Mark 11.9-10) becomes 'Hosanna to the son of David! Blessed is he who comes in the name of the Lord' (Matt. 21.9).
- Seeing Jesus' amazing cures in the temple, the children repeat the acclamation, 'Hosanna to the son of David' (21.15), another distinctive feature of Matthew's account.

Where Mark may have been hesitant to highlight Jesus' royal descent — at the climax or immediate aftermath of the Jewish revolt, Roman authorities would hardly be sympathetic towards any claimant to the throne of Israel — Matthew presumably believed that any such political fear had faded sufficiently.[217] This

---

16.28; 24.30) — he is the only Evangelist to speak of 'the coming (*parousia*) of the Son of Man' (24.27, 37, 39); see also Kingsbury, *Matthew* 113-22.

214. That 'son of David' was a messianic title would be recognized by anyone familiar with Israel's scriptures and traditions; see e.g. 2 Sam. 7.11-13; Isa. 11.1-3; Jer. 23.5-6; *Ps. Sol.* 17.21-25. See also particularly L. Novakovic, *Messiah, the Healer of the Sick: A Study of Jesus as the Son of David in the Gospel of Matthew* (WUNT II/170; Tübingen: Mohr Siebeck, 2003). Ulrich Luz (in private correspondence) also refers to L. A. Huizenga, *The New Isaac: Tradition and Intertextuality in the Gospel of Matthew* (NovTSupp; Leiden: Brill, 2009), who argues that the Gospel of Matthew has a significant Isaac typology in presenting Jesus as the decisive sacrifice.

215. Mark 2.25; 10.47-48; 12.35-37; cf. 2.25.

216. Matt. 9.27 and 20.30-31; 22.42-45; cf. Matt. 12.3.

217. J. Willitts, *Matthew's Messianic Shepherd-King: In Search of 'the Lost Sheep of the House of Israel'* (BZNW 147; Berlin: de Gruyter, 2007), finds in the motif evidence of 'the presence of a Jewish nationalism within at least one stream of Jewish Christianity of the mid to late first century' (232). See also Y. S. Chae, *Jesus as Eschatological Davidic Shepherd* (WUNT 216; Tübingen: Mohr Siebeck, 2006). Stanton finds indications of Jewish hostility to claims that Jesus is Son of David (Matt. 2.3; 9.27-28; 12.23; 21.9, 15) as well as to Jesus' exorcistic ministry (9.34; 10.25; 12.24, 27) (*A Gospel for a New People* ch. 7).

speculation is strengthened by the fact that Matthew also shows less inhibition in referring to Jesus as 'King (of the Jews)'.[218]

(4) That Jesus was the answer to the hopes and expectations of Israel is one of Matthew's great emphases, indicated particularly by his concern repeatedly to note that *Jesus fulfilled various scriptures* — scriptures whose messianic significance Jesus had brought to light:[219]

- 1.22-23 — the virginal conception and Emmanuel prophecy (Isa. 7.14);
- 2.15 — 'Out of Egypt I called my son' (Hos. 11.1);
- 2.23 — 'He will be called a Nazarene' (?);
- 4.14-16 — Galilee of the Gentiles . . . (Isa. 9.1-2);
- 8.17 — Isa. 53.4 fulfilled in Jesus' ministry of exorcism and healing;
- 12.17-21 — another Servant song fulfilled in Jesus (Isa. 42.1-4);
- 13.35 — prediction of Jesus' constant use of parables (Ps. 78.2);
- 21.4-5 — entry into Jerusalem fulfilling Zechariah's prophecy (Zech. 9.9, with Isa. 62.11);
- 26.56 — unspecified scriptures fulfilled in Jesus' arrest in the garden of Gethsemane;
- 27.9 — prophecy fulfilled in the use of Judas Iscariot's betrayal price to buy a potter's field (Zech. 11.13).[220]

The prominence of Isaiah should be noted — a confirmation of the important influence which Isaiah had on earliest Christian thinking.[221]

---

218. Matt. 2.2; 21.5; 25.34, 40; 27.11, 29, 37, 42; see Gnilka, *Matthäusevangelium* 2.538. But note also Eusebius, *HE* 3.11.1-12.1 and 3.19-20, cited below (§45.3).

219. 'In order that what had been spoken (through the prophet) might be fulfilled' is one of the hallmarks of Matthew's Gospel — 1.22; 2.15, 17, 23; 4.14; 8.17; 12.17; 13.35; 21.4; 26.56; 27.9. Note also 2.5-6, 17-18; 3.3; 11.10; 13.14-15; 21.16; 21.42; 22.43-44. 'Some are attached to the minutiae of Jesus' career, as if to emphasize that the whole of Jesus' life, down to the last detail, lay within God's foreordained plan' (Brown, *Introduction* 207). See also Luz, *Matthäus* 1.189-99 (on the theological problems of the fulfillment citations — 196-97); bibliography review in Stanton, *ANRW* II.25.3 1930-33; also *A Gospel for a New People* ch. 15; M. Konradt, 'Die Rezeption der Schrift im Matthäusevangelium in der neueren Forschung', *TLZ* 135 (2010) 919-32.

220. Matthew refers to the prophecy as Jeremiah's, presumably indicating that the Zechariah passage had become merged with Jeremiah's well-known encounter with the potter and his symbolic act in buying a field (Jer. 18–19, 32); see further my *Unity and Diversity* 100-101, 103-4, 108; M. Knowles, *Jeremiah in Matthew's Gospel: The Rejected Prophet Motif in Matthean Redaction* (JSNTS 68; Sheffield: JSOT, 1993) 52-81; C. M. Moss, *The Zechariah Tradition and the Gospel of Matthew* (BZNW 156; Berlin: de Gruyter, 2008) ch. 9.

221. It is unclear whether Matthew drew directly on the Hebrew text; as a rule he follows the LXX, but in one or two cases he may have followed other translations of the

(5) More disputed is the influence of a *Moses-prophet* expectation, rooted in Deut. 18.15, 18;[222] but Matthew does seem to present Jesus as a new Moses,[223] or as the fulfillment of Israel's divinely intended purpose.

- The opening words of Matthew's Gospel (*biblos geneseōs*) are clearly an echo of the opening of the first of Moses' books (Gen. 2.4; 5.1).[224]
- The infant Jesus is spared from the murderous wrath of King Herod (Matt. 2.16-18), just as the infant Moses had been saved from the murderous command of the Pharaoh (Exod. 1–2).
- The exodus motif is obviously a factor in Matt. 2.15: 'Out of Egypt I called my son' (Hos. 11.1).
- The temptation of Jesus in the wilderness after his forty-day fast is interpreted by reference to passages from Deut. 6 and 8, evoking the parallel with Israel's wilderness wanderings (Matt. 4.1-10).[225]
- Only Matthew gathers most of Jesus' various teachings into five blocks or sermons,[226] the first (the Sermon on the Mount) when he had gone up a mountain, presumably in some echo of the five books of Moses.[227]
- The strong affirmation of the Law (especially 5.17-19).
- Although Matthew follows Mark in his account of the transfiguration, he adds the note that Jesus' face 'shone like the sun', echoing the description of Moses in Exod. 34.29-35, and he would probably have recognized and affirmed the echo of Deut. 18.15 in the heavenly voice's command, 'Listen to him' (Matt. 17.5).[228]

Hebrew, possibly an oral collection of testimonia (Kümmel, *Introduction* 110-12; see also Brown, *Introduction* 207-8, and the tabular analysis of Davies and Allison, *Matthew* 1.33-57).

222. See *Jesus Remembered* §15.6.

223. See particularly D. C. Allison, *The New Moses: A Matthean Typology* (Minneapolis: Fortress, 1993). Kümmel unjustifiably rejected any suggestion that Matthew was trying to portray Jesus as the 'new Moses' (*Introduction* 106).

224. See Luz, *Matthäus* 1.117-19; Davies and Allison, *Matthew* 1.150-55.

225. See particularly B. Gerhardsson, *The Testing of God's Son (Matt 4:1-11 & PAR)* (CB; Lund: Gleerup, 1966).

226. Each block is concluded with the same phrase — 'And it happened when Jesus finished (these sayings)' (7.28; 11.1; 13.53; 19.1; 26.1) — in effect designating five blocks of teaching, 5.3–7.27; 10.5-42; 13.3-52; 18.1-35; 24.2–25.46.

227. B. W. Bacon, *Studies in Matthew* (London: Constable, 1930), famously suggested that Matthew's Gospel should be apportioned into five books — chs. 3-7, 8-10, 11.1-13.52, 13.53–18.35 and 19-25. Discussion in W. D. Davies, *The Setting of the Sermon on the Mount* (Cambridge: Cambridge University, 1964) 14-25. Other bibliography in Kümmel, *Introduction* 106 n.5.

228. So e.g. Gnilka, *Matthäusevangelium* 2.96-97; Hagner, *Matthew* 2.494; and further A. D. A. Moses, *Matthew's Transfiguration Story and Jewish-Christian Controversy* (JSNTS 122; Sheffield Academic, 1996).

Jesus as 'prophet' is not usually regarded as a sufficiently positive evaluation of Jesus in the NT,[229] and the identification of Jesus as the Moses prophet appears elsewhere in the NT only in Acts (3.22-23 and 7.37).[230] Within the NT, then, Matthew's use of the motif is the most positive christological affirmation along these lines, and is a strong indication of Matthew's concern that his Gospel should speak forcefully to his fellow Jews.

(6) Matthew, however, goes beyond what might be regarded as the traditional Jewish expectations. The birth of Jesus is not simply symbolical of God's presence with his people (Matt. 1.23), as in Isaiah's prophecy (7.14). Jesus himself expresses or *embodies the divine presence* — 'Emmanuel, God is with us'. Matt. 1.23 by itself would not be sufficient to make this point.[231] But it is confirmed by Jesus' extraordinary promise that 'where two or three are gathered in my name, I am there among them' (18.20), a saying utterly unique to Matthew and clear evidence of Matthew's own theology.[232] Regularly noted is the parallel with *m. 'Abot* 3.2: 'But if two sit together and words of the Law (are spoken) between them, the Divine Presence rests between them'. Although attributed by the Mishnah to a rabbi (Hananiah b. Teradion) who was killed in the Bar Kokhba revolt, the saying may well express a rabbinic commonplace (cf. *m. 'Abot* 3.3, 6).[233] Like the rabbis, the post-70 Christians were faced with the crisis that the Jerusalem temple, the expression and location of the divine presence in Israel,[234] had been destroyed. But where the rabbis saw the divine presence as relocated to the Torah, the Christians saw it as relocated to Jesus. In effect the same point is made in the final words of Matthew's Gospel (Matt. 28.20), 'And behold, I will be with you until the end of the age' — making a neat inclusio with the Emmanuel saying, 'God is with us', of 1.23;[235] the universal authority ('all authority in heaven and earth') given to the exalted Jesus (28.18) simply enhances the point. For Matthew, Jesus was not simply Son of God, son of David, Messiah, Son of Man, Moses

---

229. See again *Jesus Remembered* §15.6.

230. *Beginning from Jerusalem* 93.

231. S. Gathercole, *The Pre-existent Son: Recovering the Christologies of Matthew, Mark and Luke* (Grand Rapids: Eerdmans, 2006), reads Matt. 1.23 as asserting 'Jesus' identification with God' (75-76) without asking how Isa. 7.14 would have been understood.

232. '18.20 is almost universally regarded not as a saying of the pre-Easter Jesus but as an utterance of the risen Lord, this because it presupposes the "spiritual" presence of Jesus among his disciples' (Davies and Allison, *Matthew* 2.790).

233. Davies and Allison, *Matthew* 2.789-90; Luz, *Matthäus* 3.53.

234. E.g. 1 Kgs. 9.3; Pss. 11.4; 76.1-2; 80.1; Ezek. 43.6-9; Zech 2.10-11; Sir. 36.18-19; 11QTemple 46.12.

235. See further D. D. Kupp, *Matthew's Emmanuel: Divine Presence and God's People in the First Gospel* (SNTSMS 90; Cambridge: Cambridge University, 1996).

prophet. He embodied God's presence and universal authority in a way that no other servant of God had done before him.[236]

(7) In a similar way, Matthew seems to go beyond the Q material in regarding Jesus not simply as the spokesman of divine Wisdom, but as himself *embodying divine Wisdom*.

- Where Luke 7.35 identifies Jesus and the Baptist as the *children* of Wisdom, Matt. 11.19 identifies Jesus with *Wisdom*: 'Wisdom is justified from her works', alluding back to Matthew's distinctive reference to 'the works of the Christ' (11.2).
- In Luke 10.21-22/Matt. 11.27 Jesus speaks in language characteristic of a teacher of wisdom; in contrast, however, in Matt. 11.28-30 (unique to Matthew) Jesus echoes ben Sira's invitation to his pupils to put their necks under the yoke of *Wisdom* (Sir. 51.25-27), whereas Jesus' invitation is for his disciples to take *his own* yoke upon them.[237]
- In Luke 11.49 'the *Wisdom* of God said, "I will send them prophets..."'; but in Matthew's parallel (Matt. 23.34) it is Jesus himself who says, '*I* will send you prophets...'.
- In Matt. 23.37-38, the imagery of a mother hen ('Jerusalem, Jerusalem, ... how often have I desired to gather your children together, as a hen gathers her brood under her wings') could be as much of divine presence/protection as specifically of Wisdom.[238] If 23.38 ('your house is left to you desolate') is an allusion to the belief that the Shekinah (the divine presence) had departed from the temple,[239] then it strengthens the implication that Matthew saw Jesus as the embodiment of the divine

---

236. Matt. 28.16-20 is frequently regarded as the key to Matthew's theology, the goal to which the Gospel has been driving (see e.g. Schnelle, *History* 230-31, with bibliography). J. Schaberg, *The Father, the Son and the Holy Spirit: The Triadic Phrase in Matthew 28:19b* (SBLDS 61; Chico: Scholars, 1982), argues that the phrase is a development of the Danielic triad, Ancient of Days, one like a son of man, and angels (cf. Luke 9.26; 10.21-22; Rev. 1.4-5) (particularly 183-87, 286-90).

237. See further C. Deutsch, *Hidden Wisdom and the Easy Yoke: Wisdom, Torah and Discipleship in Matthew 11.25-30* (JSNTS 18; Sheffield: JSOT, 1987) ch. 4, summary 142; disputed by Stanton, *A Gospel for a New People* ch. 16.

238. Deut. 32.11; Ruth 2.12; Ps. 17.8; 36.7; 57.1; 61.4; 63.7; 91.4; Isa. 31.5. The imagery is used of Wisdom in Sir. 1.5. See further M. J. Suggs, *Wisdom, Christology and Law in Matthew's Gospel* (Harvard University, 1970) 67; Dunn, *Christology* 202-4. Davies and Allison, commenting on 23.37, note the rabbinic habit of referring to the conversion of a Gentile as coming under 'the wings of the Shekinah' (*Matthew* 3.320).

239. Davies and Allison, *Matthew* 3.321-22 and Luz, *Matthäus* 3.382, note the report of Josephus (*War* 6.300) that at the feast of Pentecost before the destruction of the temple the priests heard the voice of a host saying 'We are departing hence', a tradition evidently known also to Tacitus (*Hist.* 5.13).

presence/Wisdom, who had now taken the place previously filled by the Jerusalem temple.

There is a danger of reading too much into this data,[240] and even if it helps us to see from Matthew's perspective, there is a question of how much of such a thrust would have been recognized by Matthew's audiences (it only became clear to modern critics when Matthew could be read alongside Luke). However, for a motif to be recognized as part of Matthew's theology, it is not necessary to argue that it would have been obvious to his audiences (especially on a first hearing of the Gospel). And the fact that it dovetails so neatly with the more obvious motif of divine presence strengthens the probability that for Matthew Jesus = Wisdom is an entirely fair way of reading his Gospel and his intention in composing it.

(8) One other feature worthy of note confirms the conclusion that Matthew drew on and shaped the Jesus tradition to present a higher christology than his predecessors. This is the fact that Matthew uses the term *proskynein* far more frequently than either Mark or Luke.[241] The term itself is ambiguous and may be used to express submission or petition before one of high authority.[242] This arguably is how the term should be understood when Matthew uses it of various petitions made to Jesus during his mission (the leper, Jairus, the Syrophoenician woman, the mother of James and John).[243] But Matthew was certainly well aware that the same word was regularly used in the sense 'worship' — as in the temptation to worship the devil (Matt. 4.9-10/Luke 4.7-8). The sense 'pay homage' may still be most appropriate in Matthew's account of the magis' *proskynein* of the infant Jesus (2.2, 8, 11), as in Mark's account of the sham homage offered to the condemned Jesus (Mark 15.19). But in the two usages in Matthew's account of the appearances of Jesus after his resurrection, the most natural rendering is that they 'worshipped' Jesus (Matt. 28.9, 17; as also Luke 24.52). It is presumably significant, then, that Matthew uses *proskynein* so often, and that in the earlier petitioning references he elected to use or insert *proskynein* where other versions used other terms. For Matthew there was a direct continuity between the humble petitioning of Jesus during

---

240. Gathercole cautions against reading such Wisdom christology as affirming that Jesus was 'the incarnation of an actually preexistent person or being'; it would 'still only mean that he was in some sense the embodiment of God's creative and redemptive purpose' (*The Pre-existent Son* 209).

241. See above n.207.

242. There is an equivalent range of meaning and significance in the title *kyrios* ('lord/Lord'); cf. e.g. Matt. 8.2, 6, 8, and 17.15 with Matt. 8.25, 10.24-25, 14.28, 30, 17.4 and 22.43-45; discussion in Kingsbury, *Matthew* 103-13.

243. Matt. 8.2; 9.18; 15.25; 20.20; also 18.26; similarly Mark 5.6.

his mission and the worship offered to the resurrected Jesus. Such overtones are confirmed by Matthew's one other *proskynein* reference, where, as noted above, he radically departs from Mark's downbeat conclusion of the account of Jesus walking on the water (Mark 6.51-52) to read, 'Those in the boat worshipped him, saying, "Truly you are the Son of God"' (Matt. 14.33). This too is of a piece with Matthew's christology of divine presence: worship is offered to Jesus precisely because he expresses and embodies the divine presence.[244]

Intriguingly, all this elaboration of the gospel of Jesus Christ was derived from the Jesus tradition. The elaboration is quite substantial, but nothing which twists the Jesus tradition unnaturally or indeed forcedly, or bends it out of shape to make a claim for Jesus which the tradition itself could not support. Jesus as God's son was firmly rooted in the Jesus tradition. The issue of him as Messiah, and his use of 'the son of man' terminology, likewise. The son of David and Moses prophet themes were little taken up elsewhere, but were hardly foreign to the impact Jesus made during his mission. The argument from prophecy fulfilled pushed a case but used well-established tradition. The claims of Jesus as divine presence and Wisdom and worthy to be worshipped certainly reflected the absorption of the full impact made by his mission, teaching and resurrection; but they were still expressions of that impact and indicate how deep an impression that impact had made on those who followed him. Even when Matthew's shaping and elaboration of the Jesus tradition is acknowledged, the impact made by Jesus himself during his mission is still clearly evident. Matthew's Jesus is still Jesus remembered.

c. A Manual of Discipleship and Church Discipline

(1) No less than Mark was Matthew concerned to show how the Jesus tradition provided clear guidance for the believers for whom he wrote his Gospel. It is true that he does not emphasize Jesus' role as a teacher quite so much as Mark; in address to Jesus, Matthew's preference for 'Lord' in place of Mark's 'Teacher'[245] is understandable, given Matthew's more developed christology just outlined. But Matthew has his own distinctive emphasis on Jesus as teacher — notably Jesus' invitation (as Wisdom) for others to take his yoke upon them and to learn from him (11.29), and his insistence that his

---

244. For further discussion see my *Did the First Christians Worship Jesus? The New Testament Evidence* (London: SPCK, 2010), here 10-11.
245. See above n.118.

disciples have 'one teacher' (23.8).²⁴⁶ And he has more than compensated for his omission or modification of Mark's 'teacher' references by his inclusion of far more of Jesus' actual teaching than Mark was able (or chose) to include, notably in the five 'sermons' put together by Matthew.

- The Sermon on the Mount (Matt. 5–7) probably functioned as a compendium of catechesis, beginning with a list of beatitudes to describe the character to which the catechized should aspire (5.3-12),²⁴⁷ including instruction on the practice of piety and prayer (6.1-18), and ending with the parable which commends the wise man who builds his life on solid rock by hearing and acting upon what Jesus says (7.24-27). 'The Sermon on the Mount is disciples ethic'.²⁴⁸
- The fuller commissioning of Matt. 10, with the additional warnings of persecution and the exhortation to fearless confession, clearly continued to serve as a manual for mission.²⁴⁹
- The collection of parables in Matt. 13 provides a peerless elaboration of Mark's parable chapter; how many of Jesus' parables were never transcribed?
- Matt. 18 serves as a Christian equivalent to Qumran's Community Rule.
- And Matt. 24–25 provide all the exhortation and forewarning that any community could want or need in preparing for the return of Christ.²⁵⁰

(2) However, more distinctive of Matthew's parenesis is its ecclesiastical thrust — instruction not just for individual disciples but for their corpo-

---

246. See also Matt. 9.11; 12.38; 17.24; and further J. Y.-H. Yieh, *One Teacher: Jesus' Teaching Role in Matthew's Gospel Report* (BZNW 124; Berlin: de Gruyter, 2004), with comparison of Jesus' teaching role in Matthew with the Teacher of Righteousness and Epictetus (see particularly ch. 1 and 273-325).

247. 'The Beatitudes . . . are a summary description of the character of the true disciple . . . (and) serve also as a portrait of Jesus himself' — H. B. Green, *Matthew, Poet of the Beatitudes* (JSNTS 203; Sheffield: Sheffield Academic, 2001) 288, 290.

248. Luz, *Matthäus* 1.544. Davies answers the question 'whether Matthew in concentrating on the words of Jesus as a "new law" has departed from the mind of Jesus' with both 'yes and no' (*Setting* 433).

249. Luz advocates reading ch. 10 'as Matthew's basic manifesto for his view of the church' and prefers to refer to it not as the 'mission discourse' but the 'disciple discourse' (*Studies in Matthew* ch. 8, here 149).

250. The five great speeches 'are direct address to the readers and for them direct effective commands of Jesus' (Luz, *Matthäus* 1.38). Also to be noted is the far greater prominence which Matthew gives to the day of judgment (10.15; 11.22, 24; 12.36; also 5.21-22; 12.41-42; 23.33). 'It is hardly a coincidence that only in Matthew are found portrayals of the Last Judgment that serve as the motivation for the parenesis (cf. Matt. 7.21ff.; 13.36ff.; 25.31ff.)' (Schnelle, *History* 224; see also 234-35).

rate identity as church. Matthew's ecclesiological perspective is apparent at various points.[251]

- Matthew is the only Evangelist to use the word *ekklēsia* (Matt. 16.18; 18.17), presumably conscious of the fact that *ekklēsia* was the usual Greek translation for the Hebrew *qāhāl,* denoting gathered Israel as the 'assembly' of Yahweh, or 'assembly' of Israel;[252] like Paul,[253] Matthew evidently regarded the church as the continuation of Israel as the assembly of God.
- Matt. 19.28 (the twelve disciples 'will sit on twelve thrones judging the twelve tribes of Israel') obviously confirms that Matthew was conscious of the symbolism of Jesus choosing twelve disciples — representing eschatological Israel.
- Matthew also makes more of the shepherd/sheep imagery than Mark or Luke: in particular, Jesus will 'shepherd my people Israel' (Matt. 2.6); and Jesus insists that he was sent only for 'the lost sheep of the house of Israel' (10.6; 15.24).[254]
- For Matthew the new community could be characterized as a 'brotherhood',[255] grouped round the elder brother Jesus, and thus forming a new family,[256] with corresponding implications for conduct and mutual relationships.
- The parable of the tares, with its warning not to be too hasty in distinguishing wheat from weeds, is distinctive to Matthew (13.24-30, 36-43); similarly the distinctive Matthean final paragraph to the parable of the great supper (Matt. 22.11-14) — the church as a *mixtum compositum* of bad and good (22.10).
- In one of the earliest redaction critical studies Bornkamm observed that Matthew's setting of the sequence on 'following Jesus' (Matt. 8.18-22) immediately before the episode of the stilling of the storm (8.23-27) was

---

251. 'Matthew has long been recognized as the most "ecclesiastical" of the four gospels' (Stanton, *ANRW* II.25.3 1925; with review of bibliography 1926-29).

252. *Jesus Remembered* 513-14.

253. *Beginning from Jerusalem* 599-601.

254. See also Matt. 7.15; 9.36; 10.16; 12.11-12; 18.12; 25.32-33; 26.31 — most of them distinctive of Matthew. See also n.217 above.

255. So e.g. W. Trilling, *Das Wahre Israel: Studien zur Theologie des Matthäusevangeliums* (Leipzig: St. Benno, 1962) 189; E. Schweizer, *Matthäus und seine Gemeinde* (SBS 71; Stuttgart: KBW, 1974) 114-15; Overman, *Matthew's Gospel and Formative Judaism* 95. See Matt. 5.22-24, 47; 7.3-5; 18.15, 21, 35; 23.8 — again, most of them distinctive of Matthew.

256. Matt. 12.49-50; 25.40; 28.10. Note also Matthew's repeated reference to God as 'Father' (see above n.211).

Matthew's way of showing what discipleship would involve,[257] with the boat perhaps symbolizing the church surviving the storms of persecution by virtue of Jesus' presence in it.

- 10.41 and 23.34 probably imply Christian communities ministered to by itinerant prophets.
- Finally worthy of note is the climactic great commission of 28.19, including the command to baptize converts 'in the name of the Father and of the Son and of the Holy Spirit' — a formulation which indicates that the rite of admission to the church had already developed from the earlier baptism 'in the name [singular] of Jesus Christ' to reflect a burgeoning christology with a closer association between Jesus (the Son) and God (the Father).[258]

(3) Most striking in Matthew's ecclesiology is the role and status he assigns to Peter. Peter's role as the first or lead disciple of Jesus during his mission and in the early years of the Jerusalem community was well established and firm in the communal memory.[259] But while Mark certainly signals the importance of Peter during Jesus' mission, he makes surprisingly little of it.[260] And Peter is not mentioned in the Q material. But Matthew adds a number of references to Peter which highlight his leadership role.

- Matthew explicitly designates Simon Peter as the 'first' among Jesus' twelve disciples (Matt. 10.2) — the only Evangelist to do so.
- Peter is presented as spokesman for the disciples in a number of instances additional to Mark — Matt. 15.15; 17.24; 18.21.
- To Mark's account of Jesus walking on the water (Mark 6.45-52) Matthew adds the subplot of Peter asking to come to Jesus on the water, failing in faith and having to be rescued by Jesus (Matt. 14.28-31).
- Most strikingly of all, to the account of Peter's confession of Jesus as Messiah, Matthew adds Jesus' high commendation of the insight given to Peter (16.17), and both Jesus' prediction of Peter's (or his confession's) role as the rock on which Jesus would build his church and Jesus' ap-

---

257. G. Bornkamm et al., *Tradition and Interpretation* 52-57. The key was the introduction which linked the two paragraphs: 'He embarked on the boat and his disciples followed him' (8.23).

258. See n.236 above.

259. *Jesus Remembered* 508, 540 and n.250, 644-45, 843-46; *Beginning from Jerusalem* 208, 366-69, §26.

260. See above §39 n.29.

pointment of Peter to exercise the power of the keys of the kingdom of heaven (16.18-19).[261]

What precisely is intended by this great Petrine commission is not as clear as it might be.[262] But the implication is clear: Matthew's account confirms that in at least an important swathe of churches Peter was already recognized to be a foundational figure of the church as a whole. And the influence which Matthew's Gospel soon began to exercise (§44.8b) would help establish or confirm that fundamental role for Peter more and more widely through the Mediterranean world.

At the same time, this foundational role for Peter in Matthew should not be exaggerated or entirely referred to Peter alone. It is noteworthy that in the walking on the water episode, Peter is presented as representative of disciples' 'little faith' (*oligopistos*).[263] In the context of Matthew's other *ekklēsia* references, the same authority to 'bind and loose' is given to Jesus' disciples as a whole and in a slightly more fulsome way (18.17-18).[264] And in 28.10 Matthew does not follow Mark 16.7 in distinguishing Peter from the rest of the disciples. Matthew was also concerned to discourage use of what might be called titles of ecclesiastical rank. He has Jesus say emphatically, 'You are not to be called rabbi, for you have one teacher, and you are all brothers. And call no one your father on earth, for one is your Father in heaven. Nor are you to be called instructors, for (only) one is your instructor, the Christ'

---

261. 'You are Peter (*petros*) and on this rock (*petra*) I will build my church (*ekklēsia*) and the gates of hades will not prevail against it. I will give you [singular] the keys of the kingdom of heaven, and whatever [singular] you bind on the earth will be bound in heaven, and whatever [singular] you loose on earth will be loosed in heaven' (Matt. 16.18-19). Sim sees in the tradition behind the passage 'a direct response to Paul's denial of Peter's fundamental role in establishing the Christian movement' (*The Gospel of Matthew* 200-203), but bases the charge on highly tendentious inferences drawn from 1 Cor. 1.12, 3.22 and 10.4.

262. Full discussion in Davies and Allison, *Matthew* 2.625-30, 634-41. Luz summarizes the 'critical consensus' which now dominates current exegesis (most Protestant and much Roman Catholic): (1) the saying (16.18-19) is post-Easter, a *Gemeindebildung* (community formation); (2) it is concerned with 'Peter's non-juristic precedence' (without thought of Peter as visible head of the whole Church); (3) the idea of apostolic succession is not to be connected with the text (*Studies in Matthew* ch. 9, here 165-66; also *Matthäus* 2.455-59). For a restatement of the traditional Greek and Syrian (and subsequently Protestant) view (Luz, *Matthäus* 2.476-77; also *Studies* 169) that it is not Peter (*Petros*) who is the rock (*petra*) but Peter's confession, see C. C. Caragounis, *Peter and the Rock* (BZNW 58; Berlin: de Gruyter, 1990).

263. *Oligopistos* is a distinctive Matthean theme (Matt. 8.26; 14.31; 16.8; also 17.20), though he may have drawn it in the first place from a Q tradition (Matt. 6.30/Luke 12.28).

264. 'Truly I tell you, all that you [plural] bind on earth will be bound in heaven, and all that you [plural] loose on earth will be loosed in heaven' (18.18); cf. John 20.23.

(23.8-10).²⁶⁵ These qualifications, however, should not be read as calling into question Peter's foundational role. They constitute more a warning not to forget Peter's failings or not to attribute to him an exclusive authority. And they no doubt reflect the high regard ('warts and all') in which he was held (probably) in the Syrian churches of the late first century.²⁶⁶ This, we might add, strengthens the inference that Peter's role was focused particularly on the Jewish Christian mission.²⁶⁷

(4) Almost as striking within Matthew's reworking of the Jesus tradition is the composition of ch. 18, Matthew's 'community rule'.

- He begins with the (probably) well-known instruction of Jesus on true greatness (18.1-5/Mark 9.33-37/Luke 9.46-48).
- To that he adds Jesus' probably equally familiar warnings about temptations (18.6-9/Mark 9.42-48/Luke 17.1-2) and the parable of the lost sheep (18.10-14/Luke 15.3-7), with its priority given to the well-being of 'one of these little ones' (18.6, 10, 14).
- But then comes instruction on church discipline (18.15-18), which seems to be an elaboration of Jesus' teaching on forgiveness (Matt. 18.21-22/ Luke 17.3-4).
- The encouragement to agree on what may be asked in prayer,²⁶⁸ and the promise that Jesus will be in the midst even of meetings of only two or three (18.19-20) are unique to Matthew,²⁶⁹ as is the parable of the unforgiving servant (18.23-35).

This last is one of the best examples in the Synoptic Gospels of how the Jesus tradition was elaborated and extended to speak to situations which

---

265. Perhaps significant here is also the fact that, apart from Matt. 10.2, Matthew refrains from talking of the 'disciples' as 'apostles'. Davies and Allison observe that if these instructions constitute a general prohibition against ecclesiastical titles 'one could scarcely find a biblical text so little heeded' (*Matthew* 3.278).

266. Fuller discussion in Davies and Allison, *Matthew* 2.647-52 (bibliography 647 n.1); Luz, *Matthäus* 2.467-71 (bibliography 451).

267. See further *Beginning from Jerusalem* §35.

268. Does the sequence 18.15-20 suggest that vv. 18-20 have in mind specifically the member of the church and the offending brother — vv. 18-20 the product of agreed reconciliation (W. G. Thompson, *Matthew's Advice to a Divided Community: Mt 17,22–18,35* [AB 44; Rome Biblical Institute, 1970] 202)? Thompson emphasizes the importance of forgiveness and reconciliation in ch. 18.

269. 18.19 is of a piece with other encouragements on how to pray effectively (Mark 11.23-24; John 16.23-24; James 1.5-6), but 18.20 is usually regarded as a prophetic utterance in an early Christian worship gathering, heard as a word of the exalted Christ (see above n.232).

developed in the early churches and to which the Jesus tradition initially did not refer. But even so it is sufficiently clear that the elaborated motifs and emphases were of a piece with and consistent with the spirit of teaching which can be traced back to Jesus himself.[270] In this way we can see how the tradition of Jesus' mission and teaching both continued to provide instruction on following Jesus and gave the young churches a clearer sense of identity by relating them to the foundational status and example of Peter and by encouraging them to regard and act towards one another as members of the family of Christ.

d. Jousting with the Pharisees over Israel's Heritage

In discussing the date of Matthew (§39.2c) I have already referred to the broad consensus that Matthew's Gospel was written some time after 70 and reflects some degree of confrontation with the rabbinic Judaism which began to emerge in Palestine after the disastrous failure of the first Jewish revolt. But Matthew does not merely 'reflect' such confrontation. The Gospel is itself the best evidence for such confrontation, and a major reason for its being written was no doubt to engage in such confrontation.

Some of the evidence for this has already been marshaled:

- Jesus presented as Israel's Messiah, son of David, king of the Jews;
- the parallel of Jesus with Moses — Jesus as the fulfilment of the hope for a prophet like Moses;
- the repeated emphasis on Jesus as having fulfilled Israel's scriptures;
- the birth narrative asserts both that Jesus 'will save his people (*laos*) from their sins' (1.21) and that he 'is to shepherd my people (*laos*) Israel' (2.6);
- the church (*ekklēsia*) as the continuation of Israel as the assembly of Yahweh (16.18);
- Jesus' mission as to 'the lost sheep of the house of Israel' (10.6; 15.24);
- and the twelve's future role in judging the tribes of Israel (19.28).

In addition, Matthew's increased attention to the Pharisees, as Jesus' opponents and as the chief objects of Jesus' own criticisms, underscores the likelihood that all these emphases in Matthew's Gospel had a common objective: to make the case that emerging Christianity was the eschatological

---

270. Cf. particularly S. Byrskog, *Jesus the Only Teacher: Didactic Authority and Transmission in Ancient Israel, Ancient Judaism and the Matthean Community* (CBNTS 24; Stockholm: Almqvist & Wiksell, 1994).

outworking of Second Temple Judaism;[271] and to do so in opposition to a Pharisaic Judaism making the same claim.

Nothing makes this clearer than Matthew's presentation of Jesus in relation to the law. For there is no suggestion that Matthew wanted to present Jesus as rejecting the law, as, in effect, yielding the law entirely to the Pharisees. As embryonic rabbinic Judaism began to reconstitute Judaism round the law and the Halakhah, it would have been quite natural for embryonic Christianity to abandon the law altogether as a community marker, to yield the law entirely to the successors of the Pharisees. In contrast, however, Matthew was evidently concerned to demonstrate his (and his community's) *loyalty to the Torah*. To the Pharisees with whom he was in conflict, the Matthean Jesus says in effect, We are as loyal to the law as you:

> Do not think that I have come to abolish the law or the prophets; I have not come to abolish but to fulfill. For truly I tell you, until heaven and earth pass away, not one letter, not one yodh, will pass from the law until all is accomplished. Therefore, whoever breaks one of the least of these commandments, and teaches others to do the same, will be called least in the kingdom of heaven; but whoever does them and teaches them will be called great in the kingdom of heaven (Matt. 5.17-19).

Indeed, the claim is that the followers of Jesus were *more* devoted to what the law demands.

- In the same paragraph, Jesus continues: 'For I tell you, unless your righteousness exceeds that of the scribes and Pharisees, you will never enter the kingdom of heaven' (5.20). The Matthean church was as much motivated to perform 'righteousness' as any Pharisee (6.1), though the righteousness they hungered for and were to seek was God's righteousness (5.6; 6.33).[272]
- So in the rest of chapter 5, Jesus goes on to penetrate below the wording of various commandments to their deeper meaning. The commandment

---

271. Did Matthew regard the Christian brotherhood as 'the true Israel' — 'to whom this kingdom of God has been given [21.43], who "has" it, that one is Israel' (Trilling, *Das Wahre Israel* 75)? But a critique of Israel's leadership (21.45) is not best expressed in terms of true and false Israel; cf. Gnilka, *Matthäusevangelium* 2.544-45; Saldarini entitles ch. 2 of *Matthew's Christian-Jewish Community*, 'Matthew's People: Israel'.

272. G. Friedlander, *The Jewish Sources of the Sermon on the Mount* (1911; New York: Ktav, 1969), famously maintained that 'Four-fifths of the Sermon on the Mount is exclusively Jewish' (266); though he also was of the opinion that in comparison with Matt. 7.1-2, 'Pharisaic teaching [as in *m. Abot* 1.6] is infinitely superior to that of the Gospel' (214).

against murder is more fully to be understood as a warning against anger and insult and denigration of a brother (5.21-22); the commandment against adultery is more fully to be understood as a warning against lust (5.27-28). It is not so much that Jesus replaces Moses or abrogates the law at certain points (Matt. 5.33-48); it is rather that Jesus gives a definitive interpretation of the law as it bears on human relations, fulfilling its deeper intention.[273] Doing the will of the heavenly Father is what really counts,[274] with the implication that the Father's will is not to be identified with a narrow reading of the law or a superficial declaration of loyalty.[275] We may infer that Paul's view was similar in his talk of 'the law of Christ' (Gal. 6.2).[276]

- Like Hillel, so highly regarded by the rabbis, the Matthean Jesus was ready to sum up the law in a single word — 'In everything do to others what you would have them do to you' (Matt. 7.12) — a positive version of 'the golden rule', where Hillel's was a negative form.[277] Similarly, like

---

273. The antitheses which take issue with particular commandments or concessions (Matt. 5.21-42; 19.3-9) actually make responsibility before God more demanding. See further Overman, *Matthew's Gospel and Formative Judaism* 73-90; Saldarini, *Matthew's Christian-Jewish Community* ch. 6 — 'The six so-called antitheses (5:21-48) are not understood by Matthew as changes in God's law, but as more penetrating appreciation of and obedience to the law' (162); Sim, *The Gospel of Matthew* 123-39, who reads the antitheses 'as intensification rather than abrogation' (130); Luz, *Matthäus* 1.333. On 5.38-42 see also Betz, *Sermon on the Mount* 277-84.

274. Matt. 6.10; 7.21-23; 12.50; 21.31; 26.42; another motif extended by Matthew (see also n.288 below.

275. Cf. Hummel, *Auseinandersetzung* 50, 56. In contrast Luz does not hesitate to describe 5.20 as 'a classic expression of what Reformation theology terms justification by works', though he proceeds to qualify the assertion (*Studies in Matthew* ch.10, here 214).

276. See also Betz, *Sermon on the Mount* 626-27; R. Deines, 'Not the Law but the Messiah: Law and Righteousness in the Gospel of Matthew — An Ongoing Debate', in D. M. Gurtner and J. Nolland, eds., *Built upon the Rock: Studies in the Gospel of Matthew* (Grand Rapids: Eerdmans, 2008) 53-84. Sim finds in Matthew a strong 'anti-Pauline' thrust: 'doers of lawlessness' (Matt. 13.41) 'can only apply to the members of the law-free or Pauline wing of this movement'; 'Matthew openly and savagely attacks Paul and his law-free gospel' (*Gospel of Matthew* 199-213, here 204, 213). But to generalize Paul's opposition to Gentile believers being required to observe the laws of circumcision and of clean and unclean (Gal. 2), or to characterize his whole mission as 'law free', misses Paul's otherwise positive attitude to the Jewish law (*Theology of Paul* §23; *New Perspective on Paul* 51-55 [§3.3]). See also K. R. Iverson, 'An Enemy of the Gospel? Anti-Paulinism and Intertextuality in the Gospel of Matthew', in C. W. Skinner and K. R. Iverson, eds., *Unity and Diversity in the Gospels and Paul*; F. J. Matera FS (Atlanta: SBL, 2012) 7-32.

277. 'What is hateful to you, do not do to your neighbour; that is the whole Torah, while the rest is commentary thereon; go and learn it' (*b. Sabb.* 31a); see further Davies and Allison, *Matthew* 1.686-88.

Mark, Matthew depicts Jesus as summing up the law and the prophets by referring to the Shema ('You shall love the Lord your God with all your heart, and with all your soul, and with all your mind'), and by pulling out Lev. 19.18 from the sequence of commandments in Lev. 19 ('You shall love your neighbour as yourself') to give it a unique primacy: 'On these two commandments hang all the law and the prophets' (Matt. 22.37-40).[278] In the Sermon on the Mount Jesus had already rejected the current elaboration of 'You shall love your neighbour — and hate your enemy'. For Matthew's Jesus the love command should be differently extended: 'Love your enemies, and pray for those who persecute you' (5.43-44).

- At the beginning of the story of the disciples plucking and eating grain on the Sabbath Matthew adds that they did so because 'they were hungry' (12.1); thus he increases the parallel with David (12.3) and makes the disciples' action less reprehensible.
- In Matt. 15.1-20 Matthew takes up the same tradition as Mark, where Jesus teaches about purity, that the impurity of the heart is more serious than the impurity of the hands. But where Mark infers from this that Jesus thus abolished the distinction between clean and unclean foods (Mark 7.15, 19), Matthew simply underlines that inner cleanliness is much more important than the cleanliness of some foods (Matt. 15.17-20).[279] Similarly Matt. 23.25-26.
- The authority given to Peter (16.19) and the disciples (18.18) to 'bind and loose', so distinctive of Matthew's Gospel, echoes the authority traditionally claimed by the rabbis — to declare what is *not* permitted (to bind) and to declare what *is* permitted (to loose).[280] Matthew claims that the same authority was given by Jesus to Peter and his immediate disciples, and evidently believed that the scribes and Pharisees were using such authority to build walls of exclusion (23.13).
- Matthew's version of Jesus' teaching on divorce is also significant. In Mark 10.1-9 Jesus seems to deny the legitimacy of divorce, and thus

---

278. As noted in *Jesus Remembered* 584 n.182, the earliest parallel focus on Lev. 19.18 in Jewish tradition is attributed to rabbi Akiba, early second century — that Lev. 19.18 is 'the greatest general principle in the Torah' (*Sipra* on Lev. 19.18) — perhaps another indication of the post-70 interaction between emerging Christianity and emerging rabbinic Judaism.

279. Matt. 15.1-20 should not be read simply as Matthew's redaction of Mark 7; rather Matt. 15 may well be evidence that Matthew knew a different version of Jesus' teaching, the oral tradition of Jesus' teaching on purity which circulated in Jewish Christian assemblies (see further *Jesus Remembered* 573-77, with bibliography). But the contrast with Mark still stands (Sim, *Gospel of Matthew* 132-35).

280. Str-B 1.738-41. Full discussion in Davies and Allison, *Matthew* 2.635-41.

overrules the Mosaic ruling which permits divorce (Deut. 24.1-4). In Matthew, however, Jesus' teaching is presented as a contribution to the debate about how Deut. 24.1, 3 should be interpreted (Matt. 19.3-9). The Matthean Jesus in effect participates in the debate between the schools of Hillel and Shammai, and seems to side with the more rigorous Shammaite ruling, that divorce is only permitted in the case of immorality.[281]

- In the denunciation of 'scribes and Pharisees' in chapter 23, Jesus acknowledges the scribes' and Pharisees' teaching authority (they 'sit on Moses' seat — 23.2) and commands his followers to 'do whatever they teach you and follow it; but do not do as they do, for they do not practise what they preach' (23.3). Later Jesus' denunciation is that the scribes and Pharisees 'tithe mint, dill, and cumin, and have neglected the weightier matters of the law: justice, mercy and faith. It is these you ought to have practised without neglecting the others' (23.23) — a prophetic word very much in the spirit of Isaiah, Amos and Micah.[282] As with the prophetic critique of failure to observe the spirit of the law, so the Matthean Jesus' critique of Pharisaic casuistry is a critique not of the law, but of how it was being interpreted.[283]

- In the same vein we should note that only in Matthew does Jesus quote Hos. 6.6, and does so twice: 'Go and learn what this means, "I desire mercy, not sacrifice"' (Matt. 9.13; also 12.7). The twofold citation of Hos. 6.6 in Matthew probably reflects a different evaluation of the theological significance of the destruction of the temple from that of the 'Pharisees'.[284]

- To the warning of Mark 13.18, 'Pray that the catastrophe may not happen in winter', Matthew adds, 'Pray that it may not happen in winter or on a Sabbath' (Matt. 24.20). Clearly implied is the fact that the Matthean community continued to observe the Sabbath; so far as the Matthean Christians were concerned, Jesus had not called for the Sabbath law to be abrogated.[285] The implication is that the two Sabbath stories taken

---

281. Bibliography in Kümmel, *Introduction* 113 n.31; also D. R. Catchpole, 'The Synoptic Divorce Material as a Traditio-Historical Problem', *BJRL* 57 (1974) 93-127.

282. See e.g. Isa. 58.1-12; Amos 5.21-24; Micah 6.6-8.

283. K. G. C. Newport, *The Sources and Sitz im Leben of Matthew 23* (JSNTS 117; Sheffield: Sheffield Academic, 1995), argues that Matthew draws on source material for 23.2-31, which 'predates the fall of the temple and stems from an *intra muros* debate between various factions within Judaism' (182).

284. Hummel, *Auseinandersetzung* 98-99.

285. Less plausible, if indeed the ways of Matthew's community and rabbinic Judaism had already parted (but see §46.5b below), is Stanton's suggestion that 'flight on a Sabbath would provoke further hostility from some Jewish leaders' (*A Gospel for a New People* 8, ch. 8).

over from Mark (Matt. 12.1-13) were intended by Matthew not to teach that the Sabbath is no longer important, but to teach how it should be observed in the light of Jesus' fulfillment of the law.
- Probably not insignificant are the terms of the final commission of Matthew's Gospel: they are to teach the converts of the nations 'to observe all that I (Jesus) have commanded you' (28.20). Matthew did not hesitate to characterize Christian catechesis as command(ment)s to be observed.

A striking feature of Matthew's Gospel at this point is his use of two words distinctive of his own vocabulary. As already noted, Matthew is the only Gospel writer to speak of *anomia*, 'lawlessness'.[286] Clearly this is Matthew's own word. In warning against 'lawlessness', as Jesus does in these passages, Matthew was clearly proclaiming Jesus' loyalty to the law, and his own and the gospel's loyalty to the law at the same time. Again as noted above, almost as distinctive of Matthew's vocabulary is his use of the word 'righteousness', *dikaiosynē*.[287] Note again 5.20: 'Unless your righteousness exceeds that of the scribes and Pharisees, you will never enter the kingdom of heaven'.[288]

This jousting with the Pharisees may also help explain Matthew's distinctive emphasis on Jesus as the divine presence and as Wisdom (§42.3b(6,7)). For, as again we have seen, for the rabbis, in the aftermath of the temple's destruction, the focus of the divine presence in effect shifted from the temple to the Torah. And we should remember that already well before 70 Israel's wisdom

---

286. See above nn.205, 276; also Overman, *Matthew's Gospel and Formative Judaism* 16-19.

287. See above n.206.

288. B. Przybylski, *Righteousness in Matthew and His World of Thought* (SNTSMS 41; Cambridge: Cambridge University, 1980), plausibly argues that righteousness in Matthew 'is essentially a Jewish concept' (123) and is different from that in Paul, in that in Matthew righteousness 'deals solely with God's demand rather than gift' (106). More controversially he goes on to argue that Matthew uses 'righteousness' only in polemical contexts (in relation to the Pharisees), and prefers to describe discipleship obligation in terms of 'doing the will of God' (ch. 6). However, he downplays the very positive references to righteousness (5.6, 10, 20; 6.1, 33), where it is hard to see a distinction between practising righteousness and doing the will of God (see n.274 above), and his unwillingness to recognize that Matthew would think of disciples as 'the righteous' gives too little weight to 10.41; 13.43, 49; 25.37, 46. See also Overman, *Matthew's Gospel and Formative Judaism* 91-94. In some contrast, both R. A. Guelich, *The Sermon on the Mount: A Foundation for Understanding* (Waco: Word, 1982) 170-74, and J. K. Riches, *Conflicting Mythologies: Identity Formation in the Gospels of Mark and Matthew* (Edinburgh: T & T Clark, 2000) 190-96, stress that for Matthew righteousness is the outworking of relationship with God (5.6, 10; 6.33). See also F. Moloney, 'Matthew 5:17-18 and the Matthean Use of *DIKAIOSUNĒ*', in Skinner and Iverson, eds., *Unity and Diversity in the Gospels and Paul* 33-54.

tradition had identified divine Wisdom also with the Torah (Sir. 24.23; Bar. 4.1). So what Matthew was doing was in effect saying to his Pharisaic/rabbinic opponents: the line of continuity runs from Moses into and through Jesus, not the law; the focus of the divine presence now is in Jesus, not in the Torah.

We should note, then, that Matthew's taking over of the Gospel format from Mark did not mean that he saw the gospel of Jesus as set in antithesis to the law. Matthew would not have welcomed the antithesis between gospel and law which the Lutheran Reformation read too quickly into Paul.[289] And he certainly would not have welcomed the suggestion that Christianity had abandoned its Jewish heritage. The Gospel for him was a thoroughly Jewish gospel — entirely in the spirit of the law and the prophets. There was disagreement between Jesus' followers and the rabbis on how the law and the prophets should be interpreted. But there was a basic agreement with the rabbis that the law and the prophets continued to be of major importance. Jesus as the fulfillment of the law had brought home the deepest meaning of the law. His life and teaching showed how the law should be obeyed. Relation to God was now to be worked out from Jesus as the centre, with reference to the law but not the law as the centre or starting point. Fulfilment was not abrogation. It was focus on Jesus which brought the law also into focus, by being read through the lens which was Jesus and his gospel.

e. Mission to Gentiles

Despite its Jewish character and concerns,[290] a notable feature of Matthew's Gospel is its commitment that the gospel of Jesus Messiah, Son of God, should be taken to the (other) nations, linked with the thought, expressed more than once, that Israel was in danger of being replaced in God's purpose of salvation.[291]

- By tracing Jesus Messiah's genealogy back to Abraham, Matthew (1.1) may be implicitly acknowledging Paul's argument that the sons/heirs of Abraham include Gentile believers (Rom. 4; Gal. 3).

---

289. See my *The New Perspective on Paul* (Grand Rapids: Eerdmans, ²2008) 22 n.88.

290. Note that Matt. 18.17 (let the unrepentant brother 'be to you as a Gentile [*ethnikos*] and a tax-collector') reflects and retains a traditional Jewish attitude to the non-Israelite as someone to be shunned and kept separate from. Sim argues that the 'swine' of Matt. 7.6 refers to Gentiles (cf. 15.26) (*Gospel of Matthew* 237-39).

291. This is the consensus position in Matthean scholarship. Sim questions whether any texts in Matthew reflect recognition of or advocacy of a current Gentile mission (*Gospel of Matthew* 236-47), but he ignores most of the following data, finding only two verses (Matt. 24.14 and 28.19) which envisage a Gentile mission, that is, a law-observant mission (242-47).

- In Matt. 1.3-6, the only women mentioned in the genealogy of Jesus prior to Mary (Tamar, Rahab, Ruth and the wife of Uriah) are all non-Jews, a subtle reminder at the very beginning of the Gospel that Gentiles had played an integral part in Israel's own history.[292]
- In the birth narrative the central characters, apart from Mary, Joseph and Jesus, are the magi 'from the East' (2.1), who alone worship Jesus (2.11), in contrast to the current king of the Jews (Herod) who tries to eliminate him (2.16).
- John the Baptist warns against his Jewish devotees presuming on their descent from Abraham; 'God is able from these stones to raise up children to Abraham' (3.9).
- To the story of the healing of the centurion's boy, Matthew transfers Jesus' conclusion so affirmative of the centurion's faith and so despairing of Israel: 'I tell you, many will come from east and west and will eat with Abraham and Isaac and Jacob in the kingdom of heaven, while the heirs of the kingdom will be thrown into the outer darkness . . .' (8.11-12).
- Despite 10.5-6, 10.18 envisages testimony being given also to the Gentiles.
- Matthew inserts Isa. 42.1-4, one of the most positive of Israel's prophecies with regard to the Gentiles, into his description of Jesus' healing ministry, climaxing with 'And in his name the Gentiles will hope' (Matt. 12.18-21).
- Matthew cites Jesus sharply contrasting the repentance of the men of Nineveh, and the queen of the south's eagerness to learn, with the lack of response to Jesus' message evidenced by Jesus' own generation (12.41-42); the sayings are drawn from Q material (Luke 11.31-32), but in Matthew's Gospel they have a sharper bite.
- The interpretation of the parable of the tares envisages the seed ('the sons of the kingdom') being sown in the field, which is 'the world' (Matt. 13.38). Similarly 24.14 envisages 'the gospel of the kingdom' being preached 'throughout the whole world, as a testimony to all the nations'.
- The parable of the labourers in the vineyard (Matt. 20.1-16) implies that the Gentiles, though responding late to the gospel's summons, will not be disadvantaged.
- To the parable of the tenant farmers Matthew adds the shocking conclusion: 'Therefore I tell you, the kingdom of God will be taken from you and will be given to a people (*ethnos*) who produce its fruits' (21.43);

---

292. 'The four Gentile women at the beginning correspond to "all nations" at the end' (Schnelle, *History* 231).

also added is the note that the chief priests and Pharisees recognized that Jesus was speaking about them (21.45).[293]

- Matthew's elaboration of the parable of the wedding feast, with the king's angry destruction of the city of the initially invited guests (Jerusalem), includes the king's verdict, 'Those invited were not worthy. Therefore go into the main streets and invite everyone you find to the wedding' (22.8-9) — where again the clear implication is that for Matthew the Gentile mission has taken over from the unsuccessful Jewish mission.[294]
- Perhaps most significant of all, Matthew makes a point of ending his Gospel with the mission commission of the disciples: 'Go therefore and make disciples of all the nations . . .' (28.19-20). For whatever length of time the earlier commission of Jesus, not to go the way of the nations/Gentiles (10.5), was held to be valid, Matthew's conclusion with the great commission to 'all the nations' made it clear that Jesus' earlier instruction had been long superseded.[295]

Matthew's apparent pro-Gentile and anti-Jewish emphasis is strong enough for some commentators to conclude that Matthew himself was a Gentile,[296] or at least that he writes from a Gentile-Christian viewpoint. But the pro-Gentile emphasis is more accurately described as pro-Gentile *mission*, being held out as a continuing challenge to Israel.[297] As such it becomes fairly obvious that for Matthew this was the inevitable outworking of Jesus' own teaching on and practice of mission, in the light of Jesus' resurrection. Matthew faithfully retained the words which underlined the more limited objectives of Jesus' own mission (10.5-16; 15.24); but the cli-

---

293. It is from this verse that Stanton derives his title — *A Gospel for a New People*.
294. Disputed by Sim, *Gospel of Matthew* 239-42.
295. It is important that *panta ta ethnē* be translated 'all the nations' rather than 'all the Gentiles'; Matthew had not given up hope of 'making disciples' of his fellow Jews (Davies and Allison, *Matthew* 3.684; and particularly Luz, *Matthäus* 4.447-52).
296. Bibliography in Kümmel, *Introduction* 114-15; Stanton, *ANRW* II.25.3 1917-20; also *A Gospel for a New People* 131-39; Schnelle, *History* 220 n.235; 235-36. See particularly the very full discussion of Davies and Allison, *Matthew* 1.9-58, on Matthew's Semitisms (1.80-85).
297. Luz justifiably argues that the decision in favour of a Gentile mission must have been a significant turning point (cf. 10.5-6!) for the Matthean community, perhaps under the influence of Mark's Gospel (*Matthäus* 1.91-93). The fact that circumcision seems to have been (no longer) an issue suggests both that the Jewish-Christian Gentile mission reflected in Matthew was different from the Pauline mission, and that the issue had nonetheless been resolved without lasting effect either on Matthew's pro-Gentile mission or as an explicit factor in the relation of Matthew's community with current Jewish authorities; significantly, and somewhat surprisingly (in view of Matt. 18 and 23), Matthew continued to be constrained by the Jesus tradition's account of the issues confronting Jesus' mission.

max of 28.19-20 makes it clear enough that Jesus' resurrection had revolutionized everything for his disciples.[298] But not in a way that ignored or left behind Jesus' own teaching and commission. For even if 21.43 is to be assigned to Matthew's redaction, as Mark 13.10/Matt. 24.14 have to be read as expressions of early Christian conviction, and even if Matt. 12.17-21 was clearly added by Matthew, there was still sufficient in the Jesus tradition to indicate that the fresh post-Easter perspective was one which derived from Jesus and in continuity with his earlier mission. The memory of Jesus' own response to the few Gentiles to whose need he was able to minister was itself probably proof enough for Matthew. And the prospect of Gentiles being welcomed in heaven and faring better in the final judgment was one which Jesus himself was clearly remembered as affirming.[299] The retention of Matt. 10.5-6 and 15.24, however, may imply that Matthew and his community did not come very quickly to appreciate that the restriction on Jesus' mission had now been removed.

In sum, then, Matthew was a faithful tradent of the Jesus tradition, handling the memory of Jesus' mission and teaching in much the same way that it had been handled from the first time that Jesus' disciples shared their impressions of Jesus and began to formulate the Jesus tradition for worship, preaching and catechetical purposes. He followed Mark's lead in putting the tradition into a Gospel framework and slotted in the Q material to that framework. He elaborated the tradition at various points to bring out what he and his community saw to be its continuing significance. He interpreted the tradition at various points to make clearer its relevance to the situation of what most infer was a community made up primarily of Jews who believed in Messiah Jesus. He added some sentences to sharpen the point of a more ambiguous tradition. And overall the thrust of the gospel was illuminated for him by the light of Jesus' resurrection, particularly as confirming that as gospel it is also good news for the nations as a whole, Gentiles of course, but Jews not excluded. Yet all the time the outlines of the impression originally made by Jesus are quite perceptible. The Jesus of Matthew is not a different Jesus from the Jesus of Mark. The impact he made was being read slightly differently or distinctively

---

298. P. Stuhlmacher, 'Matt 28:16 and the Course of Mission in the Apostolic and Postapostolic Age', in J. Ådna and H. Kvalbein, eds., *The Mission of the Early Church to Jews and Gentiles* (WUNT 127; Tübingen: Mohr Siebeck, 2000) 17-43, argues that Matthew has taken over a very old Jewish-Christian tradition (going back to the pillar apostles in Jerusalem — Gal. 2.7-9) which advocated mission to the nations as the way in which the hope both of 'eschatological restoration of greater Israel' and of the pilgrimage of the nations to Zion will be fulfilled.

299. Matt. 8.11-12/Luke 13.28-29; Matt. 12.41-42/Luke 11.31-32.

by Matthew, but that was always how the Jesus tradition had been celebrated and transmitted, and the impact was clearly made by the person who is at the centre of his Gospel — Jesus.

We will have to postpone discussion of the reception of Matthew's Gospel till §44, but in any case, Matthew gives a clear indication of how the Jesus tradition continued to exert its influence into the final decades of the first century.

42.4 The Gospel according to Luke — and Acts

As with Mark and Matthew we proceed by asking the same two questions: (a) How did Luke contrive his Gospel from the Jesus tradition available to him? And (b) what did he hope to achieve by writing what he freely acknowledged was one of a succession of 'many', 'an orderly account (*diēgēsis*) of the events which have been fulfilled among us' (Luke 1.1)?

Both questions are given particular force by Luke's own prologue to his Gospel (Luke 1.1-4). For these earlier accounts (1.1) were 'as passed on to us (by) those who from the beginning were eyewitnesses and servants of the word' (1.2).[300] So, Luke saw himself as following in an already well established and authoritative train. He does not suggest that the former accounts were inadequate or lacking in authority. Rather, his declared intention was to 'follow everything carefully from the beginning (and) to write in orderly sequence (*kathexēs*)' (1.3). In other words, he sought not to discredit his predecessors and to make their work expendable. His intention was more to confirm, by careful investigation,[301] what was already received as the eyewitness testimony of respected preachers and teachers. So too his intention to 'write in orderly sequence' need not imply that Luke reckoned the earlier accounts disorderly or unsatisfactory. His wording may simply indicate that most of the earlier *diēgēseis* were only partial accounts of the events of Jesus' mission,

---

300. It should be noted that the 'many' are not necessarily to be wholly identified with the 'eyewitnesses and ministers'. Luke claims that the passing down of the tradition certainly began with 'eyewitnesses'. But the 'many' who composed the earlier *diēgēseis* were not necessarily eyewitnesses themselves, though able to draw on the tradition at least initially passed on by the eyewitnesses. Kümmel justifiably notes that Luke 'does not presuppose the existence of a complete gospel from the hand of an apostle, judging by his distinction between the tradition of the original witnesses (1:2) and the gospel writings which he knows (1:1)' (*Introduction* 129).

301. On *parakolouthein* ('to follow closely, follow up, investigate') see Fitzmyer, *Luke* 1.296-97; Bovon, *Lukas* 1.37-38; Alexander, *Preface* 128-30; D. P. Moessner, 'The Appeal and Power of Poetics (Luke 1:1-4)', in D. P. Moessner, ed., *Jesus and the Heritage of Israel* (Harrisburg: TPI, 1999) 84-123.

or his awareness that his own ordering of these events would differ from the sequencing of his predecessors.[302] But whatever Luke's precise intention behind the words of his prologue, they certainly sharpen the issues posed by the two questions.

a. How Did Luke Go About Composing His Gospel?

Here again the solution to 'the Synoptic problem', which won the consensus support at the beginning of the twentieth century, seems to provide the clearest answer. Like Matthew, Luke was in the happy position of having two written sources on which to draw — Mark and Q.[303] In the case of Luke's Gospel, however, the conclusions of nineteenth- and twentieth-century scholarship need to be immediately qualified by reference, once again, to Luke's prologue. For the 'many' *diēgēseis* to which Luke refers can confidently be taken to include Mark and the Q material. But the 'many' can hardly refer to only Mark and Q alone.

This should not be taken to mean, however, that there were several (many) more *written* accounts of Jesus' mission prior to Luke. For, as noted in *Beginning from Jerusalem*, *diēgēsis* refers simply to 'an orderly description of facts, events or words' and can refer not only to written narrative, but also to oral recitals.[304] It is quite likely, then, that Luke had in mind the so far limited number of written accounts (Mark, Q, and ?) but also collections of oral Jesus tradition which were substantial enough (carefully compiled) to be described as *diēgēseis*, quite possibly including oral versions of or equivalents to much of Mark, and separate collections of oral Jesus tradition which are now included in the blanket terms 'Q' and 'L'.[305] If indeed it is the case, as I believe, that most (all) apostles and teachers retained a substantial resource of Jesus tradition to inform and facilitate their congregations' worship, discipleship and witness, then any substantial performance or rendition

---

302. 'Three qualities are claimed for his investigation, completeness, accuracy, and thoroughness ("from the beginning"); and another for his composition, order ("systematically")' (Fitzmyer, *Luke* 1.289).

303. See above n.177.

304. *Beginning from Jerusalem* 115 n.253, referring to BDAG 245; Fitzmyer, *Luke* 1.292; also Bovon, *Lukas* 1.34. Likewise Luke's description of the many's endeavour (*epecheirēsan* — literally 'set their hand to') (1.1) need not imply written accounts, since *epicheirein* had long been used more broadly to describe a wider range of endeavours, including the 'attempt to prove, argue dialectically' (LSJ 672). *Paradidōmi* ('hand down, pass on') (1.2) was used regularly for the transmission of oral tradition (as in Mark 7.3; 1 Cor. 11.2, 23a; 15.3).

305. 'L' denoting earlier tradition unique to Luke; see below.

of that tradition could in principle be included in Luke's reference to many *diēgēseis* prior to his own. For, like almost all early Christians, Luke himself would no doubt have been familiar with such performances/preachings/teachings in the assemblies he himself attended. His aim was explicitly to reassure Theophilus as to the 'firmness' (*asphaleia* — 'truth, certainty') of what he had been taught (1.4),[306] that is, to provide confirmation of such (or more specific) earlier *diēgēseis*.[307]

An important corollary should not be ignored: that Luke had no thought of his having had to go around digging up unknown or hitherto unused Jesus tradition, or of searching out old apostles to secure their recollections of Jesus as for the first time. On the contrary, Luke confirms what otherwise could be presupposed. First, that Jesus tradition was well used, in orderly collections and settings, and familiar to the bulk of early Christians. In other words, Luke's opening words ('Since many have undertaken to set down an orderly account . . .') were not intended to inform his readers/audiences of something they did not already know; rather, Luke's opening words referred to what they all were already familiar with, and gave that familiar practice as the reason for his own endeavours — to give a still clearer and more soundly based account.[308]

Second, it could be generally assumed that the tradition was as first passed on by the original disciples of Jesus. Here it is significant that 1.2 comes before 1.3: that is, that the talk of eyewitness tradition is not Luke's proud claim as something distinctive of his own *diēgēsis*, but refers to the well-known character of all the preceding *diēgēseis* to which he refers in 1.1. *The importance of both these points for our appreciation of how the Jesus tradition was used in the pre-Gospels period, and of its accepted character as the eyewitness testimony of Jesus' own disciples, has been too much played down in Gospels scholarship and in the quest of the historical Jesus.*

The upshot is that, as with Matthew, we can envisage five different collections of Jesus tradition (or categories of such collections) on which Luke was able to draw.

---

306. Cf. Acts 22.30 and 25.26; see also Bovon, *Lukas* 1.40-41.

307. The appeal to 'eyewitnesses' was conventional, but there is no reason to doubt that Luke intended it as an accurate description of the reliability of the Jesus tradition, which he himself had checked out, so that Theophilus could rely on Luke's *diēgēsis*. See further S. Byrskog, *Story as History — History as Story* (WUNT 123; Tübingen: Mohr Siebeck, 2000); Bauckham, *Jesus and the Eyewitnesses*.

308. Luke's preface strongly suggests to Alexander that what follows was intended not as an introduction for outsiders, but as a reminder for people already well aware of much of the contents (*Preface* 142, 188-93).

1. Mark's Gospel. Again I refer to a series of passages in Luke where the closeness of wording between Mark and Luke is best explained in terms of Luke's literary dependence on Mark.[309] Here redaction criticism can be practised with good effect.[310]
2. Tradition which Mark has transcribed but which Luke probably knew in an independent and somewhat different oral form or which he told in his own way.[311] Here redaction criticism is more problematic, since the detail of the tradition being used by Luke is unclear.
3. Written Q tradition. Again I acknowledge that much of the Q material common to Matthew and Luke is so closely parallel in form and wording that a shared literary source (Q) provides the best solution.[312]
4. Q material which was in oral form, hence the divergences between the Matthean and Lukan versions.[313]
5. Tradition which is unique to Luke (L), most of which is probably best explained by the inference that Luke's stock or collection of oral Jesus

---

309. Luke 5.33-39 (Mark 2.18-22); Luke 9.22-27 (Mark 8.31–9.1); Luke 18.15-17 (Mark 10.13-16); Luke 18.31-34 (Mark 10.32-34); Luke 20.1-8 (Mark 11.27-33); Luke 21.7-33 (Mark 13.3-32) (*Jesus Remembered* 144 n.15). Strong dependency on written Mark is also visible in Luke 4.33-35; 5.12b-14, 20-24; 6.1-11; 8.16-18, 26-39; 9.18-21, 28-30, 33b-35; 18.18-30; 19.28-38; 20.9-47; 21.1-4, 7-11, 29-33; 22.7-14.

310. Pioneered by Conzelmann, *The Theology of Saint Luke*.

311. I instance

Luke	Mark	Luke	Mark	Luke	Mark
3.19-20	6.17-18	7.36-50	14.3-9	13.18-19	4.30-32
3.21-22	1.9-11	8.19-21	3.31-35	16.18	10.11-12
4.14-15	1.14-15	8.22-25	4.35-41	19.47-48	11.18-19
4.31-32	1.21-22	9.10-17	6.32-44	21.5-6	13.1-2
4.40-44	1.32-38	9.37-43	9.14-29	21.12-24	13.9-20
6.12-16	3.13-19	11.29-30	8.11-12	21.25-28	13.24-27
6.17-20	3.7-13	12.11-12	13.11	24.1-12	16.1-8

See above n.182. In most of chs. 22–23 a simple comparison of the Synoptic accounts strongly suggests that Luke was able to draw on (a) variant and complementary account(s) of Jesus' passion.

312. See again *Jesus Remembered* 147 n.29 (add Luke 4.2-12; 10.21-24; 11.24-26, 34-35; 13.34-35).

313. I instance the following, though in some cases the variations could be explained as Luke's variations on written Q tradition in oral manner:

tradition, as expanded by his investigations, was still wider.[314] The 'L' material makes up between one-third and 40 percent of Luke's Gospel.

It is not necessary to argue for in effect a sixth source,[315] what has usually been referred to as 'Proto-Luke', that is, the suggestion that Luke was able

Luke	Matt.	Luke	Matt.	Luke	Matt.
6.20-23	5.3-12	11.42	23.23	15.3-7	18.12-14
6.27-30	5.38-43	11.43	23.6	16.16	11.12-13
6.31	7.12	11.47	23.29-30	16.17	5.18
6.32-36	5.44-48	11.49-51	23.34-36	16.18	5.32
6.40	10.24-25	12.2-9	10.26-33	17.3	18.15
6.43-44	7.16-17	12.33-34	6.19-21	17.4	18.21-22
6.45	12.35	12.51-53	10.34-36	17.6	17.20b
6.46	7.21	12.54-46	16.2-3	17.24	24.27
6.47-49	7.24-27	12.58-59	5.25-26	17.26-36	24.37-41
7.1-10	8.5-13	13.23-24	7.13-14	17.33	10.39
10.16	10.40	13.25-27	7.22-23	19.11-27	25.14-30
11.2-4	6.9-13	14.15-24	22.1-14	22.30	19.28
11.16	16.1	14.26-27	10.37-38		
11.39	23.25	14.34-35	5.13		

See above n.185. Note also the mingled units, where Luke's treatment seems to reflect several versions (8.16/11.33, 8.17/12.2, 8.18/6.38/19.26; 9.1-6/10.1-12; 11.14-23/Mark 3.22-27/Matt. 12.22-30; cf. 7.36-50 with Mark 14.3-9/Matt. 26.6-13/John 12.1-8). Fitzmyer's analysis does not distinguish closely parallel Q passages from not closely parallel 'Q' passages (*Luke* 1.80). See also Klein, *Lukasevangelium* 46-47, who reminds us that Luke also quotes an otherwise unknown saying of Jesus in Acts 20.35 — 'It is more blessed to give than to receive'.

314. Notably chs. 1-2; 3.10-14, 23-38; 5.1-11; 9.52-56, 60-62; 10.17-20, 38-42; 11.27-28; 12.13-15, 35-38, 47-48, 49-50; 13.1-5, 31-33; 14.7-14, 28-33; 16.10-12, 14-15; 17.7-10, 20-21, 28-32; 19.1-10, 41-44; 21.34-36, 37-38; 22.31-32, 35-38; 23.6-12, 13-16, 27-32, 39-43; 24.13-35, 36-43, 55-53. Luke provides his own introductions and adds his own material (3.1-2, 5-6; 3.15, 18; 4.1, 13, 14, 16-30; 6.24-26; 8.1-3; 9.51; 11.1; 12.35-38, 47-48, 57; 13.22; 14.25; 15.1-2; 19.39-40); he adds several healings (7.11-17; 13.10-17; 14.1-6; 17.11-19) and particularly parables (10.29-37; 11.5-8; 12.16-21; 13.6-9; 15.8-10, 11-32; 16.1-9, 19-31; 18.1-8, 9-14). Cf. the lists of 'L' passages in Fitzmyer, *Luke* 1.83-84, and C. F. Evans, *Saint Luke* (London: SCM, 1990) 26-27. Fitzmyer runs counter to the normal assumption by emphasizing that L (and M) were 'not necessarily written' (*Luke* 1.64). K. Paffenroth, *The Story of Jesus according to L* (JSNTS 147; Sheffield: Sheffield Academic, 1997), argues that the L material was drawn from a common source, probably written but retaining a high level of orality (146-49).

315. Though one could argue that the LXX served as a further source (e.g. Klein, *Lukasevangelium* 47). In contrast, J. R. Edwards, *The Hebrew Gospel and the Development of the Synoptic Tradition* (Grand Rapids: Eerdmans, 2009), implausibly argues that the Semitisms in Luke are to be explained not by Luke's imitation of the LXX, but by Luke's use of the Hebrew Gospel (often referred to in the patristic period — chs. 1-2), written in Hebrew, not Aramaic (particularly chs. 4-5).

to draw on or himself composed a document by combining Q and L material; the Gospel itself would then have been composed by inserting the Markan material into Proto-Luke.[316] Given the consistency of Luke's style, however, it is no more realistic or practical to disentangle Proto-Luke from Luke as it is to disentangle Ur-Markus from Mark. And Mark is too much of a framework, for Luke as well as for Matthew, with the result that the hypothesized Proto-Luke lacks much coherence as single document.[317] It makes better sense, then, to envisage Luke having access to a range of collections of Jesus tradition, including stories about Jesus and parables of Jesus which may have been part of earlier 'orderly accounts' but which no other of the canonical Evangelists knew or drew on.

As with the other Synoptic Gospels, the best way to get a real feel for Luke's intentions (including his theology) in his version of the Jesus tradition is a combination of redaction and composition criticism.[318] In the case of Matthew, the degree of closeness between Mark and Matthew strongly suggested that Matthew's editing of Mark was an obvious way to begin to answer the question of how Matthew had handled the Jesus tradition (§42.3a). With Luke, however, and not least because the L material is so extensive (but also to vary procedure!), Luke's use of the Jesus tradition is more readily discerned from the fresh material he has introduced.[319] In particular the following should be noted:

- 1.5-80 — the strong link affirmed between John the Baptist and Jesus;
- chs. 1-2 — the inclusion of the strongly Jewish-Christian canticles;
- 2.1-20, 41-52 — the stories of the shepherds and of the youthful Jesus;

---

316. A particularly British contribution to the resolution of the Synoptic problem: Streeter, *The Four Gospels* 199-222; V. Taylor, *Behind the Third Gospel: A Study of the Proto-Luke Hypothesis* (Oxford: Oxford University, 1926).

317. See particularly Kümmel, *Introduction* 131-37; Fitzmyer, *Luke* 1.90-91. Paffenroth finds 'an identifiable structure' in the L material (*The Story of Jesus* 144-46, 159-65), but it could equally consist of several different groupings of Jesus tradition with common themes; e.g., the Lukan parables could conceivably have been drawn from a well-ordered collection of parables.

318. Luz (private correspondence) thinks questions need to be answered like, 'Why has Luke simply alternated Markan blocks and non-Markan blocks? How far has he composed the non-Markan blocks himself? Why are sections of Mark missing? Why is his history of the passion so markedly different from Mark?' I prefer to note the differences and the significance of the differences in presentation of what is essentially the same material; in many/most cases the full explanation for the differences becomes more speculative than useful.

319. The non-Markan material in Luke is usually reckoned as 60-65 percent of Luke (e.g. Kümmel, *Introduction* 131; Brown, *Introduction* 263). Both Kümmel (*Introduction* 137-39) and Brown (*Introduction* 263-65) document Lukan redaction of Mark. And see further Fitzmyer, *Luke* 1.66-73, 92-96, 107-8; Evans, *Saint Luke* 17-20, 30-33, 38-40.

- 3.10-14 — the Baptist's exhortation to ethical integrity;
- 4.16-30 — a much extended account of Jesus' preaching in Nazareth;
- 5.1-11 — Peter's confession that he is a 'sinner' (5.8);
- 6.24-26 — the addition of the 'woe' sayings to the beatitudes;
- 7.11-17 — Jesus' compassion for a widow bereft of her only son;
- 7.36-50 — Jesus' acceptance of the ministrations of a woman sinner;
- 8.2-3 — prominence given to the women who supported Jesus;
- 9.51 — the early beginning of the journey to Jerusalem which provides the framework for a much larger proportion of Jesus tradition than the other Synoptics (9.51–19.27);[320]
- 9.52-56 — the first event on the journey as an encounter with Samaritans;
- 10.1-12, 17-20 — the mission of the seventy, implying a larger vision of mission than that of the twelve (9.1-6);
- 10.29-37 — the parable of the Good Samaritan;
- 10.38-42 — Mary and Martha;
- 12.13-21 — danger of greed and reliance on abundance of possessions;
- 13.1-9 — the parable of the barren fig tree;
- 14.1-6 — Jesus' logic of grace in healing on the Sabbath;
- 14.7-14 — the importance of humility;
- 15.8-32 — the priority of Jesus' concern for the lost;
- 16.19-31 — the parable of the rich man and Lazarus;
- 17.11-19 — only the Samaritan grateful for healing;
- 18.1-8 — the parable of the unjust judge;
- 18.9-14 — the parable of the Pharisee and the tax collector praying in the temple;
- 19.1-10 — the salvation of Zacchaeus.

When we allow this distinctively Lukan material to signal what Luke saw the Jesus tradition as saying to his own day, how he read the gospel of Jesus Christ for his own time and circumstances, we find that its emphases accord well with what we find also in the rest of Luke (indeed of Luke-Acts).

In turning to our second question — What did Luke hope to achieve in writing his Gospel? — we need once again to bear in mind that Luke wrote two books, and that he presumably saw them as closely connected. Moreover, it is sufficiently clear that when he wrote his Gospel, Luke already had the intention to write a second volume. That is to say, he did not intend his Gospel

---

320. As Bovon notes (*Lukas* 1.20), all references to the journey are redactional (Luke 9.51; 10.38; 13.22, 33; 14.25; 17.11; 18.35; 19.28). The travel narrative joins Mark again at 18.15. See further Kümmel, *Introduction* 141-42; Evans, *Saint Luke* 34-36; and particularly D. P. Moessner, *Lord of the Banquet: Literary and Theological Significance of the Lukan Travel Narrative* (Minneapolis: Fortress, 1989).

to be complete in itself, as we might say Mark and Matthew saw their Gospels as complete in themselves. Rather Luke saw his two volumes as two parts of the one story, set within world history (Luke 3.1-2). This was his own attempt to give substance to what he subsequently records as Paul's affirmation that the story he was about to tell 'was not done in a corner' (Acts 26.26). So Luke began his second volume by referring to his first volume (his 'first word') as the narrative of 'what Jesus began to do and teach' (Acts 1.1).[321] The point is that themes and motifs run through both volumes. Their development is only half-completed by the end of the Gospel. In consequence, to answer our second question we will be able also to take account of Luke's second volume, since it can be presumed that the aims of Acts were an extension of those in the Gospel or at least consistent with them. Here we will be able to draw on the extensive analysis of Acts, including its aims, in *Beginning from Jerusalem*.

b. The Significance of Jesus[322]

(1) Luke enhances Mark's christology of Jesus as the *Son of God* by his account of the virginal conception (Luke 1.32, 35),[323] and strengthens the tradition of Jesus speaking of God as his Father,[324] but otherwise he simply retains the 'Son/Father' references of Mark[325] and Q.[326] More noticeably, Luke leaves Jesus' response to the high priest's question, 'Are you the Son of God?', with the ambiguous 'You say that I am' (Luke 22.70). And surprisingly, he turns Mark's climactic confession by the centurion ('Truly, this man was God's Son') into what is more of an admission, 'Certainly this man was just' (23.47). Evidently Luke strongly believed that Jesus was God's son, but he did not give it the sort of emphasis it had in Mark, a conclusion confirmed by the modest role the title plays in Acts (Acts 9.20; 13.33).

---

321. See *Beginning from Jerusalem* 142 and n.38.

322. Discussion of Lukan christology from 1950 to 2005 is reviewed by F. Bovon, 'Christology', *Luke the Theologian* (Waco: Baylor University, ²2006) 123-223, 532-36.

323. Gathercole presses the case for reading Luke 1.78 ('the *Anatolē* will visit us from on high') as an affirmation of Jesus' pre-existence (*The Pre-existent Son* 238-42), even though he recognizes that it is a 'poetic statement' (296) and that in Zechariah (3.8; 6.12) *anatolē* is the translation of *ṣemach* ('branch'), a standard way of referring to the hoped-for son of David.

324. Luke 2.49; 22.29; 23.34(?); 23.46; 24.49.

325. Luke 3.22 (Mark 1.11); Luke 4.41 (Mark 1.34/3.11-12); Luke 8.28 (Mark 5.7); Luke 9.35 (Mark 9.7); Luke 20.13 (Mark 12.6); Luke 22.42 (Mark 14.36); Luke 22.70 (cf. Mark 14.61). But he omits Mark 13.32 (the confession of the Son's ignorance).

326. Luke 4.3, 9; 10.21-22; 11.13. 11.2 begins the Lord's Prayer with the bare 'Father' (*pater, abba*?).

(2) Jesus as *Messiah* and *son of David* is also enhanced by the birth narrative (Luke 1.69; 2.11, 26) and added at 4.41, but otherwise the Markan emphasis is retained.[327] In the final scenes of the Gospel, the tempo picks up. The crowd on Palm Sunday hail Jesus as 'king' (19.38 — unique to Luke); and Luke helpfully explains to his readers that the charge against Jesus required judgment by the Roman procurator, since 'Christ' means 'king', 'king of the Jews' (23.2-3/Mark 15.2). Luke's version of the mockery of Jesus on the cross has the Jewish leaders saying, 'He saved others; let him save himself, if he is the Christ of God, the chosen one' (Luke 23.35). And the climax of the two resurrection appearances is Jesus' repeated exposition of the scriptures as demonstrating that the Christ must suffer before rising from the dead (24.26, 46), preparing for a central feature of the earliest Christian preaching.[328] Mark's 'messianic secret' motif is largely trimmed down,[329] but the implication remains that Jesus' messiahship can be properly understood only in the light of Jesus' passion and resurrection. This is what Luke implied in the prologue in reminding his readers that this theme of 'fulfilment' was common to all earlier accounts as well (Luke 1.1). However, important as the theme of fulfilment of scripture is for Luke,[330] it is not structurally so important as in Matthew, and is part of his larger, though not very prominent, theme of eschatological fulfilment.[331] More distinctively Lukan is his emphasis on the divine necessity (*dei*) of what Jesus did and what happened to him.[332]

(3) Distinctively Lukan is the emphasis Luke places on the role of the *Holy Spirit* in his christology — in Jesus' conception (1.35), at the beginning of Jesus' mission (4.1, 14) and in his anointing for mission (4.18; Acts 10.38). Since the other Synoptic Evangelists show little of the same interest, we may infer that Luke deemed it important to show how the Jesus of his Gospel models the outworking of the gospel and how Jesus' own experience of the Spirit foreshadowed the crucial role of the Spirit in Acts.

(4) This also links into the strand of Moses-*prophet* christology which Luke retains: provision of food in the wilderness (9.12-17); in the Transfigu-

---

327. Luke 9.20 (Mark 8.29); Luke 18.38-39 (Mark 10.47-48); Luke 20.41 (Mark 12.35); Luke 22.67 (Mark 14.61).

328. Acts 2.31, 36; 3.18; 8.32-35; 9.22; 17.3; 18.5, 28; 26.23.

329. See above §42.2b(3).

330. Luke 4.21; 18.31; 22.37; 24.44; Acts 1.16; 3.18; 10.43; 13.27, 29. See further Bovon, 'The Interpretation of the Scriptures of Israel', *Luke the Theologian* 87-121.

331. Luke 1.1; 9.31, 51; 21.24; 22.16; but hardly evident in Acts apart from Acts 2.16-17 and 3.18-21 (cf. 14.26).

332. Luke 2.49; 4.43; 9.22 (Mark 8.31); 11.42 (Matt. 23.23); 13.16, 33; 15.32; 17.25; 19.5; 21.9 (Mark 13.7); 22.7, 37; 24.7, 26, 44; Acts 1.16, 21; 3.21; 4.12; 5.29 etc.; see also *Beginning from Jerusalem* 73 n.82.

ration story, Moses and Elijah speak with Jesus about Jesus' 'exodus' (9.31); Jesus casts out demons 'by the finger of God' (11.20; echoing Exod. 8.19).[333] In a passage unique to Luke, Jesus affirms that as a prophet it was inevitable that he would be killed in Jerusalem (Luke 13.33). And the two disciples on the road to Emmaus characterize Jesus as 'a prophet mighty in deed and word', who they had hoped 'was the one to redeem Israel' (24.19, 21).[334]

(5) Luke takes over most of the *Son of Man* references in his material, but has some distinctive references, perhaps best explained as performance variations in recitals of Jesus tradition.[335] The most noticeable of these are in the section where Jesus speaks four times somewhat enigmatically of 'the day(s) of the Son of Man' (Luke 17.22-30).[336] Interestingly, the eschatological role of the Son of Man is prominent in these Lukan Son of Man sayings. So Luke certainly embraced and affirmed the tradition that Jesus spoke of himself as the Son of Man, particularly its eschatological character.[337] At the same time, as the only one of the Evangelists who carries his account (and emphases) beyond the ministry of Jesus on earth it is notable that Luke includes only one isolated use of the phrase in his second volume (Acts 7.56), thus confirming that the reference to Jesus as 'the Son of Man' did not have a living context outside the Gospel tradition.

(6) Another feature highlights the transition which Jesus' resurrection formed between his mission and his post-resurrection exalted state, or, as we may say, between volume 1 and volume 2 of Luke's two-volume work. This is Luke's careful use of the title *kyrios* for Jesus. What is notable is that Luke refrains from having Jesus spoken of as the Lord during his mission by other actors in the drama that Luke unfolds.[338] In Luke's Gospel, Jesus is referred

---

333. If the journey to Jerusalem (9.51–18.14) is ordered in a 'Deuteronomistic sequence' (see above n.320), then Luke has placed much of Jesus' teaching 'in a Mosaic, i.e. prophetic setting' (Evans, *Luke* 70).

334. Note also 7.16, climax of an episode unique to Luke (7.11-17), echoing the famous miracles of Elijah and Elisha (1 Kgs. 17.17-24; 2 Kgs. 4.32-37). In Luke 9.62 there may also be an allusion to 1 Kgs. 19.19-21. See further Fitzmyer, *Luke* 1.213-15, 656, 834. See also C. A. Evans, 'The Function of the Elijah/Elisha Narratives in Luke's Ethic of Election', in C. A. Evans and J. A. Sanders, *Luke and Scripture: The Function of Sacred Tradition in Luke-Acts* (Minneapolis: Fortress, 1993) 70-83.

335. Luke 6.22 = 'me' in Matt. 5.11; Luke 12.8 = 'I' in Matt. 10.32; Luke 18.8; 19.10; 21.36; 22.48; 24.7.

336. See *Jesus Remembered* 754-55; Bovon, *Lukas* 3.169-71.

337. See also C. M. Tuckett, 'The Lukan Son of Man', in C. M. Tuckett, ed., *Luke's Literary Achievement: Collected Essays* (JSNTS 116; Sheffield: Sheffield Academic, 1995) 198-217.

338. During his mission Jesus is regularly addressed as '*kyrie*' (19x — references in Fitzmyer, *Luke* 1.203, but in narrative terms this could be readily understood as a polite form of address (= 'sir'), even if Christian users of Luke's Gospel would presumably see in

to as 'the Lord' by those of his immediate circle for the first and only time in Luke 24.34, that is, after his resurrection.³³⁹ Luke evidently took seriously the early expression of *resurrection* faith which he attributes to Peter: 'God has made him both Lord and Messiah, this Jesus whom you crucified' (Acts 2.36). Of course, in Acts, post-Easter affirmation of Jesus as Lord is a regular (though somewhat confusing)³⁴⁰ feature; so the affirmation of Jesus' exaltation as Lord following his resurrection, which Acts 2.36 indicates, evidently became the norm for early Christian faith.³⁴¹ And of course, Luke himself, as the narrator in the Gospel, refers to Jesus as 'the Lord', for Luke could tell the story from his post-Easter perspective.³⁴² But Luke evidently took some care to preserve and reflect the striking transformation which Jesus' resurrection brought to the faith of the first disciples.³⁴³

(7) Ironically, this reinforced emphasis on Jesus' resurrection reflects also a shift in emphasis regarding the function of *the cross* as well as the resurrection in the Gospel according to Luke. For Mark's passion narrative with an extended introduction included the prominent emphasis of Jesus' death as 'a ransom for many' (Mark 10.45), his blood 'poured out for many' (14.24). But Luke (22.24-27) does not follow Mark 10.35-45 and prefers a different version of Jesus' teaching on greatness, climaxing in the thought of Jesus as 'one who serves' (Luke 22.27). And although in Luke's account of the last supper (a few verses earlier — Luke 22.19-20) the first word over the bread is close to Paul's version ('This is my body which is [given] for you' — 1 Cor. 11.24), the emphasis in the second word shifts from atoning sacrifice

---

the address anticipation or expression of their own veneration. C. K. Rowe, *Early Narrative Christology: The Lord in the Gospel of Luke* (BZNW 139; Berlin: de Gruyter, 2006), presses the narrative logic beyond individual pericopes: since Luke regards and refers to Jesus as 'the Lord' (n.342 below), he would expect his readers/audiences to take the vocative as 'Lord' (particularly 208-16).

339. C. F. D. Moule, 'The Christology of Acts', in L. E. Keck and J. L. Martyn, eds., *Studies in Luke Acts* (Nashville: Abingdon, 1966) 159-85, was the first to draw attention to this feature (here 160-61). The references to Jesus as 'Lord' in the birth narrative (Luke 1.43, 76; 2.11), Luke presumably regarded as a foreshadowing of Jesus' exalted state.

340. See my '*KYRIOS* in Acts', in C. Landmesser et al., eds., *Jesus Christus als die Mitte der Schrift*, O. Hofius FS (Berlin: de Gruyter, 1997) 363-78.

341. See further *Beginning from Jerusalem* 217-21.

342. Fitzmyer lists 18 or 19 cases, though including 24.34 (*Luke* 1.203). Rowe presses the significance of this feature for Luke's own christology: that e.g. Luke 5.17 represents the God of Israel's presence through Jesus (*Early Narrative Christology* 92-105), though to express this in terms of 'shared identity' (201), rather than, e.g., exercise of Yahweh's lordship (as in Ps. 110.1) is more confusing than helpful; cf. my *Did the First Christians Worship Jesus?* 141-44.

343. In Acts, Jesus' resurrection is the central thrust of the message preached by the first Christians (e.g. Acts 2.24-32; 4.1-2, 33; 10.40-41; 13.30-37; 17.18, 30-31).

('for many') to a covenant sacrifice ('the new covenant in my blood').[344] This alone might not amount to much, but when we include the evidence of Acts the picture becomes clearer. For the references to Jesus' death in Acts lack the emphasis on atonement ('for many', 'for sins'); there are no references to Jesus' death as an atoning sacrifice.[345] The few brief allusions to Jesus as the Servant (of second Isaiah) pick up the theme of vindication following suffering, not of vicarious suffering as such.[346] Similarly the allusion to Deut. 21.22-23 in Acts 5.30 and 10.39 ('hanging him on a tree'; cf. 13.29) seems to be intended (by Luke) to highlight Jesus' shame and disgrace, and so to serve the same humiliation-vindication motif.[347] And even 20.28 ('the church of the Lord — or of God — which he obtained with his own blood — or with the blood of his own Son') remains more than a little puzzling and obscure.[348] In short, a rather remarkable feature of Luke-Acts is that the theology of Jesus' death as atoning sacrifice is almost completely absent. The thought is much more of the wonder of Jesus' resurrection, and (as we shall see) of the resultant power of the Spirit. This *sotto voce* character of Luke's allusions to what was elsewhere spoken of as Jesus' death as atoning sacrifice may reflect an early hesitation on the subject among the first believers (reflecting Jesus' own perspective?) — an early hesitation (if that is the appropriate way to describe it) which was resolved by a fresh Hellenist willingness to assert that Jesus' death as atoning sacrifice had brought an end to any further need of temple cult and sacrifice.[349] If so, we may have to give Luke a good deal more credit for his faithfulness in reflecting (in both Gospel and Acts) an early theological perspective soon left behind (1 Cor. 15.3).[350]

344. See also *Jesus Remembered* 812-18; and further H. J. Sellner, *Das Heil Gottes: Studien zur Soteriologie des lukanischen Doppelwerks* (BZNW 152; Berlin: de Gruyter, 2007) 453-64. Fitzmyer finds in the distinctively Lukan account of Jesus on the cross saying to one of the thieves crucified with him, 'Today you shall be with me in Paradise' (Luke 23.43) 'a highly literary way (of saying) something about the salvific character of Jesus' death' (*Luke* 1.23; further 219-21).

345. Cf. Acts 2.23, 36; 3.13-15; 4.10; 5.30; 7.52; 10.39; 13.27-28.

346. Acts 3.13, 26; 4.27, 30; so also 8.30-35.

347. Cf. Evans, *Luke* 75-77.

348. Discussion in Sellner, *Das Heil Gottes* 467-76.

349. See my 'When Did the Understanding of Jesus' Death as an Atoning Sacrifice First Emerge?', in D. B. Capes et al., eds., *Israel's God and Rebecca's Children: Christology and Community in Early Judaism and Christianity*, L. W. Hurtado and A. F. Segal FS (Waco: Baylor University, 2007) 169-81; also *Beginning from Jerusalem* 230-37 — on 20.28, see 237 with n.328, and 950-51 with n.398.

350. There is no inconsistency in the fact that Luke is the only one of the Synoptic Evangelists to speak of Jesus as 'Saviour', though only in Luke 2.11 (also Acts 5.31 and 13.23). For the thought in Luke is not so much of Jesus 'saving his people from their sins'

In regard to the significance attributed to Jesus, then, Luke's overall handling of the Jesus tradition seems to be more constrained than Mark's and Matthew's.[351] He follows Mark in retaining Mark's orderly account climaxing in Jesus' death and resurrection, and though Luke does not press for Jesus' death to be understood as 'for sin', he maintains the 'gospel' emphasis on the necessity of Jesus' death and on the crucial difference made by his resurrection. But he is equally clear that the significance of Jesus was not to be attributed solely to his death and resurrection. He was God's Son and Messiah already during his mission, indeed, as from his birth. And the Jesus tradition which gave substance to that pre-passion gospel character of Jesus' mission did not need to be greatly enhanced, far less transformed into something else, for the significance of Jesus to be clear. For Luke there was no embarrassing hiccup or awkward transition from pre-Easter Jesus to post-Easter Jesus, from Gospel to Acts. Luke was very much at ease in passing on his thoroughly investigated Jesus tradition, because it dovetailed so closely into the story of his second volume, and there was no need for him to create substantial new motifs, or to air-brush out disconcerting features, in order for his Gospel to be both gospel and an authoritative account of how Jesus had indeed lived and taught.

c. The Character of the Gospel

(1) It is perhaps not so surprising that Luke alone of the Synoptic Evangelists has Jesus referred to as 'Saviour' (Luke 2.11). For integral to the gospel for Luke is that it '*saves*'.[352] This is most obvious in Acts. He describes believers as 'those who are being saved' (Acts 2.47). Peter affirms remarkably early on that

---

(as in Matt. 1.21), as of a 'leader' (*archēgos*) whose own victory makes possible the salvation of his people (Acts 5.31; Heb. 2.10; 12.2). We will return to this theme below.

351. A point well illustrated by the diminution of Mark's 'messianic secret' and by the fact that Matthew's Wisdom christology seems to have been achieved by Matthew's distinctive reading of the Q material he shared with Luke (see above §42.3b).

352. I. H. Marshall, *Luke: Historian and Theologian* (Exeter: Paternoster, 1970), saw the idea of salvation as the key to the theology of Luke (92). Bovon commends him for demonstrating 'that the theme of salvation forms the center of Luke's thought' (*Luke the Theologian* 296). See also Sellner, *Das Heil Gottes*. It is this that makes it appropriate to speak of Luke's theology as a theology of 'salvation history' (Fitzmyer, *Luke* 1.181; also 222-23). See also *Beginning from Jerusalem* 69 n.59; and my 'The Book of Acts as Salvation History', in J. Frey, S. Krauter and H. Lichtenberger, eds., *Heil und Geschichte: Die Geschichtsbezogenheit des Heils und das Problem der Heilsgeschichte in der biblischen Tradition und in der theologischen Deutung* (WUNT 248; Tübingen: Mohr Siebeck, 2009) 385-401. For a review of the discussion of Luke and 'salvation history' see Bovon, 'The Plan of God, Salvation History and Eschatology', *Luke the Theologian* 1-85.

'There is salvation in no one else; for there is no other name under heaven... by which we must be saved' (4.12). The centurion Cornelius is told to send for Peter 'who will speak words to you by which you and all your household will be saved' (11.14). The first Christians have been commissioned to 'bring salvation to the ends of the earth' (13.47). The Philippian jailor asks piteously, 'What must I do to be saved?', and Paul replies, 'Believe on the Lord Jesus Christ and you will be saved, and your household' (16.30-31).[353] Not surprisingly, then, Luke emphasizes the hope of 'salvation' in the song of Zechariah (the Benedictus — Luke 1.69, 71, 77). Equally striking is the fact that as well as taking over the Markan passages which speak of Jesus' saving/healing work,[354] Luke adds further references to Jesus' saving/healing work in other passages,[355] and includes still more references in the material unique to Luke.[356] Typical of this characteristically Lukan motif is the question put to Jesus, *Kyrie*, will only a few be saved?' (13.23), and the conclusion to Luke's unique Zacchaeus story: 'For the Son of man came to seek and to save the lost' (19.10).[357]

(2) Equally significant is the emphasis Luke puts on *forgiveness* — and the *repentance* that results in forgiveness.[358] The opening words of the account of Jesus' mission follow Mark closely: John comes in the wilderness 'preaching a baptism of repentance for the forgiveness of sins' (Mark 1.4/Luke 3.3). But Luke has already struck this note, again in the Benedictus, that John is destined 'to give knowledge of salvation to his [the Lord's] people by the forgiveness of their sins' (1.77). Luke again highlights the same emphasis in the story of the woman with the ointment unique to his Gospel (7.47-49; also 6.37). And, very striking, Luke provides what is probably an intended inclusio by highlighting the climax of Jesus' mission in the same terms as the Baptist's message: the consequence of Jesus' resurrection is 'that repentance and forgiveness of sins is to be proclaimed in his [the Messiah's] name to all nations'; and the disciples are commissioned and promised 'power from on high' to fulfill this mission (24.47-49). And the subsequent account of the disciples' mission has the same focus.[359] The prominence Luke gives to this dimension

---

353. See also Acts 2.21, 40; 13.26; 15.11; 16.17; Jesus as 'Saviour' (5.31; 13.23).

354. Luke 6.9; 8.48; 9.24; 18.26, 42; 23.35; cf. 21.19.

355. Luke 8.12, 36, 50; 23.37.

356. Luke 7.50; 13.23; 17.19; 19.10; 23.39.

357. Bovon is drawn to the thought that 'in the Zacchaeus story lies the quintessence of the whole gospel' (*Lukas* 3.277). See also Fitzmyer's response to those who accused Luke of spoiling the kerygma (*Luke* 1.12-14).

358. *Metanoia* ('repentance') — Matt. 2x; Mark 1x; Luke 5x; *metanoeō* ('repent') — Matt. 5x; Mark 2x; Luke 9x. Note Luke 5.32; 13.3, 5; 15.7, 10; Acts 3.19; 11.18; 17.30; 26.20.

359. Acts 2.38; 3.19; 5.31; 10.43; 13.38; 26.18; note also 8.22; 11.18; 13.24; 17.30; 19.4; 20.21; 26.20.

of the gospel is often lost to sight. For it features quite strongly also in the other Synoptics.[360] But the repentance to forgiveness dimension of the gospel is almost entirely passed over in John's Gospel (only John 20.23), and in comparison with Paul's emphasis on faith, the theme of repentance to forgiveness hardly features at all in the Pauline writings.[361] For Luke, however, the gospel is summed up most fully as the promise of sins forgiven. At the same time he hardly plays down the importance of *faith*, using tradition shared with Mark and Matthew,[362] but also drawing on other material known to us only from his Gospel,[363] and maintaining the emphasis into Acts.[364]

(3) *Peace* is also a characteristic effect of the gospel for Luke. This too is a distinctive theme in Luke.[365] The Benedictus climaxes in the hope that the promised light will 'guide our feet into the way of peace' (1.79). The heavenly host hold out the same prospect — 'peace on earth among those whom he [God] favours' (2.14). The disciples are sent out with a message of peace (10.5-6). The risen Jesus brings a greeting of peace to the terrified disciples (24.36). The mission of Jesus is recalled as 'preaching peace' (Acts 10.36).[366]

(4) Equally significant is the prominence which Luke gives to the theme of *'sinners'*: the gospel brings hope to sinners. He uses the term far more than the other Evangelists.[367] Mark and Matthew both give prominence to Jesus' affirmation that he had been sent 'to call sinners' (Mark 2.15-17/Matt. 9.10-13). But Luke adds a whole sequence of references:

- 5.8 — Peter's confession that he was a sinner;
- 7.34 — he draws from Q the jibe that Jesus was 'a friend of tax collectors and sinners';

---

360. Mark 2.5, 7, 9-10/Matt. 9.2, 5-6/Luke 5.20-21, 23-24; Mark 3.28/Matt. 12.31-32/Luke 12.10; Mark 11.25/Matt. 6.14-15; Matt. 6.12/Luke 11.4; Matt. 18.21-22/Luke 17.3-4; only Mark 4.12 and Matt. 18.35 are distinctive.

361. Repentance — Rom. 2.4; 2 Cor. 7.9-10; 12.21; 2 Tim. 2.25. Forgiveness — Rom. 4.7; Eph. 1.7; Col. 1.14.

362. Luke 5.20; 7.9; 8.25, 48; 17.6; 18.42.

363. Luke 7.50; (17.5); 17.19; 18.8; 22.32; note also 8.12-13, 50; 22.67; 24.25. See also Klein, *Lukasevangelium* 57.

364. Acts 3.16; 6.5, 7; 11.24; 13.8; 14.9, 22, 27; 15.9; 16.5; 20.21; 24.24; 26.18. Acts' usage well reflects the early Christian self-designation as 'believers' (*Beginning from Jerusalem* 9-10).

365. *Eirēnē* ('peace') — Luke 13x; Acts 7x; Matt. 4x; Mark 1x; John 6x.

366. See also Luke 2.29; 7.50; 8.48; 19.38, 42; Acts 9.31; 15.33; though note also Luke 12.51 (from oral Q? — cf. Matt. 10.34).

367. *Hamartōlos* — Matt. 5x; Mark 6x; Luke 18x; John 4x. See also D. A. Neale, *None but the Sinners: Religious Categories in the Gospel of Luke* (JSNTS 58; Sheffield: Sheffield Academic, 1991).

- 7.37, 39 — the woman with ointment who receives Jesus' forgiveness is identified twice as a sinner;
- 15.1-2 — the parables of the lost things and the lost son are told to Pharisees and scribes grumbling that Jesus welcomed and ate with sinners;
- 15.7, 10 — the parables illustrate the joy in heaven over one sinner who repents;
- 18.13-14 — the gospel is well summed up in the parable of the Pharisee and tax collector; it is the latter, who simply prays, 'God be merciful to me, a sinner', who is justified;
- 19.7 — Jesus goes to be a guest of Zacchaeus, the well-known sinner, again illustrating whom the gospel is for.

This gospel concern which goes beyond the normal bounds of social convention and religious tradition is illustrated also in the distinctive Lukan parables of the Good Samaritan (10.29-37), the barren fig tree (13.1-9) and the unjust judge (18.1-8), not to mention Luke's additional story of a sabbath healing (14.1-6). In his Gospel Luke does not use the Pauline term 'grace' in a gospel way, but his story of Jesus certainly illustrates well the characteristic of the gospel which Paul enshrined in the word 'grace'.[368]

(5) Also distinctive of Luke's Gospel portrayal of Jesus and of significance for his understanding of the gospel is the added emphasis he gives to the *Holy Spirit*.[369]

- 1.15, 17 — John the Baptist is filled with the Holy Spirit from birth.
- 1.35 — the conception of Jesus is due to the Spirit coming upon Mary.
- 1.67 — Zechariah is filled with the Spirit and prophesies.
- 2.25-27 — the Spirit is particularly active in and on Simeon.
- 4.1 — Jesus returns from the Jordan, 'full of the Holy Spirit'.
- 4.14 — He returns to Galilee 'in the power of the Spirit'.
- 4.18 — In his sermon in Nazareth he claims to be the one spoken of in Isa. 61.1: 'the Spirit of the Lord is upon me, because he has anointed me to preach good news to the poor'.
- 10.21 — On the return of the seventy from mission Jesus rejoices in the Holy Spirit.

---

368. In Acts see 4.33; 6.8; 11.23; 13.43; 14.3, 26; 15.11, 40; 18.27; 20.24, 32. It is somewhat surprising that Luke does not extend the concern for 'sinners' (*hamartōloi*) into Acts, even though Paul gave him opportunity to do so (especially Rom. 5.8; Gal. 2.15, 17).

369. Luke also takes over Mark's references to the Spirit (Luke 3.16, 22; 12.10, 12). Unexpectedly, however, whereas Matthew (Q?) has Jesus attributing his power as an exorcist to the Spirit (Matt. 12.28), Luke attributes it to 'the finger of God' (Luke 11.20).

- 11.13 — Luke turns the 'good things' promised to God's children into the same promise of the Holy Spirit.

The relative lack of reference to the Spirit in all the Gospels is somewhat surprising. But Luke does enough to prepare for the importance which he evidently attached to the gift of the Spirit in Acts. Only with Luke-Acts can we see that the Baptist's prediction of one who will baptize in Spirit and fire (Mark 1.8 pars.) was taken seriously and became a crucial factor in equipping the disciples for effective mission and in convincing them that the gospel was for Gentiles too (Acts 1.5, 8; 11.15-16). The outpouring of the Spirit at Pentecost launches the mission of the church in Acts (1.8; 2.4), just as Jesus' anointing by the Spirit at the Jordan launched his mission in the Gospel (Luke 3.22; 4.1, 14, 18).[370] The promise of the Spirit is the essential complement to forgiveness of sins (Acts 2.38; 10.43-48; 11.14-18). The gift of the Spirit is what completes baptism and belief (8.14-17; 19.1-6). It should simply be added that Luke was particularly impressed by the tangibility of the Spirit[371] — as of other spiritual phenomena[372] — which implies that he provides more of a precedent for 'enthusiasm' (*Schwärmerei*) and present-day Pentecostalism than most churchmen seem either to appreciate or to relish.[373]

(6) The evident concern which Luke had to correlate the Gospel's good news with the gospel as it worked out in Acts is further illustrated by the care which Luke takes to carry over the focus of Jesus' preaching on the *kingdom of God* into Acts. Mark and Matthew, of course, leave us in no doubt that Jesus' proclamation of the kingdom of God was central to Jesus' mission. But Paul seems to take few pains to indicate that the message of the kingdom provided a continuum between Jesus' good-newsing and his own gospel.[374] And the fact that John ignores Jesus' teaching on the kingdom as much as he does[375] suggests that it did not translate well to John's constituency. But Luke was obviously intent on demonstrating that Jesus' message of the kingdom of

---

370. 'The Spirit poured out on Pentecost inaugurates a new age — that is the whole point of the Pentecost-experience narrated in Acts 2. That is also the reason why one must reckon with a three-phase view of salvation-history in Lucan theology' (Fitzmyer, *Luke* 1.230). See also M. Turner, *Power from On High: The Spirit in Israel's Restoration and Witness in Luke-Acts* (Sheffield: Sheffield Academic, 1996).

371. Luke 3.22 ('in bodily form'); Acts 2.2-4; 8.18; 10.44-46; 19.6.

372. E.g. Luke 9.32; 24.37-43; Acts 1.3; 10.41; 12.9. See further my *Unity and Diversity in the New Testament* §44; 'Enthusiasm', *Enc.Rel.* 5.118-24.

373. This opinion is critiqued by Bovon, 'The Holy Spirit', *Luke the Theologian* 225-72 (here 270-71).

374. Though note particularly Rom. 14.17; 1 Cor. 4.20; 15.24; Col. 1.13; 4.11; 1 Thess. 2.12; 2 Thess. 1.5.

375. Only the Synoptic-like John 3.3, 5 and the distinctive 18.36.

§42.4 *Retelling the Story of Jesus*

God remained a major element in early Christian preaching. Not only do his references to 'the kingdom of God' in the Gospel match, and to some extent exceed, those of Mark and Matthew,[376] but Luke also takes pains to insist that the message of the kingdom was prominent in the preaching of Philip (Acts 8.12) and particularly the preaching of Paul (19.8; 20.25; 28.23). Very strikingly, Luke deliberately 'book-ends' Acts with references to the kingdom: this was the subject of the risen Christ's teaching after his resurrection (1.3); and Acts ends with Paul still 'proclaiming the kingdom of God' to all who came to him (28.30-31).

The Lukan distinctives on the kingdom of God, however, leave his understanding on the subject somewhat confused or confusing:

- he omits Mark's headline text — 'Jesus came into Galilee . . . saying, "The time is fulfilled and the kingdom of God has drawn near"' (Mark 1.15);
- 9.27 — Jesus assures his disciples that some will not taste death before they see the kingdom of God (Mark 9.1 — 'before they see the kingdom of God has come in power');
- 9.60 — Jesus exhorts a hesitant disciple that his top priority is to 'go and proclaim the kingdom of God';
- 9.62 — to another Jesus says, 'No one who puts his hand to the plough and looks back is fit for the kingdom of God';
- 16.16 — since John the Baptist 'the good news of the kingdom of God is being proclaimed, and everyone takes it [or tries to take it] by force';
- 17.20-21 — the coming of the kingdom is not observable, 'for the kingdom of God is among you';
- 18.29 — Luke replaces Mark's 'for the sake of the gospel', with 'for the sake of the kingdom of God';
- 19.11 — Jesus tells the parable of the pounds (19.12-27) 'because they [the listeners] supposed that the kingdom of God was about to appear immediately';
- 21.8 — whereas the disciples were sent out on a mission to proclaim, 'the kingdom of God has come near' (10.9, 11), they are warned not to follow those who will say, 'The time has come near';
- 21.31 — in the parable of the fig tree, which Luke shares in detail with Mark and Matthew, Luke makes it clear that what is 'near' is not the

---

376. Luke 32x; Mark 14x; Matt. kingdom of God 5x + kingdom of heaven 32x. Unique to Luke are Luke 4.43; 9.11, 60, 62; 12.32; 13.28; 14.15; 17.20, 21; 18.24, 29; 19.11; 21.31; 22.29, 30; 23.42.

coming of the Son of Man (as implied in Mark 13.26-29/Matt. 24.30-33) but 'the kingdom of God';

- 22.16, 18 — at the last supper with his disciples Jesus vows not to eat the Passover 'until it is fulfilled in the kingdom of God', and not to drink from the fruit of the vine 'until the kingdom of God comes';
- Acts 1.6 — during the risen Jesus' time with his disciples, they ask one question, 'Lord, is it at this time that you will restore the kingdom to Israel?'
- 14.22 — Paul encourages the disciples, 'It is through many persecutions that we must enter the kingdom of God'.

What is somewhat confusing is not the tension between the kingdom's presence (Luke 11.20; 16.16; 17.20-21) and the kingdom's future (22.18), for that tension was evident in Jesus' own proclamation of God's kingdom.[377] To be sure, the question of the kingdom's imminence remains. The nearness is still affirmed (9.27; 10.9, 11; 21.31), but there seems to be equal concern lest the nearness be exaggerated (19.11; Acts 1.6). This was already a concern in Mark: 'but the end is not yet' (Mark 13.7). Luke strengthens the cautionary note: 'but the end is not immediately' (Luke 21.9). He omits Mark's further caution, 'the gospel must first be preached to all the nations' (Mark 13.10). But he seems to distinguish the fall of Jerusalem (Luke 21.20-24a) from the (still future) coming of the Son of Man (21.25-28),[378] by adding the further intervening phase during which 'Jerusalem will be trampled on by Gentiles, until the times of the Gentiles are fulfilled' (21.24b).[379] Thus, in his own way, Luke makes room for the phase of early Christian mission which he will go on to narrate in Acts.[380]

---

377. *Jesus Remembered* §12.

378. 'By his omission of . . . "in those days" (Mark 13.24), Luke clearly distinguishes what Mark had linked together, the "end" of Jerusalem and the "end" of the world. What is still to come will not happen "in those days", i.e. right after the destruction of Jerusalem' (Fitzmyer, *Luke* 2.1348).

379. 'The times of the Gentiles' should not be taken simply as a reference to Roman domination of Judaea following the failure of the Jewish revolt (as Fitzmyer, *Luke* 2.1347). As the *kairoi* ('times') suggests, the phrase is an expression of Luke's eschatology (as in Acts 1.7 and 3.20), perhaps in some echo of Dan. 12.7, denoting the unfolding of the divine plan and provision (as also Acts 14.17 and 17.26). So there is a history of salvation dimension here and the parallel with Rom. 11.25 (also 11.11-12) cannot be ignored; see also Evans, *Saint Luke* 752; Bovon, *Lukas* 4.185.

380. The central point of the more elaborate thesis of Conzelmann, *Theology of Saint Luke* 16-17 and *passim*, that Luke makes theological room for the period/epoch of the church, in succession to the periods/epochs of Israel and of Jesus' ministry, is still valid, even if over-worked by Conzelmann (treated sympathetically by Fitzmyer, *Luke* 1.18-19, 182-87;

The fact, however, that Luke continued to regard the preaching of the kingdom as still an important aspect of the post-Easter gospel suggests that he was less concerned about the timing of the kingdom. The assumption that Luke framed his historical narrative as a way of resolving 'the delay of the parousia' is a preoccupation more of the twentieth century than of Luke.[381] His concern was rather that expectation or anxiety about the timing of the kingdom might well distract from what mattered. What mattered was not the dates and times which remained in the hands of the Father, but that the good news of Jesus' death and resurrection must be attested to the end of the earth by those empowered by the Spirit (Acts 1.6-8). What mattered was not looking for the kingdom as though something observable, but living out the kingdom (Luke 17.20-21) and being committed to God's rule (9.62), whatever persecutions such commitment would entail (Acts 14.22).[382]

Here again, then, we can see clearly how Luke has worked with the Jesus tradition, and how the Jesus tradition provided him with key motifs both for his telling the story of Jesus and for his account of the beginnings of Christianity. He elaborates (or draws from a wider pool of tradition) Jesus' emphasis on salvation and forgiveness. He highlights Jesus' mission for sinners, without extending it into Acts. But he gives greater emphasis to the role of the Spirit in Jesus' mission than his predecessors and thus prepares more fully for the importance of the Spirit's role in Acts. And most intriguingly he gives 'the kingdom of God' full emphasis in Jesus' preaching and does not hesitate to carry that emphasis over into Acts, even though others were more constrained on the carry-over of that emphasis into early church preaching. In none of this did Luke rework the Jesus tradition radically or introduce emphases which were foreign to the Jesus tradition. Creative performance of the Jesus tradition gave him all the scope he needed to present a Jesus whose mission and teaching were still more relevant than ever to his own day.

d. Israel and the Gentiles

One of the most intriguing aspects of each of the Gospels is how the Evangelist handles the fact that already by the time he wrote his Gospel, it had become well established that the good news of Jesus was as much for Gentiles as for Israel. The issue is of particular importance for Luke, since he probably

---

but see e.g. the critique of Schnelle, *History* 252-53, 255-57). The double account of Jesus' ascension (Luke 24.51; Acts 1.9) means that the ascension has the double function of marking the end of Jesus' earthly ministry and the beginning of the epoch/story of the church.

381. Cf. Kümmel, *Introduction* 142-45.
382. See also Fitzmyer, *Luke* 1.231-35.

intended from the beginning that the 'first word' of his Gospel should be followed by a 'second word' (Acts 1.1). It is fascinating, then, to note how the issue which arose so sharply in the period covered by Acts (how the message of a Jewish Messiah related to non-Jewish believers) is already recognized in the Gospel and its resolution already foreshadowed.

There are two aspects of the theme in Luke-Acts: (1) the Jewish character of Jesus' mission and of the gospel proclaimed by Jesus and the first disciples; (2) this gospel, as good news for Israel, is also good news for the (other) nations. Putting the two together, what becomes ever clearer as first Gospel and then Acts unfold is the continuity which Luke saw between Israel and both the mission of Jesus and the evangelistic outreach to Gentiles in Acts.[383]

(1) We note first the Israel-focus and Jewish character of the gospel/Gospel according to Luke.

- The narrative in the opening chapters of the Gospel begins and ends in the Jerusalem temple (Luke 1.5-23; 2.25-50).[384]
- John the Baptist is predicted to 'turn many of the sons of Israel to the Lord their God' (1.16), and Jesus to 'reign over the house of Jacob forever' (1.33).
- The chief characters in these opening chapters are entirely admirable in terms of Jewish piety:
    ◦ particularly, Zechariah, the father of John the Baptist, descended from Aaron, 'righteous before God, living blamelessly according to all the commandments and regulations of the Lord' (1.5-6);
    ◦ Mary, mother of Jesus, highly favoured by God (1.30);
    ◦ Simeon, 'righteous and devout, looking forward to the consolation of Israel' (2.25);
    ◦ and Anna, who 'never left the temple but worshipped there with fasting and prayer night and day' (2.37).
- The songs sung by Mary and Zechariah are typical of traditional Jewish piety. Mary's song, the Magnificat (Luke 1.46-55), is modeled closely on Hannah's prayer in 1 Sam. 2.1-10. It ends with the words:

---

383. In recent scholarship the one who has most fully appreciated Luke's understanding of the people of God is J. Jervell, *Luke and the People of God: A New Look at Luke-Acts* (Minneapolis: Augsburg, 1972); also *The Theology of the Acts of the Apostles* (Cambridge: Cambridge University, 1996). See also Sellner, *Das Heil Gottes* ch. 9. Typical of later Christian perspective is Bovon's treatment of this theme under the chapter heading 'The Church' (*Luke the Theologian* ch. 7), with critique of Jervell (377-81).

384. The Lukan preoccupation with Jerusalem is also reflected in Luke's ordering of Jesus' temptations, which climax with Jesus on the pinnacle of the temple (4.9-12).

> He has helped his servant Israel, in remembrance of his mercy, according to the promise he made to our fathers, to Abraham and to his descendants forever (1.54-55).

- Likewise the song of Zechariah, the Benedictus (Luke 1.68-79), echoes Psalmist and prophet in almost every line.[385] For example,

> Thus he has shown the mercy promised to our fathers, and has remembered his holy covenant, the oath that he swore to our father Abraham.... [John the Baptist] will go before the Lord to prepare his ways, to give knowledge of salvation to his people by the forgiveness of their sins (1.72, 76-77).

These chapters have been valued for almost all generations of Christians for the wonderful Christmas story which they provide, and for the canticles which have become so traditional in Christian liturgy. But the intensity of their Jewish character is much less appreciated and is often missed.

- Luke alone depicts Jesus as making explicit claim to be the one in whom the prophecy of Isa. 61.1-2 is fulfilled, the anointed one prophesied for Israel (Luke 4.16-21).
- Already noted (§42.4b) is the Moses-prophet and Jesus-prophet emphasis which Luke has retained.[386]
- In an early summary section, parallel to Mark 1.35-38, Luke portrays Jesus as insisting that he must move beyond Capernaum, 'to proclaim the good news of the kingdom of God to other towns; for I was sent for this purpose' (Luke 4.42-43).
- Luke adds to Jesus' teaching about new wine having to be put into fresh wineskins the further comment: 'no one drinking the old wine desires the new, for he says, "The old is good"' (5.39).
- Luke is not so uniformly critical of the Pharisees as Matthew, but includes accounts of Pharisees sympathetic or open to Jesus.[387]
- Luke omits Mark 6.45–8.26, and so ignores the record of Jesus' mission to Bethsaida, Tyre and Sidon, and the Decapolis (Mark 6.45; 7.24, 31).
- As the one sent to seek out and to save the lost (Luke 19.10) Jesus fulfils

---

385. As the marginal notes in the Nestle-Aland *Novum Testamentum Graece* illustrate.

386. Luke 9.12-17, 31; 11.20; 13.33; 24.19, 21.

387. Luke 7.36; 11.37; 13.31; 14.1; cf. Acts 5.33-39; 23.6.

the promised purpose of Yahweh to seek out and save the scattered and lost sheep of the flock of Israel (Ezek. 34.11-16).
- Unlike the other Synoptics, but like Paul (1 Cor. 11.25), Luke emphasizes the new covenant dimension of the last supper (Luke 22.20).
- Luke retains the shared tradition (with Matthew) of Jesus promising that his disciples will sit on thrones judging the twelve tribes of Israel.[388]
- As the birth narratives are marked by devout Jewish characters, so the closing scene of Jesus' life features Joseph of Arimathea, 'who was waiting expectantly for the kingdom of God' (23.51).

The theme continues into Acts.

- As already noted, Luke's second volume begins with the disciples asking the risen Jesus, 'Lord, is this the time when you will restore the kingdom to Israel?' (Acts 1.6) — a concern which Jesus does not dismiss. And it ends with Paul claiming that 'it is for the hope of Israel' that he has been imprisoned (28.20; note also 26.6-7).
- The compulsion to replace Judas and thus to complete the twelve apostles (1.15-26) implies the continued thought of the twelve as representing the twelve tribes of eschatological Israel.[389]
- Peter's first sermon in Jerusalem concludes that the promise (of the Spirit from the Father God) is 'for you, for your children, and for all who are far off, everyone whom the Lord our God calls to him' (2.39). Those who are 'far off' are probably the Jews of the diaspora, and the echo is of Isa. 57.19.[390]
- In his second sermon Peter looks for 'times of refreshing' to come from God and 'the time of universal restoration' that God announced through the prophets (Acts 3.20-21).[391] And he concludes by reminding the Jerusalemites that 'You are the descendants of the prophets and of the covenant that God gave to your fathers, saying to Abraham, "And in your descendants all the families of the earth shall be blessed"' (Gen. 12.3; Acts 3.25).
- The earliest Christian mission was defined as 'beginning from Jerusalem'

---

388. See also C. A. Evans, 'The Twelve Thrones of Israel: Scripture and Politics in Luke 22:24-30', in Evans and Sanders, *Luke and Scripture* 154-70.

389. *Beginning from Jerusalem* 153. M. E. Fuller, *The Restoration of Israel: Israel's Re-gathering and the Fate of the Nations in Early Jewish Literature and Luke-Acts* (BZNW 138; Berlin: de Gruyter, 2006), maintains that 'Luke's primary interpretative frame for understanding the Twelve is the exilic model of restoration' (239-45; here 241).

390. *Beginning from Jerusalem* 226 n.279.

391. *Beginning from Jerusalem* 92-93.

(Luke 24.47; Acts 1.8), and even when the gospel reaches far beyond the land of Israel, Luke's telling of the story maintains the centrality of Jerusalem in the gospel's expansion.[392]
- The continuity of the gospel with Israel's history and hopes is stressed in Paul's first recorded sermon (Acts 13.16-41).
- And even after 'the turn to the Gentiles' has taken place,[393] Luke's telling of the story continues to have the gospel preached to both Jew and Gentile, and 'the kingdom of God and the Lord Jesus Christ' is preached to all (Jew as well as Gentile) who come to Paul in the closing sentence of the book (28.30-31).[394]

So even though Luke does not treat it so explicitly as Matthew, the fulfillment motif in Luke is as strong as it is in Matthew; the gospel's continuity with and realization of the hopes of Israel are central themes for Luke.

(2) Equally noticeable, however, is Luke's repeated indication that this good news is not for Israel alone, that is, that Israel's good news is for Gentiles as well, and again both in the Gospel and in Acts.[395]

- Already in the intensely Jewish birth narratives, Simeon in his prayer, the Nunc Dimittis (Luke 2.29-32), extends the vision more widely. He praises God for the salvation which he has seen in the child Jesus, the salvation 'which you have prepared in the presence of all peoples, a light for revelation to the Gentiles and for the glory of your people Israel'. The echoes of Isaiah's commission of the Servant — 'I have given you as a covenant to the people, a light to the nations' (Isa. 42.6); 'I will put

---

392. Acts 8.14-25; 9.26-30; 11.1-18, 22-24; 15.1-29; 21.15–23.31. In *Beginning from Jerusalem* it was noted that Luke deliberately restricted his account of Jesus' resurrection appearances to Jerusalem (138-39).

393. Acts 13.46-47; 18.6; 28.25-28.

394. See *Beginning from Jerusalem* 1005-9, with further bibliography (n.222); also Klein, *Lukasevangelium* 59; M. Wolter, 'Israel's Future and the Delay of the Parousia, according to Luke', and R. C. Tannehill, 'The Story of Israel within the Lukan Narrative', both in Moessner, ed., *Jesus and the Heritage of Israel* 307-24, 325-39; Sellner, *Das Heil Gottes* 368-78. Schnelle inappropriately speaks of 'the displacement of Israel from its favored place in the history of salvation' (*History* 244; others in *Beginning from Jerusalem* 1007 n.225), but he ignores the closing scene (28.30-31), misses the importance of 15.15-17 (see below), and in citing Luke 21.21-24 ignores the parallel between 21.24 and Rom. 11.25. On the question whether Luke was 'anti-Semitic' see *Beginning* 1006-7 n.225; also C. A. Evans, 'Prophecy and Polemic: Jews in Luke's Scriptural Apologetic', in Evans and Sanders, *Luke and Scripture* 171-211.

395. Cf. S. G. Wilson, *The Gentiles and the Gentile Mission in Luke-Acts* (SNTSMS 23; Cambridge: Cambridge University, 1973); T. J. Lane, *Luke and the Gentile Mission: Gospel Anticipates Acts* (Frankfurt: Lang, 1996).

salvation in Zion, for Israel my glory' (Isa. 46.13); 'I will give you as a light to the nations, that my salvation may reach to the end of the earth' (Isa. 49.6) — are certainly deliberate and foreshadow the consistent thrust Luke maintains through his two volumes.
- In his account of John the Baptist Luke follows Mark (and Q?) in quoting Isa. 40.3, but he alone continues the quotation for a further two verses (40.4-5) to end with 'and all flesh shall see the salvation of God' (Luke 3.4-6).[396]
- Luke uses the Q tradition of the Baptist's preaching to remind Israel that descent from Abraham in itself does not secure divine favour; 'God is able from these stones to raise up children for Abraham' (Luke 3.8).
- Whereas Matthew begins his genealogy of Jesus with Abraham (Matt. 1.2), Luke begins with Adam, son of God (Luke 3.38).
- Obviously deliberate is Luke's expansion of the account of Jesus preaching in Nazareth: Jesus contrasts the querulous response of the residents by pointing out that Elijah was sent not to his own people but to a widow at Zarephath in Sidon, and that the only leper cleansed by Elisha was Naaman the Syrian (4.25-27); Luke also notes the outraged response of the locals (4.28-29).
- Somewhat surprisingly Luke omits one of Mark's main examples of Jesus' mission as reaching beyond Israel (Mark 7.24-30), but he retains others: both the Q story of the Gentile centurion as an example of faith more than Jesus had found in Israel (Luke 7.9), and Jesus' expectation that many (non-Jews) would come from east and west, from north and south to partake in the table-fellowship of the kingdom of God, while evil-doing Israelites would be excluded (13.28-29).
- Luke's unique doubling of Jesus' mission-commission of his disciples (Luke 9.1-6; 10.1-16) suggests the double mission of the early Jesus-sect — to circumcision and to uncircumcision (Gal. 2.7-9). The same feature appears in Luke's version of the parable of the great dinner, in the double response of the host when his guests refused to come: first one mission to recruit participants for his dinner, then another (Luke 14.21-23).
- Equally notable is the prominence which Luke uniquely gives to Samaritans in his Gospel:
    ◦ Jesus rebukes James and John for desiring vengeance on an un-

---

396. This is the kind of detail which suggests that quotations from scripture were not plucked arbitrarily from their context but often presupposed their context. This was the case argued by C. H. Dodd, *According to the Scriptures* (London: Nisbet, 1952) 126, but it has been a contested issue since then.

welcoming Samaritan village (9.52-55) — the first event on the lengthy journey to Jerusalem (9.51);
- Jesus cuts across centuries of Jewish prejudice against Samaria by telling the parable of the good Samaritan, contrasted with the lack of concern shown by the priest and Levite (10.30-35);
- the only one of ten lepers cleansed by Jesus to return to thank him was a Samaritan (17.11-19).

Thus Luke indicates how the subsequent mission to Samaria by Philip (Acts 8) was foreshadowed and in a degree anticipated by Jesus during his own mission.[397]

- In emphasizing Jesus' mission as mission to and for 'sinners' (*hamartōloi*),[398] it is striking that Luke makes so much of Jesus' protest against the categorization (by Pharisees?) of fellow Jews as 'sinners'. He makes a point of Jesus' acceptance and forgiveness of a woman whom his Pharisee host disowns as a 'sinner' (Luke 7.39-50). And he introduces the three parables of lost sheep, lost coin, and lost son by noting that 'sinners' drew near to listen to Jesus in the face of the criticism of Pharisees and scribes, that 'This man welcomes sinners and eats with them' (Luke 15.1-2). Luke here shows himself very much aware of the boundary-breaking character of Jesus' mission.[399] The implication, as Luke no doubt intended, is that 'the lost' whom Jesus came to save (19.10) include those whom devout Israelites assumed were beyond the pale of God's concern.
- A similar inference may be drawn from the added emphasis Luke gives to Jesus' mission to and for 'the poor' (*ptōchoi*).[400] Here a feature particularly worth noting, so distinctive of Luke's account, is the repeated emphasis in Luke 14.13, 21 that those to be invited to the banquet of the new age are 'the poor, the crippled, the lame and the blind'. The language echoes the list of those who are excluded from the priestly community of Qumran[401]— and echoes it so closely that it must be re-

---

397. Contrast Matthew's only reference to Samaritans (Matt. 10.5).

398. Luke 5.8, 30, 32; 7.34, 37, 39; 15.1-2, 7, 10; 18.13; 19.7.

399. *Jesus Remembered* 605-7. It is important here to remember that 'sinner' was a factional term, dismissive of others of whom the righteous did not approve (*Jesus Remembered* 528-32). Luke's references show that he (or the tradition on which he drew) was well aware of this factional usage.

400. Luke 4.18 (citing Isa. 61.1); 6.20 and 7.22 (echoing Isa. 61.1); 14.13, 21; 16.20, 22; 18.22; 19.8; 21.3.

401. 1Q28a 2.3-10; 1QM 7.4-6; 4QCD⁶; 11QT 45.12-14.

garded as probable that Luke recalls Jesus as rejecting such exclusion from the divine presence. Neither sinners nor the disabled are to be treated as unfit to feast with the saints and worship with the angels.[402]

In Acts I need recall only a few passages.

- Already quoted is the conclusion to Peter's second sermon, where he quotes the verse on which Paul built so much (Gen. 12.3):[403] God's promise to Abraham that 'in your descendants all the families of the earth shall be blessed' (Acts 3.25).
- Central to Paul's conversion is his commission to fulfill Servant Israel's commission to be a light to the world.[404]
- In Acts 10–11 Peter learns that the laws of clean and unclean do not mean that he should regard any *person* as profane or unclean (10.28).[405]
- Finally we should note how James, the brother of Jesus, and leader of the Jesus messianists in Jerusalem, resolves the problem of the increasing number of non-Jews who were coming to faith in Messiah Jesus, but without being circumcised. He resolves the problem in two steps. First, he quotes from Amos 9.11-12:

> Afterwards I will return and I will rebuild the tent of David that has fallen down, and I will rebuild its ruins and I will raise it up, in order that the rest of humanity may seek the Lord, even all the Gentiles upon whom my name has been named (Acts 15.16-17).

The combination — restoration of Israel, and Gentiles owned by God — sums up the double emphasis of Luke more clearly than anywhere else (cf. particularly Luke 2.32).[406]

- And then James issues what has become known as 'the apostolic decree' (Acts 15.20). This requires Gentile believers in Jesus to 'abstain from

---

402. *Jesus Remembered* §14.8a; and my earlier article, 'Jesus, Table-Fellowship and Qumran', in J. H. Charlesworth, ed., *Jesus and the Dead Sea Scrolls* (New York: Doubleday, 1992) 254-72.
403. Particularly Gal. 3.8; see *Beginning from Jerusalem* 93 and n.166, 535, 734.
404. Acts 9.15; 13.47; 22.21; 26.17-18, 20.
405. *Beginning from Jerusalem* 394-96.
406. It may be, as Bovon suggests (*Lukas* 1.15-16), that Luke has placed the parable of the lost son exactly at the centre of the Gospel (Luke 15.11-32 — younger and older sons) just as he placed the Jerusalem conference at the centre of Acts (15.1-35 — Gentiles and Israel) — each providing a hermeneutical key to the whole work. Surprisingly Fuller, *The Restoration of Israel*, ignores what is one of the clearest expressions of Luke's understanding of Israel's restoration.

things polluted by [contact with] idols, from fornication (*porneia*), from that which is strangled (*pnikton*), and from blood [the kosher laws]'. What has often been missed here is that the principal source of 'the apostolic decree' seems to be the legislation regarding 'the resident alien', that is, the non-Jews who were permanently resident in the land of Israel, 'in the midst of' the people (Lev. 17.8-9, 10-14; 18.26).[407] This was presumably the solution to 'the Gentile problem' of which Luke himself approved, and probably also the Jerusalem church. That is, the 'problem' is resolved by treating such Gentiles in effect as 'resident aliens', Gentiles in the midst of the people, while retaining their identity as Gentiles.

Here then was an insistence by Luke that the gospel is not foreign to Israel. The gospel is not in opposition to Israel, is not to be set in antithesis to the law. On the contrary, the gospel looks for the restoration of Israel, for the fulfillment of the hopes of Israel's prophets, and for the inclusion of Gentiles within and as part of that fulfilled hope. Unlike Mark, the Gospel of Luke does not focus on the discontinuities between the law and a message fully open to Gentiles. Unlike Matthew, the Gospel of Luke is not fighting with the rabbinic survivors of the catastrophe of 70 over the inheritance from Moses and the prophets. For Luke, *the Gospel is not gospel except as it works for the fulfillment of Israel's hope, as including Gentiles within that hope.*[408]

Given the existence of a verse like Matt. 10.5, it is hardly unfair to ask whether Luke has added these emphases to the Jesus tradition. Could the developments to be narrated in Acts really claim to be rooted in Jesus' own mission, in his own vision and in the emphases of his teaching? In fact, as has just been demonstrated, a good case can be made for answering that latter question in the affirmative. Indeed, it very much looks as though Luke framed his Gospel not only with the continuation of Acts in view from the first, but also with a view to drawing out the continuity between the two books and the (single) story they narrate. The one caution to be noted is that the continuity was not simply from Israel to Gentiles, as though Israel was now left behind. The continuity was in terms, as I have tried to insist, of Israel's hope being fulfilled precisely by the inclusion of Gentiles in that realized hope.

In this case, then, we may say that Luke saw implications and hints in the Jesus tradition which he was able to draw out and make more explicit in the

---

407. See further my *Beginning from Jerusalem* 461-69.

408. Does Luke then portray the destruction of Jerusalem as marking 'the end of Israel as a bearer of the promise' (Koester, *Introduction* 2.315), or the church 'as the true Israel' (Schnelle, *History* 253)? Such judgments come across as an over-simplification of a more complex hope; 'supersessionism' is a too easy resolution of this early Christian enigma, and one which too quickly led to anti-Judaism and subsequently to anti-Semitism.

material over which he had fuller control. It should be noted that he did *not* create new material or inject his own concerns freely into the Jesus tradition itself. He was content that the Jesus tradition pointed in the direction he saw the gospel as having gone since the first Easter, and he drew on its few explicit features but also did not hesitate to adapt his use of the Jesus tradition to make the points which he saw now needed to be made. The *Jewishness* of Jesus' background and mission and of the gospel hope still being proclaimed by Paul (and Luke as one of his successors), but the gospel as also *open to Gentiles*, these were the red lines Luke was able to begin to draw in his account of Jesus' life and mission and to continue into his second word.

e. Discipleship Priorities

One of the surprising, not to say disappointing, features of Luke's Acts is his failure to take the opportunity to describe the ethical issues and priorities of the new churches whose foundation he was describing. The sort of teaching given by Jesus, for example, in the Sermon on the Plain (Luke 6.20-49), or the issues dealt with by Paul in, say, his letters to Corinth, are notable for their absence in Acts. To be sure, there is reference to the community of goods of the first Jerusalem church (Acts 2.44-45; 4.32-37), and to concern in the church of Antioch about the impact of a predicted famine on the believers in Judaea (11.27-30). And Paul's farewell speech in Miletus strikes some strong ethical notes (20.33-35). But otherwise brief summary descriptions like 11.23, 13.52 and 20.37-38 tell us next to nothing about how the first Christians lived and their ethical priorities. One of the most striking examples of this unwillingness on Luke's part to maintain the same continuity between Gospel and Acts as he did on the Israel-Gentile issue is the complete absence of any reference to or talk of 'love' in Acts. Presumably Luke was able to assume that the paraenesis provided in his Gospel carried over in instruction and encouragement to the congregations to whom his volumes were read.[409] But the strange silence of Acts on this front remains a puzzle.

Unlike Matthew, the Gospel of Luke also seems to lack an explicit teaching concern.[410] This, however, should not lead us to underplay the sev-

---

409. Evans, *Saint Luke* 93-94. Curiously (despite what was noted in n.278 above), Luke puts the exceptional abstraction of Lev. 19.18 in the mouth of the lawyer asking Jesus the question (Luke 10.27), though this is probably just a pedagogical technique shifting the focus to Jesus' exposition of Lev. 19.18 in the parable of the Good Samaritan (10.29-37).

410. 'The Third Gospel lacks the pedagogical structure of the Matthean Gospel, with its deliberate alternation of narrative episodes and catechetical discourses' (Fitzmyer, *Luke* 1.162). Bovon observes little interest in Luke's moral teaching (*Luke the Theologian*

eral pastoral and ethical themes and emphases which Luke does maintain in his Gospel.

- An early indication of Luke's concern in this area is the brief paragraph he alone includes in *the preaching of the Baptist*, where John exhorts those who gathered round him to be generous, honest and just (Luke 3.10-14).
- Luke gives more prominence to the theme of *humility* than the other Evangelists,[411] and in his version of the story of the centurion it is his sense of unworthiness on which Luke focuses (7.4, 6). This coheres with the familiar teaching on true greatness, modeled by a little child, and not by those who lord it over others.[412] The parable of the Pharisee and the tax collector is addressed to some who regarded others with contempt (18.9).[413]
- More prominent, however, is Luke's repeated warnings against *the perils of wealth*, distinctive of his Gospel:[414]
    - God 'has sent the rich away empty' (1.53);
    - 'woe to you who are rich' (6.24);
    - whereas Mark cites 'deceitfulness of wealth' as one of the things that chokes the word (Mark 4.19), Luke speaks simply of wealth as that which chokes the word (Luke 8.14);
    - Jesus' blunt warning against greed (12.15) is followed by the parable of the rich fool (12.16-21), which together provide a more fitting sequence to Jesus' teaching on anxiety than Matthew's (12.22-31/Matt. 6.25-33);
    - discipleship is conditional on giving up all one's possessions (Luke 12.33; 14.33), as illustrated by the first disciples (5.11, 28; cf. 18.22);
    - the Pharisees are dismissed as 'lovers of money' (16.14);

435-36). Evans points out that Jesus is only addressed as 'Teacher' by non-disciples and that only in 22.11 does Jesus refer to himself as 'Teacher' (*Luke* 67), though Luke does speak consistently of Jesus' 'disciples' and carries the designation over into Acts (*Beginning from Jerusalem* 8-9).

411. Luke 1.48, 52; 14.11; 18.14.

412. Luke 9.46-48; 18.16-17; 22.24-27.

413. Luke also reproduces the Jesus tradition's concern for 'the little ones' (Luke 7.28; 9.48; 17.2), perhaps strengthening the motif with the encouragement to the 'little flock' (12.32) and the story of 'little' Zacchaeus (19.1-10).

414. Bovon reviews other literature (*Luke the Theologian* 546-51). Paul Trebilco (in private correspondence) reminds me that there is other material in Luke which seems to presuppose some rich readers — who can invite people to meals (Luke 14.12-14), can give generously (6.30, 35; 11.41; 12.33-34) or buy a sword (22.35-38).

- the parable of the rich man and Lazarus sums up the urgency of such priorities (16.19-31);
- Luke, of course, takes over the Markan saying of Jesus that 'it is easier for a camel to pass through the eye of a needle than for a rich man to enter the kingdom of God' (18.25), but also in the preceding episode he sharpens the challenge which Jesus made to the rich ruler, 'Sell *all* that you have' (18.22);
- and Zacchaeus's promise to give to the poor and to compensate generously any he had defrauded draws Jesus' response, 'Today salvation has come to this house' (19.8-9).[415]

• A natural corollary, indicated in the same passages, is Luke's *concern for the poor*; the Magnificat also celebrates that God has 'filled the hungry with good things' (1.53); the first beatitude is addressed to 'you poor' (6.20; in some contrast to Matthew's 'poor in spirit'); and the second beatitude is addressed to 'you who are hungry now', with the complementary woe addressed to those 'who are full now, for you will be hungry' (6.21, 25).

• Also notable, in a patriarchal society, is the prominence Luke gives to the attention which Jesus paid to *women* and the role of women in his mission — again a distinctive feature of Luke's Gospel:
  - Elizabeth, Mary and Anna in Luke 1–2;
  - the special notice given to the female sinner in 7.36-50;
  - the ministry of women in 8.2-3 (highlighted much earlier than Mark's equivalent — Mark 15.40-41);
  - the support given by Martha and Mary (10.38-42) and by the woman in the crowd (11.27);
  - Jesus' concern specifically for the widow of Nain (7.13) and the crippled woman (13.10-17);
  - the persistent petitioner of the unjust judge (18.2-5);
  - the prominence of women in the final acts (Luke adds 23.27-29).

Luke thus certainly prepares the way for Acts,[416] though the prominence he gives to women in Acts hardly reflects the importance of women in Paul's mission team which we learn from Paul's letters.[417]

• The only other feature distinctive of Luke's Gospel deserving of notice here is the prominence he gives to Jesus *praying*. He follows Mark in narrating the Gethsemane scene (22.40-41, 45-46) and draws 6.28 from

---

415. The parable of the dishonest manager suggests a hands-off attitude to money (16.1-9). See further Fitzmyer, *Luke* 1.247-51.

416. Particularly Acts 9.36-42; 12.12; 13.50; 16.14-15; 17.4, 12, 34; 18.2, 18, 26; 21.5.

417. *Beginning from Jerusalem* §29.6 — at least 20 percent of Paul's mission teams (571).

material shared with Matthew. But he greatly enlarges the theme and the importance of prayer in the Gospel and for Jesus:
- the Gospel begins in a prayer setting (1.10; as does Acts — Acts 1.14; 2.42);
- the Spirit came upon Jesus at Jordan while he was praying (3.21-22);
- Luke notes Jesus' habit of withdrawing to deserted places to pray (5.16);
- Jesus spends a whole night in prayer before choosing the twelve disciples (6.12-13);
- Luke notes that Jesus was in prayer prior to Peter's confession (9.18-20);
- Jesus goes up the mountain to pray and while praying he is transfigured (9.28-29);
- his practice of prayer leads the disciples to ask him to teach them to pray (11.1);
- the parable of the persistent friend is told to encourage persistence in prayer (11.5-8, introducing the Q passage 11.9-13);
- similarly, Luke gives the reason that Jesus told the parable of the unjust judge as to bring out 'the need to pray always and not to lose heart' (18.1);
- the parable of the Pharisee and tax collector is a parable on effective prayer (18.10-14).

All these are once again distinctive of Luke's Gospel. An obvious deduction is that Luke chose so to emphasize the theme in order to provide in Jesus' life and teaching a pattern of praying for the audiences who heard his Gospel read to them.

The comparison between Luke and the other Synoptics is interesting at this point. For Mark and Matthew both seemed to relish the opportunity afforded by transcribing the gospel to provide a manual of discipleship. In some contrast Luke uses his Gospel to bring home features of the mission of Jesus which have continuing relevance for the values and priorities of the gospel life which he in effect commends. He follows Mark in recording Jesus' 'terms of discipleship' (9.23-27) and underlines the point with further material (9.59-62; 14.25-33), and he shares much of the tradition which Matthew put together in the Sermon on the Mount, though the fact that it is much more scattered in Luke suggests that he was content for the paraenetical teaching to come across more episodically than in concentrated sections. But otherwise he preaches his ethical and pastoral message by allusion and by introducing parables, many of which were not known to or used by the other Evangelists. This presumably was a pedagogical decision in that he wanted Theophilus and his wider audiences to be jerked into attention by the stories he told about Jesus and the stories of Jesus which he told. Luke appreciated the effectiveness of the parable as a teaching tool and told his story of Jesus as the parable of Jesus.[418]

Here again we can see how an expert re-teller of the Jesus tradition could be effective simply by retelling episodes of Jesus' mission and parables from his mission. His focusing on particular aspects of the tradition was entirely appropriate and proper. His strengthening of chosen emphases already in the Jesus tradition was entirely to be expected. There was no point that Luke made, explicitly or by allusion, which he could not have shown to be deeply rooted in the wider Jesus tradition known to his fellow disciples. Luke's Gospel was a sustained performance of the Jesus tradition whose character as a performance would have been familiar to most of his fellow Christians.[419]

In short, Luke's 'orderly account' (Luke 1.3) was probably in character no different from the 'orderly accounts' (1.1) of his predecessors, in that the way in which Luke handled the Jesus tradition was fairly typical of the way his predecessors handled it and the way it was handled (in smaller segments, of course) in the weekly gatherings of the Christians for worship and teaching. The fact that Luke describes the work of his predecessors and his own in similar terms — *diēgēsis*, 'orderly account' (1.1); *kathexēs*, 'orderly sequence' (1.3) — is probably sufficient indication that Luke saw his work as of the same kind as his predecessors, climactic in the sequence, perhaps, but part of the same sequence. Had Luke envisaged himself as bringing in new and previously unknown material, or as creating a portrayal of Jesus at odds with earlier portrayals, he could have hardly hoped to reassure Theophilus of the *asphaleia*, 'certainty, truth', of what he had previously been taught by such predecessors, by such earlier 'orderly accounts' (1.4). It was *confirmation* of earlier instruction that Luke was endeavouring to achieve, not a wholly new and different account. The way he went about that has been sufficiently documented in this section for us to be able to appreciate how Luke hoped to

---

418. Klein illustrates the point by noting that Jesus responded to the question, 'Who is my neighbour?' (Luke 10.29), by telling a parable. 'The question is neither resolved nor explained. Reader and hearers are taken up into an event which they resonate with as they reflect on it, and out of such reflection should they then determine the question for themselves in each respective instance' (*Lukasevangelium* 1.52).

419. Fitzmyer's comment on Luke's attitude to material wealth could be applied more generally: it 'did not originate with Luke himself. There is no need to think that it is not rooted in the preaching of the historical Jesus. But for his own reasons Luke has chosen to accentuate it, and he sees it as an imperative need in the Christian community for which he writes' (*Luke* 1.248).

achieve his goal. Above all, it has become clearer that the aspects which Luke brings to the fore can be recognized as aspects of the Jesus tradition, that is, aspects of the fuller memory of Jesus' mission formulated by his first disciples and passed on through instruction and worship, and familiar to the Christians of Luke's time in varied format, presentation and interpretation. Luke's Jesus too is still Jesus remembered.

42.5 Jesus Remembered Becomes the Gospel of Jesus Christ

In this chapter, then, we have been examining the next stage in how Jesus was remembered.[420] We have already examined *what* was remembered — the *Jesus* who was *Remembered* (vol. 1). And in §§23.4-5 we noted what could be regarded as key earliest beliefs about Jesus. Now we have looked at *how* he was remembered, how the earliest beliefs about Jesus shaped the way he was remembered. We have seen how the *gospel* formulated by Paul in particular, and given the fuller shape (by Mark) of an account (Gospel) of Jesus' ministry, climaxing in his death and resurrection, was elaborated in writing across the first sixty or so years of Christianity (§41). The very fact that the good news about Jesus could be written down, in an extensive and coherent form, giving a clear portrayal of his ministry, climaxing in his death and resurrection, and that this was done within the lifetime of Jesus' immediate disciples, is a key fact whose significance is not given the attention which it deserves. And the fact that the first three accounts of Jesus' ministry, death and resurrection, the first three Gospels, are so inter-related and in effect provide such a coherent account of Jesus' ministry, showing clearly how he was remembered, gives us confidence that these are the memories of Jesus' own disciples in the years after his death and resurrection — the impact made by Jesus extending through the oral period of the traditions of Jesus' ministry and teaching and leaving its clear mark on the material which is integral to the Synoptic Gospels. It was this continuing impact made by Jesus as expressed in the first Gospels written which made it possible both to outline the earliest beliefs about Jesus and to recapture the historic impact made by Jesus himself.

What has become so clear in this chapter is that there was an extensive range of memories of Jesus' mission shared by his first followers, an extensive range of shared memories of what Jesus did and taught. The first disciples shared the same faith — the faith evoked by the 'gospel' and expressed in

---

420. I should perhaps stress again that this has been the primary task in this chapter, not to cover all aspects which go to make up the typical introductions to the New Testament Gospels.

the gathering of the traditions which make up the first three Gospels. But, of course, the faith could be and was expressed differently, with the same but also different stories about Jesus, with memories of the same teachings of Jesus but formulated differently in relation to what we can deduce were different settings.

So, the fuller g/Gospel shape provided by Mark brought out the good news of Jesus in terms of his relation to God (the Son of God), his healing and exorcistic ministry, and his role in relation to Israel as Messiah and (to the wider world) as the Son of Man. As we have seen, Mark's Gospel provided a manual of discipleship, both underlining the authority of Jesus as a teacher and indicating the content of his teaching.

Mark was followed by Matthew — the significance of this should not be overlooked — in the shape which the latter too gave to writing his Gospel, both in elaborating the significance of Jesus for Israel which he drew out, and in using his Gospel to provide a manual of discipleship and church discipline. The relevance of Matthew's Gospel to the strains of his own time (post-70) is indicated by the jousting he engaged in with the immediate heirs of the Pharisees over Israel's heritage, and by his own wrestling to portray a mission directed primarily to Israel as also of immediate challenge to Gentiles.

And Luke did the same, taking over the same range of traditions regarding Jesus' mission — probably involving wider and more careful research (Luke 1.1-4) than was possible to Mark and Matthew. Presumably it was this wider research which enabled him to draw out the significance of Jesus with his own emphases. Even more so, probably with the benefit of his wider research, he was able to highlight the character of the gospel, not least in terms of 'sinners' and the gift of the Spirit, the latter making a vital link with his ongoing story in his second volume. As important for Luke were evidently the emphasis that the gospel of Jesus was also for Gentiles and the stressing of gospel priorities.

What remains striking in all this is the unity in the diversity of these first three Gospels, the shared character of 'same yet different' in the ways Jesus was reflected on and presented. This is the important thing — what made it possible to write *Jesus Remembered:* that the rich diversity of the Synoptic Gospels provided such clear indication of the different lessons which could be brought out from what were the same memories, or, more accurately, from the differing memories of the same man and his mission. To demonstrate the other side of this remembering, that the differing memories also indicate what was important for those engaged in and responsible for the remembering, as indicated in and by the Synoptic Gospels, has been the task of this chapter.

We could round off the chapter by reflecting further on the reception of the Synoptic Gospels. But we are not yet ready to do so. Of course, we could briefly discuss the reception of Mark's Gospel above (§42.2e), because Matthew and Luke marked the beginning of that reception process, and so the brief discussion was an integral part of §42. But to go beyond that, to discuss the reception of all the Synoptic Gospels, takes us well into the second century and is better left till §44. Nor should we forget that we have not yet examined all the NT Gospels. John's Gospel has yet to be studied in detail (§43). Only then will we be in a position to ask how Jesus was remembered into the second century.

CHAPTER 43

Reshaping the Gospel of Jesus: John and Thomas

Two other documents with the title 'Gospel' share similar but contrasting features — the Gospel of John and the *Gospel of Thomas*. That is, they both draw extensively (but differently) on the early Jesus tradition as attested in the Synoptic tradition. But they also diverge markedly from that tradition in the content and the character of their material; the diversity in the use they make of the earlier tradition is so different from the diversity evident in the Synoptic tradition of Mark, Matthew and Luke that they both might legitimately be regarded as a different species from that of the Synoptics. For those familiar with the New Testament, and with both the canonical status of John and the non-canonical status of *Thomas*, this may be a very questionable comment to make. But a dispassionate judgment of these Gospels is likely to be surprised both by the *divergence* of John's treatment of Jesus from that of the other canonical Gospels and by the *closeness* of much of *Thomas*'s account to the Synoptic tradition. By treating both separately from the other canonical Gospels and side by side here, my hope is to bring home both features and to achieve a more fully informed appreciation of both. Not least, it will be important to understand better why one of the two was accepted within the New Testament canon, and the other rejected, and to ask whether, in view of the new wave of interest in the *Gospel of Thomas*, that earlier judgment should be revised or qualified.[1]

---

1. The issue posed, for example, by Funk et al., *the Five Gospels*, and H. Taussig, *A New New Testament: A Bible for the 21st Century Combining Traditional and Newly Discovered Texts* (New York: Houghton Mifflin Harcourt, 2013). An essay of Moody Smith poses the issue nicely: 'John and the Apocryphal Gospels: Was John the First Apocryphal Gospel?', *The Fourth Gospel in Four Dimensions* (University of South Carolina, 2008) 156-65. For the case to be argued here cf. particularly L. T. Johnson, 'John and *Thomas* in Context: An Exercise in Canonical Criticism', in J. R. Wagner et al., eds., *The Word Leaps the Gap:*

43.1 The Gospel according to John

When those who are unfamiliar with the NT Gospels turn from the Synoptic Gospels to John's Gospel they might well experience something of a shock. The Synoptic Gospels, despite their distinctive features, are largely of a piece, cut from the same cloth. When the three Gospels are set out synoptically the degree of sameness and overlap is very striking. John's Gospel, on the other hand, seems to be so different. There are a similar 'Gospel' structure, as we have seen (§41), and still a fair degree of overlap. But, as we shall see in a moment, the character and content are so very different.

The difference is such that it poses a major question for our exploration of the way the Jesus tradition was remembered and used in the last decades of the first century and into the second. For with the Synoptics there is a remarkable similarity in the way they show the Jesus tradition to have been used and developed. But with John's Gospel a major question arises, What has happened to the Jesus tradition? Has John departed from the Jesus tradition familiar to us from the Synoptics? Has John so developed the Jesus tradition that its beginnings in Jesus' own mission have become obscure? The Synoptic Gospels made it clear that the Jesus tradition was flexible in the use made of it, in the way it was retold and in the interpretation given to it. But always they retained the same basic character and structure of the Jesus tradition — 'the same, yet different' — so that it was quite feasible to discern the impression of the one who had made the impact which resulted in and was expressed by that tradition.[2] With John, however, 'the same yet different' is hardly applicable. And the question arises whether the controlling influences which maintained the basic sameness of the Jesus tradition in the Synoptics ceased to be effective in the case of John's Gospel. Alternatively, were there other influences shaping the earlier Jesus tradition into very different forms, transforming its character, changing the impression it gave into something very different from the impact first made by Jesus himself? Or again, was the stream of Synoptic tradition only one stream of tradition emerging from Jesus' mission? In other words, did Jesus make very different impacts on different individuals and groups, so that no single Gospel or group of Gospels can claim to have retained and to represent the full measure of Jesus' mission? These are questions, it will be appreciated, which run on into the non-canonical Gospels (§44). But it cannot but be significant that they are first raised by John's Gospel.

Essays on Scripture and Theology in Honour of Richard B. Hays (Grand Rapids: Eerdmans, 2008) 284-309.

2. This was the basis for the attempt to present the mission of Jesus in *Jesus Remembered*. See also my collected essays, *The Oral Gospel Tradition*.

a. The Puzzle of John's Gospel

With the first three NT Gospels a natural first step was to explore the interrelationships, some literary, some probably oral, between them. With John's Gospel, however, the differences with the Synoptic Gospels are so great that it is difficult to compare John so directly with the Synoptics. Since familiarity with the NT Gospels can make readers and Christian congregations somewhat blind to the differences between the Synoptics and John, it will be well, first, to indicate just how extensive and how deeply rooted these differences are.

On the other hand, there are a good many indications that the tradition behind John's Gospel is also deeply rooted, that John has been able to draw on good historical tradition in his composition. Most fascinating will be the indications that the Johannine discourses, so very different from the Synoptic memory of Jesus' teaching, are also rooted in Synoptic or Synoptic-like tradition.

i. The Differences between the Synoptic Gospels and John's Gospel

The differences can be summed up and typified in the following terms:[3]

Synoptics	John
Matthew and Luke begin with virgin conception/birth.	John begins with the incarnation of the pre-existent Logos.
Jesus goes to Jerusalem only for the last week of his mission.	Jesus is active in Judaea for a large part of his mission.[4]
Only one Passover is mentioned.	Jesus' mission extends over three Passovers.[5]
Jesus' last meal with his disciples is a Passover meal.	Jesus is crucified on the day of preparation for the Passover.[6]
Jesus speaks little of himself — nothing quite like John's 'I am's.	Jesus speaks much of himself — notably the 'I am' statements.[7]
Jesus calls for faith in God.	Jesus calls for faith in himself.
The central theme of Jesus' preaching is the kingdom of God.	The kingdom of God barely features in Jesus' speech.[8]
Jesus speaks of repentance and forgiveness quite often.	Jesus never speaks of repentance and of forgiveness only in 20.23.
Jesus speaks typically in aphorisms and parables.	Jesus engages in lengthy dialogues and circuitous discussions.

---

3. It was the differences of John from the Synoptics to which those in the early Christian period who disputed the authorship of John appealed in justification (see §39.2d(i)).

4. See also at n.48 below.

5. More detail, e.g., in Kümmel, *Introduction* 200.

6. Contrast Mark 14.12-16 pars. with John 18.28 and 19.14, 31. See further below n.47.

Synoptics	John
Jesus speaks only occasionally of eternal life.[9]	Jesus speaks regularly of eternal life.[10]
Jesus shows strong concern for the poor and sinners.	Jesus shows little concern for the poor and sinners.[11]
Jesus is notable for his ministry of exorcism.	There are no exorcisms.[12]
Distinctive of John and without real parallel in the Synoptics is John's dualism.[13]	

7. John 6.35, 48 — 'I am the bread of life'
     6.41 — 'I am the bread that came down from heaven'
     6.51 — 'I am the living bread that came down from heaven'
     8.12 — 'I am the light of the world'
     8.24, 28 — 'I am'
     8.58 — 'Before Abraham was, I am'
     10.7, 9 — 'I am the gate for the sheep'
     10.11, 14 — 'I am the good shepherd'
     11.25 — 'I am the resurrection and the life'
     13.19 — 'I am'
     14.6 — 'I am the way, and the truth, and the life'
     15.1, 5 — 'I am the true vine'

'Practically all the words of Jesus in John are *assertions about himself*' (Bultmann, *Theology* 2.63).

    8. Matt. 47x; Mark 18x; Luke 37x; John 5x in only two passages (John 3.3-5; 18.36).

    9. Mark 10.17 pars.; 10.30 pars.; Matt. 25.46; but note also references to entering into life (Mark 9.43, 45 par.).

    10. John 3.15-16, 36; 4.14, 36; 5.24, 39; 6.27, 40, 47, 54, (68); 10.28; 12.25, 50; 17.2-3.

    11. Texts like Matt. 5.3/Luke 6.20; Matt. 11.5/Luke 7.22, and Mark 10.21, 12.42-43 ('the poor'); and Mark 2.15-17 pars. and Matt. 11.19/Luke 7.34 ('sinners') have been sufficient to indicate to most of the last two generations of treatments of the historical Jesus that these were strong concerns of Jesus. John 12.5-8 and 13.29, and 9.16, 24-25, 31 would never have given that impression.

    12. Similarly John nowhere speaks of 'unclean spirits', and the term 'demon' is limited to accusations against Jesus (7.20; 8.48-49, 52; 10.20-21). See further n.88 below.

    13. Particularly 'above/below' (3.3, 7, 31; 8.23; 19.11); 'light/darkness' (1.5; 3.19-21; 8.12; 11.10; 12.35, 46), and the heavy emphasis on 'truth' (see below n.194) in implied antithesis to error. In reaction to the older view that John's dualism indicated Gnostic influence, the parallels with Qumran dualism were overstated; as C. K. Barrett, *The Gospel of John and Judaism* (London: SPCK, 1975), noted, 'The similarities between the Fourth Gospel and the Qumran literature have been overstated at the expense of their differences, which are almost or quite as important' (56); see also Bauckham, *Testimony* ch. 6. Brown documents other distinctive features of John's style — inclusion, chiasm, twofold meaning, misunderstanding, irony, and explanatory notes (*John* 1.cxxxv-cxxxvi). And note how distinctive the Johannine vocabulary is — see e.g. the list in Barrett, *John* 5-6; examples below in nn.186, 194, 204, 210.

Older harmonizing explanations, keen to affirm that John's Gospel is as historical in its presentation as the Synoptics, tried to explain such differences in terms of the different audiences to whom Jesus spoke — for example, the Synoptics recalling Jesus' teaching to the crowds, John recalling Jesus' teaching to his disciples.[14] But as David Friedrich Strauss pointed out long ago,[15] the style of Jesus' speech in John's Gospel is consistent, whether Jesus is depicted as speaking to Nicodemus, or to the woman at the well, or to 'the Jews', or to his disciples. And the style is very similar to that of the Baptist, as indeed to that of 1 John. The inference is inescapable that the style is that of the *Evangelist* or of the Evangelist's tradition, rather than that of *Jesus*.[16] And it can hardly be judged other than scarcely credible that Jesus was remembered as having uttered the 'I am' assertions, so vividly descriptive and self-assertive, and yet *not one* of the Synoptic Evangelists bothered to recall or use them. How could such self-identifying assertions made by Jesus during his mission have been so ignored or blanked out by the earlier Gospel writers? The only obvious conclusion is that the 'I am' sayings, so characteristic of John's Gospel, and so distinctive of John's Gospel, cannot be traced back as such to Jesus himself. This is Jesus tradition developed well beyond its roots in Jesus' own mission.

ii. The Historical Value of John's Gospel

Despite these differences there are many indications that John's Gospel is well rooted in the historical events of Jesus' mission.

One often-cited instance is the various geographical details which are scattered throughout John's account. Since they serve no discernible literary or theological purpose, they probably belong to the historical reminiscences from which the passages containing the references originated. For example,[17]

---

14. Cf. e.g. those referred to in my 'Let John Be John: A Gospel for Its Time', in P. Stuhlmacher, ed., *The Gospel and the Gospels* (Grand Rapids: Eerdmans, 1991) 293-323 (here 298 n.11); Anderson, *Fourth Gospel* 61; C. S. Evans, 'The Historical Reliability of John's Gospel: From What Perspective Should It Be Assessed?', in Bauckham and Mosser, eds., *John and Christian Theology* 91-119 (here 109-14). More discriminating is C. L. Blomberg, 'The Historical Reliability of John', in Fortna and Thatcher, eds., *Jesus in the Johannine Tradition* 71-82. The relation of history to theology in John is the main theme of Anderson et al., eds., *John, Jesus and History* vols. 1 and 2. Earlier phases of the debate are summarized by Kümmel, *Introduction* 198-99.

15. Already noted in *Jesus Remembered* 166. Robinson acknowledged the point (*Priority* 307, 311).

16. As Anderson recognizes (*Fourth Gospel* 58-59). See further J. Verheyden, 'The De-Johannification of Jesus: The Revisionist Contribution of Some Nineteenth-Century German Scholarship', in Anderson et al., eds., *John, Jesus and History* vol. 1, 109-20.

17. See further Anderson, *Fourth Gospel* 3, 5, 80-81; Bauckham, *Testimony* 95-100.

- 1.28 — Bethany across the Jordan
- 2.1 — Cana in Galilee (also 4.46)
- 3.23 — Aenon near Salim
- 4.5-6 — Jacob's well near Sychar
- 5.2 — the pool of Bethzatha
- 9.7 — the pool of Siloam[18]
- 11.54 — a town called Ephraim
- 18.1 — across the Kedron valley
- 19.13 — Pilate's juridical seat on 'the Stone Pavement' (*Gabbatha*).

All these are unique to John's Gospel and are best explained as historical details adhering to the earliest formulation of these traditions.

Equally striking are the various overlaps between John's Gospel and the Synoptic tradition. A very good example are the traditions regarding John the Baptist:

- that the mission of Jesus' immediate predecessor was characterized by a (once-only) baptism (Mark 1.4 pars.), that he was known as 'the Baptizer' or 'the Baptist'[19] and that he practised his mission of baptizing in the Jordan River;[20]
- clearly stated or implied is the success of the Baptist's mission in attracting so many to be baptized;[21]
- the quotation from Isa. 40.3 — the Baptist identified as 'the voice crying out in the wilderness: "Make straight the way of the Lord"';[22]
- the contrast made by the Baptist between his own status and that of the one to come — 'I am not worthy to untie the thong of his sandal';[23]

---

18. See now U. C. von Wahlde, 'The Pool of Siloam: The Importance of New Discoveries . . .', in Anderson et al., eds., *John, Jesus and History* vol. 2, 155-73.

19. *ho baptizōn* — Mark 6.14; cf. 1.4; *ho baptistēs* — Matt. 3.1; 11.11-12; etc.; Mark 6.25; 8.28; Luke 7.20, 33; 9.19; see further *Jesus Remembered* 355-57.

20. Mark 1.5, 9; Matt. 3.5-6, 13; Luke 3.3; John 1.28.

21. Mark 1.5/Matt. 3.5; Luke 3.21; cf. John 1.19-25; 3.25.

22. John 1.23; Mark 1.3; Matt. 3.3/Luke 3.4. Mark gives the quotation a headline role, combined with Exod. 23.20; Luke extends the quotation (Isa. 40.3-5), presumably to round it off with the reference to 'the salvation of God' (Luke 3.4-6); John abbreviates the Isa. 40.3 quotation, combining the last two lines in one (John 1.23).

23. John 1.27; Mark 1.7; Luke 3.16; Matt. 3.11. The variations are typical of oral variation in retelling the same tradition: John uses *axios* ('worthy'), while the others use *hikanos* ('qualified/competent'); in Matthew's version the Baptist says 'I am not qualified/competent to *carry* his sandals'; John has singular 'sandal', while the others have the plural ('sandals').

- the Baptist's contrast between his own mission of baptizing in water and the coming one's baptizing in the Holy Spirit;[24]
- that Jesus was baptized by the Baptist is taken for granted, though John does not actually say so explicitly, whereas the event is described by the others (John 1.31; Mark 1.9 pars.);
- all four are clear that the central and climactic event of the encounter between the Baptist and Jesus is that the Holy Spirit descended 'like a dove' upon him (John 1.32-33; Mark 1.10 pars.);[25] this is the real beginning of the gospel (cf. Acts 10.38);
- the descent of the Spirit is tied in to Jesus' status as the Son of God: in the Synoptics by the declaration of the heavenly voice which accompanied the descent of the Spirit ('You are my son, the beloved one, with you I am well pleased' — Mark 1.11 pars.); in John by the Baptist's testimony that because he saw the Spirit descending and remaining on Jesus, therefore he could 'bear witness that this man is the Son of God' (John 1.34);
- the imprisonment of the Baptist (John 3.24; cf. particularly Luke 3.19-20).

There can be little doubt that all four Evangelists were drawing on the same tradition — the memory of Jesus' first disciples that his mission emerged out of the successful mission of the Baptist and from what happened at the Jordan when Jesus was baptized by the Baptist, that is, with the descent of the Holy Spirit on him, confirming his status as God's Son.[26] Almost the only part of the Baptist's teaching recalled by all four Evangelists is the Baptist's contrast between his own baptizing in water

---

24. John 1.26, 33; Matt. 3.11/Luke 3.16; Mark 1.8. In Matthew the Baptist baptizes with water 'for/into repentance' (Matt. 3.11); Matthew/Luke have the Baptist predicting that the one to come will baptize in Holy Spirit *and fire*' (Matt. 3.11/Luke 3.16), whereas Mark and John have the Baptist speaking only of baptizing in Holy Spirit (Mark 1.8; John 1.33); the Synoptics predict that the one to come 'will baptize in Holy Spirit', whereas John has it as a defining characteristic of the one to come — 'the one who baptizes in the Holy Spirit'.

25. Mark indicates that the Spirit descended 'into' Jesus (Mark 1.10), whereas Matthew/Luke describe the Spirit descending 'upon' Jesus (Matt. 3.16/Luke 3.22), and John emphasizes that 'the Spirit descended and remained on him' (John 1.33); Mark also gives the event an apocalyptic character — the heavens split (*schizomenous*); Luke notes that the Spirit descended while Jesus was praying (Luke 3.21); and John has the Baptist admitting that he did not know him until he saw the Spirit descend upon him (John 1.33).

26. The Evangelists generally seem to think of Jesus as Son of God without giving too much weight to language which seems to imply that Jesus *became* Son of God at any time — at the Jordan? (Mark 1.10-11); at birth? (Matt.1-2/Luke 1-2); at resurrection? (Acts 13.33; similarly Heb. 1.5; 5.5); from eternity? (John).

and the coming one's baptizing in the Spirit, which strongly suggests that their consciousness of having been given the Spirit was one of the self-defining characteristics of the early Christians across the range of churches represented by the four Gospels, a claim to being the beneficiaries of the promised baptism in the Spirit predicted by the Baptist. Both emphases, that Jesus' mission began with the Spirit's descent on him after he had been baptized by the Baptist, and that the first Christians were those who were experiencing the Spirit directly for themselves, explain why the great body of earliest Christians had to begin their account of the gospel with the preaching and mission of the Baptist.[27] We can take it for granted that this memory and this basic story were integral to the oral tradition of the first disciples and churches from the first.[28]

Other substantial overlaps include:[29]

- 2.14-22 — the cleansing of the temple, though located by John at the beginning of Jesus' mission (Mark 11.15-17 pars.);
- 4.46-54 — the healing of the royal official's son (cf. Matt. 8.5-13/Luke 7.1-10);[30]
- 6.1-21 — the combination of the two miracles, feeding of the five thousand and Jesus walking on the water (Mark 6.32-52 par.);[31]
- 6.68-69 — the confession of Peter (Mark 8.29 pars.);
- 12.1-8 — the anointing at Bethany (Mark 14.3-9 pars.);[32]
- The Johannine passion narrative shares the same structure as its Synoptic equivalents, each of them with its own distinctive features and

---

27. This would seem to include the Q material (Robinson et al., *Q* 4-21); note also Acts 10.37-38.
28. See also Robinson, *Priority* ch. 4.
29. See also Schnelle, *History* 497-98.
30. See below n.91.
31. See *Jesus Remembered* 683-89. The fact that John has retained the close sequence between the feeding of the five thousand and the walking on water miracles (6.1-21; Mark 6.32-52 pars.), even though the accompanying discourse develops the significance only of the former, strongly suggests that these two miracles were already so firmly attached to each other in the various forms of the tradition that it would have raised more questions to omit the latter than it did to retain it as the undeveloped twin. See also P. N. Anderson, *The Christology of the Fourth Gospel: Its Unity and Disunity in the Light of John 6* (Valley Forge, PA: TPI, 1996).
32. See *Jesus Remembered* 522-24; also Dodd, *Historical Tradition in the Fourth Gospel* 162-73, and my 'John and the Oral Gospel Tradition', in H. Wansbrough, ed., *Jesus and the Oral Gospel Tradition* (JSNTS 64; Sheffield: Sheffield Academic, 1991) 351-79 (here 365-67). I draw heavily on this essay and on its sequel (n.33) in what follows. Both essays are reprinted in *The Oral Gospel Tradition*.

characteristics, though once again John shows how varied at least some re-presentations of the final part of Jesus' mission could be;[33]
- The account of the miraculous catch of fishes in 21.1-14 may be a reworking of the tradition which Luke uses in Luke 5.1-11.[34]

These all share the Synoptic-like character of the oral Jesus tradition — the same yet different — pointing to the same conclusion: that these are variations of the same core tradition which can be traced back to the beginnings of the Jesus tradition.[35] Evidently different members of the initial disciple group drew somewhat varying emphases from what was a shared stream of tradition, each with memories of the same period, events and teachings, but distinctively their own memories on individual details.

Still more striking, however, are the further historical details which John gives, not least in regard to the tradition which he shares with the Synoptics. Here again the Baptist tradition is the most illuminating. For John seems to have been able to draw on *tradition which the others had either set to one side or did not know about*. He does not hesitate to include reference to a period prior to the Baptist's imprisonment (3.24), during which Jesus' mission overlapped with the Baptist's (John 3.22-36) and during which Jesus' mission was apparently of the same character as the Baptist's (3.22-26), though John takes care to deny that Jesus himself practised baptism (4.2).[36] This tradition almost

---

33. See also my 'John's Gospel and the Oral Gospel Tradition', in A. Le Donne and T. Thatcher, eds., *The Fourth Gospel in First-Century Media Culture* (LNTS 426; London: T & T Clark, 2011) 157-85; reprinted in *Oral Gospel Tradition* 164-95. Note the somewhat surprising fact that John retains the note of suffering from the Gethsemane scene (John 12.27; 18.11), even though it contrasts with John's own portrayal of the calmness with which Jesus faced the prospect of the cross (for John, part of Jesus' 'glorification'). Dodd concludes his lengthy discussion of the passion narrative: 'there is cumulative evidence that the Johannine version represents (subject to some measure of "writing up" by the evangelist) an independent strain of the common oral tradition, differing from the strains of tradition underlying Mark (Matthew) and Luke, though controlled by the same general *schema*' (*Historical Tradition* 150). See also Schnelle, *History* 500-502. For a recent attempt to reconstruct the pre-Johannine passion narrative see F. Scherlitt, *Der vorjohanneische Passionsbericht: Eine historisch-kritische und theologische Untersuchung zu Joh 2,13-22; 11,47–14,31 und 18,1-20, 29* (BZNW 154; Berlin: de Gruyter, 2007).

34. M. Labahn, 'Peter's Rehabilitation (John 21:15-19) and the Adoption of Sinners: Remembering Jesus and Relecturing John', in Anderson et al., eds., *John, Jesus and History* vol. 2, 335-48, prefers to speak of 'memory' rather than 'tradition' (335 n.1), and sees 21.1-14 as a Johannine oral retelling of Luke 5.1-11, an example of 'secondary orality' (341).

35. See also A. J. B. Higgins, *The Historicity of the Fourth Gospel* (London: Lutterworth, 1960).

36. A. T. Lincoln, '"We Know That His Testimony Is True": Johannine Truth Claims and Historicity', in Anderson et al., eds., *John, Jesus and History* vol. 1, 179-97, suggests that

certainly goes back to the first disciples, since it includes the detail that some of Jesus' own key disciples had earlier been the Baptist's disciples (1.35-42).[37] Neither detail nor emphasis was likely to have been invented given the degree of embarrassment indicated elsewhere in the Jesus tradition over the extent to which Jesus could be counted as himself a disciple of the Baptist.[38]

Deserving of note is the clear evidence of how the oral Jesus (and Baptist) tradition could be and was handled:

- by omitting a not unimportant aspect of the tradition in order to prevent any confusion between the two missions and to highlight the distinctiveness of Jesus' mission (Synoptics);[39]
- or by focussing the retold tradition on the Baptist's witness-bearing to Jesus and on his inferior significance to that of Jesus (John).[40]

The fact that the Synoptic tradition ignored or suppressed the overlap period, of course, makes it difficult for us to evaluate the Johannine tradition in the usual way (by comparing John's version with that of the Synoptics). But we can be sufficiently confident that *the Johannine tradition too goes back to the first disciples*, and indeed, in this case, *has retained a clearer memory of the overlap period than we could have deduced from the Synoptic tradition*. A simple uniform rule that the Synoptic tradition is always more reliable than John's is immediately ruled out.[41] John's version of the beginning of Jesus' mission is itself an example of how the memory of that overlap was handled in at least one strand of earliest Christianity or in some churches.

Other examples of the extra detail given by John:[42]

- In the cleansing of the temple episode, John has Jesus saying, 'Destroy this temple, and in three days I will raise it up' (John 2.19), the very words which Mark and Matthew attribute to *false* testimony at Jesus' trial (Mark 14.58/Matt. 26.61). It is hard to avoid the conclusion that Jesus was remembered as having said something like this, and that while

---

there may be 'slightly fewer difficulties' with the hypothesis 'that the discussion of Jesus baptizing is the result of the creativity of the Fourth Evangelist or his tradition' (187-91).

37. See also Dodd, *Historical Tradition* 279-87, 302-5.
38. Note again particularly Matt. 3.14-15.
39. See *Jesus Remembered* 350-53.
40. See below §43.1c(1).
41. On this point certainly Anderson's protest against the 'de-historicization of John' and the 'de-Johannification of Jesus' is valid (*Fourth Gospel* 2).
42. See also D. Moody Smith, 'Jesus Tradition in the Gospel of John', *The Fourth Gospel in Four Dimensions* ch. 7.

the way it was turned against Jesus at his trial amounted to false witness, Jesus did in fact predict the destruction of the temple (cf. Mark 13.2 pars.) and possibly/probably also spoke about its rebuilding (whatever he meant by that).[43] In which case, *John is a better witness to Jesus than the Synoptics, and shows how the oral memory of what Jesus had said was retained in the Jesus tradition, despite the way it was used against Jesus* (a similar conclusion can be drawn from Acts 6.14).[44] John's version also strengthens the probability that Jesus gave this teaching in the context of his cleansing of the temple, and that it was the combination of the two (the event and the teaching) which determined the temple authorities to take action against him.[45]

- Between the two miracles in John 6.1-14, 16-21, John has inserted the note that the crowd wanted to 'take Jesus by force to make him king' (6.15). This is very plausible as recalled historical data (understandably passed over by other tradents), not least because it helps explain the oddities of Mark's account at the same point.[46]
- Some maintain that John's dating of Jesus' crucifixion to the day before the Passover is more accurate than that of the Synoptics, though I personally doubt it.[47]

One of the most striking differences between the Synoptics and John is that whereas the Synoptics focus on Jesus' mission in Galilee, the bulk of John's narrative focuses on Judaea and Jerusalem — 2.13–3.36; 5.1-47; 7.10 onwards. It is not unlikely that Jesus did pay more visits to Jerusalem or did spend longer time in Judaea and Jerusalem than the Synoptic tradition allows:[48]

---

43. See again discussion in *Jesus Remembered* 630-33; also J. F. McGrath, '"Destroy This Temple": Issues of History in John 2:13-22', in Anderson et al., eds., *John, Jesus and History* vol. 2, 35-43.

44. See further *Beginning from Jerusalem* §24.2c.

45. Cf. E. P. Sanders, *Jesus and Judaism* (London: SCM, 1985) 61, 72-76.

46. See *Jesus Remembered* 645-47.

47. John's dating probably reflects his theology of Jesus' death as that of the Passover lamb (John 1.29; 19.33 fulfilling the regulations regarding the Passover lamb — Exod. 12.46). 'The Johannine date of the last supper and crucifxion seems to be due to John's determination to make clear that Jesus was the true Paschal Lamb of God' (Barrett, *John* 51). See e.g. discussion in Lincoln, *Saint John* 44-46. Contrast Koester: 'John has preserved the more original and historically accurate date' (*Ancient Christian Gospels* 255); and for a recent restatement of the case for dating the crucifixion according to John's chronology, see M. A. Matson, 'The Historical Plausibility of John's Passion Dating', in Anderson et al., eds., *John, Jesus and History* vol. 2, 291-312.

48. See also *Jesus Remembered* 323-24. See also Robinson, *Priority* ch. 3 ('The Chronology of the Ministry'), and the essays by B. D. Johnson and S. Freyne, in Anderson et al., eds., *John, Jesus and History* vol. 2, 117-29, 139-54.

- The early period of overlap between the missions of the Baptist and Jesus suggests early mission in Judaea (cf. John 3).
- Luke records the close discipleship of Mary and Martha (Luke 10.38-42), and though he locates them in a village passed through on the journey to Jerusalem, John is clear that the village was Bethany, close to Jerusalem (John 11.1, 18; 12.1-8).[49]
- The 'How often' of Jesus' lament over Jerusalem in Matt. 23.37-38/Luke 13.34-35 suggests more frequent mission trips to Jerusalem.
- The fact that the Synoptics omitted such an important element of Jesus' mission as its beginnings within the Baptist movement heightens the likelihood that they have done something the same with regard to a mission of Jesus in Judaea and Jerusalem. That is to say, it is quite possible that John's focus on such mission of Jesus is more firmly rooted than the Synoptics allow.
- That Jesus had close disciples in Jerusalem or in the near environs is suggested by the (secret?) disciples who provided the donkey for his entry into Jerusalem (Mark 11.2-3 pars.) and the room for the last supper (Mark 14.12-16 pars.).

In that case, why did the Synoptic tradition ignore or set to one side Jesus' earlier Jerusalem visits? The fact that they deliberately excluded the overlap period with the Baptist is evidence enough that they felt free to do so. And perhaps Mark or the tradition on which he drew wanted to make the (final) visit to Jerusalem the climax of the Jesus story, and Matthew and Luke in doing so simply followed him (or their main stream of tradition). Since the leadership of the earliest Jerusalem community of believers in Messiah Jesus were all Galileans, one could understand why the tradition which they began and taught focused on the Galilean mission.

John, of course, does not ignore the Galilean mission, even though Jesus' coming and going to Galilee in the early chapters of his Gospel does read rather awkwardly.[50] The miracles included in that material (4.46-54; 6.1-21) are, as noted above, the closest to the Synoptic miracle tradition. But the likelihood grows throughout John's Gospel that John had a source for the mission of Jesus which was different from, or rather in addition to, the remembrances of Peter — the figure indicated (and obscured) by the reference to him as 'the

---

49. Jesus lodged in Bethany during his last week (Mark 11.11-12 par.; 14.3 par.). The depiction of Martha and Mary in John 12.1-2 (Martha served; Mary focused attention on Jesus) echoes the similar presentation of Luke 10.39-42. See also R. J. Bauckham, 'The Bethany Family in John 11-12: History or Fiction', *Testimony* ch. 8; also in Anderson et al., eds., *John, Jesus and History* vol. 2, 185-201.

50. John 2.1, 12, 13; 4.1-3, 43-46; 5.1; 6.1, 59; 7.1, 9, 10.

one whom Jesus loved' (13.23; 19.26; 21.7).[51] If that disciple is also referred to in 1.35-39, then he would have been a good source for the overlap period between the Baptist's and Jesus' missions (including the recruitment of the Baptist's disciples to become followers of Jesus). Similarly if that disciple is also referred to in 18.15-16, then he had good contacts in Jerusalem (he was known to the high priest!). This suggests that this disciple could have known or cherished memories of Jesus' mission in Jerusalem on one of his brief visits to the capital, as also episodes and contacts (like Nicodemus and Joseph of Arimathea) which the other tradents largely ignored,[52] since the Galilean tradition was more familiar and so full in itself.[53] With only John's attestation for the Judaean mission, and given the freedom with which the tradition he used or drew upon has represented the memories of Jesus' overall mission, it is difficult to draw firm conclusions. But the most likely explanation is that *John has drawn on good memories of one or more visits to Jerusalem by Jesus, even if he has treated them in his own distinctive parabolic or symbolic terms.*

iii. The Teaching of Jesus

The contrast between on the one hand the Synoptics' aphoristic sayings and parables, and on the other hand the Johannine discourses can be overdrawn. For, as we shall see, Jesus' teaching in John includes some parabolic material. And, most intriguing, the Johannine discourses often seem to grow out of or to be based on more aphoristic teaching of Jesus as evidenced by the Synoptic tradition.[54]

- 3.5 — 'Very truly I tell you, unless a person is born from water and Spirit he cannot enter into the kingdom of God'; Matt. 18.3 — 'Truly I

---

51. See above §39 n.150.

52. Joseph is mentioned by all the Gospels at the end (Mark 15.43 pars.; John 19.38); but Nicodemus appears only in John (3.1-9; 7.50; 19.39). Note Bauckham's interesting speculation that Nicodemus belonged to the wealthy and powerful Gurion family (*Testimony* ch. 7).

53. Similarly with regard to any mission in Samaria (John 4), whereas the Synoptics show why such mission might have been excluded (Matt. 10.5; Luke 9.52-54). See also S. Miller, 'The Woman at the Well: John's Portrayal of the Samaritan Mission', in Anderson et al., eds., *John, Jesus and History* vol. 2, 73-81.

54. See further Dodd, *Historical Tradition* 335-65 (particularly 347, 349, 360-61); Dunn, 'John and the Oral Gospel Tradition' 356-58. See also C. M. Tuckett, 'The Fourth Gospel and Q', and E. K. Broadhead, 'The Fourth Gospel and the Synoptic Sayings Source', in Fortna and Thatcher, eds., *Jesus in the Johannine Tradition* 280-90 and 291-301 respectively; Bauckham, *Testimony* 106-12. A much briefer sequence in Schnelle, *History* 497-98. But about 70 verses in the Johannine discourses can be said to have Synoptic parallels. See also Anderson, *Fourth Gospel* 52-53, 60-62, 131-32.

tell you, unless you turn and become like children, you will never enter into the kingdom of heaven'. This is the only passage in which John has retained a Synoptic-like reference to 'the kingdom of God' (Matthew — 'of heaven'). In John the entry-requirement is stated in similar but more radical terms and is the base point for the more extended teaching of 3.3-15/21.[55]

- 3.29 — likening Jesus' presence to the presence of the bridegroom, as marking the difference between Jesus and the Baptist, echoes Mark 2.19-20 pars.
- 5.19-30 — the exposition of the close relationship between the Father and the Son and of the authority given by the Father to the Son may well have grown out of teaching like Matt. 11.27/Luke 10.22 (cf. also John 3.35).
- 6.20 — the close similarity with Mark 6.50 suggests that John's distinctive 'I am' sayings may have been suggested to him by the story of Jesus' epiphanic appearance walking on the water.[56]
- 6.26-58 — the great bread of life discourse reads like an extensive reflection on Jesus' words at his last supper with his disciples — 'This is my body', 'This is my blood' (Mark 14.22, 24 pars.).
- 8.31-58 — the lengthy discussion on the significance of Jewish descent from Abraham could have grown out of the Baptist's warning to his fellow Jews not to rely on having Abraham as their ancestor (Matt. 3.7-10/Luke 3.7-9).
- 10.1-18 — Jesus' elaborated claim to be the good shepherd is most simply explained as growing out of Jesus' use of the imagery of sheep, particularly his parable of the lost sheep.[57]
- 12.24-26 — perhaps a slight elaboration of Jesus' own teaching, as in Mark 8.35, about the cost of discipleship.
- 13.13-16 — the account of Jesus washing his disciples' feet (13.1-11) could well be an extension and 'visual aid' to illustrate teaching like Matt. 10.24-25.
- 14.16-17, 15.26-27 and 16.4-15 — the repeated promise that the Holy

---

55. See also C. C. Caragounis, 'The Kingdom of God: Common and Distinct Elements Between John and the Synoptics', in Fortna and Thatcher, eds., *Jesus in the Johannine Tradition* 125-34. Anderson observes that John has a number of 'king' references (*Fourth Gospel* 54), but the point of comparison is with Jesus' preaching of the kingdom of God. Although Koester deserves great credit for his emphasis on the oral Jesus tradition, he has not taken the point that in oral tradition talk of 'the original form' of a saying is at best misleading — as here in *Ancient Christian Gospels* 258.

56. Cf. Anderson, *Fourth Gospel* 56-58.

57. Matt. 18.12-13/Luke 15.4-7; also Mark 6.34; Matt. 10.6; 15.24; Luke 12.32.

Spirit would teach the disciples probably began with the elsewhere remembered assurance of Jesus that the Spirit would inspire what they should say (Mark 13.11 pars.).

- We should add that the *'Amēn, Amēn'* introductory formula so regularly used by John[58] is obviously drawn from the tradition, well-known in the Synoptics, of Jesus' introducing a saying with 'Amen'.[59]
- Note also that several enriched versions of Synoptic-like exhortations pepper chs. 13-16:
    - 13.16 — Matt. 10.24/Luke 6.40;
    - 13.20 — Matt. 10.40/Luke 10.16;
    - 13.34-35 — Mark 12.28-31 pars.;
    - 15.14-15 — cf. Mark 3.35 pars.;
    - 15.16 — Mark 11.23-24 pars.;
    - 15.18-21 — Mark 13.13 pars.;
    - 16.1-4 — Mark 13.9, 12-13 pars./ Matt.10.17-18, 21-22;
    - 16.23-24 — Matt. 7.7/Luke 11.9;
    - 16.32 — Mark 14.27 par.[60]

It should also be noted that the discourses contain a number of parables not dissimilar to the more characteristic Synoptic form,[61] and three sequences of sayings again closer to the Synoptic pattern.[62] Not least of significance is the fact that the overlap with the Synoptic tradition at point after point in-

---

58. John 1.51; 3.3, 5, 11; 5.19, 24, 25; etc.

59. *Jesus Remembered* 700-701 and n.418. B. Lindars, *Behind the Fourth Gospel* (London: SPCK, 1971), claims that the 'Amen, Amen' formula is 'a recurring sign that John is making use of a saying of Jesus from his stock of traditional material' (44). See further R. A. Culpepper, 'The Origin of the "Amen, Amen" Sayings in the Gospel of John', in Fortna and Thatcher, eds., *Jesus in the Johannine Tradition* 253-62.

60. J. Beutler, 'Synoptic Jesus Tradition in the Johannine Farewell Discourse', in Fortna and Thatcher, eds., *Jesus in the Johannine Tradition* 165-73, boldly concludes 'that John 13-17 is pervaded by early Jesus tradition, mostly tradition of a synoptic character and perhaps even derived from the Synoptics themselves', though 'no single coherent discourse source can be uncovered. Rather, there has been creative use of the traditional material, forging it into a new form that expresses F(ourth)E(vangelist)'s peculiar view of Jesus . . .' (173).

61. John 3.29; 5.19-21; 8.35; 10.1-5; 11.9-10; 12.24; 16.21; see Dodd, *Historical Tradition* 366-87; also Lindars, 'Tradition' 33. Robinson notes 13 or 14 Johannine parables (*Priority* 319-20).

62. John 4.31-38; 12.20-26; 13.1-20; see Dodd, *Historical Tradition* 388-405. Tom Thatcher, 'The Riddles of Jesus in the Johannine Dialogues', in Fortna and Thatcher, eds., *Jesus in the Johannine Tradition* 263-77, notes the substantial body of riddles in the Johannine dialogues. Since riddles are a widely attested oral form, he suggests that at least some of these sayings circulated orally in Johannine circles before the Fourth Gospel was written,

dicates an independent awareness of the teaching which the early churches all remembered as Jesus' teaching.[63] The relative lack of reworking by John at these points is both what allows us to recognize the parallel (the shared memory of the same teaching) and what enables us to say with confidence that John's discourses are rooted in the memories of what Jesus taught during his mission, in Galilee or in Judaea.

In short, for all their difference in style, and the elaboration and enrichment of individual sayings and motifs, it would appear that several of the discourses of John's Gospel are deeply rooted in Synoptic-like tradition. In addition, the possibility should not be excluded that John knew other Synoptic-like tradition, not picked up in the Synoptic tradition itself, and treated it in similar manner — as a theme to be developed and elaborated in similar discourse style. Are the Johannine discourses then simply an example of how radically and extensively the Jesus tradition could be elaborated within the churches of the emerging Christianity of the late first century?[64]

b. How Did John Go About Composing His Gospel?[65]

It can be assumed that the production of John's Gospel in its final form was the end-result of a lengthy process. The beginning and ending of the process are fairly clear. We have seen enough evidence that a fair amount of the content of John's Gospel can be traced back to first-generation believers, to eye- and ear-witnesses who belonged to Jesus' own close disciples; the Baptist tradition in John's Gospel alone is sufficient indication and illustration of that conclusion. It is equally evident that a final redaction added both John 21 and the final third-party attestation of 21.24.[66] Between that beginning and ending, however, the character of the process is obscure and open to many varied speculations. Has the final version undergone very substantial

---

and that some of the larger dialogues may also have circulated orally as riddling sessions (he refers particularly to John 8.12-58). See also Kümmel, *Introduction* 201.

63. See further Schnackenburg, *St. John* 1.26-43.

64. 'The formation of the sayings of Jesus into the Johannine discourses represented a profound theological synthesis' (Brown, *John* 1.xlix).

65. As in the previous sections, 'John' here denotes the author of John's Gospel. In this case 'John' may best be identified as the one who gave the Gospel of John its distinctive character, though not the final redactor. See also above §39.2d.

66. John 20.30-31 marks an obvious conclusion, that is, to an earlier draft or edition. See further Kümmel, *Introduction* 207-15; Schnelle, *History* 490-92. J. Ashton, *Understanding the Fourth Gospel* (Oxford: Clarendon, 1991), concludes: 'the only major sections of the Gospel that cannot be directly accredited to the evangelist are (a) the signs source which he took over and adapted [see below n.68] and (b) the concluding chapter in its present form' (166).

editing, as Rudolf Bultmann famously argued?[67] Was the author able to draw on different sources? — the most plausible suggestion being that he was able to draw on a 'Signs source'.[68] Can the stages of development or composition be disentangled from the finished product, even different editions be envisaged?[69] For example, was there a Samaritan phase of development?[70] Was the prologue of John's Gospel (John 1.1-18) a relatively late addition?[71] Might it be the case that the final form of John's Gospel was not actually intended to be the final form, in which some of the anomalies and disjunctions would have been ironed out?[72] Or indeed, is it possible that the Gospel was never intended to be 'finished', but consists actually of a number of 'moving parts' within the Gospel structure, allowing a flexibility and variation in use of the Gospel in worship and meditation?[73]

Perhaps the longest running debate has been whether John knew one or more of the Synoptic Gospels — perhaps reckoning with their inadequacies and attempting to make good the defects. The argument that John did know and owed a debt to one or more of the Synoptics has some substance — the

---

67. R. Bultmann, *The Gospel of John* (1941, 1964; ET Oxford: Blackwell, 1971) xiii and Index, 'Redaction' (736); critique in D. M. Smith, *The Composition and Order of the Fourth Gospel* (Yale University, 1953); brief critique in Schnelle, *History* 485-86.

68. Particularly R. T. Fortna, *The Gospel of Signs* (SNTSMS 11; Cambridge: Cambridge University, 1970); idem, *The Fourth Gospel and Its Predecessor* (Philadelphia: Fortress, 1988); Fortna and Thatcher, eds., *Jesus in the Johannine Tradition* chs.17-20; critique in Lindars, *Behind the Fourth Gospel* 31-42; other bibliography in Schnelle, *History* 494 n.167, 513-15, and critique 494-96 and n.169. Ashton's discussion of John's notion of Messiah (*Understanding* ch. 7) is too dominated by his assumption that John had a Signs source. On the OT as a 'source' see e.g. Schnackenburg, *St. John* 121-24; Barrett, *John* 27-30 — 'an essential element in the background of the gospel' (30).

69. E.g. Brown, *John* 1.xxxii-xxxix; Lindars, *Behind the Fourth Gospel* 43-60; idem, *The Gospel of John* (NCB; London: Oliphants, 1972) 47-48, 51-54; Lincoln, *Saint John* 50-55.

70. Brown, *Community* 36-40; idem *Introduction* 363-64; Ashton, *Understanding* 294-99; other bibliography in J. F. McGrath, *John's Apologetic Christology: Legitimation and Development in Johannine Christology* (SNTSMS 111; Cambridge: Cambridge University, 2001) 17 n.45.

71. M. Theobald, *Die Fleischwerdung des Logos* (Münster: Aschendorff, 1988); also '"Der älteste Kommentar zum Johannesevangelium" (R. F. Collins)', *Studien* 41-75 (here 50-51).

72. The most commonly referred to instances are the abrupt transition from Jerusalem (ch. 5) to Galilee (6.1) and the fact that 14.31 ('Rise, let us be on our way') is followed by two more chapters of discourse (chs. 15-16). It is generally agreed that John 7.53–8.11 was a later addition. See further Schnackenburg, *St. John* 1.44-58; Brown, *John* 1.xxvi-xxviii; Kümmel, *Introduction* 204-7, 216-17; Barrett, *John* 21-26; Koester, *Ancient Christian Gospels* 246-50; Schnelle, *History* 486-89.

73. There is a parallel, perhaps, in the Worship or Order Book of many churches today, which allow a variation of content/liturgy within a fixed frame.

parallels noted above certainly give grist for the mill — and continues to be maintained with some force.⁷⁴ Unfortunately the argument is in part at least a product of the same literary mind-set which has skewed so much of the discussion of the Gospels over the last century and a half. For most of this period, the dominant working hypothesis has been that any similarity between the Gospels indicates a literary influence of one on the other, or a literary influence from a common (written) source.⁷⁵

The working hypothesis of the present study is different: that there was a lengthy period (20-30 years) during which the Jesus tradition was known and used almost entirely in oral form; and that during that period the Jesus tradition was celebrated, taught, transmitted in various forms, the variety much as we still find it in the Synoptic tradition.⁷⁶ Here we need simply add that the Synoptic tradition, while typical of the way the Jesus tradition was known and used, should not be regarded as the sum total of the Jesus tradition.⁷⁷ The corollary of that hypothesis in the case of John is then clear: that John knew much Synoptic-like tradition; or the Johannine tradition began from Synoptic-like material. Since there is no clear case of literary copying by John of Synoptic tradition, it makes better sense of John, in the context of a predominantly oral society and predominantly oral Christian community, to conclude that Synoptic-like tradition was part of the bedrock material on which the Johannine presentation of Jesus was founded.⁷⁸

---

74. Kümmel, *Introduction* 202-4; Barrett, *John* 15-18, 42-54; A. Denaux, ed., *John and the Synoptics* (Leuven: Leuven University, 1992); Lincoln, *Saint John* 29-38; Thyen, *Johannesevangelium* 4. For other bibliography see D. M. Smith, *Johannine Christianity* (Columbia: University of South Carolina, 1984) chs. 6 and 7; also *John Among the Gospels: The Relationship in Twentieth-Century Research* (Minneapolis: Fortress, 1992).

75. Kümmel argues that John knew Mark and Luke from memory (*Introduction* 204); Bultmann (*John* 6) and Schnelle (*History* 499-502) deduce from the fact that John uses the Gospel format that he must have been aware of the Gospel of Mark; other bibliography supporting the view that John knew one or more of the Synoptic Gospels in Schnelle, *History* 502 n.184. Gregory concludes that the parallels and affinities between Luke and John (notably Luke 24.12/John 20.3-10) can be as readily explained by common sources or common oral tradition (*Reception of Luke and Acts* 69).

76. See also J. Dewey, 'The Gospel of John in Its Oral-Written Media World', in Fortna and Thatcher, eds., *Jesus in the Johannine Tradition* 239-52.

77. The fact that, for example, Luke was able to draw on so much tradition unknown to or unused by the other Synoptic Evangelists (§42.4a n.314) points in the same direction; and note again John 21.25.

78. I acknowledge the debt which I particularly owe here to Dodd, *Historical Tradition*; also Lindars, *Behind the Fourth Gospel*. P. Gardner-Smith, *St John and the Synoptic Gospels* (Cambridge: Cambridge University, 1938), is to be credited as the first to make effective protest against the dominant thesis of the Fourth Gospel's dependence on the Synoptics (other bibliography in Robinson, *Priority* 11 n.27). Brown was heavily influenced

So far as the final form of the Gospel itself is concerned, it would appear that John felt free to mould the tradition available to him in his own distinctive way.

i. The Frame of Jesus' Mission

So far as the frame of Jesus' mission is concerned, John differs quite markedly from the Synoptics. Luke, for example, used Jesus' sermon in the synagogue of Nazareth to provide a window into the character of Jesus' mission which Luke wanted to highlight (Luke 4.16-30). In contrast, John provides a double *opening bracket*:

- *The marriage at Cana* (John 2.1-11) — a tradition totally unknown to the Synoptics, though possibly illustrating the point made in the earlier tradition, about the wedding-like character of Jesus' mission (Mark 2.18-19 pars.), by telling it as a story rather than as formal teaching.[79] The symbolism is obvious: water intended for Jewish rites of purification (2.6) transformed into high quality wine (2.10), illustrating the transformation brought by Jesus' mission, quite probably once again as a way of making the same point as in Mark 2.21-22 pars.
- *The cleansing of the temple* (2.14-22). Most probably this is John's version of the tradition shared by the Synoptics, but placed by them at the *end* of Jesus' mission. It is highly unlikely that there were two such episodes in Jesus' mission, one at the beginning and the other at the end. Apart from anything else, the two accounts have precisely the same character — the sellers of animals and doves are expelled from the temple precincts, and the tables of the money-changers are overturned, with some variation in detail as one would expect in an oral tradition.

The conclusion which follows most naturally is that John has elected to begin his account of Jesus' mission with the cleansing of the temple episode, because, together with the wedding at Cana, it *foreshadowed and epitomized*

---

by Dodd (*John* 1.xliv-xlvii). In charting the lengthy debate on John's relationship to the Synoptic Gospels, Smith seems still to favour Dodd's solution (*John Among the Gospels*); see also B. Witherington, *John's Wisdom* (Louisville: Westminster John Knox, 1995) 5-9. When sources cannot be readily distinguished and characterized, the image of 'trajectory' is at best conjectural and probably misleading — as in Robinson, 'The Johannine Trajectory', in Robinson and Koester, *Trajectories* ch. 7 (see also n.207).

79. Dodd notes that Jesus is recalled as telling several parables featuring wedding feasts (he refers to Matt. 22.1-14; 25.1-13, and Luke 12.35-36) and suggests that 'the traditional nucleus of this *pericope* may have been a parable' (*Historical Tradition* 226-27). See also Lincoln, "We Know That His Testimony Is True" 191-95.

the effect of Jesus' mission in relation to his native Judaism:[80] he would transform the Jewish purity ritual into new wine; he would replace the temple with his own body (John 2.21) — just as subsequently, the water he gave is far superior to the water of Jacob's well (4.12-14); and as the bread of life from heaven, he far transcends the bread which Moses gave (6.30-35); etc.[81] Somewhat as Luke moved Jesus' preaching in the synagogue at Nazareth to the forefront of his account, to indicate the character of what was to follow, so John felt free (evidently) to move the climactic cleansing of the temple likewise to set the scene and epitomize what was to follow.[82] This may seem an overbold move, but only if we assume that the Evangelists were bound to order their material in strict chronological order, an assumption which we have no reason to make and which runs counter to too much evidence to be followed without question.[83]

If John felt free to shape the beginning of his account of Jesus' mission, he felt equally or more free to construct the *closing bracket*, the event which sparked off the decision to do away with Jesus. In the Synoptics it was the symbolical 'cleansing of the temple' which set off the final spiral of opposition to Jesus,[84] and led directly to the arrest of Jesus made possible by Judas's betrayal (Mark 14.10-11 pars.). John, however, provides a quite different trigger. In John's Gospel, it is *the recalling of Lazarus from the dead* which is the immediate trigger to the final moves against Jesus. The signs which Jesus had performed, climaxing in the recall of Lazarus to life, led the high priest himself to the conclusion that it was better for one man to die than for the whole nation to be destroyed (John 11.47-53, 57). John reinforces the point by narrating how famous the raising of Lazarus became, and how threatening to the status quo the resulting support for Jesus and his message quickly became (12.9-11, 17-19).

---

80. Cf. A. R. Kerr, *The Temple of Jesus' Body: The Temple Theme in the Gospel of John* (JSNTS 220; London: Sheffield Academic, 2002).

81. See further, e.g., Lincoln, *Saint John* 76-78.

82. Anderson is the most recent to argue that Mark's chronology for the cleansing of the temple is wrong; it is John who gave the temple incident its proper historical context and thus was correcting Mark (*Fourth Gospel* 32, 48, 67, 70-71, 111-12, 158-61). But the episodes of John 4-5 hardly presuppose or depend on the temple incident, and, if an early 'cleansing' evoked opposition such as Anderson sees in John 5.18, then the time interval between the 'cleansing' and Jesus' arrest is entirely surprising. See further John Painter's review of Anderson in *RBL* (http://www.bookreviews.org/bookdetail.asp?TitleId=5879). See also M. A. Matson, 'The Temple Incident: An Integral Element in the Fourth Gospel's Narrative', in Fortna and Thatcher, eds., *Jesus in the Johannine Tradition* 145-53.

83. The words of Papias are regularly quoted on this point: that Mark 'wrote accurately all that he remembered, not, indeed, in order, of the things said or done by the Lord' (Eusebius, *HE* 3.39.15).

84. Mark 11.18/Luke 19.47-48; Mark 12.12 pars.; 14.1-2 pars.; cf. Matt. 21.15-16.

Of this raising of Lazarus from the dead (11.1-44), none of the other Evangelists show any awareness.[85] One could conceive that the earlier tradition set that episode on one side, for fear that the authorities might act against Lazarus (cf. John 12.10). But the Synoptics were most probably written about forty or more years after the event. Would that still be a factor then, when the vicinity of Jerusalem had been devastated during the siege and conquest of Jerusalem, and its residents widely scattered? Moreover, the Johannine presentation seems to reflect the beliefs and concerns of the later Johannine churches: the sign of Lazarus's recall to life prefiguring Jesus' own resurrection (11.4-5, 23-27); the high priest unwittingly confessing that Jesus died 'for the nation . . . and to gather into one the dispersed children of God' (11.51-52); many of the Jews believing in Jesus (12.11); the expanding influence of Jesus being counteracted by expulsion from the synagogue of those who believed in Jesus (12.42); all this reflecting the high and distinctive Johannine christology.[86]

It is hard to avoid the conclusion that John moved the account of the cleansing of the temple to the beginning of his Gospel to provide a window through which the unfolding of Jesus' mission and revelation should be seen. And that he did so also to make room for his own version of the climax to Jesus' mission, the climax which triggered the decisive action against Jesus. More has to be said about the raising of Lazarus, but it is best said in the context of John's account of Jesus' signs.

ii. Jesus' Mission of Healing

Equally striking is the way John has structured Jesus' mission of healing (John 3–12), in what C. H. Dodd designated as 'the Book of Signs'.[87] John seems to work to a pattern of a characteristic miracle which highlights an aspect of Jesus' mission and its significance. No type of miracle is repeated. It appears to be the case that John has taken six characteristic miracles, perhaps even miracle types, in order to draw out the significance of each. That significance is typically brought out by *the often lengthy discourse or dialogue which is attached to the miracle*, before or after. The point is underlined by the term which John uses consistently for the miracles — 'sign',[88] a sign-ificant event which conveys a meaning

---

85. The character Lazarus appears only in John (John 11.1-44; 12.1-2, 9-10, 17). The only other Lazarus in the NT is the beggar by that name in Jesus' parable of the rich man and Lazarus (Luke 16.20-25).

86. John 11.4, 25-26; 12.27-36, 44-50.

87. C. H. Dodd, *The Interpretation of the Fourth Gospel* (Cambridge: Cambridge University, 1953).

88. John 2.11, 23; 3.2; 4.48, 54; 6.2, 14, 26, 30; 7.31; 9.16; 10.41; 11.47; 12.18, 37; 20.30. Despite traditions like Matt. 12.28/Luke 11.20 and Mark 3.27 pars., exorcisms did not func-

far larger than the event itself.[89] The most persistent themes are new life[90] and light from darkness, as already signalled in the prologue (1.4-5, 7-9, 13):

- 2.1-11 — water to wine, first sign (2.11) — significance indicated by the clues (third day, 2.1; wedding; water of purification rites; a sign which revealed his glory, 2.11);
  - 3.1-21 — dialogue with Nicodemus on new birth (3.3-8, 15-16, 19-21);
- 4.46-54 — saving a royal official's son from death — emphasis on life (4.50-53), second sign (4.54), though also a warning against a faith based solely on signs (4.48; cf. 2.23-25);
  - corollary to the water of life discourse with the Samaritan woman (4.7-26, especially 4.10, 14), and reaping the fruit for eternal life (4.35-36) already in Samaria (4.29-30, 39-43);
- 5.1-9 — healing of a paralyzed man — a more traditional format (healing on a Sabbath);
  - 5.10-47 — dialogue with 'the Jews' focusing on the christological significance of Jesus so acting on the Sabbath (the theme returned to in 10.11-39), but also on Jesus' working as indicating the life which is in the Son and granted by the Son (5.24-26, 40);
- 6.1-14 — feeding of five thousand, attached to the walking on water (6.16-21);
  - 6.25-65 — the great bread of life discourse (particularly 6.27, 33, 35, 40, 47, 48, 51, 53-54, 57-58, 63; rounded off by Peter's confession, 6.68);
- 9.1-7 — healing of a blind man;
  - led into by preceding discussion begun with Jesus' promise of the light of life (8.12), and leading into extensive discourse on blindness and sight (9.8-41);
- 11.1-44 — recalling Lazarus from death — significance emphasized from the beginning (11.4);
  - discourse on eternal life despite and through death (particularly 11.23-26), prior to the miracle itself.

---

tion sufficiently as 'signs' for John; see also G. H. Twelftree, 'Exorcisms in the Fourth Gospel and the Synoptics', in Fortna and Thatcher, eds., *Jesus in the Johannine Tradition* 135-43.

89. See also U. Schnelle, *Antidocetic Christology in the Gospel of John* (1987; ET Minneapolis: Fortress, 1992) ch. 3.

90. See further M. Labahn, *Jesus als Lebensspender: Untersuchungen zu einer Geschichte der johanneischen Tradition anhand ihrer Wundergeschichten* (BZNW 98; Berlin: de Gruyter, 1999): 'the Fourth Evangelist presents the wonder working Jesus, occasionally more implicit but often explicit, simply as the life-giver' (501).

One of the questions which this raises is whether John draws the actual miracles which he relates from his tradition. Or does he provide a sequence of miracle types, (a) partly drawn from specific tradition (feeding of the five thousand, healing a child at a distance), (b) partly illustrating types of healing for which Jesus was famous (of paralysis and blindness), and (c) partly stories which express the richest significance of Jesus even if not actually rooted in specific events (water of Jewish purification into abundant and high quality wine, recalling Lazarus to life).

(a) The first of these possibilities is already intriguing, since John's account of the healing of the royal official's son is so different from the parallel in Matthew and Luke,[91] and since virtually the only significant points of agreement between John and the Synoptics, on what is obviously the same tradition of the feeding of the five thousand, are the actual numbers (5,000, 200 denarii, 5 loaves and 2 fishes, 12 baskets of fragments).[92] Here is *important evidence of the degree to which the same memory and tradition could be diversely retold.*

(b) The second of the possibilities suggests that John or his tradition had no qualms in telling the story of Jesus using *types* of his healing ministry rather than any particular instances.[93]

(c) The third possibility cannot be excluded, since it is so hard to locate both the water into wine miracle[94] and the recalling of Lazarus to life[95] within Jesus' mission, and since they so powerfully illustrate the effect of Jesus' mission. This could suggest that *John or his tradition felt free to document Jesus'*

---

91. The possibility that the healing of the royal official's son is a variation of Matthew's and Luke's account of the healing of the centurion's boy certainly cannot be excluded (see Dodd, *Historical Tradition* 188-95; and my 'John and the Oral Gospel Tradition' 359-63; also *Jesus Remembered* 212-16). See also P. J. Judge, 'The Royal Official and the Historical Jesus', in Anderson et al., eds., *John, Jesus and History* vol. 2, 83-92, with Craig Koester's response (102).

92. See also 'John and the Oral Gospel Tradition' 363-65. Anderson also concludes that the contacts between Mark and John have to be traced back to the oral stages of their tradition (*Fourth Gospel* 29-30).

93. Similarly Dodd, *Historical Tradition* 174-88; see also my 'John and the Oral Gospel Tradition' 374.

94. The provision of 480-720 litres of wine would certainly be grotesque as a historical event; but as a symbolical parable it was very powerful. See also n.79 above and Lincoln, "We Know That His Testimony Is True" 196-97.

95. If we assume that John knew one or more of the raisings from the dead miracles attributed to Jesus by the earlier tradition (Jairus's daughter — Mark 5.35-43 pars.; Luke 7.11-15), he presumably thought they were not climactic enough for his purpose. He may also have known the tradition that Jesus himself claimed to raise the dead (Matt. 11.5/Luke 7.22). So a parabolic story of Jesus raising a dead person was hardly unjustified especially when it could serve as such a fitting climax to his own retelling of Jesus' mission. See further the careful discussions of Dodd, *Historical Tradition* 228-32; and Lincoln, *Saint John* 531-35.

mission with parabolic stories and not only actual remembered events. If this is the case, it would be quite wrong and a serious misunderstanding of John and his purpose to accuse him of deception. That is to say, *the evidence of John's Gospel itself suggests that we should not assume that he saw his role as simply recalling memories of actual events of Jesus' mission, or simply reciting the earlier tradition, in the fashion of the Synoptics.*[96] John may have concluded that to bring out the full significance of Jesus' mission he had to retell the tradition in bolder ways which brought out that significance more clearly.

iii. The Johannine Discourses

As to the Johannine discourses, it is the rootage of the Johannine discourses, in tradition which echoes and parallels Synoptic tradition, which suggests the most plausible way to understand these discourses — viz. that they are discourses and themes which express reflection over some time on things Jesus said and taught and enacted, reflection in the light of the richer christology which Jesus' resurrection and exaltation had opened up to them.[97] In other words, they exemplify not simply the passing on of Jesus tradition, but the way that tradition stimulated their understanding of Jesus in the light of what had happened subsequently.[98]

John himself attests and justifies this very process.

- Twice he explicitly notes that Jesus' disciples did not understand what Jesus was saying or doing, but that they remembered it and later understood it in the light of Jesus' resurrection and glorification.[99] This makes precisely the point that the claims regarding Jesus were rooted in Jesus' own mission as illuminated by Easter. His immediate disciples already had a true knowledge of Jesus during his mission (6.69; 17.7-8), but they did not fully understand; their knowledge was still imperfect.[100]

---

96. Anderson's criticism that I claim Baur and Strauss are correct in disparaging John's Gospel as a historical source (*Fourth Gospel* 2 n.4) ignores what I actually say, that 'John's Gospel cannot be regarded as a source for the life and teaching of Jesus of the same order as the Synoptics' (*Jesus Remembered* 166).

97. Cf. Beutler, 'Synoptic Jesus Tradition in the Johannine Farewell Discourses', *Neue Studien* 89-97, sums up: 'John 13–17 is pervaded by early Jesus tradition, mostly tradition of a synoptic character and perhaps even derived from the Synoptics themselves' (97).

98. Koester finds evidence in the *Dialogue of the Saviour* that 'dialogues were initially developed in the process of the interpretation of sayings of Jesus' (*Ancient Christian Gospels* 173-81, 256-57); see further below §44.5a.

99. John 2.22; 12.16; similarly 13.7; 14.20; 16.4. 'Stemming from the Johannine theology of the incarnation, such misunderstanding has become a studied literary technique' (Brown, *Introduction* 335-36, referring also to 3.3-4; 4.10-11; 6.26-27; 8.33-35; 11.11-13).

100. John 8.28, 32; 10.6, 38; 13.28; 14.9. See also T. Thatcher, 'Why John Wrote a

- To the same effect is the role ascribed to the Spirit/Paraclete. During Jesus' mission 'the Spirit was not yet', that is, presumably, not yet given (7.39). But when the Spirit came he would teach Jesus' disciples everything and remind them of all that Jesus had said to them (14.26); he would guide them into all truth and declare more of Jesus' truth that they were as yet unable to bear (16.12-13).[101] This is the same balance, between revelation already given and received, and fuller revelation still to come, a fuller revelation which makes the revelation already given clearer and which enables it to be more fully grasped.[102]

In short, it is hard to doubt that *John's version of Jesus' teaching is an elaboration of aphorisms, parables, motifs and themes remembered as characteristic of Jesus' teaching, as attested in the Synoptic tradition*. At the same time, John's version was not pure invention, nor did it arise solely out of Easter faith. Rather it was elaboration of typical things that Jesus was remembered as saying. Unlike the later 'Gospels', John does not attribute the fuller insight into who Jesus was to secret teaching given to a few following Jesus' resurrection. Rather, he roots it in the Jesus tradition which he shared with other churches (who presumably knew mainly the Synoptic tradition) and which was

---

Gospel: Memory and History in an Early Christian Community', in A. Kirk and T. Thatcher, eds., *Memory, Tradition, and Text: Uses of the Past in Early Christianity* (Semeia Studies 52; Atlanta: SBL, 2005) 79-97 (particularly 82-85); also *Why John Wrote a Gospel: Jesus — Memory — History* (Louisville: Westminster John Knox, 2006) 24-32.

101. In his review of Anderson's *Fourth Gospel* (n.82 above), Painter observes: 'the historical tradition in John has been thoroughly shaped by deep theological reflection from a perspective that makes difficult the separation of the tradition from the later theological development. It is the degree to which this has happened in John that separates it from the Synoptics. That need not rule out continuity between the tradition and the interpretation, but it does not mean that the interpretation is in some sense already present in the tradition, even if it is rooted there and in some way grows out of it. The experience of the resurrection and the Spirit created Johannine interpretation that was not foreseen or foreseeable beforehand'. See further Painter, 'Memory Holds the Key: The Transformation of Memory in the Interface of History and Theology in John', in Anderson et al., eds., *Jesus, John and History* vol. 1, 229-45 (especially 238-45). Thatcher draws on social memory theory to explain *Why John Wrote a Gospel*. Theobald quotes J. Zumstein: 'the remembering consists not simply of holding unalterable and complete facts in the memory, but of arranging them from a perspective which allows their true meaning to emerge' ('"Erinnert euch der Worte, die ich euch gesagt habe . . ." [Joh 15, 20]', *Studien* 256-81 [here 279]).

102. The dialectic of the Johannine conception of revelation here is summed up in the word *anangellō*, which John uses three times in 16.13-15, and which can have the force of 're-announce', 're-proclaim', but also denote the announcing of new information/revelation in 16.13. Arthur Dewey, 'The Eyewitness of History: Visionary Consciousness in the Fourth Gospel', in Fortna and Thatcher, eds., *Jesus in the Johannine Tradition* 59-70, speaks of 'anticipatory memory' (65-67).

itself rooted in the memory of Jesus' mission. This was the truth of Jesus for John — not a pedantic repetition of Synoptic-like tradition, but the significance of that tradition brought out by the extensive discourses which John or his tradition drew out of particular features of Jesus tradition as exemplified in the Synoptic Gospels.[103] To criticize John's procedure as inadmissible is to limit the task of the Evangelist to simply recording deeds and words of Jesus during his mission.[104] But John evidently saw his task as something more — the task of drawing out the fuller meaning of what Jesus had said (and done) by presenting that fuller understanding as the Spirit both *reminding* Jesus' disciples of what Jesus had said and *leading them into the fuller understanding of the truth* made possible by Jesus' resurrection and ascension.

c. The Good News about Jesus

As in §42, we turn from the question 'How' to the question 'Why': Why did John compose his Gospel? What did he hope to achieve? Almost uniquely among the NT Gospels, John provides a precise answer to that question: 'These (things) are written in order that you might believe that Jesus is the Christ, the Son of God, and that believing you might have life in his name' (20.31).[105] John's first goal was evangelistic and christological: to persuade those who heard his Gospel read to them that they should believe[106] in Jesus Christ, the Son of God.

i. Jesus Is Messiah

More than a little intriguing is the fact that John is the only NT writer who refers to Jesus as 'Messiah' (*Messias*). One of the Baptist's disciples, Andrew, finds his brother and makes the second Christian confession:[107] '"We have

---

103. 'The "I am" sayings sum up and express insights which can only have been reached through a profound reflection on the essence of Jesus' message, a reflection culminating in the realization that what Jesus came to bring was nothing other than himself' (Ashton, *Understanding* 187).

104. 'The discourses in John cannot and do not intend to be historical reporting or a word for word record' (Schnackenburg, *St. John* 1.23; and more fully, 19-25).

105. The textual uncertainty — whether *pisteuēte* or *pisteusēte* should be read (Metzger, *Textual Commentary* 256) — leaves some uncertainty as to whether the objective was simply evangelistic ('that you might come to believe'), or also pastoral/catechetical ('that you might go on believing'). Brown (*John* 1.lxxviii) and Kümmel (*Introduction* 229) strongly favour the latter alternative; in that case Luke 1.4 would provide a parallel.

106. On the twofold sense, 'believe *that*' and 'believe *in*', see below §43.1d(i).

107. In literary sequence, the first *de facto* Christian confession was that of the Baptist: 'This is the Son of God' (1.34).

found the Messiah (*Messias*)", which [John adds] is translated Christ (*Christos*)' (1.41). And the Samaritan woman at the well expresses the hope: 'I know that Messiah is coming who is called Christ' (4.25); to which Jesus responds, 'I am (he), the one speaking to you' (4.26).[108] What is so intriguing is the fact the Hebrew term 'Messiah' is used for the first time in the NT, in what is generally regarded as one of the latest of the NT writings. And yet the evidence was already clear in the earliest NT writings (those of Paul) that 'Christ' had largely lost its titular significance ('the Christ/Messiah')[109] and become more or less equivalent to a proper name ('Jesus Christ').

The significance of this is twofold. First, we have further confirmation that much of the tradition drawn on by John bears the stamp of very early concerns in the embryonic Christian movement, as also well reflecting pre-70 Jewish expectation.[110] Here the two conversations recorded are a reminder that one of the primary concerns of the first disciples after Easter was to affirm and demonstrate that Jesus was indeed Messiah, the Christ.[111] Second, still more intriguing, is the fact that John, writing late in the first century, regarded it as necessary to continue to assert that Jesus *was* Messiah. This presumably indicates that *the question of Jesus' messiahship was still a live issue* for those whom John was seeking to reach by means of his Gospel.

The ways in which John adapts the Jesus tradition to make this claim are fascinating. Here again the use made of the traditions regarding the Baptist provides an excellent illustration of the way the Jesus tradition functioned in John's Gospel. So, first here, we notice how John presents *the Baptist as witness par excellence* to Jesus, and does so by *narrowing* the Baptist tradition so that it focuses almost exclusively on that role (already signalled in John 1.6-8):[112]

- the contrast between the Baptist and Jesus (1.27)[113] is heightened (already in 1.15; also 1.30, and elaborated in 3.27-36);
- Jesus' baptism by John is passed over, as also any reference to John's

---

108. This in fact is the first of the 'I am' sayings, though here it could be more colloquially translated: 'It is me'.

109. 'Largely' is a key term here; Paul Trebilco reminds me of my *Theology of Paul* 198-99.

110. Bauckham, 'Jewish Messianism according to the Gospel of John', *Testimony* ch. 10.

111. *Beginning from Jerusalem* 214-16.

112. John 1.7-8, 15, 19, 32, 34; 3.26, 28; 5.33-34, 36. The point was made very effectively by W. Wink, *John the Baptist in the Gospel Tradition* (SNTSMS 7; Cambridge: Cambridge University, 1968) 87-106.

113. See above n.23.

as a baptism of 'repentance' (the word never occurs in John's Gospel), and so also any embarrassment at Jesus submitting to such a baptism;[114]
- the Baptist makes a triple confession ('he confessed and did not deny it, but confessed' — 1.20) that he was not the Messiah, not even Elijah or the prophet (1.20-21);
- the Baptist attests of Jesus that he is 'the Lamb of God who takes away the sin of the world' (1.29, 36), already foreshadowing Jesus' death;
- the Baptist emphasizes that the main, or indeed only, purpose of his own mission was to reveal Jesus to Israel, his true status as the Son of God (1.31, 34).[115]

It is fascinating, then, to see how the same basic tradition was and could be retold and elaborated, or curtailed, to bring out the different emphases that the Evangelists wanted brought out. Nothing tells against this already happening during the time when the Jesus tradition was almost entirely in oral mode. To be sure, John's use of the tradition suggests that he was consciously combating what he regarded as a too high evaluation of the Baptist.[116] Hence, we may deduce, the sustained downgrading of the Baptist in relation to Jesus:

- he was not the light but came only to testify to the light (1.6-8, 31);
- the Messiah always ranked before him (1.15, 30);
- he was not the Messiah, as he himself triply confessed (1.20; 3.28);
- he had to decrease while Jesus increased (3.30);
- he came from the earth, whereas Jesus came from above, from heaven (3.31).

This we should note comes in typically Johannine language, so that we can certainly speak of the Johannine elaboration of the earlier tradition, whether that elaboration is to be traced to the Evangelist himself or to the (elaborated) traditions on which he drew. But we should also note that *the distinctive Johannine emphasis is rooted in the earlier tradition* — of the Baptist speaking of the one to come as of a far higher status than his own ('I am not worthy to untie the thong of his sandals' — Mark 1.7 pars.).

---

114. Cf. again Matt. 3.13-15.

115. Thus he also omits other aspects of the Baptist's message, particularly his fierce warnings of imminent judgment (Matt. 3.7-10, 12/Luke 3.7-9, 17).

116. This is an old hypothesis usually traced back to W. Baldensperger, *Der Prolog des vierten. Evangeliums: sein polemisch-apologetischer Zweck* (Tübingen: Mohr, 1898); see also e.g. Schnackenburg, *St. John* 167-69; Brown, *John* 1.lxviii-lxx. The indication of groups of Baptist disciples in Ephesus (Acts 19.1-7) implies that the influence of the Baptist's mission (independently of that of Jesus) was quite widespread for some time.

The Johannine version of the Baptist tradition can thus be seen as a good example of a tradition deeply rooted in the memory of the first disciples, a tradition which was retold in different ways, all drawn from these earliest memories: some *abbreviating* the tradition selectively, presumably in order that it might speak more meaningfully to the new audiences; others *elaborating* it, but as an elaboration of early emphases rather than as an invention and insertion of entirely new emphases. *The elaboration created new material, but only to reinforce the earlier emphasis*, perhaps against a new and challenging evaluation of the Baptist's mission. John's version of the Baptist tradition, therefore, illustrates both the fixity and core material in the Baptist tradition, and the way in which key elements in that tradition could be developed and retold in unexpected ways as the language and needs of the Johannine churches changed.

A second intriguing feature is the prominence of the Messiah/Christ issue in ch. 4, what might be categorized as Jesus' mission in Samaria. This presumably reflects the fact that the Samaritans had a similar hope and expectation as Israel — for the coming of a 'Messiah' or Taheb, who would introduce 'a period of divine favour, a second kingdom', by uniting all Israel, crushing her enemies and exalting the Samaritan people.[117] This again suggests that the passage may well be rooted in a historical episode in which the issue of Jesus' messiahship was raised in reference to Samaritan hope and expectation, whether in the course of a passage through Samaria by Jesus himself (cf. Luke 9.52), or in the early Hellenist expansion (Acts 8).[118] John uses the passage in developing his own plot, particularly as posing the hesitant question: 'Could this possibly be the Christ?' (4.29).[119]

A third intriguing feature of John's Gospel is the way he develops the plot signalled by this last question of the Samaritan woman. For the question of Jesus' messiahship re-emerges in ch. 7 as a major motif. The crowd ask anxiously, 'Can it possibly be that the authorities know that he is the Christ?' (7.26). They weigh the options: 'We know where this man

---

117. J. Macdonald, *The Theology of the Samaritans* (London: SCM, 1964) 74-75, 79-80, 359-71. The Samaritan documents on which Macdonald's survey is drawn derive from a much later period, but John 4.19-26 is probably sufficient evidence that such hopes were already current in the first century. Macdonald also notes that 'Pontius Pilate lost his office in Palestine because of the savage way in which he quelled a riot in Samaria which arose as a result of one claiming to be the expected "Messiah"' (361, citing Josephus, *Ant.* 18.85-89).

118. O. Cullmann, *The Johannine Circle* (London: SCM, 1976), made much of John 4.38 at this point (46-49); see also M. Theobald, 'Die Ernte ist da! Überlieferungskritische Beobachtungen zu einer johanneischen Bildrede (Joh 4,31-38)', in *Studien* ch. 6.

119. Or, translated as denoting even more uncertainty, as the Greek implies, 'He cannot be the Messiah, can he?' (NRSV).

comes from; but when the Christ comes no one will know where he comes from' (7.27). Yet, 'when the Christ comes will he perform more signs than this man has done?' (7.31). And again the question of where he comes from: some say 'He is the Christ'; but others point out that the Christ will surely not come from Galilee, since scripture expects the Davidic Messiah to come from Bethlehem (7.41-42). The debate continues through the rest of the Book of Signs, with some believing and confessing Jesus as the Christ (9.22; 11.27), but others still swithering in uncertainty (10.24; 12.34). This motif, we may fairly infer, was well rooted in the earliest memories of Jesus' mission. For the question whether Jesus was/could be Messiah was almost certainly a live issue during Jesus' mission. The impact he made would naturally have aroused the hopes of many (and suspicions of others).[120] So John is again drawing on good tradition, and his dramatization of the issue in this way is wholly understandable and should be uncontroversial. Moreover, the further implication seems to be that John was pitching his presentation of Jesus as the Messiah/Christ precisely with a view to those represented by 'the crowd' — those still asking, Could it be that Jesus is, after all, the Messiah?[121] He still cherished the evangelistic hope of persuading them 'that Jesus is the Christ' (20.31). We will have to return to this subject later (§46.5c).

John does not hesitate to include the thought that Jesus is 'king of Israel' (1.49; 12.13), though he is more hesitant on the assertion that Jesus is 'the king of the Jews',[122] and he has Jesus make it clear that his kingdom is 'not from here', that is, not of this world (18.36). The claim to be Israel's royal Messiah is affirmed but transcended, and any this-world political overtones are defused.[123]

The claim that John still perceived the possibility of persuading his fellow Jews of Jesus' messiahship, and wrote his Gospel with that aim, also helps explain why he consistently presents the central tenets and praxis of Israel's religion as pointing to Jesus and completed in him[124]— so much so, this is the unspoken corollary, that there is no longer any need of them. We have already noted some of the data.

---

120. *Jesus Remembered* §15.3.
121. See further below §43.1d.
122. John 18.33-37, 39; 19.3, 14-15, 19-22.
123. Presumably this was also a factor in John's ignoring the kingdom of God as a major feature of Jesus' message.
124. See also M. J. J. Menken, 'Die jüdischen Feste im Johannesevangelium', in M. Labahn et al., eds., *Israel und seine Heilstradition im Johannesevangelium* (Schöningh: Paderborn, 2004) 269- 86.

- The theme is announced in the prologue. 'The law was given through Moses; grace and truth came through Jesus Christ' (1.17).
- Jesus is the (Passover) lamb that takes away the sins of the whole world (1.29); also 19.33-36.
- The water reserved for the rites of purification is transformed into an abundance of quality wine (2.6-10).
- The temple is to be destroyed and replaced by the temple of Jesus' risen body (2.19-21); that is, Jesus is now the locus of the divine presence.
- Moses' bronze serpent giving life to those bitten by serpents in the wilderness (Num. 21.6-9) is surpassed by the lifting up of the Son of Man to give eternal life to all who believe in him (3.14-15).
- The water of Jacob's well is far surpassed by the living water provided by Jesus (4.10-14).
- The scriptures testified of Jesus, and Moses wrote about Jesus, calling the listeners to come to him and believe in him and to have life (5.39-47).
- Jesus is more than a/the prophet (6.14),[125] greater than Moses who gave bread from heaven — the fathers who ate the manna died (6.49, 50, 58) — for Jesus is the true bread from heaven (6.32-35) which gives eternal life to all who eat it (6.50-51, 58).
- The importance of water rituals in the Feast of Tabernacles (*sukkoth*)[126] and the imagery of Zech. 14.8 are the context in which Jesus claims to be the source of the living water which will flow from within the believer (7.37-38)[127]— Jesus fulfilling the anxiety for rain for which prayers were offered at the feast.[128]
- Descent from Abraham is trumped by the double claim that Abraham rejoiced at the prospect of Jesus' day and that Jesus was ('I am') before Abraham (8.56-58).
- The feast of Dedication, commemorating the rededication of the temple by Judas Maccabeus (1 Macc. 4.41-46), after the disastrous course

---

125. The hope for a prophet like Moses (Deut. 18.15, 18) was an important part of Jewish expectation and played a role in earliest christology (see my *Christology in the Making* 138-41).

126. See e.g. Brown, *John* 1.326-27. 'That it was called simply "The Feast" shows that Tabernacles was the most popular of all Jewish feasts' (Barrett, *John* 310, on 7.2, and citing Josephus, *Ant.* 8.100).

127. Depending on how 7.37-38 is punctuated, the one from whom the rivers of living water flow could be either Jesus or the believer (discussion in Brown, *John* 1.320-23; Barrett, *John* 326-27), but either way the assumption would be that Christ himself is the source of the 'living water' (as in 4.10, 14).

128. See again Barrett, *John* 327-28. See also M. B. Spaulding, *Commemorative Identities: Jewish Social Memory and the Johannine Feast of Booths* (LNTS 396; London: T & T Clark, 2009).

followed by high priests Jason and Menelaus (2 Macc. 4.7-50), may well already have used readings with the theme of sheep and shepherds (particularly Ezek. 34)[129]— an appropriate setting (John 10.22) for Jesus' claim to be the good shepherd in succession to the thieves and bandits who had preceded him (10.1-18).

- Ironically it is Caiaphas, the high priest, who prophesies that Jesus was to die for the nation, 'and not for the nation alone, but to gather into one the dispersed children of God' (11.49-52) — Israel's hope for the restoration of the dispersed tribes being absorbed into John's understanding of the effective outcome of Jesus' death.
- Jesus' claim to be 'the true vine' (15.1) would almost certainly evoke in Jewish ears the familiar imagery of Israel as a vine.[130] As with the other similar claims — 'the true light' (1.9), 'the true bread from heaven' (6.32) — Jesus is presented as the true claimant to that description over against others for whom the claim could be made (the Baptist, the manna, even Israel itself).

In short, the belief that Jesus is the Christ, which John hoped to inculcate in and by means of his Gospel, was not the belief that Jesus was the Messiah that 'the Jews' probably hoped for (cf. John 6.15). It was the Messiah as attested by the Baptist, the Messiah who fulfilled Israel's hopes but who also transcended them, and in so doing redefined those hopes. The preparation and prefigurement had reached their intended goal in Jesus the Christ. So, the Jews who hesitated and disputed whether Jesus met all the expectations for the Messiah should hesitate no longer. Jesus was indeed the Messiah, the Christ who both met and exceeded their expectations.

Very little of all this is drawn from the earlier Jesus tradition, though there are various points of contact, as previously noted. But this whole theme is more obviously to be seen as the fruit of lengthy reflection on the life and mission of Jesus and on their significance for Israel's scriptures and for its convictions, hopes and praxis. The earlier 'messianic secret' motif of Mark in particular, with its own modest elaboration of the Jesus tradition (if John knew of it), is almost entirely left behind.[131] In John, Jesus is now openly and boldly presented as the Messiah/Christ from the very beginning. Characteristic of Johannine elaboration is the degree to which old stories of Sabbath controversy have been submerged in chs. 5 and 9 by the christological implications now drawn from them — with

---

129. Brown, *John* 1.388-89.
130. Ps. 80.8-16; Isa. 5.1-7; 27.2-6; Jer. 2.21 ('I planted you as a choice vine, all of it true seed'); 12.10-13; Ezek. 15.1-8; 17.5-10; 19.10-14.
131. Cf. Barrett, *John* 71.

the fact that a healing took place on the Sabbath day[132] being almost redundant and merely incidental to the main christological thrust of the passages.

ii. Jesus Is the Son of God

The reinterpretation of Israel's messianic hope is continued and sharpened in the theme of Jesus as the Son of God. For in 20.31, 'the Son of God' is an explanatory addition to the primary assertion, 'Jesus is the Christ'. Rich as 'Messiah' was in meaning for a Jewish audience, it was more obscure for a wider audience. In contrast, 'Son of God' had much greater resonance and richer overtones, both for a Jewish audience, accustomed to the thought both of the king and of Israel as God's son, and for a wider audience accustomed to kings and iconic figures lauded as sons of God, betokening an intimacy of divine favour and authority.[133]

This indeed is John's principal means of identifying Jesus and his significance — that Jesus is God's Son. Although the title was important for the Synoptics, it does not feature much in their Gospels. Only in Matthew is the Father-Son language extended. But in John the imagery becomes a cascade.[134] 'The Father who sent me' becomes the most regular way in which Jesus speaks of and identifies God.[135] Notable features of John's Son christology include:

- The clearest confessions in John's Gospel are those of the Baptist (1.34 — 'he is the Son of God'), of Nathanael (1.49 — 'You are the Son of God'),[136] and of Martha (11.27 — 'You are the Christ, the Son of God . . .').
- The uniqueness of Jesus as 'the one and only (*monogenēs*) Son' is repeated in the opening chapters (1.14; 3.16, 18; also 1.18).[137] This too trumps Israel's sense of being God's favoured child.[138]

---

132. John 5.9-10, 16, 18; 9.14, 16; contrast Mark 2.23–3.6 pars.; Luke 13.10-17; 14.1-6.

133. See e.g. my *Christology in the Making* 14-16. That Messiah was also understood to be God's son was implied in the use of 2 Sam. 7.14 and Ps. 2.7 as messianic texts; so already at Qumran (1QSa/1Q28a 2.11-12; 4QFlor/4Q174 1.10-18).

134. Jeremias noted the tremendous expansion of references to God as 'Father' in the words of Jesus within the Jesus tradition — Mark 3, Q 4, special Luke 4, special Matthew 31, John 100 (*Prayers of Jesus* 30, 36).

135. John 4.34; 5.23, 24, 30, 37; 6.38, 39, 44; 7.16, 18, 28, 33; 8.16, 18, 26, 29; 9.4; 12.44, 45, 49; 13.20; 14.24; 15.21; 16.5; also 3.17; 3.34; 5.36, 38; 6.29, 57; 7.29; 8.42; 10.36; 11.42; 17.3, 8, 18, 21, 23, 25; 20.21.

136. Nathanael has just been hailed by Jesus as being 'truly an Israelite' (1.47).

137. 'Though *monogenēs* means in itself "only of its kind", when used in relation to *father* it can hardly mean anything other than only(-begotten) son' (Barrett, *John* 166). See further BDAG 658; F. Büchsel, *monogenēs*, *TDNT* 4.740-41; and below §49.3b.

138. Exod. 4.22; Jer. 31.9; Hos. 11.1; see also e.g. Deut. 14.1; Isa. 43.6; Hos. 1.10.

- The sending motif is probably drawn from the Jewish and Greco-Roman convention of the envoy or ambassador, having plenipotentiary authority; and particularly from the Jewish understanding of the prophet as sent by God (used also in 1.6; 3.28), though since Jesus' messianic status transcends that of (the) prophet, so the divine agency of Jesus' mission from the Father also transcends that of the prophet.[139]
- The motif includes the thought of Jesus' authorisation from the Father: 'he sent the Son into the world to judge the world' (5.22, 27); 'the Father placed all things in his hands' (3.35); 'the Son can do nothing on his own, but only what he sees the Father doing' (5.19); 'the Father has granted the Son to have life in himself' (5.26).
- In John 'the Son of Man' motif is aligned with that of the Son of God:[140]
  - the apocalyptic Son of Man 'coming on the clouds of heaven' disappears from view, and the Son of Man 'descending from heaven' (3.13) complements the Son of God sent by the Father;[141]
  - in 5.27 it is the Son of Man to whom God gives the authority to judge, when Jesus has just said that the Father has given all judgment to the Son (5.22);
  - in 9.35-38 the belief invited by Jesus from the erstwhile blind man is belief 'in the Son of Man';
  - and the more modest way in which the Synoptics link the confession of Jesus as Son of God to his crucifixion (Mark 15.39/Matt. 27.54) is left well behind in John's theme that the Son of God (11.4), or more typically the Son of Man, is 'lifted up' and 'glorified' in his death and resurrection.[142]

---

139. See particularly P. Borgen, 'God's Agent in the Fourth Gospel' (1968), in J. Ashton, ed., *The Interpretation of John* (Edinburgh: T & T Clark, ²1997) 83-95; J.-A. Bühner, *Der Gesandte und sein Weg im 4. Evangelium* (WUNT 2.2; Tübingen: Mohr Siebeck, 1977) 181-267. 'Jesus' relationship with God continues throughout to be conceived on the analogy of the prophetic mission and the law of agency' (Ashton, *Understanding* 316). 'The Sent One not only represents the Sender, but the sending is as though the Sender himself has come; he not only brings a message, but is himself the message' (Schnelle, *Theology* 681). See also McGrath, *John's Apologetic Christology* 89-95.

140. 'The titles of Son of Man and Son of God have become interchangeable for John' (Ashton, *Understanding* 339, citing J. L. Martyn, *History and Theology in the Fourth Gospel* [Nashville: Abingdon, ²1979] 134 n.193).

141. See also 6.33, 38-42, 50-51, 58, 62; cf. 1.51. The somewhat surprising assertion of 3.13 — 'No one has ascended into heaven, except the one who descended from heaven' — may be directed against the characterization of the patriarchs and prophets as those who in effect ascended into heaven to hear (first hand) what God said, as suggested originally by H. Odeberg, *The Fourth Gospel* (Stockholm: Almqvist & Wiksell, 1929) 72-98.

142. John 3.14; 8.28; 12.23; 13.31, 34. Ashton comments: 'In the case of the Fourth

This Son of God/Son of Man christology of John's Gospel has certainly to be regarded as a substantial development within the Jesus tradition. But here not least the roots of the development are still very clear:

- Jesus' repeated talk of himself as *the Son* to God as Father is an obvious elaboration of the much more limited early memory of Jesus' praying to God as 'Abba', perhaps already elaborated in the Synoptic tradition;[143]
- Similarly Jesus' repeated talk of his having been *sent* by the Father is an obvious elaboration of the memory of Jesus' occasional self-reference in similar terms;[144]
- Similarly the elaboration of Jesus' undoubted use of the phrase 'the son of man',[145] by adding the thought of his *descent and ascent* and of his *being lifted up glorified*.
- It should perhaps be added that John includes the thought of Jesus as God's *only* (*monogenēs*) Son only in his own editorial work and does not present Jesus as making the claim for himself.

One of the most interesting aspects of the way the Jesus tradition was thus developed is that so many who knew the Synoptic Gospels also welcomed John's Gospel. We cannot assume that the issue of historicity was a factor for them. Even so, however, it is significant that a presentation so different, so developed and so shaped by editorial design and skill commended itself to the extent that John's Gospel did. By the third generation of Christianity, we may deduce, Christians were not concerned only to know what Jesus said and did, but wanted to think through its deeper significance. This was presumably the need and desire to which John responded, and his Gospel was the result.

iii. Jesus Is the Divine Word and Wisdom

The most distinctive feature of John's christology catches immediate attention in the Gospel's prologue — so simple in formulation, so profound in the claim it makes.

(1) The Gospel begins:

> In the beginning was the Word, and the Word was with God, and the Word was God. He was in the beginning with God. All things came into being through him, and without him not one thing that has come into being came

---

Gospel "passion" is a misnomer; Jesus controls and orchestrates the whole performance' (*Understanding* 489).

143. *Jesus Remembered* 711-24.
144. Mark 9.37 pars.; 12.6 pars; Matt. 15.24; Luke 4.18; 10.16.
145. *Jesus Remembered* §§16.4-5.

into being.¹⁴⁶ In him was life, and the life was the light of humankind. And the light shines in the darkness, and the darkness has not overcome it (John 1.1-5).

It is very likely that John chose to open his Gospel by focusing on the 'Word' (*logos*) because this term would speak with meaning to both Jews and Greeks.¹⁴⁷

'The word of God' would have been very familiar to all religious Jews, not least as a phrase regularly used in Israel's scriptures, usually in reference to inspired prophecy — 'the word of Yahweh came to Abr(ah)am', to Moses, Joshua, and the prophets.¹⁴⁸ Central to the thought was that an utterance of Yahweh had power to accomplish what it asserted, because it was the word of God. In creation, 'God said, "Let there be . . ."; . . . and it was so' (Gen. 1.3, 6-7, etc.). So the Psalmist naturally writes, 'By the word of Yahweh the heavens were made' (Ps. 33.6). And in the oracle of Isaiah God declares, 'The word that goes forth from my mouth shall not return to me empty, but it shall accomplish that which I purpose' (Isa. 55.11).¹⁴⁹

Logos, however, was also a very familiar term to the wide range of Greeks who thought seriously about their world and their place in it. In Stoicism, one of the principal philosophies of the time, *logos* was the term used for the divine reason which Stoics believed was immanent in the world, permeating all things. As such it was present also in man, as the seminal logos (*logos spermatikos*), so that man's highest good was to live in accordance with and by assenting to this divine reason.¹⁵⁰ Particularly helpful for John was the fact that the basic meaning of *logos* embraces both 'thought, reason' and 'speech, utterance'. And the Stoics were accustomed to distinguish two aspects or phases of *logos* — *logos* = the unexpressed thought, the thought within the mind (*logos endiathetos*), and *logos* = the uttered thought, the thought expressed in speech (*logos prophorikos*).¹⁵¹

---

146. The punctuation is unclear (early mss would have lacked punctuation); the text could be translated, 'without him nothing came into being. What came into being in him was life'. Cf. NRSV and REB; discussion with differing conclusions in Brown, *John* 1.6-7, and Barrett, *John* 156-57.

147. See e.g. H. Kleinknecht and O. Procksch, *legō*, *TDNT* 4.80-100; Barrett, *John* 152-55; Schnelle, *Theology* 688-89.

148. Gen. 15.1; Deut. 5.5; Josh. 8.27; 2 Sam. 7.4; 1 Kgs. 13.20; etc.; see further *Christology in the Making* 217.

149. See also e.g. Pss. 107.20; 147.15, 18; Wisd. 18.14-16; and further *Christology in the Making* 217-19. This concept lies at the root of modern speech-act theory.

150. Kleinknecht, *TDNT* 4.84-85. Philo regularly counseled his readers to live in accordance with 'right reason' (*Opif.* 143; *Leg. All.* 1.46, 93; 3.1, 80, 106, 148, 150, etc.).

151. The distinction was basic in Philo's thought: e.g., '. . ."logos" has two aspects,

So, when John began his Gospel with 'In the beginning was the *logos*', it would speak immediately to a wide spectrum of any audience listening to his Gospel being read. Jewish listeners would think not simply of a prophetic word which made God's will known, but also of the powerful utterance of God by which he made the world and actually brought his will to effect. Greek listeners would similarly think of the divine reason which permeated and sustained the world and by living in accordance with which they could direct their lives to best effect. Likewise, when John continued, 'The *logos* was with God and was God', both sets of listeners would find this unexceptional. For the *logos* was God's own thought and utterance. And John's further claim that 'All things came into being through (the *logos*)' would similarly accord with the presuppositions of most of his audiences. This was how the divine was present in the world and to humankind. This was how God interacted with his creation and his people Israel. The Alexandrian Jewish philosopher Philo shows clearly how fruitfully Jewish and Greek (Platonic and Stoic) understanding of the *logos* could be combined, to envisage the Word/*Logos* almost as a divine agent of God, a plenipotentiary who made the invisible, transcendent God knowable and immanent.[152]

What John's audiences would have found unexpected was the climax of the prologue:

> And the Word became flesh and dwelt (*eskēnōsen*) among us, and we have seen his glory, the glory as of a father's only son, full of grace and truth.... No one has ever seen God. The only begotten God who is closest to his Father's heart, has made him known (John 1.14, 18).

Greeks could well envisage the gods taking the appearance of human beings. Jews were more than familiar with the word of God inspiring and speaking through a man. Even Philo, the most imaginative in his talk of the *Logos*, could not do more than regard various great historical figures as allegorical symbols of the Word. But the thought of the Word *becoming* flesh was a step far too far for the generality of any audience, and abhorrent, even repulsive, to the Greek mind. This, however, is precisely the step which the prologue takes.

---

one resembling a spring, the other its outflow; "logos" in the understanding resembles a spring, and is called "reason", while utterance by mouth and tongue is like its outflow, and is called "speech" . . .' (*Migr.* 70-85; *Christology in the Making* 223).

152. See further *Christology in the Making* §28.3, with its denial that Philo thought of the *Logos* as an independent deity; to speak of a 'hypostatization' is also anachronistic and misleading. For Philo the *Logos* was the thought of God coming to expression, God making himself as knowable to humankind as humankind at its best is able to apprehend. For Philo's understanding of how God created the cosmos see his *Opif.* 16-44.

And to ensure that there could be no confusion on the claim, John integrates the prologue's assertions with his presentation of Jesus as only Son of the Father. The claim was astounding: that the utterance by which God created the world and brought his purpose to effect had become incarnate in Jesus.

1.18 presses home the point. John takes for granted the fundamental 'given' of most current sophisticated theistic systems: that God, or the ultimate God, was beyond human conception. Certainly the assertion that 'No one has ever seen God' was a fundamental axiom of Israel's religion[153] and the basis of its abhorrence of idolatry. But Logos theology had already provided a way of envisaging how the unseen God had nevertheless made himself known — through the word that he uttered, in creation, in revelation, in redemption. And John simply(!) takes that thought one step further in claiming that *Jesus* was now the one who made the unseen God visible, the unknowable God knowable (cf. Col. 1.15). As God, one might say, making a projection of himself,[154] as God's Word incarnate, 'he has made God known'.[155] Hence again, later, John interweaves this thought with his Father-Son christology: 'Whoever has seen me has seen the Father' (14.9; also 8.19; 12.45). Similarly 12.41: Isaiah saw the glory of God (cf. 1.14) — the Logos as that which is visible of God. But the thought is essentially an extension of the double meaning of *logos*, as both the hidden, unarticulated thought, and the utterance which brings that thought to expression so that others may appreciate it. Jesus is the self-expression of God.[156]

(2) Since the Logos christology of John is not explicit in the rest of the Gospel, despite the links to his dominant Son christology, it is important to recognize that the prologue could be more accurately described as Wisdom christology.[157] The reason why John preferred the prologue's focus on the

---

153. E.g. Exod. 33.20; Deut. 4.12; Sir. 43.31; Philo, *Post* 168-69; Josephus, *War* 7.346.

154. The text of 1.18 is not finally certain. The most probable reading is *monogenēs theos* ('the only-begotten G/god'); *monogenēs huios* ('the only S/son') looks to be secondary, presumably on the ground that *huios* was the obvious correlate with *monogenēs*, not *theos*. See e.g. discussion by Metzger, *Textual Commentary* 198. It should be noted that Philo did not hesitate occasionally to refer to the Logos as god — particularly *Qu. Gen.* 2.62, 'the second God, who is his Logos'.

155. One could almost translate (or transliterate!) the final verb (*exēgēsato*) as 'he has exegeted' God.

156. Cf. Robinson, *Priority* ch. 8; 'to be true to John, we should say that the Word of God subsisted in the man Jesus, *utterly and completely*, that he was *totus deus*, God all through, his perfect reflection and image, but not that he was *totum dei*, all there is of God' (396).

157. There is a wide consensus on the point; see e.g. Barrett, *John* 153-54; Stuhlmacher, *Biblische Theologie* 2.235-36; Strecker, *Theology* 473-74; Lincoln, *Saint John* 95-97. DeConick questions such a linking of the Logos of John 1 with Wisdom traditions; 'Sophia

Word could be simply that he preferred the masculine *Logos* to the feminine *Sophia* ('wisdom'), though the wider familiarity with *logos* outside Judaism was probably a decisive factor too.

The fact is, however, that apart from Philo, Wisdom was the more commonly used term in early Judaism's reflection on God's interaction with his creation and his people Israel.[158] The parallels between the Johannine prologue and the reflection on Wisdom are more extensive than those with the Logos.

1.1 — With you is wisdom, who knows your works and was present when you made the world (Wisd. 9.9; Prov. 8.23, 27, 30);

1.3 — The Lord by wisdom founded the earth (Prov. 3.19);

1.4 — Whoever finds wisdom finds life (Prov. 8.35);

1.4 — All light comes from her (wisdom) (Aristobulus in Eusebius, *Praep. Evang.* 13.12.10; Bar. 4.2);

1.5 — Wisdom's light prevails over the night and evil (Wisd. 7.29-30);

1.11 — Wisdom went forth to make her dwelling place among the children of men (Wisd. 9.10; Bar. 3.37), but found no dwelling place (*1 Enoch* 42.2);

1.14 — The one who created me assigned a place for my tent (*skēnēn*). And he said, "Make your dwelling place (*kataskēnōson*) in Jacob"' (Sir. 24.8).[159]

Obviously *logos* and *sophia* were equivalent or alternative or overlapping ways of speaking about God's interaction with the world he made and with his people — as illustrated, for example, by Wisd. 9.1-2: 'O God . . . who made all things by your word and by your wisdom formed humankind'.[160] But there seems to have been something like a Wisdom myth in early Judaism,[161] proba-

---

traditions cannot explain the identification of a pre-existent Logos with God' (*Voices of the Mystics* 113-14). Philo, for one, would find the remark baffling; see e.g. my *Christology* 171-73 and 326 n.34.

158. See also A. Strotmann, 'Relative oder absolute Präexistenz? Zur Diskussion über die Präexistenz der frühjüdischen Weisheitsgestalt im Kontext von Joh 1,1-18', in Labahn et al., eds., *Israel* 91-106.

159. See further C. A. Evans, *Word and Glory: On the Exegetical and Theological Background of John's Prologue* (JSNTS 89; Sheffield: JSOT, 1993) 83-94 (with bibliography in 83 n.1) — on parallels with Philo (100-13); McGrath, *John's Apologetic Christology* 136-43.

160. See also *Christology in the Making* 326 n.34.

161. The relevant data provided the basis for the otherwise fanciful mid-twentieth-century thesis that there existed a widely known pre-Christian Gnostic Redeemer myth on which early christology was built. This was the classic argument of Bultmann, *Theology* 1.164-83; Bultmann believed that John drew on a Gnostic discourse source and that John's dualism

bly alluded to or reflected in the passages just cited: that divine wisdom, sought by all who wished to live good lives, was impossible to discover by one's own effort (Job 28); but God had granted her to Israel. Ben Sira and Baruch made the claim explicit: that the wisdom, so necessary and desirable to right-thinking human beings, had been given to Israel in the Torah (Sir. 24.23; Bar. 4.1-4). In a sense, John's prologue was simply extending the same theological logic: as the practitioners of the Wisdom tradition in early Judaism claimed that the divine wisdom so unattainable elsewhere was now to be found in the Torah, so John in effect made the same claim with reference to Jesus. As valuable as was the Torah, it was in Jesus, God's only Son, that the creative, revelatory, redemptive Word had come to humankind, that the divine Wisdom had made God known; 'the law was given through Moses, but grace and truth came through Jesus Christ' (John 1.17).

Not least of the value of recognizing the Wisdom structure of John's prologue is that it makes clearer the degree to which the prologue is integrated with the rest of the Gospel, indeed, that the prologue is intended as a window through which the rest of the Gospel should be read.[162] For the richer Jewish Wisdom tradition seems to have provided much of the inspiration for the way John crafted his christology.[163] For example:

- 1.38-39 — Wisdom makes a daily round to gather in those who seek her (Wisd. 6.12-16);
- 2.6-10 — such generous provision is typical of Sophia (Sir. 1.16; 24.19-21; Wisd. 7.8-14);
- 3.13 — Wisdom sent from heaven (Wisd. 9.16-17; Bar. 3.29);

---

was Gnostic in origin (*John* 7-9; *Theology* 2.17). But Bultmann had already demonstrated the strong Wisdom background to the prologue — 'The History of Religions Background of the Prologue to the Gospel of John' (1923), ET in Ashton, ed., *Interpretation* 27-46. A significant course-correction in the quest for a pre-Christian Gnostic Redeemer myth was the demonstration of MacRae, 'The Jewish Background of the Gnostic Sophia Myth', that it was precisely the Jewish form of the Wisdom myth which the Gnostics used. Koester maintains that John would have known quite well that the myth of Wisdom is 'always docetic, because she is never really human', and infers that 1.14 'is pointedly anti-docetic' (*Ancient Christian Gospels* 271). See further below §49.3.

162. Beutler ('Der Johannes-Prolog — Ouvertüre des Johannesevangeliums', *Neue Studien* 215-38) and Schnelle (*Antidocetic Christology* 226) agree; contrast n.71 above.

163. 'The fourth evangelist saw in Jesus the culmination of a tradition that runs through the Wisdom Literature of the OT; . . . in John, Jesus is personified Wisdom' (Brown, *John* 1.cxxii-cxxv). See also particularly J. M. C. Scott, *Sophia and the Johannine Jesus* (JSNTS 71; Sheffield: JSOT, 1992); idem, 'John', in J. D. G. Dunn and J. W. Rogerson, eds., *Eerdmans Commentary on the Bible* (Grand Rapids: Eerdmans, 2003) 1161-1212; M. E. Willett, *Wisdom Christology in the Fourth Gospel* (San Francisco: Mellen, 1992); Witherington, *John's Wisdom* 18-27.

- 3.16-17 — Wisdom sent into the world to bring eternal life and salvation (Wisd. 8.13; 9.10, 17-18);
- 4.10, 14 — living water as especially the gift of Sophia (Sir. 15.3; 24.21, 30-31; Bar. 3.12);
- 6.30-58 — Sophia as the provider of both bread and drink (Prov. 9.5; Sir. 15.3);[164]
- 7.25-36 — Sophia's origins as a matter of speculation (Job 28.12-28; Bar. 3.14-15);
- 8.12-30 — the righteous man, who calls himself a child of God, on trial before his accusers (Wisd. 2.12-24);
- 8.58 — Wisdom makes a first-person claim to have been with God from the beginning (Prov. 8.22; Sir. 24.9);
- 10.1-18 — Wisdom as Israel's protector and saviour (Wisd. 10);
- 11.17-44 — Wisdom as the life-giver (Prov. 8.35);
- 12.44-50 — could almost be Sophia speaking (cf. Sir. 24.19-22);
- The 'I am's echo the kind of imagery and self-presentation characteristic of Wisdom (Prov. 8; Sir. 24),[165] but also as elaborations of John 1.18 — Jesus as the exposition of the 'I am' of Exod. 3.14.[166]

The christology of John's Gospel should therefore not be divorced from the christology of the prologue.[167] On the contrary, the Logos/Wisdom christology of the prologue may provide the way to read the claims made for Jesus in the rest of the Gospel. That is to say, the dominant Father-Son christology should not be read as a distinct christology but should perhaps be better seen as a blending of the earlier divine agent–(prophet) christology and the ad-

---

164. See also McGrath, *John's Apologetic Christology* ch. 11.

165. 'All of them [the "I am"s] except the "good shepherd" are explicitly associated with Wisdom ("bread" in Sir. 24:21; the "vine" in Sir. 24:17, 19; the "way" in Prov. 3:17; 8:32; Sir. 6:26; "light" in Wisd. Sol. 7:26; . . . "truth" in Prov. 8:7; Wisd. Sol. 6:22; "life" in Prov. 3:18; 8:35; and even "gate of the sheep" . . . in Prov. 8:34-35)' — S. H. Ringe, *Wisdom's Friends: Community and Christology in the Fourth Gospel* (Louisville: Westminster John Knox, 1999) 61.

166. Note also Isa. 41.4; 43.10, 25; 45.18-19; 46.4; 51,12; 52.6. See also C. H. Williams, '"I Am" or "I Am He"? Self-Declaratory Pronouncements in the Fourth Gospel and Rabbinic Tradition', in Fortna and Thatcher, eds., *Jesus in the Johannine Tradition* 343-52; McGrath, *John's Apologetic Christology* 109-115; H. Hübner, 'EN ARCHĒ EGŌ EIMI', in Labahn et al., eds., *Israel* 107-22.

167. See also G. R. O'Day, 'The Gospel of John: Reading the Incarnate Words', in Fortna and Thatcher, eds., *Jesus in the Johannine Tradition* 25-32; M. Hengel, 'The Prologue of the Gospel of John as the Gateway to Christological Truth', in Bauckham and Mosser, eds., *John and Christian Theology* 265-94; also *Theologische, historische und biographische Skizzen: Kleine Schriften VII* (WUNT 253; Tübingen: Mohr Siebeck, 2010) 34-63.

vanced Wisdom/Logos christology of the Johannine prologue. Alternatively expressed, John would no doubt have been well aware of the first person self-assertions made by Wisdom and the vivid imagery used to describe the revelatory and redemptive significance of Wisdom. He may even have been aware of the still more vivid imagery and language used for the Logos by Philo. So perhaps he crafted together Son of God and Logos/Wisdom in order that the highly personal and intimate language and imagery of Father-Son should serve as a still richer elaboration of the now revealed mystery of the *Logos* unuttered and the *Logos* uttered than anything previously suggested, and all impelled by the revelatory significance which was Jesus Messiah.[168]

There may be a significant corollary here worthy of further reflection. For if John's Son christology is in effect essentially a large-scale metaphorical elaboration of the prologue's Logos christology (more ambitious than any metaphorical elaboration of Philo), then the Son christology should be read as part of the Logos christology. That is, various aspects of the Son christology should not be read independently of the Logos christology, but rather as intended to serve the Logos christology. I am thinking not simply of the accusation that Jesus was making himself equal with God (5.18) and Jesus' striking claim to be one with the Father (10.30); for such claims are an obvious expression of Logos/Wisdom christology — Logos/Wisdom being the self-expression of the otherwise invisible God. Nor am I thinking only of the sending motif, where the Son sent is wholly representative of the Father who sent him (e.g. 10.36; 12.45). I am thinking more of the features of John's Son christology normally referred to as the Son's 'subordination' to the Father — summed up by 14.28, 'The Father is greater than I'.[169] In fact, however, the thought is not so much of subordination, as though that was already an issue. The issue is not the *relation* between the Father and the Son (as later), but the authority and validity of the Son's *revelation* of the Father, the continuity between the Father and the Son, between the *logos* unuttered and the *logos* uttered.[170] So, for example,

---

168. See further *Christology in the Making* xxvi-xxviii.

169. C. K. Barrett, '"The Father is greater than I" (John 14. 28): Subordinationist Christology in the New Testament' (1974), *Essays on John* (London: SPCK, 1982) 19-36; Stuhlmacher, *Biblische Theologie* 2.225.

170. More strongly brought out in Barrett's preceding essay, 'Christocentric or Theocentric? Observations on the Theological Method of the Fourth Gospel' (1976), *Essays on John* 1-18; see also M. L. Appold, *The Oneness Motif in the Fourth Gospel* (WUNT 2.1; Tübingen: Mohr Siebeck, 1976): 'John's christology leaves no room for even incipient subordinationism' (22). Relevant is also M. Theobald's observation that 'The Johannine Jesus never says of himself in the passive: "*I* have been sent", but speaks of his "*Father*, who sent him" or regularly only of "the one who has sent him"' ('Gott, Logos und Pneuma: Trinitarische Rede von Gott im Johannesevangelium', *Studien* 349-88, here 366; he speaks also

- 'The Father loves the Son and has given everything in his hand' (3.35);
- Jesus' claim that the Son can do nothing on his own, but only what he sees the Father doing (5.17-19);
- 'Just as the Father has life in himself, so he has granted the Son also to have life in himself' (5.26);
- 'I can do nothing on my own . . . I seek to do not my own will but the will of him who sent me' (5.30);
- 'I have come down from heaven, not to do my own will, but the will of him who sent me' (6.38);
- 'I live because of the Father' (6.57);
- 'My teaching is not mine but his who sent me' (7.16);
- 'It is not I alone who judge, but I and the Father who sent me' (8.16);
- 'I do nothing on my own, but I speak these things as the Father instructed me' (8.28-29);
- 'I did not come on my own, but he sent me' (8.42);
- 'I have received this command from the Father' (10.17-18);
- 'What my Father has given me is greater than all else, and no one will snatch it out of the Father's hand' (10.29);
- Doing the works of the Father demonstrates that 'the Father is in me and I am in the Father' (10.38; 14.10-11);
- 'What I speak, I speak just as the Father has told me' (12.49-50; 14.31);
- 'I am not alone because the Father is with me' (16.32).

In all these cases it would be most accurate to say, This is the Logos-Son speaking. Similarly, the worship offered to Jesus (20.28), from John's perspective, is the worship of God as manifest in the Logos (1.1, 18; 10.33-36).[171] The intimacy of 'I and the Father are one', of the mutual indwelling of Father and Son, of the immediate continuity in message and works between Father and Son, are all alternative (and more personally vivid) ways of indicating that the incarnate Logos is the self-expression of God.[172] It is only when the

---

of 'the Johannine mutation of Jewish monotheism' — 358). See also P. W. Meyer, '"The Father": The Presentation of God in the Fourth Gospel', in R. A. Culpepper and C. C. Black, eds., *Exploring the Gospel of John: In Honor of D. Moody Smith* (Louisville: Westminster John Knox, 1996) 255-73; J. Schröter, 'Trinitarian Belief, Binitarian Monotheism, and the One God: Reflections on the Origin of Christian Faith in Affiliation to Larry Hurtado's Christological Approach', in C. Breytenbach and J. Frey, eds., *Reflections on the Early Christian History of Religion* (Ancient Judaism and Early Christianity 81; Leiden: Brill, 2013) 171-94 — 'it is possible to speak of a "proto-Trinitarian thinking" in Johannine theology' (193).

171. Philo also spoke of the Logos and its component parts as worthy of veneration and praise (*Spec. Leg.* 1.209).

172. Ernst Käsemann's famous characterization of John's presentation of Jesus, as 'naïve docetism' (*The Testament of Jesus* [ET London: SCM, 1968] 26), misses the subtlety of

early church's Logos christology is supplanted by the Son christology of Nicaea, and the Son christology becomes detached from the Logos christology that the issue of personal relationships within the Godhead arises and talk of 'subordination' becomes necessary to maintain the balance within the by then much-refined monotheism of the Fathers.

(3) It cannot, should not and need not be denied that in thus developing his presentation of Jesus, Messiah and Son of God, John has moved far beyond the Jesus tradition as most clearly attested in the Synoptic Gospels. Yet even here we can see the seeds out of which John grew the more exotic expressions of his christology.

- Jesus as the 'word' is in a degree foreshadowed by Luke's prologue, where Luke speaks of 'those who from the beginning were eyewitnesses and servants of the word' (Luke 1.2). Here Luke was no doubt thinking in terms of his regular reference to the gospel (Acts 2.41; 4.4, 29, 31; etc.), but the thought of Jesus as embodying that word is not far distant.
- The thought of Jesus as child of and spokesman for Wisdom is rooted in the Synoptic tradition (Luke 7.35; Jesus' aphoristic teaching); the link between Jesus as teacher of wisdom and Son of the Father is already made in the most Johannine statement of the Synoptics (Matt. 11.25-27/Luke 10.21-22);[173] and, as already noted (§42.3b(7)), Matthew had already taken the step of identifying Jesus the teacher of wisdom with Wisdom herself.
- Even the 'I am's are rooted in the earlier Synoptic tradition of Jesus walking on the water, and his numinous self-identification, 'I am; do not be afraid' (Mark 6.50 par.), which John also records (John 6.20).

It is quite possible, then, to envisage how the Johannine Word/Wisdom christology is the product of long reflection on such features of the

---

John's Logos/Wisdom Christology; note the protest of M. M. Thompson, *The Humanity of Jesus in the Fourth Gospel* (Philadelphia: Fortress, 1988). As also Bauckham who reads John as affirming 'that Jesus belongs to the unique identity of the one and only God' (*Testimony* 252); but 'identity' is as much misleading as informative (see my *Did the First Christians Worship Jesus?* 141-44). Schnelle cites T. Söding, '"Ich und der Vater sind eins" [Joh 10,30]: Die johanneische Christologie vor dem Anspruch des Hauptgebotes Dtn 6,4f', *ZNW* 93 (2002) 192: 'Just as the Logos is by no means identified with *ho theos*, the God and Father of Jesus, the Logos is nonetheless fully participant in his deity' (*Theology* 673 n.35). And by drawing in references to the Spirit/Paraclete (14.16-17, 26; 15.26; 16.7-11), Schnelle, 'Trintarisches Denken im Johannesevangelium', in Labahn et al., eds., *Israel* 367-86, is able to push for his final exclamation: 'Johannine thought is Trinitarian thought!' (386).

173. See also M. Theobald, 'Das sog. "johanneische Logion" in der synoptischen Überlieferung (Mt 11,25-27; Lk 10,21f.) und das Vierte Evangelium', *Studien* 165-89.

earlier Jesus tradition. In the light of Jesus' resurrection and exaltation to the right hand of God, as they believed, it was natural to see fuller and deeper significance in such features, and natural to develop a richer expression of them within the Gospel framework already established by the Synoptic Gospels.[174] Were the question of historicity a real one for John and his audiences, in the same way as is the case today, he would probably have confirmed that he was not attempting to provide a historical record of what Jesus did and said. His concern was rather to bring out the truth of Jesus as they now perceived it, the fuller significance of the historical life and mission of Jesus which only became clear to them with the passing of some decades.[175] For John the truth of Jesus was much fuller and richer than the historical facticity of what he said and did during the three years of his mission.[176] To miss this probable conclusion and to insist that John has to be read on the same terms and level as the Synoptics is most likely to miss what John saw himself as doing.

d. The Good News That Belief in Jesus Brings

John expressed his evangelistic and pastoral aim clearly in the same verse which led us into his exposition of the good news of Jesus — 20.31: 'These (things) are written in order that you might believe that Jesus is the Christ, the Son of God, and that believing you might have life in his name'. The invitation is to believe the good news about Jesus. The promise is of life in his name.

i. A Summons to Believe

Curiously, John never uses the word 'faith'. But he uses the verb 'believe' far more than any other NT writer.[177] His summons to believe is more insistent than any other NT Evangelist. For example:

---

174. McGrath's thesis is that 'the Fourth Evangelist adapted and developed the traditions which he inherited as part of a defence of his (and his community's) beliefs against objections raised by Jewish opponents' (*John's Apologetic Christology* 230).

175. Note again John 16.12-15 and n.101 above.

176. Moody Smith coined the phrase 'John's unique metahistorical presentation of Jesus' (*Johannine Christianity* 184); note also several essays in his *Fourth Gospel in Four Dimensions*. See also M. M. Thompson, 'The Historical Jesus and the Johannine Christ', in Culpepper and Black, eds., *Exploring the Gospel of John* (Louisville: Westminster John Knox, 1996) 21-42; A. T. Lincoln, *Truth on Trial* (Peabody, Mass.: Hendrickson, 2000) 354-454; and briefly, his *Saint John* 48-49.

177. Matt. 11x; Mark 14x; Luke 9x; Acts 37x; Paul 54x; John 98x.

- 1.7 — The Baptist came to bear witness in order that all might believe through him;
- 1.12 — God gave the right to become children of God to those who believe in his (the Logos's) name;
- 2.11 — the signs Jesus did prompted people to believe in him (also 2.23; 4.53; 7.31; 10.38, 41-42; 11.45; 12.11, 42; 14.11-12); his words too (4.41; 8.30; 13.19; 14.29); contrast 12.37-39;
- 3.15 — the Son of Man will be lifted up 'in order that everyone who believes in him might have eternal life' (also 3.16, 36; 5.24; 6.40, 47);
- 3.18 — he who believes in him is not subjected to judgment (also 5.24);
- 6.29 — 'This is the work of God, to believe in the one he has sent';
- 6.35 — in the bread of life discourse it becomes clear that eating the bread/Jesus' flesh and drinking his blood are images for coming to and believing in him (6.37, 44-45, 51, 53);[178]
- 6.69 — 'we have come to believe and know that you are the holy one of God';
- 8.24 — 'Unless you believe that I am, you will die in your sins' (also 13.19);
- 10.26 — 'you do not believe because you do not belong to my sheep';
- 11.25-26 — 'I am the resurrection and the life; he who believes in me will never die';
- 12.36 — 'While you have the light, believe in the light, in order that you might become children of light' (also 12.46);
- 12.44 — 'Whoever believes in me believes not in me but in him who sent me' (also 14.1);
- 14.10-11 — 'Believe me that I am in the Father and the Father in me';
- 16.9 — sin is described as failing to believe in Jesus;
- 16.27, 30-31 — the importance of believing that Jesus has come from God (also 17.8, 21);
- 20.8, 25, 29 — believing in the resurrected Jesus.

Three points are particularly worthy of attention. First, although John gives his aim as seeking to inculcate or strengthen belief '*that* Jesus is the Christ, the Son of God' (20.31), in fact he hoped for more, that people would '*believe in*' Jesus, that is, entrust themselves to this Jesus. In fact, however, John seems to use *pisteuein hoti* ('believe that')[179] and *pisteuein eis* ('entrust

---

178. C. R. Koester, *Symbolism in the Fourth Gospel* (Minneapolis: Fortress, ²2003) 99-104, 301-9. 'To "come" to Jesus means neither more nor less than to believe in him (5:40; 6:37, 44f., 65)' (Bultmann, *Theology* 2.70).

179. 11x (e.g. 6.69; 8.24; 11.27; 13.19; 16.27, 30; 17.21; also believing Jesus (e.g. 2.22; 5.46, 47; 6.30; 14.11).

oneself to')[180] more or less synonymously.[181] The fact that John could put his objective solely in terms of 'believing *that*' assuredly implies that he could not conceive of a genuine persuasion or conviction which did not express itself in commitment to the one believed to be the Messiah, Son of God. Belief for John included an intellectual persuasion, that Jesus had indeed been sent by God, but also the enactment of that belief in entrusting or committing oneself to the Son sent by the Father.[182]

The distinction between 'belief *that*' and 'belief *in*', however, was important for John. For, secondly, in several passages he makes it clear that there is an inadequate level of belief. In particular, the belief on the basis of signs/miracles, John evidently wanted his audiences to be cautious about, even though he presents the signs as belief-creating (2.11, etc. above). Thus early on he notes that though many believed in Jesus' name because they saw his signs, 'Jesus himself did not entrust himself to them' because he knew them too well (2.23-25). He rebukes the royal official: 'Unless you see signs and wonders you will not believe' (4.48; but then 4.41, 53). Following the feeding of the five thousand, the crowd demand another sign so that they may believe him (6.30). And the bread of life discourse ends with the note that some did not believe and that many of his disciples turned back and no longer went about with him (6.64, 66). Without belief *in*, belief *that* was not enough.[183]

Thirdly, it is noticeable that the call to believe is the only demand that John makes, the only response his Gospel seeks for. A call to 'repent' or for 'repentance' never crosses his lips, not even in describing the Baptist's mission — a central feature in the equivalent references to the Baptist in the Synoptics.[184] Equally striking, John seems to make little or nothing of *baptism* as part of the response for which the gospel of Jesus calls. He passes over Jesus' own baptism by the Baptist and makes a point of noting that although Jesus' mission originally overlapped with that of the Baptist, Jesus himself did not practise or demand baptism (4.1-2). The one passage which may refer to baptism as essential to being born again (3.5 — 'No one can enter the kingdom of God without being born of water and Spirit') could be John's way of speaking

---

180. 37x — 'believe in him' (examples in the text) but also 'believe in his name' and 'believe in (*en*) him' (3.15).

181. Note 11.25-27; 14.10-12; 17.20-21; also 3.15-16.

182. Beutler emphasizes that John's objective was not simply to lead to faith in Christ and to strengthen that faith but 'to deepen the faith of Christians in Jesus as Son of God and Giver of life, even under circumstances in which the confession would endanger their social position or even their lives' ('Faith and Confession: The Purpose of John', *Neue Studien* 101-13; here 113).

183. See also Stuhlmacher, *Biblische Theologie* 2.251-57.

184. Mark 1.4 par.; Matt. 3.8/Luke 3.8; also Acts 13.24; 19.4.

of the two births necessary — natural birth 'from the flesh' (associated with the breaking of the mother's water) and birth 'from the Spirit' (3.6).[185] It is certainly the latter of which John was primarily thinking (3.3, 7-8) — the Spirit as the giver of life.

ii. That You Might Have Life

'Life' (*zōē*) is another characteristically Johannine term.[186] In contrast 'forgiveness' is never mentioned; 20.23 is surprisingly exceptional in John' Gospel. And the language of 'salvation' and 'being saved' appears far less frequently in John than in the other Gospels.[187] As John summed up his challenge in terms of 'belief', so he sums up the promise of his Gospel in terms of 'life':[188]

- 3.15, 16, 36 — 'Whoever believes in him has eternal life' (also 6.40, 47);
- 3.3, 5-8 — to enter the kingdom of God, new birth (from above) is necessary;
- 4.10, 14 — the living water that Jesus gives will be a spring welling up to eternal life;
- 6.27, 33, 35, 48, 53, 54 — Jesus as the bread of life; those who eat his flesh and drink his blood have eternal life;
- 8.51-52 — 'Whoever keeps my word will never see/taste death';
- 10.10 — 'I came that they might have life and have it abundantly';
- 11.25 — 'I am the resurrection and the life';
- 14.6 — 'I am the way, the truth and the life';
- 17.3 — 'This is eternal life, that they may know you, the only true God, and Jesus Christ whom you have sent'.

A notable feature is the way John ties in the thought of the Spirit of God as the instrument of life: the mystery of new birth is attributed to the Spirit (3.5-8); the 'living water' (4.10, 14) is explicitly identified with the Spirit which

---

185. Witherington, *John's Wisdom* 97; Thyen, *Johannesevangelium* 192-93, citing M. Pamment, 'John 3.5: "Unless One Is Born of Water and the Spirit, He Cannot Enter the Kingdom of God", *NovT* 25 (1983) 192. Barrett (*John* 209) notes the possibility, citing Odeberg, *Fourth Gospel* 48-71, but is not persuaded. More typical is Schnelle (*Antidocetic Christology* 68, 186), who presupposes rather than exegetes his opinion that 'apparently baptism was highly important in the Johannine school as the locus of the gift of the Spirit (see 1 John 2:27; 3:24; 4:1-3, 13; John 1:33; 3:5)'; similarly Stuhlmacher, *Biblische Theologie* 2.277. See also my *Baptism in the Holy Spirit* (London: SCM, 1970) ch. 15.

186. *Zōē* ('life') — John 36x; other NT Gospels 16x. *Zaō* ('live') — John 17x; rest of Gospels 18x. 'Eternal life' — John 17x; other Gospels 8x (see above n.10).

187. *Sōtēria* ('salvation') — John 1x; Matt. 0; Mark 0; Luke 4x. *Sōzō* ('save') — John 6x; Matt. 15x; Mark 15x; Luke 17x.

188. See also Ashton, *Understanding* 214-20.

those who believed in him were to receive (7.39); the Spirit is identified as 'the life-giver' (6.63); and on the evening of Jesus' resurrection Jesus says, 'Receive the Holy Spirit', and breathes (*enephysēsen*) on his disciples in an act of new creation (20.22).[189] Here the traditional imagery of the Spirit as refreshing and life-restoring water in a land often plagued with drought is drawn on to express the equivalent experience of new life which the first Christians usually referred to the gift of the Spirit.

A second striking feature is the eschatology implied in the claim that to belief in Jesus God gives eternal life *now*. 'Eternal life' for John is not typically something still awaited and to be inherited in the future, though he may not exclude that thought.[190] It is something which the believer already *has* — John's typical way of speaking on the subject.[191] 'Whoever keeps my word will never see/taste death' (8.51-52).[192] This would no doubt be an immense comfort to the band of brothers feeling themselves to be in the midst of a hostile world.

iii. Knowing Reality

John uses the language of 'knowing' a lot, but despite the twentieth-century tendency to read John's Gospel in terms of Gnosticism, John does not give the theme of 'knowing' particularly strong emphasis,[193] and he does not use the term 'knowledge' (*gnōsis*) even once. More typical and distinctive of John is the emphasis on the *truth* of Jesus and on the beneficial effect of knowing

---

189. This verb is used only twice in the Greek version of the Hebrew Bible to denote the divine creative breath (I first drew attention to this in *Baptism* 180). (i) Gen. 2.7 — God 'breathed into the nostrils [of Adam] the breath of life; and the man became a living being'. (ii) Ezek. 37.9 in Ezekiel's great vision of an exiled Israel as a valley of dry bones, where Ezekiel is instructed to prophesy: 'Come from the four winds, O breath (or wind or Spirit), and breathe upon these slain, that they may live'. See also G. M. Burge, *The Anointed Community: The Holy Spirit in the Johannine Tradition* (Grand Rapids: Eerdmans, 1987) ch. 3.

190. Cf. John 4.14, 36; 6.27; 8.12; 12.25.

191. '. . . has eternal life' — 3.15, 16, 36; 5.24, 40; 6.40, 47, 53, 54; 10.10; 20.31.

192. This does not imply that the future eschatology passages of John's Gospel (particularly 5.25-29) were later additions. The earlier Jesus tradition had a similar tension between the kingdom of God as both presently active and expected to come in the future (*Jesus Remembered* §12). 'On substantive grounds it is highly improbable that the futuristic eschatological passages are interpolated, because futuristic eschatology is found also in uncontested places (3:5; 10:9; 12:32; 14:3; 17:24) and is theologically indispensable' (Kümmel, *Introduction* 209-10); similarly Barrett, *John* 67-70; further bibliography in Schnelle, *History* 512 n.217.

193. Cf. e.g. *oida* ('know') — 4.25; 7.28-29; 10.4-5; 14.5. *Ginōskō* ('know') — 6.69; 8.32; 10.14, 38; 14.17, 20; 17.3. See also Brown, *John* 1.513-14; and on the verbs denoting seeing, 1.501-3.

this truth.[194] John could call for belief regarding and in Jesus because he was confident that what he said about Jesus was true — as confirmed also by those who could vouch for him (19.35; 21.24) — and that Jesus himself was the truth and the measure of reality. For example:

- 1.9 — the Logos (now incarnate in Jesus) was 'the true light which enlightens everyone';
- 1.14, 17 — He was 'full of grace and truth' and 'grace and truth came to be through him';
- 4.42 — the Samaritans confessed that Jesus was 'truly the Saviour of the world';
- 5.33 — John the Baptist 'bore testimony to the truth' (also 10.41);
- 6.32 — Jesus 'the true bread from heaven' given by the Father;
- 8.31-32 — 'If you continue in my word . . . you will know the truth and the truth will make you free';
- 14.6 — 'I am the way, the truth, and the life';
- 14.17, 15.26, 16.13 — Jesus promises (to send to) them 'the Spirit of truth';
- 15.1 — 'I am the true vine';
- 18.37 — 'For this I came into the world, in order that I might bear witness to the truth; everyone who belongs to the truth listens to my voice'.

To spread knowledge of the truth of Jesus was the best thing that John could hope to accomplish by his Gospel.[195]

The thought of illumination, coming to see something to which one was previously blind, was another motif that John employed — linked also with the contrast between *light* and darkness.[196] The note is struck repeatedly in the Gospel's opening verses:

- 1.4, 9 — the life in the Logos was the true light of humankind;
- 1.5 — 'the light shines in the darkness and the darkness has never overcome it';
- 1.7-8 — the Baptist came to bear witness to the light.

But even more striking is the description of the effect that the shining of the light (Jesus, the incarnate Word) had:

194. *Alētheia* ('truth') — John 25x; other Gospels 7x. *Alēthēs* ('true') — John 14x; rest of NT 12x. *Alēthinos* ('true, authentic') — John 9x; rest of NT (apart from Rev.) 9x. *Alēthōs* ('truly') — John 7x; rest of Gospels 8x.
195. See also Schnelle, *Theology* 675-76.
196. Ashton, *Understanding* 208-12.

- 3.19-21 — 'This is the judgment: the light has come into the world, but people preferred darkness to light because their deeds were evil. Everyone who does what is worthless hates the light and does not come to the light, lest their deeds should be exposed. But he who does the truth comes to the light, in order that it may be made manifest that his deeds are done in God'.

As we shall see, this passage becomes determinative of the way John develops the plot of his Gospel drama.[197] And one of the most vivid 'I am' sayings extends the thought further:

- 8.12 — 'I am the light of the world; he who follows me shall not walk in darkness but shall have the light of life' (also 9.5; 12.35-36, 46).

The message, its challenge and its attraction, is plain: as the world now is, those in it are caught up in darkness; their sight is dimmed; they cannot see properly. But now Jesus has entered the world, the light which all humankind need if they are to live lives adequately or properly; so the invitation is to believe in him, that he is the light of the world, and to discover that the way of seeing and living in the world which this belief opens up is true life and freedom.[198]

iv. Where Are the Gentiles?

Since the development of a Jewish messianic sect into a religion whose devotees were mainly Gentile was the major feature of the initial growth of Christianity,[199] one would expect John's Gospel to have reflected this development in large measure. As we saw above, it was a major feature in the shaping of all the Synoptic Gospels (§42). But John seems to have little or no interest in the subject.[200] He uses the word 'nation' (*ethnos*) only of Israel itself (11.48-52; 18.35), and never uses the plural, 'nations/Gentiles'. He mentions 'Greeks' only twice (7.35; 12.20). In the latter case 'some Greeks' wanted to see Jesus, but when Andrew and Philip tell Jesus this, Jesus seems to show no interest and makes no obviously direct response, simply taking up one of the discourse themes which characterize the Gospel (12.21-23). There is a possible reflection of the subsequent mission to the Gentiles, when 'the Jews' wonder whether Jesus 'intends to go to the Diaspora among the Greeks and to teach the Greeks' (7.35). And in ch. 11 John glosses the high priest's 'prophecy' that

---

197. See below §46 n.217; but also Schnelle, *History* 484 n.140.
198. See also Koester, *Symbolism in the Fourth Gospel* ch. 4.
199. *Beginning from Jerusalem* §§27-33.
200. As noted, e.g., by J. A. T. Robinson, 'The Destination and Purpose of St. John's Gospel', *Twelve New Testament Studies* (London: SCM, 1962) 107-25.

Jesus would die 'for the people', that is, for the nation (11.50-51), by adding, 'and not for the nation only, but to gather into one the dispersed children of God' (11.52). The passage recalls the good shepherd discourse of ch. 10: 'I have other sheep which do not belong to this fold; them also I must bring . . . so that there will be one flock, one shepherd' (10.16).

Both the latter passages take up themes which would be familiar to John's Jewish audiences — particularly the image of Israel as a flock of scattered sheep[201] gathered into one (Ezek. 34.23; 37.24). But in both instances John seems to have in view others beyond 'the nation' of Israel, beyond the sheep who 'belong to this fold'. The most obvious inference is that John had in mind the Gentiles who would come to believe,[202] those who would believe in the name of the incarnate Logos and thus become children of God (1.12), also distinguished from the incarnate Logos's 'own people' (1.11). In other words, John does what so many of the other NT writers did, that is, take up images and themes which were part of Israel's understanding of its own status and hope for its own future, and apply them to believers in Messiah Jesus, Gentile as well as Jew.[203]

At the same time, however, one of the most frequently used terms in the Johannine literature is *kosmos*, the 'world'.[204] This is not merely equivalent to 'Jews and Gentiles'. The 'world' in John is where humankind live their lives (John 1.9), a realm of darkness (1.5; 3.19) in which those who belong to the world dwell (12.35-36; 1 John 2.9-10). Satan is the ruler of this world.[205] But it is just this world that God loves (John 3.16); he has sent his Son to save the world,[206] to give his life for the world (6.33, 51); Jesus is the lamb of God who takes away the sin of the world (1.29); he is the light of the world (8.12; 9.5). So, for John as much as for Paul, the good news of Jesus reaches far beyond the nation of Israel and reaches out to all the dark world. The particular issues which framed and shaped Paul's expression of the gospel have changed, but the concept of a good news which embraces a much wider realm than Israel alone is the same message dressed in different clothes.

True as this is, it remains a surprise that John does not make more of embryonic Christianity's movement out from within Judaism into the Gentile

---

201. Jer. 23.2-3; Ezek. 34.12; 37.21.
202. Brown, *John* 1.440, 442-43; Barrett, *John* 407-8.
203. E.g. Rom. 8.28; Eph. 2.19; Col. 1.12.
204. Brown provides the following statistics (*John* 1.508):

Synoptics	John	1-3 John	Revelation	Total Johannine	Total NT
14	78	24	3	105	185

205. John 12.31; 14.30; 16.11.
206. John 3.17; 4.42; 12.47; 1 John 4.14.

world. As we shall see later, his hope still seemed to be largely focused on the confrontation with 'the Jews', his hope, despite the threat of expulsion from the synagogue (9.22; 12.42; 16.2), still to win 'the Jews' who were still wondering whether Jesus was the Messiah (§46.5c). But the Jew/Gentile dynamic, that so motivated Paul, Luke and Matthew, seems to have been replaced by a believer/world confrontation, which includes the former but which largely loses the focus on the Jew/Gentile issue that contributed so much to the emergence of Christian (and Jewish!) identity. It was a drawing back from the specific issue of whether emerging Christianity was or was not a form of Judaism, and a universalizing of it into an issue of 'in the world but not of the world' which made John so amenable to second-century Gnostics.[207]

e. Loving the Brothers

In comparison with the Synoptic Gospels, John's Gospel does not provide much guidance for living.[208] John's focus is more on the knowing and believing, and in contrast little on the doing and living which should follow from the knowing and believing.[209] The main exception is the emphasis he puts on *love*.

i. The New Commandment

'Love' is another distinctively Johannine theme in which he far surpasses the other NT Gospels. Indeed, the theme of 'love' is one of the most distinctive features of the Johannine literature (John's Gospel and the Johannine epistles) in the NT.[210] In the Gospel it is clear that the love of Son and Father for each other is central and ties in the love-theme closely to the christology of close intimacy between God and his Logos.[211] And the Father's and the Son's

---

207. But to place the Gospel of John on 'a gnosticizing trajectory' (Robinson, 'The Johannine Trajectory', in Robinson and Koester, *Trajectories* ch. 7 — here 266) is to miss the distinctiveness of the gospel which John expresses (see also §49.3 below).

208. Cf. W. A. Meeks, 'The Ethics of the Fourth Evangelist', in Culpepper and Black, eds., *Exploring the Gospel of John* 317-26; J. G. van der Watt and R. Zimmermann, eds., *Rethinking the Ethics of John: "Implicit Ethics" in the Johannine Writings* (WUNT 291; Tübingen: Mohr Siebeck, 2012).

209. Barrett notes that John never uses the words 'obedience' or 'obey' (*John* 86).

210.

	Matt.	Mark	Luke	John	1-3 John	Paul	rest of NT
agapē	1	1	0	7	21	75	11
agapaō	8	5	13	36	31	33	15

211. John 3.35; 10.17; 11.4; 14.31; 15.9; 17.23, 24, 26.

love for the world and the disciples is equally important;[212] the Son's love for them providing the model for their love.[213] Otherwise the most explicit teaching is as follows:

- 13.34 — 'I give you a new commandment, that you love one another, as I have loved you, that you also love one another' (also 15.12, 17);
- 13.35 — 'By this shall everyone know that you are my disciples, if you have love among yourselves';
- 14.15 — 'If you love me you will keep my commandments' (also 14.24);
- 14.21 — 'He who has my commandments and keeps them, he it is who loves me. And he who loves me will be loved by my Father, and I will love him and reveal myself to him' (similarly 14.23);
- 15.10 — 'If you keep my commandments you will abide in my love';
- 15.13 — 'No one has greater love than this, that someone should lay down his life for his friends';
- 17.26 — 'I made your name known to them . . . so that the love with which you have loved me may be in them, and I in them'.

Apart from the both explicit and implicit call to reflect Jesus' love, there are two striking features. One is that the command is to 'love one another'. This is described as 'a new commandment' and is at some distance from the second great commandment of the Synoptic tradition — to 'love your neighbour as yourself' (Mark 12.31 pars.). It stands equally in contrast with John's own assertion that 'God loved the world' (John 3.16).[214] As noted above, however (at n.205), for the audience reflected in John's Gospel, the world is a hostile place, and is not to be loved, either in opposition to love of God or for the sake of the world (as in 3.16). The implication is that John wrote for

---

212. John 3.16; 13.1; 14.21, 23; 15.9; 17.23; the disciple whom Jesus loved (13.23; 19.26; 21.7, 20).

213. Jesus' washing of the disciples' feet (John 13.1-11) is presented as the key illustration (13.12-17; also 13.34; 15.12; and 15.13). J. C. Thomas, *Footwashing in John 13 and the Johannnine Community* (JSNTS 61; Sheffield: JSOT Press, 1991), deduces from the text the probability that the Johannine community practised footwashing as a religious rite or practice, and that in all likelihood this practice served as a sign of forgiveness of post-conversion sin. Bauckham is unconvinced by the suggestion that the episode was an imaginative construction based on Luke 22.27 (as Barrett, *John* 436), but notes that the passage is a striking illustration of how Jesus (might have?) enacted his model of leadership as servant (*Testimony* 197-203). J. Clark-Soles, 'John 13: Of Footwashing and History', in Anderson et al., eds., *John, Jesus and History* vol. 2, 255-69, attempts to demonstrate the historical plausibility of the incident, but separates it from John's interpretation of the episode.

214. See also John 1.29; 3.17; 4.42; 6.33, 51; 8.12; 9.5; 12.46-47; 1 John 4.14 — the 'world' too being a distinctively Johannine term (see above n.204).

a community under hostile threat, and turning in upon itself, its members having to cling to each other for support. Such a narrowing down of 'love your neighbour' to 'love one another' is an understandable reaction to a threatening situation, but is nevertheless a somewhat depressing reworking of one of the most distinctive elements of Jesus' teaching.[215]

The second notable feature is that the love called for will be shown by keeping Jesus' commandments.[216] Presumably commandments beyond 'love one another' are referred to. But what (again apart from 15.13) is referred to remains unclear. Presumably, again, those for whom the Gospel was primarily intended would know the sort of teaching in view, but John did not think it necessary to describe or illustrate it. Probably we should think of the sort of catechetical teaching which Matthew's Gospel contains. But the fact that John did not think it necessary to clarify what commandments he had in mind again suggests a somewhat introverted community, where patterns of conduct and discipline were familiar and did not need to be rehearsed.

ii. *John's Individualism*

A peculiarity of John's Gospel is what might be called its lack of ecclesiology. In fact, it would be more appropriate and more accurate to speak of the 'individualism' of John.[217] For John the 'vertical' relationship with God is essentially an individual affair. There is a mutual belonging to Christ, but not a mutual interdependence in that belonging: each sheep hears the shepherd's voice for him/herself (10.3-4, 16); each branch is rooted directly in the

---

215. See *Jesus Remembered* §14.5, and further on 1 John below §49.4a. However, R. Burridge, 'Imitating Jesus: An Inclusive Approach to the Ethics of the Historical Jesus and John's Gospel', in Anderson et al., eds., *John, Jesus and History* vol. 2, 281-90, warns against caricaturing John's attitude at this point: 'following Jesus' example in the footwashing and obeying his "new commandment" means that the community of those who "love one another" must always be inclusive and open to the rest of the world' (288). Cf. Robinson's earlier protest (*Priority* 329-39); Strecker, *Theology* 515.

216. John 14.15, 21-24; 15.10.

217. E. Schweizer, *Church Order in the New Testament* (1959; ET London: SCM, 1961) 122-24; C. F. D. Moule, 'The Individualism of the Fourth Gospel' (1962), *Essays in New Testament Interpretation* (Cambridge: Cambridge University, 1982) 91-109 (especially 102-5); J. Roloff, *Die Kirche im Neuen Testament* (Göttingen: Vandenhoeck, 1993) 299-300. Brown provides an alternative reading (*John* 1.cv-cxi). R. J. Bauckham takes up Moule's theme in a 2010 lecture, 'The "Individualism" of the Gospel of John', now to be published as ch. 1 in *Gospel of Glory: Aspects of John's Theology* (Grand Rapids: Baker Academic, 2015). He concludes his study of the 'aphoristic sayings about the individual's relationship with Jesus': 'the life of the community, the disciples' mutual love, stems from the relationship between each individual and Jesus. The latter entails the former, but individual relationship to Jesus has priority. The community is constituted by individual relationship with Jesus and subsists only through individual relationship with Jesus'.

vine (15.4-7). Each munches Jesus' flesh and drinks his blood for her/himself (6.53-58); each drinks the water from his side as an individual (7.37-38). Each is encouraged to abide in Jesus' love, just as Jesus abides in the Father's love (15.9-10). And even the thought of the believers being 'one' retains the pattern of the mutual indwelling of Father and Son (17.11, 21-23) — a oneness achieved not so much by mutual cooperation (the unity through diversity of Paul's conception of the body of Christ) as by believers each abiding in Christ.

Notable is the fact that the Johannine Jesus looks for a worship which is not tied to a cultic centre (Jerusalem or Gerizim) but a worship in Spirit and truth (4.20-24).[218] It should be no surprise, then, that there is little concept of different ministries within a community of believers. Like Paul, there is no mention of priests. But unlike Paul, there is no mention of 'apostles',[219] and no hint of 'prophets' with a ministry in John's time. Even the role of 'witness', so highlighted as the role of the Baptist,[220] is referred to the disciples only once (15.27).[221] Perhaps, still more striking, there is no role for 'teachers' — and not just in the Gospel (which would be understandable), but also in the Johannine letters. In contrast, the implication is that each will be taught by God immediately and directly (John 6.45), and that all believers, having been anointed by the Holy One, have knowledge and do not need anyone to teach them, since the anointing teaches them about all things (1 John 2.20, 27). This no doubt was understood as the fulfillment of Jesus' promise that the *Paraklētos*, the Holy Spirit, would teach them all things (John 14.26). In fact, the only clearly conceptualized ministries come at the end of the Gospel. In 20.23, the authority to forgive sins is bestowed on the disciples; though it is not clear whether 'the disciples' in 20.19-23 are only 'the twelve' (referred to only in 6.67-71), or whether they represent all disciples,[222] so that the authority to forgive sins is bestowed on all who receive the life-giving Spirit. And in John 21, the appendix to the Gospel, regularly assumed to have been added to the Gospel subsequent to its completion, the risen Christ commissions Peter for pastoral ministry, to feed and tend his sheep and lambs (21.15-17).[223] It should

---

218. Ashton speaks here of 'the interiorization of the cult implied in this saying' (*Understanding* 465-66).

219. John 13.16 is not an exception.

220. See above n.112; the Samaritan woman is also presented as a good example of witness-bearing (4.39).

221. But implied also in 17.18, 20; and see 1 John 1.2; 4.14; 5.11.

222. Note Barrett's lengthy citation (*John* 568) from F. J. A. Hort, *The Christian Ecclesia* (London: Macmillan, 1897) 33. See also Brown, *John* 2.1039-45; Thyen, *Johannesevangelium* 767-68.

223. Several commentators draw attention to 'the ecclesiological imagery of the great catch of fishes' (21.1-14); see e.g. R. A. Culpepper, 'Designs for the Church in the Imag-

perhaps be added that the status and role of 'the elder' who writes 2 and 3 John are too obscure to cause the otherwise larger picture to be redrawn.

Finally, we should consider the role which John attributes to ritual. Like Paul, John seems to take for granted the sacraments of baptism and eucharist (or Lord's Supper). But like Paul he seems to retain some reservations about the significance which might be attached to them.[224] Curiously, he does not mention Jesus' baptism, only the descent of the Spirit on Jesus (John 1.32-34). Nor does he mention Jesus' last supper with his disciples. He may well refer to baptism as integral to the experience of birth from above: 'no one can enter the kingdom of God without being born of water and Spirit' (John 3.5). But, as already noted,[225] it is also clear from the immediate context that it is birth from the Spirit which is the central thought (3.6, 8). And of course, John also emphasizes as strongly as one could imagine that it is only those who consume the flesh of the Son of Man and drink his blood who have eternal life (6.53-58). But he also makes a point of portraying Jesus adding the qualification: 'It is the Spirit that gives life; the flesh is of no value. The words which I have spoken to you are Spirit and are life' (6.63).[226] Certainly one could speak of John as seeing a sacramental universe.[227] But, as already noted, the most common imagery, the diversity of water references, is presented as imaging the dynamic life-giving activity of the Spirit, not as imaging baptism.[228]

John's Gospel leaves me with the impression of a kind of conventicle or convention Christianity, not feeling at all at home in the wider society, but more threatened by it and having to strengthen the bonds of mutual affection because they were so uneasy with life in the wider world.[229] Although they

---

ery of John 21:1-14', in J. Frey et al., eds., *Imagery in the Gospel of John* (Tübingen: Mohr Siebeck, 2006) 369-402.

224. Cf. Barrett, *John* 83-85.

225. See above at n.185.

226. See my 'John 6 — A Eucharistic Discourse?', *NTS* 17 (1971) 328-38. Brown argues that in 6.63 'Jesus is not speaking of eucharistic flesh' (*John* 1.300), but it is surely impossible to divorce the 'flesh' of 6.63 from the 'flesh' of 6.51-56. See also Barrett, *John* 304.

227. Classic exposition in O. Cullmann, *Early Christian Worship* (London: SCM, 1953) ch. 2.

228. John 4.10, 14; 7.37-39; 19.34; see further *Unity and Diversity* §41. See also Burge, *Anointed Community* ch. 4. For a moderate 'sacramental reading' see Brown, *John* 1.cxi-cxiv; also *New Testament Essays* (London: Chapman, 1965) chs. 4 and 5.

229. 'Are we not threatened here with the danger of the pious conventicle that either dissolves in pure individualism in which everyone listens only to "his" witness of the Spirit, or vegetates in mere orthodoxy and in one way or another can only dismiss the world . . . and direct his love towards the brethren only?' (Schweizer, *Church Order* 129, in reference to the Church in the Johannine Letters). Cf. E. Käsemann, 'Ketzer und Zeuge', *Exegetische Versuche und Besinnungen* (Göttingen: Vandenhoeck, 1970) 168-87; idem *Testament* 39-41, 65-67, 73; Thyen professes a growing skepticism (over 50 years) to such a theory (*Johannes-*

celebrated a Messiah who came for the sake of the world, they seem to have had little sense of themselves having a mission for the sake of the world, even of sharing Christ's mission. Their spirituality was rather sustained by turning their back on the world, dependent on their own close-knit community for strength and fed by the reassurances of the Johannine tradition that they were of the light despite the surrounding darkness, they knew the truth, and they had eternal life.

f. Conclusion

In short, John's Gospel cannot be and should not be simply paralleled to the other three Gospels. Although all four Gospels can be set in parallel, as in the Aland *Synopsis*, the first three Gospels are clearly parallel in a way and to a degree that is not true of John's Gospel; that is why Matthew, Mark and Luke can be referred to collectively as 'the Synoptic Gospels'. John's Gospel is not a synoptic Gospel.

The distinctiveness of John's portrayal of Jesus should not be diminished or ignored. The older attempt to harmonize all four Gospels should be recognized to be wrong-headed. John was evidently *not* attempting to do the same thing as the Synoptic Evangelists. And though we should recognize that all Evangelists had theological axes to grind, *the briefest of comparisons is sufficient to show that the Synoptic Evangelists were much more constrained by the forms of their tradition than ever John was*. The closeness of the Synoptic parallels cannot be explained otherwise. And contrariwise, it is equally impossible to make sense of John's Gospel on the assumption that he was attempting to do the same as the Synoptic Evangelists.

We should not hesitate to draw the unavoidable corollary: that *to read and interpret John's Gospel as though John had been trying to do the same as the Synoptics is to misread and misinterpret his Gospel*. This remains the challenge for those who approach John's Gospel from a conservative perspective: by so doing, they may be missing and distorting John's message! The truth of Jesus, the story of his mission and its significance, was not expressed in only one way, as though the Gospel of Jesus Christ could be told only by strictly limiting the interpretation of the earliest Jesus tradition, the ways in which Jesus was remembered. It proved also acceptable that *the character and themes of Jesus' mission provided the basis for fuller and deeper reflection on what Jesus stood for and achieved* — still the Gospel of Jesus Christ.

---

evangelium 3). Cf. also W. A. Meeks, 'The Man from Heaven in Johannine Sectarianism' (1972), in Ashton, ed., *Interpretation* 169-205: 'It is a book for insiders' (193).

At the same time, it is equally important to note that John clearly knew the same sort of tradition known to and used by the Synoptic Evangelists.

- He follows the same Gospel format in giving his account of Jesus' mission.
- He had sources of/access to earliest memories of close disciples of Jesus which filled out parts of Jesus' mission that the other Evangelists passed over, for understandable reasons — the overlap period with the Baptist, and Jesus' earlier trips into Judaea and Jerusalem being probably the most obvious.
- The indications that John had good sources of tradition (Baptist tradition, attempt to make Jesus king in Galilee, contacts in Jerusalem), of which we would not have known had John not retold them, suggests that other parts of John's Gospel are better rooted in historical tradition than we now can tell (the Synoptists did not include all the traditional material available to them); John 21.25 speaks for all the Gospels.
- John's use of the tradition of Jesus' miracles was selective, but the types of miracle he described and which he encompassed by profound discourse and teaching were mostly familiar as types of Jesus' healing ministry.[230]
- Again and again the elaborate discourses and teaching give evidence of being rooted in Synoptic-like tradition or seem to be an elaboration of particular sayings/parables of Jesus known from the Synoptic tradition.
- John evidently knew the final passion of Jesus at first hand or from first-hand sources, a claim which is emphasized at 19.35 and 21.24 in particular; the beloved disciple and Mary Magdalene may be identified as such sources.

The most obvious way to explain and understand the distinctiveness of John's portrayal of Jesus is that John knew well the tradition which he shared with the Synoptics, and that *he wove his much more refined fabric from the same stuff as the Synoptics* — the product and expression of many years of reflection on the significance of what Jesus had taught and done, and on the significance of the revelation he had brought and constituted in his life and mission.[231] While we should not understate the distinctiveness of John's Gospel, given the many echoes and parallels in John, neither should we exaggerate the difference. *John in his own way was telling the same story as the other Evangelists*. That he chose to do so by elaborating that story in his own way should be

---

230. Contrast e.g. *The Infancy Gospel of Thomas* 2-5, and the apocryphal *Acts* (see below, e.g. §§47.4 and 48.6).

231. See also my conclusion to 'John and the Oral Gospel Tradition' 378-79.

acknowledged and properly appreciated. John's Gospel should be valued for what it is, not for what it is not.

In terms of the oral Jesus tradition, *John's Gospel shows just how diverse and varied the Jesus tradition could become in its various retellings*. The elaboration which John provided made his version of the Jesus tradition controversial; he sailed near the edge of what was acceptable. But the facts that John retained the Gospel character, and that its rootage in the earlier oral tradition was clear, were presumably sufficient to ensure that John's Gospel would be recognized as one of the four Gospels to be designated as canonical.

What then of the *Gospel of Thomas*?

43.2 The *Gospel of Thomas*

When they turn from the Gospel of John to the *Gospel of Thomas* readers might well experience a feeling of surprise similar to what they experienced when they first turned from the Synoptic Gospels to the Gospel of John — though in reverse! With John, the surprise is that the Johannine presentation of Jesus is so different from that of the Synoptics. In contrast, with *Thomas* we seem to move back from the substantially developed Jesus tradition of John, with its strongly marked christology, to material much closer in form to that of the Synoptics. As we saw above, the case for seeing John's presentation of Jesus' miracles and particularly his teaching as rooted in Synoptic-like Jesus tradition was not self-evident and had to be demonstrated with care. In contrast, even a brief consultation of *Thomas* can hardly fail to observe that the links between *Thomas* and the Synoptic Jesus tradition are clear and substantial.[232] This indeed is the paradox of John and *Thomas*, and why they make such interesting bedfellows here in the same chapter: that John is part of the NT canon, but *Thomas* is regularly closer to the Synoptic tradition than John!

One of the major consequences of the discovery of *Thomas* was that the hypothesized Q document suddenly became a more realistic hypothesis.[233] For here was a document which, like the hypothesized Q document, consists entirely of sayings attributed to Jesus. Unlike the Synoptics, but like Q, there is no narrative framework holding the whole together, and no passion narrative. From almost first glance, in fact, the *Gospel of Thomas* poses the question:

---

232. As observed also, e.g., by I. Dunderberg, '*Thomas*' I-sayings and the Gospel of John', in Uro, ed., Thomas *at the Crossroads* 33-64 (here 33).

233. Which also explains why interest in Q blossomed in the last two decades of the twentieth century; see particularly the writings of Kloppenborg in the bibliography of *Jesus Remembered*.

Is this a developed form of the Q document? And as soon as that question is raised a sequence of corollary questions follows hard on its heels. What was the undeveloped or less developed form of *Thomas*?[234] Was it the same as the Q constructed from the non-Markan close parallels between Matthew and Luke? Or does *Thomas* provide evidence of early Jesus tradition which Matthew and Luke (and Mark) ignored or deliberately omitted?[235] In other words, does *Thomas* provide proof of a more diverse response to Jesus than is evidenced by the diversity of the Synoptics? Is *Thomas* evidence that a different kind of Christianity emerged from the impact made by Jesus — a different kind from that of Paul and the Synoptic Evangelists? Such has been the conclusion of many scholars who have studied Q and *Thomas*,[236] and it cannot be dismissed lightly. So the issues posed by the *Gospel of Thomas* are both substantial and potentially of major importance.

We begin, then, by asking the same two questions: From where did the *Gospel of Thomas* derive its Jesus tradition? And what were the objectives of the one or the several who were ultimately responsible for its compilation?

a. *Thomas* and the Synoptic Tradition

As already indicated, the parallels between *Thomas* and the Synoptic tradition are numerous and clear (clearer than those between John and the Synoptics). So, as with the canonical Gospels we start by cataloguing and examining the parallels between *Thomas* and the Synoptic Gospels. Do they indicate knowledge of the Synoptic Gospels themselves? Do the links between *Thomas* and the Q tradition indicate a literary dependence?[237]

---

234. The Oxyrhynchus parallels are of course a major factor in such a discussion; see §40.4b above.

235. E.g. S. J. Patterson suggests the possibility that *Thomas* 'has its own roots, which reach deeply into the fertile soil of early Christian tradition' (*The Gospel of Thomas and Jesus* 9); also *The Gospel of Thomas and Christian Origins: Essays on the Fifth Gospel* (Leiden: Brill, 2013) 93-118.

236. So e.g. Crossan in his various writings listed in the bibliography of *Jesus Remembered*; Ehrman, *Lost Christianities* 58.

237. The most useful listing of *Thomas* and Synoptic interdependence is DeConick, *The Original Gospel of Thomas in Translation*, with an Appendix on 'Verbal Similarities between *Thomas* and the Synoptics' (299-316); see also Elliott, *ANT* 133-35. For wider surveys of parallels with other ancient literature see J. D. Crossan, *Sayings Parallels: A Workbook for the Jesus Tradition* (Philadelphia: Fortress, 1986); W. D. Stroker, *Extracanonical Sayings of Jesus* (Atlanta: Scholars, 1989); M. Meyer, *The Gospel of Thomas: The Hidden Sayings of Jesus* (San Francisco: Harper Collins, 1992). In this section (§43.2) I usually follow DeConick's translation and sub-verse division of the *Thomas* logia.

Thomas's Knowledge and Use of Synoptic Tradition

GospThom	Close Synoptic parallels	Less-close parallels with the Synoptics
2.1-4		Matt. 7.7-8/Luke 11.9-10
3.1-3		Luke 17.20-21
4.2-3	Mark 10.31 pars.	
5.1-2		Mark 4.22 pars.
6.4-5	Mark 4.22 (Matt. 10.26/ Luke 8.17)	
8.1-3		Matt. 13.47-48[238]
8.4, 21.11, 24.2, 63.4, 65.8, 96.3	Mark 4.9 + Matt. (3x), Luke (3x)	
9.1-5	Mark 4.3-8 pars.	
10		Luke 12.49
14.4		Luke 10.8-9
14.5	Mark 7.15 (Matt. 15.11)	
16.1-2	Luke 12.51/Matt. 10.34	
16.3	Luke 12.52-53 (Matt. 10.35-36)	
20.1-4	Mark 4.30-32 pars.	
21.5 cf. 103	Matt. 24.43 (Luke 12.39)	
21.10	Mark 4.29	
22.1-3		Mark 10.15 pars.
24.3		Matt. 5.14, 6.22-23
26.1-2	Matt. 7.3-5/Luke 6.41-42	
30.1-2		Matt. 18.20(?)
31.1-2	Luke 4.23-24 (Mark 6.4 par.)	
32		Matt. 5.14
33.1	Matt. 10.27 (Luke 12.3)	
33.2-3	Luke 11.33, 8.16 (Matt. 5.15, Mark 4.21)	
34	Matt. 15.14 (Luke 6.39)	
35.1-2	Mark 3.27 (Matt. 12.29; Luke 11.21-22)	
36.1-3	Matt. 6.25-30/Luke 12.22, 27-30	
38.1		Matt. 13.17/Luke 10.24
39.1-2	Matt. 23.13/Luke 11.52	
39.3	Matt. 10.16	

---

238. See also Patterson, *Gospel of Thomas and Christian Origins* 197-209.

GospThom	Close Synoptic parallels	Less-close parallels with the Synoptics
40.1-2		Matt. 15.13
41.1-2	Mark 4.25 pars.	
44.1-3	Matt. 12.31-32/Luke 12.10 (Mark 3.28-30)	
45.1-4	Luke 6.44-45/Matt. 7.16, 12.34-35	
46.1-2		Matt. 11.11/Luke 7.28
47.1-2		Matt. 6.24/Luke 16.13
47.3-4	Mark 2.22 pars.	
47.5	Mark 2.21 pars.	
48 cf. 106.1-2		Mark 11.23 pars.
54	Luke 6.20 (Matt. 5.3)	
55.1-2 cf. 101.1	Luke 14.26-27/Matt. 10.37-38	
57.1-4	Matt. 13.24-30	
61.1		Matt. 24.40-41/Luke 17.34-35
62.1		Mark 4.11 pars.
62.2		Matt. 6.3
63.1-3	Luke 12.16-21	
64.1-11	Matt. 22.2-10/Luke 14.16-24	
65.1-7	Mark 12.1-9 pars.	
66	Mark 12.10 pars.	
68.1	Luke 6.22 (Matt. 5.10-11)	
69.2	Luke 6.21 (Matt. 5.6)	
71	Mark 14.58 par. John 2.19	
72.1-3		Luke 12.13-14
73	Matt. 9.37-38/Luke 10.2	
76.1-2	Matt. 13.45-46	
76.3	Luke 12.33/Matt. 6.19-20	
78.1-3	Matt. 11.7-8/Luke 7.24-25	
79.1-3	Luke 11.27-28 and 23.29	
86.1-2	Matt. 8.20/Luke 9.58	
89.1-2	Luke 11.39-40 (Matt. 23.25-26)	
90.1-2	Matt. 11.28-30	
91.1-2		Matt. 16.1-3 (Luke 12.54-56)
92.1-2		Matt. 7.7-8/Luke 11.9-10
93.1-2	Matt. 7.6	
94.1-2	Matt. 7.7-8/Luke 11.9-10	

GospThom	Close Synoptic parallels	Less-close parallels with the Synoptics
95.1-2		Luke 6.34
96.1-2	Matt. 13.33/Luke 13.20-21	
99.1-3	Luke 8.19-21 (Mark 3.31-35 par.)	
100.1-4	Mark 12.13-17	
104.1-2		Mark 2.18-20; Luke 5.33-35
107.1-3	Matt. 18.12-13/Luke 15.4-7	
109.1-3		Matt. 13.44
113.1-4		Luke 17.20-21

By 'close parallels' I indicate a verbal similarity indicating a variation of the same saying. Since the *Thomas* tradition provides an excellent test case of what I have maintained to be characteristic of the oral Jesus tradition (the same yet different),[239] and of how varied were the forms taken by the oral Jesus tradition in use and transmission, I give more examples than is probably necessary:[240]

Thomas 9	Mark 4.3-8 pars.
Jesus said, 'Look! The sower went out. He filled his hands (with seeds). He cast (them). Some fell on the road. The birds came and gathered them up. Others fell on the rock and did not take root in the earth or put forth ears. And others fell among thorns. They choked the seeds and the worms ate them. And others fell on the good earth, and it produced good fruit. It yielded sixty per measure and a hundred and twenty per measure'.	Listen! A sower went out to sow. And as he sowed, some seed fell on the path, and the birds came and ate it up. Other seed fell on rocky soil, where it did not have much soil, and it sprang up quickly, since it had no depth of soil. And when the sun rose, it was scorched; and since it had no root, it withered away. Other seed fell among thorns, and the thorns grew up and choked it, and it yielded no grain. Other seed fell into good soil and brought forth grain, growing up and increasing and yielding thirty and sixty and a hundredfold.

---

239. Cf. DeConick, who also sees *Thomas* as a good test case for discerning how the Jesus tradition (was) developed (*Recovering the Original* Gospel of Thomas 36-37). Contrast the views referred to by S. J. Patterson, with J. M. Robinson and H.-G. Bethge, *The Fifth Gospel: The Gospel of Thomas Comes of Age* (Harrisburg: TPI, 1998) 71-72.

240. In the following tables I cite the Synoptic passage closest in parallel to the *Thomas* logion, indicating when there are also parallels in the other Synoptics, but indicating by parentheses if the parallel is not so close.

Thomas 16.1-2	Luke 12.51/Matt. 10.34
Jesus said, 'Perhaps people think it is peace that I have come to cast upon the world. And they do not know it is division that I have come to cast upon the earth — fire, sword, war'.	Do you think that I have come to bring peace to the earth? No, I tell you, but rather division (Luke)/ but a sword (Matt.).

Thomas 20.1-4	Mark 4.30-32 pars.
The disciples said to Jesus, 'Tell us what is the kingdom of heaven like?' He said to them, 'It is like a mustard seed, smaller than all seeds. But when it falls on cultivated soil, it puts forth a large branch and becomes a shelter for birds of the sky'.	He also said, 'With what can we compare the kingdom of God, or what parable will we use for it? It is like a mustard seed, which, when sown upon the ground, is the smallest of all the seeds on earth; yet when it is sown it grows up and becomes the greatest of all shrubs, and puts forth large branches, so that the birds of the air can make nests in its shade'.

Thomas 21.5[241]	Matt. 24.43/(Luke 12.39)
For this reason I say, 'If the owner of a house knows that a thief is coming, he will keep watch before he arrives. He will not allow him to break into his house, part of his estate, to steal his furnishings'.	But understand this: if the owner of the house had known in what part of the night the thief was coming, he would have stayed awake and would not have let his house be broken into.

Thomas 26.1-2/P. Oxy. 1.1-4	Matt. 7.3-5/Luke 6.41-42
Jesus said, 'The speck in your brother's eye, you see. But the plank in your eye, you do not see! When you remove the plank from your eye, then you will see clearly to take the speck out of your brother's eye'.	Why do you see the speck in your brother's eye, but do not notice the plank in your own eye? Or how can you say to your brother, 'Let me take the speck out of your eye, while the plank is in your own eye? You hypocrite, first take the plank out of your own eye, and then you will see clearly to take the speck out of your brother's eye.

241. *Thomas* 103 is very similar.

Thomas 31.1-2/P. Oxy. 1.9-14	Luke 4.23-24/Mark 6.4 par.
Jesus said, 'A prophet is not received hospitably in his own village. A doctor does not heal the people who know him'.	He said to them, 'Doubtless you will quote to me this proverb, "Doctor, cure yourself!" And you will say, "Do here also in your own village what we have heard you did in Capernaum"'. And he said, 'Truly I tell you, no prophet is received hospitably in his own village'.

Thomas 39.1-3/ P. Oxy. 655 ii.11-19	Matt. 23.13; 10.16	Luke 11.52
Jesus said, 'The Pharisees and the scribes have taken the keys of knowledge. They have hidden them. Neither have they entered nor have they allowed those who want to enter to do so. You, however, be as prudent as serpents and as guileless as doves'.	But woe to you, scribes and Pharisees, hypocrites! For you lock people out of the kingdom of heaven. For you do not enter yourselves, and you do not allow those who want to enter in to do so. Be therefore as prudent as serpents and as guileless as doves.	Woe to you lawyers! For you have taken away the key of knowledge. You did not enter yourselves, and you hindered those who were entering.

Thomas 45.1-4	Luke 6.44-45/(Matt. 7.16, 12.34-35)
Jesus said, 'Grapes are not harvested from thorn trees, nor are figs picked from thistles, for they do not produce fruit. A good person brings forth good from his treasury. A bad person brings forth evil from his wicked treasury in his heart, and speaks evil. For from the excessiveness of the heart, he brings forth evil'.	Figs are not gathered from thorns, nor are grapes picked from a bramble bush. The good man out of the good treasure of his heart produces good, and the evil man out of his evil treasure produces evil. For out of the abundance of the heart his mouth speaks.

Thomas 47.3-5	Mark 2.21-22 pars.
No one drinks old wine and immediately wants to drink new wine. Also, new wine is not put into old wineskins so that they may burst. Nor is old wine put into a new wineskin so that it may spoil. An old patch is not sewn onto a garment because a tear would result.	No one sows a piece of unshrunk cloth on an old garment; otherwise, the patch pulls away from it, the new from the old, and a worse tear is made. And no one puts new wine into old wineskins; otherwise, the wine will burst the skins, and the wine is lost and the skins; but new wine is for fresh skins.

Thomas 55.1-2[242]	Luke 14.26-27/Matt.10.37-38
Jesus said, 'Whoever does not hate his father and mother cannot become a disciple of mine. And whoever does not hate his brothers and sisters and carry his cross as I do is not worthy of me'.	If anyone comes to me and does not hate his father and mother and wife and children and brothers and sisters, yes, and even his own life, he cannot be my disciple (Luke)/ is not worthy of me (Matt.). Whoever does not carry his own cross and come after me, cannot be my disciple (Luke)/ is not worthy of me (Matt.).

Thomas 76.3	Luke 12.33/Matt. 6.19-20
You too, seek his imperishable and enduring treasure where neither moth draws near to eat nor worm destroys.	Make purses for yourselves that do not wear out, an unfailing treasure in heaven, where no thief comes near and no moth destroys.

Thomas 79.1-3	Luke 11.27-28; 23.29
A woman in the crowd said to him, 'Blessed is the womb that bore you and the breasts that nourished you'. He said to her, 'Blessed are the people who have heard the word of the Father and have truly kept it. For there will be days when you will say, "Blessed is the womb that has not conceived and the breasts that have not given milk"'.	. . . a woman in the crowd raised her voice and said to him, 'Blessed is the womb that bore you and the breasts that nursed you'. But he said, 'Blessed rather are those who hear the word of God and obey it!' For the days are surely coming when they will say, 'Blessed are the barren, and the wombs that never bore, and the breasts that never nursed'.

Thomas 86.1-2	Matt. 8.20/Luke 9.58
Jesus said, 'Foxes have their holes and birds have their nests, but the son of man has nowhere to lay his head and rest'.	And Jesus said to him, 'Foxes have holes, and birds of the air have nests; but the son of man has nowhere to lay his head'.

Thomas 90.1-2	Matt. 11.28-30
Jesus said, 'Come to me, for my yoke is mild and my lordship is gentle. And you will find rest for yourselves'.	Come to me, all who labour and are heavy laden, and I will give you rest. Take my yoke upon you, and learn of me; for I am gentle and lowly in heart, and you will find rest for your souls. For my yoke is easy, and my burden is light.

---

242. *Thomas* 101.1-2 seems to be a more developed version.

Thomas 93.1-2	Matt. 7.6
Do not give what is holy to dogs, lest they toss them on the manure pile. Do not toss the pearls to pigs, lest they break(?) them.	Do not give what is holy to dogs; and do not throw your pearls before pigs, lest they will trample them under foot and turn to attack you.

Thomas 96.1-2	Matt. 13.33/Luke 13.20-21
Jesus said, 'The Kingdom of the Father is like a woman. She took a little yeast; she buried it in dough; and made the dough into large bread loaves'.	The kingdom of heaven is like yeast that a woman took and buried in three measures of flour until it was all leavened.

Thomas 99.1-3	Luke 8.19-21/(Mark 3.31-35 par.)
The disciples said to him, 'Your brothers and your mother are standing outside'. He said to them, 'Those here who do the will of my Father, they are my brothers and my mother. They are the people who will enter the Kingdom of my Father'.	Then his mother and his brothers came to him, but they could not reach him for the crowd. And he was told, 'Your mother and your brothers are standing outside, wanting to see you'. But he said to them, 'My mother and my brothers are those who hear the word of God and do it'.

Those who recall the equivalent tables in *Jesus Remembered* documenting the parallels between the Synoptic Gospels[243] should hardly need persuading that the *Thomas*/Synoptic parallels just listed show very much the same variations as were evident in the Mark/Matthew/Luke parallels — the same, yet different. A further interesting feature, less necessary to document in a table, is that the *Thomas* version is significantly briefer than the Synoptic parallels to the *Thomas* logia 36.1-3 (on anxiety), 57.1-4 (parable of the darnel), 63.1-3 (parable of the rich fool), 100.1-4 (on paying tribute to Caesar), and 107.1-3 (parable of the lost sheep). This could suggest that the lengthier Synoptic versions are elaborations of a sparer framework; but probably it is simply a reminder that traditional material could be abbreviated, or expanded, without the main point being lost.[244] Certainly, 64.1-11 with its parallels (the parable of the dinner guests) shows how varied a story could be in different tellings, all making the same basic point and using the same structure.[245]

243. *Jesus Remembered* §§8.4-5 and *passim*.
244. Cf. again Sanders (§39 n.58). See also J. Frey, 'Die Lilien und das Gewand: EvThom 36 und 37 als Paradigma für das Verhältnis des *Thomasevangeliums* zur synoptischen Überlieferung', in Frey, ed., *Das Thomasevangelium* 122-80 (127-40, 176-80).
245. See also discussion in J. D. Crossan, *Four Other Gospels* (Minneapolis: Seabury, 1985) 39-52; and further G. E. Sterling, '"Where Two or Three Are Gathered": The Tra-

What is noticeable in all these cases is that while the parallels are close, they still pose the question whether they are close enough to suggest literary dependence, or to suggest that *Thomas* was derived by copying and editing one of the Synoptics.[246] I am less sure.[247] In each case, the tradition is undoubtedly the same,

---

dition History of the Parable of the Banquet (Matt 22:1-14/Luke 14:16-24/*GThom* 64)', in J. Frey, ed., *Das Thomasevangelium* 95-121, though I hesitate to speak of one version (or aspects) as 'more authentic' (111).

246. Two of the most recent treatments of the issue argue strongly for *Thomas*'s dependence on Matthew and Luke, as evidenced by *Thomas*'s knowledge of distinctively redactional features of the two Evangelists. Gathercole instances dependence on Matthew in *Thomas* 13 (not least its reference to Matthew as such), 14.5 and 44, and dependence on Luke in 5, 31, 33, 47, 65, 66, 99, 104 (*Composition* chs. 7, 8), though the indications of literary dependence are flimsier than in the weaker cases for literary interdependence in the Synoptic tradition. M. Goodacre, *Thomas and the Gospels: The Case for Thomas's Familiarity with the Synoptics* (Grand Rapids: Eerdmans, 2012) 30-44, notes the close verbal agreement between *Thomas* and Synoptic tradition — 3.1-3, 4.2-3, 5.2, 14.5, 26, 39.3, 73, 86; though in most cases the verbal agreement is restricted to the sort of proverbial saying which was most likely to be fairly fixed in the oral tradition (4.2-3, 5.2, 14.5, 39.3, 73, 86); his strongest case is *Thomas* 26. His further examples of Matthean redaction in *Thomas* (20 and 54, 57 — ch. 4), and of Lukan redaction in *Thomas* (31, 63, 72 — ch. 5) are hardly impressive; the strongest case is *Thomas* 79 (Luke 11.27-28 and 23.29) (ch. 6). The lack of agreement between Gathercole and Goodacre on evidence of *Thomas*'s knowledge of Matthean and Lukan redaction is interesting. Goodacre criticizes me for underestimating the importance of literacy among the early tradents (*Thomas* 130), but misses the point that in my discussion of the Synoptic tradition in *Jesus Remembered* I was focusing attention on the oral period of transmission (the first twenty or thirty years) and allowing the possibility that the Synoptic tradition in *Thomas* goes back to that period. Gathercole also argues that the influence of Paul on *Thomas* is evident in *Thomas* 3 (Rom. 10.7), *Thomas* 17 (1 Cor. 2.9, and especially *Thomas* 53 (Rom. 2-3) (*Composition* 227-49).

247. Given the likelihood that Jesus tradition was widely circulated and known, it is not enough simply to say that 'The similarities between *Thomas* and the Synoptics are extensive, and so a literary explanation is more probable' (Gathercole, *Composition* 139). Likewise to claim that 'an extant literary source' trumps a 'rather speculative . . . appeal to an unknown oral tradition' (*Composition* 146; also 214-21) both overstates the degree of similarity ('source'?) and ignores the fact that the Synoptic tradition must have been well established in oral form before it was transcribed, and that it continued to be known and used in oral form for several decades into the second century (§44). I continue to insist that the Synoptic tradition is itself sufficient proof of the way in which Jesus was remembered in the decades before the Jesus tradition was transcribed; the alternative is to regard the decades of 30-70 not so much as a 'tunnel period' and more as a black hole. To limit the discussion of the Synoptic/*Thomas* parallels to whether they support any of the differing (literary) resolutions of 'the Synoptic problem' is at best blinkered thinking.

R. Uro, '*Thomas* and Oral Gospel Tradition', in Uro, ed., *Thomas at the Crossroads* 8-32, argues strongly for indirect literary influence: 'secondary orality' is 'a noteworthy alternative in the source-critical analyses of the sayings in the *Gospel of Thomas*' (21); 'the suggestion that *Thomas* had access to some "pure" oral traditions, uninfluenced by any written records of Jesus' sayings is simply unrealistic' (19-20); further bibliography partic-

but in almost all the cases the variations can be well explained as the variations typical of diverse oral performances of what is basically the same tradition. This is not to say that one form or version of the tradition was more original than others, closer to what Jesus actually said when he first delivered the teaching or saying.[248] It simply underlines what became evident in the first volume of *Christianity in the Making*: that the Jesus tradition was varied from the first, that Jesus may well have delivered his more important teaching on several occasions, in varied form and wording, and that in many cases the argument for one version to be regarded as necessarily more authentic than another may well be simply wrong-headed.[249]

The less close parallels probably do not really need to be illustrated here, since even a casual look will make clear that while the *Thomas* logion has some link with the Synoptic tradition, in almost every case the link is much more tangential than the logia illustrated above, and the Synoptic parallel is more of a distraction from *Thomas*'s intention. But I note some examples below.[250]

---

ularly on 9-10, and Gathercole, *Composition* 157-58. Uro illustrates his case by reference to *Thomas* 14.4-5 (22-32). The only problem is that 'secondary orality' merges into and in effect becomes hard to distinguish from the thesis of a broad oral Jesus tradition on which the Synoptic tradition drew and to which it contributed; in many/most cases it may become almost meaningless to speak of specific or direct Markan or Matthean or Lukan influence on the *Thomas* tradition. Similarly the judgment of Patterson in *The Fifth Gospel*, that 'The genesis of the *Gospel of Thomas* probably lies in the last decades of the first century' (45), can apply with any confidence only to the tradition shared with the Synoptics.

248. Contrast Koester, who maintains that 'in a number of instances Thomas has clearly preserved a more original form of the saying' and who argues that *Thomas* preserves an early form of the Q tradition which lacked an apocalyptic orientation (*Ancient Christian Gospels* 89-99, also 145-46, 150, 157-58, 170; earlier '*GNOMAI DIAPHOROI*' 130-32). Much more plausible is DeConick's argument that the failure of early eschatological expectations to be realized ('the Non-Event') resulted in a 'collapse of the apocalypse' and a shift from apocalypticism to an encratic form of mysticism (*Recovering* chs. 6-9); similarly in 'Mysticism and the *Gospel of Thomas*' 209-12; see also Goodacre, *Thomas* 184-87; contrast Patterson, *Gospel of Thomas and Christian Origins* 232-36. Similarly Koester's assertion that *Thomas* 9 is 'more original' than Mark 4.3-9 (*Ancient Christian Gospels* 102) misses the point that both versions are simply variations of the same parable; similarly with other parallels which Koester draws with Mark (108-12).

249. See also J. Schröter, *Erinnerung an Jesu Worte: Studien zur Rezeption der Logienüberlieferung in Markus, Q und Thomas* (WMANT 76; Neukirchen-Vluyn: Neukirchener, 1997) 136-43, 236-37, 295-96, 373-75, 412-14, 432-34, 459-69.

250.

Thomas 3.1-3/P. Oxy. 654.9-16	Luke 17.20-21
Jesus said, 'If those who lead you say to you, "Look! The kingdom is in heaven", then the birds of heaven will precede you; if they say, "It is under the earth", then the fish of the sea will precede you. But the kingdom of heaven is within you and outside you'.	The kingdom of God is not coming with signs to be observed; nor will they say, 'Look, here it is!' or 'There!', for look, the kingdom of God is within/among you.

To be more specific, the above tabulation reveals a number of important features.

1. Of the 114 *Thomas* logia, 42 contain close parallel material — that is, 36.8%. The percentage is misleading, since the *Thomas* logia vary in length, and in some cases only part of the whole logion has closely parallel material (e.g. *Thomas* 21, 61, 68). I have not counted the multiple occurrences of 'Whoever has ears should listen' (8.4, etc.).
2. When the less-close parallels are included, the figure goes up to about 63, that is, 56.2% (with the same qualification).[251] This assuredly indicates that *Thomas* shared a great deal of the Jesus tradition known to us from the Synoptics.[252] And if the Synoptic tradition has the best claim to express the impact made by Jesus himself and the way he was remem-

Thomas 5.1-2/P.Oxy. 654.27-31	Mark 4.22 pars.
Jesus said, 'Understand what is in front of you, and what is hidden from you will be revealed to you. For nothing is hidden that will not be manifested'.	For there is nothing hidden except to be revealed, nor is anything hidden but that it might come to the light.

Thomas 10	Luke 12.49
Jesus said, 'I have cast fire upon the world. And look! I am guarding it until it blazes'.	I came to cast fire upon the earth. And how I wish that it were already kindled.

Thomas 32/P.Oxy. 1.36-41	Matt. 5.14
Jesus said, 'A city built on a high mountain and fortified cannot fall nor be hidden'.	You are the light of the world. A city set on a hill cannot be hidden.

Thomas 47.1-2	Matt. 6.24/Luke 16.13
Jesus said, 'It is impossible for a man to ride two horses and to bend two bows. Also it is impossible for a servant to serve two masters, or he will honour the one and insult the other'.	No one can serve two masters. For either he will hate the one and love the other, or he will be devoted to one and despise the other.

Thomas 92.1-2	Matt. 7.7-8/Luke 11.9-10
Jesus said, 'Seek and you will find. However, the questions you asked me previously, but which I did not address then, now I want to address, yet you do not seek (answers)'.	Ask, and it will be given you. Seek, and you will find. Knock and it will be opened to you. For everyone who asks receives, and he who seeks finds, and to him who knocks it will be opened.

251. Cameron maintains that 'no fewer than 68 of the 114 sayings in the text have biblical parallels' (*ABD* 6.536). Gathercole agrees with Koester (with slight differences) that 67 of the *Thomas* logia overlap significantly with the Synoptics; he includes 13, 25, 102 and 106 (*Composition* 153).

252. *Thomas*'s dependence on Synoptic tradition 'touches on every strand of Synoptic data. No group of material is absent' (Goodacre, *Thomas and the Gospels* 20-24).

bered by the earliest Christian disciples,[253] then it follows that *Thomas* is also a witness to that impact and to the way Jesus was remembered. Whether this is true of the rest of *Thomas* is a question to be discussed after taking into consideration the rest of the *Thomas* material.

3. The parallels with Q material (that is, the non-Markan tradition shared by Matthew and Luke) are particularly notable, 29 in all (25.4%).[254] But it is also notable that at other times *Thomas* seems to share the tradition with only one of the Synoptics — Mark (21 instances),[255] Matthew (11 in all, 9.6%),[256] and Luke (9 in all, 7.9%).[257] The extent of the parallels certainly confirms that *Thomas* shared much of the Q material, but gives no support to the possibility that *Thomas* knew the Q material in a document the sequence of whose sayings Luke may have preserved.[258] Even if there was a distinctive Q collection (or a Q document), *Thomas*'s knowledge of the Jesus tradition as represented by the Synoptic tradition was much broader than Q.[259]

4. The same is true for the indications that *Thomas* knew tradition otherwise known to us only from one Synoptic Gospel (e.g. 39.1-2, 90.1-2, 93.1-2). The parallels do not demonstrate literary dependence, and therefore need not imply a knowledge of that Gospel as such. The impression is thus strengthened that the oral Jesus tradition was wide-

---

253. As argued in *Jesus Remembered*.

254. Q parallels — *Thomas* 2, 16, 21.5, 26.1-2, 33.1, 2-3, 34, 36.1-3, 39.1-2, 44, 45.1-4, 46.1-2, 47.2, 54, 55.1-2, 61.1, 64.1-11, 68.1, 69.2, 73, 76.3, 78.1-3, 86.1-2, 89.1-2, 91.1-2, 92.1-2, 94.1-2, 96.1-2, 107.1-3. Koester reckons that of 79 sayings of *Thomas* with Synoptic parallels, 46 have parallels in Q; he includes *Thomas* 5, 6.3, 10, 17, 24.3, 43, 61.3, 69, 79.1, 95, 103 (*Ancient Christian Gospels* 87-89); but assignation of most of these to Q is highly disputable. See also T. Zöckler, *Jesu Lehren im Thomasevangelium* (NHMS 47; Leiden: Brill, 1999) 53-98. Goodacre, of couse, protests against the suggestion that *Thomas* provides support for the existence of a Q document (*Thomas and the Gospels* 9-14).

255. But perhaps the parallels noted as Mark par(s). should be included, since it is quite possible that the other Synoptists were dependent on Mark at these points, which would add another 10 or so to the list (notably *Thomas* 9, 20, 41). Koester notes 27 sayings and parables shared with Mark (*Ancient Christian Gospels* 107), mostly as indicated above.

256. Specifically Matthean parallels — *Thomas* 8.1-3, 32, 39.3, 40.1-2, 57.1-4, 62.2, 76.1-2, 90.1-2, 93.1-2, 109.1-3.

257. Specifically Lukan parallels — *Thomas* 3.1-3, 10, 14.4, 63.1-3, 72.1-3, 79.1-3, 95.1-2, 101.1, 113.1-4. Surprisingly, Koester thinks that special Lukan material occurs only once in *Thomas* (*Ancient Christian Gospels* 107).

258. It is generally recognized that Matthew has grouped the Q material according to his own editorial strategy.

259. B. Chilton, 'The Gospel according to Thomas as a Source of Jesus' Teaching', in D. Wenham, ed., *Gospel Perspectives* vol. 5, *The Jesus Tradition outside the Gospels* (Sheffield: JSOT, 1984) 155-75 (here 159).

spread and known in varying amounts, in diverse sequences in different centres and with variety in wording similar to what we have already seen in the Synoptic tradition. And the earlier issue is again posed: whether any of the Evangelists or *Thomas* used all the Jesus tradition available to them.

5. Since so much of the *Thomas* tradition shares so many features with the Synoptic tradition, we may infer that distinctive characteristics given to the Jesus tradition in the Synoptic tradition, or already established in the material represented by the Synoptic tradition, had become more widely established — finger-prints of what thus appears to have been the main stream of oral Jesus tradition.[260] Or perhaps we should use a more contemporary image to suggest that such features form a large part of the 'genome' of the Jesus tradition. Of some interest here is the indication that the custom of inserting the exhortation, 'Whoever has ears should listen', to reinforce other logia, as attested in the Synoptic tradition,[261] is also a feature of the *Thomas* tradition (*Thomas* 8.4, etc.). Notable too is the fact that the parallels in several cases indicate that particular *groupings* of Jesus' sayings had become established, that is, as a regular feature of the oral Jesus tradition (*Thomas* 16, 33-34, 47, 65-66, 68-69, 92-94).[262] It should occasion no surprise that particular associations of sayings of Jesus became a common feature of Jesus tradition as used in perhaps widely ranging congregations — perhaps due to the influence of a particular apostle or influential teacher. And as human genes link one generation back to its ancestors, its genetic makeup in very large part the result of what its ancestors were and did, so we might deduce that the 'genetic makeup' of the Jesus tradition is evidence of the impact made by Jesus, indeed *is* itself an enduring part of the impact made by Jesus.

---

260. To be noted is the fact that *Thomas* 90.1-2 was familiar with what can almost certainly be regarded as Matthew's elaboration of the Jesus tradition (see §42.3b(7) above); that is, not necessarily that he knew Matthew's Gospel as such, but that some at least of the elaboration by individual teachers entered into the wider pool of oral tradition.

261. *Jesus Remembered* 462 n.379.

262. Cf. Cameron, *ABD* 6.537. It is not enough to argue that the association of the parable of the wicked tenants and Ps. 118.22 in *Thomas* 65-66 is evidence of literary dependency on Mark 12.1-11/Luke 20.9-17 (Gathercole, *Composition* 188-94), since the Synoptic tradition indicates that the association had become an established part of the (oral) Jesus tradition. However, J. P. Meier, 'The Parable of the Wicked Tenants in the Vineyard: Is the Gospel of Thomas Independent of the Synoptics?', in Skinner and Iverson, eds., *Unity and Diversity in the Gospels and Paul* 129-45, finds four redactional changes in Luke's version (Luke 20.9-18) that are clearly mirrored in *Thomas* 65-66.

b. The Distinctive *Thomas* Tradition

The parallels between *Thomas* and the Synoptic tradition are fascinating and important. At the same time, however, 52 of the 114 *Thomas* logia are not included in the above table. That is, on the same basis of calculation used above, 45.6% of *Thomas* logia lack parallel with the Synoptic tradition. The figure is still higher, since of the logia included in the above table, other parts of the same logia are not listed in the table.[263] So a fairer reckoning would be that something over 50% of *Thomas* lacks parallel with the Synoptic tradition.

To give a feel for this material I cite some examples:

- 7.1-2 — Jesus said, 'Blessed is the lion that the person will eat, and the lion becomes man. And cursed is the person whom the lion eats (and the lion becomes man?)'.
- 11.1-4 — Jesus said, 'This heaven will pass away, and the one above it will pass away. And the dead are not alive, and the living will not die. In the days when you ate what is dead, you made it something living. When you are in the light, what will you become? On the day when you were one, you became two. When you are two, what will you become?'
- 18.1-3 — The disciples said to Jesus, 'Tell us, how will our end come about?' Jesus said, 'Have you discovered the beginning that you seek the end? Because where the beginning is, the end will be also. Whoever will stand in the beginning is blessed. This person will know the end, yet will not die'.
- 27.1 — (Jesus said), 'If you do not fast from the world, you will not find the kingdom'.
- 42 — Jesus said, 'Be passers-by'.
- 51.1-2 — His disciples said to him, 'When will the dead rest, and when will the new world come?' He said to them, 'What you look for has come, but you have not perceived it'.
- 64.12 — Buyers and merchants (will) not enter the places of my Father.
- 69.1 — Blessed are those who have been persecuted in their hearts. They are the people who truly have known the Father.
- 74 — He said, 'Lord, many people are around the well(?), but no one is in the well(?)'.
- 97.1-4 — Jesus said, 'The kingdom of the (Father) is like a woman carrying a jar filled with meal. While she was walking (on the) road still a long way out, the handle of the jar broke. Behind her, the meal leaked

---

263. *Thomas* 3.4, 3.5, 4.1, 4.4, 6.1, 6.2-3, 14.1-3, 64.12, 68.2, 69.1 (using DeConick's sub-division of the logia).

out onto the road. She did not realize it. She had not noticed a problem. When she arrived at her house, she put the jar down and found it empty'.
- 98 — Jesus said, 'The kingdom of the Father is like someone who wished to kill a prominent man. While at home, he drew out his knife. He stabbed it into the wall to test whether his hand would be strong (enough). Then he murdered the prominent man'.
- 102 — Jesus said, 'Woe to the Pharisees because they are like a dog sleeping in the cattle trough. For the dog neither eats nor lets the cattle eat'.
- 110 — Jesus said, 'Whoever has found the world and become wealthy, he should disown the world'.
- 113.1-4 — His disciples said to him, 'When will the kingdom come?' 'It will not come by waiting. It will not be said, "Look! Here it is!" or "Look! There it is!" Rather, the kingdom of the Father is spread out over the earth, but people do not see it'.

Nothing here is directly parallel to Synoptic tradition, but there are not a few echoes of Synoptic-like sayings (e.g. *Thomas* 51.1-2, 69.1, 102, 113.1-4), and the repeated references to the kingdom are strong indications that this central feature of Jesus' own preaching has been retained[264]— as indeed Jesus' practice of telling provocative parables to illustrate the kingdom (*Thomas* 97, 98) — even when much/most of the teaching provided the challenge laid down in the opening logion: 'Whoever finds the meaning of these words will not die' (*Thomas* 1).

Also interesting are the number of logia which may echo or reflect the more distinctive *Johannine* language.[265]

Thomas 1	John 8.51
And he said, 'Whoever finds the meaning of these words will not taste death'.	Truly, truly, I say to you, if anyone keeps my word, he will never see death.

Thomas 13.5	John 4.14
After you drank, you became intoxicated from the bubbling fount which I had measured out.	... the water that I shall give him will become in him a well of water bubbling up to eternal life.

---

264. *Jesus Remembered* §12. But all note that the future eschatological note so typical of the Synoptic teaching on the kingdom is lacking (e.g. Blatz, *NTA* 1.114). See also Chilton, 'Thomas' 162-66.

265. See further R. E. Brown, 'The Gospel of Thomas and St John's Gospel', *NTS* 9 (1962-63) 155-77; also Koester, *Ancient Christian Gospels* 113-24; Dunderberg, '*Thomas* I-sayings' 33-35.

Thomas 15	
Jesus said, 'When you see the one who was not born of woman, fall on your face and worship him. That one is your Father'.	Cf. John 1.14; 10.30; 14.9; 20.28.

Thomas 24.1	
His disciples said, 'Teach us about the place where you are, because we must seek it'.	Cf. John 7.33-34; 8.21; 13.33, 36-37; 14.3-5.

Thomas 25.1-2	John 15.12
Jesus said, 'Love your brother like your soul. Watch over him like the pupil of your eye'.	This is my commandment: love one another, as I have loved you. Also 13.34-35; cf. 1 John 2.10; 3.10, 14-16; 4.20-21.

Thomas 28.1[266]	John 1.14
Jesus said, 'I stood in the midst of the world and I appeared to them in flesh'.	And the Logos became flesh and dwelt among us.

Thomas 38.2	John 7.34
There will be days when you will seek me, (but) will not find me.	You will seek me and you will not find me. Where I am going you cannot come.

Thomas 43.1-3[267]	John 8.25; 14.9
His disciples said to him, 'Who are you to say these things to us?' 'From what I say to you, you do not know who I am'.	8.25 — They said to him, 'Who are you?' Jesus said to them, 'Why do I speak to you at all?' 14.9 — Jesus said to him, 'Have I been with you so long, and yet you do not know me, Philip?'

---

266. Discussion in Dunderberg, *'Thomas'* I-sayings' 46-49, concluding that no direct contact between *Thomas* tradition or Johannine tradition is evident (49).

267. Discussion in Dunderberg, *'Thomas'* I-sayings' 61-62.

Thomas 61.2-5[268]	
Salome said, 'Who are you, sir? That is, from (whom)? You have reclined on my couch and eaten at my table'. Jesus said to her, 'I am he who comes from the one who is an equal. I was given some who belong to my Father'. 'I am your disciple'. 'Therefore I say, when a person becomes (equal) (with me), he will be filled with light. But if he becomes separated (from me), he will be filled with darkness'.	Cf. John 3.19-21; 5.18; 6.37; 10.29-30.

Thomas 77[269]	
Jesus said, 'I am the light which is above all things. I am everything. From me, everything came forth, and up to me, everything is reached'.	Cf. John 1.3-5, 9; 8.12; 9.5.

Thomas 92.1-2	John 16.4-5
Jesus said, 'Seek and you will find. However, the questions you asked me previously but which I did not address then, now I want to address, yet you do not seek (answers)'.	I did not say these things to you from the beginning, because I was with you. But now I am going to him who sent me, yet none of you asks me, 'Where are you going?'

These logia can be fairly described as echoing distinctive Johannine tradition. But any question of literary dependence, that Thomas knew the Gospel of John, can certainly be answered with a firm negative.[270] If knowledge of such distinctive features was dependent exclusively on familiarity with written tradition, then a more positive answer might be argued for. But in a culture where familiarity with Jesus tradition would still depend to a considerable extent on oral and aural transmission, it is much the more likely that such often quite faint echoes provide evidence that John's distinctive treatment of the

---

268. Discussion in Dunderberg, '*Thomas*' I-sayings' 49-56, noting that in contrast to *Thomas*, John's Gospel 'speaks of equality with God only in connection with Jesus' (55).

269. Discussion in Dunderberg, '*Thomas*' I-sayings' 58-60, concluding that the similarities between *Thomas* 77 and John are 'more likely due to their common background in Wisdom Christology than to a literary relationship' (60). J. Schröter, 'Die Herausforderung einer theologischen Interpretation des *Thomasevangeliums*', in Frey, ed., *Das Thomasevangelium* 435-59, notes that in *Thomas* Jesus is not 'the light of the world' but 'the light which is over all' (454-55).

270. Brown, 'Gospel of Thomas' 175; see also Dunderberg, '*Thomas*' I-sayings' 41-43, 63-64.

oral Jesus tradition became an element in the wider Jesus tradition.[271] John, in other words, should not be regarded as a sidetrack going off at a tangent from the main stream of Jesus tradition. The authority claimed by John's Gospel, with its source in the 'beloved disciple', would ensure that John's formulation of the Jesus tradition would be widely respected and influential.[272] Another illustration of this may be the fact that *Thomas* refers to God most often as 'the Father' (in 17 logia), though *Thomas* never follows John in speaking of Jesus as 'the Son'.

A further feature of *Thomas* relevant to the issue of where his tradition came from is the sequence of references to the Jewish concerns which dominated the early decades of embryonic Christianity — notably Sabbath observance, circumcision and ritual slaughter:

- 27.2 — If you do not observe the Sabbath day as a Sabbath, you will not see the Father.
- 43.2 — You are like the Jews, for they love the tree (but) hate its fruit, or they love the fruit (but) hate the tree.
- 52.1-2 — His disciples said to him, 'Twenty-four prophets have spoken in Israel, and all of them have spoken about you'. He said to them, 'You have left out the Living One who is in your presence and you have spoken about the dead'.[273]
- 53 — His disciple said to him, 'Is circumcision profitable or not?' He said to them: 'If it were profitable, their father would beget them circumcised from their mother. But the true circumcision in Spirit has found complete advantage'.
- 60 — A Samaritan was carrying a lamb as he was going into Judea. He

---

271. The alternative, as argued by Koester (*Ancient Christian Gospels* 113-24, 260-63), that John knew the *Thomas* tradition and adapted it, eliminating aspects he did not agree with, is at best tendentious; while not in essence implausible, in practice it assumes the thesis that Koester is attempting to demonstrate (*petitio principii*). DeConick, *Voices of the Mystics* 26-32, argues that some of the theology in John's Gospel is a direct response to visionary mystical traditions, 'a "faith mysticism" as a polemical response to the mystical ascent soteriology such as that found in the *Gospel of Thomas*' (131); see further below §49. For reviews of the debate on possible interconnections between the John and the *Thomas* traditions, see Dunderberg, '*Thomas*' I-sayings' 35-40, and DeConick 26-32.

272. Cf. S. L. Davies, *The Gospel of Thomas and Christian Wisdom* (New York: Seabury, 1983).

273. M. Moreland, 'The Twenty-four Prophets of Israel Are Dead: *Gospel of Thomas* 52 as a Critique of Early Christian Hermeneutics', in J. M. Asgeirsson et al., eds., *Thomasine Traditions in Antiquity: The Social and Cultural World of the Gospel of Thomas* (Nag Hammadi and Manichaean Studies 59; Leiden: Brill, 2006) 75-91: 'The Thomasine community did not want to search the scriptures in order to link Jesus to the Hebrew past' (88).

said to his disciples, '(What will) that one (do) with the lamb?' They said to him, '(He comes) in order to kill it and eat it'. He said to them, 'As long as it is alive, he will not eat it, but (only) if he kills it and it becomes a corpse'. They said, 'He is not permitted to do it any other way'. He said to them, 'You yourselves must also seek a place within for rest, lest you become a corpse and be consumed'.

To be noted also are the striking references to James —

- 12 — The disciples said to Jesus, 'We know that you are going to leave us. Who will be our leader?' Jesus said to them, 'In the place to which you have come, you will go to James the Just, for whose sake heaven and earth came into existence'.

and those to the Pharisees (*Thomas* 39 and 102, cited above), which indicate that the *Thomas* tradition had strong roots in circles where Sabbath was still of great importance and where James was highly revered.[274] We cannot infer that all the *Thomas* tradition went through a traditionalist Jewish-Christian phase, but we can infer that *Thomas* absorbed and retained early traditions in which the concerns represented by James were prominent. The fact that *Thomas* did continue to give place to such tradition, even though its own characteristic concerns had moved on to a different plane, indicates that *Thomas* did respect these roots and concerns.[275]

In short, while *Thomas* reflects different phases of the developing Jesus tradition,[276] there is nothing in the *Thomas* tradition to suggest that the dis-

---

274. A. Marjanen, '*Thomas* and Jewish Religious Practices', in Uro, ed., Thomas *at the Crossroads* 163-82, however, notes that logion 13 succeeds logion 12, perhaps implying that Thomas with his secret teaching (*Thomas* 13) has superseded the earlier authority of James (181-82).

275. Marjanen sees a critical distancing from Jewish religious practices ('*Thomas* and Jewish Religious Practices'), but it would be more accurate to say that the *Thomas* material, on circumcision (*Thomas* 53 above) and on fasting, prayer and almsgiving (*Thomas* 6.1, 14.1-3, 27.1, 104.1-2), reflects more the sort of debate which must have been common among the first-generation believing Jews (cf. Mark 2.18-20; Matt. 6.1-6; Luke 11.39-40/Matt 23.25-26/ *Thomas* 89.1-2; Rom. 2.28-29; Phil. 3.3).

276. Including possible knowledge of or influence from Paul — S. Gathercole, 'The Influence of Paul on the *Gospel of Thomas* (§§53.3 and 17)', in J. Frey, ed., *Das Thomasevangelium* 72-94 — cf. *Thomas* 53.3 and Rom. 2:25–3:2; *Thomas* 17 and 1 Cor. 2.9. Koester argues on the basis of 1 Cor. 2.9/*Thomas* 17 that a Corinthian faction knew a number of sayings (of Jesus) which they understood as the revelation of hidden wisdom and life-giving knowledge (*Ancient Christian Gospels* 55-62). But a postulated link between Corinth and Q is extremely tenuous; and see Gathercole 88-93.

tinctive material can be traced back to the beginnings of the Jesus tradition, that is, to the impact made by Jesus himself.[277] But this is an issue which will require a fuller examination of the message of *Thomas*.

c. The Good News for *Thomas*

To bring out the parallels and differences from the canonical Gospels the treatment here will follow roughly the same pattern as with them.

i. The Christology of Thomas

The most immediate feature for any comparison on this point with the canonical Gospels is the absence of titles and names for Jesus familiar from these other Gospels. Jesus is never spoken of as Messiah or Christ.[278] The issue of whether he was Israel's Messiah is never even alluded to. There is one reference to 'the son of man' (*Thomas* 86), but it is not even very clear whether the phrase is a title referring to Jesus, or simply a reference to 'the human being', lacking any sense of belonging to this world, in contrast to foxes and birds.[279] Jesus is referred to only once as God's 'Son' (*Thomas* 37)[280] and never as 'Lord'.

One of the most interesting logia is *Thomas*'s equivalent of the Synoptic pericope where Jesus inquires as to who people think he is. In the Synoptics, the reply is in terms of a prophet, and Peter confesses Jesus to be Messiah (Mark 8.27-29 pars.). In *Thomas* 13, Peter replies that Jesus is 'like a righteous angel', and Matthew replies that he is 'like a sage'. But Thomas confesses that he cannot even begin to answer the question properly. Jesus takes him aside and 'told him three words'. When Thomas returns to the rest and they ask him what Jesus had said, Thomas replies, 'If I tell you one of the words which he told me, you will pick up stones and throw them at me. Then fire will come out of the stones and burn you up'. Clearly the context of the question and answer session has shifted, from a very Jewish context to a different context of reference. At the same time it looks as though the revelation given secretly to Thomas is that Jesus shares the divine name.[281] In other words, the Thomas logion may have been trading

---

277. The opinion cited by Koester, that 'the entire (or almost entire) tradition contained in the *Gospel of Thomas* (is derived) from an independent early stage of the sayings tradition' (*'GNOMAI DIAPHOROI'* 132) is both a gross exaggeration and fanciful.

278. Though *Thomas* 52.1 reports the disciples saying to Jesus, 'Twenty-four prophets have spoken in Israel, and all of them spoke about you'.

279. DeConick, *Thomas* 251-52.

280. Jesus refers to God as 'my Father' in *Thomas* 61 and 99 (Davies, *Thomas* 85).

281. As DeConick notes, the *Acts of Thomas* alludes to *Thomas* 13 in ch. 47, and in ch. 133 states that the Name given to Jesus is 'the exalted Name that is hidden from all' (*Thomas* 85).

on the speculation regarding the angel in whom God put his name (Exod. 23.21) and correlated it with the Johannine elaboration of the same speculation (John 17.11). This would tie in also with *Thomas* 15, cited above (§43.2b): Jesus can be identified with the Father (cf. John 10.30; 14.9). Also with *Thomas* 61.2-5, also cited above (§43.2b): Jesus as equal with the Father (cf. John 5.18).

For *Thomas* the most characteristic way of referring to Jesus is as 'the Living One' (*Thomas* Incipit, 52, 59, 111), though also as 'the Son of the Living One' (37). Either way, Jesus is presented as the embodiment of 'the light which is above all things. I am everything' (77). He is everywhere in the world: 'Lift the stone and you will find me there. Split the wood and I am there' (30.3-4). To be far from him is to be far from the kingdom (82). 'Jesus said, "Whoever drinks from my mouth will become as I am. I myself will become that person, and what is hidden will be revealed to him"' (108).

This last reference takes us back to the main distinctive of *Thomas*'s christology: that Jesus is valued and reverenced in the *Thomas* tradition, not because of his death or resurrection.[282] He is the Living One because he represents the Father so completely. His significance for *Thomas* is primarily that he has brought the (saving) revelation.[283] Like the Johannine Christ he is the Revealer.[284] But whereas John takes pains to correlate Jesus' role as Revealer with the gospel of his death and resurrection, *Thomas* focuses almost exclusively on the revelation — 'the secret words which the living Jesus spoke and which Didymus Judas Thomas wrote down' (Incipit).

ii. The Alternative Gospel

A strong underlying assumption is that those for whom *Thomas* has been written and circulated were people who believed that their *true nature and spiritual home is different from their existence in this world.*

- 3.3-4 — Jesus said . . . 'The kingdom is within you and outside you. When you know yourselves, then you will be known; and you will know that you are sons of the living Father'.

---

282. 'The only mention of the crucifixion occurs in an indirect reference to his disciples carrying a cross as does Jesus (Saying 55)' (R. Valantasis, *The Gospel of Thomas* [London: Routledge, 1997] 8-9).

283. See also Schröter, 'Theologische Interpretation des *EvThom*' 444-53.

284. Davies observes that *Thomas* 'has no Christology, properly so called' and suggests the possibility that 'Thomas derives from a time' when terms like Christ, Son of Man, Messiah, Saviour, Son of God 'were not yet common in reference to Jesus' (99), though earlier he had observed that in *Thomas* Jesus is not merely a messenger or friend of Wisdom, but 'is Wisdom itself, creating, illuminating, permeating all things' (with reference to logion 77) (87), which suggests a parallel with Matthew rather than the earlier Mark.

- 18 — The disciples said to Jesus, 'Tell us how our end will come about'. Jesus said, 'Have you discovered the beginning that you seek the end? Because where the beginning is, the end will be also. Blessed is he who will stand at the beginning. He will know the end and will not taste death'.
- 19.1 — Jesus said, 'Blessed is he who was before he was born'.
- 49 — Jesus said, 'Blessed are the celibate people, the chosen ones, because you will find the kingdom. For you are from it. You will return there again'.
- 50 — Jesus said, 'If they say to you, "Where did you come from?", say to them, "we came from the light" — the place where the light came into being of its own accord and established (itself) and became manifest through their image. If they say to you, "Is it you?", say, "We are its children, and we are the chosen people of the living Father". If they ask you, "What is the sign of your Father in you?" say to them, "It is movement and rest"'.
- 67 — Jesus said, 'He who knows everything but fails (to know) himself, has missed everything'.
- 83 — Jesus said, 'The images are visible to man, but the light which is within them is hidden in the image of the Father's light. The light will be revealed, but his image is concealed by his light'.
- 84 — Jesus said, 'When you see the likeness of yourselves, you are delighted. But when you see the images of yourselves which came into being before you — which neither die nor are visible — how much you will suffer'.[285]
- 111.2-3 — Jesus said . . . 'He who lives from the Living One will not see death'. Does not Jesus say, 'He who finds himself, of him the world is not worthy'?

Such people may be ignorant of their true nature and origin, and *unaware* of, *lacking knowledge* of the real contrast between their true nature and their present existence.

- 3.5 — Jesus said . . . 'When you know yourselves, you will know that you are sons of the living Father. But if you do not know yourselves, then you are in poverty, and you are poverty'.
- 28 — Jesus said, 'I stood in the midst of the world, and I appeared to

---

285. On *Thomas* 83 and 84 see particularly E. E. Popkes, 'The Image Character of Human Existence: *GThom* 83 and *GThom* 84 as Core Texts of the Anthropology of the Gospel of Thomas', in Frey, ed., *Das Thomasevangelium* 416-34 (with further bibliography in the notes).

them in flesh. I found all of them drunk. I found none of them thirsty. And my soul suffered pain for the sons of men, because they are blind in their hearts and do not see that they have come into the world empty, seeking to go out of the world empty again. But now they are drunk. When they shake off (the effects of) their wine, then they will repent'.
- 29 — Jesus said, 'If the flesh existed for the sake of the Spirit, it would be a miracle. If the Spirit (existed) for the sake of the body, it would be a miracle of miracles! But I marvel at how this great wealth settled in this poverty'.
- 56 = 80 — Jesus said, 'Whoever has come to know the world has found a corpse. And he who has found a corpse, of him the world is not worthy'.
- 70 — Jesus said, 'That which you have will save you if you bring it forth from yourselves. That which you do not have within you [will] kill you if you do not have it within you'.
- 87 — Jesus said, 'Wretched is the body crucified by/which depends on a body. Wretched is the soul crucified by these together/that depends on both'.
- 112 — Jesus said, 'Woe to the flesh crucified by/which depends on the soul! Woe to the soul crucified by/which depends on the flesh!'[286]

Consequently the process of salvation is perceived quite differently from the NT writings — not as a change of status or a redeeming transformation, but as a realisation of one's true nature.[287]

Bound up with this is what seems to be a form of Adam theology, that the *original divine image was androgynous* (a way of reconciling the two creation stories — Gen. 1.26-27 and 2.7, 22), so that restoration to primal purity was a return from the two to the one, and women becoming men.

- 11.3-4 — Jesus said . . . 'When you are in the light, what will you become? On the day when you were one, you became two. But when you are two, what will you become?'
- 22.4-7 — Jesus said to them, 'When you make the two one, and make the outside like the inside, and the above like the below. And when you make the male and the female into a single being, with the result that the male is not male nor the female female. When you make eyes in place

286. For the variant translation see DeConick, *Thomas* 253-54.
287. A. Marjanen, 'The Portrait of Jesus in the *Gospel of Thomas*', in Asgeirsson et al., eds., *Thomasine Traditions in Antiquity* 209-19: 'The role of the Savior . . . is in a way assigned to the elect themselves in *Thomas*. . . . For *Thomas*, the final outcome of a human being's attempt to be saved does not depend on any act of Jesus, but on something which a human being has in him/herself (70)' (217).

of an eye, and a hand in place of a hand, and a foot in place of a foot, and an image in place of an image, then you will enter (the kingdom)'.[288]
- 85 — Jesus said, 'Adam came into being from a great power and great wealth. But he was not worthy of you. For had he been worthy (he would) not (have) died'.
- 106.1 — Jesus said, 'When you make the two one, you will become sons of man'.
- 114 — Simon Peter said to them, 'Mary should leave us because women are not worthy of life'. Jesus said, 'Look, I shall lead her, in order to make her male, so that she too may become a living spirit, resembling you males. For every woman who will make herself male will enter the kingdom of heaven'.[289]

The ethical consequence seems to have been a *strongly ascetic* code of practice, including a high regard for celibacy. In consequence, *Thomas* is frequently regarded as emanating from encratite circles,[290] but notably lacking in community or ecclesiastical concerns,[291] that is, even more individualistic than the Gospel of John.

- 4.2-4 — Many who are first will be last, and they will become a single one.
- 16.4 — ... they will stand alone/as celibate people.[292]
- 21.1-4 — Mary said to Jesus, 'What are your disciples like?' He said, 'They are like little children who dwell in a field which does not belong to them. When the owners of the field come, they will say, "Leave our

---

288. Discussion in R. Uro, 'Is *Thomas* an Encratite Gospel?', in Uro, ed., Thomas *at the Crossroads* 140-62 (here 149-56), with reference to the parallels in *2 Clem.* 12.2, 6 and the *Gospel of Egyptians*, cited by Clement of Alexandria in his *Stromateis* 3.13.92; the texts are quoted in H. Koester, *Synoptische Überlieferung bei den apostolischen Vätern* (Berlin: Akademie-Verlag, 1957) 102; see also Koester, *Ancient Christian Gospels* 357-60.

289. A. Marjanen, 'Women Disciples in the *Gospel of Thomas*', in Uro, ed., Thomas *at the Crossroads* 89-106, suggests that the saying reflects a tendency towards a more rigid lifestyle among some Thomasine Christians, and perhaps a conflict between two strongly ascetic positions, one insisting on the complete exclusion of women, the other maintaining that the hope of salvation included women.

290. Uro notes that '*Thomas* praises those who have broken with their families and have become "solitary", but never directly rejects marriage and sexual intercourse'; he concludes that *Thomas* does not derive from a strictly encratite sect as such, 'even though encratite tendencies must have occurred in *Thomas*' environment' ('Is *Thomas* an Encratite Gospel?' 161). See also Valantasis, *Gospel of Thomas* 21-24.

291. Blatz, *NTA* 1.114.

292. For the variant translation see DeConick, *Thomas* 98-99.

field to us!" In front of them, they strip naked in order to abandon it, returning their field to them'.
- 23.2 — . . . they will stand as a single one.
- 37 — His disciples said, 'When will you appear to us? When will we see you?' Jesus said, 'When you strip naked without shame, take your garments, put them under your feet like little children, and trample on them. Then (you will see) the son of the Living One, and you will not be afraid'.
- 75 — Jesus said, 'Many are standing at the door, but those who are celibate are the (only) ones who will enter the bridal chamber'.
- 105 — Jesus said, 'He who is acquainted with his father and mother will be called "the child of a prostitute"'.

The narrative underlying all this is fairly clear, familiar particularly from Gnostic literature. It is of individuals who perceive their real selves and true home to be other than this world, of a spirituality entirely uncomfortable with existence in the material world.[293] Not all for whom this is the case are aware of their true spiritual selves, their true spiritual origin and home.[294] The good news is that Jesus came from there, the kingdom of the Father, his teaching bringing the secret wisdom which is the revelation of their true being and counsel on how to act now to ensure return to that kingdom.[295] Whether this should be described as ' Gnostic' depends on one's definition of Gnosticism.[296]

---

293. On the intriguing *GospThom* 42, see P. H. Sellew, 'Jesus and the Voice from Beyond the Grave: *Gospel of Thomas* 42 in the Context of Funerary Epigraphy', in Asgeirsson et al., eds., *Thomasine Traditions in Antiquity* 39-73: 'When Jesus urges the readers of *Thomas* to become passers-by, he tells them not to linger in this world, not to be caught in the trap of conversation, or better, relations with the "living dead" all around them. . . . the "living who will not die" must recognize the world for the corpse it truly is and refuse to be caught up in its ways (*Gos.Thom.* 27, 50, 86)' (72-73).

294. A striking parallel here is 'the Hymn of the Pearl' in the *Acts of Thomas* 108-13; see §40.6e above.

295. Cf. Robinson, *Nag Hammadi Library* 1-10; Koester, *Ancient Christian Gospels* 124-28. DeConick argues that 'the Thomasine Christians were mystics seeking visions of God for the purpose of immortalization'; the encratite lifestyle was 'the way to be in a state of continual purification and sinlessness, a state of readiness for the dangerous journey' (*Voices of the Mystics* 107-8).

296. See above §38.4c. R. Uro, 'The Social World of the *Gospel of Thomas*', in Asgeirsson et al., eds., *Thomasine Traditions in Antiquity* 19-38, critiques attempts to deduce the social world of the *Gospel of Thomas* as 'often built on a rather simplistic reading of *Thomas*'s religious symbolism and ethical teaching' (37). S. L. Davies, *The Gospel of Thomas and Christian Wisdom* (New York: Seabury Press, 1983) ch. 2: 'Thomas has almost no gnostic characteristics' (23). And in Gathercole's opinion, 'any idea of *Thomas* being "Gnostic" should almost certainly be abandoned' (*Composition* 148).

But if 'Gnostic' can properly be used for a widespread spirituality which assumed a basic dualism between spirit and matter, which felt itself to be not at home in and at odds with the world, and which looked for an answer which resolved the paradox of human existence (in terms of knowledge of their true identity and an accordingly ascetic life-style), then *Thomas* can be described as 'Gnostic'.[297]

43.3 Comparing John and *Thomas*

The defining characteristic of John's Gospel is its unfolding the fuller truth now evident in Jesus' teaching and mission as known to the Johannine community from the earlier Synoptic-like Jesus tradition. Particular sayings and parables had been reflected on and their fuller meaning developed in sometimes lengthy discourses. Characteristic miracles of Jesus were seen as 'signs' and the sign-ificance teased out in other discourses. With *Thomas*, in contrast, the Synoptic-like tradition is mostly drawn in more or less as such, and *Thomas*'s good news is not so much drawn from the earlier tradition but attached to or set alongside the earlier Jesus tradition. This is particularly clear in a number of instances.

Both John and *Thomas* take up the episode of Peter's confession of Jesus (Mark 8.27-30 pars.). In John 6.68-69, Peter responds to Jesus' question, 'Do you also wish to go away?' (6.67), by saying, 'Lord, to whom can we go? You have the words of eternal life. We have come to believe and know that you are the Holy One of God'. Peter's confession of Jesus as Messiah fitted into the Johannine plot (the separating effect of Jesus) and is expressed in not uncharacteristic Jewish language. In *Thomas* 13, in contrast, as we saw above (§43.2c(1)), the episode becomes a way of relativising the status of Peter

---

297. See also Cameron, *ABD* 6.539; Popkes, 'Image Character' 431-33; cf. Ehrman, *Lost Christianities* 59-63. Although a similar argument could be made for calling John's Gospel 'Gnostic' (Uro, Thomas *at the Crossroads* 5), the distinctive features of John's Gospel, unlike the distinctive *Thomas* tradition, are firmly rooted in the earlier Jesus tradition. See further A. Marjanen, 'Is *Thomas* a Gnostic Gospel?', in Uro, ed., Thomas *at the Crossroads* 107-39. DeConick reflects the recent revisionary attitude to 'Gnosticism' in maintaining that the term 'Gnostic' is misleading, since different traditions were too casually lumped together and lost their distinctiveness; 'there was not an umbrella religion called "Gnosticism" in which these groups participated'. She argues instead that *Thomas* is a text which echoes early Syrian religiosity; 'the study of Syrian Christianity has been relegated to the deviant, the Gnostic, rather than heir to Jerusalem'; 'a form of Christianity in Syria which was encratic, honouring the solitary life over the marital', which can be traced back to a form of Christian Judaism (*Thomas* 1-6).

and of highlighting the claim that Thomas had been given special and secret revelation, too dangerous for him to pass on.[298]

In John 3 we have noted how John elaborates the condition which the Jesus tradition had laid down for entry into the kingdom (Matt. 18.3): 'No one can enter the kingdom of God without being born of water and Spirit' (3.5). Here again *Thomas* 22 goes off at a sharp angle, not elaborating the principal thought, like John, but tacking it on to its own narrative and sloganizing motifs.[299]

> Jesus saw little babies nursing. He said to his disciples, 'These little ones nursing are like those who enter the Kingdom'. They said to him, 'Will we enter the Kingdom as little babies?' Jesus said to them, 'When you make the two one, and when you make the inside like the outside, and the outside like the inside, and the above like the below. And when you make the male and the female into a single being, with the result that the male is not male nor the female female. When you make eyes in place of an eye, and a hand in place of a hand, and a foot in place of a foot, and an image in place of an image, then you will enter (the Kingdom)'.

In John 14-16 Jesus responds to his disciples' anxiety about his going away by talking about his relationship with the Father and promising that the Spirit will deal with all their concerns. In contrast *Thomas* 37 again directs readers' attention to its own distinctively gnostic gospel:[300] 'His disciples said, "When will you appear to us? When will we see you?" Jesus said, "When you strip naked without shame, take your garments, put them under your feet like little children, and trample on them. Then (you will see) the son of the Living One, and you will not be afraid"'.

In John 16.23-24 Jesus' encouragement to ask, seek and knock (Matt. 7.7/Luke 11.9) is taken up in Jesus' encouragement to the disciples to ask when he has left them. *Thomas* 2 also draws on the Synoptic tradition but adds a quite different theme: 'Jesus said, "He who seeks should not stop (seeking until) he finds; and when he finds, he will be amazed; and when he is amazed, he will marvel, and will be king over all/he will rest"'.

In John the theme of the coming of Jesus as the shining of light which separates good from evil (John 3.19-21) is the key to the thought of Jesus as 'the light of the world' (8.12), separating believing Jews from unbelieving Jews (chs. 8-19). In contrast, in *Thomas* 77 there is no room for the idea of Jesus as

---

298. See also above §40 at n.198.
299. See also DeConick, *Thomas* 115-18.
300. See again DeConick, *Thomas* 153-54.

the light of the world, and the thought is limited to Jesus' cosmological significance: 'Jesus said, "I am the light which is above all things. I am everything. From me, everything came forth, and up to me, everything reached"'.

There seems, then, to be a fairly fundamental difference between the ways in which John and *Thomas* deal with the earlier Jesus tradition. John lives and breathes in the atmosphere of that tradition. He reflects on it at length and, always keeping in visible contact with that tradition, presses into it, drawing out its deeper meaning and significance. *Thomas*, on the other hand, has taken over a good deal of similar Synoptic-like tradition, tradition with the sort of variation we are already familiar with in the Synoptic tradition itself. Indeed, the Synoptic-like tradition in *Thomas* is much more recognizable than it is in John. But, and this is what matters, the distinctive message of *Thomas* is *not* drawn from that tradition, as is John's.[301] It is drawn from a *different* analysis of the human condition and a *different* solution. There are points of contact, of course; otherwise *Thomas* could not have drawn in as much Jesus tradition as it has. Themes of light and life provide a common currency. That Jesus was the principal inspiration for so much of such language in Christian circles meant that he was a good peg on which to hang the different message, supported as it was to at least some extent by a significant portion of the Jesus tradition. But the *central* message was *not* that of Jesus or of the Jesus tradition, on which both John and *Thomas* were able to draw.

43.4 Is *Thomas* a 'Gospel'?

The correlation of *Thomas* tradition with Synoptic and Johannine tradition is particularly intriguing. For, as we have seen, there are plenty of points of contact, and clear indications of continuity particularly between the *Thomas* and Synoptic traditions. The essential point, however, is that the *basic narrative* which holds the *Thomas* tradition together is distinctly other than what we find in the Synoptic and even the Johannine traditions. The distinctive message of *Thomas* comes from a source and an explanation of the human condition which is not to be found elsewhere in the Jesus tradition thus far examined. It is an import into that tradition. There are sufficient elements in the Synoptic

---

301. The nearest example we have of *Thomas* drawing its message from Jesus tradition is probably *Gosp.Thom.* 3 (cf. Luke 17.20-21): 'Jesus said, "If those who lead you say to you, Lo the kingdom is in heaven, then the birds of heaven will precede you. If they say, It is in the sea, then the fish will precede you. But the kingdom is within you and outside you. When you know yourselves, then you will be known; and you will know that you are sons of the living Father. But if you do not know yourselves, then you are in poverty, and you are poverty'.

tradition which *Thomas* was able to use and to blend into its underlying narrative. But it is hard to see the distinctive *Thomas* message as drawn from the Jesus tradition as attested in the Synoptic (and the Johannine) Gospels. The *Thomas* message has a very different 'take' on human existence, even though Jesus drawn into that milieu was evidently believed to be the one whose teaching brought them the message which the *Thomas* community needed. Quite a number of Jesus' sayings could be heard as speaking to their situation.³⁰² But the recognizable Jesus tradition was essentially a bolt-on addition to a framework which originated in a different perception of reality from that of the Jewish scriptures and of the Jesus tradition so far reviewed.³⁰³

It is not that *Thomas* originated from the initial impact made by Jesus, and simply disagreed with or abandoned the eschatology and soteriology of the Jesus tradition as evidenced in the canonical Gospels, but otherwise maintained a direct line of tradition from Jesus himself.³⁰⁴ Unlike even the Q traditions, despite the reference to John the Baptist in *Thomas* 46, the Synoptic tradition taken over by *Thomas* has been almost entirely separated from any association with Jesus' actual life (and death).³⁰⁵ It is free-floating teaching, without substantive historical anchor. Nor are there any indications that *Thomas*'s distinctive message was itself part of the immediate impact made by Jesus.³⁰⁶ *The basic narrative of Thomas is too distinctive and too different from the other first-century indications of the impact made by Jesus for us to find a root for the Thomas perspective in Jesus' mission or the early oral Jesus tradition.*³⁰⁷ Much the more likely is that the *Thomas* community, or direct

---

302. E.g. *Thomas* 3, 5, 39, 76, 86, 92. For Valantasis, *Thomas*'s 'sayings work at constructing a new and alternative subjectivity' (*Gospel of Thomas* 10-12).

303. Cf. DeConick's analysis of sayings which she regards as 'secondary accretions', and which cohere with characteristic vocabulary and themes (*Recovering* 71-76).

304. Cf. again DeConick, *Recovering* 78-85.

305. But *Thomas* 55 draws on the Q saying (Luke 14.26-27/Matt.10.37-38) that a follower of Jesus should expect to carry his cross as Jesus did.

306. It is noticeable that the several quotations of Jesus in the *Acts of Thomas* quote only Synoptic tradition and not any of the distinctive Thomasine material — *ActsThom* 28 (Matt. 6.34, 26, 30), 36 (Matt. 19.23; 11.8; 6.25), 53 (Matt. 7.7), 79 (cf. Matt. 7.15), 80 (Matt. 19.28), 82 (Mark 8.18; Matt. 11.15, 28), 86 (Matt. 26.52-53), 94 (cf. Matt. 5.5-8), 144 (Matt. 6.9-13). 'The whole of c.46 is based on Lk. 11:23-23' (Drijvers, *NTA* 2.407 n.80); Drijvers lists many other echoes (405-11). Echoes of *Gosp.Thom.* can be discerned in 10 (*GT* 1), 39 and 47 (*GT* 13), 92 (*GT* 22), 136 (*GT* 2), 147 (*GT* 22) and 170 (*GT* 52), though the echoes are light in comparison with the quotations from Matthew. Klauck wonders if the author knew the Gospel tradition from Tatian's *Diatessaron* and discusses whether the echoes of the *Gospel of Thomas* indicate the existence of a 'Thomas school' (*Apocryphal Acts* 146, 147-48).

307. It is this feature which tells most strongly against Koester's thesis that *Thomas* preserves 'the theological perspective (of the Jesus tradition known to *Thomas*) that must have dominated its initial stage', in contrast to John (*Ancient Christian Gospels* 123; also

predecessors, were influenced by the Synoptic tradition known to them, but found it attractive because it helped to fill out their own instinctive narrative, because it spoke to a self-understanding which they derived from elsewhere than Jesus. The Jesus tradition, including its Johannine tendency, provided a figure whose teaching contained revelation which brought the *Thomas* community enlightenment,[308] and which allowed them to expand that tradition's revelatory significance by elaborating it well beyond its earlier thrust and focus. In effect, the Jesus tradition which appealed to them was simply co-opted to their basic 'Gnostic' world-view and spirituality.[309]

Whether this happened in direct opposition and hostility to the gospel as established by Paul, and embodied in the gospel-structure of Mark and the other canonical Gospels, it is now impossible to say. The omission of such emphases as are readily evident in the canonical Gospels could simply indicate a stream of Jesus tradition taken over selectively and wedded to the 'Gnostic' narrative. The absence of any explicit polemic against a Pauline alternative gospel strongly suggests the existence of (a) group(s) who found enough in the Jesus tradition to link it into a story explanatory of their identity derived from elsewhere. To call this a Gospel (the *Gospel of Thomas*)[310] is understandable because of the substantial use of Jesus tradition; and patristic references to

---

Introduction 2.150-54). The issue does not depend on whether 'Gnosticism' can be dated to the first century (*Ancient Christian Gospels* 83); the issue is whether the 'gnostic' narrative, whenever it emerged, can be attributed to Jesus or to the immediate impact of his mission and of the early Jesus tradition.

308. I use the term 'community' without attempting to specify the character or locations of those significantly influenced by *Thomas*.

309. DeConick reviews the history of the debate on the tradition-history behind *Thomas*, rightly, in my opinion, emphasizing its character as 'an orally-derived text', a 'rolling corpus' which, in her view, began with the *ipsissima verba* of Jesus (*Recovering* 55-56, 61-62; see also her contribution on 'The *Gospel of Thomas*' to Foster, ed., *Non-Canonical Gospels* 13-29 (here 20-24). She goes on reconstruct a 'kernel *Gospel of Thomas*' (*Recovering* Part Two; *Thomas* ch. 2), as the first phase in the development of *Thomas*. However, the 'kernel *Gospel*' contains none of the material which I regard as giving *Thomas* its distinctive message (§43.2b above). A rolling corpus model representing the *Thomas* history of tradition, therefore, should not expect to find a single (oral) source (the Jesus tradition) (as in *Recovering* 56). A more accurate model, in my view, would show *two* different originating sources, the 'Gnostic' world view and the Jesus tradition, drawn together where they could be meshed into one, and elaborated and expanded in community usage. DeConick's further observation, that the wisdom traditions in *Thomas*, regarded by several as the Q-root of *Thomas*, are 'made subservient to the dominance of mysteries, in much the same way as Paul appears to be doing in 1 Corinthians' (referring to 1 Cor. 1.20-25; 2.6-13) (*Voices of the Mystics* 207-8), is nearer the truth. See also Frey's brief critique of DeConick in 'Die Lilien und das Gewand' 140-43.

310. 'The Gospel according to Thomas' is the colophon at the end of the Coptic text.

other Gospels are a salutary reminder that the Markan Gospel form had not so established itself as to prevent other non-Markan forms from being conveniently designated as 'Gospel'. The decisive point, however, whether recognized explicitly or not, is that in the hands of Mark and the other canonical Evangelists the Jesus tradition was held within the gospel framework, 'Gospel' as given its Christian definition by Paul, that is, as an account of the mission of Jesus climaxing in his death and resurrection (§41). *Thomas*, as a handbook of teaching for an encratite or 'Gnostic' group, which, on the strength of much of his (expanded) teaching, counted Jesus as the great revealer of their true state, should not be regarded as a 'Gospel' as defined by the first-century Christians.

In short, in terms of genre and literary form, 'Gospel' may seem to be the most natural title for *Thomas*. But *Thomas*'s structure and content are so different from the 'gospel' as given definition by Paul and the canonical Gospels, that the '*Gospel of Thomas*' can and should be judged a misnomer. And if the title persists, as now well established, *Thomas* has to be judged to be a very different gospel from the Gospels of the NT. Its exclusion from the canon of the NT, the canon of the fourfold Jesus tradition, is both understandable and was entirely appropriate.

43.5 Two Different Gospels, Two Different Hermeneutical Strategies[311]

In John's Gospel we see a presentation of Jesus' mission and of Jesus' teaching whose roots can readily be traced back to the earliest impact made by Jesus as attested in the Synoptic tradition. The early tradition has evidently been reflected on for many years. The Gospel of John is the fruit of that reflection. In effect John has stripped that tradition down to what he regarded as its principal features, and these have been the focus of that reflection. In what stands as the final stage of that reflection, we see these principal features of the earlier tradition expanded and elaborated, well beyond what the Synoptic Evangelists allowed themselves to do in their Gospels — notably characteristic 'signs' whose significance is expounded, and the meaning of treasured sayings and parables elaborated. We see elements which were present but not prominent in the earlier tradition brought into the spotlight and their significance brought out at length, notably the call to faith and the promise of life eternal. And we see elements which one or more of the earlier Gospels had already

---

311. See also my 'The Earliest Interpreters of the Jesus Tradition: A Study in Early Hermeneutics', in S. E. Porter and M. R. Malcolm, eds., *Horizons in Hermeneutics*; A. C. Thiselton FS (Grand Rapids: Eerdmans, 2013) 119-47.

reflected on and developed, even if modestly, similarly brought to centre stage and given a prominence which showed how much more light could be shed on the significance of Jesus' mission and teaching, notably the Father-Son imagery and the reinforcement of Jesus' divine authority. Because the roots of this can be clearly identified in the earlier Jesus tradition I characterize it as a development of the earlier Jesus tradition *from within*.

In contrast, the distinctive *Thomas* material does not appear as an unfolding of the Synoptic material on which *Thomas* draws. The *distinctive* gospel of *Thomas* is an add-on to the Synoptic-like tradition; it has another source. The Synoptic tradition could be read in the light of *Thomas*'s analysis of the human condition, but the reading was not drawn from that tradition; it was imposed upon it. If John's can be characterized as a development of the earlier Jesus tradition *from within*, *Thomas*'s would have to be described as a development *from without*.

There are various parallels between John and *Thomas*, notably in the presentation of Jesus as a revealer, who can be identified with God, and in the above-below dualism. But the content of the good news revealed is very different; the attitude to the world is very different; the response called for is very different; the degree of rootedness in the earlier Jesus tradition is very different. It can certainly be argued that the *Thomas* community, or its direct predecessors, were influenced by the Synoptic tradition known to them, but not because they could unfold it to bring out its message, as did John, not because they could draw out their distinctive message from it, as did John. Rather the *Thomas* people found the earlier Jesus tradition attractive because it helped to fill out their own instinctive narrative, because it spoke to a self-understanding which they derived from elsewhere than Jesus. Not entirely unlike John, *Thomas* found in the Jesus tradition a figure whose teaching contained revelation which they could add to their own instinctive insights. But in effect, the Jesus tradition which appealed to them was simply tacked on to their basic 'Gnostic' world-view and spirituality.

In short, John developed the Synoptic Jesus tradition as it were *from the inside*, expanding the meaning of the inherited Synoptic tradition, with a message still rooted in the Old Testament and still of immediate relevance to 'the Jews'. In contrast, *Thomas* worked on the early Jesus tradition more *from the outside*, drawing on it and adapting it to a very different understanding of the human situation and a very different understanding of the good news which humanity needed. By tacking on a range of early Jesus tradition, which could be read in the light of that other philosophy, presumably *Thomas* hoped to enlarge the appeal of his message. But *Thomas*'s use of the early Jesus tradition is more like a hostile takeover, whereas John's is like an heir exploring the richness of the inheritance which had come to him from Jesus through the Jesus tradition.

All this makes clearer why John was preserved within the canon of the New Testament by the great church, and why *Thomas* was rejected. The different hermeneutical strategies made the difference. And the corollary for church tradition — and for translating scripture into other languages — should not be ignored. If John is a precedent and model, then the acceptable hermeneutic is one which draws out from within the earlier tradition (scripture) what it sees to be of continuing or newly perceived significance. If *Thomas* is the warning precedent, then the hermeneutic which should be regarded with suspicion is one which makes a philosophy with different roots the key to understanding the earlier tradition (scripture), or which simply attaches elements from scripture on to a frame or narrative drawn from elsewhere.

CHAPTER 44

The Jesus Tradition in the Second Century

44.1 Introduction

We have now seen something of the impact made by the Jesus tradition and how it functioned and was handled in the first seventy or so years of the Christian movement. The bulk of it circulated in oral form for twenty to thirty years. Evidence that it was well-known in that period is implicit in the fact that when it was first put into writing in substantial terms (Q and Mark, followed by Luke and Matthew) there was a large pool, or large pools of Jesus tradition on which the writers could draw. This pool, or these pools, we can safely presume was/were the living oral tradition, which was derived from Jesus' earliest disciples and the apostles who founded a widening circle of churches, and which was used in various combinations and groupings. This was the Jesus tradition which gave these congregations their identity, and from which they gained inspiration for their worship, instruction for their lives and resources for witness and apologetic. This was the tradition which the Evangelists were able to shape in ways that no doubt reflected characteristic and typical ways of presenting Jesus, of performing, celebrating, teaching and transmitting the traditions about Jesus in the various churches with which they were associated. The Gospel of John and the *Gospel of Thomas* give added testimony to the extent to which the oral Jesus tradition was known in a wide range of territory. And several of the NT letters (Romans, 1 Corinthians, 1 Thessalonians, James, 1 Peter)[1] strengthen the likelihood that already within the first fifty years so

---

1. See *Jesus Remembered* 181-84; *Beginning from Jerusalem* 1135, 1154. *Pace* J. Schröter, *Vom Jesus zum Neuen Testament: Studien zur urchristlichen Theologiegeschichte und zur Entstehung des neutestamentlichen Kanons* (WUNT 204; Tübingen: Mohr Siebeck, 2007) 81-104, I continue to maintain that when passages in these letters demonstrate close similarity to and some measure of interdependence with sayings attributed to Jesus in the

much of the oral Jesus tradition had entered the life-blood of the string of churches stretching round the north-east quadrant of the Mediterranean that it could be assumed and alluded to as theirs, as how Christians characteristically thought and acted.

What happened to the Jesus tradition in the second century? The Gospels which became integral to the canon of the NT were already written, and their (spreading) influence and the course of progress towards their canonization will be traced in the following pages. But it should not be inferred that the scribalization of the oral Jesus tradition brought its oral phase to an end. Both John and *Thomas* bear witness to a widely known oral tradition with many overlaps and parallels with the oral tradition enscripted in the Synoptic tradition,[2] and they also imply knowledge of oral tradition unrecorded in the Synoptic Gospels. It is probably a natural inference that Jesus tradition continued to be known and circulated orally, even when the written Gospels were becoming established well beyond the recipients for whom they were initially intended. But this will need to be tested.[3] And if John and *Thomas* demonstrate that the Jesus tradition could be elaborated well beyond what the Synoptic tradition was familiar with, we also need to ask whether and if so how much further the Jesus tradition was developed in the second century, and how acceptably.

In particular, should the NT Gospels be regarded as the only true inheritors of the oral Jesus tradition, the only authoritative written expressions of the Jesus tradition? It is well known that Irenaeus, Bishop of Lyons, writing between 175 and 185, made the first public commitment to an exclusive four Gospel canon.[4] But other Gospels were already in circulation, as Irenaeus himself was well aware. Why did Irenaeus insist on only four — Matthew, Mark, Luke and John — and with what justification? The last generation of scholarship has been almost overwhelmed by the realization that the number of other documents known as Gospels raises afresh the old (already second-century)

Synoptic tradition, the most obvious inference is that the epistolary passages were drawing on already familiar Jesus tradition (which did not need to be explicitly attributed to Jesus since the writers could assume that it was familiar as such to the audiences); rather than that the (later) parallel Synoptic material was derived from such early Christian teaching (drawn from more diverse sources) as the epistles attest.

2. See above §§42-43.

3. In acknowledging that the content of oral tradition as such cannot be examined (our sources are all literary), Gregory rightly argues that discussion should not be limited to what is accessible to the methods of modern scholarship; the possibility that oral tradition explains points of contact between second-century texts and the Jesus tradition should not be discarded or ignored (*Reception of Luke* 15).

4. 'It is not possible that the Gospels can be either more or fewer in number than they are', using the analogy of the 'four zones of the world' and 'four principal winds' (*adv. haer.* 3.11.8).

question, Why these Gospels (NT) and not the others (so-called apocryphal)?[5] The controversy over the so-called *Secret Gospel of Mark*,[6] the publicity given to the pseudo-historical claims made in Dan Brown's *The Da Vinci Code*[7] and the recent discovery of the *Gospel of Judas*[8] have all highlighted the issues afresh and ensured that they cannot be confined to scholars' studies or university lecture halls. Was Walter Bauer correct in suggesting that the beginnings of Christianity in various centres were much more varied than previously assumed, and that 'orthodoxy' was simply the faction which (eventually) won in each centre, condemning the other factions as 'heretical'?[9] And were these victories and condemnations reinforced by the suppression and destruction of the other factions' beliefs? Were there other Gospels which were initially as authoritative and influential as the NT Gospels, but which were suppressed by the mainstream of Christianity which decided to focus only on Matthew, Mark, Luke and John?[10] Did Irenaeus start a new trend by insisting that only these four should be recognized as 'Gospels' or did he rescue them (John in particular) from the claims made for them by other or gnostically inclined Christians?

The issues here can be summed up by the provocative title of Bart Ehrman's recent *Lost Christianities* (2003). That is, were there in the second century movements which were as much influenced by Jesus and the Jesus tradition as the 'Christianity' so named by Ignatius,[11] and which have as much justification to the name 'Christianity' as the form advocated by Ignatius? This is precisely why this third volume of *Christianity in the Making* is entitled *Neither Jew nor Greek: A Contested Identity*. For it was in the second century that this contest became real and virulent, and at its centre were the claims made about and for Jesus by the different 'Christianities', and not least the claims made on and use made of the Jesus tradition.

So the objectives of this chapter are straightforward:

---

5. The most recent and forthright attempt to address this question is C. E. Hill, *Who Chose the Gospels? Probing the Great Gospel Conspiracy* (Oxford University, 2010).

6. See above §40 n.256.

7. D. Brown, *The Da Vinci Code* (New York: Doubleday, 2003).

8. See above §40 n.233.

9. See above §38.n.26.

10. W. L. Petersen, 'The Diatessaron and the Fourfold Gospel', in C. Horton, ed., *The Earliest Gospels: The Origins and Transmission of the Earliest Christian Gospels* (London: T & T Clark, 2004) 5-68, identifies nine non-canonical Gospels which existed before 175 — *Gospel of the Ebionites, Gospel of the Egyptians, Gospel of the Hebrews, Gospel of the Nazoraeans, Gospel of Thomas, Gospel of Peter*, Unknown Gospel (P.Egerton 2), *Gospel of Judas* and *Infancy Gospel of James* (51); cited by Hill, *Who Chose the Gospels?* 7-8. But, as we shall see, there are several other documents, which may have originated in the second century, for which the title 'Gospel' is used.

11. See *Beginning from Jerusalem* 5-6.

- to investigate the evidence that the Jesus tradition was still known orally, and what that tells us about the continuing influence of the Jesus tradition, independently of the written Gospels. We will examine both the Apostolic Fathers (early second century) — a famous comment by Papias will require careful consideration — and the Apologists (mid-second century) (§§44.2-3).
- to investigate what the apocryphal Gospels were doing with the Jesus tradition and, bearing in mind our findings on *Thomas,* what that tells us about any controls (or lack of controls) which the Jesus tradition itself exerted on the process (§§44.4-7).
- to investigate what happened to the four NT Gospels as such, particularly their spreading influence; also why they were distinguished from other Gospels and other uses made of the Jesus tradition, and whether such distinction was justified (§44.8).

44.2 The Oral Jesus Tradition into the Second Century — The Apostolic Fathers

The fact that second-century Christian writers show familiarity with Jesus tradition has fascinated scholarship at least since the nineteenth century.[12] In the period when the dominant concern was to uncover the written sources of the Gospels, it was natural to think of the Apostolic Fathers' knowledge and use of Jesus tradition in terms of their knowledge of and dependence on one or more of the Gospels, and subsequently as attesting the existence of a Q document. J. B. Lightfoot, for example, in his commentary on a passage to be examined below (*1 Clem.* 13.2), observes that 'as Clement's quotations are often very loose, we need not go beyond the Canonical Gospels for the source of this passage. . . . The hypothesis therefore, that Clement derived the saying from oral tradition or from some lost Gospel, is not needed'.[13] This was typical of the apparent unhappiness

---

12. See particularly Oxford Society of Historical Theology, *The New Testament in the Apostolic Fathers* (Oxford: Clarendon, 1905) = *NTAF*; Koester, *Synoptische Überlieferung bei den apostolischen Vätern*; D. A. Hagner, 'The Sayings of Jesus in the Apostolic Fathers and Justin Martyr', in D. Wenham, ed., *Gospel Perspectives* vol. 5: *The Jesus Tradition outside the Gospel* (Sheffield: JSOT, 1985) 233-68; A. Gregory and C. Tuckett, eds., *Trajectories through the New Testament and the Apostolic Fathers* (Oxford: Clarendon, 2005), Part II: 'Gospels and Gospel Traditions in the Second Century', 27-68; also *The Reception of the New Testament in the Apostolic Fathers* (Oxford: Clarendon, 2005); Young, *Jesus Tradition in the Apostolic Fathers,* whose ch. 2 provides 'a brief history of scholarship on the sources of the Jesus tradition in the Apostolic Fathers', with extensive bibliography, but who limits his own study to passages which appeal explicitly to Jesus tradition (29).

13. J. B. Lightfoot, *The Apostolic Fathers:* Part I: *S. Clement of Rome,* vol. 2 (London:

with any thought that Jesus tradition had been derived from an oral source. The rationale, presumably, was that the validity of the reference depended on being able to identify a written source, with the implication that anything else would mark the saying as suspect or render it inauthentic. The fact that the enterprise could be described as the second-century knowledge and use of 'the New Testament' already biased the discussion unhelpfully. And the typical category 'non-canonical', used of some versions of Jesus tradition, carried with it the overtone of 'not to be trusted' — a shadow from which the more recent preference for the category 'extra-canonical' does not fully escape.

Despite that, it will soon become evident that there was a growing readiness in the twentieth century to recognize the likelihood that most of the early second-century quotations of or allusions to Jesus tradition are best explained as attesting a still well-known, much used and living oral tradition of Jesus' teaching. Credit is particularly due to Helmut Koester for cutting the Gordian knot of distrust of oral tradition by emphasizing that the Jesus tradition existed in oral streams ('free tradition') well into the second century, and by repeatedly warning against the assumption of a purely literary and linear development of the Jesus tradition.[14] His examination of the evidence from the Apostolic Fathers is well worth following.

a. What Constitutes a Quotation of or Allusion to Jesus Tradition?

Before turning to particular texts it might be helpful to remind ourselves of the difficulties in assessing whether a text is dependent on an earlier text, and whether it therefore constitutes knowledge of and possibly respect for that earlier text. The options are more extensive than most previous studies have appreciated.

- Literary dependence — that is, use of and quotation from one of the NT Gospels, though not necessarily signaled as a formal quotation. A surprising amount of the early discussion of second-century knowledge of Jesus tradition was effectively restricted to this kind of knowledge/dependence.
- Literary dependence — quotation from a NT Gospel, read and perhaps

---

Macmillan, 1890) 52. D. A. Hagner, *The Use of the Old and New Testaments in Clement of Rome* (NovTSupp 34; Leiden: Brill, 1973), refers to those who argued for dependence on a written source ('Sayings of Jesus' 148-49).

14. *Synoptische Überlieferung*; also 'Written Gospels or Oral Traditions?', *JBL* 113 (1994) 293-97; also 'Gospels and Gospel Traditions in the Second Century', in Gregory and Tuckett, eds., *Trajectories* 27-44; see also Hagner, 'Sayings of Jesus'.

studied earlier, but now quoted from memory. This enabled knowledge/ use of an earlier written text to be recognized, even when the quoted material was at some variance from the written text which has come down to us.

- Literary dependence — quotation from a variant text of the NT Gospels. The variations in the text of the NT writings have been made abundantly clear by decades of careful textual criticism. But are the variations known to us the total sum of the variant texts used in the second century? The possibility that a quotation was from a text of a NT Gospel no longer known to us cannot be ignored or dismissed.
- The same range of possibilities apply also to the broader category of allusion or echo. What constitutes an allusion or echo is, of course, always liable to some dispute.[15] In our case, a major and often decisive factor will be indication (or lack of indication) that the putative allusion/echo shows awareness of distinctive features of the related text — particularly important when the issue is whether an allusion is to or is an echo of a particular NT Gospel.
- Non-literary dependence, that is, knowledge and use of Jesus tradition in oral form — an aspect of the whole debate which has been of particular importance in these volumes. Although focus inevitably has to be on written documents, the likelihood that much/the majority of the Jesus tradition would have continued to circulate in oral form well into the second century, and the possibility that second-century writers were drawing on knowledge of the oral Jesus tradition, as known through liturgy, preaching and catechesis, can certainly not be excluded. This includes 'second orality', that is, written Gospels known only through hearing them read, perhaps often, but perhaps also some time ago.
- A further possibility which will become apparent as we proceed is that distinctive features of one or another NT Gospel had been absorbed into the wider oral Jesus tradition. Consequently, what appears to be an allusion to a specific NT Gospel may simply be drawn from that wider oral Jesus tradition. That is, it need not provide evidence of the writer's own use of the NT Gospel itself, though the very fact that a distinctive feature of a NT Gospel has become more widely known is itself firm testimony of the influence of that Gospel.
- Nor should the likelihood be ignored that much of the Jesus tradition had entered into the thought processes and social intercourse of the

---

15. R. B. Hays, *Echoes of Scripture in the Letters of Paul* (Yale University, 1989), suggests seven tests — availability, volume, recurrence, thematic coherence, historical plausibility, history of interpretation, satisfaction (29-32).

second-century Christians.[16] That is to say, just as many of the phrases and verbal images of Shakespeare and the King James Bible became part of every-day English language,[17] so it should be possible to recognize second-century language and imagery which are not quotations or even allusions, but which were drawn from Jesus tradition and attest that this particular tradition of Jesus' words or deeds was well known.

b. Jesus Tradition in the Letters of the First Century

I begin with a brief reference to a few of the passages (already mentioned) in the letters of Paul, James and 1 Peter which are generally regarded as echoes of or allusions to the oral Jesus tradition of the time. This is simply to gain a clearer idea of what can count as a mid-to-late first-century allusion to the Jesus tradition, and what these allusions tell us about the way in which the Jesus tradition functioned in congregations where we cannot assume that the written Gospels were known or were the source for such allusions. These passages can then function as a precedent for early second-century use of the Jesus tradition and a comparator to the ways in which the Jesus tradition functioned in the third and fourth generations of the infant Christian movement.

Rom. 12.14	Luke 6.27-28
Bless those who persecute (you), bless and do not curse (them).	Love your enemies . . . bless those who curse you.

1 Cor. 13.2	Matt. 17.20
If I . . . have all faith so as to remove mountains . . .	Truly I say to you, if you have faith . . . you will say to this mountain, 'Go there from here', and it shall go.

16. I made a case for this in reference to Paul's knowledge and use of the Jesus tradition (*Jesus Remembered* 181-84). What was certainly true of the scriptural (OT) language and imagery, which must have come naturally to Paul in his own speech and teaching, can almost as certainly be presupposed with regard to the degree to which Jesus tradition had become part of his life-blood and shaped the themes of his preaching and letter-writing.

17. As Robert McCrum pointed out in an article in the Sunday *Observer* (Sunday, 21 November, 2010):

'As well as selling an estimated 1bn copies since 1611, the *KJB* went straight into our literary bloodstream like a lifesaving drug. Whenever we put words into someone's mouth, or see the writing on the wall, or go from strength to strength, or eat, drink and be merry, or fight the good fight, or bemoan the signs of the times, or find a fly in the ointment, or use words such as "long-suffering", "scapegoat" and "peacemaker" we are unconsciously quoting the *KJB*. More astounding, compared to Shakespeare's prodigal 31,000-word vocabulary, the *KJB* works its magic with a lexicon of just 12,000 words.'

1 Thess. 5.2	Matt. 24.43/Luke 12.39
You know that the day of the Lord comes thus like a thief in the night.	You know this, that if the householder knew at what watch of the night the thief was coming, he would have kept awake . . .

James 5.12	Matt. 5.34-37
Above all, my brothers, do not swear, either by heaven or by earth or by any other oath, but let your 'Yes' be 'yes' and your 'No' be 'no' . . .	But I say to you, Do not swear at all, either by heaven . . . or by earth . . . But let your word be, 'Yes, yes' and 'No, no'; anything more than these comes from the evil one.

1 Peter 2.12	Matt. 5.16
Conduct yourselves praiseworthily among the Gentiles, in order that . . . from your praiseworthy works observing, they may glorify God in the day of visitation.	Let your light so shine before men that they may see your good works and glorify your Father in heaven.

If these are among the best examples of traditions of Jesus' teaching which evidently influenced the paraenesis which is a feature of the NT letters,[18] the examples which follow in the Apostolic Fathers will demonstrate two distinctive features. One is that the later paraenesis drew more closely on the Jesus tradition; the dependency on teaching which we know particularly from the Synoptic Gospels to have been derived/remembered from Jesus' mission is more marked and more easily recognized. Should we regard this as an indication that the writing down of the oral Jesus tradition in the NT Gospels was already giving a firmer and more stable shape to the Jesus tradition being quoted or drawn on? The other is that whereas the NT letters had simply absorbed the Jesus tradition into their Christian exhortation, without making a point that it had been derived from Jesus, in some of the Apostolic Fathers there is much more of a concern to recall that this was the teaching of the Lord Jesus.

In recalling that the Jesus tradition was often alluded to in NT documents other than the Gospels, we should also note two agrapha of Jesus[19] which are recorded elsewhere in the NT:[20]

18. See again nn.1 and 16 above.

19. Agrapha = isolated sayings of or attributed to Jesus and not attested elsewhere; see further below §44.4a.

20. Are there other agrapha in the NT textual tradition? Elliott refers also to 1 Cor. 7.10; 9.14 and 1 Thess. 4.15ff. as other agrapha found in the NT (*ANT* 28). But 1 Cor. 7.10 more obviously alludes to Jesus' teaching as in Mark 10.11 pars., as does 1 Cor. 9.14 to Luke 10.7; and the 'word of the Lord' referred to in 1 Thess. 4.15 is probably a prophetic word

- Acts 20.35 — ... remembering the words of the Lord Jesus, that he said, 'It is more blessed to give than to receive';
- Luke 6.4 codex D adds — The same day, seeing a certain man working on the Sabbath, he (Jesus) said to him, 'Fellow, if you know what you are doing, blessed are you; but if you do not know, you are accursed and a transgressor of the law'.

If they are indeed recollections of particular sayings of Jesus, they are a reminder:

- that not all of Jesus' teaching can be assumed to have been available to each of the NT Gospel writers;
- that the Jesus tradition within the earliest churches was more extensive than has been recorded in the NT Gospels;
- and that the Jesus tradition was maintained in a living oral form after it had begun to be transcribed in written collections and Gospels.

But now we must move on to the phase following (most of) the NT writings, including the writing of the NT Gospels.

c. *1 Clement*

Discussion of *1 Clement* naturally focuses on two passages[21]— *1 Clem.* 13.2 and 46.8[22]— each quoting a sequence of Jesus' words: 'Remember the words of the Lord Jesus, for he said:'[23]

---

intended to assuage the anxieties of the Thessalonian believers (see my *Theology of Paul* 303-4). Other agrapha attested in the textual tradition of the NT Gospels are probably best seen as glosses and elaborations added to the text in the course of transmission; e.g., the D reading in Matt. 20.28 appears to be a variant drawn from Luke 14.8-10.

21. So *NTAF* 58-62; Koester, *Synoptische Überlieferung* 12-19; Hagner, *Use* 135-64; Young, *Jesus Tradition* chs. 4-6.

22. For other possible allusions to Jesus tradition in *1 Clement* (particularly 24.5 and 15.2) see E. Massaux, *The Influence of the Gospel of Saint Matthew on Christian Literature before Saint Irenaeus* (1950; ET 3 vols., Macon, GA: Mercer University, 1990) 1.12-32; Hagner, *Use* 164-71; A. F. Gregory, '*1 Clement* and the Writings That Later Formed the New Testament', in Gregory and Tuckett, eds., *Reception* 129-57 ('The Synoptic Gospels' 131-39), here pp. 137-39.

23. For convenience I add here also the parallels in Polycarp.

i. 1 Clement 13.2

1 Clement 13.2	NT Gospel tradition		Polycarp, *Phil.* 2.3
1. Show mercy, that you may be shown mercy;	Matt. 5.7; cf. 18.33	Blessed are those who show mercy, for they will be shown mercy.	3. Show mercy that you may be shown mercy;
2. forgive, that it may be forgiven you.	Mark 11.25; cf. Matt. 6.12, 14; 18.35; Luke 6.37c	Forgive if you have anything against anyone, that the Father . . . may also forgive you . . .	2. Forgive and it will be forgiven you;
3. As you do, so it will be done to you;	Matt. 7.12/ Luke 6.31	(Everything, as much) as you wish that people would do for you, thus you also do to them.	
4. as you give, so it will be given to you;	Luke 6.38a	Give, and it will be given to you.	
5. as you judge, so you will be judged;	Matt.7.2a/ Luke 6.37a	With what judgment you judge, you will be judged.	1. Do not judge, lest you be judged;
6. As you show kindness, so will kindness be shown to you;	Cf. Luke 6.35c	He is kind to the ungrateful and the wicked.	
7. With what measure you measure, by the same measure it will be measured to you.	Matt.7.2b/ Mark 4.24/ Luke 6.38b	With what measure you measure, it will be measured to you.	4. With what measure you measure, it will be measured to you in return.

Since all seven of the sayings quoted in *1 Clem.* 13.2 have some degree of parallel with Luke 6.31, 36-38 (four of the seven sayings have parallels in Matthew), it is possible to imagine Clement with a copy of Luke's Gospel to hand, or recalling what he had heard and retained from readings of Luke's Sermon on the Plain (or Matthew's Sermon on the Mount). But, apart from no. 7, the wording is not particularly close to that of either Matthew or Luke, and the ordering of the seven units hardly suggests their derivation from one or another of the written Gospels. In fact, hardly anything suggests a literary dependency. A more plausible explanation is that Clement was familiar with one of the no doubt many varied groupings of Jesus' teaching, perhaps one he had put together himself, for preaching or teaching purposes, on the theme of 'As you . . . so to you'.[24] *1 Clem.* 13.2, in other words, provides a very good

---

24. Massaux concludes that Clement drew from a 'catechism' whose author was inspired by Matthew (*Influence* 1.12). See Hagner's full discussion (*Use* 135-51, especially 137-38); 'The form of the citation is eminently suitable for material designed to be handed

example of how oral Jesus tradition could be, and no doubt was, put together in different combinations, with format adapted to a particular teaching emphasis or theme.[25]

Polycarp, *Phil.* 2.3, is very similar to *1 Clem.* 13.2, with four of the same sayings introduced by a similar call to remember what the Lord said in his teaching. This suggests to some that Polycarp knew *1 Clement* and was directly dependent on *1 Clem.* 13.2.[26] But the variation in order of the sayings points rather to a familiar grouping of Jesus' teaching in the preaching and teaching of the churches concerned.[27]

---

down by memory' (151); also 'Sayings of Jesus' 238 — 'The emphasis here, as in 13.2, on "remembering" is particularly suitable for material derived from oral tradition' (238, noting also Acts 20.35). 'Clement does not yet quote the text of a Gospel literally, because he feels bound up with the teaching of Jesus through the living oral tradition' (Hengel, *Four Gospels* 128-30). See also W.-D. Köhler, *Die Rezeption des Matthäusevangeliums in der Zeit vor Irenäus* (WUNT 2.24; Tübingen: Mohr Siebeck, 1987) 67-71; H. E. Lona, *Der erste Clemensbrief* (KAT 2; Göttingen: Vandenhoeck, 1998) 215, with further bibliography.

25. Gregory reviews recent discussion and notes that the majority opinion is that *1 Clem.* 13.2 is evidence of 'a pre- rather than a post-synoptic collection of sayings ascribed to Jesus' ('*1 Clement*' 133), that is, pre-synoptic oral tradition; see also his *Reception of Luke* 125-29.

26. Notably Lightfoot, *Apostolic Fathers* I.2.52; Koester, *Synoptische Überlieferung* 117-18. J. B. Bauer, *Die Polykarpbriefe* (KAV 5; Göttingen: Vandenhoeck, 1995), gives a full list of the Polycarp passages which have suggested his use of *1 Clement* (28-30). The word for word parallel of *1 Clem.* 13.2 in Clement of Alexandria, *Stromateis* II.18.91 (see *NTAF* 59) can be confidently explained as Clement of Alexandria drawing directly from the earlier Clement (Hagner, *Use* 140-46).

27. Massaux, *Influence* 2.29-30 (see n.24 above); Young, *Jesus Tradition* 160-73; Hartog, *Philippians* 58-60. The variations in Polycarp are 'more easily explainable as variations in the development of oral tradition than as Polycarp's poor attempt at recalling Clement's citation' (Hagner, *Use* 151; also 'Sayings of Jesus' 235-36); similarly Köhler, *Rezeption* 108. See also M. W. Holmes, 'Polycarp's *Letter to the Philippians* and the Writings That Later Formed the New Testament', in Gregory and Tuckett, eds., *Reception* 187-227 (here 190-93).

ii. 1 Clement 46.8

1 Clement 46.8	Matt. 18.7, 6	Mark 14.21; 9.42	Luke 17.1, 2
Woe to that person!	7 Woe to the person through whom the cause of stumbling comes.	14.21 Woe to that person through whom the Son of Man is betrayed.	... woe through whom it comes.
It would have been good for him if he had not been born than cause one of my elect to stumble. It would have been better for him to have a millstone put around him and be drowned into the sea than to pervert one of my elect.	6 Whoever causes one of these little ones who believe in me to stumble, it would be an advantage for him that a heavy millstone were hung round his neck and he were drowned in the depths of the sea.	It were good for him if that person had not been born. 9.42 Whoever causes one of these little ones who believe to stumble it would have been good for him rather if a heavy millstone were placed round his neck and he had been cast into the sea.	It would be to his advantage if a stone from a mill were placed round his neck and he had been thrown into the sea than that he caused one of these little ones to stumble.

1 Clem. 46.8 shows clear familiarity with a theme of Jesus' teaching attested in all three Synoptics. Again the variation of wording makes it less likely that Clement was quoting any written Gospel as such.[28] The probability is rather that a warning given by Jesus (more than once?) against causing a disciple to stumble, using the fearful imagery of drowning under the weight of a millstone, was remembered and cited quite widely in early Christian exhortation with the slight variations typical of orally used and transmitted tradition.[29] The drawing in of a phrase ('better that he had not been born'), more familiar in the tradition in reference to Judas (Mark 14.21), is the sort of interactive or allusive variation that one could expect in oral tradition.[30]

We can conclude, therefore, with Koester, that '1 Clement never refers to a written Gospel. ... the author of 1 Clement makes use of none of our Synoptic Gospels'.[31] But it is equally clear that Jesus tradition, as attested in

---

28. *Pace* Massaux, *Influence* 1.22-24, who in general assumes too readily that parallels and allusions are to be explained only in terms of literary dependence.

29. See further Hagner, *Use* 162-63; Köhler, *Rezeption* 63-64; Gregory, '*1 Clement*' 135-37; Lona, *Clemensbrief* 498.

30. Koester, *Synoptische Überlieferung* 19. Hermas, *Vis.* 23(IV.2).6, shows that the words used of Judas were applied more broadly (see further Hagner, *Use* 156-59).

31. *Synoptische Überlieferung* 23. Young is equally emphatic (*Jesus Tradition* 113-18,

the Synoptic tradition, was well known in different groupings and valued as integral to Christian catechesis and paraenesis.

d. Ignatius

There are a few possible allusions to Jesus tradition in the seven letters of Ignatius. Since he also shows little interest in the scriptures (OT),[32] that is less of a surprise. We need look at only six examples.[33]

i. Ephesians 5.2

Ephesians 5.2	Matthew 18.19-20
If the prayer of one or two has such power, how much more will that of the bishop and the entire church?	If two of you agree on earth about anything you ask, it will be done for you by my Father in heaven. For where two or three are gathered in my name, I am there among them.

It is certainly plausible to infer that Ignatius was taking his lead from teaching recalled as given by Jesus.[34] But the lack of closeness in wording between the two texts makes it very unlikely that Ignatius was quoting Matthew. At most we can say that Ignatius knew a version of the saying also used by Matthew.[35]

149-50, 190-91). Köhler leaves open the question of *1 Clement*'s use of Matthew — in no way clearly demonstrable, but not to be excluded (*Rezeption* 72).

32. *Eph.* 5.3 (Prov. 3.34); *Magn.* 12 (Prov. 18.17); *Trall.* 8.2 (cf. Isa. 52.5).

33. Massaux lists seven texts 'where literary influence [from Matthew] is certain' — *Eph.* 5.2; 14.2; *Trall.* 11.1; *Philad.* 3.1; *Smyrn.* 1.1; *Polyc.* 1.2; 2.2 (*Influence* 1.87-91). Hagner limits his study of Ignatius to four cases ('Sayings of Jesus' 239-40); Young considers only *Smyrn.* 3.2a (*Jesus Tradition* 229-32). As noted above (§41 n.39) references to 'the gospel' (*Philad.* 8.2; 9.2; *Smyrn.* 7.2) are probably not to a written Gospel. See also W. R. Schoedel, 'Ignatius and the Reception of the Gospel of Matthew in Antioch', in Balch, ed., *Social History* 129-77.

34. W. R. Inge confidently asserts that 'the reference is clearly to the saying recorded in Matthew — "probably a well-known saying" of Christ (Zahn)' (*NTAF* 77).

35. 'It is evident that the reference to "one or two" in Ignatius reflects a tradition independent of Matthew' (Schoedel, *Ignatius* 56 n.11). Meier refers to the 'lyrical passage' (*Eph.* 19.2-3) developing Matthew's story of the Magi and the star, which 'may indicate that Ignatius had meditated on, preached upon, and reworked Matt 1–2 for some time' (in Brown and Meier, *Antioch and Rome* 25).

ii. Smyrneans 1.1

Smyrneans 1.1	Matthew 3.13-15
... baptized by John, in order that all righteousness might be fulfilled by him.	Jesus came ... to John to be baptized by him.... Jesus said to him, 'Let it be so now, for thus it is fitting for us to fulfill all righteousness'.

Since Matt. 3.15 is unique to Matthew, including the distinctively Matthean emphasis on 'righteousness' and 'fulfillment',[36] Ignatius here is obviously echoing Matthew's distinctive treatment of Jesus' baptism. This strongly suggests that Ignatius either had access to a copy of Matthew's Gospel, or had a good memory of hearing a reading from Matthew's Gospel, or that Matthew's distinctive 'take' on Jesus' baptism had entered into the more widely known Jesus tradition.[37] When the language is so distinctive of Matthew, Occam's razor suggests that to hypothesize a source or version used by Matthew is unnecessarily complex.[38]

iii. Smyrneans 3.2

Smyrneans 3.2-3	Luke 24.39, 42-43
... he said to them, 'Reach out, <u>touch me and see</u> that I am not a bodiless demon'.... And after his resurrection he ate and drank with them as a fleshly being ...	He said to them ... '<u>Touch me and see</u>, for a spirit does not have flesh and bones as you see that I have'.... They gave him a piece of broiled fish, and he took it and ate it before them.

An allusion to Luke's Gospel is certainly possible. However, the quotation is attested elsewhere in early Christianity, but not attributed to Luke's Gospel. Origen attributes it to 'the Doctrine of Peter', Jerome to 'the Gospel according to the Hebrews',[39] and Eusebius quotes *Smyr.* 3.2 but confesses that he

---

36. See §42 at n.219 above; Koester largely ignores the combination of the two characteristic Matthean motifs (*Synoptische Überlieferung* 59).

37. Cf. *NTAF* 76-77; Koester, *Synoptische Überlieferung* 59; R. Bauckham, 'The Study of Gospel Traditions outside the Canonical Gospels: Problems and Prospects', in Wenham, *Jesus Tradition* 369-403 (here 395).

38. *Smyr.* 1.1 'clearly indicates that Ignatius knew Matthew' (Köhler, *Rezeption* 79); 'this is the one passage in which Matthew's own redaction of synoptic materials seems clearly evident in Ignatius' (Schoedel, *Ignatius* 222). Cf. Davies and Allison, *Matthew* 1.327; P. Foster, 'The Epistles of Ignatius of Antioch and the Writings That Later Formed the New Testament', in Gregory and Tuckett, eds., *Reception* 159-86 (here 174-76, 180-81), including a justifiable critique of Koester, *Synoptische Überlieferung* 57-59; also Gregory and Tuckett, eds., *Trajectories* 329 nn.16, 17; also J. P. Meier, 'Matthew and Ignatius', in Balch, ed., *Social History* 178-86 (citing also *Philad.* 3.1, *Pol.* 2.2 and *Eph.* 19.2-3).

39. Full quotations in Koester, *Synoptische Überlieferung* 45-46.

does not know what source Ignatius was quoting (*HE* 3.36.11). That Ignatius knew the *same tradition* which Luke has produced is clear enough, but it was probably a tradition known independently of Luke's Gospel. And the facts that Ignatius includes elements not in Luke (he makes specific mention of Peter), and that he ignores elements in Luke (that Jesus showed them his hands and feet) which would have strengthened Ignatius's point (that Jesus was in the flesh even after the resurrection), almost certainly indicate Ignatius's knowledge and use of oral tradition independent of Luke.[40]

iv. Smyrneans 6.1

Smyrneans 6.1	Matthew 19.12
Let the one who receives (this) receive it.	Let the one who is able to receive (this) receive it.

Although the wording is close, the teaching to which the exhortation is appended is very different.[41] The exhortation, indeed, sounds similar to the more regularly used, 'Let the one who has ears to hear, hear' (Mark 4.9; etc.), and probably is used by Ignatius at this point in similar fashion, to drive home his own teaching. In other words, it probably was a free-floating exhortation drawn in to emphasize a point being made, 'a homiletical formula used to commend hard sayings',[42] and not indicative of any particular dependency.[43]

v. Polycarp 2.1

Polycarp 2.1	Luke 6.32
If you like good disciples, <u>it is</u> no <u>credit to</u> you (singular).	If you love those who love you, what <u>credit is</u> that <u>to</u> you (plural)?

An allusion derived by copying a written text seems less than likely, but an exhortation crafted by memory of Jesus tradition is certainly plausible, whether the memory was from oral Jesus tradition or from hearing a reading from Luke's Gospel.[44]

---

40. See also *NTAF* 79-80; Schoedel, *Ignatius* 226-27; Foster, 'Ignatius of Antioch' 182, drawing on Gregory, *Reception of Luke* 69-75; Young, *Jesus Tradition* 230-32.

41. Whereas the verbal similarity in Justin's *1 Apol.* 15.4c is not so close, but the context so closely follows Matt. 19.12a that an echo of Matthew is very probable.

42. Schoedel, *Ignatius* 236; similarly *NTAF* 77; Koester, *Synoptische Überlieferung* 35.

43. See also Foster, 'Ignatius of Antioch' 179-80.

44. 'The similarity . . . to Luke 6:32 . . . suggests an indebtedness to common tradition (presumably reflected also in 1 Pet 2:18-19; cf. *Did.* 1.3; *2 Clem.* 13.4)' (Schoedel, *Ignatius* 262).

vi. Polycarp 2.2

Polycarp 2.2	Matthew 10.16/*Thomas* 39.3
Be <u>wise</u> (singular) <u>as</u> a <u>serpent</u> in all things <u>and</u> always <u>pure as the dove</u>.	Be <u>wise</u> (plural) <u>as</u> the <u>serpents</u> <u>and pure as the doves</u>.

The variation of singular/plural is what can be expected in the use made of Jesus tradition in different preaching/teaching contexts. The saying's proverbial character suggests that it may well have had much wider circulation,[45] whether as an independent proverb, or as oral Jesus tradition, or as remembered from a reading of Matthew's Gospel (second orality).[46]

Several other possible allusions in Ignatius's letters to Matthew's Gospel in particular are regularly cited.[47] But in no case can they serve as evidence of a literary dependency of Ignatius on Matthew. A knowledge of the tradition which Matthew also used can be readily inferred, but realistically, nothing more.[48] For example, in both *Trall.* 11.1 and *Philad.* 3.1 Ignatius speaks of evil growths as 'not a planting of the Father'. An allusion to Matt. 15.13 ('Every plant that my heavenly Father has not planted will be uprooted') is possible.[49] But the imagery is a good biblical one (the people of God as God's planting)[50] and not distinctive of Matthew, so that a regular use of such imagery in the exhortations of typical Christian assemblies can be easily envisaged, without any thought of attribution to Matthew (or to Jesus) as such.[51]

Eph. 11.1 uses the phrase 'the wrath about to come', a phrase which appears also in the Q version of John the Baptist's preaching (Matt. 3.7/Luke 3.7). But Ignatius talks of fearing the wrath about to come, while the Baptist

---

45. Cf. not only *GThom.* 39.3, but also Canticles Rabbah 2.14, the Nag Hammadi *Teaching of Silvanus* 95.7-11 and Rom. 16.19 (see Davies and Allison, *Matthew* 2.180-81; DeConick, *Thomas* 160). Schoedel refers to the Midrash on the Song of Songs 2.14 (*Ignatius* 263).

46. Cf. Koester, *Synoptische Überlieferung* 43; Hagner, 'Sayings of Jesus' 239; see also Foster, 'Ignatius of Antioch' 178-79.

47. Others cited by Inge and Foster as implausible are *Eph.* 5.2/Matt. 18.19-20; *Eph.* 6.1/Matt. 10.40; *Magn.* 5.2/Matt. 22.19; *Magn.* 9.3/Matt. 27.52; *Rom.* 9.3/Matt. 10.40-41; *Pol.* 1.2-3/Matt. 8.17 (*NTAF* 77-79; Foster, 'Ignatius of Antioch' 180). Koester's examination is still more extensive (*Synoptische Überlieferung* 26-61). Köhler regards *Eph.* 15.1/Matt. 23.8; *Eph.* 19/Matt.2.2, 9; *Philad.* 2.2/Matt. 7.15; *Philad.* 6.1/Matt. 23.27; *Polyc.* 1.2-3/Matt. 8.17 as good possibilities of Matthean dependence (*Rezeption* 80-86).

48. See also J. S. Sibinga, 'Ignatius and Matthew', *NovT* 8 (1966) 262-83. Schoedel is inclined to agree with Koester 'that it was oral material to which Ignatius was indebted' (*Ignatius* 9).

49. Köhler, *Rezeption* 80.

50. Davies and Allison, *Matthew* 2.532.

51. Foster, 'Epistles of Ignatius' 177-78.

exhorted his hearers to flee from the wrath about to come; so a close dependence on Baptist tradition as such is not indicated. 'Wrath' as a way of speaking of future/eschatological divine retribution was familiar in the OT and early Jewish literature[52] and elsewhere in the NT.[53] So if the phrase itself ('the wrath about to come') is sufficiently distinctive of the Baptist's preaching, that phrase, originated by the Baptist, may simply have become part of Christian exhortation, or could be attributed to a wider knowledge of or impact of the oral tradition of the Baptist's preaching. Specific knowledge of a Q document as such or of Matthew in particular is not required to explain Ignatius's use of the phrase.

Eph. 14.2 also may indicate some knowledge or influence of tradition shared by Matthew and Luke (Matt. 12.33b/Luke 6.44a), though in this case the Matthean/Lukan parallel more likely indicates a shared oral rather than a written tradition.

Ephesians 14.2	Matthew 12.33	Luke 6.43-44
No one who professes faith sins, nor does anyone hate after acquiring love. The tree is plainly to be seen from its fruit.	Either make the tree good and its fruit good, or make the tree bad and its fruit bad. For from the fruit the tree is known.	No good tree makes bad fruit, nor again does a bad tree make good fruit. For each tree is known from its own fruit.

The thought is proverbial,[54] so an echo of Jesus tradition is certainly plausible though not compelling; but nothing indicates literary dependence.[55]

Eph. 17.1 refers to the anointing of Jesus' head. The allusion to the episode, differently recalled in the Synoptics (Mark 14.3 pars.) and John 12.3, is clear. But the different versions are sufficient evidence of a story retold quite widely and differently, that is, in the oral Jesus tradition. A dependence on a specific Gospel cannot be claimed with any assurance.[56]

In addition, there are two possible instances of Ignatius knowing John's Gospel, or Johannine tradition.[57] The first is *Rom.* 7.2-3, where Ignatius uses the phrase 'living water also speaking in me' (cf. John 4.10, 14),[58] and goes on

---

52. *TDNT* 5.401, 415.
53. Note particularly 'the coming wrath' (1 Thess. 1.10; also Eph. 5.6; Col. 3.6); also Rom. 2.5, 8; 5.9; 9.22; Rev. 6.16-17; 11.18; 14.10; 16.19; 19.15.
54. Cf. Sir. 27.6; *b. Ber.* 48a.
55. On the last two passages, cf. Foster, 'Ignatius of Antioch' 181-82.
56. Koester, *Synoptische Überlieferung* 56-57; Köhler, *Rezeption* 82.
57. *NTAF* 82-83 looks at five other cases of which only *Magn.* 7.1 and 8.2 (cf. John 8.28-29) impress; Foster is less impressed ('Ignatius of Antioch' 183); C. E. Hill, *The Johannine Corpus in the Early Church* (Oxford University, 2004) 434-37, is more impressed; he refers also to *Philad.* 9.1-2 and *Smyrn. praescr.* 1.1-2 (438-40).
58. But note also the parallel with/reminiscence of *Odes of Solomon* 11.6-7 — 'And speaking waters touched my lips from the spring of the Lord generously. And so I drank

to talk of 'the bread of God which is the flesh of Jesus Christ . . . and for drink I desire his blood, which is imperishable love' (cf. John 6.41-58). The close combination of the two themes is probably sufficient to indicate that Ignatius knew and had been influenced by John's reworking of Jesus tradition.[59]

The second is *Philad.* 7.1: 'the Spirit is not deceived, since it comes from God. For it knows whence it comes and where it goes . . .'. The clause 'whence it comes and where it goes' is verbatim with the same clause in John 3.8, except that in John it is a general 'you' (Nicodemus) who knows this, whereas in Ignatius it is the Spirit which knows (cf. John 8.14).[60] Since Ignatius's reference to the Spirit at this point is so different from John's, any suggestion of a quotation is implausible. At best we can speak of a way of characterizing the mystery of the Spirit's working which may well have originated with John but which had become detached from any specific context and used to describe other workings of the Spirit.[61]

In all this, of course, it has to be remembered that Ignatius was writing his letters while he was on his way through Asia Minor to martyrdom in Rome. His ability to transport written texts with him was presumably limited, so that such echoes of Jesus tradition as there are in his letters were most probably derived from his memory. Overall both the number of echoes and their difference or relative independence from the wording of the canonical Gospels suggest more a living tradition which had become the life-blood of early churches, a tradition in part deriving from Jesus, known mostly through oral usage, or into which Jesus tradition had fed, but which was valued more for its continuing relevance (impact) than because it could be specifically attributed to Jesus as such. That still discernible are the roots of these allusions to or influence from the Jesus tradition also attested in the Synoptic tradition, or indeed even the distinctive features which Matthew and John introduced to the Jesus tradition, should occasion no surprise, but simply remind us that the Jesus tradition was indeed living tradition. From such evidence we can discern some confirmation of the influence of Matthew and John in the development of that tradition. That still does not allow us to conclude from the evidence

---

and became intoxicated, from the living water that does not die' (cf. *Thomas* 13.5) (cf. Schoedel, *Ignatius* 185).

59. 'The whole passage is inspired by the Fourth Gospel' (Lightfoot, *Apostolic Fathers* II.2.224); *NTAF* 81-82. Massaux is uncertain (*Influence* 1.103-4); but Hill makes a strong case (*Johannine Corpus* 432-34). Ignatius's emphasis on Christ's flesh may be more motivated by his anti-Docetic concern (*Trall.* 8.1; *Rom.* 7.3; *Philad.* 4; 5.1; *Smyrn.* 7.1).

60. 'The coincidence is quite too strong to be accidental' (Lightfoot, *Apostolic Fathers* II.2.266); 'Here we have the strongest possibility in Ignatius of a dependence directly on the Fourth Gospel' (Schoedel, *Ignatius* 206); Hill, *Johannine Corpus* 437-38.

61. See also Foster, 'Ignatius of Antioch' 184.

with any confidence that Ignatius knew any written Gospel as such.[62] But it does confirm that at least Matthew and John were either well known or were already influential, that is, most probably in Syria, from which Ignatius came, and in Asia Minor, where he wrote his letters.

e. Polycarp

In Polycarp's letter to the Philippians there are several allusions to Jesus tradition. The most obvious one, *Phil.* 2.3, we have already looked at above, on *1 Clem.* 13.2.[63] But Polycarp continues, still recalling what 'the Lord said when he taught':

Phil. 2.3	Matt. 5.3, 10	Luke 6.20
. . . and, 'Blessed are the poor	Blessed are the poor in spirit, for theirs is the kingdom of heaven. Blessed are those who have been persecuted for righteousness' sake, for theirs is the kingdom of heaven.	Blessed are you poor for yours is the kingdom of God.
and those who are persecuted for righteousness' sake, for theirs is the kingdom of God'.		

The differences make a quotation of Matthew unlikely, but the reference to Matthew's distinctive motif of 'righteousness' again suggests at least some knowledge of or influence from Matthew. Perhaps it would be simplest to infer that Matthew's formulation of Jesus tradition had become part of the oral Jesus tradition, a version of Jesus' teaching on this point more widely circulated and known.[64]

Phil. 7.2 is also interesting: 'Through our entreaties asking the all-seeing God not to bring us into temptation, just as the Lord said, "The spirit is willing, but the flesh is weak"'. The echo of the Lord's Prayer in the first half is obvious (Matt. 6.13), but even more striking is the echo of Jesus' words in Mark 14.38/ Matt. 26.41 — 'Watch and pray lest you enter into temptation; the spirit is willing, but the flesh is weak' — where the final clause is precisely as Polycarp quotes. However, a literary dependency on Matthew (or Mark) is not the most

---

62. Köhler concludes that it is a 'probability bordering on certainty' that Ignatius knew Matthew or at least Matthean material (*Rezeption* 95-96); Hill is equally confident regarding Ignatius's familiarity with John's Gospel (*Johannine Corpus* 440-41).

63. See above §44.2c(i).

64. See also Köhler, *Rezeption* 99-100; Gregory, *Reception of Luke* 134-35; Holmes, 'Polycarp's *Letter*' 193-94; Young, *Jesus Tradition* 168-72.

plausible explanation.⁶⁵ It looks rather as though Polycarp's exhortation has grown out of meditation on the Lord's Prayer, which would of course have been well known from regular liturgical usage. To this Polycarp attached a proverbial saying which could be readily detached from its original placing in the story of Jesus' Gethsemane experience and used in other settings.⁶⁶ As such we may regard *Phil.* 7.2 as a typical example of how the oral Jesus tradition could be and was often merged into an exhortation appropriate to the circumstances addressed.⁶⁷

Phil. 6.2 also draws on the Lord's Prayer: 'If we ask the Lord to forgive us, we ought also to forgive'. The exhortation probably echoes the kind of reflection which the Lord's Prayer petition for forgiveness (Matt. 6.12/Luke 11.4) evoked, as in Matt. 6.14-15, Mark 11.25 and Col. 3.13. Here again the evidence points to the continuing influence of Jesus' teaching on prayer, as known through regular liturgical usage.⁶⁸

Other suggested allusions to particular Synoptic texts are still less persuasive —

- *Phil.* 5.2, 'servant of all' (Mark 9.35; cf. Matt. 20.28);
- *Phil.* 12.3, 'Pray . . . for those who persecute and hate you' (Matt. 5.44/ Luke 6.27)⁶⁹—

but indicate how language and sentiments originating with Jesus became part of subsequent Christian paraenesis.

Polycarp also seems to have known key members of the Johannine corpus:

---

65. Koester is surprisingly confident that 'Polycarp must have known one of these two Gospels' (*Synoptische Überlieferung* 115); contrast Young, *Jesus Tradition* 232-37.

66. Cf. *NTAF* 103; Hagner, 'Sayings of Jesus' 240; Holmes notes how many think the passage demonstrates Polycarp's dependence on or knowledge of Matthew but is himself uncertain ('Polycarp's *Letter*' 195-96). The contrast between flesh and spirit was characteristically Jewish; see W. D. Davies, 'Paul and the Dead Sea Scrolls: Flesh and Spirit', *Christian Origins and Judaism* (London: DLT, 1962) 145-77.

67. Massaux characteristically protests: 'Why turn to an oral tradition or to a parent document of the gospels, whose existence is hypothetical?' (*Influence* 2.32).

68. Koester, *Synoptische Überlieferung* 120; cf. Holmes, 'Polycarp's *Letter*' 194.

69. Koester again infers that Matthew and Luke were known and used in Polycarp's community (*Synoptische Überlieferung* 119-20), but see also Köhler, *Rezeption* 101-2, and Gregory, *Reception of Luke* 135. Holmes notes that the command to 'pray for one's enemies' was widespread and took subtly different forms in early Christian writings (e.g. *Did.* 1.3; Justin, *1 Apol.* 14.3; 15.9; *Dial.* 96.3; 133.6; Athenagoras, *Leg.* 11.2; Theophilus, *Ad Autol.* 3.14; *Ap. Const.* 1.2.2; P.Oxy. 1224); he suggests that the tradition which was incorporated in the Gospels also had a life of its own ('Polycarp's *Letter*' 197).

For anyone who does not confess that Jesus Christ has come in the flesh is an antichrist [cf. 1 John 4.2-3; 2 John 7]; and whoever does not confess the witness of the cross is from the devil [cf. 1 John 3.8]; and whoever distorts the words of the Lord for his own passions . . . this one is the firstborn of Satan [cf. John 8.44]. And so let us leave behind the idle speculation of the multitudes and false teachings and turn to the word that was delivered to us from the beginning [cf. 1 John 1.1; 2.7, 24; 3.11; 2 John 5] . . . (*Phil.* 7.1-2).

This suggests a knowledge of John's Gospel.[70] In addition, *Phil.* 5.2 ('inasmuch as he promised to raise us from the dead') could reflect a promise first formulated in John (6.40, 44, 54), but does not carry with it the necessary implication that Polycarp drew it from his own reading of John's Gospel.[71]

Holmes also notes that *Phil.* 6.1 ('. . . knowing that we are all in debt with respect to sin') seems to imply reference to a familiar and authoritative saying, but one whose source is unknown.[72] This adds some strength to the probability that Polycarp had a greater store of catechetical teaching which came to him through oral tradition, not all derived from Jesus tradition as such.

Here again, then, we can speak of influence from the Gospels of Matthew and John, confirming their already established status in Asia Minor in the early second century.

f. Didache

The Teaching of the Twelve Apostles is introduced as 'The teaching of the Lord through the twelve apostles to the nations/Gentiles'. The very wording indicates the understanding of the distinctive teaching that was to follow: it had originated with the Lord (Jesus Christ); and it had been passed down through the apostles. There is already something of an idealization here (an active role for the twelve) which is hardly supported in other Christian literature up till then. But the basic claim being made should not be overly discounted. For it reflects much of what has become apparent in our study of the Jesus tradition: that there were leading disciples (apostles) who from the beginning took responsibility to pull together, formulate, rehearse regularly, translate and transmit the teaching which they had received from Jesus and which had so impressed them that such formulation as Jesus tradition and use and spread of it were natural compulsions. It is perhaps worth noting that this responsibility

---

70. Hill, *Johannine Corpus* 418-19; also 354-57.
71. *NTAF* 104; Hill, *Johannine Corpus* 420; Holmes, 'Polycarp's *Letter*' 198-99.
72. 'Polycarp's *Letter*' 188-89.

is attributed to all twelve apostles, and no mention is made of the one or two or more who had carried the process further by transcribing the Jesus tradition into Gospels. Though, as we shall see, it is probable that *Didache* was able to draw on at least Matthew's Gospel, or drew on tradition much influenced by Matthew,[73] this title (*The Teaching of the Twelve Apostles*) reflects more the larger task of using and transmitting the Jesus tradition which must have been carried on in oral terms, a task which was the responsibility of more than the Evangelists. The likelihood, then, is that the Jesus tradition on which *Didache* draws was known to its compiler through different channels and versions of the oral Jesus tradition, even when the most immediately traceable version was that of Matthew's Gospel.[74]

(1) *Didache* begins with a familiar paraenetic technique — an exposition and contrast of 'the two ways' (*Did.* 1-6).[75] 'The way of life' begins with a whole sequence of Jesus' teaching ('the teaching of the Lord').

Didache 1.2-5	(chiefly) Matthew	
² First, 'you will love the God' who made you, second 'your neighbour as yourself'.	Mark 12.29-31 pars. First . . . you will love the Lord your God . . . second, you will love your neighbour as yourself.	*Barn.* 19.2 *Barn.* 19.5
And whatever you do not want to happen to you, do not do to another.	Matt. 7.12 Whatever you want that people should do for you, do you thus also for them.	Luke 6.31

---

73. H. van de Sandt, ed., *Matthew and the Didache: Two Documents from the Same Jewish-Christian Milieu* (Assen: Van Gorcum, 2005), contains the papers of the Tilburg Conference (April 2003) discussing whether the significant agreements between *Didache* and Matthew are to be explained by *Didache*'s knowledge and use of Matthew, or by their use of common tradition, or origin in the same milieu; the contributors were almost equally divided between these options.

74. The questions whether the texts we now have of *Didache* (and Matthew) include redactional elements and chronologically distinct layers (see §40.1e above) make the issue of possible influence (either way) much more complicated than can be dealt with here (cf. Niederwimmer, *Didache* 76-77). But the key questions for us are posed in any case by the texts as they now stand.

75. The theme of 'two ways' was familiar in both Jewish and non-Jewish literature, so that dependence on Jesus tradition (e.g. Matt. 7.13-14) need not be implied here; see further §45.5b below; also C. M. Tuckett, 'The *Didache* and the Writings That Later Formed the New Testament', in Gregory and Tuckett, eds., *Reception* 83-127 (here 96). See also J. S. Kloppenborg, '*Didache* 1.1–6.1, James, Matthew and the Torah', in Gregory and Tuckett, eds., *Trajectories* 193-221.

Didache 1.2-5	(chiefly) Matthew	
... ³ 'Bless those who curse you' and 'pray for your enemies', and fast for those who persecute you.	5.44, 46-47 Love your enemies, [bless those who curse you], pray for those who persecute you . . .	Luke 6.27 Rom 12.14 Bless those who persecute you, bless and do not curse.
For what credit is it if you love those who love you? Do not the Gentiles also do this? But love those who hate you, and you will not have an enemy.	For if you love those who love you, what reward do you have? . . . Do not also the Gentiles do the same?	Luke 6.32
⁴ Abstain from fleshly passions. If someone 'gives you a slap on the right cheek, turn to him the other also', and you will be perfect.	5.39 whoever slaps you on your right cheek, turn to him the other also. 5.48 Be perfect as your heavenly Father is perfect.	1 Pet 2.11 I urge you . . . to abstain from fleshly passions. Lk 6.29a
If someone 'will force you to go one mile, go with him two'.	5.41 Whoever will force you to go one mile, go with him two.	
If someone takes away your cloak, give him also your shirt. If someone takes from you what is yours, do not ask for it back (you could not get it back anyway!).	5.40 to him who wants to sue you and to take your shirt, yield to him also your cloak.	Luke 6.29b
⁵ 'Give to everyone who asks you, and do not ask for it back'.	Luke 6.30 Give to everyone who asks you, and from him who takes away what is yours, do not ask for it back.	Matt 5.42

Then follows an elaboration, commending the attitude taught by Jesus, but warning the recipient of such generosity that his need should be real (1.5).

Didache 1.5-6	(chiefly) Matthew	
	5.25-26 Come to terms quickly with your accuser while you are on the way to court with him, or your accuser may hand you over to the judge, and the judge to the guard, and you will be thrown into prison; truly I tell you, you will by no means get out from there until you have repaid the last penny.	Luke 12.57-59
Being in jail he will be interrogated about what he did; and 'he will not get out from there until he has repaid the last penny'. ⁶ But it has also been said concerning this: 'Let your almsgiving sweat in your hands, until you know to whom to give it'.	?	

Several interesting features call for comment:

- the degree of parallel with the Q material common to Matthew's Sermon on the Mount and Luke's Sermon on the Plain is striking;
- apart from Luke 6.30, the closest parallels are with Matthew;
- the degree of disorder from Matthew's sequence does not suggest a close literary dependence;
- the additional material in *Didache* (the parallel with 1 Pet. 2.11 in *Did.* 1.4, the elaboration in 1.5 and the unknown saying used in 1.6) suggests a Jesus tradition which has been expanded in the course of usage.

It is likely, then, that *Didache* knew Matthew's Gospel, or more precisely the Jesus tradition on which Matthew drew.[76] If Matthew was responsible for gathering Jesus tradition in just this collection, then the conclusion would have to be that *Didache* did know Matthew as such, or at least was

---

76. The argument, frequently made, that linking the commands to love God and love the neighbour was already familiar in non-Christian Judaism (e.g. Koester, *Synoptische Überlieferung* 135; Hagner, 'Sayings of Jesus' 241; Tuckett, *'Didache'* 97) ignores the fact that Jesus' abstraction of Lev. 19.18 ('love your neighbour as yourself') from the welter of commandments and his giving it such special prominence ('second') were unprecedented. It is this distinctive feature of the Jesus tradition which *Did.* 1.2 reflects. The point can be made more plausibly in the case of *Did.* 1.2b/Matt. 7.12 (see *Jesus Remembered* 588-89).

well able to recall the formulation that Matthew gave to this collection of Jesus tradition.[77]

It is certainly possible that Matthew at this point had been able to draw on teaching material which had already been grouped — as may also be suggested by the Lukan parallels.[78] Furthermore, the differences of *Didache* from Matthew, even when Matthew is closest, the evidence of Rom. 12.14 and 1 Pet. 2.11, the parallels with *Barnabas* and the elaborations provided by *Didache* strongly suggest material which was more widely used in Christian paraenesis and which had been shaped in the process of oral usage and transmission (cf. Justin, *1 Apol.* 15-16).[79] Even so, however, it remains probable that *Didache* reflects in some degree Matthew's contribution to and influence on the oral Jesus tradition, its catechetical and paraenetical usage.[80]

In the rest of the paraenetical section (*Did.* 1-6) there is only one other clear echo of Jesus tradition:[81] *Did.* 3.7 — 'Be meek, since "the meek will inherit the land/earth"' (Matt. 5.5), though, of course, the quoted passage is also a quotation from Ps. 37.11.[82]

(2) In the section on baptism, fasting, the Lord's prayer and the eucharist (*Did.* 7-10), there are several other references which reflect influence from Matthew in particular:

---

77. Cf. Koester, *Synoptische Überlieferung* 240; 'definite literary contacts with the Sermon on the Mount' (Massaux, *Influence* 3.151).

78. C. N. Jefford, *The Sayings of Jesus in the Teaching of the Twelve Apostles* (Leiden: Brill, 1989), concludes that 'the section consistently is dependent upon Synoptic texts that are derived from the Sayings Gospel Q' (52).

79. See J. Draper, 'The Jesus Tradition in the Didache', in Wenham, ed., *Jesus Tradition* 269-87 (here 273-79); W. Rordorf, 'Does the Didache Contain Jesus Tradition Independently of the Synoptic Gospels?', in H. Wansbrough, ed., *Jesus and the Oral Gospel Tradition* (JSNTS 64; Sheffield: JSOT, 1991) 394-423 (here 408-9, 411). Koester regards 'the interpretation of the traditional sayings of Jesus . . . now tied to the developing Christian catechism' as 'a momentous step' (*Introduction* 2.158). J. Schröter, 'Jesus Tradition in Matthew, James, and the Didache: Searching for Characteristic Emphases', in van de Sandt and Zangenberg, eds., *Matthew, James and Didache* 233-55, concludes from a study of the theme of 'perfection' in the three writings that 'the so-called "Jesus traditions" in the Didache, then, are taken from a multitude of early Christian catechetical traditions which James and Matthew had access to as well' (253); but to describe the evidence of *Did.* 1.2-6 as 'so-called "Jesus tradition"' comes across as unjustifiably tendentious.

80. On Justin, *1 Apol.* 15-16, see below §44.3b(ii).

81. Quite a lot of attention is given to the parallels between *Did.* 2.2-3 and Matt. 19.18-19 pars., but the *Didache* text could be as well rooted in Exod. 20.13-16 and Deut. 5.17-20; see also §45.5b below.

82. Cf. Jefford, *Sayings of Jesus* 73-81. Tuckett finds it unlikely that the Didachist derived this exhortation from Matthew, but concludes that *Did.* 6.2 ('you will be perfect' — repetition of *Did.* 1.4; cf. Matt. 5.48) seems 'to indicate a close link between the *Didache* and Matthew's gospel' ('*Didache*' 99-102).

Did. 7.2-3	Matt. 28.19
Baptize in the name of the Father and of the Son and of the Holy Spirit ... pour water on the head three times in the name of Father and Son and Holy Spirit.	... make disciples of all nations, baptizing them in the name of the Father and of the Son and of the Holy Spirit.

This baptismal formula is distinctive to Matthew; elsewhere in the NT baptism is performed 'in the name of the Lord Jesus'.[83] So either *Didache* reflects direct dependence on Matthew as such. Or, since in this section *Didache* is dealing with matters of regular liturgy, *Did.* 7.2-3 reflects the fact that Matthew's formulation was soon absorbed into wider liturgical practice.[84] It is, of course, possible that Matt. 28.19 reflects an already established baptismal formula. But given the other Matthean-type quotations and echoes of the Jesus tradition, influence, direct or indirect, from Matthew becomes harder to deny. On the evidence of this passage, along with the others, it is safe to conclude that Matthew's Gospel was already written, and already exercising a widening influence.

(3) *Did.* 8 follows the sequence of instruction regarding fasting and prayer in Matt. 6.1-18:

Did. 8.1-2	Matt. 6.2, 5, 9-13, 16
1 Do not keep your fasts with the hypocrites....	2 Whenever you give alms, do not sound a trumpet, just as the hypocrites do in the synagogues ... 16 And whenever you fast, do not be like the hypocrites ...
2 Nor pray like the hypocrites, but as the Lord commanded in his gospel, pray thus: Our Father who is in heaven, hallowed be your name;	5 And whenever you pray, do not be like the hypocrites ... 9 Therefore pray thus: Our Father who is in heaven; hallowed be your name;
your kingdom come; your will be done, as in heaven, also on earth;	10 your kingdom come; your will be done, as in heaven, also on earth;
give us today our daily bread; and forgive us our debt, as we also forgive our debtors;	11 give us today our daily bread; 12 and forgive us our debts, as we also have forgiven our debtors;
and do not bring us into temptation, but deliver us from the evil one; for yours is the power and the glory for ever.	13 and do not bring us into temptation, but deliver us from the evil one.

83. Acts 2.38; 8.16; 10.48; 19.5; implied in 1 Cor. 1.13, 15.

84. Draper points out that the earlier form, 'baptized in the name of the Lord', has survived in *Did.* 9.5, and infers that 7.1 'is probably a later redactional retouch', in any case 'taken from current liturgical practice and not from any written source', which, however, may well have been influenced by the text of Matthew ('The Didache' 272 and n.16).

The indications of direct influence from Matthew here are strong. It is true, of course, that the Lord's prayer would be familiar from regular liturgical usage.[85] But we know from Luke's version (Luke 11.2-4) that different versions of the Lord's prayer were current among the early churches. And as the above translation makes clear, *Didache*'s version is almost word for word in agreement with Matthew's. Moreover, *Didache*'s warning against hypocrites, in regard both to fasting and prayer, complementing the instruction on the Lord's prayer, is too close to the same sequence in Matt. 6 to be accidental — especially in view of the fact that 'hypocrite' is a characteristic and almost distinctive Matthean word, and it is only Matthew who uses it in this context. The fingerprints of Matthew's usage, sequence and version of the Lord's prayer make either knowledge of Matthew's Gospel or influence directly from Matthew's Gospel much the most obvious conclusion to draw.[86]

Two other features also deserve note. One is the clause, 'as the Lord commanded in his gospel'. This hardly indicates 'gospel' in the sense of 'gospel book'.[87] But it does indicate that 'gospel' as including Jesus' teaching was a well-established understanding of the Christian 'gospel' (see also 11.3 and 15.3-4).[88]

The other is that *Didache*'s conclusion to the Lord's prayer provides clear evidence of a natural liturgical tendency to add an appropriate doxology to the prayer that Jesus was remembered as teaching.[89] This also further demon-

---

85. The point is pressed by Niederwimmer (*Didache* 170), but he passes over too lightly the points of contact with distinctive features of Matt. 6.

86. Massaux, *Influence* 3.154-55; Köhler, *Rezeption* 35-36. 'Is this dependent upon Matthew? Despite some recent scholars who have answered in the negative, we find an affirmative answer irresistible. . . . One could hardly hope for more evidence of direct literary borrowing' (Davies and Allison, *Matthew* 1.597-98). Cf. Tuckett, '*Didache*' 103-6; and contrast Koester, *Synoptische Überlieferung* 208-9; Young plays down or ignores the complementary material in *Did.* 8.1-2 (the references to fasting and 'hypocrites') (*Jesus Tradition* 218-25).

87. 'Best understood as a reference to the (oral) preaching of the Lord, although the interpretation of (a reference to) a Gospel writing is not quite impossible' (Koester, *Synoptische Überlieferung* 203). The case for reference to a Gospel writing (Matthew — Jefford, *Apostolic Fathers* 21 n.27) could be made more strongly in the other *euangelion* passages in *Didache* (11.3; 15.3-4) (Köhler, *Rezeption* 26-27, 55); on 11.3 see n.91 below; 15.3-4 speaks of teaching 'as you have it in the gospel', possibly with allusion to Matt. 18.15-17 (cf. Koester 11, 240); see further §41 n.39 above.

88. Cf. Niederwimmer, *Didache* 168-70; and see n.91 below.

89. 'The absence of any ascription in early and important representatives of the Alexandrian (B), the Western (D and most of the old Latin), and the pre-Caesarean (f^1) types of text, as well as early patristic commentaries on the Lord's Prayer (those of Tertullian, Origen, Cyprian), suggests that an ascription, usually in a threefold form, was composed (perhaps on the basis of 1 Chr 29.11-13) in order to adapt the Prayer for liturgical use in the early church' (Metzger, *Textual Commentary* 16-17).

strates that the oral Jesus tradition, including what could be regarded as the more stable liturgical tradition, retained a flexibility which allowed addition or completion to what was no doubt already regarded as sacred tradition.[90]

(4) Other echoes of/allusions to Matthean tradition simply strengthen the case which is already clear:

Did. 9.5	Matt. 7.6
The Lord has spoken concerning this: 'Do not give what is holy to the dogs'.	Do not give what is holy to the dogs; and do not throw your pearls before swine . . .

Did. 11.1-4	Matt. 10.40-41
He who comes and teaches you all these things . . . welcome him . . . welcome him as the Lord. As for the apostles and prophets, act thus in accordance with the ordinance of the gospel.[91] Let every apostle who comes to you be welcomed as the Lord.	He who welcomes you welcomes me, and he who welcomes me welcomes him who sent me. He who welcomes a prophet in the name of a prophet will receive a prophet's reward; and whoever welcomes a righteous person in the name of a righteous person will receive a righteous person's reward.

Did. 11.7	Matt. 12.31
Do not test or condemn every prophet speaking in the Spirit; for every sin will be forgiven, but this sin will not be forgiven.	Therefore I say to you, every sin and blasphemy will be forgiven to people, but the blasphemy against the Holy Spirit will not be forgiven.

Did. 13.2	Matt. 10.10
So too a true teacher is worthy, just like the worker, of his food.	Worthy is the worker of his food.

Each of these is distinctive to Matthew. Once again there is no indication of quotation or copying from Matthew's Gospel.[92] But when *Didache* so consistently echoes distinctive features of Matthew it is hard to doubt that *Didache* has been influenced by Matthew, at the very least through the influ-

---

90. The point is even more clearly demonstrated by the much elaborated words which *Didache* attaches to the thanksgiving meal/eucharist (*Did.* 9.2-4).

91. The phrase 'ordinance of the gospel' *(to dogma tou euangeliou)* suggests a reference to a written text. 'If so, then the likeliest candidate is again the gospel of Matthew, with perhaps the text of Matt. 10.40-41 in mind' (Tuckett, *'Didache'* 107). Note again the other references to the 'gospel' (8.2 and 15.3, 4).

92. E.g. Draper notes the different applications of 9.5 and 11.3; he thinks it more likely that *Didache* has taken 9.5 from Jewish usage and that 13.2 may be rooted in Jewish wisdom tradition (*The Didache* 273).

ence of Matthew's version of Jesus tradition on the Jesus tradition as used by *Didache*.[93]

Finally, worth noting is the degree to which *Did.* 16 seems to reflect knowledge of the apocalyptic discourse of Mark 13 pars., again particularly the Matthean version:[94]

Didache	Matthew	*Didache*	Matthew
16.1	24.42	16.6	24.30
16.4	24.10-12	16.6	24.31
16.5	24.10, 13	16.8	24.30

In short, *Didache* may well have drawn on a living oral tradition, familiar from catechesis, preaching and regular worship.[95] But the associations with distinctive features of Matthew's Gospel are too strong to be ignored. Either the composition of *Didache* demonstrates immediate knowledge of Matthew's Gospel as such, or Matthew's Gospel had a very substantial influence on shaping the liturgical and paraenetical material familiar to an already wide range of Christian congregations.[96] Even if various strands of *Didache* can be attributed to different authors/sources, the distinctively Matthean character of the tradition (*Did.* 7.2-3; 8.1-2; 9.5; 11.1-4, 7; 13.2) suggests that all sources/

---

93. Köhler regards dependence on Matthew in the cases of 9.5, 11.7, 1.1-2 and 15.3-4 as 'very possible' (*Rezeption* 36-39).

94. Massaux confidently claims literary dependence on Matthew (*Influence* 3.167-73). The language of *Did.* 10.5 also echoes Matt. 24.31. For the view that *Didache* bears testimony to an independent, earlier tradition, see Draper, *The Didache* 280-83. See the full discussion in Tuckett, '*Didache*' 110-19, who concludes: 'The pattern of parallels may be most easily explained if the *Didache* here presupposes Matthew's finished gospel' (119).

95. Koester concludes that *Did.* 7.1, 8.2, 9.5 and 15.3 'stem not from a written Gospel but from the free tradition' (*Synoptische Überlieferung* 240); Hagner also concludes that 'the phenomena [the parallels between Matthew and *Didache*] can be readily explained as the result of dependence upon oral tradition' ('Sayings of Jesus' 242); similarly Jefford with regard to the *Did.* 1-5 and 16 material: 'the Didachist and the Matthean redactor have shared a common sayings source' (*Sayings of Jesus* 91); the Didachist knew the milieu in which Matthew emerged (Köhler, *Rezeption* 55); Rordorf, 'Jesus Tradition'; Niederwimmer, *Didache* — independent tradition (91), proverbial tradition (101-2), an apocryphal sayings collection (104), liturgical tradition (160, 170), etc. For further bibliography see Tuckett, '*Didache*' 95 n.51.

96. Too much of the discussion (as in *NTAF* 27-30) has focused too narrowly on the question whether the *Didache* texts are 'quotations' of Matthew or dependent on Matthew as such. Between random 'oral tradition' and 'quotation', *tertium datur*: an oral tradition which has been significantly influenced by Matthew's version of the Jesus tradition. See again the extensive bibliography in Tuckett, '*Didache*' 95 n.51. The case for seeing distinctive Lukan influence on *Didache* depends largely on the Lukan parallels to *Did.* 1.3-5 (particularly Luke 6.29-30); see discussion in Tuckett 119-25 and Gregory, *Reception of Luke* 120-24.

authors shared a Jesus tradition which had been strongly influenced by the Matthean version;[97] quite possibly the shared Matthean influence was a factor in the different strands being drawn together. Whatever ways *Didache* came together, its content strongly suggests that Matthew was the best known and most influential of the Gospels already current in the churches of the eastern Mediterranean region.

g. *Barnabas*

Beside the many quotations from the OT (§45.5c), the number of references to Jesus tradition in *Barnabas* are few. Most striking is *Barn.* 4.14: '... as it is written, "Many of us were found called, but few chosen"'. A quotation from or allusion to Matt. 22.14 ('Many are called, but few chosen') is certainly possible.[98] In which case the reference would be to the written Gospel of Matthew. But the 'as it is written' formula usually introduces a scriptural quotation,[99] and such a reference to Jesus tradition is without parallel in the Apostolic Fathers, though it should be recalled that 2 Pet. 3.16 includes the letters of Paul as 'scripture',[100] and, as is noted below, *2 Clem.* 2.4 refers to Mark 2.17 pars. as 'scripture'. A further possibility is that the reference is to an apocalyptic writing, unknown to us, where the 'many/few' proverbial antithesis might well be familiar, as *4 Ezra* 8.3 suggests.[101]

Otherwise the possible links are even more tenuous.[102]

---

97. *Pace* A. J. P. Garrow, *The Gospel of Matthew's Dependence on the* Didache (JSNTS 254; London: T & T Clark, 2004), who thinks dependence of the different layers of *Didache* on Matthew or common tradition to be less plausible than Matthew's dependence on the *Didache*. His over-ambitious division of *Didache* into different layers includes a redactional 'Gospel layer: 8.2b; 11.3b; 15.3-4', which allows him to accept the probability that *euangelion* in these passages refers to Matthew's Gospel (ch. 8) without it undermining his principal thesis.

98. 'Not compelling, but a good possibility' (Köhler, *Rezeption* 113); 'quite likely' (Hvalvik, *Struggle* 33-34).

99. Prostmeier notes that *Barnabas* uses the term *gegraptai* regularly (8 times) to draw on the writing's authority (*Barnabasbrief* 91).

100. Massaux, *Influence* 1.66, and J. Carleton Paget, 'The *Epistle of Barnabas* and the Writings That Later Formed the New Testament', in Gregory and Tuckett, eds., *Reception* 229-49 (233), justifiably warn against the assumption that *Barnabas* could *not* have been referring to Matthew as scripture.

101. Koester notes that *Barn.* 4.3 and 16.5 also treat as scripture what we know now as *1 Enoch*; and that *Barnabas*'s two uses of the word *euangelion* refer to the gospel as preached, not a written Gospel (*Synoptische Überlieferung* 126-27). See also Prostmeier, *Barnabasbrief* 226-27 n.154.

102. Massaux reviews other possible links where Matthean literary influence is at best doubtful (*Influence* 1.67-74).

- The reference in *Barn.* 5.9, that Jesus 'did not come to call the righteous but sinners', obviously draws (verbatim) upon the Jesus tradition attested in Mark 2.17 pars.; but knowledge of that tradition was evidently wider than the written Gospels (cf. Gal. 2.14-17; 1 Tim. 1.15).[103]
- *Barn.* 5.12 — 'God speaks of the blow they delivered against his flesh: "When they smite their own shepherd, then the sheep of the flock will perish"' — echoes Matt. 26.31/Mark 14.27 ('I will strike the shepherd, and the sheep of the flock will be scattered'), but *Barnabas* seems to be referring to the scripture quoted (Zech. 13.7).[104]
- Even more clearly *Barn.* 6.6 is a verbatim quotation of Ps. 22.18 (LXX 21.19) — 'They cast lots for my clothing' — which is different from Mark 15.24 pars.
- *Barn.* 7.3 refers to the drink offered to Jesus on the cross as 'mixed with gall'; only Matt. 27.34 refers to 'gall', but such a reference could quite readily have become part of the liturgical remembrance of Jesus' crucifixion.
- The quotation of Ps. 110.1 in *Barn.* 12.10 was likely drawn from the arsenal of OT texts used in early Christian apologetic,[105] even though 12.11 shows awareness of Jesus' own handling of the Psalm passage, as recalled in Mark 12.37 pars.

In short, *Barnabas* shows clearly enough that the story of Jesus' passion was well known in early Christian assemblies and that the tradition of what Jesus taught about his mission was familiar. But it tells us nothing reliable as to whether the Jesus tradition was already in written form. On the other hand, the fact that such allusions can be recognized confirms the significant degree of stability in the oral Jesus tradition.[106]

h. *Shepherd* of Hermas

Hermas is rather disappointing from our perspective. Although probably one of the latest of the Apostolic Fathers, when one or more of the NT Gospels would certainly have been becoming better and more widely known,[107] Her-

---

103. See also P.Oxy. 1224. But, as just noted, *2 Clem.* 2.4 cites the saying as 'scripture'; and Justin, *1 Apol.* 15.8, also quotes the same saying, perhaps dependent on Luke's version (Luke 5.32).

104. Koester, *Synoptische Überlieferung* 128-29; Köhler, *Rezeption* 117.

105. *Beginning from Jerusalem* 218.

106. Cf. Koester, *Synoptische Überlieferung* 156-58; Hagner, 'Sayings of Jesus' 242-43; Carleton Paget, '*Barnabas*' 238-39.

107. J. Verheyden, '*The Shepherd of Hermas* and the Writings That Later Formed the

mas makes no explicit quotation of or allusion to any NT Gospel (or to Paul's letters).[108] And as the lengthiest of those accounted as Apostolic Fathers, one might have expected much greater scope for echoes of Jesus tradition.[109] In fact, however, they are few and far between.[110]

- *Mand.* 29(IV.1).6 on divorce (If a divorced man marries another, he commits adultery) could echo Mark 10.11/(Matt. 19.9) and/or Luke 16.18/(Matt. 5.32); or at least it demonstrates how, as with Paul (1 Cor.

New Testament', in Gregory and Tuckett, eds., *Reception* 293-329 (here 293-94). However, the references to a couch with 'four legs' (*Vis.* 23(III.13).3) and a tower with 'four courses' (*Sim.* 81(IX.4).3) can hardly be taken with any confidence as references to four Gospels (see *NTAF* 117-18); when the numbers used are interpreted nothing is made of the 'four' (*Sim.* 93(IX.15).4). Verheyden reviews the debate of the last 150 years on whether allusions to NT writings can be discerned in Hermas (*Shepherd* 296-322), noting that the interpretation of the 'four legs' as the four canonical Gospels has been rejected unanimously and often ridiculed (322).

108. That Hermas valued books is clear from *Vis.* 3(I.3)-4(I.4), 8(II.4).3; in *Vis.* 5(II.1).3-4 Hermas sees an elderly woman (later revealed as the church (*Vis.* 8(II.4).1) reading a little book, and in response to her question says, 'Lady, I cannot remember so many things. Give me the book that I might copy it', which he then proceeds to do (see also *Vis.* 25(V).5-7). But unlike most of the Apostolic Fathers he does not even quote from the OT; his only use of the 'as it is written' formula is a reference to the Book of Eldad and Modat (*Vis.* 7(II.3).4; cf. Num. 11.26), a lost apocalyptic work.

109. E.g.
- the commandments given Hermas, though ordered in sequence, bear no relation to and make no allusion to Jesus' commandments (*Mand.* 26(I)ff.), although referring to 'the commandment of the Lord' (*Mand.* 28(III).2);
- talk of evil spirits indwelling someone (*Mand.* 33(V.1), 34(V.2).7) could easily have alluded to Matt. 12.43-45/Luke 11.24-26;
- unlike the *Didache*, treatment of the two ways (*Mand.* 35(VI.1)) makes no attempt to draw in Jesus tradition;
- the vice-catalogues of *Mand.* 38(VIII) 3-5 bear no relation to Mark 7.21-22 par.;
- the warning against doubting (double-mindedness) when praying (*Mand.* 39(IX)) certainly echoes Jas. 1.8, but hardly Mark 11.23-24 and only faintly Luke 18.1;
- guidance on fasting (*Sim.* 54(V.1), 56(V.3)) makes no attempt to draw on Jesus tradition;
- the parable of the master going on a journey and leaving his vineyard to be cared for by a slave (*Sim.* 55(V.2)) shows no awareness of the comparable Jesus parables (Matt. 25.14-30/Luke 19.11-27; Mark 12.1-12 pars.);
- in the vision of twelve mountains (*Sim.* 97(IX.20).1-2) the thistles and thorns of the third mountain could echo the parable of the sower (Mark 4.18-19 pars.; cf. also *Vis.* 14(III.6).5), but there is no allusion to the parable itself.

See also n.28 above.

110. None, even of Massaux's list of 'definite or very probable' cases of Matthean influence, is persuasive, apart from *Sim.* 97(IX.20).2-3 (*Influence* 2.111-20). Snyder finds 30 allusions to the Synoptics (*Shepherd of Hermas* 162-63).

7.12-16), the original dominical teaching on divorce was the basis for continued reflection and refinement.[111]
- Is Hermas's confession of his lack of understanding and of his heart as hardened (*Mand.* 30(IV.2).1) an allusion to Mark 6.52?[112]
- The criticism of those who like 'seats of honour' (*Mand.* 43(XI).12; cf. *Vis.* 17(III.9).7) could echo Mark 12.39 pars.
- The thought of *Mand.* 49(XII.6).3 may have been slightly influenced by Matt. 10.28 (and Jas. 4.12).[113]
- *Similitudes* speaks of entering the kingdom of God frequently (e.g. 89(IX.12).4; 92(IX.15).2; 93(IX.16).2-4; 108(IX.31).2). However, only 97(IX.20).2-3 closely echoes a saying of Jesus — rich people 'will enter the kingdom of God with difficulty' (close to Mark 10.23 pars.).[114] And since talk of entering the kingdom of God had evidently become detached from specific contexts, that is, had entered the common vocabulary of paraenetic exhortation, the particular warning of Jesus recalled in Mark 10.23 pars. may simply have become an element in such exhortation, without reference to a particular text or incident in Jesus' mission. The same holds true for attempts to detect influence from John's Gospel — in particular, *Sim.* 93(IX.16).2-4 (entry into the kingdom of God through going down into the water and rising up to new life) as influenced by John 3.3-5.[115]
- *Sim.* 106(IX.29).1-3 could be or reflect a brief meditation on or elaboration of Mark 10.14 pars. or Matt. 18.3; but there is no specific allusion or reference.

At best, then, Hermas indicates how (and confirms that) language and themes from the Jesus tradition had become part of the vocabulary and motifs used in Christian preaching and teaching, without it being thought necessary to attribute them to Jesus, or to any written Gospel.[116] Hermas in fact shows how readily exhortation within Christian communities could be (almost entirely) in-

---

111. See further Verheyden, '*Shepherd*' 323-29.
112. 'It is as if Hermas said, "I am like those men who are reproached in the Gospel"' (*NTAF* 120).
113. Koester, *Synoptische Überlieferung* 247-48.
114. *NTAF* regards this as a quotation (121).
115. Hill finds three possible traces of influence from John (3.5, 10.7, 14.6) in *Sim.* 89-93(IX.12-16), but accepts that the evidence is 'not too impressive', and is content to note that lack of formal citation of John does not imply that he avoided John (*Johannine Corpus* 376-78).
116. Cf. Koester, *Synoptische Überlieferung* 254-56. 'Any similarity between parables in *Hermas* and those in the Gospels is better explained on the basis of a common oral tradition' (Osiek, *Hermas* 26).

dependent of the Jesus tradition.¹¹⁷ The fact that Hermas is much inferior to the Jesus tradition, laboured, pedantic, narrowly focused and over-elaborate in its visions, indicates that the loss of more direct influence from the Jesus tradition may have been a factor in diminishing the quality of the writing and its message.

i. *2 Clement*

2 Clement is quite unlike Hermas in that it regularly draws in quotations from (Israel's) scripture with introductory phrases like, 'The scripture says', 'the Lord says'.¹¹⁸ The three most interesting quotations of Jesus tradition are *2 Clem.* 2.4, 8.5 and 13.4.

2 Clem. 2.4	Mark 2.17 pars.
Another scripture says, 'I came not to call the righteous, but sinners'.	I came not to call the righteous but sinners.

This follows a quotation from Isa. 54.1 (*2 Clem.* 2.1a) which is then expounded line by line (2.1b-3). So the quotation of Mark 2.17 pars. is 'another scripture' like the prophetic scripture of Isaiah. It is most unlikely that *Clement* would refer to a saying of Jesus which he knew only through oral tradition as 'scripture' (= 'writing'). The most obvious deduction is that *Clement* refers to Jesus tradition not just transcribed in a written collection of Jesus' teaching, but in a written form which had already achieved the authoritative and sanctified status of 'scripture'.¹¹⁹ And the most obvious

---

117. 'For him what was required was precisely new revelation and not just reference back to the tradition' (Köhler, *Rezeption* 128).

118.
- 3.5 — 'he/it also says in Isaiah' (Isa. 29.13);
- 6.8 — 'the scripture says in Ezekiel' (Ezek. 14.14-20);
- 7.6 — 'he/it says' (Isa. 66.24);
- 11.2 — 'the prophetic word also says' (?; cf. *1 Clem.* 23.3-4);
- 13.2 — 'the Lord says' (Isa. 52.5);
- 13.2 — 'and again (he says)' (?);
- 14.1 — 'the scripture that says' (Jer. 7.11);
- 14.2 — 'the scripture says' (Gen. 1.27);
- 15.3 — 'God who says' (Isa. 58.9);
- 17.4 — 'the Lord says' (Isa. 66.18).

The heavy dependence on and influence of Isaiah is noteworthy. See further K. P. Donfried, *The Setting of Second Clement in Early Christianity* (NovTSupp 38; Leiden: Brill, 1974) 49-56.

119. Koester, *Synoptische Überlieferung* 64-65, 71; Kelhoffer, '"Gospel" as a Literary Title' 405-6. C. M. Tuckett, '*2 Clement* and the Writings That Later Formed the New Testament', in Gregory and Tuckett, eds., *Reception* 251-92, concludes that some dependence

corollary is that *Clement* knew and was familiar with one or more of the NT Gospels.[120]

2 Clem. 8.5	Luke 16.10
The Lord says in the gospel, 'If you do not keep what is small, who will give you what is great? For I say to you that the one who is faithful in very little is faithful also in much'.	The one who is faithful in very little is faithful also in much.

Does 'gospel' here refer to a written Gospel?[121] The fact that the first half of the saying quoted has no parallel in any of the NT Gospels may well suggest that *Clement* here is drawing on oral tradition.[122] But it is also possible that the 'gospel' referred to is the Gospel of Luke, and that *Clement* quotes an elaborated (orally elaborated) version of the Lukan text (second orality);[123] the fact that *Clement* has already quoted a Jesus saying whose closest parallel is Luke 16.13 (*2 Clem.* 6.1) may well indicate that a copy of Luke's Gospel was close to hand or that he had recently heard it being read from. In any case, the implication is that such Jesus tradition, whether oral or written, was often extended or interpreted with the interpreted/extended saying being regarded as a version of the saying itself.

2 Clem. 13.4	Luke 6.32-35/(Matt. 5.43-46)
God says, 'It is no credit to you if you love those who love you; but credit to you if you love your enemies and those who hate you'.	If you love those who love you, what credit is that to you? . . . But love your enemies . . .

---

on Matthew (direct or indirect) is the most likely explanation of the text, since there is no other evidence that *2 Clement* used Mark, and *2 Clem.* 2.4 lacks the distinctive Lukan addition of the phrase 'for repentance' which Justin, *1 Apol.* 15.8, does have (254-55). Contrast Donfried, who questions whether *Clement* used 'scripture' in such a clear-cut way and concludes that the saying was probably drawn from a written collection of 'community tradition' (*Second Clement* 57-60, 79-81); similarly Young, *Jesus Tradition* 241-42. See also above n.103.

120. Cf. Köhler, *Rezeption* 136. Massaux is much too confident: 'In any hypothesis, it must be acknowledged that 2 Clement depends on Mt.' (*Influence* 2.5).

121. *NTAF* suggests 'a single Evangelic source . . . a sort of combined recension of two or more of our Synoptists . . . an earlier local type of harmony than Tatian's *Diatessaron*' (125; but further 133), with 6.1-2 and 9.11 illustrating a possible fusion of Matthew and Luke (133-34). Koester, *Synoptische Überlieferung* 11, 65, Tuckett, '2 Clement' 269, Pratscher, *zweite Clemensbrief* 35, and Kelhoffer, '"Gospel" as a Literary Title' 408-10, likewise infer reference to a written text.

122. Donfried, *Second Clement* 72-73.

123. Cf. Gregory, *Reception of Luke* 137.

It is unclear what the christological weight of the introduction to the saying is.[124] The saying comes as part of a sequence of sayings of 'the Lord', the first from Isa. 52.5, and it could be that the saying was regarded as just as much 'word of God' as the earlier sayings (the second from an unknown source). That is, the introduction need not mean that Jesus was being regarded as God, but simply that what he said could also be cited as God's word, because Jesus spoke the word of God as much as Isaiah.[125] In ether case the introduction indicates how prized and authoritative was the Jesus tradition for the second-century Christians. The saying itself obviously draws on a version of Jesus' teaching most like Luke's version (Luke 6.32-35). But it is elaborated in ways similar to the elaborations by Matthew and Luke of the tradition which they shared (Q?),[126] and confirms that still towards the middle of the second century there was no compulsion or particular desire or felt necessity to quote Jesus' teaching in fixed form even if already transcribed.[127] The Jesus tradition was still living tradition, flexible and adaptable to the specific nuances and emphases of particular teachers.

Most of the quotations of Jesus tradition are introduced with introductory phrases, such as 'the Lord says'.[128]

2 Clem. 3.2	Matt. 10.32/(Luke 12.8)
He himself says, 'The one who confesses me before men, I will confess him before my Father'.	Everyone who confesses (in) me in front of men, I will confess (in) him in front of my Father who is in heaven.

2 Clem. 4.2	Matt. 7.21; cf. Luke 6.46
(The Lord) says, 'Not everyone who says to me, "Lord, Lord" will be saved, but only he who does righteousness'.	Not everyone who says to me, 'Lord, Lord', will enter into the kingdom of heaven, but only he who does the will of my Father who is in heaven.

124. Pratscher reminds us that *2 Clem.* 1.1 calls on audiences to 'think about Jesus Christ as we think about God' (*zweite Clemensbrief* 33).

125. 'Here God is conceived as speaking in Christ, who elsewhere is Himself cited as the authority behind the Gospel' (*NTAF* 124-25).

126. *Did.* 1.3 and Justin, *1 Apol.* 15.9, confirm that the exhortation to 'love those who hate you' had become a regular elaboration of the Jesus tradition at this point.

127. Gregory concludes that the saying provides insufficient evidence that *2 Clement* was drawing on Luke's Gospel (*Reception of Luke* 138-39); but Tuckett thinks that the language 'appears to presuppose Luke's redactional work, and hence Luke's finished gospel' ('2 Clement' 271-72).

128. Tuckett reviews other possible allusions to or dependence on Synoptic tradition ('2 Clement' 256, 273-76). The passages listed by Grant and Graham, *First and Second Clement* 134, are not so persuasive.

2 Clem. 5.2	Luke 10.3/Matt. 10.16
The Lord says, 'You will be like sheep in the midst of wolves'.	Behold, I am sending you like sheep in the midst of wolves.

2 Clem. 6.1	Luke 16.13/Matt. 6.24
The Lord says, 'No house slave can serve as the slave of two masters'. If we wish to serve God and Mammon, it is disadvantageous to us.	No house slave can serve as the slave of two masters. . . . you cannot serve God and Mammon.

2 Clem. 6.2	Matt. 16.26 pars.
What is the advantage if someone gains the whole world, but forfeits his soul?	What will a person be advantaged if he gains the whole world and forfeits his soul?

2 Clem. 9.11	Matt. 12.50/Mark 3.35
The Lord said, 'My brothers are these who do the will of my Father'.	Whoever does the will of my Father who is in heaven, he is my brother and sister and mother.

The fact that *2 Clement* introduces Jesus tradition in the same way that it introduces quotations from the OT could suggest that these quotations of Jesus tradition were also drawn from written Gospels. But the quotations of the OT are mostly closer to the Greek translations of the Hebrew Bible than the quotations of Jesus tradition are to the texts of the NT Gospels.[129] The quotations are sufficiently close to equivalent Synoptic versions for us to be confident that they are drawn from the same fountainhead. But the variations are entirely similar to the variations already noted between the Synoptic Gospels.[130] That is to say, *2 Clement* either demonstrates that the oral tradition of

---

129. *2 Clem.* 14.2 refers to 'the books and the apostles'. *NTAF* took this as a reference to the OT, *2 Clement*'s Bible, and the apostolic writings, though perhaps, 'he thought only of the sayings of the Lord in such narratives as the authoritative element' (124). But the reference is probably to the books of the Jewish scriptures, and to the Jesus tradition generally as attributed to the apostles (see also Koester, *Synoptische Überlieferung* 67-69; Donfried, *Second Clement* 93-95; Pratscher, *zweite Clemensbrief* 182-83).

130. Koester maintains that 3.2, 4.2, 6.2 and 9.11 provide sufficient evidence that the quotations, and all the other Matthew-like quotations, stem from Matthew's Gospel, and that Lukan redaction in 4.5, 5.4 and 9.11 similarly leads back to Luke's Gospel; but he concludes finally that *2 Clement* did not use Matthew and Luke directly, rather a written collection of the Lord's words, based on Matthew and Luke, but including apocryphal pieces and elaborations of Synoptic logia (*Synoptische Überlieferung* 109-10; see further *Ancient Christian Gospels* 349-56). Donfried concludes that seven out of the nine quotations he examines were based on independent non-canonical tradition, probably oral, though he agrees that 2.4 and 6.1 may have been dependent on Mark and Luke respectively (*Second Clement*

Jesus' sayings was still a major current resource for Christian catechesis and paraenesis.[131] Or, if *2 Clement*'s sources included one or more of the Synoptic Gospels, the author continued to handle them with the same flexibility with which the Jesus tradition had always been handled from the first. Passing on the teaching of the written Gospels was little different in style from the passing on of the oral Jesus tradition prior to its inscription. Second orality was little different from first orality.

Most intriguing is what appears to be a quotation from the *Gospel of Thomas*:

2 Clem. 12.2	*Thomas* 22.1-5
When the Lord himself was asked by someone when his kingdom would come, he said, 'When the two are one, and the outside like the inside, and the male with the female is neither male nor female'.	(In response to a question about entering the kingdom) Jesus said to them, 'When you make the two one, and when you make the inside like the outside ... And when you make the male and the female into a single being, with the result that the male is not male nor the female female.'

Here is evidence that what we now know as quite distinctively *Thomas* tradition[132] either was more widely known within the communities which cherished Jesus tradition and understood to be a saying of Jesus, or distinctive *Thomas* tradition had entered into the more widely known Jesus tradition. Probably significant is the fact that *2 Clement* goes on to expound the saying (12.3-6) and does so in what was presumably already traditional Christian terms (no hypocrisy between Christians, outward expression consistent with inward reality, Gal. 3.28) — that is, quite differently from the distinctive strand of *Thomas* teaching. Presumably *2 Clement* valued the saying, and if the author knew of it

---

79). Köhler thinks dependence on Matthew is probable in 3.2, 4.2, and 6.2; 9.11 is sufficiently explained as a free citation of Matt. 12.50 (*Rezeption* 131-35, 138). Not untypical of the whole discussion, Tuckett is too quick to infer from small variations which parallel Matthean and Lukan variations that *2 Clement* presupposes their redactional activity and therefore their finished Gospels ('*2 Clement*' 260, 263, 266, 268, 270-71, 278-79; similarly Gregory, *Reception of Luke* 146-49); but the variations of the Jesus tradition in oral circulation and use should not be limited to Matthew's and Luke's as such. Pratscher leaves the question open — dependence on a canonical Gospel, on oral tradition, on a sayings collection or on an apocryphal Gospel (*zweite Clemensbrief* 33-36). Young concludes that *2 Clem.* 6.1-2 and 9.11 provide the strongest case for dependence on the finished form of the (NT) Gospels, but questions whether it is strong enough (*Jesus Tradition* 269-72).

131. Hagner presses the possibility of dependence on oral tradition ('Sayings of Jesus' 245-46); in contrast to Massaux, who remains confident that literary influence of Matthew can be detected (*Influence* 2.3-10).

132. See above §43 n.288.

as used in a *Thomas* context, he may have thought it desirable to thus rescue it from a more Gnostic context and interpretation.[133] In any case, the saying confirms that the Jesus tradition continued to flow in a broadening stream and that early attempts were made to restrict it within more traditional boundaries.

Finally, it should not pass mention that *2 Clement* also quotes, with the same introductory formulae, from sources unknown to us:

- 4.5 — The Lord has said, 'Even if you were gathered together with me in my bosom but did not do what I have commanded, I would cast you away and say to you, "Leave me! I do not know where you are from, you who do what is lawless"' (cf. Matt. 7.22-23/Luke 13.26-27).[134]
- 5.4 — Jesus said to Peter, 'After they are dead, the sheep should fear the wolves no longer. So too you: do not fear those who kill you and then can do nothing to you; but fear the one who, after you die, has the power to cast your body and soul into the hell of fire' (cf. Luke 12.4-5/Matt. 10.28).[135]
- 14.3 — He says, 'Protect the flesh that you may receive the Spirit'.

Here again some discomfort may be experienced that the Jesus tradition had expanded and broadened so far as to include such material. That the first two may have some rootage in the Synoptic tradition eases the disquiet; and the third may well reflect the more typical second-century reaction against Paul's disparagement of the flesh. But the implication seems impossible to avoid, that round the large core of Jesus tradition, familiar to us from the Synoptic material, but also from the Gospel of John and the *Gospel of Thomas*, swirled a more extensive body of tradition attributed to Jesus and about Jesus and almost certainly in process of being expanded. Presumably the awareness of such a process was a factor in the initial impulse to transcribe the Jesus tradition into written Gospels, and a major factor in the focus of the (authoritative) Jesus tradition being narrowed progressively to these written Gospels.

In view of this awareness of more extensive Jesus tradition,[136] it is note-

---

133. Cf. Clem. Alex., *Strom.* 3.13.92, cited below §44.4a.

134. The fact that *2 Clem.* 4.2, 5 reflects the same sequence as Matt. 7.21-23 could suggest a more direct dependence on Matthew's Gospel. Donfried thinks it more likely that *2 Clement* draws on the Q tradition which Matthew and Luke also used (*Second Clement* 62-68). See also Tuckett's full discussion, concluding that *2 Clement* may well presuppose the finished Gospel of Luke (260-63).

135. Again the fact that *2 Clem.* 5.2, 4 may reflect Matt. 10.16, 28/Luke 10.3, 12.4-5 could strengthen the possibility of direct dependence on Matthew, or that *2 Clement* presupposes the finished forms of Matthew and Luke (Tuckett, '*2 Clement*' 264-66).

136. See my conclusions drawn from use of the above material in '2 Clement and

worthy that possible allusions to John's Gospel, or the Johannine slant on the Jesus tradition, are minimal. The references to being 'gathered together with me in my bosom' (4.5) as an allusion to John 13.23 and to Jesus as 'first a spirit and then became flesh' (9.5) as an echo of John 1.14 can hardly be described as quotations from John and could as or more readily be explained as simply using language which had become part of common Christian reflection, even if the 'became flesh' phrase originated with John.[137]

j. Papias

Papias is known only in fragments, as quoted particularly by Eusebius. But since he was active in the first few decades of the second century (his dates are traditionally given as 60-135), and his five-volume *Expositions of the Sayings of the Lord* is most likely to be dated in the later decades of his life (§40.1i), he serves as a valuable witness to the way the Jesus tradition was being received during the first half of the second century. We have already drawn heavily on what Papias says about the Gospels of Mark, Matthew and Luke (§39.2). Here it is the testimony he gives to the value he placed on eyewitness testimony. Eusebius introduces his citation (*HE* 3.39.2-4, 7, 11, 14):

> [2]Papias himself, in the preface of his discourses, makes it clear that he himself was never a hearer or eyewitness of the holy apostles. Instead, he explains by the language he uses that he received the matters of faith from those acquainted with them:
> [3]'I will not hesitate to set out for you, along with these interpretations, all that I ever carefully learned and have carefully remembered from the elders, certifying their truth. For unlike most people, I took no pleasure in hearing those who had a lot to say, but only those who teach the truth; and not those who remembered commandments which came from someone else, but only those (who remembered) the commandments which came from the Lord faithfully/to faith and which proceed from the truth itself. [4]But if someone chanced to come who had been associated with the elders, I inquired about the words of the elders, what Andrew or Peter had said, or what Philip or what Thomas (had said), or what James or what John (had said) or Matthew or any other of the Lord's disciples, and what things Aristion and the elder

---

the Jesus Tradition', in M. Lang, ed., *Ein neues Geschlecht? Entwicklung des frühchristlichen Selbstbewusstseins* (Festschrift for Wilhelm Pratscher; NTOA 105; Göttingen: Vandenhoeck, 2014) 153-69.

137. Tuckett concludes that it is 'very unlikely that *2 Clement* shows any knowledge of the gospel of John at all' ('*2 Clement*' 253).

John, disciples of the Lord, were saying. For I did not suppose that what came out of books (*biblion*) would benefit me as much as that which came from a living and abiding voice'.¹³⁸ . . .¹³⁹

⁷This Papias, whom we have just been discussing, acknowledges that he received the words of the apostles from those who had been associated with them, but he also says that he himself was an actual hearer of Aristion and the elder John. And so he often remembers them by name, and in his writings he sets forth their traditions. . . . ¹¹And he sets out other matters that came to him from the unwritten tradition, including some strange parables of the Saviour and his teachings, and several other rather fictive tales. . . . ¹⁴And in his own writing he passes on other accounts of the sayings of the Lord from the previously mentioned Aristion, as well as traditions from the elder John.

Several features in this fascinating passage invite comment. First, Papias gives clear testimony to the oral tradition, 'unwritten tradition' (11 — *paradosis agrapha*) with which he was made familiar, presumably in his earlier or youthful years (80s?).¹⁴⁰ Interestingly at these points he does not mention, or is not remembered as mentioning, written collections of Jesus' teaching, or written Gospels,¹⁴¹ even though his testimony elsewhere is probably the earliest concerning the Gospels of Mark, Matthew and John (§39.2). It is all the more striking, when he is making a point about the truth and authority for his teaching (3), that he evidently felt no pressure to validate that authority by demonstrating that it had come to him in written form.¹⁴²

Second, a chain of tradition is clearly in view — 'he received the words of the apostles from those who had been associated with them' (7).¹⁴³ This implies a three-link chain — apostles, companions, Papias.¹⁴⁴ Some confusion

---

138. This last paragraph is also quoted by Jerome, *Lives of Illustrious Men* 18, cited in Ehrman, *Apostolic Fathers* 2.107.

139. Here Irenaeus notes and tries to explain the two 'Johns'.

140. Bauckham, *Eyewitnesses* 14, 17-19.

141. *Biblia* referred to in 4 could include written documents and scrolls (BDAG 176).

142. Hengel overstates his point: 'Papias is writing at a time when oral tradition has become the problematical exception, and a written text has almost come to be taken for granted' (*Four Gospels* 65). His judgment is sounder when he claims that 'Between AD 70 and 180 there was no opposition between the Gospel preached by word of mouth and the Gospel set down in writing' (132).

143. Ehrman translates *parēkolouthēkōs* in 4 as 'who had been a companion' of (one of) the elders, but the same verb, *parēkolouthēkotōn* in 7, as 'who had been their followers'. The latter is misleading, since the verb *parakoloutheō* means 'to be closely associated with, attendant upon' (BDAG 767).

144. Cf. Irenaeus's testimony that in his childhood he had been able to listen to 'the

enters at this point, since it is not clear whether Papias distinguishes the 'elders' who were disciples of the Lord (John the elder) (7) from elders whom he was able to consult and learn from directly himself (3).[145] But certainly Papias implies that much/most/all of what he was taught (as a younger Christian) came to him orally and aurally.

Third, part of the confusion focuses on Aristion and the elder John. Papias obviously gives special attention to these two (also 'disciples of the Lord', like the twelve). The tenses he uses (4) — the apostles 'had said' (*eipen*), but Aristion and the elder John 'were saying' (*legousin*) — imply that Papias himself never met or heard the apostles,[146] but that Aristion and the elder John were still actively teaching, probably in the province of Asia, during his earlier years. Indeed, according to Eusebius, Papias claimed that he himself had heard Aristion and the elder John with his own ears and that his writings contained their traditions (7). This must mean that Papias could recall the teaching of Aristion and the elder John which he himself remembered from early encounters (80s, 90s), but that he still relished encountering people who had been closely associated with them (as well as with the apostles) for their own memories of what these first-generation disciples had passed on.[147]

Fourth, worth noting also is the wide circle of apostles whom Papias cites as sources for knowledge of Jesus' teaching, a wider circle than we learn from other early sources — Andrew, Peter, Philip, Thomas, James, John, Matthew — seven of the twelve.[148] It is noticeable that Papias felt no pressure to focus on one or two, above all Peter, as the source of the authoritative teaching of Jesus tradition. Nor did he think it necessary or desirable to include the names of all the twelve.[149] But he adds Aristion and the elder John, presumably be-

---

blessed Polycarp', 'how he reported his conversations with John and with the others who had seen the Lord, and how he remembered their words and some things concerning the Lord which he had heard from them' (Eusebius, *HE* 5.20.6).

145. See discussion in Bauckham, *Eyewitnesses* 16-17.

146. Bauckham infers that the tense means the apostles were already dead (*Eyewitnesses* 17), which would be awkward if Papias was indeed speaking from the perspective of the 80s, since if the Gospels of Matthew and John are to be associated with Matthew and John, then they were being written most probably in the 80s and 90s (§39.2).

147. Bauckham questions the report that Papias heard Aristion and the elder John personally (*Eyewitnesses* 19), which seems unnecessary.

148. The list may be influenced by John 1.40-44 and 21.2 (Bauckham, *Eyewitnesses* 20-21). Also notable is the fact that in addition to Peter, John and Matthew, the other four (Andrew, Philip, Thomas and James) appear as the authorities in subsequent apocryphal traditions.

149. No writings are attributed to James (son of Alphaeus), Thaddeus or Simon the Cananean, though some literature is attributed to Bartholomew (Elliott, *ANT* 652-72), and Origen knew of a Gospel according to Matthias (*ANT* 19-20); the Gnostic Basilides

cause he had had personal contact with them. The impression he gives is that many/most of the original disciples of Jesus (more than the twelve) were active in spreading Jesus' message or passing on his teaching.[150] This adds weight to the scenario sketched in earlier volumes of *Christianity in the Making*: that the traditions about Jesus and his teaching were put into oral form by the first disciples and that they probably already gave it the form and shape which it still maintains in the Synoptic tradition — the 'living and *abiding* voice' (4).

Fifth, the contrast Papias draws between 'what came out from books' and 'what came from a living and abiding voice' certainly picks up a proverbial contrast between what we today might call 'book-learning' and 'the living voice'.[151] But it should not be transformed into a contrast between 'a lengthy chain of oral tradition' and direct personal experience of a teacher'.[152] The contrast Papias makes is between first-hand information and information from books; oral tradition is not in view here. To draw from Papias's statement an inference that Papias distrusted oral tradition is at best tendentious. Rather we should infer, in my view, that what Papias knew about these earlier days, he knew through the oral tradition of the communities — the tradition which stemmed from those who had been Jesus' disciples. It was entirely natural and understandable that he should cherish the opportunity provided by occasional visits from eyewitnesses or disciples with first-hand experience and information from the first generation — not necessarily because they told him something he had never heard before but because they confirmed what

---

claimed that his doctrines were derived from a private tradition going back to Matthias (*ODCC* 1058).

150. Bauckham stresses that 'the oral traditions had not evolved away from them [named eyewitnesses] but continued to be attached to them' (*Eyewitnesses* 20). But the implication is more of a broad array of eyewitnesses; Papias mentions seven names and adds, 'or any other of the Lord's disciples' (4). The thought is more of the direct connection with first generation disciples, 'those who remembered the commandments given by the Lord faithfully/to faith' (3), (eyewitness testimony, certainly), rather than a concern to be able to attach particular traditions to particular individuals. The great reassurance for Papias was that the oral tradition constituted and secured that connection with the first disciples. As Bauckham observes later, 'Papias assumes that the value of oral traditions depends on their derivation from still living witnesses who are still themselves repeating their testimony' (29) — though he should put the statement in the past tense, as referring to Papias's experience in the 80s. But again he weakens Papias's point by adding that 'Papias's whole statement implies that the value of oral tradition decreases with distance from the personal testimony of the eyewitnesses themselves' (29), since Papias's point is surely that the chain of tradition (disciples, elders, Papias) has ensured the faithful transmission of the teaching of Jesus, as confirmed by the occasional visits of individuals who were closer to the first disciples.

151. Alexander, 'The Living Voice'.

152. Bauckham, *Eyewitnesses* 22-24, 27.

he already knew through the oral tradition.¹⁵³ What person who was an eager and well-instructed disciple would not cherish the opportunity to hear even familiar stories and teaching from such highly regarded disciples of his Lord? Just as anyone today might well want to hear the first-hand account of an encounter with some great historic figure, even though the story itself was well known. To repeat: for Papias the value of the visitors was not that they brought unknown Jesus tradition, but that their testimony confirmed so much of what he had known only through oral tradition.¹⁵⁴

Sixth, we should note also that Papias was implying the desirability of expounding Jesus' sayings (3). Does that imply an exposition of written material, or of oral teaching? It could imply (for Papias) an initial collection and writing down of oral tradition in order to expound Jesus' teaching hitherto passed down predominantly in oral form. It is somewhat surprising that at this point Papias gives no hint of awareness of others who had already taken it in hand to transcribe the Jesus tradition (notably Matthew). We should probably deduce from this that Papias was conscious that he was on what we might call the cusp between oral tradition and its transcription, and was more typical of the generation (like Matthew) who began to see the value of transcribing the oral Jesus tradition, without feeling the need to acknowledge dependence on any literary predecessor.

Finally it should not escape notice that Papias was conscious of other teachings; he was not interested in 'those who remembered commandments which came from someone else' (*allotrias*), but only in 'those who remembered the commandments which came from the Lord' (3). No doubt we should see here an awareness of competitors to the message of/about Jesus, and perhaps

153. Bauckham repeats his (not Papias's) contrast between eyewitness accounts and the oral tradition in *Eyewitnesses*, p. 294, though he goes on to note: 'There is no reason, then, why the tradition Papias knew from local transmission should have been any less closely connected with named eyewitnesses than those he collected from his visitors'. Bauckham's concern is to highlight the difference between oral history and oral tradition, but he seems to be unconcerned by the implication that churches depended for the vitality of their knowledge of Jesus tradition on occasional visits by those closer to the first disciples and that in the absence of such visits they lacked reliable Jesus tradition. My point is different: that given the beginning of the traditioning process in the eyewitness testimony of the first disciples, the character they gave it in their various retellings and reusings was essentially the same as the character it retained in subsequent retellings and reusings; consequently, whether the Synoptic tradition (as we now have it) was drawn directly from eyewitnesses themselves or from the subsequent retellings and reusings in one or more churches, the essential character of the Jesus tradition remained the same — as a synopsis of the first three Gospels still demonstrates.

154. Worth noting here is Papias's repeated reference to 'remembering' (3, 3, 7). See also R. Cameron, *Sayings Traditions in the Apocryphon of James* (HTS 34; Philadelphia: Fortress, 1984) ch. 3 ('Remembering the Words of Jesus').

an awareness of teaching added to the Jesus tradition, as I have suggested the *Gospel of Thomas* did — though it should also not escape notice that Papias refers to *Thomas* with no qualms as a source for the Lord's teaching (4).

I have concentrated here on eyewitness testimony. But we should also recall that Papias provides the earliest testimony to the writing of Mark's Gospel and Matthew's Gospel (*HE* 3.39.15-16).[155] Moreover, in Andrew of Caesarea's fifth- or sixth-century *Commentary on the Apocalypse*, Papias is quoted as citing Luke 10.18 ('I saw Satan fallen from heaven like a lightning bolt').[156] He seems to have known the story of Jesus and the woman taken in adultery (John 7.53–8.11) and may have quoted a version of it.[157] And a strong argument can be made that when Irenaeus attributes quotation of John 14.2 ('In my Father's house are many mansions') to 'the elders, the disciples of the apostles' (*adv. haer.* 5.36.2), he is drawing from Papias; and that Papias is referring to the generation before him ('the elders, the disciples of the apostles').[158] In short, it is entirely likely that Papias knew all four NT Gospels as providing authoritative records of Jesus' teaching.[159]

k. Conclusions

This survey of the Apostolic Fathers, the first decades of the second century, has been very revealing as regards the Jesus tradition. There have been several important findings:

- With one or two exceptions, the Jesus tradition, particularly the sayings of Jesus, was often cited and constituted an important element in catechetical and paraenetic teaching.
- This was true across quite a wide spectrum of churches as attested by the documents reviewed. Clement could cite Jesus tradition on the assumption, presumably, that it would be as well known in Corinth as in Rome — as indeed had Paul when writing from Corinth to Rome. Ignatius, coming from Syria, could assume that his allusions would be recognized by churches in Asia Minor and Rome. *Didache* could present teaching material which would presumably have been more widely known and

---

155. See again §39.2 above.
156. F. Siegert, 'Unbeachtete Papiaszitate bei armenischen Schriftstellern', *NTS* 27 (1981) 605-14.
157. See Holmes, *Apostolic Fathers* 308-11, 317.
158. J. B. Lightfoot, *Essays on Supernatural Religion* (London: Macmillan, 1889) 194-202; Hill, *Johannine Corpus* 385-86, 407-8, and further 386-94.
159. See also Hill, *Who Chose the Gospels?* ch. 10.

liturgical order which must have been widely practised. *2 Clement* quotes and echoes a substantial amount of Jesus tradition.

- Some of the use of the Jesus tradition is explicitly attributed to 'the Lord'. But much more seems to have simply been absorbed into the lifeblood of these early churches. We may safely assume that such allusions would have been widely recognized and would have reverberated in an echo chamber with other and related teaching recalled as handed down from Jesus.
- While several features within the echoed Jesus tradition can be linked to distinctive features of one of the already written Gospels, particularly Matthew, but also John, the references do not demand to be interpreted as quotations or dependent on the writers having a written Gospel to hand.[160] The references need not even be examples of poorly remembered readings of the written Gospel in question. As likely or more likely, the allusions are cases of second orality — knowledge of the distinctive element of the written Gospel recalled from hearing that Gospel read at some earlier juncture. Or indeed they may simply indicate that some distinctive features of one or more written Gospel had been absorbed into the more widely circulating oral tradition — a performance variation which had taken hold among a wider range of performers (teachers, worship leaders) of the Jesus tradition. What can be inferred with greater confidence when distinctive features, say of Matthew's Gospel, are echoed, is that such echoes demonstrate both the strong likelihood that Matthew's Gospel was already written, and that it was already exercising a widening influence.[161]
- The Papias testimony in particular confirms that oral Jesus tradition was still a lively resource for the early churches. Word of mouth and personal testimony were greatly prized (Papias would hardly be alone in this), and prized more highly than what came only in writing. The fact that all the items reviewed in this section are documents indicates that there was no hostility to transcribing Jesus tradition, but probably suggests that the early decades of the second century marked a growing transition from dependence on oral tradition to realization that as eyewitnesses became more remote in time and as Christianity spread still wider, the transcrip-

---

160. See also P. Foster, 'The Text of the New Testament in the Apostolic Fathers', in C. E. Hill and M. J. Kruger, eds., *The Early Text of the New Testament* (Oxford University, 2012) 282-301.

161. G. N. Stanton, '5 Ezra and Matthean Christianity in the Second Century', *JTS* 28 (1977) 67-83, reprinted in *A Gospel for a New People* 256-77, finds clear allusions in *5 Ezra* (= *4 Ezra*) 1.24 to Matt. 21.43, in *5 Ezra* 1.32-33 to Matt. 23.37-38 and in *5 Ezra* 2.20ff., 34-35 to Matt. 25.32ff. (264-72).

tion of the oral gospel was becoming more desirable and necessary. This suggestion seems to be borne out by what we can learn about the use made of the Jesus tradition in the Apologists.

44.3 The Oral Jesus Tradition into the Second Century — The Apologists

Although those usually accounted 'Apologists' (§40.2) would take us into the third century (notably Tertullian), we will restrict our study here to Aristides, Justin Martyr, Tatian, Athenagoras, Theophilus of Antioch, and Melito of Sardis, here including Irenaeus, but leaving to one side the *Epistle to Diognetus*.[162]

a. Aristides

The most striking feature in Aristides' *Apology* is the invitation to the king (Hadrian?)[163] to read for himself in 'what is called the holy gospel writing' (15.1 Greek).[164] Aristides also refers to 'the writings of the Christians' (16.1 Greek), referring back to what he had been saying in *Apol.* 2, 14-15 about Jesus' life, death, and ascension.[165] But the evidence of specific knowledge and use of Jesus tradition is slight, nothing on which any substantial argument could be built. Massaux refers only to *Apol.* 16.2 (Syriac): the reference to one finding a treasure and concealing it could conceivably be an echo of Matt. 13.44.[166] And Hill offers 2.5 (Syriac) — 'he himself was pierced by the Jews,

---

162. The *Epistle to Diognetus* shows no interest in Jesus tradition, although an echo of Mark 3.4 pars. is perceptible in the critique of the Jewish idea of God 'forbidding anything good to be done on the sabbath' (4.3). Richardson finds a sequence of 'parallels' with John's Gospel (*Early Christian Fathers* 207-8 n.3), but the only plausible echo is 8.5 (cf. John 1.18). The *Epistle*'s modest logos christology (11, 12.9), unlike Justin's, shows no dependence on the prologue to John's Gospel, and anyway, chs. 11-12 are usually regarded as of a different document from chs. 1-10 (see below §45 n.190). See also Jefford, *Diognetus* 72-93, who suggests that there was a primitive narrative behind chs. 1-10, delivered in oral recitation (125).

163. See above §40.2b.

164. In the Syriac (2.4) 'the gospel' is also referred to as recently preached among the Jews, but also as something which the king could read (in the Greek at 15).

165. The Syriac refers to the Christian 'writings' more frequently (15.1; 16; 17); see further Hill, *Johannine Corpus* 398-402.

166. Massaux, *Influence* 3.6-7; Köhler refers cursorily to other cases of possible influence (*Rezeption* 493), to which might be added the negative form of the golden rule (*Apol.* 15), though it is not distinctively Christian (see *Jesus Remembered* 588-89 n.202).

and he died and was buried' — as 'necessarily' evoking John 19.37,[167] though here again we could have an element from John which had been drawn or absorbed into the wider Jesus tradition. In which case the reference would again confirm the influence of John but not necessarily knowledge and use of John itself.

b. Justin Martyr

As already noted (§41.5), Justin Martyr clearly knew the Gospel in written form (*Dial.* 10.2; 100.1) and of more than one 'Gospel' (*1 Apol.* 66.3; *Dial.* 88.3). He could invite the Emperor to 'examine our writings' (*1 Apol.* 28.1), rebuke Crescens that he had not 'encountered the teachings of Christ' (*2 Apol.* 8.3) and assume that Trypho had 'read what our Saviour taught' (*Dial.* 18.1). From Justin we also learn that 'the memoirs of the apostles' were regarded as equally/(equivalently?) suitable for readings at Sunday Christian gatherings as 'the writings of the prophets' (*1 Apol.* 67.3).[168] And since Justin quotes Synoptic tradition, or Synoptic-like tradition, more extensively than any other of the second-century texts prior to Irenaeus, it is probably simplest to note where Justin's quotations/allusions provide evidence of dependence on or of the influence of specifically one or another of the written (NT) Gospels.[169]

---

167. *Johannine Corpus* 400-401.

168. As G. N. Stanton, *Jesus and Gospel* (Cambridge University, 2004), notes, 'This is the earliest extant reference to the reading of "the gospels" in the context of Christian worship. . . . The liturgical setting provides further evidence that status of the memoirs was very high indeed' (100); see also Hengel, *Four Gospels* 37; Minns and Parvis, *Justin* 259. That Justin knew 'the memoirs of the apostles' in writing is also clear from *Dial.* 88.3; 101.3; 103.6; 104.1; 105.6; 106.3; 107.1 (cf. Köhler, *Rezeption* 259-60). Hagner draws attention to the fact that 'the references to the memoirs occur in a section devoted mainly to narrative rather than the sayings of Jesus (*Dial.* 100-107)' ('Sayings of Jesus' 248). See also L. Abramowski, 'Die "Erinnerungen der Apostel" bei Justin', in P. Stuhlmacher, hrsg., *Das Evangelium und die Evangelien* (WUNT 28; Tübingen: Mohr Siebeck, 1983) 341-53 = ET *The Gospel and the Gospels* (Grand Rapids: Eerdmans, 1991) 323-35.

169. W. Sanday, *The Gospels in the Second Century* (London: Macmillan, 1876), summarizes the evidence of Gospel quotations in Justin: 'The total result may be taken to be that ten passages are substantially exact, while twenty-five present slight and thirty-two marked variations' (116). A. J. Bellinzoni, *The Sayings of Jesus in the Writings of Justin Martyr* (NovTSupp 17; Leiden: Brill, 1967), notes two other sayings of Jesus in Justin Martyr (*Dial.* 35.3b and 47.5) which have no parallels in any of the Gospels (131-34); see also Koester, *Ancient Christian Gospels* 361-62.

i. Mark

The allusions to Jesus tradition in Justin which can be seen as indicating dependence on Mark as such are very few —

1 Apol. 16.7/*Dial.* 101.2	Mark 10.17-18
1 Apol. 66.3	Mark 14.22-23[170]

Dial. 106.3 refers to details 'recorded (by Peter) in his Memoirs',[171] confirming that Justin thought of the Gospel of Mark as Peter's 'memoirs'.

ii. Matthew

In contrast, the evidence of Justin's use of or dependence on Matthew or distinctively Matthean tradition can be readily illustrated:[172]

1 Apol. 15.1-2	Matt. 5.28, 29
1 Apol. 15.4	Matt. 19.12, 11
1 Apol. 15.11	Matt. 6.19-20
1 Apol. 15.15	Matt. 6.31-33
1 Apol. 15.17	Matt. 6.1
1 Apol. 16.1-2	Matt. 5.39-40, 16

---

170. Here, in speaking of the eucharist, Justin quotes the distinctive Luke 22.19 ('Do this in remembrance of me'), but the 'words of institution' themselves are quoted in the briefer Markan/Matthean form ('This is my body; this is my blood'), rather than the fuller Lukan/Pauline form.

171. Abramowski, 'Erinnerungen' 353 (ET 334-35); the details are that Jesus gave Simon the name 'Peter' and James and John the name 'Boanerges, that is, "sons of thunder"' (Mark 3.17). Bellinzoni found more Markan elements in *1 Apol.* 16.6, 99.2 and *Dial.* 93.2 (*Sayings* 47), though the evidence is less impressive, and he concludes that Justin never derived material from Mark alone (140).

172. The examples are principally from Bellinzoni, *Sayings* 28-30, 33-37, 60-67, 120-23, and Hagner, 'Sayings of Jesus' 247, who draws on Sanday, *The Gospels in the Second Century* 113-16. Bellinzoni also finds a goodly number of cases which show 'features of harmonization of Matthew and Luke' or of Matthew with Mark (76-88), though the variations are well within the compass of a tradition in second orality phase. Massaux is characteristically more confident of many other literary contacts with Matthew in *1 Apology* (*Influence* 11-41) and in *Dialogue* — no less than 42 'definite' instances (49-82). Köhler is equally confident in finding many more passages where dependence on Matthew is probable (*Rezeption* 166-235). *Biblia Patristica: Index des Citations et Allusions Bibliques dans la Littérature Patristique, des Origines à Clément d'Alexandrie et Tertullian* vol. 1 (Paris, 1975) lists more than 170 citations and allusions to the Gospel of Matthew in the writings of Justin. See also J. R. C. Cousland, 'Matthew's Earliest Interpreter: Justin Martyr on Matthew's Fulfilment Quotations', in T. R. Hatina, ed., *Biblical Interpretation in Early Christian Gospels* vol. 2: *The Gospel of Matthew* (LNTS 310; London: T & T Clark, 2008) 45-60.

1 Apol. 16.5	Matt. 5.34, 37; (Jas. 5.12)
1 Apol. 16.9	Matt. 7.21[173]
Dial. 17.4	Matt. 23.23, 27
Dial. 35.3	Matt. 7.15
Dial. 51.3	Matt. 11.12-15
Dial. 49.5	Matt. 17.10-13
Dial. 76.4; 120.6; 140.4	Matt. 8.11-12
Dial. 76.5	Matt. 7.22-23; 25.41
Dial. 78.1-8; 102.2; 103.3	Matt. 1-2
Dial. 96.3	Matt. 5.45
Dial. 100.3	Matt. 16.16-17
Dial. 105.6	Matt. 5.20
Dial. 107.1	Matt. 16.4
Dial. 108.2	Matt. 28.13
Dial. 112.4-5	Matt. 23.27, 23, 7
Dial. 115.6	Matt. 7.2
Dial. 120.6; 140.4	Matt. 8.11-12
Dial. 125.2	Matt. 25.18

iii. Luke

Of particular interest is the fact that several of Justin's quotations of Jesus tradition include distinctively Lukan material. The point can be illustrated best by referring to quotations of tradition which only Luke attests, and to passages where Lukan redaction is evident.[174] Examples of the former are:

1 Apol. 17.4	Luke 12.48
1 Apol. 33.4-5	Luke 1.35, 32[175]
Dial. 51.2, 76.7, 100.3	Luke 24.7
Dial. 76.6	Luke 10.19
Dial. 100.5	Luke 1.26, 35
Dial. 103.4	Luke 23.7
Dial. 105.5	Luke 23.46

---

173. Justin provides a concentrated epitome of Jesus' teaching in *1 Apol.* 15-17, a medley of teaching probably drawn as much from catechetical material or oral/liturgical usage, as from particular Gospels.

174. Here I follow Gregory, who reviews a larger number of examples, most of which are less demonstrably dependent on Luke (*Reception of Luke* 226-63). Bellinzoni's review of 'sayings that reflect dependence on Luke only' focuses on *1 Apol.* 15.3; 16.1, 10; 17.4 (*Sayings* 70-76).

175. Here we find an intriguing merger of Luke 1.35, 32 with Matt. 1.21 (also *1 Apol.* 33.8).

Examples of the latter are:

1 Apol. 15.8	Luke 5.32/Mark 2.17/Matt. 9.13
1 Apol. 15.9	Luke 6.27-28/(Matt. 5.44)
1 Apol. 16.1	Luke 6.29/(Matt. 5.39-40)
1 Apol. 19.6	Luke 18.27/(Mark 10.27/Matt. 19.26)
Dial. 51.3	Luke 16.16/(Matt. 11.12-15)
Dial. 81.4	Luke 20.35-36/(Mark 12.25/Matt. 22.30)

We need not go into further detail.[176] The two facts hang together: the fact that Justin knew several Gospels, and the fact that he draws on distinctively Lukan features when alluding to or quoting the Jesus tradition. The implication has to be that Luke's Gospel was one of the Gospels which Justin knew and with which he was familiar. The possibility, or better, likelihood, remains strong that some at least of Justin's knowledge comes from catechetical and liturgical collections of Jesus' teaching.[177] And, once again, it should hardly be inferred that tradition ceased to be passed on by word of mouth or through liturgical practice now that written Gospels were well known. But as there was a tendency to harmonize the texts of the Gospels, so there would doubtless have been a tendency to bring the oral tradition into more recognizable conformity to the written texts of the Gospels already so prized within congregations like those familiar to Justin.[178]

iv. John

Somewhat surprisingly, Justin nowhere quotes explicitly from John's Gospel,[179] though 1 Apol. 61.4 with its strong echo of John 3.3, 5 calls for attention:[180]

---

176. Gregory also infers the likelihood 'that Justin knew at least the Lukan passion narrative, and this might suggest that he knew the rest of the gospel as well' (*Reception of Luke* 274-91).

177. Cf. Justin, *1 Apol.* 15-17, with *1 Clem.* 13, *Did.* 1-6 and *Barn.* 18-20. See further Koester on 'Harmonizations of the Texts of Matthew and Luke' (*Ancient Christian Gospels* 365-75); 'Justin Martyr is the first Christian writer who is aware of the fact that the written gospels have become a "text"' (402). Stanton thinks that 'these ten sets of sayings of Jesus [*1 Apol.* 15-17] were almost certainly collected and arranged by Justin himself for catechetical purposes in his school in Rome' (*Jesus and Gospel* 96).

178. Cf. Koester's judgment: Justin's 'writings permit insights into the work of a school of scriptural exegesis in which careful comparison of written gospels with the prophecies of scripture endeavored to produce an even more comprehensive new gospel text' (*Ancient Christian Gospels* 378); with further examination of the birth narratives, John the Baptist and the narrative of Jesus' baptism, and the passion narrative (379-402).

179. Bellinzoni concludes that 'Justin's quotations of the sayings of Jesus show absolutely no dependence on the Gospel of John' (*Sayings* 140).

180. Grant, *Greek Apologists* 58-59; Hill, *Johannine Corpus* 325-28. 'Justin must have obtained this saying through the tradition of the baptismal liturgy, and is not dependent

> *1 Apol.* 61.4 — Unless you have been born again you shall by no means enter into the Kingdom of heaven;
>
> John 3.3, 5 — Unless someone has been born from above/from water and Spirit, it is not possible [for him] to see/enter into the kingdom of God.

And *Dial.* 88.7 includes a quotation from John 1.20, woven into the Synoptic account of John the Baptist.[181] But a strong argument can be made that John's Gospel 'played a formative role in, perhaps was the impetus for' Justin's Logos christology: according to Justin, 'the pre-existent Logos himself became man, and was called Jesus Christ'.[182] Justin explicitly states that he 'learned from the memoirs' his knowledge that Jesus was *monogenēs*, who 'became man through the virgin' (*Dial.* 105.1) — evidently a blend of Matthew's and Luke's birth narratives with John 1.14, 18.[183]

In short, there is sufficient evidence that Justin did know and use all four of the NT Gospels. It is likewise clear that Justin regarded these writings as having the same status as the words of scripture (Old Testament).[184] Not only so, but 'there is no clear evidence for Justin's knowledge of any gospels other than the canonical four'.[185] So Justin attests not only high regard for the NT Gospels individually (Matthew, Mark, Luke, John) but attests also that these were the only writings regarded as authoritative for the churches which he represented.[186]

c. Tatian

There are only a handful of passages in which Tatian in his *Address to the Greeks* can be shown to be influenced by Gospel tradition as such. In 4.1 he

---

upon a written gospel' (Koester, *Ancient Christian Gospels* 361); see also Minns and Parvis, *Justin* 239.

181. Stanton, *Jesus and Gospel* 76.

182. Hill, *Johannine Corpus* 316-20, citing *1 Apol.* 5.4 and 32.10 (John 1.14); also *1 Apol.* 63.15 (John 1.1), *1 Apol.* 60.7 (cf. John 1.1, 14) and *1 Apol.* 46.2 (cf. John 1.9); also *1 Apol.* 21.1, 22.2 and 23.2, and *Dial.* 61.1, 3 and 76.2 (cf. John 1.18).

183. Hill, *Johannine Corpus* 320-24. Hill also observes that Justin knew details contained only in John's accounts of Jesus' baptism and of Jesus' crucifixion (328-35).

184. Stanton, *Jesus and Gospel* 97-99.

185. Stanton, *Jesus and Gospel* 76, and further 75-78, 100-103; similarly Köhler, *Rezeption* 256; see also Hill, *Who Chose the Gospels?* ch. 6.

186. 'When speaking of the life of Christ, Justin sometimes uses materials that are not to be found in the "Memoirs". At no place does he quote this material as coming from the "Memoirs"' (Shotwell, *Justin Martyr* 25).

affirms that 'God is a Spirit', probably quoting from John 4.24. In 13.1 he quotes 'the saying, "The darkness does not comprehend the light"', that is, probably a quotation from John 1.5. 19.4 'All things were made by him, and without him not one thing was made' looks very much like a quotation from John 1.3. And in 30.1 he speaks of the 'hidden treasure', possibly an allusion to Matt. 13.44. Clement of Alexandria also may attribute to Tatian various quotations from the NT, from the Pauline corpus and from the Gospels,[187] though it is unclear how far Clement's reference to Tatian extends.[188]

The most interesting feature of Tatian's evidence, however, must undoubtedly be his *Diatessaron*,[189] in which he weaves together into a single account all four Gospels — the first harmonization[190]— beginning, it is worth noting, with John 1.1 and ending with John 21.25. Justin's tendency to harmonize Jesus tradition may have encouraged his pupil to attempt a complete harmonization. So even if the *Diatessaron* was not compiled till after Justin's martyrdom and Tatian's return to Syria, it nevertheless constitutes very solid testimony to the fact that the four NT Gospels, *all four*, were already established, by early in the second half of the second century, as the authoritative records of Jesus' life, mission and teaching — and *only these*, since Tatian evidently made no effort and had no desire to incorporate other accounts of Jesus' mission or of his teaching into his harmonization. As a pupil of Justin Martyr, Tatian's *Diatessaron* probably confirms that already in Rome in the middle of the second century the four Gospels were well-known and accorded the equivalent of scriptural status.[191] And as one who came to be regarded as a heretic, Tatian's non-use of other Gospels is a factor to be borne in mind when we turn to the next range of second-century evidence.

d. Athenagoras

Here we are back with material rather more similar to that of *1 Clement* or *Didache*, where appeal is made to teachings in which Christians were brought up:

187. Matt. 6.19, 24; 23.9; Luke 14.20; 20.34, 35; John 3.6; 6.27 (*Stromata* 3.12).
188. See also Massaux, *Influence* 3.110-13; Köhler, *Rezeption* 499; Hill, *Johannine Corpus* 299-301.
189. See W. L. Peterson, 'Tatian's Diatessaron', in Koester, *Ancient Christian Gospels* 403-30.
190. Justin's use of harmonized Jesus tradition does not indicate any desire on his part to provide a full harmonization, still less that he intended such a harmonization to replace the Synoptic Gospels (Stanton, *Jesus and Gospel* 103).
191. See also Hill, *Who Chose the Gospels?* 103-12.

Plea 11.1	Matt. 5.44-45
What, then, are those teachings in which we are brought up? 'I say to you, Love your enemies; bless those that curse you; pray for those that persecute you; that you may be the sons of your Father who is in heaven, who causes his sun to rise on the evil and the good, and sends rain on the just and the unjust'.	I say to you, Love your enemies Luke 6.28a and pray for those who persecute you; that you may be sons of your Father who is in heaven, for he causes his sun to rise on the evil and the good, and sends rain on the just and the unjust.

Plea 12.3	Matt. 5.46, 42	Luke 6.32, 34
'If you love', he says, 'those who love you, and lend to those who lend to you, what reward will you have?'	If you love those who love you, what reward do you have? Cf. 5.42b	If you love those who love you, what credit is that to you? If you lend to those from whom you hope to receive, what credit is that to you?

Plea 32.2	Matt. 5.28
'For he who looks', he says, 'on a woman to lust after her has already committed adultery in his heart'.	He who looks on a woman to lust after her has already committed adultery with her in his heart.

Plea 33.2	Mark 10.11
'For whoever puts away his wife', says he, 'and marries another, commits adultery'.	Whoever puts away his wife and marries another, commits adultery against her.

The degree of verbal similarity is such that, were it to be found between the Synoptic Gospels, we would conclude that they provide good evidence of literary dependence. In other words, it makes best sense to infer that Athenagoras knew and was able to draw on Matthew's Gospel. Even if we should rather infer that Athenagoras drew his teaching from familiar catechesis and paraenesis,[192] it was teaching which had drawn on or been shaped by the written Matthew. In the case of *Plea* 33.2, it is possible, of course, that Athenagoras drew on Matt. 19.9 but omitted the exception clause ('except for adultery').[193]

It is also possible that Athenagoras drew on John's Gospel. In his treatise *On the Resurrection* 10.2-3 he refers to the Son of God as 'the Word of the Father': 'through him all things came into existence' (John 1.3); 'the Father and the

---

192. As suggested also by Rom. 12.14 and *Did.* 1.3, it would appear that Luke 6.28a ('Bless those who curse you') had become a well-quoted maxim, more widely integrated into Jesus' teaching on love of enemies.

193. See also Massaux, *Influence* 3.120-25; Köhler, *Rezeption* 494-98.

Son are one' (John 10.30); 'the Son is in the Father and the Father in the Son' (John 10.38; 14.10; 17.21); 'he is the first begotten of the Father' (John 1.14). These cannot be described as quotations of John, but it is hard to deny their distinctively Johannine character. Athenagoras was almost certainly influenced by John's Gospel, either directly or at some remove (second orality). Not least of importance is Athenagoras's testimony to the use made of John by one who can be regarded as an apologist for the mainstream of second-century Christianity.[194]

e. Theophilus of Antioch, *To Autolycus*

Somewhat curiously, the little use made of the Jesus tradition by Theophilus is very similar to that of Athenagoras:[195]

Autolycus 3.13	Matt. 5.28, 32; 19.9
Autolycus 3.14	Matt. 5.44, 46; 6.3
Autolycus 2.22	John 1.1, 3[196]

The similarity suggests that issues of chastity and responses to hostility were major apologetic concerns in the latter decades of the second century; also that John 1.1-3 was providing a much valued way of integrating Christian belief about Christ into wider philosophic reflection on the cosmos. It should be noted that both of the first two groups of quotations are introduced as 'the voice of the Gospel', 'the Gospel says'. Since, like the passages similarly used by Athenagoras, they can be regarded as quotations, the implication is that Theophilus uses the term 'Gospel' with reference to Matthew in particular, or perhaps generically to the message of the written Gospels.[197] At the same time, it is clear that the Gospel tradition is only one element in his teaching, drawn more richly from the OT, and he quotes more easily from the Greek philosophers and playwrights than from the 'Gospel'. Theophilus's brief use of John confirms that, like Athenagoras, he was not at all embarrassed so to use it; he gives no hint that it had been taken over by the Gnostic factions within still adolescent Christianity.[198]

194. See also Hill, *Johannine Corpus* 81-83.
195. See also Massaux, *Influence* 3.134-39; Köhler, *Rezeption* 500-504.
196. Is the sentence in *Autolycus* 2.13, 'For the things which are impossible with men are possible with God', a quotation of Luke 18.27?
197. In the preface to his *Commentary on Matthew* (398), Jerome refers to a commentary on Matthew by Theophilus.
198. See further Hill (*Johannine Corpus* 78-80), who also argues strongly that 'well before Irenaeus wrote, Theophilus in Antioch was using the Apocalypse of John as a textual, religious authority' (80-81).

In addition, we should note Jerome's report that Theophilus composed a book in which he 'put together in one work the words of the four Evangelists' (*Ep.* 121.6.15);[199] that is, he produced a harmony of the four NT Gospels, presumably much like the more famous *Diatessaron* of Tatian.[200] Again of significance are the two facts: that *all* four NT Gospels were regarded as having a proto-canonical status; and that *only* the four NT Gospels were so used, others evidently not being considered as appropriate to be so included.

f. Melito of Sardis

Melito of Sardis need not detain us long, since he had no concern or reason to quote or allude to particular sayings and events in Jesus' mission beyond his suffering and death. Jesus' birth from a virgin is simply a fact of the faith (66, 70, 104) and required no more elaborate reference. His miracles of healing and raising from the dead are alluded to on several occasions (72, 78, 86, 89-90, 101), but only the healing of the man with the withered hand (Mark 3.1-5 pars.) and the raising of one who had been lying in the tomb for four days (John 11) are identifiable (78). The only allusion to a saying of Jesus is the laudatory description in 102 of Jesus, that he 'bound the strong one' (Mark 3.27 pars.). But Matthew's distinctive testimony is alluded to on several occasions — 86 (Matt. 17.24-27), 92 (Matt. 27.24), 98 (Matt. 27.51). And, as 79, 92-93 and 95-97 make clear, Melito certainly knew the details of the tradition of Jesus' final suffering and death. There are some signs of influence from John's Gospel,[201] but they are at best faint.

g. Irenaeus

It is hardly necessary to cite Irenaeus's familiarity with the Jesus tradition as enscribed in the written (NT) Gospels, since he committed himself so explicitly and emphatically to the four NT Gospels, and only four (*adv. haer.* 3.11.8).[202]

---

199. Cited by Hill, *Johannine Corpus* 78-79.

200. Hill, *Who Chose the Gospels?* 92-93, 108-9.

201. Hall, *Melito* 98; Hill, *Johannine Corpus* 295-96, 362-64. 'While the refined and highly poetic Asiatic rhetoric of Melito's work on the passion prevents direct quotations from the Gospels, he does work in/works on the Fourth Gospel with the Synoptics in a harmonizing way', with many illustrations (Hengel, *Johannine Question* 141 n.16; *johanneische Frage* 23 n.29).

202. Osborn, *Irenaeus* 175-77. See e.g. Hill's documentation of Irenaeus's use of the Johannine corpus (*Johannine Corpus* 96-101, more fully 95-118).

What is worth noting is that Irenaeus in using the NT Gospels did not find it necessary to defend his use as though it was an innovation.[203] He uses all four, though not so much Mark, but not as something new, nor as a tactic to be defended. His high regard for and use of the four NT Gospels, including John, is simply the climax of the trend we have seen through the second century, as knowledge and use of the oral Jesus tradition gave way steadily to dependence on one or more of the written NT Gospels in particular. The ease with which Irenaeus cites and correlates Gospel texts (as also OT and Pauline texts) also shows that he was thoroughly familiar with their content and detail, no doubt by reason of long and careful study. In other words, it is clear that by the end of the second century the four NT Gospels were deeply rooted in the liturgies and reflections of the great church.

It should be noted that unlike most of his predecessors, Irenaeus does not merely quote Gospel texts but expounds them — as in *adv. haer.* 3.8.1-2 (Matt. 22.21; 6.24; 12.29), 3.9.2 (Matt. 2.11), 4.36.1-2, 5-6 (Matt. 21.33-44; 22.1-14).[204] Even more noteworthy is Irenaeus's indication of how the Valentinians used the Gospel tradition.[205] He rebukes the Valentinians that 'they gather their views from other sources than the scriptures' (1.8.1). Thus the interpretation of the parable of the woman who mixes yeast with three measures of flour (Matt. 13.33) in terms of the Valentinian three types of men, spiritual, psychical and material, is hardly drawn from the parable itself (1.8.3). And Irenaeus complains of the Marcosians that 'whatever they find in the scriptures capable of being referred to the number eight, they declare to fulfill the mystery of the Ogdoad' (1.18.3); the fact that Jesus was baptized at age thirty (Luke 3.23) points them to the thirty aeons (2.12.1);[206] the twelve apostles are a type of the twelve aeons (1.21.1), and according to their system Jesus can only have preached for twelve months after his baptism (1.20.1; 1.22.1). Such use of the Jesus tradition well illustrates that the referential system being used

---

203. 'His line of argument strongly suggests that he is not making a case for a recent innovation. But underpinning what he and others had long accepted, i.e. that the church had been given one Gospel in fourfold form — four authoritative writings, no more, no less' (Stanton, *Jesus and Gospel* 105, and further 105-9). Similarly Hill, *Who Chose the Gospels?* chs. 2-3: 'Irenaeus writes as if the church had been nurtured by these four Gospels from the time of the apostles' (41).

204. Osborn's observation, that 'His ideas are formed through an understanding of the theology of Paul and John rather than from an accumulation of texts' (*Irenaeus* 14), applies also to his use of other Gospel texts.

205. A fragment of Valentinus's teaching (in Clement's *Stromateis*) contains quotations from Matt. 5.18 and 19.7 (Dunderberg, 'School of Valentinus' 73 n.41).

206. The parable of the labourers in the vineyard (Matt. 20.1-16), with labourers hired at different times of the day, gave similar scope for playing with numbers (1+3+6+9+11 = 30) (*adv. haer.* 1.1.3).

was drawn from elsewhere, with the Jesus tradition material simply drawn on to the extent that it could fit with the system.

What is particularly interesting in comparing the testimony drawn from the Apostolic Fathers with the testimony of the apologists is the transition from a knowledge of the Jesus tradition primarily in *oral* terms (through regular liturgical and catechetical usage) to a greater awareness of and reliance on *written Gospels*. Also evident is little or no use of or reliance on the sort of tradition attributed to Jesus by the *Gospel of Thomas* and the apocryphal Gospels to be reviewed below — even though catechetical and apologetic presentations did not hesitate to elaborate the Christian teaching and claims by drawing on other sources. Together these facts strongly suggest: (1) that the oral Jesus tradition was steadily being conformed to the written versions in the NT Gospels — the NT Gospels were well on the way to providing the main body of Christians with the norm for what counted as Gospel; and (2) that the inscribing of the Jesus tradition was seen as a way of bracketing it off from the other Gospels which were beginning to appear in this period — a way of preventing the Jesus tradition from being elaborated in ways which drew it too far away from its original inspiration in the life, teaching, death and resurrection of Jesus.

44.4 Other Streams of Jesus Tradition

It is already clear from the *Gospel of Thomas* that there were other streams of Jesus tradition than those preserved in the New Testament Gospels. And we have already noted that there were many other Gospels or Gospel-like documents circulating in the second century (§40.4). So, what other attestation is available regarding the Jesus tradition? How valuable is the source material either as further testimony to the remembered Jesus or as testimony to the development and developing character of the Jesus tradition? And what does that material say about the way second-century Christianity was itself developing? The issues have become of substantially greater importance since in the later decades of the twentieth century it became fashionable in some scholarly circles to find in these 'other Gospels' expressions of Jesus tradition which were *earlier* than the tradition of the NT Gospels. This was partly a follow through from the great quest for the pre-Christian Gnostic Redeemer myth, which featured so strongly (and failed) in the middle decades of the twentieth century.[207] Partly also the effect of a weariness with a quest for the historical

---

207. See above §38.4b.

§44.4   *The Jesus Tradition in the Second Century*

Jesus which had become bogged down in endless debates about particular passages and features of the NT Gospels; and a dissatisfaction with having to depend so much on the traditional sources (particularly Acts) for knowledge of Christianity's beginnings.[208] So the possibility that other writings from the second or even later centuries could contain forms of tradition about Jesus which were earlier than the NT traditions and could even provide a source for some of the NT Gospel material became a great incentive for fresh investigation and speculation.[209] We have already seen what is, or may be, at stake in discussion of the *Gospel of Thomas*. But the discussion has embraced a good number of other Gospels, and interaction with and examination of the resulting claims will be a major concern in this section (§44.4).

In fact, some of what I have casually referred to as 'streams of Jesus tradition' would be better imaged as pools or puddles than rivers — agrapha, and fragmentary papyri particularly. But others are parts of more extensive writings, or the writings themselves, containing extensive teaching attributed to Jesus or further stories particularly of his birth and infancy and of his ministry and passion. Overall, as will become clear, the value of the material for historical knowledge of Jesus is almost nil. But the material does show clearly that Jesus was a figure of fascination, whose teaching and life became an increasing focus of reflection and hope for those seeking a spiritual answer to their sense of disorientation and search for peace. So the material also provides rich and sometimes penetrating insights into the spirituality of the period. In this section we will focus on the 'pools' rather than the 'streams' and leave the other Gospels to §§44.5 and 6.

a. Agrapha

For more than a century close attention has been paid to the fact that various sayings of Jesus or attributed to Jesus are attested in the variant textual traditions of the NT Gospels and in the church fathers, sayings which are without parallel in the NT Gospels and which would otherwise be unknown.[210] Their description as 'agrapha' ('unwritten') is a further re-

---

208. See *Beginning from Jerusalem* 87 n.135.

209. Notably, Robinson and Koester, *Trajectories*; and Koester, *Ancient Christian Gospels*. But note also Cameron, ed., *The Other Gospels*; J. D. Crossan, *Four Other Gospels: Shadows on the Contours of Canon* (Minneapolis: Winston, 1985); also *The Historical Jesus*; Ehrman, *Lost Christianities*; also *Lost Scriptures*.

210. See the collections made by J. Jeremias, *Unknown Sayings of Jesus* (London: SPCK, 1958, ²1964), by O. Hofius in Schneemelcher-Wilson, *NTA* 1.88-91 (with bibliography), and by Elliott, *ANT* 26-30 (with bibliography). Massaux lists 22 'unauthentic

minder of the mind-set which envisaged the transmission of Jesus' teaching only in literary terms. The very few which have impressed or appealed to twentieth-century scholars as probably 'authentic' (teaching which Jesus himself gave) are a reminder of the richness, diversity and durability of the oral Jesus tradition.[211] But their credibility as sayings which Jesus was remembered as uttering depends largely on their compatibility with the more familiar Synoptic traditions, and that credibility is minimal.[212] So while the agrapha attest the developing character of what can still be included under the title 'Jesus tradition', their value lies in demonstration that the late Jesus tradition was a stream which was becoming more and more remote from the Jesus tradition of the first century.

All that is necessary here, then, is to note the most striking 'unknown sayings' to illustrate the character and potential value of the agrapha as a whole.

- Jerome, *on Eph.* 5.4, quotes from 'the Hebrew Gospel' Jesus as saying to his disciples, 'Never be glad unless you are in charity with your brother'/'Only then shall you be glad, when you look on your brother with love'.[213]
- Epiphanius, *Pan.* 30.16.5, quotes the Gospel of the Ebionites recording Jesus as saying, 'I have come to abolish the sacrifices: if you do not cease from sacrificing, the wrath [of God] will not cease from weighing upon you'.[214]

Clement of Alexandria, *Stromata*, records two sayings from the *Kerygma Petri*[215] which seem to be elaborations of the traditions of Jesus' (post-resurrection) missionary commissions:

- *Strom.* 6.5.43 notes that in the *Kerygma Petri*, Peter records Jesus saying to the disciples, 'If then any of Israel will repent and believe in God

---

agrapha . . . which have been composed under the influence of Matthew' (*Influence* 2.249-61); and W. D. Stroker amasses no less than 266 *Extracanonical Sayings of Jesus* (Atlanta: Scholars, 1989). See also P. Nagel, 'Apokryphe Jesusworte in der koptischen Überlieferung', in Frey and Schröter, eds., *Jesus in apokryphen Evangelienüberlieferungen* 495-526.

211. On Acts 20.35 and Luke 6.4 D see above §44.2b.

212. See *Jesus Remembered* 172. E.g., Hofius lists only seven sayings, and counts as possibly authentic only Jerome, *on Eph.* 5.4, *GospThom* 82 and P.Oxy. 1224 (see §44.4b below) (*NTA* 91).

213. First rendering by Elliott, *ANT* 9; second by Hofius, *NTA* 91.

214. Elliott, *ANT* 15.

215. In the next six examples I follow Elliott, *ANT* 23, 9, 18 and 30.

through my name, his sins shall be forgiven him;²¹⁶ and after twelve years go out into the world lest any say, "We did not hear"'.
- *Strom.* 6.6.48 has a somewhat similar but more extensive missionary commission by the Lord after his resurrection.²¹⁷

Clement of Alexandria seems also to draw on the more gnostically inclined teaching which came to be attributed to Jesus:

- *Strom.* 2.9.45 — As it is also written in the Gospel of the Hebrews, 'He who wonders shall reign, and he who reigns shall rest'.
- *Strom.* 3.9.1 — according to the Gospel of the Egyptians Jesus said, 'I have come to undo the works of the female', to which Clement adds the note: 'by the "female" meaning lust, and by "the works" birth and decay'.
- *Strom.* 3.13.92 also refers to the Gospel of the Egyptians quoting the Lord as saying, 'When you tread under foot the covering of shame and when out of two is made one, and the male with the female, neither male nor female'.
- *Strom.* 5.14.96 — 'He that seeks will not rest until he finds; and he that has found shall marvel; and he that has marveled shall reign; and he that has reigned shall rest' (but not attributed to Jesus).

The first seems to echo and the last to quote *Gosp. Thom.* 2;²¹⁸ and the third echoes *Gosp. Thom.* 37.2 and 22.4-5, as did *2 Clem.* 12.2.²¹⁹ But another saying of Jesus drawn from *Thomas* (82) has attracted much support as probably authentic, even though Origen, who says he read it somewhere (*In Jer. Hom.* 3.3), may show some uncertainty on the matter:²²⁰

>He who is near me is near the fire.
>He who is far from me is far from the kingdom.

---

216. Schneemelcher here compares Luke 24.27; Acts 5.31; 10.43 (*NTA* 2.41).

217. I have not included the somewhat similar elaboration of the risen Christ's missionary commission in what is known as the Freer logion preserved in Codex W (fifth century) after Mark 16.14, that is, a probably scribal elaboration of the longer ending to Mark's Gospel, itself an addition to Mark's Gospel; see e.g. Metzger, *Textual Commentary* 124-25.

218. Vielhauer and Strecker see here the influence of 'mystic-gnostic religiosity' (*NTA* 1.175). Stroker indicates a range of parallels from Gnostic writings (*Extracanonical Sayings* 116-19). See also Klijn, *Jewish-Christian Gospel Tradition* 47-51.

219. See above §43 n.288; also Stroker, *Extracanonical Sayings* 12-16.

220. S. C. Carlson, 'Origen's Use of the *Gospel of Thomas*', in Charlesworth et al., eds., *Sacra Scriptura* 137-51, concludes that Origen thought *Gosp. Thom.* 82 was a genuine saying of Jesus (143-44). Carlson also finds allusions to *Gosp. Thom.* 1 and 23 in other writings of Origen.

This material adds little to our inquiry about the continuing impact of the Jesus tradition, except that it confirms that the Gnostic elaboration of the Jesus tradition (as in *Thomas*) was more widely known. It is also of some interest that by the end of the second century the Jesus tradition seems to have been known only in written form.

b. Fragmentary Papyri[221]

We have already noted the value of the Oxyrhynchus papyri in the evidence they provide that the *Gospel of Thomas* was known in Greek (§40.4b). But other papyri from Egypt indicate that the Jesus tradition was widely known and was being elaborated in different ways.

In Papyrus Egerton 2, only the front and back of fragment 1 and the front of fragment 2 invite comment.[222]

P.Egerton 2 frag. 1 verso	John 5.39, 45; 9.29; 5.46
... Then [tu]rn[ing] to the rulers of the people, he spoke this word, 'Sea[rch] the scriptures in which you th[ink] you have life; it is they [which be]ar witness concerning me. Do not thi[nk th]at I have come to accuse [you] to my Father; the one [who acc]uses you is Moses, on whom [you] have set your hope'. When they s[ai]d, 'We well know that God sp[oke] to Moses; but as for you, we do not know [where you come from]'. Jesus answered and sa[id to th]em, 'Now stands accused [your failure] to believe (those who have [been attest]ed by him. For if you had bel[ieved Moses] you would have believed [me], for he [wrot]e about me to your fathers').	You search the scriptures because you think that in them you have eternal life; and it is they which bear witness concerning me.... Do not think that I will accuse you to the Father; the one who accuses you is Moses, on whom you have set your hope.... We know that God has spoken to Moses; but as for this man, we do not know where he comes from. If you believed Moses, you would believe in me, for he wrote about me.

---

221. Most of this material could have been included under §44.4a as agrapha; but the different categories are convenient, so I follow the now customary practice as in Elliott, *ANT* 31-45, and Schneemelcher, *NTA* 92-105. See also T. J. Kraus, M. J. Kruger and T. Nicklas, eds., *Gospel Fragments* (Oxford University, 2009).

222. In the translations below the fragmentary nature of the texts is indicated by the square brackets; the contribution of P.Köln 255 is indicated by the round brackets at the end of the two sides of fragment 1.

§44.4   *The Jesus Tradition in the Second Century*

P.Egerton 2 frag. 1 recto	John 10.31; 7.30; 10.39
... take up] stones together to s[to]ne [hi]m. And the [rule]rs laid their ha[nds] on him [in or]der to arrest him and hand [him over] to the crowd; and they were not [able] to arrest him, because the hour of his betrayal had not yet c[ome]. But the L[or]d himself escaped [from their han]ds and withdrew from [them].	Again the Jews took up stones to stone him. Therefore they sought to arrest him, and no one laid his hand on him, because his hour had not yet come. Therefore they sought again to arrest him, and he escaped from their hand.
	Luke 5.12-14 pars.
And behold a leper ca[me to him], saying, 'Teacher, ... If then [you are willing], I am cleansed'. And the Lord [said to him], 'I am willing; be cleansed'. [And immediately] the lep[rosy] left him. But the Lord said to him, 'Go, show [your]self to th[e priests], (and make an offering [for your clea]nsing, as Moses co[mmanded, and] sin no more ...)'.	And there came to him a leper, beseeching him and saying to him, 'If you are willing, you can cleanse me'. And he stretched out his hand and touched him, saying, 'I am willing; be cleansed'. And immediately the leprosy left him. And he ordered him to tell no one, but 'Go, show yourself to the priest, and make an offering for your cleansing, as Moses commanded, for a testimony to them'.

P.Egerton 2 frag. 2 recto	John 3.2; Mark 12.14-15 pars.; Luke 6.46; Matt. 15.7-9 par.
Coming to him they tested him with a [probing en]quiry, s[aying], 'Teacher Jesus, we know that you have come [from God], for what you do bears w[itness] beyond all the prophets. [Tell] us then, Is it lawful to [pay] to the kings what relates to their rule? Should we p[ay th]em or not?' But Jesus, knowing their [way of] thinking, said to t[hem] indig[nantly]: 'Why do you call me [with your mo]uth "teacher" and do n[ot list]en to what I say? Well has I[saiah] prophesied [concerning y]ou, saying, "Th[is people] with their [li]ps [honours] me, but their [hear]t is [far fr]om me; in vain do th[ey worship me], (teaching human) command[ments"]'.	Nicodemus came to him by night and said to him, 'Rabbi, we know that you are a teacher come from God; for no one can do the signs which you do, unless God is with him'. 'Is it lawful to pay tribute to Caesar or not?' But he, knowing their hypocrisy, said to them ... 'Why do you call me, "Lord, Lord", and do not what I say?' 'Well has Isaiah prophesied concerning you, saying, "This people with their lips honours me, but their heart is far from me; in vain do they worship me, teaching as instructions human commandments"'.

There are several striking features here:

- The influence of John's Gospel, particularly on fragment 1, is hard to deny. This would be all the more striking if P.Egerton 2 can be dated to the middle of the second century (or earlier), and may be ranked almost

as valuable as p^{52} as a testimony to the circulation and influence of John's Gospel in the second century.[223]
- The mixture of distinctive Johannine features hardly suggests a copying direct from the written Gospel of John. They suggest much more an extensive familiarity with John's Gospel, either from personal study of the written Gospel or from hearing it read regularly, so that passages and phrases from John's Gospel came naturally to mind as the papyrus codex was being composed. In other words, the Johannine character of P.Egerton 2 is probably best explained as another case of second orality — but with the implication, it should not be ignored, that John's Gospel was in substantial use and well known.[224]
- Equally striking is the influence from Synoptic tradition on the recto of fragment 1 and in fragment 2.[225] Again, it is unlikely that the parallels are to be explained as literary dependency. The Jesus tradition in which the stories featured was well known in close but varied Synoptic tradition. So it is impossible to decide whether P.Egerton 2 derived them from oral Jesus tradition or from one (or more) particular Gospel(s) recalled in oral mode.[226]
- The fact that there is no significant feature of the P.Egerton 2 material for whose source we have to look beyond the Jesus tradition, as known to us from the Synoptics and John's Gospel,[227] suggests a deep familiarity with this Jesus tradition making possible varied combinations in reuse.
- The mixing of what can properly be called Synoptic and Johannine tradi-

223. See above §39.2d(iii).
224. Koester's argument that P.Egerton 2 'is older than the Gospel of John' and 'belongs to a stage of a tradition that preceded the canonical gospels' (*Introduction* 2.182; similarly *Ancient Christian Gospels* 207-11; cf. Cameron, ed., *The Other Gospels* 73; Crossan, *Four Other Gospels* 74-75) fails to give weight to characteristically and distinctively Johannine features (searching the scriptures, witness-bearing, the contrast with and testimony of Moses, Jesus' origin questioned, failed attempts to arrest and stone Jesus, Jesus' hour still to come; Koester agrees that 'the language is "Johannine" throughout' — *Ancient Christian Gospels* 209), and also exaggerates the significance of differences ('life' instead of 'eternal life') which are typical of second orality (and of oral tradition, as indicated by the Synoptic tradition); see also D. F. Wright, 'Apocryphal Gospels: The "Unknown Gospel" (Pap. Egerton 2) and the Gospel of Peter', in Wenham, ed., *Jesus Tradition* 207-32 (here 210-15); Barrett, *John* 110, 268, 270; Hill, *Johannine Corpus* 302-6.
225. 'The influence of Lk. is beyond doubt' (Massaux, *Influence* 2.182).
226. Cf. Koester, *Ancient Christian Gospels* 213-15, noting that 'there is nothing in this pericope [frag. 2] that clearly reveals redactional features of any of the gospels in which parallels appear' (215). The use of the plural ('priests') in P.Egerton 2 frag. 1 recto, where Luke 5.14 pars. uses the singular ('priest'), is hardly significant; as Luke 17.14 indicates, either usage was appropriate as an ending to the telling of a story of leprosy being cleansed. See also Wright, 'Apocryphal Gospels' 216-20.
227. Frag. 2 verso is too obscure to allow a clear decision as to its source.

tion indicates that different inputs were absorbed into the Jesus tradition with the result that the developed Jesus tradition could be used without any sense that the source and authority for particular traditions or for diverse features of particular traditions should be or need be distinguished. John's Gospel was being treated as straightforwardly as the Synoptic Gospels.

Other papyri fragments do not provide much help to forward the discussion.[228]

- The Fayyum Fragment (third century) is a briefer version of Mark 14.27, 29-30/Matt. 26.31, 33-34.
- The Merton Papyrus 51 (*P.Mert.* 51) (third century) is a small fragment recounting response to John the Baptist and a saying about a tree, its fruit and the treasure of the heart (cf. Luke 6.43-45/Matt. 7.17-20; 12.33-35).
- P.Oxy. 1224 (beginning of the fourth century) has fragments of two pages. One has a brief summary of the tradition attested in Mark 2.16-17 pars., and the second combines elements of the tradition attested in Matt. 5.44/Luke 6.27-28 and Mark 9.40 par.
- P.Oxy. 840 (fourth or fifth century) has a story of Jesus being criticized by a Pharisee for failing to perform the required ritual washing before entering the temple. Jesus replies by contrasting the Pharisee's purity gained by washing in dirty water with himself and his disciples having bathed 'in the living water which comes down from (heaven)'. The story has no parallel in the NT Gospels, but could have been inspired by the awareness of the many confrontations which they attest between Jesus and Pharisees, and particularly by Jesus tradition such as Mark 7.1-23 par.,[229] Matt. 23.25/Luke 11.39 and John 4.10, 14.[230]
- The Strasburg Fragment (fourth–sixth centuries) shows the influence particularly of the Gethsemane tradition (Mark 14.34, 38, 41 par.).
- *P.Berolinensis* 11710 (sixth century) contains a snatch of conversation between Jesus and Nathanael, which echoes John 1.49 and 1.29.
- *P.Cairensis* 10735 (sixth or seventh century) shows awareness of Luke 1.36 and 76 and Matt. 2.13.

228. See Schneemelcher, *NTA* 94-95, 100-105; Elliott, *ANT* 31-34, 35-37, 41-45; also Massaux, *Influence* 2.249-61; Köhler, *Rezeption* 453-58. For the Greek texts of the papyri see again Aland, *Synopsis* 584 (index) and Bernhard, *Other Early Christian Gospels* 98-127.

229. Cf. Cameron, who on the basis of the 'close parallels' with Mark 7.1-23 pars. dates it in the second half of the first century (*Other Gospels* 53).

230. See also M. J. Kruger, 'Papyrus Oxyrhynchus 840', in Foster, ed., *Non-Canonical Gospels* 157-70, who argues for its association with the historical Jewish-Christian sect of the Nazarenes (169); Evans, 'The Jewish Christian Gospel Tradition' 258-64.

The best we can say is that even in the later centuries, when the fourfold Gospel was established scripture, reference to and use made of the Gospel tradition in homily and reflection show little concern for precision of quotation or for the careful ordering of passages alluded to. These papyri also provide no substantive evidence of knowledge of or reliance on non-canonical Gospels.

c. *Epistula Apostolorum*

The *Epistula Apostolorum* (§40.5e) has many quotations from and echoes of a wide range of NT writings. Notable are knowledge of distinctive features of the NT Gospels:[231]

- 3 — the first attempt to interweave John's account of the Logos becoming flesh (John 1.13-14) with the Lukan birth narrative (Luke 2.7);
- 5 — the wedding at Cana (John 2.1-12);
- 5 — the Markan or Lukan accounts of Jesus healing the woman with a haemorrhage (Mark 5.25-34/Luke 8.43-48) and the Gerasene demoniac (Mark 5.6-13/Luke 8.28-33);
- 5 — Matthew's distinctive episode about paying the temple tax (Matt. 17.24-27);
- 11 — John's account of Thomas being convinced of Jesus' resurrection (John 20.27);
- 14 — Luke's account of the annunciation by the angel Gabriel to Mary (Luke 1.26-38);
- 17 — the mutual indwelling of Jesus with his Father (as in John 10.38, 14.11 and 17.21);
- 18 — the new commandment to love one another (John 13.34);
- 41 — the parable of the wise and foolish virgins (Matt. 25.1-13);
- 48 — the Matthean counsel on reproving one's brother (Matt. 18.15-18).

Indeed, it is quite likely that *Ep.Apost.* knew all four NT Gospels as such, and provides evidence, perhaps even earlier than Justin, that the four Gospels were already highly regarded and well used by those who were resisting gnostic elaboration of the Jesus tradition.[232]

---

231. The only other Gospels drawn on (in *Ep.Apost.* 4) are the *Infancy Gospel of Thomas* (6.3; 14.2) and/or Pseudo-Matthew, *Infancy Gospel* 38.1.
232. See particularly D. D. Hannah, 'The Four-Gospel "Canon" in the *Epistula Apostolorum*', *JTS* 59 (2008) 598-633; also below n.248.

d. Jewish-Christian Gospels (§40.4a)

The references to the so-called Jewish-Christian Gospels in Clement of Alexandria, Origen, Jerome and other Church Fathers contain a fair number of passages which include versions of episodes or teaching of Jesus more familiar from the NT Gospels, particularly Matthew. Whether the passages come from one or more actual Gospels, perhaps even a Hebrew/Aramaic version of Matthew, is unknowable.[233] But at least we can say with some confidence that they provide insufficient evidence of a pre-Matthean or proto-Matthean version of the Jesus tradition quoted, since the variations are well within the scope which could be expected in use made of Matthew itself. They thus provide further indications that the Jesus tradition as known to us in the Synoptic/Matthean tradition was more widely known, was packaged and repackaged in different ways and was supplemented by further material.[234] The most obvious variant parallel material is as follows:

i. The Gospel according to the Hebrews[235]

Clement, *Strom.* 2.9.45	cf. Matt. 7.7/Luke 11.9
Jerome, *on Isa.* 11.2	Mark 1.9-11 pars.
Jerome, *de Vir. Ill.* 2	resurrection appearance to James[236]

ii. The Gospel of the Nazaraeans

Origen, *on Matt.* 15.14	Matt. 19.16-24/Mark 10.17-25
Eusebius, *Theophania* 4.22	Matt. 25.14-30
Jerome, *de Vir. Ill.* 3	quotes Matt. 2.15 and 23
Jerome, *on Matt.* 12.13	Matt. 12.9-14 pars.
Jerome, *adv. Pelag.* 3.2	Matt. 3.13-14; 18.21-22

iii. The Gospel of the Ebionites[237]

Epiphanius, *Pan.* 30.13.2-3	Mark 1.16-20 par.; 3.13-19 pars.
Epiphanius, *Pan.* 30.13.4-5	Mark 1.4-6 par.[238]

---

233. See above §40.4a.
234. The extracts and quotations can be conveniently consulted in Cameron, *Other Gospels* 85-86, 99-102, 104-6; Ehrman, *Lost Scriptures* 9-16; see also §40 n.174 above.
235. See also above §44.4a; and Origen, *on John* 2.12, cited below in n.268.
236. Cited in *Jesus Remembered* 863 n.171.
237. Köhler cites all the following passages as evidencing clear Matthean influence (*Rezeption* 272-84).
238. The further references to the Baptist's ministry (*Pan.* 30.13.6; 30.14.3) seem

Epiphanius, *Pan.* 30.13.7-8 Matt. 3.14-15
Epiphanius, *Pan.* 30.14.5   Mark 3.31-35 pars.
Epiphanius, *Pan.* 30.22.4-5 cf. Mark 14.12-16 pars.[239]

Such brief extracts make it impossible to build up a coherent picture of these Gospels (or this Gospel). But it does appear that the extracts are from versions of one or more of the NT Gospels, most likely the Gospel of Matthew, but versions which have drawn in elaborated Jesus tradition[240] and which have been adapted to express Ebionite views.[241]

In short, this scatter of knowledge and use of Jesus tradition provides some further evidence that the Jesus tradition was elaborated and added to in a Gnostic direction (agrapha), but otherwise adds to the increasing evidence that from about the middle of the second century quotation of and allusion to Jesus tradition indicate knowledge and use of the written (NT) Gospels.

44.5 Gnostic Gospels 1 — The Issue of Early Source Material

I will look first at the material which purports to preserve teaching of Jesus; for elaborations of the narrative Jesus tradition, see §44.7 below.

Here the discussion broadens once again from the straightforward issue of second-century writers' knowledge of the written NT Gospels to the question whether later apocryphal Gospels have preserved early Jesus tradition, earlier than (much of) the Synoptic tradition. This question has been posed by the Nag Hammadi codices in particular, and has already been discussed in relation to the most plausible instance of such early Jesus tradition (the *Gospel of Thomas*) (§43). In addition, Helmut Koester has made a bold attempt to find evidence of other source material, in particular, sources used by John's Gospel in two 'dialogue gospels' in the Nag Hammadi codices, the *Dialogue of the Saviour* (*NHL* III.5) and the *Apocryphon of James* (*NHL* I.2).[242] How-

---

to blend details from Matthew, Luke and John (Gregory, 'Jewish-Christian Gospels' 63-65), perhaps reflecting a 'Gospel harmony' similar to Tatian's *Diatessaron* (Lührmann, *Die apokryph gewordenen Evangelien* 31, 233).

239. Jesus' affirmation that he did not want to eat the meat of the Passover may reflect an Ebionite vegetarianism or objections to sacrifice, as in 30.16.5, cited above in §44.4a (Gregory, 'Jewish-Christian Gospels' 66).

240. See e.g. Gregory, 'Jewish-Christian Gospels' 61-66.

241. See further below §44.8a, b.

242. Koester, *Ancient Christian Gospels* 173-200, particularly 180 and 200. For the texts, see B. Blatz and D. Kirchner in Schneemelcher-Wilson, *NTA* 1.300-12 and 285-99 respectively; and Robinson, *NHL* 244-55 and 29-37 respectively; also Cameron, *Other Gospels* 40-48 and 57-64 respectively; and Meyer, *Gnostic Gospels of Jesus* 221-39 and 187-207

ever, the evidence Koester cites hardly supports his case; the links are at best tenuous and the supporting arguments tendentious.

a. The *Dialogue of the Saviour*

The *Dialogue of the Saviour* certainly has parallels with the Gospel of John — reference to the Father's 'only-begotten son' (2), and emphasis on light (14, 27, 34, 50). But the parallel of the dialogue form itself tells us little or nothing. The dialogue form is persistent and sustained throughout the *Dialogue* (Matthew, Judas and Mary the dominant dialogue-partners). In John the dialogue form is much more episodic and with a wider range of characters (Nicodemus, Samaritan woman, the Jews, disciples, Martha, Pilate). Without substantive closer parallels between the *Dialogue* and John, however, it is impossible to determine whether one has influenced the other.

So far as the *Dialogue* is concerned, the stronger parallels are with the *Gospel of Thomas*. As with both John and *Thomas*, there are clear echoes of and influence from Jesus tradition as attested in the Synoptic Gospels. The most obvious examples are:

- *Dial. Sav.* 8 — 'The lamp [of the body] is the mind'; cf. Matt. 6.22-23;
- *Dial. Sav.* 9-12, 20 — 'He who seeks [. . .] reveals . . .; cf. Matt. 7.7/Luke 11.9;
- *Dial. Sav.* 14 — 'In that place [there will] be weeping and [gnashing] of teeth over the end of [all] these things; cf. Matt. 8.12;
- *Dial. Sav.* 35 — 'How will someone who does [not] know [the Son] know the [Father]?'; cf. Matt. 11.27/Luke 10.22;
- *Dial. Sav.* 53 — Mary said . . . 'the labourer is worthy of his food' and 'the disciple resembles his teacher'; cf. Matt. 10.10/Luke 6.40.

But the passages which Koester suggests as parallels with John (*Dial. Sav.* 25-30/ John 14.2-12) simply do not fit the category of parallel; so that, once again, the attempt to argue for influence either way lacks a necessary foundation. Much more striking are the *Thomas*-like features which, as with *Thomas*, shift the line of thought into a quite different and Gnostic-like narrative — talk of 'this impoverished cosmos' (26), 'carrying flesh around' (28) and '[Everyone] who has known himself' (30).[243] The *Thomas*-like character of the *Dialogue*

---

respectively. Elliott includes 'the Letter (Apocryphon) of James' in his section on 'Apocryphal Apocalypses' (*ANT* 673-81).

243. Koester's tendentiousness here is evident in his assertion that in John 14 the

is confirmed by further references to what I have referred to as a Gnostic (or Gnostic-like) narrative, usually in parallel to *Thomas*:[244]

- *Dial. Sav.* 34 — 'you are from [that] place'; cf. *Gosp. Thom.* 50;
- *Dial. Sav.* 37 — the Son of Man greeted them and said to them, 'A seed from a power was deficient and it went down to [the] abyss of the earth. And the Greatness remembered [it] and he sent the [Word to] it. It brought it up into [his presence] so that the First Word might not fail';
- *Dial. Sav.* 50 — '. . . you will clothe yourselves in light and enter the bridal chamber'; cf. *Gosp. Thom.* 75;
- *Dial. Sav.* 55 — He said to them, 'You are from the fullness and you dwell in the place where the deficiency is';
- *Dial. Sav.* 84-85 — Judas said to Matthew, 'We [want] to understand the sort of garments we are to be [clothed] with, [when] we depart the decay of the [flesh]'. The Lord said, '. . . you will become [blessed] when you strip [yourselves]'; cf. *Gosp. Thom.* 37;
- *Dial. Sav.* 92, 95 — Matthew said, 'Pray in the place where there is [no woman]', he tells us, meaning, 'Destroy the works of womanhood', not because there is any other [manner of birth], but because they will cease [giving birth]. . . . Judas said [to Matthew], '[The works] of [womanhood] will dissolve . . .'; cf. *Gosp. Thom.* 114.

Nor should it cause any surprise that *Dial. Sav.* 57, like *Gosp. Thom.* 17, seems to regard 1 Cor. 2.9 as a saying of Jesus,[245] or that the theme of 'rest' is common in the *Dialogue* (1, 2, 65, 68) as in *Thomas* (50.3, 60.6, 86.2, 90.2), or that being 'solitary' (*monachos*) is an ideal commended in both (*Gosp. Thom.* 16, 49, 75; *Dial. Sav.* 1, 2).[246]

In short, the most obvious way to interpret the *Dialogue of the Saviour* is along the lines suggested for interpretation of the *Gospel of Thomas*. The association between the Synoptic-like Jesus tradition and the *Dialogue of the Saviour* is much more flimsy than in the case of *Thomas*. But like *Thomas*, the *Dialogue of the Saviour* has a Gnostic-like perspective[247] to which Jesus and

---

more original reference to self-knowledge (*Dial. Sav.* 30) has been 'replaced quite surprisingly by a reference to knowledge of Jesus', 'a deliberate christological reinterpretation of the more traditional Gnostic dialogue' (*Ancient Christian Gospels* 180).

244. Koester notes that *Dial. Sav.* 'reveals a surprising familiarity with the sayings of the *Gospel of Thomas*' (*Ancient Christian Gospels* 185).

245. See also §43 n.276.

246. See again Uro, 'Is *Thomas* an Encratite Gospel?' 159-60.

247. 'The programme of the Dialogue of the Saviour may be seen in the saying about

his disciples have been recruited, but in the case of the *Dialogue*, with little to no purchase from the earlier Jesus tradition.[248]

b. *Apocryphon of James*

With the *Apocryphon of James* the case made by Koester for the Gospel of John evidencing some influence from or reaction to the *Apocryphon* is even less persuasive.[249] There are certainly indications of influence from early kerygmatic formulations:

- 6.2-4 — 'Verily I say unto you, none will be saved unless they believe in my cross';
- 8.11-15 — 'as to the word, its first part is faith; the second, love; the third, works; for from these comes life';
- The frequent talk of being 'filled' and 'full' (2.35–4.19) and references to the Spirit ('full of the Spirit' — 4.19; 5.22; 6.20; 9.28) echo the language of Luke and Paul;
- 13.23-25 — 'For your sakes I have placed myself under the curse, that you may be saved'; cf. Gal. 3.13;
- 14.30-31 — 'Today I must take (my place at) the right hand of the Father'.

More to the point, there is certainly some evidence of knowledge of or influence from Jesus tradition:

- There are several references to 'the kingdom of God/heaven' (3, 6-9, 12-14), though in each case the link with the Synoptic material is at best tenuous.[250]
    - 2.30-33 — 'No one will ever enter the kingdom of heaven at my bidding, but (only) because you yourselves are full'.[251]

---

seeking and finding, marveling, ruling and resting, as different stages in the attainment of *gnosis*' (B. Blatz, in Schneemelcher-Wilson, *NTA* 1.302).

248. Tuckett concludes: 'DialSav appears to presuppose certainly Matthew's, and probably Luke's finished gospels. There is no support here for Koester's theories about links between DialSav and synoptic tradition being at a pre-redactional stage so far as the synoptic gospels are concerned' (*Nag Hammadi* 134-35).

249. Koester draws heavily on Cameron, *Sayings Traditions*.

250. Cf. Köhler, *Rezeption* 383-84. A comment of Pheme Perkins on the *Gospel of Mary* is relevant here: 'Its incorporation of kingdom sayings of Jesus into the canonical framework of resurrection appearances suggests that the canonical Gospels played a crucial role in determining what could be credibly attributed to the Lord' (*Gnosticism* 183).

251. Koester infers that this passage presupposes a saying attested also in Mark 10.15

- 3.30-34 — 'Blessed are they who have not been ill, and have known relief before falling ill; yours is the kingdom of God'.
- 6.5-7 — 'those who have believed in my cross, theirs is the kingdom of God'.
- 7.22-23 — 'Do not allow the kingdom of heaven to wither'.
- 8.23-27 — 'So also can you yourselves receive the kingdom of heaven; unless you receive this through knowledge, you will not be able to find it'.
- 9.32-35 — 'Can you still bear to sleep, when it behooved you to be awake from the first, so that the kingdom of heaven might receive you?'
- 12.14-15, 22-30 — 'Do you think that many have found the kingdom of heaven? . . . For the kingdom of heaven is like an ear of grain after it had sprouted in a field. And when it had ripened it scattered its fruit and again filled the field with ears for another year. You also, hasten to reap an ear of life for yourselves that you may be filled with the kingdom!'
- 13.17-19, 26-36 — 'Do not make the kingdom of heaven a desert within you'. . . . Peter . . . said, 'Sometimes you urge us on to the kingdom of heaven, and then again you turn us back, Lord; sometimes you persuade and draw us to faith and promise us life, and then again you cast us forth from the kingdom of heaven'.
- 14.14-19 — 'Verily I say unto you, he who will receive life and believe in the kingdom will never leave it, not even if the Father wishes to banish him'.

- 4.23-30 — James answered, 'Lord, we can obey you if you wish, for we have forsaken our fathers and our mothers and our villages and followed you. Grant us, therefore, not to be tempted by the devil, the evil one'; cf. Mark 10.28-29 pars. and Matt. 6.13.
- 8.6-10 refers to a sequence of parables — 'The Shepherds' and 'The Seed' and 'The Builders' and 'The Lamps of the Virgins' and 'The Wage of the Workmen' and 'The Didrachmae' and 'The Woman' — which could readily be linked with Synoptic parables,[252] though if the parable

---

and John 3.3, 5 (*Ancient Christian Gospels* 190-91; cf. Cameron, *Sayings Traditions* 66-71), but it is only the motif of 'entering the kingdom' which is traditional.

252. Koester identifies the parables as Luke 16.4-6, Mark 4.3-9 pars., Matt. 7.24-27/ Luke 6.47-49, Matt. 25.1-12, Matt. 20.1-15, Luke 16.8-9 and Luke 18.2-8. Since the parables appear in all three Synoptic Gospels he concludes that 'this list of parables . . . is the only strong indication for use of canonical gospels in this writing', but the passage is probably an interpolation into the text of the *Apocryphon* (*Ancient Christian Gospels* 196-97).

which follows is an example of the *Apocryphon*'s parables they could have been quite different from the Synoptic parables.

- 8.16-23 — 'The word is like a grain of wheat; when someone has sown it, he had faith in it; and when it sprouted, he loved it because he had seen many grains in place of one. And when he had worked, he was saved because he had prepared it for food, (and) again he left (some) to sow. So also can you receive the kingdom of heaven . . .' — somewhat like the kingdom parable in Mark 4.26-29.
- The risen Jesus speaking of his descent and of his (the Son) ascending 'to the place from whence I came' (8-10, 13-15) parallels the Johannine descent/ascent of the Son of Man, but dependence on or derivation from one or the other is hardly demonstrable.
- 12.41–13.1 — 'Blessed will they be who have not seen, [yet have believed]!' may have been influenced by John 20.29, but the context is quite different.

That there are some connections here is evident, but they can best be described as remote, a connectedness at some remove from the Synoptic and Johannine Jesus tradition.[253] Any argument that the *Apocryphon* is evidence of forms of the Jesus tradition earlier than the Synoptic and Johannine versions is again tendentious,[254] even more so than in the case of the *Dialogue of the Saviour*. Absence of Synoptic or redactional features in particular echoes of Jesus tradition[255] is itself no evidence of pre-Synoptic/Johannine tradition, since the *Apocryphon* material is always bonded with traits at some remove from the Synoptic/Johannine parallels, and since the oral Jesus tradition must have been known and provided stimulus to different reflection in other circles. The impression given by the *Apocryphon* is rather of distant echoes and fading influence.[256]

---

253. Koester offers some other parallels between the *Apocryphon* and John, but the parallels are thin (*Ancient Christian Gospels* 195-96); Koester notes that there is no evidence of dependence of the *Apocryphon* on John, but is willing to argue that John 14.9 is a polemical rejection of the belief expressed in *Apoc. Jas.* 12.35-40, and that John 16.26 is a similar rejection of *Apoc. Jas.* 9.4-6, even though Jesus as intercessor and advocate is a thoroughly Johannine motif (John 17; 1 John 2.2).

254. Cameron maintains that the echoes of Jesus-tradition suggest 'that the *Ap. Jas.* is based on independent sayings collections that were contemporary with other early Christian writings' (*Sayings Traditions* 130). Koester finds Cameron's arguments convincing (*Ancient Christian Gospels* 189 n.5, 200). Tuckett finds it likely that *Apoc. Jas.* knew Matthew and Luke (*Nag Hammadi* 87-97).

255. An observation on which Cameron builds too much (*Sayings Traditions* 10, 53-54, 125-26).

256. The structural parallel between *Apoc. Jas.* 5.33–6.7 and Mark 8.31-33 (Cameron, *Sayings Traditions* 85-90) is a good example.

The influences of a Gnosticizing Jesus tradition, as in *Thomas* and the *Dialogue*, are equally thin: 'your heart is drunken; do you not, then, desire to be sober?' (3.9-10); reference to 'what to say before the archons' in context of talk of descent and implied ascent (8.35–9.4); 'none of those who have worn the flesh will be saved' (12.12-13); 'I shall strip myself that I may clothe myself' (14.35-36). In fact, the *Apocryphon* is better regarded as exemplifying a syncretistic spirituality which drew from various sources and which the Nag Hammadi community would have found sufficiently of interest and relevance to be included in their codices.

One of the most intriguing features of the *Apocryphon* is that it combines the confession of its character as 'a secret book' with the claim to be 'remembering' what the Saviour had taught during the 550 days of his resurrection appearances (1.8-10, 2.8-21). The tension between a 'secret' book and 'remembered' teaching is obvious and is most simply explained as a rather ineffective strategy to overcome the inherent paradox of the claim: the writer was conscious that his teaching was somewhat remote from what was usually understood as Jesus tradition, and could only hope to pass it off as Jesus' teaching on the grounds that it had been given secretly to James and Peter (1.10-12).[257]

Equally interesting is another indication of the transition from oral tradition to written book (2.10-15): the revelation given to the twelve disciples in the prolonged period of post-resurrection appearances was being recalled and written down. This suggests that the teaching of the *Apocryphon* was recognized to be too distant from the oral Jesus tradition so that it could only hope to become established in and by means of a written document.

c. Other Revelation Dialogues

Other revelation dialogues, purporting to be dialogues between Jesus and one or more of his disciples, have even less, indeed no visible rootage in the Jesus tradition and reflect later spiritual reflections novelistically attached to the names of Jesus' disciples.[258] They are indicative of the fascination which

---

257. The 'remembering' here is notably different from the 'remembering' of *1 Clem.* 13.2 and Polycarp, *Phil.* 2.3, where the Jesus tradition being remembered is clear, allowing for the usual variation of oral transmission. *Apoc. Jas.* 2.8-15 is not evidence for the acceptability of free creation of Jesus tradition (*pace* Cameron, *Sayings Traditions* ch. 3), but rather evidence of the *Apocryphon*'s attempt to claim the authority of Jesus' teaching 'remembered'.

258. 'The persistent appeal to *secret* teachings of Jesus given to one or another of the apostles is a tacit admission that not very much support could be gained from his acknowledged *public* teachings' (Hill, *Who Chose the Gospels?* 235).

§44.6   *The Jesus Tradition in the Second Century*

the reputation of Jesus exercised in wider circles of second- and third-century spirituality, but little more.²⁵⁹ For example, the *Gospel of the Egyptians*, known to us only in fragments cited by Clement of Alexandria,²⁶⁰ seems to be a dialogue between Jesus and Salome, but evidences no rootage in the earlier Jesus tradition. The *Book of Thomas the Contender* introduces itself as 'The secret words that the Saviour spoke to Judas Thomas and which I Matthew wrote down'. But it shows almost no relation to Jesus tradition known from elsewhere; 'the overwhelming mass of the material clearly represents traditions and ideas that are of a quite different nature and essentially non-Christian, and even alien to Christianity'.²⁶¹ Similarly with *The First Apocalypse of James*: 'apart from the importance attributed to James the Just there is little in the writing that can with any confidence be attributed to the influence of Jewish Christianity in particular. There is a good possibility, then, that the figure of James was chosen by a circle of Gnostics as a convenient peg on which to hang their teaching'.²⁶²

44.6 Gnostic Gospels 2

We need refer only briefly to other documents more justly described as Gnostic Gospels, since they become increasingly remote from the early Jesus tradition.²⁶³ Their content is clearly late, and it is almost impossible to mount an argument of any weight that the content derives from variant forms of first-

---

259. The *Epistula Apostolorum* may be an exception since it draws on the Gospel of John (Hill, *Johannine Corpus* 367-69; and above §44.4c), but it is an anti-Gnostic work that deals with the kind of questions on christology and eschatology which must have provided the grist of theological reflection in the second century (Koester, *Introduction* 2.236-38). The *Epistula Apostolorum* 'mimics a form of revelation literature which was popular among many Gnostics, attempting to combat its opponents with their own theological weapons' (Cameron, *Other Gospels* 132).

260. See above §44.4a. On the *Gospel of the Egyptians* (not the Nag Hammadi Gospel of the same name) see further Cameron, *Other Gospels* 49-52; Schneemelcher, in Schneemelcher-Wilson, *NTA* 1.209-15; Elliott, *ANT* 16-19. Cameron boldly concludes: 'If an Egyptian provenance is granted, the Gospel of the Egyptians shows that the Jesus movement there was, from the outset, influenced by gnosticism' (*Other Gospels* 50).

261. H.-M. Schenke, in Schneemelcher-Wilson, *NTA* 1.239; full text 241-47; also Tuckett, *Nag Hammadi* 83-87; J. D. Turner, in Robinson, *NHL* 201-7; Meyer, *Gnostic Gospels* 205-18.

262. W. R. Schoedel and D. M. Parrott, in Robinson, *NHL* 260; full text in 262-68; also W.-P. Funk, in Schneemelcher-Wilson, *NTA* 1.320-27.

263. See those cited in H.-C. Puech and B. Blatz, in Schneemelcher-Wilson, *NTA* Part IX.

century Jesus tradition. I will limit examination to what may be considered the most interesting.

a. The *Gospel of Philip*

The *Gospel of Philip*[264] is best described as a *florilegium*, a miscellany or anthology of sayings,[265] with something of the character of the commonplace books of early modern Europe,[266] or subsequently almanacs. Its inspiration can be called Christian: unusually the word 'Christian' appears several times in self-reference (as in 49, 59, 95); and it talks much about Jesus, the Nazorean, the Christ (e.g. 9a, 19, 47, 70, 81a, 83), though it does not attribute its teaching to Jesus. However, one of the sources from which it draws material was certainly early Christian tradition, though used for *Philip*'s own end:[267]

23b	—	1 Cor. 15.50 and John 6.53;
60	—	cf. Eph. 5.32;
69d	—	cf. Matt. 6.6;
72a	—	Mark 15.34;
74	—	cf. John 3.5-8;
76	—	cf. John 4.23;
89	—	Matt. 3.15;
110a	—	John 8.34 and 1 Cor. 8.1;

264. For the text see Isenberg, *NHL* 141-60; II.-M. Schenke, 'Gospel of Philip', in Schneemelcher-Wilson, *NTA* 1.179-208; Meyer, *Gnostic Gospels* 45-87; Ehrman, *Lost Scriptures* 38-44. I follow the verse numbers given by Schenke. Koester does not treat *GPhil* and *Gosp. Truth*, since they are 'not to be counted as Gospels' (*Ancient Christian Gospels* 47).

265. See particularly M. L. Turner, *The Gospel according to Philip: The Sources and Coherence of an Early Christian Collection* (Nag Hammadi and Manichaean Studies 38; Leiden: Brill, 1996), who notes that notebooks and miscellanies were common features of classical society. Wilson describes it as 'a Christian form of Gnosticism adhered to by former Jews', but 'anti-Jewish, if largely on a metaphysical level' (*Related Strangers* 201, 207).

266. 'Such books were essentially scrapbooks filled with items of every kind: medical recipes, quotes, letters, poems, tables of weights and measures, proverbs, prayers, legal formulas. Commonplaces were used by readers, writers, students, and humanists as an aid for remembering useful concepts or facts they had learned. Each commonplace book was unique to its creator's particular interests' (Wikipedia, 'Commonplace book').

267. 'It is clear that the author of *GPhil* uses Matthew only where it could be made serviceable to his intentions' (Köhler, *Rezeption* 399). See also Tuckett, *Nag Hammadi* 72-81. G. Röhl, *Die Rezeption des Johannesevangeliums in christlich-gnostischen Schriften aus Nag Hammadi* (Frankfurt: Europäische Hochschulschriften: Reihe 23, 1991), finds *Philip*'s use of Johannine material to be incidental and unreflective of the actual content of John's Gospel (162-63).

§44.6   *The Jesus Tradition in the Second Century*

111b —Luke 10.34 and 1 Pet. 4.8;
123b —Matt. 3.10;
123c —John 8.32;
126a —Matt. 15.13.

Its curiosities include:

- 17a — Some said: 'Mary conceived by the Holy Spirit'. They are in error! They do not know what they are saying! When did a woman ever conceive by a woman?[268]
- 17c — The Lord [would] not [have] said: 'My F[ather who art] in heaven' if [he] had not (also) [ano]ther father; but he would have said simply:['My Father'].
- 26a — Jesus deceived everyone. For he did not show himself as he was; but he showed himself as [they would] be able to see him.
- 31 — The perfect conceive through a kiss and give birth.
- 33 — 'The Father' and 'the Son' are simple names; 'the Holy Spirit is a double name'.
- 42 — Cain was begotten in adultery. For he was the son of the serpent.
- 44 — You saw the Spirit and became spirit. You saw Christ and became Christ. You saw the [Father] and will become Father.
- 55b — The S[aviour lov]ed [Ma]ry Mag[da]lene more than [all] the disciples and kissed on her [mouth] often.
- 72a — Jesus' cry of dereliction seems to be interpreted as the human Jesus' sense of abandonment by the heavenly Christ who left him before his death.
- 78 — If the woman had not separated from the man, she would not have died with the man. The separation from him became the origin of death.
- 90a — Those who say that they will die first and (only then) rise again are in error. If they do not first receive the resurrection while they are still alive, when they die they will receive nothing.
- 95 — The chrism is superior to baptism. For from the chrism we were called 'Christians', not from the baptism.

The *Gospel of Philip* also contains characteristic Gnostic, specifically Valentinian themes,[269] though not all its material by any means can be described

---

268. Cf. Origen, *on John* 2.12: 'If any should lend credence to the Gospel according to the Hebrews, where the Saviour himself says, "My mother, the Holy Spirit . . .", he will have difficulty in explaining how the Holy Spirit can be the mother of Christ' (Elliott, *ANT* 9).

269. Notably the intriguing mystery of the bridal chamber, which has the character of the innermost initiation (following baptism, chrism and eucharist) of a mystery cult (particu-

as Gnostic.[270] If composed by a Gnostic, it was a Gnostic open to a wider range of teachings. If an expression of a wider syncretistic spirituality, it contained sufficient Gnostic teaching to commend itself to the Nag Hammadi compositors. But if Christian 'Gospel' is defined either by its content of teaching which derived from Jesus (Jesus tradition) or by its account of the mission of Jesus in Galilee-Judea climaxing in his death and resurrection, then the *Gospel of Philip* hardly justifies the title 'Gospel', or can be only so described in a sense quite remote from the original use of the word as a Christian term.

b. *The Gospel of Truth*

The Gospel of Truth,[271] somewhat similarly, echoes the Christian gospel and draws on earlier Jesus tradition, particularly the Johannine tradition:[272]

> 18.16-21 — Jesus the Christ . . . showed (them) a way; and the way is the truth which he taught them (cf. John 14.6).
> 20.11-14 — Jesus was patient in accepting sufferings . . . since he knows that his death is life for many.
> 20.25 — He was nailed to a tree.
> 31.28-29 — He became a way for those who had gone astray.
> 31.35–32.4 — He is the shepherd who left behind the ninety-nine sheep which were not lost. He went searching for the one which had gone astray. He rejoiced when he found it . . . (cf. Matt. 18.12-13/Luke 15.4-6).
> 32.18-25 — Even on the Sabbath, he labored for the sheep which had fallen into the pit. . . . (cf. Matt. 12.9-13).
> 33.15-16 — Do not return to what you have vomited to eat it (cf. 2 Pet. 2.22).

---

larly 61a, 66, 68, 76, 79, 98, 122a-d, 125a, 127); in 39 we find a distinction between Echamoth and Echmoth ('Echamoth is simply Wisdom, but Echmoth is the Wisdom of death . . . "the little Wisdom"') evidently drawing on the Valentinian myth of the lower Sophia, 'Achamoth'. See further Schenke, 'Gospel of Philip', *NTA* 1.186-87; Turner, *Gospel of Philip* chs. 8-9, who reviews the material associated with the 'Thomas' traditions (206-26); P. Foster, 'The Gospel of Philip', in Foster, ed., *Non-Canonical Gospels* 68-83.

270. It is unclear whether the Nag Hammadi *Gospel of Philip* is the same as the *Gospel of Philip* attested by Epiphanius, which he describes as revealing what the soul must say as it ascends to heaven (see again Schenke, *NTA* 1.180-81).

271. Text in H. W. Attridge and G. W. MacRae, *NHL* 38-51; Meyer, *Gnostic Gospels* 91-112; Ehrman, *Lost Scriptures* 45-51.

272. Tuckett argues that the sole source for *Gosp. Truth*'s Synoptic material was Matthew (*Nag Hammadi* 57-68).

38.7-24 — The Son makes visible the invisible name of the Father; similarly 27.7-8 (cf. John 1.18).[273]

But the characteristic notes are the same Gnostic features as we noted in the case of the *Gospel of Thomas*: repeated emphasis on knowledge, as bringing enlightenment to those shrouded in a fog, lost in ignorance and darkness, drunk, sunk in sleep,[274] and bringing them to rest, the resting-place of the Father.[275] Two passages illustrate the essential message:

- 21.11-18 — If one has knowledge, he receives what are his own and draws them to himself. For he who is ignorant is in need, and what he lacks is great, since he lacks that which will make him perfect.
- 22.13-20 — He who is to have knowledge in this manner knows where he comes from and where he is going. He knows as one who having been drunk has turned away from his drunkenness, (and) having returned to himself, has set right what are his own.

It is probable, then, that the Gospel of John was well known and appreciated in the Valentinian community from which the *Gospel of Truth* came.[276] But that does not imply that John had a Valentinian tendency. For it is sufficiently clear that the Johannine tradition used was being drawn into a different conception of human need and of the answering good news.[277] Given the already high regard in which Christians held Jesus, there was a natural, probably unavoidable tendency for him to be drawn into other systems and to be presented as the bearer of the alternative good news. But the good news thus presented answered the very different analysis of the human condition and is only tangentially aligned with the gospel of the NT letters and Gospels.

---

273. For other possible echoes of John's Gospel see Barrett, *John* 113-14; and more fully, 'The Theological Vocabulary of the Fourth Gospel and of the Gospel of Truth', in W. Klassen and G. F. Snyder, eds., *Current Issues in New Testament Interpretation* (London: SCM, 1962) 210-23, 297-98, reprinted in *Essays on John* (London: SPCK, 1982) 50-64; also Schnackenburg, *John* 1.146-48; J. A. Williams, *Biblical Interpretation in the Gnostic Gospel of Truth from Nag Hammadi* (SBLDS 79; Atlanta: Scholars, 1988).

274. *Gosp. Truth* 17.10-13, 30-31; 18.4-22; 22.16-20; 24.32–25.3; etc.

275. *Gosp. Truth* 22.9-12; 24.14-20; 42.21-25; 43.1.

276. Barrett's carefully argued conclusion in his 'Theological Vocabulary' was that the great weight of probability indicated that the author of the *Gospel of Truth*, possibly Valentinus himself, had read John's Gospel.

277. If this is the same *Gospel of Truth* to which Irenaeus refers, his judgment is sound: 'it agrees in nothing with the Gospels of the Apostles' (*adv. haer.* 3.9.11). See further Hill, *Johannine Corpus* 264-70.

c. *The Gospel of Mary*

The Gospel of Mary,[278] so far as we are concerned, has only one significant echo of earlier Jesus tradition, which, however, incorporates a cluster of echoes: Jesus 'greeted them all, saying, "Peace be with you. Receive my peace to yourselves. Beware that no one leads you astray, saying, 'Lo here!' or 'Lo there!' For the Son of Man is within you. Follow after him! Those who seek him will find him. Go and preach the gospel of the kingdom"' (8.13-22).[279] It reflects also some of the early Angst in early Christian circles: the disciples 'were grieved. They wept greatly, saying, "How shall we go to the gentiles and preach the gospel of the kingdom of the Son of Man? If they did not spare him, how will they spare us?"' (9.5-12). But these are incidental to the vision of the Lord which was granted to Mary Magdalene and which climaxes (several pages are missing) in a description of the soul ascending to heaven overcoming the four powers which would block the way to rest (15.1–17.7).

Most fascinating is the concluding section in which Peter and Andrew are depicted as denying that Jesus said these things, and to a woman. Levi intervenes and protests on Mary's behalf, pointing out what Peter had already acknowledged, that the Saviour loved Mary more than the rest of women, 'more than us' (10.1-3; 17.10–18.21). This can plausibly be seen as reflecting tensions within second-century Christianity — Andrew and Peter representing the main line of the Jesus tradition, while the woman, Mary Magdalene, interestingly, is presented as the spokesperson of a different understanding of the gospel, also claimed to be from Jesus, but doubted by Andrew and Peter.[280] That leadership of the mainline second-century Christians was somewhat embarrassed by the fact that the first witness to the risen Christ was Mary Magdalene, *apostolos apostolorum* (John 20.1-18),[281] is not at all unlikely; but if so, it is equally worthy of note that Gnostic Christians attributed their version of the salvation process to Mary — though the fact that it was some of the early

---

278. Text in G. W. MacRae and R. McL. Wilson, *NHL* 524-27 (but it is not one of the Nag Hammadi codices); Ehrman, *Lost Scriptures* 35-37; and particularly Tuckett, who sets out the three papyrus texts separately (*Gospel of Mary* Part II). See also R. Griffith-Jones, *Beloved Disciple: The Misunderstood Legacy of Mary Magdalene, the Woman Closest to Jesus* (New York: Harper, 2008).

279. 8.14-15 (John 20.19, 21, 26); 8.15-17 (Mark 13.5, 21 pars.); 8.18-19 (Luke 17.21); 8.19-20 (cf. Mark 8.34 pars.); 8.20-21 (cf. Matt. 7.7/Luke 11.9); 8.21-22 (cf. Matt. 24.14). *Gosp.Mary* 7.8-9 and 8.10-11 also uses the familiar 'He who has ears to hear, let him hear'. See further Tuckett, *Nag Hammadi* 36-38; also *Gospel of Mary* ch. 5.

280. K. L. King, *NHL* 524; Lührmann, *Die apokryph gewordenen Evangelien* 122-23.

281. Paul, after all, had omitted any mention of the women witnesses of the risen Christ in the early creedal statement of 1 Cor. 15.5-7.

Gnostics who reacted against an overly patriarchal mainstream may not be counted as good news.[282]

d. *The Gospel of the Saviour*

The Gospel of the Saviour is not of great significance.[283] It certainly shows knowledge of the NT Gospels — notably

- 17-19 — For it is written, 'I will strike the shepherd, and the sheep of the flock will be scattered'. So I am the good shepherd. I lay down my life for you (Matt. 26.31; John 10.11);
- 48 — O my [father], if it be [possible], let this [cup] pass from me (Matt. 26.39);
- 70 — Do not touch me until I ascend to [my Father and your Father], to [my God and] your God . . . (John 20.17);
- 75 — A little while I am among you (John 7.33; 13.33; 14.19; 16.16-19);
- also 42 has a clear echo of Rev. 4.10.

The document's principal curiosity is that it concludes with the Saviour addressing the cross ('O cross'), calling on the cross not to be afraid and assuring it that he was rich and would fill the cross with his wealth (104-19)[284] — a personification of the cross similar to what we find in the *Acts of Andrew* 349, and not far from *Gosp.Peter* 9.39.[285]

Apart from the evident knowledge of Matthew and John (the above passages have more the character of direct quotations, particularly from John's Gospel, than sayings drawn from an independent oral tradition), the *Gospel of the Saviour* simply illustrates the sort of syncretistic religious speculation to which the Jesus tradition contributed and into which some of it was drawn.

e. *The Gospel of Judas*

The Gospel of Judas, despite the publicity which its publication received, is of little relevance to us since its thought is characteristically Gnostic, in particular

---

282. Note the similar prominence apparently given to Salome in the *Gospel of the Egyptians* (not to be confused with the Nag Hammadi text with the same title; see Elliott, *ANT* 16), as also the prominence of women in the apocryphal Acts (§40 nn.284, 285).
283. The text is most conveniently accessible in Ehrman, *Lost Scriptures* 52-56.
284. Hedrick and Mirecki, *Gospel of the Savior* 54-57, 115-16.
285. See below §44.7a.

Sethian,[286] and the motivation driving *Judas* has moved far from the first-century Jesus tradition. The opening words — 'the secret revelatory discourse in which Jesus spoke with Judas Iscariot for eight days, three days before he celebrated Passover' (33.1-6) — are typical of a message which cannot claim to be drawn from earlier Jesus tradition and can only attribute its teaching to Jesus by claiming to have been secretly given.[287]

One example should suffice.[288] In a parody of the Synoptic tradition of Peter's confession of Jesus as Messiah (Mark 8.27-30 pars.), the disciples confess Jesus to be 'the son of our God' (*Judas* 34.11-13)[289]— Jesus is never referred to in *Judas* as Messiah (his Jewish manhood was of no relevance).[290] But Jesus then rebukes them that they do not know him (34.14-18) and they 'curse him in their hearts' (34.21-22);[291] whereas Judas goes on to give the truer confession, 'You came from the immortal Aeon of Barbelo, and the one who sent you is he whose name I am not worthy to speak' (35.17-20).[292]

The second part of *Judas* (47-57) is largely devoted to a typically Gnostic

---

286. The Sethian character of the *Gospel of Judas* is generally agreed; see particularly J. D. Turner, 'The Place of the *Gospel of Judas* in Sethian Tradition', in Scopello, ed., *The Gospel of Judas in Context* 187-237. Of the most Sethian passage (47-57), M. Meyer observes, 'Except for one brief aside in the text, there is nothing whatsoever that is specifically Christian in the revelation' ('Interpreting Judas: Ten Passages in the *Gospel of Judas*', in Scopello, ed., *Judas* 41-55 [here 49]).

287. Cf. the prologues to the *Gospel of Thomas* and *Thomas the Contender*.

288. For other possible indications of *Judas*'s knowledge of or influence from Matthew see Gathercole, *Judas* 134-38. J. M. Robinson, 'The Sources of the *Gospel of Judas*', in Scopello, ed., *Judas* 59-67, finds evidence that *Judas* knew Luke's Gospel (60-61). See also U.-K. Plisch, 'Judasevangelium und Judasgedicht', in Frey and Schröter, eds., *Jesus in apokryphen Evangelienüberlieferungen* 387-96.

289. 'The reference to "*our* God" is a reference to the Demiurge Ialdabaoth, the lesser god, the creator and biblical god whom the Sethian Gnostics believed apostolic Christians worshipped' (DeConick, *Thirteenth Apostle* 97).

290. 'Jesus' credentials as Jewish Messiah have been swept aside in preference for his role as Gnostic redeemer' (S. Gathercole, 'The *Gospel of Judas*: An Unlikely Hero', in Foster, ed., *Non-Canonical Gospels* 84-95 [here 93]).

291. 'Such a picture of the twelve disciples would have completely spoiled the authority of the twelve, upon which rested the faith of the entire apostolic church, a faith and a church that the Sethians wished to undermine and defeat' (DeConick, *Thirteenth Apostle* 100). The attack on the twelve is most explicit in 38.1–41.6, where they are depicted as corrupt priests offering useless sacrifices; see also Gathercole, *Judas* 77-80. E. Pagels and K. L. King, *Reading Judas: The Gospel of Judas and the Shaping of Christianity* (London: Allen Lane, 2007) are content to view *Gosp.Judas* as 'only one more retelling of a much-told tale, but it gives this story a radical new twist, one that turns the tables on "the twelve"' (31).

292. DeConick, 'The *Gospel of Judas*: A Parody of Apostolic Christianity', in Foster, ed., *Non-Canonical Gospels* 96-109, argues strongly that Judas is presented negatively and not positively; with further bibliography (108-9; see also §40 n.233 above).

(Sethian) attempt to explain how the world in all its imperfections derived ultimately from 'the great invisible spirit' — that is, by an almost limitless sequence of descending orders of being, until there is some illegitimacy in the line of descent, here identified with Ialdabaoth and Saklas (51.8-17), who creates Adam and Eve (52.14-21).[293] Such an elaborate cosmology almost certainly marks a later stage in Gnostic systems than the 'revelation of true nature' exemplified by the *Gospel of Thomas* and the *Dialogue of the Saviour*, which suggests a date no earlier than the middle of the second century.

f. *Secret Mark*

Finally mention should be made of *Secret Mark*.[294] As already noted, the putative letter of Clement of Alexandria contains two citations from a longer text of the Gospel of Mark, following Mark 10.32-34 and 10.46a. However, the brief text seems to be made up of a mélange of phrases from and echoes of the NT Gospels.[295] So even if authentic, and not a forgery, it can hardly be regarded as an earlier version of Mark's Gospel.[296] Its implication of a

---

293. See further Gathercole, *Judas* 86-103; DeConick, *Thirteenth Apostle* 32-39.

294. Text in Cameron, *Other Gospels* 69-71; Ehrman, *Lost Scriptures* 88-89; Elliott, *ANT* 149.

295. Echoes are discernible from Mark 1, 4, 5, 9, 10, 14, Matt. 7 and John 3, 11 and 20.

296. Koester argues tortuously that the extant text of canonical Mark is a secondary redaction of 'the original Mark' known to Matthew and Luke, that *Secret Mark* is the work of the same redactor, and that 'the canonical Mark . . . is an abbreviated version of the *Secret Gospel of Mark*' (*Ancient Christian Gospels* 293-303, here 302; similarly Cameron, *Other Gospels* 68). But here too Koester builds far too much on differences in the Synoptic tradition, which are more readily explained in terms of oral tradition variations. Crossan also argues 'that "canonical" Mark was a purified version of the "secret" Gospel' (*Four Other Gospels* 107), but infers with similar implausibility that 'canonical Mark scattered the dismembered elements of those units [of *Secret Mark* which canonical Mark had eliminated] throughout his gospel' (108, 111). On the contrary, it is much more likely that *Secret Mark* was composed drawing phrases and material from elsewhere in NT Mark, than that an editor produced NT Mark by scattering phrases from *Secret Mark* through his revision. H. Merkel, *NTA* 1.106-9, only slightly overstates his case: 'Anyone who reads the text impartially will rather gain the impression that here the raising of Lazarus in Jn. 11 is adapted in an abridged form, with the admixture of numerous echoes of Synoptic pericopes' (107). Marcus sums up his brief treatment of the 'Secret Gospel' by concluding that 'Contrary to Koester, Secret Mark is more likely a redaction of Canonical Mark than the other way around' (*Mark 1-8* 47-51).

Similarly, Koester's claim, that the absence of distinctive Johannine features shows it to be 'impossible that *Secret Mark* is dependent upon John 11' (296), is an absurd overstatement since use and adaptation of an older story (as in John 11) can abbreviate and allude to as well as repeat and expand, as many Synoptic parallels illustrate. Presence of an Evangelist's distinctive characteristics probably do imply influence from that Evangelist;

mystery-type initiation of 'the young man', and/or of a homosexual relationship between the young man and Jesus[297] reflects more the kind of speculation with which Clement elsewhere shows himself to be familiar.[298] It confirms that Mark's Gospel was well-known and used (as also John's Gospel), but it provides no further information about the Jesus tradition or about its influence in the second century.

In sum, the Gnostic Gospels show awareness of and reliance on the Jesus tradition as known to us from the NT Gospels, but provide no evidence of Jesus tradition which might have been known to but unused by the NT Gospel writers. They provide evidence only of Jesus tradition elaborated and adapted to fit with anthropological and soteriological claims, which, as with the *Gospel of Thomas*, had been drawn from a different perception of the human condition. Not least of interest are the number of indications that some groups saw in the special relationship between Jesus and Mary Magdalene opportunity to contest the patriarchal leadership of the great church.

44.7 Narrative Gospels

There are also Gospels or closely related writings which develop the narrative tradition of the first-century New Testament Gospels. They are almost all novelistic, speculative and often fantastical elaborations of parts of the Gospel accounts which were too brief or left many questions unanswered.

a. *Gospel of Peter*

The most striking is the *Gospel of Peter*, which seems to be an elaboration of early traditions of the crucifixion, burial and resurrection of Jesus.[299] There has been a notable attempt to find embedded in the *Gospel of Peter* an early,

---

but absence of such characteristics provides an argument from silence and proves nothing. We have found too many variant echoes and allusions to Jesus tradition and to tradition specific to particular Gospels in the above pages for such another tendentious argument (regrettably typical of Koester on this subject) to be persuasive.

297. See further Foster, *Non-Canonical Gospels* 178-80.
298. See §40 n.256 above.
299. I follow the translation used by Elliott, *ANT* 154-58; for explanation of the numbering of the text, see Schneemelcher, *NTA* 1.217. For introductory matters see above §40.4d.

indeed the original, passion narrative.³⁰⁰ But dependence of the *Gospel of Peter* on the NT Gospels, perhaps only through second orality, is clearly to be seen — for example, Pilate's washing his hands at Jesus' trial and the guard set on Jesus' tomb from Matthew (*Gosp.Pet.* 1.1/Matt. 27.24; *Gosp.Pet.* 8.29–11.49/ Matt. 27.62-66; 28.11-15),³⁰¹ and the repentant thief from Luke (*Gosp.Pet.* 4.13/Luke 23.40-41).³⁰² The variations from the NT Gospel tradition are partly to be explained in terms of the variations within the Jesus tradition on Jesus' passion: greater awareness of the phenomenology of oral tradition has made clear that variation in tradition is to be explained more likely by social variables affecting different performances than by literary-type redaction;³⁰³ the NT Gospels themselves provide clear testimony that there was no single (written) version of Jesus' passion from which the different passion narratives were derived.³⁰⁴ But no doubt the *Gospel of Peter*'s version is also to be explained

300. Crossan, *Four Other Gospels* 125-81; also *The Cross That Spoke: The Origins of the Passion Narrative* (San Francisco: Harper & Row, 1988); also *Historical Jesus* 385-87; also 'The *Gospel of Peter* and the Canonical Gospels', in Kraus and Nicklas, eds., *Evangelium nach Petrus* 117-34. Crossan dates what he calls the *Cross Gospel* to the first stratum of Jesus tradition, in which he includes also the *Gospel of Thomas*, P.Egerton 2, and P.Oxy. 1224, as well as the early Pauline letters and Q (*Historical Jesus* 427-29). Crossan's thesis is taken further by P. A. Mirecki in *ABD* 5.280-81.

301. P.Oxy. 4009 also clearly draws on Matt. 10.16. Massaux (of course) finds evidence of definite literary influence from Matthew (*Influence* 2.201-7). For a more measured assessment see Köhler, *Rezeption* 437-48, and J. Verheyden, 'Some Reflections on Determining the Purpose of the "Gospel of Peter"', in Kraus and Nicklas, eds., *Evangelium nach Petrus* 286-90.

302. 'The *G.Pet.* . . . at least presupposes the material worked up in the canonical Gospels and has developed it further' (Köhler, *Rezeption* 442). 'In reality, the Gospel of Peter offers free novelistic elaborations of an earlier Gospel tradition from the collection of the four Gospels' (Hengel, *Four Gospels* 218 n.50). See further particularly R. E. Brown, 'The *Gospel of Peter* and Canonical Gospel Priority', *NTS* 33 (1987) 321-43; also *The Death of the Messiah* (2 vols.; New York: Doubleday, 1994) 2.1325-36. Koester also finds major problems with 'Crossan's ingenious hypothesis' (*Ancient Christian Gospels* 218-20). Foster critiques Mirecki as well as Crossan ('*Gospel of Peter*' 38-40).

303. See particularly A. Kirk, 'Tradition and Memory in the *Gospel of Peter*', in Kraus and Nicklas, eds., *Evangelium nach Petrus* 135-58 (here particularly his critique of Koester, 137-38, 154-56). Kirk in fact provides a more than adequate response to Crossan's final offer: 'If anyone can show me how a person who knows the canonical versions either as scribal documents or oral traditions got from them to the present *Gospel of Peter*, I would withdraw my proposed solution' ('*Gospel of Peter*' 134).

304. Koester, however, follows Crossan to the extent that he concludes that 'the *Gospel of Peter* has preserved the most original narrative version of the tradition of scriptural interpretation' (*Ancient Christian Gospels* 230). He bases his argument on the opinion of Philipp Vielhauer, that a description of Jesus' suffering using passages from the OT 'without quotation formulae' is 'older than the explicit scriptural proof' (quoted in *Gospels* 218). But it can be equally and more persuasively argued that a narrative making almost explicit use

by the curiosity which, for example, Matthew's story of the guard presumably provoked, and particularly by curiosity about the resurrection of Jesus itself. The fact that Jesus' resurrection is not described in the earlier Gospels would have provided sufficient incentive for an imaginative attempt to provide such an account.[305] Hence the striking and rather fantastical account of the stone rolling away 'of itself' from the mouth of the tomb, of 'two men' coming down from heaven and entering the tomb, and of the watching guard seeing 'three men come out from the sepulcher, two of them supporting the other and a cross following them, and the heads of the two reaching to heaven, but that of him who was being led reached beyond the heavens' (*Gosp.Pet.* 9.36–10.40).

There may be a docetic tinge in the document, as Serapion concluded: it is suggested that Jesus felt no pain on the cross (4.10); and Jesus cries out from the cross, 'My power, O power, you have forsaken me' (5.20). But even so, *Peter* can hardly be called a Gnostic Gospel.[306] Moreover, it implies that the Jews were responsible for the crucifixion itself (6.21) and attempts to exonerate Pilate (11.46), strengthening a tendency already evident in the NT Gospels, but probably also reflecting the increasing hostility towards Jews in second-century Christianity.[307] In any case, there is no real evidence in the *Gospel of Peter* of an account of Jesus' passion earlier than and independent

---

of Psalm passages, as in the Synoptic Gospels, was the more necessary from the first telling of the story of Jesus' passion if fellow Jews were to be persuaded that Jesus' death was 'in accordance with the scriptures' (see *Jesus Remembered* 777-79). As Swete noted, several of the allusions to the OT psalms and prophets are only recognizable when compared with the direct quotations in other writers (*Akhmim Fragment* xxvi-xxvii). See also T. Nicklas, 'Das Petrusevangelium im Rahmen antiker Jesustraditionen', in Frey and Schröter, eds., *Jesus in apokryphen Evangelienüberlieferungen* 223-52.

305. 'Tatian's *Diatessaron* shows that there was a tendency in the 2d cent. to create one consecutive story . . . , and the *Protevangelium of James* gives an imaginative recasting of the infancy stories from echoes of Matt and Luke combined with imaginative popular developments. Therefore, the work . . . would not have been an oddity in the early days of Christianity' (Brown, *Death of the Messiah* 2.1335).

306. As Brown observes, 'The passages cited . . . are capable of a nondocetic interpretation' (*Death of the Messiah* 2.1338); '. . . the question of the docetic or Gnostic character of the work is to be answered with an unambiguous negative'; 'Everything speaks for the view that the Gos.Pet. originated in a community which cannot be characterized by any description of heretics, whether old or new' (Schneemelcher, *NTA* 220, 221). See also M. Myllyoski, 'Die Kraft des Herrn: Erwägungen zur Christologie des Petrusevangeliums', in Kraus and Nicklas, *Evangelium nach Petrus* 301-26; with more bibliography, Verheyden, 'Purpose' 290-91.

307. See further Verheyden, 'Purpose' 291-98, with review of recent discussion. Several of the contributions to Kraus and Nicklas, *Evangelium nach Petrus*, discuss the possibility that the *Gospel of Peter* influenced other early (second- and third-century) Christian literature. But *Gosp.Pet.* is probably more representative of a second-century trend than itself particularly influential.

of the NT Gospels and of the traditions which they embody; and there is sufficient evidence of *Peter*'s dependence on distinctive features of the NT Gospels. The *Gospel of Peter* simply is a further demonstration that the story of Jesus' passion, and no doubt the claims made concerning it in the second-century churches, stirred a much wider interest in Jesus and in the claims made regarding his death and resurrection.

The same novelistic interest in expanding the story of Jesus' passion is evident in other documents named as Gospels, which may have included material which originated in the second century, particularly the *Acts of Pilate*.[308] But even if the *Acts* can be traced back to the second century the document is primarily an elaboration of the NT Gospels' passion narrative. It draws on John's account of Jesus' encounter with Pilate (John 18.30-38; *ActsPilate* 3; 4.3), the accusation that Jesus said he would be able to destroy the temple and build it in three days (Mark 14.58 pars.; *ActsPilate* 4.1), and Matthew's account of the Jewish crowd replying, 'His blood be on us and on our children' (Matt. 27.25; *ActsPilate* 4.1). Nicodemus features prominently (hence presumably the mediaeval title, the *Gospel of Nicodemus*), the two others crucified with Jesus are named, Dysmas and Gestas (9.4; 10.2), as also the soldier who pierced Jesus' side with a spear, Longinus (16.7), and, significantly, 14.1 quotes the long ending of Mark (Mark 16.15-18). But the motivation lies more in feeding the curiosity and imaginations of believers and other interested parties of later centuries. And the main interest of the *Acts* lies in the more developed christology (for example, the images on the Roman standards bow down and worship Jesus — 1.5, 6), the development of the charge that Jesus was born of fornication (2.3-5), and the more sympathetic portrayal of Pilate at the expense of the Jews.[309]

b. Other Infancy Gospels

The other more obvious gap for anyone interested in the full story of Jesus' life was the almost complete absence of information about his infancy and childhood. Here the NT Gospels, with only the birth narratives of Matthew and Luke and the isolated story of the young Jesus in Luke 2.41-51, could not help but provoke curiosity and prompt questions about the silent years. Thus with the *Protevangelium of James*,[310] although knowledge of the Matthew/

---

308. Text in Schneemelcher-Wilson, *NTA* 1.505-21; Elliott, *ANT* 169-85; Cameron, *Other Gospels* 165-82.

309. No more need be said about the *Gospel of Bartholomew* and the *Gospel of Gamaliel* (see §40 at nn.249 and 250).

310. Text in Schneemelcher-Wilson, *NTA* 1.426-39; Elliott, *ANT* 57-67; Cameron, *Other Gospels* 109-21; Ehrman, *Lost Scriptures* 64-72.

Luke birth narratives can certainly be assumed,[311] the further information it provides about Mary's parents (Joachim and Anna) is unlikely to be based on reliable information and is probably fanciful.[312]

The *Infancy Gospel of Thomas*[313] begins with the delightfully childish story of the five-year-old Jesus moulding twelve clay sparrows and bringing them to life (2). But it continues with stories of a petulant Jesus causing the death of playmates who offended him and the blindness of those who complained about him (3-5; also 14). The child Jesus not only knows his letters, but goes on to expound the mysteries of the first letter, Alpha (6-7). And, following several other striking miracles, he is worshipped (9, 10, 18). This narrative probably fulfilled the same role as cartoon strips in the twentieth century, and functioned at the same level.[314]

The same curiosity about the hidden years of Jesus presumably explains the subsequent traditions that Jesus spent seventeen years in India and Tibet, studying with Buddhist and Hindu holy men,[315] a variation on the superficially more plausible suggestion that Jesus had learned his wisdom and healing/(magical) techniques from his time in Egypt. And no sooner had the discovery of the Dead Sea Scrolls been publicized than the suggestion was advanced that Jesus had spent his hidden years at Qumran.[316]

What we learn from all such speculation, already in the second century, is that a fascinating figure like Jesus, whose impact was so manifest and enduring, was bound to stimulate questions as to his 'unknowns' and the source and explanation for the impact he made. But that is what we learn — that Jesus was perceived to be so important and his teaching so significant that it provoked such speculation, and that the various speculations were valued by some for some time — not that the speculations themselves were well rooted in reliable historical sources or the Jesus tradition, or that the speculations provide a lasting insight into Jesus.

Interesting as all these other Gospels are, then, there is no reason to rank them with the NT Gospels, or even with the *Gospel of Thomas* as witnesses to the

---

311. Cf. Massaux, *Influence* 2.228-36.

312. 'The *Protevangelium* contains no material of independent historical value and very little of historical value even where it parallels the canonical accounts' (Foster, '*Protevangelium*' 124).

313. Text in Schneemelcher-Wilson, *NTA* 1.444-51; Elliott, *ANT* 75-83; Cameron, *Other Gospels* 124-30; Ehrman, *Lost Scriptures* 58-62.

314. 'Probably written as Christian children's literature' — Hill, *Who Chose the Gospels?* 87, referring to R. Aasgaard, *The Childhood of Jesus: Decoding the Apocryphal Infancy Gospel of Thomas* (Eugene: Cascade Books, 2009) 168, 203.

315. N. Notovitch, *The Unknown Life of Jesus Christ* (Sydney: Axiom, 2007); see further 'Lost Years of Jesus' in Wikipedia.

316. C. F. Potter, *The Lost Years of Jesus Revealed* (1958; Fawcett, 1985).

continuing impact of the Jesus tradition. They certainly attest the significance attributed to Jesus and the fascination which his life and mission provoked, particularly in filling out with novelistic enthusiasm the gaps in the early forms of the tradition. They indicate that in the second century Jesus became such a focus of revelation and salvation that other analyses of the human condition were eager to draw him into their scheme and to credit some of their own insights to him, crediting and using the earlier Jesus tradition where they could. And one of the most interesting features of this (second half of the) second-century interaction with the Jesus tradition is the degree to which it attests less a continuing, living oral Jesus tradition (even with the agrapha), and indicates more a consistent dependence on knowledge and use of written Gospels, the NT Gospels as such. But overall, even when echoes and use of Jesus tradition are evident, the impression which the material gives is of an increasing remoteness from the earlier Jesus tradition, as elements in the Jesus tradition were attached to a distinctively different message of salvation, or human curiosity elaborated the earlier tradition to fill in gaps left by it. Particularly notable is the fact that the Gnostic Gospels typically had to base their claim for their distinctive message on teaching given secretly by Jesus, but previously unknown — in effect an admission that they could not base that message on the earlier Jesus tradition. Attempts to discern still earlier forms of the Jesus tradition in these sources both demonstrate the tendentiousness of those no longer willing to give credence to the NT Gospels and consistently lack credibility themselves.

44.8 The Recognition of the Four (Canonical) Gospels

The echoes of and allusions to Jesus tradition in the letters of the NT indicated clearly enough that the memory and use of Jesus' teaching was a lively feature of the worship and paraenesis of the churches represented in and by these letters. In the latter decades of the first century the use made of Mark's Gospel by both Matthew and Luke is manifest proof that at least one of the written Gospels (Mark) had become more widely known than the immediate circles from which it emerged. But the close study of the Christian documents from the first decades of the second century (§44.2) was surprisingly more ambiguous on what these documents revealed about the actual knowledge and use made of the Jesus tradition. That Jesus' teaching was still known orally and aurally was the most obvious conclusion. But there were sufficient indications that the Gospel of Matthew and probably also the Gospels of Luke and John were known and had influenced, by their own contributions, the character and content of the Jesus tradition. The inference which emerged was that the first half of the second century was a transition phase in the transmission and knowledge of the Jesus tradition, from a knowledge derived primarily from the still lively oral Jesus tradition, to a greater influence of and dependence on the written Gospels.

This transition phase is probably also indicated by the way in which the term *euangelion* may already have begun to feature during this period as a reference to a written g/Gospel.[317] Somewhat of a supporting consideration is the fact that Jesus tradition begins to be referred to in the same way as the (Jewish) scriptures, indeed possibly cited as scripture (*Barn.* 4.14; *2 Clem.* 2.4), where once again the probability is that one or another of the Gospels already in writing was the source of the quotation. We also recall that Aristides invited the king to read for himself in 'what is called the holy gospel writing' (15.1 Greek; 2.4 Syriac). Justin Martyr's knowledge of the Gospel in written form (*Dial.* 10.2; 100.2) and of more than one 'Gospel' (*1 Apol.* 66.3) is therefore quite characteristic for the middle of the second century.[318] And his report that 'the memoirs of the apostles' were read at Sunday Christian gatherings, and given the same reverence as was due to 'the writings of the prophets' (*1 Apol.* 67.3), reflects the same respect shown for the teaching of Jesus throughout that period.

If, then, Justin can be regarded as representative, it is clear that the Jesus tradition was known and used with the same sort of flexibility as before — whether drawn from oral tradition (liturgical or catechetical), or in second orality memory of readings, or hearing read one or another of the written Gospels. In all this we should still not think in terms of written Gospels either superseding (rendering redundant) the oral Jesus tradition or fixing the Jesus tradition in final written form. Nevertheless, it is the growing evidence of knowledge of and dependence on the written Gospels on which we will focus. By this I mean primarily the NT Gospels, since the evidence reviewed above in §44.4-7 is that the other documents known as Gospels were either increasingly sectarian versions of one of the NT Gospels (Matthew) or were primarily intent to promulgate a message which was quite different from the Jesus tradition even when added to it.

The simplest and most straightforward procedure is to summarize the evidence of knowledge and use of each of the four NT Gospels in turn as reviewed above.

317. See above (431, 439) on *Did.* 11.3 and 15.3-4; *2 Clem.* 8.5.
318. Hengel, however, notes that it is only after the time of Irenaeus (c. AD 180) that 'the church fathers speak without embarrassment of four "Gospels" in the plural' and that up until the middle of the second century 'they were quite strict in using the singular and never the plural'. 'Even in Irenaeus the use of the singular "Gospel" far exceeds that of the plural' (*Four Gospels* 3, 10).

a. Mark

There is in fact surprisingly little indication that the Gospel of Mark was known and used. However, such a finding is not really surprising. For Mark's Gospel had been so much absorbed into Matthew's Gospel that it is very difficult to distinguish any allusion to Jesus tradition as distinctively Markan. Since features of Mark, distinctive when it was first written (notably, its character as 'a passion narrative with an extensive introduction' — §41.2), were taken over by the subsequent Gospels, it is almost impossible to recognize such features as 'distinctively Markan'.

In fact, given that Matthew was in effect a second edition of Mark, it is more surprising that Mark's Gospel survived as a separate Gospel worth preserving in its own right. After all, if there was a Q document current in the middle of the first century, even if not so large as usually inferred from the non-Markan traditions shared by Matthew and Luke, then it was not preserved as a document, and so, presumably, was not thought worth preserving in its own right. The (complete?) takeover of Q's content by Matthew and Luke gave the material its enduring context, the context which provided what Luke and Matthew perceived to be the clearest meaning for the material, so that there was no need felt to retain the Q document itself. And if the *Gospel of Thomas* drew not dissimilarly on a Q document, then once again Q itself was not retained.

But Mark was retained, to be hailed by Irenaeus as one of the church's four core Gospels. The reason probably is that indicated by Papias: that Mark's Gospel was seen as derived from Peter, as the record of Peter's recollection and use of the Jesus tradition in his preaching.[319] The argument is somewhat convoluted, but nevertheless has merit: that the retention of Mark (largely hidden from modern perception) was itself a demonstration that Peter was (increasingly) venerated as Jesus' lead disciple. Mark was treasured because it was regarded as Petrine, the gospel according to Peter.

Always allowing that the knowledge shown may be of Matthew's or Luke's version of a shared tradition, we should at least note the possible allusions to Mark:

1 Clem. 13.2	Mark 11.25
1 Clem. 46.8	Mark 9.42; 14.21
Ign., *Eph.* 17.1	Mark 14.3
Polyc., *Phil.* 7.2	Mark 4.38
Polyc., *Phil.* 5.2	Mark 9.35
Barn. 5.9; *2 Clem.* 2.4; Justin, *1 Apol.* 15.8; P.Oxy. 1224	Mark 2.17

---

319. M. Hengel, *Der unterschätzte Petrus* (Tübingen: Mohr Siebeck, 2006) 164-65.

Hermas, *Mand.* 29(IV.1).6	Mark 10.17
Hermas, *Mand.* 30(IV.2).1	Mark 6.52
Hermas, *Mand.* 43(XI).12	Mark 12.39
Hermas, *Sim.* 97(IX.20).2-3	Mark 10.23
Papias	
Athenagoras, *Plea* 33.2	Mark 10.11
Justin, *1 Apol.* 16.7/*Dial.* 101.2	Mark 10.17-18
P.Egerton 2 frag. 2 recto	Mark 12.14-15
Fayyum Frag.	Mark 14.27, 29-30
P.Oxy. 1224	Mark 9.40
Strasburg Frag.	Mark 14.34, 38, 41
Epistula Apostolorum 5	Mark 5.6-13, 25-34
Gospel of Hebrews	Mark 1.9-11
Gospel of Ebionites	Mark 1.4-6; 3.31-35
Apoc. Jas. 8.16-23	cf. Mark 4.26-29
Gosp.Phil. 72a	Mark 15.34
Secret Mark	

Nor should it be forgotten that a longer ending was added to Mark, probably in the first half of the second century (attested also by *ActsPilate* 14.1), and that Tatian (and Theophilus) took it for granted that Mark's Gospel should be interwoven with the others in his *Diatessaron*. So, whether directly, or through Matthew, we can fairly conclude that the Jesus tradition inscribed by Mark was certainly well known, well used and well respected in the second century.

b. Matthew

It is clear from §§44.2-3 that a strong case can be made for the Gospel of Matthew being known and exerting a strong influence on the catechetical and paraenetic teaching of the Christian assemblies in the first three or four decades of the second century. Clear evidence for direct dependence on Matthew, that one of the Apostolic Fathers drew a sentence directly from his own reading of Matthew, is not there. But it is most unlikely that passages such as Ignatius, *Smyrn* 1.1, Polycarp, *Phil.* 2.3, *Did.* 1.2-6, 7.2-3 and 8.1-2 could have been written had Matthew not already been in writing and either was familiar to Ignatius, Polycarp and the Didachist or had influenced the shape of the traditional (oral) teaching material known to and used by many Christian churches.[320] *2 Clement*, Athenagoras, Theophilus and especially Justin Martyr,

---

320. See also above on Ign., *Eph.* 5.2; *Smyrn.* 6.1; Polyc., *Phil.* 2.2; 7.2; 12.3; *Did.* 9.5; 11.1-4, 7; 13.2; 16; *2 Clem.* 3.2; 4.2; 6.2; 9.11.

but also *Epistula Apostolorum*, the Jewish-Christian Gospels, the *Gospel of the Saviour*, the *Gospel of Philip*, the *Gospel of Truth* and especially the *Gospel of Peter* and the *Protevangelium of James* all bear testimony to knowledge of and influence from Matthew's Gospel.[321] It is no surprise, then, that so much attention has been focused on determining the influence of Matthew in particular on second-century Christianity,[322] since the Jesus tradition reviewed above displayed so many distinctively Matthean features.

In the light of such evidence of knowledge of or influence from Matthew there can be little doubt that the Gospel of Matthew was well known and well used long before the middle of the second century. The evidence, however, does not support any suggestion that the Jesus tradition had been finally encapsulated and fixed in Matthew or in any other written Gospel. Even where Matthean influence is evident, the variations from the text form of Matthew which has come down to us suggest rather that the Jesus tradition was still flexible, that the influence of Matthew's Gospel on the Jesus tradition was steadily growing, but also that Jesus' teaching and mission were still remembered and spoken about in the way that the Jesus tradition had always been known and used more or less from the first — the substance or gist of particular teachings or events relatively constant but the verbal detail and groupings very diverse. It is unnecessary, then, to argue that even Justin drew all his material either directly from known written Gospels or from 'extra-canonical' written collections of Jesus tradition. The natural variations in use of a living tradition (including a Matthean-shaped tradition) in the worship and teaching of predominantly oral communities are sufficient to explain all the data.

c. Luke

In contrast with Matthew, the early second-century evidence even of oral or paraenetical tradition with distinctive Lukan features is slight.[323] But as we move into the middle of the second century, further evidence can be cited.[324]

---

321. The same is noticeably true of the *Apocalypse of Peter* (see e.g. the quotations and allusions, particularly Matt. 17 and 24, noted by Tuckett, *Nag Hammadi* 117-24, and Elliott, *ANT* 600-12). In the *Acts of John* there is clear dependency on Matt. 7.7 (22), 6.19 (34), and probably on Matthew's account of Jesus' transfiguration (90) and on Matt. 27.45 (97). In the system of Ptolemaeus, according to Irenaeus, there is frequent reference to Matthew (*adv. haer.* 1.3.1-4; 6.1; 7.4); and the *Letter of Ptolemaeus to Flora* is a rather sophisticated discussion of Matthew's teaching on the law (Foerster, *Gnosis* 1.154-61).

322. Notably Massaux, *Influence*, and Köhler, *Rezeption*.

323. Notably *1 Clem.* 13.2; Ignatius, *Smyrn.* 3.2-3; *Polyc.* 2.1; *Did.* 1.5; *2 Clem.* 8.5.

324. Particularly Athenagoras, *Plea* 11.1; P.Egerton 2 frags. 1 and 2; *Epist. Apost.* 3, 5, 14; *Gosp.Phil.* 111b; and *Gosp.Pet.* 4.13; and n.288 above.

Special mention should again be made of Justin Martyr — several of whose quotations of Jesus tradition, as noted above, include distinctively Lukan material — and the four-Gospel harmonizations of Tatian and Theophilus.

Still more noteworthy is the testimony provided by Marcion who devised his system in Rome in the 140s and 150s. Basic to his system was the Gospel of Luke and epistles of Paul, which he edited to accord with his own assumptions and designs, or as Irenaeus describes it, 'mutilating the Gospel according to Luke and the epistles of Paul'.[325] This is usually understood to indicate that Marcion used an abridged version of Luke's Gospel, though the issue is made more complex by the variations in the manuscript traditions of the text of Luke. It is unnecessary to go into the details of the discussion.[326] What is clear is that Marcion knew and made intensive use of Luke's Gospel to promote his version of the Christian message. Whether he knew other of the NT Gospels and selected Luke, dispensing with the others, is a matter for speculation. But in any case, Marcion certainly is a somewhat embarrassing witness to the fact that Luke's Gospel was an established authority for the teaching of Jesus in the middle of the second century.[327]

d. John

The question whether John's Gospel was known and its use reflected in the second-century Christian literature is much debated. For a long time the dominant opinion was that John was little known or used by the mainstream, proto-orthodox churches, and that it was more strongly favoured by the Gnostics, with the implication that it was more acceptable to the latter and regarded with some suspicion by the former.[328] But Charles Hill in particular has torpedoed

---

325. Irenaeus, *adv. haer.* 3.12.12. Tertullian uses similar language to describe Marcion's use of Luke (*adv. Marc.* 4.2.4). See further below §47.5b.

326. Gregory discusses the issue at length (*Reception* 174-96).

327. Gregory sums up his investigation: 'Not only is he [Marcion] the first witness to the use of a gospel text which in content and order is demonstrably Lukan, albeit in a shorter form than the *Luke* known to us today, but by virtue of his early date he is in fact the first witness to *any* Gospel text treated as an independent and free-standing whole' (*Reception* 196). Gregory goes on to question the common view that Marcion chose Luke because Marcion was a Paulinist, and Luke's Gospel could be regarded as written by someone who had been a companion and strong supporter of Paul. He concludes, 'We simply do not know why Marcion made use of *Luke*, or even in fact that he chose it — it is possible . . . that *Luke* was simply the gospel that Marcion knew best, perhaps because *Luke* was the first Gospel to reach Pontus' (205).

328. Influential in this view was J. N. Sanders, *The Fourth Gospel in the Early Church: Its Origin and Influence on Christian Theology up to Irenaeus* (Cambridge University,

that view rather effectively.³²⁹ For, as we have seen, knowledge and influence of John's Gospel can be regarded as firmly attested as early as Ignatius, *Rom.* 7.2-3, Polycarp, *Phil.* 7.1-2, and *Epist. Apost.* 5, 11, 17, 18. The Apologists most likely knew and were influenced by John — Justin, *1 Apol.* 61.4, and Tatian, *Address* 4.1, 13.1, Athenagoras, *Plea* 10.2-3, Theophilus, *Autolycus* 2.22 — not forgetting that Tatian and Theophilus went on to include John in their Gospel Harmonies.³³⁰ In addition, a good case can be made that the longer ending to Mark's Gospel (added probably in the first half of the second century) knew and used John (its opening paragraph summarizes John 20's account of Mary Magdalene's discovery that Jesus' tomb was empty).³³¹ On a broader frame, P.Egerton 2 frag. 1 certainly drew on John's Gospel, and it is more likely that any line of influence between John and the more Gnostically-inclined Gospels (the *Dialogue of the Saviour*, the *Gospel of Philip* and the *Gospel of Truth*) runs from John to these later documents rather than vice-versa.³³² The older view

---

1943). Even Hengel thought that 'for a long time it [the Fourth Gospel] was not regarded as "on the same level" as the other Gospels' (*Four Gospels* 137). Chapter 5 of Culpepper's *John* is entitled 'Obscurity: The Apostle in the Second Century'. It was regarded as particularly significant that the earliest commentary on John's Gospel was written by a Gnostic, Heracleon; see E. H. Pagels, *The Johannine Gospel in Gnostic Exegesis: Heracleon's Commentary on John* (SBLMS 17; Nashville: Abingdon, 1973); 'the earliest interpreters of John, as a matter of fact, were gnostics' (Cameron, *Other Gospels* 88). I was greatly influenced by this view in my earlier writing — particularly 'John and the Synoptics as a Theological Question', in Culpepper and Black, eds., *Exploring the Gospel of John* 301-13.

329. He entitles the first chapter of his *Johannine Corpus*, 'The Orthodox Johannophobia Theory' (sparked off by Sanders), and summarizes his critique of the view that John was particularly favoured by the Gnostics under the heading 'the Myth of Gnostic Johannophilia' (466-68), even though Irenaeus acknowledged that the Valentinians made copious use of John (*adv. haer.* 3.11.7; 1.9.1-3) (107-8). It cannot be assumed that Heracleon regarded John's Gospel as scripture 'before the orthodox'; rather Heracleon tried to draw John into Valentinianism (208-11); see also E. Thomassen, 'Heracleon', in T. Rasimus, ed., *The Legacy of John: Second-Century Reception of the Fourth Gospel* (NovTSupp 132; Leiden: Brill, 2010) 173-210. Hill credits also particularly Hengel, *Johannine Question*, and T. Nagel, *Die Rezeption des Johannesevangeliums im 2.Jahrhundert* (Leipzig, 2000), for challenging the previous consensus.

330. See also N. Perrin, 'The *Diatessaron* and the Second-Century Reception of the Gospel of John', in Rasimus, ed., *Legacy of John* 301-18; and further, on second-century knowledge and use of John, see Culpepper, *John* 108-14, 119-32.

331. Hill, *Johannine Corpus* 402-6; citing Hengel, *Johannine Question* 11; and particularly J. A. Kelhoffer, *Miracle and Mission: The Authentication of Missionaries and Their Message in the Longer Ending of Mark* (WUNT 2.112; Tübingen: Mohr Siebeck, 2000). Hengel was of the opinion that in Mark 16.9-20 all four Gospels are used (*Four Gospels* 134). See also T. K. Heckel, *Vom Evangelium des Markus zum viergestaltigen Evangelium* (WUNT 120; Tübingen: Mohr Siebeck, 1999) 283-85.

332. E.g. the *Gospel of Truth* possibly echoes John 14.6 in *NHL* I.18.19-20, almost certainly draws on the parable of the shepherd and the sheep (Matt. 18.12-14/Luke 15.1-7;

(of J. N. Sanders, etc.), however, is true to the extent that it was Irenaeus who most effectively contested the Gnostic attempts to make their own use of the Johannine prologue (John 1.1-18), and who ensured that the Gospel of John would provide a firm basis for subsequent Christian reflection on Jesus and the Godhead and a strong bulwark against Gnostic alternatives.[333]

e. Papyri and Codices

In responding to the claim that the second century was flooded with Gospels, and that there were a good many other Gospels which were as widely known, highly regarded and as well used as the NT Gospels, Hill points to the data provided by the early papyri finds. For the period before 200, there have been discovered between seven and thirteen possible manuscripts of one of the four NT Gospels (apart from Mark). In contrast, there are only between two and five possible second-century manuscripts of non-canonical Gospels (Egerton Gospel, *Gospel of Peter*, *Gospel of Thomas*). The proportions are similar for the third century, though more numerous in each case.[334] For these periods it should be recalled that no Christian faction was strong enough to suppress other factions across the Empire; they were all much more liable to

---

more than John 10.1-18), and on Matt. 12.11 (*NHL* I.31.35–32.30), and speaks often of the Father and the Son ('the name of the Father is the Son' — I.38.7; I.39.19-20, 24-28); but all in the context of a Gnostic understanding of the human condition as drunkenness, or sleep, or ignorance to be resolved by the coming of or coming to knowledge. Note again Barrett's conclusion that the great weight of probability indicates that the author of the *Gospel of Truth*, possibly Valentinus himself, had read John's Gospel (n.276 above). Hill's thesis is supported by P.-H. Poirier, 'The *Trimorphic Protennoia* (NHC XIII,1) and the Johannine Prologue: A Reconsideration', in Rasimus, ed., *Legacy of John* 93-103, concluding that the *Trimorphic Protennoia* was a polemical reinterpretation of the Johannine prologue 'through the use of allusions intended to convince the reader that the Logos-Protennoia is superior to the incarnated Logos of the Fourth Gospel' (101). Similarly with the *Apocryphon of John*; cf. J. D. Turner, 'The Johannine Legacy: The Gospel and *Apocryphon of John*', in Rasimus, ed., *Legacy of John* 105-44. In the *Acts of John* a clear echo of Johannine language, as in John 14.10-11, is evident in Jesus' words, 'Know that I am wholly with the Father, and the Father with me' (*ActsJohn* 100); and probably allusions to Johannine christology, particularly the 'I am' sayings, in *ActsJohn* 98 (cf. 109). See also Hill's summing up in regard to Gnostic use of John in *Johannine Corpus* ch. 5 and 466-67; and further below §49.7.

333. B. Mutschler, 'John and His Gospel in the Mirror of Irenaeus of Lyons: Perspectives of Recent Research', in Rasimus, ed., *Legacy of John* 319-43: John 1.3 and 1.14 'as theological shibboleths or dogmatic guard-rails' (340). See further §49.3d below.

334. L. W. Hurtado, *Early Christian Artifacts: Manuscripts and Christian Origins* (Grand Rapids: Eerdmans, 2006) 20-23, 29-35; Hill, *Who Chose the Gospels?* 9-25. Contrast the overstatement of Koester quoted above (§39 n.30).

be persecuted and suppressed themselves by hostile or suspicious authorities. So second- or third-century manuscripts were as likely to be retained or hidden away, whatever the faction. And the relative spread of papyri manuscripts can the more probably serve to indicate the likely spread of the views expressed therein.

A second point worthy of note is the 'curious fact that all of our early copies of the Gospels of Matthew, Mark, Luke, and John were written on codices'.[335] Most of these were of a size which would be most suitable for public reading, that is, in services of worship, which may explain why the early Christians adopted the codex form.[336] In contrast, only the Egerton Gospel and one of the three copies of the *Gospel of Thomas* could be plausibly claimed to have been written for public reading. Indeed, most of the apocryphal Gospels were probably produced for private rather than public reading — some more mythological to answer a different understanding of the human condition, or more novelistic than serious history, to feed or stimulate curiosity, fulfilling a similar function to that of popular folktales.[337]

If Christians began to use the codex (rather than the roll) for their Gospels early in the second century, or even earlier,[338] we can probably assume that Justin and his successors were able to consult a codex containing two or more of the NT Gospels.[339] There is no evidence, however, that any 'fifth' Gospel was ranked alongside the 'canonical four' or ever included in any codex containing two or more Gospels.[340] So if the evidence already reviewed is

---

335. 'With only one possible exception [p^{22} = P.Oxy. 1228], every single papyrus copy of the gospels is from a codex' (Stanton, *Jesus and Gospel* 82, and further 82-91). 'The Gospels were probably written on codices from the beginning' (Hengel, *Four Gospels* 50, and further 116-27). Scholarship was alerted to the importance of the codex-book format for early Christianity by the publication of the Chester Beatty Biblical papyri, the third-century codex p^{45} containing all four Gospels and the book of Acts (F. G. Kenyon, *The Chester Beatty Biblical Papyri: Descriptions and Texts of Twelve Manuscripts on Papyri of the Greek Bible* [London: Emery Walker, 1933-37]). Influential has been C. H. Roberts and T. C. Skeat, *The Birth of the Codex* (London: British Academy, 1983).

336. Hill quotes Stanton's phrase 'pulpit edition' (*Who Chose the Gospels?* 119-21). On the debate as to why the early Christians preferred the codex, see further Stanton, *Jesus and Gospel* 165-91; Hurtado, *Early Christian Artifacts* 61-83.

337. Hill, *Who Chose the Gospels?* 25-33.

338. 'The earliest known New Testament papyrus, p^{52} of about A.D. 125, was written as a codex' (Aland and Aland, *Text* 76).

339. As well as p^{45}, the early third-century p^{75} contains substantial portions of Luke and John.

340. As Hengel points out, although Clement of Alexandria displayed 'a relatively generous attitude towards apocryphal Gospel tradition', 'even for him the apostolic origin and special church authority of the four Gospels was already unassailable' (*Four Gospels* 15, 19).

sound for the recognition of the four NT Gospels as solely authoritative for mainstream Christianity,[341] then it becomes more likely that when Irenaeus referred to the four Gospels as a coherent and defining group, he was thinking of these Gospels perhaps already contained in a single codex, a fourfold Gospel codex (like p[45]).[342] In short, the status implied in the use of the codex form, the status already attributed to the four NT Gospels, and the possibility that the fourfold Gospel codex was already a feature of late second-century Christianity, anticipate the subsequent formal recognition that the Gospels of Matthew, Mark, Luke and John were integral members of the canon of the New Testament.[343]

We can conclude with confidence, therefore, that all four of the NT Gospels were known, highly valued and used during the first half of the second century. Despite the uncertainties occasioned regarding oral tradition, second orality and quoting from memory, there are sufficient indications, in Ignatius, Polycarp, Papias and Justin in particular, not only that the Jesus tradition contained variously in all four NT Gospels was widely known, but also that all four Gospels themselves were familiar and treated as authoritative sources for the mission and teaching of Jesus. That Matthew and John were particularly valued can be readily explained by the fact that both could be and were attributed to immediate disciples of Jesus, two of the twelve apostles. Luke was somewhat less used, but was still highly regarded, presumably because Luke was esteemed as a spokesman for Paul, the apostle. And Mark's Gospel, though it had been superseded by Matthew, and though its influence and use are much harder to detect, was probably also highly regarded, particularly as being the spokesman for Peter. But equally significant are the facts that Justin shows no awareness of or interest in Gospels other than the canonical four, and that Tatian and Theophilus evidently took it for granted that only the four

---

341. See further Heckel, *Vom Evangelium des Markus* 266-355; D. Hannah, 'The Four-Gospel "Canon" in the *Epistula Apostolorum*', *JTS* 59 (2008) 598-633.

342. Stanton, however, overstates the case: 'Well before the end of the second century there was a very well-established tradition of four-gospel codices'; Justin 'may well have had a four-gospel codex in his catechetical school in Rome by about AD 150' (*Jesus and Gospel* 74, 77). But Hengel concluded from the papyri evidence that 'before Constantine the Gospels were predominantly disseminated as individual codices' (*Four Gospels* 45-46, though see also 50-51). And note the critique by P. M. Head, 'Graham Stanton and the Four-Gospel Codex: Reconsidering the Manuscript Evidence', in J. Willitts et al., eds., *Jesus, Matthew's Gospel and Early Christianity: Studies in Memory of Graham N. Stanton* (LNTS 435; London: T & T Clark, 2011) 93-101, who questions Stanton's linking of the four-Gospel canon, which 'certainly seems to have existed by the end of the second century', with the four-Gospel codex, which does 'not seem to have become common until the fourth century' (100).

343. See further below §50.2c.

NT Gospels should be included in their harmonies. In short, one can speak of a 'four-Gospel canon' in effect and already widely acknowledged before Irenaeus effectively sealed the issue. In contrast, even when other Gospels drew on earlier Jesus tradition, they never achieved such a widespread effect and authority.[344]

44.9 Conclusions

(a) It is very likely that the Jesus tradition continued to be known orally well into the second century. The writing down of the Jesus tradition by Mark and his successors did not bring the oral tradition to an end. Since the large proportion of any Christian congregation would be illiterate, their knowledge of the Jesus tradition would be oral and aural, including the second orality of having heard one of the written Gospels read aloud. If Papias is typical of the more literate Christians, they would cherish visits of those who could tell them the version of stories and teachings that the latter themselves had heard from first or second generation eye- and ear-witnesses. They would cherish such visits not simply, or not so much, for any new stories or teachings which such visitors brought with them, but for the confirmation and possibly correction of the stories and teachings they already knew and which already provided the resource for their worship and living as Christians.

(b) There is sufficient indication that the inscribing of the Jesus tradition by Matthew and John in particular influenced the wider (oral) Jesus tradition, so that often the echo of or allusion to Jesus tradition, or the more widespread catechetical, liturgical and apologetic tradition, would bear the stamp of features introduced to the Jesus tradition by the versions which Matthew and John recorded.

(c) As the second century progressed, it would appear that dependency on the oral tradition as such diminished as the NT Gospels became more widely known and influential. A dependency on oral tradition continuing into the fourth generation anyway would be surprising. But in any case, the combined testimony of Justin, Tatian, Theophilus and Irenaeus indicates that reference to Jesus' mission and teaching was most likely to the already acknowledged NT Gospels. And if Clement of Alexandria is typical, it would suggest that the transition from knowledge of Jesus' teaching through oral tradition to knowledge dependent on written Gospels was more or less complete by the end of the second century.

(d) The other (non-canonical) Gospels also attest the influence of the

---

344. See also Hill, *Who Chose the Gospels?* 99-101.

first-century Jesus tradition. But characteristically the more gnostically oriented Gospels weave earlier Jesus tradition into a diagnosis and narrative of the human condition which is not drawn from the earlier Jesus tradition but from elsewhere. It is the alternative narrative which provides 'the other gospel'. Jesus tradition is drawn in when it can serve that other gospel, but is not allowed to correct that other gospel. What constituted the 'gospel' for Paul, the first Christians and the NT Gospel writers has been almost wholly ignored; the death and resurrection is not, or is no longer, the *gospel*. The distinctive DNA has been abstracted from the first-century Jesus tradition, and what seemed usable out of the Jesus tradition has been grafted in as best as possible to a different species.

With the other Gospels any pretence to be drawing on or building upon the early Jesus tradition has been abandoned. Jesus still provides a magnetic attraction, but the distinctive message (gospel) attributed to him is drawn entirely from elsewhere, usually from that other (Gnostic) narrative. And it can only be attributed to Jesus by being presented as secret teaching, known only to the sect which promulgated it.

(e) It is wholly understandable, therefore, that Irenaeus should see in the four NT Gospels both the foundation documents for Christianity and the bulwark against the distortions and perversions of the gospel content and format which were the other Gospels. In this Irenaeus was not taking an unusual step, or trying single-handedly to withstand a torrent of other Gospels causing confusion among the mainstream of Christians. He was simply summing up the trends that had always been there, from the late first century, and bringing to appropriate conclusion what had been the main thrust of the Jesus tradition into the second century.

In Part Eleven (§§41-44), then, we have traced the influence of the remembered Jesus from the fall of Jerusalem (70 CE) to nearly the end of the second century.

This has also been a study of how the concept of 'gospel' became, in the early years of Christianity, and particularly under Paul's influence, a fundamental way of expressing what Jesus was believed to have accomplished, the story of Jesus' historic mission and its significance (§41). Fundamental was the transition from 'gospel' to 'Gospel', the written account of Jesus' mission in Galilee and Jerusalem, climaxing in his death and resurrection — fundamental to the good news for the first believers.

Very striking were the coherence and integration of what appear to have been the first Gospels written (Mark, Luke, Matthew) (§42). The basic structure is shared — the gospel as the climax of the Gospel — and there can be little doubt that this was the same Jesus who was being remembered, even if differently, no doubt for different contexts and subsidiary aims. The possibility of drawing a clear delineation of the Jesus who was thus remembered (vol. 1) was readily confirmed, even when the different emphases of each of the three Evangelists could be as readily set out.

The difference of the Fourth Gospel (John) from the first three would seem to pose a problem, especially when set alongside the *Gospel of Thomas*, since so much of the latter has more immediate parallel with the Synoptic tradition than does John. But closer examination (§43) revealed the extent to which John's Gospel is essentially an elaboration of the same traditions which the earlier Evangelists used. Whereas the distinctive message/gospel of *Thomas* was drawn from elsewhere, however much Synoptic-like tradition was brought in to strengthen the impression that Jesus had taught this gospel. The use of Jesus tradition gives some justification for *Thomas* to be counted as a *Gospel*, but it was not 'gospel' as defined by Paul and confirmed by both the Synoptics and John's Gospel.

The prominence given, understandably, to the *Gospel of Thomas* in recent years has cloaked the evidence of the principal second-century figures whose voices still reverberate in tradition. The fact that Jesus was seen as a teacher of tremendous significance is attested in almost everything looked at in §44. It was probably inevitable that he attracted other ways of understanding and resolving what was seen as the essential human need and dilemma. And inevitable too that much of the teaching and significance thus attributed to him could be melded to some extent with the Jesus tradition preserved particularly by the Synoptic Evangelists. But the ways in which the remembered Jesus was configured into the Jesus of the NT Gospels are readily traceable through the second century. At the same time the growing focus on the NT Gospels as (in effect) alone fully deserving the title 'Gospel' becomes ever sharper, with the other Gospels more curiosities (or threats) than serious contenders in the worship and teaching of the great majority of Christians.

So, now, having examined in detail the way in which the first great factor (the impact of Jesus and the Jesus tradition) shaped earliest Christianity, we turn to the impact of Jesus' brother, James (§45), and to the sad story of the parting of the ways (§46).

PART TWELVE

JEWISH CHRISTIANITY AND THE PARTING OF THE WAYS

There is something of an oddity about the title 'Jewish Christianity'. For in a very important sense, that is what Christianity is — at least in its beginnings, and integrally in its character. In an important sense, often lost to view, the adjective 'Jewish' is quite unnecessary, since Christianity, with a Jewish Messiah as its central figure, and its holy scripture predominantly written by Jews, can hardly be anything other than 'Jewish' in a crucially defining sense. The oddity, rather, at least arguably, is that Christianity so quickly lost sight of its Jewish roots and character, that 'Jewish Christianity' became just one form of Christianity, almost a primitive form to be lost increasingly to view as Christianity became more international and less definitively Jewish in character. The increasing loss of distinctively Jewish identity is one of the most striking features of the first two centuries of Christianity. The growth of a contradictory *adversus Iudaeos* tradition which came to dominate Christianity more or less up to the present day has a self-contradictory character. To reckon seriously with this fact is still one of the great challenges facing twenty-first-century Christians, when the memory of the Holocaust is still unspeakably raw.

If, then, James, the brother of Jesus, was one of the principal figures to emerge in the first generation of Christianity, it is important to re-express his significance, his enduring significance, and to clarify why it is that 'Christianity' can no longer be defined as 'Jewish Christianity'. This is the task of the next two chapters.

CHAPTER 45

Jewish Christianity

45.1 Introduction

As already implied (§38.3b), the term 'Jewish Christianity' is more problematic than helpful. It has been used traditionally to refer to the 'Jewish-Christian' sects dismissed by Irenaeus, Epiphanius and the other early Christian heresiologists. So much so that it is questionable whether there is much point in continuing with a term so confusing and misleading, too much stained by the history of its usage.[1] Other terms have been tried, like Judaeo-Christianity and Christian Judaism, but they have their own problems and may be as confusing and as contentious as the term they replace.[2] 'Jewish believers in Jesus', as a

---

1. See the illuminating essay by J. C. Paget, 'The Definition of the Terms *Jewish Christian* and *Jewish Christianity* in the History of Research', in Skarsaune and Hvalvik, eds., *Jewish Believers in Jesus* 22-52; also S. C. Mimouni, *Early Judaeo-Christianity: Historical Essays* (Leuven: Peeters, 2012) chs. 5-6; Broadhead, *Jewish Ways of Following Jesus* ch. 2.

2. Daniélou worked with a definition of Jewish Christianity, as distinct from Hellenistic Christianity and Latin Christianity, as fundamentally 'characterised by the fact that its imagery is that of the dominant Jewish thought-form of the time, namely apocalyptic' (*Theology of Jewish Christianity* 4). An influential essay by R. Murray, 'Defining Judaeo-Christianity', *Heythrop Journal* 15 (1974) 303-10, in contrast suggested that 'Jewish Christianity' should be used for the sociological phenomenon of Jews who were also Christians, whereas 'Judaeo-Christianity' should be used for Daniélou's ideological definition. See also J. E. Taylor, 'The Phenomenon of Early Jewish Christianity: Reality or Scholarly Invention', *VC* 44 (1990) 313-34. Brown reminded us of how complex the actual situations would have been by distinguishing four groups of 'Jewish Christians and their Gentile converts': (1) those 'who insisted on *full observance of the Mosaic Law, including circumcision*, for those who believed in Jesus'; (2) those 'who did *not* insist on circumcision but did require converted Gentiles to keep *some Jewish observances*'; (3) those 'who did *not* insist on circumcision and did *not* require observance of the Jewish ("kosher") food laws'; and (4) those 'who did not insist on circumcision or observance of the Jewish food laws and who *saw no abiding significance*

further alternative referent, may not be as helpful as it at first appears, since it leaves unclear whether such believers maintained or abandoned their Jewish lifestyle — an issue which was already causing division in Paul's time (Rom. 14.1-15.6), and which was even more contentious for Ignatius (*Magn.* 8.1-2; *Magn.* 10.1-3).[3] And switching from the defining marker of ethnicity ('Jews who believed in Jesus') to one of belief or praxis ('Jewish ways of following Jesus')[4] allows the definition to include judaizing Gentiles (Godfearers) who believed in Jesus, and Christians who adopted a Jewish frame of reference,[5] but probably confuses the category still further.[6] It may be simplest, then, to stick with the term 'Jewish Christianity', despite its inadequacies, since it expresses so straightforwardly the paradox which is at the centre of Christianity's identity:

- that it is a Jewish sect which has become predominantly non-Jewish, and traditionally dismissive of and antagonistic to the religion of the Jews;
- that more than three-quarters of its sacred scriptures are the scriptures of Israel, the Hebrew Bible and its Greek version (LXX);
- that the God it worships is the God of these scriptures, that is, the God of Israel;
- that the Saviour it exalts is Jesus Christ, that is, Messiah Jesus, whom the first Christians regarded as the emissary from God long-expected by Israel's prophets and seers;
- all the apostles, on whom the Christian church is built, were Jews.

Closely bound up with the paradox that is 'Jewish Christianity' are the tensions which were already evident in the first generation, in the mission of Paul to Gentiles and in the reactions of traditionalist Jewish believers-in-Jesus to that mission —

---

in Jewish cult and feasts' (R. E. Brown and J. P. Meier, *Antioch and Rome: New Testament Cradles of Catholic Christianity* [London: Geoffrey Chapman, 1983] 2-8).

3. Mimouni, 'Pour une définition nouvelle du judéo-christianisme ancien', *NTS* 38 (1991) 161-86, translated in his *Early Judaeo-Christianity* 25-53, wants to restrict the term 'Jewish Christian' to those Jews who believed in Jesus as messiah and who continued to observe the Torah (4, 51). But O. Skarsaune, 'Jewish Believers in Jesus in Antiquity — Problems of Definition, Method, and Sources', in Skarsaune and Hvalvik, ed., *Jewish Believers in Jesus* 3-21, prefers the term 'Jewish believer in Jesus' to include also Jewish believers who did not retain a Jewish lifestyle (9).

4. Broadhead's title.

5. Broadhead includes a chapter on 'Judaizers' (*Jewish Ways* ch. 10). Cf. R. W. Longenecker, *The Christology of Early Jewish Christianity* (London: SCM, 1970) 3. And see also Mimouni, *Early Judaeo-Christianity* 126-32.

6. See Paget, 'Jewish Christianity' 733-42.

- an identity determined by ethnicity or by praxis or by belief;
- the necessity and role of ritual markers which define identity (circumcision, baptism);
- and the terms of association between groups who practise different rituals and life-styles as an expression of their identity.

Paul tried to hold the paradox together and to encourage a churchmanship which embraced the tensions. But the question remains unresolved as to whether he had any real hope of succeeding in his endeavour, with most of the evidence pointing to a negative answer. His theology could not trump social relationships and praxis; so is his theology at this point still valid or relevant?

The question for us now is, How did the same paradox and tensions work out in the period following the catastrophic failure of the first Jewish revolt and through the second century? The best way to explore this question, I suggest, is to take the two parts of the title, 'Jewish Christianity', with due seriousness:

- to consider how *Jewish* in character Christianity remained, including the Christianity which distanced itself from Judaism;
- and to note how *Christian* were the Jews who believed in Messiah Jesus, including those who were dismissed as heretics by the Christian heresiologists.

As with Part Eleven, we want to trace the continuing impact of the forces which were so determinative in first-generation Christianity. In this case we recall both that one of the principal tensions, probably *the* principal tension in the first generation, was the tension between Paul and James, and that the Jerusalem church seems to have been the centre and principal focus of what might be best described as 'Christian Judaism' ('Judaism' in the same way as Pharisaic Judaism or Essene Judaism was also 'Judaism'). So the influence of James, running into the second century, is a primary concern. Also the form of Christianity (Jesus-discipleship) which he represented; so what happened to the Jerusalem and Judaean (and Galilean) assemblies? And how, more broadly, did the Jewish interests and emphases of first-generation Christianity extend into the post-70 period and the second century?

45.2 The Enigma of James[7]

a. The New Testament James

James, the brother of Jesus, we recall, was the principal figure in the community of believers-in-Jesus in Jerusalem from about 40 till his judicial execution in 62.[8] The impression from Acts 15.13-21, that he edged ahead of Peter as recognized leader and 'chief executive' for the (Jewish) believers-in-Jesus, is confirmed by Paul's naming him as first of the 'pillar apostles' (Gal. 2.9 — James, Cephas and John) and by Paul's account of Peter complying with the 'certain people who came from James' in withdrawing from table fellowship with the Gentile believers (2.12). There is also the possibility that in the creedal statement in 1 Cor. 15.3-8 the second list of witnesses ('to James, then to all the apostles' — 15.7) had been put together as a complement to, or even to rival, the first list ('to Cephas, then to the twelve, then to more than five hundred' — 15.5-6), to give the resurrection appearance to James as much authorizing legitimacy as the appearance to Cephas.[9] Add to that the tension between James and Paul, implicit in the parenthesis of Gal. 2.6, in how the Antioch incident came about (2.12-16), and in Rom. 15.31 and Acts 21.20-21; even in the relative calm of the NT accounts the picture which emerges is of a significant degree of factionalism within the earliest Christian movement, a factionalism to which James was integral.

The letter attributed to James strongly suggests that he was highly regarded among diaspora Jews who believed in Jesus, as highly regarded as he was among Jesus-believers in Jerusalem itself. Indeed, the suggestion is highly plausible that the letter of James consists of the teaching/preaching which James gave to diaspora Jewish believers (and other Jewish pilgrims?) on their pilgrimage visits to Jerusalem.[10] The fact that such a letter was prized and made it into the NT canon,[11] despite its characteristic Jewishness, and despite its lack of distinctively

---

7. On James see particularly W. Pratscher, *Der Herrenbruder Jakobus und die Jakobustradition* (FRLANT 139; Göttingen: Vandenhoeck, 1987); and J. Painter, *Just James: The Brother of Jesus in History and Tradition* (University of South Carolina, 1997); also B. Chilton and C. A. Evans, eds., *James the Just and Christian Origins* (NovTSupp 98; Leiden: Brill, 1999); B. Chilton and J. Neusner, eds., *The Brother of Jesus: James the Just and His Mission* (Louisville: Westminster John Knox, 2001); D. R. Nienhuis, *Not by Paul Alone* (Waco: Baylor University, 2007) 121-50 ('James of Jerusalem in History and Tradition').

8. See *Beginning from Jerusalem* 210, 411, §36.1.

9. See discussion in Pratscher, *Herrenbruder* 35-46. See also below Jerome, *de vir. ill.* 2 and *Gosp. Thom.* 12.

10. *Beginning from Jerusalem* §37.2c.

11. See the summary treatment in Kümmel, *Introduction* 405-7. 'Origen is the first early theologian to make clear use of the letter of James' (Nienhuis, *Not by Paul Alone* 55-60).

Christian emphases,[12] must indicate that it was highly regarded across a wide range of second- and third-century churches. In particular, we could speculate that a letter addressed to the diaspora (Jas. 1.1) would have been most highly prized among diaspora Jews who were believers in Messiah Jesus; and that its acceptance by the wider circle of predominantly Gentile churches must imply that the Jewish believers-in-Jesus were genuinely respected by the predominantly Gentile churches. This, despite the letter's reassertion of the traditional Jewish interpretation of Gen. 15.6 with its qualification of one of the fundamental arguments put forward by Paul in defence of his gospel (Jas. 2.18-26).[13]

In the NT records, then, the impression given in regard to James is rather confused and mixed. This may help to explain why, when we look beyond the first century, the significance attributed to James is even more mixed, with James himself quite neglected in patristic literature.

b. The Patristic James

We have already noted Eusebius's lengthy quotation from the early second-century Hegesippus, an extensive account of James's character as 'the Just' and of his execution (*HE* 2.23.4-9, 13-18).[14] The only description of Jesus' resurrection appearance to James is provided by Jerome who notes that 'the Gospel called "according to the Hebrews", which was recently translated by me into Greek and Latin, which Origen frequently uses, records after the resurrection of the Saviour':[15]

> And when the Lord had given the linen cloth to the servant of the priest, he went to James and appeared to him. For James had sworn that he would not eat bread from that hour in which he had drunk the cup of the Lord until he should see him risen from among them that sleep. And shortly thereafter the Lord said: 'Bring a table and bread!' And immediately it is added: he took the bread, blessed it and brake it and gave it to James the Just and said to him: 'My brother, eat thy bread, for the Son of man is risen from among them that sleep' (Jerome, *de vir. ill.* 2).

---

12. Though Niebuhr (in private correspondence) reminds me of the strong opening of the letter (1.1 — 'servant of God and of the Lord Jesus Christ'), of the strong christological language in 2.1, of the fact that *pistis* occurs so frequently in the letter (16x) and of the strong use of Jesus tradition in 2.8-13 (see also *Beginning from Jerusalem* §37.2c).

13. See *Beginning from Jerusalem* 1142-44.

14. Quoted in *Beginning from Jerusalem* 1088-89, 1093-95.

15. I follow the translation of Vielhauer and Strecker, *NTA* 1.178.

Worth noting is the implication that James was present at the last supper and 'had drunk the cup of the Lord', also that James's conversion to become a follower of his brother must have happened before Jesus' death and resurrection. Is the implication also that the first resurrection appearance was to James? — perhaps another indication that 1 Cor. 15.7 began as an account of the risen Lord's priorities in commissioning his apostles which was different from that enshrined in 1 Cor. 15.5-6, and suggestive of some rivalry between Peter and James on the point.[16]

Probably the earliest patristic reference to James comes in Irenaeus, who in quoting Acts 15 makes a point of the agreement reached by Paul, Peter, James and John, noting that the apostles were acting scrupulously 'according to the dispensation of the Mosaic law, showing that it was from one and the same God' (*adv. haer.* 3.12.14-15). The polemical *en passant* no doubt reflects Irenaeus's reaction to the way the historical tensions between these apostles were being exploited, and particularly his rejection of the Marcionite attempt to set Paul (and others) over against the Mosaic law. That James is explicitly included, as Acts 15 demanded, is an intriguing example of James being brought in to refute a Marcionite Paul. Tertullian similarly responds to Marcion's use of Gal. 2.13-14, that is, Paul's critique of Peter for 'not walking uprightly according to the truth of the gospel', by arguing that Paul was only censuring Peter's inconsistency, 'practising somewhat different from what he taught' (*adv. Marc.* 4.3).[17] It was evidently of crucial importance to be able to maintain that Paul, Peter, John *and James* all taught the same gospel.

Eusebius quotes Clement of Alexandria in books six and seven of his *Hypotyposes* (now lost to us):

> After the resurrection the Lord gave the tradition of knowledge to James the Just and John and Peter, these gave it to the other apostles, and the other apostles to the seventy, of whom Barnabas also was one. Now there were two Jameses, one James the Just, who was thrown down from the pinnacle of the temple and beaten to death with a fuller's club, and the other who was beheaded (*HE* 2.1.3-5).

---

16. Painter, *Just James* 185-86.

17. The sharp confrontation between Peter and Paul in Gal. 2.11-14, and the account of Paul rebuking Peter in condemnatory terms, gave many a headache to the church fathers; as classically outlined in F. Overbeck, *Über die Auffassung des Streits des Paulus mit Petrus in Antiochien (Gal. 2, 11ff.) bei den Kirchenvätern* (1877; Darmstadt: Wissenschaftliche Buchgesellschaft, 1968); see also A. Wechsler, *Geschichtsbild und Apostelstreit: Eine forschungsgeschichtliche und exegetische Studie über den antiochenischen Zwischenfall (Gal 2,11-14)* (BZNW 62; Berlin: de Gruyter, 1991).

As so often with Clement, he shows himself willing to flirt with talk of 'knowledge' and the thought of a (secret?) 'tradition of knowledge', but again he takes care to attribute it not simply to James, but to John and Peter as well, and to 'the other apostles'. James is again portrayed as belonging to the same team as Peter, John and the other apostles.[18]

However, the principal way in which James was retained within the tradition of the great church was by fitting him into its developing ecclesiology, that is, by clothing him in episcopal robes.[19] This is most clearly signaled by Eusebius who more or less begins his principal account of the history of the church by recording that James, the brother of Jesus, 'to whom the men of old had also given the surname of "Just" for his excellence of virtue, is narrated to have been the first elected to the throne of the bishopric of the church in Jerusalem' (*HE* 2.1.2). He goes on to quote Clement's *Hypotyposes* to the same effect: 'For Peter and James and John after the Ascension of the Saviour did not struggle for glory, because they had previously been given honour by the Saviour, but chose James the Just as bishop of Jerusalem' (HE 2.1.3). Similarly, when Eusebius's story returns to James it is with the reminder that it was to him that 'the throne of the bishopric in Jerusalem had been allotted by the apostles' (*HE* 2.23.1). And subsequently the reference is further elaborated: 'The throne of James, who was the first to receive from the Saviour and the apostles the episcopate of the church at Jerusalem . . . has been preserved to this day' (*HE* 7.19).[20]

In addition, of course, we should include mention of the *Protevangelium of James*.[21] The James intended is almost certainly the brother of Jesus, an elder brother by a previous marriage (*Prot. Jas.* 17.1-2), who wrote the story after the death of Herod (25.1), which would make him much older than Jesus. Whatever the reasons for attributing it to James, the attribution itself speaks highly of the regard in which he was held in the circles in which the veneration of Mary grew.

All this suggests an interest in James determined by his status as Jesus' brother, by 1 Cor. 15.7, by the memory of his role in Jerusalem as attested

---

18. See further Pratscher, *Herrenbruder* 186-99.
19. See Pratscher, *Herrenbruder* 178-86.
20. 'What does emerge clearly in his *History of the Church* is the fact that Eusebius wishes to restrict James' sphere of influence to one place only, namely, Jerusalem' (S. Freyne, *Retrieving James/Yakov, the Brother of Jesus: From Legend to History* [Bard College, 2008] 23) — that is, no doubt, in response to the Jewish-Christian exaltation of James as bishop of the whole Church (see below). Eusebius's assertion that James received the episcopate not only from the Saviour, but also the apostles, would have the same motivation. See also Painter, *Just James* 154-56.
21. See above §40 at n.251 and §44 at n.310.

by Acts ('ecclesiasticized' as bishop), by the tradition of his piety, and by the records of his violent execution. An enduring concern was to ensure that the Acts portrayal of James as at one with the other apostles was maintained, despite (presumably) claims that were being made regarding James elsewhere. Beyond that, however, there is no indication of continuing influence or of a faction within the circles represented by Hegesippus and the Church Fathers which venerated James or regarded him as its founder or leader.[22]

c. The Jewish-Christian James

James appears in stronger profile in the documents most obviously linked with what the Fathers regarded as Jewish-Christian (heretical) sects.

In the passage already cited from Jerome, James has a prominent role in the accounts of the resurrection appearances in the 'Gospel according to the Hebrews'. What the relation of this Gospel was to the Gospel of Matthew remains obscure,[23] but the contrast is striking, since James is not mentioned except in passing in any of the NT Gospels. In the Hebrews Gospel, however, James seems to have been picked out as given special attention by the risen Jesus, in a context which suggests that James was given prominence in a eucharistic setting.

More striking is the testimony of Hegesippus, according to Eusebius (*HE* 4.22.8), a Jewish believer in Jesus. According to Hegesippus, 'The charge of the Church passed to James, the brother of the Lord, together with the Apostles' (*HE* 2.23.4), by which he may mean that James was the *primus inter pares* in the leadership not merely of the Jerusalem community but of the whole church.[24] Hegesippus goes on in the same passage (HE 2.23.4-9)[25] to describe James not only as the 'Just', perhaps in echo of Jesus as 'the just one',[26] but also as having a priestly role in protecting and praying for forgiveness for his people and as the 'gate of Jesus', presumably through which access

---

22. Painter observes with regard to Epiphanius's account of James (*Pan.* 78.14.1-6; see *Beginning from Jerusalem* 1089 n.46), that he makes no reference 'to James as the recipient of a significant post-resurrection revelation, either in reference to his call or in terms of an ongoing secret revelation. From the perspective of Epiphanius, the fighter of heresy, this theme gave too much away to the enemy to be taken on board in his own treatment of James' (*Just James* 213).
23. See above §40.4a.
24. Pratscher, *Herrenbruder* 107-8.
25. Cited in *Beginning from Jerusalem* 1088-89.
26. Matt. 27.19; Luke 23.47; Acts 3.14; 7.52; 22.14; 1 Pet. 3.18; 1 John 2.1.

to salvation is made possible.[27] Hegesippus is hardly reliable as a historical source, but his account is probably indicative of the very high esteem in which James was held by the Jewish believers in the period between the two Jewish revolts against Rome.

Equally striking is what we find in the fourth-century *Pseudo-Clementine* literature, generally regarded as Jewish-Christian or as at least containing strong Jewish-Christian features, which derive from an earlier period.[28] Notable here are the Letter of Peter to James (*Epistula Petri*) and the Letter of Clement to James (*Epistula Clementis*) which preface the Clementine *Homilies*. The *Epistula Petri* begins:

> Peter to James, the lord and bishop of the holy church. . . . Knowing well that you, my brother, eagerly take pains about what is for the mutual benefit of us all, I earnestly beseech you not to pass on to any one of the Gentiles the books of my preachings which I (here) forward to you, nor to any one of our own tribe before probation. But if some one of them has been examined and found to be worthy, then you may hand them over to him in the same way as Moses handed over his office of a teacher to the seventy.

The concern in what follows is that 'our word of truth' will be misinterpreted and distorted.

> For some from among the Gentiles have rejected my lawful preaching and have preferred a lawless and absurd doctrine of the man who is my enemy. And indeed some have attempted, whilst I am still alive, to distort my words by interpretations of many sorts, as if I taught the dissolution of the law . . .

On reading the letter, James accedes to Peter's request

> that we should pass on the books of his preachings that have been forwarded to us not indiscriminately, but only to a good and religious candidate for the position of a teacher, a man who as one who has been circumcised is a believing Christian . . .

and there follow careful instructions regarding the terms on which the books could be passed on.

The following *Epistula Clementis* is similarly addressed to 'James, the lord

---

27. See also Pratscher, *Herrenbruder* 110-21; and Bauckham quoted in *Beginning from Jerusalem* 1089.
28. See above §40.6g.

and bishop of bishops, who governs the holy church of the Hebrews at Jerusalem and those which by the providence of God have been well founded everywhere, together with the presbyters and deacons and all the other brethren'. Clement purportedly goes on to recount his commissioning by Simon Peter to be Peter's successor, with the instructions and exhortations which Peter gave him at that time, with the request that Clement send a summary of Peter's teaching to James.

The esteem in which James is held in these documents is clearly evident — 'the lord and bishop of bishops', whose episcopal governance extends well beyond Jerusalem; he 'governs . . . the churches founded everywhere'.[29] No wonder the question is asked, whether there were many who regarded James as, in effect, 'the first pope'.[30] Besides this, the great church's attribution to James of the bishopric of Jerusalem may be counted as a compromise which history could at least justify without conceding the claims of Jewish-Christian devotees. The contrast between Peter and Clement is evident too. Peter writes as an equal, Clement more as a subordinate ('my lord James'; similarly *Recog.* 3.74).

Notable in the exchange with Peter is the wariness and suspicion of Gentile (believers), and the fact that the only ones regarded as potential teachers are Jewish believers-in-Jesus ('one who has been circumcised' and 'a believing Christian'). Also that 'the man who is my enemy', that is, Paul (as becomes clear elsewhere in the Clementine *Recognitions*), is regarded with antagonism because of his lawless teaching which distorts Peter's teaching as though he (too) 'taught the dissolution of the law'. All this looks very much like an extension of the situation and tensions which we learn from Paul and Acts: that James had succeeded Peter as in effect the leader of the Jerusalem church, and that James presided over a church whose members were all(?) Jewish believers-in-Jesus and who were deeply suspicious of Paul's Gentile mission and its disregard for and denigration of the law.[31] The implication is strong that a fairly direct line can be drawn from that first-century Jerusalem community of Jewish believers-in-Jesus to the individuals and communities reflected in the pseudo-Clementine *Homilies*.

29. Note also *Recog.* 1.43 — the church in Jerusalem 'was governed with most righteous ordinances by James, who was ordained bishop in it by the Lord'; 1.68 — Caiaphas addresses James 'the chief of the bishops'.

30. H. J. Schoeps, *Jewish Christianity* (ET Philadelphia: Fortress, 1969), notes that Theodor Zahn called James 'the Pope of Ebionite fantasy' (40). See also M. Hengel, 'Jakobus der Herrenbruder — der erste "Papst"?' (1985), *Paulus und Jakobus: Kleine Schriften III* (Tübingen: Mohr Siebeck, 2002) 549-82. With reference to a marble fragment from the church of St. John in Ephesus, which may refer to James as *prōtopapa(s)*, 'first pope' (*I. Eph.* IV.1290), Painter wonders whether 'the Eastern church submitted the name of James as the first pope in the face of growing claims of the primacy of Peter from the Western church in Rome' (*Just James* 113).

31. Cf. Acts 21.20-21; Gal. 2.6, 11-14; Rom. 15.30-31.

The *Ascents of James* (*Anabathmoi Iakōbou*), for long regarded as a principal source drawn into the Pseudo-Clementine *Recognitions* (1.33.3–1.71.6),[32] contains further fascinating material.

> The church of God founded in Jerusalem was abundantly multiplied and grew through James, who was ordained bishop in it by the Lord and governed it with most righteous administrations (1.44.3);

> James the chief of the bishops (1.68.2).

James's success in persuading all the people and the high priest to receive baptism is interrupted by 'a certain hostile man' who accuses them of being 'deceived by a magician' (1.69.8–1.70.2). Despite being 'overcome by James the bishop' the same man reacts violently and begins a murderous assault (1.70.3-6). During a confused flight, 'that hostile man attacked James and threw him down headlong from the top of the steps', nearly killing him (1.70.8). Three days later news comes from Gamaliel, a leader of the people and a secret brother, who brought news 'that the hostile man had received authority from Caiaphas the high priest to pursue all who believe in Jesus and travel to Damascus with his letters, so that there also by using the help of unbelievers he might bring ruin to the faithful. Another reason why he was especially hastening to Damascus was that he believed Peter had fled there' (1.71.3-4).

There are several noteworthy features here:

- James is again treated as a high status figure in the beginnings of the new movement — 'ordained bishop by the Lord', 'chief of bishops';
- The latter account is drawn directly from Acts, or from the sources on which Acts drew — Gamaliel (Acts 5.34-39), the savage persecution by Saul of Tarsus, and his commissioning by Caiaphas to pursue the Jesus-believers to Damascus (Acts 8.3; 9.1-2);[33]
- Saul/Paul is clearly the 'hostile man' and his initial response to James

---

32. See particularly Van Voorst, *The Ascents of James*, from whom I draw the following translations of the late fourth- or early fifth-century Latin translation by Rufinus of Aquila (d. 410). See also Jones, *An Ancient Jewish Christian Source* index 'James'; and further §45.8d below.

33. See further F. S. Jones, 'An Ancient Jewish Christian Rejoinder to Luke's Acts of the Apostles: Pseudo-Clementine *Recognitions* 1.27-71', in Stoops, ed., *Apocryphal Acts* 223-45.

takes up what became (Justin, *Dial.* 69.7; *b.Sanh.* 43a), and probably had already become, a standard Jewish dismissal of Jesus as a 'magician';[34]
- Paul's (subsequent) animosity(?) to James is prefigured in the violent attack which the 'hostile man' makes on James;
- James's success as an evangelist among his own people is integral to the plot (the conflict with Saul/Paul — *Recog.* 1.69.8–1.70.1), perhaps implying a contrast with the lack of success of (the later) Paul among his own people;[35]
- Paul's hostility to James is paralleled by an equal hostility between Paul and Peter: 'the man who is my enemy' in *Epistula Petri* (above) is no doubt equally an allusion to Paul, where the hostility is put in the present-day terms of Peter writing to James; Paul, even after his conversion, was still 'my enemy'.

This last is of a piece with *Homilies* 17.18-19 where it is most obviously Paul who is being attacked under the figure of Simon Magus, and it is Paul's claim to have seen the risen Christ (and so also Paul's claim to an apostolic commissioning) which is being dismissed. Peter speaks to Simon Magus of the revelation given to him, referring explicitly to Matt. 16.13-17, from which he

> learned that revelation is knowledge gained without instruction, and without apparition and dreams. . . . The declaration of anything by means of apparitions and dreams from without is a proof, not that it comes from revelation, but from wrath. . . . [with justification drawn from Num. 12.6-8] . . . You see how the statements of wrath are made through visions and dreams, but the statements to a friend are made face to face [as to Moses], in outward appearance, and not through riddles and visions and dreams, as to an enemy. If, then, our Jesus appeared to you in a vision, made himself known to you, and spoke to you, it was as one who is enraged with an adversary (17.18-19).

Here, clearly, it is Paul who is in view in the guise of Simon Magus,[36] and it is not the persecuting Saul who is under attack, but the Paul who claimed on the basis of the resurrection appearance made to him that he had been commissioned as an apostle. In other words, the pseudo-Clementine literature represents a form of Christianity which set itself over against Paul and did so

---

34. G. N. Stanton, 'Jesus of Nazareth: a magician and a false prophet who deceived God's people', *Jesus and Gospel* (Cambridge University, 2004) 127-47.

35. See also n.285 below.

36. See also below n.296; but also §48 n.83. It is of some interest that Luke has Paul describing his Damascus road experience as a 'heavenly vision' (Acts 26.19).

by putting Paul in outright antagonism with both James and Peter.[37] As we shall see later (§48), Peter remains at the pinnacle of veneration among Jesus' own disciples. But the literature also represents the attempt to link James and Peter tightly together, and to do so not least by setting both in antagonistic relation to Paul, so much so that Paul's claims to be an apostle, and so by implication his mission to Gentiles, can be dismissed as unauthorized and mistaken. This coalition between James and Peter and its united opposition to Paul were presumably vital to the self-understanding and self-justification of the Jewish believers-in-Jesus who saw James as their founder and leader.[38]

What should also not escape notice is that in the *Homilies'* identification of Paul with Simon Magus, they began to enter the rather different world of Gnostic Christianity, in which Simon Magus featured strongly.[39] Which brings us to the fourth and most enigmatic aspect of the revered James.

d. The Gnostic James

One of the most intriguing features to emerge from the Nag Hammadi codices is that James features as often as he does. He is given almost as much prominence in the *Gospel of Thomas* as in the traditions already cited (though not as a bishop): *Thomas* 12 — 'The disciples said to Jesus, "We know that you are going to leave us. Who will be our leader?" Jesus said to them, "In the place to which you have come, you will go to James the Just, for whose sake heaven and earth came into existence"'. Here we may have an indication that *Thomas* was drawing on a Jewish-Christian belief that it was James who really filled the place which the earlier tradition attributed to Peter;[40] though, if so, we should also recall the suggestion that since logion 13 succeeds logion 12, perhaps the implication is that Thomas with his secret teaching has superseded the earlier authority of James.[41]

Noticeably, three other Nag Hammadi tractates are attributed to James. The *Apocryphon of James* presents itself as a letter from James, the brother

37. '. . . a form of Jewish Christianity that is anti-Pauline but with a universalist strain, anticultic but with a legalistic strain, and above all obsessed with James' (Wilson, *Related Strangers* 153-54). See also J. Wehnert, 'Antipaulismus in den Pseudoklementinen', in *Ancient Perspectives on Paul,* ed. T. Nicklas, A. Merkt and J. Verheyden (SUNT 102; Göttingen: Vandenhoeck, 2013) 234-62.

38. See also Schoeps, *Jewish Christianity* 47-58; Pratscher, *Herrenbruder* 126-50.

39. See above §38.4a and below §§48.5-6. In ps.-Clem. *Hom.* 18.1, for example, Simon insists that the creator of the world is not the highest God.

40. Pratscher, *Herrenbruder* 152.

41. See above §43 n.274; though if Thomas was also a brother/twin (Didymos) of Jesus then it could imply some tension in the Thomasine view of Jesus' two brothers (Painter, *Just James* 163).

of Jesus, written, perhaps, to Cerinthus (the name is illegible).[42] It introduces itself as 'a secret book which was revealed to me and Peter by the Lord', so typical of a Gnostic-type genre which claims to pass on secret knowledge. That James is signalled out as the recipient of this secret teaching[43] tells us that once again the memory of James was revered across a wide spectrum of second-century Christianity (or Christianities), so much so that those who wanted to promote a teaching which was diverging from the Jesus tradition of the first century[44] saw James as a figure who commanded respect across the board. Also noticeable is the way James and Peter are held in close association, again suggesting a tactic to claim the accreditation of the two most prominent close associates of Jesus from the first generation.[45]

In the *First Apocalypse of James* (§40.7a), James is acknowledged to be the Lord's brother, but addresses him throughout as 'Rabbi'. James himself is named 'James the Just' (32.2-4), confirming that James's reputation as 'the Just' was widely spread. Curiously, the Lord commands him to leave Jerusalem (25.15), it would appear, prior to the Roman siege of Jerusalem (36.16-19), presumably joining the flight to Pella — this despite the firm record of James's execution in 62. Most notable is the inclusion of Addai among those to whom James is to pass on the secret teaching (36.15-24), indicating another link with Syria, as a likely melting pot or crossroads between Jewish-Christian tradition and Gnostic speculation.[46] That the presentation of James reflects some Jewish-Christian characteristics[47] strengthens the case that second-century Gnostic systems had some Jewish-Christian roots.

In the *Second Apocalypse of James* the 'discourse that James the Just spoke in Jerusalem' ends with an account of James's execution by stoning;[48] but otherwise it portrays a James who thought and spoke in Gnostic terms (§40.7b). Again the most relevant feature here is that James was regarded as a figure of esteem and authority, so that associating teaching with his name presumably was intended to give the teaching a wider appeal to those who also revered the name of James the Just.[49]

---

42. Text in *NHL* 29-37; Elliott, *ANT* 673-81.
43. Cf. again Clement of Alexandria quoted above (Eusebius, *HE* 2.1.3).
44. See above §44.5b.
45. But Painter maintains that the *Apocryphon* goes on to 'set James apart and on a level of his own' (*Just James* 165-66).
46. See below §45.8f.
47. Painter, *Just James* 169-70, with particular reference to A. Böhlig, 'Der Jüdische und judenchristlichen Hintergrund in gnostischen Texten von Nag Hammadi', in Bianchi, ed., *Le Origini dello Gnosticismo* 109-40, esp. 130-40.
48. Cited in *Beginning from Jerusalem* 1095.
49. 'James, who held a position of special prominence in Jewish-Christian circles, is regarded as the possessor of a special revelation from Jesus and is assigned a role in the

In addition, according to Hippolytus, the Naasenes attributed their teachings to James, the brother of the Lord, handed down to Mariamne (*Ref.* 5.2).

So Gnostic regard for James reflects something of the high Jewish-Christian esteem for James, setting him up in some rivalry to Peter, though not reflecting Jewish-Christian antipathy to Paul. But the Gnostic James can claim no roots in earlier James-tradition and prospers only as a mediator of secret revelation, that is, as a prototype Gnostic.[50]

So, here is the enigma of James:

- he is generally remembered as close to the Lord Jesus, the principal leader of the first Jerusalem church, and generally revered for his righteousness (James the Just);
- but apart from his leadership of the Jerusalem church being recast according to the later model of monarchical episcopacy, James was not regarded as a figure of continuing influence by the Church Fathers;
- among Jewish believers in Jesus James was regarded rather as a champion, together with Peter, against the increasingly Gentile membership of the churches;
- and, somewhat surprisingly, he was also presented as a sponsor and authoritative spokesman for more Gnostic teaching.

This suggests an unwillingness on the part of the recognized spokesmen for 'the great church' to recognize James as fully one of them,[51] as one to defend as they would Peter and Paul, a James who in the end was too unrepresentative of the Christianity which was emerging in the second and third centuries, and a James who could in effect be surrendered to the Jewish-Christian and gnostic wings of emerging Christianity without too much regret.

Gnostic tradition that rivals, and perhaps exceeds, that of Peter in the canonical tradition' (Hedrick, *NHL* 269). Pratscher notes that in *2 Apoc.Jas.* Jesus kisses James (56.14-15) and addresses him as 'my beloved' (56.16; 57.5), and wonders whether the unknown beloved disciple of John's Gospel has become the known beloved disciple of a certain Gnostic group (*Herrenbruder* 168-69).

50. Pratscher, *Herrenbruder* 176-77.

51. P.-A. Bernheim, *James, Brother of Jesus* (London: SCM, 1997): 'The pre-eminence of James as it emerges from an impartial reading of the New Testament and other traditions does not fit well with the primacy of Peter and other apostles' (271). Painter also observes that 'the emerging orthodoxy of the early church tended to isolate Jesus from all [of his family] but Mary, his virgin mother' (*Just James* 151; see also 181).

45.3 What Happened to the Jerusalem Church?

The Jerusalem assembly of believers-in-Jesus had been the mother church of all the churches which became established in the eastern Mediterranean up to 70. But it had also been the heart and centre of a traditionalist Jewish understanding and practice of the young faith, as again Acts 21.20-21 reminds us. So the question of what happened to the Jerusalem church in and as a result of the war against Rome and its catastrophic outcome is of first importance for this chapter. We have already looked at the question in *Beginning from Jerusalem* §36.3, and there is no need to repeat what was discussed there. The 'flight to Pella' tradition (that the main body of believers in Jerusalem fled across the Jordan to the city of Pella, before the siege of Jerusalem) will have to be taken up below, in view of Epiphanius's report which linked the Nazoraean heresy with Pella (*Pan.* 29.7.7-8). And the question whether Jewish believers-in-Jesus are attested in rabbinic tradition subsequently in Palestine will have to be attended to below also. For the moment our question relates to Jerusalem in the aftermath of the Jewish war.

Here we are almost entirely dependent on Eusebius, which hardly gives much cause for confidence. He gives quite a full account, but without indicating his sources, and with some notes of reserve ('the story goes', 'so it is said', 'an ancient story').[52]

> After the martyrdom of James and the capture of Jerusalem which immediately followed, the story goes that those of the Apostles and of the disciples of the Lord who were still alive came together from every place with those who were, humanly speaking, of the family of the Lord, for many of them were then still alive, and they all took counsel together as to whom they ought to adjudge worthy to succeed James, and all unanimously decided that Symeon the son of Clopas, whom the scripture of the Gospel also mentions [Luke 24.18], was worthy of the throne of the diocese there.[53] He was also, so it is said, a cousin of the Saviour, for Hegesippus relates that Clopas was the brother of Joseph, and in addition that Vespasian, after the capture of Jerusalem, ordered a search to be made for all who were of the family of David, that there might be left among the Jews no one of the royal family and, for this reason, a very great persecution was again inflicted on the Jews (*HE* 3.11.1–12.1).

---

52. Note also the unwillingness to recognize that there were birth brothers of Jesus. See e.g. J. A. Brashler, 'Jesus, Brothers and Sisters of', *ABD* 3.819-20.

53. On the list of Jerusalem bishops and on Symeon in particular, see Bauckham, *Jude and the Relatives of Jesus* 70-94.

Domitian gave orders for the execution of those of the family of David and an ancient story goes that some heretics accused the grandsons of Judas (who is said to have been the brother, according to the flesh, of the Saviour) saying that they were of the family of David and related to the Christ himself. Hegesippus relates this exactly as follows. "Now there still survived of the family of the Lord grandsons of Judas, who was said to have been his brother according to the flesh,[54] and they were delated as being of the family of David" (*HE* 3.19.1–20.1). (The grandsons demonstrate that they were simple peasants and the story continues.) "They were asked concerning the Christ and his kingdom, its nature, origin, and time of appearance, and explained that it was neither of the world nor earthly, but heavenly and angelic, and it would be at the end of the world, when he would come in glory to judge the living and the dead and to reward every man according to his deeds. At this Domitian did not condemn them at all, but despised them as simple folk, released them, and decreed an end to the persecution against the church. But when they were released they were the leaders of the churches, both for their testimony and for their relation to the Lord, and remained alive in the peace which ensued until Trajan" (*HE* 3.20.4-6).

Eusebius goes on to record more fully that these members of the Lord's family survived until the reign of Trajan (98-107), and 'presided over every church', during a time of 'complete peace in every church' (*HE* 3.32.5-6). During Trajan's reign, however, the same Symeon/Simon, son of Clopas, second bishop of the Jerusalem church, was martyred — at the age of 120! Eusebius, still quoting Hegesippus, recounts that Symeon was accused of being a descendant of David and a Christian by 'certain heretics',[55] was 'tortured for many days' and finally crucified (*HE* 3.32.1-6). Eusebius also notes that Hegesippus 'makes extracts from the Gospel according to the Hebrews, and from the Syriac and particularly from the Hebrew language, showing that he had been converted from among the Hebrews, and he mentions points as coming from the unwritten tradition of the Jews' (*HE* 4.22.8).

If Eusebius is reliable on all this,[56] then Hegesippus could provide

---

54. On the ancient question of whether James and Jude/Judas were children of Joseph and Mary (full brothers of Jesus) see Bauckham, *Jude and the Relatives of Jesus* 19-32; on the passage here (30-32); Bernheim, *James, Brother of Jesus* ch. 1.

55. On the 'certain heretics' see below. But since the accusers of Symeon were themselves arrested as members of the 'royal house of the Jews' (*HE* 3.32.4), Smallwood 'suggests that Symeon's enemies were members of his own family who had not adopted Christianity and were trying, unsuccessfully, to divert attention from themselves' (*Jews* 352).

56. See below at n.61. 'Some of the earlier traditions contain legendary or improbable material but can still be used, with the help of modern critical methods, to aid in putting

good testimony on the post-70 history of the Jerusalem community of Jewish believers-in-Jesus — Hegesippus being himself, according to Eusebius, a Jewish believer-in-Jesus. That James was succeeded by a cousin, Symeon,[57] certainly fits with the suggestion that James himself gained his leadership role because he was Jesus' brother, perhaps already reflecting the caliphate tradition of succession through brother or cousin rather than son.[58] The later story (the late 80s or early 90s) of grandsons of another brother, Judas, brought before emperor Domitian, maintains the implication of a family dynasty, though those referred to are described simply as 'leaders of the churches'[59] and as 'simple folk'.[60] It is far from clear how this relates to the earlier report which Eusebius drew from the early third-century Julius Africanus, that those known as *'desposyni*, because of their relation to the family of the Saviour', went about the rest of the land (Palestine) from the Jewish villages of Nazareth and Kokhaba, expounding the genealogy of their descent (*HE* 1.7.14).[61] But it is at least likely that communities of Jewish believers in Jesus continued to flourish or at least persist in Palestine, under the continuing leadership of the family of Jesus at least till the second decade of the second century.[62]

Still more intriguing is the fact that Hegesippus traces 'the seven heresies . . . among the people' (that is, the Jewish believers-in-Jesus) to Thebouthis, 'because he had not been made bishop'.

---

together reconstructions of early Christian history' (G. F. Chesnut, 'Eusebius of Caesarea', *ABD* 2.675).

57. The dating is at best confused, since according to Hegesippus Vespasian began the siege of Jerusalem immediately after the execution of James (*HE* 2.23.18); so when and where Symeon took over the leadership of the Jerusalem believers is hardly clear.

58. Discussion in Bauckham, *Jude and the Relatives of Jesus* 125-30.

59. Presumably assemblies of Jewish believers-in-Jesus in Judaea.

60. See further Bauckham, *Jude and the Relatives of Jesus* 94-106.

61. See further Bauckham, *Jude and the Relatives of Jesus* 60-70. 'In fact, the relatives of Jesus are the only early Christian leaders we can confidently locate in Galilee' (131); Bauckham goes on to resist the thesis that Jerusalem and Galilee had different forms of Christianity (131-32). The archaeological evidence is unhelpful: J. Taylor concludes her 'Parting in Palestine', in H. Shanks, ed., *Partings: How Judaism and Christianity Became Two* (Washington: Biblical Archaeology Society, 2013) 87-104, 312-17: 'there is currently no archaeological evidence for Jewish-Christianity in Galilee' (104); E. M. Meyers, 'Living Side by Side in Galilee' in the same volume (133-50; notes 326-29), deals mainly with the later situation, but concludes that 'before Constantine, we have very little material evidence for the existence of Christianity in the Holy Land' (149).

62. On the list of Jerusalem bishops and on Symeon in particular, see Bauckham, *Jude and the Relatives of Jesus* 70-94. Bauckham concludes his study of Symeon: 'Symeon was therefore the leader of the Jerusalem church and probably the most important figure in Jewish Christianity for nearly forty years, perhaps even longer' (93).

After James the Just had suffered martyrdom for the same reason as the Lord, Symeon, his cousin, the son of Clopas was appointed bishop, whom they all proposed because he was another cousin of the Lord. For this cause they called the church virgin, for it had not yet been corrupted by vain messages, but Thebouthis, because he had not been made bishop, begins its corruption by the seven heresies, to which he belonged, among the people. Of these were Simon, whence the Simonians, and Dositheus, whence the Dosithians, and Gorthaeus, whence the Goratheni and the Masbothei. From these come the Menandrianists and the Marcianists and the Carpocratians and the Valentinians and the Basilidians and Saturnilians; each of these puts forward in its own peculiar way its own opinion, and from them come the false Christs and false prophets and false apostles who destroy the unity of the church by their poisonous doctrine against God and against his Christ (*HE* 4.22.4-6).[63]

This is an early expression of Eusebius's view that heresy was a late corruption of the originally 'virgin church', the traditional view which Bauer so sharply questioned.[64] But it is very striking that Hegesippus attributes the rise of heresy to members of the mother church, or perhaps more accurately, to disaffected members of the mother church. The heresies named are mostly those of the standard (principally Gnostic) heretics — Simon (Magus), Menander, Marcion, Carpocrates, Valentinus, Basilides and Saturninus. But it is notable that Dositheus, a Samaritan, is depicted more as a Jewish heretic,[65] and that the Masbothei are listed also as a Jewish sect.[66] It would appear, then, that

---

63. Eusebius goes on to quote Hegesippus's description of 'the sects which once existed among the Jews' — 'Essenes, Galileans, Hemerobaptists, Masbothei, Samaritans, Sadducees, and Pharisees'.

64. See above §38.2.

65. The traditions regarding Dositheus are very confused and may refer to more than one individual. For example, he is described by Pseudo-Tertullian as one of 'Judaism's heretics, ... Dositheus the Samaritan, who was the first who had the hardihood to repudiate the prophets'; the Sadducees arose 'from the root' of Dositheus's error (*adv. haer.* 1); he is depicted as a follower of John the Baptist, and the first to deny the resurrection of the dead (Ps. Clem., *Recog.* 1.54.1-3); the relation of Dositheus and Simon is unclear, which one was the initial leader of the sect (Ps.Clem., *Recog.* 2.8; *Hom.* 2.24); according to Origen, Dositheus claimed to be 'the Christ prophesied by Moses' and 'son of God' (*c.Celsum* 1.57; 6.11); the Nag Hammadi tractates include 'The Three Steles of Seth', revelation given to Dositheus (*NHL* VII.5). See further S. J. Isser, *The Dositheans: A Samaritan Sect in Late Antiquity* (SJLA 17; Leiden: Brill, 1976); A. D. Crown, *The Samaritans* (Tübingen: Mohr Siebeck, 1989) 41-43.

66. From the references to the Goratheni, in Epiphanius and Theodoret, we learn no more than we do from Hegesippus. Notable is the fact that so many of those named are designated in one place or another as Samaritans — Simon, Dositheus, Gortheus(?), Menander, Saturninus.

Hegesippus did not see any clear distinction between Jewish sects and early Gnostic-type or proto-Gnostic groups.[67] For all the question marks which must be attached to Hegesippus's testimony, such accounts give further strength to the likelihood that Jewish influence played a significant part in the emergence of groups subsequently described simply as Gnostic.[68] At any rate, it would be highly questionable to portray the great church as a main trajectory with 'Jewish-Christian' and 'Gnostic' trajectories each going off at a tangent separately, on either side of the main trajectory. The development of Christianity was much messier than that, a criss-crossing of muddy tracks rather than clear distinct paths diverging from each other.[69]

We will pause at this point, since it would appear that after the second Jewish revolt and the foundation of Aelia Capitolina, the local Jerusalem church was purely Gentile in composition.[70] Interestingly, Hegesippus's report of the emergence of the 'seven heresies' makes no link with the later reports which identify the beginning of the Ebionites in Pella, and the tradition of the Jerusalem believers fleeing to Pella before the siege of Jerusalem. Without being able to do more than highlight these curiosities we will return to the tradition of Pella as the source of the Jewish-Christian 'heresies' below.

45.4 The Jewish Christian Writings of the New Testament

If we are to appreciate how Jewish was the mainstream of Christianity which began to emerge through the final decades of the first century, we must pay particular attention to the documents, particularly the NT documents, of course, which emerged during that period. The point being made, I should repeat, is that 'Jewish' should not be regarded as describing a separate stream, far less simply a divergent, even renegade stream running into the second century and beyond — 'Jewish Christianity' in the old sense of *Jewish*-Christian 'heresy'. The core founding documents of what became catholic Christianity

---

67. We will have to give further attention below to Simon, Marcion, Valentinus and Basilides (see below particularly §46.6i and §47.5b).

68. In patristic opinion Cerinthus and the Ebionites were closely associated (Irenaeus, *adv. haer.* 1.26.1-2; Hippolytus, *refutatio* Prol. 7.7-9; 7.34.1; 10.22.1; pseudo-Tertullian, *adv. omn. haer.* 3; Epiphanius, *anacephalaiosis* t.2 30.1; Jerome, *ep.* 112.13) — 'Cerinthus and his successor Ebion' (Jerome, *adv. Luc.* 23). The same story, of the apostle John rushing from a bathhouse in Asia to escape from the presence of a heretic, is told with reference both to Cerinthus (Irenaeus, *adv. haer.* 3.3.4) and to Ebion (Epiphanius, *anacephalaiosis* t.2 30.24.1-5).

69. See above §38 at n.47.

70. Eusebius, *HE* 4.6.4; *ODCC* 869.

were also Jewish through and through, deeply rooted in Jewish scriptures, faith and ethics, so much so that it is not inaccurate to describe mainstream Christianity as directly continuous with Second Temple Judaism, and catholic Christianity itself as Jewish Christianity, since the Jewish character of Christianity is integral to its identity.[71]

a. The New Testament Gospels

i. Mark

The Gospel according to Mark is arguably the least Jewish of the four canonical Gospels. But even there the Jewish context and character of Jesus' mission is clearly presupposed.

- The Gospel is introduced with the quotations from Exod. 23.20 and Isa. 40.3 (Mark 1.2-3).
- The opening Judaean context and subsequent Galilean context are made clear from the beginning (1.5, 14, 28, 39).
- The initial focus on mission in the synagogues is equally clear (1.21, 39; 3.1; 6.2).
- Jesus insists that the healed leper should go to the priest and follow the instructions laid down by Moses for such a case (1.44).
- His dispute with Pharisees regarding the Sabbath is not about *whether* the Sabbath should be observed, but *how* it should be observed (2.27; 3.4).
- His disciples are all fellow Jews, twelve of them appointed, with obvious (twelve tribes) symbolism (3.14-19).
- Jesus' explanation of why he speaks in parables is drawn from Isa. 6.9-10 (Mark 4.11-12).
- He brings new life to the daughter of the leader of the synagogue (5.35-43).
- He speaks of himself as a prophet (6.4) and is widely regarded as a prophet (6.15; 8.28).
- He debates with Pharisees and scribes and instructs his disciples on the nature of purity, again quoting Isa. 29.13 to justify his stance (7.1-23).
- He is confessed by Peter to be 'the Messiah' of Israel's hopes (8.29).
- He experiences the company and by implication the affirmation of Mo-

---

71. Cf. and contrast Daniélou's definition of 'Jewish Christianity' as encompassing '"all Christian theology of Jewish expression" from the beginnings of Christianity to the middle of the second century' (Mimouni, *Early Judaeo-Christianity* 29).

ses and Elijah on the mountain (9.4), and affirms that the hope for Elijah to come (from heaven) has been realized (by implication) in the ministry of the Baptist (9.13).
- Jesus discusses divorce with Pharisees, justifying his view on the basis of Gen. 1.27 and 2.24 (Mark 10.6-8), and responds to the man asking what he must do to inherit eternal life by referring him to the (ten) commandments (10.19).
- He is hailed by the blind man as 'son of David' (10.47, 48), and on his entry into Jerusalem the crowd hails him in the words of Ps. 118.25, as 'the one who comes in the name of the Lord' (Mark 11.9).
- He justifies his controversial action in 'cleansing the temple' by citing Isa. 56.7 and Jer. 7.11 (Mark 11.17).
- In the parable of the vineyard tenants he takes up the imagery of Israel as God's vineyard (Isa. 5.1-7) and justifies the parable's judgmental outcome by reference to Ps. 118.22-23 (Mark 12.10-11).
- He affirms the Pharisaic hope of resurrection of the dead over against the Sadducees (12.18-27), affirms the priority of the Shema (Deut. 6.4-5) (Mark 12.29-30), selects Lev. 19.18 as indicating the next most important priority (Mark 12.31) and echoes Hos. 6.6 on love as more important than sacrifice (Mark 12.33).
- He is keen to celebrate the Passover with his disciples and depicts his coming death as a covenant sacrifice (14.12-15, 24).
- In the hearing before the High Priest he affirms that he is the Messiah (14.61-62) and is crucified as 'the king of the Jews' (15.26).
- On his death the veil of the temple is torn in two, from top to bottom (15.38), leaving the reader to reflect on its significance.[72]

Mark was well aware that he was writing for a Gentile Christian audience. He knew he had to explain, for example, such niceties as that the Greek term *koinos*, which in everyday Greek meant 'common', was the term used in Greek-speaking Jewish circles to denote 'defiled', that is, not having been ritually purified (7.2). In other words, he knew he had to explain the Jewish context and character of Jesus' mission. He did not hide or obscure either context or character. He simply took it for granted that this Jewish context and character were integral to the story of Jesus. So much so, that even Jesus' rendering the laws of unclean food null (7.19), his warning that responsibility for the vineyard of Israel would be passed to others (12.9) and his prediction

---

72. For the influence of the OT, especially the Psalms, in shaping the account of Jesus' death, see *Jesus Remembered* 777-81; now also K. O'Brien, *The Use of Scripture in the Markan Passion Narrative* (LNTS 384; London: T & T Clark, 2010).

that the temple would be destroyed (13.2, 14) were to be seen as qualifications of the overall portrayal, not as attempts to extricate Jesus from his context or to deny the character of his mission.[73]

ii. Luke

The Gentile orientation of the Gospel according to Luke and of Luke-Acts is much clearer, articulated as early as Simeon's paean of praise in Luke 2.29-32. But Luke takes even more pains to ensure that the Jewishness of Jesus' person and mission is clear beyond peradventure. For example,

- the canticles of Luke 1-2 are shot through with Jewish sentiment and hope now to be fulfilled, the evocation of Hannah's prayer (1 Sam. 2.1-10) in Mary's *Magnificat* being particularly noticeable (Luke 1.46-55).
- That what had happened, in the birth of the Baptist, and in the raising up of Jesus Messiah and Mosaic prophet, was in fulfillment of God's covenant promise to Abraham is emphasized early in each volume (Luke 1.72; Acts 3.25).
- Jesus was circumcised and the offering for purification was performed in accordance with the law (Luke 2.21-24).
- Simeon looked for 'the consolation of Israel' (2.25) and Anna spoke for all who look for 'the redemption of Jerusalem' (2.38), just as Paul at the end of Acts could say that his imprisonment in Rome was 'for the sake of the hope of Israel' (Acts 28.20).

So also,

- Jesus was the one who fulfilled the prophetic hope of Isa. 61.1-2 (Luke 4.17-21).
- Jesus fulfils the hopes for the age to come expressed by Isaiah (7.22).
- Referring to the disciples as the 'little flock' (12.32) echoes the popular image of Israel as God's flock.[74]
- Jesus sets his mission wholly within the context of the mission of former prophets (13.33-34).
- The twelve disciples, Jesus predicts, 'will sit on thrones judging the twelve tribes of Israel' (22.30).

---

73. See now J. G. Crossley, 'Mark's Christology and a Scholarly Creation of a Non-Jewish Christ of Faith', in J. G. Crossley, ed., *Judaism, Jewish Identities and the Gospel Tradition: Essays in Honour of Maurice Casey* (London and Oakville, CT: Equinox, 2010) 118-51.
74. See *Jesus Remembered* 511 n.107.

- The risen Christ explains that what had happened to Jesus was fully in accord with prophetic expectation (24.25-27, 44-47).

So far as Acts is concerned, we could give as further examples the felt need to restore the twelve by finding a replacement for Judas (Acts 1.20-26);[75] the fulfillment of other prophecies (2.16-21, 25-28, 34-35; etc.); as with Paul, the covenant made with the patriarchs includes the promise of Abraham's seed as a blessing to all the families of the earth;[76] the solution to the Gentile problem in terms of the resident aliens within Israel (15.14-20);[77] and the way Paul could legitimately claim that he was on trial for the hope of the resurrection which Pharisees shared (23.6).[78]

Luke too, then, takes for granted the Jewish character of the story he is telling. That he tells the story with particular reference to the incoming of the Gentiles is clear. But he seeks to integrate this outreach to non-Jews wholly with the Jewish character of covenant promise and prophetic hope; it was just that the promise and the hope had been realized in the Gentile mission.

iii. Matthew

With the Gospel according to Matthew, the Jewishness of his presentation need hardly be argued for, since Matthew is the most Jewish of the Gospels.[79] In fact the demonstration of how Matthew handled the Jesus tradition (§42.3a) was very largely a demonstration of Jesus' significance for Israel, as Messiah and Son of David, and in fulfillment of various Jewish scriptures (§42.3b). We noted that Matthew is alone in reporting Jesus' insistence that he was sent only for 'the lost sheep of the house of Israel' (10.6; 15.24). And in presenting Jesus as jousting with the Pharisees over Israel's heritage (§42.3d), Matthew went out of his way to insist that Jesus, and by implication the Matthean congregations, was wholly loyal to the law, and indeed, more righteous than the Pharisees (5.17-20). It is not too much of an exaggeration to infer that Matthew was determined to present Jesus in the form of and with the effect of a new Moses.[80] Matthew's Jewish mindset is probably nowhere more

---

75. That Luke related the replacement of Judas and thus regarded the restoration of the twelve as of first importance should not be ignored (see §42 n.389 above).

76. Acts 3.25, quoting Gen. 12.3/18.18, as had Paul in Gal. 3.8.

77. See again *Beginning from Jerusalem* 461-68.

78. See further Keener, *Acts* 1.473-77, 477-91.

79. Sim insists that it is mistaken to label the religion of the Matthean community as 'Christianity'; 'their religious tradition is most aptly described as Christian Judaism' (*Gospel of Matthew* 299); see further below §46.5b.

80. See §42 n.223 above.

evident than in his understanding of sin as 'debt' and in the emphasis he gives to judgment and reward — a trait which some would regard as unchristian.[81]

iv. John

As for the Gospel according to John, the perspective is almost as clear. Again the point need hardly be elaborated here since, as with Matthew, the way in which John handled the Jesus tradition tells a very similar story (§43.1c). So, for example, it was still important for John to be able to insist that Jesus was Messiah (1.41; 4.25-26).[82] It is the precedents from Israel's history which explain and make sense of Jesus' mission:

- the (Passover) lamb of God that takes away the sins of the whole world (John 1.29; 19.33-36);
- Moses' bronze serpent giving life to those bitten by serpents in the wilderness (Num. 21.6-9), foreshadowing the lifting up of the Son of Man to give eternal life to all who believe in him (John 3.14-15);
- the water of Jacob's well foreshadowing the living water provided by Jesus (4.10-14), accompanied by the assertion unique to John that 'salvation is from the Jews' (4.22);
- Moses wrote about Jesus (5.46), and the manna from heaven foreshadowed Jesus as the true bread from heaven (6.32);
- and Jesus' claim to be 'the true vine' (15.1) evoking the familiar imagery of Israel as a vine.

It is clear, even from this brief resume, that John could not conceive of Jesus apart from his Jewish context and the Jewish character of his mission. Unless Jesus was the fulfiller of Israel's hopes he would have been nothing for John, or at least, John would have been unable to spell out Jesus' significance. Of course, with John, and Matthew in particular, there is more to be said and we will have to return to the subject to look at the data provided from a different angle in the next chapter (§46.5).[83] But too much of the discussion of these texts, in particular in the last few decades, has been dominated by the issue to which we will return in §46, the partings of the ways, and indeed, by the question whether anti-semitism is expressed, as well as rooted, in Matthew

---

81. See particularly N. Eubank, *Wages of Cross-bearing and Debt of Sin: The Economy of Heaven in Matthew's Gospel* (BZNW 196; Berlin: de Gruyter, 2013).

82. John, we recall, is the only NT writer to refer to Jesus as *Messias*.

83. The question of John's relation to Gnosticism, of course, complicates the issue. See e.g. Barrett, who signals the possible confusion by noting that 'this gospel contains Judaism, non-Judaism, and anti-Judaism', followed by 'John combines Gnosis and anti-Gnosticism' (*The Gospel of John and Judaism* 71-72).

and John.[84] So it has been important to make clear that these documents, whatever role they played or did not play in the pulling apart of Christianity from Judaism, were themselves thoroughly Jewish in character, and that they did not even begin to entertain the idea that Jesus could have been other than Israel's Messiah, the one who fulfilled Israel's hopes and the expectations of Israel's prophets.

b. The Later Paulines

When we turn to the post-Pauline letters which belong to the Pauline corpus, it would be easy to fall into the assumption that a pro-Gentile trajectory which began with the Pauline mission would by then have veered well away from the Jewish beginnings of Christianity. But that is far from the case.

i. Ephesians

Starting with Ephesians, we have already noted that even if written after Paul, it provides one of the clearest statements of Paul's own priorities, in taking a Jewish gospel to non-Jews.[85] Even so, one might easily be surprised by its overtly Jewish character. This is clear from the outset.

- The recipients are described as 'saints' twice in the opening verses (1.1, 4) and there is more talk of the 'saints' than in any other Pauline letter (10 times).[86]
- The blessing in 1.3-14 uses characteristic Jewish language throughout: for example, 'Blessed are you',[87] 'chosen',[88] 'the beloved',[89] 'the mystery of his will',[90] and 'God's possession'.[91]
- And the following prayer, 1.17-19 in particular, is full of semitic phrases — 'the Father of glory', 'a spirit of wisdom and revelation in the knowl-

---

84. See below §46.5e.
85. See *Beginning from Jerusalem* §37.1.
86. 'The saints' = Israel (e.g. Pss. 16.3; 34.9; Isa. 4.3; Dan. 7.18, 21-22; Tob. 8.15; Wisd. Sol. 18.9; 1QSb 3.2; 1QM 3.5; 10.10) — a characteristic feature of Paul's address (1 Cor. 1.2; 2 Cor. 1.1; Phil. 1.1; Col. 1.2).
87. 1 Kgs. 8.15; 1QS 11.15; Luke 1.68-75.
88. Deut. 7.6-8; 14.2.
89. Deut. 32.15; 33.5, 26; Isa. 44.2; Dan 3.35 LXX; Sir. 45.1; 46.13.
90. Dan. 2.18-19, 27-30; and further R. E. Brown, *The Semitic Background of the Term 'Mystery' in the New Testament* (Philadelphia: Fortress, 1968).
91. Exod. 19.5; Deut. 14.2; 26.18; Mal. 3.17.

edge of him',[92] 'your heart having been enlightened',[93] 'the riches of his glorious inheritance among the saints',[94] and 'greatness of his power . . . the working of his mighty strength'.[95]

None of this can be put down simply to a contrived or even learned familiarity with the Jewish scriptures. Rather we have to speak of a writer whose own thought processes were thoroughly impregnated with characteristic Jewish thought and idiom.

The same is true of the latter half of the letter, the paraenesis in particular. There are over 20 quotations and echoes (of differing strengths) of LXX passages, including Torah, Prophets and Writings.[96] Here again we cannot speak of literary artifice so much as of a mode of thought and speech whose very language and metaphors have been shaped by life-long familiarity with the Jewish scriptures.[97]

Overall the impression given by the letter is of a native (Hellenistic) Jewish perspective, assumed from within rather than from without.[98] This is particularly noticeable in the author's strongly Jewish attitude to non-Jews, that is, to Gentiles. The readership envisaged is clearly Gentile (2.11; 3.1). So the description of their pre-Christian state is significant — 'dead in trespasses and sins' (2.1, 5), under the domination of evil powers (angels) who led them astray (2.2),[99] 'sons of disobedience' (2.2; 5.6), 'by nature children of [divine] wrath, like the rest' (2.3), 'once you were in darkness' (5.8). Similarly the exhortation of 4.17-19, where the words associated with 'Gentiles' express a native Jewish perspective — 'futility', 'darkened', alienated from the life of God, 'ignorance', 'licentiousness', 'uncleanness'. In

---

92. Cf. Isa. 11.2; Wis. 7.7; 1QS 4.3-5.

93. 1QS 2.3; 11.3-6.

94. Cf. 1QS 11.7-8; for anyone familiar with the Jewish scriptures, this phrase would immediately evoke the characteristic talk of the promised land of Israel as God's inheritance (see e.g. W. Foerster and J. Herrmann, *TDNT* 3.759-61, 769-76).

95. Cf. Isa. 40.26; and further K. G. Kuhn, 'The Epistle to the Ephesians in the Light of the Qumran Texts', in J. Murphy-O'Connor, ed., *Paul and Qumran* (London: Chapman, 1968) 115-31.

96. Details in my 'Deutero-Pauline Letters', in J. Barclay and J. Sweet, eds., *Early Christian Thought in Its Jewish Context* (Cambridge University, 1996) 130-144 (here 137), from which I draw most of the treatment here of Ephesians and the Pastorals.

97. See also A. T. Lincoln, 'The Use of the OT in Ephesians', *JSNT* 14 (1982) 16-57. Note also, in particular, the use of Pss. 110.1 and 8.6 in Eph. 1.20-22 and the striking interpretation of Ps. 68.18 in Eph. 4.8.

98. Cf. e.g. V. P. Furnish, 'Ephesians, Epistle to the', *ABD* 2.538-39; A. T. Lincoln, 'The Theology of Ephesians', in A. T. Lincoln and A. J. M. Wedderburn, *The Theology of the Later Pauline Letters* (Cambridge University, 1993) 73-166 (here 89-90).

99. Cf. particularly *Jub.* 15.31.

such passages the author speaks quite naturally as one who views the world through Jewish eyes.

It is within this context that the key passage (2.11-22) gains its fullest significance. The perspective is again wholly Jewish: the readers are called 'Gentiles in the flesh, called "uncircumcision" by those who called themselves "circumcision"' (2.11). Previously they had been 'without Christ, alienated from the body politic of Israel, and strangers to the covenants of promise, having no hope and without God in the world' (2.12). Correspondingly, the blessings received by these Gentiles, who have now responded to the gospel of Christ, are the same covenant blessings of Israel — peace, access to God as Father,[100] 'no longer strangers and resident aliens, but fellow-citizens with the saints and members of God's household . . .' (2.17-19). The symbolism of the (Jerusalem) temple as the place of God's dwelling transposed to the community as a whole (2.18-22), is fully in line with the Jewish ideal implied, for example, in Exod. 19.6, Lev. 26.11-12 and Ezek. 37.27, and is parallel to a similar move at Qumran (1QS 8-9).

As already indicated (§37.1), the author captured well the high Pauline priority, to reassure Gentile believers-in-Jesus that they fully participated in blessings previously understood as limited to Israel. The 'mystery' had been unveiled, that 'Gentiles are fellow heirs [that is, with the Jews]' (3.6). Insofar as the law had presented a barrier separating Jew from Gentile, it had been abolished (2.14-15), with the consequence that what were previously two (Jew and Gentile) are now 'one new human being' (2.15). This is the language not of Gentile triumphalism over ethnic Israel, but of an Israel universalized by recourse to the larger category of new creation (1.22; 4.22-24). But it is also the language of a Gentile Christianity which could not understand itself except in terms of the category of Israel and of Israel's blessings.

ii. The Pastoral Epistles

In some contrast, when we turn to the Pastoral Epistles, the issues of Jewish context seem to be a degree or two more remote. Paul's apostleship to the Gentiles has none of the centrality which it had in the earlier Paulines — 'a teacher of the Gentiles' (1 Tim. 2.7), 'that all the Gentiles might hear the message' (2 Tim. 4.17). The 'mystery', so prominent in the earlier Pauline expositions of the same theme,[101] has become something more formalized — 'the mystery of faith', 'the mystery of our religion' (1 Tim. 3.9, 16). The

---

100. Cf. Rom. 5.2; 1QS 11.13-15.
101. Rom. 11.25; Col. 1.26-27; Eph. 3.3-6.

challenges confronted in the two letters to Timothy seem to be lacking in anything distinctively Jewish in character — 'myths and genealogies', 'godless and silly myths' (1 Tim. 1.4, 20; 4.7), 'knowledge' (1 Tim. 6.20), 'dispute about words', 'godless chatter', 'holding the resurrection is past' (2 Tim. 2.14, 16, 18), 'stupid, senseless controversies' (2 Tim. 2.23). That said, however, we should also recall the strong possibility that Jewish elements ('Jewish myths' — Tit. 1.14) were drawn into and acted possibly as a catalyst to early Gnostic speculation.[102] So the possibility that the Pastorals indicate more of the elements in that mixed bag should certainly not be ruled out.

More striking is the positive attitude to the law in 1 Tim. 1.7-9 — 'desiring to be teachers of the law' (a good ambition in itself), 'the law is good', 'the law is for the lawless' — which echoes the positive role ascribed to the law in Rom. 2.12-16, 7.12-13 and 13.3-4. Only with 1 Tim. 4.3-5, warning against those 'who forbid marriage and enjoin abstinence from foods which God created to be received with thanksgiving . . .', with its echoes of 1 Cor. 7, 10.25 and Rom. 14.6, do we see reflected the more critical sensitivities of Paul the Jew wrestling with the law as a problem for Christian praxis. Similarly in 2 Tim. 1.9 and Tit. 3.5 the talk of salvation not because of works but in virtue of God's mercy seems even more dispassionate and formulaic than Eph. 2.8-9. In somewhat more marked contrast to earlier Pauline letters, the emphasis on 'good works' as a desirable goal is a consistent and regular theme in the Pastorals.[103] But characteristic of Paul the Jew is the strong affirmation of 2 Tim. 3.16 that 'all scripture is inspired by God' and is useful for teaching, for reproof, for correction, and for training in righteousness'.

Only in the case of Titus can we speak with assurance of an engagement with distinctively Jewish issues.[104] In Tit. 1.10-11 the author castigates 'those of the circumcision', who are presumably also in view in the dismissive talk of 'Jewish myths' and 'commands of men who reject the truth' (1.14), and again in warnings against 'quarrels relating to the law' (3.9). Even if the teaching was syncretistic, it was both predominantly Jewish in character and promulgated by (Christian?) Jews. Perhaps, then, in this case a conflict between church and synagogue lies in the background, possibly a competition for adherents and sympathizers (God-fearers)[105] who were attracted to the

---

102. See above §39 at n.210.

103. Twelve times; cf. 2 Cor. 9.8; Phil. 1.6; 2 Thess. 2.17; Col. 1.10; Eph. 2.10.

104. The Jewish character of the Pastorals is often missed, subsumed into a discussion of the (Jewish?) character of the opposition in view (e.g. Kümmel, *Introduction* 378-79; Marshall, *Pastoral Epistles* 46).

105. See B. Chilton, 'The Godfearers: From the Gospels to Aphrodisias', in Shanks, ed., *Partings* 55-71, with earlier bibliography in the notes (309-10).

various house groups/synagogues/churches which evidently still operated in a not altogether undifferentiated or at least overlapping way at this time.[106] Hence also, perhaps, the more substantial echo of Pauline language in 3.1-3 and reminder of Pauline soteriology in 3.5-7, indicating a sense on the part of the author of the need to recall his readers to teaching which had originally been forged in the fiercer fires of controversy stirred by Paul's mission to the Gentiles.

We will delay discussion of the Pastorals' christology till §47.2a. But here we should also note the degree to which the thought world and language of the Pastorals draws often unconsciously on Jewish categories. 1 Timothy provides several examples:

> 2.2 — the expression of the political prudence learned by Jewish minorities over decades of existence in the diaspora, often under hostile authorities;[107]
> 2.13-15 — the use of Adam and the fall narratives (Gen. 1-3);
> 3.15 — the talk of 'the household of God, which is the assembly (*ekklēsia*) of the living God', echoing the Jewish understanding of the community as God's dwelling place,[108] and the regular LXX reference to the assembly (*ekklēsia*) of Israel;[109]
> 4.3-4 — the obvious allusions to Gen. 9.3 and 1.31;
> 5.18-19 — the citation of Deut. 25.4 and 19.15;
> 6.7 — the reflection of sober day-to-day wisdom as in Job 1.21 and Eccles. 5.15.

Likewise in 2 Timothy Jewish categories are assumed: 'Paul' speaks positively of his ancestors (1.3); he endures 'for the sake of the elect' (2.10); he affirms the central importance of the holy (that is, Jewish) scriptures (3.15-16). And several passages draw on scriptural and Jewish language and themes:

- 2.7 — Prov. 2.6;
- 2.19 — Isa. 28.16 again, with quotations from Num. 16.5 and Isa. 26.13;
- 3.8 — Jannes and Jambres (Exod. 7.11, 22; cf. CD 5.18-19);
- 3.11 — Ps. 34.19; *Pss. Sol.* 4.23;
- 3.15 — Ps. 119.98;
- 4.8 — Wis. 5.16;

106. On the question of the legal status of the early Christian groupings, see below §46 at n.53.
107. Cf. Ezra 6.10; Jer. 29.7; Bar. 1.11; Rom. 12.15-21.
108. See above on Ephesians (§45.4b).
109. *Beginning from Jerusalem* §30.1.

- 4.14 — Ps. 62.12; Prov. 24.12; etc.;
- 4.17 — Ps. 22.21; 1 Macc. 2.60.

The same positive affirmation of Jewish categories and faith is evident also in Titus: the addressees are 'God's elect' (1.1); the purpose of God's saving act in Christ was to 'redeem us from all lawlessness and cleanse for himself a people of his own, zealous for good works' (2.14);[110] and there are various echoes of typically Jewish language in the hymn-like passage in 3.4-7.[111] Whether in all this we see here evidenced a still living relationship with the broader Judaisms which survived the catastrophe of the first Jewish revolt it is not possible to say. But even if the language is simply inherited Christian tradition, it remains significant that that inheritance retains such a thoroughly Jewish character, and that the language is used so instinctively. The Christianity thus expressed is still Jewish through and through.

c. The Rest of the New Testament

Here we will focus primarily on Hebrews, Jude and Revelation.

i. Hebrews

It would seem to be hardly necessary to demonstrate the Jewishness of Hebrews, since it must appear fairly obvious. But since the letter might well be regarded as expressing the first clear anti-Judaism sentiments in the NT (§46.5d), it is all the more important to appreciate its own intensely Jewish character.

More than any other NT writing, Hebrews is structured round regular and repeated use of and reference to the Jewish (OT) scriptures:[112]

---

110. The resonance with Exod. 19.5; Deut. 7.6; 14.2; Ps. 130.8 and Ezek. 37.23 is clear; see H. Preisker, *TDNT* 6.57-58.

111. Particularly Deut. 9.5; Ps. 31.21; Joel 2.28; Wis. 1.6.

112. I follow the quotations identified in Nestle-Aland[26] and Nestle-Aland[28]. For the variations in reckoning the number of quotations or references see e.g. Lane, *Hebrews* 1.cxvi. Schnelle reckons 35 direct quotations (exclusively from the LXX) and about 80 allusions to OT passages (*History* 375). 'The interpretation of Scripture is certainly the key for understanding Hebrews' (Koester, *Introduction* 273-74). See also Attridge, *Hebrews* 23-25; Koester, *Hebrews* 115-18, both with further bibliography; A. Gheorghita, *The Role of the Septuagint in Hebrews: An Investigation of Its Influence with Special Consideration to the Use of Hab 2:3-4 in Heb 10:37-38* (WUNT 2.160; Tübingen: Mohr Siebeck, 2001); A. Rascher, *Schriftauslegung und Christologie im Hebräerbrief* (BZNW 153; Berlin: de Gruyter, 2007).

1.5a	Ps. 2.7	6.14	Gen. 22.17
1.5b	2 Sam. 7.14	7.1-2	Gen. 14.17-20
1.6	Deut. 32.43	7.4	Gen. 14.20
1.7	Ps. 104.4 LXX	7.17	Ps. 110.4
1.8-9	Ps. 45.6-7 LXX	7.21	Ps. 110.4
1.10-12	Ps. 102.25-27 LXX	8.5	Exod. 25.40
1.13	Ps. 110.1 LXX	8.8-12	Jer. 31.31-34
2.6-8	Ps. 8.4-6 LXX	9.20	Exod. 24.8
2.12	Ps. 22.22 LXX	10.5-9	Ps. 40.6-8
2.13a	Isa. 8.17; 12.2	10.16-17	Jer. 31.33-34
2.13b	Isa. 8.18	10.28	Deut. 17.6
3.5	Num. 12.7	10.30	Deut. 32.35-36
3.7-11	Ps. 95.7-11	10.37-38	Hab. 2.3-4
3.15	Ps. 95.7-8	11.18	Gen. 21.12
4.3	Ps. 95.11	11.21	Gen. 47.31
4.4	Gen. 2.2	12.5-6	Prov. 3.11-12
4.5	Ps. 95.11	12.26	Hag. 2.6, 21
4.7	Ps. 95.7-8	12.29	Deut. 4.24; 9.3
5.5	Ps. 2.7	13.5	Deut. 31.6
5.6	Ps. 110.4	13.6	Ps. 118.6

Such an intense usage of the Jewish scriptures underlines just how much the writer saw faith in Christ as dependent on and as fulfilment of Israel's profoundest hopes and traditions.[113] The arguments put forward regarding the significance of Christ and of what he has done are Jewish through and through, dependent not on the concept and practice of every cult or of any other cult but premised entirely on Israel's worship, traditions and hopes.

- Heb. 1.1-3 is a classic expression of early Wisdom christology, reflecting knowledge and influence of the sort of reflection on divine Wisdom and Logos which we find in Second Temple Judaism.[114]
- 1.5-14: the Son (Jesus) as far superior to the angels, the argument built entirely on the Jewish scriptures referred to above.[115]
- 2.5-18: Ps. 8.4-6, with its reference to human beings ('man, son of man'), interpreted as fully realized only in Jesus, not as transcending the humanity of which Ps. 8 spoke, but as ensuring Jesus' solidarity with hu-

---

113. See also Koester, *Hebrews* 56-57 and cf. 76-77, 109-15, 119-22.
114. See above §39 n.241; and see further my *Christology* §25.3.
115. See also K. L. Schenck, 'A Celebration of the Enthroned Son: The Catena of Hebrews 1', *JBL* 120 (2001) 469-85.

mankind ('the seed of Abraham') so that his suffering and death provided their salvation.
- 2.17–3.2: the first mention of the letter's principal theme — Jesus as high priest 'to make sacrifice of atonement for the sins of the people' (2.17).
- 3.1-6: Jesus as Son worthy of more honour in God's house than Moses as servant.
- 3.7–4.11: Israel's wilderness wanderings seen as a prototype for the process of salvation;[116] the 'rest' symbolized in the seventh day of creation (4.4), and not fully entered into in the promised land (4.5), and therefore still open to the present generation to 'enter in' (4.6-11); Jesus as the new Joshua (*Iēsous*) completing where the first Joshua fell short (4.8).[117]
- 4.14–5.10: the high priesthood of Christ, on the basic model of the Aaronic priesthood (5.1-4), but Jesus was 'designated by God a high priest according to the order of Melchizedek' (5.10) — the mysterious Melchizedek of Gen. 14.18-20 and Ps. 110.4.
- 6.13-20: the promise of descendants to Abraham (6.14) linked to the high priestly role as a hope that enters the Holy of Holies (6.19-20), into which only Israel's high priest could enter on only one day each year, the day of atonement.
- 7.1-10: the fact that Abraham paid tithes to Melchizedek indicates the superiority of the Melchizedek priesthood to that of Levi, who as a descendant of Abraham was in effect included in the tithe-paying to Melchizedek.[118]
- 7.11-28: contrast between the levitical/Aaronic priesthood and the priesthood of Melchizedek, for which only Jesus qualifies — eternal (7.3, 16, 23-24), sinless and thus not needing to sacrifice first for his own sins (7.27).

116. Käsemann focused on this theme in his *The Wandering People of God*.
117. B. Whitfield, *Joshua Traditions and the Argument of Hebrews 3 and 4* (BZNW 194; Berlin: de Gruyter, 2013), takes up a suggestion of Rendel Harris that the clue to the transition from Heb. 2 (angels and high priest) to Moses and Israel's wilderness experience in Heb. 3-4, which does not seem to fit into the letter's great Jesus as High Priest theme, lies in the allusion to Joshua (*Iēsous*) in Num. 13-14, and the link which the name provides to the Joshua (*Iēsous*) of Zech. 3, who thus provides the link back into the theme of a high priest in the divine presence.
118. For the Jewish reflection on Melchizedek (Qumran, Philo and Josephus) of which Hebrews can be counted a distinctive part, see F. L. Horton, *The Melchizedek Tradition: A Critical Examination of the Sources to the Fifth Century A.D. and in the Epistle to the Hebrews* (SNTSMS 30; Cambridge University, 1976) ch. 2; G. L. Cockerill, 'Melchizedek without Speculation: Hebrews 7.1-25 and Genesis 14.17-24', in R. Bauckham et al., eds., *A Cloud of Witnesses: The Theology of Hebrew in Its Ancient Contexts* (LNTS 387; London: T & T Clark, 2008) 128-44.

- 8.1-5: Israel's earthly sanctuary only an imperfect copy of the heavenly sanctuary (the actual presence of God).
- 8.6-13: the first covenant similarly imperfect (8.7), but now superseded by the promised new covenant of which Jesus is the mediator.
- 9.1-28: the imperfections demonstrated by the necessity for an endless repetition of sin offerings (9.6-7, 25); but Christ's sin offering (his death) is effective once for all because he has entered the heavenly Holy of Holies with his own blood (9.11-12, 24).
- 10.1-25: the law and Israel's sacrificial cult only a shadow of what was to come in Christ (10.1); his sacrificial death and exaltation to heaven as the single cleansing and perfecting offering (10.12-18); entry into the heavenly sanctuary now possible for all thus cleansed (10.19-22).
- 10.26-39: warnings against apostasy drawn from scripture.
- 11.4–12.2: the roll-call of men (and women) of faith, providing 'a great cloud of witnesses' to those still in the race, is drawn entirely from Israel's history.[119]
- 12.3–13.16: other exhortations drawn from Israel's scriptures and history, reinforcing the claim that the new covenant brings them to the heavenly (not the earthly) Jerusalem.

In short, this letter is clearly written by someone whose whole understanding of salvation was determined by Israel's scriptures and cult. The Christ that he presents is garbed entirely in the robes provided by Israel's priesthood, sanctuary and sacrificial system. Christ is depicted as qualified, the only one so qualified, to meet Israel's deepest cultic yearnings and hopes. The terms of salvation are premised entirely on Israel's cult. Hebrews is one of the most Jewish documents in the NT. And it was most probably written for those deeply attracted to or hitherto dependent on the Jerusalem cult, the very features of the Jerusalem cult which attracted them providing the starting point and basis for the author's argument and plea (§39.3c(ii)). The fact that the author regarded the cult as passé (chs. 8-10) may well have been a factor in the slowness of its acceptance in the West, where, if *1 Clement* is any guide, the OT cult was seen as the pattern for Christian ministry.[120]

---

119. M. Bockmuehl, 'Abraham's Faith in Hebrews 11', in Bauckham et al., eds., *Hebrews and Christian Theology* 364-73, notes 'the remarkable fact that aside from Jesus himself no exemplars of New Covenant faith are singled out anywhere in the letter.... the exemplars of faith are taken not from the apostolic churches of Jerusalem, Antioch or Rome, but exclusively from the Old Testament' (365-66).

120. Brown thinks it likely that Hebrews was sent to Rome but was never enthusiastically accepted by the Roman church (Brown and Meier, *Antioch and Rome* 143-49); see also n.148 below.

ii. The Other New Testament Epistles

We need to say little more about James than to repeat what was already noted in *Beginning from Jerusalem* §37.2: that for all its inclusion in the NT, 'the letter is so characteristically Jewish and so undistinctively Christian'. In that chapter I demonstrated particularly how deeply rooted James is in the Jewish wisdom tradition, drawn particularly from Proverbs, ben Sira and the Wisdom of Solomon — a wisdom into which Jesus' wisdom teaching was fully integrated. Notable, as by comparison with Paul, for example, is the very positive attitude to the Jewish law, with the typically Jewish emphasis on doing the law. A church which included the letter of James in its de facto canon clearly cherished its Jewish character and heritage.

With 1 Peter, though much closer to Paul, the same sense as in James (1.1) of a letter written to those living in exile in the diaspora is equally evident (1 Pet. 1.1). If, as most conclude,[121] the intended recipients were Gentile believers (cf. particularly 4.3), then the point is still highly effective in demonstrating that for 1 Peter Christian identity was Jewish identity.[122] In 1 Peter the rootedness of Christian faith in the Jewish scriptures is as evident as anywhere else in the NT, particularly in the strong claim that Christ is the fulfilment of Israel's prophecies and in effecting the salvation which the prophets looked for (1.10-11). The clearly evident quotations from and allusions to the Jewish scriptures[123] are surrounded by many more less clear allusions to Torah, Prophets and Writings.[124] The instruction for their faith

---

121. The consensus among modern commentators; see e.g. D. G. Horrell, *1 Peter* (New Testament Guides; London: T & T Clark, 2008) 47-48; D. F. Watson and T. Callan, *First and Second Peter* (Paideia; Grand Rapids: Baker Academic, 2012) 7-8. In *Beginning from Jerusalem* §37.3c I argue that 1 Peter was written for Jewish believers.

122. See particularly R. Feldmeier, *Die Christen als Fremde: Die Metapher der Fremde in der antiken Welt, im Urchristentum und im ersten Petrusbrief* (WUNT 64; Tübingen: Mohr Siebeck, 1992); L. Doering, 'First Peter as Early Christian Diaspora Letter', in K.-W. Niebuhr and R. W. Wall, eds., *Catholic Epistles and Apostolic Tradition* (Waco: Baylor University, 2009) 215-36, 441-57.

123. Note particularly

1.16	Lev. 11.44-45; 19.2	2.22	Isa. 53.9
		2.24-25	Isa. 53.4-6, 12
1.24-25	Isa. 40.6-8	3.10-12	Ps. 34.13-17
2.3	Ps. 33.9 LXX	3.14-15	Isa. 8.12-13
2.6	Isa. 28.16	4.8	Prov. 10.12
2.7	Ps. 117.22 LXX	4.14	Isa. 11.2
2.8	Isa. 8.14	4.18	Prov. 11.31
2.10	Hos. 1.6, 9; 2.25	5.5	Prov. 3.34
2.12	Isa. 10.3	5.8	Ps. 22.14

124. J. H. Elliott, *1 Peter* (AB 37B; New York: Doubleday, 2000), lists approximately

in Christ and consequential living was drawn from their Jewish heritage and was Jewish in character.

Even more striking, the letter of Jude draws all its warning examples from Jewish history:[125]

- 5 — the destruction of the wilderness generation (Num. 14.29-37);
- 6 — the rebellious angels (Gen. 6.1-4);
- 7 — Sodom and Gomorrah (Gen. 19.4-25);
- 9 — the archangel Michael as the great contender against and rebuker of the devil (Dan. 10.13, 21; Zech. 3.2);[126]
- 11 — Cain, Korah and Balaam (Gen. 4.8; Num. 16, 22-24);
- 12 — clouds without rain (Prov. 25.14);
- 13 — wild waves (Isa. 57.20);
- 14 — Enoch (Gen. 5.21-22);
- 14 — the Lord coming with myriads of his holy ones (Deut. 33.2);
- 16 — bombastic speech (Dan. 11.36 Theod.);
- 16 — partial judgment (Lev. 19.15);
- 18 — mockers (*empaiktēs*) predicted (Isa. 3.4);
- 23 — a brand snatched from the fire (Amos 4.11; Zech. 3.2);
- 23 — filthy clothes (Zech. 3.4).

Particularly interesting are the indications of knowledge of and influence from the Enoch traditions influential in late Second Temple Judaism:[127]

---

46 OT citations and allusions (excluding iterative allusions and biblicisms). 'The letter employs a diversity of OT texts, motifs, and themes in order to illustrate the ancient heritage to which the Christian brotherhood is heir and to provide scriptural and hence authoritative substantiation for its message of affirmation and exhortation' (12-17). 'Such is the abundance of references to and motifs from the OT that virtually all of the imagery of 1 Peter is drawn from its writings' (P. J. Achtemeier, *1 Peter* [Hermeneia; Minneapolis: Fortress, 1996] 12). Of the further bibliography Achtemeier and Elliott refer to, see particularly W. L. Schutter, *Hermeneutic and Composition in First Peter* (WUNT 2.30; Tübingen: Mohr Siebeck, 1989).

125. 'The letter of Jude contains probably the most elaborate passage of formal exegesis in the manner of the Qumran pesharim to be found in the New Testament. . . . Such exegesis must have flourished especially in the early Palestinian church' (Bauckham, *Jude and the Relatives of Jesus* 233). 'There is a remarkable use of the traditions of ancient Judaism that in its intensity is unique in the New Testament' (Schnelle, *History* 420; see also 420-21). See also Neyrey, *2 Peter, Jude* 32-36.

126. The tradition that Jude was quoting from the *Assumption of Moses* in verse 9 goes back to Gelasius of Cyzicus (fifth century); see e.g. H. F. D. Sparks, *The Apocryphal Old Testament* (Oxford: Clarendon, 1984) 600-601. Jude 16 may also reflect *T.Moses* 7.7, 9. For full discussion see Bauckham, *Jude and the Relatives of Jesus* ch. 5.

127. See also Bauckham, *Jude and the Relatives of Jesus* 137-41.

Jude	1 Enoch	Jude	1 Enoch
4	cf. 48.10	14	60.8
6	10.4-6; 12.4	14-15	1.9
13	cf. 18.15-16	16	cf. 5.4

Here again are strong indications of the Jewish character of the paraenesis, and of the hopes and fears of early Christian congregations. If Jude was thought, like James, to be closely related to Jesus (§39.3e(i)), then it would imply that the strong Jewish character of Jesus' own teaching and that of his close relatives was especially cherished in the last decades of the first century and the early decades of the second — long enough, certainly, for the letter to become more and more esteemed by a widening circle of churches and to be included in the canonizing process which became stronger in the second half of the second century.

More distinctively Christian than James (Jesus referred to explicitly six times), it is nevertheless significant that such a strongly Jewish writing could gain the acceptance that it evidently did and become part of the NT canon, even if in a more deutero-canonical status for many. That such a little and, it would appear, such an inconsequential letter should gain that level of widespread acceptance attests the widespread acknowledgment in early Christianity of its distinctively Jewish character. Wherever it originated, it attests the strength of the Jewish character of the early Christian communities from which it emerged and who cherished it.[128]

With regard to 2 Peter it will be sufficient to note its very Jewish character as a 'farewell speech' or 'testament',[129] its dependency on the very Jewish letter of Jude (§39.3f), particularly the similar way in which it draws on traditionally Jewish eschatological hopes and fears,[130] and its rather close links with the Gospel of Matthew.[131] The Jewish character of the NT writings extends to their latest member.

---

128. See also A. Gerdmar, *Rethinking the Judaism-Hellenism Dichotomy: A Historiographical Case Study of Second Peter and Jude* (CBNTS 36; Stockholm: Almqvist & Wiksell, 2001).

129. Bauckham, *Jude, 2 Peter* 131-34.

130. Bauckham, *Jude, 2 Peter* 138-40; 'The connection between flood, final judgment with water as the means of punishment, and fire in 2 Pet. 3.5-7, 10, 12, 13 has parallels in the *Life of Adam and Eve* 49.3; Josephus, *Antiquities* 1.70-71; *SibOr* 4.172ff.; 5.155ff., 512ff.; *1 Enoch* 83.3-5' (Schnelle, *History* 430).

131. Schnelle notes the transfiguration story (2 Pet. 1.17/Matt. 17.5), the common interest in the figure of Peter, and cites as further examples 2 Pet. 2.6/Matt. 10.15 (Sodom and Gomorrah), 2 Pet. 2.21/Matt. 21.32 ('the way of righteousness'), and 2 Pet. 2.22/Matt. 7.6 (dogs and swine). He cites the judgment of P. Dschulnigg, 'Der theologische Ort des Zweiten Petrusbriefes', *BZ* 33 (1989) 161-77, that the author of 2 Peter is at home in the

The influence of the OT on the Johannine letters is less obvious. Given the strongly Jewish character of John's Gospel the lack of more obviously distinctive Jewish features is a surprise.[132] Probably the most significant feature is that the belief that 'Jesus is the Christ', Christ as still a title, was evidently of continuing definitive significance for the communities represented (1 John 2.22; 5.1; 2 John 9), and Jesus is still remembered as 'the righteous (one)'.[133]

iii. Revelation

The final NT writing to be considered is Revelation, the Apocalypse of John, which, together with Matthew, John, Romans, Hebrews, James and Jude, is one of the most Jewish of the NT writings and expressive of the Jewish milieu from which it came. The fact that it is an 'apocalypse', an account of heavenly realities invisible to normal vision, unveiled to a seer through angelic mediation, the only apocalypse properly speaking in the NT, sets it immediately within the apocalyptic tradition of Second Temple Judaism. Its predecessors were Daniel and the Enochic apocalypses.[134] Its emergence in the late decades of the first century puts it in the company of *4 Ezra* and *2 Baruch*, both indicative and expressive of the crisis into which the destruction of the Jerusalem temple tipped early Judaism. Indeed, like these two classic Jewish apocalypses (*4 Ezra* and *2 Baruch*), the Apocalypse of John may be the best indication in the NT that the catastrophic climax of the first Jewish war against Rome initiated a crisis for the early Jewish believers in Christ as well. Also, that as with *4 Ezra* and *2 Baruch*, the book of Daniel became a reference point and a resource for renewal of faith and hope among those most troubled by the loss of the temple.

Most striking is the degree to which Revelation's christology is influenced by earlier apocalyptic language and categories. The opening vision of

---

Jewish Christianity of the Gospel of Matthew, 'whose theology he defends all along the line' (177) (*History* 429-30).

132. 'In contrast to the Gospel, which cites the Old Testament 19 times, not a single quotation from the Old Testament is found in 1 John; in fact the reference to Cain in 1 John 3.12 is the only allusion to the Old Testament in the letter' (Schnelle, *History* 456). The same is true of 2 John and 3 John. E. E. Ellis, *The Old Testament in Early Christianity* (Grand Rapids: Baker, 1992), refers to only three verses from the Johannine letters — 1 John 2.18, 2.28 and 5.20, none of them as allusions. There may be some echoes of OT phrasing (as in 1 John 1.9/cf. Deut. 32.4; 1 John 3.5/cf. Isa. 53.4-5, 9, 11-12; 2 John 8/cf. Ruth 2.12), but they could simply reflect early Christian usage and need not imply direct dependence on these scriptures as such.

133. 1 John 2.1, 29; 3.7; an early way of referring to Christ (Acts 3.14; 7.52; 22.14; Jas. 5.6).

134. Revelation's rather bizarre imagery is also characteristic of Jewish apocalypses. See further, e.g., the articles on 'Apocalypses and Apocalypticism', in *ABD* 1.279-88.

§45.4   *Jewish Christianity*

'one like a son of man' is drawn entirely from Dan. 7.9, 13, but also Ezek. 1.24, 26, 8.2 and Dan. 10.5-6:[135]

> Rev. 1.12-16: '... *one like a son of man, clothed with* a long robe and with a *golden girdle* round his breast; *his head and his hair were white as white wool, white as snow*; *his eyes were like a flame of* fire, his feet were *like burnished bronze* ... and *his voice* was *like the sound of many waters* ...'.

> Dan. 7.9, 13: 'As I looked, thrones were placed and one that was Ancient of Days took his seat; his raiment was *white as snow*, and *the hair of his head like pure wool*; his throne was *fiery flames*, its wheels were burning *fire*. ... I saw in the night visions, and behold, with the clouds of heaven came *one like a son of man*, and he came to the Ancient of Days ...'.

> Dan. 10.5-6: 'I lifted up my eyes and looked, and behold, *a man clothed in linen*, whose loins were *girded with gold* of Uphaz. ... *his eyes like flaming torches*, his arms and legs like the gleam of *burnished bronze*, and the sound of *his words like the noise of a multitude*'.

> Ezek. 1.24-27: In his vision of the chariot throne of God, Ezekiel heard the sound of the wings of the living creatures '*like the sound of many waters*'; 'and seated above the likeness of a throne was *a likeness as it were of a human form*. And upward from what had the appearance of his loins I saw as it were *gleaming bronze*, like the appearance of a *fire* enclosed round about ...'.

> Ezek. 8.2: 'Then I beheld, and lo, a form that had *the appearance of a man*; below what appeared to be his loins it was *fire*, and above his loins it was like the appearance of brightness, *like gleaming bronze*'.

What is so striking here is that John drew his imagery entirely from this rich resource of descriptions of heavenly visions in Jewish apocalyptic writings. And that in so doing, he entered entirely into the speculation about glorious angelic beings seen in such visions. Since these glorious angels were not just heavenly messengers, but expressed the majesty of the divine presence and served in one degree or other to represent God,[136] it was inevitable that there

---

135. See also Beale, *Revelation* 220-22; also 297-301, 366-69. In the following quotations the italics highlight the phrases borrowed from or certainly influenced by the OT passages.

136. The possibility of confusion goes back to the early stories about epiphanies of 'the angel of the Lord' (e.g. Gen. 16.7-13; Exod. 3.2-6; 23.20-21), and is well illustrated by

would be some confusion between the glorious angel and God himself.[137] John did not hesitate to exploit that confusion: his description of the exalted Jesus drew on both Dan. 7.9, the description of the Ancient of Days, and on 7.13, 'one like a son of man'; he drew on both the hesitant description of the one who rode the chariot throne in Ezek. 1.24-27, and on the similar descriptions of the glorious angel in Ezek. 8.2 and Dan. 10.5-6. So John did not hesitate either to describe the 'mighty angel' of Rev. 10.1 in similar language, or to indicate that the Lamb shares the throne of God (7.15-17; 22.1, 3).[138]

The other principal ways of referring to Christ are equally, and equally manifestly, derived from Jewish imagery and usage. Christ as 'the Lion of the Tribe of Judah' (Rev. 5.5) alludes to Gen. 49.9, and Christ as 'the Root of David' (Rev. 5.5; 22.16) is an allusion to Isa. 11.1, 10, both indicating that for John the apocalyptic significance of Christ is as the expression of Judah at its best and as fulfillment of Israel's messianic hopes.[139] More prominent are the 28 references to Jesus as a 'lamb' (*arnion*). Such animal imagery is familiar in apocalyptic literature, though not usually in reference to a Messiah. But as a metaphor for one whose death was seen as a sacrifice — the imagery is introduced in ch. 5, the Lamb 'standing as if it had been slaughtered' (5.6, 12) — it was deeply rooted in Israel's sacrificial tradition. In context, however, it is not the image of a weak victim which emerges. For the lamb is also described as 'having seven horns and seven eyes' (5.6), 'horn' being a familiar symbol of royal power (as in Dan. 7.7-8, 11-12), and the 'seven eyes' alluding to Zech. 4.10, symbolizing divine omniscience. The choice of *arnion* for 'lamb', rather than the more familiar *amnos*, may also indicate that John had in mind the sense 'ram' as well, since the lamb of Revelation shares God's throne, exercizes judgment (6.16) and conquers his enemies (17.14).[140]

Like most other NT writings, Revelation is heavily dependent on the OT.[141] One of the most striking features of the Apocalypse of John is the degree of his indebtedness in particular to Ezekiel:

---

the glorious angel Yahoel (probably a combination of Yahweh and Elohim) in *Apoc. Ab.* 10.3; see also *Apoc. Zeph.* 6.11-15; and below §49 at n.126.

137. See particularly C. Rowland, 'The Vision of the Risen Christ in Rev. 1.13ff.: The Debt of an Early Christology to an Aspect of Jewish Angelology', *JTS* 31 (1980) 1-11; also *The Open Heaven: A Study of Apocalyptic in Judaism and Christianity* (London: SPCK, 1982).

138. See further below §49.5a.

139. See further Aune, *Revelation* 1.350-51.

140. Lambs are used in *1 Enoch* 90 as an image for the Maccabeans. See further Aune, *Revelation* 1.353-54, 367-73; Beale, *Revelation* 350-57.

141. 'The seer's major source is provided by the Old Testament. His work is characterized by an enormous number of allusions and by echoes of extensive passages. Fragmentary citations and even direct quotations from the Old Testament are found in Rev. 1.7; 2.27; 4.8; 6.16; 7.16, 17; 11.11; 14.5; 15.3, 4; 19.15; 20.9; 21.4, 7. Quotations and allusions are

- 4.6-9 — the four 'living creatures' round the throne of God (Ezek. 1.5-11);
- 7.2-4 — divine marks or seals as providing protection from divine judgment (Ezek. 9.3-6);
- 10.9-10 — the command to eat the scroll (Ezek. 3.1-3);
- 11.1-2; 21.9-21 — the command to measure the temple and the measuring of Jerusalem (Ezek. 40-42);
- 18.1–19.2 — the description of Babylon as 'the great whore' (cf. Ezek. 23, 27);
- 20.8 — Gog and Magog (Ezek. 38-39).

John, not unjustifiably, can be described as 'a new Ezekiel'.[142]

In short, John in writing his Apocalypse evidently saw his writing not just as a (Christian) adaptation of Jewish apocalyptic tradition, but as part of that major stream of reflection which emerged from Second Temple Judaism, in the wake of Jerusalem's destruction. If his writing was a Christian response to the crisis or impending crisis for the future of early Christianity, it was also a Jewish response to the far more severe crisis for Jewish hope and identity.[143]

To sum up, two features of this survey of the post-70 NT writings stand out as most striking. One is the consistent Jewishness of the language, thought forms and emphases of the religion they express. A Christianity which regards these writings as canonical cannot, or should not, fail to recognize and to affirm the Jewish character of the Christianity which they represent. If second-century Christianity began to distance itself from Judaism, it is all the more significant that the same Christianity could and did embrace writings like James, Jude and Revelation. The Jewish roots and Jewish character of Christianity could be neither ignored nor disputed, however uncomfortable some evidently found this to be.

The other is that for the most part this acknowledgment and de facto affirmation of the Jewishness of Christianity is not made as a claim which disowns or

---

influenced in part by the LXX or other later translations, but often reflect the author's own knowledge of Hebrew or Aramaic texts. Continual reference is made to Ezekiel, Isaiah, Jeremiah, Daniel, and the Psalms' (Schnelle, *History* 531). See the full analysis of Charles, *Revelation* 1.lxv-lxxxvi; Beale, *Revelation* 76-99.

142. D. Frankfurter, in the *Jewish Annotated New Testament* (New York: Oxford University, 2011) 473.

143. Fiorenza observes that when she started her work on Rev. 'the majority of scholars agreed that the book was an only slightly redacted Jewish apocalypse. The theology of Rev. was therefore held to be Jewish rather than genuinely Christian and as such to be of little significance for the reconstruction of early Christian theology and life' (*Revelation* 25).

denies the religion of Israel. The one exception is, arguably, the letter to the Hebrews, and, as we shall see, a dispute with other heirs of Second Temple Judaism is evident particularly in Matthew and John (§46.5). But the Jewishness of the inheritance is never in dispute, and the Christian claims to that heritage are rooted deeply in Israel's own scriptures. In the subsequent discussion of 'the parting of the ways' (§46) this key characteristic of Christianity should never be downplayed.

45.5 The Jewish Character of Second-Century Christian Writings

The Jewishness of the second-century Christian writings is not as consistent as in the first-century (NT) writings, but it is as clear in several important instances.

a. *1 Clement*

1 Clement draws more extensively on the scriptures (OT) than any earlier Christian document. From ch. 3 to ch. 57 there are quotations, often extensive quotations in almost every chapter,[144] not to mention various allusions.

1 Clement	quotation	*1 Clement*	quotation
3.1	Deut. 32.15	15.5	Ps. 31.18
4.1-6	Gen. 4.3-8	15.5-6	Ps. 12.4-6
4.10	Exod. 2.14	16.3-14	Isa. 53.1-12
6.3	Gen. 2.23	16.15-16	Ps. 22.6-8
8.2	Ezek. 33.11	17.2	Gen. 18.27
8.4	Isa. 1.16-20	17.3	Job 1.1
10.3	Gen. 12.1-3	17.4	Job 14.4-5 (LXX)
10.4-5	Gen. 13.14-16	17.5	Exod. 3.11; 4.10
10.6	Gen. 15.5-6	17.6	?
12.1-7	Josh. 2	18.1	1 Sam. 13.14
13.1	Jer. 9.23-24	18.2-17	Ps. 51.1-17
13.4	Isa. 66.2	20.7	Job 38.11
14.4	Prov. 2.21-22	21.2	Prov. 20.27
14.5	Ps. 37.35-37	22.1-7	Ps. 34.11-17, 19
15.2	Isa. 29.13	22.8	Ps. 32.10
15.3	Ps. 62.4	23.3-4	?
15.4	Ps. 78.36-37	23.5	Isa. 13.22 (LXX); Mal. 3.1

144. Grant and Graham, *First and Second Clement* 101-3, and Lona, *erste Clemensbrief* 46, have similar lists; see further Lona 42-48.

§45.5 *Jewish Christianity*

1 Clement	quotation	1 Clement	quotation
26.2	Ps. 28.7	36.5	Ps. 110.1
26.2	Ps. 3.5	39.3-9	Job 4.16-18; 15.15; 4.19–5.5
26.3	Job 19.26		
27.5	Wisd. 12.12	42.5	Isa. 60.17 (LXX)
27.7	Ps. 19.1-3	46.2	?
28.3	Ps. 139.7-8	46.3	Ps. 18.25-26
29.2	Deut. 32.8-9	48.2-3	Ps. 118.19-20
29.3	Deut. 14.2; Num. 18.27	50.4	Isa. 26.20; Ezek. 37.12
30.2	Prov. 3.34	50.6	Ps. 32.1-2
30.4-5	Job 11.2-3 (LXX)	52.2	Ps. 69.30-32
32.2	Gen. 22.17; 26.4	52.3	Ps. 50.14-15
33.5	Gen. 1.26	52.4	Ps. 51.17
33.6	Gen. 1.28	54.3	Ps. 24.1
34.6	Dan. 7.10; Isa. 6.3	56.3-4	Prov. 3.12
35.7-12	Ps. 50.16-23	56.5	Ps. 141.5
36.3	Ps. 104.4	56.6-15	Job 5.17-26
36.4	Ps. 2.7-8	57.3-7	Prov. 1.23-33

In his rebuke of the factionalism of the 'young Turks' in the Corinthian church Clement draws his most telling examples, both good and warning examples, from Israel's scriptures — Abel murdered by Cain; Jacob and Joseph, Moses, Aaron and Miriam, victims of jealousy; Dathan and Abiram examples of factional jealousy (4); good examples of Noah and Jonah (7), of Enoch, Noah, Abraham, Lot and Rahab (9-12), of Elijah and Elisha, also Ezekiel, of Abraham, Job and Moses (17), of David (18), of Abraham, Isaac and Jacob (31), of Daniel and the three Jews cast into the fiery furnace (45); again of the rebels against Moses and Pharaoh (51), and again of Moses (53), and finally of Judith and Esther (55).

Here is someone who was deeply familiar with the whole range of the scriptures, not least the Writings (Psalms, Job and Proverbs). They are Israel's scriptures, but Clement simply takes it as a given that they are his scriptures, his churches' scriptures. He assumes as completely self-evident that there is a direct continuum with the history of Israel's good and bad examples and that of the Christians in Rome and Corinth; it is their history too. In the same way he thinks of those from whom he is writing and for whom he is writing as the 'called' (prescript), as God's 'loved ones',[145] as 'God's elect',[146] as the 'holy people' to whom Ezekiel spoke (8.3), all terms characteristically used of

---

145. *1 Clem.* 1.1; 7.1; 12.8; etc.
146. *1 Clem.* 1.1; 2.4; 6.1; 49.5; 58.2; 59.2.

God's people Israel. All this without any sense of taking over language (and identity) which was exclusive to ethnic Israel, or of somehow replacing all these patriarchs, prophets and sages in the purpose of God.[147]

In some ways most significant for the Christianity which he seeks to inculcate, Clement draws his ecclesiology from Israel's priestly orders and sacrificial ritual (40-41), assuming too that the continuum with Israel included Christian ministry as the continuation of Israel's priestly cult.[148] And this without any thought that with the loss of the temple, the Christianity which was emerging might take a different religious form from the priestly and sacrificial cults so familiar in the religions of the time. And without paying any attention to the teaching of Hebrews on the subject, even though he seems to have known and used the document![149]

In short, *1 Clement* is more aware of the Jewishness of Christianity than almost any other writer from the period — both of Christianity's deep roots in Israel's history, and of Israel's scriptures as a/the primary resource for Christian exhortation and discipline.[150]

b. *Didache*

Unlike *1 Clement*, the *Teaching of the Twelve Apostles* is not built round extensive quotations from the early Christian scriptures (OT). But it is very like the letter of James, in that it blends its extensive use of Jesus tradition (§44.2f) with typically Jewish wisdom and ethics. That is to say, it treats the Jesus tradition as a natural continuation and extension of traditional Jewish teaching.[151]

---

147. The opinion of W. K. Lowther Clarke, *The First Epistle of Clement to the Corinthians* (London: SPCK, 1937), that Judaism is 'completely discarded in the Epistle' (10), is without foundation and belongs to a bygone age.

148. 'Why does *1 Clement* place such admiring emphasis on the divinely assigned order in the Jerusalem cult and in its personnel [*1 Clem.* 40.1-5; 41.2]? Chap. 42 gives a clear answer: because there is a similar divinely designed order in the Christian ministry' (Brown in Brown and Meier, *Antioch and Rome* 170).

149. 'While Clement does not identify the presbyters as those who presided at the eucharist (which is never mentioned) or call them priests, his work reflects a tendency at the turn of the first century that will coalesce and develop through the second century until the bishop, presbyters, and deacons are pictured as the Christian high priests, priests, and levites, centred around their role in the eucharist as the Christian sacrifice' (Brown in Brown and Meier, *Antioch and Rome* 171; see also 176-83).

150. K. Beyschlag, *Clemens Romanus und der Frühkatholizismus* (Tübingen: Mohr Siebeck, 1966), argued that the author of *1 Clement* 'depended on a Hellenistic-Jewish apologetic tradition that had stamped itself on Roman Christianity' (Schoedel, 'Apostolic Fathers' 460).

151. J. Weiss, *Earliest Christianity* (1937; New York: Harper Torchbook, 1959), saw

This becomes clear at once, by its setting out its paraenesis as the choice between 'two ways, one of life [chs. 1-4] and one of death [ch. 5]' (1.1). This was a characteristic Jewish way of spelling out ethical options,[152] probably rooted in Moses' putting before the wilderness Israelites the options of life and death, blessings and curses, and urging them to choose life, that they may live (Deut. 30.19). Jer. 21.8 had already transposed it into a choice between two ways, the way of life and the way of death. And typically Ps. 1.6 contrasts 'the way of the righteous' and 'the way of the wicked'.[153] But it was the discovery of the Dead Sea Scrolls which brought home the importance of the motif in Jewish thought — the contrast between those who 'walk on the paths of light' and those who 'walk on the paths of darkness' (1QS 3.20-21).[154] The Jesus tradition's contrast between the narrow gate/hard road that leads to life and the wide gate/easy road that leads to destruction (Matt. 7.13-14) draws on the same tradition. Indeed, the fact that one of the earliest self-references of the sect of the Nazarene was as 'the Way' (Acts 9.2), parallel to one of the self-designations of the Qumran community,[155] indicates that both sects thought of themselves as having made a definitive choice between the alternative ways set before them. The explicit life/death, light/darkness choice as between two ways became a regular feature of early Christian paraenesis, in documents also indicative of the influence of Jewish tradition.[156]

---

the baptismal catechesis of chs. 1-6 as 'a combination of Jewish requirements — the basis is a Jewish proselyte catechism — and of the sayings of Jesus' (2.558). M. Del Verne, *Didache and Judaism: Jewish Roots of an Ancient Christian-Jewish Work* (London: T & T Clark, 2004): 'As a matter of fact, some institutions present in the *Didache* appear to be a mere adaptation or transposition to the new Christian environment of institutions typically Jewish' (75-76).

152. See Kraft, *Barnabas and the Didache* 4-16, 134-62; Niederwimmer, *Didache* 48-63, 83-88; and particularly H. van de Sandt and D. Flusser, *The Didache: Its Jewish Sources and Its Place in Early Judaism and Christianity* (Assen: Van Gorcum, 2002) 1-190: 'The composer of *Did.* 6:2-3 was an exponent of a group of Jewish-Christians who remained within the ambit of Tora-observance. Compliance with the entire Tora is an ideal but the text shows a tolerant attitude to those who are not capable of bearing "the whole yoke of the Lord"' (269).

153. Similarly e.g. Ps. 119.29-30; 139.24; Prov. 4.18-19; 14.12; 15.9-10.

154. See also particularly *1 Enoch* 94.1-4; *2 Enoch* 30.15 ('the two ways — light and darkness'); *T. Asher* 1.3; *T. Ab.* 11.2-3; *Sib. Or.* 8.399-401; and further in W. Michaelis, '*hodos*', *TDNT* 5.48-65; rabbinic parallels in SB 1.461-64. 'Given the absence of distinctively Christian language in the teaching of the two paths and its clear parallel now in the *Manual of Discipline*, it is generally thought that the document underlying all these documents was originally Jewish' (Ehrman, *Apostolic Fathers* 408). See also Schoedel, 'Apostolic Fathers' 467; Draper, *Didache in Modern Research* 13-16.

155. See *Beginning from Jerusalem* 13-14 and nn.59, 61.

156. Particularly *Barn.* 18.1–20.2; *Apostolic Constitutions* 7. See also Barnard, 'The Dead Sea Scrolls, Barnabas, the *Didache* and the Later History of "The Two Ways"', *Studies* 87-107.

The Jewish character of the *Didache* is evident from the first.[157]

- The path of life begins thus: 'First, love the God who made you, and second your neighbour as yourself' (1.2). The combination of Deut. 6.5 and Lev. 19.18 in the way that Jesus expressed it (Mark 12.29-31 pars.) was no doubt conscious and deliberate.
- The mélange of Jesus tradition in the rest of ch. 1 merges into 'the second commandment of the teaching' in ch. 2, which consists of an elaboration of Exod. 20.13-17, probably with conscious echoes of Matt. 19.18 and 5.33.
- The warnings against idolatry in ch. 3 are characteristically Jewish, and the encouragement to 'Be meek, since the meek will inherit the earth' (3.7) was probably drawn equally from Matt. 5.5 and Ps. 37.11.
- The exhortation to follow the way of life climaxes with the appeal: 'Do not abandon the commandments of the Lord, but guard what you have received, neither adding to them nor taking away' (4.13), where the echo of Deut. 4.2 (cf. 12.32) was no doubt deliberate.[158]
- The encouragement 'if you can bear the entire yoke of the Lord, you will be perfect' (6.2), linked to a warning against 'food sacrificed to idols' (6.3), suggests the Jewish thought of the yoke of the law,[159] and possibly the influence of James.[160]
- The urging to fast twice a week indicates a conscious maintenance of a Jewish practice, even allowing for the attempt to distinguish their practice from that of 'the hypocrites' (cf. Matt. 6.5) — Wednesday and Friday, not Monday and Thursday (8.1-2)![161] And the urging to pray the Lord's prayer three times a day (8.3) echoes traditional Jewish spiritual discipline.[162]
- Equally significant are the several Jewish motifs in the instructions re-

---

157. There was a broad consensus as to the *Didache*'s character as a Jewish-Christian document from the first (Draper, *Didache in Modern Research* 8-10).

158. Niederwimmer, *Didache* 145.

159. Draper pushes the point: 'In a Jewish Christian milieu it seems likely that "the yoke of the Lord" refers to the Torah and that becoming "perfect" refers to full conversion to Judaism, including circumcision on the part of Gentile converts' (*NIDB* 2.122). Contrast H. Lietzmann, *A History of the Early Church* (4 vols.; Cleveland and New York: Meridian, 1961): 'The *Didache* gives the clearest possible outline of a type of Christianity entirely free from the Mosaic law. . . . The document lauds Jesus as the teacher of a higher ethic and as victor over Judaism' (1.205) — which should be ranked with Lowther Clarke's opinion in n.147 above.

160. Bernheim, *James, Brother of Jesus* 263.

161. See §46 n.261 below.

162. Jeremias, *The Prayers of Jesus* 69-72.

garding the eucharist: 'We give you thanks, our Father, for the holy vine of David, your child, which you made known to us through Jesus your child' (9.2); 'We give you thanks, holy Father, for your holy name.... You, O Master Almighty, created all things for the sake of your name, and gave both food and drink to humans for their refreshment, that they might give you thanks' (10.2-3);[163] the echo in 9.4 and 10.5 of Israel's prayer[164] for the gathering in of those scattered among the nations (Deut. 30.3-5); the repeated ascriptions of glory to God (9.2, 3, 4; 10.2, 4, 5); the use of Jewish prayer language ('Hosanna to the God of David') and the continued use of Aramaic in echo of 1 Cor. 16.22 ('Maranatha! Amen').[165]

- The awareness of the dangers of false prophecy (ch. 11) reflects both ancient Jewish and more recent Christian experience of prophecy.[166]
- Perhaps most striking of all is the transposition in chs. 13-14 of the provision Israel should make for priests (the first fruits) and of the sacrificial imagery to the prophets, 'for they are your high priests' (13.3), justified by a quotation from Mal. 1.11, 14 (14.3); prophet had replaced priest, but the related obligations (to support the priest) had continuing force.

As with *1 Clement*, therefore, *Didache* gives clear evidence that the early Christians whose ethical principles, liturgical practice and experience of ministry are reflected in its chapters had a characteristically Jewish mindset and instinctively drew on Jewish law and tradition. Still more, so Jewish in character is the *Didache* that it raises the question whether 'Jewish' and 'Christian' were separate categories for the communities which the *Didache* represents, whether they would have thought to distinguish the categories from each other. In fact, the *Didache* is probably more deserving of the title 'Jewish Christianity' than any other writing of the period.[167]

---

163. 'According to a wide scholarly consensus these Eucharistic prayers are grafted on the Birkat Ha-Mazon, the Jewish meal prayer' (van de Sandt, ed., *Matthew and the Didache* 8); Wilson, *Related Strangers* 226-27, and further 228-29.

164. As in Shemoneh 'Esreh 10.

165. Note also that in *Did.* 9-10 the eucharist takes place in the context of a meal (cf. *Did.* 10.1 with 1 Cor. 11.25), as earlier (cf. Acts 20.7; Jude 12; 2 Pet. 2.13).

166. Classically in 1 Kgs. 13 and 22 and in Jeremiah's self-doubt (Jer. 20.7); in early Christianity note Matt. 7.15; 1 Thess. 5.19-22; 1 John 4.1; Hermas, *Mand.* 11.7, 11, 16.

167. Del Verne concludes that the *Didache* 'documents the "cohabitation" of "Christian Judaism" with contemporary strands of Judaism — in Syria-Palestine and probably in the region of Antioch in the 1st century C.E.' (*Didache and Judaism* 266). G. Vermes, *Christian Beginnings from Nazareth to Nicaea AD 30-325* (London: Allen Lane, 2012): 'the Didache envisages a rather primitive and rudimentary form of Jewish-Christianity, not

c. The *Epistle of Barnabas*

Somewhat like *1 Clement*, *Barnabas* quotes and draws on scripture (the OT) extensively (see table on opposite page).[168]

As already noted, the final chapters (18-20) provide another example of 'two-ways' paraenesis, and may well be based on *Did.* 1-6, or at least drew on the same material; that is, a very Jewish pattern of teaching.[169]

Different from *1 Clement*, however, is the polemical exposition which *Barnabas* brings to these texts, as we shall see below (§46.6b). That factor, however, should not blind us to the evident fact that *Barnabas* owned the scriptures as his and drew his teaching directly from them, drawing with equal facility on the five rolls of the Torah, on the major prophets, and on the Psalms. The knowledge 'Barnabas' sought to impart (1.5) was contained in (the right understanding of) the scriptures; it was to the scriptures that he turned because they were the source of knowledge.[170] Without the foundation and resource which they supplied, indeed, he would have had very little to say.

But because they were also the scriptures of others, *Barnabas* recognized the need to establish that they could and should be understood as foreshadowing Christianity. Hence his extensive use of typology in 7.3–8.1 and 12: the sacrifice of Isaac, the scapegoat of the Day of Atonement ritual, the sacrifice of the red heifer (Num. 19), the bronze serpent all being types of Jesus' sacrifice.[171] Similarly his numerological interpretation of the 318 whom he deduces were circumcised as members of Abraham's household (9.8): 18 consists of 'I' (= 10) and 'E' (= 8), the first two letters of 'Jesus' (*Iēsous*), and 300 is represented by 'T', the sign of the cross (9.8). So too his spiritualizing of the laws of clean and unclean: avoid unclean animals means avoid people who are like pigs, or lamprey-eels, or hares, or hyenas; Moses gave these teachings 'in the Spirit' and was not really speaking

---

unlike, and doctrinally even less developed than, the church described in the first twelve chapters of the Acts of the Apostles' (137).

168. See also tabulation in Kraft, *Barnabas and the Didache* 179-81, 184-85; Hvalvik, *Struggle* 336-41.

169. See nn.152-154 above. '*Barnabas* shows fewer traces of the Christian revision of the Jewish catechism than the *Didache*, and is thus more closely related to the Jewish original' (Koester, *Introduction* 2.279).

170. 'The events of the past — that is, of Jewish religious history — hold the key to what is happening and what will happen (see 1:7; 5:3; 17:1-2). The very language employed throughout Barnabas to describe the *Christian* hope is directly and thoroughly rooted in the language of God's dealings with Israel' (Kraft, *Barnabas and the Didache* 33); 'There can be no doubt that Barnabas held "the Scriptures" to be his highest and only authority' (Hvalvik, *Struggle* 103-5), scripture especially as predictive prophecy (108-9); 'a central issue for the author is *the right interpretation of Scripture*' (204).

171. See also Hvalvik, *Struggle* 114-19.

Barnabas	OT	Barnabas	OT
2.5	Isa. 1.11-13	9.5	Jer. 9.26
2.7	Jer. 7.22	9.8	Gen. 17.23; 14.14
2.8	Zech. 8.17	10.1	Lev. 11.7-15; Deut. 14.8-14
2.10	Ps. 51.17		
3.1-5	Isa. 3-10	10.2	Deut. 4.10, 13
4.4	Dan. 7.24	10.4	Lev. 11.13-16
4.5	Dan. 7.7-8	10.5	?
4.7	Exod. 31.18; 34.28	10.6	Lev. 11.6
4.8	Exod. 32.7	10.7	?
4.11	Isa. 5.21	10.10	Ps. 1.1
5.2	Isa. 53.5, 7	10.11	Lev. 11.3; Deut. 14.6
5.4	Prov. 1.17		
5.5	Gen. 1.26	11.2-3	Jer. 2.12-13
5.12	Zech. 13.7	11.4	Isa. 45.2-3
5.13	Ps. 22.20, 16	11.5	Isa. 33.16-18
5.14	Isa. 50.6-7	11.6-7	Ps. 1.3-6
6.1-2	Isa. 50.8-9	11.10	Ezek. 47.12
6.2-3	Isa. 28.16	12.1	*4 Ezra* 4.33; 5.5
6.3	Isa. 50.7	12.2	cf. Exod. 17.8-13
6.4	Ps. 118.22, 24	12.4	Isa. 65.2
6.6	Ps. 22.16; 118.12	12.6	Lev. 26.1
6.6	Ps. 22.18	12.7	Num. 21.8
6.7	Isa. 3.9-10	12.9	Exod. 17.14
6.8	Exod. 33.1, 3	12.10	Ps. 110.1
6.12	Gen. 1.26, 28	12.11	Isa. 45.1
6.13	?	13.2	Gen. 25.21-23
6.13	Exod. 33.3	13.4	Gen. 48.11, 9
6.14	Ezek. 11.19	13.5	Gen. 48.14, 19
6.16	Ps. 42.4	13.7	Gen. 15.6; 17.4
6.16	Ps. 22.22, 25	14.2	Exod. 24.18; 31.18
6.18	Gen. 1.28	14.3	Exod. 32.7-19
7.3	Lev. 23.29	14.7	Isa. 42.6-7
7.4	Cf. Lev. 16	14.8	Isa. 49.6-7
7.6-8	Lev. 16.7-10, 20-22	14.9	Isa. 61.1-2
9.1	Ps. 18.44	15.1	Deut. 5.12
9.1	Cf. Isa. 33.13	15.2	cf. Jer. 17.24-25
9.1	Isa. 33.13; Jer. 4.4	15.3	Gen. 2.2-3
9.2	Deut. 5.1; Ps. 34.12; Isa. 50.10	15.4	Ps. 90.4
		15.8	Isa. 1.13
9.3	Isa. 1.2, 10	16.2	Isa. 40.12; 66.1
9.3	Isa. 40.3	16.3	cf. Isa. 49.17
9.5	Deut. 10.16	16.5	cf. *1 En.* 89.54-56

about food (ch. 10).¹⁷² In so doing, of course, *Barnabas* was anticipating the future Christian technique of dealing with awkward OT passages by means of spiritualizing or allegorizing them. But, even so, the *Letter of Barnabas* does underline how important the scriptures of Israel continued to be in early Christianity. And if indeed the author was a converted Gentile (§40.1f(i)) it is all the more striking that the Christianity which he espoused was so conscious of (if somewhat embarrassed by!) its Jewish heritage, and indeed eager to embrace that heritage.¹⁷³

d. *2 Clement*

2 Clement deserves some notice since it is a homily which draws substantially on the (OT) scriptures,¹⁷⁴ particularly Isaiah.¹⁷⁵ Its initial exposition of Isa. 54.1, for example, by referring it to 'us' (*2 Clem.* 2), is similar to the exposition of Habakkuk at Qumran. Equally significant is the fact that, somewhat like James and *Didache*, *2 Clement* takes it for granted that Jesus tradition is an equal resource for exhortation;¹⁷⁶ 'the books [of the prophets] and the apostles' are conjoint authorities for the church (14.2).¹⁷⁷

e. The Remaining Apostolic Fathers

The remaining Apostolic Fathers do not give such good examples of the Jewishness of their faith or of their dependence on scripture (OT). Presumably their own particular priorities and the occasions on which they wrote did not give any particular stimulus to draw on Jewish material.

---

172. See also Wilson, *Related Strangers* 129-31; Hvalvik, *Struggle* 119-22.

173. Horbury regards Barnabas and Justin's writings as 'Jewish as much as Christian documents' which 'could properly be assigned to a Christian sub-section of Jewish literature' ('Barnabas' 345).

174. See §44 n.118 above; also Grant and Graham, *First and Second Clement* 133-34. 'The importance of the work lies simply in its reflection of rather ordinary Christian (essentially Jewish-Christian) life and thought in the early second century' (Grant and Graham 110).

175. *2 Clem.* 2.1-3 (Isa. 54.1), 3.5 (Isa. 29.13), 7.5 (Isa. 66.24), 13.2 (Isa. 52.5), 14.1 (Jer. 7.11), 15.3 (Isa. 58.9), 16.3 (Mal. 4.1; Isa. 34.4), 17.4 (Isa. 66.18), 17.6 (Isa. 66.18, 24). *2 Clement* also regularly stresses the importance of keeping the commandments, but they are 'the commandments of the Lord (Jesus Christ)' (3.4; 4.5; 6.7; 8.4; 17.3, 6).

176. See again §44.2i above.

177. Koester quotes the frequently repeated characterization of Hans Windisch: 'The theological basis of *2 Clement* is, stated briefly, a Synoptic-Gospels Christianity understood in terms of contemporary Judaism' (*Introduction* 2.235).

- Ignatius was primarily concerned to strengthen the position of the bishop of the churches to which he wrote, though his occasional quotations from scripture provide sufficient demonstration of his knowledge of the scriptures and his assumption that they provided authoritative instruction.[178]
- Polycarp in his *Letter to the Philippians* begins by rejoicing that their faith was 'proclaimed from ancient times' (*Phil.* 1.2), and echoes Eph. 2.8-9 ('saved by grace, not from works') rather than the more typical Pauline contrast of faith with works of the law (1.3). His repeated emphasis on God's commandments[179] and righteousness[180] is characteristically Jewish, and his reference to their being 'well trained in the sacred scriptures' (12.1) indicates an assumption of their (the OT's) fundamental importance.[181]
- The *Shepherd* of Hermas, however, makes no quotations from the (Jewish) scriptures,[182] and only occasional allusions can be detected, particularly to the Psalms and the Wisdom literature.[183] The writer makes great play of 'commandments' (the section known as the *Mandates* consists of exposition of twelve commandments),[184] and was evidently influenced by the two

---

178. *Eph.* 5.3 (Prov. 3.34); 15.1 (cf. Ps. 33.9); *Magn.* 12 (Prov. 18.17); *Trall.* 8.2 (cf. Isa. 52.5); the bishop of Philadelphia is commended because 'he is attuned to the commandments like a lyre to the strings' (*Philad.* 1.2); and 'we should also love the prophets, because their proclamation anticipated the gospel' (5.2; 9.2); 'the words of the prophets' and 'the law of Moses' are authoritative teaching (*Smyrn.* 5.1; 7.2). Somewhat surprisingly, however, Ignatius's exhortations to fellow bishop Polycarp do not draw at all on OT paraenesis. Daniélou regarded Ignatius as a representative of Jewish Christianity (*Theology* 39-43); but apart from *Eph.* 19 having roots in a form of Jewish apocalyptic (*Ascension of Isaiah*), Schoedel concludes that 'little that is specifically Jewish Christianity can be found in Ignatius' (*Ignatius* 16). More interesting is the contribution of Ignatius in §46 below.

179. *Phil.* 2.2; 3.3; 4.1; 5.1; (6.3).

180. *Phil.* 2.3; 3.1, 3 ('the commandment of righteousness'); 4.1; 5.2; 8.1; 9.1, 2.

181. He alludes to and draws on scriptural passages as a natural reflex — 6.1 (Prov. 3.4), 10.2 (Prov. 3.28), 10.3 (Tob. 4.10), 10.3 (Isa. 52.5). Schoedel finds echoes of Psalms, Proverbs, Isaiah, Jeremiah, Ezekiel and Tobit (*Polycarp* 5); in contrast, the *Martyrdom of Polycarp* makes no effort to draw on the OT. O. Skarsaune, 'Evidence for Jewish Believers in Greek and Latin Patristic Literature', in Skarsaune and Hvalvik, eds., *Jewish Believers in Jesus* 505-67, suggests that Polycarp was himself Jewish (522-24). See also Hartog, *Polycarp's Epistle to the Philippians* 226-31.

182. The only explicit and direct reference is to the lost apocryphal work, the Book of Eldad and Modad (*Vis.* 2.3.4).

183. See the marginal listings in Lake, *Apostolic Fathers* 2.6-305; Snyder finds about 50 allusions, half from the Psalms (*Shepherd of Hermas* 161-62).

184. The *Mandates* is 'mostly composed of traditional Jewish materials', and the *Similitudes* 'is based on a collection of parables which certainly has a Jewish origin' (Koester, *Introduction* 2.259). 'There is also growing agreement that *Herm.* is much indebted to

ways tradition, but at no great depth and rather simplistically, without any awareness of Pauline-like angst over the law and how it can be obeyed.[185] So we can speak of the influence of biblical tradition on him,[186] but with the least profundity of any of the documents so far examined.

- From the preserved fragments of Papias we can glean very little since almost all of the patristic references to or citations from Papias focus on his testimony about the early days of Christianity. But it is probably significant that his speculation about the abundant and supernatural fruitfulness of the age to come (Irenaeus, *adv. haer.* 5.33.3) is very similar to what we find in *2 Bar.* 29.5-6, and that he is remembered as interpreting the accounts of creation and Paradise as referring to Christ and the church.[187] The implication is that his mind-set was largely determined by the scriptures (OT).[188]

In sum, it is clear that the (Jewish) Bible was central to the thinking and teaching of several of the Apostolic Fathers, and assumed to be of importance by the others. At this stage biblical and Jewish mind-set were still more or less synonymous, Christians, as much as Jews generally (not just the successors of the Pharisees), drawing fully and freely on the scriptures (what became for Christians the OT) as fundamental documents for faith and morally responsible living. This Christianity was still intensively Jewish in that sense at least.

f. Aristides' *Apology*

In his *Apology*, Aristides describes Jews and Christians as distinct entities, so we should not expect much if any indications of Jewish influence.[189] And in his critique of idolatry (*Apol.* 3, 13) and affirmation of the oneness of God (13), a perspective obviously rooted in earlier Jewish polemic, his failure to draw

---

Judaism ... (though) the importance of Judaism for *Herm.* may, however, have been exaggerated' (Schoedel, 'Apostolic Fathers' 470).

185. In fact, popular pagan representations were more influential on Hermas (Lampe, *Paul to Valentinus* 227-31).

186. Osiek, *Hermas* 25.

187. Anastasius of Sinai (seventh century), *Contemplations on the Hexameron* 1, 7 (quoted in Ehrman, *Apostolic Fathers* 110-13).

188. 'The Jewish-Christian substance of Papias's thought has also received strong emphasis' (Schoedel, 'Apostolic Fathers' 472).

189. 'Later Christians liked to see quotations from Scripture, but Aristides supplied none' (Grant, 'Aristides', *ABD* 1.382). The *Kerygma Petrou*, however, even in the brief extracts, refers to the scriptures on several occasions and notes, 'we say nothing without [the testimony of] scripture' (Clement of Alexandria, *Strom.* 6.15.128).

on or show any obvious influence from Jewish arguments and affirmations is striking. On the other hand, it is true that his description of the ethical integrity of Christians draws on the decalogue, without doing so explicitly.

g. *Epistle to Diognetus*

Rather like Aristides, the *Epistle to Diognetus* regards Christians as a 'new people (*genos*) or way of life' (1) and dismisses the idolatry of non-Jews and non-Christians (2), but again with little or no evident influence from the long-running Jewish polemic against idolatry. There is a near-quotation from Ps. 146.6 (3.4), and an interesting reflection on the close proximity of the 'tree of knowledge' and the 'tree of life in the middle of paradise' (12.3-8). 'The fear of the law' and 'the grace of the prophets' are listed in a sequence with 'the faith of the Gospels', 'the tradition of the apostles' and 'the grace of the church' (11.6).[190] He also echoes the fundamental Jewish observation that no one (even Moses) has ever seen God (8.5; Exod. 33.20-23) and concludes with a reference to 'the Passover of the Lord' (12.9). But the Jewish milieu of Christianity is at best implicit.

h. Justin Martyr

Justin Martyr, however, is very different. It was of first importance that his belief in Jesus as Christ was firmly rooted in and could be demonstrated to be fully in accord with the scriptures — as he has Trypho observe, 'You are anxious to draw your proofs from them [the scriptures]' (*Dial.* 56.16). His argument with Trypho was that his claims about Christ 'were plainly proclaimed in the scriptures' (76.6). He does not hesitate to affirm that 'out of fear we endeavour for our part to discourse in accordance with the scriptures' (82.3); they are 'the word of God' (58.4).[191] It is not surprising, then, that in his first *Apology* he gives priority to demonstrating that the (OT) prophecies speak of Christ (*1 Apol.* 32-42, 48-53). But it is particularly in his *Dialogue with Trypho* that Justin pulls out all stops to demonstrate that Christian faith is entirely proved and substantiated by scripture, and that Jews are at fault in failing to recognize that (Jesus) Christ was the one for whom the scriptures were

---

190. The difference in style and content (from the negative attitudes to the Jews in chs. 3-4) has led most to conclude that chs. 11-12 are from a different hand from that of the author of chs. 1-10 (Ehrman, *Apostolic Fathers* 2.123-24; Jefford, *Diognetus* 43-51).

191. See also e.g. *Dial.* 58.1; 65.2; 67.3; 68.1; 73.6; 80.1. See also Shotwell, *Justin Martyr* chs. 1-2.

looking.[192] Since the evidence is overwhelming, I will restrict the references to what appears to have been the first day of the dialogue (1.1–74.3),[193] ignoring the many references in addition to the quotations, and not including the quotations attributed to Trypho.

Dialogue	Scripture quoted
11.1	Deut. 5.15
11.3	Isa. 51.4-5; Jer. 31.31-32
12.1	Isa. 55.3-5
13.2-9	Isa. 52.10–54.6
14.4-7	Isa. 55.3-13
15.2-6	Isa. 58.1-11
16.1	Deut. 10.16-17; Lev. 26.40-41
16.5	Isa. 57.1-4
17.2	Isa. 5.18-20
19.2	Jer. 2.13
19.3	Gen. 5.24
19.6	Ezek. 20.12, 20
20.1	Exod. 32.6; Deut. 32.15
20.6	Deut. 32.20
21.2-4	Ezek. 20.19-26
22.2-5	Amos 5.18-6.7
22.6	Jer. 7.21-22
22.7-10	Ps. 50
22.11	Isa. 66.1
23.4	Gen. 17.14
24.2	Isa. 26.2-3
24.3-4	Ps. 128.4-5; Isa. 2.5-6; Jer. 3.17; Isa. 65.1-3

192. 'In the OT exegesis of the *Apology*, Justin used "testimony sources" with texts already chosen by Christians, whereas in the *Dialogue* he used texts transmitted by Jews. He thought that the testimony texts were authentic, while the other version(s) had been corrupted. When he claimed in the *Dialogue* that Jews had cut predictions of Christ out of their text he was comparing their version(s) with his own Christian book' (Grant, 'Justin Martyr', *ABD* 3.1133-34, referring to O. Skarsaune, *The Proof from Prophecy: A Study in Justin Martyr's Proof-Text Tradition* [NovTSupp 66; Leiden: Brill, 1987]; see also Horbury, 'Barnabas' 337-38; Wilson, *Related Strangers* 270-71). 'It has been demonstrated recently that the numerous special readings in Justin's quotations from the Old Testament derive from a Jewish tradition of textual revision in which the Greek text was brought into closer agreement with the further developments of the Hebrew text' (Koester, *Introduction* 2.342). 'He [Justin] uses Old Testament Haggada in the same way as he uses Christian Haggada. In fact, he incorporates haggadic material into his own material in exactly the same way the rabbis used the Haggada' (Shotwell, *Justin Martyr* 89). See further Skarsaune, *Proof from Prophecy*.

193. See above §40.2e at n.136.

Dialogue	Scripture quoted
25.1-5	Isa. 63.15–64.12
26.2-4	Isa. 62.10–63.6
27.2-3	Isa. 1.23; 3.16
27.4	Deut. 32.20; Isa. 29.13
28.2	Jer. 4.3-4
28.3	Jer. 9.25-26
28.5	Mal. 1.10-12
31.2-7	Dan. 7.9-28
32.3	Dan. 7.25
32.5	Jer. 4.22; Isa. 29.14
32.6; 33.1-2	Ps. 110
33.1	Isa. 6.10
34.1	Ps. 19.7
34.2-6	Ps. 72
36.2	Jer. 4.22
36.3-6	Ps. 24
37.1	Ps. 47.5-9
37.2-4	Ps. 99
38.3-5	Ps. 45
39.1	1 Kgs. 19.10, 14, 18
39.4	Ps. 68.18
39.5	Isa. 5.21; 29.18
41.2	Mal. 1.10-12
42.1	Ps. 19.4
42.2	Isa. 53
43.3	Isa. 53.8
43.5-6	Isa. 7.10-16
44.2	Ezek. 14.20
44.3	Isa. 66.23-24
49.6	Num. 27.18
49.8	Exod. 17.16
50.3-5	Isa. 40.1-17
52.2	Gen. 49.8-12
52.4	Isa. 1.8
53.3	Zech. 9.9
53.6	Zech. 13.7
55.3	Isa. 1.9
56.2	Gen. 18.1-3
56.6	Gen. 18.14
56.7	Gen. 21.9-12

Dialogue	Scripture quoted
56.12	Gen. 19.23-25
56.14	Ps. 110.1; Ps. 45.6-7
56.17-18	Gen. 18.13-14, 16-17, 20-23
56.19-21	Gen. 18.33–19.1, 10, 16-25
58.4-5	Gen. 31.10-13
58.6-7	Gen. 32.22-30
58.8-9	Gen. 35.6-10
58.11-13	Gen. 28.10-19
59.2	Exod. 2.23; 3.16
60.4	Exod. 3.2-4
61.3-5	Prov. 8.22-36
62.1	Gen. 1.26-28
62.3	Gen. 3.22
62.5	Josh. 5.13–6.2
63.2	Isa. 53.8; Gen. 49.11
63.3	Ps. 110.3-4
53.4-5	Ps. 45.6-11
64.4	Ps. 99.1-7
64.6	Ps. 72.1-19
64.8	Ps. 19.1-6
65.4-6	Isa. 42.5-13
66.2-3	Isa. 7.10-16
68.4	Isa. 53.8
68.6	Isa. 7.14
69.5	Isa. 35.1-7
70.2-3	Isa. 33.13-19
71.3	Isa. 7.14
72.2	Jer. 11.19
73.1–74.2	Ps. 96

Justin's command of scriptural knowledge is evident throughout the *Dialogue*; he often quotes extensive passages, complete Psalms for example. He is well able to point out that such as Abel, Enoch, Noah, Lot and Melchizedek were pleasing to God 'without circumcision' (*Dial.* 19.3-4), and that there are scriptures which demonstrate that God does not commend or need Israel's sacrifices or temple.[194] He is the first to use the patriarchal narratives' ambiguity between the angel of God and God[195] to make the argument that the

194. *Dial.* 21-22, citing at length Ezek. 20.19-26, Amos 5.18–6.7, Jer. 7.21-22 and Ps. 50; also *Dial.* 117.1 citing Mal. 1.10-12.
195. Gen. 18.31-32; Exod. 3.2-4; Josh. 5.13–6.2.

presence of Christ, also God, explains the ambiguity,[196] to explain the 'us' of the creation narrative christologically (Gen. 1.26-28; *Dial.* 62.1-3) and to draw on Prov. 8.22-36 for an explicit Wisdom christology (*Dial.* 61, 129). He is the first to meet the (Trypho's) objection that the Hebrew does not support the LXX reading of Isa. 7.14 as referring to a 'virgin' (*Dial.* 67.1; 71.3; 84.1-4).[197] And his extended exposition of Ps. 22 in reference to the cross is impressive (*Dial.* 97.3–106.4). Trypho's acknowledgment to Justin 'that you do your utmost to be careful by keeping close to scripture' (80.1) is thus justified. It was evidently the fact that Christianity was so deeply rooted in Israel's ancient religion and that Christ was so much in accord with these scriptures which persuaded Justin to abandon his Platonism for Christianity.

In short, Justin was keen to demonstrate the integral continuity of Christianity with the religion of Israel.[198] Justin and Trypho worshipped the same God (11.1). There was no doubt that Jesus was of the race of David (45.4). Justin was able to claim that 'every day some (Jews) are [still] becoming disciples unto the name of his (God's) Christ' (39.2). He saw types of Christian beliefs and practices in various characteristic elements of Israel's religion (40-42). As Justin himself affirms, 'We, who have come to know the true worship of God from the law, and the word that went forth from Jerusalem by the apostles of Jesus, have fled for refuge to him who is God of Jacob and God of Israel' (110.2).[199]

i. Athenagoras

Athenagoras in his *Plea for the Christians* was not concerned to demonstrate Christianity's ancient roots in the religion and scriptures of Israel. But he takes it for granted that his appeal to Moses, Isaiah, Jeremiah and the other prophets, those inspired by the Spirit as a flute-player breathes into his flute, will carry weight with his distinguished addressees. He quotes from Isaiah to substantiate his belief in the oneness of God (*Plea* 9),[200] and finds in Prov. 8.22 a reference to the Logos (10); but apart from a passing quotation from

---

196. *Dial.* 56, 58, 60.4; 62.4-5; 125.5; 126-129; so also *1 Dial.* 63. See also D. C. Trakatellis, *The Pre-existence of Christ in the Writings of Justin Martyr* (Harvard Dissertations in Religion 6; Missoula: Scholars, 1976) ch. 2.

197. See also Horner, *Listening to Trypho* 158-62.

198. See above n.173; and Wilson, *Related Strangers* 274-78.

199. Tatian, though a pupil of Justin, showed nothing of the same interest in demonstrating Christianity's deep roots in Israel's scriptures beyond his assertion that Moses anticipated Homer and other venerated philosophers and heroes (*Address* 36-41).

200. Isa. 43.10-11; 44.6; 66.1; also drawing on 41.4.

Prov. 21.1 (*Plea* 18) he makes no other reference to Jewish thought, with references to Homer far in excess (especially 18, 21). His treatise *On the Resurrection* at no point draws on scripture, and indeed includes only one quotation from NT writings — 1 Cor. 15.54 (*Res.* 18).

j. Theophilus

Theophilus drew much more regularly on 'the sacred scriptures of the holy prophets' (*Autolycus* 1.14): in demonstrating that God is known by his works (1.6-7),[201] in his extensive description of God creating the world in six days (2.10-18) and in his account of paradise, the fall and its consequences (2.19-31), giving explanations nowhere else to be found (2.33).[202] A sequence of confessional affirmations and precepts drawn from the law and the prophets (2.34-35)[203] finds some confirmation in the teachings of the poets and philosophers (2.36-38). The familiar dismissal of false accusations against the Christians (promiscuity and cannibalism — 3.4), and denigratory comparisons with common beliefs concerning the gods (3.5-8), are followed by positive affirmations of Christian values and conduct, drawn primarily from 'the holy scriptures' 'inspired by one Spirit of God' (3.9-14; here 3.11, 12),[204] with Gospel teaching interspersed (3.13, 14)[205] as entirely of a piece. In contrast to the uncertain conjectures of the philosophers, Theophilus has no hesitation in claiming that 'we [the Christians] know the truth', being 'instructed by the holy prophets who are instructed by the Holy Spirit of God' (3.17), and going on to expound the deluge (3.18-19), the antiquity of Moses and Solomon's temple (3.20-22), the prophets being more ancient than any Greek writers (3.23-26), demonstrating that Christian beliefs were not new or recent but ancient and true, precisely because they were those of 'the prophetical writings' (3.29).

---

201. Job 9.9; Pss. 135.7; 33.6.

202. See also Grant, *Greek Apologists* 157-61. In his 'Theophilus of Antioch to Autolycus', in *After the New Testament* (Philadelphia: Fortress, 1967), Grant observes that 'almost everything in his exegesis can be paralleled in Jewish haggadic literature' (136).

203. Exod. 20.14-17; Prov. 4.25; Deut. 4.19; Isa. 42.5-6; 45.12; 40.28; Jer. 10.12-13; 51.17-18; Ps. 14.1, 3; Hab. 2.18.

204. Exod. 20.3-4, 12-17; 23.6-8; 22.21; Isa. 55.6-7; Ezek. 18.21-23; Isa. 31.6; Jer. 6.9; Isa. 1.16-17; 58.6-8; Jer. 6.16; Hos. 12.6; Joel 2.16; Zech. 7.9-10; Prov. 4.25; Matt. 5.28, 32; Prov. 6.27-29; Isa. 66.5; Matt. 5.44, 46; 6.3.

205. See above §44.3e.

k. Melito of Sardis

Melito of Sardis certainly knew his scripture: Eusebius quotes the preface to one of his writings in which he makes what appears to be the earliest known 'list of the recognized scriptures of the Old Testament', encourages his brother Onesimus in his desire 'to know the accurate facts about the ancient writings' and sends him 'extracts from the law and prophets concerning our Saviour' (*HE* 4.26.12-13).[206] In his *Peri Pascha* Melito refers in detail to the regulations for the Passover (*Peri Pascha* 11-15), followed by melancholy reflection on the death of Egypt's first-born (16-29). He describes the creation and fall of man (47-48) and reflects in equally melancholic spirit on the disastrous consequences for humankind (49-56). He sees predictions of Christ's sufferings in episodes in the lives of Abel, Isaac, Joseph, Moses and David (59, 69) and quotes various scriptures in elaborating his point.[207] His principal point, as already noted, is that the Passover and various other events and individuals in the OT are types of Christ and his sacrificial death. Although he plays down the continuing value of the type (§46.6h), there is no question that it was important for Melito to be able to demonstrate the continuity between his faith in Christ and the (Jewish) scriptures, and the significant lessons which could be drawn from the types for Christian understanding of the paschal mystery of Christ's death.[208]

l. Irenaeus

It is hardly necessary to document or illustrate Irenaeus's dependency on scripture, that is, the OT.[209] He was well aware that his opponents made use of scripture, parables in particular being vulnerable to misinterpretation (*adv. haer.* 2.27-28), but he insists that what was not plain should always be interpreted by the plain (2.28.3). And in his central argument against the Valentinians and Marcionites he is able repeatedly to draw on the OT to show that there is no other God 'except him who is called God and Lord of all, who also said to Moses, "I am that I am"' (Exod. 3.14); and that the God of Abraham, Isaac, Jacob and Israel is the Father of our Lord Jesus Christ (*adv. haer* 3.6).

---

206. Although referring to the LXX, the list of OT writings he appends (*HE* 4.26.4) includes only the writings of the Hebrew Bible.

207. Deut. 28.66 (61), Ps. 2.1-2 (62), Jer. 11.19 (63), Isa. 53.7 (64), Ps. 35.12, 4 and Isa. 3.10 LXX (72).

208. Melito uses the term 'mystery' 16 times in 1-65.

209. Osborn notes that A. Benoit, 'Ecriture et tradition chez S. Irénée', *RHPR* 40 (1960) 33, finds 629 references to the OT in *adv. haer.*, but 1,065 to the NT (*Irenaeus* 162 n.1).

'Only he who made all things is rightly called "God" and "lord" (3.8.3). . . . No human mind can penetrate beyond him; indeed, it would be foolish to try (2.25.4). Any such attempt leads to the fallacy and futility of infinite regress (1.16.3; 4.19.1)'.[210] The fact that the OT scriptures foretold the advent and passion of God's Son is clear indication that they were inspired by one and the same God (4.10). His attitude is well indicated in the way he draws on the provision made by God in the garden of Eden to indicate God's desire that Christians should be nourished by the 'the Lord's scriptures': 'For the Church has been planted as a garden (*paradisus*) in this world; therefore says the Spirit of God, "Thou mayest freely eat from every tree of the garden" (Gen. 2.16), that is, Eat ye from every scripture of the Lord' (*adv. haer.* 5.20.2). With Irenaeus we see the transition from Jewish scripture to Christian Bible.[211]

m. Quartodecimans

In Asia Minor the tradition was to observe the feast of the Saviour's Passover (Last Supper) on the fourteenth day of the moon (Nisan 14), which was the day when the Passover lambs were killed (Exod. 12.6), and the day on which, according to John, Jesus had celebrated the Last Supper. 'Thus it was necessary to finish the fast on that day, whatever day of the week it might be' (Eusebius, *HE* 5.23.1). Elsewhere the practice was to finish the fast on the Sunday (Easter Sunday), however that related to Nisan 14. The Quartodeciman practice was believed to stem from the apostle John, according to whose account Jesus was crucified on 'the day of preparation for the Passover' (John 19.14), when the Passover lambs were killed (hence John 19.36 quoting Exod. 12.10, 46 LXX).[212] And it was strongly supported by Polycarp and Melito. When Victor, bishop of Rome, tried to suppress the Quartodecimans, Irenaeus was among those who sharply rebuked him, pleading irenically that diversity of

---

210. Osborn, *Irenaeus* 28-29; and further 27-34, 52-57: 'Irenaeus attacked Gnostics for their lack of consistent argument. The one all-embracing God provided a rational first principle. Irenaeus required that any argument, about man or God, should not contradict itself. Since God is the highest and all-embracing reality, there can be no other God beside God (2.1.2)' (34); 'Against Gnostic and Marcionite claims Jesus brought a message from a strange unknown God, Irenaeus insists that the son makes the father visible. In Jesus Christ there is no new God but a new manifestation of the only God' (112); *invisibile filii pater, visibile autem patris filius* (*adv. haer.* 4.6.6).

211. 'Irenaeus provides the first clear evidence of a Christian Bible' (Osborn, *Irenaeus* 162; see further ch. 8).

212. The Jewish day began at sunset, so the Last Supper and crucifixion would have taken place on the same day; for discussion on the difference between the Synoptic and Johannine timing of Jesus' crucifixion, see Barrett, *John* 48-51.

practice should be tolerated (*HE* 5.24.11-18).[213] The point is, of course, that we see a substantial body of second-century Christians clinging to the Passover character of the Last Supper (and so also of the Christian eucharist)[214] and of Jesus' death.[215]

In short, the Jewishness of the Christian faith was still largely taken as a given by the Apostolic Fathers and the Apologists, and although a growing sense of the distinctiveness of Christianity from Judaism is evident in their writings there is no effort made to deny that the scriptures quoted are the Jewish scriptures.

45.6 The Heritage of Second Temple Judaism

The claim that Christianity was more genuinely the heir of Second Temple Judaism than rabbinic Judaism would seem at first sight to be absurd. The rabbinic Judaism which developed slowly out of the catastrophes of the two Jewish revolts, and which became the classic pattern of Judaism through to this day, would seem to most to be the obvious, and indeed the only obvious heir of Second Temple Judaism. As we have seen, early Christianity, as well as rabbinic Judaism, can obviously lay claim to be a genuine heir of the religion of Israel, as expressed normatively in Israel's scriptures. But the real heir of the Judaism which emerged from the Maccabean resistance to Syrian dominance and to the pervasive influence of Hellenism is unquestionably rabbinic Judaism.

However, the fact remains that Second Temple Judaism was more diverse than the Pharisaic Judaism of the pre-Christian Paul.[216] The Judaism of the Sadducees was of a different order, more to be regarded as normative Judaism in the pre-70 period. The Judaism of the Essenes was the clearest example of a pre-70 sectarian Judaism. And the Judaisms of the apocalyptists and of the diaspora were different again, though more difficult to characterize to any great extent. Embryonic Christianity, the sect of the Nazarenes, is prop-

---

213. See more fully Wilson, *Related Strangers* 235-41.
214. Paul also refers to 'Christ sacrificed as our *pascha*' (1 Cor. 5.7).
215. 'At a later date the Quartodecimans organized themselves as a separate Church. They survived as a sect down to the 5th century' (*ODCC* 1355).
216. It will be recalled that the NT uses *Ioudaismos* only twice, in Gal. 1.13-14, where it is clear that what Paul was referring to was not the diversity of what modern historians call 'Second Temple Judaism', but the zealotic and separatist Pharisaic Judaism, to which the pre-Christian Paul had been committed, and which he disowned as a result of his conversion; see further *Beginning from Jerusalem* §25 and §29.2a.

erly described as yet another form of Second Temple Judaism, overlapping at various points with several of its competing alternatives.[217]

The critical factor, which gives weight to the claim referred to at the beginning of this section, is that *it was Christianity rather than rabbinic Judaism which preserved so much of the heritage of this diverse Second Temple Judaism, which might otherwise have been lost.* Rabbinic Judaism drew heavily on the earlier (particularly) Pharisaic halakhoth and traditions, but effectively nothing more. And Christianity had no interest in Sadducean or Essene traditions. But it was Christianity which preserved the LXX, so that a distinguishing feature between Christianity and rabbinic Judaism became the forms in which their common scriptures were preserved and used — LXX for the Christians, Hebrew Bible for the rabbis.[218] Arguably the two greatest sequences of Jewish writings, by Philo and Josephus, are known to us today not because they were preserved, copied and continued to be studied by the rabbis, but because they were valued by the early Christians. Philo undoubtedly influenced early christology through his extensive concept of the Logos as God's self-manifestation in creation and revelation,[219] and has indeed been called 'the first Christian theologian'.[220] And it would appear that Josephus's brief references to Jesus[221] were readily elaborated to provide a firm testimony (by Josephus!) that Jesus 'was the Messiah' and appeared to his disciples 'on the third day... restored to life' (*Ant.* 18.63-64).[222] Other writings usually

---

217. The point is made repeatedly in *Beginning from Jerusalem* — e.g. 16-17, 238-40.

218. A classic illustration is the disagreement between Justin and Trypho on the Greek translation of Isa. 7.14 — Justin defending the LXX rendering (*parthenos* –'virgin') and Trypho arguing that the translation of the Hebrew *'almâ* ('young maiden') is more accurately rendered by the Greek *neanis* ('young girl'), the agreed translation of Aquila, Symmachus and Theodotion (*Dial.* 67.1; 71.1-3; 84.1-4). See further M. Hengel, *The Septuagint as Christian Scripture* (Edinburgh: T & T Clark, 2002) particularly 43-44. It is arguable that the alternative Greek versions, Theodotion, Aquila and Symmachus, which probably emerged in the second century, were products of the overlap between Judaism and Christianity (Eusebius calls Symmachus an Ebionite [Eusebius, *dem. evang.* VII.1; *HE* 5.17; similarly Theodoret, *prol. lib.* 2], and Theodotion and Aquila 'both Jewish proselytes' [*HE* 5.8.10]; similarly Jerome, *in Hab.* 3.10-13; according to Augustine some called the Nazoreans Symmachians [*contra Faustum* 19.4]). They probably represented attempts to find a Greek translation of the Hebrew scriptures more acceptable to most Jews; cf. J. M. Dines, *The Septuagint* (London: T & T Clark, 2004) 81-93.

219. See e.g. J. N. D. Kelly, *Early Christian Doctrines* (London: A & C Black, ^{2}1960) 19-22.

220. G. E. Sterling, *EDEJ* 1069.

221. See *Jesus Remembered* 141.

222. The elaborated account is usually known as the *Testimonium Flavianum*, attested by Eusebius, *HE* 1.11.7-8; see e.g. S. Mason, *Josephus and the New Testament* (Peabody: Hendrickson, ^{2}2003) 226-36; and further H. Schreckenberg, 'The Works of Josephus and the Early Christian Church', in L. H. Feldman and G. Hatai, eds., *Josephus, Judaism and Christianity* (Leiden: Brill, 1987) 315-24.

referred to as the Jewish pseudepigrapha, some of which were also more widely valued, as at Qumran, became more directly influential in parts of Christianity. The most obvious example is the Enoch writings gathered together as *1 Enoch*, whose influence is evident in some NT texts,[223] and which as the *Book of Enoch* became part of the canon of the Ethiopian Orthodox Church.[224]

Still more interesting are the indications that the early Christians used some Jewish writings as a template for their own compositions.[225]

- It is generally recognized that books 7 and 8 of the fourth-century *Apostolic Constitutions and Canons*, an early church manual of liturgical and ecclesiastical regulations, drew heavily on Hellenistic synagogal prayers, by inserting references to Jesus Christ, his birth, crucifixion, the Lord's day, the Church, and so on. Otherwise, the prayers have a distinctively Jewish character and may be dated as early as the middle of the second century.[226]
- The *Testaments of the Twelve Patriarchs* have been so christianized that it is almost impossible to disentangle a pre-Christian version. Nevertheless the presence of fragments of the Testaments of Levi and Naphtali discovered at Qumran makes it most likely that the Christian document was based on an earlier Jewish document or model, whose messianic ideas

---

223. E.g. Matt. envisages "the Son of Man seated on the throne of his glory" in judgment, which may echo *1 Enoch* 62:5; 69:29 (cf. 45:3; 55:4; 61:8; 62:3); see further J. Theisohn, *Der auserwählte Richter: Untersuchungen zum traditionsgeschichtlichen Ort der Menschensohn der Bilderreden des äthiopischen Henoch* (Göttingen: Vandenhoeck, 1969) ch. 6. See also above on Jude (n.125).

224. See particularly M. A. Knibb, 'Christian Adoption and Transmission of Jewish-Pseudepigrapha: The Case of 1 Enoch', *JSJ* 32 (2001) 396-415, reprinted in M. A. Knibb, *Essays on the Book of Enoch and Other Early Jewish Texts and Traditions* (Leiden: Brill, 2009) 56-76. As part of the canon of a Christian church *1 Enoch* was included in *Eerdmans Commentary on the Bible* (ed. J. D. G. Dunn and J. W. Rogerson, 2003).

225. In what follows I draw particularly on Charlesworth, 'Christian Additions to the Apocryphal Writings'. See also Wilson, *Related Strangers* 97-98, 107-8; T. Elgvin, 'Jewish Editing of the Old Testament Pseudepigrapha', in Skarsaune and Hvalvik, eds., *Jewish Believers in Jesus* 278-304, who reviews also Christian interpolations in the *Lives of the Prophets* (Christian interpolation most obviously at 2.8-9, 12-13), *Fourth Baruch* (a Christian ending added — 9.14-32) and the *Apocalypse of Abraham* 29.3-13.

226. See D. A. Fiensy and D. R. Darnell, 'Hellenistic Synagogal Prayers', *OTP* 1.671-97, with the likely Christian insertions in the composition of the *Apostolic Constitutions* clearly noted. Charlesworth notes that the self-definition indicated by the insertions 'probably became fully polemical as the Jewish-Christian community that continued to recite these prayers disassociated itself from the vast majority of Jews' ('Christian Additions' 33). See also Wilson, *Related Strangers*: 'Judaism is dismissed, curiously, as a heresy and the Jews as the killers of Christ' (102).

(as at *T. Levi* 17 and *T. Jud.* 24.1) provided an obvious link and stimulus to Christian elaboration.[227]

- Again, it is generally recognized that chaps. 1-5 of the *Martyrdom and Ascension of Isaiah* is a document appropriately entitled the *Martyrdom of Isaiah*, within which 3.13–4.22 is a manifestly Christian interpolation. Stories of martyrdom were familiar from the accounts of the Maccabean martyrs (2 Macc. 7), and Heb. 11.37 contains an allusion to the account of Isaiah's execution by being sawn in two (*Martyrdom* 5.14). So the Jewish *Martyrdom* may well have been current at the turn of the first century, at which time the Christian interpolation could already have been made.[228]

- The first two chapters and the last two chapters of *4 Ezra* are best regarded as Christian additions to *4 Ezra*, the former more properly designated *5 Ezra*, and the latter *6 Ezra*.[229] *4 Ezra* is usually dated to about 100 CE, and its wrestling with the question why God had delivered his people into the hands of their enemies may well have appealed to the redactor. *5 Ezra* may well have emerged as a reflection prompted by *4 Ezra* on the experiences of the second Jewish revolt.[230] In a Christianity looking for its own identity, it would have been an attractive option to attribute the catastrophes of the two Jewish revolts to Israel's failure to keep the covenant (*4 Ezra* 2.5-7; 15.25) and to present Ezra as turning to the Gentiles, rather as had Paul (1.24; 2.33-34). But those represented continued to reprise classic prophetic rebuke, to set themselves within Israel's history, the patriarchs and prophets given them as leaders (1.38-40; 2.18), and to define themselves in characteristically Jewish terms as those who keep God's commandments and precepts (1.24; 2.20-22; 16.76).[231]

---

227. Text by H. C. Kee in *OTP* 1.775-828. The most prominent researcher on the *Testaments* has been M. de Jonge; see his 'Patriarchs, Testaments of the Twelve', *ABD* 5.181-86. Charlesworth notes ten undeniably Christian passages ('Christian Additions' 36-40). 'The evidence points to a Jewish-Christian interpolator (or author) belonging to a mixed community of Jews and Gentiles, or to a Jewish Christian community with open lines to Gentile brethren, shortly after the Bar Kokhba revolt' (Elgvin, 'Jewish Editing' 292; other bibliography 286 n.22). Wilson notes 'their unrestrained universalism' (*Related Strangers* 105-7).

228. M. A. Knibb, 'Martyrdom and Ascension of Isaiah', *OTP* 2.143-76 (here 149); Wilson, *Related Strangers* 99-101; Elgvin, 'Jewish Editing' 292-93. On the interpolation see Charlesworth, 'Christian Additions' 41-46.

229. The whole document appears in the NT Apocrypha as '2 Esdras'. I will cite all the references as *4 Ezra* (= *2 Esdras*).

230. Stanton, '5 Ezra' 262-63; Elgvin, 'Jewish Editing' 301.

231. See also Wilson, *Related Strangers* 92, 95-97; Charlesworth, 'Christian Additions' 46-48. The clearest Christian feature is the reference to 'a young man of great stature' in Ezra's vision, identified as 'the Son of God whom they confessed in the world' (*4 Ezra* 2.43-47).

§45.6 *Jewish Christianity*

- *Sibylline Oracles* were a popular genre in the ancient world, a form of political propaganda warning of woes and disasters predicted to come upon humankind.[232] Jewish writers began to use the genre in the second century BCE; *Sib. Or.* 3-5, and 11 are the clearest examples.[233] Christian insertions in these writings are modest,[234] but book 1 seems to be a Christian reworking of an originally Jewish oracle,[235] and book 2 is probably a Christian composition though drawing on a Jewish original.[236] The Christian redaction of books 1 and 2 is probably to be dated no later than 150 CE.[237]
- We should probably add here the *Odes of Solomon*, but not because they are a Christian revision or adaptation of an earlier Jewish writing. Rather the *Odes* seem to draw their primary inspiration from the (OT) Psalms, as did the additional Qumran Psalms, not to mention the Qumran hymns and the *Psalms of Solomon*. What is of equal interest for us is that the *Odes* are clearly Christian in inspiration, speaking regularly of the Son, the Messiah (§40.1j), and the echoes of John's Gospel are particularly noticeable (§49.6). There is also a degree of antipathy to Gentiles (as in *Odes* 10.5 and 29.8). So in all probability the *Odes* were written by a Jewish believer in Jesus.[238]

What is noticeable in all this is the familiarity of the early Christians with what were distinctively Jewish writings; and not just a familiarity, but also what we might call a sense that these were also their writings, whose relevance and value to Christians could be naturally and readily brought out by elaboration and addition. The medium through which such Jewish writings came to Gentile believers was most probably Jewish believers, who were still in close connection with, perhaps even part of, Jewish communities, and who saw their specific belief in Messiah Jesus as the natural outworking and extension of their Jewish faith. It is equally arguable that early second-century writings which are regarded as entirely Christian, I

---

232. The sixteenth-century *Prophecies* of Nostradamus aroused a similar fascination.

233. J. J. Collins, 'Sibylline Oracles', *ABD* 6.3-4.

234. Charlesworth notes only two Christian additions in book 3 — *Sib. Or.* 3.776 and 5.256-59 ('Christian Additions' 48-49).

235. The final section, on the incarnation and life of Christ (1.324-400), is clearly a Christian addition. See also Wilson, *Related Strangers* 102-3; see also 103-5.

236. J. J. Collins, 'Sibylline Oracles', *OTP* 1.317-472 (here 330). See particularly O. Wassmuth, *Sibyllinische Orakel 1-2: Studien und Kommentar* (AJEC 76; Leiden: Brill, 2011). *Sib. Or.* 8 may well have a Jewish underlay, though books 6 and 7 are clearly Christian compositions (Collins, *ABD* 6.5).

237. Collins, *OTP* 1.331-32.

238. Emerton, *AOT* 684. See also §49.6 and §50.1e below.

think particularly of the *Didache*, are to be attributed to such groups of Jewish believers in Jesus, groups who might subsequently have been regarded as heterodox.[239]

Another striking feature is that the writings indicated above seem to have come from quite a wide spectrum of countries — Philo in Egypt, Josephus in Rome, the Hellenistic synagogal prayers and the *Testaments* perhaps from Syria, the *Martyrdom* and *4 Ezra* probably from Palestine, and the *Sibylline Oracles* variously attributed to Egypt, Phrygia and Syria — with the likely corollary that they attest that Jewish believers were widespread throughout the western diaspora and that Jewish Christianity was a fertile seed-bed for Christianity's own distinctive identity.

45.7 The *Minim*

Probably the most fascinating evidence relating to Jewish believers in Jesus are the *minim*. Many rabbinic traditions refer to the *minim*, that is, individuals of whom the rabbis disapproved or toward whom they were antagonistic. They are usually thought to be Jews who did not conform to the Judaism which was being reconstructed by the rabbis, though some think that others including the Romans were the target. Why they were designated as *minim* is also disputed: were they simply nonconformists regarded as disruptive of the community ethos which the rabbis were striving to nurture,[240] or were doctrinal issues at stake, with the rabbis pushing for a form of orthodoxy which counted other views false and a threat to their Judaism? There has been a strong tendency to identify at least many of the *minim* as Christians, and to identify the issues separating them from the rabbis as the beliefs about Jesus concerning which the early Christians had become more outspoken.[241] To this aspect of the subject we will return in §46. Here the task is simply to make the case that many at least of the *minim* were in fact Christians, that is, Jewish believers in Jesus,

---

239. Cf. Mimouni, *Early Judaeo-Christianity* 82, 161-69. Mimouni also reckons *Barnabas* to be Judaeo-Christian (197-213), but in that case we would have to envisage a different kind of 'Judaeo-Christianity', influenced by the more Hellenized Judaism of Alexandria, and reacting against the tightening focus on the law of Palestinian rabbinic Judaism.

240. Particularly A. Schremer, *Brothers Estranged: Heresy, Christianity, and Jewish Identity in Late Antiquity* (Oxford University, 2010).

241. The classic collection of data is R. T. Herford, *Christianity in Talmud and Midrash* (London: Williams & Norgate, 1903); for references to Jesus himself (rather than Jewish believers in Jesus) see 35-96, 344-60. For further bibliography see P. S. Alexander, 'Jewish Believers in Early Rabbinic Literature (2d to 5th Centuries)', in Skarsaune and Hvalvik, eds., *Jewish Believers* 659-709 (here 659 n.1), and Schremer, *Brothers Estranged*.

and that the references provide clear indication that there were many such Jewish believers in Jesus in Syria-Palestine in the second century.²⁴²

The clearest evidence is two passages, both in *Tosefta Hullin* 2, which are more or less universally recognized as referring to a Christian, and as providing evidence of Jewish believers in Jesus among the Jewish communities being rabbinized.

> There was a case with Rabbi Eleazar ben Dama, who was bitten by a snake, and Jacob of Kefar Sama came to heal him in the name of Jesus ben Pantera; but Rabbi Ishmael did not allow him. He said to him, 'You are not permitted, Ben Dama!' He said to him, 'I will bring you proof that he may heal me', but he did not manage to bring the proof before he died. Rabbi Ishmael said, 'Happy are you, Ben Dama, for you have expired in peace, and you did not break down the hedge of the Sages. For whoever breaks down the hedge of the Sages calamity befalls him, as it is said, "He who breaks down a hedge is bitten by a snake" (Eccl. 10.8)' (*t. Hull.* 2.22-23).²⁴³
>
> There was a case with Rabbi Eliezer, who was arrested on account of *minut*, and they brought him up to the tribunal for judgment. (The case was dismissed.) And when he left the court he was distressed to have been arrested on account of *minut*. His disciples came in to comfort him but he did not take comfort. Rabbi Akiba entered and said to him, 'Rabbi, may I say something to you so that you will not be distressed? . . . Perhaps some one of the *minim* told you a teaching of *minut* that pleased you'. He said to him, 'By heaven, you reminded me! Once I was strolling in the street of Sepphoris, and I met Jacob of Kefar Sikhnin, and he said a teaching of *minut* in the name of Jesus ben Pantiri, and it pleased me. And I was arrested for words of *minut*, for I transgressed the words of Torah, "Keep your way far from her and do not go near the door of her house" (Prov. 5.8; 7.26)' (*t. Hull.* 2.24).²⁴⁴

Jesus of Nazareth was evidently referred to in rabbinic tradition as Jesus ben Pantera/Pantiri (or ben Stada), his father assumed to have been an otherwise unknown person (Roman soldier?) known as Pantera or Stada.²⁴⁵ The passages confirm the presence in Galilean villages of those who acted or

---

242. 'While not all *minim* are Jewish Christians, it does appear that Jewish Christians are, in the eyes of some rabbis, *minim*' (Broadhead, *Jewish Ways* 290).

243. Herford, *Christianity* 103-8 (with parallel versions); here and in the following extract I follow Schemer's translation (*Brothers Estranged* 87-88).

244. Herford, *Christianity* 137-45 (with parallel versions); Bauckham, *Jude and the Relatives of Jesus* 106-21.

245. Herford, *Christianity* 36-40. But note Broadhead's hesitations (*Jewish Ways* 286-87); and see further Wilson, *Related Strangers* 186-89.

taught in the name of Jesus — that is, Jewish believers in Jesus — here two, both named Jacob, from different villages. They were evidently members of the communities in view, conversing freely with and able to offer help to fellow members of the village community.[246] Equally interesting is the concern shown by the rabbis illustrated in the two passages over possible influence from such believers: in one case the concern was that the hedge being constructed round the Torah (the oral halakhoth) was being disregarded or broken through; in the other the *minut* referred to was a teaching in the name of Jesus. The concern is attributed to two of the principal rabbinic teachers in the period 120-140 (Ishmael and Akiba), suggesting that rabbinic hedge-building was also boundary drawing between the rabbis and their fellow Jews who believed Jesus to be Messiah, and that the process was already well advanced by the fourth decade of the second century.

The most persuasive evidence that the rabbis took offence at Christian claims for Jesus is the 'two powers heresy'. Again we will look at this more closely in §46.4c. The point to be made here is simply that the most obvious target for any denial that there are 'two powers in heaven' is the Christian claim that Jesus had been exalted to the right hand of God and been granted divine or semi-divine honours, as already in Phil. 2.10-11. Given the evidence already of John 5.18 and 10.33, it is hard to doubt both that those who denounced the 'two powers' (as above) affirmations aimed the rebuttal at Christians, and, more to the point here, that there were those Jews within the Jewish communities of Syria-Palestine who made such affirmations about Jesus.

Particularly intriguing here is the fact that subsequently Jerome was able to refer to 'the Minaeans' (= *minim*) who were active in synagogues cursed by the rabbis.

> What shall I say of the Ebionites who claim to be Christians? Until now there exists a sect (*haeresis*) among the Jews throughout all the synagogues of the East, which is called '(the sect) of the Minaeans (*Minaeorum*)', and is condemned by the Pharisees up till now. Usually they are called Nazarenes; they believe in Christ, the Son of God, born of Mary the virgin; and they say that he it is who suffered under Pontius Pilate and rose again, in whom we

---

246. L. H. Schiffman, *Who Was a Jew? Rabbinic and Halakhic Perspectives on Jewish-Christian Schism* (Hoboken: Ktav, 1985): 'The tannaim did not see the earliest Christians as constituting a separate religious community' (51-52). R. A. Pritz, *Nazarene Jewish Christianity: From the End of the New Testament Period Until Its Disappearance in the Fourth Century* (Jerusalem: Magnes, 1988): 'Jacob may be seen as more than just an isolated individual; he is representative, a type of Jewish Christian evangelist-healer which post-70 Jewish communities in Palestine may have encountered frequently' (107).

also believe. But while they desire to be both Jews and Christians, they are neither Jews nor Christians (*Ep.* 112.13).

Since Jerome spent so long in Palestine — the final thirty years of his life in a hermit's cell near Bethlehem — his reference is further and good evidence that the large Jewish communities which stayed close to the promised land included a significant number of believers in Jesus. Were all outspoken, and regarded as *minim*, disruptive of the Judaism which the rabbis sought to nurture? Or were there others, neither outspoken nor disruptive, but still believers in Jesus as an appropriate expression of their Judaism? Not least of the significance of the rabbinic traditions and Jerome's reference are their indications that the *minim* (= Jewish believers-in-Jesus) continued to function in Jewish synagogues in Syria/Palestine as late as the late fourth century.

45.8 Jews Who Also Followed Jesus

One of the most intriguing features of Justin Martyr's *Dialogue with Trypho* is his attestation that Christians in Asia Minor were confronted with a situation similar to that which troubled Paul: that there were two kinds of Jewish believers in Jesus as the Christ. On the one hand were those who wished to continue observing the law, but who did not insist that Gentile believers should live in accordance with the law; they, Justin assured Trypho, would be saved and Justin envisages having 'communion with them in all respects, as being of one family and as brothers' (*Dial.* 47.1-2). On the other hand, Justin could not accept Jewish believers in Jesus who tried to compel Gentile believers to keep the commandments as they (the Jewish believers) did; but he was unwilling to deny that they could be saved, unless they abandoned their belief that Jesus was the Christ (47.3-4).[247]

The situation envisaged by Justin seems to foreshadow the more complicated data provided by subsequent patristic sources on what the Christian heresiologists regarded as Jewish-Christian sects — Ebionites, Nazoraeans, and Elkesaites. We are entirely dependent on the references to those movements made by the patristic authors, whose antagonism to them makes it very unclear as to how much their evidence should be trusted. The confusion and uncertainties regarding the Jewish-Christian Gospels, *The Gospel according to the Hebrews*, *The Gospel of the Nazareans*, *The Gospel of the Ebionites*, already discussed (§40.4a), underline the problems. And Jerome, for one, seems to

---

247. Cf. Paget, 'Jewish Christianity' 756-57.

have thought that Nazoraeans was another name for Ebionites (*Ep.* 112.13).[248] But we can at least be confident that there were groups who were Jewish believers-in-Jesus, known by these names; so the evidence should be at least reviewed, even if in summary fashion, to see what further information or clues it provides about Jewish Christianity in the second century.

a. Ebionites

There is a general recognition that the term 'Ebionites' denotes the 'poor ones',[249] though several assume that they were so called after a founder named Ebion,[250] and there is an understandable tendency to take the title as an indication of their poverty of understanding.[251] Epiphanius reports that Ebion's preaching originated in Pella in Perea, the city of the Decapolis to which the believers in Christ (Nazoraeans?) had fled from Jerusalem after

---

248. Quoted above in §45.7, and more fully in A. F. J. Klijn and G. J. Reinink, *Patristic Evidence for Jewish-Christian Sects* (NovTSupp 36; Leiden: Brill, 1973) 200-201. Origen corrects Celsus, who criticized the followers of Jesus for leaving the law of their fathers; 'he failed to notice that Jewish believers in Jesus have not left the law of their fathers. For they live according to it . . .' (*c. Celsum* 2.1). Jerome tells us that he was taught Hebrew by 'a believing brother among the Hebrews' (*ep.* 125.12). See also Wilson, *Related Strangers* 89-90 and again 143-59.

249. E.g. Origen, *de princ.* 4.3.8; similarly *c. Celsum* 2.1; Jerome, *in Esaiam* 66.20. *Ebionim* is a positive term within a Jewish context; 'the name of the Ebionites must surely be connected in some way with the long Jewish tradition of referring to the pious poor' (R. Bauckham, "The Origin of the Ebionites', in P. J. Tomson and D. Lambers-Petry, eds., *The Image of the Judaeo-Christians in Ancient Jewish and Christian Literature* [WUNT 158; Tübingen: Mohr Siebeck, 2003] 162-81), referring particularly to Ps. 37.11, linked to 'the poor' in Matt. 5.3-5, and interpreted at Qumran as a self-reference, 'the congregation of the poor' (3Q171 2.9). The *Ascents of James* 1.62.2 'probably preserves for us the Ebionites' self-designation as "the poor", its derivation from the opening words of the Matthean beatitudes, . . .' (177-80). No attempt, however, is made to link the *Ebionim* with 'the poor among the saints at Jerusalem' (Rom. 15.26). Similarly O. Skarsaune, 'The Ebionites', in Skarsaune and Hvalvik, *Jewish Believers* 419-62 (here 421, 424-27). See also Wilson, *Related Strangers* 148-49; S. Häkkinen, 'Ebionites', in Marjanen and Luomanen, *Companion* 247-78.

250. E.g. Tertullian, *de praes. haer.* 32.3-5; 33.11; Epiphanius, *Pan.* 30.1.1 — sects were usually named after their originator (Justin, *Dial.* 35.6). 'The ancients quite properly called these men Ebionites, because they held poor and mean opinions concerning Christ' (Eusebius, *HE* 3.27.1). M. A. Jackson-McCabe, 'Ebionites and Nazoraeans: Christians or Jews?', in Shanks, ed., *Partings* 187-205: 'Though this Ebion would eventually become a fixture in the tradition, it is all but certain that no such person ever existed' (190).

251. E.g. Origen, *de princ.* 4.3.8; Eusebius, *HE* 3.27.6; Epiphanius, *Pan.* 30.17.1, 3; 30.18.1; Jerome, *in Esaiam* 1.3.

the capture of Jerusalem (*Pan.* 30.2.1, 7),[252] and Jerome locates them firmly in Syria,[253] though Epiphanius also thought that Ebion had preached in Asia and Rome.[254]

The earliest reference to the Ebionites is provided by Irenaeus, *adv. haer.* 1.26.2:[255] 'Those who are called Ebionites agree that the world was made by God. . . . They use the Gospel according to Matthew only and repudiate the apostle Paul, saying that he was an apostate from the Law. . . . they practise circumcision, persevere in the customs which are according to the Law and practise a Jewish way of life, even adoring Jerusalem as if it were the house of God'. The features which Irenaeus focuses on appear in subsequent references.[256] For example, Hippolytus reports that 'They live conformably to Jewish customs saying that they are justified according to the Law, and saying that Jesus was justified by practising the Law' (*refutatio* 7.34.1);[257] Origen observes that there are 'those who seem to have accepted the name of Christ but nevertheless believe that the rule of carnal circumcision has to be accepted, like the Ebionites' (*hom. in Gen.* 3.5); and Jerome speaks of 'the snares of Hebion who decides for them who believe among the Jews, that the Law has to be observed' (*ep.* 112.16).[258] Eusebius notes that the Ebionites observed the Sabbath, but also celebrated the Lord's day 'as a memorial of the resurrection

---

252. Schoeps calls Pella 'the Jamnia of Ebionitism' (*Jewish Christianity* 28). On the historical value of the Pella tradition see Wilson, *Related Strangers* 145-48; and on the lack of confirmation from archaeological evidence see P. Watson, 'The Christian Flight to Pella? The Archaeological Picture', in Shanks, ed., *Partings* 73-86, 310-12.

253. Jerome, *de situ et nom. loc. hebr. liber* 112; similarly Eusebius, *onomasticon* p. 172, 1-3. 'The derivation of the Greek term used by the Fathers from Aramaic shows that the Ebionites lived mainly in primarily Aramaic-speaking areas' (Bauckham, 'Origin' 177).

254. Epiphanius, *Pan.* 30.18.1 ('also in Cyprus'); cf. Jerome, *ep.* 112.13 (Ebionites were to be found 'among the Jews throughout all the synagogues of the East'). A. Schmidtke, *Neue Fragmente und Untersuchungen zu den judenchristlichen Evangelien* (Leipzig: Hinrichs, 1911), 'has shown convincingly that in mentioning Asia and Rome Epiphanius is transferring to Ebion something he knew about Cerinthus' (Skarsaune, 'Ebionites' 451).

255. I draw the following quotations from Klijn and Reinink, *Patristic Evidence for Jewish-Christian Sects.*

256. Particularly *adv. haer.* 3.15.1. Broadhead produces a useful tabular summary of the beliefs and practices attributed to the Ebionites; but he also notes that 'the representation of the Ebionites, like that of the Gnostics, is a broad swamp into which flow all sorts of poisons and pollutions and heresies' (*Jewish Ways* 197-98, 199-202, 205-6).

257. See also Justin, *Dial.* 67.2; Tertullian, *de prae. haer.* 32.5; Origen, *hom. in Gen.* 3.5; Eusebius, *HE* 3.27.2. 'We can be quite certain that Ebionite doctrine claimed that Jesus was elected to be anointed as Messiah because of his perfect observance of the Law' (Skarsaune, 'Ebionites' 435).

258. Epiphanius draws attention to the fact that 'they have elders and *archisynagōgoi*, and they call their church a synagogue and not church and honour Christ in name only' (*Pan.* 30.18.2).

of the Saviour' (*HE* 3.27.5).²⁵⁹ Origen also notes that the Ebionites 'do not accept the letters of Paul' (*c. Celsum* 5.66);²⁶⁰ similarly Eusebius notes that the Ebionites rejected all the epistles of the Apostle 'whom they called an apostate from the Law' (*HE* 3.27.4; likewise Theodoret, *prol. lib.* 2.1); and similarly Jerome, that they 'rejected Paul as a transgressor of the Law' (*in Matth.* 12.2).²⁶¹

More confusing is the Ebionites' christology. The most common report is that the Ebionites believed Jesus 'was born of man and woman in the same way as we also are born'.²⁶² But Origen recognizes two opinions among Ebionites: that Jesus was 'born of Mary and Joseph, as well as that he is from Mary only and the divine Spirit' (*in Matth.* 16.12; similarly *c. Celsum* 5.61). Eusebius similarly notes that there were different kinds of Ebionism: that others 'did not deny that the Lord was born of a virgin and the Holy Spirit, but . . . also refused to confess that he was God, Word and Wisdom' (*HE* 3.27.3). Epiphanius suggests that Ebion's followers 'started to think differently about Christ' (under the influence of Elxai?), that he was also the first man, Adam, 'created before all things, that he is a spirit and stands above the angels and is lord of all' (*Pan.* 30.3.3-5; similarly John Damascene, *de haer.* 30).²⁶³ And Theodoret similarly notes that the Ebionites said 'that the Lord Jesus Christ was born of Joseph and Mary, who as man excelled all others in virtue and purity', but that 'another group with the same name' 'say that the Saviour and Lord was born of a virgin' (*prol. lib.* 2).²⁶⁴

The patristic data is thus very confusing, suggesting that, for the most part, there was little personal experience of or communication with Ebionite

---

259. The transition from the Sabbath to the Lord's day as the prime day of worship is more obscure than we like to admit; cf. Rev. 1.10; *Did.* 14.1; Ignatius, *Magn.* 9.1; *Gos. Pet.* 35, 50. Wilson simply confesses: 'How the transition from Sabbath to Sunday took place we do not know'; but he thinks that 'a gradual transition . . . perhaps makes the best sense'; and he concludes by noting 'the unavoidable but awkward recognition that in abandoning the Sabbath, Christians were abandoning one of the fundamental Mosaic commands' (*Related Strangers* 232-35).

260. Origen also contested the Ebionite appeal to Matt. 15.24 ('I was sent only to the lost sheep of the house of Israel') by arguing that 'there is one Israel according to the flesh and another according to the Spirit' (*de princ.* 4.3.8).

261. According to Epiphanius the Ebionites claimed that Paul was a Greek, who went up to Jerusalem and wanted to marry the daughter of a priest; in order to do so he became a proselyte and was circumcised; but since his suit was rejected he became angry and wrote against circumcision and the Sabbath and the law (*Pan.* 30.16.9).

262. Origen, *hom. in Luc.* 17; similarly *in epist. ad Titum*; also Irenaeus, *adv. haer.* 5.1.3; Tertullian, *de virg. vel.* 6.1; *de carne Chr.* 14; Eusebius, *HE* 5.17; *de eccl. theol.* I.14; Epiphanius, *Pan.* 30.2.2; 51.2.3; Jerome, *de. vir. ill.* 9, 54.

263. See further Klijn and Reinink, *Patristic Evidence* 33-34.

264. See also Jackson-McCabe, 'Ebionites and Nazoraeans' 197.

groups,[265] though Origen, who spent many years in Caesarea, and Jerome, who spent his latter years near Bethlehem,[266] probably had direct knowledge of Jewish believers. But we can certainly take it for granted that there were such groups, particularly in Syria. The evidence reads as though they were full heirs of James and the Jewish believers in Jesus referred to in Acts 21.20;[267] that is, they were indeed Jewish believers in Jesus who maintained a Jewish way of life (circumcision and law observance), and who reinforced the earlier antipathy to Paul and his law-free (or law-light) Gentile mission. If the majority of Ebionites, at least at the earliest (second century) stage, believed that Jesus was the natural son of Mary and Joseph, that is, Messiah in accordance with the belief which Trypho espoused (Justin, *Dial.* 48.4; 49.1; 67.2), then we should envisage a group which early on had refused to accept the higher christology already well established in the earliest churches, in Palestine as well as in the diaspora, according to the NT evidence. In any case we should avoid thinking of 'the Ebionites' as a monolithic body, and hesitate before we envisage Ebionites widely spread across the western diaspora.[268] Rather we should envisage a (wide) variety of Jewish groupings, particularly in Syria-Palestine, who regarded Jesus as Messiah, but were probably largely independent of each other, and who used a variety of ways to highlight the significance they saw in Jesus. They were probably more integrated into the Jewish communities and synagogues than they were with the more distinctively Christian groups in the same vicinity, more sub-sects within the still diverse Judaism of the second century than breakaways into a more distinctive form of Christianity.

In short, the Ebionites well represent the continuum which must have still existed across the spectrum of second-century Judaism and Christianity, standing somewhere in the middle of the spectrum, who in Jerome's words wanted to be both Jews and Christians, but were regarded by both rabbis and Christian leaders as 'neither Jews nor Christians' (*ep.* 112.13) — 'Ebion that

---

265. 'Patristic observations on Jewish Christianity have no great historical value. One writer usually copies his predecessor or combines what has been written by a number of earlier writers' (Klijn and Reinink, *Patristic Evidence* 67; similarly Skarsaune, 'Ebionites' 461). 'By the time Epiphanius was writing the Panarion Jewish-Christian movements had long become a marginal phenomenon, and they certainly represented no threat for the Great Church' (J. Verheyden, 'Epiphanius on the Ebionites', in Tomson and Lambers-Petry, eds., *The Image of the Judaeo-Christians* 182-208 (here 205)).

266. Mimouni describes Jerome as 'a figure who lives in daily contact with the Judaeo-Christians of his time, in their multiple forms' (*Early Judaeo-Christianity* 124).

267. J. Willitts, 'Paul and Jewish Christians in the Second Century', in Bird and Dodson, eds., *Paul and the Second Century* 140-68, cautions against reading a too simple continuity between Acts 21.20 and the later Pauline opponents (147-49).

268. 'Especially in the Western part of the Roman Empire, the church fathers seem to have had no personal contacts with Jewish-Christian Ebionites' (Häkkinen, 'Ebionites' 253).

archheretic, half-Christian and half-Jew (*semi-Christianus et semi-Judaeus*)' (*in Gal.* 3.13-14).

b. Nazoraeans[269]

The patristic testimony regarding the Nazoraeans is almost wholly limited to the unreliable Epiphanius (e.g. *Pan.* 19.5.1, 4; 29.6.1),[270] and to Jerome, who certainly was familiar with the *Gospel of the Nazoraeans* (§40.4a). As to the name itself, Epiphanius was well aware that Jesus had been known as 'the Nazoraean (*Nazōraios*)' because he came from Nazareth, and inferred that the Nazoraeans had accepted this name 'because of Christ' (29.6.7-8);[271] also that 'all Christians were called Nazoraeans once'.[272] This certainly ties in with the other available evidence: Acts 24.5, that the first believers-in-Jesus in the land of Israel were known as 'the sect of the Nazarenes (*Nazōraioi*)';[273] that the developed form of the *birkat ha-minim* includes a curse on 'the Nazarenes (*notzrim*)';[274] that 'Nazarenes' became the established name for Syrian Christians;[275] and that *notzrim* has been the standard term for Christians in rabbinic Judaism since the Middle Ages.[276]

---

269. There are different spellings of the name — *Nazarēnoi* (Eusebius, *onomasticon* p. 138, 24-25); *Nazōraioi* (*Pan.* 19.5.4). But *Nasaraioi* (Epiphanius, *Pan.* 19.5.1) should not be confused with *Nazōraioi* (Pritz, *Nazarene Jewish Christianity* 17-18, 45-47). Some modern commentators prefer to use the term 'Nazarene' consistently — notably the specialist study of Pritz, *Nazarene Jewish Christianity*, and Paget, 'Jewish Christianity' 760-61.

270. Verheyden thinks that 'the Nazoraeans of *Pan.* 29 may well be to a large degree the product of Epiphanius' imagination' ('Epiphanius' 184). Similarly P. Luomanen, 'Nazarenes', in Marjanen and Luomanen, eds., *Companion* 279-314: 'The heresy of the Nazarenes as it is depicted in *Panarion* 29 is pure fiction' (308).

271. Similarly Tertullian, *adv. Marc.* 4.8; Eusebius, *onomasticon* p. 138, 24-25; Jerome, *de situ* 143.

272. *Pan.* 29.1.3; 29.6.2, 5; similarly Jerome, *de situ* 143.

273. 'It is important to note that the name Nazarenes was at first applied to all Jewish followers of Jesus. . . . This should be borne in mind when considering the total absence of the name from extant Christian literature between the composition of Acts and 376, when [Epiphanius's] *Panarion* was written' (Pritz, *Nazarene Jewish Christianity* 15; also 44-45).

274. See below §46.4b. Epiphanius also reports that the Jews 'three times a day say: "May God curse (*epikatarasai*) the Nazoraeans"' (*Pan.* 29.9.2; cf. Jerome, *ep.* 112.13; *in Amos* 1.11-12; *in Es.* 5.18-19; 52.4-6).

275. See *Beginning from Jerusalem* 15 n.67.

276. W. Kinzig, 'The Nazoraeans', in Tomson and Lambers-Petry, eds., *Image of the Judaeo-Christians* 463-87 (here 471). Pritz notes that Jesus *ha-notzri* is mentioned five times in the Babylonian Talmud and Christians as *ha-notzrim* a further two or three times (*Nazarene Jewish Christianity* 95-102). See also Herford, *Christianity* 344-47; M. de Boer, 'The Nazoreans: Living at the Boundary of Judaism and Christianity', in Stanton and Stroumsa,

Epiphanius gives some brief details:[277]

- 'by birth they are Jews and they dedicate themselves to the Law and submit to circumcision' (29.5.4);
- 'after having heard the name of Jesus only and having seen the divine signs performed by the hands of the apostles, they also believed in Jesus' (29.5.6);
- 'actually they remained wholly Jewish and nothing else' (29.7.1);
- they 'live according to the preaching of the Law as among the Jews' (29.7.2);
- 'there is no fault to find with them apart from the fact that they believe in Christ' (29.7.2);
- 'They also accept the resurrection of the dead . . . (and) proclaim one God and his Son Jesus Christ' (29.7.3);
- 'They have a good mastery of the Hebrew language' and read the scriptures in Hebrew (29.7.4);
- 'Only in this respect they differ from the Jews and Christians: with the Jews they do not agree because of their belief in Christ; with the Christians because they are trained in the Law, in circumcision, the Sabbath and the other things' (29.7.5);
- 'They emphatically declare that he (Christ) was born of the Holy Spirit from Mary' (29.7.6);
- 'They proclaim as Jews that Jesus is the Christ' (29.9.3), but Epiphanius dismissed them as 'Jews and nothing else' (29.9.1);
- 'They have the entire Gospel of Matthew in Hebrew' (29.9.4)'.
- In addition, Jerome succinctly describes the Nazoraeans (*Nazaraei*) as those 'who accept Christ in such a way that they do not cease to observe the old Law' (*in Es.* 8.11); but he also notes that they affirmed that Paul was the last of the apostles and that (his) preaching of the gospel reached to the whole world (9.1).[278]
- And Augustine notes that 'although the Nazoraeans confess that the son of God is Christ, they nevertheless observe everything of the old Law which Christians learned by the apostolic tradition not to observe carnally but to understand this spiritually'; whereas 'the Ebionites also say that Christ is only a man' (*de haer.* 9-10).

---

eds., *Tolerance and Intolerance in Early Christianity and Judaism* 239-62 (here 247-52); Luomanen, 'Nazarenes' 279-314.

277. Pritz quotes the whole of *Panarion* 29 (*Nazarene Jewish Christianity* 30-35, the Greek text — 113-19). See also Luomanen, 'Nazarenes' 288-89, 293-96.

278. Pritz, *Nazarene Jewish Christianity* 64-65. On Jerome's view of the Nazarenes see further Luomanen, 'Nazarenes' 296-307.

Epiphanius also asserts that 'this heresy of the Nazoraeans exists in Beroea in the neighbourhood of Coele Syria' (similarly Jerome, *de vir. ill.* 3),[279] and that 'it took its beginning after the exodus from Jerusalem when all the disciples went to live in Pella' (*Pan.* 29.7.7-8). 'There the Nazoraean heresy had its beginning' (29.7.8).[280]

The question posed by Epiphanius's view of the Nazoraeans, the silence about the Nazoraeans prior to Epiphanius and the evidence regarding the Nazarenes/*notzrim* can be expressed thus: When did the Nazarenes become a 'heresy'? Was the name one of the names used for Christians generally, particularly espoused by Jewish believers in Jesus? Were the Jewish believers in Jesus of whom Justin spoke positively (§45.8a) called by others or did they call themselves 'Nazarenes/Nazoraeans'?[281] Even when we take Epiphanius seriously, it would appear that the only really distinguishing feature of the Nazoraeans was that they continued to observe the Law (and read the scriptures in Hebrew). Probably, however, they were more open to the expansion of their faith through Paul and did not expect Gentile believers to observe the Law.[282] Rabbinic tradition mentions that the day after the Sabbath was the day of the *notzrim*.[283] And their christology was faithful to the Gospel testimony of Jesus' virgin birth and did not seem to attract opposition from Christian leaders like Epiphanius and Jerome, though devotion to the Law (and maintaining a distinctively Jewish way of life) seem to have been sufficient cause for them to be regarded as heretics.[284] As those who continued to be known by one of the earliest names for the new Jewish sect ('Nazarenes') we may infer that they resisted the sort of developments in theology and christology which are evident in the NT writings and saw no need or cause to move on

279. 'Jerome bears witness to a group of Jewish followers of Jesus who are active in Syria in the late 4th century CE' (Broadhead, *Jewish Ways* 174).

280. See also Luomanen, 'Nazarenes' 289-91. Confusingly Epiphanius believed that 'the heresy of the Nazaraeans (*Nazōraioi*) existed before Christ' (29.6.1), probably confusing Nazoraeans with Naziraeans (*Naziraioi*) (30.1.3), like Samson and John the Baptist, despite distinguishing the two terms earlier (29.5.6-7). Jackson-McCabe notes tartly: 'Why references to a Nazoraean "heresy" that had supposedly existed since the first century suddenly appear only in these late fourth-century works is a question' ('Ebionites and Nazoraeans' 198).

281. 'In most respects the Nazarenes look like a mainstream Christian group' (Wilson, *Related Strangers* 156).

282. Pritz, *Nazarene Jewish Christianity* 64-65, 109; Kinzig, 'Nazoraeans' 476-78. It is worth noting that Matthew's Gospel bears witness to a Gentile mission which was Petrine rather than Pauline in character (cf. Schnelle, *History* 225).

283. Herford, *Christianity* 171-73.

284. Paget notes that Jerome's use of the Nazarene commentary on Isaiah indicates a greater sympathy with the Nazarenes ('Jewish Christianity' 761); and Broadhead finds no hint of critique in Jerome's use of the same Nazarene commentary (*Jewish Ways* 171).

from the basic beliefs of the first Jewish believers in Jesus.[285] Their continued retention of the name 'Nazarene/Nazoraean', when developing Christianity (apart from Syria) largely abandoned it, can be regarded as a claim to direct continuity with the first-century Jerusalem/Palestinian church.[286] And the fact that the name was maintained in reference to Syrian Christianity suggests the strength (and primitiveness) of the Jewish character of Syrian Christianity.

c. Elkesaites

There is some uncertainty as to whether the Elkesaites should be included in the list of Jewish-Christian sects, since Epiphanius did not regard them as typically Jewish (*Pan.* 53.1.4). They were also known as Sampsaeans or Ossaeans and linked with the Ebionites.[287] But Eusebius reports that they 'reject certain parts of every scripture', and use 'portions of the entire old (scripture/ Testament) and of the Gospel but reject the Apostle altogether' (*HE* 6.38). Theodoret, *prol. lib.* 2.7, ascribes to them views similar to those attributed to the Ebionites by Epiphanius (*Pan.* 30.3.3-5) and John of Damascus (*de haer.* 30). Epiphanius locates them in the region of Perea, the other side of the Dead Sea (*Pan.* 19.1.2; 53.1.1), where a 'remnant' still remained (19.2.2), and John of Damascus reports that 'they still live in Arabia, above the Dead Sea' (*de haer.* 53).

The heresy is attributed to a teacher called Elxai or Elxaios or Elchasai or Elkesai (Theodoret, *prol. lib.* 2.7), who apparently joined the alternatively named sects some time after their foundation in the time of Emperor Trajan and probably influenced their christology (Epiphanius, *Pan.* 19.1.4; see

---

285. 'An ossified form of the type of Jewish Christianity associated with Peter and James' (Paget, 'Jewish Christianity' 761); see also the earlier views reviewed by Luomanen, 'Nazarenes' 279-81. Jackson-McCabe concludes his study of 'Ebionites and Nazoraeans': 'The presence of such groups throughout antiquity underscores the fact that Judaism and Christianity became two neither as a consequence of some single, finally decisive event, nor as the inevitable result of inexorable inner forces of essentially different religions. Indeed, the interpretation of historical events and the very notion that there are such essential, static realities underlying the terms "Judaism" and "Christianity" are themselves part of the ongoing rhetoric of Jewish and Christian identity. "Religions" do not part ways with each other as much as particular groups of people do' (205).

286. The suggested line of continuity between Nazoraeans (or Ebionites) and the original Jerusalem believers in Jesus does not depend on the Pella tradition, but the latter certainly strengthens the case for the continuity having a historical foundation; see again *Beginning from Jerusalem* §36.3; also Pritz, *Nazarene Jewish Christianity* 122-27.

287. Epiphanius, *ancoratus* 13.5; *Pan.* 19.2.2; 30.3.3.2; 53.1.1; Augustine, *de haer.* 10, 32; John of Damascus, *de haer.* 30.

also 19.5.4; 30.3.2; 30.17.5).²⁸⁸ Hippolytus speaks of 'his apparent adhesion to the Law' (*refutatio* Prol. 9.4) and according to Epiphanius, 'although he originated among the Jews and was Jewish minded, he did not live according to the Law' (*Pan.* 19.1.5). His influence is attributed to a book,²⁸⁹ which Elkesaites say 'fell from heaven' (Eusebius, *HE* 6.38), and in which the (false) prophet revealed 'astonishing, ineffable and great mysteries' (*Pan.* 19.15.2; see further 19.3-4).²⁹⁰ According to Epiphanius, two sisters descended from his family were highly revered ('worshipped as gods') up to the time of Constantine (19.2.5).

The groups known variously as Elkesaites, Sampsaeans and Ossaeans are probably a good indication of the melting pot of religious beliefs and practices which sprang up in the early centuries CE, usually under the stimulus or inspiration of a prophetic or visionary individual, which gained a number of adherents in one or more particular vicinities, and which flourished only for a limited period.²⁹¹ They are also a reminder that more distinctively Jewish and Christian beliefs and practices were part of that melting pot, the named groups operating on the fringes of the more established religions and causing perplexity and problems to both synagogue and church.

d. The Pseudo-Clementine Literature

If indeed underlying the pseudo-Clementine literature is a source which can be identified in *Recog.* 1.27-71 (§40.6g), then it becomes a valuable witness to views which can be characterized as distinctive of Jewish believers in Jesus.²⁹² Its most striking features include:

---

288. Klijn and Reinink, *Patristic Evidence* 29-30, 33. But Skarsaune thinks Epiphanius's naming Elxai as a major teacher of the Ebionites is his own invention ('Ebionites' 452-53); see also Pritz, *Nazarene Jewish Christianity* 36-37; Wilson, *Related Strangers* 149-50.

289. Hippolytus, *refutatio* 9.13.1; 10.29.1; Epiphanius, *Pan.* 19.1.4; 53.1.3. See also F. S. Jones, 'The *Book of Elchasai* in Its Relevance for Manichaean Institutions', *Aram* 16 (2004) 179-215.

290. The fragments contained in Hippolytus and Epiphanius advocate prayer towards Jerusalem and that the Sabbath should be honoured, but they also urge a second baptism for impurity and reject sacrifices and priestly rites. See J. Irmscher, 'The Book of Elchasai', *NTA* 2.685-90; and further G. P. Luttikhuizen, 'Elchasaites and Their Book', in Marjanen and Luomanen, eds., *Companion* 334-64.

291. See also G. Hällström and O. Skarsaune, 'Cerinthus, Elxai and Other Alleged Jewish Christian Teachers or Groups', in Skarsaune and Hvalvik, eds., *Jewish Believers* 488-502 (here 496-502).

292. Stanton prefers the title of the proposed source, 'An Apologia for Jewish Believers in Jesus' ('Jewish Christian Elements' 317-23).

- high regard for James — 'The church of God founded in Jerusalem was abundantly multiplied and grew through James, who was ordained bishop in it by the Lord and governed it with most righteous administration' (43.3; also 66.2, 5; 68.2; 70.3);[293]
- central to the christology is the conviction that Jesus is the prophet predicted by Moses (36.2; 40.4; 41.2; 43.1-2; 44.5-6; 58.3; 69.5), the true prophet who had previously appeared to Abraham and Moses (33.1-2; 34.4), the (eternal) Christ (44.2, 4; 52.3; 59.3; 60.4; 63.1; 69.3), God's Son incarnate (45.4; 60.7; 63.2; 69.6-7 — not two g/Gods), who will come again (49.2-5);[294]
- baptism (54.1; 55.3; 69.8) should be performed in the triune name (63.3; 69.5);
- a clear sense of distinction and distance from unbelieving Jews (43.1-2; 53.1), also from the Samaritans (57.1-5) and the disciples of John the Baptist (60.1-4). The issue is the significance of Jesus, and the accusation that Jesus was a magician is noted and dismissed (42.4; 58.1-2; 70.2). The baptized believers 'will be preserved unharmed from the destruction of the war that is impending on the unbelieving nation and the place itself. But the nonbelievers will be exiled from the place and the kingdom' (39.3 Latin).
- Notable is the rejection of sacrifices (36.1; 37.2-4); 'Jesus is the one who by the grace of baptism extinguished the fire that the high priest had lit for sins' (48.5; 54.1).[295]
- Notable also is that Saul/Paul is introduced as 'a certain hostile person' who disputed with James and then threw him from the top of the stairs, leaving him for dead (70.1-8), thereafter receiving a commission from the high priest Caiaphas to persecute all who believed in Jesus and to go to Damascus, to which he hastened 'because he believed that Peter had fled there' (71.3-4).[296]

---

293. We have already noted the high esteem for James in the pseudo-Clementine *Epistula Petri* and *Epistula Clementis* which preface the *Homilies* (§45.2c).

294. Cf. Schoeps, *Jewish Christianity* 65-73. Jesus as 'the true prophet' is the basic christological affirmation of the pseudo-Clementines (*Hom.* 3.20, 49; *Recog.* 1.16; 5.10; 8.59; 10.51). 'It is noteworthy that the *Recognitions* consciously limits the debate to the christological question: . . . whether (Jesus) . . . is the one prophet' (1.50.7) (Broadhead, *Jewish Ways* 271).

295. Skarsaune shows that the anti-sacrifice polemic is more primitive than in Barnabas and Justin (*Proof from Prophecy* 296-98, 316-18).

296. 'Paul is not opposed for his mission to the Gentiles, but rather for his intrusion into the conversion of the Jewish leaders and the people of Jerusalem' (Broadhead, *Jewish Ways* 273). Luedemann summarizes the view of the *Recog.* 1 source in one sentence: 'Paul bears the blame for the fact that James was not successful in converting the whole Jewish

- Somewhat surprisingly, however, there is a recognition that Gentiles should be called (in place of those who remained unbelievers) 'so that the number that was shown to Abraham might be filled' (42.1; 50.2; 64.2).[297]

The attitude to fellow Jews is perhaps best summed up in 64.1-2: God 'is even more angered about your sacrificing after the end of the time for sacrifices. Precisely because of this the temple will be destroyed, and they will erect the abomination of desolation in the holy place. Then the gospel will be made known to the nations as a witness for the healing of the schisms that have arisen so that your separation will occur'.

Here is clearly a writing which expresses the views of Jewish believers in Jesus,[298] mostly in a lengthy conversation between Clement and Peter (44.4–71.6), which recalls or represents the early Jerusalem church's disputes with the priestly authorities and Pharisees about Jesus. Interestingly, the members of the (reconstituted) twelve are portrayed/recalled as each taking active part in the disputes,[299] though (arch)bishop James provides the climactic apologia (68.3–69.8), provoking the attack of the Saul/Paul character. The writing also knows and draws on Matthew's Gospel (baptism in the triune name — Matt. 28.19),[300] and on Acts or the traditions on which Luke himself drew (Gamaliel — Acts 5.34-39; *Recog.* 1.65.2-3;[301] Saul's high priestly commission to go to Damascus — Acts 9.1-2; *Recog.* 1.71.3-4).[302] The reference to the destruction of the temple and the exile of unbelieving Jews (1.39.3; 64.1) suggests

---

community in Jerusalem to the Christian side' (*Opposition to Paul* 184). Note again the hostility to Paul elsewhere in the pseudo-Clementine literature (see above §45.2c). See also Stanton, 'Jewish Christian Elements' 315-17. Willitts urges caution in evaluating the testimony of the source ('Paul and Jewish Christians in the Second Century' 163-64).

297. The attitude to circumcision, and whether it was required of all believers, is unclear (Paget, 'Jewish Christianity' 763). But 'there is no question of the Gentile church replacing Israel, but only unbelieving Jews within Israel' (Stanton, 'Jewish Christian Elements' 320).

298. 'A "foundation narrative" of a community of Jewish believers in Jesus; . . . This "apologia" is one of our most important pieces of evidence for Jewish believers in Jesus' (Stanton, 'Jewish Christian Elements' 322). See also A. Y. Reed and L. Young, 'Christianity in Antioch: Partings in Roman Syria', in Shanks, ed., *Partings* 105-32; notes 317-26 (here 124-31).

299. Matthew (*Recog.* 55.4), Andrew (56.2), James and John, the sons of Zebedee (57.3), Philip (59.1), Bartholomew (59.2), James the son of Alphaeus (59.4), Lebbaeus (59.7), Simon the Canaanite (60.3), Barabbas (60.5), Thomas (61.3); Peter is the principal narrator after 45.1, part of his instruction of Clement in *Recognitions*.

300. Jones, *Ancient Jewish Christian Source* 140.

301. Gamaliel is described as 'secretly our brother in faith' (65.2; 66.4).

302. Jones, *Ancient Jewish Christian Source* 141.

a post-135 perspective, while the reference to the preservation of baptized believers (39.3) may echo the flight to Pella tradition.[303] The bolder christology and the positive attitude to Gentile evangelization seem closer to what we learned about the Nazoraeans, though the portrayal of Saul/Paul as the 'hostile person' who attacks James (and seeks out Peter) is a sharper echo of earlier antipathies. And the rejection of temple sacrifices could indicate how early Jerusalem believers and their heirs reacted to the destruction of the temple.[304] But it would probably be a mistake to look for a straightforward mesh with patristic descriptions of any of the other groups of Jewish believers in Jesus. And we should be content with the further indications that there were a good many Jewish believers in Jesus in the second century who were diverse in their beliefs in Jesus, and in their attitudes to and relations both with emerging rabbinic Judaism (the unbelieving Jews) and with the Gentile churches.[305]

e. Jewish Christianity in the Second Century

Almost all of the evidence reviewed above is later than the second century,[306] but given a basic assumption of continuity between the beginnings of Christianity ('the Nazarenes') and later 'Jewish Christianity', it is entirely appropriate to infer that 'Jewish Christianity' featured strongly in the second century. Undoubtedly there were a considerable number of Jews who believed Jesus to be Messiah and who were distinguished within or from the more widespread Christianity by their continued commitment to observe the law and their maintenance of a distinctively Jewish way of life. They would no doubt have claimed that their practice of circumcision, their observance of the Sabbath and Passover and their continued obedience of the law was a matter of

---

303. Van Voorst, *Ascents* 100-101; disputed by Stanton, 'Jewish Christian Elements' 320. The source itself records that a group of approximately 5,000 went down to Jericho (71.2).

304. 'This source provides an apology for Jewish believers in Jesus who are bewildered by the fact that sacrifices are no longer practiced in their own day' (Stanton, 'Jewish Christian Elements' 320).

305. If the *Circuits of Peter* can be identified as a *Grundschrift* for the pseudo-Clementines (§40 n.341), it should be noted that the food regulations echo the Apostolic Decree in Acts 15 and that there is indication that Jesus' dispute with Pharisees was still a lively issue (Jones, 'Jewish Christianity' 321-25).

306. We could add the *Didascalia Apostolorum*, usually dated to the first half of the third century and assumed to have been written in Greek, but known only in Syriac, which Strecker regards as a Jewish Christian document, demonstrating that in northern Syria 'Jewish Christianity occupied a dominant "orthodox" position superior to "Catholicism"' ('Jewish Christianity' 254-57).

simple loyalty to the memory of Jesus, disciples following the example of their master (Matt. 10.24-25).[307] And the fact that they knew and used the Jesus tradition in Hebrew, continuing to use a Hebrew Gospel,[308] when the great bulk of Christianity would have operated only in Greek, underlines both the primitiveness of their origins and their *de facto* determination to affirm their direct line of continuity with the 'Hebrews' of the Jerusalem church.[309] They probably held James in high regard, and a direct line of continuity can probably be drawn with the attitudes and suspicions expressed in Acts 21.20. Almost certainly a goodly number at least would have regarded with hostility the developments associated with Paul; that would be a natural corollary to their commitment to live in accordance with the law.[310] But in terms of christology we have to envisage a wider diversity of opinion. Many maintained that Messiah Jesus was simply a man, conceived and born like everyone else. Others accepted the birth narratives of the Gospels of Matthew and Luke: that Jesus was born of Mary of the Holy Spirit.[311] Others again seem to have been influenced by the more speculative systems linked with the names of Cerinthus[312] and others.

If we correlate this data with Justin's assertion that there were two kinds of Jewish believers in Jesus as the Christ (*Dial.* 47.1-4), we could identify the Jewish believers with whom Justin felt more comfortable with the Nazoraeans, and those who maintained a harder Jewish line with the Ebionites;[313] though we should also recall that there were evidently Jewish believers-in-Jesus who were influenced by (or contributed to) the more Gnostically-inclined attempts to assess the significance of Jesus. In any event, we have to envisage a wide

---

307. Broadhead, *Jewish Ways* 249.
308. See above §§40.4a and 44.4d.
309. Cf. Acts 6.1; 2 Cor. 11.22; Phil. 3.5.
310. If the fourteenth-century Gospel of Matthew in Hebrew reflects an early Jewish version of Matthew, it is probably significant that the great commission of Matt. 28.19-20 is omitted, implying an unwillingness to envisage the evangelization of Gentiles (Evans, 'Jewish Christian Gospel Tradition' 267-70).
311. Cf. Isidore of Seville: 'The Nazoraeans say that Christ is God . . . The Ebionites say that Christ is (only) man . . .' (*de haer. lib.* 10-11).
312. Irenaeus seems to have thought that the Cerinthians were Jewish Christians; but see Klijn and Reinink, *Patristic Evidence* 3-19.
313. Cf. Skarsaune, 'Ebionites' 439-40, who also notes that Origen (*c. Celsum* 2.1) seemed to think of all Jewish believers who kept the law as Ebionites (443). But those who believed in the virgin birth were probably Nazoraeans (Pritz, *Nazarene Jewish Christianity* 21-22, 28). See also Mimouni, *Early Judaeo-Christianity* 55-69, and Broadhead, *Jewish Ways* 181-87. The evidence suggests to Bauckham that the Nazarenes/Nazoreans were the group in most direct continuity with the pre-70 Jerusalem church and 'that Ebionism originated, probably some time in the second century, as an attempt to reform Jewish Christianity by revising its beliefs' ('Origin' 172-75). Similarly Kinzig, 'Nazoraeans' 481.

spectrum of beliefs among the Jewish believers-in-Jesus. And again, we cannot assume any kind of monolithic, systematic 'Jewish Christianity', but should rather infer Jewish believers-in-Jesus still functioning in synagogues while forming house groups of their own or associating with more explicitly Christian house-churches, or with groups who favoured more exotic speculation.

What happened to 'Jewish Christianity'? The most probable outcome (but given the scarcity of data, it is a modest probability) is twofold. The greater sympathy shown towards Jewish believers-in-Jesus who accepted the virgin birth suggests a form of Jewish Christianity (Nazoraeans) which remained dominant in Syria and which elsewhere eventually was probably absorbed into the more distinctive Christianity. Whereas it is more likely that the Jewish believers-in-Jesus who affirmed that the Christ was a man born ordinarily (Ebionites) were finally absorbed by the spreading influence of rabbinic Judaism.

One of the most intriguing developments in the latter decades of the twentieth century has been the re-emergence of 'Jewish Christianity' — Jews who accepted that Jesus was Messiah but who wished to retain their identity as Jews and to maintain a Jewish way of life — Messianic Jews, Jews for Jesus.[314] Ironically, but sadly, though wholly understandably, like the Jewish believers-in-Jesus who were regarded in the early centuries as neither Jews nor Christians, the latter-day Jewish believers-in-Jesus are disowned by both Jews and Christians. Yet, if the Jewish believers-in-Jesus of the second century were a vital link maintaining a continuity between Jew and Christian which otherwise is too easily lost to sight and neglected,[315] and if they actually retained a stronger link back to Jesus' own ministry and to the earliest form of Jerusalem Christianity, then the potential of these modern Jewish believers-in-Jesus to revitalize Jewish/Christian dialogue as an ecumenical dialogue within and among God's people should not be missed.

f. Syrian Christianity

We should not close this section without considering the extent to which Syrian Christianity, or at least eastern Syrian Christianity (focused in Edessa), should be regarded as the most enduring form of Jewish Christianity. One

---

314. See particularly D. Rudolph and J. Willitts, eds., *Introduction to Messianic Judaism: Its Ecclesial Context and Biblical Foundations* (Grand Rapids: Zondervan, 2013).

315. But Mimouni concludes: 'It is no longer possible to consider that Judaeo-Christianity has simply served as "a link between the Synagogue and the Church"' (Strecker) (*Early Judaeo-Christianity* 433).

could refer, of course, to Antioch.[316] Peter's 'victory' over Paul in the Antioch incident (Gal. 2.11-14), as seems most likely,[317] would have reinforced the traditional Jewish character of Antioch's emerging Christianity. That the 'apostolic decree' seems to have gone out to the churches established from Antioch (Acts 15.23) probably confirms that the church in Antioch became an influential centre for promoting a Jacobean interpretation and praxis of the new faith of 'Christians'.[318] We also noted that several of the second-generation Christian documents, characteristically Jewish-Christian documents, are quite naturally associated with Antioch (Matthew, *Didache* and the *Odes of Solomon*).[319] Ignatius's letters certainly suggest that among the conflicting currents in Antioch were docetic views of Christ (*Trall.* 10.1), though the interaction or competition with Jews (*Magn.* 8.1; 10.3; *Philad.* 6.1) was probably a more dominant concern. The fact that this tension was helping Ignatius to define 'Christianity'[320] implies that the tension was so great because 'Christianity' and 'Judaism' still overlapped for most of those involved in both.[321] We should also recall that Theophilus of Antioch's apology to *Autolycus* has a very Jewish character.[322] Serapion, bishop of Antioch (late second century), should also be mentioned, since he was 'one of the chief theologians of his age',[323] though only a few fragments of his writings survive.

But the more intriguing drama was being played out further to the east, in Edessa. According to Eusebius the message of Jesus came to Edessa very early on, indeed, just after Jesus' ascension.[324] He quotes two letters which he claims to have extracted from Edessa's own archives and to have (had) translated from the Syriac. The first is from King Abgar, 'the celebrated monarch of the nations beyond the Euphrates', who was suffering from a terrible illness, and who, having heard of Jesus' cures 'without drugs and herbs', wrote to Jesus pleading that he would come and heal him (*HE* 1.13.6-9). The second is Jesus' reply, declining to come, since he must complete the mission given to him, but promising to send a disciple to heal him after he (Jesus) had been 'taken up'

---

316. Note M. Slee, *The Church in Antioch in the First Century* CE: *Communion and Conflict* (JSNTS 244; London: Sheffield Academic Press, 2003).

317. *Beginning from Jerusalem* §27.6.

318. See further *Beginning from Jerusalem* §27.6.

319. On the *Didache* and *Odes* see §40.1e and j.

320. See below §46.6a.

321. See also Meier in Brown and Meier, *Antioch and Rome* 46-51, 53-55; and further Meeks and Wilken, *Jews and Christians in Antioch*; M. Zetterholm, *Formation of Christianity in Antioch* (London: Routledge, 2003).

322. See above §45.5j.

323. *ODCC* 1485.

324. See H. J. W. Drijvers, 'The Abgar Legend', *NTA* 1.492-99, who argues that it had an anti-Manichean purpose.

(1.13.10). Eusebius goes on to quote an account appended, also in Syriac, describing how after Jesus' ascension Judas Thomas had sent Thaddaeus, one of the seventy,[325] to Edessa. Thaddaeus, having healed many, was summoned by Abgar and healed him too, promising to preach the word of life to the citizens next day (1.13.11-22). In his second volume Eusebius summarizes Thaddaeus's mission, and concludes, 'From that day to this the whole city of the Edessenes has been dedicated to the name of Christ' (2.1.6-7).[326]

Not surprisingly it was this so very early spread of the gospel of Christ (the date given would be about 30, the year of Jesus' crucifixion — 1.13.22) which provoked Bauer to begin his challenge to the Eusebian history of Christianity.[327] He found the Abgar saga to be 'a pure fabrication, without any connection with reality, which need not have emerged earlier than the beginning of the fourth century',[328] and suggested that 'Christianity was first established in the form of Marcionism', that is 'heresy' not 'orthodoxy', not much later than 150.[329] Of the Thomasine literature Bauer knew only the *Acts of Thomas*. But with the emergence of the Nag Hammadi codices, including, of course, the *Gospel of Thomas* and the *Book of Thomas the Contender*, it became an attractive option to trace the Thomasine character of early eastern Syrian Christianity to an earlier stage.[330] If Thomas could indeed be presented as a or indeed the founding figure of Edessene Christianity, then Bauer's conclusion would still follow: that the original form of eastern Syrian Christianity was the same sort of syncretistic mix as we find in the Thomasine literature.[331]

How soon a form of Christianity reached Edessa, which is set on the eastern bank of the Euphrates and effectively in the border region between Rome and Parthia, it is impossible now to say. It is nevertheless likely that the influence of Christian ideas and teaching reached Edessa through early trading links with Antioch. But perhaps it was only when Osrhoene, with its capital Edessa, became a client kingdom of Rome in 166 that a form of Ara-

---

325. The reference is to Luke 10.1, but Matt. 10.3 names Thaddaeus as one of the twelve. 'The legend of Thaddaeus as one of the Twelve . . . belongs to the region around Hamidiya on the Syrian coast and to Beirut and Arwad, and has nothing whatever to do with Edessa' (Drijvers, *NTA* 1.494).

326. A fourth-century inscription from Ankara(?) seems to speak of James offering the city of Edessa to God (*NDIEC* 2.203-6).

327. Bauer, *Orthodoxy and Heresy* ch. 1.

328. 'A historical fiction, but not pure fantasy' (Drijvers, *NTA* 1.494).

329. Bauer, *Orthodoxy and Heresy* 11, 29.

330. See also §40.4b and §40 n.326.

331. Koester, reworking Bauer's thesis ('*GNOMAI DIAPHOROI*' 126-43), concludes: 'Thomas was the authority for an indigenous Syrian Christianity even before the formation of noticeable orthodox influence in this area' (133).

maic/Syriac-speaking Christianity became established in Edessa.[332] Whatever the historical facts, the point remains that the close association of Thomas with Syrian Christianity and the character of Thomasine literature strongly suggest that eastern Syrian Christianity was much more syncretistic in form than Eusebius would have been willing to admit.[333] To attempt to attach labels — Gnosticism, Marcionism, Manicheism or even Jewish Christianity — would not be helpful, since what is in view are not monolithic or homogeneous systems. Rather, the Thomasine character of Edessene Christianity, if that is a fair way to describe the situation, suggests that the influences which may be traced back to Jesus and the Christianity 'beginning from Jerusalem' were only one element in the syncretistic mix which was the beginning of Christianity in eastern Syria.[334]

Particularly intriguing is the thesis of April DeConick with regard to the *Gospel of Thomas*. Noting the unfamiliarity of most Western scholars with Orthodox Christianity, she observes that 'The *Gospel of Thomas*, far from representing the voice of some late generic "gnostic" heresy or some early sapiential Christianity, is quite cogent with early Syrian Christianity as described in the oldest literature from the area'. Noting also the number of *Thomas* logia (in what she calls the 'kernel gospel' of *Thomas*) which have parallels with the versions used in Tatian's *Diatessaron* and the pseudo-Clementine literature, she suggests that this does not indicate some 'new' or 'unique' or 'lost' Christianity:[335] 'Nor is the Thomasine community some previously unknown school, deviant group, or self-identifying church. Rather it represents a current in

---

332. According to F. C. Burkitt, *Early Eastern Christianity* (London: John Murray, 1904), Jewish-Christian evangelization of Edessa began in the second half of the second century. Similarly W. S. McCullough, *A Short History of Syriac Christianity to the Rise of Islam* (Chico: Scholars, 1982) 9. See also K. E. McVey, 'Edessa', *ABD* 2.284-87.

333. Relevant here, though how relevant is uncertain, is the fact that Tatian, to whom Gnostic tendencies can be ascribed (§40.2f above), was highly regarded in Syrian churches till well through the tenth century, and his *Diatessaron* 'was apparently the standard gospel used by many Syrian churches until the early fifth century' (Petersen, 'Tatian the Assyrian' 153-55).

334. Bardaisan of Edessa (c. 155-222) would further illustrate the point since his teaching seems to have been highly syncretistic (K. E. McVey, 'Bardaisan of Edessa', *ABD* 1.608-10). See further N. Denzey, 'Bardaisan of Edessa', in Marjanen and Luomanen, *Companion* 159-84.

335. DeConick, *Recovering the Original* Gospel of Thomas 238-43 (quotations from 240-41, 242); see also §40 n.205. In her contribution to Asgeirsson et al., *Thomasine Traditions in Antiquity* ('On the Brink of the Apocalypse: A Preliminary Examination of the Earliest Speeches in the Gospel of Thomas', 93-118), DeConick observes that the apocalyptic expectations and christological ideas in what she calls the kernel *Thomas* appear to be most similar to the traditions associated with conservative Christian Judaism from Jerusalem and those developed later by the Ebionites (117).

the stream of Christian traditions that ultimately became Eastern Orthodoxy. It is the voice of eastern Syrian Christianity in its earliest recoverable form'.

The fact that Eusebius records Hegesippus as attributing the beginnings of 'the seven heresies' to the earliest days of the post-70 Jerusalem church (*HE* 4.22.4-6) may therefore be a more accurate portrayal of how the character of Jewish Christianity developed as it spread eastwards than his too ready affirmation of the Abgar legend. The Assyrian Church of the East and Nabatean Christianity may be other expressions of the Jewish Christianity which spread eastwards. In particular, Thomasine Christianity should probably be regarded as a further reminder of how many diverse elements and tendencies there were in Middle Eastern spirituality and religion and that the emerging Christianity of these regions did not escape from these influences or remain virginally intact but rather demonstrated just how influential were these aspirations and seekings for salvation. And, not least, we should note that it is necessary to join Thomas to the triumvirate of first-generation Christianity (as well as John — §49) since he or the traditions associated with his name were so evidently a huge influence in eastern Syria and beyond.

45.9 Conclusions

More important than trying to unravel the various puzzles of 'Jewish Christianity' is the recognition of the Jewishness of Christianity. For most of Christianity's history 'Jewish' and 'Christian' have been regarded as contrasting, in some cases even antithetic, terms, the adjectival equivalents of 'Judaism' and 'Christianity'. But for all the common era, 'Jewish' has never been simply an ethnic referent. And in the first and second century 'Jewish' was a broader term than 'Judaism'. It is important for Christianity's self-identity that it does not forget or ignore or play-down or denigrate or deny its Jewish origins — a Jewish Messiah, Jewish apostles, Jewish scriptures (OT),[336] the God of Israel (the one God of Jew and Gentile — Rom. 3.29-30). But it is also important that Judaism recognizes the Jewishness of Christianity and engages seriously with the Jewishness of the latter's claim that Jesus is the Messiah of Jewish expectation, and that the gospel for Gentiles as well as Jews is the fulfillment of the covenant promise to Abraham that blessing would come to the nations through or because of him.

---

336. Easily done when in many Christian worship services any scheduled reading from the OT is regularly omitted.

In particular,

1. James, the brother of Jesus, should be given much more respect than he has traditionally received. As a blood relation to Jesus, he is one of the closest links which earliest Christianity had with Jesus. In Christian perspective, however, he has been all too often treated as a straw-man opponent of Paul. That trend should be reversed and James be given much more prominence and reverence, equivalent to that accorded to the other two first-generation leaders, Peter and Paul[337]— his integrity and influence recognized across a wide spectrum of second-century Christianity, and the letter attributed to him respected as an authentic expression of the early faith of the founding community of Christianity.
2. Equally, Jerusalem, not Rome or Byzantium (or Wittenberg, or Geneva, or Canterbury...), should be reaffirmed as the mother church of Christianity. It is the church of Jerusalem, not least under James's leadership, which assures Christianity's direct link back to Jesus.
3. The Jewish character of the earliest Christian writings (the NT and much of the second-century Christian writings) should not be regarded as an embarrassment but be clearly recognized and strongly affirmed — not least the degree to which the Jewish scriptures (OT) were integral to their definition and understanding of Christianity.
4. When the gap between Judaism and Christianity has been so deep for so long, both should recognize how much of the broader Second Temple Judaism's expression and character was taken up by and proved fruitful to Christianity rather than to (rabbinic) Judaism. Not least, the bridge which Philo provided, not just between Hellenistic Judaism and the sect of the Nazarenes but also with the developing Hellenistic Christianity, should be reaffirmed and explored for its further potential to strengthen Jewish/Christian dialogue.
5. Perhaps above all, the evaluation made of the *minim* and the *notzrim*, of the Nazoraeans and Ebionites,[338] should be reassessed. Where identity was being formed and contested, it is understandable that sharp differentiations were focused on, and clearly marked boundaries were drawn. But with different identities long established and boundaries perhaps now proving to be more inhibiting than affirming, it could well be argued

---

337. Schoeps can even claim that 'As far as we can tell, James the brother of Jesus, by disposition a mediator, was a guarantee of the church's unity; with his death the era of schisms began' (*Jewish Christianity* 20).

338. Still worthy of reflection is Schoeps's conclusion 'that in second- and third-century Ebionitism we have a conservative, early form of primitive Christianity which was excluded from the tradition of the Great Church' (*Jewish Christianity* 108).

that there is after all room for groups who thought they could fill the intervening spaces with integrity and honour.
6. Likewise the link which a positive evaluation of 'Jewish Christianity' can provide between western and eastern Christianity needs to be looked at afresh and its potential for the growth of ecumenical respect and mutual understanding to be further explored.
7. Not least, the re-emergence of messianic Jews in the present should be seen as opportunity for a similar growth of respect and understanding, together with a resolve that the history of condemnation and heresy-denunciation should not be repeated.

CHAPTER 46

The Parting of the Ways

46.1 The Imagery to Be Used

It is important from the outset to remind ourselves that 'Judaism' and 'Christianity' were not major factors in what is to be examined. The terms hardly occur in our literature — 'Judaism' only twice in the NT (Gal. 1.13-14) and in Ignatius (*Magn.* 8.1; 10.3; *Phil.* 6.1), and 'Christianity' also only in Ignatius.[1] The point is not simply one of semantics and the issue of anachronistic terminology. The point is rather that we must avoid thinking of 'Judaism' and 'Christianity' in the first two centuries of the common era as already clearly defined entities and clearly distinguished one from the other. For most of our period, the heirs of 'Second Temple Judaism' were reeling from the shock of the failed three revolts against Rome.[2] The rabbinic Judaism, which traced its real beginnings to the assembly of teachers at Yavneh following the disaster of 70 CE, throughout our period was only beginning to establish itself and to attempt to imprint its character on Jewish synagogues outside Palestine. The 'Judaism' of the Western diaspora, with which emerging Christianity had most to do, was still 'Hellenistic Judaism' and not yet rabbinic Judaism, with all that that meant, bearing in mind the diversity of diaspora Judaism already reflected in the 'Judaism' of the Second Temple period.[3] And in embryonic

---

1. See n.7 below.
2. See below §46.3.
3. See particularly P. Trebilco, *Jewish Communities in Asia Minor* (SNTSMS 69; Cambridge University, 1991); J. M. G. Barclay, *Jews in the Mediterranean Diaspora from Alexander to Trajan (323 BCE — 117 CE)* (Edinburgh: T & T Clark, 1996); M. H. Williams, *The Jews among the Greeks and Romans: A Diasporan Sourcebook* (London: Duckworth, 1998); E. S. Gruen, *Diaspora: Jews amidst Greeks and Romans* (Cambridge: Harvard University, 2002); cf. also Feldman, *Jew and Gentile in the Ancient World*.

Christianity, where lines of continuity had already been clearly drawn with the heritage of the religion of Israel and of post-exilic Judaea, the lines to mark out 'Christianity' as distinct within that variously claimed heritage were still being tentatively, though sometimes boldly, sketched out. The problems with defining the relation of rabbinic Judaism to diaspora Judaism were matched on the Christian side by the problems of defining the relation between Jewish and Gentile believers in Jesus, including not least the dispute as to how much of that same heritage should be claimed, and how it should be claimed.

So in this chapter especially, it must be recalled that we are not dealing with two already well defined religions relating to each other. Nor are we dealing with two bodies of people ethnically, religiously and culturally distinct from each other; even the distinguishing character of different rituals (circumcision, baptism, shared meals) proved to be not so very distinguishing in many instances. What we are dealing with are several diverse bodies of people, all in greater or less degree acknowledging their dependence on the (OT) scriptures, all basing their self-identity claims on these same scriptures, and all searching for ways to define that identity more clearly. For the Christians the claims regarding Jesus Christ, and the significance of his teaching, death and resurrection, were, of course, central; but not independent of the heritage embodied in the scriptures. Consequently, the need to justify the beliefs and praxis which focused on or stemmed from Jesus, as thoroughly Jewish/scriptural in character, was a fundamental part of the dialogue between 'Jew' and 'Christian' throughout our period.

A rather important consequence follows immediately: that the imagery of 'the parting of the ways' is more misleading than helpful. We have already noted (§38.3a above) the dissatisfaction which the imagery has provoked and need only recall the most salient points. Above all, the inadequacy of the 'parting of the ways' imagery is its assumption that the historical actuality is faithfully (or adequately) represented in the splitting of one way ('Judaism') to become two ways ('Christianity' and rabbinic 'Judaism'), or in a single-event 'parting' between two clearly defined religions. But as noted at the beginning of this study,[4] the Judaism at the beginning of the first century, better expressed as Second Temple Judaism, was not a single 'way' or single entity. There were a number of 'ways' pursued by Jews in the Second Temple period. They all confessed the one God of Israel, believed that Israel was God's elect nation, celebrated their Judaean/Jewish ethnic identity, were committed to obey the Torah and acknowledged the centrality of (Jerusalem) temple and cult.[5] But they did so in different ways. Their expression of these shared beliefs

---

4. *Jesus Remembered* §9.

5. In *Partings* §2, I characterized 'The Four Pillars of Second Temple Judaism' as monotheism, election, covenant focused in Torah, and land focused in temple.

was different. Their praxis, as or more important than their beliefs, varied significantly. So much so that many scholars, Jewish as well, think it more accurate to speak of *Judaisms* (plural) during this period.⁶ Some of these Judaisms are well known — Sadducees, Pharisees, Essenes, in particular. But there were other strands or paths followed — represented, for example, by the Enoch cycle of literature, apocalyptists, mystics, Hellenizers, diaspora Judaism, and not forgetting 'the people of the land' and the Samaritans. The Judaism of Second Temple Judaism was as factional as Judaism has ever been.

Equally problematic is the use of the term 'Christianity' for what was happening in the first century. For the word does not appear until early in the second century, first coined, so far as we can tell, by Ignatius of Antioch.⁷ Linguistically speaking, 'Christianity' did not yet exist in the first century! — though, of course, it was a natural development from the fact that believers in Jesus the Christ had been called 'Christians' for some time (Acts 11.26). As already pointed out in *Beginning from Jerusalem* §20, in the Acts of the Apostles the movement of Jesus' followers is referred to as a 'sect' (Acts 24.14; 28.22), 'the sect of the Nazarenes' (24.5). Significantly, this is the term Acts also uses, as does the Jewish historian Josephus, for the 'sects' of the Sadducees, Pharisees and Essenes.⁸ In other words, Acts regarded the early movement inspired by Jesus as one of the sects or factions which made up and were part of late Second Temple Judaism.

Equally significant is the fact that the first believers in Messiah Jesus are described as those 'who belong to the way'.⁹ The image clearly reflects the Hebrew idiom of conduct as walking (*hālak*) along a path, an imagery, untypical of Greek thought, which Paul continued to use.¹⁰ This emphasis on the right way to follow is reflected even more strongly in the Pharisaic/rabbinic understanding of 'Halakhah', as referring to the rules/rulings (derived from the written Torah) which determine how individuals should act ('walk') in

---

6. E.g. S. Sandmel, *The First Christian Century in Judaism and Christianity* (New York: Oxford University, 1969) ch. 2, 'Palestinian Judaisms'; J. Neusner et al., eds., *Judaisms and Their Messiahs at the Turn of the Christian Era* (Cambridge: Cambridge University, 1987); A. F. Segal, *The Other Judaisms of Late Antiquity* (Atlanta: Scholars, 1987); J. Murphy, *The Religious World of Jesus: An Introduction to Second Temple Palestinian Judaism* (Hoboken, NJ: Ktav, 1991) 39.

7. Ign. *Magn.* 10.1-3; *Rom.* 3.3; *Phil.* 6.1; *Mart. Pol.* 10.1; referred to already in *Beginning from Jerusalem* §20 nn.6, 120. And see further again Niebuhr, '"Judentum" und "Christentum"', in §38 n.34.

8. Acts 5.17; 15.5; 26.5; Josephus, *War* 2.119-66; *Ant.* 18.11-15.

9. Acts 9.2; see also 19.9, 23; 22.4; 24.14, 22; cf. 18.25-26; 2 Pet. 2.2; possibly reflected in 1 Cor. 12.31. Here I repeat *Beginning from Jerusalem* 13-14.

10. See my *The Theology of Paul the Apostle* (Grand Rapids: Eerdmans, 1998) 643 nn.82-84.

particular situations.[11] And the Qumran sect used the term in much the same way as it appears in Acts;[12] the Qumranites liked to think of themselves as 'the perfect of way (*derek*)', who 'walk in perfection of way (*derek*)'.[13] In other words, as Qumran was one of the 'ways' of being a Jew, one of the component parts of diverse Second Temple Judaism, so the movement which sprang from Jesus was seen as another 'way' of living out the covenant obligations of the people of Israel.[14]

The issues posed by the imagery of 'the parting of the ways' are further complicated by the fact that it is not clear, or at least cannot simply be assumed, how the rabbinic Judaism which became the normative expression of Judaism between the second and fourth centuries (and later) relates to the diverse expressions of Second Temple Judaism. As we note below, the rabbis can rightly be regarded as the direct heirs of the Pharisees. But are they the heirs of the other forms of Second Temple Judaism, of the other ways of being Jewish?[15] And is the Christianity which became the state religion of the Roman Empire in the fourth century the direct (and only) heir of 'the sect of the Nazarene', the people of 'the way' (of Jesus)? Was there a direct, linear connection in each case? Was there one way in each case which led without side-roads and bypasses to the fourth-century outcome? Or did the ways wander hither and thither?[16] Did the ways fragment? How in any case do we relate 'Jewish Christianity' within the big picture?[17] And did other ways merge into the way(s) emerging from the first century? Again as we have already seen, the issue of Gnostic Christianity at once raises its head.[18]

Of course, by late antiquity and the beginning of the Middle Ages there were two distinct entities — Christianity and Judaism. So some sort of division(s), or split(s), or parting(s) had taken place by then.[19] How to describe

---

11. See further G. G. Porton, 'Halakah', *ABD* 3.26-27; S. Safrai, 'Halakha', in S. Safrai, ed. *The Literature of the Sages* (CRINT II.3.1; Assen: van Gorcum, 1987) 121-209.

12. Note particularly the absolute use ('the way') in 1QS 9.17-18, 21; 10.21; CD 1.13; 2.6.

13. 1QS 4.22; 8.10, 18, 21; 9.5.

14. We have already noted that early Christian paraenesis shared with Qumran in particular the contrast of the 'two ways, one of life and one of death' (*Did.* 1.1); see above §45.5b.

15. See above §45.6.

16. Lieu prefers the imagery of 'a criss-crossing of muddy tracks' ('"The Parting of the Ways"' 119/29). Martin Goodman, 'Modelling the "Parting of the Ways"', reproduces nine different models, while acknowledging that to image other models is impractical (*Judaism in the Roman World: Collected Essays* [Leiden: Brill, 2007] 175-85).

17. The issue discussed in §45.

18. Already posed in §43.

19. See above §38 nn.41-43.

these divisions/splits/partings? In fact, no single imagery can adequately describe such a complex historical process or development.[20] Probably the simplest imagery to use is the processes in which the parts of a garment pull apart over time, the threads which begin to break under the stresses of 'wear and tear', or the popping of rivets as heavy seas put unbearable strain on the metal plates of a ship, and so on. Such imagery is still inadequate, but a focus on the strains and tensions between Jews and believers-in-Jesus, including not least Jewish believers-in-Jesus, seems most likely to bring to light what became the irreconcilable features which brought about the emergence of two different (and opposed) identities. And since our knowledge of Pharisaic Judaism (30-70 CE) and of the beginnings of rabbinic Judaism (70-100 CE) in relation to followers of Jesus is so thin, when drawing from rabbinic sources, we will have to depend, more than is comfortable, almost exclusively on Christian sources.

46.2 Early Strains and Stresses

We have already traced the earliest period of what became known as 'Christianity' in the preceding volumes. But it is worth recalling that some consider the split between Judaism and Christianity either to have already happened during that period, or to have been rendered unavoidable by what happened during that period.

a. Jesus' Death and Resurrection

The traditional Christian view is that the rejection of Jesus by the bulk of the Jews spelled their own rejection.[21] Alternatively, some would argue that the crucifixion and resurrection (or the earliest claims that Jesus had been raised from the dead) were already decisive factors more or less from the first.[22] Others, in emphasising the apocalyptic dimension of the first claims for

---

20. My use of the plural ('Partings') in *The Partings of the Ways between Christianity and Judaism* (London: SCM, 1991) was not always appreciated; but note also the 'Preface to the Second Edition' (2006). See again the earlier discussion in §38.3a above.

21. A. von Harnack, *The Expansion of Christianity in the First Three Centuries* (ET London: Williams & Norgate, 1904): 'By their rejection of Jesus the Jewish people disowned their calling and dealt the death-blow to their own existence' (81-82); quoted by Broadhead, *Jewish Ways* 354.

22. E.g., C. A. Evans, 'Root Causes of the Jewish-Christian Rift from Jesus to Justin', in S. E. Porter and B. W. R. Pearson, eds., *Christian-Jewish Relations through the Centuries*

Jesus' resurrection, would seem to imply thereby that Christianity was seen from the beginning to have emerged on a quite different plane, without any *heilsgeschichtlich* (salvation-history) continuity with Israel of old except as a claim made by Paul's Jewish-Christian opponents.[23]

A second potential 'parting' is often linked to the belief that Jesus' death was seen in earliest Christian circles not only as a sacrifice, but as a sacrifice which rendered all other sin-offerings in the Jerusalem temple unnecessary, null and void[24]— the argument so powerfully developed later in the letter to the Hebrews.

A third potential 'parting' can be advocated in the persecution following the judicial lynching of Stephen, according to Acts 6-7.[25] The chief self-confessed 'persecutor', Saul of Tarsus (Gal. 1.23), certainly attributed his policy to his Pharisaic 'zeal' during his 'earlier life in Judaism' (1.13-14). But we have already noted that 'Judaism' for Saul the zealous Pharisee was not the only 'Judaism' in that period, and certainly not the whole of Second Temple Judaism, however much his persecution policy had high priestly and Pharisaic(?) backing. His persecution policy was an extreme example of Second Temple factionalism at its worst.

Insofar as the issue is how soon 'the ways parted', none of the above provide evidence that the 'ways' had already 'parted' in these opening years. As noted in *Beginning from Jerusalem* (§23.5), the first Jerusalem believers continued to participate in the temple cult, including the sin-offering. The issue of a sacrifice to end all sacrifices had not yet arisen.[26] In any case, we should recall that the status and role of the temple had already been questioned by

---

(JSNTS 192; Sheffield Academic, 2000) 20-35, argues that 'the fundamental sticking points for many Jewish people were the simple facts that Jesus had been put to death and the kingdom of God had failed to materialize' (23). 'One can speak of Christianity as a sect of Judaism only for the first transitional year or two of its existence' (Hagner, *New Testament* 390).

23. Particularly J. L. Martyn, *Galatians* (AB 33A; New York: Doubleday, 1997); also *Theological Issues in the Letters of Paul* (Edinburgh: T & T Clark, 1997).

24. E.g. J. Ådna, *Jesu Stellung zum Tempel: Die Tempelaktion und das Tempelwort als Ausdruck seiner messianischen Sendung* (WUNT; Tübingen: Mohr Siebeck, 2000): the death of Jesus 'replaces and supersedes the sacrificial cult in the Temple once for all as the atoning death for the many' (429).

25. Wander thinks that the confrontation of Acts 6.1 already 'decisively prefigures' the later separation of Jews and Christians (*Trennungsprozesse* 130). The fact that Acts 6.1 refers to tensions among the first members of the Jesus sect is the first reminder that 'parting of the ways' tensions were as much internal to earliest Christianity as they came to be in relations between Jews and Christians.

26. See further my 'When Did the Understanding of Jesus' Death as an Atoning Sacrifice First Emerge?', cited above (§42 n.349).

the Qumran sect, who regarded their own community as a substitute for the corrupt temple in Jerusalem.[27]

Moreover, as again previously noted, Jewish believers in Jesus continued largely undisturbed in Jerusalem prior to the Jewish revolt of 66-70. There was a greater danger of a 'parting of the ways' between the Jewish believers in Jerusalem and the Pauline mission, than of a parting between Christianity and Second Temple Judaism. The 'parting' tensions were initially experienced more *within* earliest Christianity than *between* 'Christianity' and 'Judaism'. Most scholars accept that earliest Christianity functioned initially as a sect within Second Temple Judaism, 'the sect of the Nazarenes' (Acts 24.5, 14), so that the question whether the ways would or should part was by no means an obvious conclusion to be drawn during the first generation. And this has certainly been confirmed by the findings of the second volume, *Beginning from Jerusalem*.

b. The Opening to the Gentiles

The next most obvious strain within the fabric of Second Temple Judaism was the broadening out of the new sect's membership to non-Jews. For ethnicity has always been at the heart of Jewish identity, the (physical) seed of Abraham, the blood-line descending from Abraham, Isaac and Jacob.[28] Non-Jews could be absorbed into that line of descent, by becoming Jews (proselytes); and a widespread hope was that Gentile pilgrims would flood to Zion at the end of the age.[29] But as the core element of Jewish identity, of being a 'Jew (*Ioudaios*)', was the geographical entity 'Judaea' (*Ioudaia*), so the core element of Second Temple (and subsequent) Judaism was the ethnic Jew. Paul knew this well (Gal. 2.15) and tried to shift the definition of 'Jew', and also of 'Israel', to include those who were not ethnic Jews: 'Jew' denoted inner disposition towards God, not something physical (Rom. 2.28-29); and 'Israel' denoted

---

27. See particularly CD 3.12–4.12; 4QFlor. 1.1-7; and further B. Gärtner, *The Temple and the Community in Qumran and the New Testament* (SNTSMS 1; Cambridge: Cambridge University, 1965) chs. 2 and 3; G. Klinzing, *Die Umdeutung des Kultus in der Qumrangemeinde und im NT* (Göttingen: Vandenhoeck & Ruprecht, 1971) part II.

28. See particularly Schiffman, *Who was a Jew?*; also S. Cohen, *The Beginnings of Jewishness: Boundaries, Varieties, Uncertainties* (Los Angeles: University of California, 1999).

29. Pss. 22.27-28; 86.9; Isa. 2.2-4 = Mic. 4.1-3; Isa. 45.20-23; 56.6-8; 66.19-20, 23; Jer. 3.17; Zeph. 3.9-10; Zech. 2.11-12; 8.20-23; 14.16-19; Tob. 13.11; 14.6-7; *1 En.* 10.21; 90.30-36; *Sib. Or.* 3.715-19. See further J. Jeremias, *Jesus' Promise to the Nations* (London: SCM, 1958) 56-62; T. L. Donaldson, 'Proselytes or "Righteous Gentiles"? The Status of Gentiles in Eschatological Pilgrimage Patterns of Thought', *JSP* 7 (1990) 3-27; also *Judaism and the Gentiles: Jewish Patterns of Universalism (to 135 CE)* (Waco: Baylor University, 2007).

those called by God, which could include Gentiles as well as Jews (Rom. 9.6-12, 24).[30] But did he succeed in such redefinitions?[31] Could he succeed? Understandably, Paul's defence of his mission strategy (1 Cor. 9.19-23 — to Jews, as a Jew; to those outside the law, as one outside the law) has been as much denigrated as it has been admired. But the question is whether the influx of Gentiles in itself inevitably changed the character of the sect of the Nazarene and accelerated any pulling apart from both mainline Judaism and the diversity of Second Temple Judaism. Paul himself certainly saw his mission as of a piece with the Servant of Yahweh's mission, to be 'a light to the Gentiles', and likewise he saw the gospel of Messiah Jesus to the Gentiles as the fulfillment of the promise to Abraham that in him all the nations would be blessed (Gal. 3.8).[32] But did that apologia ever convince more than a few of his fellow Jews? Even so, the tearing apart of the Jesus sect (increasingly Gentile in membership) from (or within) Second Temple Judaism did not happen within the lifetime of Paul. And the fact that he was so successful in making a collection from his largely Gentile churches for the poor among the saints in Jerusalem, even though its actual delivery in Jerusalem is shrouded in some mystery,[33] is sufficient indication that Paul himself was determined that the tensions between Jewish and Gentile believers should not become more serious.

Since we have already noted that the tensions which eventually pulled Christianity and Judaism apart were also tensions *within* the Jesus movement, it is salutary to remind ourselves that the acceptance of Gentiles was not in itself a divisive factor for the Jesus sect. For it would appear that more traditionalist Jewish believers like James seemed also very ready to incorporate Gentile believers within the covenant people — at least, according to Acts 15.[34] So ethnicity was no barrier, or breaking point. Nor, it would appear, was even circumcision a make-or-break point for the leading Jewish believers within the Jesus movement itself (Gal. 2.7-9). And although there was clearly a severe tension between the most traditionalist Jewish believers and Paul, on whether distinctively Jewish laws could be ignored,[35] Paul himself did not see the gospel and the law as mutually exclusive opposites. On the contrary,

---

30. See further my *Romans* (WBC 38, 2 vols.; Dallas: Word, 1988) 127-28, 546-49.
31. The accompanying argument that the primary circumcision was circumcision of the heart (Rom. 2.28-29; Phil. 3.3) had some good scriptural precedent (Deut. 10.16; Jer. 4.4; 9.25-26; Ezek. 44.9), but it presumably cut as little ice with Paul's main Jewish interlocutors as his redefinitions of 'Jew' and 'Israel'.
32. *Beginning from Jerusalem* 533-36.
33. *Beginning from Jerusalem* §33.4, §34.1e.
34. *Beginning from Jerusalem* §27.3e.
35. E.g. Gal. 2.11-14; Acts 21.21.

he saw faith, and the Spirit, and love as the keys to fulfilling the law,[36] and keeping the commandments of God as still of first importance (1 Cor. 7.19).[37]

A more decisive breaking point was probably not Paul's gospel or theology or mission as such, so much as the practices he encouraged in the diaspora congregations which he founded or regarded as part of the Gentile mission. For in both Corinth and Rome,[38] Paul attempted to build single communities embracing both traditionalist Jews and Gentiles, including many Gentiles who had not much respect for such Jewish scruples. He defended the right of such traditionalist Jews to maintain their scruples, but made it clear that he thought such scruples were no longer necessary. He urged the less scrupulous to willingly limit their freedom to make room for the more scrupulous. But such communities must have found it hard to get along as partners with any local synagogues. There are strong indications of this in Col. 2.16-23, where it would appear that the local synagogue regarded the Christian congregation as disqualified from any claim on Israel's heritage.[39] It was all very well to claim that in Christ 'there is no longer Jew or Greek' (Gal. 3.28), but for those who saw their identity as 'Jew', the consequent strain and undermining of identity would probably have been too much. Was it inevitable that the more Gentile Paul's churches became, the less Jewish they became too?[40]

c. A New Name

To what extent did the sharpening of the identity of the first believers in Jesus, the sect of the Nazarene, as 'Christians' provide evidence of a growing distinction between Jew and Christian or of separation between Jew and Christian? To what extent did the creation and use of such an identity marker contribute to the 'parting'?

At first sight the designation of the new sect as 'Christians' (Acts 11.26) should be significant, especially if it indicated that 'Christian' was seen to be distinct and different from 'Jew'. But, again as noted in *Beginning from Jeru-*

---

36. Rom. 3.27-31; 8.1-4; Gal. 5.6.

37. See further *Theology of Paul* ch. 8. The Lutheran setting of gospel and law in sharp antithesis was not as well founded in Paul's letters as it was thought to be.

38. 1 Cor. 8, 10; Rom. 14.1–15.6.

39. See my *The Epistles to the Colossians and to Philemon* (NIGTC; Grand Rapids: Eerdmans, 1996) 29-33.

40. Cf. particularly W. Meeks, *The First Urban Christians: The Social World of the Apostle Paul* (Yale University, 1983) 97, 168; J. M. G. Barclay, "'Do We Undermine the Law?' A Study of Romans 14.1–15.6', in J. D. G. Dunn, ed., *Paul and the Mosaic Law* (WUNT 89; Tübingen: Mohr Siebeck, 1996) 287-308 (here 303-8).

salem, the name (*Christianoi*) was almost certainly coined by the Roman authorities in Antioch, on the analogy of Herodians (*Hērōdianoi*) or Caesarians, the party of Caesar, or possibly members of Caesar's household (*Kaisarianoi*). The 'Christians' were so called because they were perceived to be partisans of 'Christ', followers of 'Christ', members of the Christ-party.[41] Those so referred to would not be 'Christians' as distinct from Jews. Rather, the term would refer to Jewish synagogue communities or sub-groups which had embraced Gentile believers, that is, Jews as well as Gentiles. What distinguished them, from the authorities' perspective, was not their ethnicity but their commitment to Messiah/Christ Jesus.

Here too we need to consider the expulsion of the Jews from Rome by Emperor Claudius, probably in 49. The famous Suetonius reference (the expulsion was Claudius's response to disturbances involving Chrestus)[42] implies that the disturbances took place *within* the Jewish community in Rome, presumably between members of one or more of the several synagogues in Rome, and presumably occasioned by the Jewish believers in Messiah/Christ Jesus causing controversy with and offence to some of their fellow Jews. Some think that the expulsion of 49 effected the separation of the believers-in-Jesus from the Roman synagogues.[43] But, even considering Acts 18.2, there is nothing to suggest that only Jews who believed in Messiah Jesus were expelled; those who were expelled were expelled as Jews. And Paul subsequently (c. 57) wrote to Roman believers who included Jews as well as Gentiles: as many as half of those named and greeted in Rom. 16 were probably of eastern origin and very likely Jewish;[44] and Rom. 14.1–15.7 seems to reflect a situation in which more traditionalist Jewish believers, who had been expelled from Rome, had been returning, following Claudius's death, and were receiving a cool or cold reception from the more liberal Gentile believers who had been undisturbed by the Claudius decree and now formed the majority of the new movement.[45] As for the puzzling account of Paul's time in Rome (Acts 28), the only reason which makes sense of Luke's failure to explicitly include believers-in-Jesus

---

41. *Beginning from Jerusalem* 303-6.

42. Suetonius, *Divus Claudius* 25.4; see again *Beginning from Jerusalem* 58-60.

43. E.g. Schnelle: the expulsions of 49 'accomplished the final separation between the Christian community and the synagogue' (*History* 112); S. Spence, *The Parting of the Ways: The Roman Church as a Case Study* (Leuven: Peeters, 2004) 117.

44. Lampe, *From Paul to Valentinus* 167-70; *pace* A. A. Das, *Solving the Romans Debate* (Minneapolis: Fortress, 2007), who argues that Paul was writing to an exclusively Gentile audience.

45. I follow the influential argument of W. Wiefel, 'The Jewish Community in Ancient Rome and the Origins of Roman Christianity', *Judaica* 26 (1970) 65-88, reprinted in K. P. Donfried, ed., *The Romans Debate* (Peabody, MA: Hendrickson, 1991) 85-101. See also *Beginning from Jerusalem* 923-29, with further bibliography.

in his description of Paul's final entry to and imprisonment in Rome is that the believers-in-Jesus were included in the description of Paul's continuing contacts with the Jewish community in Rome (28.17-24).[46] No less than when Paul wrote Romans, when also he reached Rome (60) and lived there for two years, there seem to have been still close links between the groups of Jesus-believers and the synagogues in Rome.

The next possible rent also depends on the explicit use of the designation 'Christians'. I refer to Tacitus's description of the persecution of Christians in Rome by Emperor Nero in 64 CE, following the great fire of Rome. According to Tacitus, Emperor Nero, in an attempt to divert suspicion from himself (as the possible arsonist), 'substituted as culprits, and punished with the utmost refinements of cruelty a class of men, loathed for their vices, whom the crowd styled Christians' (*Annals* 15.44.2). Most infer from Tacitus' description that the Christians were already widely recognized as a body distinct from the Roman synagogues;[47] but the reference suggests rather that Nero's agents looking out for plausible scapegoats became aware of the Christians from market-place gossip.[48] There is no hint that they were regarded as 'Christians' as distinct from Jews, or that the Jewish synagogues played any part in inciting the persecution.[49] The fact that early accusations against Christians (hatred of the human race, and atheism) were standard charges against Jews,[50] and the fact that Sulpicius Severus (beginning of fifth century) was able to report[51] that a few years later, Titus determined to de-

---

46. *Beginning from Jerusalem* 1002-9.

47. E. A. Judge, 'Judaism and the Rise of Christianity: A Roman Perspective', *TynB* 45 (1994) 355-68, points out that Romans 'seem to have been unaware of the links between Jews and Christians', and deduces that 'a socially clear-cut separation from an early stage must be assumed' (366). See also Spence in particular (*Parting* 119-37, 170; though see also 235-37); G. Jossa, *Jews or Christians? The Followers of Jesus in Search of Their Own Identity* (WUNT 202; Tübingen: Mohr Siebeck, 2006) 133-35; and Cook, *Roman Attitudes* ch. 2.

48. One can readily envisage that the surge of evangelistic activity presumably referred to in Phil. 1.12-18 drew increasing numbers into the movement — Tacitus speaks of 'vast numbers' of those 'whom the crowd styled Christians (*Chrestianos*)' (*Annals* 15.44.2) — and made the populace at large more aware of the movement.

49. E. M. Smallwood, *The Jews under Roman Rule from Pompey to Diocletian* (Leiden: Brill, 1981), discusses whether there was any Jewish involvement in the denunciation of the 'Christians' (218-19). Luz, however (in private correspondence), notes that it was the 'Christians' and not the rest of the Jews who were made 'scapegoats', so a recognizably distinct group, whether or not they belonged to the Roman synagogues; 'under Nero the Jews were left in peace, but the Christians were persecuted'.

50. *Beginning from Jerusalem* 57 and n.23. Jossa also notes that the accusation which Tacitus levels against the Christians, of 'hatred of the human race' (*Ann.* 15.44.4), is the same accusation that he levels against the Jews (*Hist.* 5.5.1) (*Jews or Christians?* 134).

51. A report for which Tacitus is possibly the source (Stern, *GLAJJ* 2.64-67) — the

stroy the Jerusalem temple 'in order that the religion [singular] of the Jews and Christians should be more completely exterminated' (*Chronicle* 2.30.7),[52] imply that from an outsider's perspective the religions of Jew and Christian, though different, were not yet disentangled.

Here too we need to ask what would have been the *legal status* of the different groupings of believers-in-Jesus. The Roman authorities were notoriously suspicious of unauthorized groups, or *collegia*, voluntary associations. Jewish synagogues were a recognized exception, their rights of assembly and national practices permitted. Any development of particular interest groups within the synagogue would raise no eyebrows, and even some breach with a particular synagogue community was likely to be regarded by the authorities as an internal dispute, Jews with Jews, as in the famous case in Corinth recorded by Luke (Acts 18.12-17). In the highly sensitive context of the capital city itself, there would be all the greater motivation for the new groups of Jesus-believers, including Gentiles, to shelter under the protection of the legal status of the synagogue, to avoid drawing unfavourable attention to themselves.[53] Such a policy would certainly have been consistent with the quietist social policy which Paul himself urged on the recipients of his letter to Rome (Rom. 12.14–13.7). And even if the Roman authorities perceived the early Christians as a distinct body, that may tell us little about many/most early Christians' sense of identity.

In short, within Jewish communities in the period prior to 70, there is evidence of plenty of strains and stresses between Jewish believers in Jesus and other Jews. But clear and explicit reference to a parting of the ways between Jews and Christians, as having already happened, in Jerusalem or elsewhere, prior to 70 (the end-point of *Beginning from Jerusalem*) there is not. In the period 30-70, the great bulk of Jews certainly refused to accept the proclamation that Jesus was Messiah, but there is no indication that they regarded their fellow Jewish believers as 'Christians' and no longer 'Jews'. And if the in-

---

manuscript of Tacitus's *Annals* breaks off in book 16, when his account had reached the year 66, before the outbreak of the Jewish revolt.

52. Referred to by Jossa, *Jews or Christians?* 134 n.27. The account continues: 'those religions [plural], though opposed to one another, derive from the same founders; the Christians stemmed from the Jews (*Christianos ex Judaeis*) and the extirpation of the root would easily cause the offspring to perish'. The ambivalence ('religion'/'religions') suggests that Christian identity emerging in that period was both confused and confusing: were 'Christians' the same as Jews, or a separate religion? Had Gentile converts become members of a Jewish sect?

53. See further my 'The Legal Status of the Earliest Christian Churches', in M. Zetterholm and S. Byrskog, eds., *The Making of Christianity: Conflicts, Contacts and Constructions*; Bengt Holmberg FS (Winona Lake: Eisenbrauns, 2012) 75-93.

flux of Gentiles into the new sect caused them any problems they could well have regarded such converts as aberrant God-fearers, only part-way towards proselyte status.

For the period from 70 onwards, however, the simple question about the parting of the ways between Christianity and Judaism gains new complexity. It can best be tackled under three heads: Roman policy towards Israel and Jews; the developments within Judaism; and the evidence of early Christian writings.

46.3 Rome Changes Everything

On almost any reckoning, the catastrophe of 70 CE, the effective end of 'the (first) Jewish War' against Rome and the destruction of the Jerusalem temple, changed the whole character of the process towards the 'parting of the ways' between Judaism and Christianity. The 'Judaism', within which 'Christianity' had begun to emerge, itself began a process of self-definition which inevitably contributed to the earlier strains and stresses. 'Christianity' effectively lost its mother church, and Jerusalem and the land of Israel played little or no part in what proved to be the decisive developments in Christianity's search to define its own identity. These are the two main areas of inquiry in this chapter: the developments in the formation of identity of both 'Judaism' and 'Christianity' in the period 70-180, especially as these developments interacted with each other; and particularly the extent that identity formation on both sides was determined by each distancing itself from the other. But first we set the political scene within which these developments and distancings took place, bearing in mind that the political scene-setting was bound to play a part in the developments.[54]

a. The Loss of the Jerusalem Temple

The large-scale destruction of Jerusalem in 70[55] was a blow to Jews of epochal significance.[56] Although Jerusalem had not been under independent Jewish

---

54. See also Wilson, *Related Strangers* 3-10; he reviews the Roman attitude to Jews over the period (11-19), and Jews and Christians in Roman society thereafter (20-25, 25-33, 33-35).

55. The destruction of the city was so complete 'as to leave future visitors to the site no ground for believing that it had ever been inhabited' (Josephus, *War* 7.3).

56. 'For the historian also 70 is the end of an epoch. Apart from Josephus' account of the reduction of the fortresses, there is no continuous history of Palestine after 70 . . .' (Smallwood, *Jews* 331).

control since its capture by Pompey in 63 BCE, the Herodian dynasty and rule by the high priestly families meant that for most of the time Jewish control was still largely effective for regulating daily existence. But from 70 onwards effective rule of Jerusalem was no longer under Jewish control[57] and passed through an amazing succession of hands — Romans, Byzantines, Muslims, Crusaders, Mamluks, Ottomans and British — and it was not till nearly nineteen centuries had passed that Jews gained full and independent control of Jerusalem once again (1967).[58] It should occasion no surprise, then, that, after these nineteen centuries, the reconstituted nation of Israel should be so determined to retain full control of Jerusalem as its capital, even though the policy in effect gives no recognition to the rights of the people who have resided in what has been known as Palestine since the Roman period.

The destruction of Jerusalem and devastation of Judaea, however, were not so serious for Jews living further afield,[59] even in Galilee.[60] Agrippa II, who had tried to prevent the war, was allowed to retain rule of his toparchies (Tiberias, Tarichaeae, Abila and Livias-Julias) and granted further territory,[61] and Jews (there were many) who had opposed the war could still come and go to Jerusalem.[62] For Judaism the more fundamental loss was the destruction of the temple. The anguish at the loss is expressed most poignantly by the

---

57. See J. Choi, *Jewish Leadership in Roman Palestine from 70 CE to 135 CE* (Ancient Judaism and Early Christianity 83; Leiden: Brill, 2013), who concludes: 'Post-70 Judaea was a power vacuum without any dominant Jewish leadership, but with plenty of potential candidates' (220), thinking of the Herodian kings who 'failed to achieve control of *provincia Judaea*, and thus disappeared some time late in the first century' (210-11); 'Priests — especially High Priests — failed to regain their previous honours' (211); and rabbinic influence was 'fairly limited, most likely only among their followers' (211). See further ch. 4, 'The Extent of the Realization of Jewish Ideals of Leadership between 70 CE and 135 CE'.

58. See S. S. Montefiore, *Jerusalem: The Biography* (London: Phoenix, 2011). It is unclear whether Simon bar Kochba gained control of Jerusalem for any length of time during the second Jewish revolt (132-135).

59. G. Alon, *The Jews in Their Land in the Talmudic Age* (2 vols.; Jerusalem: Magnes, 1980, 1984) 1.5-8, 59-64; L. I. A. Levine, 'Judaism from the Destruction of Jerusalem to the End of the Second Jewish Revolt: 70-135 C.E.', in H. Shanks, ed., *Christianity and Rabbinic Judaism: A Parallel History of Their Origins and Early Development* (Washington: Biblical Archaeology Society, ²2011) 139-66: 'culturally, economically and socially, Jewish life outside of Jerusalem and its environs was not seriously interrupted between the pre- and post-destruction era' (141).

60. Sepphoris, for example, had remained loyal to Rome.

61. Schürer, *History* 1.477-78. M. Goodman, *Rome and Jerusalem: The Clash of Ancient Civilizations* (London: Penguin, 2007): 'Agrippa's personal links with the new imperial regime were exceptionally close' (458-59); see also Levine, 'Judaism' 144-45.

62. 'References in rabbinic literature give the impression that much Jewish land remained in or soon reverted to private ownership' (Smallwood, *Jews* 341-43).

apocalyptists, writing probably in the decades following 70 and setting their lament in the context of the first destruction of the temple in 587 BCE. For example, *2 Baruch*:

> O that my eyes were springs,
> and my eyelids, that they were a fountain of tears.
> For how shall I be sad over Zion,
> and lament over Jerusalem?
> For at the place where now I am prostrate,
> the high priests used to offer sacrifices,
> and placed thereon incense of fragrant spices.
> Now, however, that of which we are proud has become dust,
> And that which our soul desired is ashes (*2 Bar.* 35.2-4 *OTP*).[63]

The anguish was hardly surprising, since the temple had been at the heart of the religion of Israel and of Second Temple Judaism. It was the place where God had chosen to put his name, the focal point for the divine-human encounter and the sacrificial cult on which Jewish well-being and salvation depended.[64] Of course, the hope was initially strong that the temple would be rebuilt, although, unusually, given Rome's normal respect for national religions, Vespasian did not grant permission for its rebuilding[65]— presumably the zealotic passions which the second temple had inspired were sufficient warning. But given that the post-exilic Judaeans had restored the temple after the destruction of the first temple, Jews were bound to cherish the hope that the same would happen again. *2 Baruch*, written probably about 100, again illustrates the hope: 'And at that time, after a short time, Zion will be rebuilt again, and the offerings will be restored, and the priests will again return to their ministry. And nations will again come to honor it. But not as fully as before' (*2 Bar.* 68.5-6 *OTP*).

We have already seen, in connection with the *Epistle of Barnabas*, the likelihood that the arousal of anticipation of a rebuilt temple was a factor in

---

63. See also *Apoc. Abr.* 27; *4 Ezra* 3.1-3, 28-36; *4 Bar.* 3.

64. *Jesus Remembered* 287-88; and further *Partings of the Ways* §2.4. 'The destruction of the Temple ... rendered *impossible* the practice of whole areas of his [the Jew's] religion, especially in the field of communal ritual ... a gaping vacuum' (Alon, *The Jews in Their Land* 1.50).

65. See also Smallwood, *Jews* 345-48. 'It is worthwhile emphasizing the enormity of this refusal in the context of ancient religious practice, and the extent to which it revealed a special prejudice against the Jews. . . . Everyone else in the empire was free to continue to worship in the ways hallowed by their ancestors' (Goodman, *Rome and Jerusalem* 449, 463-64).

the outbreak of the second Jewish war against Rome (132-135).⁶⁶ The fact that Hadrian, in the wake of the Bar Kokhba rebellion, went ahead with his plans to raze the site of Jerusalem, build there a new city, Aelia Capitolina, and build a temple to Jupiter Capitolinus on the site of the Jewish temple, must have been an effective deathblow to that hope. And although today Jerusalem itself is back in Jewish hands, the presence of the Islamic Noble Sanctuary, Dome of the Rock, the Haram al-Sharif, on the site of the temple, realistically rules out any prospect of the Jewish temple being restored within the foreseeable future.⁶⁷

To what extent diaspora Judaism was affected by the disaster of 70 is not as clear as one would wish. Early in the campaign against Rome, the Jews of Antioch suffered grievously, along with many of the God-fearers who had judaized too far for the local populations; and in 70-71 they were accused of starting a serious fire which destroyed many public buildings (Josephus, *War* 7.41-62).⁶⁸ And Jewish extremists (*sicarii*) who escaped from the disaster in Palestine attempted to stir trouble in Alexandria and Cyrene, but without much success (*War* 7.409-19, 437-41).⁶⁹ But there is no indication of troubles elsewhere, in the large Jewish communities in Rome⁷⁰ and Asia Minor, in particular. If Justin's Trypho is a good witness, his testimony would be that Jews in Asia were undisturbed and able to thrive even with the second Jewish war under way.⁷¹ All, however, would have been affected by the 'Jewish tax' which Vespasian levied on all Jews, as we shall see.

We have already noted how much the Jerusalem believers in Jesus were affected by the 70 catastrophe (§45.3). But the impact on other Christian churches is much harder to detect. Apart from the Matthean version of the parable of the wedding banquet (Matt. 22.2-14), with its clear allusion to the destruction of Jerusalem (22.7-8), there are only hints and possible allusions to the destruction of Jerusalem and temple. Notably, there are no Christian

---

66. See above §40.1f.
67. As we shall see (§46.4a), however, the loss of the temple for Judaism was not as devastating as it must have first appeared.
68. See Smallwood, *Jews* 358-64.
69. Smallwood, *Jews* 366-71; Goodman, *Rome and Jerusalem* 461-62. The response to the troubles in Alexandria included the demolition of the Jewish temple at Leontopolis, at the southern end of the Nile delta, which had flourished for more than 240 years (Josephus, *War* 7.421, 433-36).
70. The fact that Berenice, sister of Agrippa II, became Titus's mistress in Rome (Cassius Dio 66.15.3-5; 66.18.1 [*GLAJJ* 2.378-79]; Schürer, *History* 1.479; Smallwood, *Jews* 385-88) would no doubt have made things easier for the local Jews. And Jews of Rome felt free enough to bring accusations against Josephus, who retained imperial patronage (Josephus, *Life* 428-29; Goodman, *Rome and Jerusalem* 463).
71. See §40.2e above.

heart-rending laments over the disasters which had befallen the Jewish people and the destruction of the temple, such as we find in *4 Ezra* and *2 Baruch*. The implication is that the fall of Jerusalem and destruction of the temple made little impression among the diaspora groupings of believers-in-Jesus — presumably since they were both geographically remote from and, probably as a consequence of continuing Hellenist influence, spiritually remote from the Jerusalem cult — other than as providing a way to make sense of Jesus' death. Since the history of diaspora Jewish communities following the failure of the first Jewish revolt is unclear,[72] prior to their coming under the influence of emerging rabbinic Judaism,[73] it is also unclear whether Christian disinterest in the fall of Jerusalem and the loss of the temple was a significant factor in determining relations between Jews and Christians in the western diaspora. But here too the *fiscus Judaicus* may well have played a significant part.

b. *Fiscus Judaicus*

The *fiscus Judaicus* was the tax levied by Emperor Vespasian following the failure of the Jewish revolt, the equivalent of the former temple tax (two drachmas), still to be paid by all male Jews, but now (the Jerusalem temple having been destroyed) to be paid to the temple of Jupiter Capitolinus in Rome (Josephus, *War* 7.218).[74] By so doing, Vespasian was both able to recharge his treasury, much diminished by his wars, and to punish the Jewish nation appropriately, reinforcing his unwillingness to see the Jerusalem temple being rebuilt. As depressing as this must have been for all Jews, Roman diaspora Jews as well, since the widely supported payment of the temple tax had been a major bonding commitment for diaspora Jews, the situation became more serious following the first two members of the Flavian dynasty (Vespasian and Titus). For under the emperor Domitian (81-96), this tax was strictly enforced and exacted 'with utmost vigour' (*acerbissime*).[75] That is, according to Suetonius, people who had previously been exempt from the tax were now compelled to pay it. Suetonius identifies those affected: 'those who without publicly acknowledging that faith yet lived as Jews, as well as

---

72. Apart from the Jewish uprising in north Africa in 115-17 (see §46.3c below).

73. But we cannot assume that this happened before the third century; see §38 n.51 above.

74. Schürer, *History* 2.271-72; Smallwood, *Jews* 371-78 — 'the Temple tax had been paid only by men between the ages of twenty and fifty, including freed slaves and proselytes. The tax in its new form was payable by both sexes from the age of three.... The extension of liability quadrupled the total sum previously paid to the Temple in Jerusalem' (373-74).

75. On Domitian's ascent to power see Goodman, *Rome and Jerusalem* 464-68.

those who concealed their origin and did not pay the tribute levied upon the people' (*Domitian* 12.2), that is, judaizing Gentiles and non-religious Jews.[76] Cassius Dio confirms that under Domitian many 'who drifted into Jewish ways were condemned' on the charge of atheism, and suffered severe penalties (*Historia Romana* 67.14.2).[77] This would presumably have come as a shock to any Jewish believers-in-Jesus who were trying to disown their Jewish identities (concealing their origin).[78] But it would almost certainly have provided a strong motivation to many Gentile believers-in-Jesus to deny that they had converted to Judaism and to distinguish themselves more clearly as non-Jews to avoid paying the tax.

The issue became more complex, since Domitian's successor, Nerva, countermanded Domitian's unpopular action by reforming the *fiscus Iudaicus* in 96, and, according to Dio, quashed the practice of permitting slaves and freedmen to accuse others 'of adopting the Jewish mode of life' (68.1.2). Nerva's coins proclaim: *Fisci Iudaici calumnia sublata*, 'the malicious accusation with regard to the Jewish tax has been removed'.[79] The point is that Nerva's reform gave a fresh scope both to those who wished to affirm a Jewish identity and to those who wished to deny that they were Jews; the latter being exempt from false denunciations. Proselytes and even God-fearers who wished to identify with Judaism could pay the tax. But those who were unwilling to pay the tax, even though their religion was very Jewish in character (Gentile Christians), could deny their Jewish roots by claiming exemption from the tax. Such encouragement to pull apart Christian and Jewish identity endured for perhaps as long as ten years, and may well help to explain how the early second-century Roman writers Tacitus (*Ann.* 15.44.2) and Suetonius (*Life of Nero* 16.2), not to mention Pliny the Younger (*Ep.* 10.96),[80] could refer to 'Christians' (for the first time in non-Christian writings) as a clearly identifiable and distinct body (religious practitioners, similar to Jews, but non-payees

---

76. Text and fuller details in *GLAJJ* 2.128-30. See further Smallwood, *Jews* 376-78; M. Goodman, 'Nerva, the *fiscus Judaicus* and Jewish Identity', *JRS* 79 (1989) 40-44; and further M. Heemstra, *The* Fiscus Judaicus *and the Parting of the Ways* (WUNT 2.277; Tübingen: Mohr Siebeck, 2010). 'There can be little doubt that Suetonius is describing individuals who were actually living a Jewish life and who refused to publicly admit it in order that they could avoid the tax' (Cook, *Roman Attitudes* 124).

77. Text in *GLAJJ* 2.379-80.

78. Full discussion in Heemstra, Fiscus Judaicus ch. 2.

79. 'The coins commemorate the abolition, not of the tax itself, but of *calumnia*, false charges, which had arisen in connection with it' (Smallwood, *Jews* 378).

80. Quoted in full in *Beginning from Jerusalem* §21.1e, but less relevant here since Jews are not mentioned (Pliny the Younger's *Epistles* are not included in *GLAJJ*). See also Cook, *Roman Attitudes* ch. 4.

of the Jewish tax).[81] Perhaps then, ironically, it was an issue of economics and taxation which finally made the legal status of Christians clearly distinct from that of Jews in the eyes of the Roman authorities.

c. The Jewish Revolt of 115-117

Mention should be made of the Jewish revolt under Trajan in Cyrenaica and Egypt,[82] although its origins and causes are far from clear, with only brief accounts provided by Cassius Dio (68.32.1-3)[83] and Eusebius (*HE* 4.2.1-5).[84] It would appear that racial conflict between Jews and Greeks in Egypt[85] — there had been a long history of tension between Greeks and Jews in Alexandria in particular — boiled over into outright Jewish revolt against Rome.[86] It inevitably gained a nationalist dimension, with the Jewish antagonists seeking independence and probably intending to march, through Egypt, to accomplish return to the promised land.[87] The Roman suppression was, as usual, ruthless

---

81. 'From the year 96 onwards it was possible for Roman authorities to recognize Christians, because they were exclusive monotheists, who did not pay the Jewish tax' (Heemstra, *Fiscus Judaicus* 196). 'By the time Pliny wrote to Trajan about legal action against the Christians (*Ep.* 10.96-97) in the year 112 CE, there is no doubt about their distinct identity in Roman eyes' (Wilson, *Related Strangers* 16). M. H. Williams concludes her 'Jews and Christians at Rome: An Early Parting of the Ways', in Shanks, ed., *Partings* 151-78: 'To all intents and purposes, the break between Jews and Christians at Rome was complete by the early second century C.E.' (177).

82. Schürer, *History* 1.529-34. Detailed discussion in M. P. Ben Zeev, *Diaspora Judaism in Turmoil 116/117 CE* (Leuven: Peeters, 2005).

83. Text with commentary in *GLAJJ* 2.385-89.

84. Dio refers also to serious disturbances in Cyprus, and Eusebius to severe repression of Jews in Mesopotamia as linked to the north African revolt. On the latter, and on serious disorder/unrest in Judaea, see Ben Zeev, *Diaspora Judaism* chs. 8 and 9, who concludes that the Jewish revolts of this period disrupted Roman policy towards Parthia, helping to ensure that the Jews of Mesopotamia were able to remain outside the Roman world (264-66).

85. Dio records that 220,000 Gentiles perished in Cyrene and 240,000 in Cyprus (68.32.2). 'The appalling casualty figures may well be exaggerated. But comments by contemporaries confirm the extreme violence' (Goodman, *Rome and Jerusalem* 477-79).

86. Possible explanations for the revolt of 115-117 'all rest on the primary assumption that Jews in the Roman empire hated Roman rule. . . . It would be unsurprising if Jewish frustration at Roman attacks on Judaism manifested itself in a war against the religion of the oppressive state' (Goodman, *Rome and Jerusalem* 480).

87. See Smallwood's full analysis (*Jews* ch. 15; here 397). W. Horbury, 'The Beginnings of the Jewish Revolt under Trajan', in P. Schäfer, ed., *Geschichte — Tradition — Reflexion; Festschrift für Martin Hengel* vol. I: *Judentum* (Tübingen: Mohr Siebeck, 1996) 283-304, argues that the revolt was influenced by messianism from the start (295-303).

— 'a massacre on such a scale that the blood of the slain stained the sea as far as Cyprus'.[88] The events provide a grim reminder of the sort of tensions between Jews, and their neighbours and rulers, which must have been a feature of many diaspora Jewish communities, though elsewhere they did not boil over (Alexandria had always been a flashpoint), and which no doubt contributed to the buildup to the second Jewish war in Palestine.[89] The consequence was that previously numerous Jewish communities in Cyrenaica and Alexandria (and Cyprus) declined drastically in numbers and significance.[90] According to Dio, no Jew was allowed to set foot in Cyprus, and 'if one of them is driven upon its shores by a storm he is put to death' (68.32.3).

Of interest for us is the fact that Christians are nowhere mentioned in these accounts of the north African and Cyprus disturbances, even though the Jesus sect had spread early to Cyprus (Acts 13.4-12; 15.39),[91] and must have made some impact in Alexandria by the early second century. Such lack of reference to Christians may be simply due to the brevity of the accounts, though one would have expected Eusebius to make something of it if the Jewish revolutionaries had attacked Christians. The only obvious deduction to make, otherwise, is that the Christians were not yet regarded (by the bulk of Jews) as a group already distinct from the Jewish community.[92] The alternative, that the Christians were identified with 'the Greeks' (and so suffered in the Jewish violence against the Greeks), is less likely, since the Jewish revolutionaries would almost certainly have regarded such Christians as particularly hateful in view of the claims the latter made on what the former would have regarded as distinctively Jewish heritage; but there is no hint of such a feature in the revolt.

d. The Bar Kochba Revolt — 132-135

The continued suspicion among the Roman rulers in Palestine, attested in Eusebius,[93] about the possibility of messianic pretenders arising in Judaea to

---

88. Smallwood, *Jews* 404; Levine, 'Judaism' 159.
89. See also Schürer, *History* 1.529-34; Smallwood, *Jews* 421-27. 'As far as the Romans were concerned, disaffection among Jews in one part of the empire necessarily threw under suspicion those in another, as they had shown consistently ever since Vespasian adopted his policy of hostility to Judaism in 70' (Goodman, *Rome and Jerusalem* 481).
90. Smallwood, *Jews* 409-12, 414-15.
91. Nor in the even briefer references in the early 5th century Orosius, *Historiarum Adversum Paganos* 7.12.6-8.
92. See also R. A. Kraft and A. M. Luijendijk, 'Christianity's Rise after Judaism's Demise in Early Egypt', in Shanks, ed., *Partings* 179-85.
93. See above §45.3.

head up further trouble, and the revolt in north Africa, is sufficient indication that the imperial authority must have felt itself to be walking on egg shells in the administering of Jewish affairs.[94] As already suggested (§40.1f), during his visit to Judaea in 130, Hadrian probably planned or announced his intention to build a new city on the site of Jerusalem (Aelia Capitolina)[95] and to erect a temple to Zeus on the site of the Jerusalem temple destroyed in 70. Whether this was in response to Jewish longing for Israel's temple to be restored or provoked a reactive wave of passion for the restoration of Herod's temple, we need not decide (cf. *Barn.* 16.1-4). But it is not hard to envisage how both the endless frustration at the absence of the temple cult, and any suggestion that a Gentile temple would make the realization of the dream of the restoration of Herod's temple impossible, were strong breezes which fanned the smouldering flame of Jewish resentment into the fire of renewed rebellion.[96]

The revolt was led by Simon ben Kosiba, regarded by some, including the famous rabbi Akiba, as 'son of the Star' (Num. 24.17), bar Kokhba, that is, as the Messiah.[97] Those who dismissed Akiba's attribution of messianic status called him rather bar Koziba, son of the lie = Liar.[98] The revolt was initially successful, with coins and documents itemizing up to four years marking 'the Liberation of Israel' and naming the revolt's leader as 'Nasi (Prince) of Israel'.[99] It swept through Palestine and probably reached beyond its borders,[100] and was so serious that Hadrian himself took charge of its suppression for a time.[101] Whether Jerusalem itself was captured by the rebels remains un-

---

94. The governors appointed for Judaea and Syria-Palestine post-70 were of a much higher calibre, from the senatorial class, than their pre-70 equestrian predecessors. For lists see Schürer, *History* 1.514-19; Smallwood, *Jews* 546-57.

95. 'The discovery of a coin from Aelia Capitolina, dated to the year 131, strengthens Dio's explanation as it shows that plans for this city were well underway before the onset of conflict' (Levine, 'Judaism' 163).

96. See §40 nn.66, 67 above, and further Smallwood, *Jews* 432-36; Goodman, *Rome and Jerusalem* 483-88 — 'Aelia Capitolina was not to be refounded as a Greek city in which Jews might settle and be "civilized", but as a Roman colony, inhabited by gentiles, from which Jews were to be excluded' (485).

97. Though Levine points out that the messianic component in Bar Kokhba's leadership has been called into question ('Judaism' 161-62).

98. Schürer, *History* 1.543-44 nn.130, 131.

99. Smallwood, *Jews* 439-40, 441, 443-44.

100. 'All Judea had been stirred up, and the Jews everywhere were showing signs of disturbance, and giving evidence of great hostility to the Romans . . . ; many outside nations, too, were joining them through eagerness for gain, and the whole earth, one might almost say, was being stirred up over the matter' (Cassius Dio 69.13.1-2; see *GLAJJ* 2.391-405, with full commentary; also Goodman, *Rome and Jerusalem* 488-90).

101. Smallwood, *Jews* 450-51.

clear;[102] the city was the headquarters of the Tenth Legion, and even if Bar Kokhba controlled it for a time, its complete lack of defence walls made it entirely vulnerable to any strong Roman force.[103] Otherwise, by remorseless reduction of rebel strongholds and, finally, refuges, the Romans ground the revolt to its inevitable end.[104] The last battle was over the strong mountain fort of Bether, southwest from Jerusalem, which was captured in the eighteenth year of Hadrian (134/135 CE): 'the siege lasted a long time before the rebels were driven to final destruction by famine and thirst, and the instigator of their madness paid the penalty he deserved' (Eusebius, *HE* 4.6.3).

The revolt must have shattered any association between the rebels and the Jewish believers in Messiah Jesus.[105] To follow Akiba in acknowledging Bar Kokhba as Messiah would have been impossible to them.[106] And the passions which began and sustained the revolt for the three or four years would almost certainly have meant that Jewish believers in Jesus were regarded as traitors and apostates.[107] But for the Jews in Palestine the outcome was far worse. With the foundation of Aelia Capitolina Jews had no place in their former capital; Gentile colonists took their place. 'From then on no Jew was permitted to enter the city area; any Jew seen there was punished with death'.[108] That would presumably have included Jewish believers in Jesus; not

---

102. 'The prominence given to a priest (Eleazar the Priest) on the coinage was surely connected with the rebels' aim of restoring the Temple and its cult' (Smallwood, *Jews* 440-41, 443).

103. Schürer, *History* 1.550-51; see also Goodman, *Rome and Jerusalem* 490-91.

104. '"The whole of Judaea was practically a desert". Fifty forts were destroyed and 985 villages, 580,000 Jews(?) fell in battle and those who succumbed to illness or starvation were uncounted' (Schürer, *History* 1.553, drawing on Cassius Dio 69.14.1-2). See Smallwood's account of the later stages of the revolt (*Jews* 451-57).

105. Horbury notes that the degree to which Christians shared in Jewish hopes and Jewish hostility to Rome, as evidenced in Barnabas and Justin, may initially have encouraged the Bar Kokhba rebels to look to the Jewish believers for support, and heightened their anger when they did not do so ('Barnabas' 338-39); similarly 'Messianism Among Jews and Christians in the Second Century', in *Messianism Among Jews and Christians: Twelve Biblical and Historical Studies* (London: T & T Clark, 2003) 275-88 (here 287).

106. 'It was precisely because of the Messianic nature of the movement that Christians were unable to participate in it without denying their Messiah' (Schürer, *History* 1.545). R. Bauckham, 'Jews and Jewish Christians in the Land of Israel at the Time of the Bar Kochba War, with Special Reference to the *Apocalypse of Peter*', in Stanton and Stroumsa, eds., *Tolerance and Intolerance* 228-38, finds in *Apoc. Pet.* 16 indication that the Palestinian Jewish believers-in-Jesus were opposed to Bar Kochba's central aim of rebuilding the temple (232-35); similarly Wilson, *Related Strangers* 6-7; Broadhead, *Jewish Ways* 277-78.

107. According to Justin Martyr, Bar Kochba 'gave orders that Christians alone should be led to cruel punishments, unless they would deny Jesus Christ and utter blasphemy' (*1 Apol.* 31.6).

108. Schürer, *History* 1.553.

simply Jews, but Jewish believers in Jesus could no longer regard Jerusalem as their headquarters and spiritual home. In contrast, no doubt non-Jewish believers took the opportunity to settle in Jerusalem; the church of Jerusalem became wholly Gentile in composition and character (Eusebius, *HE* 4.6.4). The impact of all this on Jewish communities of the Roman diaspora and their relations to Christians around them is unclear — we recall that Justin had his dialogue with Trypho while the revolt was in progress.[109] But so far as relations in Palestine itself are concerned, both the revolt, under the leadership of 'the son of the Star', and its outcome must have opened a gaping wound which could hardly be healed, even if for most rabbis Bar Kokhba was better referred to as Bar Koziba.

e. Subsequent Roman Policy

The end of an era was marked by several symbolic events of profound significance: particularly, the 'ploughing up' of Jerusalem and the temple site;[110] also Hadrian's decision to ban Jews from entering Jerusalem and, unusually in such circumstances, to change the name of the province from Judaea to Syria Palestina.[111] In many ways, however, the most distressing outcome of the failed revolt was Hadrian's banning of circumcision as a barbaric custom, on a par with castration.[112] Although circumcision was more widely practiced among the Semitic nations, it is hard to doubt that the ban was directed specifically at Judaism,[113] since circumcision had come to be understood to be such a central Jewish identity marker; 'the prohibition of circumcision was, to the Jewish mind, tantamount to a ban on Judaism itself'.[114] The prohibition was subsequently removed by Antoninus Pius (138-161), possibly following another period of Jewish disturbance — the Roman authorities recognizing that unless they tolerated Jewish traditions and allowed their religious rites they would be confronted with endless trouble. But it was the effective annihilation of Israel as a political entity which opened the door to the epochal development of rabbinic Judaism.[115] The all too well proven futility of rebellion against Rome

---

109. Justin refers to the desolation of Jerusalem in *1 Apol.* 47 and *Dial.* 16, 25.
110. 'Possibly the plough was driven across the city . . . to signify its utter destruction, and even across the Temple site to symbolize the supersession of Yahweh by Jupiter' (Smallwood, *Jews* 459).
111. Smallwood, *Jews* 463-64; Goodman, *Rome and Jerusalem* 493-94.
112. Schürer, *History* 1.536-39; Wilson, *Related Strangers* 7-8.
113. *Pace* Schürer, *History* 1.539-40. See also Smallwood, *Jews* 429-31, 465.
114. Schürer, *History* 1.555; Smallwood, *Jews* 465.
115. Schürer, *History* 1.555.

ensured that in the sustained period of peace which ensued, the rabbis could concentrate on their supreme mission of re-creating Judaism.

46.4 Development of and Developments within Judaism

Before 70 the question was whether we could or should speak of a parting of the ways between believers in Jesus and Second Temple Judaism. But with the destruction of the Jerusalem temple, that is, the *de facto* end of Second Temple Judaism, the question inevitably changes. If no longer the question is of a parting from Second Temple Judaism, then the question has to be rephrased — parting from what?[116] The complementary question is, of course, that if the parting was in part at least instigated from within Judaism, then from what was it parting? But let us take one step at a time.

a. The Beginnings of Rabbinic Judaism

In the aftermath of the destruction of Jerusalem in 70 there does not seem to have been any attempt to re-establish it as a religious centre; in the absence of the temple the primary motivation was lacking. And after the further devastation of 135, Jews were forbidden to settle in Jerusalem. The focus shifted instead to the coastal town of Yavneh. According to rabbinic tradition Yohanan ben Zakkai survived the disaster of 70 and was given permission by Vespasian to gather a group of Torah scholars at Yavneh (Jamnia), near the Judaean coast.[117] With rabbinic hindsight this gathering marked the beginning of the attempt to reconstruct Judaism without a temple, later known as the Yavnean academy and later still as the 'council of Yavneh'.[118] But how much was actually accomplished there, in the aftermath of 70 CE (the revolt continued at Masada until early 74), is much disputed (as indeed even the fact of a Yavnean rabbinate).[119] Yohanan, already an old man, was succeeded by

---

116. As Wilson notes: 'A common error... is to assume that rabbinic Jews = Judaism' (*Related Strangers* 170).

117. J. Neusner, *A Life of Yohanan ben Zakkai* (Leiden: Brill, ²1970); also *First Century Judaism in Crisis* Part III; Alon, *The Jews in Their Land* ch. 5; Schürer, *History* 1.525-26; 2.109-10. On the question whether, and if so, to what extent Essenes and Sadducees survived as such in the post-70 period, see M. Goodman, 'Sadducees and Essenes after 70 CE', in *Judaism in the Roman World* 153-62.

118. J. P. Lewis, *ABD* 3.634-37.

119. P. Schäfer, 'Die sogenannte Synode von Jabne: Zur Trennung von Juden und Christen im ersten/zweiten Jh. n. Chr.', *Studien zur Geschichte und Theologie des Rabbi-*

Gamaliel II, who was evidently regarded as posing a sufficient threat to be condemned to death early in the Bar Kochba revolt, as was rabbi Akiba, imprisoned for some time before being tortured to death.[120] Subsequently, later in the second century, the school of rabbinic scholarship moved to Galilee, to Sepphoris and then to Tiberias, which had been largely untouched by the devastation caused by the Bar Kochba revolt.

The principal factor in this reconstitution of Judaism was the transfer from temple to Torah. What devastated Second Temple Judaism beyond repair was the cessation of the sacrificial cult of the Jerusalem temple. This is less obvious than it might be, since the rabbis continued to give rulings on the administration of the temple cult as though it was still in operation[121]— presumably because they saw themselves as legislating for a pattern of religion which would soon (or eventually) be restored, though it should be noted that both Josephus and post-70 Christian writings similarly used the present tense in referring to the temple sacrifices.[122] But now the real focus was on the Torah, the impetus being to formulate a Judaism which could thrive without a temple: to take over the responsibility previously exercised by the priests in determining the calendar and 'rabbinizing' the liturgy;[123] and to gather and extend the halakhic rulings (the oral Torah) which had already been well developed particularly by the Pharisees[124]

---

nischen Judentums (Leiden: Brill, 1978) 45-64; other bibliography in Saldarini, *Matthew's Christian-Jewish Community* 216 n.11.

120. Smallwood, *Jews* 465-66.

121. Schürer, *History* 1.521-23; Alon, *The Jews in Their Land* 1.114-18. 'In fact, the detailed prescriptions for the sacrifices to be found in the Mishnah, redacted around 200 CE, presuppose that even at that date rabbis expected, or at least hoped, that the Temple could and would be rebuilt.... There is not a shred of evidence that any ordinary Jew at this time thought of the cessation of sacrifices as desirable. On the contrary, all Jews were waiting impatiently for God to be worshipped properly again, "speedily, in our days"' (Goodman, *Rome and Jerusalem* 448-49, echoing the Kaddish prayer).

122. See above §39 n.258; as noted there, it is this slightly surprising practice which means that the letter to the Hebrews' failure to mention the destruction of the temple provides no clear evidence of a pre-70 date. Levine points out that neither the Fourth Sibyl (writing about 80 CE) nor pseudo-Philo's *Liber Antiquitatum Biblicarum* (which he dates to the late first century) shows any particular concern over the destruction of the Jerusalem temple ('Judaism' 145).

123. One of the primary concerns at Yavneh was evidently to establish the dates for the feast-days, and thus resolve the calendrical disputes which had racked Second Temple Judaism (Alon, *The Jews in Their Land* 1.108-12).

124. We know that the development of halakhoth (to show how the Torah applied to everyday life) was already well under way by the beginning of the first century CE. Both *Jub.* 2.17-33; 50.8-12 and CD 10.14–11.18 indicate how far the Sabbath law had been elaborated halakhically; and 4QMMT B gives a good example of the sort of concerns which became life and breath for the early rabbis.

in the latter decades of the Second Temple.[125] These were the rulings, debated and ordered, which were transcribed into the Mishnah at the end of the second century, under the leadership of Judah the Patriarch/Prince (Nasi). In the process Judaism had been transformed from a religion of sacrificial cult to one of Torah compliance, where the central ministry was no longer that of priest but that of rabbi — 'a new Judaism in which good deeds and prayer would take the place, at least in terms of theological efficacy, of the Temple cult'.[126]

What happened to the other sects within Second Temple Judaism is much less clear, but Qumran had been destroyed by the Romans in 68, and never resettled, and the rule and influence of the power-broking Sadducees had been fatally undermined by the disaster of 70. But even with the loss of the temple, priests would almost certainly have retained their traditional status (and expected their traditional rights to be honoured) in local communities.[127] Village elders would have retained authority and synagogues would have been governed by local community leaders.[128] And the complete disappearance of Sadducees and Essenes after 70 is hardly likely.[129] Apocalyptic and mystical strands of Second Temple Judaism also maintained their existence, though their influence in shaping post-70 Judaism was probably no more than marginal. The factor of long-term significance, however, was that the Yavnean rabbis and their successors seem to have followed a deliberate policy of defining the identity of Judaism more tightly, in accordance with their reading of the Torah. They would no doubt have thought they were simply clarifying what Judaism should always have been. But those who did not conform were in effect shut out from the rabbinic Judaism being developed. The diversity of a Judaism in which Sadducee flourished alongside Pharisee and Essene, in which diaspora Judaism had a range of affiliation with those within the homeland of Israel and in which there was a place for apocalyptic and mystical strands was largely lost within the attempts of

---

125. Alexander, 'Jewish Believers' 671-76. The known rulings of Yohanan were 'quite limited in scope and marginal to Jewish life generally', presumably because the shock of 70 took quite some time to absorb and his scope for adapting traditional practices was limited; but Gamaliel's reformation seems to have been more extensive, particularly in liturgical matters, prayers, holidays and the calendar (Levine, 'Judaism' 148-58). On Gamaliel see also Alon, *The Jews in Their Land* 1.119-24.

126. Goodman, *Rome and Jerusalem* 448.

127. Alon, *The Jews in Their Land* 1.101.

128. M. Goodman, *State and Society in Roman Galilee, AD 132-212* (Totowa: Rowman & Allanheld, 1983). 'In the first two centuries . . . no evidence points to rabbinic control over synagogues' (Saldarini, *Matthew's Christian-Jewish Community* 13).

129. M. Goodman, 'Sadducees and Essenes after 70 CE', *Judaism in the Roman World* ch. 13.

emerging rabbinic Judaism to achieve a more coherent and sustainable, a narrower self-definition.

It is repeatedly emphasized in studies of Jewish communities and of Judaism in the early centuries of the common era that rabbinic Judaism did not emerge overnight,[130] however highly Yohanan ben Zakkai, Gamaliel II and Judah the Prince are regarded in Jewish commemoration — Christians need think only of their own hagiographical traditions for the point to be made. Nor was the pattern of Judaism developing at Yavneh, Sepphoris and Tiberias taken up with any immediacy by Jewish communities outside Syria-Palestina.[131] The Judaism of the Roman diaspora encountered by the Christian communities through the second century was not yet rabbinic Judaism.[132] All of which makes more intriguing the question of how embryonic Christianity fared in this process. For the attitude of emerging rabbinic Judaism to the sect of the Nazarene and emerging Christianity can hardly be separated from the attitude of rabbinic Judaism to the other Judaisms of Second Temple Judaism. Was the sect of the Nazarenes simply another of the strands of Second Temple Judaism which emerging rabbinic Judaism disowned? Or to put the issue more provocatively: given that rabbinic Judaism effectively disentangled itself from the other forms of Second Temple Judaism, was it the only Second Temple sect to make legitimate (and exclusive) claim to the heritage of Second Temple Judaism? Was indeed the emergence of rabbinic Judaism itself the decisive factor in the 'parting of the ways'?

b. The *Birkat ha-Minim*

The most intriguing indication that the Yavnean rabbis acted to exclude Christians from their reconstituted Judaism is the *birkat ha-minim*, 'the blessing (or

---

130. E.g. Wilson, *Related Strangers* 19. 'The specific cases in which rabbis are portrayed as judges almost all concerned very limited areas of religious law — issues involving purity, the food laws, the annulment of vows, the observance of fasts in time of drought, and so on — and the rabbinic texts themselves assume that rabbinic rulings were disregarded by the many Jews termed either neutrally *ammei haaretz* (those who do not fulfil rabbinic injunctions on purity and tithing) or in more hostile terms as *minim* (heretics)' — M. Goodman, *The Roman World: 44 BC – AD 180* (London: Routledge, 1997) 313-14.

131. See above §39 n.122.

132. Pritz notes that Nazarene familiarity with the names of second-century Jewish leaders displayed in Jerome's *in Es.* 8.14 indicates that 'the Nazarenes must have remained on intimate terms with rabbinic Judaism' (*Nazarene Jewish Christianity* 58-62). Similarly Broadhead, *Jewish Ways* 167-68.

malediction) against the heretics', inserted in the twelfth benediction of the *Shemoneh 'Esreh*, the eighteen benedictions, also known as the Amidah.[133]

> And for apostates let there be no hope; and may the insolent kingdom be quickly uprooted, in our days. And may the Nazarenes and the heretics (*minim*) perish quickly; and may they be erased from the Book of Life; and may they not be inscribed with the righteous. Blessed art thou, Lord, who humblest the insolent.

There is a tradition in the Babylonian Talmud (*b. Ber.* 28b)[134] to the effect that the benediction relating to the *minim* was composed by Samuel the Small during the period when Rabban Gamaliel was head of the rabbinic academy in Yavneh (c. 80-c. 115). This has been related to the expulsion of believers in Messiah Jesus from the synagogue, referred to in John 9.22,[135] and to the 'cursing in your synagogues them that believe on Christ' to which Justin refers Trypho repeatedly.[136] The reasoning would presumably be that no follower of Jesus could take part in the recitation of the *Shemoneh 'Esreh*, since the twelfth benediction would be pronouncing a curse on himself and his fellow Christians. If this were the case, even as early as the 80s of the first century, it would provide the first indication, from the Jewish side, of action taken to divide Christian from Jew, to make it impossible for Jewish believers-in-Jesus to continue functioning as Jews, acceptable members of the Jewish community.

The issue is fraught, since it is likely that the specific reference to the Christians (the *Notzrim*) was a later addition to the *birkat ha-minim*. The revision of the twelfth benediction may well have taken place later, and it is very questionable whether the explicit reference to Christians (the Nazarenes) was part of the original formulation.[137] Even so, the tradition probably reflects an early Yavnean rabbinic decision to count other forms of Second Temple Judaism, what could be described roughly as non-Pharisaic understandings and

---

133. Wander observes that most NT research sees the break between Judaism and Christianity as effectively documented in the *birkat ha-minim* (*Trennungsprozesse* 3).

134. Herford, *Christianity* 125-37.

135. See below §46.5c.

136. See below n.309.

137. See now Boyarin, *Border Lines* 67-73; R. Langer, *Cursing the Christians? A History of the Birkat Haminim* (Oxford University, 2011) ch. 1; both with further bibliography, including particularly P. W. van der Horst, 'The Birkat ha-minim in Recent Research', in *Hellenism-Judaism-Christianity: Essays on Their Interaction* (Kampen: Pharos, 1994) 99-111. Wilson points out that 'if the reference to Christians (*notzrim*) had been there from the start the malediction would most likely have been called the *Birkat ha-notzrim*' (*Related Strangers* 180; see further 179-83).

praxis of Judaism, as unacceptable, what came to be referred to as *minut*, and its practitioners as *minim*.[138] Moreover, John 9.22 does indicate some formal decision on the part of synagogue authorities to expel believers in Messiah Jesus, and Justin's *Dialogue with Trypho* certainly indicates active denunciation (cursing) of both Jesus and his followers in the middle of the second century. So even if the dating of the *birkat ha-minim* directed explicitly against Christians is uncertain, the tradition adds strongly to the sense that the early leaders of rabbinic Judaism sought to make a clear dividing line between them and their reconstituted Judaism on the one side and Christians on the other.[139] If we can properly speak of a parting of the ways in this connection, then it was a parting sought as much from the Jewish as from the Christian side.[140] And if the rabbis referred to all Christians as *notzrim*,[141] then it constituted a recognition on the part of the rabbis that Christians were a Jewish heresy. At the very least it is worth noting that the *minim* and the *notzrim* are clear evidence that a good many Jews resisted the rabbis in their attempt to reconstitute Judaism.

c. Christians as *Minim*

Min denotes 'sectarian', in the classic church/sect sociological pattern — that is, the dominant, mainstream, formally recognized body (church) over against the minority, more narrowly focused group (sect). *Minim* is the disparaging term used by the main body for the nonconformist group, with overtones of 'apostate' or 'heretic' gathering quickly around it. In the perspective of rabbinic Judaism (where we find the language of *minim* and *minut*), a represen-

---

138. 'Though attested only much later, there are strong grounds for accepting the basic accuracy of the Bavli's report that the cursing of the heretics was introduced under rabbinic auspices into the Amidah in the late first/early second century C.E.' (Alexander, 'Jewish Believers' 674); Alexander also 'wonders whether the rabbinic version of the Amidah may not have been a response to Jewish Christians attempting to introduce the Paternoster into the synagogue service' (674). 'The struggle between the rabbinic party and the Jewish Christians was probably fought out in the synagogue' (676).

139. See particularly W. Horbury, 'The Benediction of the *Minim* and Early Jewish-Christian Controversy', *JTS* 33 (1982) 19-61; also *Jews and Christians in Contact and Controversy* ch. 2 and 240-42. Cf. Mimouni, *Early Judaeo-Christianity* 133-57; Broadhead, *Jewish Ways* 290-96.

140. Horbury notes that concerns to maintain Jewish unity put limits on communal tolerance from an early period (Paul's persecution, 2 Cor. 11.24, John 9.22) and argues that the *birkat ha-minim* would have been consistent with that (*Jews and Christians* 11-13).

141. Kinzig, 'Nazoraeans' 484-86. 'To the rabbis, Christians were part of a wider heretical tendency in which the existence of "two powers" in heaven was espoused' (Wilson, *Related Strangers* 194).

tative Judaism which had been accorded some recognition from the Roman authorities, those who did not conform to or who dissented from the Judaism being constituted were *minim*. Even though the rabbis did not represent the majority of (Palestinian) Jews for some time, nevertheless they were the most organized body within second-century Palestinian Judaism, and saw themselves as formulating normative Judaism.[142] Integral to that task was the categorization of nonconforming Jews as outsiders, as *minim*. Ironically, the 'separatism' which had been lauded in pre-70 Judaism came to be regarded as a sign of dissent and apostasy in post-70 Judaism. Israel had understood itself as separated for God and with an obligation to separate from the (other) nations (as classically in Lev. 20.24-26); and Pharisees were so named because they were deemed and deemed themselves to be 'separatists' (*perushim*).[143] But with the boot on the other foot, with the most direct heirs of the Pharisees able to regard themselves as the mainstream, a defining feature of *minut* was deemed to be failure or refusal to conform to the new self-expression of Judaism, regarded as separation from (rabbinic) Judaism and thus as *minut*.[144] *Perushim* became one of the terms used for *minim*![145]

The rabbis no doubt designated all non-rabbinic dissent and factionalism as *minut*. But it is sufficiently clear in the sources that only Jews were designated as *minim*,[146] and that prominent among the *minim* were Jewish believers in Jesus.[147] We have already noted the clearest evidence of this in

---

142. In *Brothers Estranged*, Schremer justifiably protests against the suggestion that rabbinic Judaism was the product of an encounter with the competing claims of Christianity, a suggestion which vastly overrates the extent and influence of Christianity in the second century (see further 122-24).

143. See *Beginning from Jerusalem* 472 at nn.248, 249.

144. So particularly Schremer, *Brothers Estranged* chs. 2-3. The dismissive terms 'denote opponents of the rabbinic party, whom the rabbis want to suggest do not belong to the community of Israel' (Alexander, 'Jewish Believers' 668; see also 677-79). See also M. Goodman, 'The Function of Minim in Early Rabbinic Literature', in P. Schäfer, ed., *Geschichte — Tradition — Reflexion; Festschrift für Martin Hengel* vol. I: *Judentum* (Tübingen: Mohr Siebeck, 1996) 501-10, reprinted in *Judaism in the Roman World* 163-73.

145. Alexander, 'Jewish Believers' 666-67.

146. In *Shem. R.* 19.4 it is assumed that *minim* are circumcised; before they go down to Gehinnom their circumcision will be effaced, according to R. Berachjah (Herford, *Christianity* 191-92). As Herford observes: 'It is important to notice that as late as the fourth century [in Palestine] there were Jewish Christians who were being circumcised' (192).

147. See again the discussion in Wilson, *Related Strangers* ch. 6 ('Jewish Reactions to Christianity'). Alexander thinks the relative silence in rabbinic literature on Christianity can be interpreted either as a lack of interest in Christianity (the rabbis were focused almost exclusively on their introverted concerns), or as a polemical device (pointedly to ignore it). He nevertheless concludes 'that the rise of Christianity had a decisive impact on the development of Judaism after 70 — despite the "silence" of the rabbinic sources'. The specific

t. Hull. 2.22-24, evidence from the first half of the second century (§45.7). What was striking about these passages was that acting or teaching in the name of Jesus was itself regarded as *minut*. Jesus was evidently regarded as the author of or as responsible for *minut*. Even to be seen talking to a believer in Jesus was to run the risk of being accused of heresy. So, more or less by definition, any follower of Jesus, any believer in Jesus, would be regarded as a *min*.

Given that the written Gospels were becoming more established and known during the first half of the second century (§44.8), it is of particular interest to note the rabbinic rulings which have been preserved regarding 'the *gilyonim* and the *sifrei minim*', and their status in relation to the already canonical scriptures. The key issue was whether the former 'defiled the hands' (that is, were inspired, sacred), and whether they should be saved from burning (as being of canonical value).[148] The *gilyonim* are frequently taken to be Christian Gospels, though the point is disputed,[149] and the *sifrei minim* probably at least included Christian writings or Christian Torah scrolls in particular.[150] At any rate, the rulings attest a period during which many Jews probably read and prized documents written by Christians.[151] That is, they probably thought of the Christian writings as in the same category as ben Sira. It was the leaders who regarded it as of importance to ban these writings, probably because they disapproved of some of their teachings, but probably also simply because they had been written by Christians.

Here we should probably add that the closing of the Hebrew canon by the rabbis probably had an anti-heretical, that is, anti-Christian motivation: not only the *gilyonim* (Gospels) but the OT apocryphal writings, including ben Sira, known to be valued by the Christians, were not to be regarded as inspired, however much they might have been used.[152]

One of the principal 'heresies' attributed to the *minim* is the belief that there are two powers in heaven, regarded by the rabbis, naturally, as a denial

---

term *Notzrim* (Nazarenes) is rarely used in rabbinic sources ('Jewish Believers' 660-61, 665, 666, 668). See also Schremer (*Brothers Estranged* 8), who repeatedly argues that none of the references to *minim* 'need to be understood as denoting Christians' (e.g. 79, 86, 88). The hermeneutical judgment, however, is one of probability, not of judgments which are 'definite', 'beyond doubt' (104), or 'possible, but nonprovable' (107).

148. *t. Yad.* 2.13; *t. Sabb.* 13(14).5; in Herford, *Christianity* 155-61.

149. '*Gilyonim* is most plausibly explained as a deliberate deformation of the word *euangelion*, "Gospel" (cf. *b. Sabb.* 116a)' (Alexander, 'Jewish Believers' 681); similarly Hengel, *Septuagint* 44-45.

150. Alexander, '"Parting"' 11-15; 'Jewish Believers' 679-82.

151. To what extent were the Jewish-Christian writings noted above in §45.6 valued and used by Jews?

152. Hengel, *Septuagint* 44-47.

of the unity of God (monotheism).[153] The roots of this belief seem to be the reflection and speculation on glorious angelic beings seen in visionary heavenly journeys in apocalyptic literature and probably mystical experience; the name of the angel in *Apoc. Ab.* 10.3, Yaoel, is probably derived from Exod. 23.20-21.[154] Key stimulative passages were Ezekiel's vision of the chariot throne of God (Ezek. 1) and the visions of Isaiah (Isa. 6) and Daniel (Dan. 7 and 10.5-6). There are indications, indeed, that Yohanan ben Zakkai was himself greatly interested in the chariot chapter of Ezek. 1 and probably practised meditation on it (*t. Hag.* 2.1 pars.).[155] Closely related was speculation about exalted human figures, notably Enoch (already in *1 Enoch* 71.14).[156] Most famous is the tradition of the four sages who 'entered the garden (*pardes*)' (*t. Hag.* 2.3-4 pars.). One of them is remembered as an arch-heretic, because in his vision of heaven he mistook the glorious figure sitting on a great throne (Metatron) as a second power in heaven, thus denying the unity of God.[157] One of the starting points of the 'two powers heresy' seems to have been speculation on the plural thrones in Dan. 7.9;[158] even rabbi Akiba, another of the four, is remembered as being rebuked for his speculation regarding the occupant of the second throne.[159]

That this so disturbing event is related to the early decades of the second century, the same period as the *minim* believers in Jesus just referred to, suggests that early Christian reflection about Jesus would have been one of the targets in rabbinic dismissal of the two powers *minut*. For, from the earliest days of the new sect, Jesus had been revered as the one now sitting at God's right hand (Ps. 110.1),[160] on the second throne! And the most obvious candidates for exponents of what the rabbis regarded as the 'two powers heresy' are probably the Christians in their developing christology. The alternative

---

153. A. F. Segal, *Two Powers in Heaven: Early Rabbinic Reports about Christianity and Gnosticism* (Leiden: Brill, 1977), reviews the key passages — *Mekhilta of R. Simeon b. Yohai* p.81 pars.; *Mekhilta Bahodesh* 5; *b. Hagigah* 15a; *Genesis Rabba* 1.14 pars.; *Sifre Deuteronomy* 379; *Sifre Zuta Shalah* 15.30 (chs. 2-5).

154. See particularly I. Gruenwald, *Apocalyptic and Merkabah Mysticism* (Leiden: Brill, 1979); Rowland, *The Open Heaven*.

155. See Neusner, *Yohanan ben Zakkai* 134-40; Gruenwald, *Apocalyptic* 75-86; Rowland, *Open Heaven* 282-305.

156. Convenient surveys of the range of reflection are provided by L. W. Hurtado, *One God One Lord: Early Christian Devotion and Ancient Jewish Monotheism* (Philadelphia: Fortress, 1988); and A. Chester, *Messiah and Exaltation: Jewish Messianic and Visionary Traditions and New Testament Christology* (WUNT 1.207; Tübingen: Mohr Siebeck, 2007).

157. *b. Hag.* 15a; *3 Enoch* 16.

158. Segal, *Two Powers* 33-67, 148-49.

159. *b. Hag.* 14a; *b. Sanh.* 38b.

160. See *Beginning from Jerusalem* 218-21.

hypotheses, that the 'heresy' had in view Gnosticism,[161] or the Roman imperial cult,[162] do not make so much sense of the data, since *minim* were, almost by definition, Jews, since the 'heresy' seems to have grown out of Jewish reflection on divine epiphanies and divine agency, and since the alarm seems to have been raised by the claim (or implication) that there was a second divine power in heaven, rather than by claims that there were many divine powers.[163] It was the Christians who could be particularly targeted for the claim that there is another power in heaven, beside God — that is, the Lord Jesus Christ.[164] So, probably we can identify the two powers *minut* with the second-century Christian teaching about Jesus. We may think particularly of the strong Logos christology which is clearly expressed in the Christian Apologists,[165] though as we shall see, there is evidence in John's Gospel (§46.5c) that early christological claims for Jesus were rousing rabbinic hostility before the end of the first century.[166]

Worth noting here is the case recently made by Daniel Boyarin that Christianity's developing Logos christology should be seen as closely parallel to Judaism's (the Targums') Memra theology.[167] He argues, indeed, that 'Logos theology (and hence trinitarianism) emerges as a difference between Judaism and Christianity only through the activities of heresiologists on both sides of the divide'. Rabbinic theology chose to name what had been the traditional Logos (or Memra) doctrine of God as a heresy, indeed, *the* heresy, the

---

161. Segal addresses this issue and concludes that 'opposition to Christian exegesis preceded opposition to extreme gnostic exegesis.... In all the earliest traditions, the second figure is always seen as a complementary figure, suggesting that the notion of a divine helper who carried God's name is the basic concept which developed into heresy ...' (*Two Powers* 262). Otherwise Schremer, *Brothers Estranged* 84.

162. Schremer, *Brothers Estranged* particularly ch. 5; rabbinic Judaism's discourse of *minut* was born out of the crisis of faith caused by Rome's crushing defeats (ch. 1).

163. 'The rabbis are unlikely to have polytheistic paganism in mind. It is not credible to imagine that pagans would have defended paganism to Jews by citing in detail the Jewish Scriptures. Rather we should be looking for *Jewish* groups who may have argued that the different theophanies of the Hebrew Bible were evidence for a plurality of divine powers.... The precise wording "two powers" seems very precise. At bottom the issue is monotheism' (Alexander, 'Jewish Believers' 685; though see also 701-4).

164. Herford concluded that the doctrine of the two powers in heaven is the Jewish description of the teaching of the Epistle to the Hebrews on the relation of Christ to God (*Christianity* 264-66).

165. Justin, *1 Apol.* 5, 12, 21-23, 32, 36, 46, 63 (see Minns and Jarvis, *Justin* 61-66); Tatian, *Address* 5, 7, 13; Athenagoras, *Plea* 4, 6, 10, 12, 18, 24, 30; Theophilus, *Autolycus* 2.10, 22.

166. Cf. Ashton, *Understanding* 158.

167. Boyarin, *Border Lines* Part II. On the significance of Boyarin's contribution to the debate see above §38.3a.

archetypal 'two powers in heaven' heresy, and thus in effect labelled Christianity a heresy. The Christian heresiologists for their part named Monarchianism and Modalism a heresy by calling it 'Judaism'![168] The claim is provocative, but it makes good sense of the rather confusing christological controversies of the early centuries.[169] More to the present point, it strengthens the view that early christology was an extension of late Second Temple reflection on God and his chief (angelic) agents, and that it was that extension, the claims being made for Jesus in particular, which caused the rabbis to draw back into a more clear-cut understanding of the unity of God. Moreover, if Boyarin is right, the pulling apart of Christianity and Judaism was effected from both sides, the heresiologists on both sides attempting to clarify their identity by drawing a clear border dividing them from the other most direct heir of Second Temple Judaism.

Whatever the finer details, and the many disputed aspects, there seems to be further evidence here of, if not a parting of the ways, at least a conscious concern on the part of those shaping the identities of Christianity and of Judaism to do so by each distancing themselves from the other.[170]

46.5 The New Testament Writings

What can we learn about the strains and stresses between emerging Christianity and emerging Judaism in the post-70 period from the Christian side? In fact, the bulk of the NT writings span the last few decades of the first century. So they are promising sources in which to seek for indications of further stress points between Christianity's Jewish matrix and its developing identity. As we have seen, most of these NT writings have a strongly Jewish character. The letter of James is addressed to 'the twelve tribes who are in the diaspora' (Jas. 1.1); and 1 Peter is not dissimilarly addressed to the 'elect sojourners/exiles of the diaspora' (1 Pet. 1.1). At the other end of the spectrum, in the book of Revelation, the letters to the churches in Smyrna and Philadelphia refer dismissively to 'those who say they are Jews and are not', but are a/the 'synagogue of Satan' (Rev. 2.9; 3.9) — indicating a serious rupture between

---

168. Boyarin, *Border Lines* 92, 145-46. His response to Hurtado is noteworthy: 'I believe that the binitarianism is not specifically Christian; only its association with Jesus is' (283 n.97).

169. Cf. my undeveloped reflections in the Foreword to *Christology in the Making* (London: SCM, ²1989 = Grand Rapids: Eerdmans, 1996) xxx-xxxi.

170. See also Wilson's final 'Overview' (*Related Strangers* 285-301). I responded to his critique of my *Partings of the Ways* (1991) (*Related Strangers* in 285-86) in the Preface to the second edition of *Partings* (2006), particularly xviii-xxi.

at least these particular churches and the synagogues in the same city.[171] Yet in the last members of the Pauline corpus, the Pastoral Epistles, the issues provoked by Paul's insistence on a Jewish gospel for Gentiles seem to have largely faded into the past. But there are plenty of indications that the issues which are at the heart of the parting of the ways question were still more lively in other of the NT writings. We focus on Acts, the Gospels of Matthew and John and the letter to the Hebrews.[172]

a. Acts

With Luke's Acts a case can be made that Luke presents 'the Jews' generally as 'irredeemably resistant to God's will and his offer of salvation', as 'the murderers of Jesus', and as 'by nature and congenitally obstreperous and opposed to the will and purpose of God'.[173] And it is true that in the speeches of Acts Jews are blamed for the death of Jesus,[174] and in the narrative are regularly depicted as hostile to the Christian mission.[175] But many of the references to 'the Jews' are to the Jewish community in places where Paul preached — 'the Jews' of Antioch (13.45, 50), or Iconium (14.4), or Thessalonica (17.5), or Corinth (18.12, 14), or Ephesus (18.28). Besides which there are various positive references to Jews: particularly Jews who believed and responded positively to Paul's message;[176] Jews who speak well of such as Cornelius and Ananias (10.22; 22.12); and Paul affirms his own Jewish identity ('I am a Jew' — 21.39; 22.3). So it is doubtful whether Luke's Acts can legitimately be described as

---

171. *Pace* Koester who suggests that those in view may have been 'Jewish-Christian gnostics' (*Introduction* 2.253), and Wilson who suggests that they were Gentile Judaizers (*Related Strangers* 162-63); but see Satake, *Offenbarung* 159-60. Satake also notes that 'the conflict with the synagogue in Smyrna (2.9) and Philadelphia (3.9) allows the presumption that the separation of the Christian communities from the synagogue and their independence had not long happened' (103). At the same time we should not fail to notice that the 144,000 whose robes have been washed in the blood of the Lamb are identified as 'sealed out of every tribe of the people of Israel' (Rev. 7.4, 14; also 21.12). See particularly P. L. Mayo, *"Those Who Call Themselves Jews": The Church and Judaism in the Apocalypse of John* (PTMS 60; Eugene, OR: Pickwick, 2006), who argues that John viewed the church as God's new spiritual Israel. See also Satake, *Offenbarung* 104-7; and §49.5b below.

172. See also Wilson, *Related Strangers* ch. 2 ('Jews and Judaism in the Canonical Narratives' — Mark, Matthew, Luke-Acts and John). I draw on the following material in 'From the Crucifixion to the End of the First Century', in Shanks, ed., *Partings* ch. 2 (here 45-51).

173. Notably Sanders, *Jews in Luke-Acts* 49, 54, 63; 'Christian enmity towards Jews becomes a public affair' (Wilson, *Related Strangers* 71).

174. Particularly Acts 2.36; 4.10; 5.30; 10.39; 13.27-28.

175. Acts 14.2, 19; 17.5, 13; 18.6; 20.19; 28.19.

176. Acts 13.43; 14.1; 21.20; 28.24.

anti-Jewish. The attempt to shift the responsibility for Jesus' crucifixion from the Romans and to place it entirely on the temple authorities was more an apologetic tactic (to avoid criticism of Roman power) than born of antagonism to Jews as such. And the description that Jews often (but not always) took the lead in resisting a message initially preached in their synagogues was probably not an unfair generalisation of what often took place.[177]

The issue is probably posed most sharply by the final scene of Acts (Paul under house arrest in Rome): whether it marks a decisive and final break between Paul and his fellow Jews, with the gospel now seen as solely for the Gentiles (Acts 28.28).[178] But so to argue would cut across the solution to the problem of Jewish/Gentile fellowship to which Luke had given prominence in Acts 15, and which he presumably presented as the way forward for future Jew/Gentile fellowship in Christian assemblies.[179] Moreover, Luke speaks of a turn to the Gentiles on two occasions prior to Acts 28 (13.46-47; 18.6), and on both occasions Paul continues his normal practice of preaching first in the local Jewish synagogue. There is nothing to indicate that Paul (or Luke!) was altering his tactics in that final scene. Rather, Luke depicts Paul as speaking positively of 'the ancestral customs' (28.17), of 'my nation' (28.19) and of his imprisonment as 'for the sake of the hope of Israel' (28.20). Hardly irrelevant is the fact that the quotation from Isa. 6.9-10 (28.26-27), passing judgment on the deafness and blindness of the people, came as part of Isaiah's own commission, which he then went on to carry out by prophesying to that people. And Luke, we recall, had restricted his account of Paul's time in Rome to his social intercourse and communication with the Jews of Rome (28.17-28). The implication of the closing verses (28.30-31 — Paul 'welcomed all who came to him, proclaiming the kingdom of God and teaching about the Lord Jesus Christ'), therefore, is that the 'all' who came to Paul would have included the only people with whom he had communicated when he first arrived.[180] Luke's picture, then, is entirely consistent with a mission which continued, and should continue, to reach out to both Jews and Gentiles despite repeated Jewish obduracy.[181]

---

177. See further my 'The Question of Anti-semitism in the New Testament Writings', in Dunn, ed., *Jews and Christians* 177-211 (here 187-91).

178. As again argued by Sanders, who quotes regularly from E. Haenchen, 'The Book of Acts as Source Material for the History of Early Christianity', in L. E. Keck and J. L. Martyn, eds., *Studies in Luke-Acts* (Philadelphia: Fortress, 1966) 258-78, Haenchen's judgment that 'Luke has written the Jews off' (278).

179. *Beginning from Jerusalem* 461-69.

180. It is not irrelevant to note that Acts ends with 28.30-31, *not* with 28.26-28.

181. See further my 'The Question of Anti-semitism' 191-95; and *Beginning from Jerusalem* 1006-9 (both with further bibliography); Keener, *Acts* 1.459-91.

An intriguing feature of Acts is the significantly elaborated text of Acts as it appears in what is usually referred to as the 'Western text', as exemplified particularly by Codex Bezae (D). Whether the Western text is a revised text or an interpolated text, the important point for us is that it was the text of Acts possessed and used by many western churches.[182] It is usually dated to the second century, quite likely the first half of the second century.[183] Its relevance here is what has been characterized as the 'anti-Judaic tendencies' of the Western text.[184] This may be something of an overstatement; the Western text may simply have strengthened tendencies already present in the earlier text.[185] In other words, the D-text may be an indication of how the dialogue between Christian and Jew, left suspended at the end of Acts, was being continued through the second century. Was it more like the factional disputes between the 'sects' of Second Temple Judaism,[186] than the blunt dismissals of Judaism which became prominent in Christian writers as the second century progressed?[187] Whatever the precise details of the case, the fact that the Western text strengthens the expression of more negative attitudes to

---

182. The Western text is most clearly attested in the Old Latin translation from the Greek; and also in quotations from certain second- and third-century Christian writers, including Cyprian, Tertullian and Irenaeus.

183. J. H. Ropes, *The Text of Acts* (= Vol. III of *BCAA*, 1926) ccxliv-ccxlv; C. Tuckett, 'How Early Is "the" "Western" Text of Acts?', in T. Nicklas and M. Tilly, eds., *The Book of Acts as Church History* (BZNW 120; Berlin: de Gruyter, 2003) 69-86; J. Rius-Camps and J. Read-Heimerdinger, *The Message of Acts in Codex Bezae: A Comparison with the Alexandrian Tradition* (LNTS, 4 vols.; London: T & T Clark, 2004-2009) 1.10.

184. Particularly E. J. Epp, *The Theological Tendency of Codex Bezae Cantabrigiensis in Acts* (SNTSMS 3; Cambridge University, 1966) ch.2; also 'Anti-Judaic Tendencies in the D-Text of Acts: Forty Years of Conversation', in Nicklas and Tilly, eds., *The Book of Acts as Church History* 111-46. Epp sums up his arguments: 'The D-text portrays the Jews and their leaders as more hostile toward Jesus and assigns them a greater responsibility for his death than does the B-text.... The D-text minimizes the response of the Jews and the importance of Judaism and its institutions to the new faith.... The D-text portrays the Jews, especially their leaders, as more hostile toward the apostles and as persecuting them more vigorously' (*Theological Tendency* 165-66).

185. C. K. Barrett, 'The Acts and the Origins of Christianity', *New Testament Essays* (London: SPCK, 1972) 101-15, observes that 'the chief tendency of the Western Text is simply to exaggerate. The editor does not so much introduce new tendencies into Acts as make clearer and more emphatic tendencies that were already there' (104).

186. 'The negative criticism of Jewish individuals and institutions that is intensified in Codex Bezae is conveyed in terms that were above all meaningful to Jews of the first century.... The book of Acts and more especially the Bezan text of the book, is "hostile" to Jews in the same way that the biblical prophets are hostile to Jews (and it makes little sense to say that the vehemence and insistence of their denunciations were "anti-Jewish")' (Rius-Camps and Read-Heimerdinger, *Message* 1.38).

187. See below §46.6.

Jews does imply that the dialogue was becoming more strained as the second century proceeded.

b. Matthew

More intriguing is Matthew's Gospel. Here there has been a long-running debate as to whether Matthew wrote *intra muros* or *extra muros*, that is, as one who regarded himself and his community as still within the Judaism of the 80s or as already outside its walls.[188] Given its post-70 date, the question can be rephrased: Was Matthew's Gospel written from within the walls already beginning to be built round emerging rabbinic Judaism, 'the hedge of the Sages' (*t. Hull.* 2.23)? Or was the Matthean community already outside the walls, a church (in Antioch's back streets?) sniping at the quite separate (much more established) synagogue across the road or round the corner?[189] The difficulties in getting a firm hold on a question like this are obvious. The frequent schisms within the history of Christianity raise just the same issues. Are Roman Catholic, Orthodox, Protestant, Pentecostal all parts of the same religion, or are they really different religions? And what of Seventh Day Adventists and Mormons? The often internecine rivalry between Sunni and Shia Muslims, like the similar rivalry of Christian denominations in earlier centuries, raises the same issue. When the focal point and chief defining marker of a subgroup or faction within a religion becomes different from the focal point and chief defining marker of another subgroup or faction purportedly within the same religion, should we really be talking about two factions or two different religions?

In this case a major problem with the view that Matthew's community had already separated from Judaism is that the view seems to assume an already clearly defined 'Judaism', a well-bounded identity. But as we noted in the opening remarks of this chapter (§46.1), the 'Judaism' against which Matthew could react was not (yet) clearly defined. The point is so important for the discussion here that it is well worth repeating: in the final decades of the first century we do not as yet have clearly defined 'Judaism' and 'Christianity', but a whole diverse range of religious Jews seeking to maintain and practise

---

188. See particularly Stanton, *A Gospel for a New People* Part II: 'The Parting of the Ways', especially chs. 5-6 and 124-31. 'Matthew's community is Extra-Muros yet still defining itself over against Judaism' (Stanton, *ANRW* II.25.3 1914-15, 1921). See also M. Konradt, *Israel, Kirche und die Völker im Matthäusevangelium* (WUNT 215; Tübingen: Mohr Siebeck, 2007).

189. Davies argues that the *birkat-ha-minim* lay behind Matthew's hostility to the Pharisees/rabbis (*Sermon on the Mount* 275-82). See also Overman, *Matthew's Gospel and Formative Judaism* 48-56.

their religious devotion to God (the God of Israel) more fully. Matthew's community/ies were among these Jews, and though they were more committed to non-Jewish mission, their commission to make disciples of all nations did not exclude Jews and may have been part of their hope for the restoration of Israel and the incoming to Zion of the eschatological Gentile proselytes.[190]

In Matthew's case there are various factors to be considered. Does the fierce polemic against 'scribes and Pharisees' in Matt. 23 indicate a sharp break between the church(es) for which Matthew was writing, and the rabbis attempting to reconstitute Judaism after 70? Or should we rather speak of a continuation of the often equally acerbic disputes of the Second Temple period? Again, does Matthew's repeated reference to 'their synagogues' (distinctive of Matthew) imply a sharp distancing by Matthew of the synagogue from the church(es) for which he was writing? Or are the references simply to the synagogue(s) of the people in the town or area being visited,[191] or to 'their' or 'your synagogues' as distinct from 'our synagogues' (10.17; 23.34)?[192] The prospect of being flogged 'in their synagogues' (10.17; cf. 23.34) implies that Matthew's audiences continued to acknowledge the authority of the synagogue to exert such punishment (cf. 2 Cor. 11.24).[193] Matthew also speaks of 'their scribes' (7.29), but in 8.19 and 23.34 scribes are portrayed in a positive light, and 13.52 may well be a self-reference to Matthew himself as a scribe.[194] So once again the contrast could be simply between *their* scribes' and 'ours'. In other words, the language may be no more than that of subgroups or factions *intra muros* trading blows with each other or speaking somewhat dismissively of the other.

More striking are the passages which seem to indicate that the Jewish people as a whole have been rejected by God.[195] But the first reference (8.11-12) is again more reminiscent of the warnings made within the factionalism of

---

190. See also above §42 at n.291.
191. Matt. 4.23; 9.35; 12.9; 13.54.
192. The assembly of believers-in-Jesus is referred to by James as a 'synagogue' (Jas. 2.2).
193. Hummel, *Auseinandersetzung* 30-31; similarly for Hummel, 'the paying of the temple tax [17.24-27] is an expression of the conscious belongingness to the Jewish community' (32); see also 159-61. 'Coming in the last decades of the first century, Matthew's polemic against "*their* synagogues" cannot be understood as having broken away from the established order of Judaism in Jesus' day. Rather it was generated within the context and convulsions of an emerging new order, with both theological and social implications' (L. M. White, 'Crisis Management and Boundary Maintenance: The Social Location of the Matthean Community', in D. L. Balch, ed., *Social History of the Matthean Community: Cross-Disciplinary Approaches* [Minneapolis: Augsburg Fortress, 1991] 211-47 [here 217]).
194. See above §39 n.99.
195. Particularly Matt. 8.11-12; 21.43; 22.7-8; 23.37-39.

the Second Temple period, that other factions were betraying their covenant obligations and in danger of losing their status as belonging to God's favoured nation.[196] The second reference (21.43), Matthew makes clear, was directed against the chief priests and scribes (21.45), a not untypical prophetic warning that the leaders of the people were failing in their responsibility.[197] And the last two (22.7-8; 23.37-39) are more readily understandable as allusions to the catastrophe of 70 than as a rejection of the people as such.[198]

To press the point, the condemnation in Matthew is not of Israel, but of Israel's leadership, and is reminiscent of Ezekiel's similar condemnation of Israel's leadership (Ezek. 34).[199] The several warnings of rejection echo earlier prophetic warnings to Israel (e.g. Amos 9.7-8). And even the infamous Matt. 27.25 ('All the people answered [Pilate]: "His blood be on us and on our children"') is more an indication of the failure of 'the chief priests and elders' in leading the people astray (27.20), and echoes the terms of God's covenant with Israel — 'visiting the iniquity of the fathers upon the children and the children's children, to the third and fourth generation'.[200] We should not forget that the rebuke, polemic and dismissal characteristic of the in-fighting between the various factions of Second Temple Judaism was much more vitriolic than modern dialogue is accustomed to.[201] And as David Flusser noted, 'all motifs of Jesus' famous invective against the Pharisees in Matt. 23 are also found in rabbinical literature'.[202]

On the more positive side we should recall, for example, that Matthew has retained the strong note that Jesus saw his mission as restricted to Israel (Matt. 10.5-6; 15.24);[203] he insists more strongly than any other of the Evan-

---

196. See e.g. my 'Pharisees, Sinners and Jesus', in *Jesus, Paul and the Law* (London: SPCK, 1990) 61-86 (here 73-77); also *Jesus Remembered* 528-32.

197. Sim, *Gospel of Matthew* 148-49.

198. See further my 'The Question of Anti-semitism' 207-8.

199. See further Saldarini, *Matthew's Christian-Jewish Community* ch. 3; Sim, *Gospel of Matthew* 118-23. Cf. Stanton's analysis of Matthew's 'anti-Jewish polemic' (*A Gospel for a New People* ch. 6).

200. Exod. 20.5; 34.7; Num. 14.18; Deut. 5.9. See further my 'The Question of Anti-Semitism' 208-9; Saldarini, *Matthew's Christian-Jewish Community* 32-34. Overman draws attention to the unnoticed parallels between 27.25 and 1 Sam. 26.9 and 2 Sam. 1.16 (*Matthew's Gospel* 151 n.3). H. Kvalbein, 'Has Matthew Abandoned the Jews?', in Ådna and Kvalbein, eds., *Mission* 45-62, notes that 'in the law it is important that the "whole people" is involved in a curse or a capital punishment' (50-51).

201. L. T. Johnson, 'The New Testament's Anti-Jewish Slander and the Conventions of Ancient Polemic', *JBL* 108 (1989) 419-41: 'By the measure of contemporary Jewish polemic, the NT's slander against fellow Jews is remarkably mild' (441).

202. Cited in my *The Partings of the Ways* (2006) 213 n.82.

203. Luz (private correspondence) refers particularly to 10.23: the mission to Israel

gelists that Jesus was a devout Jew whose faithfulness to the law, or to the spirit of the law, exceeded that of the Pharisees (5.17-20);[204] there is a degree to which he presents Jesus as the new Moses;[205] and the extended mission of the final 'great commission' is to '*all* nations' (28.19).

It is fairly clear, then, and generally agreed, that the communities which Matthew represented or for which he wrote were at loggerheads with the emerging rabbinic leadership of post-70 Judaism.[206] What is not clear, however, is whether this was an in-house debate, an extension of Jesus' own disagreements with various Pharisees, part of the sequence of disagreements not untypical of the factional disputes which marred Second Temple Judaism; and whether we can speak of the rabbinic opponents ejecting the believers-in-Jesus from the synagogue, whether they even had the power or authority to do so. In fact, Matthew himself was obviously strongly motivated to present Jesus as wholly within any boundaries which could/should be drawn round Judaism. Implied is his hope still to win his fellow Jews for Jesus. So far as Matthew himself was concerned, the debate was still *intra muros*.[207] For Matthew and his church the question had not been finally answered. There was still the possibility that 'the people' might come to believe that Jesus had been raised from the dead (27.64). The story of his empty tomb was still being told among the Jews to the time of Matthew (28.15). For Matthew, the church was still in continuity with the 'assembly' (*ekklēsia*) of Israel (16.18; 18.17). Jesus' twelve disciples were still expected to sit on thrones judging the twelve tribes of Israel (19.28). Matthew presumably still held out the gospel as hope for the lost sheep of the house of Israel (10.5-6).[208] He still regarded Jesus' fulfillment and interpretation of the law as guidance for disciples (5.17-20). Even if the (Yavnean) rabbis regarded Matthew's church as outsiders, Matthew still evi-

---

continues to the parousia (see also his *Matthäus* 2.113-17)! Note also Matt. 18.17 cited in §42 n.290.

204. The antitheses of Matt. 5 are hardly a critique of the law but a deepening of it (see further §42.3d).

205. See §42 n.223 above.

206. So particularly Davies, *Sermon on the Mount* 256-315. On the significance of Yavneh note also Overman, *Matthew's Gospel* 38-43. Luz notes some striking similarities between Yohanan and Matthew (*Matthäus* 1.98-99).

207. A. F. Segal, 'Matthew's Jewish Voice', in Balch, ed., *Social History* 3-37, proposes 'that the hostility to Pharisees one sees in the First Gospel provides one piece of evidence that Christians were still concerned with what was happening in Jewish communities and synagogues, still found there, and greatly vexed by some of the positions they heard from Christian Pharisees inside and outside of synagogues' (35).

208. Stanton notes that Matthew makes more of the similarities between Jesus and John the Baptist (*Gospel for a New People* 81). Would that be because the Baptist was more universally admired in Jewish communities than Jesus?

dently regarded himself as an insider, his church still *intra muros*,²⁰⁹ probably still understanding itself as a 'sect' within the religion of Israel, like the 'sects' of Second Temple Judaism (Pharisees, Sadducees, Essenes),²¹⁰ and like them hoping to reconfigure Israel in accord with the fresh understanding of Israel's destiny which had been (differently) revealed to them.²¹¹ The defining/ excluding walls of rabbinic Judaism were being built, but were still far from complete. The pressure for a 'parting of the ways' was coming from the side of the Yavnean rabbis. But whatever the post-70 rabbis wanted to bring about, for Matthew himself the ways had not yet parted.

c. John

Still more intriguing is the Gospel of John.²¹² John seems to go out of his way to present the traditional icons of the religion of Israel as passé. In particu-

---

209. Dunn, 'The Question of Anti-semitism' 209; similarly e.g. Kilpatrick, *Origins* ch. 6; Bornkamm: 'the struggle with Israel is still a struggle within its own walls' (*Tradition and Interpretation in Matthew* 39); Kümmel: 'his opposition is [not to Judaism but] to unbelieving Judaism' (*Introduction* 117); Schnelle: 'a liberal Hellenistic Diaspora Jewish Christianity that had engaged in Gentile mission for some time' (*History* 221; see further 236-37); and of recent detailed studies, particularly Overman, *Matthew's Gospel and Formative Judaism* 141-61; Saldarini, *Matthew's Christian-Jewish Community* particularly ch. 2; and Sim, *Gospel of Matthew* 142-63 — 'an internal Jewish debate . . . The religion of the Matthean community was not Christianity but Judaism' (163); J. D. Kingsbury sums up a general agreement of the papers in Balch, ed., *Social History*, that 'the Matthean community is best thought of as a sect within Judaism' (265). Luz's counter judgment, that 'Matthew does not reckon with non-Christian Jewish readers of his Gospel', does not give enough weight to what he also recognizes to be the Matthean community's 'double' or 'split identity' (*Matthäus* 1.96-98). Hagner's depiction of a community which shared two worlds is probably nearer the mark (*Matthew* lxix-lxxi); he notes that in Jesus' saying about the new wine and wineskins, Matthew adds the ending: 'and so both are preserved' (Matt. 9.17) (lxxi).

210. Perhaps more like a modern Seventh Day Adventist community in relation to modern Christianity than a Mormon community. 'When Martin Luther began protesting against Roman Catholicism, he had no intention of founding a new church — but his attack was not the less vigorous for that' (Davies and Allison, *Matthew* 1.23).

211. A. J. Saldarini, 'The Gospel of Matthew and Jewish-Christian Conflict', in Balch, ed., *Social History* 39-61: 'One cannot be deviant unless one is a member of the community. . . . Matthew is deviant not because of disagreement with a normative Judaism but because he is a minority against the majority and because he recommends a more fundamental reorientation of the tradition than many other Jewish movements' (48-50).

212. For extensive discussion see R. Bieringer et al., eds., *Anti-Judaism and the Fourth Gospel* (Assen: Royal Van Gorcum, 2001). E.g., R. A. Culpepper, 'Anti-Judaism in the Fourth Gospel as a Theological Problem for Christian Interpreters' (68-91), concludes that 'John is both thoroughly Jewish and trenchantly anti-Jewish' (90); but S. Motyer,

lar, John interprets the disputed saying of Jesus, 'Destroy this temple and in three days I will raise it up', as a reference to 'the temple of his [Jesus'] body', which his disciples only realized after Jesus' resurrection (John 2.19-22). The implication is obvious, that for his first disciples, Jesus himself had replaced the temple. In the same spirit is the preceding story, of Jesus transforming the water reserved for the Jewish rites of purification into high quality wine (2.6-10). Similarly, in the encounter with the Samaritan woman, the water from Jacob's well is contrasted unfavourably with the living water which Jesus offers the woman (4.6-15). And, not least, in the great bread of life discourse, Jesus far outshines Moses, since Moses only gave bread which provided temporary nourishment, whereas Jesus himself is the bread from heaven which gives life to the world (6.32-35, 48-51, 58). All these, however, are claims drawn up within Israel's own terms of reference and hopes for the future. So are they to be interpreted as a disparagement of Israel's icons, a distancing of the Jesus movement from its native Judaism? Or are they rather invitations to the Jews of John's time to see in Jesus the fulfillment of Israel's prophetic visions and hopes?

The issue is sharply posed by John's talk of 'the Jews'. For 'the Jews' are regularly depicted as hostile to Jesus, and in John 8 in particular, 'the Jews' are scarified by Jesus as children of the devil, not children of Abraham (8.39-44). It is easy to draw from this that from John's perspective 'the Jews' are sharply to be distinguished from Jesus and his disciples; the ways have already parted between the Johannine believers-in-Jesus and the Jews.[213] However, the situation reflected is not quite so clear-cut. For one thing, in many passages 'the Jews' seems to be a way of referring to the Jewish authorities.[214] And in many other references 'the Jews' seem to denote the Jewish/common people, 'the crowd'.[215] What is particularly striking about the central section of the Gospel is that this crowd of Jews is divided about Jesus, who he is, and whether he should be believed in, some of them explicitly coming so to believe.[216] In this section a strong impression is given that 'the Jews'/the crowd are divided, and

---

'The Fourth Gospel and the Salvation of Israel: An Appeal for a New Start' (92-110), argues that the Fourth Gospel cannot fairly be charged with hatred of these Judean Jews who opposed Jesus' (107-8).

213. Wilson notes 'the insidious, indiscriminate use of "the Jews" in chapters 18-19 to describe those primarily responsible for Jesus' death' (*Related Strangers* 75; also 80).

214. John 5.10, 15, 16, 18; 7.1, 13; 8.48, 52, 57(?); 9.18, 22; 10.31, 33; 11.8. In 5.15; 7.13; 9.18, 22; 11.8 an individual or individuals who are themselves Jews are distinguished from 'the Jews'.

215. John 6.41, 52; 7.11-12, 15, 31, 35; 8.22, 31; 10.19, 24; 11.19, 31, 33, 36, 42, 45, 54; 12.9, 11.

216. John 6.52; 7.11-12, 31, 35, 40-44; 10.19; 12.11, 17-19; 12.34. See also Lincoln, *John* 70-72.

§46.5 *The Parting of the Ways*

have not yet made up their minds with regard to Jesus[217]— 'the Jews' = 'the crowd' in the middle between 'the Jews' = the authorities and the disciples. All this raises the question whether John saw this still to be the case, that although 'the Jews' (authorities) were set against Jesus and his disciples, 'the Jews' (the crowd) were still open to persuasion.[218]

The question is posed afresh by the unique Johannine use of the term *aposynagōgos*, 'expelled from the synagogue'. The parents of the blind man 'were afraid of the Jews; for the Jews had already agreed that anyone who confessed Jesus to be the Messiah should be put out of the synagogue' (9.22); 'many, even of the rulers, believed in him, but because of the Pharisees did not confess it lest they be put out of the synagogue' (12.42); Jesus' disciples should anticipate being put out of the synagogue (16.2).[219] As already noted, this distinctive Johannine feature has invited the hypothesis that the *birkat ha-minim*, 'the blessing (or malediction) against the heretics,' had already been pronounced by the post-70 rabbinic authorities.[220] The hypothesis is problem-

---

217. It was C. H. Dodd who pointed out that what he called 'the Book of Signs' (ch. 3-12) is constructed with a view to bringing out the divisive effect of Christ, the escalating process of separation (*krisis* — 3.19; 5.22, 24, 27, 29, 30; 7.24; 8.16; 12.31) and division (*schisma* — 7.43; 9.16; 10.19) which was the inevitable effect of the light shining (3.19-21) (*Interpretation* 352-53). See also Ashton, *Understanding* 229-32; M. Theobald, 'Das Johannesevangelium — Zeugnis eines synagogalen "Judenchristentums"?', *Studien* 204-53 (particularly 225-26).

218. For a recent discussion, with bibliography, see W. E. S. North, '"The Jews" in John's Gospel: Observations and Inferences', in J. G. Crossley, ed., *Judaism, Jewish Identities and the Gospel Tradition: Essays in Honour of Maurice Casey* (London: Equinox, 2010) 206-26. She concludes: John's usage 'stems from his desire to promote his own group as an alternative and authentic form of Judaism' (221). Von Wahlde suggests that in the first edition of the Gospel 'Jews' denoted 'Judeans', whereas in the second edition 'the Jews' denoted 'official Judaism' (*Gospel and Letters of John* 1.51-52, 70-73, 145-49). In Bieringer et al., eds., *Anti-Judaism*, six essays are devoted to the subject of 'the Jews'. E.g., H. J. de Jonge, 'The "Jews" in the Gospel of John' (239-59), suggests that the Jews against whom John polemicizes are Christians who do not share John's high christology (258); and M. C. de Boer, 'The Depiction of "the Jews" in John's Gospel: Matters of Behavior and Identity' (260-80), concludes that '"The Jews" are those who claim to be arbiters of a genuinely Jewish identity', a claim which caused Johannine Jewish Christians 'to abandon the term "the Jews" for themselves as Jewish disciples of Jesus even as they sought in their own way to remain faithful to Moses and the scriptures of Israel', noting also that the Nazoreans apparently did the same (279 and n.64).

219. An appropriate reminder may be that there is no indication of such expulsions of believers in Jesus from synagogues in pre-70 Palestine. J. Bernier, Aposynagōgos *and the Historical Jesus in John: Rethinking the Historicity of the Johannine Expulsion Passages* (Leiden: Brill, 2013), argues implausibly that the Johannine expulsion passages could describe events that occurred during Jesus' lifetime.

220. See above §46.4b. The thesis that the *birkat-ha-minim* lay behind John 9.22 was

atic since, apart from anything else, the specific reference to the Christians (the *Notzrim*) was most likely a later addition to the *birkat ha-minim*.[221] Even so, it is likely that Jewish believers-in-Jesus were early on regarded as *minim* by the progenitors of rabbinic Judaism.[222] And we need not settle the issue of when the *birkat ha-minim* began to be said and in what form in rabbinic synagogues, to acknowledge the testimony of John 9.22 that some synagogue authorities (in Syria-Palestine) were already, before the end of the first century, acting to expel Jewish believers in Jesus from the synagogues which they controlled. However local the historical context of John 9.22, it provides a further indication that the early pressures towards a parting of the ways came primarily from the side of the Jewish/rabbinic authorities.

The other most relevant feature of John's Gospel at this point is the strong indication of what it is that the post-70 Jewish authorities (referred to in the Gospel) objected to so strongly in regard to the Jewish believers in Jesus. A negative reaction to the assertions mentioned in the opening paragraph can certainly be inferred.[223] But it is clear from John that it was the Christian claims for Jesus which seem to have become, it would appear for the first time, a breaking-point for some/many Jews. This is clearest in two passages:

- John 5.18, where 'the Jews' seek to kill Jesus 'because he . . . was calling God his own Father, thereby making himself equal to God';
- John 10.30-31, where 'the Jews' take up stones to stone Jesus in response to Jesus asserting that 'The Father and I are one'.

In all the earlier tensions caused by early Christian beliefs in Jesus, there are no indications that any provoked such a fierce reaction from Jewish authorities.[224] But here claims being made for Jesus by his followers seem to have been recognized for the first time as a threat to the unity of God, to the fundamental Jewish creed (*Shema*) that God is one (Deut. 6.4).[225]

Why the claims for Jesus made by the first Christians did not seem to

---

given influential statement by Martyn, *History and Theology in the Fourth Gospel*. See also Wengst, *Bedrängte Gemeinde* ch. 5.

221. See above n.137.
222. See above nn.138-139.
223. Note particularly John 5.10, 16, 18; 7.1.
224. The negative responses to Paul's christology are indicated in 1 Cor. 1.23 and implied in Gal. 3.13; no negative response is indicated or hinted at in reference to Paul's affirmation of the *Shema* in the same breath as his affirmation of Jesus as Lord in 1 Cor. 8.4-6 (see *Beginning from Jerusalem* 339-40, 579-80, 804-5; also *Did the First Christians Worship Jesus?* 113-16).
225. Similarly Theobald, 'Das Johannesevangelium', *Studien* 249-51.

create a negative reaction from Jewish authorities prior to the post-70 reaction indicated in John's Gospel, is a question insufficiently asked, but is probably answered by what was referred to earlier as the chief reason why the Christians came to be regarded as *minim* (§46.4c). For so much of John's christology can be best seen in the context of late Second Temple Jewish reflection on divine epiphanies and divine agency.[226] Note particularly:

- The Wisdom/Logos christology of John 1.1-18 is essentially of a piece with the Wisdom theology of Jewish Wisdom tradition (Prov. 8; Sir. 24; Bar. 3-4) and the Logos theology of Philo;[227]
- God appearing in human form (Ezek. 1.26) is not so very far from the thought of God appearing in human flesh (John 1.14, 18);
- John 3.13 appears to be a direct rebuttal of claims to revelation received in heavenly journeys of apocalyptic vision or mystical experience;[228]
- The Son of Man descending/ascending (3.13; 6.62) is an extension of the reflection stimulated by Dan. 7.13-14 as indicated also in the *Similitudes of 1 Enoch* (37-71) and *4 Ezra* 13;
- The motif of Jesus the one 'whom God sent' (6.29) plays on the theme of 'the prophet who has come into the world' (6.14) but transcends the traditional role of Moses and prophet;[229]
- The famous 'I am' sayings of John's Gospel[230] and the claims to Jesus' pre-existence (as in John 8.58) would not ring oddly to anyone familiar with the 'I' claims of Wisdom.[231]

So, it was not that the Johannine christology expressed a theological reflection which was foreign to the Judaism of the period. It was rather that the reflections of the believers in Jesus were pressing the earlier lines of reflection too far.[232] The rabbinic reaction against revelatory claims derived from apocalyptic vision or mystical practice included also a reaction against the christology put forward in John's Gospel. And presumably it was the christological claims

---

226. See my *Partings* §11.6; and earlier, 'Let John Be John: A Gospel for Its Time', in P. Stuhlmacher, ed., *The Gospel and the Gospels* (Grand Rapids: Eerdmans, 1991) 293-322.

227. See my *Christology* chs. 6-7; and above §43.1c(3).

228. First noted by H. Odeberg, *The Fourth Gospel* (Uppsala, 1929) 72-98.

229. See further W. A. Meeks, *The Prophet-King: Moses Traditions and the Johannine Christology* (NovTSupp 14; Leiden: Brill, 1967); Bühner, *Der Gesandte und sein Weg*.

230. See above §43 n.7.

231. See e.g. Brown, *John* 1.cxxii-cxxv; Scott, *Sophia and the Johannine Jesus* ch. 3; McGrath, *John's Apologetic Christology*, particularly ch. 5.

232. *4 Ezra* 8.20-21 seems to be directed against claims to be able to see and describe God's throne (Rowland, *Open Heaven* 54-55); and there are explicit cautionary notes concerning the chariot chapter (Ezek. 1) in the Mishnah (*m. Hag.* 2.1; *m. Meg.* 4.10).

made about Jesus which was the principal factor which predisposed post-70 rabbis to determine that these Jewish believers-in-Jesus were *minim*, and consequently to be expelled from the synagogue. Even then the matter was not final, since, as already indicated, it is quite likely that the second-century christological controversies were in part at least controversies between a Christianity and a Judaism which were attempting to define themselves over against each other.[233] The point here is that John's Gospel indicates that this reaction was already under way before the end of the first century.

d. Hebrews

Finally we should consider the letter to the Hebrews. The main theme of this letter is twofold. It presents the tabernacle and cult which Moses was commanded to set up during Israel's wilderness wanderings as copies and shadows of the way into the divine presence in heaven. The instruction to Moses to furnish the tabernacle 'according to the pattern/archetype shown you in the mountain'[234] quite naturally suggested a link to Plato's conception of the heavenly world of ideas that form the archetypes of which earthly equivalents are but imperfect copies,[235] a foreshadowing of 'the good things to come' (Heb. 10.1).[236] Particularly in mind was the Day of Atonement ceremony, the only day of the year when the High Priest could enter into the Holy of Holies in the tabernacle where the presence of God was most real (Lev. 16). Here the writer's claim is clear, that what happened to Christ, his death and his exaltation to heaven, was the real enactment of what in the earthly Jewish cult and the Day of Atonement ritual was a mere copy and shadow (Heb. 9.6-14). That is, Jesus was the real High Priest; Jesus' death was the real Day of Atonement sacrifice; and his entry into heaven was the entry into the divine presence itself (9.24-26; 10.10-12). His priesthood was unique — an order of priesthood, the order of the mysterious figure Melchizedek (Gen. 14.17-20; Ps. 110.4), a priestly order for which only one who was 'without father, without mother, without genealogy, having neither beginning of days nor end of life . . . a priest for ever' could qualify (Heb. 7.3). Only Jesus the Son of God (1.2-3) was thus

---

233. See above at §46.4c. Schnelle maintains, with supprt from Hengel, that the early 'conflicts with the Jewish environment . . . no longer play a decisive role for the Johannine school at the *current* situation when the Gospel of John was composed' (*History* 480). But the earlier debates transposed in the Johannine tradition into christological issues certainly did play a decisive role in the current situation of the Johannine community.
234. Exod. 25.40; cf. 1 Chron. 28.19.
235. Heb. 8.5; 9.23-24.
236. See above §39.3c.

qualified for that priesthood. Which meant that his sacrifice had a similarly eternal character, which meant that what it achieved was once-for-all (*hapax*) and valid for all time (9.26-28). This meant that all other sacrifices had been made redundant and were no longer necessary (9.8-10; 10.1-4). For Christ's entry into the real Holy of Holies, before the heavenly throne of God, meant that the way into the very presence of God had been opened up once for all, so that all who came in Christ's train could 'draw near to the throne of grace' for themselves, without any further priestly mediation.[237]

As noted in §39.3c, the date of the letter is disputed. But it looks as though it was written for Jewish believers ('to the Hebrews') grieving over loss of the Jerusalem temple,[238] though perhaps also for Gentile God-fearers who had initially been attracted to Judaism by its temple ritual. This would explain why the letter-writer focuses on the tabernacle. He does not make his case on the grounds that the temple had been destroyed. He goes to the scriptural basis and the instructions which governed both the pre-temple tabernacle and the two temples which followed. By so doing, he could focus entirely on the scriptural blueprint for the priestly and sacrificial cult, without any distraction regarding the geographical site and what had happened there. The only Jerusalem he was concerned with was the heavenly Jerusalem (12.22).

The consequences for relations between what Jesus had brought into effect and traditional Judaism were substantial. By limiting the function of the Jerusalem cult to the past, to what was merely a copy, indeed, an imperfect copy and (fore)shadowing of the heavenly reality, the writer was in effect dismissing the traditional cult as passé and finished. Christ's sacrifice was the real thing for which Israel's traditional cult had only prepared. Christ had once-for-all and for ever opened the way into the very presence of God in heaven, for others to follow and 'draw near' — in pointed contrast to Israel's high priest who alone could enter into the Holy of Holies, and only on one day each year, and then have to withdraw back to where the veil intruded. Consequently there was no need for that frustratingly only annual ceremony to be endlessly repeated. The 'new covenant' for which Israel had longed[239] was now in operation and had made the first covenant 'antiquated; and what is antiquated and growing old will soon disappear' (8.13). Christ was the High Priest who made all priests, all orders of priesthood, redundant (no one else could qualify for the Melchizedek priesthood). Christ's sacrifice made the

237. The fact that its readers could now 'draw near' (*proserchesthai*) to the throne of grace, to God, to the heavenly realities, through the veil into the heavenly Holy of Holies each for him/herself, to the heavenly Jerusalem (Heb. 4.16; 7.25; 10.1, 19-22; 11.6; 12.22; also 6.19-20; 7.19; 9.24), sums up the letter's argument and plea.

238. See above at §39 n.260.

239. Heb. 7.22; 8.7-12; 9.15; 12.24.

continuation of a sacrificial cult unnecessary. The Christianity which Hebrews promulgated superseded the Judaism of tabernacle and temple.

For most commentators, this sustained argument sounded the first note of the 'supersessionism' which, from the second century onwards, became mainstream Christianity's attitude to Judaism.[240] The issue has focused particularly on Heb. 8.13, regularly translated in terms stronger than used just above: 'In speaking of a new (covenant) he has made the first (covenant) *obsolete*. And what is *obsolete* and growing old is near *destruction*'.[241]

But should Hebrews be read in quite such a vitriolic and dismissive way?[242]

1. The critique is very narrowly focused — on the rubrics and practice of the ancient tabernacle cult, and by implication on the Jerusalem cult of Second Temple Judaism. It may take a parting swipe at Israel's food laws (13.9),[243] but there is nothing of Paul's critique of circumcision or of the law, and nothing of Matthew's polemic against Jewish leaders. Is 'supersessionism' or replacement theology the best way to describe a call to 'run the race' where it is the heroes of Israel's faith (11.4-40) who make up the 'great cloud of witnesses' (12.1) cheering on those to whom the letter is addressed?

2. Critique of the Jerusalem cult was hardly unusual within the Judaisms of the period.[244] Qumran in particular regarded the Jerusalem cult as so corrupt that it could be disregarded in favour of the participation in the worship of the angels experienced in the sect's own worship.[245] And the Yavnean rabbis quickly found it necessary to put forward alternatives to the Jerusalem sacrifices while the temple site remained desolate.[246] So even a

---

240. See below §46.6, particularly on the *Epistle of Barnabas* and Melito of Sardis (§§46.6b and h). 'There can be little doubt that the negative impulses of the author would have encouraged his readers . . . to form a clear and unambiguous judgment: Judaism is defunct, because it has been surpassed' (Wilson, *Related Strangers* 122-23).

241. BDAG 155, 751 (my emphasis); contrast Attridge — 'In speaking of a new covenant he has made the first one antiquated, and that which becomes antiquated and aged is close to vanishing' (*Hebrews* 225).

242. In what follows I draw in particular on R. B. Hays, '"Here We Have No Lasting City": New Covenantalism in Hebrews', in Bauckham et al., eds., *Hebrews and Christian Theology* 151-73.

243. Though see Attridge, *Hebrews* 394-96.

244. Hays ('No Lasting City' 154 n.9) cites S. J. D. Cohen, 'The Significance of Yavneh: Pharisees, Rabbis, and the End of Jewish Sectarianism', *HUCA* 55 (1984) 27-53: 'A common feature of Jewish sectarianism is the polemic against the Temple of Jerusalem: its precincts are impure, its cult profane, and its priests illegitimate' (43).

245. See particularly C. Newsom, *The Songs of the Sabbath Sacrifice* (Atlanta: Scholars, 1985).

246. According to the *Fathers According to Rabbi Nathan* A4, when confronted by R. Joshua lamenting over the destruction of the temple, 'That this, the place where the

late first-century critique of the tabernacle cult and suggestion of a superior alternative, in terms which both Alexandrian Jews and Jewish apocalyptists would recognize and potentially find attractive, should not be read as though it was a mid-second-century Christian writing.[247] The vision of what was now to be set over against the Jerusalem cult was unique within the factionalism of late Second Temple Judaism, but could still be regarded and regard itself as a necessary part of the reassessment which all those who had looked to the Jerusalem temple as the centre of their faith and religious practice were now called on to make.

3. In building on the promise of a 'new covenant' the writer quotes Jer. 31.31-34 at length — including the fact that the promise of the new covenant is made to 'the house of Israel', a promise that 'I will be their God and they will be my people' (8.10). At no point does the writer indicate that the new covenant is no longer with (ethnic) Israel.[248] 'Nowhere does Hebrews suggest that the Jewish people have been replaced by a new and different people of God'.[249] The writer looks for a continuation, a realization of a long foreshadowed reality, a transformed perspective on long hallowed practice (though one for which Israel's scriptures should have prepared Israel); but not really for a 'replacement' of a Jewish Israel by another (Gentile) Israel.

4. The issue can be summed up in the translation of 8.13. Did the writer regard the Jerusalem cult as 'obsolete' or simply as old — the logical antonym to the *new* covenant, but with no more dismissive tone than Jeremiah's? And did he indicate or imply that the cultic practice of the Jerusalem temple was 'near to destruction', or near to 'disappearance'? 'Destruction', of course would hardly be inappropriate in a post-70 context. But Harold Attridge notes that the term (*aphanismos*), which is used only here in the NT, 'recalls tech-

---

iniquities of Israel were atoned for, is laid waste!', Yohanan ben Zakkai replied, 'My son, be not grieved; we have another atonement as effective as this. And what is it? It is acts of loving kindness, as it is said "I desire mercy and not sacrifice" (Hos. 6.6)'; see also Neusner, *Yohanan ben Zakkai* 113-14; Levine, 'Judaism' 152.

247. Hays, 'No Lasting City' 162.

248. Hays can even argue that 'in light of the pervasive "new exodus" imagery throughout Hebrews, it seems more probable that Hebrews represents a form of Jewish "restoration eschatology"'. . . . 'Hebrews is no more supersessionist than Jeremiah' ('No Lasting City' 161-62, 165). Luz (in private correspondence) thinks it self-evident and important to note that Hebrews speaks of a new covenant, but not of a new people of God.

249. Hays, 'No Lasting City' 154; 'The Qumran texts . . . provide a clear precedent for the use of "new covenant" language by a Jewish sectarian community to describe their own system of teachings and practices over against other Jewish interpretative options' (161). See CD 6.18-19; 8.20-21; 19.33-34; 20.11-13. Hays refers to the discussion by S. Lehne, *The New Covenant in Hebrews* (JSNTS 44; Sheffield: JSOT, 1990) 43-54.

nical legal language for a law that has fallen out of use'.[250] In which case the term could simply be another way of making the new/old contrast: when the new has come, for which the house of Israel has long longed, the old can be left behind; 'it belongs to the realm of the earthly-transitory'.[251] Who would want to stick with the old when the full effectiveness of the new is open to them? Is the claim that the hope and ideal of Israel's cult has been realized a denigration of the cult, or, like Jesus' teaching on individual commandments of the law (according to Matt. 5), a pressing through to the deepest significance of the cult? And was that so very different, in principle, from the way in which the Yavnean rabbis responded to their now destroyed temple cult?

How are we to read a document which has been read since early days in the context of a Christian *adversus Judaeos* tradition, but which was written before that tradition became established and which may not have been intended to be read as so antipathetic to and disdainful of the Jerusalem temple cult?[252] The fact that Hebrews still worked with the imagery of priest and cult, and on the blueprint of the Torah tabernacle (Heb. 8.5), is a reminder of just how Jewish was the mental and social world which the writer and the recipients of his letter inhabited — a reminder too that the Torah's language and praxis gave the writer the language he needed to express his beliefs about Jesus and the significance of his death and exaltation. Does the way the letter came to be read cancel out a reading which can make serious claim to be the reading intended? Would traditionalist Jews wrestling with the consequences of the temple's destruction for their assurance of sins forgiven (their conscience)[253] have found the transition in perspective to the heavenly reality, imaged by the traditional but now desolate cult, so offensive? Be that as it may, the fact that doubts remained over the apostolicity of Hebrews for some centuries in the West[254] could suggest that many Christians were uncomfortable with what could so easily come across as a dismissive attitude to what still counted as Christianity's mother faith and praxis. And, ironically, the fact that Christianity itself reverted to being a religion which came to focus in a sacrifice-offering priest could also imply that the vision of Hebrews was too unsettling for many Christians as well.

---

250. Attridge, *Hebrews* 228-29; further J. Moffatt, *Hebrews* (ICC; Edinburgh: T & T Clark, 1924) 111.

251. Weiss, *Hebräer* 447.

252. 'It is appropriate to talk about Christian anti-Judaism only at a later period when statements from the NT were detached from their context and were misinterpreted as anti-Judaic' (Lane, *Hebrews* 1.cxxvi).

253. See again §39 at n.260.

254. See e.g. von Campenhausen, *The Formation of the Christian Bible* 232-33.

e. Christian Anti-Judaism?

It will not have escaped notice that most of the material reviewed above has raised the question for many whether the NT is anti-Jewish, or even anti-semitic, or expresses such views and attitudes.[255] The discussion provides (I hope) sufficient considerations against the appropriateness of a Yes answer to that question. The key consideration is the vital importance of setting these several late first-century texts (as also Christian writings before and after) in their historical context. There is all the difference in the world between two well-established institutions (or ethnic groups, or religions) despising and dismissively rubbishing long-term opponents, and two groups beginning to emerge within the same heritage struggling to clarify their identities in relation to each other. It is, of course, the latter which applies in this case. Where what became known as 'Christianity' and '(rabbinic) Judaism' were only beginning to emerge in the distinctiveness of their identities, the polemic and name-calling have more the character of the sharp tensions between the different factions of Second Temple Judaism. The embarrassment of the anti-Jewish or anti-semitic charge against the NT for Christians only arises when the historical character and context of the NT writings are forgotten or ignored.[256] When, for example, Rev. 2.9 ('synagogue of Satan') becomes an excuse for a Chrysostom to condemn synagogues as dwelling places of demons,[257] or present-day Christian sermons take a text like John 8.44 as a timeless 'word of God' and thus as a continuing judgment against 'the Jews', then the anti-Jewish and anti-semitic sentiments can be justly attributed to the preacher, not to the text.

In short, in late first-century Christian literature (post-70 NT writings) there are a number of indications of the strains and stresses between the Jewish believers in Jesus and the other Jewish survivors of the catastrophe of the first Jewish revolt. There are clear indications that the Christians pressed for a fresh understanding of faith and practice in the light of what had happened to Jesus the Christ, but saw themselves as still operating within the terms and categories given in Second Temple Judaism. And there are several indications

---

255. See again my 'The Question of Anti-semitism', with bibliography there.

256. I may refer to my contribution to Bieringer et al., eds., *Anti-Judaism and the Fourth Gospel* — 'The Embarrassment of History: Reflections on the Problem of "Anti-Judaism" in the Fourth Gospel' 47-67. See also Ulrich Luz's sensitive consideration of 'Anti-Judaism in the Gospel of Matthew as a Historical and Theological Problem: An Outline', *Studies in Matthew* 243-61.

257. Chrysostom, 'Homily 1 Against the Jews' 6 (in Meeks and Wilken, *Jews and Christians in Antioch* 97-98).

that the Yavnean rabbis began a process of redefinition of Judaism which increasingly marginalized and shut out Jewish believers in Jesus as well as other Second Temple sectarians. But to speak of a parting of the ways, even if the imagery were fully acceptable, (or of Christian anti-Judaism) is at this stage far from being justified.

46.6 Second-Century Christian Literature

A striking feature immediately meets us when we turn to the Apostolic Fathers and the Apologists. In §43 and §44 there was much to be discussed in regard to the influence of the Jesus tradition. In §45 there was equally much to be noted regarding the Jewish character of the understanding of Christianity which the documents contained. But when our attention turns to evidence of strains and breaches between emerging Christianity and emerging (rabbinic) Judaism, the evidence is much more limited. For example, *1 Clement* is wholly absorbed in dealing with the internal problems among the Corinthian believers. Clement never mentions 'Jews', and his references to 'Israel' are all historical. Since *1 Clement* must reflect in some degree the late first-century contexts within which the churches in Rome and Corinth were functioning (§40.1a), the lack of any indication that relations with Jews or between Jewish and Gentile Christians were a factor in these contexts is not of a little interest. Similarly, the *Shepherd* of Hermas reflects situations of social conflict, almost certainly in Rome itself,[258] but again there is no indication that relations with Jews or between Jewish and Gentile Christians were a factor. We cannot deduce from this silence, of course, that relations were positive, or that church and synagogue were in harmony, with overlapping membership. But certainly the lack of any indication that ways were parting or that in Rome at any rate synagogue and church were in competition or in sullen dismissal of the other, should make us pause before rushing to conclusions on the evidence about to be examined, where, for some Christians, Jews were the 'other', and where antagonism and confrontation are explicit.

In the Apostolic Fathers we need focus only on two of the letters of Ignatius and the *Epistle of Barnabas*. The letter of Polycarp, like the other letters of Ignatius, adds nothing to the present inquiry. It is true that the *Martyrdom of Polycarp* accuses 'the Jews' in particular for their part in Polycarp's burning (13.1; 17.2; 18.1), which certainly indicates a high degree of rupture and hostility between synagogue and church in Smyrna, though it is reminiscent of the hostility displayed by 'the Jews' in the Acts accounts of Paul's mission, and

---

258. Lampe, *Paul to Valentinus* 90-99; and further above §40.1g.

like them may not be universalized into a widespread and generally recognized disowning of Christianity by diaspora Jews.[259] And *Did.* 8.1-2, in referring to 'hypocrites', certainly has Jewish practice in mind (fasting on Mondays and Thursdays), and indicates a desire on the side of the Jewish believers in Christ to distinguish the all too similar Christian practice (fasting on Wednesday and Friday) from the traditional Jewish equivalent. But since the passage clearly draws on Matt. 6.5, 16, to describe it as 'anti-Jewish polemic'[260] is something of an overstatement; the use of Matthew's 'boo-word' 'hypocrite' speaks more of a jostling for space than an outright polemic, as in Matthew.[261]

More attention needs to be given to the Apologists, but even so only Aristides, the *Epistle to Diognetus*, Justin Martyr, Melito of Sardis and Irenaeus call for attention. Of the other Apologists, the issue of Tatian's anti-Judaism is limited to the exaggerated responsibility placed on the Jews for the crucifixion of Jesus (as in *Diatessaron* 51.15), which simply reflects the way the story is told in the canonical Gospels and in the early Acts sermons (Acts 2.23; 3.14-15; etc.). In his *Address*, 'Jews' are mentioned only in brief historical references in his attempt to demonstrate the priority of Moses (*Address* 36-38). Among the writings of Apollinarius, bishop of Hierapolis, were two books *Against the Jews* (Eusebius, *HE* 4.27.1). Since there was a strong and well-established Jewish community in Hierapolis,[262] the situation may well have been similar to that confronting Melito in Sardis, and the occasion and effect of Apollinarius's polemic may have been similar to that of Melito (see §46.6h below). Athenagoras has nothing to contribute to the discussion; Christians' relationship with Jews were not relevant to what he was writing. And as we have seen (§45.5j), Theophilus quotes extensively from the OT, but without any sense that he was taking over something strange to Christianity or denying it to the Jews.[263]

---

259. See above §46.5a. It is perhaps significant that in referring to Polycarp's arrest (on Friday), the *Martyrdom* uses the Jewish terms 'Preparation' (7.1; as also *Did.* 8.1), and 'great Sabbath' (8.1), probably in echo of John 19.31 (Schoedel, *Polycarp* 60-61), and implying a rejection of Polycarp similar in character to that of Jesus, but nevertheless thinking in Jewish terms. See also Hartog, *Philippians* 226-31. Paul Trebilco refers me to C. R. Moss, *Ancient Christian Martyrdom: Diverse Practices, Theologies and Traditions* (Anchor Yale Bible Reference; New Haven: Yale, 2012) who questions whether the involvement of Jews in Polycarp's martyrdom is historical.

260. Ehrman, *Apostolic Fathers* 409.

261. Vermes suggests that 'others' in the case of the *Didache* were other Jewish believers in Jesus; he conjectures 'that the "hypocrites" of the Didache were Jewish-Christians who remained attached to Pharisaic customs' (*Christian Beginnings* 140-41).

262. See Grant, *Greek Apologists* 86.

263. His references to the Jews are purely historical (3.9, 20, 22, 25, 29), and he knew and speaks in commendatory terms of Josephus's writings (3.23).

a. Ignatius

The immediately relevant passages are found in Ignatius's letters to the *Magnesians* and the *Philadelphians*.

> *Magn.* 8.1-2 — Do not be deceived by false opinions or old fables that are of no use. For if we have lived according to Judaism until now, we admit that we have not received God's gracious gift. For the most divine prophets lived according to Jesus Christ.

> *Magn.* 9.1 — And so those who lived according to the old ways came to a new hope, no longer keeping the Sabbath but living according to the Lord's day...

> *Magn.* 10.1-3 — For this reason, since we are his disciples, let us learn to live according to Christianity. For whoever is called by a name other than this does not belong to God. So lay aside the bad yeast, which has grown old and sour, and turn to the new yeast, which is Jesus Christ.... It is outlandish to proclaim Jesus Christ and practise Judaism. For Christianity did not believe in Judaism, but Judaism in Christianity — in which every tongue that believes in God has been gathered together (cf. Isa. 66.18).

> *Philad.* 6.1 — But if anyone should interpret Judaism to you, do not hear him. For it is better to hear Christianity from a man who is circumcised than Judaism from one who is uncircumcised.

Several features call for attention here.

- As already noted earlier, this is the first use of the term 'Christianity' known to us. Apart from Gal. 1.13-14 this is also the first use of the term 'Judaism' in a Christian document. Evidently Ignatius could conceive of two different religious systems, which he could distinguish from each other. The significance of this is heightened by the fact that Ignatius came from Antioch (where 'Christians' were first so designated),[264] and was travelling through Asia Minor.
- Ignatius had in mind that Christians had hitherto 'lived according to Judaism' (*Magn.* 8.1) and that Jews who had become Christians had changed their religious practice accordingly (9.1); Judaism believed in Christianity (10.3).

---

264. Acts 11.26. See *Beginning from Jerusalem* 303-6.

- He was concerned that Christians wanted to 'practise Judaism' (*Magn.* 10.3), that is, possibly that Christian Jews wanted to continue with their Jewish praxis, and/or that Gentile Christians were (still) attracted to Judaism.[265] But that was to get things the wrong way round: 'Christianity did not believe in Judaism'; it was Judaism which believed in Christianity.[266]
- He wanted to discourage Gentile Christians from inquiring about Judaism, discouraging them especially from being beguiled by other Gentiles who had already succumbed to the attraction of Judaism (Judaizers). At the same time he was very ready to acknowledge that Christian Jews had a better understanding of Christianity (than Gentile Christians) (*Philad.* 6.1).
- His attitude to 'Judaism' was negative ('false opinions [*heterodoxiai*]', 'old fables', 'old ways',[267] 'bad yeast, old and sour') but not strongly antagonistic.[268]

What emerges from this is that in the early second century, there was a widespread perception (in Syria and Asia) that Judaism and Christianity were conjoint religions, that 'Christianity' was a descendant from and close kin to

---

265. See discussion in C. K. Barrett, 'Jews and Judaizers in the Epistles of Ignatius', *Essays on John* 133-58; and Wilson, *Related Strangers* 163-65. Barrett thought it possible 'to trace in Justin's position an earlier situation in which Jewish Christians had attempted to impose their Jewish customs upon Gentile Christians' (*The Gospel of John and Judaism* 68). Wilson questions whether the Judaizers were promoting Judaism in general; 'rather, the Judaizers had a particular view of the scriptures, and were especially inclined to dispute any Christian beliefs that they could not find in them (*Philad.* 8:1-2; 9:1)' (165). P. J. Donahue, 'Jewish Christianity in the Letters of Ignatius of Antioch', *VC* 32 (1978) 81-93, argued that Ignatius was confronting Christians who continued to follow the lead and model provided by James. Sim argues that the Christian Jewish opponents of Ignatius were members of the later Matthean community (*Gospel of Matthew* 272-86), though to describe Jews as 'judaizing' hardly reflects the original use of the term (*Beginning from Jerusalem* 473-74).

266. 'To confess Christ and to "Judaize" are mutually exclusive for Ignatius' (Koester, *Introduction* 2.286).

267. R. M. Grant, *Ignatius of Antioch* (R. M. Grant, ed., *The Apostolic Fathers* vol. 4; London: Nelson, 1966): 'The words for "old" or "antiquated" occur in Ignatius only here (*Magn.* 8.1; also 9.1; 10.2) and in *Eph.* 19.3. Evidently he regards Judaism as the primary expression of "antiquity" in contrast to the "newness" (*Magn.* 9.1; *Eph.* 19.2-3) of the gospel' (62). The prophets are highly regarded ('the most divine prophets') because they 'lived according to Jesus Christ' (*Magn.* 8.2).

268. Barrett, however, made the somewhat disturbing observation that 'Ignatius himself finds the Judaizers easier to define sociologically than theologically', accusing the church, as represented by Ignatius, of falling out of theology and into sociology, 'adopting the common [that is, generally negative] Hellenistic attitude [to Jews]' ('Jews and Judaizers in the Epistles of Ignatius' 155).

'Judaism', that, indeed, they were two forms of the one religion.[269] To see 'Judaism' and 'Christianity' thus closely interrelated, allowing an overlapping practice, was, however, not or no longer acceptable to Ignatius, who was keen to draw a clear boundary between 'Judaism' and 'Christianity'.[270] He readily acknowledged that 'Christianity' began in 'Judaism', that the one body of the church was composed of Jews and Gentiles (*Smyrn.* 1.2), that Jewish believers had the best understanding of Christianity. But the (many) Christians who saw 'Judaism' and 'Christianity' as two peas in the same pod should be discouraged from acting from that perception; members of the small apartment-church groups should refuse the attraction of the long-established and well-regarded synagogue rituals and festivals; to hanker after 'Judaism' was to devalue the grace they had received; 'Christianity' was the 'new hope' towards which 'Judaism' only looked. In short, in Ignatius we see the beginning of attempts by Christian leaders to define Christianity by distinguishing it more clearly from Judaism. This tension between Christians who saw Judaism as a twin religion and leaders who wanted to define the identity of Christianity over against Judaism (or the Jews) reappears regularly through the second century and beyond — a contested identity indeed.

b. *Epistle of Barnabas*

With *Barnabas* the picture grows darker.

> 2.4-6 — Through all the prophets he has shown us that he has no need of sacrifices, whole burnt offerings, or regular offerings. For he says in one place, 'What is the multitude of your sacrifices to me? says the Lord. I am sated with whole burnt offerings, and have no desire for the fat of lambs....

---

269. Mimouni infers that the Christian communities addressed by Ignatius 'still function on the model of Jewish communities of the Roman diaspora (notably in Asia Minor), that is: there is a core of Christians of Jewish origin around which gravitate the proselytes and sympathizers, themselves of Pagan origin' (*Early Judaeo-Christianity* 94).

270. See also T. A. Robinson, *Ignatius of Antioch and the Parting of the Ways: Early Jewish-Christian Relations* (Peabody: Hendrickson, 2009). It is possible that Ignatius's attitude was partially at least in reaction to the situation he had left behind in Antioch, where relations between Jews and Christians seem to have remained positive following Paul's probable failure in the Antioch incident (Gal. 2.11-14) (cf. Meeks and Wilken, *Jews and Christians in Antioch* 18). That is, Ignatius may have reacted negatively to such positive relations, and his departure from Antioch may even have been something of a relief to the Antioch church; cf. C. Trevett, *A Study of Ignatius of Antioch in Syria and Asia Minor* (Lewiston: Mellen, 1992) 60-61. Ignatius's strenuous advocacy of monarchical episcopacy may have been part of the same reaction.

Trample my court no longer.... I cannot stand your new moons and sabbaths' (Isa. 1.11-13). And so he nullified these things with the new law of our Lord Jesus Christ...

4.6-8 — do not become like some people by piling up your sins, saying that the covenant is both theirs and ours. For it is ours. But they finally lost it... (quoting Exod. 31.18 and 32.7). Moses understood and cast the two tablets from his hands (Exod. 32.19). And their covenant was smashed — that the covenant of his beloved, Jesus, might be sealed in our hearts...

4.14 — Israel was abandoned even after such signs and wonders had occurred in it.

5.7-8 — (The Lord) allowed himself to suffer in order to redeem the promise given to the fathers and to show, while he was on earth preparing a new people for himself.... Moreover, while teaching Israel and doing such wonders and signs, he preached to them and loved them deeply.

6.16 — we are the ones he has brought into the good land (of milk and honey).

9.1, 4, 9 — he has circumcised our hearts.... But even the circumcision in which they trusted has been nullified. For he has said that circumcision is not a matter of the flesh. But they violated his law, because an evil angel instructed them.... For the one who has placed the implanted gift of his covenant in us knew these things.

10.2 — 'I will establish a covenant with this people in my righteous demands' (cf. Deut. 4.10, 13). So then the commandment of God is not a matter of avoiding food; but Moses spoke in the Spirit.

10.12 — We speak as those who know the commandments in an upright way, as the Lord wished. For this reason he circumcised our hearing and our hearts, that we might understand these things.

11.1 — It is written about the water that Israel will not at all accept the baptism that brings forgiveness of sins.

14.1-7 — (in response to the question 'whether the covenant is for us or them' — 13.1): He has given it, but they were not worthy to receive it because of their sins.... So Moses received the covenant, but they were not worthy. . . . Moses received it as a servant, but the Lord himself gave it to us, as a people of the inheritance, by enduring suffering for us. He was made manifest so that those people might be completely filled with sins, and that we might receive the covenant through the Lord Jesus who inherited it. He was prepared for this end, that when he became manifest he might make a covenant with us by his word . . . 'I have given you as a covenant of the people, as a light of the nations . . .' (Isa. 42.6).

Here too several features call for attention:

- There is an evident 'us' and 'them' attitude in *Barnabas*,[271] with a deliberate attempt to distinguish (not so much distance) the Jewish 'them' from the Christian 'us'.[272]
- The antipathy to the temple cult (2.4-6) of course is in tune with prophetic rebuke of superficial worship (Isa. 1.11-13); but it is both similar to some Jewish-Christian rejection of sacrifices,[273] and not so distant from a rabbinic Judaism which grew accustomed to having no temple; and its degree of hostility to the temple cult may reflect reaction to the possibility of the temple being rebuilt (ch. 16).[274]
- There is a genuine concern that members of *Barnabas*'s community were being attracted to fully embrace Israel's traditional religion: God 'made all things plain to us beforehand [having quoted Isa. 58.3-10 at length] that we should not be shipwrecked as newcomers/proselytes[275] to their law' (3.6).[276]
- The attitude to Israel is somewhat ambivalent: it has been 'abandoned' (4.14); but God had done wonders and signs among them and 'loved them deeply' (5.8). Are the Christians 'Israel' — 'we are the ones he has brought into the good land (of milk and honey)' (6.16) — or 'a new people' (5.7)?[277]

---

271. E.g. 2.9; 3.1-3; 4.6; 8.7; 10.12; 14.4-5; 15.8-9; see also Hvalvik, *Struggle* 113, 137-40.

272. But we recall that *Barnabas* never uses the terms 'Judaism', 'Jew', 'Christianity' or 'Christian'.

273. Ps-Clem., *Recog.* 1.36.1; 37.2-4; see above §45.8d at n.295.

274. See above §40.1f(iii).

275. See §40 n.55.

276. 'Fear of Christian Assimilation to the Jews' (Horbury, 'Jewish-Christian Relations in Barnabas' 323-27). See further Paget, *Barnabas* 56-58.

277. Paget refers to Skarsaune's observation (*Proof* 332) that *Barnabas* 'is the only apostolic father to use *laos* ("people") in relation to both Jews and Christians' (*Barnabas* 59 n.305; cf. Hvalvik, *Struggle* 144).

- Israel had received the covenant[278] but 'they finally lost it' (4.7),[279] because 'they were not worthy' (14.4). But when *Barnabas* says that it is sinful to say that the covenant 'is both theirs and ours. It is ours' (4.6-7), it is not entirely clear whether he means that the Christians have taken over Israel's covenant — 'the Lord himself gave it to us, as a people of the inheritance' (14.4) — the same covenant (14.4);[280] or whether it was another covenant which was in mind — 'the covenant of his beloved, Jesus' (4.8), 'the implanted gift of his covenant' (9.9). There is evidently a line of continuity through Jesus — 'that we might receive the covenant through the Lord Jesus who inherited it' (14.5); and the 'covenant with us' is presented as the 'covenant of the people' in which the Servant of Isaiah would also be 'a light of the nations' (Isa. 42.6) (14.7).[281] So whether the same or a new covenant, the point is that it is in direct continuity with and in fulfillment of Israel's covenant destiny, to be also 'a light of the nations'.[282]
- The continuity is strongly marked also by the references to circumcision: the significance of circumcision is misunderstood if the focus is on the circumcision of the flesh (9.4);[283] what counts is the circumcision of the heart which the Christians have received (9.1; 10.12).
- Similarly the commandments of the law are misunderstood if they are understood to refer only to food (ch.10): the ritual laws should never have been interpreted literally — 'Moses spoke in the Spirit' (10.2); the

---

278. Paget notes that the term 'covenant' occurs 13 or 14 times in *Barnabas* and only twice in the rest of the 'sub-apostolic' literature (*Barnabas* 59).

279. *Barnabas* refers only to the smashing of the two stone tablets in Exod. 32.19 and ignores the report that two fresh tablets of stone were cut out in Exod. 34; 'the history of Israel — as a people — starts and ends at Sinai' (Hvalvik, *Struggle* 146; and further 154-57).

280. *Barnabas* 'holds to the view that there is one covenant; regards the one covenant as containing the right laws if only interpreted correctly; and is strongly opposed to the idea that that covenant is anything other than the possession of the Christians' (Paget, *Barnabas* 196). Paget finds strong parallels between the covenant theology of *Barnabas* and that of Qumran (196-200), concluding, e.g., that 'Both are strongly opposed to any notion of a shared covenant' (199); but he notes also the differences from Hebrews' covenant theology (218-20, 225).

281. Cf. Hvalvik, *Struggle* 148-52.

282. 'The recurrence of the covenant theme, the allusion to Christians who favored the concept of a joint inheritance, and the radical (and unbiblical) denial of the covenant to Israel — all of these suggest that the issue was not simply antiquarian, theoretical, or even scriptural, but an urgent and pressing matter which had already made disturbing inroads into the church' (Wilson, *Related Strangers* 138).

283. *Barn.* 9.4 evidently interpreted Gal. 3.19 (the law ordained through angels) in an entirely negative way ('an evil angel instructed them').

understanding of those circumcised in the heart sees in them instruction on righteous living (10.12).[284]

Much of the material used by *Barnabas* reflects a period when Judaism was continuing to attract Gentile (potential) proselytes (3.6). We should envisage an established Jewish community, in relation to which the newer movement of Christians was much less influential and respected. The issue of Christianity's origins in the religion of Israel was not simply an academic issue, as scholarship at the turn of the nineteenth/twentieth centuries maintained, but a matter of defining and defending an emerging (distinctive) identity in face of the more obvious claims and identity of the local Jewish community.[285] Although it is hard to avoid the impression of a theology regarding Israel heading into supersessionism,[286] *Barnabas* is more regretful that Israel 'finally lost it', than denunciatory or derogatory in his language.[287] Its attitude to Israel is rooted in the prophetic call for the deeper reality of worship and righteous living to be realized. And its claim for the Christianity it represents reflects the ambivalence in Israel's own theology as to whether Israel's hope was for a new covenant or for a fuller realization of the first covenant, and ambivalence too on how Israel's commission to be a light of the Gentiles should be fulfilled. Given the sharpness of many prophetic rebukes of Israel's religious practice in the past, *Barnabas* can still be heard as the voice of someone more concerned to recall Israel to its destiny and to see the development of Gentile Christianity as a fulfilling of Israel's destiny, rather than as one who simply dismissed Israel as no longer to be considered as having a place in God's affections and purpose.[288]

---

284. '... the "new law of our Lord Jesus Christ" (2.6) ..., which is in fact *the true law*, and is "new" only by way of contrast to the incorrect, literal (cultic) interpretation of Mosaic law which prevailed in Israel' (Kraft, *Barnabas and the Didache* 34).

285. See particularly Paget, *Barnabas* 52-66; *Barnabas* 'seeks to give the Christian community for whom he is writing a clear identity over against the majority Jewish community' (69).

286. Horbury observes that 'a Christian sense of accepted separation from the Jewish community seems first clearly detectable in writings from about the end of the first century onwards, notably the Epistle of Barnabas' (*Jews and Christians* 11-13). For those who think *Barnabas* was fighting 'Judaistic' tendencies among his addressees or perceived Judaism as itself a threat, see Paget, *Barnabas* 52 nn.267, 268. Others play down *Barnabas*'s 'anti-Judaism' (52-53); see also §40 n.66 above.

287. '*Barnabas*' description of the Jews (focuses) on two concepts: "sin" and "error"' (Hvalvik, *Struggle* 141). Hvalvik denies that *Barnabas* expresses a "replacement theology": 'the Church did not take over the place and status of the Jews, but they got the place *meant for* the Jewish people' (147).

288. Horbury begins his essay on 'Jewish-Christian Relations in Barnabas and Justin Martyr' (in *Jews and Christians*, ed. Dunn): "the Ways have parted already, for the writers

c. 5 Ezra, Sibylline Oracles

Of the Christian redactions or additions to Jewish writings, we should note particularly *5 Ezra* and the *Sibylline Oracles*.[289]

Although *5 Ezra* is clearly Jewish in character, and probably Jewish Christian in origin, its warnings go beyond the typical warnings of the biblical prophets:

- *4 Ezra* 1.25 — 'Because you have forsaken me, I also will forsake you. When you beg mercy of me, I will show you no mercy';
- *4 Ezra* 1.30-31 — 'I will cast you out from my presence. When you offer oblations to me, I will turn my face from you';
- *4 Ezra* 2.10 — 'Tell my people that I will give them the kingdom of Jerusalem, which I was going to give to Israel'.

The rebuke and rejection are notably different from other post-biblical Jewish writings which explain the judgment on Israel as Yahweh's discipline, as distinct from the destruction meted out to sinners: 'He never withdraws his mercy from us. Although he disciplines us with calamities, he does not forsake his own people' (2 Macc. 6.16).[290] Jewish believers-in-Jesus were beginning to think of themselves as God's people, but as other than Israel.[291]

In the redaction of the *Oracles*, the most notable passage is probably *Sib. Or.* 1.365-75 and 1.387-400, in which the death of Jesus is attributed to Israel acting 'with abominable lips and poisonous spittings', 'smitten in breast and heart with an evil craze' (1.365-66, 368-69). The consequence is that 'the Hebrews reap the bad harvest' and 'will be driven from their land; wandering,

---

considered here' (315); similarly Vermes, *Christian Beginnings* 148-52. 'The intra-Jewish problematics of Paul and the Gospel of Matthew have become vituperative and caricaturing polemics' (King, *Gnosticism* 41). But Horbury concludes: 'Yet, for all their contribution to the Christian inheritance, the Epistle of Barnabas and Justin's works in their second-century setting are Jewish as much as Christian documents. Despite and partly because of their anti-Judaism, they attest the overshadowing spiritual power of the Jewish polity, and could properly be assigned to a Christian sub-section of Jewish literature' ('Barnabas' 345).

289. See above §45 at nn. 229, 234, 235.

290. The distinction between Israel being disciplined and the ungodly/sinners being judged/destroyed is a particular theme of the *Psalms of Solomon* (3.4-12; 7.1-10; 8.23-34; 13.5-12) and the *Wisdom of Solomon* (11.9-10; 12.22; 16.9-10).

291. 'The replacement of Israel by the "coming people" is the main theme of 5 Ezra' (Stanton, '5 Ezra' 260). Stanton thinks that *5 Ezra* stressed 'the finality of the separation of the church from Israel' (262), 'a complete rupture between the church and Israel' (268), but that the community was 'primarily concerned to establish its continuity with Israel in spite of a recent final rupture' (270).

being slaughtered, they will mix much darnel in their wheat' (1.387, 395-96).[292] In *Sib. Or.* 6.21 the land of Israel is referred to as the 'land of Sodom'.[293] There is an enmity here which, if expressed by Jewish believers-in-Jesus, indicates a disillusionment with Israel and a self-distancing from the 'Hebrews' which can no longer be called 'Jewish-Christian' without difficulty.

In both these writings the sense of a disowning of Israel is palpable, even while the authors draw on earlier intra-Jewish laments for and denunciations of Israel's failures — seeking to establish their identity by distancing their community from much that had previously been integral to that identity.

d. Aristides

The most striking feature of Aristides is his clear distinction between Jews and Christians as two (distinct) 'classes of men' (*Apol.* 2). He commends the Jews' perception of God as closer to the truth than all the nations, but criticizes them because 'by their mode of observance it is to the angels and not to God that their service is rendered — as when they celebrate sabbaths and the beginning of the months, and feasts of unleavened bread, and a great fast; and fasting and circumcision and the purification of meats, which things, however, they do not observe perfectly' (*Apol.* Syriac 14).[294] Here there is some respect for Jews,[295] but no acknowledgment that Christianity owed anything to the ancient religion of the Jews, despite his affirmation that Christianity began from 'Jesus the Messiah', 'born of the race of the Hebrews' and 'from a Hebrew virgin' (*Apol.* 2). Here wrote a Gentile who had no conception of or at least readiness to acknowledge Christianity's strongly Jewish heritage.

e. *Kerygma Petrou*[296]

From what appear to be extracts in Clement of Alexandria it is evident that the *Kerygma* sought to distinguish the Christians from both Greeks and Jews.

---

292. 'The redactor clearly distinguishes himself from Israel; he holds a vile hatred for Israel . . .' (Charlesworth, 'Christian Additions' 50).
293. 'The redactor here identifies himself with a type of Christianity that has moved far away from Judaism' (Charlesworth, 'Christian Additions' 51).
294. Here the Greek version focuses rather on their (the Jews') betrayal of the Son of God and denial that Christ is the Son of God.
295. The *Apology* also evinces knowledge of the patriarchs and the time in Egypt (Syriac 2), and of the deliverance by Moses from Egypt (Greek 14).
296. See above §40.2c.

Christians worship God, not in the 'old way' of the Greeks and the Jews, but 'in a new way, by Christ', 'in a new way, in a third form' (*Strom.* 6.5.39-41):[297]

> we have found in the scriptures how the Lord says: Behold, I make with you a new covenant, not as the covenant with your fathers in mount Horeb. He has made a new one with us, for the ways of the Greeks and Jews are old, but we are they that worship him in a new way in a third race, even Christians. For clearly, as I suppose, he showed that the one and only God was known by the Greeks in a gentile way, by the Jews in a Jewish way, and by us in a new and spiritual way. . . . not that the three peoples are separated by time, so that one might suppose three natures, but rather trained in different covenants of the one Lord, by the word of the one Lord.

That comes across in rather even-handed and generous terms. But the denigration of Greek religion as mere idol worship is paralleled by an equivalent dismissal of Jewish worship:[298]

> Neither worship him as do the Jews, for they, who suppose that they alone know God, do not know him, serving angels and archangels, the month and the moon, and if no moon be seen they do not celebrate what is called the first sabbath, nor keep the new moon, nor the days of unleavened bread, nor the feast, nor the great day [of atonement].[299]

Here the Christian attempt to achieve self-definition by distancing itself from its nearest neighbours is already reaching for the concept of a third race, neither Greek nor Jewish, but Christian. Such a self-distinction could be said to have been heralded by Paul,[300] but Paul saw the new entity as made up of Jews and Greeks.[301] Here the self-presentation could only be achieved, evidently, by denigrating its maternal or sibling religion. Such polemic is not so very different from Qumran's self-justifying polemic against mainstream Second Temple Judaism. The difference is that such polemic was essentially within the bounds of Second Temple Judaism, a conscious distancing from 'the multitude of the people' (4QMMT C7). Here, however, the distancing is

---

297. This passage 'contains one of the clearest assertions of a Christian sense of self-identity and the way in which this is bolstered by denigration of the alternatives' (Wilson, *Related Strangers* 93).

298. The *Kerygma* refers also to Jesus' 'death, and cross, and all the rest of the tortures (*kolaseis*) which the Jews inflicted on him' (*Strom.* 6.15.128).

299. Origen, *On John*, cites the same passage (Elliott, *ANT* 24).

300. 1 Cor. 1.22-23; 10.32.

301. 1 Cor. 1.24; cf. Eph. 2.14-16.

of Christian from Jew. The concern for Israel[302] echoes that of Paul in Rom. 10.14-21, but without the intensity and existential anguish expressed by Paul in the same chapters.

f. *Epistle to Diognetus*[303]

Again, rather like Aristides and the *Kerygma Petrou*, the *Epistle to Diognetus* distinguishes Christians clearly from Jews: 'the Christians do not worship like the Jews' (3.1). Also like Aristides and the *Kerygma*, the critique of idolatry is followed by a critique of Jewish worship, in which the latter is seen as little different from the former.[304] In ch. 4, Jews are repeatedly scorned for their *alazoneia* ('boasting, arrogance') in regard to circumcision,[305] for their 'telling lies about God as forbidding anything good to be done on the sabbath' (4.3), and for 'the sham of their fasting and new moon festival — ridiculous and unworthy of argument' (4.1), 'the vulgar silliness, deceit, fussiness and arrogance of the Jews' (4.6).[306] Here too the protest of a Paul has been turned into a denigratory dismissal of fundamental Jewish identity-markers.[307]

In these last three writings there is clearly evident a desire to distance Christianity from Judaism and no real willingness to acknowledge Christianity's origins within early Judaism and its Jewish character.

---

302. 'Wherefore Peter says that the Lord said to the apostles: If anyone of Israel then wishes to repent and by my name to believe in God, his sins shall be forgiven him. After twelve years go forth into the world so that no one may say: We have not heard' (*Strom.* 6.5.43).

303. See above §40.2d.

304. 'Those who suppose they are performing sacrifices of blood and fat and whole burnt offerings, and thereby to be bestowing honor on him by these displays of reverence, seem no different to me from those who show the same honor to the gods who are deaf...' (3.5).

305. 'Not worthy of scorn to boast in the mutilation of the flesh as a testimony to their election, as if because of it they were especially loved by God' (4.4).

306. 'In the Epistle of Barnabas and in the Letter to Diognetus the repulsion to Judaism is so violent that one step further would have carried the writers into Gnostic or Marcionite dualism' (Lightfoot, *Clement* 1.9).

307. M. F. Bird, 'The Reception of Paul in the *Epistle of Diognetus*', in Bird and Dodson, eds., *Paul and the Second Century* 70-90: 'the Paulinism of *Diognetus* stands at a point between proto-orthodoxy and Marcion', but Bird notes several features which distance *Diognetus* from Gnostic interpretation of Paul — more akin to *Barnabas* than to Marcion (88-90).

g. Justin Martyr[308]

Much more interesting is the evidence of Justin's *Dialogue with Trypho*. He regularly attests that Jews in their synagogues curse Christ and Christians,[309] and accuses them of persecuting Christians when they have the power to do so.[310] But he also knows that some Jews acknowledge Jesus to be Christ, though they 'declare that he was man of merely human origin' (*Dial.* 48.4; cf. 49.1). And he is confident that Jewish believers who continue to practise as Jews will be saved, but only if they do not try to persuade Gentile believers to live in accordance with the law (46.1–47.3; 120.2). But, notably, Justin also asserts that 'they who conducted their lives in accordance with the law of Moses should equally be saved', and 'saved by means of this Christ of ours, in the resurrection equally with the righteous who were before them, Noah and Enoch and Jacob . . . ; together with those who recognize this Christ as the Son of God' (45.3-4).[311]

Interestingly, in another passage Justin refers to 'those who are Christians in name',[312] and 'so-called Christians', and in the same breath refers also (by implication) to so-called Jews, enumerating seven (heretical) sects — Sadducees, Genistae, Meristae, Galileans, Hellenians, Pharisees and Baptists — who acknowledge 'God with their lips, yet their heart is far from him'.[313] This suggests that Justin thought of Jews and Christians in the same terms. It also suggests an awareness of the diversity of second-century Judaism, and a rather confused understanding of Judaism, probably mostly informed by experience of diaspora Judaism in the Roman empire — he knows that the LXX was read in synagogue services (72.3).[314] We can infer that rabbinic Judaism, as it established itself more and more firmly in Palestine, was beginning to stretch its authority to the western diaspora, for example, warning Jews not to have conversations with such as Justin (38.1). But since such as Trypho seem to

---

308. See above §40.2e.
309. *Dial.* 16.4; 47.4; 93.4; 95.4; 96.2; 108.3; 123.6; 133.6; 137.2. See above §46.4b.
310. *Dial.* 16.4; 95.4; 110.5; 131.2; 133.6; see also *1 Apol.* 31.5-6; 36.3; cf. *M. Polyc.* 13.1; 17.2; 18.1; *Diogn.* 5.17. Horbury talks of 'an organized Jewish rebuttal of the apostolic preaching' and a 'corporate Jewish rejection of Christianity' ('Barnabas' 341-43).
311. His criticism of Jewish practices, as in 117.1, draws on the earlier criticisms of the prophets (in this case, Mal. 1.10-12).
312. Presumably at least Marcion (they 'blaspheme the God of Abraham . . .') and Gnostics (they say 'that there is no resurrection of the dead . . .').
313. *Dial.* 80.3-4, alluding to Isa. 29.13.
314. How much Justin's knowledge of Judaism (and of Christianity) came from his upbringing in Samaria (§40.2e) is unclear. As Kraft notes: 'Unfortunately, we cannot tell what role (if any) his homeland played in the development of his Christian thought' (*Barnabas and the Didache* 50).

have ignored this counsel, and since Justin's awareness of the sort of concerns being displayed in the halakhic debates within early rabbinic Judaism seems to be limited (112.4; 117.2-4),[315] we may infer that (western) diaspora Judaism was still much more open to the Christian claims about Jesus — many Jews were becoming disciples of Christ (39.2) — than the rabbis in Syria-Palestine.

For his part Justin has no hesitation in claiming that Christians are the true Israel: 'We are the true and spiritual Israelitish nation, and the race of Judah and of Jacob and Isaac and Abraham . . .' (11.5).[316] But he does not take the title 'Israel' away from his Jewish dialogue partners. His criticism is rather that they deceive themselves, 'as though you alone were Israel' (123.6). His case is rather that as 'your whole nation was addressed as Jacob and Israel, so also we who keep the commandments of Christ, are, by virtue of Christ who begat us unto God, both called and in fact are, Jacob and Israel and Judah and Joseph and David, and true children of God' (123.9).[317] In his typological exposition of the two wives of Jacob in Gen. 29-30, 'Leah is your people and the synagogue; but Rachel is our church. And Christ still serves for these and for his servants that are in both' (134.3). And his expectant hope is that 'Jesus the Christ will turn the dispersion of the people' (113.3).[318]

Not surprisingly Justin also disputes that circumcision is really necessary (19.3). But his real point is that circumcision in the flesh is 'a type of the true circumcision' (41.4); the second circumcision, of the heart, is effected by the words of Jesus (113.6; 114.4). In this, as in the other matters above, Justin's criticism of Jewish practice is not very far from that of the prophets. And his claims that 'Israel' has broadened to include Gentile believers, who need neither to be circumcised nor to observe the law's commandments, is in direct continuity with similar arguments of Paul. Justin's *Dialogue with Trypho* certainly indicates a notable degree of separation between (Gentile) Christians

---

315. See also n.73 above. Williams, *Justin Martyr* xxx-xxxiv, and Shotwell, *Justin Martyr* 71-93, argue that Justin's knowledge of Palestinian Judaism was more extensive: 'Justin had at least a good working knowledge of post-Biblical Judaism' (Williams xxxiii); Shotwell speaks of 'a large body of evidence that points to a wide variety of acquaintance with Jewish lore. . . . (a) surprising knowledge of contemporary Jewish thought' (88-89). Horner, however, observes that 'Trypho's connection to Judaism does not show a strong attachment to the rabbinic written tradition as we know it', and adds that 'during the second century C.E. this is not a surprising phenomenon and it should not compromise Trypho's standing as a legitimate Jew' (*Listening to Trypho* 145).

316. See also 119.5; 130.3-4; 'Israel means all who flee by him (Christ) to the Father' (125.5); 'Israel is also Christ' (134.6–135.3); cf. 110.4; 119.3-5; 122.6.

317. There were 'two seeds of Judah, and two races, as two houses of Jacob, the one born of flesh and blood, and the other of faith and spirit' (135.6).

318. Note also *1 Apol.* 52.10-12, drawing on Isa. 11.12; 43.5, 6, 17; 64.11; Joel 2.13; Zech. 2.6; 12.10-12.

and traditionalist Jews. But it also attests a considerable spectrum of Jewish believers in Jesus: those who believed Christ was only a man, those who insisted that Gentile believers should observe the law and those who presumably mingled and worshipped freely with Gentile believers in Christ.[319] And, in contrast to *Barnabas* and *Diognetus*, there is clear evidence of an openness to traditionalist Jews, as illustrated by the *Dialogue* itself, and an openness on Justin's part to recognize that God will honour Jews who practise righteousness, as he honoured Enoch, Noah and those who preceded Moses.

In short, Justin attests a growing separation between a predominantly Gentile Christianity and the Judaism of the western diaspora, but also a still considerable overlap in Jews who variously recognized Jesus to be the Christ, and an ongoing dialogue across the spectrum of claims to Israel's scriptures and heritage.[320]

h. Melito of Sardis[321]

In his *Peri Pascha*, Melito follows *Barnabas* (7.3–8.1) and Justin[322] in his use of typology, but he makes it central to his apology.[323] Unusually, but valuably, Melito sets out the schematic rationale of his use of the term. Everything needs a pattern, a prefiguration, a model (35-37): 'Is not that which is to come into existence seen through the model which typifies it?' (36). The corollary, however, is clear: once that which the model prefigured has come into being, the model itself has fulfilled its role and can be dispensed with.

> So whenever the thing arises for which the model was made, then that which carried the image of that future thing is destroyed as no longer of use, since it has transmitted its resemblance to that which is by nature true. Therefore, that which once was valuable, is now without value because that which is truly valuable has appeared. For each thing has its own time: there is a dis-

---

319. See also above §45.8a and e.

320. MacLennan characterizes the *Dialogue* as 'a "friendly exchange" between two persons discussing the meaning of the tradition of Israel in the light of the Christian claims as Justin understood them' (*Early Christian Texts* 85). G. N. Stanton, 'Justin Martyr's Dialogue with Trypho: Group Boundaries, "Proselytes" and "God-fearers"', in Stanton and Stroumsa, *Tolerance and Intolerance* 263-78, concludes: 'Justin's *Dialogue* indicates that in the middle of the second century both Judaism and Christianity were concerned to maintain tight boundaries'; but also that 'there is movement across both boundary lines' (274).

321. See above §40.2j.

322. *Dial.* 40.1 ('the passover was a type of Christ'); 41.1, 4; 42.4; 90.2; 91.2, 3, 4; 111.1, 2; 114.1; 120.5; 131.4; 134.3; 140.1.

323. 'Type' appears some fifteen times in *Peri Pascha* 1-58; the near synonym of 'model' is used intensively in 36-40, and 'image' in 37, 38 and 42.

tinct time for the type, there is a distinct time for the material, and there is a distinct time for the truth. You construct the model. You want this, because you see in it the image of the future work. You procure the material for the model. You want this, on account of that which is going to arise because of it. You complete the work and cherish it alone, for only in it do you see both type and the truth (37-38).

The application of the schema to Melito's principal subject is clear: the Passover lamb is a type of the death of Christ (1-10, 32-33); but with the realization or fulfillment of the type, in the death of Christ, the type itself has no more value (44).[324] The same is true in other cases:

> the people had value before the church came on the scene, and the law was wonderful before the gospel was brought to light. But when the church came on the scene, and the gospel was set forth, the type lost its value by surrendering its significance to the truth, and the law was fulfilled by surrendering its significance to the gospel. Just as the type lost its significance by surrendering its image to that which is true by nature, . . . so indeed also the law was fulfilled when the gospel was brought to light, and the people lost their significance when the church came on the scene, and the type was destroyed when the Lord appeared. Therefore, those things which once had value are today without value, because the things which have true value have appeared. . . . . . The temple here below once was valuable, but now it is without value because of the Christ from above. The Jerusalem here below once had value, but now it is without value because of the Jerusalem from above (41-45).

The key indicators of Melito's view of the Israel which still existed are clear: when the fulfillment has come, 'the model is destroyed as no longer of use', what was once valuable is no longer of value (37); the law and the people have lost their significance now that the gospel and the church have come (42-43), 'the type was destroyed when the Lord appeared' (43). But the tone is not so much denunciatory as pointing out what seemed to Melito to be obvious: who would want to stick with the model when the reality had already come to be? who would want to hold on to the type when the truth itself had been revealed and the fulfillment had been so fully realized?[325]

---

324. Melito also identifies Christ with other types: 'This is the one who was murdered in Abel . . .' (69); despite his devaluation of the type relative to that which it foreshadowed, the type still retains value in that it is (and continues to be) a type.

325. 'Judaism and all it signifies is defunct. The positive assessment belongs solely

The theological logic is similar to that of Paul in his letter to Galatia: the role of the law was temporary, epoch-limited until the coming of Christ (Gal. 3.23-25); the present Jerusalem had been left behind by the Jerusalem above (4.25-26).[326] But Paul never expressed his point by inferring that what Israel counted as of central importance was worthless and should be 'destroyed'; his attitude in Rom. 9.4-5 and 11.29 is much more affirmative. Melito's attitude to the fundamentals of Israel's religion is closer to that of Hebrews, with Melito's typology replacing Hebrews' Platonic world-view of earthly copy of heavenly ideal.[327] But his denunciation of Israel (he never speaks of 'the Jews') for denying, renouncing and killing the Lord is expressed more in sorrow than in anger,[328] and less fiercely and dismissively than several of his predecessors.[329] It was Israel's blindness in failing to recognize the first-born of God which cut Melito to the quick, its ingratitude to the one who had watched over them in the past and had healed so many during his mission.

> O lawless Israel, why did you commit this extraordinary crime of casting your Lord into new sufferings — your master, the one who formed you, the one who made you, the one who honored you, the one who called you Israel? (81)

> O ungrateful Israel, come here and be judged before me for your ingratitude (87).

And even when he says, 'you were found not really to be Israel, for you did not see God . . .' (82), Melito is playing on the meaning of 'Israel' as interpreted by Philo, 'man seeing God' (Is-ra-el),[330] which was subsequently taken up by

---

to Israel's past, the negative to their present' (Wilson, *Related Strangers* 246; and further 241-56).

326. Note also the 19th and 20th century German referent for Second Temple Judaism: *Spätjudentum* — 'late Judaism' because its role was seen to be only preparatory for Jesus and Christianity, so in effect 'late Judaism' = last Judaism, as having no more role within the divine purpose.

327. See §39 n.245 above. 'There is little doubt that Melito's concern with Old Testament is due to controversy with Marcionite and Gnostic groups about the origin and authority of the ancient Scriptures. He would wish to affirm their authority and at the same time exculpate himself from any insinuation of Judaizing' (Hall, *Melito* xli).

328. *Peri Pascha* 73-81, 86, 92-93, 96, 99.

329. 'The *Homily* was not directed against the Jews of Sardis, or any other Jewish group in particular, but was written to Christians who defined themselves against the Israel of the Bible' (MacLennan, *Early Christian Texts* 112; see also 151).

330. See LCL, *Philo* 10.234; e.g. *Abr.* 57-58; *Legat.* 4.

Clement of Alexandria and other church fathers.³³¹ It was Israel's failure to see God in Christ which caused Melito such puzzlement and distress. Unlike Paul, he apparently saw no hope for Israel; the disasters of the two Jewish revolts had destroyed the type — 'You dashed the Lord to the ground; you, too, were dashed to the ground, and lie quite dead' (99). How that translated into his attitude towards and any interaction with the Jews of Melito's time, not least in a city where the synagogue had such a prominent place in the city's life,³³² remains obscure.³³³

i. Irenaeus

When we turn to Irenaeus we move into a quite different atmosphere. The denunciations of *Barnabas* and Melito are left behind. 'The Jews' are referred to regularly, but only rarely in a dismissive manner. The Jews even now put demons to flight by invoking the name of God (*adv. haer.* 2.6.2). Jesus acted in accordance with the practice of the Jews (2.22.3). In defending the integrity of the LXX rendering of Isa. 7.14, against that of Theodotion and Aquila, 'both Jewish proselytes', he points out that the LXX translation was done by Jews themselves, well before the birth of Christ and therefore uninfluenced by Christian use of the LXX text (3.21.1). Instruction of the Jews was an easy task, because they were in the habit of hearing Moses and the prophets (4.24.1).

In Book 3.12 Irenaeus takes pains to point out to the followers of Simon Magus and Marcion that the Christian belief in God was entirely in accord with Moses' teaching on the Creator God. The apostles did not preach to the Jews 'another greater or more perfect Father'. Peter did not preach that the God of the Jews was one and the God of Christians another. They preached to Jews and Greeks the same message — one God and Jesus Christ his Son.³³⁴

---

331. *PGL* 678.

332. Trebilco (in private correspondence) notes that the debate about the dating of the Sardis synagogue continues, with special reference to J. Magnes, 'The Date of the Sardis Synagogue in Light of Numismatic Evidence', *American Journal of Archaeology* 109 (2005) 443-75, who argues for a mid-sixth-century date for the construction of the synagogue.

333. In the apocryphal *Acts* there is very little evidence of anti-Judaism. The most striking instance is the *Acts of John* reference to Jesus' arrest 'by the lawless Jews, who received their law from a lawless serpent' (94).

334. It is noticeable that Irenaeus directs 90 percent of his polemic against the Valentinians and Marcionites and other views stemming from Simon Magus. The references to the Ebionites are much fewer, more *en passant* and less vitriolic (*adv. haer.* 1.26.2; 3.15.1; 3.21.1-8 [on LXX as the most reliable translation of Isa. 7.14]; 4.33.4; 5.1.3). Irenaeus evidently did not regard 'Jewish Christianity' as such a serious threat to the great church.

In Book 4.9-16 Irenaeus makes it clear that for him there was but one author of the old and the new law. The purpose of God was to lead men by successive covenants gradually to attain to perfect salvation. He distinguishes the natural law (the Decalogue) from the Mosaic law. Christ did not abrogate the natural precepts of the law but fulfilled and extended them (4.13), drawing particularly on Matt. 5.[335] 'The true God (Jesus) did confess the commandment of the law as the word of God, and called no one else God besides his own Father' (4.9.3). As for the law regarding tabernacle and temple, 'by means of types they learned to fear God, and to continue devoted to his service' (4.14.3). Other laws were added 'on account of their hardness of heart' (4.15.2). But 'the law never hindered them [Israel] from believing in the Son of God' (4.2.7; also 4.8.2-3).

The Jews are condemned as 'slayers of the Lord' (3.12.6; 4.28.3), but more in regret than in condemnation. So far as sacrifices are concerned, the church offers a pure oblation, unlike the Jews whose 'hands are full of blood; for they have not received the Word, through whom it is offered to God' (4.18.4). This latter is Irenaeus's chief complaint: that the Jews do not accept the word of liberty, they pretend to serve with observances beyond those required by the law and they do not recognize the advent of Christ (4.33.1); they do not realize that the new covenant has come in with the Lord's advent (4.34.4). The critique is very similar to that of Paul in 2 Cor. 3: 'when the law is read to the Jews, it is like a fable; for they do not possess the explanation of all things pertaining to the advent of the Son of God . . . ; but when it is read by the Christians, it is a treasure, hid indeed in a field, but brought to light by the cross of Christ' (4.26.1). And echoing the argument of Rom. 9-11, Irenaeus draws a parallel from Israel's history: 'As they [the Jews] were saved by the blindness of the Egyptians, so are we, too, by that of the Jews' (4.28.3; cf. 4.30.1, 3).

In short, the emphasis in Irenaeus is certainly on continuity and hardly at all on discontinuity. In the face of the 'heresies' of Simon Magus, Marcion and the others, it was of vital importance to him that the God and Father of the Lord Jesus Christ was the God proclaimed by Moses, of vital importance that the law and the prophets were the word of God and of such vital importance that his look back to the history of the Jews majors on the positives rather than the negatives. Their rejection of Christ and of the gospel was a matter of profound regret, though in the spirit of Paul he probably did not give up hope for what the second advent of Christ might accomplish. If *Barnabas* and Melito are the voices of supersessionism, Justin and Irenaeus give hope for a more positive dialogue.[336]

---

335. The argument of 4.13 echoes that of Paul in Gal. 3, and of 4.19 that of Hebrews.
336. Osborn's observation — 'Eusebius' claim that Irenaeus was a peacemaker in

There is clear evidence, then, in the second-century Christian writings, which have been preserved in one form or another, that there were repeated attempts by Christian leaders to define the identity of Christianity by distinguishing it and distancing it from the religion of the Jews, by denying that ethnic Israel was still the chosen people of God, by claiming Israel's heritage for their own. But the attitude was by no means uniform. While there were supersessionist dismissals of Judaism's own claims to that heritage, there were also expressions of regret at Israel's failure to appreciate the character of its own heritage, and traditional-style prophetic rebuke of Israel for that failure.

More to the point, the self-definition by distinguishing and distancing from the closest sibling (second-century Judaism), a distinguishing and distancing from the 'other' which was probably inevitable (psycho-sociologically speaking), should not be taken as the whole story or true of all Christians by any means. Here I need simply refer again to what was outlined in §38.3a above: that the Christian leadership insisted on a clear separation between Christianity and the religion of the Jews precisely because the separation was not clear; it was not even clear that there should be a separation. There were Jewish and Gentile Christians who regularly attended the synagogue on Saturday and observed the traditional Jewish feasts and customs, Jewish believers in Jesus and judaizing Gentile believers in Jesus.[337] This can only be because these believers in Jesus saw their belief as part of a broader Jewish heritage, including one God, an un-imageable God (except insofar as Jesus Christ had made the invisible God visible), high moral standards and care for the poor. There must have been many Jewish believers-in-Jesus who regarded themselves still as Jews, and many Gentile converts who thought they were entering an offshoot of the very venerable religion of the Jews. These were not alternative ways of being religious; they ran together; they overlapped. The evidence briefly reviewed in §38.3a goes well beyond the second century; but if the problem for leaders and synods ran well into the fourth century, then the overlaps must certainly have been well established and common all through the second century. If we listen only to the Ignatiuses and the Melitos, we would have to say that the ways between Christianity and Judaism had already parted — or, probably more accurately, they wanted to enforce such a separation. But it is almost certainly more accurate to conclude that such voices were loudest and most insistent, in claiming in effect that the ways had

---

name and nature (*HE* 5.24.18) is not simply a play on words but a fact borne out by Irenaeus' life and work (*HE* 5.23-25)' (*Irenaeus* 5) — applies more broadly than to his peace-making role in the Quartodeciman controversy.

337. See also Broadhead, *Jewish Ways* ch. 10.

§46.7 *The Parting of the Ways*

parted, precisely because the ways had not yet parted.[338] To which voice should we listen most carefully?

46.7 Conclusion

Several conclusions become clear from these last two chapters:

- the principal 'other' for early Christianity was early Judaism, and the principal 'other' for early Judaism was early Christianity;
- both Christianity and (rabbinic) Judaism were entirely dependent on Israel's scriptures and foundation beliefs to define their own identities;
- while rabbinic Judaism reacted to the disasters of the two Jewish revolts against Rome by effectively sloughing off those expressions of Second Temple Judaism which were no longer in tune with their distinctive focus on Torah, Christianity retained and built on the wider expressions of Second Temple Judaism;
- nor should it be forgotten that despite the first Jewish revolt, Judaism was widely recognized and respected as an ancient national religion, with synagogues often in prominent positions in Mediterranean cities; in contrast, the Christian house-groups and tenement-churches were, throughout this period, effectively minor players in back-streets rather than on main thoroughfares — and probably (in the face of Roman suspicion of voluntary associations and new cults, especially from the east) to at least some extent sheltering under the relative protection of the status accorded to the Jews and their synagogues;
- Jewish believers in Jesus continued to be part of Jewish communities in Syria and Palestine for some generations, probably a puzzle and an embarrassment to both rabbis and Christian leaders;
- leading figures both in the increasingly Gentile-dominated 'great church' and in emerging rabbinic Judaism, probably from after the failure of the Bar Kokhba revolt, made increasing attempts to identify and define their religion by drawing boundary lines which distinguished and distanced it from their significant 'other';
- somewhat surprisingly, the developing christology within the great church was not such a dividing line initially as it became later, with the

---

338. Pritz observes that 'The separation process was no sudden tear but a slow parting of company'. But he goes on to conclude: 'By the middle of the second century, the rift was probably complete' (*Nazarene Jewish Christianity* 58-62, 102, 109).

Ignatiuses and Melitos not so characteristic of Christianity as they were seen to be later, and not dissimilar from Jewish reflections about God;[339]
- at the same time many within the areas which leaders were attempting to so define did not think in terms of two clearly distinct religious movements but saw themselves as part of a heritage stretching back to Israel's patriarchs and living in an area where Jews and Christians were fellow sharers in that heritage.[340] Irenaeus points a more positive way forward.

These findings simply strengthen the evidence reviewed at the beginning of this investigation (§38.3a) that Christianity and Judaism did not become clearly distinct in the eyes of many diaspora Jews and Gentile Christians at any time in the second century, and probably not till after the Constantinian settlement gave Christianity a sense of superiority and establishment status with which Judaism could not compete. Even then, however, the common ground which lay between them could not but invite bolder souls to reach beyond the boundaries in search of co-religionists and kindred spirits. It is true of course, that the mainstream of establishment Christianity developed an often virulent anti-Jewish policy, with horrific outcomes in the twentieth century. But such developments as the Council for Christians and Jews (UK) and the reappearance, after centuries in which Jewish Christianity was a dim memory, of Messianic Jews and Jews for Jesus are a reminder that bonds are for many more important and more enduring than boundaries.

---

339. See again §38.3a above.
340. Skarsaune sums up well the sense that for many Christian Jews and Christian Gentiles there was no sense of a clear boundary between Christianity and Judaism ('Jewish Believers in Jesus in Antiquity' 8).

PART THIRTEEN

THE CONTINUING INFLUENCE OF PAUL AND PETER

CHAPTER 47

Paul

47.1 Introduction

Of the three principal figures in the formation of first-generation Christianity, it is Paul who made and has made the most lasting impact. James, as we have seen, has been largely ignored by the great church; apart from his conveniently filling the ecclesiastical role of first bishop of Jerusalem, in accord with Eusebian hindsight, he was effectively squeezed out by second-century leaders who found it necessary to define the identity of Christianity by distancing it from Judaism, and so also in effect from the form of Judaeo-Christianity that James most exemplified. And Peter, so much the focus of developing Catholic Christianity, seems to have made little explicit impact on the writings (the NT) which through our period came steadily to be more and more prized as central to the definition of Christian identity. We will have to devote §48 to an examination of the continuing impact of Peter. It was Paul, however, who made and leaves the strongest impression from the first generation of Christian leadership. 'The second founder of Christianity'[1] is an accolade of which Paul is not unworthy.

What made his impact so decisive was not simply his role in widening the appeal of the Jewish messianic sect to draw in increasing numbers of Gentiles — and thus, despite his best intentions, accelerating the development of Christianity away from Judaism and from its Jewish roots. The letter to Ephesians, as we saw in §37.1, summed up well the central significance of Paul's role in bringing the gospel to the Gentiles (Eph. 3.1-10). And without a doubt, it is principally due to Paul that the Jewish messianic sect, led by James, developed increasingly in the second century into a religion in its own right, a religion of

---

1. See *Beginning from Jerusalem* §29 n.8.

Gentile and Jew, but increasingly Gentile in membership and already in the second century becoming increasingly and predominantly Gentile.

In addition, however, it is hardly possible to ignore the influence of Paul in shaping the writings which became the NT. Of the twenty-seven writings which make up the NT, no fewer than thirteen are attributed to his authorship. Of these no one really disputes seven to be genuinely Pauline,[2] with opinion more or less equally divided on another two.[3] But the four others are in the canon of the NT precisely because they were attributed to Paul.[4] And Hebrews seems to have secured its otherwise disputed place in the NT canon primarily because the belief became established that it too had been written by Paul (§39.3c). More persuasive is the fact that the Acts of the Apostles are in fact predominantly the Acts of Paul, with Paul the dominant figure (Acts chs. 9, 13-28) and principal hero of the history. Add to that the strong impression that the Gospel of Mark was heavily influenced by Paul: it is Mark who takes Paul's technical term 'gospel' and turns it into a 'Gospel', an account of Jesus' mission which builds up to and climaxes in his death and resurrection, in direct accord with the Pauline gospel.[5] Since all the canonical Gospels follow Mark's lead in telling their Gospel in Paul's gospel form, including the Gospel of John (§41.4), it can be fairly said that it was the influence particularly of Paul which determined the canonical Gospel form. Finally we should add that of the other letters in the NT, 1 Peter is widely regarded as very Pauline in language and character.[6] The letter of James can be regarded as in some degree provoked by Paul (James 2.18-26),[7] but 1 Peter seems to have fallen under Pauline influence! Since this brief survey covers about three-quarters of the NT, it may fairly be concluded

---

2. Romans, 1 and 2 Corinthians, Galatians, Philippians, 1 Thessalonians, Philemon. See *Beginning from Jerusalem* §§32, 33 and 34 for treatments of these letters.

3. Colossians and 2 Thessalonians, which I regard as written by Paul or with his approval (*Beginning from Jerusalem* §§31.6 and 34.6).

4. Ephesians can be characterized as quintessentially Pauline (*Beginning from Jerusalem* §37.1); on the Pastoral Epistles (1 and 2 Timothy, and Titus), see above §39.3b and below §47.2a.

5. See above §§41.1-2 and further §42.2. The association of Mark with Paul was well rooted in the tradition (Acts 13.5; Col. 4.10; 2 Tim. 4.11; Phlm. 24).

6. *Beginning from Jerusalem* 1150-51; see also Brown in Brown and Meier, *Antioch and Rome* 134-39.

7. *Beginning from Jerusalem* 1141-44. See also D. C. Allison, 'Jas 2:14-26: Polemic against Paul, Apology for James', *Ancient Perspectives on Paul* (ed. Nicklas et al.) 123-49: as well as rebutting Paul's teaching, with a view to Jewish Christian auditors, Allison concludes that James 'was likely trying to correct a misinterpretation of Christianity that he knew to be current among some outsiders' (147), so that when read by non-Christian Jews, '2:14-26 . . . would function . . . as apologetics' — not so much a refutation of Paul 'but proper perception of and sympathetic appreciation for the Jewish Christianity of James' (148).

that of the three first-generation Christian leaders it is Paul's influence which has been most dominant in the formation of the NT writings.[8]

How then should we describe and evaluate the continuing influence of the impact made by Paul through the second generation and the second century of Christianity? The issue is more tantalizing than might be expected since it does not gel readily with the first two first-generation influences: Paul's own dependence on and interaction with the Jesus tradition is only modestly explicit and has to be argued for; and he was regularly regarded as a hostile and negative force by the Jews who believed in Jesus, as we saw in §§45 and 46. So a key question is, How was Paul looked back on and his contribution valued in the second century? The believing (Christian) Jews had very mixed feelings about Paul, but how was he regarded in other developing forms of Christianity? How much were his letters valued? Was his influence as formative of the great church as it was of the NT? Was he seen as precedent for and instigator of much more radical forms of Christianity?

We will look, then, at the way in which Paul was presented and his apostolic significance firmly established in the second generation (Pastorals, Acts) (§47.2a). The degree to which his letters were used and the development of a collection of Paul's letters, already effectively a basic canon, should be documented and discussed (§47.3). The development of Pauline legends and his influence on Gnostic groups also call for attention (§47.4). And the question whether Marcion was the most Pauline follower of Paul can hardly be ignored (§47.5). Did Irenaeus rescue Paul for the great church or was it more that he recognized a formative theological genius whose influence had been more contentious up till then (§47.6)?

47.2 Paul as Depicted in Second-Generation NT Documents

We have already looked at the way Paul is presented in what was probably the earliest of the post-Pauline Pauline letters — Ephesians (§37.1). That was a presentation which summed up well what we know to have been Paul's own priorities, though perhaps a little more vaingloriously than Paul himself would have wished. But he is also depicted in the Pastoral epistles to Timothy and Titus, and by Luke in Acts. What do these writings tell us about the way Paul was perceived and his contribution evaluated in the latter decades of the first century?

---

8. However, J. D. Tabor, *Paul and Jesus: How the Apostle Transformed Christianity* (New York: Simon & Schuster, 2012), overstates 'the dominance of pro-Pauline writings within the New Testament canon.... Even the order and arrangement of the New Testament books reflects the dominance of Paul's perspectives'. 'The entire New Testament canon is largely a post-Paul and pro-Paul production' (7, 19).

a. The Pastoral Epistles

Assuming that the Pastorals were written by one who had been a disciple or associate of Paul's, and that his objective was to 'contemporize' or promote the influence of Paul for his own generation (§39.3a-b), the question is, How did he see Paul fitting into or contributing (apostolically) to the developing situations of the final decades of the first century? The reverence for Paul is obvious: Paul was a heroic figure whose conversion expressed the power and character of the gospel (1 Tim. 1.12-17), and who could certainly be presented as a model and example of a lifetime of committed service (2 Tim. 4.6-8). His calls for discipline, dismissals of those who had failed him, and warnings against false teaching, not uncharacteristic of his earlier letters, could be echoed to reinforce both his image as a stern disciplinarian and the strictness with which the Christian communities needed to safeguard their organization and identity.[9]

But the most striking features are the ones which most clearly mark out the distinctiveness of the Pastorals, as already noted briefly in §39.3b: 'increasing institutionalization' and the 'crystallization of faith into set forms'. Both are indicative of a second-generation movement, where the freedom of the charismatic pioneer to create and experiment with fresh forms and formulations comes increasingly to be seen as a threat to the forms and formulations which had proved to be most effective in the first generation — where it becomes more important to conserve than to explore afresh. This has been the universal experience of spiritual renewal movements down the centuries, as illustrated by the Reformation in the sixteenth century and Pentecostalism in the twentieth, and the Pastorals are clear examples of the same sociological development.[10]

(1) So far as ecclesiastical organization is concerned, the most obvious contrast is between the Pastorals and 1 Corinthians. In writing 1 Corinthians, Paul was fully aware that he was confronted with a calamitous lack of self-discipline and good order. But at no time does he appeal to 'elders' or 'overseers' or 'deacons' to exercise authority and to bring order to the disorder. He appeals to the Corinthians' good sense (1 Cor. 5), he hopes that the charism of wisdom will be granted and exercised (1 Cor. 6.5), he urges them to respect those who have taken initiative in service (1 Cor. 16.15-18). But he does not assume that elders or leaders should be appointed (contrast Acts 14.23). His concept of 'church order' seems to be much more charismatic, dependent on the immediacy of the Spirit's direction and enabling (1 Cor. 12, 14).[11]

---

9. 1 Tim. 1.19-20; 4.1-3; 5.1-16; 6.20-21; 2 Tim. 1.15; 2.14-18; 3.1-9; 4.3-4, 14; Tit. 1.10-16.

10. See particularly MacDonald, *The Pauline Churches*.

11. See my *Jesus and the Spirit* ch. IX.

It can, of course, be argued that 1 Corinthians was written relatively early in Paul's missionary career, and that the experience of the Corinthian church in particular made Paul realize that he had to exercise more discipline and require more order in his assemblies. But he had already been engaged in apostolic mission for about twenty years when he wrote 1 Corinthians; and his own execution took place less than ten years later. And there are no indications in his later letters that he had reacted to the Corinthian crises with a determination to demand greater organization in his churches. The Pastorals read rather as written from the perspective of disciples of Paul who were determined to curtail or shut down the charismatic freedom, a freedom which Paul had so valued even when it got out of hand. So the roles of Timothy and Titus are presented as more authoritarian than Paul had ever been, with a power to ordain and appoint (1 Tim. 5.22; Tit. 1.5) which Paul had never exercised.[12] *Charisma* was no longer (to be) seen as a gracious gift and enabling for all members of Christ's body (Rom. 12; 1 Cor. 12), but as a formal empowering for office (1 Tim. 4.14; 2 Tim. 1.6).[13] And formally recognized 'elders' and formally appointed overseers and deacons are integral to the structure of the assemblies.[14]

One could still argue that an older Paul had himself turned away from and revised his earlier vision of the church as the charismatic body of Christ. But given the differences of style and circumstances reflected, it is more plausible to see a later hand in effect surmising how Paul would or should have reacted to these changing circumstances. Either way, the Paul of the Pastorals is presented as one who was much more concerned with ecclesiastical structures for good order than ever had been the case with the earlier Paul. He has become Paul the good churchman, significantly different from Paul the innovative apostle.[15]

(2) So far as the crystallization of the faith is concerned, the picture is similar — a dominant desire to consolidate and secure a more objectified identity. Faith is much less the living means by which individuals are in communication with God and by which they live, than that by which they

---

12. Paul had even held back from becoming too involved in baptizing his converts (1 Cor. 1.14-16).

13. 'Perhaps the clearest deficit of the Pastorals over against the Pauline theology is to be seen in that they no more reckon with a living presence of the Spirit in the community. The work of the Spirit appears to be restricted to the holder of office, to whom it has been assigned by ordination with the laying on of hands' (J. Roloff, *Der erste Brief an Timotheus* [EKK XV; Zürich: Benziger, 1988] 381).

14. 1 Tim. 3.1-7, 8-13; 5.(1), 17, 19; Tit. 1.5, 7-9.

15. Cf. Marshall, *Pastoral Epistles* 94.

believe.[16] It is now 'the faith', that which is to be believed,[17] 'the standard of sound teaching' (2 Tim. 1.13), a deposit once entrusted and now to be 'guarded'[18] lest it be 'blasphemed' (1 Tim. 6.1). Paul is still thought of as a preacher of the gospel,[19] but apart from 2 Tim. 4.5, Timothy and other leaders are characterized more as teachers of 'faithful sayings' and 'sound words'.[20] Illustrative of the perspective so different from Paul's confidence in the imminence of the parousia[21] is the command to Timothy envisaging an extended period in which the teaching will be passed on: 'what you have heard from me through many witnesses entrust to faithful people who will be able to teach others as well' (2 Tim. 2.2). As Raymond Brown justly observes: 'The Pastorals reflect what will become increasingly characteristic of Christianity in the second through the fourth centuries: an ever-sharpening insistence on orthodoxy (correct faith content), combined with orthopraxy (correct behavior)'.[22]

Quite what this consolidation of the faith implies for the faith itself is less clear than we might have hoped. We have already noted (§45.4b) that the issues which had featured so largely in Paul's own time seem to have faded. The references to Jew/Gentile tensions seem to be more echoes of the past and formulaic in character than the living issues which so racked Paul existentially. And the references to alternative teachings seem to be more generalized and vaguer in content, for example, 'foolish tales such as are told by elderly women' (1 Tim. 4.7), than what Paul had to counter. As 'the faith' became more firmly defined, the alternatives became the more easily dismissed in sweepingly dismissive terms.

However, the only detail about the faith which is clearly defined is the christology. And here we find the fascinating feature of a faith which is developing but which is still being held within or in relation to the Jewish monotheism within which Christianity came to maturity. The traditional faith remained firm, but the belief in Christ so fundamental to the faith was stretching its traditional terms. Thus, on the one hand we note the remarkably strong reaffirmation of Jewish monotheism which is a feature particularly of 1 Timothy:

16. E.g. Gal. 2.20; Rom. 14.23.
17. 1 Tim. 1.19; 3.9; 4.1, 6; 5.8; 6.10, 12, 21; 2 Tim. 3.8; 4.7; Tit. 1.13; 2.2.
18. 1 Tim. 6.20; 2 Tim. 1.14.
19. 1 Tim. 1.11; 2 Tim. 1.8; 2.8.
20. 1 Tim. 4.9-11, 13, 16; 5.17; 6.3; Tit. 1.9. 'Teaching' (*didaskalia*) occurs 15 times in the Pastorals, as compared with twice in Romans and once each in Ephesians and Colossians; typically characterized as 'sound' teaching (1 Tim. 1.10; 6.3; 2 Tim. 1.13; 4.3; Tit. 1.9, 13; 2.1, 2).
21. E.g. 1 Thess. 4.15-17; 1 Cor. 7.29-31; Phil. 4.5.
22. Brown, *Introduction* 649-50.

- 1.17 — 'To the King of ages, immortal, invisible, the only God, be honour and glory for ever and ever';[23]
- 2.5 — 'There is one God',[24] which the one mediatorship of 'the man Christ Jesus' does not detract from but rather confirms and enhances;
- 6.15-16 — 'The blessed and only Sovereign, the King of kings and Lord of lords, who alone has immortality and dwells in unapproachable light, whom no man has ever seen or can see'.[25]

On the other hand, and at the same time, the Pastorals' christology would seem to encroach to a substantial degree on this monotheism. A favourite phrase is 'God our Saviour'.[26] That the God of Jewish monotheism is meant is clear.[27] But the role of Saviour is now shared by Christ;[28] and more strikingly, Christ is now understood as 'the glory of our great God and Saviour' (Tit. 2.13),[29] and perhaps as 'the goodness and loving kindness of God our Saviour' (Tit. 3.4).[30] In view of the tensions indicated and discussed at the end of §45.4b and in §46.4c, it is notable that the Pastorals do not, like Ignatius, call Jesus 'God' *simpliciter*, but weave their faith in Jesus into their reaffirmed monotheistic heritage in what we can fairly call Logos theology terms — Jesus as the embodiment of God's glory and decisive expression of his saving power.

Here, then, is a striking example of the way in which christological claims developed, in direct dependence on Jewish faith in the one God and yet without any sense of awkwardness for or tension with that prior faith. Whether this is because the writer(s) was/were Gentile, for whom the monotheistic affirmations were simply part of Christianity's Jewish heritage taken on board with their conversion to Jesus as Saviour, or because this is the voice of traditional Jewish conviction before a high christology became too controversial for more traditional Jews (and Jewish believers-in-Jesus), we cannot tell. Either way, it

---

23. Cf. e.g. Jer. 10.10; 2 Macc. 1.24-25; *Ep. Arist.* 132; see further G. Delling, '*MONOS THEOS*', *TLZ* 77 (1952) 469-76.

24. The central Jewish confession, the *Shema* (Deut. 6.4).

25. Cf. e.g. Exod. 33.20; Deut. 10.17; 2 Macc. 12.15; 3 Macc. 5.35; see further Roloff, *Erste Brief an Timotheus* 355-57.

26. 1 Tim. 1.1; 2.3; 4.10; Tit. 1.3; 2.10; 3.4.

27. E.g. Deut. 32.15; Ps. 24.5; Mic. 7.7; Wis. 16.7; 1 Macc. 4.30; further G. Fohrer and W. Foerster, *TDNT* 7.975-78, 1012-14.

28. 2 Tim. 1.10; Tit. 2.13; 3.6.

29. See V. Hasler, 'Epiphanie und Christologie in des Pastoralbriefen', *TLZ* 33 (1977) 193-209; G. D. Fee, *Pauline Christology: An Exegetical-Theological Study* (Peabody: Hendrickson, 2007) 442-46.

30. 'The Christology is newly formulated in terms of epiphany' (Marshall, *Pastoral Epistles* 78) — referring to 1 Tim. 6.14; 2 Tim. 1.10; 4.1, 8; Tit. 2.13.

is striking that this first clear attempt to consolidate Christianity's faith took some pains to emphasise its continuing Jewish character, and the integration between faith in Jesus and faith in the one God as of continuing importance and indeed taken for granted.

This then is the Paul who is presented in the Pastoral Epistles — a Paul for whom the priority was to consolidate the faith, to guard it unflinchingly and to pass it on faithfully. This was Paul as his disciple(s) evidently wanted him remembered — as equipping his churches for what would be a threatened and challenging future. That the christology was not a static entity or simply a recall of faithful sayings, but itself developing fresh expression, probably indicates that, alongside the development of church hierarchy, it was the growing reverence for Christ which most clearly marked out the second-generation churches (of the Aegean) as they moved into the second century.

b. The Paul of Acts

There is indeed little question that Paul is the principal hero of Luke's history of Christianity's beginnings.[31] As already noted, his account of Paul's conversion and subsequent mission activity takes up well over half of the book. Luke is also entirely at one with Paul's own self-evaluation in the prominence he gives to Paul's vocation as missionary to the Gentiles, although, unlike Paul, he does seem somewhat hesitant about ranking Paul as an apostle alongside the twelve apostles.[32] There are the unresolved puzzles of why Luke does not mention Paul's letter-writing, and why he almost entirely ignores the presence of Christians already in Rome prior to Paul's entry in captivity to Rome. But it is perhaps understandable that he wanted to make the climax of his account Paul's final success — despite trials and tribulations, Paul succeeds in bringing the gospel to the heart of the Roman empire.

However, the Paul who emerges from the pages of Acts is a much more eirenic figure, particularly in his relations with the mother church of Jerusalem, than would ever appear to have been the case when we rely solely on the testimony of Paul's own letters. We may recall some of the striking features which emerged in *Beginning from Jerusalem*.

---

31. J. C. Lentz, *Luke's Portrait of Paul* (SNTSMS 77; Cambridge University, 1993), argues that Luke presents Paul as a man of high social status: 'Luke's intention is to emphasize that Paul's social credentials and virtuous character place him in elite company', 'no mere "rank-and-file" citizen, but an individual one could not dismiss lightly or punish without regret' (104, 138).

32. *Beginning from Jerusalem* 361-63, 437.

- Not long after his conversion in Damascus Paul goes up to Jerusalem and meets with the apostles (Acts 9.23-27). In contrast, Paul himself seems to be explicitly and emphatically denying reports, quite possibly, to the same effect: he did *not* immediately go up to Jerusalem to those who were apostles before him, and when he did go to Jerusalem, three years later, he stayed with Peter and otherwise saw only 'James, the Lord's brother' (Gal. 1.17-20).[33]
- As already noted, Luke depicts Paul as appointing elders in his early congregations (Acts 14.23), even though elders are never mentioned in the Pauline corpus prior to 1 Timothy and Titus.[34] In contrast, Paul gives no hint that he did appoint or might have appointed his first converts in Achaia, Stephanas and his family, to a leadership role, even though they displayed obvious leadership potential (1 Cor. 16.15-16).
- In the controversy as to whether believing Gentiles should be circumcised, the decisive testimony is that of Peter (Acts 15.6-11), and the final ruling is that of James (15.13-21); and James is the principal mover behind the 'apostolic decree' (15.20, 29) which Paul then delivered to the (Galatian) churches which he and Barnabas had previously established (15.23, 30-31; 16.4). In contrast, in Paul's account of the resolution of the issue, it was his testimony and argumentation which was decisive (Gal. 2.1-9), and thereafter he never makes mention of an 'apostolic decree'.[35]
- Luke makes no reference to the incident at Antioch, which was instigated by representations from James in Jerusalem, and in the course of which Paul denounced Peter (Gal. 2.11-14). Paul's breach with Barnabas, which was probably the result of Barnabas's failure to back Paul in the incident, is put down by Luke to a more personal and somewhat trivial dispute about Mark's suitability for the mission team (Acts 15.36-39).
- Luke says nothing of the interventions of Jewish believers-in-Jesus which disrupted Paul's mission in Galatia, Corinth and Philippi, which probably took their inspiration from Jerusalem, and to which Paul responded with some vitriol.[36] In contrast Luke seems to make a point of drawing

---

33. See further my 'The Relationship between Paul and Jerusalem according to Galatians 1 and 2', *New Testament Studies* 28 (1982) 461-78; also *Beginning from Jerusalem* 362-69.

34. 1 Tim. 5.(1-2), 17, 19; Tit. 1.5.

35. *Beginning from Jerusalem* §27.3.

36. Gal. 1.6-9; 5.1-12; 2 Cor. 2.17–3.1; 11.3-6, 12-15; Phil. 3.2. See further *Beginning from Jerusalem* §31.7, §32.7b and g, and §34.4f.

parallels between Peter and Paul,[37] and of depicting them as preaching the same message.[38]

- Luke gives no hint of Paul's readiness to act 'as if outside the law' (1 Cor. 9.21), but makes a point of noting Paul's readiness to have Timothy circumcised (Acts 16.3), his undertaking a Nazirite vow on the way to Jerusalem (18.18-23) and his willingness to follow James's recommendation that he should go through purification rites in the temple to counter the rumours that he taught Gentile believers not to observe the law (21.21-26). Paul might well have done all these things,[39] but the fact that Luke makes a point of recounting Paul's compliance with the law, when he also ignores the sort of advice Paul gives in Romans 14 and 1 Corinthians 10, strongly suggests a tendentious motivation on Luke's part.
- Similarly his failure to give a clear account of Paul's motivation in making his final trip to Jerusalem — to deliver the collection (Rom. 15.25-28) — or of Paul's fears that the collection might not be acceptable to the Jerusalem leadership (15.31), suggests something of a cover-up. Had this attempt of Paul to heal the breach with Jerusalem been successful, Luke would hardly have ignored it. That he did ignore it, strongly suggests that the collection failed to achieve what Paul had hoped. Luke's failure to mention any support given to Paul by the Jerusalem leaders, including the highly respected James, during Paul's two-year imprisonment is probably confirmation that the breach was not mended. Rather than end his account of Paul's relations with Jerusalem on a negative note Luke presumably decided to say nothing.[40]

It is likely, then, that Luke was following Jerusalem's version of all or most of these episodes.[41] It is not necessary to argue that Luke deliberately

37.

Peter		Paul
3.1-10	Healing of a crippled man	14.8-10
5.15	Miraculous healings	19.12
8.14-24	Denouncing imposters	13.6-12
9.36-41	Reviving a dead person	20.9-12

38. Acts 2.22-40; 13.26-41. Luke's parallelism of Peter with Paul was first noticed by M. Scheckenburger, *Über den Zweck der Apostelgeschichte* (Bern, 1841).

39. *Beginning from Jerusalem* 663-64, 751-52, 961-62.

40. *Beginning from Jerusalem* 970-72.

41. See my 'Luke's Jerusalem Perspective', in S. Walton et al., eds., *Reading Acts Today: Essays in Honour of L. C. A. Alexander* (LNTS 427; London: T & T Clark, 2011) 120-36. See also J. Jervell, *The Unknown Paul: Essays on Luke-Acts and Early Christian History* (Minneapolis: Augsburg, 1984) ch. 4; Jervell maintains that Paul the Jew 'has been preserved in the oral tradition that lies behind the Acts of the Apostles' (59).

corrupted and perverted his account in order to synthesize two diverging strands of earliest Christianity (Jerusalem and Pauline).[42] Since Baur, this has been a common line of explanation for such curiosities of the Lukan account.[43] But even if Luke was simply following the Jerusalem version of events, that is itself sufficient to make the point that his presentation of Paul was tempered by the strong impulse to depict him as compliant with the leadership of James, his mission closely paralleling that of Peter, and his relationship with Jerusalem unbroken.

The point is, then, that it was Luke's portrayal of Paul which, together with the Pastoral Epistles, probably exemplified or dominated the view of the churches which received and circulated these writings. The second-generation Paul was quite a different character from the Paul of the earlier letters. The Pastorals and Acts brought Paul into the comfort zone of a Christian leadership seeking to consolidate Christianity's faith and order and to retain its Jewish character, while keeping it distinct from emerging rabbinic Judaism. Paul was no longer a controversial character, outspoken, pushing back boundaries, dealing innovatively with changing circumstances. He was the safe Paul, the ecclesial Paul.

c. 2 Peter

The most astonishing feature of 2 Peter's testimony on this point is that it regards Paul's letters as scripture:

> 3.15-16 — '. . . consider the patience of our Lord as salvation, just as our beloved brother Paul wrote to you in accordance with the wisdom given to him, as he does in all his letters, speaking in them concerning these matters. In them there are some things hard to understand, which the ignorant and unstable twist to their own destruction, as they do the other scriptures'.

This is very striking since, as already noted, such a status (scripture) is not otherwise accorded to NT writings till *2 Clement* and Justin.[44]

---

42. A. J. Thompson, *One Lord, One People: The Unity of the Church in Acts in Its Literary Setting* (LNTS 359; London: T & T Clark, 2008), sets the theme within concerns for unity as documented in other ancient literature.

43. See e.g. W. W. Gasque, *A History of the Criticism of the Acts of the Apostles* (Grand Rapids: Eerdmans, 1975) chs. II and V. For a broader survey of Luke's portrayal of Paul see S. E. Porter, 'The Portrait of Paul in Acts', in S. Westerholm, ed., *The Blackwell Companion to Paul* (Chichester: Wiley-Blackwell, 2011) 124-38.

44. See above §44.2i and §44.3b.

Two other features, however, should not be missed. One is that the author of 2 Peter was familiar with a number of Paul's letters ('all his letters') and regarded them all to be ranked with 'the other scriptures', that is, presumably, primarily the OT/LXX writings already regarded as scripture.[45] This suggests that already ('all' = many/most of) Paul's letters had been collected and circulated more widely among churches which cherished his memory (in this case Rome?). The other feature is that the letters were being taken up by those whom 2 Peter regarded as 'ignorant and unstable', probably the 'false teachers' referred to in 2.1. Unfortunately it is not at all clear which themes or emphases of Paul's letters were being so 'twisted' — perhaps drawing antinomian corollaries from his teaching on freedom from the law (cf. 2 Pet. 2, particularly 2.19), or distorting his eschatology (cf. 2 Pet. 3).[46]

Thus already in 2 Peter, perhaps early in the second century, two trends become evident: both an increasing reverence for Paul and the fact that his letters stimulated or provided material for a wider range of teaching and conduct than the leaders of the great church found acceptable. Both trends will be well exemplified in what follows.

47.3 The Reception of Paul in the Second Century

We already know how Paul was regarded among the second-century groups of Jewish believers in Christ. An Ebionite tendency set Paul in the sharpest antithesis with James,[47] though a Nazoraean tendency seems to have been more sympathetic to or accepting of the Gentile expansion most associated with Paul (§45.8b).[48] And it is probably unsurprising that the most Jewish-Christian writing among the Apostolic Fathers, *Didache*, shows the least influence from Paul.[49] Nor should it probably occasion much surprise that the *Shepherd* of Hermas shows about as little interest in or influence from Paul, since its quality of thought is so different, and influence from

---

45. As indicated in n.44, the canonical Gospels were regarded as 'scripture' by the time of *2 Clement* and Justin. For what letters may have been in mind in 2 Peter see the brief discussion of Bauckham, *Jude, 2 Peter* 330-31.

46. See again Bauckham, *Jude, 2 Peter* 332-33.

47. See above §§45.2c, 45.8a, d.

48. Willitts presses too hard the argument that anti-Paulinism was 'not a central or even near-central element of Jewish Christian identity in the second century' ('Paul and Jewish Christians in the Second Century' 165, 167-68).

49. Tuckett, '*Didache*' 91-93.

Jewish tradition and from James is more readily arguable.⁵⁰ But how was he regarded and his letters received elsewhere and by what eventuated as more mainstream groups?

a. *1 Clement*

Clement regarded Paul very highly — of that there is no doubt:

> *1 Clem.* 5.5-7 — 'Because of jealousy and strife Paul showed the way to the prize for endurance. Seven times he bore chains; he was sent into exile, he was stoned; he became a herald in both the East and the West; and he received the noble fame for his faith. He taught righteousness to the whole world, came to the limits of the West, and bore witness before the rulers. And thus he was set free from this world and taken up to the holy place, having become the greatest example of endurance'.

The passage reflects a clear impression of Paul towards the end of the first century, in Rome, an impression based on some knowledge of Paul's teachings and of his life as a missionary and of his death. The emphasis on 'endurance' (*hypomonē*) perhaps reflects Paul's own regular use of the term.⁵¹ And the focus of his teaching on 'righteousness' (*dikaiosunē*) may well reflect the importance of the term for Paul, particularly in his letter to Rome.⁵² This suggests that Clement was able to draw on a living memory of Paul's teaching. Similarly, the information about Paul's sufferings overlaps to a small extent with Paul's self-testimony in 2 Cor. 11.23-27, but certainly was not drawn from there. Likewise, the reference to Paul's witness 'before the rulers' and his death

---

50. 'His thought is determined from extra-Christian, especially Jewish traditions and presentations. The law is (regarded) as a moral, and thus before God the powerful salvation creating norm, without the question of the relationship between Judaism and Christianity appearing to be relevant. Signs of a positive reception of Paul in the theology are lacking, as also indications of the author's critical engagement with Paul' (A. Lindemann, *Paulus im ältesten Christentum* [Tübingen: Mohr Siebeck, 1979] 289-90). The only plausible interaction with Paul is *Mand.* 4.4.1-2 (cf. 1 Cor. 7.39-40) (Verheyden, 'The *Shepherd of Hermas*' 324-29; who also notes that 'the *Shepherd* shows no interest in the subtleties of Paul's argument' — 219). For possible echoes of James see J. Drummond, *NTAF* 108-13. See also Osiek, *Hermas* 24-27.

51. *Hypomonē* appears 16 times in the Pauline corpus.

52. *Dikaiosunē* is used 33 times in Romans. Hagner thinks the evidence of *1 Clement*'s familiarity with Romans is 'unassailable' (*Use* 220); see also Brown in Brown and Meier, *Antioch and Rome* 166-67.

probably presupposes information not available from Paul's letters, and so equally derived from memories of Paul's final years in Rome.[53]

Firsthand knowledge of Paul's letters is also clear. Most strikingly from 1 Corinthians to which Clement refers directly:

> *1 Clem.* 47.1-3 — 'Take up the epistle of the blessed Paul, the apostle. What did he first write to you, at the beginning of his proclamation of the gospel? Truly, inspired by the Spirit, he wrote to you concerning himself and Cephas and Apollos, because even then you had engaged in partisan strife'.

This certainly indicates knowledge of 1 Cor. 1-4 and that the letter was well known both in Corinth and Rome — a further indication that Paul's letters to particular churches had been circulated to other churches, a practice probably instituted at an early stage among churches which reverenced Paul (cf. again Col. 4.16).

Beyond that the evidence is more open to the possibility of shared tradition or oral memory. However, the fact that Clement was obviously familiar with 1 Corinthians increases the likelihood that similar passages or echoes in 1 Corinthians and *1 Clement* are to be explained by Clement's writing his letter in the light of the precedent which 1 Corinthians provided in dealing with Corinthian factionalism. In addition, there is a substantial measure of agreement that Clement knew Romans as well as 1 Corinthians,[54] and possibly also Galatians, Philippians, Colossians and Ephesians.[55]

1 Clement	Certain	Very probable	Quite likely
13.1		1 Cor. 1.31	
24.1		1 Cor. 15.20, 23	
24.4-5			1 Cor. 15.36-37
34.8		1 Cor. 2.9	
37.5–38.2		1 Cor. 12.20-26	
47.1-3	1 Cor. 1.12		
49.5		1 Cor. 13.4-7	
32.2			Rom. 9.5

---

53. On the testimony that Paul 'came to the limits of the West', see *Beginning from Jerusalem* 1055-56.

54. A. J. Carlyle in *NTAF* 37-44; Lindemann, *Paulus* 177-99; Gregory, '1 Clement' 144-51; also E. Dassmann, *Der Stachel im Fleisch: Paulus in der frühchristlichen Literatur bis Irenäus* (Münster: Aschendorff, 1979) 79-91.

55. See Carlyle 51-54 and particularly Hagner, *Use* 221-29, whose conclusion, however, that 'the greater part, if not the whole, of the Pauline corpus was probably known to him [Clement] and was present in his mind' (237) is overbold.

1 Clement	Certain	Very probable	Quite likely
32.4–33.1			Rom. 5.21–6.2
35.5-6		Rom. 1.29-32	
50.6-7			Rom. 4.7-9

Particularly intriguing is the possibility that Clement was able to draw also on the Pastorals. He uses a number of terms distinctive to the Pastorals,[56] and there are a number of shared themes:[57] for example, concern for the elder and the deportment of women,[58] readiness for good works,[59] the portrayal of Paul,[60] what is approved by God,[61] and God not lying.[62] Whether this indicates knowledge of the Pastorals or simply paraenetical concerns common to the early churches probably is neither here nor there. What is more relevant is that *1 Clement* shares with the Pastorals a deep ecclesiastical conviction that the churches need to be more disciplined and more tightly organized — a striking feature when *1 Clement* is set alongside the charismatic perspective of its predecessor, 1 Corinthians. Clement goes further than Acts (14.23) in depicting the apostles as appointing 'the first fruits of their ministries as bishops and deacons' (*1 Clem.* 42.1-5). And he goes further than the Pastorals in reverting to distinctions between priest and laity and depicting the bishop as a sacrifice-offering priest (*1 Clem.* 40-41; 44.1-4). Insofar as there was influence from Paul, therefore, this was Paul or the Pauline heritage being conformed to the pattern of religion as it was normally understood, organized and practised.[63]

b. Ignatius

As with *1 Clement*, it is clear that Ignatius venerated the apostle Paul:

> *Eph.* 12.2 — 'you are fellow initiates with Paul, who was sanctified, who was attested, deservedly blessed, in whose footsteps may I be found when I attain to God, who in every epistle makes mention of you in Christ Jesus'.

---

56. 'Of the 175 words in the Pastoral epistles, which are lacking in the rest of the NT, 16 come before us in 1 Clement' (Lona, *erste Clemensbrief* 50).
57. Lona, *erste Clemensbrief* 50.
58. Cf. *1 Clem.* 1.3 with 1 Tim. 5.17 and Tit. 2.4-5 (*NTAF* 50-51).
59. Cf. *1 Clem.* 2.7 with Tit. 3.1 and 2 Tim. 2.21.
60. Cf. *1 Clem.* 5.6 with 1 Tim. 2.7 and 2 Tim. 1.11.
61. Cf. *1 Clem.* 7.3 with 1 Tim. 2.3.
62. Cf. *1 Clem.* 27.2 with Tit. 1.2.
63. Lindemann concludes: 'The author of 1 Clement is no representative of an explicit "Paulinism"; but his letter is an important testimony for the considerable influence which Paul and his letters have exercised on theology and the church in Rome at the end of the first century' (*Paulus* 199).

Rom. 4.3 — 'I do not order you as did Peter and Paul. They were apostles; I am a convict. They were free; I up till now have been a slave'.

Here again, as with 2 Pet. 3.16, we have not only attested knowledge that Paul wrote several letters, but also knowledge of what he wrote in them, even if the claim that the Ephesian Christians were mentioned in every letter is rather hyperbolic.[64] This strengthens the impression that Paul's letters had already, in the first decade or two of the second century, been circulated quite widely (Ignatius would have known them in Syrian Antioch), and most probably as a collection of his letters.

That Ignatius was familiar with a number of these letters is clear enough from his own letters. There are no direct quotations or references, as in *1 Clem.* 47.1-3, but echoes of Pauline language and phrases are sufficiently common to substantiate the case that Ignatius had known and used several of Paul's letters.[65]

Ignatius		**Probable echoes**	**Possible echoes**
Eph.	8.2	Rom. 8.5; 1 Cor. 3.1-3	
	10.1		1 Thess. 5.17
	15.3		1 Cor. 3.16
	16.1		1 Cor. 6.9-10
	18.1	1 Cor. 1.18, 20, 23	
	18.2; 20.2	Rom. 1.3-4	
	19.3		Rom. 6.4
Magn.	10.2		1 Cor. 5.7-8
Trall.	9–10		1 Cor. 15.12-14, 32
	12.3		1 Cor. 9.27
Rom.	5.1	1 Cor. 4.4	
	6.1		1 Cor. 9.15
	7.2		Gal. 6.14
	9.2	1 Cor. 15.8-9	
Philad.	3.3		1 Cor. 6.9-10
	7.1		1 Cor. 2.10

64. Ephesus is mentioned only in 1 Cor. 15.32; 16.8; Eph. 1.1 (v.l.); 1 Tim. 1.3; 2 Tim. 1.18; 4.12. But references to the churches in Asia could be included (1 Cor. 16.19; 2 Tim. 1.15; cf. Rom. 16.5; 2 Cor. 1.8; 8.18-19, 23-24), as could Paul's references to his care for his churches generally (as in 2 Cor. 11.28; cf. Rom. 16.4; 1 Cor. 7.17; 11.16; 14.33-34; 2 Cor. 12.13; 2 Thess. 1.4). See also Dassmann, *Stachel* 129-32.

65. W. R. Inge in *NTAF* 64-75; Lindemann, *Paulus* 199-221; Dassmann, *Stachel* 132-49; Foster, 'Ignatius' 164-72.

§47.3   *Paul*

Ignatius	Probable echoes	Possible echoes
Smyrn. inscrip.		1 Cor. 1.7
10.2		2 Tim. 1.16
11.3		Phil. 3.15
Polyc. 1.2		Eph. 4.2
5.1		Eph. 5.25, 29
6.2		2 Tim. 2.4; Eph. 6.14-17

Of course, we can hardly think of Ignatius, restrained by his captors, able to carry with him a collection of scrolls containing copies of Paul's letters, from which he was able to quote. But the uncontrived way Ignatius seems to draw on Pauline terminology and phrases[66] strongly suggests that he had studied and reflected on at least several of Paul's letters during his own ministry in Antioch.[67] Significantly it would appear once again to be 1 Corinthians with which Ignatius was especially familiar[68]— which suggests that this Pauline letter was particularly valued in these decades, presumably for the way he (Paul) had handled the various pastoral issues put to him. But the impression is hard to escape that Ignatius had so steeped himself in Paul's letters that his own thought and concerns, perhaps unconsciously, were shaped by Pauline language and imagery.

This is all the more interesting for two reasons. One is that it is far from obvious that Ignatius was a Paulinist in theology.[69] But it can quite readily be argued that Ignatius's emphases represent understandable developments from Paul's theology.[70] This would be true particularly in regard to christology: the insistence that Jesus was God in the flesh, both truly divine and truly human

---

66. Particularly clear are the echoes of 1 Cor. 1.20 in *Eph.* 18.1 ('Where is the wise man? . . . Where is the debater?') and the use of *ektrōma* ('abortion') in *Rom.* 9.2 (1 Cor. 15.8).

67. Foster concludes that there is a strong case for Ignatius's usage of four epistles, in declining order of likelihood — 1 Corinthians, Ephesians, 1 Timothy and 2 Timothy ('Ignatius' 172). I would be inclined to add Romans. Schoedel notes that A. E. Barnett, *Paul Becomes a Literary Influence* (Chicago: University of Chicago Press, 1941) 107, was confident regarding 1 Corinthians, Romans and Ephesians, and thought it probable that Ignatius also knew Galatians, Philippians and Colossians (*Ignatius* 9-10). Jefford is 'clear that the bishop falls well within the influence of the letters of Paul, particularly since his letters to Ephesus and Rome are so closely modeled upon those of the apostle' (*Apostolic Fathers* 12).

68. Inge infers that 'Ignatius must have known this Epistle [1 Corinthians] almost by heart' (*NTAF* 67).

69. 'Ignatius obviously considers Paul to be the theologian who had most truly understood the salvation proclaimed in Christ's cross and resurrection'; 'the many allusions to the Pauline correspondence demonstrate that Ignatius repeatedly returned to those letters to find guidance and instruction' (Koester, *Introduction* 2.283, 284). The absence in Ignatius of allusions to Paul's teaching on justification naturally catches attention (Lindemann, *Paulus* 217-18).

70. Cf. C. B. Smith, 'Ministry, Martyrdom and Other Mysteries: Pauline Influence on Ignatius of Antioch', in Bird and Dodson, eds., *Paul and the Second Century* 37-56.

(flesh),[71] can readily be explained as a Pauline understanding of Christ developed in the face of the emergence of docetist teaching;[72] even though Ignatius's insistence that Christ's resurrection was also 'in the flesh' (*Smyrn.* 3.1) leaves behind Paul's differentiation of flesh and body in his conceptualization of the resurrection in 1 Cor. 15.35-50.[73] Likewise Ignatius's ecclesiology, with its persistent insistence on mono-episcopacy,[74] could be seen as continuing the trend set in the Pastorals; though his insistence that only a eucharist authorized by the bishop is valid (*Smyrn.* 8.1-2) would most likely have jarred with Paul. On the other hand, his strong polarization of Christianity and Judaism, and insistence on their clear distinction (§46.6a), would probably have cut at the heart of Paul's still sustained hopes for Israel (Rom. 11).

The other reason why Paul's influence on Ignatius is so interesting is that after the Judaean churches, probably the Syrian churches were most distant from Paul and most critical of his Gentile mission as carried out in Pauline terms.[75] It could, of course, be the case that Ignatius shared an Antiochene tradition, which had also helped shape Paul's thought.[76] But possibly it was Ignatius himself who brought the Pauline letters into the worship and teaching of the church in Antioch.[77] Nor should it be forgotten that Ignatius was writing his letters to churches which had probably all been established by Paul himself or by the missions sent out by Paul from Ephesus to other cities in Asia. In any case it would not be stretching the evidence too far to describe Ignatius as a protégé of Paul.[78]

c. Polycarp

Polycarp in his letter to the *Philippians* likewise venerated Paul:

> *Phil.* 3.2 — 'Neither I nor anyone like me is able to attain the wisdom of the blessed and glorious Paul. When he was with you in the presence of the men at that time he taught the word of truth accurately and reliably. And when

---

71. Especially *Eph.* 7.2; 18.2; 19.3; *Rom.* Inscrip.; 6.3.
72. *Trall.* 10; *Smyrn.* 2; 4.2; 5.2.
73. *Beginning from Jerusalem* 827-29.
74. E.g. *Eph.* 2.2; 4.1; 5.3; 6.1; *Magn.* 6.1-2; 7.1; 13.2; *Trall.* 2.1-2; 3.1; 7.2; 13.2; *Philad.* 3.2; 7.1-2; *Smyrn.* 8.1-2; 9.1; *Polyc.* 6.1.
75. The breach with Jerusalem probably included a breach with Antioch (*Beginning from Jerusalem* §27.6).
76. Again, see *Beginning from Jerusalem* §24.9.
77. Lindemann, *Paulus* 221.
78. Smith, 'Ministry' 56.

he was absent he wrote you letters. If you look closely into them you will be able to be built up in the faith that was given to you' (see also 9.1; 11.2-3).

Like Clement, Polycarp was well acquainted with the letter(s) which Paul had written to Philippi.[79] This again suggests that Paul's letters had been circulated and were well known in other churches (Polycarp was writing from Asia to Macedonia), again possibly in a collection. The allusions made to Paul's ministry, both in person and by letter (3.2; 9.1; 11.3), also suggest that Polycarp's knowledge of Paul's relationship with Philippi was not drawn solely from Paul's letter to Philippi but also from oral traditions concerning Paul's ministry which presumably circulated among the churches established by or as a result of Paul's Aegean mission.

The indications that Polycarp, like Ignatius, was steeped in the sentiments of Paul's letters are manifold; I mention only the more likely instances.[80]

Polycarp, *Philippians*	Probable echo	Possible echo
1.3	Eph. 2.5, 8-9	
2.2		2 Cor. 4.14
3.3		Gal. 4.26; 1 Cor. 13.13
4.1	1 Tim. 6.7, 10	
5.1	Gal. 6.7	
5.3	1 Cor. 6.9-10	
6.2		Rom. 14.10,12; 2 Cor. 5.10
9.2		Phil. 2.16; 2 Tim. 4.10
11.2	1 Cor. 6.2	
12.1	Eph. 4.26	
12.3		Phil. 3.18

---

79. The plural 'letters' (3.2) could imply that Paul wrote more than once to Philippi (Phil. 2.19-30 implies several contacts between Paul and the church there); or it could strengthen the quite popular hypothesis that Philippians is made up of more than one letter (*Beginning from Jerusalem* 1011-12). But it should also be noted that Polycarp refers the Philippians to 'the beginning of his [Paul's] epistle' (*Phil.* 11.3), which could equally suggest that the plural in 3.2 was a slip of Polycarp's pen. See the brief review of the discussion in Holmes, 'Polycarp's *Letter to the Philippians*' 201-2 n.55).

80. P. V. M. Benecke, *NTAF* 85-86, 89-98, 101 (citing 50 passages); Lindemann, *Paulus* 221-32; Dassmann, *Stachel* 149-58; K. Berding, *Polycarp and Paul* (Leiden: Brill, 2002) 33-125, 191-206; Holmes, 'Polycarp's *Letter to the Philippians*' 201-18; see also Hartog, *Polycarp's* Epistle 65-68.

Particularly notable is what appears to be a direct quotation in *Phil.* 11.2 from 1 Cor. 6.2:

1 Cor. 6.2 — 'Or do we not know that the saints will judge the world?'

Phil. 11.2 — '"Or do we not know that the saints will judge the world?", as Paul teaches'.

But the others are more in the nature of echoes, probably some at least conscious and deliberate. Equally notable is the fact that Polycarp seems to refer to Eph. 4.26 as scripture: 'As it is written in these scriptures, "Be angry and do not sin", and "Let not the sun go down on your anger"' (*Phil.* 12.1). The first quotation could be taken from Ps. 4.4, but the two together, given as (a) quotation(s) from written scripture, can hardly have been taken from anywhere else than Eph. 4.26.[81] That 1 Corinthians was well known is hardly a surprise, following Clement and Ignatius. But the probability that Polycarp also knew several other Pauline letters,[82] including those generally regarded as post-Pauline (Ephesians and 1 Timothy),[83] is a striking testimony to the acceptability of what the post-Pauline authors were doing.[84]

The implications are obvious. One is that by the earliest decades of the second century a substantial number of Paul's letters had been circulated among the churches of the Aegean region — presumably valued by the churches which owed their existence to Paul's Aegean mission. As already noted, such circulation may have been in accordance with Paul's own intention and so practised from the first (Col. 4.16). But even if this was done irregularly and erratically at first (some have been lost), by the time of Ignatius and Polycarp the practice had probably become regular and more organized, with the

---

81. Cf. M. F. Wiles, *The Divine Apostle: The Interpretation of St Paul's Epistles in the Early Church* (Cambridge University, 1967) 4; Lindemann, *Paulus* 227-28; M. W. Holmes, 'Paul and Polycarp', in Bird and Dodson, eds., *Paul and the Second Century* 57-69 (here 61).

82. Holmes concludes Polycarp's use of 1 Corinthians, Ephesians, 1 and 2 Timothy is 'highly probable', and use of Romans, Galatians and Philippians is 'probable' ('Polycarp's Letter to the Philippians' 226). See also his 'Paul and Polycarp' 59-61.

83. Hartog, *Philippians* 61. 'For Polycarp there is no apostolic authority other than Paul, and the letter demonstrates how a bishop could conduct his office of directing and ordering the affairs of the Christian churches in the spirit of Paul, namely, in the spirit of the Pastoral Epistles' (Koester, *Introduction* 2.307). Jefford finds 'a close association between Polycarp and the Pastoral Epistles of the New Testament' in language and style, and is intrigued but unconvinced by von Campenhausen's suggestion that Polycarp may have edited the Pastoral Epistles (*Apostolic Fathers* 15 and n.15).

84. Or to the success of their deception if pseudepigraphy is taken as deceitful and intended to deceive; but see §39.3a above.

letters already put together in some sort of collection for ease of distribution to new churches for their own teaching and preaching.[85]

The other, which also strengthens the first, is that not only the memory and reputation of Paul were sanctified, but also his letters were so highly valued that it did not cause surprise or protest when his letters were referred to in the same breath as the scriptures. Again it should be underlined that this was already happening early in the second century, only about fifty years after Paul's martyrdom. It should also be noted that Paul was not a controversial figure,[86] and, in contrast to the evidence from the groups of Jewish believers in Jesus, there is no evidence that his heritage was contested, even if some of its key emphases were not reinforced.[87]

d. *Epistle of Barnabas*

Given that the very Jewish-Christian *Didache* displays no real influence from Paul, it is more surprising that the *Epistle of Barnabas* also seems to reflect little influence from or use of Paul.[88] This is surprising, since one might have thought that Paul's critique of Israel and of the emphasis Israel placed on circumcision would have been grist to *Barnabas*'s anti-Judaism tendency — as Marcion demonstrated to an extreme.

However, the most plausible echo may help explain *Barnabas*'s failure to exploit Paul as a potential ally. In *Barn.* 13.7 the Lord is quoted as saying, 'See, Abraham, I have made you a father of the nations who believe in God while uncircumcised'. This is hardly a quotation from Gen. 17.4, though the allusion to Gen. 17.4 is clear enough. But it does very much echo Paul's exposition of the same covenant promise to Abraham in Rom. 4.9-17. The difference is that Paul presses the case that uncircumcised Gentiles are included along with the circumcised (4.11-12), whereas *Barnabas* presses the opposite case that circumcised Israel is now excluded from the covenant (*Barn.* 4.6-8, 14;

---

85. Cf. Holmes, 'Polycarp's *Letter to the Philippians*' 226-27.

86. The fact that Papias, regarded by Irenaeus as 'a companion of Polycarp' (Eusebius, *HE* 3.39.1), makes no reference to Paul or any quotation from Paul should not be taken as a sign of any opposition to Paul or to the way Paul was being used (as suggested by C. M. Nielsen, 'Papias: Polemicist against Whom?', *TS* 35 [1974] 529-35, cited by Lindemann, *Paulus* 291-92). The quotations from Papias are too fragmentary and focused on the Jesus tradition and Evangelists (§44.2j) for such a far-reaching conclusion to be drawn.

87. See Lindemann, *Paulus* 230-32; Berding, *Polycarp and Paul* ch. 5; Holmes, 'Paul and Polycarp', 66-69: 'it would not be inaccurate to say that Polycarp is more overtly influenced by Pauline parenesis ("exhortation") than he is by Pauline theology' (69).

88. J. V. Bartlet, 'The Epistle of Barnabas', *NTAF* 3-6, 11-14; Lindemann, *Paulus* 274-82; Paget, '*Barnabas*' 239-45.

13.1; 14.1, 4-5).[89] It is probably significant, then, that in an earlier passage *Barnabas* may well echo Paul's reference to circumcision as a 'seal' (of the covenant) (*Barn.* 9.6; Rom. 4.11); but he does so only to treat the thought rather dismissively, since 'every Syrian and Arab and all the priests of the idols are circumcised as well. So then, do those belong to their [Israel's] covenant?' (*Barn.* 9.6). *Barnabas*, then, echoes Paul only to rebut Paul's line of argument. So presumably, insofar as *Barnabas* was aware of Paul and of Paul's letters, it was with the realization that Paul was much more inclusive of Gentile as well as Jew, or, as *Barnabas* presumably saw it, of Jew as well as Gentile, much too inclusive for *Barnabas* to accept.[90] Rather than engage with Paul in any explicit way *Barnabas* chose to ignore him almost entirely.[91] This in itself may be something of a testimony to the continuing influence of Paul in encouraging positive relations between Jews and Christians in the second century, an influence which *Barnabas* could only attest by trying to silence it. But that, of course, is itself an argument from silence.

e. 2 Clement

2 Clement does not advance the discussion at all, since none of the possible echoes of Paul's letters can be classified above the 'possible' category. Gregory and Tuckett sum up their own findings:

> There is now a widespread consensus that although 'Clement' employed imagery used by Paul, nevertheless the evidence suggests that at no point did he make conscious and deliberate reference either to Paul or to his writings, and that no direct citations of, or allusions to, Paul's letters are to be found in *2 Clement*. This need not mean that he had no acquaintance with Pauline traditions . . . but it is possible that such 'Pauline' parallels that he displays were already part of the common discourse of early Christianity, regardless of whether or not they are likely to have originated with Paul.[92]

---

89. Paget, '*Barnabas*' 240.

90. Cf. the use of Gen. 25.21-23 in *Barn.* 13.2-3 and Rom. 9.7-13 — '*Barnabas* seeing in it a prophecy of the Christian people, Paul citing it simply for the principle of sovereign election' (Bartlett, *NTAF* 4).

91. Further discussion in Paget, *Epistle of Barnabas* 207-14; contrast the earlier view that *Barnabas* was a representative of Paulinism (207).

92. Tuckett, '*2 Clement*' 279; in agreement with Lindemann, *Paulus* 270-71. It would be unfair to set *2 Clement*'s emphasis on *antimisthia* ('recompense, exchange' — *2 Clem.* 1.3, 5; 9.7; 11.6; 15.2) in contrast to Paul's teaching, as Pratscher implies — 'Already the talk of *antimisthia* presupposes a religious self-understanding, which is dominated by thought of

The most plausible echoes[93] are:

2 Clement

1.8	Rom. 4.17
2.1	Gal. 4.27
7.1	1 Cor. 9.24-25
8.2	Rom. 9.21
9.3	1 Cor. 3.16; 6.19
11.7	1 Cor. 2.9
13.2	Rom. 2.24
14.2	Eph. 5.23

Such a lack of interest in and influence from Paul is somewhat surprising, considering the close relation of *1 Clement* and *2 Clement* (§40.1h). On the other hand we should not assume that explicit references to Paul were regarded as a necessary warrant for the integrity or authority of such a letter. If the NT letter writers had simply absorbed Jesus tradition into their own paraenesis, without deeming it necessary to attribute the teaching explicitly to Jesus,[94] then it would be hardly surprising if influence from Paul had been similarly absorbed into the preaching and teaching of churches which, without necessarily saying so explicitly, nevertheless venerated his memory. But such an argument is only a little stronger than an argument from silence.

f. Odes of Solomon

As for the *Odes of Solomon*, we need only note the clearest echo of Paul in *Odes* 11.1-3:

> My heart was pruned and its flower appeared,
> Then grace sprang up in it,
> And it produced fruits for the Lord.
> For the Most High circumcised me by his Holy Spirit,
> Then he uncovered my inward being toward him,
> And filled me with his love.

---

achievement' (*zweite Clemensbrief* 237) — since Paul was also concerned that his converts produce 'good works' (2 Cor. 9.8; Col. 1.10) and prove themselves worthy of their Lord (Col. 1.10; 1 Thess. 2.12), and he looked for 'the harvest or fruit of righteousness' in their lives (2 Cor. 9.9-10; Phil. 1.11).

93. J. V. Bartlet, *NTAF* 126-27, 128-29; Donfried, *Second Clement*, particularly 192-200; Lindemann, *Paulus* 265-69; Tuckett, '2 *Clement*' 280-89.

94. See above §44 n.1.

And his circumcising me became my salvation,
And I ran in the Way in his peace,
In the Way of truth.

The echoes of Paul's emphasis on 'grace',[95] of Paul's insistence that believers had been circumcised in their hearts by the Spirit,[96] and of his talk of the fruit of the Spirit (Gal. 5.22) and of God's love poured into believers' hearts through the Spirit (Rom. 5.5) can hardly be coincidental, but rather suggest a hymn-writer and community for whom Paul's letters were food and drink.

g. Aristides

Turning to the Apologists, Aristides probably warrants a brief mention. His polemic against idolatry and Greek religion could contain echoes of Paul's (cf. *Apol.* 3.2 and 8.2 with Rom. 1.25, 22);[97] his reference to the Greek convert confessing that 'I did these things in ignorance' (*Apol.* 17.4) could be counted as an echo of 1 Tim. 1.13; and the reference to Christian 'writings' which the king may read for himself (*Apol.* 16.5 Syriac) presumably includes some at least of Paul's letters.[98] But Aristides evidently was not concerned (or perhaps better, was concerned not) to demonstrate his dependence on earlier writings, though his sustained critique of traditional religions can be regarded as a climax of such earlier critiques, both Jewish and philosophical. That he did not draw on Paul, even though Paul was his most significant Christian predecessor, probably tells us more about Aristides than it does about the influence of Paul on second-century Christian thinking.

h. The *Epistle to Diognetus*

The *Epistle to Diognetus* has more interest at this point. The most recent study notes a clear citation from Paul and suggests a sequence of allusions and echoes — of which only the most persuasive need mentioning.[99]

---

95. *Odes* 4.6; 5.3; 6.6; 7.10, 22, 26; 9.5; etc.
96. Rom. 2.29; Phil. 3.3.
97. Including the hostility to homosexuality (see §40 n.114 above).
98. Lindemann, *Paulus* 351-52.
99. Bird, 'The Reception of Paul in the *Epistle of Diognetus*'. *Diogn.* 10.6/Gal. 6.2 could be added.

§47.3 Paul

Diognetus	Citation	Allusion	Echo
2.1		Eph. 4.23-24	
4.1, 5		Col. 2.16	
5.8-9		Rom. 8.12-13; Phil. 3.20	
6.5			Gal. 5.17
7.2		Col. 1.16	
8.10-11		Rom. 16.25; Eph. 3.5	
9.2-5			2 Cor. 5.21
10.4		Eph. 5.1	
10.7		1 Cor. 2.1; 4.1	
11.1, 3		1 Tim. 2.7; 3.16	
12.5	1 Cor. 8.1		

The allusions to and echoes of Paul's writings are clear —

- the talk of a 'new man' (2.1),
- warnings against emphasis on circumcision, Sabbath and calendrical fussing over feasts (4.1, 4-5),
- the hazards of the flesh (5.8-9; 6.5),
- the sending of Christ, agent in creation and Son, making God known (7.2, 4; 8.1, 5-6),
- the mystery long hidden but now unveiled (8.10-11; 10.7; 11.2),
- the righteous Son given to justify the lawless (9.2-5).

The evidence is sufficiently strong to warrant the conclusion that Paul was 'clearly the most formative intellectual force in the theology of the apologist'.[100] That Paul is never mentioned may be all the more significant in that, as with the earlier lack of reference of Jesus tradition to Jesus himself, it may well indicate that Paul's teaching, independently of his writings as such, had become so much meat and drink to mid-second-century catechesis and preaching that no such reference was deemed necessary to give the teaching added weight.

i. Justin Martyr

Justin Martyr is the most puzzling of the mid-second-century apologists, so far as perceptible influence from Paul is concerned. For Paul is never men-

---

100. Bird, 'Reception' 87.

tioned,[101] and echoes of Pauline teaching are mostly rather faint. This is surprising, since Justin provides such solid testimony for the fact that the NT Gospels were already well established in Christian assemblies (§44.3b). And certainly, in Rome, where Justin had settled, Paul would have been known and had been venerated for fifty years already, if *1 Clement* is any guide. Moreover, one would have thought that Paul, as the principal predecessor for any dialogue between Jews and believers in Jesus, would have provided much grist for Justin's principal work, his *Dialogue with Trypho*. However, a survey of possible echoes of Paul in the *Dialogue* has overall disappointing results.[102]

The one exception is probably Justin's frequent references to circumcision: a full recognition that circumcision of the flesh was a fundamental identity marker for Jews (*Dial.* 16, 18-19); circumcision as a 'sign',[103] indeed 'a sign that you (Jews) should be separated from other nations and from us' (12.2); the affirmation that Abraham was justified by faith when he was 'in uncircumcision' (23.4; 92.3), and that (therefore) circumcision is no longer necessary (24.1; 29.1); and the insistence that Christians had received a 'second' or 'true circumcision', the circumcision of the heart.[104] Quite likely these had become standard strategies in Christian discussions with or in regard to Jews. But it is hard to doubt that the line of thought stems from passages like Rom. 2.28-29, 4.10-11 and Col. 2.11.[105] Not surprisingly, then, Justin's assertion that we (Gentiles) are children of Abraham because we share the like faith (*Dial.* 119.5-6) comes across as an echo of Gal. 3.6-7.

Beyond that, however, the echoes become fainter. The references to the curse of the law (*Dial.* 95.1) and to the crucified man as cursed according to Deut. 21.23 (*Dial.* 89.2; 96.1) could well be an echo of Gal. 3.10-13[106]— strengthening the likelihood that Justin knew and had been influenced by Paul's letter to the Galatians. The catena of texts from the Psalms and Isaiah in *Dial.* 27.3 seems to be drawn from Rom. 3.13-17,[107] though possibly from

---

101. Peter is referred to in *Dial.* 100.3 and 106.3; John in 81.5; and the sons of Zebedee also in 106.3.

102. Lindemann, *Paulus* 353-67; Massaux, *Influence* 3.96-100; Skarsaune, *Proof from Prophecy* 92-100; P. Foster, 'Justin and Paul', in Bird and Dodson, eds., *Paul and the Second Century* 108-25.

103. *Dial.* 23.4; 28.4; 137.1.

104. *Dial.* 12.3; 18.2; 41.4; 43.2; 92.4; 113.6-7; 114.4.

105. Cf. Massaux, *Influence* 3.97-98; Foster, 'Justin and Paul' 117-19.

106. Lindemann, *Paulus* 365-66; Skarsaune, *Proof from Prophecy* 94; but Massaux justifiably notes that Justin's putting the objection in the mouth of Trypho may well indicate that it was a traditional objection among Jews (*Influence* 3.98).

107. Lindemann, *Paulus* 360. Lindemann also notes that the quotation from 1 Kgs. 19 in *Dial.* 39.1 is closer to the wording used in Rom. 11.3 than to the wording of the LXX;

a previous collection known to Paul.[108] And the interpretation of Ps. 68.18 as a reference to Christ's ascension could well be an echo of Eph. 4.8 (*Dial.* 39.4; 87.6). But does Trypho's comment that some Christians eat idol food (*eidōlothyton*) as being harmless (*Dial.* 35.1) count as an allusion to 1 Cor. 8?[109] Should the reference to Isa. 1.9 in *Dial.* 55.3 be attributed to the influence of Rom. 9.29? Should the references to Christ as the 'firstborn of all creatures'[110] be attributed to Col. 1.15? And are the references to Christ's subjection of the principalities and powers[111] to be attributed to 1 Cor. 15.24 and Col. 2.15?[112]

So it is possible to agree that Justin knew some at least of Paul's letters, or at least was influenced by their teachings.[113] But the evidence is still surprisingly slight, and still poses the question: Why is Paul not paraded by Justin as a Jew whose arguments with respect to the gospel and Jews could surely be drawn on? One possible answer is that he ranked Paul's letters less highly than the OT and the Jesus tradition/Gospels,[114] though that would be somewhat surprising if the attitude expressed in 2 Pet. 3.16 was more widespread. Alternatively, perhaps he was conscious that while Paul had been arguing that uncircumcised Gentile believers could nevertheless be included in the seed of Abraham (Rom. 4; Gal. 3), Justin was rather more dismissive of Jewish status before God (§46.6g). Paul's relative positiveness towards his own people was

---

in his opinion 'there can be no doubt that Justin has taken over this citation immediately from Rom. 11' (*Paulus* 362). So also Massaux, *Influence* 3.96.

108. Cf. L. E. Keck, 'The Function of Romans 3:10-18 — Observations and Suggestions', in J. Jervell and W. A. Meeks, eds., *God's Christ and His People* (Oslo-Bergen Tromsö: Universitetsforlaget, 1977) 141-57.

109. Lindemann, *Paulus* 360.

110. *Dial.* 84.2; 85.2; 100.2; 116.3; 125.3; 138.2; see also *1 Apol.* 23.2; 33.6; 46.2; 53.2; 63.15.

111. *Dial.* 41.1; 49.8; 111.2; 121.3; 131.5.

112. On possible echoes of Justin's *Apologies*, see Lindemann, *Paulus* 355-58; Foster, 'Justin and Paul' 113-17. Massaux is unusually negative in his findings: 'not one text appears with certainty to be literarily dependent on the apostle' (*Influence* 3.48). Similarly Foster 117.

113. Lindemann, *Paulus* 366, and Skarsaune, *Proof from Prophecy* 100, agree that Justin knew and used Romans and Galatians in particular. Worthy of note is the opinion of L. W. Barnard, *Justin Martyr: His Life and Thought* (Cambridge University, 1967): 'He made an outstanding contribution to the intellectual tradition of Christian thought by his interpretation of the logos. He was moreover the first thinker after St. Paul to grasp the universalistic element in Christianity and to sum up in one bold stroke the whole history of civilization as finding its consummation in Christ' (169).

114. '*Apol* and *Dial* show Justin's principled disinterest in the church tradition. For him there were only two authorities: the Old Testament (LXX) and the teaching of Jesus' (Lindemann, *Paulus* 363); similarly Foster, 'Justin and Paul' 124.

perhaps something of an embarrassment for Justin.[115] Another possibility is that Justin was all too aware that Paul was being made use of by Marcion and gnosticizing groups (§47.5) and regarded Paul as a lost cause.[116] Consequently, although Justin cannot be regarded as a strong witness to second-century reverence for Paul and to the influence of his writings, at the same time he cannot be regarded as a negative testimony on the same point, far less as a witness that Paul was regarded as a dangerous precedent in Christian tradition.

j. The Other Apologists

We need not dally over the other apologists who have contributed to earlier chapters. There are some possible echoes of Paul in Tatian's *Address*, but more to the point are references to Tatian by Irenaeus, Clement of Alexandria and Jerome which make it clear that they understood him to have (mis)interpreted various Pauline texts.[117] It is certainly possible to see that Athenagoras's understanding of the resurrection was drawn directly from 1 Corinthians 15.[118] And Theophilus in his apology to *Autolycus* makes several quotations from and allusions to Paul.[119] Melito of Sardis does not seem to echo Paul as such, though his argument in the *Peri Pascha*, including Christ as the Passover lamb (*Peri Pascha* 65), would not have been particularly dependent on Paul anyway.[120] We hardly need to say more about the epistolary compositions which Paul sparked off (§40.5), but should just note that the *Epistula Apostolorum* makes much of Paul as preacher to the Gentiles, drawing heavily on the Acts account of his conversion, but also with clear knowledge of Paul's own account.[121]

---

115. Alternatively Matthew Thomas suggests that Justin was alert to the fact that Paul was too much of an embarrassment to his fellow Jews, regarded as disloyal to his nation — 'a toxic anti-authority in Trypho's eyes' (private correspondence).

116. 'To have mentioned the apostle to the Gentiles explicitly would thus have brought Justin too close to Marcion and have made the dialogue with the Jews more difficult' (Lüdemann, *Opposition to Paul* 153).

117. Irenaeus, *adv. haer.* 3.23.8 (1 Cor. 15.22); Clement of Alexandria, *Strom.* 3.12.81 (1 Cor. 7.5); Jerome, *Com. in Ep. ad Gal.* 6 (Gal. 6.8). See Massaux, *Influence* 3.113-14. 'Some, like Tatian, rejected "some epistles of Paul" although in practice drawing upon his writings in the exposition of their own teaching' (Wiles, *Divine Apostle* 5).

118. *Plea* 31 (1 Cor. 15.44); *Resurrection* 18 (quoting from 1 Cor. 15.53); Massaux, *Influence* 3.130-31.

119. *Autolycus* 1.14 (Rom. 2.7-9 and 1 Cor. 2.9); *Autolycus* 3.14 (Rom. 13.7-8 and 1 Tim. 2.2); Massaux, *Influence* 3.140-41. See further R. M. Grant, 'The Bible of Theophilus of Antioch', *JBL* 66 (1947) 173-96.

120. For what can be said see Dassmann, *Stachel* 286-92.

121. *Ep.Apost.* 31, 33 — Gal. 1.13, 16, 23; Phil. 3.5. On Irenaeus see below §47.6.

In sum, the survey of second-century regard for Paul and of knowledge and use of his letters provides somewhat mixed results.

- The strong reverence for Paul shown by *1 Clement*, Ignatius and Polycarp, at the beginning of the second century, is not much reflected in later writings. Was this because Paul became something of an awkward or embarrassing figure? — regarded as something of an apostate and traitor by many groups of Jewish believers in Jesus, and taken up too enthusiastically by Marcion and Gnosticizing groups, for him to be cited and drawn on explicitly and without question?
- The relative ignoring of or failure to draw explicitly on Paul by such as *Barnabas, 2 Clement*, Aristides and Melito may be a pointer in the direction just suggested. At the same time, their relative silence regarding Paul should not be read as evidence of disregard for Paul, or that Paul was not known or uninfluential, since in each case there may not have been sufficient desire or incentive to draw on the distinctive arguments or teachings of Paul.
- The stronger impression, from *1 Clement*, Ignatius, Polycarp, the *Odes of Solomon* and most of the apologists is that most of Paul's letters were known and used, probably read in Christian assemblies and used for teaching and catechesis, and quite likely already in one or more collections, codices. The evidence stretches from Rome, through Asia Minor to Antioch, suggesting the growing influence of Paul's letters, particularly in what was the heartland of Gentile Christianity.
- Although quotations and direct allusions are relatively few, the sum of likely allusions and echoes stretches across most of Paul's letters and of the other letters ascribed to Paul. The fact that Paul is not often cited as the authority for the teaching or instruction being echoed, does not imply a disrespect for Paul, but may rather indicate that his teaching had become so interwoven in the characteristic teaching of the churches that no attribution to Paul was thought to be necessary. As already suggested, there may be a parallel here with the Jesus tradition in the letters of the first and early second century: that the teaching had so entered the lifeblood of the Christian communities that explicit attribution to Paul was unnecessary for the teaching to have the authority it embodied.

A closing tabulation of the possible echoes of Paul in the most prominent second-century Christian literature may serve as a helpful summary of Paul's influence during that period.

	Rom	1 Cor	2 Cor	Gal	Eph	Phil	Col	1 Th	2 Th	1 Tim	2 Tim	Tit	Phm
1 Clem.	×	×	?	?	?	?				×	×	×	
Ignatius	×	×		?	×	?	?	?		×	×		
Polycarp	?	×	?	×	×	?				×			
Barnabas	×												
2 Clem.	?	?		?	?								
Odes of Solomon													
Aristides	?									?			
Diognetus	×	×			×	×	×			?			
Justin	×			×	×		×						
Tatian		×	×										
Athenagoras					×								
Theophilus	×	×								×			
Melito													

47.4 The Legendary Paul

As well as the references to Paul and the echoes of or allusions to his teaching, it was quite natural that his life and teaching would be subjects of speculation and imaginative reconstruction. Paul, after all, had been such a pivotal figure in the development of Christianity that curiosity would inevitably have been aroused, particularly about parts of his life where tradition was rather threadbare and about aspects of his teaching which stimulated further reflection. As with Jesus, and James, more literature inevitably appeared which was about Paul or attributed to Paul.

a. The *Acts of Paul*

The *Acts of Paul* (§40.6a), with its account of Paul's travels, seems to show awareness of the itinerary of Paul's mission attested in the Acts of the Apostles. Fragments begin with his conversion outside Damascus, and the command that he go to Damascus and then to Jerusalem.[122] The next centre of his

---

122. Bauckham returns to the question of *ActsPaul*'s possible dependence on Acts (§40 n.277) by focusing on the one clear overlap (the narrative of Paul's conversion) — 'The *Acts of Paul*: Replacement of Acts or Sequel to Acts?', in Stoops, ed., *Semeia* 80 (1997) 159-68.

activity is Antioch, then Iconium, where he first encounters Thecla, then Myra, Sidon, Tyre, Ephesus, Philippi, Corinth and Rome. All these are mentioned in Acts and though they are not in the same sequence, they could reflect Paul's movements on his first missionary journey (Acts 13-14) and subsequent return to the eastern seaboard of the Mediterranean prior to his Aegean mission. The stoning and expulsion of Paul from Antioch (*ActsPaul* 2) echoes the similar stoning and expulsion of Paul from Lystra (Acts 14.19-20). Another echo of the NT Acts is the decision of the governor of Iconium to imprison Paul 'until he had time to hear him more attentively', which sounds like an echo of the way Felix dealt with Paul in Caesarea (Acts 24.25-26). The outraged response of the goldsmiths of Ephesus to Paul's attack on idolatry (*ActsPaul* 7) has strong echoes of the near riot in Ephesus occasioned by Paul's preaching and provoked by the silversmiths (Acts 19.23-41). And Paul's encounter with the wild beasts in the amphitheatre of Ephesus is presumably based on 1 Cor. 15.32.[123] The same episode underlines how many women were attracted to Paul's preaching, which provides another echo of Acts.[124] In the Philippi episode the prophecy of Cleobius and the resulting lamentation (*ActsPaul* 9) echo the equivalent prophecy of Agabus and the similar lamentation of Acts 21.10-14.[125] And the *Martyrdom of Paul* contains an episode where Nero's cupbearer Patroclus, sitting on a high window to hear Paul, falls down and dies, only for Paul to encourage those present to make prayerful lament to Christ that the boy may live, which is what happens (*ActsPaul* 11.1). The echo of the Eutychus episode in Acts 20.7-12 is fairly obvious. None of these echoes can be regarded as providing good historical information, but they do show knowledge of the Lukan Acts, quite possibly supplemented by oral traditions otherwise unknown to us.[126]

Equally interesting is that in the *Acts of Paul and Thecla* false disciples are immediately introduced under the names of Demas and Hermogenes (*ActsPaul* 3.1, 4, 12, 14, 16), contrasted with faithful supporters by the name

123. See also Klauck, *Apocryphal Acts* 64-67.
124. Acts 16.13-15; 17.4, 12, 34.
125. Possibly the name given to the captain of the ship to take Paul to Rome, Artemon (*Artemōn*), was suggested by the reference to the *artemōn* ('foresail'?) in Acts 27.40.
126. Schneemelcher, *NTA* 2.232 (full discussion 218-33); MacDonald, *Legend* 19-26; Klauck, *Apocryphal Acts* 74. On Thecla and Queen Tryphaena, the latter a known historical figure, MacDonald wonders whether behind the *Acts* stories are 'the memories of these two respected Anatolian women', and notes that 'no author from the first millennium of the church ever doubted Thecla's existence' (*Legend* 21). Burrus hypothesizes stories originally told by and for Christian women and with some roots in oral sources (*Chastity as Autonomy* 58, 98, 108). See also W. Rordorf, 'Tradition and Composition in the *Acts of Thecla*: The State of the Question', in D. R. MacDonald, ed., *Semeia* 38: *The Apocryphal Acts of Apostles* (1986) 44-52.

of Onesiphorus (in whose house Paul meets Thecla) and Titus (3.2-5, 7, 15, 23-26). Since all four are mentioned in 2 Timothy, with similarly negative and positive comments (1.15-16; 4.10, 19), it is most likely that the names were drawn from there, or from the traditions which fed into 2 Timothy.[127] To Demas and Hermogenes is attributed the teaching that 'the resurrection has already taken place', which sounds like another borrowing from 2 Tim. 2.18. In the *Martyrdom of Paul* Titus and Luke are prominent together, somewhat as in 2 Tim. 4.10-11.

3 Corinthians, incorporated within the *Acts*, has a strong echo of 1 Corinthians:

> 1 Cor. 15.3 — 'I handed on to you as of first importance what I in turn had received';

> *ActsPaul* 8.3.4 — 'I delivered to you first of all what I received from the apostles'.

And the use of the image of 'adoption' and reference to 'the spirit of Christ' (*ActsPaul* 8.3.8, 10) may contain an echo of Rom. 8.9, 15. Other echoes of Paul's letters in *3 Corinthians* are audible in the sentence, 'I have these bonds on me that I may win Christ, and I bear his marks that I may attain the resurrection of the dead' (*ActsPaul* 8.3.35); I refer to Gal. 6.17 and Phil. 3.8, 11.[128]

At the same time, it is evident that Paul's teaching has been taken to an extreme and in ways he would not have welcomed. In particular, the teaching on chasteness which dominates the story of Paul and Thecla could have been inspired by Paul's reservation about marriage:

> 1 Cor. 7.29 — 'let those who have wives be as though they had none';

> *ActsPaul* 3.5 — 'blessed are those who have wives as not having them'.

But Paul was much more understanding of and sympathetic to the desire for marriage and active sexual relations within marriage (1 Cor. 7.3-5, 9, 36-38). And in *3 Corinthians* the teaching on the resurrection echoes 1 Cor. 15, as what had been received from the apostles (*ActsPaul* 8.3.4), but the insistence

---

127. Hermogenes is described as 'the coppersmith' (*ActsPaul* 3.1), although in 2 Timothy 'the coppersmith' is the equally hostile Alexander (2 Tim. 4.14).

128. See also P. Herczeg, 'New Testament Parallels to the Apocryphal Acta Pauli Documents', in Bremmer, ed., *Apocryphal Acts of Paul* 144-49.

that resurrection will be of the flesh (8.3.6, 24) abandons Paul's assertion that the resurrected body will be a 'spiritual' body, not of flesh and blood which 'cannot inherit the kingdom of God' (1 Cor. 15.44, 50). Paul's argument that what is sown is not the body that is to be (15.37) is contradicted by the counter assertion that God raises 'the body which is sown' (*ActsPaul* 8.3.27). Here the insistence, first attested in Ignatius, that Christian hope is for the resurrection of the flesh (Ignatius, *Smyrn*. 3.1), has abandoned the subtle distinction introduced by Paul, between 'body' and 'flesh'.[129] No doubt, as with Ignatius, this was a reaction, or better an over-reaction, to a docetist christology which denied that Christ came in the flesh. But the consequence was disastrous for patristic and subsequent Christianity's evaluation of physical and sexual function.

Nevertheless, it is clear from the *Acts of Paul* that Paul was revered, as apostle, teacher, miracle-worker and martyr, that the first record of his mission and travels (Acts of the Apostles) was well known, and that his letters were known and drawn on, even if at times in ways contrary to Paul's own intention. The hyperbole regarding his mission is kept within bounds — neither of Thecla's miraculous deliverances are attributed to Paul — and the portrayal of Paul as one whose teaching captivated various women is a welcome alternative to the more typical traditional view of Paul as a misogynist.[130] Of some interest also is that the Jew/Gentile issue so central to Paul's mission, and to the NT Acts' negative references to Jews, leaves only the faintest echo in the legendary *Acts* (*ActsPaul* 6; 8.3.9-10). It is Paul the famous preacher and teacher who is being lauded here rather than the apostle to the Gentiles.[131]

A comparison of the way Paul is presented in the *Acts of Paul* and in the Pastoral Epistles is also appropriate, for each present a tendentiously slanted picture of Paul, partly building on features of Paul's ministry and partly introducing divergent features. The Pastorals present a positive view of marriage[132] and reflect Paul's liberal attitude to food,[133] but also suppress Paul's relatively positive attitude to the role of women in worship and leadership,[134] stressing an exclusively male hierarchy. In contrast, the *Acts of Paul* values virginity

---

129. See *Beginning from Jerusalem* §32.5i.

130. The misunderstanding of 1 Cor. 7 (see *Beginning from Jerusalem* §32.5d) seems to be endemic in most evaluations of Paul.

131. 'Paul is not theologically evaluated, but hagiographically received for popular piety' (Dassmann, *Stachel* 279).

132. Church leaders should marry (1 Tim. 3.2, 12; Tit. 1.6), in contrast to Paul's hesitation on the desirability of marriage (1 Cor. 7.28-38).

133. Cf. 1 Tim. 4.3-4 and Tit. 1.15 with Rom. 14.14 and 1 Cor. 10.26-27.

134. The fact that 1 Cor. 14.34-36 links with 1 Tim. 2.11-12 should not be allowed to silence the other data referred to in *Beginning from Jerusalem* 633-35, 811-13.

and celibacy far higher than Paul ever did, but like Paul gives prominence to a charismatic (unofficial) ministry, in particular that of a woman; it is Paul who commissions Thecla: 'Go, and teach the word of God' (3.41).[135] Much as the *Acts of Paul (and Thecla)* were lauded in the churches of late antiquity and the mediaeval period, it is clear that it was the Paul of the Pastorals who won the day and made the most effective and lasting impact on Christian ecclesiology.[136]

b. The *Acts of Peter*

The *Acts of Peter* (§40.6b) should be mentioned here too, since Codex Vercellensis begins with Paul in Rome preparing for his mission to Spain and going to Spain (*ActsPeter* 1-3, 6).[137] It is only after his departure that Simon Magus arrives in Rome, followed by Peter sent by the Lord from Judaea to counter Simon. It should be noted that no attempt is made to present Peter as the first apostle to visit Rome, far less as the founder of the Christian community in Rome. Rather their belief is 'in him whom Paul preached' to them (4). It is Paul who had commended Peter to them (6). Paul is described as Peter's 'fellow-apostle' (10), and, remarkably, Peter challenges Simon Magus to recall how he had fallen at Peter's feet 'and those of Paul' (23), despite the total absence of Paul from the Acts 8 episode in Samaria. And the *Acts of Peter* ends with the expectation of Paul's return to Rome after the death of Peter (40). It is somewhat curious that in the *Acts of Peter* it is references to Paul at the beginning and end which form an inclusio. Far from the account of Peter's miraculous mission providing an occasion to mark his pre-eminence above Paul, the intention seems to be rather to emphasize their collegiality, both in preaching the same faith and in contesting the same corruption of the

---

135. 'The Christian women who appealed to Thecla and kindled Tertullian's ire surely understood one of the author's intentions correctly' (Klauck, *Apocryphal Acts* 75). See also S. L. Davies, *The Revolt of the Widows: The Social World of the Apocryphal Acts* (Southern Illinois University, 1980); P. N. Hogan, 'Paul and Women in Second-Century Christianity', in Bird and Dodson, eds., *Paul and the Second Century* 226-43; S. J. Davis, *The Cult of St. Thecla: A Tradition of Women's Piety in Late Antiquity* (Oxford University, 2001).

136. MacDonald argues that the *Acts of Paul* consist of 'old wives' tales' (1 Tim. 4.7), stories told primarily by celibate women outside the household (*Legend* ch. 2, here 53), and that the reference in 1 Tim. 4.7 indicates that the Pastorals were written to counter such popular legends (ch. 3). However, it is not necessary to establish such a direct link for the thesis to be probable that the Pastorals were reacting against memories of a Pauline mission which was more encouraging of women in ministry and leadership.

137. Included is the promise that Paul would be 'perfected' (martyred) 'under the hands of Nero' (1).

gospel.[138] That it accomplishes such an intention while refraining from setting them in personal encounter and cooperation in the same place at the same time may, however, be significant — an echo of the awareness that Paul and Peter did not always see eye to eye.

Other writings attributed to Paul, but written after the second century, should at least be mentioned since they indicate something of how his letters were received and how he was regarded in later antiquity. Although they fall outside the period on which we focus, their character and content are not specific to the later dates and can be regarded as possibly illustrative of how Paul was perceived from the late second century onwards.

c. The *Epistle to the Laodiceans*

The *Epistle to the Laodiceans* as a letter putatively from Paul (§40.5b) is disappointing. Indeed, what is of most interest is that it is so uninteresting: it pushes in no particular direction and simply repeats Pauline sentiments and concerns.[139] It throws no fresh light on any aspect of Paul's mission or his theology or the reception of his letters, and simply shows clear knowledge of Paul's letters as well as respect for the apostle and for what he had recorded as his motivation and hope. It also follows that such respect may have been sufficient reason for its composition rather than any attempt to deceive or promote a tendentious view of Paul.

d. The Correspondence of Paul and Seneca

The correspondence of Paul and Seneca (§40.5c) is not of great interest,[140] although the description of the fire of Rome and of Nero's persecution in letter 11 may reflect some source or oral tradition otherwise unknown to us.[141] The inspiration for the composition may have come from the Acts account of Paul's encounter with Epicurean and Stoic philosophers in Athens (Acts 17). To imagine not simply Paul's encounter with Seneca, but a friend-

---

138. But was this a later perspective (see above §40 n.302)? The failure to present Peter as the founder of the church in Rome is all the more significant if the insertion of Paul into the document was later.

139. See above §40 n.259.

140. 'The philosophy of the two outstanding personalities of their time does not find expression in a single sentence' (Römer, *NTA* 2.46), though letter 14 has some echoes of Pauline language.

141. Probably Paul had already been executed (*Beginning from Jerusalem* §34.7).

ship between them, with Seneca speaking admiringly of Paul (letter 12),[142] and ready to show Nero Paul's letters and evoke Nero's sympathy (letter 7), must have been attractive to a fourth-century Christian, when an emperor had emerged who was indeed favourable to Christianity. At any rate, the correspondence shows a regard and respect for Paul, with the confidence that at least his moral exhortations (letter 1) could reverberate positively in the highest philosophical circles.

e. The *Apocalypse of Paul*

What is of interest to us in the *Apocalypse of Paul* (§40.7c) is the high regard shown for Paul. The souls in hell are given the 'great grace of a day and a night's refreshment [from their torment] on the Lord's Day for the sake of Paul the well-beloved of God' (44), and Paul is greeted by the Virgin Mary, Moses, Noah and others with blessings called upon Paul and the generation and nation which came to faith through him (46, 48-51).[143] This confirms that Paul was remembered as the great apostle to the nations, and with nothing of the (Jew/Gentile) tensions which were such a feature of his mission retained or any resolution of them offered.

The common feature of the four apocryphal works about Paul or attributed to Paul is that they were inspired by aspects of his known mission (his ministry to and with women; his engagement with classic philosophy) and by an impulse to fill in gaps in what was known of Paul (his lost letter to the Laodiceans; his heavenly journey). Of course a fuller picture of the esteem in which Paul was held in the patristic period is better gained from the great patristic figures — Ambrosiaster, Augustine, etc. — but the fact that the apocryphal literature relating to Paul was so rooted in the Acts account of Paul and in Paul's letters, and that he was recalled with such esteem and affection, is a tribute to the lasting impact which he made.

47.5 'The Apostle of the Heretics'?

This is how Tertullian refers to Paul in his extensive polemic against Marcion.[144] For the impression was already widespread that Marcion had built his

---

142. Though Seneca is portrayed as wanting to improve Paul's style (letters 9, 13).

143. See also T. Nicklas, 'Gute Werke, rechter Glaube: Paulusrezeption in der *Apokalypse des Paulus*?', *Ancient Perspectives on Paul* (Nicklas et al., ed.) 150-69.

144. Tertullian, *adv. Marc.* 3.5 ('haereticorum apostolus'); see also *adv. haer.* 23-24.

system principally on the letters of Paul. But not only Marcion, also different Gnostic systems, particularly Valentinianism, drew heavily on Paul. So much so that a century ago, at the heydey of the History-of-Religions approach to the NT and the beginning of the quest for pre-Christian Gnosticism,[145] Richard Reitzenstein could refer to Paul as perhaps 'the greatest of all the gnostics'.[146] Whereas most of the Jewish believers-in-Jesus probably regarded Paul with suspicion, and his Gentile mission as the stage where things began to go wrong, there were other religious ideologies or systems which found much in Paul amenable to them. Indeed, the issue cannot be sidestepped: that the two responses to Paul, the different ways in which he was received and in which his impact worked out in the second century, may in fact be related. Was 'the Gnostic Paul' a confirmation that Paul had led emerging Christianity in a direction too far away from its roots in Second Temple Judaism, so that his fellow Jewish believers were right to turn their backs on him? Alternatively posed, was the great church's increasing rejection of the Jewish Christian 'sects' a *de facto* affirmation that if Christianity was going to establish itself as a truly international religion, within the prevailing culture of the Greco-Roman world, it had to become a different kind of religion from Judaism?

We will look, then, first at the ways in which those generally regarded as Gnostics received and used Paul, and second at Marcion.

a. The Gnostic Paul

It is an interesting, not to say a somewhat uncomfortable, fact that much in Paul proved so attractive to so many Gnostics.[147] At not a few points, indeed, Paul affirmed views which commended him more to the 'heretical' Gnostics than to the 'orthodox' Fathers.[148] Indeed, according to Clement of Alexandria, Valentinus's disciples claimed that he had been taught by Theudas, a pupil

---

145. *Beginning from Jerusalem* 36-42.

146. R. Reitzenstein, *The Hellenistic Mystery-Religions* (^{3}1927; ET Pittsburgh: Pickwick, 1978) 84.

147. 'The real attraction of Gnosticism to Christianity was not, then, the figure of Jesus; it was the theology of Paul, which contained "the basic outlook of its own piety"' (King, *Gnosticism* 99, quoting Bousset) — an observation much diminished by the Nag Hammadi texts, particularly the *Gospel of Thomas*.

148. The point is made forcibly by E. H. Pagels, *The Gnostic Paul* (Philadelphia: Fortress, 1975) 1-12: 'Valentinus himself often alludes to Paul . . . ; his disciples Ptolemy, Heracleon, and Theodotus — no less than Irenaeus, Tertullian, and Clement — revere Paul and quote him simply as "the apostle"' (2). She concludes her opening chapter with the challenge: 'If the apostle were so unequivocally antignostic, how could the Gnostics claim him as their great pneumatic teacher?' (10). See also Dassmann, *Stachel* 196-222.

of Paul (*Strom.* 7.17), and Paul was even spoken of as 'in the form of the Paraclete' (*Exc. ex Theod.* 23.2).[149] The Nag Hammadi texts confirm that for many of those responsible for the tracts, Paul was simply 'the Apostle', or 'the great apostle',[150] and *The Teachings of Silvanus* alludes to a statement of Paul (1 Cor. 11.1) 'who has become like Christ' (108.30-32). The Nag Hammadi texts include a brief *Prayer of the Apostle Paul*, 'heavily indebted to . . . the Pauline letters',[151] and a Coptic *Apocalypse of Paul*.[152]

Not least of significance was the fact that Paul denied that he was dependent on the earlier apostles and Jerusalem leaders for his gospel. His insistence that his gospel came to him by direct revelation from God, 'not of human origin nor from a human source' (Gal. 1.11-12), would have been more appealing to those who claimed secret revelation from the risen Christ in distinction from the ecclesiastical tradition of the heresiologists.[153] What was so offensive to many Jewish believers in Jesus, in the Clementine *Homilies*,[154] was precisely what made Paul appealing to Gnostics. According to Hippolytus, the Naasenes were able to draw on 2 Cor. 12.4 and 1 Cor. 2.13-14 as precedent for their claims to secret and higher wisdom (*Ref.* 5.3).[155] Epiphanius reports

---

149. Lindemann, *Paulus* 98. See further J. L. Kovacs, 'Grace and Works: Clement of Alexandria's Response to Valentinian Exegesis of Paul', *Ancient Perspectives on Paul* (ed. Nicklas et al.) 191-210.

150. *Treat. Res.* 45.25-28 echoes Rom. 8.17 and Eph. 2.6, and 46.25-27 echoes Rom. 8.27. *Hypost. Archons* 86.20 quotes Eph. 6.12 and Col. 1.13. *Exeg. Soul* 131.2-13 quotes 'Paul, writing to the Corinthians', cites 1 Cor. 5.9-10 and Eph. 6.12, and in 134.1-2 echoes 2 Cor. 3.6 (*NHL* 194, 196). Note also that the *Gospel of Philip* quotes 1 Cor. 15.50 (56.31-34), alludes to 1 Cor. 8.1 (77.25-26) and echoes Rom. 7.14-19 (83.25-29); and *The Dialogue of the Saviour* also echoes the much echoed 1 Cor. 2.9 (140.1-4) (*NHL* 144, 155, 158, 252).

151. D. Mueller, *NHL* 27-28. 'The major motifs of the prayer are gnostic commonplaces' (H. W. Attridge, 'Paul, Prayer of the Apostle', *ABD* 5.205).

152. Not to be confused with the *Apocalypse of Paul*; see §40.7c and d.

153. Pagels, *Paul* 102. The typical claim that Jesus gave secret instruction to disciples during his appearances following his resurrection — the *Apocryphon of James* indicating that the appearances continued for 550 days (*Apoc. James* 2.19-21 — *NHL* 30); similarly Ptolmaeus (Irenaeus, *adv. haer.* 1.3.2) — of course made more room for the resurrection appearance to Paul (1 Cor. 15.8), long after the forty days of appearances asserted by Luke (Acts 1.1-11).

154. Ps.Clem., *Hom.* 17.18-19, cited above in §45.2c.

155. The Valentinians maintained that Paul 'made use of the basic concepts of their system in his letters in a manner sufficiently clear to anyone who can read. . . . The teaching of Valentinus is just as inconceivable without the letters of Paul as without the prologue to the Fourth Gospel, and it is no accident that Paul is preferred by all Valentinians as the preacher of the hidden wisdom who speaks out most clearly' (T. Zahn cited by Bauer, *Orthodoxy* 224-25). Wiles similarly notes that Valentinus and Basilides found in Paul's letters 'valuable evidence for their ideas about the nature of man and esoteric knowledge' (citing Irenaeus, *adv. haer.* 1.8.3, and Hippolytus, *Elenchus* 7.26.3), and that Basilides is reported

that the Cainites had fabricated a book which they called the *Ascent of Paul*, expressing the 'ineffable words' which Paul claimed to have heard during his journey to the third heaven (2 Cor. 12.4) (*Pan.* 38.2.5). And the Valentinian exegetes could cite 1 Cor. 2.13-14 and 15.48 to enlist Paul's support for their threefold distinction between pneumatics, psychics and choics (Irenaeus, *adv. haer.* 1.8.3).[156] It is little surprise that W. Schmithals, the most prominent advocate of the view that Paul encountered Gnosticism during his mid-first-century mission, could seize on two passages in Galatians and 1 Corinthians in promoting his thesis:

> The argument [of Gal. 1.12] is genuinely Gnostic. The Gnostic apostle is not identified by means of a chain of tradition, by the apostolic succession, but by direct pneumatic vocation.[157]

> What is found in [1 Cor.] 2.6-3.1 could be the precise exposition of a Gnostic.[158]

Similarly the Valentinians valued Ephesians as unfolding 'the mystery of the pneumatic redemption',[159] and seem to have attributed their speculation about the aeons to Ephesians and Colossians.[160] And Irenaeus reacts dismissively against the use of 2 Cor. 4.4 to maintain that 'the god of this world' is other than God (*adv. haer.* 3.7.1).[161]

Of course much of this disputation was tendentious — on both (or all) sides. Paul did not claim that he derived his gospel exclusively or entirely from his encounter with Christ on the Damascus road. He freely affirms that the gospel which he preached had been passed down to him by those already believers in Christ (1 Cor. 15.3). It was rather his 'take' on that gospel, his interpretation of it as also for non-Jews ('his gospel' indeed), which he attributed to the risen Christ (Gal. 1.15-16), and which he was anxious should be approved

---

to have quoted 1 Cor. 2.13 as 'scripture' (again citing Hippolytus, *Elenchus* 7.26.3) (*Divine Apostle* 5-6, 4).

156. On the distinction see above §38 at n.119. The Valentinians interpreted Paul's discussion of Jews and Gentiles in Romans as referring allegorically to different groups of Christians, the psychic and the pneumatic respectively (Pagels, *Paul* 6, 19-21).

157. W. Schmithals, *Paul and the Gnostics* (ET Nashville: Abingdon, 1972) 29.

158. W. Schmithals, *Gnosticism in Corinth* (^{3}1969; ET Nashville: Abingdon, 1971) 151.

159. Pagels, *Paul* 115; see also Rudolph, *Gnosis* 300-302.

160. Bauer, *Orthodoxy* 234; see e.g. Irenaeus, *adv. haer.* 1.3.4; Clem. Alex., *Exc. Theod.* 43.2; Hippolytus, *Ref.* 6.29; further Zahn, *Geschichte des Neutestamentlichen Kanon* 1.751-53.

161. Similarly Tertullian responding to Marcion's use of 2 Cor. 4.4 (Tertullian, *adv. Marc.* 5.11). See also Lindemann, *Paulus* 384-85; N. Perrin, 'Paul and Valentinian Interpretation', in Bird and Dodson, eds., *Paul and the Second Century* 126-39 (here 129-32).

by the Jerusalem leadership years later (Gal. 2.2). That revelation was very different from the revelations claimed by the later Gnostics. We have already noted how the unutterable words Paul heard during his heavenly journey (2 Cor. 12.1-4) were equally as open to an imaginative creation from within the 'great church' (*Apoc. Paul*) as they were to Gnostic invention (§40.7c, d) — neither being exegetically justifiable.

Similarly, the Pauline term 'mystery' readily lent itself to transposition into a way of referring to the Gnostic narrative of creation and redemption.[162] But apart from some everyday usage,[163] the heavy weight of theological significance which Paul put on the term was in his use of it to refer to God's purpose for the salvation of Gentiles as well as Jews, a purpose long hidden from the ages and only now revealed.[164] And Paul's use of *pneumatikoi, psychikoi* and *sarkinoi/sarkikoi* cannot be transposed into the Valentinian threesome, since Paul rebukes the Corinthians as 'fleshly' (*sarkinoi/sarkikoi*) in reference not to their given character, but for their factionalism (1 Cor. 3.1-4); he laments that he himself is *sarkinos* (Rom. 7.14). And the hope held out in 1 Cor. 15 is that the psychical body (*sōma psychikon*) will be transformed into a spiritual body (*sōma pneumatikon*) (1 Cor. 15.44, 46).[165]

On the other hand, it could well be argued that the Gnostic dualism between creation and redemption was able to draw strength from Paul's conception of the resurrected body as 'spiritual'. Presumably because they recognized this, the Fathers argued intensely that it was the *flesh* which would be resurrected. Already Ignatius insists: 'I know and believe that Jesus was in the flesh even after the resurrection' (*Smyrn.* 3.1). The argument could be built on Luke 24.39, but not readily on Paul. Irenaeus and Tertullian were clearly concerned at the capital which their opponents were able to make out of 1 Cor. 15.50 ('flesh and blood cannot inherit the kingdom of God'),[166] but their attempts to wrest a favourable meaning from the passage are hardly convincing.[167] And Epiphanius rants at the Valentinians, somewhat amusingly at this point, in the following terms: 'They deny the resurrection of the dead,

---

162. Cf. 1 Cor. 15.51; Eph. 5.32.
163. 1 Cor. 13.2; 14.2.
164. Rom. 11.25; (16.25); Col. 1.26-27; well caught by Eph. 3.3-10. This would have been the primary thought behind other references — 1 Cor. 2.1, 7; 4.1; Col. 2.2; 4.3; Eph. 1.9; 6.19.
165. To be noted also is that, according to Origen, Basilides interpreted Paul's 'I died' (Rom. 7.9) as a reference to reincarnation (see Pearson, 'Basilides the Gnostic' 18).
166. As by the Ophites in Irenaeus, *adv. haer.* 1.30.13 (Foerster, *Gnosis* 1.93), and in the *Gospel of Philip* 23b (*NTA* 1.191) = 56.32-34 (*NHL* 144). 'This is [the passage]', complains Irenaeus, 'which is adduced by all the heretics in support of their folly' (5.9.1).
167. Irenaeus, *adv. haer.* 5.9-14; Tertullian, *de res. carn.* 48-50. See below §47.6; also Wiles, *Divine Apostle* 44; Pagels, *Paul* 85-86.

saying something mysterious and ridiculous, that it is not this body which rises, but another rises from it, which they call spiritual' (*Pan.* 31.7.6). But it is clear that Paul did indeed conceive of the resurrection body as 'spiritual', as different from the body which goes into the ground (1 Cor. 15.37), and as different from the mortal, perishable, flesh and blood body which dies (15.42-50).[168]

What has been missed here is the neatness of Paul's solution to the question, 'With what kind of body do (the resurrected) come?' (15.35); that is, the distinction he makes between 'body' and 'flesh'. By maintaining belief in a resurrection *body* Paul retained the Hebrew understanding of material creation as made by God and good, while, at the same time, he in effect diverted the more typically Hellenistic antipathy to the material into his own warnings, we might even say antipathy, to the flesh.[169] To ignore and lose that distinction is to miss the subtlety of Paul's treatment of the resurrection and to lose its potential for response to the Gnostics.

In contrast, by ignoring Paul's distinction, and returning to the more Greek identification of body and flesh, the early Fathers may have refuted the Gnostic disparagement of the physical and material.[170] But at the same time, by abandoning Paul's distinction between flesh and body they opened the door to Paul's warnings against living in accord with the flesh being understood as antipathy to the body and to the natural functionings of the corporality of God's creation. Most notably, with the later Fathers, Augustine and Jerome, sexual function became fleshly, negative, the means of transmitting original sin — with virginity and celibacy exalted to a degree that a more biblical creation theology (God made man and woman for each other) could never have allowed.[171]

So Paul was preserved by the great church as a spokesman for 'orthodoxy' against Gnostic 'heresy' by dumbing down the subtlety of his anthropology and conception of the resurrection body, with disastrous long-term effects for Christian evaluation of sexuality. To bring in Paul as the great champion against the Gnostics was something of a Pyrrhic victory.[172]

---

168. As noted in *Beginning from Jerusalem* 827–30, in the extended sequence of two antithetical columns set up by Paul in 1 Cor. 15.42-54, 'flesh and blood' belong in the (negative) column along with 'corruption' (15.42, 50), 'dishonour' (15.43), 'weakness' (15.43), 'natural body' (15.44-46), 'earthly' (15.47-49), 'the dead' (15.52), 'corruptible' (15.53-54) and 'mortal' (15.54), which are set antithetically over against the (positive) column consisting of 'incorruption', 'glory', 'power', 'spiritual body', 'heavenly', 'incorruptible', 'incorruption', and 'immortality'.

169. As e.g. in Rom. 7.18; 8.7; Gal. 5.16-17; 6.8; see further *Theology of Paul* §§3.2–3.4.

170. Cf. Wiles, *Divine Apostle* 26-29.

171. Ironically, they shared an antipathy to ordinary sexual function with most Gnostics.

172. One might also wonder whether the patristic church's two-nature christology reflects something of a Gnostic dualistic world-view (cf. Rudolph, *Gnosis* 372).

b. Marcion — the Radical Paulinist

We have left Marcion till now, since it was his use of Paul in particular which made him such a challenge and threat both to the 'great church' and to the continuing status of Paul as apostle of the 'great church'.[173] Harnack could even describe Marcion as 'the first Protestant'.[174] And Stephen Wilson notes that 'During its heyday in the second century the Marcionite church was one of the dominant forms of Christianity'.[175]

Marcion is remembered as initially a disciple of Cerdo, who, according to Irenaeus, 'took his system from the followers of Simon' and 'taught that the God proclaimed by the law and the prophets was not the Father of our Lord Jesus Christ, . . . the one was righteous, but the other benevolent' (Irenaeus, *adv. haer.* 1.27.1).[176] Marcion evidently took up and developed Cerdo's teaching: the God proclaimed by the law and the prophets was the author of evils who took delight in war.[177] But Jesus, 'derived from that Father who is

---

173. J. Knox prefaces his *Marcion and the New Testament* (University of Chicago, 1942, reprinted 1980) by quoting Theodore Zahn: 'No Christian teacher of the second century holds so significant a place in the history of the ecclesiastical canon as the heretic Marcion' (vii). Hoffmann concludes (acknowledging it as oversimplification) 'that for Marcion Paul commands papal authority. He is the sole infallible teacher' (*Marcion* 308).

174. King, *Gnosticism* 66. Harnack has often been criticized for regarding Marcion as a second-century Luther; see e.g. T. D. Still, 'Shadow and Light: Marcion's (Mis)construal of the Apostle Paul', in Bird and Dodson, eds., *Paul and the Second Century* 91-107 (here 95 and n.23).

175. Wilson, *Related Strangers* 208; Wilson provides a helpful analysis of Marcion's teaching (211-12).

176. Quoted also by Eusebius, *HE* 4.11.2. Similarly Justin Martyr, *1 Apol.* 26.5, on whom Irenaeus probably drew (*adv. haer.* 4.6.2). More fully, according to Tertullian, Cerdo 'introduces two first causes, that is, two Gods — one good, the other cruel: the good being the superior; the latter, the cruel one, being the creator of the world. He repudiates the prophecies and the Law; renounces God the Creator; maintains that Christ who came was the Son of the superior God; affirms that he was not in the substance of flesh; states him to have been only in a phantasmal shape, to have not really suffered, but undergone a quasi-passion, and not to have been born of a virgin, nay, really not to have been born at all' (Tertullian, *adv. haer.* 6).

177. See also Tertullian, *adv. Marc.* 1.2 (Marcion quoted Isa. 45.7); Still, 'Shadow and Light' 96-99. Marcion is probably not to be described as a Gnostic: he borrowed or agreed with the Gnostic concept of the Creator, the Demiurge, as a second and inferior God, and thought of Jesus in docetic terms; but he did not engage in the characteristically Gnostic dualistic speculation about how the (material) world was created, nor did he make a great play of saving *gnosis* (Hoffmann, *Marcion* 175-89); discussion of the issue is briefly reviewed by Lindemann, *Paulus* 387-89; see also §38 n.157 above. 'Marcion did not want to be a prophet proclaiming a new revelation, nor did he ever try to publish his thoughts in a pseudepigraphical book under the pseudonym of Paul' (Koester, *Introduction* 2.330).

above the God that made the world, ... was manifested in the form of a man to those who were in Judaea, abolishing the prophets and the law, and all the works of that God who made the world' (1.27.2).

According to Tertullian, Cerdo also accepted only a diminished Gospel of Luke and several of Paul's epistles, 'neither all the epistles, nor in their integrity', but he rejected the Acts of the Apostles and the Apocalypse (*adv. haer.* 6). If so, this would help explain Irenaeus's report that Marcion too 'mutilated' the Gospel according to Luke, setting aside Jesus' teaching in which he confesses that the Maker of the universe is his Father; and that he dismembered Paul's epistles in like manner and removed all of Paul's quotations from the prophets (Irenaeus, *adv. haer.* 1.27.2).

Whether Marcion drew his inspiration directly from Paul, or simply elaborated his inheritance from Cerdo,[178] the fact remains that Paul provided Marcion's primary authority for his teaching and for his claim in effect to be the truest follower of Paul.[179] Tertullian indeed notes that although Marcion ascribed no author to his Gospel, he might well have 'published his Gospel in the name of St. Paul himself, the single authority of the document' (*adv. Marc.* 4.2).[180] Marcion's starting point was probably the antithesis between the law and the gospel, which he could derive fairly readily from Paul,[181] and which was evidently the basis for writing his *Antitheses*, intended to exploit and work out the ramifications of that basic antithesis.[182] Significant here is the fact that Marcion seems to have placed Paul's letter to the Galatians first in his collection of Paul's letters (Tertullian, *adv. Marc.* 5.2), the most sustainedly polemical

---

178. Moll disputes the claim that Marcion was a disciple of Cerdo (*Marcion* 41-43). Räisänen also thinks the claim that Marcion had close connections with Cerdo is dubious ('Marcion' 104).

179. Against Harnack's view that Marcion made the early church aware of a largely unknown Paul (*Marcion* 12), the evidence already reviewed in this chapter speaks otherwise; 'Marcion did not make Paul an authority, he made use of his authority' (Moll, *Marcion* 86). 'One wonders whether Marcion's radicalized Paulinism could have had the success it had, unless Paul's letters already had an acknowledged status in many existing parts of Christendom' (Räisänen, 'Marcion' 116).

180. On 'Marcion's Paulinism' see also Hoffmann, *Marcion* ch. 7.

181. E.g. Rom. 3.20; 7.4-6; 2 Cor. 3.6; Gal. 2.19; 3.13; 5.1; Col. 2.20-23; and as typified by Paul's repeated confrontations with what are usually referred to as 'Judaizers' in Galatians, 2 Corinthians 3, 10-13 and Philippians 3. It is somewhat unnerving to recall that Lutheranism built its own system largely round the same law/gospel antithesis.

182. Tertullian, *adv. Marc.* 1.19; 4.1. Moll thinks the *Antitheses* was a rather brief collection of contradictory passages from the OT and NT which functioned as a kind of Marcionite catechism; it was not an extensive commentary and has been overrated in previous scholarship (*Marcion* 107-14, 120). E. W. Scherbenske, *Canonizing Paul: Ancient Editorial Practice and the* Corpus Paulinum (Oxford University, 2013), argues that the *Antitheses* was an introductory work to guide readers of the biblical text to a proper reading (74-85).

of Paul's letters in which the gospel/law antithesis is most clearly expressed.[183] And since law characterized the Old Testament, it followed that the OT itself fell on the wrong side of the antithesis, and the God of the OT as well.[184] By the same logic, all that drew upon or derived from the OT should be disentangled from the gospel. That included the OT itself and all NT quotations from and dependencies on the OT. Hence Irenaeus's declaration that 'This man is the only one who has dared openly to mutilate the scriptures' (*adv. haer.* 1.27.4). And Tertullian's caustic comment that 'Marcion expressly and openly used the knife, not the pen, since he made such an excision of the scriptures as suited his own subject-matter' (*de praescr. haer.* 38). Thus he drew only on a mutilated Luke, traditionally the follower of Paul, and used Galatians (Gal. 2.6-9, 13-14) and 2 Cor. 11.13 to insinuate the untrustworthiness of other apostles (and the Gospels which derived from them),[185] while also removing what he regarded as the adulterations which had been added to the text of Paul's letters (Tertullian, *adv. Marc.* 4.2-5).[186]

There was an attractive simplicity about Marcion's gospel — a resolution of the endless tensions between the punitive God of the OT and the gracious God of Jesus and Paul. No wonder Marcion proved to be so influential for those who wanted a faith which was clear-cut and from which such tensions had been removed.[187] And for such a simplistic faith the sharpness of Paul's contrasts between old covenant and new, between 'letter' and 'Spirit' (as in 2 Cor. 3), could not fail to be attractive as providing the key to a complete religious system. The tensions between the leaders of a Jewish messianic sect and the Pauline mission to Gentiles were never so radically exploited.[188] Was this indeed what the Jewish believers in Jesus, hostile to Paul and his mission, had feared? Was this the inevitable end for a movement to break embryonic Christianity free from its Jewish matrix? Marcion demonstrated that just such a trajectory could be drawn from Paul, and it is not entirely clear that those who dismissed Marcion understood Paul all that much better.[189]

183. Hoffmann, *Marcion* 75-76.
184. Ehrman, *Lost Christianities* 104-7; though see §38 n.160 above.
185. See also Hoffmann, *Marcion* 101-5, 135-39, 146-53.
186. Still, 'Shadow and Light' 102. See further U. Schmid, *Marcion und sein Apostolos* (Berlin: de Gruyter, 1995). Scherbenske discusses examples of Marcion's 'textual manipulation' (*Canonizing Paul* 94-115).
187. See above §38 n.161.
188. Knox sees an undoubted 'historical continuity between Paul's conflicts with the Judaizers . . . and Marcion's struggle with the Roman church' (*Marcion* 15).
189. Wiles notes that 'E. Hoffmann-Aleith concludes a study of Chrysostom's interpretation of Paul [*ZNW* 38 (1939) 138] by declaring that he is a striking example of how the theologians of the early Church combined an admiration for Paul with an unconscious failure to understand him' (*Divine Apostle* 3). See also Wilson, *Related Strangers* 218-21.

Of course, a system built on a mutilated Paul and an adulterated Luke was vulnerable to obvious challenge.[190] And Tertullian had little difficulty in undermining Marcion's claims.[191] Paul preached no new God, even though he abrogated some of God's ancient laws; the God whom Christ revealed was the Creator (*adv. Marc.* 1.21); to deny the reality of Christ's sufferings and death (because of the denial of his flesh) was to deny Christ's resurrection and thus to subvert Paul's argument in 1 Cor. 15.12-19 (*adv. Marc.* 3.8). Paul's conflict with Peter (Gal. 2.13-14) should not be exaggerated, since Peter might simply have been acting according to Paul's own principle of becoming all things to all men (1 Cor. 9.22) (*adv. Marc.* 4.3). Likewise with Luke's Gospel, in what we would now call 'a careful reading' of the Gospel, Tertullian is able to argue effectively that the connection of Christ with the Creator is clearly to be seen (*adv. Marc.* 4.13-43). And in Book 5 he does the same with Paul's epistles: demonstrating that 'they were in perfect unison with the writings of the Old Testament, and therefore testified that the Creator was the only God and that the Lord Jesus was his Christ'.[192] For example, Marcion's teaching makes no sense of 1 Corinthians 1.18-25 (*adv. Marc.* 5.5), or of Christ as our Passover (1 Cor. 5.7; *adv. Marc.* 5.7); Marcion alters 'last Adam' of 1 Cor. 15.45 to 'last Lord', because 'last Adam' connects Christ to the Creator of the first Adam (*adv. Marc.* 5.10); 2 Cor. 3 can hardly be understood as envisaging two Gods (*adv. Marc.* 5.11); the intensity of Marcion's mutilation of Romans shows how unPauline Marcion's gospel is (*adv. Marc.* 5.13); Rom. 8.3, Jesus sent 'in the likeness of sinful flesh', cannot be understood in docetic terms, since the 'likeness' refers not to the 'flesh' but to the 'sinful' (*adv. Marc.* 5.14); and Col. 1.15-17 clearly envisages Christ as bound up with creation and as making the Creator visible (*adv. Marc.* 5.19).[193]

As vulnerable as Marcion's exposition of Paul is to critique,[194] then, the uncomfortable fact remains that Marcion exposes the problem of Paul in an acute way. The problem was the complexity and subtlety of Paul's theology, too often 'resolved' in an unbalanced way, by 'orthodox' as much as 'heretic'.[195] The problem arose because Paul had been trying to hold together in a consis-

---

190. Moll provides a list of Marcion's deletions from the Gospel of Luke (*Marcion* 92-98).

191. See also A. M. Bain, 'Tertullian: Paul as Teacher of the Gentile Churches', in Bird and Dodson, eds., *Paul and the Second Century* 207-25 (here 209-15).

192. ANF 3.429.

193. See also Still, 'Shadow and Light' 105-6.

194. 'His editing of Romans was the most drastic of all' (Wilson, *Related Strangers* 214). But see also J. M. Lieu, '"As much my apostle as Christ is mine": The Dispute over Paul between Tertullian and Marcion', *Early Christianity* 1 (2010) 41-59.

195. Cf. Wiles, *Divine Apostle* 132-39.

tent way what he regarded as earlier revelation (the religion of Israel and the scriptures of Israel) and the new revelation through and of Christ which had found him and transformed him. He had been trying to proclaim a distinctively Jewish faith to a widespread non-Jewish audience. He had been conscious of the need to translate old terms into new language, to say intelligibly what had never been said before. No wonder 2 Peter found 'some things in them [Paul's letters] hard to understand' and easy to twist (3.16). And still to this day commentators and theologians either find Paul inconsistent or take a particularly important feature of his theology and make it the key to the whole, subordinating all other features to the one or sloughing them off because they confuse the clear and straightforward insight of the chosen item.[196] Marcion's Paulinism is the classic example of an aspect of and emphasis in a more complex system being abstracted from the system and pressed to an extreme.[197] As Tertullian and the others demonstrated, to so oversimplify a theology as profound as Paul's was to be unfaithful to it and effectively to destroy it. At the same time, however, it was probably Marcion who drove Christian apologists and theologians to engage in depth with Paul, to probe into his theology, and not simply to quote him or allude to him.[198]

47.6 Paul and Irenaeus

Irenaeus marks the beginning of serious engagement with Paul, 'the first great exponent of Paul'.[199] He was obviously highly familiar with the whole Pauline corpus, quoting from his letters regularly and easily.[200] Irenaeus thus provides irrefutable proof that by the end of the second century Paul's letters had been

---

196. The enduring problems, for example, of making coherent sense of Paul's attitude to the law and of the tension between his teaching on justification by faith and not works and his teaching on judgment according to works illustrate the point all too well; see e.g. H. Räisänen, *Paul and the Law* (WUNT 29; Tübingen: Mohr Siebeck, 1983); Dunn, ed., *Paul and the Mosaic Law*; J. D. G. Dunn, 'If Paul could believe both in Justification by Faith and Judgment according to Works, why should that be a problem for us?', in A. P. Stanley, ed., *Four Views on the Role of Works at the Final Judgment* (Grand Rapids: Zondervan, 2013) 119-41.

197. The same is true of Mani; Manichaeism being regarded by many as a 'Pauline heresy' (*ODCC* 1027).

198. Lindemann, *Paulus* 395.

199. Osborn, *Irenaeus* 189.

200. Irenaeus quotes from or clearly draws on all the letters attributed to Paul, apart from Philemon, particularly Romans and 1 Corinthians, but with similar familiarity with 2 Corinthians, Galatians, Ephesians, Philippians and Colossians. See B. C. Blackwell, 'Paul and Irenaeus', in Bird and Dodson, eds., *Paul and the Second Century* 190-206 (here 192-93).

§47.6 *Paul*

collected, were widely circulated (Irenaeus was based in Gaul) and were well known and used. There is no embarrassment in his usage. As is clear particularly from his Book One, he knew that the Valentinians and Marcion[201] also made use of Paul in building their systems; but he was entirely confident that he could demonstrate the confusion and invalidity of their use. Whatever the claims and despite the claims made by his opponents regarding Paul, for Irenaeus there was no doubt that Paul was 'the apostle' whose teaching established the faith of the great church.

Moreover, Irenaeus engaged with Paul and theologized with and through Paul. He did not simply quote passages from Paul as though a straightforward quotation would be sufficient to demonstrate the misunderstanding of the 'heretics'. In *adv. haer.* 3.7.1-2, for example, he engages in careful exegesis of 2 Cor. 4.4, Gal. 3.19 and 2 Thess. 2.8. In a sequence of passages in Book Four he demonstrates a clear understanding of Paul's arguments in Gal. 3.5-9 (4.21.1), Rom. 9.10-13 (4.21.2), Rom. 4 (4.25.1-3) and 2 Cor. 3 (4.26.1); his reliance on Paul is emphasized in the closing paragraph of Book Four (4.41.4). Particularly interesting is his lengthy attempt in Book Five to refute what he regards as the misuse and misunderstanding of 1 Cor. 15.50 — 'flesh and blood cannot inherit the kingdom of God' (5.9-14) — by interpreting 'flesh and blood' as 'those who have not the Spirit of God in themselves' (5.9.1); 'the flesh, when destitute of the Spirit of God, is dead, not having life, and cannot possess the kingdom of God' (5.9.3); 'man without the Spirit is not capable of inheriting the kingdom of God' (5.10).

However, Irenaeus most clearly demonstrates that he was a Paulinist, building his own theology on Paul, in his thesis of recapitulation: that Christ, the Word, the Son of God, recapitulated Adam in himself.[202] He builds particularly on Rom. 5.14 and 1 Cor. 15.20-22 (3.22.3, 4); in Christ the one God 're-formed the human race' (4.24.1); the Word, 'having become united with the ancient substance of Adam's formation, rendered man living and perfect, receptive of the perfect Father, in order that as in the natural [Adam] we all were dead, so in the spiritual we may all be made alive' (5.1.2); he 'summed up human nature in his own person . . . recapitulating in himself . . . that original handiwork of the Father' (5.14.2).[203] This enabled Irenaeus to refute those who denied Adam's salvation: 'inasmuch as man is saved, it is fitting that he

---

201. The Marcionites 'allege that Paul alone knew the truth, and that to him the mystery was manifested by revelation' (*adv. haer.* 3.13.1).

202. *Adv. haer.* 3.21.10–23.8; 4.24.1; 6.1.2; 14.1-3; 20.2; 21.1-3.

203. Irenaeus thus resolved one of the points of tension in Paul's christology: that Jesus was Lord not simply by virtue of Ps. 110.1, but also in fulfillment of Ps. 8.4-6. That the two roles merged in Paul's thought is indicated by the fact that the final lines of Ps. 8.6 and Ps. 110.1 said the same thing (*Beginning from Jerusalem* 897-98 n.165).

who was created the original man should be saved'; 'for Adam showed his repentance by his conduct'; 'when therefore the Lord vivifies man, that is, Adam, death is at the same time destroyed' (3.23.2, 5, 7).[204] More to the point, however, Irenaeus's recapitulation thesis was at the heart of his refutation of the soteriologies of the Valentinians and Marcion: it was one and the same God who made Adam and sent his Son; salvation has been achieved by the Word combining with flesh; it is the Son's assumption of flesh which ensures the resurrection of the flesh; 'if the flesh were not in a position to be saved, the Word of God would in no wise have become flesh' (5.14.1).[205] It was not least the genius of Irenaeus that in his theology of recapitulation he managed to blend the Adam christology of Paul and the incarnation christology of John to provide a truly biblical theology.[206]

A not insignificant corollary is that while the death of Christ is still a major point of conflict between Irenaeus and his Gnostic opponents, the Pauline emphasis on the cross as an atoning sacrifice for sin is sidelined; the emphasis is rather on the reality of Christ's death as the destruction of death and thus the reversal of Adam's corruption, as already indicated by Paul in Rom. 5.12-21 (2.20.3; 3.18.7).[207] But more significant was the fact that Irenaeus did not succumb to the great church's perspective in reading Paul through the Pastoral Epistles and Acts. His theology was formed by direct interaction with Paul's principal letters, particularly Romans and 1 Corinthians, and ensured that the theology of Paul and theologizing with Paul would form a fruitful dynamic for subsequent Christianity.

It is Irenaeus, therefore, who put Paul at the centre of Christian theology, so that it is in no way surprising that following Irenaeus we find sustained exegetical commentary on and exposition of Paul's letters, beginning with Tertullian and Origen, followed at some remove by Chrysostom, Theodore of Mopsuestia, and in the west by Marius Victorinus, Ambrosiaster, Jerome and Augustine. And it was probably Irenaeus who secured for Paul the adulation

---

204. This was in reaction to Tatian's denial of Adam's salvation (*adv. haer.* 1.28.1, cited above in §40.2f).

205. 'For Irenaeus the incarnation was physically necessary to save humanity from death and corruption'; 'God and man are united in Christ where the sin of Adam is reversed and the perfection of Christ is fulfilled' (Osborn, *Irenaeus* 101, 110-11; see further ch. 5). See also Blackwell, 'Paul and Irenaeus' 200-204.

206. 'R. Seeberg identified Irenaeus as the first great representative of biblicism. Nothing could be further from the truth, because Irenaeus analyses the theology of scripture more rigorously than most theologians. His own theology blends Paul and John in a way which is beyond proof-texts and based on a profound understanding' (Osborn, *Irenaeus* 172). See also below §49 at n.69.

207. Cf. Osborn, *Irenaeus* 118-21; 'John does not oppose the centrality which Paul gives to Christ crucified but joins it with the incarnation' (186).

in which he was held thereafter by Origen and his successors as expositors of Paul.[208]

47.7 In Sum

The fact is that Paul remains a contrary and troublesome figure within the history of Christianity, his letters as provocative as they are confirmatory. But that is precisely why his letters are such valuable members of the NT canon. Paul (as does Jesus) prevents a Christianity which acknowledges the NT canon from becoming too self-satisfied and conformist, too content with a comfortable identity or with a nicely coherent system of theology or practice. The fact that a Jewish believer in Jesus could condemn Paul as an apostate, or that a Valentinus or Marcion could find him so inspirational for their divergent systems, should be a constant warning that a simplistically coherent theology or a too comfortable church has lost Paul. At the same time, the fact that Paul could inspire an Irenaeus, an Augustine and a Luther should be sufficient rejoinder. A Pauline-type church or theology will always have inner tensions, be rather lumpy, allow or encourage diverse forms and expressions. That was Paul's initial role, to prick presuppositions and presumptions and to remind the church(es) of all generations that the heart of the matter is always a bare trust in the grace and mercy of the God and Father of the Lord Jesus Christ. It is a role which he still fulfills.

---

208. See also M. W. Elliott, 'The Triumph of Paulinism by the Mid-Third Century', in Bird and Dodson, eds., *Paul and the Second Century* 244-56. The esteem for Paul from the third century onwards is illustrated by Wiles, *Divine Apostle* 19-25; see also King, *Gnosticism* 99-100.

CHAPTER 48

Peter

48.1 Introduction

When it comes to assessing the continuing influence of the three leading figures of first-generation (embryonic) Christianity, Peter proves to be the most intriguing. Of the enduring impact of Paul there can be little doubt, both in the growth of churches he established in Asia Minor and elsewhere, and in the letters he in effect bequeathed to Christianity, so sharply defining its character and theology. And even with James, a clear impression is evident, both of his significance in the first generation, as indicated in Acts and by inference from Paul's letters, and of his continuing influence as a foundational figure, as indicated in the letter ascribed to him (James), and particularly in the Jewish-Christian writings. But with Peter, the first- and second-century mists gather more densely and it becomes very hard to pick out salient features.

It is clear from the Gospel tradition, already current in the first generation, that Peter/Cephas was remembered as the first named, leader and spokesman of the twelve,[1] first mentioned of Jesus' three most intimate disciples (Peter, James and John).[2] Paul cites as recognized creedal tradition that the risen Jesus had appeared first to Cephas (1 Cor. 15.5), obviously recognized to be a mark of honour and a confirmation of an especially favoured

---

1. Mark 3.16-19 pars.; 8.29, 32 pars.; 9.5 pars.; 10.28 pars.; 11.21; 14.29 pars.; 16.7.
2. Mark 5.37 par.; 9.2 pars.; 13.3; 14.33 par. O. Cullmann, *Peter: Disciple, Apostle, Martyr* (London: SCM, ²1962), notes that 'even within this innermost circle it is almost always Peter who stands in the foreground' (25, and 25-28). So also P. Perkins, *Peter: Apostle for the Whole Church* (1994; Minneapolis: Fortress, 2000) 72, 102. M. Bockmuehl, *Simon Peter in Scripture and Memory* (Grand Rapids: Baker Academic, 2012), notes that 'Peter is the only disciple whom Jesus addresses by name in all four Gospels' (25).

relationship with Jesus, now exalted.[3] And Luke was undoubtedly able to draw on good tradition to the effect that Peter had been the earliest leader of what became the Jerusalem church (Acts 1-5; Gal. 1.18).[4]

Thereafter, however, the mists begin to gather more thickly. Luke reports that Peter was active in consolidating the first mission to Samaria (Acts 8), that he had an active (and healing) ministry among the groups of believers on the Judaean coast (Acts 9.32-43), and, most notably, that he gave an unexpected lead in opening the gospel to non-Jews (Acts 10-11). But beyond that his movements become obscure. During the persecution by Herod Agrippa he disappears from Jerusalem, 'to another place' (12.17), whose identity is never revealed.[5]

Both Paul and Luke report variously Peter's participation in the Jerusalem conference regarding the influx of Gentile believers, and his agreement with the resulting policy that Gentile believers did not need to be circumcised (Gal. 2.1-10; Acts 15). If the Acts account reflects a Jerusalem version of the discussion and decision, then it is important to note that the decisive arguments were made by Peter, but that the concluding ruling was given by James. According to Paul, James was indeed the *primus inter pares* (Gal. 2.9),[6] but Peter's responsibility, as agreed at that meeting, was for mission to his fellow Jews (Gal. 2.8-9). And the most obvious inference to be drawn from his subsequent conduct at Antioch (withdrawing from table fellowship with Gentile believers — Gal. 2.12) is that Peter was all too conscious of his primary mission responsibility (to the circumcized) and accordingly was anxious not to offend his fellow Jews unnecessarily.[7] In that case it would appear that he sided with James in a more restrictive policy as regards full fellowship with Gentile believers (quite possibly the policy designated as 'the apostolic decree').[8]

Otherwise we learn from Paul that Peter (Cephas) went on mission accompanied by his wife (1 Cor. 9.5), and that his influence was a factor in the potential factionalism in the church of Corinth (1 Cor. 1.12; 3.22), even though there is no firm evidence of any visit Peter made to Corinth or of time he spent

---

3. Though we also noted in §45.2a that 1 Cor. 15.3-7 may have incorporated a rival account in which it was remembered that Jesus had appeared to James either first or as specially favoured (1 Cor. 15.7), a tradition cherished by circles of Jewish believers in Jesus.

4. Hengel notes that Peter, under his diverse names (Peter, Simon, Cephas), appears in the Synoptics 75 times and in John 35 times. Overall in the NT he is referred to in person 181 times, whereas Paul/Saul has 177 mentions (*Der unterschätzte Petrus* 16).

5. See *Beginning from Jerusalem* §26n.130.

6. Though it should be noted that D reverses the order, putting Peter before James, in Gal. 2.9, presumably reflecting the Western assumption that Peter was the most eminent of the three (see also Metzger, *Textual Commentary* 592).

7. See *Beginning from Jerusalem* §§27.4-6.

8. See again *Beginning from Jerusalem* 461-69.

with the Corinthian church.⁹ Of course, if Peter had not visited Corinth, then the fact that his name became a rallying cry for some in Corinth is itself testimony to the high esteem in which he was held more widely beyond the areas in which he personally worked.¹⁰

So the evidence to be drawn from first-generation sources regarding Peter and his influence is at best patchy and leaves an ambiguous picture. In particular, where did he stand on the issue which most pulled the first generation apart — the issue whether Gentile believers should be regarded as fully part of the eschatological people of God without taking on what had become crucial identity markers of the covenant people (circumcision, and laws of clean and unclean)? Did he position himself somewhere between James and Paul and in effect, for that first generation at least, hold them together by his stature and policy (sometimes backing the one, sometimes following the lead of the other)? The absence of Peter from the final chapters of Acts heightens immeasurably the sense of intrigue which envelops Peter in the buildup to the catastrophe of 70 CE. Would he have counseled acceptance of the collection brought by Paul? Or would he have washed his hands of Paul as the Jerusalem believers may well have done?¹¹ Or . . .

To probe further into the continuing influence of Peter into the second century we need to look at what evidence is available to us: the Petrine letters in the NT; the evidence of Peter's significance as reflected in the other second-generation NT writings; the now familiar route through the Apostolic Fathers and Apologists; the apocryphal Peter; and the almost as familiar route through the Peter of Jewish-Christian and Gnostic texts and the legendary Peter.

48.2 The Epistles of Peter

The letters attributed to Peter, 1 Peter and 2 Peter, do not provide as much of a start as might have been hoped for. In Paul's case there are a number of letters, seven at least, which are almost universally accepted as from his own hand or in his own words. So we gain clear information about his movements and clear insight into his thought. In the case of James, the probability is sufficiently strong that the letter attributed to him is a fair representation of his teaching, both in content and style, so that it can be justifiably regarded as providing a clear indication of how he was remembered and how influential his teaching continued to be. And even if the link with the person of James

---

9. See also §48.5 below.
10. Perkins, *Peter* 114, 118.
11. See again *Beginning from Jerusalem* 970-78.

himself is less than sure, in any case the letter provides an expression of a distinctively Jewish belief in Jesus which must have been influential among Jewish believers in Jesus in the post-70 period.

With the letters attributed to Peter, however, the case is rather different.

a. 1 Peter

The frustration with 1 Peter is fairly intense. I included it in §37 as the legacy of Peter, implying that it played the same role with regard to Peter as did Ephesians for Paul, and the letter of James for James. But of the three, 1 Peter came across as the least convincing as a representation of the distinctive teaching of the one to whom it was attributed. Ephesians certainly represented well what we know to have been distinctive of Paul's self-understanding and mission. And the distinctiveness of the letter of James presumably reflects the distinctive character of James's teaching. But we know so little of what was distinctive about Peter's preaching and teaching from our other NT sources that it remains also unclear as to whether we can regard 1 Peter as representing the distinctiveness of Peter.[12]

Yet, perhaps that is a clue as to why the letter was written and why it was attributed to Peter. Perhaps it was precisely because it was *not* distinctive within the range of teaching among the earliest churches that it was treasured. It expressed beliefs about Jesus which were integral to Christian faith and united believers across a wide range of Roman provinces;[13] it spoke for as well as to Christians conscious of living in a hostile world and liable to suffer persecution; and it provided a model of how believers should be church.[14] Is that indicative of how Peter was seen in the post-70 period — not as a factional leader emphasizing the distinctive emphases of the faction, but as one who emphasized the characteristic features of Christian faith and praxis, the features which believers shared and which bound them together?[15] Such an

---

12. 'The portrayal of Peter in this letter is particularly striking in that no special Petrine privilege is either assumed or asserted. . . . what marks 1 Peter is its basic *compatibility* and catholicity rather than its distinctiveness within early Christian literature' (Bockmuehl, *Simon Peter* 130).

13. *Beginning from Jerusalem* 1154-55.

14. See again *Beginning from Jerusalem* 1160-66.

15. '1 Peter should be seen as evidence for the universalizing of Peter as a leader for the whole church' (Perkins, *Peter* 120) — even though '1 Peter does not appeal to the example of Peter directly' (121). See also L. Goppelt, *Der erste Petrusbrief* (KEK; Göttingen: Vandenhoeck, 1978) 30-37.

inference can be drawn only tentatively, but it may be strengthened by two other features of the letter.

One is the puzzle as to whether the letter was written to Jewish believers or to Gentile believers.[16] If the former, it would correlate well with the earlier tradition that Peter's primary mission was to his fellow Jews. In that case, it would provide evidence that Peter was remembered as strengthening Jewish believers in areas (Pontus, Galatia, Cappadocia, Asia and Bithynia) where the Gentile mission was probably the major expression of early Christianity. In addition, since the letter gives no indication of tension or factionalism with other believers, it could probably be inferred that 1 Peter was valued not least because of its emphases on the commonalities rather than the diversities which might have pulled believers in these regions in different directions.

If, alternatively, 1 Peter was written with Gentile believers in view, its most striking feature is the use of characteristic Israel motifs to describe the letter's recipients — particularly 'a chosen race, a royal priesthood, a holy nation, a people for God's own possession' (1 Pet. 2.9).[17] Add to this the heavy influence of Jewish (OT) language and thought evident in the letter, and the emphasis on OT prophecy fulfilled by Jesus,[18] and again the inference is clear: that the letter was written to draw Gentile believers into a characteristically Jewish pattern of belief. This would have been highly eirenic, and with, once again, no hint of factional tensions with other (Jewish) believers, the inference can again be drawn that 1 Peter was most valued for its ability to make Gentile believers feel that they fully belonged to this new religious movement with its distinguishing features so characteristically Jewish. If so, then, once again, Peter was being remembered and his influence still felt as a unifying figure and not a divisive figure, such as the reputations of James and Paul did not hide.

The other interesting feature of 1 Peter at this point is the very Pauline character of the letter — for example, the 'in Christ' language,[19] the same understanding of 'charisms' as community gifts of service and speech (4.10-11), and the same conception of sharing Christ's sufferings (4.13).[20] The striking character of this feature should not be downplayed. For it runs counter to the inferences which might be drawn from passages like Gal. 2.12 and 1 Cor. 1.12,

---

16. I argue for the former alternative, but am in a small minority on the point (*Beginning from Jerusalem* 1158-60).

17. Drawing on Exod. 19.6; Isa. 43.20-21; Mal. 3.17. See further *Beginning from Jerusalem* 1158. Interestingly, Irenaeus asserts, presumably with 1 Pet. 2.5, 9 in mind, that 'all the righteous possess the sacerdotal rank. And all the apostles of the Lord are priests' (*adv. haer.* 4.8.3).

18. *Beginning from Jerusalem* 1153, 1160; and above §45 nn.123, 124.

19. 1 Pet. 3.16; 5.10, 14.

20. *Beginning from Jerusalem* 1150-51, 1161.

that Paul and Peter were at odds in the emphases they gave in their preaching and teaching. And perhaps deliberately so: the Peter who was set aside for apostolic ministry to his fellow Jews in fact speaks the same language as the Paul who was set aside for apostolic ministry to Gentiles! Moreover, the fact that, like Paul, 1 Peter interweaves Jesus tradition into its paraenesis[21] further suggests that 1 Peter was put forward and valued for the powerful way in which it bonded together the founding influence of Jesus with the potentially divergent strands of Jewish and Gentile mission. And Peter, to whom this consolidating letter is attributed, is thus again portrayed as a unifying figure holding together the diverse groups who shared belief in Jesus.

b. 2 Peter

Quite what to make of 2 Peter is not at all clear: its pseudonymity is more or less taken for granted by all serious students; and there is no evidence of its being known and used in the second century.[22] What it tells us about the regard for and influence of Peter in the second century, therefore, is inferential and speculative at best. Nevertheless, it remains highly probable that 2 Peter was written some time in the first half of the second century; the fact that it was sufficiently esteemed to be included eventually in the recognized canon of the NT assuredly rules out a later date. In which case it still does tell us something of the esteem in which Peter was held in the second century.

Here the reaching back to recall early traditions of Peter's close relationship with Jesus should be noted: the Synoptic tradition of Peter (with James and John) sharing in the experience of Jesus' transfiguration, as a personal testimony;[23] and the Johannine tradition of the risen Jesus predicting Peter's death, again as a personal testimony.[24] Both are highly honorific reminiscences, especially when other traditions of Peter's faithlessness and denial of Jesus[25] could also or alternatively have been recalled. 2 Peter's reminder of them hardly suggests that a more negative reputation of Peter had to be countered. It suggests rather that Peter was esteemed precisely because (notwithstanding less laudatory reminiscences preserved in the Gospel tradition) the closeness of Peter's relation with Jesus and the honour which Jesus bestowed

---

21. *Beginning from Jerusalem* 1154.
22. §39 n.284.
23. 2 Pet. 1.17-18: 'We ourselves heard this voice come from heaven, while we were with him [Jesus] on the holy mountain' — drawing on Matt. 17.1-9 (referring to 17.5-6) pars.
24. 2 Pet. 1.14: 'I know that I will soon be divested of my body, as our Lord Jesus Christ made clear to me' — drawing on John 21.8-19.
25. Matt. 14.29-31; Mark 14.66-72 pars.

on Peter in such intimate exchanges were what marked him out and set him so high in the esteem of the believers in Jesus whose views are represented or reflected by 2 Peter.

A second feature worthy of note is the striking fact that 2 Peter has incorporated so much of the epistle of Jude in its composition (§39.3f). Jude will have been valued because of its attribution to the brother of Jesus, and brother of James; and it possibly relates to Jude as the epistle of James relates to James, that is, as containing at least some authentic reminiscences of Jude's teaching (§39.3e). This would integrate 2 Peter firmly with the family of Jesus, the family of Jesus round which the Jerusalem believers gathered in the pre-70 period and round which they seem to have rallied in the post-70 period.[26] It would also confirm that Peter was remembered as having retained a close relationship and having maintained a bond of trust with the early leaders of the Jewish believers in Jesus. The apocalyptic character of the exhortations, both of Jude and of 2 Peter, is typically Jewish, and may indeed reflect some of the reactions of the Jewish believers in Palestine in the wake of the double calamity of the two failed revolts against Rome.

The third relevant feature is the esteem in which Paul is held — 'our beloved brother Paul' (2 Pet. 3.15). Not only so, but Paul's letters are clearly regarded as authoritative texts for preaching and teaching, 'scriptures' indeed (3.16). This would hardly have been so had the emphases of the gospel and theology so clearly expressed in most of these letters been regarded with suspicion, still less with hostility, by the group behind 2 Peter or who cherished 2 Peter. On the contrary, the group who regarded Paul's letters as scripture must have approved the Pauline mission to the Gentiles and the terms in which Paul had carried out that mission. At the same time, the recognition that Paul's letters were being misinterpreted by 'false teachers' (2.1; 3.16) may well indicate awareness of the use of Paul's letters by early Gnostic or gnosticizing groups or even by Marcion (§47.5). Here 2 Peter can be heard as the voice of the great church trying to retain Paul as one of its spokesmen and to prevent Paul from being taken over by a more radical gnosticizing tendency; the significance of such high praise of *Paul* being attributed to *Peter* should not be missed. If 2 Peter can be given some credit for retaining Paul's own radicalism within the spectrum of orthodoxy (as Christian 'scripture'), then the debt which Christianity owes to 2 Peter was probably sufficient to secure 2 Peter's place within the NT canon.

Despite the differences between 1 and 2 Peter, therefore, 2 Peter does a similar job to that of 1 Peter and strengthens the impression that Peter was seen already in the second century as a bridge-builder (*pontifex*!), holding together the other three formative influences stemming from the first generation

---

26. See §45.3 above.

— the Jesus tradition, James and Paul.[27] Each of the other three was being pulled away from the others by parasitical ideologies or polarizing forces. Not so Peter, or only to a minimal extent. This is perhaps the principal reason for the relative silence regarding Peter — that he or rather his influence was a stabilizing force, not so interesting because not so controversial, the link which helped prevent the chain which constituted the great church from sundering into the still greater diversity of hard-line Jewish Christianity and Gnostic Christianity. But this is too great a conclusion to draw simply from study of the Petrine epistles. We must inquire further.

48.3 Peter in the Rest of the New Testament

(Simon) Peter/Cephas is named elsewhere in the NT (apart from 1 and 2 Peter) only in the four Gospels, Acts and Paul's letters (1 Corinthians and Galatians). We have already noted the last information, but it is appropriate to remind ourselves that:

- Paul in effect acknowledged that Peter had been accorded a certain primacy in the establishment of the gospel (1 Cor. 15.5);
- by his recourse to Peter (Gal. 1.18), Paul in effect acknowledged Peter's role as leader of the first disciples of Jesus, and therefore, presumably, the best resource for Paul's re-education regarding Jesus' mission;
- Paul also freely acknowledged Peter's own role in mission;[28]
- evidently Paul's respect for Peter was not seriously or lastingly undermined by their disagreement in Antioch (Gal. 2.12-16) and by the later tensions in Corinth, whatever precisely they were.[29]

But now we need to take note of the testimony of the Gospels and Acts.

27. I echo a reflection which emerged from my study of *Unity and Diversity in the New Testament* (1977, ³2006), to explain why Peter became the focal point of unity in the great church: 'For Peter was probably in fact and effect the bridge-man (*pontifex maximus*!) who did more than any other to hold together the diversity of first-century Christianity' (430). The suggestion is taken up, for example, by Perkins: 'Peter as an Ecclesial Centrist' (*Peter* 9-14). 'The key to Peter's ecclesiastical utility in his lifetime may have been his ability to hold the Christian middle together, being acknowledged as an apostle by Paul, yet not alienating James' more conservative backers' (Brown in Brown and Meier, *Antioch and Rome* 210). In his *The Remembered Peter* (WUNT 262; Tübingen: Mohr Siebeck, 2010) Markus Bockmuehl gently chides me for failing to follow through my 1977 reflection in the first two volumes of *Christianity in the Making* (58-60).
28. Gal. 2.7-9; 1 Cor. 9.5.
29. *Beginning from Jerusalem* §32 n.170 and §35.1c.

a. Mark

Here we must recall the Papias tradition that Mark was Peter's interpreter (§39.2a(i)). The tradition itself attests the importance attributed to Peter in the early second century as a or indeed the primary witness for the story of Jesus' mission and for the account of his teaching. The fact that Mark himself does not give any indication of this may be because his dependence on Peter was too well known to require emphasis. But arguably such dependence is reflected in the prominence which Mark gives to Peter in his narrative,[30] with Peter first and last mentioned (Mark 1.16; 16.7) forming an *inclusio*.[31] That almost the last word of the Gospel is the angelic message explicitly for Peter ('Go, tell his disciples and Peter that he is going ahead of you into Galilee; there you will see him') reassures the reader/audience that Peter's denial of Jesus was neither held against him, nor weakened his position of leadership among the twelve.

Of course, if indeed Mark drew his portrayal of Peter directly from Peter himself, that could also carry the somewhat unattractive corollary that Peter himself gave prominence to his own role in his preaching and retelling the story of Jesus,[32] though also not sweeping his failures (particularly his denial of Jesus) under the carpet. Whatever Mark's sources were — an individual disciple of Jesus (Peter), or oral traditions, already established among and by a broader sweep of Jesus' first disciples, and of consistently firm character despite the diversity of different tellings[33]— the most salient feature to emerge in and from that testimony and tradition is that Peter was the most prominent of Jesus' disciples (the twelve).[34] That this prominence is attributed to Mark, who is elsewhere remembered for his association with both Peter and Paul,[35] adds a further element of intrigue into the possibility that Peter proved to be and was remembered as a reconciling figure, in this case through Mark.

---

30. See nn.1 and 2 above. The argument that Mark told the story of his Gospel predominantly 'from Peter's perspective' and to convey this perspective is pushed by Bauckham (*Jesus and the Eyewitnesses* ch. 7). Bockmuehl makes the more modest claim that 'Mark's Gospel implies a degree of narrative proximity to Peter that would mutually reinforce rather than undermine memories of their actual association in the city' (*Simon Peter* 141).
31. Bauckham, *Jesus and the Eyewitnesses* 124-27.
32. Was the prominence of Peter in the Jesus tradition due to Peter's own testimony, or simply an established feature of the Jesus tradition, as told by whomever, more or less from the first, reflecting the shared memory that Peter was in fact the most prominent of the first disciples?
33. My thesis in *Jesus Remembered*.
34. As again already indicated in the first two notes of §48.
35. 1 Pet. 5.3 — 'my son Mark'; Col. 4.10; 2 Tim. 4.11 — 'useful in my ministry'.

b. Matthew

Given that other testimony regarding Peter has a somewhat mixed character, it is probably the Gospel of Matthew which really established the stature of Peter and ensured his primacy among the first disciples of Jesus.[36] For it is in Matthew alone that we find the fuller account of Peter's confession of Jesus at Caesarea Philippi. Mark 8.29 has the bare account that Peter confessed: 'You are the Christ/Messiah' (similarly Luke 9.20). But in Matt. 16.16-19 we read:

> Simon Peter answered and said: 'You are the Christ/Messiah, the son of the living God'. Jesus answered and said to him, 'Blessed are you, Simon son of Jonah, because flesh and blood has not revealed it to you, but my Father who is in the heavens. And I say to you that you are Peter (*Petros*) and on this rock (*petra*) I will build my church and the gates of Hades will not prevail against it. And I will give you the keys of the kingdom of heaven, and whatever you bind on earth will be bound in the heavens, and whatever you loose on earth will be loosed in the heavens'.

Here Peter is designated as a 'rock'. The play on words in the Greek is self-evident (*Petros, petra*). But it should not be forgotten that the play was equally effective in Aramaic (*Cephas, kepha'* = 'rock'). That Peter was well known by the nickname Cephas ('Rock/Rocky') is well attested by Paul and confirmed by John.[37] So he must have been so designated during the first generation, and there is no reason to doubt that it was Jesus who first so designated him or made the play on his name. John 1.42 puts the nicknaming of Peter at the beginning of Peter's discipleship, and quite apart from the context given it by Matthew. But undoubtedly it was Matthew's version of how the nickname was bestowed on Peter which established the name and its significance from the second generation onwards.

In this key passage Peter/Cephas is given the status by Jesus of being the rock on which the church is founded.[38] The fact that the use of 'church'

---

36. Though Matthew also includes the story of Peter venturing to walk on the water but demonstrating not so much his boldness in faith as his 'little faith' (Matt. 14.28-31). As R. E. Brown, K. P. Donfried and J. Reumann, *Peter in the New Testament* (London: Geoffrey Chapman, 1974), observe: 'In both his strength and his weakness he is a lesson for Christian disciples' (83).

37. 1 Cor. 1.12; 3.22; 9.5; 15.5; Gal. 1.18; 2.9, 11; John 1.42.

38. The play on words (*Cephas, kepha', Petros, petra*) would seem to rule out an alternative view which became the particularly Protestant riposte to Roman Catholic exegesis, that the 'rock' in Matt. 16.18 was intended by Matthew to refer to Peter's confession rather than to Peter himself. Cullmann's *Peter* marked the demise of that response: 'there is no

(*ekklēsia*) almost certainly reflects the subsequent ecclesiological vocabulary (already familiar in Paul's letters) does not alter the effect of the basic image. Nor should the possible clash with 1 Cor. 3.11 (the 'foundation is Jesus Christ') be exaggerated; in Eph. 2.20 the foundation is 'the apostles and prophets, with Christ himself as the cornerstone'. And use of the singular suggesting thought of the universal church (whereas Paul thought more of churches) takes us beyond the first generation (though note Col. 1.18). But the overall effect is to underline the effectiveness of Matthew's text: that Matt. 16.18 established Peter's claim to be Jesus' first disciple, *numero uno*, and his person as the basis on which the Christian church was built.

Moreover, in the same passage Jesus gives Peter 'the keys of the kingdom of heaven'. It is true that the following authorization ('whatever you bind on earth will be bound in the heavens, and whatever you loose on earth will be loosed in the heavens') is given later to Jesus' disciples as a whole (Matt. 18.18), which makes Peter more a *primus inter pares* than a mono-authority.[39] But the 'power of the keys' is mentioned only in the commissioning of Peter, and even if the power to bind and loose is intended as the explication of the power of the keys, it would nevertheless have been significant that the authority and responsibility of the keys was explicitly given only to Peter.[40]

It is when we recall that the Gospel of Matthew was the most influential in the second century (§44.8b), that the full weight which Matt. 16.16-19 brought to bear on the significance of Peter in the post-70 circles of believers

---

essential difference in meaning between *Petros* and *Petra*' (*Peter* 20-21); and see further Part Two, particularly 212-17, including the argument that the foundation 'rock' applies only to Peter with no thought of its application to successors. See also Meier in Brown and Meier, *Antioch and Rome* 66-68, who also notes that Matthew was 'obviously concerned about a type of nascent "clericalism" that is threatening his church' (Matt. 23.1-12) (70-71); Gnilka, *Matthäusevangelium* 2.63-65; Davies and Allison, *Matthew* 2.626-27; Luz, *Matthäus* 2.472-83; Bockmuehl similarly notes the importance of not misreading Peter's appointment 'in monarchic or autocratic terms' (*Simon Peter* 76; see also 85-86, 181-83). Hengel, *Petrus* 30-39, however, reminds us that neither James, nor Paul, nor John is regarded as having such a 'fundamental' role for the future of the church, and that this basic role was already attributed to Peter, in the early apostolic time of the first generation, and indeed before Easter (50, 52).

39. On Matthew's portrayal of Peter as a or the representative disciple of Jesus, see *Beginning from Jerusalem* 1066. 'In the perspective of Mt 16.18f lies perhaps a Petrine office as representing the whole Church, but not as its pinnacle' (Luz, *Matthäus* 2.482).

40. 'The power of the key of the Davidic kingdom [with reference to Isa. 22.22] is the power to open and to shut, i.e., the prime minister's power to allow or refuse entrance to the palace, which involves access to the king.... Does Matthew have to remind the Jewish Christians in his own community that the power of admitting to the church and excluding from it (binding/loosing) was given to Peter who stands behind the decision to admit Gentiles?' (Brown-Donfried-Reumann, *Peter* 97, 99-100).

in Jesus becomes clear. However venerated were James and Paul by their different factions within embryonic Christianity, the Gospel of Matthew would have been sufficient in itself to ensure that Peter was accorded a significance and stature which went beyond that of either James or Paul.

c. Luke-Acts

Luke follows Mark in highlighting Peter's leading role among Jesus' disciples. But he has his own distinctive emphasis which sharpens the focus on Peter to a significant extent. Where Mark and Matthew begin their account of Jesus' mission by narrating Jesus' call of Simon Peter and Andrew, James and John,[41] Luke tells the story only of Peter's call (Luke 5.1-11), in the context of a miracle of Jesus (the miraculous draught of fishes), in which the climax is Peter's humble confession before Jesus, 'Depart from me, Lord, for I am a sinful man' (5.8).[42] James and John are then introduced, but the commissioning which follows is addressed only to Simon: 'From now on you will catch people'.[43]

Significant also is the extra paragraph which Luke has in addition to the other Gospels in his account of Peter's denial being foretold. Jesus says to Peter (Luke 22.31-32):

> Simon, Simon, listen! Satan has demanded to sift you (plural) like wheat, but I have prayed for you (singular) that your own faith may not fail; and you (singular), when once you have turned back, strengthen your brothers.

This commissioning for what Luke's audiences would recognize as a post-Easter ministry[44] is a somewhat eerie complement[45] to John's more explicit post-Easter commissioning of Peter to act as shepherd of Jesus' sheep (John 21.15-17).[46]

---

41. Mark 1.16-20/Matt. 4.18-22.

42. See also Bockmuehl, *Simon Peter* 115-17.

43. Luke 5.10; cf. Mark 1.17/Matt. 4.19. 'Thus the apostolic sending of Peter and his success in missionary endeavor (of which we read in Acts) is grounded in the pre-Easter intention of Jesus' (Brown-Donfried-Reumann, *Peter* 119).

44. See also Fitzmyer, *Luke* 2.1422-23; and particularly Brown-Donfried-Reumann *Peter* 121-25.

45. This may be another indication of John's knowledge of the distinctive Lukan tradition — or vice-versa (cf. Luke 24.22-24 with John 20.1-10).

46. 'The overlap between Luke and John also serves to confirm the persistence of some such memory, however diversely expressed, of Peter as uniquely commissioned by the Lord to a ministry beyond Easter' (Bockmuehl, *Simon Peter* 122). But Perkins also points out

Luke also adds the note in his account of Peter's denials of Jesus that 'The Lord turned and looked at Peter', prompting Peter's recollection of Jesus' prediction that Peter would deny him three times, and causing him to weep bitterly (Luke 22.61-62). The implication is, once again, of a special bond between Jesus and Peter. And, rather strikingly, in his account of the first Easter Sunday, Luke includes the report that 'The Lord has risen indeed and has appeared to Simon' (Luke 24.34), the only Gospel to confirm that the first appearance of the risen Jesus was to Simon Peter (1 Cor. 15.5). That Peter is given such distinctive prominence at the beginning and end of Luke's account of Jesus' mission (Luke 5.8; 24.34) is a more impressive *inclusio* than can be seen in Mark (1.16; 16.7).[47] Neither *inclusio* necessarily signifies direct dependence for these Petrine traditions on Peter himself. But both certainly indicate that next to Jesus himself, Peter was remembered as the most prominent and most important of Jesus' disciples, particularly because of the closeness of his relationship with Jesus.

In Acts the emphasis given to Peter's leadership is sustained and accentuated.[48] And while Peter and John are associated as close companions in chs. 3-5 and 8, John is a shadowy figure with the spotlight falling on Peter.[49] More interestingly, the tensions between Paul and Cephas/Peter, which can hardly have been unknown among the first believers,[50] are in effect countered by Luke, in that he sets their missions in parallel:[51]

- they preach the same message — 2.22-39; 13.26-41;
- they both heal a lame man — 3.1-10; 14.8-11;
- their preaching is inspired by the Spirit — 4.8; 13.9;
- they both deal harshly with deceit — 5.1-11; 13.6-12;
- both have amazing healing powers — 5.15; 19.12;
- through both the Holy Spirit is bestowed — 8.17; 19.6;
- they both triumph over magicians — 8.18-24; 19.13-20;
- they both cure bed-ridden men — 9.32-34; 28.8;
- they both restore to life someone who had died — 9.36-41; 20.9-12;
- they both have to restrain individuals who want to worship them — 10.25; 14.11-13; 28.6;
- they both have miraculous release from prison — 12.6-11; 16.25-34.

---

that 'neither Luke nor John provide any evidence to support the claim that Peter is shepherd or successor to Jesus in a way that other apostles are not' (*Peter* 103).
47. Cf. again Bauckham, *Jesus and the Eyewitnesses* 126.
48. Acts 1.15; 2.14, 38.
49. Acts 3.4, 6, 12; 4.8; 5.3, 8-9, 29; 8.20.
50. Gal. 2.11-16; cf. 1 Cor. 1.12.
51. As first noted by M. Schneckenburger, *Über den Zweck der Apostelgeschichte* (Bern, 1841); see *Beginning from Jerusalem* §21 n.119; and further Keener, *Acts* 561-74.

Evidently, for Luke, Peter and Paul were not antagonists, but were in effect partners in a shared mission. This is all the more striking in view of the fact that Paul, in dominating more than half of Luke's narrative, seems to overshadow Peter. But Luke, it would appear, took some pains to depict Peter and Paul as following more or less the same course, and with the same effectiveness in their mission. The fact that Peter fades from Acts to the extent that he does, therefore, should not be given too much prominence. Indeed, the parallelogram which Luke draws for their common mission may well have been intended to prevent the impression that Paul overshadowed Peter.

Most striking of all, of course, is that Luke, even though fully recognizing that Paul had been especially commissioned by the risen Christ to take the gospel to Gentiles,[52] makes a point of attributing to Peter the breakthrough of the gospel to Gentiles (chs. 10-11). The precedent of Philip evangelizing the Ethiopian eunuch is passed over relatively briefly (8.35-38). And narration of the breakthrough in Antioch is postponed till after Peter's encounter with Cornelius, and again treated relatively briefly (11.19-26). But Peter's success at Caesarea is given five or six times more attention. Not only so, but in the crucial Jerusalem conference, at which the problems posed by the success of the Gentile mission were resolved, Luke attributes the decisive contribution to Peter, referring to his success at Caesarea (15.7-11), with Barnabas and Paul (note the order) playing only a supportive role (15.12). That was not how Paul recalled the crucial debate (Gal. 2.1-10). But the Acts account was presumably, like the other Peter/Paul emphases, meant to provide a balance for Paul's domination of the second half of the book.[53] The old Baur thesis that Acts was a late writing intended to reconcile two opposing parties, a Peter party and a Paul party, which had dominated the early history of Christianity, was much too tendentious. But one of its roots was well grounded: that Acts sought to draw a veil over historical tensions between Peter and Paul; and that it did so by portraying Peter and Paul as near identical twins so far as the growth and expansion of Christianity were concerned.

Luke-Acts does not seem to have been as influential as Matthew in the second century. But the volumes, jointly or separately, may well have been widely known and influential; Luke's Acts of the Apostles provides the most obvious inspiration for the second- and third-century *Acts of Paul*, etc. (§40.6). So it is quite in order to infer that Luke-Acts would add substantial weight to the profile of Peter as it entered the second century:

---

52. Acts 9.15; 22.21; 26.17-18.

53. The analysis of the Jerusalem conference in *Beginning from Jerusalem* 461-69 focused on the historical issues raised by the account. Here the concern is with Luke's purpose and the influence of his account into the second century.

- the leading disciple of Jesus, especially close to Jesus;
- the first leader of the Jerusalem church;
- as much a pioneer of the expansion of Christianity beyond Palestine to embrace non-Jews as Paul;
- and much more a reconciling than a divisive force.

The bridge-role (*pontifex*) of Peter between Jesus' mission and the beginnings of Christianity, and between the two principal and potentially divergent strands of emerging Christianity, is further enhanced.

d. John

As regards the portrayal of Jesus' disciples in John's Gospel, a primary concern of John seems to have been the provision of a counterpoise to the elsewhere dominant theme of Peter's precedence, in terms of closeness to Jesus ('the beloved disciple' — John 13.23, 25) and as prime witness to Jesus.[54] Not to be ignored either is the principal role given to Mary Magdalene as *apostolos apostolorum* (John 20.1-18), an intriguing foreshadowing of the prominence given to Mary, particularly in relation to Peter, in the *Gospel of Mary* (*Gosp. Mary* 17.7–18.21), and to ministry of women, for example, in the *Acts of Paul* and in the Montanist movement (§49.8). But it is still the case that John gives prominence to Peter. Although Andrew is mentioned first, he is introduced as 'the brother of [the well-known] Simon Peter' (John 1.40).[55] John alone has Simon (Peter) renamed as Cephas ('rock') by Jesus at their first encounter (1.42). And it is Peter who makes the Johannine equivalent to the confession of Jesus as Messiah: 'You are the Holy One of God' (6.68). On the other hand, it is John who has the somewhat embarrassing scenes of Peter unwilling to let Jesus wash his feet, and then misunderstanding the symbolism (13.4-10), and of Peter's vainglorious attempt to defend Jesus (18.10-11). In the Last Supper discourses, Peter is just one of Jesus' interlocutors (13.36-37), like Thomas, Philip and Judas (14.5, 8, 22), whose role is simply to maintain the discourse's

---

54. See above §39 at n.141 and below §49 n.22; though Cullmann notes that if the emphasis on the beloved disciple is in some reaction to the elsewhere prominence of Peter, it is an indirect confirmation of the 'peculiarly representative position' of Peter (*Peter* 31); and see Brown-Donfried-Reumann, *Peter* 134-39; also K. Quast, *Peter and the Beloved Disciple: Figures for a Community in Crisis* (JSNTS 32; Sheffield: JSOT, 1989).

55. 'Peter's position is a point of reference that can be taken for granted from the outset. . . . The Fourth Evangelist sees Simon Peter as a familiar character before the narrative even begins' (Bockmuehl, *Simon Peter* 58).

momentum. And though the account of Peter's denials is somewhat elaborated, it is no different in effect from the Synoptic accounts (18.15-18, 25-27).

The real interest is in the resurrection narratives. John records that Peter was the first witness of Jesus' tomb being empty (20.2-7), an account also attested by Luke 24.12, though he does not go on to confirm that Peter was the first to see the risen Jesus. What we do find is, in what was probably an addendum to the Gospel (ch. 21), an account of an appearance of Jesus to a group of disciples in Galilee, when they had returned to their fishing practice. The story of a miraculous draught of fishes is similar to Luke 5.1-11, but the opportunity is not taken to develop the theme of Peter having a particularly close relationship with Jesus (John 21.5-8).[56] Subsequently, however, Peter is given the risen Jesus' full attention. Jesus draws out a threefold confession by Peter of his love for Jesus, each time Jesus' response being the commission to 'Feed my sheep', 'Tend my sheep', 'Feed my sheep' (21.15-17). Here Peter is set up as the shepherd of the flock, on which Jesus had spoken so movingly in ch. 10, presumably under Jesus as the chief shepherd.[57] And then Jesus predicts the form of death that Peter will suffer (21.18-19), which may be an allusion to the tradition of Peter's own crucifixion.[58] But, in any case, it adds further to the implication that Peter was specially appointed and favoured by Jesus — the concluding line, 'After this he [Jesus] said to him [Peter], "Follow me"' (21.19), a fitting slogan for Peter the pre-eminent follower of Jesus.[59]

48.4 Peter in the Apostolic Fathers and Apologists

Since the portrayal of Peter is maintained at such a consistently high level throughout the NT Gospels, the implication is that his prestige was also very high among the first-century post-70 assemblies of believers in Jesus. It would be the most natural corollary to infer that Peter continued to rank highly and

---

56. 'Simon Peter remains important, but he is not the one really attuned to Jesus' (Brown-Donfried-Reumann, *Peter* 141).

57. 1 Pet. 5.1-5 makes a point of warning that such a role was not an occasion for self-glorification or arbitrary exercise of power: those addressed should think of themselves as no more than under-shepherds, Christ himself being the chief shepherd (5.4). Bockmuehl observes that 'there is no implication here that Peter is the *only* proper shepherd; nor is there any hint of a succession of Petrine ministry so defined' (*Simon Peter* 65; but note also 66-67). But the parallel between John 21.15-17 and 1 Pet. 5.1-5, which can hardly be explained in terms of literary dependency, probably indicates a common tradition about the pastoral role of Peter (Brown-Donfried-Reumann, *Peter* 154; similarly Perkins, *Peter* 37).

58. *Beginning from Jerusalem* 1074 n.55.

59. 'The leading role of Peter in all four Gospels corresponds to the significance of the "rock-man" for the whole Church from the beginning' (Hengel, *Petrus* 73).

be referred to often with the same level of respect in the writings which were or came to be regarded as in effect most representative of the first half of the second-century mainstream Christianity. Surprisingly, that is not the case. The references to Peter himself are fewer than those to Paul (apart from Papias),[60] and evidence of allusions to 1 Peter are much more dubious in comparison with the allusions to the (of course, many more) Pauline epistles.

a. References to Peter

The search for such references in the Apostolic Fathers starts well but then disappoints.

1 Clement has only one reference to Peter:

> We should consider the noble examples of our own generation. Because of jealousy and envy the greatest and most upright pillars were persecuted, and they struggled in the contest even to death. We should set before our eyes the good apostles. There is Peter, who because of unjust jealousy bore up under hardships not just once or twice, but many times; and having thus borne his witness he went to the place of glory that he deserved. Because of jealousy and strife Paul showed the way to the prize for endurance . . . (*1 Clem.* 5.1-5).

Here the most notable feature is twofold: that only two individuals are picked out and named as 'the greatest and most upright pillars' — Peter and Paul; and that Peter is mentioned first, even though the link between Rome and Corinth on which Clement builds was established by Paul.[61] This tells us that already, before the end of the first century, Peter was regarded as the leading apostle and highest authority in Rome.[62]

---

60. 'We appear to have rather more documents [which "deal with Peter"] from the close of the second century and beyond than from the preceding decades, which seem largely silent' (Bockmuehl, *Remembered Peter* 75), echoing C. Grappe, *Images de Pierre aux deux premiers siècles* (Paris: Universitaires de France, 1995) 19-20.

61. Does the 'many times' of 5.4 imply a much fuller knowledge of Peter's history than is now available to us?

62. 'The fact that these two apostles are reconciled with each other and named together reflects an important development in the ecclesiastical-political situation' (Koester, *Introduction* 2.290). On the implications of the double reference to 'jealousy', that both Peter and Paul suffered from internal rivalry within the Roman church(es), see Cullmann, *Peter* 91-110; Brown in Brown and Meier, *Antioch and Rome* 124-25. For discussion on the testimony of *1 Clem.* 5 to Peter's ministry (and death) in Rome, within living memory, see Bockmuehl, *Remembered Peter* 124-30.

Ignatius refers to Peter twice in his letters — the first already quoted in reference to Paul (§47.3b):

> *Rom.* 4.3 — I do not order you as did Peter and Paul. They were apostles; I am a convict. They were free; I up till now have been a slave.

> *Smyrn.* 3.2-3 — And when he [the risen Jesus] came to those who were with Peter, he said to them, 'Reach out, touch me and see that I am not a bodiless daimon' [cf. Luke 24.39]. And immediately they touched him and believed, having been intermixed with his flesh and spirit. For this reason they also despised death, for they were found to be beyond death. And after his resurrection he ate and drank with them [cf. Acts 1.4] as a fleshly being, even though he was spiritually united with the Father.

Here too it is of some significance that Ignatius refers first to Peter, even though the course of his travel, his sequence of letters and his expectations mirrored Paul's more closely. Not insignificant is the fact that he describes Jesus' appearance 'to those who were with/around (*peri*) Peter' — Peter as the central figure round whom the others gathered.[63] Equally of note is the fact that in alluding to the Lukan account of Jesus' resurrection appearance (Luke 24.39), Ignatius takes it for granted that the disciples were gathered round Peter, even though Peter is not mentioned in Luke's account of the scene. This is the sort of assumption that the Gospel narratives would have prompted. So it is rather surprising that this is the only example of such an assumption to be found in the Apostolic Fathers.

In the Apostolic Fathers the only other explicit references to Peter are to be found in the selections from Papias which Eusebius and others quote. Papias, of course, has the famous tradition that Mark was Peter's interpreter (or translator), as already noted in §39.2a.[64] Intriguing, however, is the fact that in listing the sources and authorities for other traditions Papias makes no attempt to single out Peter: 'what Andrew or Peter had said, or what Philip, or what Thomas had said, or James or John or Matthew or any of the other disciples of the Lord, and what things Aristion and the elder John, disciples of the Lord, were saying' (*HE* 3.39.4).[65] Papias, of course, is remembered as hav-

---

63. Bockmuehl concludes rather strongly: 'Evidently Simon Peter represents the center of the gospel tradition like no other figure in the early church' (*Simon Peter* 48); similarly *Remembered Peter* 90-91.

64. Eusebius, *HE* 3.39.15-16; and see further §39 n.20 above.

65. Eusebius, *HE* 3.39.4; Jerome, *Lives of Illustrious Men* 18. In Philip of Side's *Ecclesiastical History* Papias is quoted as listing the apostles: 'after Peter and John, Philip and

ing personally heard the apostle John speaking,[66] and that seems to have been ranked more highly than his testimony regarding Peter. But it is still somewhat surprising that he is not remembered as having highlighted the importance of Peter in establishing the chain of authoritative tradition on which he drew.[67]

The Apologists do not seem to have made anything of the status and authority of Peter — they did not have any particular reason or occasion for doing so. The one exception is Justin Martyr, who in his *Dialogue with Trypho* twice refers to Simon being surnamed Peter by Jesus (100.3; 106.3). What is noticeable is that Justin obviously had in mind Matthew's account of Peter's confession of Jesus ('when he [Simon] recognized him as Son of God, even Christ, according to the revelation of his Father, he [Christ] surnamed [him] Peter' — cf. Matt. 16.16-17). This is the passage in which Peter (*Petros*) is named by Jesus as the 'rock' (*petra*) on which he would build his church, and the allusions by Justin confirm that this passage would have been known and reflected on in the second century, as confirmation of the status of Peter.[68] Otherwise it is rather surprising that Justin makes no reference to Peter's residence or martyrdom in Rome.

It is notable that Irenaeus hardly mentions Peter. As with Justin, he recalls Matt. 16.17 on two occasions,[69] but otherwise reference is to Peter along with Paul,[70] and it is Paul who, for Irenaeus, is pre-eminently 'the apostle'. He does recognize the importance of Acts 10 in the story of Peter, using it to make his regular anti-Marcionite point that Peter certainly did not preach that the God of the Jews was one, and the God of the Christians another (*adv. haer.* 3.12.7).[71] And of the various references to Peter in Origen's *contra Celsum* Books 1, 2 and 6 ('as it were the firstfruits of the apostles', 2.65), the most interesting is his appeal to the same Acts 10 passage,[72] that 'Peter seems

---

Thomas and Matthew, he indicated that Aristion and another John, whom he also called an elder, were disciples of the Lord'.

66. Irenaeus, *adv. haer.* 5.33.4; Eusebius, *HE* 3.39.1.

67. In some contrast to a principal thesis of Bauckham, *Jesus and the Eyewitnesses*.

68. Bockmuehl justifiably deduces from Justin's description of the (NT) Gospels as 'memoirs of the apostles' (see above §44 at n.168) that Justin probably regarded Mark as the memoirs of Peter (*Simon Peter* 45-46).

69. *adv. haer.* 3.13.2; 3.21.8.

70. *adv. haer.* 1.13.6; 1.25.2; 3.3.2; 3.13.1-3; 4.35.2; though 3.12.1-7 consists of extensive quotations from Acts 1-5 and 10, in which Peter, of course, features strongly.

71. In his thesis regarding the 'living memory' of the first generation still evident in the second century (*Remembered Peter* 15-30), Bockmuehl suggests that Irenaeus (with his link through Polycarp to John) marks the final phase of such personal memory (23-27); 'Christian memory did remain for 150 years an important point of reference for Simon Peter's public "persona" in diverse and even competing Christian circles' (76-77).

72. Acts 10.9-15; also Gal. 2.12.

to have kept the customs of the Mosaic law for a long time, as he had not yet learnt from Jesus to ascend from the letter of the law to its spiritual interpretation' (2.1-2). This is part of Origen's recognition, *contra Celsum*, that 'Jewish believers in Jesus have not left the law of their fathers' (2.1) — Peter, or at least his earlier history, providing a link to such Jewish believers.

One other intriguing testimony should be mentioned, from Clement of Alexandria, *Stromata* 7, cited by Eusebius, *HE* 3.30.2:

> They say that the blessed Peter when he saw his own wife led out to death rejoiced at her calling and at her return home, and called out to her in true warning and comfort, addressing her by her name, 'Remember the Lord'. Such was the marriage of the blessed and the perfect disposition of those dearest to them.[73]

Without concerning ourselves about the source and possible historicity of the report, what remains of interest is that 'the blessed Peter' and his marriage were being held up as an example to be followed — first strains of subsequent hagiography.

b. Possible Echoes of 1 Peter

The strongest indications of knowledge of and dependence on 1 Peter are to be found in Polycarp's *Philippians*. Eusebius indeed reports that Polycarp in his letter to the Philippians 'has made some quotations from the first Epistle of Peter' (*HE* 4.14.9). And this is borne out in three clear instances:[74]

Phil. 1.3	1 Pet. 1.8, 12
Phil. 8.1	1 Pet. 2.21-24
Phil. 10.2	1 Pet. 2.12

Elsewhere the evidence is at best unpersuasive, any modest sharing in themes or vocabulary probably more indicative of communal liturgical and catechet-

---

73. Eusebius cites it as coming from *Stromata* 7, but in ANF 2.541 it appears in *Stromata* 11. In the same passage, Eusebius quotes Clement as referring to Peter's children (*HE* 3.30.1); see also Hengel, *Petrus* 207-17.

74. *NTAF* 86-89; Massaux, *Influence* 2.42-45 (who both also list four other likely cases — *Phil.* 2.1/1 Pet. 1.13; *Phil.* 2.2/1 Pet. 3.9; *Phil.* 5.3/1 Pet. 2.11; *Phil.* 7.2/1 Pet. 4.7); J. H. Elliott, *1 Peter* (AB 37B; New York: Doubleday, 2000) 143 (who lists eleven other 'virtually certain citations'); Holmes, 'Polycarp's *Letter to the Philippians*' 220-22. *Mart. Polyc.* 10.2 may also contain an echo of 1 Pet. 2.13; and see again Elliott, *1 Peter* 144.

ical usage than of knowledge of 1 Peter in particular. In *1 Clement* several possible echoes of or some allusive dependencies on 1 Peter have been noted, but none carries conviction.[75] Similarly with Ignatius, possible echoes of or dependency on 1 Peter are as tantalizingly faint as in the case of *1 Clement*.[76] Whether or not Clement and Ignatius knew 1 Peter, the evidence of their letters provides little or no confidence on the point. Unlike Paul, the reputation of Peter did not depend to any noticeable extent on what he had written. None of the possible instances of literary influence from 1 Peter on the *Didache*[77] or *Barnabas*[78] or the *Shepherd* of Hermas[79] or *2 Clement*[80] are persuasive enough to be relied on. The same is even truer of the Apologists.[81] The first explicit quotations from 1 Peter are in Irenaeus.[82]

75. I draw the data from *NTAF* 55-57; Massaux, *Influence* 1.38-39; see also Brown in Brown and Meier, *Antioch and Rome* 166-69; Elliott, *1 Peter* 139-40. Gregory, '1 Clement', does not consider any examples.

1 Clement	1 Peter	1 Clement	1 Peter	1 Clement	1 Peter
1.3	3.1-4	7.7	2.25	49.5	4.8
2.2	4.19	21.7	3.1-5	57.1	5.5
2.4	2.17; 5.9	30.1	1.15-16; 2.1	59.2	2.9
5.7	2.21	30.2	5.5	61.3	2.25
7.2, 4	1.18-19	36.2	2.9		

76. Again I draw the data from *NTAF* 76, which mentions only Eph. 5.3 as a real possibility, and Massaux, *Influence* 1.117-18, who marshalls the data without much enthusiasm. Foster, 'The Epistles of Ignatius of Antioch', does not consider any examples.

Ignatius	1 Peter	Ignatius	1 Peter
Eph. 5.3	5.5	Magn. 9.2	3.19; 4.6
Eph. 9.1	2.5	Trall. 9.2; Smyrn. 7.1	1.21
Magn. 8.2; Philad. 5.2	1.10	Rom. 9.1	2.25; 5.2
		Polyc. 5.2	4.11

77. *Did.* 1.4/1 Pet. 2.11; *Did.* 4.11/1 Pet. 2.18 — *NTAF* 33-34; Massaux, *Influence* 3.177-78; Tuckett, 'The *Didache*' 90-91.

78. *Barn.* 4.12/1 Pet. 1.17; *Barn.* 5.1/1 Pet. 1.2; *Barn.* 5.5, 6; 6.7/1Pet. 1.10-11; *Barn.* 6.2-4/1 Pet. 2.6-8; *Barn.* 16.10/1 Pet. 2.5 — *NTAF* 9, 11-12, 14-16; Massaux, *Influence* 1.80-81; Paget, 'The *Epistle of Barnabas*' 248 (references are confused).

79. *Vis.* 3.3.5/1 Pet. 3.20-21; *Vis.* 3.11.3/1 Pet. 5.7; *Vis.* 4.3.4/1 Pet. 1.7; *Sim.* 9.12.2-3/1 Pet. 1.20; *Sim.* 9.14.6 and 9.28.5/1 Pet. 4.13-16; *Sim.* 9.29.1, 3/1 Pet. 2.1-2 — *NTAF* 115-17; Massaux, *Influence* 2.159-61; Verheyden, 'The *Shepherd of Hermas*' 297-98.

80. *2 Clem.* 14.2/1 Pet. 1.20; *2 Clem.* 16.4/1 Pet. 4.8 (but *2 Clement* could have drawn the phrase from *1 Clem.* 49.5) — *NTAF* 56, 128; Massaux, *Influence* 2.22-23; Gregory and Tuckett, '*2 Clement*' 291 and n.143.

81. But see Elliott, *1 Peter* 144-46.

82. 1 Pet. 1.8 (*adv. haer.* 4.9.2; 5.7.2); 1 Pet. 2.16 (*adv. haer.* 4.16.5; 4.37.4); 1 Pet. 2.23 (*adv. haer.* 3.16.9; 4.20.2). 1 Pet. 1.12 is also drawn on in *adv. haer.* 2.17.9, 4.34.1 and 5.36.3; 1 Pet. 3.20 in *adv. haer.* 1.18.3; and 1 Pet. 4.14 in *adv. haer.* 4.33.9.

Consequently, we can conclude that 1 Peter was probably known and taken to be a letter of Peter, and that it may well have contributed somewhat to the liturgical and paraenetic language of the second-century churches. But we can have little confidence that it was well used, far less that it was regularly referred to or cited as such, and so such evidence as there is adds little or nothing to our understanding of how Peter was regarded and whether the esteem for him continued to grow through the second century.

48.5 The Jewish-Christian Peter

Here we turn most naturally to the pseudo-Clementine literature. We have already noted several features of the portrayal of Peter in the Letter of Peter to James which introduces the *Homilies* (§45.2c).

- Peter writes to James, 'the lord and bishop of the holy church' (*Epistula Petri* 1.1), soliciting his help. Peter is thus presented as in a subordinate role to James.
- He is concerned that his preaching will be misunderstood by Gentiles (1.2; 2.3), including his interpretation of scripture (1.3-5), but particularly that he (Peter) is being represented as teaching 'the dissolution of the law' (2.4), an opinion which Peter firmly refutes (2.5-6). This suggests that Peter was seen as a somewhat ambiguous figure after his death (2.7), claimed by Gentile believers as supporting a less strict commitment to law-observance. The letter would then amount to an attempt by Jewish believers in Jesus to reclaim Peter as consistently faithful to the law and acknowledging the lead given by James. The implication of James's response (4) is that the books containing Peter's preachings were considered to be rather dangerous, perhaps as stretching too far the boundaries of Christianity as understood by traditionalist Jewish believers, and were thus to be severely restricted in their circulation.
- To the same effect is the reference to 'the man who is my enemy' (2.3), almost certainly Paul. The parallel with *Homilies* 17.18-19 in which Paul is merged with the figure of Simon Magus, Peter's arch enemy (cited in §45.2c),[83] serves to distinguish Peter from Paul as sharply as early Chris-

---

83. Much of the tale told in *Homilies* and *Recognitions* is of Peter's preaching against or debating with Simon, indicating how popular was this tradition within the Petrine legend-mongering. Klauck notes that Simon Magus 'can be interpreted as a cipher for Paul in some scenes, but certainly not in every passage' and glimpses 'behind Simon the outlines of the figure and teaching of Marcion' (*Apocryphal Acts* 227). Bockmuehl swims against the main

tian tradition could imagine. Since Paul is probably also the one to be identified as the 'hostile man' who attacks James in *Recog.* 1.69.8–1.71.4 (§45.2c), the effect is even stronger to set Peter and James in close association in their opposition to Paul.

The Letter of Clement to James consists principally of Peter's commissioning of Clement, in terms reminiscent of the Pastorals and Ignatius. Its introduction, however, includes a most laudatory reference to Peter.

> Simon, who because of the true faith and the most secure basis of his teaching was appointed to be a foundation stone of the Church, and for that very reason was surnamed Peter by the mouth of Jesus which cannot lie [Matt. 16.17-18], the first-fruit of our Lord, the first of the apostles, to whom the Father first revealed his Son [1 Cor. 15.5], whom Christ with good reason called 'blessed', the called and chosen, table companion and fellow-traveller, the good and proven disciple, who as the most capable of all was commanded to enlighten the darkest part of the world, the West [cf. *1 Clem.* 5.7], and was enabled to achieve it . . . (*Epistula Clem.* 1.2-3).

Peter proceeds to appoint Clement as bishop and to entrust him with Peter's teacher's chair. 'He has accompanied me from the beginning even to the end, and so has heard all my homilies'. To him Peter conveys 'the authority to bind and to loose, that all that he ordains on earth shall be decreed in heaven . . . as one who knows the canon of the Church'.[84] Clement proceeds to narrate Peter's homilies in *Homilies*, but the two affirmations regarding Peter in these opening paragraphs of *Epistula Clementis* raise two intriguing possibilities. One is that those represented by the pseudo-Clementines wanted to credit Peter with the Pauline mission to bring light to Gentiles living in darkness (Acts 26.18); in *1 Clem.* 5.7 it was Paul who was said to have reached the limits of the West. The other is that as Peter supplanted Paul, so Clement may have been represented as in effect supplanting Mark; it was Clement (not Mark, à la Papias)[85] who was Peter's faithful companion and recorder of Peter's teaching. Here again, in other words, Peter was being claimed for a more traditionalist Jewish understanding of emerging Christianity.

More enduring, however, the esteem in which Peter was held is again shown to be due, primarily, to his specially favoured status as attested by Matt.

---

stream in questioning whether the identification of Simon with Paul is sound (*Remembered Peter* 101-13).

84. *Epist. Clem.* 2.2-4; Matt.16.19; John 20.23.
85. See above §39.2a(i).

16.17-19. And the instructions Peter gives to Clement set him firmly in that stream which flows through the Pastorals and Ignatius to 'the great church'. The strong affirmation that Clement, bishop of Rome, was appointed by Peter, is a major step towards the establishment of the dogmatic traditions of apostolic succession and the pope as Peter's successor. In the same connection, it is worth noting the interesting contrast with the Paul of both the NT and the apocryphal Acts, in that 'there are no women among the disciples of Peter nor among the ecclesiastical office-bearers whom he appoints'.[86] Given the popularity of the pseudo-Clementines, as indicated by the large number of Latin manuscripts, their influence must have been substantial in establishing the dominance of Peter in the ecclesiology of the great church.

48.6 The Apocryphal Peter

The range of writings which have Peter in their title initially provoke suspicion, since they suggest that the motivation was, 'If others have Gospels and Acts and Apocalypses attributed to them, then surely Peter should have them too'. If that was indeed the case, of course, it would imply that Peter was regarded as such a pre-eminent figure among the founders of Christianity that it would seem to many as simply a matter of honour that such writings should be attributed to him also. In which case, it is not so much a question of whether the content of these documents reflected the beliefs and teachings of Peter himself as a question of what teaching was thought appropriate to have Peter's name appended to it, and what *that* tells us about the esteem in which Peter was held by groups of believers in Jesus through the second century.

a. *Kerygma Petrou*

We start with the curious *Kerygma Petrou*, which Clement of Alexandria, notoriously uncritical, evidently thought was a genuine account of Peter's preaching, though, as noted earlier, Origen questioned it.[87] In the extracts cited by Clement Peter is certainly portrayed as a missionary, recalling that the Lord (Jesus) commissioned his disciples to preach in his name to Israel, and in

---

86. Klauck, *Apocryphal Acts* 228.
87. See above §40.2c and n.118. Origen also refers to a book which he calls *The Doctrine of Peter*, which he dismisses as 'neither by Peter nor by any one else who was inspired by the spirit of God' (*de Principiis*, praef. 8), but it is unclear whether the two books are the same (Schneemelcher, *NTA* 2.36-37).

language reminiscent of Rom. 10.14-18 (*Strom.* 6.5.43). But in 6.6.48 it is the universal mission (of Matt. 28.19) on which Jesus sends the twelve, to win men to the belief that there is one God, as well as to faith in Christ. And, as became clear in §46.6e, in the *Kerygma* Peter distances Christians as 'a third race' from both Greeks and Jews (6.5.41), and is as dismissive of Jewish religion as he is of Gentile idolatry — 'they [who] suppose that they alone know God, do not know him, serving angels and archangels, the month and the moon' (6.5). To that extent, then, Peter's responsibility for mission to his fellow Jews is recalled but has in effect been left behind, and Peter now stands for a universal mission, finding its identity in distinction from both Gentiles and Jews. If the *Kerygma Petrou* did indeed emerge in the first decades of the second century (§40.2c), that was quite a dramatic reconfiguring of Peter's significance, pulling him away from his Jewish context and aligning him more firmly with a Christianity self-consciously taking an independent stand within the Hellenistic world. To secure Peter, Jesus' own leading disciple, as spokesman for that stand was in itself something of a coup, and indicative of the importance which the Christianity of the 'third race' evidently placed on presenting Peter as its spokesman.

b. The *Gospel of Peter*

The *Gospel of Peter* (§40.4d) contains no additional information regarding Peter. The account of Jesus' execution and of his resurrection is presented as first-person testimony by Peter himself (*Gosp.Pet.* 26, 60 — 'But I, Simon Peter and my brother Andrew . . .'). But the account itself is clearly derived from and elaborated from the earlier (NT) Gospels,[88] including the two 'I' (Peter) passages — *Gosp.Pet.* 26 (John 20.19) and *Gosp.Pet.* 60 (John 21.1-2). Notably, it leaves Peter out from the empty tomb story,[89] and evidently had no interest in promoting Peter as a disciple or witness of the risen Lord.[90] Given that the *Gospel of Peter* most probably had a limited circulation, it tells us nothing of significance as to the regard in which Peter was held in western Syria in the second half of the second century, beyond the fact that Peter was deemed a natural choice to be narrator in such a novelistic presentation — an attribution to Peter which may have persuaded Serapion to regard *Peter* initially as acceptable for church use.[91] More significant is the high regard for

---

88. See above §44.7a.
89. Mark 16.7; Luke 24.12; John 20.3-10.
90. J. Verheyden, 'Some Reflections on Determining the Purpose of the "Gospel of Peter"', in Kraus and Nicklas, ed., *Evangelium nach Petrus* 281-99; for the above references see 285-86.
91. See above §40.4d.

Peter attested by Serapion: 'we receive both Peter and the other apostles as Christ' (Eusebius, *HE* 6.12.3).[92]

c. The *Acts of Peter*

The *Acts of Peter* (§40.6b) also falls short of adding anything to our knowledge of Peter. It certainly draws on the Acts 8 tradition of Peter's denunciation of Simon Magus — the heart of the document — though it introduces the new confrontation by recalling Peter's 'expulsion' of Simon from Judaea (*ActsPet.* 5; also 12, 28).[93] It also has Peter recalling his experience of walking on the water (7), though his loss of faith in the event (Matt. 14.25-33) is recalled only by Simon (*ActsPet.* 10). Peter recalls also his denial of Jesus (*ActsPet.* 7), refers to 'my fellow disciple and co-apostle Judas' (8) and echoes his first encounter with Jesus, 'I am a sinner' (28; cf. Luke 5.8). The talking dog in *ActsPet.* 9, 12 may have been suggested by 2 Pet. 2.16's reference to the talking donkey in the story of Balaam (Num. 22).[94] In *ActsPet.* 20, rather like 2 Pet. 1.17-18, Peter refers to his experience of seeing Christ's majesty 'on the holy mountain; but when I with the sons of Zebedee saw his brightness I fell at his feet as dead, closed my eyes, and heard his voice in a manner which I cannot describe'. The quotation from Isa. 53.4 also in *ActsPet.* 20 may have been inspired by 1 Pet. 2.22-25. And the same passage seems to echo John's Gospel: 'He is in the Father and the Father in him'; 'This Jesus you have, brethren, the door, the light, the way, the bread, the water, the life, the resurrection . . .'

We have already noted some parallels between Peter and Paul which seem to have been deliberately introduced into the *Acts of Peter* (§47.4b). We should note something of the same motivation in the *Acts of Paul*. In particular, the captain of the ship on which Paul embarked to be taken to Italy, Artemon, had been baptized by Peter (*ActsPaul* 10)[95]— suggesting a further link between the two great apostles in a mission reaching well beyond Jews. And in the following episode in *ActsPaul* 10 the Lord Jesus comes walking on the sea to encourage Paul — an echo, presumably, of the tradition concerning Peter

---

92. 'I would suggest that until about the year 200 it is legitimate to assume that this statement still bears something of the force of a living personal and communal memory in Antioch' (Bockmuehl, *Remembered Peter* 82; see further 78-83; and *Simon Peter* 43-44).

93. The pseudo-Clementine *Recognitions* 2 and 3 and *Homilies* 2-4, 16-20 use the Peter/Simon confrontation as occasion for extensive theological discussion; see also n.83 above.

94. Curiously the Eubula in *ActsPet.* 17 echoes the Eubula in *ActsPaul* 7.

95. Cf. *ActsPet.* 5, where Peter baptizes the steersman Theon on his trip to Italy. The friendly treatment offered to Peter by Theon in *ActsPet.* 5 echoes the similarly kind treatment offered to Paul by the Roman centurion on his voyage to Rome (Acts 27-28).

in Matt. 14.25-33, an episode which Peter also recalls in *ActsPet.* 7 — again in effect setting Peter and Paul in parallel. Both *Acts* indicate that the reverence for the two apostles was growing together. This is all the more significant since Peter was never deemed to have provided grist to the heretical mill, as was the case with Paul. The contrast is that Peter was the pre-eminent heresiologist, as demonstrated by his victories over Simon Magus, the arch-heretic; whereas Paul's teaching was too easily distorted. Ironically, it was the fact that Peter's role as a teacher was not particularly remembered which ensured that he was safer from dangerous interpretation than was Paul. Yet, still they were remembered together as the two most foundational apostles.

Despite its status as 'apocryphal', the *Acts of Peter* seems to have been widely used in mainstream churches for a long time, especially the *Martyrdom of Peter*, known in several Middle Eastern translations,[96] and the value placed on the document no doubt reflects the esteem and reverence with which Peter was regarded.

d. The *Acts of Peter and the Twelve Apostles*

The Acts of Peter and the Twelve Apostles (§40.6f) is of value for our purposes only in that the document confirms that Peter was regarded and esteemed as the leader of the twelve apostles and their principal spokesman. The allusion to Matt. 16.16, 18 (Jesus' naming of Peter) in *NHL* VI.1.9 also confirms the crucial role which that passage was already playing in the status accorded to Peter.

e. The *Apocalypse of Peter*

In the *Apocalypse of Peter* (§40.7e), Peter is the lead figure in the exchange with Jesus drawn from Matt. 24 (*Apoc.Pet.* 1-2), which introduces the lengthy description of the final judgment and the varied punishments of sinners. In the Akhmim text the description begins as a personal testimony of Peter. Most striking is the commission given to Peter personally by the Lord Jesus Christ to 'go to the city of the west' (Rome?) and to spread Christ's 'gospel throughout all the world in peace' (14.4-6). Here again the mission, attributed especially to Paul in the NT Acts and Pauline epistles, is transferred to Peter, with no mention of or allusion to Paul.[97] The fact that the section concludes

---

96. Schneemelcher, *NTA* 2.277, 278; Stoops, *ABD* 5.268; Klauck, *Apocryphal Acts* 82.
97. See also Bauckham, 'Apocalypse of Peter' 246-53, though allusion to Peter's martyrdom is minimal.

with an elaboration of Peter's role in Matthew's account of the transfiguration of Jesus (Matt. 17.1-8) is a further indication (cf. 2 Pet. 1.16-18) that this passage in Matthew's Gospel, along with Matt. 16.17-19, was a major factor in the developing hagiography focused on Peter.[98]

The Coptic *Apocalypse of Peter* (§40.7f) adds nothing to our inquiry, apart from the fact that it recruits Peter to the advocates of Gnostic anthropology and christology. Peter was so integral to the identity of Christianity that no claim to a true understanding or representation of Jesus' death, the core tradition of Christianity, could be made without claiming Peter as its protagonist — even if the portrayal was fanciful from beginning to end.

f. The *Letter of Peter to Philip*

The *Letter of Peter to Philip* (§40.4c) as another 'revelation dialogue', more Gnostic than distinctively Christian, adds nothing to our knowledge of the continuing influence of Peter and of second-century attitudes to him, except that it is further demonstration of the recognition among those attracted by Christian tradition that Peter was an authoritative figure to whom it was of major importance that the message of salvation (however conceived) could be attributed. A curiosity is the conclusion, where 'the apostles parted from each other into four words in order to preach' (140.23-26), where the 'four words' could be understood as an allusion to the four Gospels.[99] In which case it would be significant that the reference is to the four Gospels which were already widely recognized as constituting Christian scripture, without either suggesting that there were other Gospels of equal merit or even that there might be more than 'four words' which conveyed the message of the apostles.

g. The *Apocryphon of James*

We should recall also that in the Nag Hammadi *Apocryphon of James* (§44.5b), James identifies what is to follow as 'a secret book which was revealed to me and Peter by the Lord' (*Apocryphon James* I.1.10-12).[100] As already noted

---

98. R. Bauckham, '2 Peter and the Apocalypse of Peter', *The Fate of the Dead: Studies on the Jewish and Christian Apocalypses* (Leiden: Brill, 1998) 290-303, examines parallels between the two documents and concludes that the Apocalypse's transfiguration narrative is dependent on Matthew, but influenced by 2 Peter's account (302-3).

99. Meyer, *NHL* 432.

100. Not to be confused with the *Apocalypse of James* (see above §§40.7a, b).

(§45.2d), the association of Peter with James suggests an attempt to give the revelation attributed to James the added and weighty authority of Peter.

h. Basilides

Also to be noted is the claim made by Basilides, according to Clement of Alexandria (*Strom.* 7.17), that his teacher was Glaucias, 'the interpreter of Peter'. This should possibly be seen as 'a Basilidian counter to the Peter-Mark tradition current in Alexandrian ecclesiastical circles'.[101]

i. The *Epistula Apostolorum*

In the *Epistula Apostolorum* (§40.5e) the two passages which mention Peter are of some interest. The first (*Ep.Apost.* 2) lists the apostles as 'John, Thomas, Peter, Andrew, James, Philip, Bartholomew, Matthew, Nathanael, Judas Zelotes, and Cephas'. Not only is Peter listed after, significantly(?), John and Thomas, but Peter is distinguished from Cephas, a curiosity which gave some scope for those who wanted to distinguish the Cephas of Gal. 2.11-14 from Peter. The second (*Ep.Apost.* 11) recalls Peter's thrice denial of Jesus, but also has the risen Jesus inviting Peter to put his finger in the nail-print of his hands, and Thomas to put his hand in Jesus' side. That Peter was included in the 'some who doubted' (Matt. 28.17) presumably implied that he was representative of those who by physically touching the risen Jesus were convinced beyond doubt that 'he had risen in the flesh' and was to be worshipped (12).

j. Peter and Rome

Mention should be made also of what has to be described as the legend of Peter's foundation of the church in Rome, or, more typically, of Peter and Paul as the founding apostles of the Roman church. This seems to be first attested by Irenaeus, when he emphasizes the pre-eminence 'of the very great, the very ancient, and universally known Church founded and organized at Rome by the two most glorious apostles, Peter and Paul' (*adv. haer.* 3.3.2). But we know that there were Christian gatherings in Rome before Paul arrived there (as his letter to Rome attests), and Paul would surely have indicated if Peter had been there before him. In fact, the only apostles mentioned in connection with the

---

101. Pearson, 'Basilides the Gnostic' 4 and n.16.

§48.6 *Peter*

pre-Pauline and pre-Petrine gatherings in Rome are Andronicus and Junia (Rom. 16.7).[102] So although the historical probability of Peter's martyrdom in Rome is quite strong,[103] the attribution of the church of Rome's foundation to Peter has to be regarded with the sort of historical suspicion which attaches also to Dionysius's claim that Peter was the founding apostle of the church in Corinth,[104] and the later claim that Peter was the first bishop of Antioch.[105]

Finally we should note the further confirmation that Peter was the most highly regarded figure in what became evident as the mainstream of Christianity, in the fact that other groups seem to have seen the necessity or at least taken the opportunity to undermine or challenge the primacy being accorded to him within the great church.[106] As we saw in §48.5, the pseudo-Clementines portray Peter as in effect petitioning support from James. Earlier we saw that in *Gosp.Thom.* 13 (§43.2c(1)), Peter's confession of Jesus is much downgraded;[107] and whereas in Matt. 16.17 Peter is congratulated for the revelation given to him, in *Thomas* 13 it is Thomas who is given special and secret revelation, too dangerous even for him to pass on. And notably in the *Gospel of Mary* Peter is rebuked for doubting that the Saviour could impart secret teaching to Mary, and is reminded that the Saviour 'loved her more than us'.[108] If other

---

102. Paul's unwillingness to 'build on someone else's foundation' (Rom. 15.20; cf. 2 Cor. 10.13-16) hardly cloaks an awareness that Peter was Rome's foundation apostle.

103. See *Beginning from Jerusalem* §35.3. The fact that Ignatius could allude to Peter and Paul giving the Romans instructions (*Rom.* 4.3) suggests his awareness that both Peter as well as Paul had spent some time teaching in Rome (Bockmuehl, *Simon Peter* 48). But it is also noticeable that Ignatius, despite his strong advocacy of monarchical episcopacy, does not refer to a bishop of Rome, far less argue that Peter was Rome's (first) bishop. If 1 Peter reflects the situation in Rome, it speaks only of elders/presbyters who have an overseeing (*episkopountes*) role (5.1-2). Brown also notes that Hermas speaks of plural presbyters (*Vis.* 2.4.2) and bishops (*Sim.* 9.27.2), and that according to Irenaeus (Eusebius, *HE* 5.24.14), before Soter (eleventh in the line of succession) the church of Rome was presided over by presbyters; but he also suggests that the Roman church of *1 Clement* 'may have seen itself as the successor of the Jerusalem apostolic church in supplying direction to the missionary churches like Corinth' (Brown and Meier, *Antioch and Rome* 163-64, 175-76).

104. Dionysius, bishop of Corinth, c. 170 (Eusebius, *HE* 2.25.8); but the claim runs contrary to the self-testimony of Paul that he was the sole founder of the Corinthian church (1 Cor. 3.6; 4.15; cf. Acts 18.1-18).

105. Eusebius, *HE* 3.36.2; but if the Antioch church sided with Peter against Paul in the dispute there (Gal. 2.11-17), as seems likely, then it is more understandable that Peter should be claimed by Antioch as one of its founding apostles, even though the Antioch church was founded well before Peter came to it (Acts 11.19-26) and Peter is not included among its earliest leaders (Acts 13.1).

106. See also n.38 above.

107. Peter replies that Jesus is 'like a righteous angel'.

108. *Gosp.Mary* 17.16–18.15; cf. *Gosp.Thom.* 114. Peterson also notes that, on the ba-

groups found it necessary thus to challenge the status of Peter, in regard to his authority, the revelation given to him and his favoured relationship with Jesus, we can probably infer with justice that Peter was not only highly regarded within the great church, but also that the great church rooted its claims in the status accorded to Peter.

48.7 Conclusion

In all this it is, of course, impossible to forget that for nineteen centuries, more or less, Peter has been reverenced as the first bishop of Rome, the first pope of Catholic Christianity. Peter stands at the apex of the theology of apostolic succession, the most direct historical link with Jesus himself, and almost as much a keystone in the foundation of the Christian church as Jesus himself. The fact that the historian can no more regard Peter as the apostolic founder of the first congregations of believers in Rome, any more than he can historically be credited with the establishment of Christianity in Antioch or Corinth, is evidently neither here nor there. What counts was, and is, the status ascribed to Peter, especially in Matt. 16.17-19, Peter as the foundation rock for the church. That does attest the high esteem in which Peter was held already before the first century had passed. And what we have seen above confirms that his influence was very strong, and that it may well have played a determinative role in holding together the disparities of the Christianity which emerged into the second century and in helping his successors to remain faithful to the central heritage of the Jesus tradition and to the gospel as articulated particularly by Paul.[109]

In short, the resolution of the 'contested identity' in terms of Peter, rather than James or Paul, may owe much more to Peter, to the part he played in the controversies of the first generation, and to the 'bridge-building' character of his influence thereafter than is clearly discernible in historical analysis. In theology, theological influence, he probably has to yield the palm to Paul. But in ecclesiology, ecclesiastical influence, he is without peer.

---

sis of John 1.40-42, in the ninth century Andrew was set up as 'the First-Called of the Apostles' against Peter 'the Prince of the Apostles' and was imagined as 'founder of the Patriarchate at Byzantium in direct opposition to the Roman claim to Peter as first Bishop of Rome', a claim only recognized by the Greek and Syriac Churches (*Andrew* 47).

109. Bockmuehl's focus on tracing the 'living memory' of Peter in East and West concludes that, 'Far from polarizing or vacillating, as has sometimes been claimed, the remembered profile of Peter appears to hold the capacity to bridge the tensions between Paul's radical mission and Jerusalem Christianity's mission to Israel' (*Simon Peter* 150).

PART FOURTEEN

BEYOND THE FIRST GENERATION

CHAPTER 49

John

49.1 Introduction

Our strategy thus far has been to examine the continuing influence of the most prominent influences on first-generation Christianity — the Jesus tradition (Part Eleven), James the brother of Jesus (Part Twelve), Paul and Peter (Part Thirteen). But for anyone familiar with the New Testament that leaves an obvious gap; there is someone missing. One of the most important writings in the NT is John's Gospel. And when we add to it the three Johannine epistles, and perhaps also the Apocalypse of John (Revelation), it is evident that there is still much more to be told if we are to trace the full story of *Christianity in the Making* in the hundred or so years following the failure of the first Jewish revolt.

By 'John', of course, we refer primarily to the son of Zebedee, brother of James, who, with Peter and James, seems to have been closest to Jesus of his twelve disciples.[1] The problems begin to arise, however, when we ask whether he was a figure of influence in the beginnings of Christianity. In the Synoptic Gospels he (and James) have nothing of the prominence of Peter. In Mark and Matthew, when the Zebedee brothers are mentioned, John is always named second, regularly as 'the brother of James',[2] presumably indicating that James was remembered as the more prominent, John being known (simply) as the brother of James. John is remembered as on one occasion asking Jesus a question, about

---

1. 'Peter and James and John, the brother of James' — Mark 5.37; Mark 9.2/Matt. 17.1; Mark 13.3; Mark 14.33/(Matt. 26.37); 'Peter and John and James' — Luke 8.51; 9.28; Acts 1.13.

2. Mark 1.19, 29; 3.17; 5.37; 9.2; 10.35, 41; Matt. 4.21; 10.2; 17.1; also Luke 5.10; 6.14; 9.54. Only in Luke 8.51 and 9.28 is John named first; in Acts 12.2 Luke records the execution of James, the brother of John.

'the strange exorcist' (Mark 9.38/Luke 9.49), but otherwise is remembered only for the somewhat embarrassing episode where James and John ask Jesus for the highest honour of sitting on Jesus' right and left in his glory (Mark 10.35-37).[3] In Acts John appears for a time as Peter's faithful shadow, but then disappears altogether from the scene.[4] Even after the execution of John's brother, James (Acts 12.2), when we might have thought that the departure of the more dominant(?) brother would have allowed John to come more to the fore, his absence is still more notable, John not even being mentioned in the context of the Jerusalem council (Acts 15). Paul's sole mention of him in that same context (Gal. 2.9) at least confirms his status as one of the 'pillar' apostles in Jerusalem, but hardly implies a figure of prominence or forcefulness when compared with the other two 'pillars', Peter and (the other) James (the brother of Jesus).

The problems do not diminish when we turn to the Johannine literature in the NT. For no 'John' is ever mentioned in either the Gospel of John or the Johannine Epistles. The question whether 'the beloved disciple' in the Gospel should be identified with John, son of Zebedee, has been discussed in §39.2d(i), without a clear answer emerging, or at least one which commands wide assent. Is the 'John' of the Gospel of John, John son of Zebedee, or John the Elder, or ...? The picture is no clearer with the Johannine letters, where, once again, the name 'John' does not appear. And in the case of Revelation, the 'John', 'John the seer', can hardly be identified with the apostle John with any confidence (§39.3h(i)).

All that said, however, it can hardly be assumed that John's Gospel dropped out of the sky in the second generation, post-70, of Christianity. The degree to which it shows interaction with the first-generation Jesus tradition (e.g. §43.1a(iii)) and the fact that it provides important historical information about Jesus and his first disciples supplementary to what can be gleaned from the Synoptic tradition (§43.1a(ii)), assuredly indicates a forceful factor within first-generation Christianity which may not have blossomed (fully) during those forty years but certainly did so thereafter. The importance which Irenaeus attached to the traditions, linking both Polycarp and Papias to John,[5] confirms that it was precisely such a link back into the apostolic age which John provided. To focus thus on John, following James, Paul and Peter, then, is not so much a departure from the strategy to date, since, in the event, the role of 'John' proved to be one of the most powerful influences in the making of Christianity.

---

3. Matthew softens(?) the embarrassment by having the mother of the Zebedee brothers making the request (Matt. 20.20-21). But Matthew follows Mark in recording the sequel, that when the other ten disciples heard about it, they were angry with the brothers (Mark 10.41/Matt. 20.24).

4. Acts 3.3, 4, 11; 4.13, 19; 8.14; also Luke 22.8.

5. Irenaeus, adv. haer. 3.3.4; 5.33.4; see above §40 nn.28, 92 and 93; also §48 n.71.

49.2 Recap

In fact, John has not been absent from earlier phases of our inquiry, but thus far usually when in pursuit of other questions, particularly the role of John's Gospel in the development of the Jesus tradition (§43.1) and in the 'Jewish Christianity' question (§45.4a, §46.5c). The emphasis, however, has been the more conservative necessity to demonstrate how faithful John's Gospel has been to the earlier Jesus tradition attested in the Synoptic tradition, and to demonstrate the Jewishness of his presentation of Jesus. Although the developments on both fronts were tremendous, it was the continuities on which we focused: that the developments were, in the case of the Jesus tradition, developments from within rather than imposed from without, as in the *Gospel of Thomas*; and, in the case of 'Jewish Christianity', developments of motifs and lines of reflection about God already current in Second Temple Judaism.

Without resiling from any of these findings it is now necessary to look at John in his own terms, to 'let John be John',[6] rather than as just another canonical Gospel, like the others. For in focusing on the continuities with the matrix from which John's Gospel emerged and on which it drew, it would be all too easy to ignore the differences, the points of tension, between John's Gospel and its predecessors, too easy to forget and underplay the distinctiveness of John's Gospel within the NT. We need not repeat the list of differences between John's Gospel and the Synoptic Gospels noted at the beginning of §43.1a for it to be clear that there is more to John than the continuities elaborated in §43 and §§45, 46.

Nevertheless, we have already covered a lot of the ground at which we need to look again, and it is probably most useful to begin this chapter by recalling just how much we have already learned about the contribution made by or attributed to this John, in particular the Gospel according to John.

a. The Conservative John

We have noted that the roots of John's Gospel can assuredly be traced back to Jesus' mission and to eye- and ear-witness testimony regarding that mission. We cannot identify the source(s) for these roots with any great confidence — the beloved disciple, John son of Zebedee, the elder John, or whoever. But neither can we ignore the strong probability that John was able to draw on specialist, personal knowledge, for example, of the overlap between Jesus'

---

6. I allude to my 'Let John Be John — A Gospel for Its Time', in *The Gospel and the Gospels*, ed. P. Stuhlmacher (Grand Rapids: Eerdmans, 1991) 293-322.

initial mission and that of the Baptist, including Jesus' recruitment of several of the Baptist's disciples, and of Jesus' Judaean mission. This tradition must have been circulating orally during the same period as the Synoptic tradition was circulating. We can guess why the Synoptic tradition ignored at least some of the distinctive information which we find in John — in particular, that it was more concerned to mark the disjunction between the missions of the Baptist and of Jesus than their overlap.[7] But otherwise the overlap is too substantial to allow us to infer that communities/congregations which cherished the Synoptic tradition were quite separate from communities/congregations which cherished Johannine tradition. The passing over of some of John's details by the Synoptic tradition seems to be too deliberate for it to be attributed to ignorance. And, as we saw in §43, John's development seems again and again to be development of shared tradition rather than tradition unknown to the Synoptics. So we have to envisage a range of communities/ congregations who had richer stores of tradition than we can now be aware of, and within that range some who began to reflect on and to elaborate the Jesus tradition in ways which eventuated in the distinctive Johannine retelling of the story of Jesus.

Presumably this was happening already in Judaea/Palestine. Was there a Samaritan input, reflecting an early Samaritan stage in the development of embryonic Christianity,[8] and perhaps helping to explain the hostile references to 'the Jews'?[9] The fact that Johannine dualism is closer to that of the Dead Sea Scrolls than to subsequent Gnostic dualism[10] also could suggest some influence from Qumran or other Essenes converted to belief in Jesus Messiah, though there is no clear evidence that John's Gospel knew or drew on Qumran literature.[11] And the element of polemic against disciples of John the Baptist[12] suggests a debate most lively within the Judaea/Palestine milieu, though we can hardly forget that according to Acts 19.1-7 the influence of the Baptist had extended as far as Ephesus, with which tradition also links John. Most strikingly, the virulent opposition by and to 'the Jews' suggests that the

---

7. See above §43.1a(ii).

8. See above §43 n.118.

9. Brown, *Community* 36-40. I have found Brown's suggested reconstruction of the early history of Johannine Christianity as compelling now as when I first read it thirty years ago and, as will become evident, will mostly follow his lead. See also his *Introduction* 373-76; J. L. Martyn, 'Glimpses into the History of the Johannine Community' (1977), *The Gospel of John in Christian History* (New York: Paulist, 1979) ch. 3; Ashton, *Understanding* 166-74.

10. One of the critical responses to Bultmann which a closer examination of the Dead Sea Scrolls made evident — see e.g. the extended discussion in Schnackenburg, *John* 1.124-49.

11. Brown, *Community* 30.

12. See above §43 at n.116.

context in which the Gospel was determinatively shaped was one where Jewish synagogues had a powerful local influence. The suggestion that John's Gospel works at two levels, reflecting both the historical situation of Jesus' mission and the situation of Johannine communities/congregations, probably in the post-70 period, is highly plausible.[13] But was this happening in Syria, implying a post-70 departure from Palestine of Johannine believers? And should we envisage still more layers in the process leading to John's Gospel, perhaps the final layers reflecting a further transition of Johannine believers/congregations to Ephesus?[14] The more we stretch the time and distance beyond Jesus' mission in Galilee and Judaea, the greater the possibility that other factors have to be allowed for in explaining the developments in the Johannine account of Jesus.

b. The Jewish John

Here it is probably necessary only to recall the findings regarding John's christology (§43.1c). John clearly regarded his message 'that Jesus is the Messiah, the Son of God' (John 20.31) as the central claim of his Gospel. The distinctiveness of Jesus' messiahship was rooted in Jewish expectation of a messiah and is built round characteristically Jewish themes. The distinctiveness of Jesus as the Son of God was nevertheless an elaboration of the commission of a prophet, and Jesus as the Son of Man was sufficiently close to Jewish reflection on the human figure of Dan. 7.13-14 for it to occasion little surprise as a concept in Jewish circles. Likewise the portrayal of Jesus in terms familiar in Jewish reflection on God's immanence, as Wisdom and Word, was language which would resonate meaningfully and favourably in Jewish ears.[15] In short, there was a deliberate and sustained strategy to present Jesus as the one who fulfilled Israel's hopes in ways and to a degree which surpassed all potential previous alternatives, including Moses, the Torah and the prophet.

It is true, of course, that John's strategy vis-à-vis his fellow Jews was failing, or had already failed. 'The Jews' are too often referred to in hostile terms, and the clear indication that Johannists had been expelled from the

---

13. So particularly and influentially by Martyn, *History and Theology in the Fourth Gospel* — a 'two-level drama'.

14. See above §39.2d(ii).

15. Jesus' claims 'are made from within the Jewish tradition and *cannot be explained in any other way*' (Ashton, *Understanding* 141; and further 148-50); 'the most startling of (the claims made for Jesus) were made within a religious tradition which in the first place made them possible and continues to give them intelligibility' (159).

synagogue[16] puts the question beyond dispute. Yet, John seems to have still cherished the hope that his gospel would be heard and accepted by those who could most appreciate the terms in which he expressed it. He hoped that there were those like Nicodemus and the blind man (John 9) who believed secretly and who needed to step openly into the light and declare their belief. And there is the possibility that the Apologists' use of John's Logos theology and the two powers heresy in rabbinic Judaism reflect two sides of what was an ongoing dispute between emerging Christianity and emerging Judaism, a dispute in effect still not finally resolved.[17]

In sum, it can be fairly said that John, the author of the main body of John's Gospel, probably saw his portrayal of Messiah Jesus as fully within the boundaries set by the Jewish scriptures and by the reflection thereon within Second Temple Judaism.[18] He was pushing the boundaries back, in terms of christology, much as Paul had done in terms of a Jewish gospel for Gentiles. And, as we shall see, he was opening the gospel of Jesus to different and questionable interpretations. But John would have denied that he was ignoring or breaching the boundaries which defined Israel's heritage.

c. The Distinctive John

Our study thus far also enables us to mark out John's distinctiveness in relation to the other principal influences of the first generation, with findings which are at best confusing and pose other questions.

- We have examined the way in which John reacted to the earlier Jesus tradition, confirming that it proved to be a deeply rooted influence even when much reflected on. Yet, at the same time, very little of the typical portrayal of Jesus in the Synoptic Gospels prepares us for the characteristic reworking of the Jesus tradition in John's Gospel. As noted in §43.1a,[19] a striking feature is the way in which the balance in the Synoptic Jesus' preaching of the kingdom of God, between its already active and its still future presence, has been transformed in John into a consistent emphasis on realized eschatology.[20]
- There is nothing to link John with James, the brother of Jesus, as such,

16. See above §46.5c.
17. See above §46.4c.
18. See again my 'Let John Be John' (n.6 above); Lincoln, *John* 70-81.
19. See also §43 nn.190-92.
20. See also M. Theobald, 'Futurische versus präsentisches Eschatologie', *Studien* ch. 22.

beyond the reference in Gal. 2.9 to their shared pillar apostleship. But was John consciously moving beyond the more traditional (Jacobean) Jewish believers in Jesus (as possibly implied in passages like John 6.60-66, 7.3-5 and 8.31), and trying to persuade them, as well as half-persuaded believers, to take the next step (as possibly implied in passages like John 4.39-42 and 9.35-39)?[21]

- The question of interaction with Paul is more intriguing, in view of the tradition linking John with Ephesus, one of the major centres of Paul's mission and a church established by Paul. But, as we shall see, John seems more than ready to go beyond what in comparison seem like more tentative explorations of Paul's christology.
- Even more intriguing is John's relation to Peter, the only one with whom John was associated in the opening chapters of Acts. For the possibility that they were regarded as in some sense rival figures, and rival authorities, as suggested by John 20.1-10 and 21.20-23, cannot be ignored.[22]

So again the question arises, not so much whether there were two (or more) rival streams of Jesus tradition (which §43.1 showed to be unlikely), but whether there were rival streams within the shared Jesus tradition. If, as I suggested in §43.1e, Johannine Christianity is a kind of conventicle Christianity, then that could well have indicated a degree of reaction against the Petrine ecclesiology which was probably moving in the direction indicated by the Pastorals and Ignatius.[23] Here John's declining the opportunity to refer to the disciples of Jesus as 'apostles' (neither in John's Gospel nor in the Johannine Epistles), his surprising neglect to make explicit description of Jesus' baptism or of the institution of the Lord's Supper, his description of the worship sought by God in spiritual rather than institutional terms (John 4.23-24),

---

21. As argued particularly by Brown, *Community* 71-81; e.g. on John 7.3-5 Brown observes: 'John's claim that the brothers of Jesus . . . did not really believe in him cannot be facilely dismissed as a simple historical memory that at first some of Jesus' family did not react well to his ministry (see Mark 3:21, 34-35; 6.4). . . . I would argue that John's hostile picture of the brothers is meant to have a perduring significance' (75-76).

22. See above §39 nn.142-143. Brown refers to 'the consistent and deliberate contrast between Peter and the Beloved Disciple, the hero of the Johannine community' — referring also to John 13.23-26; 18.15-16; 19.26-27; 21.7 (*Community* 82-83). The fact that John never refers to the disciples of Jesus as 'apostles' (despite John 13.16) is also significant here.

23. 'In counterposing their hero over against the most famous member of the Twelve, the Johannine community is symbolically counterposing itself over against the kinds of churches that venerate Peter and the Twelve . . . the "Great Church". . . . The Johannine Christians represented by the Beloved Disciple clearly regard themselves as closer to Jesus and more perceptive than the Christians of the Apostolic Churches' (Brown, *Community* 83-84). See also below on 3 John (§49.4c).

and his warning that the (eucharistic) flesh is worthless ('It is the Spirit that gives life' — 6.63) all confirm that Johannine Christianity was marking out a distinctive path within the range of late first-century Christianity.[24]

At the same time we should recall our other finding that John's Gospel was known, used and respected in the second century (§44.8d). There is no evidence of a continuing rivalry between John and James, or John and Paul, or John and Peter. There is no evidence that John's Gospel was ignored or regarded with suspicion by proto-orthodox churches[25]— contrary to a view common in the twentieth century.[26] There is more to be said on this point, as we shall see, but any attempt to peel John away from the strands of Christianity represented by James, Paul and Peter has no backing in the evidence thus far reviewed.

What, then, did John's distinctiveness consist of? I will focus on the most obvious feature — John's christology — noting also how it seems to have opened the door to interpretations of which John would not have approved.

49.3 Let John Be John

When we consider John's presentation of Christ, all its firm rootage in and continuity with Jewish and early Christian theologizing should not blind us to or diminish our perception of the radical transmutation which John makes in his portrayal of Christ.

a. The Incarnate Word

It is not enough simply to point out the Wisdom and Logos language and imagery on which John drew, particularly in the prologue to the Gospel, but also elsewhere (§43.1c). The claim which John made was that the Lo-

---

24. See particularly Schweizer, *Church Order in the New Testament* ch. 11. 'The Fourth Gospel is best interpreted as voicing a warning against the dangers inherent in such developments [apostolic succession, church offices, sacramental practices] by stressing what (for John) is truly essential, namely, the living presence of Jesus in the Christian through the Paraclete. No institution or structure can substitute for that' (Brown, *Community* 88).

25. Brown also discusses whether Johannine Christianity should be described as 'sectarian' (*Community* 14-16, 61-62, 89-91), pointing out the great prayer for Christian unity was for the oneness of Johannine and Apostolic Christianity, and that John's Gospel was never regarded as sectarian by the great church (90-91).

26. But see again particularly Hill, *The Johannine Corpus in the Early Church*.

gos/Wisdom had 'become flesh' (John 1.14) — not just was manifest in poetic metaphor to describe divine action,[27] not just as symbolized in the character of Israel's heroes and heroines (as in Philo),[28] not just as a casual visitor like an angelic messenger in human appearance, but *'became flesh'*, *became* a human being who had lived a full life from birth to death in first-century Palestine.[29]

John was fully aware of the immensity of the claim he was making. He did not introduce it in ways open to varied interpretation, like Paul in Col. 2.9. He did not refer to it allusively as could be said of Matthew's Wisdom christology in Matt. 11.2, 19. He did not seek to distinguish the Logos from God, as an emanation somewhat distant from God, as in later Gnostic systems; the Logos was not only with God in the beginning, but was God (John 1.1). Nor did he attempt to play down what the Logos had become: 'that which is born of flesh is flesh' (3.6); 'the flesh is of no value' (6.63); but the Logos 'became *flesh*', its polar opposite.[30] The Johannine prologue relishes the paradox, what most thoughtful people of his time would regard as an absurdity, as nonsense, as inconceivable — that God could become a human being of flesh and blood, a man who would die, that the infinite gulf between Creator and creation could be thus spanned. The Greeks could conceive of gods appearing on earth for a short time or in disguise. They could conceive of demi-gods, the offspring of a god with a human partner, or of humans being deified. But a god becoming material and corruptible flesh, a human being and living a full human life? The sages of Israel felt it both appropriate and necessary to identify divine Wisdom with the Torah[31]— Wisdom as inscripturated; but to claim that Wisdom/Logos had *become* a particular human figure — as incarnated?[32] And the later Gnostic systems could only envisage the gap between creator and cre-

---

27. As in Wisd. 10-11 and 18.14-16.

28. Particularly Sarah (*Leg. All.* 2.82; *Cher.* 9-10, 45, 49-50; *Det.* 124; *Congr.* 9, 13, 22, 79-80, 129; *Mut.* 79-80, 151-153; *Abr.* 100).

29. The *Prayer of Joseph* (first-century CE?), in which Jacob/Israel is presented as designating himself as 'the firstborn of every living thing to whom God gives life', 'the archangel of the power of the Lord and the chief captain among the sons of God', and 'the first minister before the face of God', is more a way of glorifying Israel in the person of its eponymous patriarch than a precedent for John 1.14.

30. Cf. J. F. McHugh, *John 1-4* (ICC; London: T & T Clark, 2009) 51-53.

31. Sir. 24.23; Bar. 4.1.

32. Jewish speculation moves in a different direction in Merkavah mysticism; see e.g. I. Gruenwald, *Apocalyptic and Merkavah Mysticism* (AGJU 14; Leiden: Brill, 1980); D. J. Halperin, *The Faces of the Chariot: Early Jewish Responses to Ezekiel's Vision* (Tübingen: Mohr Siebeck, 1988); A. A. Orlov, *Heavenly Priesthood in the Apocalypse of Abraham* (Cambridge University Press, 2013).

ation being bridged through a lengthy series of aeons of decreasing divinity. But the Johannine prologue sees the gap as bridged in one step: 'the Word became flesh' (1.14).[33]

The step which the Johannine prologue took moved the theology of divine/human relationships into new territory. In further expressions of the gospel of salvation it was a potential game changer of huge significance. Should John's bold identity, God-become-flesh, be regarded as a step too far and the essential difference and distance between divine and human be reasserted by denying the reality of the Logos-Christ's flesh? Or should the logic of John's concept of incarnation be pressed further, in claiming that the incarnation had complete soteriological significance as well — that by taking flesh into God (the Godhead) flesh itself was redeemed, incarnation as theosis (divinization) — the cross and resurrection becoming something of an afterthought — salvation gained by eating the flesh and drinking the blood of the Son of Man (John 6.53-58), no longer the body broken and the blood shed as a way of dealing with sin? Whatever John's intention in these matters, the die was cast and the theological discussion moved on to a different level.

b. The Son Sent and the Son of Man Descended

Just as deliberate was John's presentation of Jesus as the Son of God as a way of transforming earlier christological debates. The firm identification of the Messiah as 'the Son of God' in describing the purpose of the Gospel (John 20.31) transformed the old debate as to whether Jesus was the Messiah, a debate still reflected in John. Even more striking is the way the Johannine prologue went out of its way to link the Logos-become-flesh assertion with the thought, evidently of equal importance, of the incarnate Logos as the Son of God. The glory evident in the incarnate Logos was 'a father's/the Father's only (begotten) son/Son' (1.14). 'The only-begotten (*monogenēs*) God[34] who is in the Father's close embrace has made him known' (1.18). This blending of the prologue's unique Logos christology with Son christology not only attached the former tightly with a christology

---

33. Schnelle, *Antidocetic Christology in the Gospel of John*, particularly 221-22; 'here *sarx* cannot be understood as merely an irrelevant factor or a necessary medium' (227). Schnelle's principal thesis is that John's Gospel presupposes the conflict reflected in 1 John (1 John predating the Gospel) and so the Gospel itself has to be understood as engaging in 'a comprehensive theological combat with Docetism' (228-29).

34. 'God' is the more strongly attested reading for John 1.18 (see e.g. Barrett, *John* 169; Metzger, *Textual Commentary* 198; Ehrman, *Orthodox Corruption* 78-82; McHugh, *John 1-4* (69-70); see also above §43 n.137.

firmly rooted in Jesus' own spirituality,[35] it also gave the Son christology a new dimension.

This concept of the Logos-Son's intimacy with the Father, as revelatory of the Father, transforms what had been a powerful image into something still more powerful. 'Son of God' is no longer simply a way of indicating that someone was especially favoured by God.[36] 'Sent' by God was no longer simply a way of denoting a divinely authorized commission.[37] In one of John's favourite ways of speaking of Jesus' mission, 'the Father who sent me', a commission from heaven has been transformed into a mission from heaven. The Son came down from heaven (6.38); here is the source for the Nicene creed's clause 'he came down from heaven'. What had not been clearly articulated in passages like Rom. 8.3 and Gal. 4.4, or Phil. 2.6-7, was now openly expressed, and its full corollary drawn out — not only that the Son knew the Father's purpose to an intimate degree, but also that the Son acted as the Father's plenipotentiary in the fullest sense. The *monogenēs* and the Logos-who-is-God-and-who-has-become-flesh are two sides of the one coin for John.

It was no doubt in the same spirit that John advanced the earlier Son of Man christology by adding the thought of the Son of Man's descending and ascending (3.13; 6.62). What had been an apocalyptic image of Christ's triumph, 'coming on the clouds of heaven', whether to heaven or from heaven, now becomes a further way of speaking of Christ's initial coming from heaven. The somewhat surprising assertion of 3.13 — 'No one has ascended into heaven, except the one who descended from heaven' — may indeed, as already noted, be directed against the characterization of the patriarchs and prophets as those who in effect ascended into heaven to hear (first-hand) what God said.[38] Here again the thought of the prophet as sent, that is, commissioned by God, has been transformed into the claim that Jesus, as the Logos-Son, was in fact one, the only one, who had really been present in the heavenly assembly such as was envisaged in Job 1-2. It is this opening of heavenly reality, not so much by means of a heavenly journey and with the help of an interpreting angel, but an opening on earth in and through Jesus to those ready to receive it which moves the Gospel of John on to a new plane.

---

35. See *Jesus Remembered* §16.2.
36. See *Christology in the Making* §3.
37. See particularly Bühner, *Der Gesandte und sein Weg im 4. Evangelium.*
38. See above §43 n.141.

c. The Revealer

Since for John Jesus is the incarnate Word, the one who has made the unseen God see-able, it was a central concern for John to bring home to audiences the truth of this very fact. In a famous *bon mot* Rudolf Bultmann highlighted the role in John's Gospel of Jesus as the revealer; but all that he reveals is that he is the revealer![39] That was an inadequate summary of John's purpose. It is true of course that Jesus as the incarnate Word and Wisdom fulfils the role previously filled in Second Temple reflection on Word and Wisdom — not least their role as revealers. But the significance of Jesus as the divine revealer for John was that he revealed *God*, the Son revealed *the Father*, the uttered Word revealed the one who uttered the word. To know this was to know the reality which Jesus was, and thus to know God, the Father. 'This is eternal life, that they know you, the only true God, and the one you sent, Jesus Christ' (17.3).

This emphasis on Jesus as the one who reveals the true reality of God is a further key element in John's transmutation of the gospel into something more daring and challenging. Christ not only brought the word of God — 'Thus says the Lord', in classic prophetic speech — he *is* the Word. He not only brought revelation from the Father, he *is* the revelation. 'No one has ever seen God . . . (but) the only-begotten God[40] . . . has made him known' (1.18); 'Whoever sees me sees him who sent me' (12.45); 'Whoever has seen me has seen the Father' (14.9). He and the Father are one (10.30). He utters the divine 'I am'.[41] That is the claim which lifted Jesus from the status of one who might finally be reckoned on a par with Moses or Mohammed, and which makes the claims of Christianity seem so intemperate in inter-faith dialogue. But the claim is nonetheless at the heart of John's presentation of Christ.

As a corollary it should not be assumed that in his talk of the Son's dependence on the Father (as in 5.19), John was already caught up in the later debates about the relationships of the two persons of the Trinity, the Father and the Son. Rather, the point[42] is that to label 14.28 ('the Father

---

39. Bultmann, *Theology* 2.66 — 'Jesus as the Revealer of God *reveals nothing but that he is the Revealer*' (his emphasis); 'in his Gospel (John) presents only the fact (*das Dass*) of the Revelation without describing its content (*ihr Was*)'. The reformulation by Bultmann's pupil, Ernst Käsemann, *The Testament of Jesus* (1966; ET London: SCM, 1968) — 'Jesus is nothing but the revealer and . . . Jesus is the only revealer of God and therefore belongs totally on the side of God even while he is on earth' (11) — typifies Käsemann's misreading of John (see also above §43 n.172). Ashton reflects at length on Bultmann's *'blosses Dass'* ('naked "that"') and concludes, 'the medium is the message' (*Understanding* ch. 14 and 553).

40. See above n. 34.

41. Particularly 8.28, 58; 13.19.

42. Already made in §43 at n.169.

is greater than I') as 'subordinationist christology' is to read John against a much later background of theological discussion than the first century. The language used by John was more an expression of his Logos christology, as a way of expressing the continuity between the Father and the Son, the authority and definitiveness of the Son's revelation of the Father, the Son as the self-expression (Logos) of the Father. This is what John wanted to get over when he has Jesus asserting that he speaks the words of God (3.34), what he heard from God (8.26), what the Father commanded him to speak (12.49); the Son did not come of his own accord (7.28; 8.42) but as the Son sent to reveal the Father. The Logos expresses primarily continuity, oneness, not distinction.[43]

d. John's Christology in Gnostic Perspective

The transmutation in christology which John achieved was so radical that it raised the question whether John had gone too far. In particular, had John gnosticized the gospel? The presentation of Jesus as the Son sent from the Father, of the Son of Man descending to earth, had striking parallels with the later Gnostic Redeemer myth, and could imply that the myth was already full blown, as some found suggested also in the Wisdom myth evidenced in Bar. 3.37 and *1 Enoch* 42. Likewise John's emphasis on Jesus as the divine revealer, who brings the truth,[44] and the characteristic Johannine light/darkness dualism,[45] would naturally carry the corollary that salvation was ignorance being dispelled by new knowledge,[46] those blind being given to see (particularly ch. 9),[47] and would almost inevitably imply that such knowing, such illumination, was the heart of the salvation being offered. The issue became acute in the twentieth century with Bultmann's drawing what for him was the obvious conclusion: that John's christology had in fact been shaped by the (pre-Christian) Gnostic Redeemer myth.[48] The summary of his conclusions expressed the claim unequivocally:[49]

    43. See also §43 n.170 above.
    44. See above §43 n.194; e.g. John 1.14, 17; 8.32; 14.6.
    45. Notably John 1.4-5; 3.19-21; 8.12; 12.36, 46.
    46. Cf. John 8.32; 14.7; 17.3.
    47. See above §43 n.193 — though we recall that John does not use the noun *gnōsis* itself.
    48. Bultmann, 'The History of Religions Background of the Prologue to the Gospel of John'. Bultmann found the evidence for John's dependence on the Gnostic myth chiefly in the Revelation-discourse source which he thought to underlie Jesus' discourses in the Gospel (*Theology* 2.13). See also above §43 n.161.
    49. Bultmann, *Theology* 2.12-13; the author's background was Judaism, but not 'orthodox' Judaism, rather 'a Gnosticizing Judaism' (13).

The figure of Jesus in John is portrayed in the forms offered by the Gnostic Redeemer-myth which had already influenced the Christological thinking of Hellenistic Christianity before Paul and then influenced him. It is true that the cosmological motifs of the myth are missing in John, especially the idea that the redemption which the "Ambassador" brings is the release of the pre-existent sparks of light which are held captive in this world below by demonic powers. But otherwise Jesus appears as in the Gnostic myth as the pre-existent Son of God whom the Father clothed with authority and sent into the world.

Bultmann's leading pupil, Ernst Käsemann, was well enough aware that a closer parallel to the Johannine dualism was to be found in the Dead Sea Scrolls,[50] but he still found it impossible to avoid the conclusion that John's Gospel was already well on the way to portraying Jesus in Gnostic terms.[51]

One can hardly fail to recognize the danger of his [John's] christology of glory, namely, the danger of docetism. It is present in a still naïve, unreflected form and it has not yet been recognized by the Evangelist or his community.

Käsemann's views were still well towards one end of the spectrum which characterized the second half of the twentieth century,[52] but his characteriza-

---

50. Bultmann, in a still early response to the Dead Sea Scrolls, saw in them proof that 'a pre-Christian gnosticizing Judaism' already existed in Palestine (*Theology* 2.13 n).

51. Käsemann, *The Testament of Jesus* 26. Unsurprisingly Käsemann concluded that John's acceptance into the church's canon was a human error but by divine providence: 'From the historical viewpoint, the Church committed an error when it declared the Gospel to be orthodox'. But he saw the reception of the Fourth Gospel into the canon as 'the most lucid and most significant example of the integration of originally opposing ideas and traditions into the ecclesiastical tradition', and a proof of his thesis that the NT canon is the basis not so much for Christianity's unity as for its diversity (*Testament* 74-76). See again §43 n.172 above.

52. The transition from Bultmann's radical view is well demonstrated by Kümmel, that John 'lays claim to the language of gnosis in order to show Christians that Jesus is the true revealer' (*Introduction* 218-28, here 230), and Koester (Bultmann's last pupil) who argues strongly that John rejects a Gnosticizing understanding of salvation (*Ancient Christian Gospels* 263-67). For the debate see also Schnackenburg, *St John* 135-49; Brown, *John* 1.lii-lvi; Barrett, *John* 81-82; and particularly Schnelle, *Antidocetic Christology in the Gospel of John*, with his more recent review in *History* 504-9; and L. R. Zelyck, *John Among the Other Gospels: The Reception of the Fourth Gospel in the Extra-Canonical Gospels* (WUNT 2.347; Tübingen: Mohr Siebeck, 2013). In British scholarship the transition from a dominant interest in the Greek/Hellenistic background of John to a focus primarily on its Jewish background was marked by the transition from Dodd's *Interpretation of the Fourth Gospel* (1953) to Barrett's *John* (1955); see Barrett's own comments on the point

tion of the dangers to which John's christology exposed itself would seem to be confirmed by the popularity which John's Gospel enjoyed among the various Gnostic groupings, particularly the Valentinians. Heracleon (c. 160-180) wrote the first commentary on John's Gospel.[53] We learn from Irenaeus and Epiphanius that Ptolemaeus offered an extensive exegesis of the Johannine prologue.[54] Irenaeus was well aware also that the followers of Valentinus made copious use of John's Gospel (*adv. haer.* 3.11.7). And the Nag Hammadi codices indicate influence from John at a number of places.[55] A curiosity is that the Alogoi, a Christian sect which flourished in Asia Minor around 170 CE, so named because they opposed Logos christology, attributed John's Gospel to Cerinthus (Epiphanius, *Pan.* 51.3-4).

What we find, however, when we consult the Valentinian exegesis of John (at least as it is available to us from Irenaeus, Clement of Alexandria and Hippolytus) is that they recoil from John's explicit assertion, that the Logos 'became flesh', from any thought that there could be such an immediate conjunction of God and the physical world.[56] Rather they bring to their reading of the prologue the assumption that the divine realm is much more complex than Jewish monotheism allowed[57] and that the transition from divine to hu-

---

(*Gospel of John and Judaism* 63-64). See also J. H. Charlesworth, 'The Dead Sea Scrolls and the Gospel according to John', in Culpepper and Black, eds., *Exploring the Gospel of John* 65-97.

53. See E. H. Pagels, *The Johannine Gospel in Gnostic Exegesis: Heracleon's Commentary on John* (Nashville: Abingdon, 1973).

54. Irenaeus, *adv. haer.* 1.1.1-8; Epiphanius, *Pan.* 31.9.1-27; extensive selection in Foerster, *Gnosis* 1.127-45.

55. See Brown, for example: 'There is a Word (*Logos*) Christology in the *Tripartite Tractate*, and "I AM" Christology in the *Second Apocalypse of James*; also in *The Thunder, the Perfect Mind*, and in the *Trimorphic Protennoia* (where it is joined with a docetic account of the death of Jesus)' (*Community* 147-48). But the influence of John on the *Second Apocalypse of James* is minimal (cf. e.g. *NHL* V.49.5-6 and V.58.2-8). And *The Thunder: Perfect Mind* echoes not so much the 'I am's of John as the self-proclamation of Lady Wisdom (Sir. 24), but in a sequence of antithetical and paradoxical contrasts which bemuse more than inform (*NHL* 295-303); cf. the *Acts of John* below. See also Culpepper, *John* 114-19.

56. 'Gnostic critics claim that the basic error of "the many" involves their preoccupation with the historical reality of Jesus' (Pagels, *Johannine Gospel* 11). If John (in Ephesus?) was engaged in a wider debate with Greek mythology (cf. John 7.35; 12.20-26), as argued by George van Kooten in a paper given in Cambridge in 2014 ('Between Mythology and Philosophy: Rereading John's Notion of Being Begotten from God in a Greek Context — Engaging with C. H. Dodd's "The Interpretation of the Fourth Gospel [1953]" Sixty Years On'), John 1.14 would be equally critical.

57. Ptolemaeus reads Isa. 45.5 as the Demiurge, 'too weak to know anything spiritual, (imagining) that he was himself the only God' (Irenaeus, *adv. haer.* 1.5.4).

man is much more tortuous than a surface reading of John 1.3[58] and 1.14[59] allowed. Thus, Ptolemaeus reads John 1.1-2 as distinguishing three — God, Beginning and Logos. And when 1.3-4 and 14 are drawn in, it is to distinguish a first Tetrad (Father, Grace, the Only-begotten, and Truth). Linked with the second Tetrad (Logos and Life, Man and Church) they make up the Ogdoad, 'the mother of all the aeons'.[60] Again, when Heracleon reads 'What was made in him was life' (John 1.3-4) he understood 'in him' as meaning 'for spiritual men' (pneumatics),[61] that is, reading into John's words the Valentinian presupposition that humanity was divided into three classes, pneumatics, psychics and choics.[62] For other illustrations, we could note Heracleon's allegorical interpretation of John 2.13-20,[63] of 4.1-42 (the awakening of the spiritual essence) and of 4.46-54 (the demiurge asking the Saviour for help, as the human being created by the demiurge was about to die).[64] And Ptolemaeus maintains that Jesus' confessions in John 10.30 and 14.6 indicate that Jesus 'was other than that which he assumed'; that John 19.34 indicated 'the outflowing of the passions'; and that in references to the Son of Man in the passion predictions 'he appears to be speaking of another person, namely, of him who experiences passion'.[65] In the *Trimorphic Protennoia* the 'I' speaks regularly of having come down to the world, as 'Word, and I revealed myself in the likeness of their shape' (*NHL* XIII.47.15-16); 'As for me, I put on Jesus. I bore him from the cursed wood, and established him in the dwelling places of his Father'.[66]

Such readings of John are typical of the Gnostic exegesis reported by Irenaeus and Clement of Alexandria, characteristic of a mind-set looking for arguments to support its given position rather than anything which might call the given in question — what is now regarded as eisegesis rather than exe-

---

58. Particularly Sophia submitting to an illegitimate passion from which matter was derived (Irenaeus, *adv. haer.* 1.2.2; 1.4.1; 1.5.1-6).

59. Ptolemaeus insisted that Christ 'was endowed with a body which had a psychic substance . . . He received nothing whatever material . . . for matter is not capable of being saved' (*adv. haer.* 1.6.1).

60. Irenaeus, *adv. haer.* 1.1.8.5; also 1.1.1-3 (Foerster, *Gnosis* 1.144-45). Similarly Clement of Alexandria, *Exc. Theod.* 1.6 (Foerster, *Gnosis* 1.223); and the *Tripartite Tractate*.

61. Fragment of Heracleon in Origen, *in Joh.* 2.21; Foerster, *Gnosis* 1.163. See also Clem. Alex., *Exc. Theod.* 1.7; 1.41.3-4.

62. See above §38 at n.119; and see also Irenaeus, *adv. haer.* 1.5.1; 1.6.1.

63. Foerster, *Gnosis* 1.166-68; though, as Pagels reminds us, Origen also practised 'spiritual exegesis' (*Johannine Gospel* 66-67).

64. Dunderberg, 'School of Valentinus' 80.

65. Clem. Alex., *Exc. Theod.* 61.1-4. We might add that the sense of alienation from the world indicated in John's Gospel (Brown, *Community* 63-66) would likely resonate with the characteristic Gnostic sense of alienation (§38 n.148).

66. *NHL* XIII.50.12-15; cf. John 14.2.

gesis.[67] By reading through the text to what they assumed was an underlying schema, the reading itself could come across as sophisticated, more appealingly subtle than a straightforward reading.[68] Irenaeus was able to refute such eisegesis by the much more straightforward exegesis of John 1.14: it was the Word of God which became flesh, the only-begotten Son of the only God; 'the apostle certainly does not speak regarding any other, or concerning any Ogdoad, but respecting our Lord Jesus Christ. . . . flesh is that which was of old formed for Adam by God out of the dust, and it is this that John has declared the Word of God became'.[69]

Käsemann's argument was, in effect, similar to that of Ptolemaeus and may indeed be said to reflect what must have been the interpretative logic of many Valentinians:[70]

> Does the statement 'The Word became flesh' really mean more than that he descended into the world of man and there came into contact with earthly existence, so that an encounter with him became possible? Is not this statement totally overshadowed by the confession 'We beheld his glory', so that it received its meaning from it. . . . Do not (the) features of his lowliness . . . represent the absolute minimum of the costume designed for the one who dwelt for a little while among men, appearing to be one of them, yet without himself being subjected to earthly conditions?

But Käsemann was being equally unfair to John. For John 'the Word became flesh' was *not* 'totally overshadowed by the confession "We beheld his glory"'. It was precisely that the glory was manifested *in and as flesh* on which John insisted.[71] The 'glory' was not only the glory of the pre-existent Word or of the ascended Christ, but Jesus' being glorified in his crucifixion; John retains the structure given to the Gospel by Mark.[72] To be sure, John sailed close to the wind, but he was never blown off course. Gnostic exegesis could only claim John's support by denying the both-and of flesh and glory, of glory-in-flesh,

---

67. Irenaeus provides good examples of Ptolemaeus's interpretation of other NT passages (*adv. haer.* 1.8.2-4).

68. See also §44 at n.328. In contrast, the Apologists' Logos christology was much closer to and a more empathetic reading of the Johannine prologue (§40.2e, f, i; §44 n.329).

69. Irenaeus, *adv. haer.* 1.9.3; see also 3.11.2-3 ('according to the opinion of no one of the heretics was the Word of God made flesh'); 3.16.2, 5-8; 3.17.4; 3.18.1, 7; 3.19.1; 5.18.2-3.

70. *Testament* 9-10.

71. Bultmann had similarly missed the point in his insistence that 'his incarnation is only a *means* to the revelation which he brings and not the revelation *itself*' (*John* 65).

72. See above §41.4. Contrast Käsemann, who notably, and surprisingly, claims that 'apart from a few remarks that point ahead to it, the passion comes into view in John only at the very end' (*Testament* 7).

the both-and of death-and-resurrection. In emphasizing the immediacy and completeness of the conjunction in John 1.14, John subverted all attempts to pull him into the Gnostic camp.[73] Irenaeus and Clement of Alexandria were right to claim that the Gnostics abused John's Gospel and to ensure that it remained as a fundamental expression of Christian belief.

At the same time, Käsemann was right to emphasize that John did sail close to the wind, and to draw the corollary that the church's recognition of John's canonical authority amounted to a recognition that proclamation of the gospel has to be inventive and creative, at times dangerously so, if it is to speak effectively to generations with changing presuppositions and world-views. The success of Irenaeus, then, in ensuring that Valentinian Gnostics would be unsuccessful in their attempt to claim John and the Johannine prologue as their own, was something of a mixed blessing since John's Gospel includes within the NT canon a degree of adaptation and inventiveness in the proclamation of Jesus which those who prefer simply to retell the old gospel story without much variation will typically find unnerving.

There is a final irony which should not escape notice — that it was John's christology which made its most lasting effect on Christian theology, whereas its ecclesiology was quickly passed over and survived or revived only on the fringes[74] of a Christianity dominated by monarchical episcopacy and a strict doctrine of apostolic succession.

49.4 1-3 John

We can assume that the three Johannine letters come from the same stable or school at about the same period as John's Gospel (§39.3g). Perhaps the most important clue to the relationship of these Johannine documents to each other is the lack of any reference to 'the Jews' in the three letters. 'The Jews' formed a crucial interactive feature in the construction of the Gospel, and probably reflects the rupturing of the continuity which went back to the context of Jesus' mission within Second Temple Judaism (§46.5c). Given the contrast with 1-3 John, from which 'the Jews' are completely missing, it makes best sense to infer that the three letters were written after the rupture with the (local?) synagogue, reflected in John 9.22, when the Johannine communities were trying to find their own feet, in independence for the most part from their

---

73. See also Thompson, *The Humanity of Jesus in the Fourth Gospel* ch. 2 ('Incarnation and Flesh').

74. See e.g. below §49.8.

Jewish matrix.[75] The degree to which 'love your neighbour' has been focused on 'love your brothers' (§43.1e) suggests a group perspective all too conscious of its need to hold together in the face of a generally hostile world.[76] The degree of reassurance previously given by the sense of belonging to the synagogue community was no longer theirs. Their reassurance came now solely from their common commitment to Christ and to one another (1 John 1.3-7).

a. 1 John

It is here that 1 John 2.19 becomes a vital clue to the new situation which had developed, we may assume, since the rupture with the synagogue. The writing (it is not really a letter) builds up to this verse. It begins by reassuring the readers of the grounds for their assurance — the blood of Christ ensuring forgiveness, cleansing and atonement (1.7–2.2). It hints that there are those who claim to know Christ but who do not obey his commandments (2.3-6), who claim to be in the light while hating their brothers (2.7-11), who love the world and the things of the world (2.15-17). Then comes the outspoken denunciation (2.18-21):

> Children, it is the last hour! As you have heard that antichrist is coming, so now many antichrists have come. From this we know that it is the last hour. They went out from us, but they did not belong to us; for if they had belonged to us, they would have remained with us. But by going out they made it plain that none of them belongs to us. But you have been anointed by the Holy One, and all of you have knowledge. I write to you, not because you do not know the truth, but because you know it, and you know that no lie comes from the truth.

It is clear what had happened. There had been a schism within the community, the group of believers in Jesus Christ. It is not just that one or two had left the fellowship, but the group itself had split. The words of 1 John are addressed to those who had remained true to the original message[77] which first bound the group together — the original (Johannine) gospel, 'the word of life'

---

75. As in Brown, *Community* 94-97; *contra* Schnelle (see n.33 above).
76. See above §43 at n.229; and nn.24 and 65 above.
77. A notable feature of 1 John is its repetition of the phrase *ap' archēs*, 'from the beginning': 'what was from the beginning' (1.1); 'the commandment which you had from the beginning' (2.7); 'you have known him from the beginning' (2.13-14); 'what you have heard from the beginning' (2.24; 3.11).

(1.1-3), the 'truth'[78] which they received and believed.[79] The complaint is that the outgoing group had not remained true to that original message. The implied charge that the outgoing group were liars and were walking in darkness (2.4, 11) is simply the writer's way of characterizing those who disagreed with him — no doubt primarily because they (forcefully) disagreed with him, with his understanding of the message 'from the beginning', which disagreement therefore constituted them as liars and walking in darkness.[80]

What the disagreement amounts to is also fairly clear. The 'liar' 'denies that Jesus is the Christ' (2.22). The spirit of the antichrist (2.18) does not confess Jesus, that is, that 'Jesus Christ has come in the flesh' (4.2-3). The faithful group confess that Jesus is the Son of God (4.15; 5.5); they believe 'the testimony that God has given concerning his Son' (5.10). What is notable here is the degree to which the writer in effect cleaves to the message delivered in the Gospel: that Jesus is the Christ, the Son of God (John 20.31), so attested by God as recorded in the Gospel. This includes the key assertion, that the Word became flesh (1.14), that it is by eating Christ's flesh that they receive eternal life and abide in him and he in them (6.54-58). It is precisely thus that the faithful group in 1 John could be reassured that they abide in Christ[81] — because they continued to believe that Jesus Christ came in the flesh, the message they had heard from the beginning (1 John 2.24).

Evidently what the writer warns against is some new or alternative teaching, which has an appealing sophistication, but which the writer denies emphatically. Those who have been anointed (with the Spirit) already know the truth (2.20, 27). The Spirit which they have received is the Spirit of truth promised in the Gospel which would confirm what they have heard 'from the beginning' (John 15.26-27) and lead them into all the truth (16.13-15); this is the Spirit whose reassurance (1 John 3.24; 4.13) is bound up with the confession that Jesus Christ came in the flesh (4.1-3, 6).[82]

To speak of it as a new teaching is probably misleading. Most likely those attacked in 1 John had derived their teaching from John's Gospel, that is, the Gospel tradition which was the common basis of the Johannine community.[83]

---

78. Another key term: *alētheia*, 'truth' — 1 John 1.6, 8; 2.4, 21; 3.18-19; 4.6; 5.6; *pseustēs*, 'liar' — 1.10; 2.4, 22; 4.20; 5.10; *pseudos*, 'lie' — 2.21, 27.

79. 'Believe' — 1 John 3.23; 4.16; 5.1, 5, 10, 13.

80. Similarly the implied accusation of not doing right (3.10), of not loving = hating = murdering (3.11-15, 23), and of not loving the brothers (4.20-21).

81. 1 John 2.6, 24, 27, 28; 3.17, 24; 4.13, 15, 16.

82. Von Wahlde maintains that different views of the Spirit outpoured on believers, and its significance, was a major factor in the crisis which divided the Johannine community (*Gospel and Letters* 345-54).

83. Brown, *Community* 103-9.

We may infer, then, that those denounced in 1 John were reacting against the straightforward interpretation of John 1.14, which was precisely the meaning that John had intended to convey: that the Word *became flesh*; to believe that Jesus is the Christ, the Son of God, is to believe precisely that,[84] and thus by eating the flesh of the Son of Man,[85] to have life (20.31). What precisely the reaction to John 1.14 was is not so clear, though quite possibly an appeal to John 6.63 ('It is the Spirit that gives life; the flesh is of no value/useless') was interpreted as making impossible a straightforward reading of 1.14.[86] Was it, then, an unwillingness on the part of Jews to believe that the Word could become flesh, that Jesus was the Word become flesh?[87] Was it an early Gnostic view that the divine could not *become* human — that Christ 'suffered only in appearance',[88] or that the Christ was distinct from Jesus and did not die on the cross?[89] Or was it, as Käsemann had in effect anticipated, or rather echoed, that the secessionists claimed the real emphasis of John 1.14 to be on the glory evident in the Word become flesh — the only significance of the flesh being as the locus and means in and by which the glory became manifest? Hence 1 John's response: Jesus Christ came not only with water (docetists could read

---

84. As Tertullian clearly saw: 'Surely he is antichrist who denies that Christ has come in the flesh. By declaring that his flesh is simply and absolutely true, and taken in the plain sense of its own nature, the scripture aims a blow at all who make distinctions in it' (*Carn. Chr.* 24).

85. See above §43 at n.178.

86. von Wahlde, *Gospel and Letters* 3.142.

87. D. R. Street, *"They Went Out from Us": The Identity of the Opponents in First John* (BZNW 177; Berlin: de Gruyter, 2011), sees the vital clue in 2.22: the opponents denied that 'Jesus is the Christ'; they were apostate Jews who rejected the fundamental claim of the early Christian movement, that Jesus is the Messiah. But his attempt to argue that the reference to 'Christ come in the flesh (4.2)' is non-polemical (204-18) ignores the negative implications in John's references to 'flesh' (as in John 3.6 and 6.63). 'As already in 2.16 the word *sarx* has been used in a negative sense. . . . The false teachers deny the fleshly existence of Jesus' (G. Strecker, *Die Johannesbriefe* [KEK 14; Göttingen: Vandenhoeck, 1989] 211-12; and further 131-39).

88. Ignatius, *Smyrn.* 2.1; 4.2; 5.2; 7.1. It is significant that Polycarp, also from (bishop of) Smyrna, explicitly quotes 1 John 4.2-3 (*Phil.* 7.1), strongly suggesting that he was also contesting a docetic view of Christ and probably assumed that 1 John had been too. On the variant reading of 1 John 4.3 ('every spirit that looses/separates Jesus') see the debate between Brown, *Epistles* 494-96, and Ehrman, *Orthodox Corruption* 125-35.

89. Or could we envisage an early Valentinian-type attempt (as above) to avoid the crudeness of the Word becoming *flesh* by attempting to blunt John's sharpness within a confusion of aeons? *Pace* Street, the fact that the diversity of Gnostic views could include thought of the Logos as come or clothed in flesh (as in *exc. Theod.* 1.1; *Gosp. Philip* 72c) (*They Went Out* 198-202) should not detract from the fact that there were docetic views which Ignatius and others sought to refute.

Jesus' anointing by the Spirit at the Jordan as the Christ coming upon the man Jesus) but with water and blood (John 19.34); he really died (1 John 5.6).[90]

Whatever the actual reason for the split in the Johannine communities, it appears to be christological in character and to have arisen from a reaction among some believers in Christ to John's attempt to re-envision the earliest Christian claims about Christ in such bold and outspoken terms — the Logos-God become man, as crucial to human salvation.[91] And if the dispute and split foreshadows the later Valentinian attempts to claim John for themselves, 1 John can be regarded as already refuting the viability and legitimacy of such a reading of the message heard 'from the beginning'. Irenaeus recognized this in his drawing on 1 and 2 John to refute any attempt to regard Jesus and Christ as distinct from each other (*adv. haer.* 3.16.8). Any attempt to use John 16.13-15 to advance a 'truth' which ran counter to the original word as in John's Gospel itself was cut off before it could gain traction. 1 John 4.1-2 had already made it clear that only the Spirit which confessed that Jesus Christ has come in the flesh is of God (3.16.8). In which case the role of 1 John as a corollary to the Gospel may well have been hugely significant, in that it invalidated any attempt to read John 1.14 in a sense other than that so clearly intended by John.[92]

The character of the community which probably emerged from the confrontation with 'the Jews' of John's Gospel is also intriguing. We noted John's 'individualism' in §43.1e(ii), and 1 John strengthens the impression that ecclesiastically the Johannine communities had something of a conventicle character. The stress is on the directness and immediacy of relation with God and Christ, that they are 'born of God',[93] 'know God'[94] and 'abide' in him.[95] The nearest we come to a description of the Johannine church(es) is in terms of their 'fellowship' (*koinōnia*) with one another, as with the Father and the Son (1 John 1.3, 6, 7). 'Brother' is the regular reference to other believers.[96] The writer addresses

---

90. Brown, *Community* 109-23, though he stresses that his reconstruction of the secessionists' thought does not fit exactly either docetist or Cerinthian thought (105); further *Epistles* 47-86; disputed by Street, *They Went Out* 284-94. See also Ehrman, *Orthodox Corruption* 182-83.

91. The only clear indications of the secessionists' views are in reference to christology. The other disputes suggested by Brown — ethics, eschatology, pneumatology (*Community* 123-44) — may only be rhetoric: to hold alternative views of the Gospel's gospel in itself laid the secessionists open to such other charges.

92. 'The ultimate contribution of the author of 1 John to Johannine history may have been that of saving the Fourth Gospel for the church' (Brown, *Community* 150).

93. 1 John 2.29; 3.9; 4.7; 5.1, 4, 18; also 3.19-22.

94. 1 John 2.3-5, 14; 3.6, 24; 4.6-8, 13; 5.20; also 2.23 and 5.12.

95. 1 John 2.6, 24, 27, 28; 3.6, 9, 24; 4.12, 13, 15-16.

96. 1 John 2.9-11; 3.10, 12-17; 4.20-21; 5.16.

his readers/audience as 'My little children'[97] and 'Beloved'[98] (2.7), though his relation to them is unclear — apostle, or exhorter? Otherwise there is no hint of an ecclesiastical hierarchy; the difference from Ignatius, repeatedly reinforcing the authority of the bishop, is striking.[99] The writer can even say that they have all the knowledge they need, from the Spirit's anointing, and need no other teacher (2.20, 27). The contrast, of course, is with the false teaching which the writer contests, but it is nevertheless notable that he is quite content that they draw their assurance from their experience of the Spirit.[100] Prophets as such are never mentioned as important ministries in the church, the only reference being a warning against 'false prophets' (4.1-3); in contrast the writer urges that it is the original message ('from the beginning') which is their security.[101]

In short, the lines of continuity with John's Gospel are obvious (notably in the emphasis on Father and Son, on mutual abiding, and on the Spirit). The developed portrayal of Jesus in John's Gospel is strongly affirmed; this is the word 'from the beginning', and includes the older image of Christ's death as an atoning sacrifice (*hilasmos* — 2.2). But a retreat from the assertion that Jesus was the Word become flesh, that Jesus Christ came in the flesh, is ruled out of order. The resulting community affirmed that God loves the world (2.2; 4.9, 14), but was entirely wary of the world,[102] and probably was predominantly introverted as they wrestled with their own internal schism. The links to John are clear, but very little of links to other forms of Christianity which were emerging at the same period. In the contested identity of the second century 1 John is something of a loner in its ecclesiology but confirmative of the christology and theology brought to expression by John's Gospel.

b. 2 John

2 John adds little to 1 John, though it has much more the character of a letter. Even if we can identify the author as 'the elder' (John the elder?), that takes

---

97. 'Little children' (*teknia*) — 1 John 2.1, (12), 28; 3.7, 18; 4.4; 5.21; 'children' (*paidia*) — 2.(13), 18; 'children (*tekna*) of God' — 3.1, 2, 10; 5.2, (19).

98. *Agapētos* — 1 John 2.7; 3.2, 21; 4.1, 7, 11.

99. Barrett insightfully observes that for Ignatius it is the ministry of the church that guarantees the carnal reality of Jesus (*Magn.* 6.1; *Trall.* 3.1; *Philad.* 7; etc.) (*John* 64).

100. 1 John 3.24; 4.13; 5.6.

101. Intriguingly the original message 'from the beginning' presumably includes the Johannine reshaping of the Gospel of Jesus which John no doubt attributed to the Spirit (John 14.26; 16.12-13) (see §43 n.101 above). The Johannine community could claim without embarrassment that John's Gospel was the original message.

102. 1 John 2.15-17; 3.1, 13; 4.3-5; 5.4-5, 19.

us no further forward.¹⁰³ The address to 'the elect lady and her children' (2 John 1, 4-5), and from 'the children of your elect sister' (13), is more of a puzzle than a help.¹⁰⁴ But the emphasis on 'truth' (1-4), on 'love' as measured by keeping the commandments (3, 6), and on remaining loyal to the message 'from the beginning' (5-6) marks 2 John out as belonging to the same camp as 1 John. The false teaching opposed is again that of the antichrist who denies that 'Jesus Christ comes in the flesh' (7).¹⁰⁵ 'All who (thus) go beyond and do not abide in the teaching of Christ, do not have God' (9). Their false teaching constitutes 'evil deeds', and any who come with this teaching is to be refused welcome and hospitality (10-11). Here speaks a defensive apologetic which is hardly confident of its ability to out-argue opposing or alternative views.

c. 3 John

3 John is more interesting. It is closer to the Pauline letters than any other of the NT epistles, insofar as the author writes to a particular person (3 John 1 — Gaius), begins with a more regular expression of prayer for the addressee (2) and of pleasure at the good news of their continuing to 'walk in truth' (3-4), closes with hopes to see Gaius soon (14) and is concerned about a turn of events in the church of Gaius (9-10). The implication is of some factional disagreement or conflict in that church. The Elder has previously written to the church, but his letter has been ignored (9). So he is writing to Gaius to encourage him to welcome and support brothers who have come to Gaius's church on mission 'for the sake of the name' (5-8).¹⁰⁶ The implication that these (Asia province?) churches were not isolated from one another, and that a significant number of believers undertook the practice (and responsibility) of maintaining links between them (cf. *Did.* 11-12), should not be ignored. We may suppose that these 'brothers' belonged to the Elder's faction.¹⁰⁷ Demetrius (12) belonged to the same faction, and was perhaps the leading figure

---

103. The title 'elder' could suggest a more traditional ecclesiology (Acts 14.23; 20.17, 28-30; 1 Tim. 3.1-7; 5.17-22; Tit. 1.5-11; Jas. 5.14; 1 Pet. 5.1; *1 Clem.* 44.5; 47.6; 54.2; 57.1), but it is more likely that the usage is more like that of Papias, indicating someone next in authority to the apostles and eyewitnesses. See further Klauck, *Der zweite und dritte Johannesbriefe* 29-33; and §39.3g above.

104. Discussion in Lieu, *Epistles* 65-67; Klauck, *zweite Johannesbrief* 33-37.

105. For the echo of 1 John 4.2, but here using the present tense ('comes'), see Lieu, *Epistles* 84-87.

106. That these missioners have 'taken nothing from Gentiles/unbelievers (*ethnikoi*)' (7) suggests a continuing link with Jewish believers in Jesus.

107. 'Brothers' — 3 John 3, 5, 10; 'friends' — 14.

among the missioning brothers. '[Favourable] testimony has been borne to him by everyone, and by the truth itself; and we bear testimony, and you know that our testimony is true' (12); the striking echo of John 21.24 would support the view that the Elder was also responsible for John 21 and that he saw the 'truth' which he advocated as wholly in line with that of John's Gospel.

The problem for the Elder, and for his faction, was that Diotrephes, who 'likes to be first/leader', had assumed a leading role in Gaius's church. He 'does not receive us', perhaps in the sense of refusing to acknowledge our authority (9),[108] and 'makes malicious or disparaging statements about us' (10). Not satisfied with mere words, he does not receive the brothers,[109] prevents those who want to do so, and expels them from the church (10).

Who then was Diotrephes and what was the cause of the serious rift? The most obvious inference is that the Elder is the champion of the Johannine understanding of the gospel. There is no use of the 'from the beginning' formula of 1 and 2 John. But appeal to 'truth' (*alētheia*) is as strong a theme in 3 John as in 1 and 2 John,[110] and the most natural assumption is that it is the 'truth' as perceived and maintained by and within the Johannine tradition. However, the rift in this case does not appear to be over theology or christology, as implied in 1 and 2 John. In 3 John the problem appears to be more a personality clash, a power play between Diotrephes and the Elder.[111] The most intriguing suggestion in this case is that Diotrephes was moving down the line of ecclesiastical development most clearly represented by Ignatius — that is, that Diotrephes was trying to exert the authority which Ignatius wanted to attribute to the local bishop.[112] Given the individualism of John and the likelihood that the Johannine assemblies saw themselves as what later became known as 'conventicles', groups of believers coming together for worship and fellowship without ecclesiastical officials, it is quite possible that 3 John was the first protest against the monarchical episcopacy which became the norm for the subsequent ecclesiology of the great church.[113] Certainly the com-

---

108. Brown, *Epistles* 718.

109. Ironically, Diotrephes was following the church discipline counseled in 2 John 10.

110. 3 John 1, 3, 4, 8, 12.

111. The history of interpretation is briefly reviewed by Klauck, *dritte Johannesbrief* 106-9.

112. Käsemann, 'Ketzer und Zeuge: zum johanneischen Verfasserproblem', provocatively argued that Diotrephes was the 'orthodox' leader of the community addressed, acting as a monarchical bishop, and defending his community against the 'Christian Gnostic' Elder!

113. An earlier expression of this theory would put it in terms of a pietistic and anti-institutional reaction to 'early catholicism' (Dunn, *Unity and Diversity* 392). Cf. Lieu, *Epistles* 154-64.

plaints against Diotrephes are a disturbing foretaste of the charges of arrogance and abuse of power which litter the later history of Christian leadership.

If there is anything in this it is something of a wonder that 3 John only just squeezed into the NT canon.[114] Perhaps Diotrephes was a rogue example of the trend so commended by Ignatius, so that such influence as he had did not avail to prevent 3 John being preserved. More likely the influence of the Elder, as representing the strong stream of Johannine tradition recognized by Papias and others, was strong enough to ensure that it was retained within the Johannine corpus. In any case, it is an important reminder of the factional diversity in emerging Christianity, and of ecclesiastical as well as christological tensions pulling the heirs of the first-generation leadership in divergent directions. If we can infer that the Johannine christology fed into the broader stream of the great church, we can probably also infer that the heirs of its conventicle form of Christianity gradually became reconciled to an increasingly dominant episcopal form of Christianity.[115]

49.5 The Apocalypse of John

The unresolved/unresolvable question whether John the seer, whose visions make up the book of Revelation, has anything to do with John the brother of James, the apostle John, or the elder John (§39.3h), should not exclude Revelation from a consideration of the influence of John into the second century. For the confusion relating to the question may simply indicate that 'Johannine influence' had a rather amorphous character, though, apparently, all stemming from Asia province or Ephesus in particular. And whoever John the seer actually was, the influence of the Apocalypse of John in shaping the chiliasm of Papias and others in the second century is well known (§40.7) — providing a fascination which the Johannine Gospel's expression of realized eschatology could never quite match, despite the latter's providing a more secure foundation for an enduring Christian eschatology. The fact that Revelation was eventually accepted into the NT canon, despite the problems which its interpretation caused in the earliest Christian centuries — and still

---

114. Lieu, *Epistles* ch. 1 (see also §39 n.299 above); briefly Culpepper, *John* 92-93.

115. Brown, *Community* 151-62; in *Epistles* 106-8, Brown suggests that the Elder was 'a Johannine purist' and that 'figures like Diotrephes may have been more perceptive about the only practical way in which the substance of the Johannine tradition could be preserved against secessionist trends. If such a theory is correct, it was not the Presbyter-author of the Epistles but an emerging Johannine church leader like Diotrephes who was responsible for leading the Johannine remnant into the Great Church' (also 738-39). Klauck agrees (*dritte Johannesbrief* 109-10). See also §44.8d above.

today!¹¹⁶ — is a reminder of how important a cosmic spiritual dimension was for the different forms of earliest Christianity, and of how dangerously volatile was (and is) the apocalyptic genre.¹¹⁷

a. The Christology of Revelation

It was the re-envisioning of Christ which demanded first attention as the principal feature of the Johannine Gospel and Epistles and as the most enduring Johannine influence on developing Christian theology. So we naturally turn initially to focus on the christology of the Johannine apocalypse.

Much of the christology is what might be expected, though in its own distinctive terms: the writing is introduced as 'the revelation (*apokalypsis*) of Jesus Christ' (Rev. 1.1); the seer 'attested the word of God and the testimony of Jesus Christ' (1.2); the introductory blessing is 'from him who is and who was and who is to come, and from the seven spirits¹¹⁸ who are before his throne, and from Jesus Christ, the faithful witness, the firstborn of the dead, and the ruler of the kings of the earth' (1.4-5). The thought of Christ as exalted to heaven, ruling with God (Ps. 110.1) and sitting in judgment is taken for granted;¹¹⁹ as also his soon coming again (22.7, 12, 20).

The dominant reference to the exalted Christ is as 'the Lamb'.¹²⁰ It is entirely significant that the initial appearance is of the Lamb 'as slaughtered' (5.6), and that the worship is offered to 'the Lamb that was slaughtered' (5.12); the Lamb is primarily the sacrificial lamb.¹²¹ In this way John the seer retains the emphasis both in Paul's and in the NT Gospels' christologies: however much Christ is associated with God in his cosmic reign, the primary focus in the christology remained on the fact that Christ had died.¹²² The cosmic sig-

---

116. I need only refer to Hal Lindsey's *The Late Great Planet Earth* (Grand Rapids: Zondervan, 1970), and Tim LaHaye's *Left Behind* series of novels (Wheaton: Tyndale House, 1995-2007).

117. See also H. H. Rowley, *The Relevance of Apocalyptic* (London: Lutterworth, 1944, ³1963).

118. On 'the seven spirits' see Aune, *Revelation* 1.33-35.

119. Rev. 11.15; 12.10; 20.4, 6; see also 1.18; 3.21; 6.16; 17.14; 19.11-13. Interestingly, Christ is referred to simply as 'Jesus' more often in Revelation than in the other non-Gospel writings of the NT — 9 times, 6 of them as 'the testimony of Jesus' (1.9; 12.17; 17.6; 19.10(2); 20.4; note also 14.12 — 'the faith of Jesus'); but 'apart from his death he [the seer] has little interest in the historical Jesus' (Satake, *Offenbarung* 81).

120. *Arnion* ('lamb') appears 29 times in Revelation, and only once elsewhere (John 21.15 — referring to Jesus' disciples as 'lambs').

121. For background see Aune, *Revelation* 1.367-73; Satake, *Offenbarung* 208-10.

122. Although the word for 'lamb' is different from that used in John 1.29 (*amnos*),

nificance which is attributed to the exalted Christ, perhaps not unexpectedly in an apocalypse, is not expressed by speaking of Christ's or the Logos's pre-existence, but by depicting the (slaughtered) Lamb as the one who unveils and determines the future (5.1–6.1ff.).[123]

The most striking feature of Revelation's christology, however, is the way in which John the seer pushes out the bounds of the earlier christologies — as striking in its degree of innovation as the christology of the Johannine Gospel and Epistles, but notably different, and by its use of apocalyptic symbolism more difficult on which to gain a clear handle.[124]

What immediately catches the eye is the seer's initial vision of the exalted Jesus — Rev. 1.12-16:

> Then I turned to see the voice that was speaking to me, and on turning I saw seven golden lampstands, and in the midst of the lampstands *one like the son of man, clothed with* a long robe and with a *golden girdle* round his breast; *his head and his hair were white as white wool, white as snow; his eyes were like a flame of fire*, his feet were *like burnished bronze*, refined as in a furnace, and *his voice was like the sound of many waters*; in his right hand he held seven stars, from his mouth came a sharp two-edged sword, and his face was like the sun shining in full strength.

Anyone familiar with Jewish apocalyptic writing would recognize that the elements in John's vision were drawn directly from the similar visions of Ezekiel and Daniel.[125] What is so striking is that the seer draws on both glimpses of God himself and on visions of glorious angels. Noticeably, perhaps shockingly, Jesus is described in terms used in Dan. 7.9, 13 not only for the son of man, but also for the Ancient of Days.[126] We are here in the apocalyptic tradition of a glorious angelic figure, where similar or the same descriptive features are prominent.[127] The most interesting feature of this tradition is

---

the image is similarly of atoning sacrifice, as Rev. 7.14 confirms: the saints 'have washed their robes . . . in the blood of the Lamb', the imagery of cleansing blood drawn from Israel's sacrificial cult (cf. e.g. Lev. 14.52; Heb. 9.14, 22; and, noticeably, 1 John 1.7) (Aune, *Revelation* 2.475).

123. Satake, *Offenbarung* 79-87; 'in the presentation of the pre-existent one he shows no interest' (80); 'the Christ event as the turning point of history' (82).

124. In what follows I draw on my *Partings* §11.4.

125. I refer to the passages from Ezekiel and Daniel already cited in full in §45.4c(iii) above.

126. 'The author has virtually equated the two figures' (Aune, *Revelation* 1.116). A degree of identification may have been anticipated in some versions of Dan. 7.13 LXX ('he came like a son of man, and like the Ancient of Days'); see further Aune 1.90-92.

127. E.g. *Apoc. Zeph.* 6.11-15; *Apoc. Ab.* 11.1-4; *Joseph and Asenath* 14.9.

that the angelic figure could so readily be mistaken for or confused with God.[128] In *Apoc. Ab.* 10.3, for example, the angel is identified as Yahoel, probably a combination of Yahweh and El, and most obviously an allusion to Israel's guardian angel in Exod. 23.20-21, in whom was God's name. This interpretation of the glorious angel of apocalyptic vision may have grown out of the older tradition of 'the angel of the Lord', an angelic messenger easily confused with God.[129] What was noticeable in the tradition, however, is the fact that the apocalyptists took some care to ensure that the visionary did *not* confuse the glorious angel with God by firmly refusing worship[130] or by joining in worship with the visionary (*Apoc. Ab.* 17.2). Similarly, in *Asc. Isa.* 8.4-5, the glorious angel refuses to be addressed as 'my lord'; 'I am not your lord, but your companion'.[131]

It is precisely at this point that John the seer broke step with his fellow apocalyptists. He followed them in making the point clearly that the angel who interprets his visions should not be worshipped: 'You must not do that! I am a fellow servant with you. . . . Worship God!' (Rev. 19.10; 22.8-9). But *Jesus* is more clearly worshipped in Revelation than anywhere else in the NT. The hymns in chapter 5, to the Lamb, are no different in character from the hymns in chapter 4, to God; note also the opening doxology 'to him who loves us and freed/washed us from our sins by his blood' (1.5-6).[132] In such passages as 5.13 and 7.10 the Lamb is linked with God in a common ascription of adoration. In other words, the inhibitions about worshipping a glorious interpreting angel, which John the seer shared with his fellow apocalyptists, he abandoned in the case of the exalted Christ, the Lamb of God.

This clearly implies that the seer's running together of the descriptions

---

128. See also §45 n.136 above.

129. Following the appearance of the angel of the Lord to Hagar and Ishmael (Gen. 16.7-12), Hagar asks, 'Have I really seen God and remained alive after seeing him?' (16.13). In Gen. 21.17-18 the angel speaks in the first person as God. In Gen. 31.11-13 the angel says, 'I am the God of Bethel'. And in Exod. 3.2-14 the angel speaking from the burning bush says, 'I am who I am'.

130. *Apoc. Zeph.* 6.15; *Asc. Isa.* 7.21; see also Tob. 12.16-20.

131. See further R. Bauckham, 'The Worship of Jesus', *Climax of Prophecy* 118-49; L. T. Stuckenbruck, *Angel Veneration and Christology* (WUNT 2.70; Tübingen: Mohr Siebeck, 1995).

132. See further, and for the following review of Revelation's christology, O. Hofius, 'Das Zeugnis der Johannesoffenbarung von der Gottheit Jesu Christi', in H. Lichtenberger, ed., *Frühes Christentum* (M. Hengel FS vol. III; Tübingen: Mohr Siebeck, 1996) 511-28; also Satake, *Offenbarung* 87-91. Here Hofius notes that 'Doxologies are valid originally only for *God*. When doxologies are referred also to Christ, that can generally happen only under the presupposition that he is worthy of the same praise as God himself' (512-13); also quoted by Satake (89 n.124).

in Ezekiel and Daniel, both of God as seen in vision and of glorious angels, was no accident. His intention was precisely to say that the exalted Jesus was *not* merely a glorious angel or to be confused with one. The glorious angel was not to be worshipped. But the exalted Christ was! This is of a piece with the fact, again no doubt deliberate on John's part, that both God and the exalted Christ say, 'I am the Alpha and Omega'.[133] John has no hesitation in referring to the exalted Christ as 'the holy one'[134] and 'king of kings and lord of lords' (17.14; 19.16).[135] And some of the descriptions of the exalted Christ's relation to the throne in the seer's vision seem to imply that the Lamb was sitting on *God's* throne (3.21; 7.17); it is 'the throne of God and of the Lamb' (22.1, 3). This should probably be seen as one of John's ways of acknowledging the fullest significance and status of Christ in relation to God without abandoning his more traditional monotheism within an apocalyptic tradition familiar with the angelic agents of God which embodied the person, majesty and authority of God.[136]

In any case, we have to recognize that in the Apocalypse of John the inhibition which presumably held back the earlier Christian writers, including Paul, from speaking of the exalted Christ as 'God', and from speaking uninhibitedly of the worship of Jesus, has been broken through. The other John(s) made a similar breakthrough,[137] though in different terms, and together they presumably represent a development in Christian self-confidence in asserting the significance of Jesus at the end of the first century, an assertion which Ignatius already took for granted and regularly expressed in more uninhibited terms.[138] Whether we can describe this as a Johannine influence on Christian thought or as two quite different strands, it is nonetheless significant that both the Johannine Logos/creation theology and the Johannine apocalyptic theology came together in such uninhibited affirmation of a theos-christology.

133. Rev. 1.8; 21.6; 22.13.
134. Rev. 3.7; cf. 6.10. '"The holy one" is used frequently of God in the LXX, often in the expression "the Holy One of Israel", which occurs twenty-nine times in Isaiah alone' (Aune, *Revelation* 2.407). The seer uses it of God in Rev. 15.4 and 16.5.
135. As a title for God see particularly Dan. 4.37, and further Aune, *Revelation* 3.953-54.
136. Stuckenbruck concludes: 'The exalted status of Christ as an object of worship alongside God was not intended as a breach of monotheism. While the Apocalypse of John may have been read by "outsiders" as a writing with a ditheistic theology, linguistic and thematic considerations suggest that the author took deliberate measures to impede such an idea' (*Angel Veneration* 272).
137. John 1.1, 18; 20.28; 1 John 5.20. On 1 John 5.20 see R. E. Brown, *Jesus God and Man* (London: Chapman, 1968) 18-19; also *Epistles* 625-26.
138. See above §40 n.25.

b. The Churches of Revelation

Probably the other most important feature of Revelation for us is the indication that John the seer was able to write with revelatory authority to the seven churches of Asia (Rev. 2-3). Equally valuable is the fact that the letters give a snapshot, from a particular perspective, of the seven churches, and therefore also of the character of the Christianity which had become established or flourished within Asia. Notably the churches seem all to be different, though confronted with different circumstances and challenges.

Perhaps the most striking is the impression of churches well established, quite likely the plantings of missions from Ephesus as early as Paul.

- The church in Ephesus — the mother church(?) first addressed — has abandoned its 'first love' and is called to repentance and to do its 'first works' (Rev. 2.4-5).
- The church in Sardis has a good reputation, but is in fact 'dead'. It is recalled to what it first received and heard, and repentance too is called for (3.1-3).[139]
- The church in Laodicea seems to be in an even more desperate state, 'neither cold nor hot' and fit only to be spewed out. The principal problem is that it is far too self-satisfied, thinking itself rich and prosperous and needing nothing, but in reality is 'wretched, pitiable, poor, blind and naked' (3.15-17).

Here is a familiar story, to be repeated over and over again in the history of Christianity — churches established with initial enthusiasm and commitment, but all too soon becoming too self-contented, their commitment slackened and the distinctiveness of their initial witness dimmed.

Particularly interesting are the indications of tensions with local synagogues.

- The church in Smyrna is experiencing slander from 'those who say they are Jews and are not but are a synagogue of Satan' (2.9).
- The church in Philadelphia is likewise confronted with 'those of the synagogue of Satan who say that they are Jews and are not, but are lying' (3.9).[140]

---

139. In contrast the 'last works' of the church in Thyatira are greater than the 'first', and the church in Philadelphia has 'kept the word' initially given them by Christ (3.8, 10).

140. See §46 n.171 above. It is unclear how the other references to Satan — Satan's throne in Pergamum (2.13), and 'the deep things of Satan' (2.24) — correlate with the 'synagogue of Satan' references in 2.9 and 3.9. It is probably typical of John the seer that

The tension in both cases reflects the fierce dismissal of 'the Jews', as children of the devil (John 8.44),[141] but the denial of the title 'Jew' to the local synagogue community presumably reflects more of a Pauline concern to retain 'Jew' as a spiritual and non-ethnic term,[142] or at least a claim that the local Jews had fallen short of their ideal and commission, as understood by Gentile believers more influenced by Paul.[143]

More serious were evidently the dangers threatening the churches from within — teachings and practices which had been embraced.

- For all that it had abandoned its first love, the church in Ephesus hated 'the works of the Nicolaitans' which Jesus (and John) also hated (2.6).
- Some of those in the church in Pergamum held to 'the teaching of Balaam', eating food sacrificed to idols and practising sexual license, which are equated with 'the teaching of the Nicolaitans' (2.14-15).
- Worse still, the church in Thyatira was 'tolerating the woman Jezebel, who calls herself a prophet and teaches and deceives my slaves to practise sexual license and to eat food sacrificed to idols' (2.20).

Here we are back in the sort of problems which Paul had to address in 1 Cor. 5-10,[144] except that the seer seems to have been more unyieldingly strict than Paul in the liberty he encouraged (1 Cor. 10.25-30). At the same time it should not escape notice that these concerns were deeply rooted in Jewish priorities and history — to avoid the *porneia*, which was socially acceptable in

---

everything which he saw as opposed to his central message was evidence of Satan's rule (cf. 2.10; 12.9, 12; 20.2, 10). Paul Trebilco points out that some think the reference is to Gentile Christian Judaizers; note particularly M. Murray, *Playing a Jewish Game: Gentile Christian Judaizing in the First and Second Centuries CE* (Waterloo: Wilfrid Laurier University, 2004) 73-74, 99.

141. Characterisation of the Jewish community as 'a synagogue of Satan' provided a precedent for the diatribes against the Jews of Chrysostom and Luther.

142. Rom. 2.28-29; Phil. 3.3.

143. A further aspect may be that since the Jewish revolt the ethnic identity of Jews was no longer recognized in some territories — a Hadrianic inscription refers to them as 'the formerly Jews' (*hoi pote Ioudaioi*) (*CIJ* 742) — so that the Smyrnean Jews had defiantly retained their identity as Jews (Hemer, *Letters* 66-67); but Trebilco (in private correspondence) notes that the inscription is highly debated, with reference to W. Ameling, *Inscriptiones Judaicae Orientis*, vol. II: *Kleinasien* (TSAJ 99; Tübingen: Mohr Siebeck, 2004), No. 40 (177-79). Hemer describes the letter to Smyrna as 'the least Jewish of the seven despite the presence of a considerable Jewish community in the city' (67).

144. Hemer concludes his examination of the Nicolaitans that they were probably 'an antinomian movement whose antecedents can be traced to the misrepresentation of Pauline liberty' (*Letters* 94); cf. Fiorenza, *Book of Revelation* ch. 4; Satake, *Offenbarung* 175-76; and see also Aune, *Revelation* 148-49.

Greek society, and the idolatry which eating idol food unavoidably involved. If the seer was not laying claim to be more Jewish than 'those who say they are Jews and are not', at least he was determined not to be less Jewish in praxis.[145]

Caught up in this concern was also the recognition that false teaching could come from within:

- 'those who claim to be apostles and are not' — the church in Ephesus commended for putting them to the test and finding them to be false (2.2);
- Jezebel called herself a prophet and was tolerated by the church in Thyatira (2.20).[146]

This has obvious parallels with those designated as (false) apostles in 2 Cor. 11.5, 13 and the *Did.* 11.3-6, and with the recognition of the dangers of false prophecy elsewhere.[147] It confirms that the early congregations in the Aegean area had far from clear borders and demarcation lines, almost certainly were open to visiting apostles and prophets of varied background, and had a changing constituency.

So far as ecclesiology is concerned, various hints suggest a churchmanship somewhere between Paul and John. Here too the absence of any idea of hierarchy and office is striking, especially when we compare the not so distant (in time or geography) contemporaries of the Pastorals and Ignatius. All believers are kings and priests (1.6; 5.10; 20.6), all are God's servants (7.3); as in Paul, 'the saints' refer to believers in general.[148] Apostles are mentioned positively (apart from 2.2), but as belonging to the founding era of Christianity (21.14; cf. 18.20). Elders appear in the heavenly throne room,[149] but if they represent human counterparts at all (rather than the OT council of Yahweh) it would be all believers and not just particular office-bearers — twelve probably representing the Israel of God of the old era, and twelve representing Christianity, the new Israel.[150] So too, the 'angels' of the churches in 1.20 and

---

145. See again §46 n.171 above.

146. The reference to Jezebel implies a concern that Lamb-focused faith would be diluted or perverted by syncretistic beliefs and practices (1 Kgs. 16.31).

147. 1 John 4.1-3, *Did.* 11.7-12 and Hermas, *Mand.* 11.

148. Most clearly in the final benediction (Rev. 22.21 — some mss omit 'saints', but it is probably the best reading; see Aune, *Revelation* 3.1239); *hoi hagioi* ('the saints') are referred to 14 times in Revelation.

149. Rev. 4.4, 10; 5.8; 11.16; 19.4; see also 7.4 and 21.12.

150. Beale, *Revelation* 322-26; but Satake points out that nowhere are the 24 understood as two groups of 12, and suggests that 1 Chron. 25.9-31 provides the background (*Offenbarung* 198). Full discussion and documentation in Aune, *Revelation* 1.287-92.

chs. 2-3 should not be taken to represent bishops (overseers) or particular leaders; since the words addressed to each angel clearly apply to each church as a whole, the angels are best taken as heavenly counterparts of the various churches.[151] In any event, there is no mention in Revelation of bishops, deacons, teachers or pastors, and 'priests' and 'elders' are designations for the whole Christian community.

The only distinctive ministries mentioned by the seer are those of *prophet*[152] and *witness* or martyr.[153] These words seem sometimes to denote particular individuals within a church,[154] but in 11.3, 10 it is probably the Christian community as a whole which is symbolized as two witnesses or prophets. It is not clear whether the twin terms 'saints and prophets/martyrs'[155] refer equally to the entire community, or distinguish prophets/martyrs from the rest of the saints (as presumably in 18.20). But certainly there is no suggestion of a prophetic hierarchy, and insofar as all believers are called upon to bear testimony to Jesus, so all experience the Spirit of prophecy.[156] Here we have something of a parallel with the Pauline concept of ministry: in principle every saint a witness and prophet, though some called to exercise that ministry in a fuller way than others. The seer of Revelation is sometimes singled out as claiming a unique authority,[157] but this is simply the authority of prophetic inspiration which any prophet would have believed belongs to his prophecy; and 22.18-19 is little more than a literary convention to ensure faithful transmission of the author's original.[158] John the seer made no effort to distinguish himself from those to whom he wrote either as a witness or as a prophet (1.2, 9; 19.10). In short, so far as ecclesiology, order and worship are concerned, Revelation depicts or assumes churches which lived through and out of prophecy.[159]

---

151. See discussion in Aune, *Revelation* 1.108-12; Beale, *Revelation* 217-19; Satake, *Offenbarung* 147-48.

152. Rev. 2.20; 10.7; 11.10, 18; 16.6; 18.20, 24; 22.6, 9. 'The whole Church is therefore understood in principle, at least in this passage [19.10], as a Church of prophets; so the same thing holds good here for the prophets as for the martyrs. . . . There is no other order. . . . thus in the last resort there is but one ministry to which everyone is bound to be called — the ministry of the witness and the prophet' (Schweizer, *Church Order* 135-36).

153. Rev. 2.13; 11.3; 17.6; cf. 1.2, 9; 6.9; 11.7; 12.11, 17; 19.10; 20.4.

154. Rev. 2.13, 20; 22.9.

155. Rev. 11.18; 16.6; 17.6; 18.24.

156. Rev. 12.11, 17; 19.10; cf. 6.9-11; 20.4.

157. Rev. 1.3; 21.5; 22.6, 18-19.

158. Cf. e.g. Deut. 4.2; *Ep. Arist.* 310-11; *1 Enoch* 104.11; *Did.* 4.13; Eusebius, *HE* 5.20.2 (citing Irenaeus). See also Aune, *Revelation* 3.1229-32; Beale, *Revelation* 1150-54.

159. See further A. Satake, *Die Gemeindeordnung in der Johannesapokalypse* (Neukirchen: Neukirchener, 1966); also *Offenbarung* 101-4.

This is another reason, then, why the Apocalypse of John can be considered alongside the Gospel and Epistles of John. For all three bodies of literature envisage forms of church which were at some odds or tension with the developing hierarchical system which Ignatius in particular pushed hard for and which became the pattern for the great church. As ever in such cases, it should not be taken for granted, by a canonical hermeneutic, or whatever, that these Johannine alternatives, like the early Pauline ecclesiology, are to be simply subsumed into a Pastorals ecclesiology without remainder.

49.6 The *Odes of Solomon*[160]

Any attempt to trace a second-century trajectory of the influence of John would have to include the *Odes of Solomon*, which contain repeated echoes of John's Gospel:

- 3.10 — 'This is the Spirit of the Lord, which is not false, which teaches the sons of men to know his ways'; cf. John 14.26;
- 7.6 — 'Like my nature he became, that I might understand him, and like my form, that I might not turn away from him'; cf. John 1.14;
- 7.12 — 'He has allowed him to appear to them that are his own'; cf. John 1.11;
- 11.7 — 'So I drank and became intoxicated, from the living water that does not die'; cf. John 4.14;
- 12.12 — 'For the dwelling place of the Word is man'; cf. John 1.14;
- 16.19 — 'the worlds are made by his word'; cf. John 1.3;
- 18.6 — 'Let not light be conquered by darkness, nor truth flee from falsehood'; cf. John 1.5;
- 30.1-2 — 'Fill for yourselves water from the living fountain of the Lord . . . And come all you thirsty and take a drink . . .'; cf. John 4.10; 7.37-38;
- 32.2 — 'And the Word from the truth who is self-originate'; cf. John 1.14.[161]

---

160. See above §40.1j and §47.3f.
161. Also *Odes* 41.11-14 —
    'And his Word is with us all our way,
    the Savior who gives life and does not reject ourselves.
    The man who humbled himself . . .
    The Son of the Most High appeared . . .
    and light dawned from the Word
    That was before time in him'.

Moreover, the passages where Christ speaks in first-person terms may also indicate influence of the Johannine 'I am' sayings.[162]

We may indeed have to locate the *Odes* on the same trajectory from John's Gospel through 1-2 John, and not far from these Johannine communities, displaying some of the same attractiveness to Gnostic spirituality as did John's Gospel, but also reflecting the importance of the Johannine prologue for their christology and soteriology, even if not with as explicit insistence on the physicality of the incarnation as the Johannine literature (though see *Odes* 7.4-6 and 19.6-10).

49.7 The Gnostic John

We have already seen how the Valentinian Gnostics interpreted John (§49.3d), and sufficient has been said on the *Gospel of Truth* in §44.6b. But it is worth also noting other examples of how John may have influenced Gnostic thought which have come down to us.[163]

a. The *Apocryphon of John*

The *Apocryphon of John* is a revelation 'of the mysteries, [and the] things hidden in silence' delivered by Jesus Christ to John — identified, as in the NT Gospels, as the brother of James, son of Zebedee — presumably after Jesus' resurrection. Irenaeus makes no mention of it, but it is probably a good representative of the kind of teaching against which he set his face.[164] It is one of the best and clearest expressions of the elaborated Gnostic myth of the decline from the supreme deity, the Invisible Spirit, through a sequence of emanations. The vital break comes, as regularly, when Sophia 'wanted to bring forth a likeness out of herself without the consent of the Spirit — he had not approved — and without her consort' (*NHL* II.9.28-31) — ironically, a parody of virginal conception. What she gives birth to is Yaltabaoth, who asserts 'I am God and there is no other God beside me',[165] and 'I am a jealous God and

---

162. See also Schnackenburg, *John* 1.144-45; Barrett, *John* 112-13; and particularly J. H. Charlesworth and R. A. Culpepper, 'The Odes of Solomon and the Gospel of John', *CBQ* 35 (1973) 298-322; Charlesworth, *Critical Reflections* 232-45.

163. See also §44.8d above.

164. F. Wisse, 'The Apocryphon of John', *NHL* 104-23, regards it as 'certain that the main teachings of the tractate existed before 185 C.E.' (104).

165. *NHL* II.11.20-21; Isa. 45.21-22.

there is no other God beside me';[166] that is, Yaltabaoth is identified with the God of the OT. It is he, the chief archon, who says to his attendant authorities, 'Come, let us create a man according to the image of God and according to our likeness, that his image may become a light for us',[167] and calls his name Adam. The second creation narrative is drawn in too, when Yaltabaoth 'blew into his face the spirit which is the power of his mother ... and the power of the mother went out of Yaltabaoth into the natural body'.[168] At which the rest of the powers, jealous, 'took him and threw him into the lowest region of all matter' (*NHL* II.20.7-9).

More intriguing is the handling of the rest of Gen. 2-3. The helper sent to Adam is 'luminous Epinoia which comes out of him, who is called Life' (II.20.17-19). She was 'taken from the power of the man ... and not, as Moses said, "his rib-bone"' (II.23.1-3). She is responsible for their eating from 'the tree of knowledge of good and evil, which is the Epinoia of the light' (II.22.4-5; II.23.28-29), which awakens them 'out of the depth of sleep' and awakens their thinking (II.23.30-31, 34-35). It is Yaltabaoth who then casts them out of paradise (II.24.7), the chief archon who brings a flood in the days of Noah,[169] and the chief archon who sent his angels to the daughters of men to have offspring with them.[170]

The evidence of reflection on the opening chapters of Genesis, and the degree of concern to maintain the infinite gulf between the Invisible Spirit and created matter, are clear, with the second creation narrative giving scope to explain the divine spark trapped within the natural body, and the tree of knowledge regarded positively as providing the awakening gnosis. But of influence from John's Gospel there is no evidence. The nearest is the first-person description of the perfect Pronoia going 'into the realm of darkness', entering 'the middle of the prison', 'the midst of darkness and the inside of Hades', 'the midst of prison which is the prison of the body'.[171] The hope of salvation is that those who hear will 'get up from the deep sleep' and be 'sealed in the light of the water with five seals' (II.31.5-6, 20-24). But this is hardly Johannine; the Johannine insistence that the Logos-God became flesh is never challenged. And though the message of the tractate is attributed to John (II.32.1-5), that can only be because John, son of Zebedee, was a highly esteemed name within the circles which laid some claim to Christian identity, a teacher of deep reflection whose teachings were proving amenable to Gnostic interpretation.

166. *NHL* II.138-39; Exod. 20.5; Deut. 5.9.
167. *NHL* II.15.1-4; Gen. 1.26.
168. *NHL* II.19.25-32; Gen. 2.7.
169. *NHL* II.28.32-35; Gen. 7.
170. *NHL* II.29.17-20; Gen. 6.1-6.
171. *NHL* II.30.17-19, 25-26; II.31.3-4.

The lack of any evidence of influence from or dependence on John's Gospel, however, is a further confirmation that the gnostic reading of John was at some remove, a critical remove, from John's Gospel itself.

b. The *Trimorphic Protennoia*

The *Trimorphic Protennoia* may provide a good example of how thought developed in the melting pot of second-century Mediterranean religiosity. It appears to have begun as a self-proclamation of the 'three-formed first thought', modeled to some extent on the Jewish Wisdom hymn (as in Sir. 24). This was taken in a Gnostic direction: she awakens those who sleep; she exists in everyone; through her, gnosis comes forth; she is the image of the Invisible Spirit; she is Barbelo; the great Demon is also called Saklas and Yaltabaoth; she is androgynous. At some point the Christ, the Perfect Son, the only-begotten God is introduced into the mix and perhaps in the talk of coming down into the world, the Word, 'a hidden Light, bearing a Fruit of Life, pouring forth a Living Water . . . the glory of the offspring of God' (*NHL* XIII.46.16-21). J. D. Turner suggests that a third stage in the composition history was 'a deliberately polemical incorporation of Christian, specifically Johannine Christian materials' and that this third stage should perhaps be assigned 'to the period of struggle over the interpretation of the Christology of the Fourth Gospel witnessed by the New Testament letters of John, perhaps the first quarter or half of the second century'.[172]

c. The *Acts of John*

The *Acts of John* strengthens the tradition that (latterly) John was centred in Ephesus.[173] It draws also on the memory of his membership of the inner circle round Jesus of Peter, James and John (*ActsJohn* 88-91). Its account of John's death (106-15) suggests that the tradition of John dying a natural death was so firmly anchored that it left no scope to develop a story of a more dramatic death as a martyr.[174] And it records that John, in preparing for his death, prays to God, 'O God, who have chosen us for the apostleship among the Gentiles' (112) — presumably betraying a Gentile mission/church perspective which

---

172. J. D. Turner, 'Trimorphic Protennoia', *NHL* 512-13.
173. See §40.6c above.
174. Klauck, *Apocryphal Acts* 38.

was keen to include one of the most famous of Jesus' disciples as (one of) the Gentile mission's chief proponents.[175]

Most striking is the christology, which represents a wrestling with the problems posed by the traditional gospel of salvation procured through Jesus' suffering, but in a religious milieu where the assertion of such bodiliness seemed to be counter-intuitive. Christ appears in varied polymorphic forms (82, 88-93) — 'his unity which has many faces' (91).[176] He had 'a material and solid body', at other times 'the substance was immaterial and bodiless'. John 'wished to see whether the print of his foot appeared upon the earth . . . but I never saw it' (93). The following hymn wrestles with the paradoxes of the Jesus story and includes reference to 'an Ogdoad' (95). But Christ is also 'the Word sent by the Father' (96) and is above the suffering of the cross (97-98). The real cross 'which has united all things by the Word . . . is not the cross of wood which you will see when you go down here, neither am I he who is upon the cross' (99). The multitude round the cross 'is the lower nature', 'the many . . . who are outside the mystery' and should be ignored and despised (100). 'You hear that I suffered, yet I suffered not; that I suffered not, yet I did suffer' (101).

> Perceive in me the slaying of the Logos, the piercing of the Logos, the blood of the Logos, the wounding of the Logos, the hanging of the Logos, the passion of the Logos, the nailing of the Logos, the death of the Logos. And thus I speak, discarding manhood. Therefore, in the first place think of the Logos, then you shall perceive the Lord, and thirdly the man, and what he has suffered (101).

'The Lord contrived all things symbolically and as a dispensation toward men, for their conversion and salvation' (102). The conclusion is, 'Let us worship him who became man apart from this body' (103). 'You therefore must also be persuaded, beloved, that it is no man that I preach to you to worship, but God unchangeable, God invincible, God higher than all authority, and all power . . .' (104).[177]

This can hardly be described as a straightforwardly Gnostic view,[178] but

---

175. Possibly, too, the account of the collapse of the temple of Artemis (*ActsJohn* 42) is presented as an implied contrast with Paul's effective failure in Acts 19.

176. Klauck tabulates the varied appearances (*Apocryphal Acts* 31-32).

177. In *ActsJohn* 43 John prays to the Lord, 'Glory to you, my Jesus, the only God of truth' (also 82).

178. Contrast Koester: 'the basic Gnostic position of the hymn (87-105) is obvious, although there are no signs of an elaborate Gnostic mythology'; 'the primary purpose of this section . . . is the validation of docetism' (*Introduction* 2.197); Klauck: *ActsJohn* 97-102 has 'a theology that must be judged gnostic' (*Apocryphal Acts* 17); cf. Elliott, *ANT* 306-7.

it displays both the kind of intellectual problems which a passion gospel posed to an intense Platonic world view, and a not unsophisticated attempt to hold together the different sides of the paradox (cf. 29). That such a degree of sophistication was offered in the name of John perhaps attests the respect in which the Gospel of John's portrayal of Christ was held in the second century, the sophistication of John's elaboration of the 'passion narrative with an extended introduction' in Logos and Wisdom terms. Also possible, however, is that the *Acts of John* attests the further development of a more docetic interpretation of John's Gospel which the Johannine epistles contested. Should the proponents of the christology of the *Acts of John* be linked to those who 'went out from us but were not of us' (1 John 2.19)?[179]

49.8 The Montanists

It is appropriate to include Montanism in this study of Johannine influence in the second century, since there is clear testimony that the movement, in its different phases, was influenced by both the Gospel and the Apocalypse of John.[180]

The beginning of the movement can be dated to the third quarter of the second century in Phrygia;[181] hence early reference to the participants as Phrygians or Cataphrygians, 'the so-called Cataphrygian heresy'.[182] Its initial most striking feature was ecstatic prophecy,[183] and the emphasis on prophecy

---

179. Klauck, *Apocryphal Acts* 41.

180. It was the fact that Montanists drew on the Johannine literature which caused the anti-Montanist Gaius to reject both John and Revelation (e.g. Culpepper, *John* 121).

181. The primary sources for our knowledge of Montanism are the hostile reports of Eusebius, *HE* 5.16.1-19.2 and Epiphanius, *Pan.* 48.1.4-13.8; in contrast the allusions in the later writings of Tertullian are more sympathetic. For an excellent brief survey see R. E. Heine, 'Montanus, Montanism', *ABD* 4.898-902; R. M. Grant, 'Montanism', *EC* 3.640-41, provides a useful collection of Montanist prophecies. See also R. E. Heine, *The Montanist Oracles and Testimonia* (Macon: Mercer University, 1989); and now A. Marjanen, 'Montanism: Egalitarian Ecstatic "New Prophecy"', in Marjanen and Luomanen, *Companion* 185-212. The classic study is P. de Labriolle, *La crise montaniste* (Paris: LeRoux, 1913). For inscriptional evidence of Montanism's continued influence into the sixth century see W. Tabbernee, *Montanist Inscriptions and Testimonia: Epigraphic Sources Illustrating the History of Montanism* (Macon: Mercer University, 1997); and see also his *Prophets and Gravestones: An Imaginative History of Montanists and Other Early Christians* (Peabody, MA: Hendrickson, 2009).

182. Hippolytus, *Ref.* 8.12; Eusebius, *HE* 5.16.1.

183. Epiphanius in particular attacked Montanists for their reliance on ecstatic prophecy (Heine, *ABD* 5.899).

as a continuing feature of Christian worship and important for guidance made it known as 'the New Prophecy'. Its progenitor was one Montanus,[184] and, as in so many other cases,[185] the movement is also named after him — Montanism — though the two other prophets who brought the ongoings in Phrygia to public attention were two women, Priscilla and Maximilla.[186] The influence of 'the New Prophecy' spread well beyond Asia, the possibility of individual experiences of inspired speech proving as attractive into the third century[187] as did Pentecostalism in the twentieth century,[188] the influence being most noted in Rome and in north Africa, winning the support of Tertullian, the father of Latin Christianity, in his latter years. 'In the third century the understanding of Montanism was ... transformed from a renewal movement of the Christian church to a heresy'.[189]

That John's Gospel provided an important scriptural warrant for Montanism is clearest in Hippolytus's report that their followers claimed Priscilla and Maximilla to be inspired by the Paraclete Spirit, and likewise Montanus (*Ref.* 8.12), the reference being, obviously, to the Paraclete promised in John 14-16.[190] The revelations did not affect doctrinal subjects; the christology of

---

184. '... a recent convert ... suddenly fell into frenzy and convulsions. He began to be ecstatic and to speak and to talk strangely, prophesying contrary to the custom which belongs to the tradition and succession of the church from the beginning' (Eusebius, *HE* 5.16.7). To Montanus is attributed the famous description of inspiration: 'Behold, man is like a lyre, and I hover over him like a plectrum; man sleeps, but I watch. Behold, it is the Lord who makes men's hearts ecstatic and gives them (new) hearts' (Epiphanius, *Pan.* 48.4; Grant, *EC* 3.640).

185. E.g. Valentinianism, Lutheranism, Calvinism.

186. '... two more women ... spoke madly and improperly and strangely, like Montanus' (Eusebius, *HE* 5.16.9).

187. 'The many other wonderful works of the grace of God which were still being wrought up to that time in divers churches produced the belief among many that they also were prophets' (Eusebius, *HE* 5.3.4).

188. Cf. C. M. Robeck, 'Montanism and Present Day "Prophets"', *Pneuma: the Journal of the Society for Pentecostal Studies* 32 (2010) 413.

189. Marjanen, 'Montanism' 193, who goes on to argue that 'it was not the *fact* that Montanists focused on prophetic activity and the expectation of an imminent end that led to a development which eventually placed Montanist communities outside the Catholic Church. Rather, it was the *way* these theological emphases came into expression in Montanism and shaped the power structures in and relationships between various early Christian communities' (195).

190. See also Marjanen, 'Montanism' 198-99. The importance of the Spirit in the *Odes of Solomon* (*Odes* 3.10; 6.7; 11.2; 13.2; 19.2, 4; 23.22; 25.8; 28.1, 8; 36.1, 3) suggests a similar influence from John through the *Odes*. The quotation from Montanus (above n.184) may indeed have been prompted by *Odes* 6.1-2 ('As the [wind] moves through the harp and the strings speak, So the Spirit of the Lord speaks through my members, and I speak through his love'); see also 14.8 and 16.5.

the Montanists seems to have been unobjectionable.[191] The revelations related more to matters of discipline: the Montanists did not permit a second marriage after the death of a spouse (Epiphanius, *Pan.* 48.9);[192] they instituted new and more frequent fasts (Hippolytus, *Ref.* 8.12); two prophecies of Montanus refused repentance for sin committed after baptism, and encouraged thought of martyrdom.[193] Irenaeus, understandably, rebuked them for paying insufficient heed to what Paul had written to the Corinthians about prophecy (*adv. haer.* 3.11.9). But Tertullian notes that 'the Bishop of Rome[194] had acknowledged the prophetic gifts of Montanus, Prisca and Maximilla, and, in consequence of the acknowledgment, had bestowed his peace on the churches of Asia and Phrygia' (*adv. Prax.* 1).[195] And though he could claim Paul's authority in not permitting women to speak in church (*Virg. Vel.* 9),[196] Tertullian himself drew confidently on John 14.26 in vigorously advocating the view that the Paraclete had not been silenced since the days of John but was active in 'the direction of discipline, the revelation of the scriptures, the re-formation of the intellect, the advancement toward the "better things"'.[197]

The influence of Revelation is also clear. The revelations just mentioned were more like the revelations which Paul attributed to prophecy (1 Cor. 14.6, 26). But prophecies attributed to Maximilla had a more apocalyptic character: 'There will be wars and revolutions' (Eusebius, *HE* 5.16.18); 'After me there will be no more prophecy, but the end' (Epiphanius, *Pan.* 48.2.4).[198] Most striking was Priscilla's vision of Christ: 'Appearing as a woman clothed in shining robe, Christ came to me; he put wisdom into me and revealed to me that this place [Pepuza] is sacred, and here Jerusalem will come down from heaven' (Epiphanius, *Pan.* 49.1).[199] Whether Tertullian thought of Pepuza in connection with the divinely-built Jerusalem 'let down from heaven' (Rev. 21.2) is

---

191. Tertullian, *Jejun.* 1; Epiphanius, *Pan.* 48.1.3-4.
192. See further Marjanen, 'Montanism' 200-202.
193. 'The church can remit sins, but I will not do so lest others also sin'; 'Do not hope to die in bed ... but in martyrdom, so that he who suffered for you may be glorified' (Robert M. Grant, *EC* 3.640). See also Heine, *ABD* 5.899.
194. Either Victor (ANF 3.630-31) or Zephyrinus (Heine, *ABD* 4.900).
195. It is entirely probable that it was in reaction to Montanist use of John (and Revelation) that the so-called Alogoi attributed both writings to Cerinthus (Epiphanius, *Pan.* 51.2-3).
196. See also Heine, *ABD* 4.991.
197. Tertullian, *Virg. Vel.* 1; also *Jejun.* 12-13, 15; *Monog.* 3. Interestingly, Irenaeus, no friend of Montanism, also makes a point of insisting that the Spirit and spiritual gifts, including prophecy, were still part of continuing Christian experience (*adv. haer.* 5.6.1; 5.8.1). See also Eusebius, *HE* 5.17.4.
198. Grant, *EC* 3.640.
199. Grant, *EC* 3.641; see also Marjanen, 'Montanism' 203-6.

hardly clear (*adv. Marc.* 3.25), but the Montanist sympathies of his later years would have made him open to the revelatory work of the Spirit.

Perhaps most striking is Tertullian's defence of the continuing role of the Spirit in the contemporary church.

> On which side, then, do you think the Spirit is confirmed as existing among us; when he commands, or when he approves, what our God has always both commanded and approved? But you again set up boundary-posts to God, as with regard to grace, so with regard to discipline; as with regard to gifts, so, too, with regard to solemnities; so that our observances are supposed to have ceased in like manner as his benefits; and you thus deny that he still continues to impose duties, because, in this case again, "the Law and the Prophets [were] until John". It remains for you to banish him wholly, being, as he is, so far as lies in you, so otiose (*Jejun.* 11).

Thus Tertullian maintained a way of interpreting John's Gospel which sought to be true to the importance which John had placed on the immediacy of the Spirit (not contained within or restrained by 'boundary-posts'), on the Spirit's continuing role in expressing the gospel and in forming the Christian life, and on the dangers of the Spirit being confined to sacrament or Bible. And, Tertullian notwithstanding, the Montanists can be credited for refusing to follow the catholic church's unwillingness to recognize the legitimacy of women in ministry (Epiphanius, *Pan.* 49.2.5).

49.9 Conclusion

The Johannine trajectory into the second century had two distinguishing features. One was its christology, providing the basis for the Logos christology which the Apologists took up in their own philosophical way. The presentation of the Logos-Son who revealed the invisible Father in a hostile world gave scope to a Gnostic narrative in which salvation was essentially a matter of spiritual persons being made aware of their heavenly origin and destiny. But John's insistence that the Logos became flesh gave too little scope to those who saw salvation as liberation from the flesh and from this material world. And attempts to weaken the starkness of John 1.14 — a becoming only in appearance or not a complete conjunction of Logos and flesh — were readily undermined by the Johannine epistles, by Justin (*1 Apol.* 63) and particularly by Irenaeus. In his attempt to ensure that the gospel of Jesus, of the Logos-become-flesh, spoke to a wider spiritual hunger and questioning, John did indeed sail close to the wind. But it would not be true that he was taken over by the Gnostic systems and that Irenaeus rescued him for the great church only with difficulty. On the contrary, it was John's own insistence on the human reality of the one who revealed God most fully and finally that was recognized from early on and given its due prominence by Irenaeus. And it was the Gospel, as also the Apocalypse of John, which ensured that the worship offered to the risen Jesus and to the Lamb was not worship of a second divine being but worship of God as revealed in Jesus.

The other distinctive feature was John's justification of his reshaping of the Jesus tradition by appeal to the Paraclete-Spirit, not only in reminding of what had been said before (John 14.26), but also in leading into truth not previously revealed and declaring (more fully) what is of Christ (16.12-14). This recognition that the Spirit not only reaffirmed old revelation but led into new insight was evidently the basis of John's conception of his task in retelling the story of Jesus. It was reaffirmed in 1 John with the assertion that the anointing of the Spirit gave believers the knowledge and the teaching they needed (1 John 2.20, 27), and in Revelation by the emphasis on the Spirit of prophecy (Rev. 19.10). This strand was less appealing to John's Gnostic sympathizers but found resonance in the *Odes of Solomon* and in Montanism.

The effect of John's boldness in his retelling the gospel of Jesus was thus twofold. It provided an insight into the divine significance of Jesus which became a fundamental emphasis in the christology of catholic Christianity. But it also held open the door to a Christianity of the Spirit, not content with traditional forms and formulae. In other words, John represents an element in the NT canon as potentially problematic as Paul. The only difference is that whereas the canonical Paul tamed the early apostle, John had no such institutionalizing qualification, and Revelation only heightened the paradox of Johannine Christianity.

CHAPTER 50

A Contested Identity

In this final volume of the trilogy *Christianity in the Making*, the concern has been to trace the emergence of Christianity's distinctive character through most of the second century. The starting point has been the year 70, the destruction of Jerusalem and its temple, which in effect marked the end of Second Temple Judaism. That was a decisive fulcrum point not only for Judaism but also for embryonic Christianity, whose first developments had taken place within the matrix of Second Temple Judaism. The end point is marked by Irenaeus who provides something of a hill-top position from which to gain a clear perspective on what had happened in the second century and who in effect marked out the character of the Christianity which would progress through the third century to its Constantinian triumph early in the fourth. But that was the end of a much more complex and troubled period in which the identity of Christianity was much more disputed than Irenaeus would have allowed. It is the issues and the competing parties in that contest which we have attempted to trace in vol. 3.

A major concern shared by all these parties was to trace their own distinctive views back to Jesus and his first disciples, to claim the support of James and Paul, Peter and John (and Thomas) for their rendition of the (Christian) gospel. Consequently the procedure followed has been to trace the continuing influence of these first-generation figures and the ways in which the competition to claim their support was central to the contest. The Jesus tradition, James (the brother of Jesus), Peter and Paul were the most obviously influential features and figures, whose ministries and teaching shaped the first generation of emerging Christianity.[1] So it made best sense, having reviewed the

---

1. As the Jesus tradition itself demonstrates (*Jesus Remembered*) and *Beginning from Jerusalem* §37 reminds us.

relevant and voluminous source material (§§39, 40), to proceed by examining how the impact of Jesus, and of James, Paul and Peter, affected the second-century claimants to their heritage. John, a kind of 'Johnnie come lately', had of course to be included, but it also became clear that the controversial figure of Thomas could not escape attention either. Having summarized how their heritage was disputed (§50.1), we can then reflect on how our findings affect our perspective on the Christianity which has endured (§50.2).

50.1 The Continuing Impact of Jesus and of the First-Generation Leaders

a. The Jesus Tradition

The most striking feature of the initial inquiry (§41) was the way in which the term 'gospel' came to include the story of Jesus' mission and teaching, and not just the account of his death and resurrection and their corollaries. The transition from 'gospel' to 'Gospel' did not switch attention away from cross and resurrection; the passion narrative remained constant as the climax of the written Gospel. It was not that Jesus became remembered primarily as a teacher or sage or miracle-worker. His mission as Saviour, through crucifixion and resurrection, remained the high point of the Gospel. It was not that his teaching became the primary means of salvation, Jesus as the conveyer of saving knowledge or wisdom. But these early Gospel writers evidently saw it as also essential that the salvation-effecting events were not separated from the pre-passion mission of Jesus. It was not simply that a salvation-effecting death and resurrection happened in some mythical context, or could be reduced to an event which took place at a point of time whose historical and geographical parameters were irrelevant. The salvation-effecting event was the death and resurrection of Jesus of Nazareth, and his mission in Galilee and Judaea was inseparable from it and integral to it. Not least, the story of how Jesus had lived a genuinely human life in his particular historical social context was evidently valued as demonstrating how a life of trust in God could and should be lived out. But it was the realization that the Gospel included the *whole* story of Jesus' mission which prevented the story from being compartmentalized, with genuine suffering and death being set apart from teaching and miracle-working, and which set a standard and definition of Christian Gospel which endured through the disputes and alternatives put forward throughout the second century.

In §42 the most intriguing feature to emerge from the study of the first three NT (Synoptic) Gospels was the clear demonstration of how the same

§50.1   *A Contested Identity*

story about Jesus could be retold with different details and emphases. It is self-evidently the same story; the portrayal of Jesus which emerges is remarkably the same, despite the variations of detail and emphasis.[2] I believe that such retellings of stories about Jesus and teachings of Jesus were how the Jesus tradition first developed and took its shape during the period of oral transmission, before the Gospels were written.[3] But the point here is that the Synoptic tradition and the Synoptic Gospels demonstrate that the story of Jesus, the same story of Jesus, could be told with such variety. Whether or not 'the same yet different' is a feature of oral tradition, the fact is that the phrase well describes the character of the Synoptic tradition and the Synoptic Gospels. As the 'gospel' in Paul, the same gospel, could be variously described as 'the gospel for the circumcized' and 'the gospel for the uncircumcized' (Gal. 2.7), with different outworkings, as the tensions between Paul, Peter and James illustrate, so the Gospel could be formulated and reformulated differently, according to Mark, according to Matthew, and according to Luke, with differences which did not always gell neatly. The point is, however, that the diversity was not unlimited; the diversity was held firmly within the G/gospel framework of 'a passion narrative with an extended introduction'. And that was to prove decisive in the war between the NT and apocryphal Gospels which was such a feature of the second century.

John's Gospel provided an obvious challenge to the claim that Mark had given the determinative definition of 'Gospel' — especially when it was compared with the *Gospel of Thomas* (§43). For so much of *Thomas* is far closer to the Synoptic tradition than is the bulk of John. The vital difference, however, was that John had retained the Markan framework, whereas *Thomas* had separated teaching from death and resurrection. Moreover, although John's retelling of the story of Jesus was much more adventuresome than the Synoptic Evangelists, he draws in what was evidently historical tradition which the Synoptics might have used but did not;[4] and his reworking of the material is a reworking and elaboration of the earlier tradition. *Thomas*, on the other hand, does not so much rework the Synoptic-like tradition with which he was familiar, as graft it on to a different story, with a different gospel presupposing a different perception of the human condition. The Johannine version of

---

    2. I have quoted too much the mature assessment of C. H. Dodd in his last significant work, *The Founder of Christianity* (London: Collins, 1971), but it makes a point which is too often overlooked and which still deserves attention: 'The first three gospels offer a body of sayings on the whole so consistent, so coherent, and withal so distinctive in manner, style and content, that no reasonable critic should doubt, whatever reservations he may have about individual sayings, that we find here reflected the thought of a single, unique teacher' (21-22).

    3. The primary thesis of *Jesus Remembered*.

    4. See particularly §43.1a(ii) above.

the Jesus tradition grows from within; whereas the Thomasine version grew from without by spatchcocking earlier Jesus tradition with material which is distinctively different. In the case of John's Gospel a line of direct continuity can be drawn from the earlier Jesus tradition, as evidenced by the Synoptic tradition, to John's elaborated version of it. In contrast, in the case of the *Gospel of Thomas*, despite the fact that much of the material has a Synoptic-like character, the distinctively Thomasine material cannot be traced back to Jesus; the gospel of *Thomas* in its distinctiveness is not derived from Jesus. The claim that the *Gospel of Thomas* is a source of historical tradition which can be traced back to Jesus applies only to the Synoptic-like material. But for the source of the material which gives *Thomas* its distinctive character we have to look elsewhere, in the direction of what became central to and characteristic of the Gnostic systems.

When we turned to look at the second-century sources more directly (§44), to examine the impact of the Jesus tradition, and the way it was handled, a clear picture again emerged. Initially, in the first half of the second century, the impression was strong that the Jesus tradition was known predominantly in oral form. This was an important finding in itself, since by then all four NT Gospels had already been written. In other words, the transcription of the Jesus tradition into written form did not bring the oral Jesus tradition to an end. Well into the second century the main access of the wide scatter of house- and apartment-churches to the Jesus tradition would have been through the teaching of teachers and elders and through catechismal and liturgical familiarity. Even when one (or more) written Gospels came into the possession of congregational leaders, the great bulk of the worshippers would know the story of Jesus from hearing it read rather than reading it themselves. And each written Gospel as it was copied and circulated would immediately begin to have the textual variations which have been the meat and drink of generations of textual critics for five hundred years; the phenomenon of 'same yet different' did not cease with the writing down of the Jesus tradition.

However, the influence of the written Gospels spread slowly and surely, so that by about the middle of the second century the evidence is clear that knowledge of Jesus tradition came primarily through the written Gospels, read at worship sessions (as Justin testifies) and quoted by the learned (as Irenaeus was to exemplify). A striking feature is that the Gospel of Matthew seems to have been the most used, most familiar and most quoted. That would help explain the prestige accorded to Peter. And though Matthew was in effect a second edition of Mark, nevertheless Mark was not dispensed with — as most assume was the case with a Q document; here again the tradition that the Gospel of Mark was the 'memoir of Peter' must have counted heavily in favour of Mark's continued use. Luke was also certainly used, and survived the exaggerated esteem and mutilation of Marcion. And despite a long-standing view that John was more beloved by the Valentinians and was something of an embarrassment to the leaders of 'the great church', the evidence is clear enough that John was also much valued and used.[5] What is more striking, in view of the semi-popular view that through the second century there were many Gospels of apparently equal or competing merit, there is little evidence that any other Gospels were as widely revered and used as the NT Gospels. For those who wanted to be able to claim that their teaching derived from Jesus, with any hope of being believed outside their own circles, the only Gospels to command widespread respect were the NT Gospels. It was not that Irenaeus arbitrarily chose the four NT Gospels as alone authoritative, out of a large selection of Gospels. The truth is that he simply confirmed what had been the case for several decades: that the four NT Gospels were the clearest form which the Jesus tradition took, the only ones to be relied on for information about Jesus and his teaching. The four NT Gospels — the one Gospel according to four different gospelers — were the enduring impact of the Jesus tradition, and ensured that the impact of Jesus from which Christianity first emerged would not be lost.

b. James and Jewish Christianity (§§45-46)

James, known as the brother of Jesus (Matt. 13.55), was the most direct line of continuity with Jesus. Although tradition did not count him as a disciple of Jesus during Jesus' mission, his subsequent conversion or affirmation by Jesus was not disputed (1 Cor. 15.7), and his emergence as leader of the Jerusalem believers, the mother church, was probably inevitable, given his blood relationship with Jesus. More to the present point, James became synonymous with an embryonic Christianity which saw itself as a sect within Second Temple Judaism, a messianic and eschatological sect, but essentially a form of Judaism. It was chiefly this emphasis which was carried forward into the second century by those who most venerated his memory and name. Some of that influence leaked over into more Gnosticizing circles — no doubt part of that melting pot into which Jewish insights and speculations also fed and on which the later Gnostic systems drew. But the principal line of influence led directly into those groupings of Jewish believers in Jesus who saw maintaining their Jewish praxis as entirely consistent with their belief in Jesus. These groupings, traditionally regarded as Jewish-Christian sects or heresies, were

---

5. I refer again particularly to Hill, *The Johannine Corpus in the Early Church*, on which I drew heavily in §44.

very active through the second century and survived for another two or three centuries. Their claim to be the most directly continuous with James and the mother church of Jerusalem was harder to deny than the heresiologists would have acknowledged. Jacobean Christianity, we could say, was the first skin of Christianity, which it sloughed off as it developed and grew out of its initial shape. In sloughing it off, the memory of James could be retained only by means of ecclesiastical rationalization (James as the first bishop of Jerusalem), though the letter attributed to him ensured that much of the priorities and praxis identified with James would be carried forward into a Christianity which in effect had disowned him.

None of this should be allowed to cloak or diminish the essentially and continuingly Jewish character of the growing Christianity. The God whom they worshipped was the God first revealed to Israel, the God of the OT; this had to be a principal line of defence against Valentinians and Marcionites who wanted to set the Christian God against the God of the OT. The Jesus whom they venerated and worshipped was Jesus Christ; although the titular form of Christ (= Messiah) had been lost to sight, it was again essential, in the face of those who wanted to distinguish Jesus from Christ, to affirm that Jesus was Christ, Christ was Jesus. The scriptures on which they drew were Israel's scriptures; a 'plain sense' reading of which gave authorization to the great church's fundamental beliefs and ruled out the apparently sophisticated finesse of Gnostic readings. The designation of the scriptures of Israel as part of the *Christian* Bible, as it increasingly emerged in the second half of the second century, did not make them any the less the scriptures of Israel, but rather reinforced the inescapably Jewish character of a Christianity which had to explain and defend itself by claiming to be the fulfillment of these scriptures. The assertion that Christianity was Israel, that the scriptures of the OT were theirs, could never succeed as an exclusivist or triumphalist claim, without undermining the character of the Christianity which made that claim.

All this means that the pulling apart of Christianity and Judaism could never be anything more than messy and protracted. The claim, often made, that Christianity and Judaism were quite distinct and already clearly separated early in the second century, may have been music in the ears of many Christian leaders, from Ignatius onwards. But it would have made little sense to the bulk of ordinary believers who thought of Saturday and Sunday, Passover and Last Supper, circumcision and baptism as variations on the same theme. When did the factional disputes and vituperation between Christian and Jew, as between Essenes, Pharisees and Sadducees, give way to the anti-Judaism which subsequently morphed into anti-Semitism? Here again the middle ground formed by traditionalist Jewish believers in Jesus and Christian *minim* is a factor which sixteen centuries of divorce by a decree of nullity has long obscured. To those who find it necessary to insist on as sharp and final as possible a disjunction between Christianity and Judaism, the Jewishness of Christianity, the Jewishness of Jesus, the Jewishness of the apostles and the Jewishness of NT as well as OT will always be a challenge and a problem, but it is a challenge and a problem at the heart of Christianity itself.

c. Paul (§47)

Paul is the *enfant terrible* of Christianity. It was because he asked so many awkward and embarrassing questions, questions as to whether the Jewishness of the faith which Jesus had inspired could incorporate Gentiles, that the infant movement changed in emphasis if not in direction. His apostolic mission, which those who were apostles before him could not deny, ensured that Christianity would break through the traditional boundaries which had hitherto defined Israel and its covenant with God. His definition of the Christian gospel provided Mark with his Gospel format and in effect determined the form of Gospel which would remain definitive for Christianity and undermine the claims of other Gospels to convey the Christian gospel. But to be prized to the full within the mainstream of Christianity his *terrible*ness had to be tamed, as it was by the Pastoral Epistles and Luke's Acts. It was this Paul who could be drawn on by the Apostolic Fathers in safety without threatening the developing emphases and structures. The apocryphal Paul proved to be a plastic Paul who could be moulded to whatever shape which his reputation could be said to justify. But it was the Valentinians and Marcion who seized on some of the most troublesome features of his letters, and who exaggerated some of his emphases, ignoring their context. And although Irenaeus and Tertullian were well able to provide a definitive answer to such misuse by the careful exegesis of proper use, the edginess of Paul within the NT canon[6] and his own attempts to explain his mission and gospel within the context of the middle decades of the first century, and not least in relation to his maternal religion, continue to provoke misunderstanding and selective emphases which simply acknowledge a failure to appreciate the subtlety and roundedness of his theology.

---

6. The point could be alternatively expressed as the tensions between the earlier Paul and the Paul of the Pastorals — an edginess which remains, whether or not the Pastorals were written by Paul himself.

d. Peter (§48)

Peter is the great enigma, who rarely appears to direct view, face to face, but whose shadow is long and lengthens through our period. His significance and influence are established by three features of his early history. The first two, of course, are his clearly remembered status as the leader and spokesman of Jesus' disciples and one of his intimates, and his highly privileged position, in the early tradition as attested by Paul, of being the first to see and be commissioned by the risen Christ. His period of leadership of the first group of believers in Jesus in Jerusalem was soon overshadowed by James's leadership. But the third decisive feature is the testimony provided by Matthew that Peter was appointed by Jesus as the 'rock' on which Jesus would build his church (Matt. 16.18-19). Peter was also widely regarded, according to Papias, as the principal source for Mark's Gospel. And since Matthew, as in effect the substantive second edition of Mark, became the dominant Gospel voice through the second century, an obvious deduction is that the reputation of Peter as the 'rock' on which Jesus was building his church would be extended as widely as Matthew was circulated. The tradition that Peter had been martyred in Rome provided a natural link for those who saw the church in the capital city of the Empire as the natural successor of the mother church in Jerusalem, providing a providential basis for later claims of apostolic succession and Roman papacy. The more historically substantive basis is probably the impression which arises from the references to Peter in Paul's letters and in Acts, and from the principal letter attributed to Peter. For the impression is of a figure who, unlike James and Paul, did not have a distinctive or uncompromising position on disputed points of doctrine and praxis. Rather he comes across as one who could see both sides in such a dispute and adapt to the circumstances. He comes across as someone in the middle, able to hold together the factions pulling in opposite directions. He comes across as the figure who defines the common ground, the consensus positions to which others hold even when they are pushing for this particular emphasis or that. Perhaps, then, Peter did more and stood for more than most Protestants allow — the greatest bridge-builder (*pontifex maximus*) of all the Christian leaders in earliest Christianity.

e. John (§49)

Just when the continuing influence of Jesus and the first-generation leaders into and through the second century seems to have thus been settled, John arrives on the scene demanding to be heard — and justifiably. For John brings before us fresh information about Jesus' mission. But he also provides a 'take' on the story of Jesus which inevitably causes the eyebrows to shoot upwards. Again he gives the Jewishness of that story an unexpected twist, and provides an insight into the tensions confronting Jewish believers in Jesus in the later decades of the first century which helps explain so much of how both Christianity and Judaism developed. Not only so, but he provides an alternative, or supplement, to the story of Peter as the dominant influence in shaping the Jesus tradition, by bringing both 'the beloved disciple' and Mary Magdalene into a focus which, it might otherwise be thought, the great church would have preferred to remain unfocused. Above all John demonstrates how the central beliefs about Jesus were developing — whether John himself made the development or was reporting a more widespread development. It was his Logos christology which proved to be unacceptable to the rabbis,[7] but which provided the way for the Christians to redefine the Jewish monotheism which they had inherited. Just as it was his insistence that the Logos had *become*, not merely appeared as, flesh which proved to be the glue which enabled Irenaeus to maintain the integration of creation with salvation against the Gnostic voices who could simply not reconcile spirit and matter. A perhaps unintended consequence was a decisive transfer of emphasis from cross and resurrection to incarnation — the divine taking human flesh into itself becoming the crucial salvific act. John himself managed to hold them together — his Gospel still works within the Markan gospel format. But the earlier theology of the cross, as a dealing with the sin which blocks the way to God, was too easily lost to a theology of theosis, of salvation as divinization. The tension here has never been satisfactorily resolved.

The other aspect of John which complicated the problems which the adjudicating Petrine influence may otherwise have resolved was the difficulty of fitting John into such an adjudication. John's individualism and perhaps conventicle format were in effect a counter and complement to the institutionalisation of monarchical episcopacy for which Ignatius, only a decade or so after John, was already pushing. His spirituality fed a wider range of devotion, as the *Odes of Solomon* illustrate, than the Ignatiuses of this world were likely to appreciate. And the Johannine emphasis on the Spirit Paraclete as the teacher on whom believers should depend, not altogether surprisingly, led to a Montanism, which itself stands as a second-century reminder that something which can justifiably be called 'spiritual Christianity' is as fully legitimate a form of Christianity as is catholic Christianity. John spreads out the spectrum of Christianity more fully than most have traditionally recognized; raising the question whether attempts to squeeze a spectrum which runs from 'Jewish Christianity' to Montanism have always been justified. And if we add

---

7. See above §49 at n.32.

the apocalypticism of the other Johannine voice in the NT, then we cannot escape the reminder that the heritage of earliest Christianity is more complex and troublesome than most Christians care to admit — or think.

f. Thomas

The inclusion of Thomas in this list might raise some eyebrows. For although John, the John of John's Gospel, cannot really be counted as one of the leading influences of first-generation Christianity, the John who is usually counted as the John of John's Gospel was one of Jesus' intimates and one of the leadership team in the earliest Jerusalem church. Whether we can speak of any impact of the Johannine form of the Jesus tradition prior to the writing of the Gospel itself, the fact remains that John's Gospel became one of the most influential in the debates which raged through the second century — probably with rabbinic Judaism over the claims of christological monotheism, and certainly in the debates with the various Gnosticizing factions as to whether the divine could incorporate the human. But Thomas, although a regular member of Jesus' twelve disciples,[8] hardly features in the Gospel story beyond his famous role in the Johannine account of Jesus' second resurrection appearance to his disciples,[9] and doesn't feature thereafter in any NT writing. And yet his name is identified with second-century literature as frequently as are the names of James, Paul and Peter.

The decisive factor was presumably the fact that Thomas was called 'Didymus', 'twin', and that was probably enough to provoke the claim that he was so called because he was, in fact, the twin of Jesus. In a growing movement which was second-century Christianity, all its variations took it for granted that it was important to be able to claim authentication from originators, in this case closeness to Jesus. So the possibility of claiming not just a closeness of discipleship, like Peter or John, or a sibling connection, like James, but the still closer relation of a twin was too huge a legitimating relationship to be ignored. These claims for the Thomasine literature did not cut much ice in the West, outside (presumably) Gnosticizing communities. But in eastern Syria Thomas was accorded a founding apostle status and remained a constitutive building block in Syriac Christianity, stretching down to India. The problem was that the basic claims for Thomas's status and authority (Jesus' twin) were dubious in the extreme. And the rootage of the *Gospel of Thomas* in early Jesus tradition was neither independent (where it accorded with Synoptic

---

8. Matt. 10.3; Mark 3.18; Luke 6.15; John 21.2; Acts 1.13.
9. John 20.24-28; also 11.16 and 14.5.

tradition) nor could it claim to derive its distinctive message from Jesus. So in the contest of and for Christian identity, the Thomasine claims were weakest of all, and apart from Syrian Christianity, Thomas had no continuing role in the formation and definition of Christian identity.

50.2 Christianity in Process of Being Defined

It would be a mistake to think that the contest over Christianity's identity was resolved by pushing aside both Jewish Christian claims that the Jewish law, ritual as well as moral, was still binding on believers in Jesus, and the Gnostic Christian claims to new revelation and knowledge, and that the outcome was a homogeneous and consistently integrated Christianity. The reality of the identity which did emerge and endured has been shown just as clearly to be much more complex than is portrayed in the traditional, Eusebian story of Christianity. As indicated in §38 there were three key elements in that story which identified Christianity and defined its distinctiveness: an ecclesiastical system built round a threefold order of bishop, priest and deacon; a New Testament defined by and defining apostolicity; and a rule of faith which functioned in effect as an apostolic creed even before creeds were formally drawn up. How does our study affect or challenge that story? And before we head down that track, we should ask whether we have found a stable centre and core in the midst of the complexity and diversity.

a. Jesus as the Defining Centre

The primary identifying feature which emerges from this study is continuity with, closeness to and dependence on the Jesus from whom the whole movement had its beginning. It was this which the NT Gospels established and which the other Gospels laid claim to but without lasting success. It was this to which Peter had an immediate and obvious claim, and John also, which gave them a foundational role for the great church, and which others tried to exploit precisely because of their foundational role, but with less justification and success. It was the same claim to a direct commission from (the risen) Jesus, and the fact that his gospel focused on Jesus' death and resurrection, which ensured that Paul's successful mission, despite the controversial character both of the claim and of the mission, did not rip the new movement apart but was counted integral to the new movement's development. On the other hand, despite being able to make one of the strongest claims to direct continuity with Jesus, as his brother, James was rather left behind in and by the same development. And despite the claim to be Jesus' twin brother, Thomas became a spokesperson for a form of Christianity which had effectively lost its line of connection with Christianity's beginnings.

In short, the identity of Christianity was defined by the *Christ* who was at its centre, the Jesus who had missioned in Galilee and Judaea, and who had been crucified and (it was believed as a fundamental conviction) raised again in Jerusalem. Christianity was the living expression and continuity of the impact made by Jesus, his mission, death and resurrection. He was the hub of the wheel, and the spokes which were most directly rooted in him, in his historical mission and in its immediate impact, supported the rim which by the end of the second century was beginning to define the wheel of Christianity and what lay beyond its rim.

b. The Ecclesiology of Christianity

So far as we can tell, the earliest ecclesiastical forms varied between a synagogue form, built round community elders, and a more charismatic form of prophet and teacher. The former is reflected in the Acts account of the Jerusalem church,[10] and, as we might expect, in James (5.14) and, less expectedly, Peter (1 Pet. 5.1, 5). The latter is reflected in Acts 13.1 and the early Pauline churches.[11] In each case the centrality of apostles is either explicit or assumed,[12] but there is no hint or indication that there could be a second generation of apostles.[13] The significance of apostles was not only that they founded churches, but that they constituted that vital link back to the beginnings with Jesus. In this connection, it can be no accident that in his list of the few significant resurrection appearances which were counted as foundational to the gospel, Paul included the appearance 'to *all* the apostles' (1 Cor. 15.7); only those who had been directly commissioned by Jesus himself could be counted as church-founding apostles.

It is noticeable that in the undisputed letters, Paul never assumes or refers to elders or leaders appointed by him,[14] not even in dealing with the

---

10. Acts 11.30; 15.2, 6, 22, 23; 16.4; 21.18.
11. E.g. Rom. 12.6-8; 1 Cor. 12.28; Eph. 4.11.
12. E.g. Acts 15.2, 6, 22, 23; not mentioned in James, but the letter is attributed to James; 1 Pet. 1.1; 1 Cor. 12.28; Eph. 4.11.
13. Ignatius seems to imply that presbyters/elders had taken the place of apostles (*Magn.* 6.1).
14. The counter evidence of Acts 14.23 and 20.17 is almost certainly to be attributed to a Lukan telling of the story from a later perspective, just as Clement could assume that Paul had appointed 'the first fruits' of his ministry (in this case Stephanas — 1 Cor. 16.15) as bishops and deacons (*1 Clem.* 42.4).

troubles in the church of Corinth. So the reference to elders in 1 Tim. 5.17, 19 and Tit. 1.5-6 may best be understood as testimony to a Pauline ecclesiology falling in line with the Jewish synagogue tradition.[15] And *1 Clement* shows that appointment of elders need not have secured good order in Corinth,[16] and may even have provoked a younger generation who harked back to the charismatic freedom of the early days.[17] The *Didache* (11-13) also indicates that other churches managed to include scope for peripatetic prophets and teachers,[18] and Hermas similarly indicates that prophets were still expected to have a function within the assembly (*Mand.* 11). The Montanist reassertion of the importance of the role of prophecy ('the New Prophecy') may not have been such a retrogression as its opponents would have liked to think.[19]

That a formal role of deacon was early on recognized in the Pauline churches is suggested by Rom. 16.1 — the first named Christian deacon, the woman Phoebe — and Phil. 1.1. The consolidation of this 'church office' is confirmed again by 1 Timothy, and by Clement and Ignatius.[20] *Episkopoi* too had an early place in some at least of the Pauline churches (Phil. 1.1), though whether the Greek should be translated as 'bishop' for some time, or as indicating a more specific oversight role (financial? — 'overseers') is less than clear.[21] Certainly by the time of the Pastorals what can be described as an 'episcopal' role (*episkopē* — 'oversight, supervision') is clearly in view (1 Tim. 3.2; Tit. 1.7), a role and 'office' attested also in the *Didache* 15, though it is notable that in the *Didache*, as in Phil. 1.1, the term is in the plural. It is with Ignatius that the idea of communities having a single 'bishop' comes to clear expression, as Ignatius insisted on the centrality of the bishop's role as the supreme authority and focus of unity of each church. That he had to press the case so strongly suggests that what he was assuming and advocating was

---

15. Cf. particularly J. T. Burtchaell, *From Synagogue to Church: Public Services and Offices in the Earliest Christian Communities* (Cambridge University, 1992).

16. *1 Clem.* 44.5; 47.6; 54.2; 57.1.

17. For Burtchaell it was obvious that the targets of the polemic of Clement (and Ignatius) 'can only have been the charismatic apostles, prophets and teachers' (*From Synagogue to Church* 322-23).

18. Given the Jewish character of the *Didache* (§45.5b) the absence of any mention of elders is surprising. See also Schweizer, *Church Order* 141-45.

19. The transition from 'charismatic organization' to the ecclesiastical office of 'early Catholicism' was more complex than R. Sohm, *Kirchenrecht* (Leipzig: Duncker & Humblot, 1892), allowed. For the debate sparked off by Sohm see E. Nardoni, 'Charism in the Early Church since Rudolph Sohm: An Ecumenical Challenge', *TS* 53 (1992) 646-62.

20. 1 Tim. 3.8, 12; 4.6; *1 Clem.* 42.4-5; Ignatius, *Eph.* 2.1; *Magn.* 6.1; 13.1; etc.

21. See e.g. J. Reumann, *Philippians* (AB 33B; Yale University, 2008) 86-89.

a not long or universally established pattern in the churches of Asia Minor;[22] we recall that he makes no reference to a bishop in Rome. Whether Ignatius was a lone voice, perhaps reacting against his experience in Antioch, or simply the most vociferous advocate of an ecclesiastical pattern which was beginning to spread, the fact remains that the pattern of monarchical episcopacy which Ignatius advocated, each congregation looking to its bishop as the focus of its unity and sacramental life, became the basic structure of the great church's ecclesiology.[23] That Irenaeus could assume so blithely that bishops were the natural (essential) successors to the apostles and constituted what could already properly be described as an 'apostolic succession'[24] owed an incalculable debt to Ignatius.

The most surprising development has already been indicated in §38.2 — the emergence of a Christian order of priesthood. The surprise is engendered by the fact that such an order was completely unknown in the first generation. Jewish priests were among the earliest converts or recruits to the Jerusalem church, according to Acts 6.7; but they evidently did not continue to function as priests in the assembly of believers in Jesus. And Paul could use the language of priestly imagery to describe a variety of Christian service;[25] but he nowhere mentions a priestly order or function in the churches he founded — the same being true even of the Pastorals. 1 Peter 2.5 and Rev. 1.6 similarly think of believers in general as a priestly people (as in Exod. 19.6), without there being any further thought that there was an order of priesthood in Christianity.[26] Most striking is the whole argument of Hebrews (as, again, already noted in §38.2) that a religious system depending on priests as intermediaries between the people and their God is what characterized the old covenant, the religion of Israel. But this system had been entirely superseded by Christ, in a priesthood which was unique and unrepeatable, for which only one who was 'without father, without mother, without genealogy, having neither beginning of days nor end of life' (Heb. 7.3) could qualify. Jesus, this solely and uniquely qualified high priest, had entered through the curtain (dividing the Holy Place

---

22. E.g. Ignatius, *Eph.* 1.3; 3.2; 4.1; 6.1; *Magn.* 3; 6.1; 7.1; *Trall.* 2.1-2; 3.1; 13.2; *Philad.* 4; 7.2; *Smyrn.* 8.1-2. See also Schweizer, *Church Order* 153-54.

23. Barrett notes Ignatius's 'tendency to attach questions of doctrine to matters of order and even of calendar'; 'The sorting out of Christian groups that took place during the second century was not carried out on a purely doctrinal basis, but was related to categories of organization and power' ('Jews and Judaizers in the Epistles of Ignatius' 154-55).

24. *adv. haer.* 3.3; cf. 4.26.2.

25. Rom. 12.1; 15.16; Phil. 2.25. *Did.* 13 does not hesitate to use the rules for the provision of Israel's priests as indicating how visiting prophets should be provided for.

26. 'It is not that there are no longer any priests: there are no longer any who are not priests' (Burtchaell, *From Synagogue to Church* 323).

from the Holy of Holies) and opened the way for his followers to follow him through the curtain, no longer simply to where the ark of the covenant was, but into the heavenly presence of God himself. Hebrews' message, then, to those who hankered for the old tangibilities of priest, altar and sacrifice, was that these were no longer necessary. Believers could now follow Christ their forerunner (6.19-20) and 'draw near' directly to the heavenly mercy-seat for themselves, without depending on priestly intermediaries (4.14-16).[27]

In contrast, and in total disregard for Hebrews, even though he probably knew it (*1 Clem.* 36.1), Clement saw Christian ministry as the continuation of the Levitical priesthood and the Levitical priesthood as the scriptural authorization for Christian ministry (40-43). This includes talk of sacrificial offerings on the altar and an acceptance of the distinction between priest and laity (40.4–41.4). Ignatius too does not hesitate to speak similarly of priests (*Philad.* 9.1) and to use the language of the altar of sacrifice (*thysiastērion*) to describe the ministry of the bishop.[28] It is hardly surprising, then, that an order of priesthood re-emerged in the Christianity of the great church, with the eucharist coming to be seen more as a priestly sacrifice, and the meal-table of the shared meal[29] coming to be regarded as an altar.[30] Perhaps this too was inevitable. For all ancient religions as such focused on their sacred spaces (temples) where their priesthood offered animal sacrifices. Such understanding and practice was more or less definitional for a religion. Consequently, the earliest Christian churches must have seemed very strange and indeed *ir*religious — no holy place, no priest, no sacrifice. For Christianity simply to be recognized as a religion the sociological pressure to conform to the religious norm must have been enormous, and in the event seems to have proved irresistible. If, then, the emergence of a church order with an overseer or supervisor was a natural sociological response to the need for order and

---

27. Schweizer sums up his study of the church in Hebrews: 'All the Old Testament ministries are fulfilled in Jesus Christ, and are therefore abolished for the Church', and concludes tersely, 'Hebrews combats the institutional Church' (*Church Order* 116). 'In the New Testament priesthood belongs to Jesus Christ alone' (173).

28. *Eph.* 5.2; *Magn.* 7.2; *Trall.* 7.1-2; *Philad.* 4.

29. See above §45 n.165.

30. Well worth noting again is Lightfoot's essay on 'The Christian Ministry' in his *Philippians*, 181-269. He notes the importance of Ignatius's influence: 'Throughout the whole range of Christian literature, no more uncompromising advocacy of the episcopate can be found than appears in these writings' (236). But he also notes that the sacerdotal view of ministry only came in with Cyprian (240): the idea was foreign to Clement (249); Ignatius 'never regards the ministry as a sacerdotal office' (250); for Justin, 'the whole Christian people . . . have become a nation of high-priests' (252); and 'Irenaeus too recognizes the whole body of the faithful under the new dispensation as the counterparts of the sons of Levi under the old' (253). See also H.-J. Klauck, 'Lord's Supper', *ABD* 4.362-72.

a focus of authority, so we should probably conclude that the emergence of a Christian priesthood, with eucharist no longer primarily a shared meal of thanksgiving but a sacrifice offered by the priest to God, was a sociological inevitability. It was not the theology which triumphed, certainly not the theology of the apostolic generation, but the social pressures to conform with the ways in which religious groups functioned.

All that acknowledged, it is important to remind ourselves that the NT canon does not include Clement and Ignatius, but it does include Hebrews — and it does include 1 Corinthians, John and Revelation. The uncomfortable fact is that the different patterns of religion expressed in these NT writings, now most commonly seen in the more charismatic churches of today, have more apostolic authorization than the traditional forms, following the Ignatian model which became the catholic model, taken for granted to be not only the norm but the only norm. Social conformity triumphed over the ecclesiastical diversity which the NT encapsulates. As Ernst Käsemann long ago observed, 'The New Testament canon does not, as such, constitute the foundation of the unity of the Church. On the contrary, as such (that is, in its accessibility to the historian) it provides the basis for the multiplicity of the confessions'[31]— which brings us to the second pillar of the great church.

c. The New Testament — Unity in Diversity[32]

As again noted in §38.2, the determinative factor in the emergence of a New Testament 'canon' was *apostolicity*. Here again the link with Jesus and to Christianity's beginnings was decisive. The theological justification for this criterion has been confirmed by our study. To be sure, the formal criterion was more of a rationalizing excuse in many cases: immediate connection with an apostle was entirely arguable in the case of Mark and Luke, but the claims for the Pastorals and 1 Peter were pushing the logic uncomfortably far, and the logic quickly broke down with Hebrews and 2 Peter. But the debate over their canonicity extended well beyond our period, and we should content ourselves with observing that the regular account of the emergence of the NT canon, which has been given repeatedly,[33] has been more or less confirmed for the phase identified with the second century.

---

31. E. Käsemann, 'The New Testament Canon and the Unity of the Church', *Essays on New Testament Themes* (London: SCM, 1964) 103.
32. I play on the title of my *Unity and Diversity in the New Testament*.
33. In addition to those cited in §38 n.19, see Kümmel, *Introduction* Part Two; B. M. Metzger, *The Canon of the New Testament* (Oxford: Clarendon, 1987); L. M. McDonald, *The Formation of the Christian Biblical Canon* (Peabody: Hendrickson, ²1995) Part Two;

So we can confirm that by the middle of the second century the four NT Gospels were already established as the authoritative expression of the apostolic Jesus tradition. Irenaeus was not the first to give them definitively authoritative status; he simply gave rhetorical flourish to explain how these four Gospels had already been recognized as effectively Christian scripture. We can confirm too that other Gospels never had the same breadth of appeal and were never accorded the same degree of authority. This was true even when other Gospels laid claim to apostolic authorship or origin — a fact which makes clear something already evident from the previous paragraph: that apostolicity was not a matter of name so much as content. It was the failure of Gospels like those of *Thomas* and *Peter* to demonstrate the apostolic sources for their distinctive messages which made them unacceptable, whatever claim their titles embodied to have come from the named apostle. The subsequent pronouncement of the canonical status of the four (NT) Gospels did not give them an authority which they had not previously possessed, but was an acknowledgment of the authority they had been exercising for decades, an authority which other (apocryphal) Gospels did not share.

We can confirm too that the other central element in what became the NT canon, the letters of Paul, must have been gathered together, circulated quite widely, and been well known and used in the main centres of Christian expansion, probably already late in the first century, and no doubt increasingly through the second century.[34] The fact that the various groups of Jewish believers reacted to Paul with hesitation or open hostility was probably a factor in their status as Christian groups being called increasingly in question. The popularity of Paul with the Valentinians and Marcionites confirmed the

---

also Nienhuis, *Not by Paul Alone*, whose subtitle is *The Formation of the Catholic Epistle Collection and the Christian Canon*.

34. A. von Harnack, *Die Briefsammlung des Apostels Paulus* (Leipzig: Hinrichs, 1926) ch. 1, maintained that the collection of the 13 letters of Paul could be traced back to about the year 100. D. Trobisch, *Paul's Letter Collection: Tracing the Origins* (Minneapolis: Fortress, 1994), argues that Paul himself collected, edited and published his four principal letters (Romans, 1 and 2 Corinthians, and Galatians) for wider circulation, thus giving birth to the conception of a Christian canon. H. Y. Gamble, *Books and Readers in the Early Church: A History of Early Christian Texts* (Yale University, 1995), argues that 'there was a collection of ten Pauline letters arranged on the principle of decreasing length and counting together letters addressed to the same community, thus emphasizing that Paul had written to seven churches' (59-62); and that it was the use of a codex for the collection which helped establish the almost exclusive preference in early Christianity for the codex (63; see the whole section on the intriguing question of the transition from the roll to the codex — 49-66). He also argues that some at least of Paul's letters were being copied and circulated during his lifetime and that the first collections were being circulated before the end of the first century (95-101).

wide recognition of his defining role in Christian tradition. But, even more impressive, is the fact that Irenaeus and Tertullian refused to cede Paul to the Valentinians and Marcionites; for the great church too Paul's letters were integral and fundamental to defining Christianity's identity. That the Paul of Acts and of the Pastorals was much more congenial to the bulk of great church leadership presumably made their affirmation of Paul that much easier, and ensured the place of Acts and the Pastorals within the NT canon.

What again needs to be appreciated is the degree to which this *de facto* canonizing process in fact canonized a degree of diversity which should have been more disturbing to the uniformity more naturally prized by catholic Christianity than is usually acknowledged. If the recognition of four canonical Gospels was in any degree a response to Marcion's regard for Luke's Gospel as *the* Gospel, then we should be grateful that the response was not to replace Luke's Gospel with Matthew's Gospel, as might have been the case since Matthew's Gospel was so much more highly valued. Another alternative could have been to respond to Marcion's Luke by insisting on a combination of the four Gospels, as in Tatian's *Diatessaron*. Presumably the status of all four (NT) Gospels was already sufficiently secure among Christian assemblies generally, so that the only answer to Marcion could be the insistence that all four Gospels must be counted as authoritative, as in Tertullian. But the recognition that the gospel of Jesus Christ could be expressed in four *different* ways — the same Gospel according to Matthew, Mark, Luke and John — had repercussions hard to control. It was hard enough to acknowledge the diversity, even contradictory adversity, among the first three Gospels. In particular, the facts that Matthew, on whom the foundational primacy of Peter largely rested, was such a Jewish Gospel, insisting that Jesus had not abrogated the Jewish law (Matt. 5.17-20), and that it warned so outspokenly against clericalism (23.2-12), must have given him a contrariness which caused considerable unease among great-church clergy, only to be dealt with by kicking such emphases 'into the long grass'.[35]

But much more problematic was John's Gospel, with its portrayal of Jesus so markedly different from that of the other (NT) Gospels. To be sure, the Johannine Jesus accorded well with the developing christology of the second century, and indeed shaped it to a far greater extent than the Synoptics. But John's Gospel also gave too much scope to more docetic and Gnostic portrayals of Jesus, even though its insistence on the fleshliness of the Logos's incarnation was enough to prevent such a takeover. Still, the boldness of its retelling of the story of Jesus, not least its attractiveness to those beyond the

---

35. As most clearly in the ignoring, indeed denying, of Jesus' clear instruction to 'call no one your father on earth, for you have one Father — the one in heaven' (Matt. 23.9).

bounds of the great church, cannot but have been disturbing to not a few in the great church. Similarly John's justification for his retelling, by reference to the Spirit-Paraclete, provided a precedent for equally bold and still bolder retellings in the future, and provided a justification for Montanist claims which Tertullian could not deny. And the ecclesiological pattern which John evidently espoused fits at best uneasily in an ecclesiology of apostolic succession and threefold ministry.[36] In short, a NT canon which includes John does not invite or encourage a straightforward conformist faith or churchmanship.[37]

The case with Paul is not dissimilar. As both Jewish believers in Jesus and Gnosticizing believers recognized, the base of Paul's authority in special revelation (resurrection appearance and commission) uniquely given to him provided a precedent for similar claims. And the fact that his gospel (Paul's gospel — Gal. 1.11; 2.2) was acknowledged by the Jerusalem apostles, despite its distinctiveness (Gal. 2.7-9), must have given those who cited his example a hope (or warning) that their claim to special revelation could prove acceptable. Although in the event such second-century claims could not claim such apostolic authenticity as had Paul's, the precedent was still somewhat unnerving. And how should one rank Paul's theology of the (charismatic) body of Christ[38] with the theology of ecclesiastical office of the Pastorals? Is 1 Corinthians as equally (and independently) canonical as 1 Timothy? Here a canonical criticism which insists on reading 1 Corinthians through the lens provided by 1 Timothy may make ecclesiastical sense, but it probably also devalues what made Paul's contribution to the beginnings of Christianity so vital and transformative. The Paul of the Pastorals is a desiccated Paul, whereas it is the Paul of the earlier letters who inspired Irenaeus and Tertullian, and subsequently some of the greatest Christian minds, even when he as often as not out-theologized them.

So a NT canon which centres on the four (NT) Gospels and the letters of Paul, as was already the case through most of the second century, includes and canonizes a diversity which is vital to the character and identity of the Christians who affirmed their canonical status. Jesus still remains at the centre, determining also the spokes of the wheel, and where and how the circumference should be drawn. But the diversity which is included within that circumference remains significant. So much so, that an insistence on conformity to one ecclesiology or a single coherent expression of Christian faith can be said to condemn itself as non-canonical — which brings us to the great church's third pillar.

---

36. But Paul Trebilco reminds me (in private correspondence) that the addition of ch. 21 to John's Gospel made quite a difference on this score.

37. See also my 'John and the Synoptics as a Theological Question', in Culpepper and Black, eds., *Exploring the Gospel of John* 301-13.

38. Rom. 12.3-8; 1 Cor. 12.

d. The Rule of Faith

That there was a common faith which united the earliest believers in Jesus is clear enough from Paul's letters. It is widely thought that in writing to the church(es) in Rome he used as his calling-card an early creedal statement of the gospel of Jesus Christ (Rom. 1.3-4), that is, a summary definition of the gospel which he could assume would be familiar to the recipients of his letter. And 1 Cor. 15.1-7 is an explicit appeal to a shared creed on which the Corinthians' faith was based and which was integral to the gospel preached by all the early evangelists (15.11). The searching out of early creedal forms, especially in the NT letters, was a fruitful project through much of the twentieth century.[39] Likewise the tracing of the emergence of the early Christian formal and ecumenical creeds through the first four centuries.[40] The latter take us beyond our own time-span, but the creedal forms already in the NT, Ephesians' talk of 'one body and one Spirit, . . . one hope . . . one Lord, one faith, one baptism, one God and Father of all' (Eph. 4.4-6), and the talk of 'the faith' so prominent in the Pastorals,[41] are sufficient indication that the recognition of the need for and desirability of a united and uniting faith was already a taken-for-granted priority.

The climax of the same concern through the second century is to be found in Irenaeus's insistence on the unity of the faith 'received from the apostles and their disciples' (*adv. haer.* 1.10.1), and Tertullian's coining of the key phrase 'the rule of faith, *regula fidei*' (*Praescript.* 13). The most striking feature of both statements was the focus, more or less exclusive, on christology: in Tertullian's terms —

> The belief that there is one only God . . . the Creator of the world,
> who produced all things out of nothing through his own Word . . . ;
> that this Word is called his Son . . .
> at last brought down by the Spirit and power of the Father into the
>   Virgin Mary,
> was made flesh in her womb, and, being born of her, went forth as
>   Jesus Christ;
> thenceforth he preached the new law and the new promise of the
>   kingdom of heaven, worked miracles;
> having been crucified, he rose again the third day;

---

39. See e.g. W. Kramer, *Christ, Lord, Son of God* (1963; ET London: SCM, 1966); and others in *Unity and Diversity* ch. 3.
40. Kelly, *Early Christian Creeds*.
41. See §39 nn.216-22. Note also Jude 3 — 'the faith that was once for all entrusted to the saints'.

> (then) having ascended into the heavens, he sat at the right hand of the Father;
> sent instead of himself the power of the Holy Ghost to lead such as believe;
> will come with glory to take the saints to the enjoyment of everlasting life . . . and to condemn the wicked to everlasting fire,
> after the resurrection of both these classes shall have happened, together with the restoration of their flesh.
> This rule, as it will be proved, was taught by Christ . . .

This accords well with our findings, as already indicated in §50.2a.[42] The most obvious area in the mapping out of the faith which united the great bulk of Christians was christology, their beliefs in and about Christ Jesus. This was the most defining, but also the most divisive issue, separating the claimants to the title 'Christian' from others, and sifting the various claimants to the title from each other. The christology of John played the crucial role. It proved divisive from the first. The Logos christology was already proving unacceptable to 'the Jews' of John, and the implications are that through the second century the same Logos christology was judged by the rabbis to be an unacceptable restatement of traditional Jewish monotheism. But it seems to have been the case that the christology of virgin birth and divine sonship was also too much even for many Jewish believers in Jesus. At the same time Valentinians tried to wrest John's Logos christology to fit with their much more elaborate theology of the Divine Spirit separated from physical matter by numerous emanations. In the face of both challenges Apologists and Irenaeus held firm. Logos christology ensured that belief in one God was secure — the Logos as the self-expression of the one God. And John's insistence that the Logos had become flesh, suffered and died, ensured that a Gnostic retelling of the story of Jesus, and of the salvation he brought, would not do. The oneness of the invisible God could not be sustained either by envisaging a multiplicity of divine beings or by maintaining that the divine could never unite with or become flesh. The first great theo-logical battle for Christianity was the battle for monotheism: how to conceive of the one God making salvation possible for physical humanity without losing the conception of God's oneness and without losing sight of the infinite gulf between divine and human, Creator and creation. It was John's Logos christology which enabled second-century Christianity to steer its way between that Scylla and Charybdis and to maintain the creedal belief in God as one.

---

42. Kelly makes the point that Irenaeus and Tertullian both believed that the unwritten *regula fidei* and scripture were identical in content (*Early Christian Doctrines* 36-41).

This outcome was at a cost, which has never been fully realized; for the simple claim that the Logos had become flesh was always going to appear too simple and simplistic. The challenges to that Logos christology led, probably unavoidably, to ever more complex creeds, climaxing in the Nicene creed and Chalcedonian definition, in which the attempt to define the indefinable, to express the inexpressible, forced metaphor and analogy beyond what they could adequately express. Irenaeus justifiably refuted the sophisticated efforts of the Valentinians to finesse the perception of the relation between divine and human in the case of Jesus. But the ecumenical creeds made a not dissimilar mistake in thinking they could find more satisfactory words to define the indefinable. Perhaps, then, the NT canon invites those who find the developed creeds as confusing as definitive (that is, not at all clear as to what the definition affirms), to return to the basic insights of the first century: that God is invisible, but Jesus has made visible the invisible God.[43]

Nor should we forget the point made in §49.3a, that John's theology of incarnation was in effect a shift in emphasis regarding the decisive saving event, from Jesus' death as atonement for sin, to his birth and incarnation as the divine taking the human into itself. Despite the Pauline insistence that central to the gospel was the affirmation that 'Christ died for our sins' (1 Cor. 15.3), the creeds shift the focus from atoning death to incarnation, content to affirm simply that he had been crucified, buried and raised from the dead, with forgiveness of sin mentioned quite separately or tied to baptism. The resultant tension between salvation as atoning death and as the human becoming divine (theosis) remains a tension to this day between Western and Eastern Christianity. And we should also recall how the insistence that the resurrection of Jesus was resurrection of the flesh, already in Ignatius, lost the subtle Pauline distinction between body and flesh, in which negative overtones were attached almost exclusively to the latter. By the return to the Greek identity of flesh and body, with the same negative sign attached to both, Paul's positive appreciation of corporeality was lost to sight and the door was opened to a Christian despising of bodily function and sexuality, an antipathy which manifested itself in encratism and misogyny.

If the bridging of the gulf between the divine and the human proved beyond the capacity of human language to express adequately, the tension between a faith rooted in a special election of a people (Israel) and a gospel for all became virtually unbearable and, again, impossible to express in a form of words which would unite all who believed in Jesus. Despite his best endeavours, Paul did not succeed in holding together the gospel for the circumcised and the gospel for the uncircumcised. And despite his bridge-building role

---

43. Col. 1.15; John 1.18.

Peter was no more successful. Justin may indicate a willingness for continued dialogue, and Irenaeus express full respect, but it was the Ignatiuses and the Melitos who set the pathway for the future. A rule of faith which held together Jewish believers in Jesus and Gentile Christians was never achieved. And the loss of regard for Christianity's Jewishness remains a feature of Christianity to this day.

50.3 Conclusion

The resolution to the contest over Christianity's identity was already clearly indicated in the second century. Jesus was the defining centre. The claim to be directly connected to and derived from Jesus of Nazareth in his mission in Galilee and Judaea in the late 20s was the decisive determinant of what counted as Christian.

Too quickly neglected, however, was the historical particularity of the revelation which was perceived to come through Jesus and which was Jesus. For it was crucial that Jesus was a Jew. It was crucial that the God he revealed was the God of Israel, that the one God whom Jesus affirmed was also the Creator of all things. It was crucial that he could be identified with the Logos which was the one God's self-expression vis-à-vis creation and humankind. It was crucial that this same Jesus had suffered and died, and had been raised from the dead and exalted to God's right hand. It was crucial that the power of God's Spirit, familiar from Israel's prophetic history, could be seen as empowering Jesus in his mission and as continuing his work after he had been exalted to heaven. All this was bound up with the historical particularity of Jesus, of Jesus the Jew, Jesus Messiah. It was when this historical particularity was played down and the story of Jesus was given a timelessness, or focused in his (post-resurrection) heavenly role, that the link to the historical Jesus was slackened and the centre lost its defining role.[44]

The neglect of the Jewishness of Jesus has meant also that the other great originating and defining force in earliest Christianity, Paul, was less fully appreciated than he had been by the first Christian generations. For only when it is fully appreciated just how Jewish the first disciples of Jesus were, and how emerging Christianity was most straightforwardly identified as a messianic sect

---

44. For further thoughts on the historical particularity of the NT texts I may refer to my 'The Embarrassment of History: Reflections on the Problem of "Anti-Judaism" in the Fourth Gospel', in Bieringer et al., eds., *Anti-Judaism and the Fourth Gospel* 47-67; and 'Biblical Hermeneutics and *Historical* Responsibility', in S. E. Porter and M. R. Malcolm, eds., *The Future of Biblical Interpretation: Responsible Plurality in Biblical Hermeneutics* (London: Paternoster, 2013) 65-78.

of Judaism, only then can the contribution of Paul be properly recognized. For it was Paul, in his insistence that the grace of God was free to all who believed, who ensured that the identity of Christianity would expand to include Gentile as well as Jew — and who ensured that reconciliation between races, and classes, has to be seen as an inescapable part of the gospel too.

If this Jesus is the defining centre, and if Paul ensured that the gospel of this Jesus was for all who respond in faith, then these are the key determinants of Christian identity. As soon as we begin to elaborate this unifying identity then diversity becomes unavoidable. Some elements are bound up closely with these key determinants.

- The model for living provided to his followers by Jesus was imbued with a Jewish ethos, with the particularity of Jesus showing how moral (and ritual) codes could and should be the expression of both love of God and love of neighbour, including the enemy.
- Jesus' practice of table-fellowship, his 'last supper', and the integration of baptism as the rite of initiation from the first.
- Paul's insistence that faith/trust in Christ crucified alone is fundamental, and that to insist on any further requirements is to destroy the basic gospel principle of faith.

But in the working out of what these involved in different settings and groupings a diversity of practice was inevitable — just as the elaboration of the defining centre was bound to create diversity since no single formulation was ever going to be adequate.

And when the elements of functioning Christianity move still further away from the unifying identity, the diversity may be expected to become more diverse still. This is true most noticeably in terms of church worship, order and ministry. The model sponsored by Ignatius was certainly becoming more widely accepted through the second century. But the alternatives enshrined within the NT canon never entirely disappeared and have re-emerged in dynamic form today.

If then the focus and centre of identity is as simple and limited as it would appear, and what proved decisive in the contest for Christian identity in the second century, then the necessary corollary is presumably that the diverse expressions of Christianity round that common core should acknowledge the legitimacy of these other, diverse expressions, and be content to unite and cooperate round the centre, content to be spokes in a wheel bigger than anything that the individual spoke has experienced.

Abbreviations

AARAS	American Academy of Religion: Academy series
AB	Anchor Bible
ABD	*Anchor Bible Dictionary.* Ed. D. N. Freedman (6 vols.; New York: Doubleday, 1992)
AD	Anno domini
AGJU	Arbeiten zur Geschichte des antiken Judentums und des Urchristentum
AJEC	Ancient Judaism and Early Christianity
ANF	Ante-Nicene Fathers
ANRW	*Aufstieg und Niedergang der römischen Welt.* Ed. H. Temporini and W. Haase (Berlin: de Gruyter, 1972-)
ANT	*The Apocryphal New Testament.* Ed. J. K. Elliott (Oxford: Clarendon, 1993)
AOT	*The Apocryphal Old Testament.* Ed. H. F. D. Sparks (Oxford: Clarendon, 1984)
BBB	Bonner biblische Beiträge
BCE	Before the Christian Era, or, Before the Common Era
BDAG	W. Bauer, *A Greek-English Lexicon of the New Testament and Other Early Christian Literature.* 3rd ed., revised by F. W. Danker (Chicago: University of Chicago, 2000)
BDB	F. Brown, S. R. Driver, and C. A. Briggs, *A Hebrew and English Lexicon of the Old Testament* (Oxford, 1907)
BETL	Bibliotheca ephemeridum theologicarum lovaniensium
BJRL	*Bulletin of the John Rylands University Library of Manchester*
BJS	Brown Judaic Studies

BNTC	Black's New Testament Commentaries
BZ	*Biblische Zeitschrift*
BZNW	Beihefte zur Zeitschrift für die neutestamentliche Wissenschaft
CBNTS	Coniectanea biblica: New Testament Series
CBQ	*Catholic Biblical Quarterly*
CE	Christian Era, or, Common Era
cf.	compare
ch(s).	chapter(s)
CIJ	*Corpus Inscriptionum Judaicarum*
CRINT	Compendia Rerum Iudaicarum ad Novum Testamentum
DLNT	*Dictionary of the Later New Testament and Its Developments.* Ed. R. P. Martin and P. H. Davids (Downers Grove: IVP, 1997)
EB	Etudes bibliques
EC	*The Encyclopedia of Christianity.* Ed. E. Fahlbusch et al. (5 vols.; Leiden: Brill/Grand Rapids: Eerdmans, 1998-2008)
ed(s).	edited by, editor(s)
EDEJ	*The Eerdmans Dictionary of Early Judaism.* Ed. J. J. Collins and D. C. Harlow (Grand Rapids: Eerdmans, 2010)
e.g.	exempli gratia, for example
EKK	Evangelisch-katholischer Kommentar zum Neuen Testament
ET	English translation
et al.	*et alii*, and others
Eusebius, *HE*	Eusebius, *Historia Ecclesiastica*
FRLANT	Forschungen zur Religion und Literatur des Alten und Neuen Testaments
FS	Festschrift, volume written in honour of
GLAJJ	*Greek and Latin Authors on Jews and Judaism.* Ed. M. Stern (3 vols.; Jerusalem: Israel Academy of Sciences and Humanities, 1976, 1980, 1984)
HKNT	Handkommentar zum Neuen Testament
HNT	Handbuch zum Neuen Testament
HTKNT	Herders theologischer Kommentar zum Neuen Testament
HTS	Harvard Theological Studies
HUCA	*Hebrew Union College Annual*
ICC	International Critical Commentary
IVF	Inter-Varsity Fellowship
JBL	*Journal of Biblical Literature*
JECS	*Journal of Early Christian Studies*
JRS	*Journal of Roman Studies*
JSHJ	*Journal for the Study of the Historical Jesus*

Abbreviations

JSJ	*Journal for the Study of Judaism*
JSNT	*Journal for the Study of the New Testament*
JSNTS	*JSNT* Supplement Series
JSOT	*Journal for the Study of the Old Testament*
JSP	*Journal for the Study of the Pseudepigrapha*
JSPSupp	*Journal for the Study of the Pseudepigrapha* Supplement Series
JTS	*Journal of Theological Studies*
KAT	Kommentar zum Alten Testament
KAV	Kommentar zu den Apostolischen Vätern
KEK	H. A. W. Meyer, Kritisch-exegetischer Kommentar über das Neue Testament
LCL	Loeb Classical Library
LNTS	Library of New Testament Studies (incorporating JSNTS)
LSJ	H. G. Liddell and R. Scott, *A Greek-English Lexicon*. Revised H. S. Jones (Oxford: Clarendon, ^{9}1940); with supplement (1968)
LXX	Septuagint
NCB	New Century Bible
NDIEC	*New Documents Illustrating Early Christianity* (Sydney: Macquarie University/ Grand Rapids: Eerdmans): vol. 1 (G. H. R. Horsley, 1981); vol. 2 (G. H. R. Horsley, 1982); vol. 3 (G. H. R. Horsley, 1983); vol. 4 (G. H. R. Horsley, 1987); vol. 5 (G. H. R. Horsley, 1989); vol. 6 (S. R. Llewelyn, 1992); vol. 7 (S. R. Llewelyn, 1994); vol. 8 (S. R. Llewelyn, 1998); vol. 9 (ed. S. R. Llewelyn, 2002); vol. 10 (ed. S. R. Llewelyn and J. R. Harrison, 2012)
NHL	*The Nag Hammadi Library in English.* Ed. J. M. Robinson (Leiden: Brill, 1988)
NHMS	Nag Hammadi and Manichaean Studies
NIDB	*The New Interpreter's Dictionary of the Bible.* Ed. K. D. Sakenfeld (4 vols.; Nashville: Abingdon, 1975-85)
NIGTC	New International Greek Testament Commentary
NovT	*Novum Testamentum*
NovTSupp	Supplement to *NovT*
NRSV	New Revised Standard Version
NT	New Testament
NTA	W. Schneemelcher and R. McL. Wilson, *New Testament Apocrypha*: vol. 1, *Gospels and Related Writings* (Cambridge: James Clarke, revised edition 1991); vol. 2, *Writings Related to the Apostles; Apocalypses and Related Subjects* (Cambridge: James Clarke, revised edition 1992)

NTAF	*The New Testament in the Apostolic Fathers* (Oxford: Clarendon, 1905)
NTL	New Testament Library
NTOA	Novum Testamentum et Orbis Aniquus
NTS	*New Testament Studies*
ODCC	*The Oxford Dictionary of the Christian Church.* Ed. F. L. Cross and E. A. Livingstone. 2nd edition (Oxford: Oxford University, 1983)
OT	Old Testament
OTP	*The Old Testament Pseudepigrapha.* Ed. J. H. Charlesworth (2 vols.; London: Darton, 1983, 1985)
PGL	*Patristic Greek Lexicon.* Ed. G. W. H. Lampe (Oxford: Clarendon, 1968)
PTMS	Princeton Theological Monograph Series
RBL	*Review of Biblical Literature*
RHPR	*Revue d'histoire et de philosophie religieuses*
SB	Sources Bibliques
SBB	Stuttgart biblische Beiträge
SBL	Society of Biblical Literature
SBLDS	Society of Biblical Literature Dissertation Series
SBLMS	Society of Biblical Literature Monograph Series
SBS	Stuttgarter Bibelstudien
Schürer, *History*	E. Schürer, *The History of the Jewish People in the Age of Jesus Christ*, revised and edited by G. Vermes and F. Millar (4 vols.; Edinburgh: T & T Clark, 1973-87)
SNTSMS	Society for New Testament Studies Monograph Series
Str-B	H. L. Strack and P. Billerbeck, *Kommentar zum Neuen Testament aus Talmud und Midrasch* (Munich, 1922-1961)
SUNT	Studien zur Umwelt des Neuen Testaments
Supp.	Supplement
TDNT	*Theological Dictionary of the New Testament.* Ed. G. Kittel and G. Friedrich (ET; Grand Rapids: Eerdmans, 1964-76)
THNT	Theologischer Handkommentar zum Neuen Testament
TLZ	*Theologische Literaturzeitung*
TS	*Theological Studies*
TSAJ	Texte und Studien zum Antiken Judentum
TynB	*Tyndale Bulletin*
UALG	Untersuchungen zur antiken Literatur und Geschichte
VC	*Vigiliae Christianae*
vol(s).	volume(s)

Abbreviations

WBC	Word Biblical Commentary
WMANT	Wissenschaftliche Monographien zum Alten und Neuen Testament
WUNT	Wissenschaftliche Untersuchungen zum Neuen Testament
ZAC	*Zeitschrift für Antikes Christentum*
ZNW	*Zeitschrift für die neutestamentliche Wissenschaft*
ZTK	*Zeitschrift für Theologie und Kirche*

Bibliography

Aasgaard, R. *The Childhood of Jesus: Decoding the Apocryphal Infancy Gospel of Thomas.* Eugene, OR: Cascade Books, 2009.
Abramowski, L. 'Die "Erinnerungen der Apostel" bei Justin', in P. Stuhlmacher, ed., *Das Evangelium und die Evangelien,* 341-53. WUNT 28. Tübingen: Mohr Siebeck, 1983; = ET *The Gospel and the Gospels,* 323-35. Grand Rapids: Eerdmans, 1991.
Ådna, J. *Jesu Stellung zum Tempel: Die Tempelaktion und das Tempelwort als Ausdruck seiner messianischen Sendung.* WUNT. Tübingen: Mohr Siebeck, 2000.
Ådna, J., and H. Kvalbein, eds. *The Mission of the Early Church to Jews and Gentiles.* WUNT 127. Tübingen: Mohr Siebeck, 2000.
Aland, K. 'The Problem of Anonymity and Pseudonymity in Christian Literature of the First Two Centuries', in *The Authorship and Integrity of the New Testament,* 1-13. SPCK Theological Collections 4. London: SPCK, 1965.
———. *Synopsis quattuor Evangeliorum.* Stuttgart: Württembergische Bibelanstalt, ^{13}1984.
Aland, K., ed. *Vollständige Konkordanz zum griechischen Neuen Testament,* vol. 2. Berlin: de Gruyter, 1978.
Aland, K., and B. Aland. *The Text of the New Testament.* ET Grand Rapids: Eerdmans, ^{2}1989.
Alexander, L. 'The Living Voice: Scepticism towards the Written Word in Early Christianity and in Graeco-Roman Texts', in D. J. A. Clines et al., eds., *The Bible in Three Dimensions: Essays in Celebration of Forty Years of Biblical Studies in the University of Sheffield,* 221–47. Sheffield: Sheffield Academic Press, 1990.
———. *The Preface to Luke's Gospel.* SNTSMS 78. Cambridge: Cambridge University, 1993.
Alexander, P. S. '"The Parting of the Ways" from the Perspective of Rabbinic Judaism', in Dunn, ed., *Jews and Christians,* 1-25.
———. 'Jewish Believers in Early Rabbinic Literature (2d to 5th Centuries)', in Skarsaune and Hvalvik, eds., *Jewish Believers,* 659-709.
Allison, D. C. *The New Moses: A Matthean Typology.* Minneapolis: Fortress, 1993.
Alon, G. *The Jews in Their Land in the Talmudic Age.* 2 vols. Jerusalem: Magnes, 1980, 1984.

Altaner, B. *Patrology*. ET Freiburg: Herder, 1960.
Anderson, P. N. *The Christology of the Fourth Gospel: Its Unity and Disunity in the Light of John 6*. Valley Forge, PA: TPI, 1996.
———. *The Fourth Gospel and the Quest for Jesus*. London: T & T Clark, 2006.
Anderson, P. N., et al., eds. *John, Jesus and History*, vol. 1: *Critical Appraisals of Critical Views*. Atlanta: SBL, 2007.
———. *John, Jesus and History*, vol. 2: *Aspects of Historicity in the Fourth Gospel*. Atlanta: SBL, 2009.
Appold, M. L. *The Oneness Motif in the Fourth Gospel*. WUNT 2.1. Tübingen: Mohr Siebeck, 1976.
Asgeirsson, J. M., et al., eds. *Thomasine Traditions in Antiquity: The Social and Cultural World of the Gospel of Thomas*. Leiden: Brill, 2005.
Ashton, J. *Understanding the Fourth Gospel*. Oxford: Clarendon, 1991.
Ashton, J., ed. *The Interpretation of John*. Edinburgh: T & T Clark, ²1997.
Audet, J.-P. *La Didache*. EB. Paris: Gabalda, 1958.
Aune, D. E. 'The Significance of the Delay of the Parousia for Early Christianity', in G. E. Hawthorne, ed., *Current Issues in Biblical and Patristic Interpretation*, 87-109. Grand Rapids: Eerdmans, 1975.
———. 'The Odes of Solomon and Early Christian Prophecy'. *NTS* 28 (1982): 435-60.
Bacon, B. W. *Studies in Matthew*. London: Constable, 1930.
Bain, A. M. 'Tertullian: Paul as Teacher of the Gentile Churches', in Bird and Dodson, eds., *Paul and the Second Century*, 207-25.
Bal, M., J. Crewe, and L. Spitzer, eds. *Acts of Memory: Cultural Recall in the Present*. Hanover, NH: Dartmouth College, 1999.
Balch, D. L., ed. *Social History of the Matthean Community: Cross-disciplinary Approaches*. Minneapolis: Fortress, 1991.
Baldensperger, W. *Der Prolog des vierten Evangeliums: sein polemisch-apologetischer Zweck*. Tübingen: Mohr, 1898.
Barclay, J. M. G. *Jews in the Mediterranean Diaspora from Alexander to Trajan (323 BCE–117 CE)*. Edinburgh: T & T Clark, 1996.
———. '"Do We Undermine the Law?" A Study of Romans 14.1–15.6', in J. D. G. Dunn, ed., *Paul and the Mosaic Law*, 287-308. WUNT 89. Tübingen: Mohr Siebeck, 1996.
Barnard, L. W. *Studies in the Apostolic Fathers and Their Background*. Oxford: Blackwell, 1966.
———. *Justin Martyr: His Life and Thought*. Cambridge University, 1967.
Barnes, T. D. 'Legislation Against the Christians'. *JRS* 58 (1968): 32-50.
Barnett, A. E. *Paul Becomes a Literary Influence*. Chicago: University of Chicago, 1941.
Barrett, C. K. 'The Theological Vocabulary of the Fourth Gospel and of the Gospel of Truth', in W. Klassen and G. F. Snyder, eds., *Current Issues in New Testament Interpretation*, 210-23, 297-98. London: SCM, 1962; reprinted in *Essays on John*, 50-64.
———. 'The Acts and the Origins of Christianity', in *New Testament Essays*, 101-15. London: SPCK, 1972.
———. '"The Father is greater than I" (John 14.28): Subordinationist Christology in the New Testament' (1974), in *Essays on John*, 19-36.
———. *The Gospel of John and Judaism*. London: SPCK, 1975.

———. 'Christocentric or Theocentric? Observations on the Theological Method of the Fourth Gospel' (1976), in *Essays on John,* 1-18.
———. *Essays on John.* London: SPCK, 1982.
———. 'Jews and Judaizers in the Epistles of Ignatius', in *Essays on John,* 133-58.
Bartlet, J. V. 'The Epistle of Barnabas'. *NTAF* 3-6, 11-14.
Barton, S. C. *Discipleship and Family Ties in Mark and Matthew.* SNTSMS 80. Cambridge: Cambridge University, 1994.
Bauckham, R. 'The Study of Gospel Traditions outside the Canonical Gospels: Problems and Prospects', in Wenham, *Jesus Tradition,* 369-403.
———. *Jude and the Relatives of Jesus in the Early Church.* Edinburgh: T & T Clark, 1990.
———. *The Climax of Prophecy: Studies on the Book of Revelation.* Edinburgh: T & T Clark, 1993.
———. 'The Worship of Jesus', in *Climax of Prophecy,* 118-49.
———. 'The Parting of the Ways: What Happened and Why', *Studia Theologica* 47 (1993): 135-51.
———. 'The *Acts of Paul* as a Sequel to Acts', in B. W. Winter and A. D. Clarke, eds., *The Book of Acts in Its Ancient Literary Setting,* 105-52. Grand Rapids: Eerdmans, 1993.
———. 'For Whom Were the Gospels Written?', in R. Bauckham, ed., *The Gospels for All Christians: Rethinking the Gospel Audiences.* Grand Rapids: Eerdmans, 1998.
———. 'Jews and Jewish Christians in the Land of Israel at the Time of the Bar Kochba War, with Special Reference to the *Apocalypse of Peter*', in Stanton and Stroumsa, eds., *Tolerance and Intolerance,* 228-38.
———. 'The *Acts of Paul*: Replacement of Acts or Sequel to Acts?', in Stoops, ed., *Apocryphal Acts of the Apostles,* 159-68.
———. *The Fate of the Dead: Studies on the Jewish and Christian Apocalypses.* Leiden: Brill, 1998.
———. 'The Apocalypse of Peter: A Jewish Christian Apocalypse from the Time of Bar Kokhba', in *The Fate of the Dead,* 160-258.
———. '2 Peter and the Apocalypse of Peter', in *The Fate of the Dead,* 290-303.
———. *James: Wisdom of James, Disciple of Jesus the Sage.* London: Routledge, 1999.
———. 'The Origin of the Ebionites', in Tomson and Lambers-Petry, eds., *Image of Judaeo-Christians,* 162-81.
———. *Jesus and the Eyewitnesses: The Gospels as Eyewitness Testimony.* Grand Rapids: Eerdmans, 2006.
———. *The Testimony of the Beloved Disciple.* Grand Rapids: Baker, 2007.
Bauckham, R., and C. Mosser, eds. *The Gospel of John and Christian Theology.* Grand Rapids: Eerdmans, 2008.
Bauckham, R., et al., eds. *A Cloud of Witnesses: The Theology of Hebrews in Its Ancient Contexts.* LNTS 387. London: T & T Clark, 2008.
———. *The Epistle to the Hebrews and Christian Theology.* Grand Rapids: Eerdmans, 2009.
Bauer, J. B. *Die Polykarpbriefe.* KAV 5. Göttingen: Vandenhoeck, 1995.
Bauer, W. *Rechtgläubigkeit und Ketzerei im ältesten Christentum* (1934, ²1964); ET *Orthodoxy and Heresy in Earliest Christianity.* Philadelphia: Fortress, 1971.

Bibliography

Baur, F. C. *Paul: The Apostle of Jesus Christ* (1845); ET, 2 vols., London: Williams & Norgate, 1873, 1875.

———. *The Church History of the First Three Centuries* (1854); ET, 2 vols., London: Williams & Norgate, 1878-79.

Beasley-Murray, G. R. *Jesus and the Last Days: The Interpretation of the Olivet Discourse.* Peabody, MA: Hendrickson, 1993.

Beck, N. A. *Mature Christianity: The Recognition and Repudiation of the Anti-Jewish Polemic of the New Testament.* London/Toronto: Associated University Presses, 1985.

Becker, A. H. 'Beyond the Spatial and Temporal *Limes*', in Becker and Reed, eds., *The Ways That Never Parted*, 373-92.

Becker, A. H., and A. Y. Reed, eds. *The Ways That Never Parted.* TSAJ 95. Tübingen: Mohr Siebeck, 2003.

Bell, H. I., and T. C. Skeat. *Fragments of an Unknown Gospel.* London: British Museum, 1935.

Bellinzoni, A. J. *The Sayings of Jesus in the Writings of Justin Martyr.* NovTSupp 17. Leiden: Brill, 1967.

Ben Ezra, D. S. '"Christians" observing "Jewish" Festivals of Autumn', in Tomson and Lambers-Petry, eds., *The Image of the Judaeo-Christians*, 53-73.

———. 'Whose Fast Is It? The Ember Day of September and Yom Kippur', in Becker and Reed, eds., *The Ways That Never Parted*, 259-82.

Ben Zeev, M. P. *Diaspora Judaism in Turmoil 116/117 CE.* Leuven: Peeters, 2005.

Berding, K. *Polycarp and Paul.* Leiden: Brill, 2002.

Bernhard, A. E. *Other Early Christian Gospels: A Critical Edition of the Surviving Greek Manuscripts.* LNTS 315. London: T & T Clark, 2006.

Bernheim, P.-A. *James, Brother of Jesus.* London: SCM, 1997.

Bernier, J. *Aposynagōgos and the Historical Jesus in John: Rethinking the Historicity of the Johannine Expulsion Passages.* Leiden: Brill, 2013.

Best, E. *Following Jesus: Discipleship in the Gospel of Mark.* JSNTS 4. Sheffield: JSOT, 1981.

Betz, H. D. *The Sermon on the Mount.* Hermeneia. Minneapolis: Fortress, 1995.

Beutler, J. 'Synoptic Jesus Tradition in the Johannine Farewell Discourse', in Fortna and Thatcher, eds., *Jesus in the Johannine Tradition*, 165-73.

———. *Neue Studien zu den johanneischen Schriften.* BBB 167. Bonn University, 2012.

Beyschlag, K. *Clemens Romanus und der Frühkatholizismus.* Tübingen: Mohr Siebeck, 1966.

Bianchi, U. *Le origini dello Gnosticismo.* Leiden: Brill, 1967.

Biblia Patristica: Index des Citations et Allusions Bibliques dans la Littérature Patristique, des Origines à Clément d'Alexandrie et Tertullian. Vol. 1. Paris, 1975.

Bieringer, R., et al., eds. *Anti-Judaism and the Fourth Gospel.* Assen: Royal Van Gorcum, 2001.

Bird, M. F., and J. R. Dodson, eds. *Paul and the Second Century.* LNTS 412. London: T & T Clark, 2011.

Bird, M. F. 'The Reception of Paul in the *Epistle of Diognetus*', in Bird and Dodson, eds., *Paul and the Second Century*, 70-90.

Black, C. C. *The Disciples according to Mark: Markan Redaction in Current Debate.* JSNTS 27. Sheffield: Sheffield Academic, 1989, ²2012.

Blackwell, B. C. 'Paul and Irenaeus', in Bird and Dodson, eds., *Paul and the Second Century,* 190-206.
Blomberg, C. L. 'The Historical Reliability of John', in Fortna and Thatcher, eds., *Jesus in the Johannine Tradition,* 71-82.
Bockmuehl, M. 'Abraham's Faith in Hebrews 11', in Bauckham et al., eds., *The Epistle to the Hebrews and Christian Theology,* 364-73.
———. *The Remembered Peter.* WUNT 262. Tübingen: Mohr Siebeck, 2010.
———. *Simon Peter in Scripture and Memory.* Grand Rapids: Baker Academic, 2012.
Bockmuehl, M., and D. A. Hagner, eds. *The Written Gospel;* G. N. Stanton FS. Cambridge University, 2005.
Bockmuehl, M., and J. C. Paget, eds. *Redemption and Resistance: The Messianic Hopes of Jews and Christians in Antiquity.* London: T & T Clark, 2007.
Bollok, J. 'The Description of Paul in the Acta Pauli', in Bremmer, ed., *Apocryphal Acts of Paul,* 1-15.
Bolt, P. G. *Jesus' Defeat of Death: Persuading Mark's Early Readers.* SNTSMS 125. Cambridge: Cambridge University, 2003.
Bolyki, J. 'Events after the Martyrdom: Missionary Transformation of an Apocalyptical Metaphor in Martyrium Pauli', in Bremmer, ed., *Apocryphal Acts of Paul,* 92-106.
Borgen, P. 'God's Agent in the Fourth Gospel' (1968), in Ashton, ed., *Interpretation of John,* 83-95.
Bornkamm, G., G. Barth, and H. J. Held, *Tradition and Interpretation in Matthew.* 1960; ET London: SCM, 1963.
Bovon, F. *Luke the Theologian.* Waco: Baylor University, ²2006.
Boyarin, D. *Dying for God: Martyrdom and the Making of Judaism and Christianity.* Stanford: Stanford University, 1999.
———. 'Semantic Differences; or, "Judaism"/"Christianity"', in Becker and Reed, eds., *The Ways That Never Parted,* 74-77.
———. *Border Lines: The Partition of Judaeo-Christianity.* Philadelphia: University of Pennsylvania, 2004.
———. *The Jewish Gospels: The Story of the Jewish Christ.* New York: New Press, 2012.
Bremmer, J. N., ed. *The Apocryphal Acts of Paul.* Kampen: Kok Pharos, 1996.
———. *The Apocryphal Acts of Peter: Magic, Miracles and Gnosticism.* Leuven: Peeters, 1998.
Bremmer, J. N. 'Magic, Martyrdom and Women's Liberation in the Acts of Paul and Thecla', in Bremmer, ed., *The Apocryphal Acts of Paul,* 36-59.
Breytenbach, C. *Nachfolge und Zukunftserwartung nach Markus.* Zürich: Theologischer, 1984.
Broadhead, E. K. *Teaching with Authority: Miracles and Christology in the Gospel of Mark.* JSNTS 74. Sheffield Academic, 1992.
———. *Naming Jesus: Titular Christology in the Gospel of Mark.* JSNTS 175. Sheffield Academic, 1999.
———. 'The Fourth Gospel and the Synoptic Sayings Source', in Fortna and Thatcher, eds., *Jesus in the Johannine Tradition,* 291-301.
———. *Jewish Ways of Following Jesus.* WUNT 266. Tübingen: Mohr Siebeck, 2010.
Brooks, S. H. *Matthew's Community: The Evidence of His Special Sayings Material.* JSNTS 16. Sheffield: JSOT, 1987.
Brown, R. E. 'The Gospel of Thomas and St John's Gospel'. *NTS* 9 (1962-63): 155-77.

———. *New Testament Essays*. London: Chapman, 1965.
———. *The Semitic Background of the Term 'Mystery' in the New Testament*. Philadelphia: Fortress, 1968.
———. *Jesus God and Man*. London: Chapman, 1968.
———. *The Community of the Beloved Disciple*. London: Chapman, 1979.
———. 'The *Gospel of Peter* and Canonical Gospel Priority', *NTS* 33 (1987): 321-43.
———. *The Death of the Messiah*. 2 vols. New York: Doubleday, 1994.
———. *Introduction to the New Testament*. New York: Doubleday, 1997.
Brown, R. E., K. P. Donfried and J. Reumann, *Peter in the New Testament*. London: Geoffrey Chapman, 1974.
Brown, R. E., and J. P. Meier. *Antioch and Rome: New Testament Cradles of Catholic Christianity*. London: Geoffrey Chapman, 1983.
Bryan, C. *A Preface to Mark: Notes on the Gospel in Its Literary and Cultural Settings*. Oxford: Oxford University, 1993.
Bühner, J. A. *Der Gesandte und sein Weg im 4. Evangelium*. WUNT 2.2. Tübingen: Mohr Siebeck, 1977.
Bultmann, R. 'The History of Religions Background of the Prologue to the Gospel of John' (1923). ET in Ashton, ed., *Interpretation*, 27-46.
———. *Theology of the New Testament*. 2 vols. ET London: SCM, 1952, 1955.
———. *The Gospel of John*. ET Philadelphia: Westminster, 1971.
Burge, G. M. *The Anointed Community: The Holy Spirit in the Johannine Tradition*. Grand Rapids: Eerdmans, 1987.
Burke, T., ed. *Ancient Gospel or Modern Forgery? The Secret Gospel of Mark in Debate*. Eugene, OR: Cascade Books, 2013.
Burkitt, F. C. *Early Eastern Christianity*. London, 1904.
Burridge, R. A. *What Are the Gospels? A Comparison with Graeco-Roman Biography*. Grand Rapids: Eerdmans, ²2004.
———. 'Imitating Jesus: An Inclusive Approach to the Ethics of the Historical Jesus and John's Gospel', in Anderson et al., eds., *John, Jesus and History*, vol. 2, 281-90.
Burrus, V. *Chastity as Autonomy: Women in the Stories of Apocryphal Acts*. Lewiston/Queenston: Edwin Mellen, 1987.
Burtchaell, J. T. *From Synagogue to Church: Public Services and Offices in the Earliest Christian Communities*. Cambridge University, 1992.
Byrskog, S. *Jesus the Only Teacher: Didactic Authority and Transmission in Ancient Israel, Ancient Judaism and the Matthean Community*. CBNTS 24. Stockholm: Almqvist & Wiksell, 1994.
———. *Story as History — History as Story*. WUNT 123. Tübingen: Mohr Siebeck, 2000.
Cameron, R., ed. *The Other Gospels: Non-Canonical Gospel Texts*. Guildford: Lutterworth, 1983.
———. *Sayings Traditions in the* Apocryphon of James. HTS 34. Philadelphia: Fortress, 1984.
Cameron, R., and M. P. Miller. *Redescribing Christian Origins*. Atlanta: SBL, 2004.
Cancik, H., ed. *Markus-Philologie*. WUNT 33. Tübingen: Mohr Siebeck, 1984.
Capes, D. B., et al., eds. *Israel's God and Rebecca's Children: Christology and Community in Early Judaism and Christianity;* L. W. Hurtado and A. F. Segal FS. Waco: Baylor University, 2007.

Caragounis, C. C. *Peter and the Rock*. BZNW 58. Berlin: de Gruyter, 1990.
———. 'The Kingdom of God: Common and Distinct Elements between John and the Synoptics', in Fortna and Thatcher, eds., *Jesus in the Johannine Tradition*, 125-34.
Carey, H. J. *Jesus' Cry from the Cross*. LNTS 398. London: T & T Clark, 2009.
Carlson, S. C. *The Gospel Hoax: Morton Smith's Invention of Secret Mark*. Waco: Baylor University, 2005.
———. 'Origen's Use of the *Gospel of Thomas*', in Charlesworth et al., eds., *Sacra Scriptura*, 137-51.
Carrington, P. *Christian Apologetics of the Second Century: In Their relation to Modern Thought*. London: SPCK, 1921.
Carter, W. *Matthew and the Margins: A Socio-Political and Religious Reading*. JSNTS 204. Sheffield: Sheffield Academic, 2000.
Casey, M. *From Jewish Prophet to Gentile God*. Cambridge: James Clarke, 1991.
———. *Aramaic Sources of Mark's Gospel*. SNTSMS 102. Cambridge: Cambridge University, 1998.
Catchpole, D. 'The Synoptic Divorce Material as a Traditio-Historical Problem'. *BJRL* 57 (1974): 93-127.
———. *The Quest for Q*. Edinburgh: Clark, 1993.
Chae, Y. S. *Jesus as Eschatological Davidic Shepherd*. WUNT 216. Tübingen: Mohr Siebeck, 2006.
Charlesworth, J. H. 'Christian and Jewish Self-Definition in Light of the Christian Additions to the Apocryphal Writings', in *Jewish and Christian Self-Definition*, vol. 2: *Aspects of Judaism in the Graeco-Roman Period*, ed. E. P. Sanders, 27-55. London: SCM, 1981.
———. *The Beloved Disciple*. Valley Forge, PA: TPI, 1995.
———. 'The Dead Sea Scrolls and the Gospel according to John', in Culpepper and Black, eds., *Exploring the Gospel of John*, 65-97.
———. *Critical Reflections on the Odes of Solomon*, vol. 1: *Literary Setting, Textual Studies, Gnosticism, the Dead Sea Scrolls and the Gospel of John*. JSPSupp 22. Sheffield Academic, 1998.
———. *The First Christian Hymnbook: The Odes of Solomon*. Eugene, OR: Wipf & Stock, 2009.
Charlesworth, J. H., et al., eds. *Sacra Scriptura: How "Non-Canonical" Texts Functioned in Early Judaism and Early Christianity*. London: Bloomsbury, 2013.
Charlesworth, J. H., and R. A. Culpepper. 'The Odes of Solomon and the Gospel of John'. *CBQ* 35 (1973): 298-322.
Chartrand-Burke, T. 'The *Infancy Gospel of Thomas*', in Foster, ed., *Non-Canonical Gospels*, 126-38.
Chilton, B. 'The Gospel according to Thomas as a Source of Jesus' Teaching', in Wenham, ed., *The Jesus Tradition outside the Gospels*, 155-75.
Clark-Soles, J. 'John 13: Of Footwashing and History', in Anderson et al., eds., *John, Jesus and History*, vol. 2, 255-69.
Clarke, W. K. Lowther. *The First Epistle to the Corinthians*. London: SPCK, 1937.
Cockerill, G. L. 'Melchizedek without Speculation: Hebrews 7.1-25 and Genesis 14.17-24', in Bauckham et al., eds., *A Cloud of Witnesses*, 128-44.
Cohen, S. *The Beginnings of Jewishness: Boundaries, Varieties, Uncertainties*. Los Angeles: University of California, 1999.

Cohn, N. *The Pursuit of the Millennium*. Secker & Warburg, 1957.
Cohn-Sherbok, D. 'Modern Hebrew Christianity and Messianic Judaism', in Tomson and Lambers-Petry, eds., *The Image of the Judaeo-Christians*, 287-98.
Colpe, C. *Die religionsgeschichtliche Schule: Darstellung und Kritik ihres Bildes vom gnostischen Erlösermythus*. Göttingen: Vandenhoeck & Ruprecht, 1961.
Conzelmann, H. *The Theology of Saint Luke*. 1953, ²1957; ET London: Faber & Faber, 1960, ²1961.
Cook, J. G. *Roman Attitudes Towards Christians: From Claudius to Hadrian*. WUNT 261. Tübingen: Mohr Siebeck, 2010.
Corwin, V. *St. Ignatius and Christianity in Antioch*. New Haven: Yale University, 1960.
Cousland, J. R. C. 'Matthew's Earliest Interpreter: Justin Martyr on Matthew's Fulfilment Quotations', in T. R. Hatina, ed., *Biblical Interpretation in Early Christian Gospels*, vol. 2: *The Gospel of Matthew*, 45-60. LNTS 310. London: T & T Clark, 2008.
Crossan, J. D. *Four Other Gospels*. Minneapolis: Seabury, 1985.
———. *Sayings Parallels: A Workbook for the Jesus Tradition*. Philadelphia: Fortress, 1986.
———. *The Cross That Spoke: The Origins of the Passion Narrative*. San Francisco: Harper & Row, 1988.
———. *The Historical Jesus: The Life of a Mediterranean Jewish Peasant*. San Francisco: Harper, 1991.
———. *The Birth of Christianity*. HarperSanFrancisco, 1998.
———. 'The *Gospel of Peter* and the Canonical Gospels', in Kraus and Nicklas, eds., *Evangelium nach Petrus*, 117-34.
Crossley, J. G. *The Date of Mark's Gospel: Insights from the Law in Earliest Christianity*. JSNTS 266. London: T & T Clark, 2004.
———, ed. *Judaism, Jewish Identities and the Gospel Tradition: Essays in Honour of Maurice Casey*. London and Oakville, CT: Equinox, 2010.
Crown, A. D. *The Samaritans*. Tübingen: Mohr Siebeck, 1989.
———. 'Judaism and Christianity: The Parting of the Ways', in A. J. Avery-Peck et al., eds., *When Judaism and Christianity Began*, 2.545-62. Leiden: Brill, 2004.
Cullmann, O. *Early Christian Worship*. London: SCM, 1953.
———. *Peter: Disciple, Apostle, Martyr*. London: SCM, ²1962.
———. *The Johannine Circle*. London: SCM, 1976.
Culpepper, R. A. *The Johannine School*. SBLDS 26. Missoula: Scholars, 1975.
———. 'Anti-Judaism in the Fourth Gospel as a Theological Problem for Christian Interpreters', in Bieringer et al., eds., *Anti-Judaism and the Fourth Gospel*, 68-91.
———. *John: The Son of Zebedee; The Life of a Legend*. Edinburgh: T & T Clark, 2000.
———. 'Designs for the Church in the Imagery of John 21:1-14', in J. Frey et al., eds., *Imagery in the Gospel of John*, 369-402. Tübingen: Mohr Siebeck, 2006.
Culpepper, R. A., and C. C. Black, eds. *Exploring the Gospel of John: In Honor of D. Moody Smith*. Louisville: Westminster John Knox, 1996.
Daniélou, J. *A History of Early Christian Doctrine before the Council of Nicaea*, vol. 1: *The Theology of Jewish Christianity*. London: Darton, Longman & Todd, 1964.
Das, A. A. *Solving the Romans Debate*. Minneapolis: Fortress, 2007.
Dassmann, E. *Der Stachel im Fleisch: Paulus in der frühchristlichen Literatur bis Irenäus*. Münster: Aschendorff, 1979.

Davies, S. L. *The Revolt of the Widows: The Social World of the Apocryphal Acts.* Southern Illinois University, 1980.

———. *The Gospel of Thomas and Christian Wisdom.* New York: Seabury, 1983.

Davies, W. D. 'Paul and the Dead Sea Scrolls: Flesh and Spirit', in *Christian Origins and Judaism*, 145-77. London: DLT, 1962.

———. *The Setting of the Sermon on the Mount.* Cambridge: Cambridge University, 1964.

Davis, S. J. *The Cult of St. Thecla: A Tradition of Women's Piety in Late Antiquity.* Oxford University, 2001.

de Boer, E. A. *The Gospel of Mary: Beyond a Gnostic and a Biblical Mary Magdalene.* JSNTS 260. London: T & T Clark, 2004.

———. 'Followers of Mary Magdalene and Contemporary Philosophy', in Frey and Schröter, eds., *Jesus in apokryphen Evangelienüberlieferungen*, 315-38.

de Boer, M. 'The Nazoreans: Living at the Boundary of Judaism and Christianity', in Stanton and Stroumsa, eds., *Tolerance and Intolerance*, 239-62.

de Boer, M. C. 'The Depiction of "the Jews" in John's Gospel: Matters of Behavior and Identity', in Bieringer et al., eds., *Anti-Judaism*, 260-80.

de Jonge, H. J. '"The Jews" in the Gospel of John', in Bieringer et al., eds., *Anti-Judaism*, 239-59.

de Labriolle, P. *La crise montaniste.* Paris: LeRoux, 1913.

de Lange, N. *Origen and the Jews: Studies in Jewish-Christian Relations in Third-Century Palestine.* Cambridge: Cambridge University, 1976.

DeConick, A. D. *Voices of the Mystics: Early Christian Discourse in the Gospels of John and Thomas and Other Ancient Christian Literature.* JSNTS 157. Sheffield Academic, 2001.

———. 'On the Brink of the Apocalypse: A Preliminary Examination of the Earliest Speeches in the Gospel of Thomas', in Asgeirsson et al., *Thomasine Traditions in Antiquity*, 93-118.

———. *Recovering the Original* Gospel of Thomas: *A History of the Gospel and Its Growth.* LNTS 286. London: T & T Clark, 2005.

———. *The Original Gospel of Thomas in Translation.* LNTS 287. London: T & T Clark, 2006.

———. *The Thirteenth Apostle: What the Gospel of Judas Really Says.* London: Continuum, 2007.

———. 'The Mystery of Betrayal: What Does the *Gospel of Judas* Really Say?', in Scopello, ed., *The Gospel of Judas in Context*, 239-64.

———. 'The *Gospel of Thomas*', in Foster, ed., *Non-Canonical Gospels*, 13-29.

———. 'The *Gospel of Judas*: A Parody of Apostolic Christianity', in Foster, ed., *Non-Canonical Gospels*, 96-109.

Deines, R. 'Not the Law but the Messiah: Law and Righteousness in the Gospel of Matthew — An Ongoing Debate', in D. M. Gurtner and J. Nolland, eds., *Built upon the Rock: Studies in the Gospel of Matthew*, 53-84. Grand Rapids: Eerdmans, 2008.

Delling, G. '*MONOS THEOS*'. *TLZ* 77 (1952): 469-76.

Del Verne, M. *Didache and Judaism: Jewish Roots of an Ancient Christian-Jewish Work.* London: T & T Clark, 2004.

Denaux, A., ed. *John and the Synoptics.* Leuven: Leuven University, 1992.

Deutsch, C. *Hidden Wisdom and the Easy Yoke: Wisdom, Torah and Discipleship in Matthew 11.25-30*. JSNTS 18. Sheffield: JSOT, 1987.
Dewey, J. 'Oral Methods of Structuring Narrative in Mark'. *Interpretation* 43 (1989): 32–44.
———. 'The Gospel of Mark as an Oral-Aural Event: Implications for Interpretation', in E. S. Malbon and E. V. McKnight, eds., *The New Literary Criticism and the New Testament*, 145–63. JSNTS 109. Sheffield: Sheffield Academic Press, 1994.
———. 'The Eyewitness of History: Visionary Consciousness in the Fourth Gospel', in Fortna and Thatcher, eds., *Jesus in the Johannine Tradition*, 59-70.
———. 'The Gospel of John in Its Oral-Written Media World', in Fortna and Thatcher, eds., *Jesus in the Johannine Tradition*, 239-52.
Dines, J. M. *The Septuagint*. London: T & T Clark, 2004.
Dodd, C. H. *According to the Scriptures*. London: Nisbet, 1952.
———. *The Interpretation of the Fourth Gospel*. Cambridge: Cambridge University, 1953.
———. *Historical Tradition in the Fourth Gospel*. Cambridge: Cambridge University, 1963.
———. *The Founder of Christianity*. London: Collins, 1971.
Doering, L. 'First Peter as Early Christian Diaspora Letter', in K.-W. Niebuhr and R. W. Wall, eds., *Catholic Epistles and Apostolic Tradition*, 441-57. Waco: Baylor University, 2009.
Donahue, P. J. 'Jewish Christianity in the Letters of Ignatius of Antioch'. *VC* 32 (1978): 81-93.
Donaldson, T. L. 'Proselytes or "Righteous Gentiles"? The Status of Gentiles in Eschatological Pilgrimage Patterns of Thought'. *JSP* 7 (1990): 3-27.
———. *Judaism and the Gentiles: Jewish Patterns of Universalism (to 135 CE)*. Waco: Baylor University, 2007.
Donelson, L. R. *Pseudepigraphy and Ethical Argument in the Pastoral Epistles*. Tübingen: J. C. B. Mohr, 1986.
———. 'The Jesus Tradition in the Didache', in Wenham, ed., *Jesus Tradition*, 269-87.
Donfried, K. P. *The Setting of Second Clement in Early Christianity*. NovTSupp 38. Leiden: Brill, 1974.
Draper, J. A., ed. *The Didache in Modern Research*. Leiden: Brill, 1996.
Dschulnigg, P. *Sprache, Redaktion und Intention des Markus-Evangeliums*. SBB 11. Stuttgart: KBW, 1986.
Dunderberg, I. '*Thomas*' I-sayings and the Gospel of John', in Uro, ed., *Thomas at the Crossroads*, 33-64.
———. 'The School of Valentinus', in Marjanen and Luomanen, *Companion*, 64-99.
———. *The Beloved Disciple in Conflict? Revisiting the Gospels of John and Thomas*. Oxford: Oxford University, 2006.
Dunn, J. D. G. 'The Messianic Secret in Mark'. *TynB* 21 (1970): 92-117, reprinted in Tuckett, ed., *The Messianic Secret*, 116-31.
———. *Baptism in the Holy Spirit*. London: SCM, 1970.
———. 'John 6 — A Eucharistic Discourse?', *NTS* 17 (1971): 328-38.
———. *Jesus and the Spirit*. London: SCM, 1975.
———. *Unity and Diversity in the New Testament: An Inquiry into the Character of Earliest Christianity*. London: SCM, 1977, ²1990, ³2006.

———. 'The Relationship between Paul and Jerusalem according to Galatians 1 and 2'. *NTS* 28 (1982): 461-78.
———. 'Let John Be John', in P. Stuhlmacher, ed., *Das Evangelium und die Evangelien*, 309-39. WUNT 28. Tübingen: Mohr Siebeck, 1983 = *The Gospel and the Gospels*, 293-322. Grand Rapids: Eerdmans, 1991.
———. *Christology in the Making*. London: SCM, ²1989/Grand Rapids: Eerdmans, 1996.
———. *Romans*. 2 vols. WBC 38. Dallas: Word, 1988.
———. 'Pharisees, Sinners and Jesus', in *Jesus, Paul and the Law*, 61-86. London: SPCK, 1990.
———. 'John and the Oral Gospel Tradition', in H. Wansbrough, ed., *Jesus and the Oral Gospel Tradition*, 351-79. JSNTS 64. Sheffield: Sheffield Academic, 1991.
———. *The Partings of the Ways between Christianity and Judaism and Their Significance for the Character of Christianity*. London: SCM, 1991, ²2006.
———. 'Matthew's Awareness of Markan Redaction', in *The Four Gospels. Festschrift for Frans Neirynck*, ed. F. Van Segbroeck, 1349-59. Leuven University Press, 1992.
———. 'Jesus, Table-Fellowship and Qumran', in J. H. Charlesworth, ed., *Jesus and the Dead Sea Scrolls*, 254-72. New York: Doubleday, 1992.
———. 'Jesus Tradition in Paul', in B. Chilton and C. A. Evans, eds., *Studying the Historical Jesus: Evaluations of the State of Current Research*, 155-78. Leiden: Brill, 1994.
———. 'Deutero-Pauline Letters', in J. Barclay and J. Sweet, eds., *Early Christian Thought in Its Jewish Context*, 130-44. Cambridge University, 1996.
———. 'Two Covenants or One? The Interdependence of Jewish and Christian Identity', in H. Lichtenberger, ed., *Geschichte-Tradition-Reflexion: III. Frühes Christentum*; M. Hengel FS, 97-122. Tübingen: Mohr Siebeck, 1996; reprinted with some additional material in *The Partings of the Ways*², 339-65.
———. *The Epistles to the Colossians and to Philemon*. NIGTC. Grand Rapids: Eerdmans, 1996.
———. 'John and the Synoptics as a Theological Question', in Culpepper and Black, eds., *Exploring the Gospel of John*, 301-13.
———. '*KYRIOS* in Acts', in C. Landmesser et al., eds., *Jesus Christus als die Mitte der Schrift*; O. Hofius FS, 363-78. Berlin: de Gruyter, 1997.
———. *The Theology of Paul the Apostle*. Grand Rapids: Eerdmans, 1998.
———. 'The Question of Anti-semitism in the New Testament Writings', in Dunn, ed., *Jews and Christians*, 177-211.
———. 'The Embarrassment of History: Reflections on the Problem of "Anti-Judaism" in the Fourth Gospel', in Bieringer et al., eds., *Anti-Judaism and the Fourth Gospel*, 47-67.
———. *Christianity in the Making*, vol. 1: *Jesus Remembered*. Grand Rapids: Eerdmans, 2003; vol. 2: *Beginning from Jerusalem*. Grand Rapids: Eerdmans, 2009.
———. *The New Perspective on Paul: Collected Essays*. Tübingen: Mohr Siebeck, 2005/Grand Rapids: Eerdmans, ²2008.
———. *A New Perspective on Jesus: What the Quest for the Historical Jesus Missed*. Grand Rapids: Baker Academic/London: SPCK, 2005.
———. 'Q¹ as Oral Tradition', in M. Bockmuehl and D. A. Hagner, eds., *The Written Gospel*; G. N. Stanton FS, 45-69. Cambridge: Cambridge University, 2005.

———. 'When Did the Understanding of Jesus' Death as an Atoning Sacrifice First Emerge?', in D. B. Capes et al., eds., *Israel's God and Rebecca's Children: Christology and Community in Early Judaism and Christianity*; L. W. Hurtado and A. F. Segal FS, 169-81. Waco: Baylor University, 2007.

———. 'Social Memory and the Oral Jesus Tradition', in S. C. Barton, L. T. Stuckenbruck, and B. G. Wold, eds., *Memory in the Bible and Antiquity: The Fifth Durham-Tübingen Research Symposium*, 179-94. WUNT 2.212. Tübingen: Mohr Siebeck, 2007.

———. 'Matthew as Wirkungsgeschichte', in P. Lampe et al., eds., *Neutestamentiche Exeges im Dialog: Hermeneutik — Wirkungsgeschichte — Matthäusevangelium*; U. Luz FS, 149-66. Neukirchen-Vluyn: Neukirchener, 2008.

———. 'Eyewitnessses and the Oral Jesus Tradition'. *JSHJ* 6 (2008): 85-91.

———. 'Reappreciating the Oral Jesus Tradition'. *Svensk Exegetisk Årsbok* 74 (2009): 1-17.

———. 'The Book of Acts as Salvation History', in J. Frey, S. Krauter, and H. Lichtenberger, eds., *Heil und Geschichte: Die Geschichtsbezogenheit des Heils und das Problem der Heilsgeschichte in der biblischen Tradition und in der theologischen Deutung*, 385-401. WUNT 248. Tübingen: Mohr Siebeck, 2009.

———. *Did the First Christians Worship Jesus? The New Testament Evidence*. London: SPCK, 2010.

———. 'John's Gospel and the Oral Gospel Tradition', in A. Le Donne and T. Thatcher, eds., *The Fourth Gospel in First-Century Media Culture*, 157-85. LNTS 426. London: T & T Clark, 2011.

———. 'Luke's Jerusalem Perspective', in S. Walton et al., eds., *Reading Acts Today: Essays in Honour of L. C. A. Alexander*, 120-36. LNTS 427. London: T & T Clark, 2011.

———. 'How Did Matthew Go About Composing His Gospel?', in D. M. Gurtner, J. Willitts and R. A. Burridge, eds., *Jesus, Matthew's Gospel and Early Christianity: Studies in Memory of Graham N. Stanton*, 39-58. LNTS 435. London: T & T Clark, 2011.

———. 'The Legal Status of the Earliest Christian Churches', in M. Zetterholm and S. Byrskog, eds., *The Making of Christianity: Conflicts, Contacts and Constructions*; Bengt Holmberg FS, 75-93. Winona Lake: Eisenbrauns, 2012.

———. 'The Earliest Interpreters of the Jesus Tradition: A Study in Early Hermeneutics', in S. E. Porter and M. R. Malcolm, eds., *Horizons in Hermeneutics*; A. C. Thiselton FS, 119-47. Grand Rapids: Eerdmans, 2013.

———. 'Biblical Hermeneutics and *Historical* Responsibility', in S. E. Porter and M. R. Malcolm, eds., *The Future of Biblical Interpretation: Responsible Plurality in Biblical Hermeneutics*, 65-78. London: Paternoster, 2013.

———. *The Oral Gospel Tradition*. Grand Rapids: Eerdmans, 2013.

———. 'If Paul Could Believe Both in Justification by Faith and Judgment according to Works, Why Should That Be a Problem for Us?', in A. P. Stanley, ed., *Four Views on the Role of Works at the Final Judgment*, 119-41. Grand Rapids: Zondervan, 2013.

———. 'From the Crucifixion to the End of the First Century', in H. Shanks, ed., *Partings: How Judaism and Christianity Became Two*, 27-53. Washington: Biblical Archaeology Society, 2013.

———. 'The Rise and Expansion of Christianity in the First Three Centuries C.E.: Why and How Did Embryonic Christianity Expand Beyond the Jewish People?', in C. K. Rothschild and J. Schröter, *The Rise and Expansion of Christianity in the First Three Centuries of the Common Era*, 183-203. WUNT 301. Tübingen: Mohr Siebeck, 2013.

———. 'Tertullian and Paul on the Spirit of Prophecy', in T. D. Still and D. E. Wilhite, eds., *Tertullian and Paul*, 72-78. London: Bloomsbury T & T Clark, 2013.

Dunn, J. D. G., ed. *Jews and Christians: The Parting of the Ways AD 70 to 135*. Tübingen: Mohr Siebeck, 1992/Grand Rapids: Eerdmans, 1999.

———. *Paul and the Mosaic Law*. WUNT 89. Tübingen: Mohr Siebeck, 1996.

Dunn, J. D. G., and J. W. Rogerson, eds. *Eerdmans Commentary on the Bible*. Grand Rapids: Eerdmans, 2003.

Dwyer, T. *The Motif of Wonder in the Gospel of Mark*. JSNTS 128. Sheffield: Sheffield Academic, 1996.

Edwards, J. R. 'The Markan Sandwich: The Significance of Interpolations in Markan Narratives'. *NovT* 31 (1989): 193-216.

———. *The Hebrew Gospel and the Development of the Synoptic Tradition*. Grand Rapids: Eerdmans, 2009.

Ehrman, B. D. *The Orthodox Corruption of Scripture: The Effect of Early Christological Controversies on the Text of the New Testament*. New York: Oxford University, 1993.

———. *Lost Christianities: The Battle for Scripture and the Faiths We Never Knew*. Oxford University, 2003.

———. *Lost Scriptures: Books That Did Not Make It into the New Testament*. Oxford University, 2003.

———. *The Apostolic Fathers*. LCL; 2 vols. Cambridge, MA: Harvard University, 2003.

Ehrman, B. D., and Z. Plese. *The Apocryphal Gospels: Texts and Translations*. Oxford University, 2011.

Eisele, W. *Ein unerschütterliches Reich: Die mittelplatonische Umformung des Parusiegedankens im Hebräerbrief*. BZNW 116. Berlin: de Gruyter, 2003.

———. *Welcher Thomas? Studien zur Text- und Überlieferungsgeschichte des Thomasevangeliums*. WUNT 259. Tübingen: Mohr Siebeck, 2010.

Elgvin, T. 'Jewish Editing of the Old Testament Pseudepigrapha', in Skarsaune and Hvalvik, eds., *Jewish Believers in Jesus*, 278-304.

Elliott, J. K. *The Apocryphal New Testament*. Oxford: Clarendon, 1993.

———. *The Apocryphal Jesus: Legends of the Early Church*. Oxford University, 1996.

Elliott, M. W. 'The Triumph of Paulinism by the Mid-Third Century', in Bird and Dodson, eds., *Paul and the Second Century*, 244-56.

Ellis, E. E. *The Old Testament in Early Christianity*. Grand Rapids: Baker, 1992.

Epp, E. J. *The Theological Tendency of Codex Bezae Cantabrigiensis in Acts*. SNTSMS 3. Cambridge University, 1966.

———. 'The Multivalence of the Term "Original Text" in New Testament Textual Criticism'. *HTR* 92 (1999): 245-81.

———. 'Anti-Judaic Tendencies in the D-Text of Acts: Forty Years of Conversation', in Nicklas and Tilly, eds., *The Book of Acts as Church History*, 111-46.

Eubank, N. *Wages of Cross-bearing and Debt of Sin: The Economy of Heaven in Matthew's Gospel*. BZNW 196. Berlin: de Gruyter, 2013.

Bibliography

Evans, C. A. *Word and Glory: On the Exegetical and Theological Background of John's Prologue.* JSNTS 89. Sheffield: JSOT, 1993.

———. 'The Twelve Thrones of Israel: Scripture and Politics in Luke 22:24-30', in Evans and Sanders, *Luke and Scripture,* 154-70.

———. 'Prophecy and Polemic: Jews in Luke's Scriptural Apologetic', in Evans and Sanders, *Luke and Scripture,* 171-211.

———. 'Root Causes of the Jewish-Christian Rift from Jesus to Justin', in Porter and Pearson, eds., *Christian-Jewish Relations through the Centuries,* 20-35.

———. 'The Jewish Christian Gospel Tradition', in Skarsaune and Hvalvik, eds., *Jewish Believers in Jesus,* 241-77.

Evans, C. A., and J. A. Sanders. *Luke and Scripture: The Function of Sacred Tradition in Luke-Acts.* Minneapolis: Fortress, 1993.

Evans, C. S. 'The Historical Reliability of John's Gospel: From What Perspective Should It Be Assessed?', in Bauckham and Mosser, eds., *The Gospel of John and Christian Theology,* 91-119.

Fee, G. D. *Pauline Christology: An Exegetical-Theological Study.* Peabody: Hendrickson, 2007.

Feldman, L. H. *Jew and Gentile in the Ancient World.* Princeton: Princeton University, 1993.

Feldman, L. H., and G. Hatai, eds. *Josephus, Judaism and Christianity.* Leiden: Brill, 1987.

Feldmeier, R. *Die Christen als Fremde: Die Metaphor der Fremde in der antiken Welt, im Urchristentum und im ersten Petrusbrief.* WUNT 64. Tübingen: Mohr Siebeck, 1992.

Fentress, J., and C. Wickham. *Social Memory.* Oxford: Blackwell, 1992.

Fiorenza, E. S. *The Book of Revelation: Justice and Judgment.* Philadelphia: Fortress, 1985.

Foerster, W. *Gnosis: A Selection of Gnostic Texts; 1. Patristic Evidence; 2. Coptic and Mandaic Sources.* Oxford: Clarendon, 1972, 1974.

Foley, J. M. *The Singer of Tales in Performance.* Bloomington: Indiana University Press, 1995.

Fornberg, T. *An Early Church in a Pluralistic Society.* Lund: Gleerup, 1977.

Fortna, R. T. *The Gospel of Signs.* SNTSMS 11. Cambridge: Cambridge University, 1970.

———. *The Fourth Gospel and Its Predecessor.* Philadelphia: Fortress, 1988.

Fortna, R. T., and T. Thatcher, eds. *Jesus in the Johannine Tradition.* Louisville: Westminster John Knox, 2001.

Foster, P. 'The Discovery and Initial Reaction to the So-called Gospel of Peter', in Kraus and Nicklas, eds., *Evangelium nach Petrus,* 9-30.

———. 'The Epistles of Ignatius of Antioch and the Writings That Later Formed the New Testament', in Gregory and Tuckett, eds., *Reception,* 159-86.

———. 'The *Gospel of Peter*', in Foster, ed., *Non-Canonical Gospels,* 30-42.

———. 'The *Gospel of Philip*', in Foster, ed, *Non-Canonical Gospels,* 68-83.

———. 'The *Protevangelium of James*', in Foster, ed., *Non-Canonical Gospels,* 122-25.

———. 'Justin and Paul', in Bird and Dodson, eds., *Paul and the Second Century,* 108-25.

———. 'The Text of the New Testament in the Apostolic Fathers', in C. E. Hill and M. J. Kruger, eds., *The Early Text of the New Testament*, 282-301. Oxford University, 2012.

Foster, P., ed. *The Non-Canonical Gospels*. London: T & T Clark, 2008.

France, R. T. *Matthew — Evangelist and Teacher.* Exeter: Paternoster, 1989.

Frankfurter, D. 'Beyond "Jewish Christianity"', in Becker and Reed, eds., *The Ways That Never Parted*, 131-43.

Franklin, E. *Luke: Interpreter of Paul, Critic of Matthew.* JSNTS 92. Sheffield: Sheffield Academic, 1994.

Frend, W. H. C. *The Early Church: From the Beginnings to 461.* London: SCM, 1965, ³1991.

Frey, J. 'Die Lilien und das Gewand: *EvThom* 36 und 37 als Paradigma für das Verhältnis des *Thomasevangeliums* zur synoptischen Überlieferung', in Frey, ed., *Das Thomasevangelium*, 122-80.

———. 'Zur Vielgestaltigkeit judenchristlicher Evangelienüberlieferungen', in Frey and Schröter, eds., *Jesus in apokryphen Evangelienüberlieferungen*, 93-137.

Frey, J., et al., eds. *Das Thomasevangelium: Entstehung — Rezeption — Theologie.* BZNW 157. Berlin: de Gruyter, 2008.

Frey, J., and J. Schröter, eds. *Jesus in apokryphen Evangelienüberlieferungen.* WUNT 1.254. Tübingen: Mohr Siebeck, 2010.

Freyne, S. *Retrieving James/Yakov, the Brother of Jesus: From Legend to History.* Bard College, 2008.

Friedlander, G. *The Jewish Sources of the Sermon on the Mount.* 1911. New York: Ktav, 1969.

Fuller, M. E. *The Restoration of Israel: Israel's Re-gathering and the Fate of the Nations in Early Jewish Literature and Luke-Acts.* BZNW 138. Berlin: de Gruyter, 2006.

Funk, R. W., et al. *The Five Gospels: The Search for the Authentic Words of Jesus.* New York: Macmillan, 1993.

Gager, J. G. 'Did Jewish Christians See the Rise of Islam?' in Becker and Reed, eds., *The Ways That Never Parted*, 361-65.

Gamble, H. Y. *Books and Readers in the Early Church: A History of Early Christian Texts.* Yale University, 1995.

———. 'The New Testament Canon: Recent Research and the Status Quaestionis', in McDonald and Sanders, eds., *The Canon Debate*, 267-94.

Gardner-Smith, P. *St John and the Synoptic Gospels.* Cambridge: Cambridge University, 1938.

Garrett, S. R. *The Temptations of Jesus in Mark's Gospel.* Grand Rapids: Eerdmans, 1998.

Garrow, A. J. P. *The Gospel of Matthew's Dependence on the* Didache. JSNTS 254. London: T & T Clark, 2004.

Gärtner, B. *The Temple and the Community in Qumran and the New Testament.* SNTSMS 1. Cambridge: Cambridge University, 1965.

Gasque, W. W. *A History of the Criticism of the Acts of the Apostles.* Grand Rapids: Eerdmans, 1975.

Gathercole, S. *The Pre-existent Son: Recovering the Christologies of Matthew, Mark and Luke.* Grand Rapids: Eerdmans, 2006.

———. *The Gospel of Judas: Rewriting Early Christianity.* Oxford University, 2007.

———. 'The Influence of Paul on the *Gospel of Thomas*. §§53.3 and 17', in J. Frey, ed., *Das Thomasevangelium*, 72-94.

———. 'The *Gospel of Judas*: An Unlikely Hero', in Foster, ed., *Non-Canonical Gospels*, 84-95.

———. *The Composition of the Gospel of Thomas: Original Language and Influences*. SNTSMS 151. Cambridge University, 2012.

Gerdmar, A. *Rethinking the Judaism-Hellenism Dichotomy: A Historiographical Case Study of Second Peter and Jude*. CBNTS 36. Stockholm: Almqvist & Wiksell, 2001.

Gerhardsson, B. *The Testing of God's Son. Matt 4:1-11 & PAR*. CB. Lund: Gleerup, 1966.

Goodacre, M. *The Case against Q*. Harrisburg: TPI, 2002.

———. *Thomas and the Gospels: The Case for Thomas's Familiarity with the Synoptics*. Grand Rapids: Eerdmans, 2012.

Goodman, M. *State and Society in Roman Galilee, AD 132-212*. Totowa: Rowman & Allanheld, 1983.

———. 'Nerva, the *fiscus Judaicus* and Jewish Identity'. *JRS* 79.6 (1989): 40-44.

———. 'Diaspora Reactions to the Destruction of the Temple', in Dunn, ed., *Jews and Christians*, 27-38.

———. *Mission and Conversion*. Oxford University, 1994.

———. 'The Function of Minim in Early Rabbinic Literature', in P. Schäfer, ed., *Geschichte — Tradition — Reflexion; Festschrift für Martin Hengel*, vol. I: *Judentum*, 501-10. Tübingen: Mohr Siebeck, 1996; reprinted in *Judaism in the Roman World: Collected Essays*. Leiden: Brill, 2007, 163-73.

———. 'Modeling the "Parting of the Ways"', in Becker and Reed, eds., *The Ways That Never Parted*, 119-29.

———. 'Sadducees and Essenes after 70 CE', in *Judaism in the Roman World*.

———. 'Modelling the "Parting of the Ways"', in *Judaism in the Roman World*, 175-85.

———. *Rome and Jerusalem: The Clash of Ancient Civilizations*. London: Penguin, 2007.

Goulder, M. D. *Luke: A New Paradigm*. JSNTS 20. Sheffield: Sheffield Academic, 1989.

Grant, R. M. *Second-Century Christianity: A Collection of Fragments*. London: SPCK, 1946.

———. 'The Bible of Theophilus of Antioch', *JBL* 66 (1947): 173-96.

———. *Gnosticism and Early Christianity*. New York: Columbia University, ²1966.

———. *After the New Testament*. Philadelphia: Fortress, 1967.

———. *Greek Apologists of the Second Century*. London: SCM, 1988.

Grant, R. M., ed. *Gnosticism: An Anthology*. London: Collins, 1961.

———. *Ignatius of Antioch*, in *The Apostolic Fathers*, vol. 4. London: Nelson, 1965.

Grant, R. M., and H. M. Graham, eds. *First and Second Clement*, in *The Apostolic Fathers*, vol. 2. London: Nelson, 1965.

Green, H. B. *Matthew, Poet of the Beatitudes*. JSNTS 203. Sheffield: Sheffield Academic, 2001.

Greenslade, S. L. *Schism in the Early Church*. London: SCM, 1953, ²1964.

Gregory, A. *The Reception of Luke and Acts in the Period before Irenaeus*. WUNT 2.169. Tübingen: Mohr Siebeck, 2003.

———. '*1 Clement* and the Writings That Later Formed the New Testament', in Gregory and Tuckett, eds., *Reception*, 129-57.

———. 'Jewish-Christian Gospels', in Foster, ed., *Non-Canonical Gospels*, 54-67.
Gregory, A., and C. Tuckett, eds. *The Reception of the New Testament in the Apostolic Fathers*. Oxford: Clarendon, 2005.
———. *Trajectories through the New Testament and the Apostolic Fathers*. Oxford: Clarendon, 2005.
Gruen, E. S. *Diaspora: Jews amidst Greeks and Romans*. Cambridge: Harvard University, 2002.
Gruenwald, I. *Apocalyptic and Merkabah Mysticism*. Leiden: Brill, 1979.
Guelich, R. *The Sermon on the Mount: A Foundation for Understanding*. Waco: Word, 1982.
———. 'The Gospel Genre', in P. Stuhlmacher, ed., *Das Evangelium und die Evangelien*, 183-219. WUNT 28. Tübingen: Mohr Siebeck, 1983 = *The Gospel and the Gospels*, 173-208. Grand Rapids: Eerdmans, 1991.
Gundry, R. H. *'EUANGELION:* How Soon a Book?' *JBL* 115 (1996): 321-25.
Haenchen, E. 'The Book of Acts as Source Material for the History of Early Christianity', in L. E. Keck and J. L. Martyn, eds., *Studies in Luke-Acts*, 258-78. Philadelphia: Fortress, 1966.
Hagner, D. A. *The Use of the Old and New Testaments in Clement of Rome*. NovTSupp 34. Leiden: Brill, 1973.
———. 'The Sayings of Jesus in the Apostolic Fathers and Justin Martyr', in D. Wenham, ed., *Gospel Perspectives*, vol. 5: *The Jesus Tradition outside the Gospel*, 233-68. Sheffield: JSOT, 1985.
———. *The New Testament*. Grand Rapids: Baker Academic, 2012.
Häkkinen, S. 'Ebionites', in Marjanen and Luomanen, eds., *Companion*, 247-78.
Halbwachs, M. *On Collective Memory*. Chicago: University of Chicago, 1992.
Hall, S. G. *Melito of Sardis:* On Pascha *and Fragments*. Oxford: Clarendon, 1979.
Hällström, G., and O. Skarsaune. 'Cerinthus, Elxai and Other Alleged Jewish Christian Teachers or Groups', in Skarsaune and Hvalvik, eds., *Jewish Believers*, 488-502.
Hanfmann, G. M. A., ed. *Sardis from Prehistoric to Roman Times: Results of the Archaeological Exploration of Sardis 1958-1975*. Harvard University, 1983.
Hannah, D. 'The Four-Gospel "Canon" in the *Epistula Apostolorum*'. *JTS* 59 (2008): 598-633.
Harnack, A. *History of Dogma*. ³1900; ET London: Constable/New York: Dover, 1961.
———. *What Is Christianity?* 1900; ET London: Williams & Norgate, 1901; 5th edition, London: Ernest Benn, 1958.
———. *The Expansion of Christianity in the First Three Centuries*. ET London: Williams & Norgate, 1904.
———. *The Mission and Expansion of Christianity in the First Three Centuries*. ET 1908; New York: Harper Torchbook, 1962.
———. *Marcion: Das Evangelium vom fremden Gott*. Leipzig: Hinrichs, 1924.
———. *Die Briefsammlung des Apostels Paulus*. Leipzig: Hinrichs, 1926.
Harrison, P. N. *The Problem of the Pastoral Epistles*. Oxford University, 1921.
Hartog, P. *Polycarp's* Epistle to the Philippians *and the* Martyrdom of Polycarp. Oxford University, 2013.
Hasler, V. 'Epiphanie und Christologie in des Pastoralbriefen'. *TLZ* 33 (1977): 193-209.
Hatina, T. R. *In Search of a Context: The Function of Scripture in Mark's Narrative*. JSNTS 232. London: Sheffield Academic, 2002.

Haverly, T. P. *Oral Traditional Narrative and the Composition of Mark's Gospel.* Ph.D. diss. Edinburgh, 1983.
Hawkins, J. C. *Horae Synopticae: Contributions to the Study of the Synoptic Problem.* Oxford: Clarendon, 1898, ²1909.
Hays, R. B. *Echoes of Scripture in the Letters of Paul.* Yale University, 1989.
———. '"Here We Have No Lasting City": New Covenantalism in Hebrews', in Bauckham et al., eds., *Hebrews and Christian Theology,* 151-73.
Head, P. M. 'Tatian's Christology and Its Influence on the Composition of the Diatessaron', *TynB* 43 (1992): 121-37.
———. 'On the Christology of the Gospel of Peter'. *VC* 46 (1992): 209-24.
———. 'Graham Stanton and the Four-Gospel Codex: Reconsidering the Manuscript Evidence', in J. Willitts et al., eds., *Jesus, Matthew's Gospel and Early Christianity: Studies in Memory of Graham N. Stanton,* 93-101. LNTS 435. London: T & T Clark, 2011.
Heckel, T. K. *Vom Evangelium des Markus zum viergestaltigen Evangelium.* WUNT 120. Tübingen: Mohr Siebeck, 1999.
Hedrick, C. W., and P. A. Mirecki. *Gospel of the Savior: A New Ancient Gospel.* Santa Rosa, CA: Polebridge, 1999.
Heemstra, M. *The* Fiscus Judaicus *and the Parting of the Ways.* WUNT 2.277. Tübingen: Mohr Siebeck, 2010.
Hemer, C. J. *The Letters to the Churches of Asia in Their Local Setting.* JSNTS 11. Sheffield: JSOT, 1986.
Henaut, B. W. *Oral Tradition and the Gospels: The Problem of Mark 4.* JSNTS 82. Sheffield: Sheffield Academic, 1993.
Hengel, M. *Judaism and Hellenism.* ET 2 vols. London: SCM, 1974.
———. *Studies in the Gospel of Mark.* London: SCM, 1985.
———. *The Johannine Question.* ET London: SCM, 1989.
———. *Die johanneische Frage.* WUNT 67. Tübingen: Mohr Siebeck, 1993.
———. *The Four Gospels and the One Gospel of Jesus Christ.* London: SCM, 2000.
———. 'Jakobus der Herrenbruder — der erste "Papst"?' (1985), in *Paulus und Jakobus: Kleine Schriften III,* 549-82. Tübingen: Mohr Siebeck, 2002.
———. *The Septuagint as Christian Scripture.* Edinburgh: T & T Clark, 2002.
———. *Der unterschätzte Petrus.* Tübingen: Mohr Siebeck, 2006.
———. 'The Prologue of the Gospel of John as the Gateway to Christological Truth', in Bauckham and Mosser, eds., *John and Christian Theology,* 265-94.
———. *Theologische, historische und biographische Skizzen: Kleine Schriften VII.* WUNT 253. Tübingen: Mohr Siebeck, 2010.
Henry, J. K. 'The Acts of Thomas as Sacred Text', in Charlesworth et al., eds., *Sacra Scriptura,* 152-70.
Herczeg, P. 'New Testament Parallels to the Apocryphal Acta Pauli Documents', in Bremmer, ed., *Apocryphal Acts of Paul,* 144-49.
Herford, R. T. *Christianity in Talmud and Midrash.* London: Williams & Norgate, 1903.
Herron, T. J. *Clement and the Early Church of Rome: On the Dating of Clement's First Epistle to the Corinthians.* Steubenville, OH: Emmaus Road Publishing, 2008.
Heschel, S. *Abraham Geiger and the Jewish Jesus.* University of Chicago, 1998.
Higgins, A. J. B. *The Historicity of the Fourth Gospel.* London: Lutterworth, 1960.

Hilhorst, A. 'Tertullian on the Acts of Paul', in Bremmer, ed., *The Apocryphal Acts of Paul,* 150-63.
Hill, C. E. *The Johannine Corpus in the Early Church.* Oxford University, 2004.
―――. *Who Chose the Gospels? Probing the Great Gospel Conspiracy.* Oxford University, 2010.
Hill, J. H. *The Earliest Life of Christ Ever Compiled from the Four Gospels Being* The Diatessaron *of Tatian.* Edinburgh: T & T Clark, 1894.
Hoffmann, R. J. *Marcion: On the Restitution of Christianity.* AARAS 46. Chico: Scholars, 1984.
Hofius, O. 'Das Zeugnis der Johannesoffenbarung von der Gottheit Jesu Christi', in H. Lichtenberger, ed., *Frühes Christentum,* 511-28. Tübingen: Mohr-Siebeck, 1996.
Hogan, P. N. 'Paul and Women in Second-Century Christianity', in Bird and Dodson, eds., *Paul and the Second Century,* 226-43.
Holmes, M. W. *The Apostolic Fathers.* Grand Rapids: Baker, 1989.
―――. 'Paul and Polycarp', in Bird and Dodson, eds., *Paul and the Second Century,* 57-69.
―――. 'Polycarp's *Letter to the Philippians* and the Writings That Later Formed the New Testament', in Gregory and Tuckett, eds., *Reception,* 187-227.
Horbury, W. 'The Benediction of the *Minim* and Early Jewish-Christian Controversy'. *JTS* 33 (1982): 19-61.
―――. 'Jewish-Christian Relations in Barnabas and Justin Martyr', in Dunn, ed., *Jews and Christians,* 315-45.
―――. 'The Beginnings of the Jewish Revolt under Trajan', in P. Schäfer, ed., *Geschichte — Tradition — Reflexion: Festschrift für Martin Hengel,* vol. I: *Judentum,* 283-304. Tübingen: Mohr Siebeck, 1996.
―――. *Jews and Christians in Contact and Controversy.* Edinburgh: T & T Clark, 1998.
―――. 'Messianism Among Jews and Christians in the Second Century', in *Messianism Among Jews and Christians: Twelve Biblical and Historical Studies,* 275-88. London: T & T Clark, 2003.
Horner, T. J. *Listening to Trypho: Justin Martyr's Dialogue Reconsidered.* Leuven: Peeters, 2001.
Horrell, D. G. *The Social Ethos of the Corinthian Correspondence.* Edinburgh: T & T Clark, 1996.
―――. *1 Peter.* New Testament Guides. London: T & T Clark, 2008.
Horton, F. L. *The Melchizedek Tradition: A Critical Examination of the Sources to the Fifth Century A.D. and in the Epistle to the Hebrews.* SNTSMS 30. Cambridge University, 1976.
Hübner, H. 'EN ARCHĒ EGŌ EIMI', in Labahn et al., eds., *Israel,* 107-22.
Huizenga, L. A. *The New Isaac: Tradition and Intertextuality in the Gospel of Matthew.* NovTSupp. Leiden: Brill, 2009.
Hummel, R. *Die Auseinandersetzung zwischen Kirche und Judentum im Matthäusevangelium.* Munich: Kaiser, 1966.
Hurst, L. D. *The Epistle to the Hebrews: Its Background of Thought.* SNTSMS 65. Cambridge University, 1990.
Hurtado, L. W. *One God One Lord: Early Christian Devotion and Ancient Jewish Monotheism.* Philadelphia: Fortress, 1988.

Bibliography

———. *Early Christian Artifacts: Manuscripts and Christian Origins*. Grand Rapids: Eerdmans, 2006.
Hvalvik, R. *The Struggle for Scripture and Covenant: The Purpose of the Epistle of Barnabas and Jewish-Christian Competition in the Second Century*. WUNT 2.82. Tübingen: Mohr Siebeck, 1996.
Incigneri, B. *The Gospel to the Romans: The Setting and Rhetoric of Mark's Gospel*. Leiden: Brill, 2003.
Isser, S. J. *The Dositheans: A Samaritan Sect in Late Antiquity*. SJLA 17. Leiden: Brill, 1976.
Iverson, K. R. *Gentiles in the Gospel of Mark*. LNTS 339. London: T & T Clark, 2007.
———. 'An Enemy of the Gospel? Anti-Paulinism and Intertextuality in the Gospel of Matthew', in Skinner and Iverson, eds., *Unity and Diversity in the Gospels and Paul*, 7-32.
James, M. R. *The Apocryphal New Testament*. Oxford: Clarendon, 1924.
Jansen, M. '"Evangelium des Zwillings?" Das *Thomasevangelium* als Thomas-Schrift', in Frey et al., eds., *Das Thomasevangelium*, 222-48.
Jefford, C. N. *The Sayings of Jesus in the Teaching of the Twelve Apostles*. Leiden: Brill, 1989.
———. *The Apostolic Fathers and the New Testament*. Peabody, MA: Hendrickson, 2006.
———. *The Epistle to Diognetus (with the Fragment of Quadratus)*. Oxford University, 2013.
Jeremias, J. *Unknown Sayings of Jesus*. London: SPCK, 1958, ²1964.
———. *Jesus' Promise to the Nations*. London: SCM, 1958.
———. *The Prayers of Jesus*. 1966. ET London: SCM, 1967.
Jervell, J. *Luke and the People of God: A New Look at Luke-Acts*. Minneapolis: Augsburg, 1972.
———. *The Unknown Paul : Essays on Luke-Acts and Early Christian History*. Minneapolis: Augsburg, 1984.
———. *The Theology of the Acts of the Apostles*. Cambridge: Cambridge University, 1996.
Johnson, L. T. 'The New Testament's Anti-Jewish Slander and the Conventions of Ancient Polemic'. *JBL* 108 (1989): 419-41.
Jonas, H. *The Gnostic Religion: The Message of the Alien God and the Beginning of Christianity*. Boston: Beacon, ²1958.
Jones, F. S. 'The Pseudo-Clementines: A History of Research'. *Second Century* 2 (1982): 1-33, 63-96.
———. 'An Ancient Jewish Christian Rejoinder to Luke's Acts of the Apostles: Pseudo-Clementine *Recognitions* 1.27-71', in Stoops, ed., *Apocryphal Acts*, 223-45.
———. *An Ancient Jewish Christian Source on the History of Christianity: Pseudo-Clementine Recognitions 1.27-71*. Atlanta: Scholars, 1995.
———. 'Jewish Christianity of the *Pseudo-Clementines*', in Marjanen and Luomanen, eds., *Companion*, 315-34.
Jossa, G. *Jews or Christians? The Followers of Jesus in Search of Their Own Identity*. WUNT 202. Tübingen: Mohr Siebeck, 2006.
Judge, E. A. 'Judaism and the Rise of Christianity: A Roman Perspective'. *TynB* 45 (1994): 355-68.

Judge, P. J. 'The Royal Official and the Historical Jesus', in Anderson et al., eds., *John, Jesus and History*, vol. 2, 83-92.

Kähler, M. *The So-Called Historical Jesus and the Historic Biblical Christ.* 1896. Philadelphia: Fortress, 1964.

Kaiser, U. U. 'Jesus als Kind', in Frey and Schröter, eds., *Jesus in apokryphen Evangelienüberlieferungen*, 253-69.

Käsemann, E. 'The New Testament Canon and the Unity of the Church', in *Essays on New Testament Themes*. London: SCM, 1964.

———. *The Testament of Jesus.* ET London: SCM, 1968.

———. 'Ketzer und Zeuge', in *Exegetische Versuche und Besinnungen*, 168-87. Göttingen: Vandenhoeck, 1970.

———. *The Wandering People of God: An Investigation of the Letter to the Hebrews.* ET Minneapolis: Augsburg, 1984.

Kazmierski, C. R. *Jesus, the Son of God: A Study of the Markan Tradition and Its Redaction by the Evangelist.* Würzburg: Echter, 1979.

Keck, L. E. 'The Introduction to Mark's Gospel'. *NTS* 12 (1966): 352-70.

———. 'The Function of Romans 3:10-18 — Observations and Suggestions', in J. Jervell and W. A. Meeks, eds., *God's Christ and His People*, 141-57. Oslo: Universitetsforlaget, 1977.

Keck, L. E., and J. L. Martyn, eds. *Studies in Luke-Acts.* Nashville: Abingdon, 1966.

Kee, H. C. *Community of the New Age.* London: SCM, 1977.

Keener, C. S. *Acts: An Exegetical Commentary.* Vol. 1. Grand Rapids: Baker Academic, 2012.

Kelber, W. H. 'Mark and Oral Tradition', in N. R. Petersen, ed., *Perspectives on Mark's Gospel*, 7-55.

———. *The Oral and the Written Gospel.* Philadelphia: Fortress, 1983.

Kelhoffer, J. A. *Miracle and Mission: The Authentication of Missionaries and Their Message in the Longer Ending of Mark.* WUNT 2.112. Tübingen: Mohr Siebeck, 2000.

———. '"How Soon a Book" Revisited: *EUANGELION* as a Reference to "Gospel" Materials in the First Half of the Second Century'. *ZNW* 95 (2004): 1-34.

———. '"Gospel" as a Literary Title in Early Christianity and the Question of What Is (and Is Not) a "Gospel" in Canons of Scholarly Literature', in Frey and Schröter, eds., *Jesus in apokryphen Evangelienüberlieferungen*, 399-422.

Kelly, J. N. D. *Early Christian Doctrines.* London: A & C Black, ²1960.

———. *Early Christian Creeds.* London: Longmans, 1960.

Kenyon, F. G. *The Chester Beatty Biblical Papyri: Descriptions and Texts of Twelve Manuscripts on Papyri of the Greek Bible.* London: Emery Walker, 1933-37.

Kermode, F. *The Genesis of Secrecy.* Cambridge, MA: Harvard University, 1979.

Kerr, A. R. *The Temple of Jesus' Body: The Temple Theme in the Gospel of John.* JSNTS 220. London: Sheffield Academic, 2002.

Kilpatrick, G. D. *The Origins of the Gospel according to Saint Matthew.* Oxford: Clarendon, 1946.

King, K. L. *What Is Gnosticism?* Harvard University, 2003.

———. 'Toward a Discussion of the Category "Gnosis"/"Gnosticism": The Case of the Epistle of Peter to Philip', in Frey and Schröter, eds., *Jesus in apokryphen Evangelienüberlieferungen*, 445-65.

Kingsbury, J. D. *Matthew: Structure, Christology, Kingdom.* Philadelphia: Fortress, 1975.

Bibliography

———. *The Christology of Mark's Gospel.* Philadelphia: Fortress, 1983.
Kinzig, W. 'The Nazoraeans', in Tomson and Lambers-Petry, eds., *Image of the Judaeo-Christians,* 463-87.
Kirk, A. 'Tradition and Memory in the *Gospel of Peter*', in Kraus and Nicklas, eds., *Evangelium nach Petrus,* 135-58.
Kirk, A. and T. Thatcher, eds. *Memory, Tradition, and Text: Uses of the Past in Early Christianity.* Semeia Studies 52. Atlanta: Scholars, 2005.
Klauck, H. J. *The Apocryphal Acts of the Apostles: An Introduction.* 2005. ET Waco: Baylor University, 2008.
Klijn, A. F. J. *Jewish-Christian Gospel Tradition.* Leiden: Brill, 1992.
———. *The Acts of Thomas.* NovTSupp 108. Leiden: Brill, ²2003.
Klijn, A. F. J., and G. J. Reinink. *Patristic Evidence for Jewish-Christian Sects.* NovTSupp 36. Leiden: Brill, 1973.
Klinzing, G. *Die Umdeutung des Kultus in der Qumrangemeinde und im NT.* Göttingen: Vandenhoeck & Ruprecht, 1971.
Kloppenborg, J. S. *Excavating Q.* Minneapolis: Fortress, 2000.
———. '*Didache* 1.1–6.1, James, Matthew and the Torah', in Gregory and Tuckett, eds., *Trajectories,* 193-21.
Knibb, M. A. 'Christian Adoption and Transmission of Jewish-Pseudepigrapha: The Case of 1 Enoch'. *JSJ* 32 (2001): 396-415.
———. *Essays on the Book of Enoch and Other Early Jewish Texts and Traditions.* Leiden: Brill, 2008.
Knowles, M. *Jeremiah in Matthew's Gospel: The Rejected Prophet Motif in Matthean Redaction.* JSNTS 68. Sheffield: JSOT, 1993.
Knox, J. *Marcion and the New Testament.* University of Chicago, 1942, reprinted 1980.
Koester, C. R. *Symbolism in the Fourth Gospel.* Minneapolis: Fortress, ²2003.
Koester, H. *Synoptische Überlieferung bei den apostolischen Vätern.* Berlin: Akademie-Verlag, 1957.
———. '*GNOMAI DIAPHOROI*: The Origin and Nature of Diversification in the History of Early Christianity', in Robinson and Koester, *Trajectories,* 114-57.
———. 'One Jesus and Four Primitive Gospels', in Robinson and Koester, *Trajectories,* 158-204.
———. *Introduction to the New Testament,* vol. 2: *History and Literature of Early Christianity.* Berlin: de Gruyter, 1982.
———. *Ancient Christian Gospels: Their History and Development.* London: SCM, 1990.
———. 'Written Gospels or Oral Traditions?', *JBL* 113 (1994): 293-97.
———. 'Gospels and Gospel Traditions in the Second Century', in Gregory and Tuckett, eds., *Trajectories,* 27-44.
Koester, H., ed. *Ephesos: Metropolis of Asia.* HTS 41. Harvard University, 2004.
Köhler, W. D. *Die Rezeption des Matthäusevangeliums in der Zeit vor Irenäus.* WUNT 2.24. Tübingen: Mohr Siebeck, 1987.
Konradt, M. *Israel, Kirche und die Völker im Matthäusevangelium.* WUNT 215. Tübingen: Mohr Siebeck, 2007.
Kraft, R. A. *Barnabas and the Didache,* in R. M. Grant, ed., *The Apostolic Fathers,* vol. 3 (1965).
———. 'The Weighing of the Parts', in Becker and Reed, eds., *The Ways That Never Parted,* 87-94.

Kramer, W. *Christ, Lord, Son of God*. 1963. ET London: SCM, 1966.
Kraus, T. J., and T. Nicklas, eds. *Das Evangelium nach Petrus: Text, Kontexte, Intertexte*. Berlin: de Gruyter, 2007.
Krosney, H. *The Lost Gospel: The Quest for the Gospel of Judas Iscariot*. Washington: National Geographic, 2006.
Kruger, M. J. 'Papyrus Oxyrhynchus 840', in Foster, ed., *Non-Canonical Gospels*, 157-70.
Kuhn, H. W. *Ältere Sammlungen im Markusevangelium*. Göttingen: Vandenhoeck, 1971.
Kuhn, K. G. 'The Epistle to the Ephesians in the Light of the Qumran Texts', in J. Murphy-O'Connor, ed., *Paul and Qumran*, 115-31. London: Chapman, 1968.
Kümmel, W. G. *Introduction to the New Testament*. London: SCM, revised edition 1975.
Kupp, D. D. *Matthew's Emmanuel: Divine Presence and God's People in the First Gospel*. SNTSMS 90. Cambridge: Cambridge University, 1996.
Kürzinger, J. 'Irenäus und sein Zeugnis zur Sprache des Matthäusevangeliums'. *NTS* 10 (1963-64): 108-15.
Kvalbein, H. 'Has Matthew Abandoned the Jews?', in Ådna and Kvalbein, eds., *Mission*, 45-62.
Kysar, R. 'The Dehistoricizing of the Gospel of John', in Anderson et al., eds., *John, Jesus and History*, vol. 1, 75-101.
Labahn, M. *Jesus als Lebensspender: Untersuchungen zu einer Geschichte der johanneischen Tradition anhand ihrer Wundergeschichten*. BZNW 98. Berlin: de Gruyter, 1999.
———. 'Peter's Rehabilitation (John 21:15-19) and the Adoption of Sinners: Remembering Jesus and Relecturing John', in Anderson et al., eds., *John, Jesus and History*, vol. 2, 335-48.
Labahn, M., et al., eds. *Israel und seine Heilstradition im Johannesevangelium*. Paderborn: Schöningh, 2004.
Lake, K. *The Apostolic Fathers*. 2 vols. LCL. London: Heinemann, 1913.
Lake, K., and J. E. L. Oulton. *Eusebius, The Ecclesiastical History*. 2 vols. LCL. London: Heinemann, 1926, 1932.
Lallemann, P. J. 'The Relation between the Acts of John and the Acts of Peter', in J. N. Bremmer, ed., *The Apocryphal Acts of Peter: Magic, Miracles and Gnosticism*, 161-77. Leuven: Peeters, 1998.
Lampe, P. *From Paul to Valentinus: Christians in Rome in the First Two Centuries*. Minneapolis: Fortress, 2003.
Lane, T. J. *Luke and the Gentile Mission: Gospel Anticipates Acts*. Frankfurt: Lang, 1996.
Langer, R. *Cursing the Christians? A History of the Birkat Haminim*. Oxford University, 2011.
Lapham, F. *Peter: The Myth, the Man and the Writings*. JSNTS 239. London: Sheffield Academic, 2003.
Lawlor, H. J., and J. E. L. Oulton. *Eusebius: Ecclesiastical History and the Martyrs of Palestine*. 2 vols. London: SPCK, 1954.
Lehne, S. *The New Covenant in Hebrews*. JSNTS 44. Sheffield: JSOT, 1990.
Lentz, J. C. *Luke's Portrait of Paul*. SNTSMS 77. Cambridge University, 1993.
Levine, L. I. A. 'Judaism from the Destruction of Jerusalem to the End of the Second Jewish Revolt: 70-135 C.E', in Shanks, ed., *Christianity and Rabbinic Judaism*, 139-66.

Lietzmann, H. *A History of the Early Church.* 4 vols. Cleveland and New York: Meridian, 1961.
Lieu, J. *The Second and Third Epistles of John.* Edinburgh: T & T Clark, 1986.
———. '"The Parting of the Ways": Theological Construct or Historic Reality?' *JSNT* 56 (1994): 101-19.
———. *Neither Jew nor Greek? Constructing Christian Identity.* Edinburgh: T & T Clark, 2003.
———. *Christian Identity in the Jewish and Graeco-Roman World.* Oxford University, 2004.
———. '"As much my apostle as Christ is mine": The Dispute over Paul between Tertullian and Marcion'. *Early Christianity* 1 (2010): 41-59.
Lightfoot, J. B. 'The Christian Ministry', in *Saint Paul's Epistle to the Philippians,* 181-269. London: Macmillan, 1868, 1885.
———. *The Apostolic Fathers: Part I. S. Clement of Rome.* London: Macmillan, ²1890.
———. *The Apostolic Fathers: Part II. S. Ignatius, S. Polycarp.* 3 vols. London: Macmillan, 1885.
———. *Essays on Supernatural Religion.* London: Macmillan, 1889.
Lincoln, A. T. 'The Use of the OT in Ephesians'. *JSNT* 14 (1982): 16-57.
———. 'The Theology of Ephesians', in A. T. Lincoln and A. J. M. Wedderburn, *The Theology of the Later Pauline Letters,* 73-166. Cambridge University, 1993.
———. *Truth on Trial.* Peabody, MA: Hendrickson, 2000.
———. '"We Know That His Testimony Is True": Johannine Truth Claims and Historicity', in Anderson et al., eds., *John, Jesus and History,* vol. 1, 179-97.
Lindars, B. *Behind the Fourth Gospel.* London: SPCK, 1971.
———. *The Theology of the Letter to the Hebrews.* Cambridge University, 1991.
Lindemann, A. *Paulus im ältesten Christentum.* Tübingen: Mohr Siebeck, 1979.
Lona, H. E. *Der erste Clemensbrief.* KAV 2. Göttingen: Vandenhoeck, 1998.
Longenecker, R. W. *The Christology of Early Jewish Christianity.* London: SCM, 1970.
Lüdemann, G. *Opposition to Paul in Jewish Christianity.* ET Minneapolis: Fortress, 1989.
———. *Heretics: The Other Side of Early Christianity.* London: SCM, 1996.
Lührmann, D. *Die apokryph gewordenen Evangelien.* NovTSupp 112. Leiden: Brill, 2004.
Luomanen, P. 'Nazarenes', in Marjanen and Luomanen, eds., *Companion,* 279-314.
Luttikhuizen, G. 'The Apocryphal Correspondence with the Corinthians and the Acts of Paul', in Bremmer, ed., *Apocryphal Acts of Paul,* 75-91.
———. 'Elchasaites and Their Book', in Marjanen and Luomanen, eds., *Companion,* 334-64.
Luz, U. *Studies in Matthew.* Grand Rapids: Eerdmans, 2005.
———. 'Anti-Judaism in the Gospel of Matthew as a Historical and Theological Problem: An Outline', in *Studies in Matthew,* 243-61.
Maccoby, H. *Judas Iscariot and the Myth of Jewish Evil.* London: Peter Halban, 1992.
MacDonald, D. R. *The Legend and the Apostle: The Battle for Paul in Story and Canon.* Philadelphia: Westminster, 1983.
MacDonald, D. R., ed. *The Apocryphal Acts of Apostles.* Semeia 38. Decatur, GA: Scholars, 1986.
Macdonald, J. *The Theology of the Samaritans.* London: SCM, 1964.

MacDonald, M. Y. *The Pauline Churches: A Socio-Historical Study of Institutionalization in the Pauline and Deutero-Pauline Writings.* SNTSMS 60. Cambridge University, 1988.

MacLennan, R. S. *Early Christian Texts on Jews and Judaism.* BJS 194. Atlanta: Scholars, 1990.

MacRae, G. W. 'The Jewish Background of the Gnostic Sophia Myth'. *NovT* 12 (1970): 86-101.

Malherbe, A. J. 'A Physical Description of Paul', in *Paul and the Popular Philosophers*, 165-70. Minneapolis: Fortress, 1989.

Marcus, J. 'Mark 4:10-12 and Marcan Epistemology'. *JBL* 103 (1984): 557-74.

——. *The Way of the Lord: Christological Exegesis of the Old Testament in the Gospel of Mark.* Louisville: Westminster John Knox, 1992.

——. 'The Jewish War and the Sitz im Leben of Mark'. *JBL* 111(1992) 441-62.

Marguerat, D. 'The *Acts of Paul* and the Canonical Acts: A Phenomenon of Rereading', in Stoops, ed., *The Apocryphal Acts of the Apostles in Intertextual Perspectives*, 169-83.

Marjanen, A. 'Women Disciples in the *Gospel of Thomas*', in Uro, ed., *Thomas at the Crossroads*, 89-106.

——. 'Is *Thomas* a Gnostic Gospel?', in Uro, ed., *Thomas at the Crossroads*, 107-39.

——. '*Thomas* and Jewish Religious Practices', in Uro, ed., *Thomas at the Crossroads*, 163-82.

——. 'The Portrait of Jesus in the *Gospel of Thomas*', in Asgeirsson et al., eds., *Thomasine Traditions in Antiquity*, 209-19.

——. 'Montanism: Egalitarian Ecstatic "New Prophecy"', in Marjanen and Luomanen, *Companion*, 185-212.

Marjanen, A., and P. Luomanen, eds. *A Companion to Second-Century Christian 'Heretics'.* Supp.VC 76. Leiden: Brill, 2005.

Markschies, C. *Valentinus Gnosticus? Untersuchungen zur valentinianischen Gnosis mit einem Kommentar zu den Fragmenten Valentin.* WUNT 65. Tübingen: Mohr Siebeck, 1992.

——. *Gnosis: An Introduction.* London: T & T Clark, 2003.

——. 'Was wissen wir über den Sitz im Leben der apokryphen Evangelien?', in Frey and Schröter, eds., *Jesus in apokryphen Evangelienüberlieferungen*, 61-90.

Marshall, C. D. *Faith as a Theme in Mark's Narrative.* SNTSMS 64. Cambridge: Cambridge University, 1989.

Marshall, I. H. *Luke: Historian and Theologian.* Exeter: Paternoster, 1970.

Mason, S. *Josephus and the New Testament.* Peabody: Hendrickson, ²2003.

Massaux, E. *The Influence of the Gospel of Saint Matthew on Christian Literature before Saint Irenaeus.* 1950. ET 3 vols. Macon, GA: Mercer University, 1990.

Martyn, J. L. *History and Theology in the Fourth Gospel.* Nashville: Abingdon, ²1979.

——. 'Glimpses into the History of the Johannine Community' (1977), in *The Gospel of John in Christian History*, ch. 3. New York: Paulist, 1979.

——. *Theological Issues in the Letters of Paul.* Edinburgh: T & T Clark, 1997.

Matson, M. A. 'The Temple Incident: An Integral Element in the Fourth Gospel's Narrative', in Fortna and Thatcher, eds., *Jesus in the Johannine Tradition*, 145-53.

——. 'The Historical Plausibility of John's Passion Dating', in Anderson et al., eds., *John, Jesus and History*, vol. 2, 291-312.

Bibliography

Mayo, P. L. *"Those Who Call Themselves Jews": The Church and Judaism in the Apocalypse of John*. PTMS 60. Eugene, OR: Pickwick, 2006.

McCullough, W. S. *A Short History of Syriac Christianity to the Rise of Islam*. Chico: Scholars, 1982.

McDonald, L. M. *The Formation of the Christian Biblical Canon*. Peabody: Hendrickson, ²1995.

———. 'The *Odes of Solomon* in Ancient Christianity: Reflections on Scripture and Canon', in Charlesworth et al., eds., *Sacra Scriptura*, 108-36.

McDonald, L. M., and J. A. Sanders, eds. *The Canon Debate*. Peabody: Hendrickson, 2002.

McGrath, J. F. *John's Apologetic Christology: Legitimation and Development in Johannine Christology*. SNTSMS 111. Cambridge: Cambridge University, 2001.

———. '"Destroy this Temple": Issues of History in John 2:13-22', in Anderson et al., eds., *John, Jesus and History*, vol. 2, 35-43.

Meade, D. G. *Pseudonymity and Canon*. WUNT 39. Tübingen: Mohr Siebeck, 1986.

Meeks, W. A. *The Prophet-King: Moses Traditions and the Johannine Christology*. NovTSupp 14. Leiden: Brill, 1967.

———. 'The Ethics of the Fourth Evangelist', in Culpepper and Black, eds., *Exploring the Gospel of John*, 317-26.

———. 'The Man from Heaven in Johannine Sectarianism' (1972), in Ashton, ed., *Interpretation*, 169-205.

———. *The First Urban Christians: The Social World of the Apostle Paul*. Yale University, 1983.

Meeks, W. A., and R. L. Wilken. *Jews and Christians in Antioch in the First Four Centuries of the Common Era*. Missoula: Scholars, 1978.

Meier, J. P. 'The Parable of the Wicked Tenants in the Vineyard: Is the Gospel of Thomas Independent of the Synoptics?', in Skinner and Iverson, eds., *Unity and Diversity in the Gospels and Paul*, 129-45.

———. 'Matthew and Ignatius', in Balch, ed., *Social History*, 178-86.

Menken, M. J. J. 'Die jüdischen Feste im Johannesevangelium', in Labahn et al., eds., *Israel*, 269-86.

Metzger, B. M. *A Textual Commentary on the Greek New Testament*. London: United Bible Societies, 1971, 1975.

———. 'Literary Forgeries and Canonical Pseudepigrapha'. *JBL* 91 (1972): 3-24.

———. *The Canon of the New Testament*. Oxford: Clarendon, 1987.

———. *The Text of the New Testament: Its Transmission, Corruption, and Restoration*. Oxford University, ³1964, ⁴2005 with B. D. Ehrman.

Meyer, M. *The Gospel of Thomas: The Hidden Sayings of Jesus*. San Francisco: Harper Collins, 1992.

———. *The Gnostic Gospels of Jesus*. New York: HarperCollins, 2005.

———. 'Interpreting Judas: Ten Passages in the *Gospel of Judas*', in Scopello, ed., *Gospel of Judas*, 41-55.

Meyer, P. W. '"The Father": The Presentation of God in the Fourth Gospel', in Culpepper and Black, eds., *Exploring the Gospel of John*, 255-73.

Miller, J. D. *The Pastoral Letters as Composite Documents*. SNTSMS 93. Cambridge University, 1997.

Miller, S. *Women in Mark's Gospel*. JSNTS 259. London: T & T Clark, 2004.

———. 'The Woman at the Well: John's Portrayal of the Samaritan Mission', in Anderson et al., eds., *John, Jesus and History*, vol. 2, 73-81.
Mimouni, S. C. 'Pour une définition nouvelle du judéo-christianisme ancien'. *NTS* 38 (1991): 2-8.
———. *Early Judaeo-Christianity: Historical Essays*. Leuven: Peeters, 2012.
Minns, D., and P. Jarvis. *Justin, Philosopher and Martyr: Apologies*. Oxford University, 2009.
Moessner, D. P. *Lord of the Banquet: Literary and Theological Significance of the Lukan Travel Narrative*. Minneapolis: Fortress, 1989.
Moessner, D. P., ed. *Jesus and the Heritage of Israel*. Harrisburg: TPI, 1999.
Moffatt, J. *Introduction to the Literature of the New Testament*. Edinburgh: T & T Clark, ³1918.
Moloney, F. J. *Mark: Storyteller, Interpreter, Evangelist*. Peabody: Hendrickson, 2004.
———. 'Matthew 5:17-18 and the Matthean Use of *DIKAIOSUNĒ*', in Skinner and Iverson, eds., *Unity and Diversity in the Gospels and Paul*, 33-54.
Moll, S. *The Arch-Heretic Marcion*. WUNT 250. Tübingen: Mohr Siebeck, 2010.
Montefiore, S. S. *Jerusalem: The Biography*. London: Phoenix, 2011.
Moreland, M. 'The Twenty-Four Prophets of Israel Are Dead: *Gospel of Thomas* 52 as a Critique of Early Christian Hermeneutics', in Asgeirsson et al., eds., *Thomasine Traditions in Antiquity*, 75-91.
Moses, A. D. A. *Matthew's Transfiguration Story and Jewish-Christian Controversy*. JSNTS 122. Sheffield Academic, 1996.
Moss, C. M. *The Zechariah Tradition and the Gospel of Matthew*. BZNW 156. Berlin: de Gruyter, 2008.
Motyer, S. 'The Fourth Gospel and the Salvation of Israel: An Appeal for a New Start', in Bieringer et al., eds., *Anti-Judaism and the Fourth Gospel*, 92-110.
Moule, C. F. D. 'The Christology of Acts', in Keck and Martyn, eds., *Studies in Luke-Acts*, 159-85.
———. 'The Individualism of the Fourth Gospel' (1962), in *Essays in New Testament Interpretation*, 91-109. Cambridge: Cambridge University, 1982.
Murphy, J. *The Religious World of Jesus: An Introduction to Second Temple Palestinian Judaism*. Hoboken, NJ: Ktav, 1991.
Murphy-O'Connor, J. *Paul: A Critical Life*. Oxford University, 1996.
Murray, R. 'Defining Judaeo-Christianity'. *Heythrop Journal* 15 (1974): 303-10.
Musurillo, H., ed. *The Acts of the Christian Martyrs*. Oxford University, 1972.
Mutschler, B. 'John and His Gospel in the Mirror of Irenaeus of Lyons: Perspectives of Recent Research', in Rasimus, ed., *Legacy of John*, 319-43.
Myllyoski, M. 'Die Kraft des Herrn: Erwägungen zur Christologie des Petrusevangeliums', in Kraus and Nicklas, *Evangelium nach Petrus*, 301-26.
Nagel, P. 'Apokryphe Jesusworte in der koptischen Überlieferung', in Frey and Schröter, eds., *Jesus in apokryphen Evangelienüberlieferungen*, 495-526.
Nagel, T. *Die Rezeption des Johannesevangeliums im 2.Jahrhundert*. Leipzig, 2000.
Nardoni, E. 'Charism in the Early Church since Rudolph Sohm: An Ecumenical Challenge'. *TS* 53 (1992): 646-62.
Neale, D. A. *None but the Sinners: Religious Categories in the Gospel of Luke*. JSNTS 58. Sheffield: Sheffield Academic, 1991.
Neusner, J. *A Life of Yohanan ben Zakkai*. Leiden: Brill, ²1970.

———. *First Century Judaism in Crisis*. Nashville: Abingdon, 1975.
Neusner, J., et al., eds. *Judaisms and Their Messiahs at the Turn of the Christian Era*. Cambridge: Cambridge University, 1987.
Newport, K. G. C. *The Sources and Sitz im Leben of Matthew 23*. JSNTS 117. Sheffield: Sheffield Academic, 1995.
Newsom, C. *The Songs of the Sabbath Sacrifice*. Atlanta: Scholars, 1985.
Nicklas, T. 'Papyrus Egerton 2', in Foster, ed., *Non-Canonical Gospels*, 138-49.
———. 'Das Petrusevangelium im Rahmen antiker Jesustraditionen', in Frey and Schröter, eds., *Jesus in apokryphen Evangelienüberlieferungen*, 223-52.
Nicklas, T., A. Merkt, and J. Verheyden, eds. *Ancient Perspectives on Paul*. SUNT 102. Göttingen: Vandenhoeck, 2013.
Nicklas, T., and M. Tilly, eds. *The Book of Acts as Church History*. BZNW 120. Berlin: de Gruyter, 2003.
Niebuhr, K. W. '"Judentum" und "Christentum" bei Paulus und Ignatius von Antiochien'. *ZNW* 85 (1994): 218-33.
Niederwimmer, K. 'Johannes Markus und die Frage nach dem Verfasser des zweiten Evangeliums'. *ZNW* 58 (1967): 173-88.
———. *Die Didache*. KAV. Göttingen: Vandenhoeck, ²1993.
Nienhuis, D. R. *Not by Paul Alone*. Waco: Baylor University, 2007.
North, W. E. S. '"The Jews" in John's Gospel: Observations and Inferences', in J. G. Crossley, ed., *Judaism, Jewish Identities and the Gospel Tradition: Essays in Honour of Maurice Casey*, 206-26. London: Equinox, 2010.
Notovitch, N. *The Unknown Life of Jesus Christ*. Sydney: Axiom, 2007.
Novakovic, L. *Messiah, the Healer of the Sick: A Study of Jesus as the Son of David in the Gospel of Matthew*. WUNT 2/170. Tübingen: Mohr Siebeck, 2003.
O'Brien, K. *The Use of Scripture in the Markan Passion Narrative*. LNTS 384. London: T & T Clark, 2010.
O'Day, G. R. 'The Gospel of John: Reading the Incarnate Words', in Fortna and Thatcher, eds., *Jesus in the Johannine Tradition*, 25-32.
Odeberg, H. *The Fourth Gospel*. Stockholm: Almqvist & Wiksell, 1929.
O'Leary, A. M. *Matthew's Judaization of Mark: Examined in the Context of the Use of Sources in Graeco-Roman Antiquity*. LNTS 323. London: T & T Clark, 2006.
O'Loughlin, T. *The Didache: A Window on the Earliest Christians*. Grand Rapids: Baker Academic, 2010.
Orton, D. E., ed. *The Composition of Mark's Gospel*. Leiden: Brill, 1999.
Osborn, C. D. 'The Christological Use of 1 Enoch 1.9 in Jude 14'. *NTS* 23 (1976-77): 334-41.
Osborn, E. *Irenaeus of Lyons*. Cambridge University, 2001.
Osiek, C. *The Shepherd of Hermas*. Hermeneia. Minneapolis: Fortress, 1999.
Overbeck, F. *Über die Auffassung des Paulus mit Petrus in Antiochien (Gal. 2, 11ff.) bei den Kirchenvätern*. 1877. Darmstadt: Wissenschaftliche Buchgesellschaft, 1968.
Overman, J. A. *Matthew's Gospel and Formative Judaism. The Social World of the Matthean Community*. Minneapolis: Fortress, 1990.
Oxford Society of Historical Theology. *The New Testament in the Apostolic Fathers*. Oxford: Clarendon, 1905.
Paffenroth, K. *The Story of Jesus according to L*. JSNTS 147. Sheffield: Sheffield Academic, 1997.

Pagels, E. H. *The Johannine Gospel in Gnostic Exegesis: Heracleon's Commentary on John*. SBLMS 17. Nashville: Abingdon, 1973.
——. *The Gnostic Paul*. Philadelphia: Fortress, 1975.
Pagels, E., and K. L. King. *Reading Judas: The Gospel of Judas and the Shaping of Christianity*. London: Allen Lane, 2007.
Paget, J. Carleton. *The Epistle of Barnabas*. WUNT 2.64. Tübingen: Mohr Siebeck, 1994.
——. 'Jewish Christianity', in W. Horbury et al., *The Cambridge History of Judaism*, vol. 3: *The Early Roman Period*, 731-75. Cambridge University, 1999.
——. 'The *Epistle of Barnabas* and the Writings That Later Formed the New Testament', in Gregory and Tuckett, eds., *Reception*, 229-49.
——. 'The Definition of the Terms *Jewish Christian* and *Jewish Christianity* in the History of Research', in Skarsaune and Hvalvik, eds., *Jewish Believers in Jesus*, 22-52.
Painter, J. *Just James: The Brother of Jesus in History and Tradition*. University of South Carolina, 1997.
——. 'Memory Holds the Key: The Transformation of Memory in the Interface of History and Theology in John', in Anderson et al., eds., *Jesus, John and History*, vol. 1, 229-45.
Parker, D. C. *The Living Text of the Gospels*. Cambridge: Cambridge University, 1997.
Parkes, J. *The Conflict of the Church and the Synagogue*. Jewish Publication Society, 1934; reprinted New York: Macmillan.
Patterson, S. J. *The Gospel of Thomas and Jesus*. Sonoma, CA: Polebridge, 1993.
——. *The Gospel of Thomas and Christian Origins: Essays on the Fifth Gospel*. Leiden: Brill, 2013.
Patterson, S. J., H.-G. Bethge, and J. M. Robinson. *The Fifth Gospel: The Gospel of Thomas Comes of Age*. London: T & T Clark, 2011.
Pearson, B. A. 'Christians and Jews in First-Century Alexandria', in G. W. E. Nickelsburg and G. W. MacRae, eds., *Christians Among Jews and Gentiles*; K. Stendahl FS, 206-16. Philadelphia: Fortress, 1986.
——. 'Gnosticism as a Religion', in *Gnosticism and Christianity in Roman and Coptic Egypt*, 201-23. New York: Continuum, 2004.
Perkins, P. *Peter: Apostle for the Whole Church*. 1994. Minneapolis: Fortress, 2000.
Perrin, N. *What Is Redaction Criticism?* Philadelphia: Fortress Press, 1969.
——. *Thomas and Tatian: The Relationship between the* Gospel of Thomas *and the* Diatessaron. Atlanta: SBL, 2002.
——. *Thomas, the Other Gospel*. London: SPCK, 2007.
——. 'The *Diatessaron* and the Second-Century Reception of the Gospel of John', in Rasimus, ed., *Legacy of John*, 301-18.
——. 'Paul and Valentinian Interpretation', in Bird and Dodson, eds., *Paul and the Second Century*, 126-39.
Pervo, R. *Profit with Delight: The Literary Genre of the Acts of the Apostles*. Philadelphia: Fortress, 1987.
Pesthy, M. 'Thecla among the Fathers of the Church', in Bremmer, ed., *Apocryphal Acts of Paul*, 164-78.
Petersen, N. R., ed. *Perspectives on Mark's Gospel*. Semeia 16. Missoula, MT: Scholars, 1979.
Petersen, W. L. 'The Diatessaron and the Fourfold Gospel', in C. Horton, ed., *The*

Earliest Gospels: The Origins and Transmission of the Earliest Christian Gospels, 5-68. London: T & T Clark, 2004.

———. 'Tatian the Assyrian', in Marjanen and Luomanen, *Companion*, 125-58.

Peterson, P. M. *Andrew, Brother of Simon Peter.* NovTSupp 1. Leiden: Brill, 1963.

Pétrement, S. *A Separate God: The Christian Origins of Gnosticism.* San Francisco: HarperCollins, 1994.

Plisch, U.-K. 'Judasevangelium und Judasgedicht', in Frey and Schröter, eds., *Jesus in apokryphen Evangelienüberlieferungen*, 387-96.

Poirier, P.-H. 'The *Trimorphic Protennoia* (NHC XIII,1) and the Johannine Prologue: A Reconsideration', in Rasimus, ed., *Legacy of John*, 93-103.

Pokorny, P. *From the Gospel to the Gospels: History, Theology and Impact of the Biblical Term 'Euangelion'.* BZNW 195. Berlin: de Gruyter, 2013.

Popkes, E. E. 'The Image Character of Human Existence: *GThom* 83 and *GThom* 84 as Core Texts of the Anthropology of the *Gospel of Thomas*', in Frey, ed., *Das Thomasevangelium*, 416-34.

———. 'Das Thomasevangelium als *crux interpretum*: die methodischen Ursachen einer diffusen Diskussionslage', in Frey and Schröter, eds., *Jesus in apokryphen Evangelienüberlieferungen*, 271-92.

Porter, S. E. 'The Portrait of Paul in Acts', in S. Westerholm, ed., *The Blackwell Companion to Paul*, 124-38. Chichester: Wiley-Blackwell, 2011.

Porter, S. E., and B. W. R. Pearson, eds. *Christian-Jewish Relations through the Centuries.* JSNTS 192. Sheffield Academic, 2000.

Potter, C. F. *The Lost Years of Jesus Revealed.* 1958. Fawcett, 1985.

Powell, M. A. *What Is Narrative Criticism?* Minneapolis: Fortress, 1990.

Pratscher, W. *Der Herrenbruder Jakobus und die Jakobustradition.* FRLANT 139. Göttingen: Vandenhoeck, 1987.

———. *Der zweite Clemensbrief.* KAV. Göttingen: Vandenhoeck, 2007.

Pritz, R. A. *Nazarene Jewish Christianity: From the End of the New Testament Period until Its Disappearance in the Fourth Century.* Jerusalem: Magnes, 1988.

Prostmeier, F. R. *Der Barnabasbrief.* KAV 8. Göttingen: Vandenhoeck, 1999.

Pryke, E. J. *Redactional Style in the Markan Gospel.* SNTSMS 33. Cambridge: Cambridge University, 1978.

Przybylski, B. *Righteousness in Matthew and His World of Thought.* SNTSMS 41. Cambridge: Cambridge University, 1980.

Quast, K. *Peter and the Beloved Disciple: Figures for a Community in Crisis.* JSNTS 32. Sheffield: JSOT, 1989.

Quasten, J. *Patrology*, vol. 1: *The Beginnings of Patristic Literature.* Westminster, MD: Newman, 1962.

Räisänen, H. *Paul and the Law.* WUNT 29. Tübingen: Mohr Siebeck, 1983.

———. *The 'Messianic Secret' in Mark's Gospel.* Edinburgh: T & T Clark, 1990.

———. 'Marcion', in Marjanen and Luomanen, *Companion*, 100-124.

———. *The Rise of Christian Beliefs: The Thought-World of Early Christians.* Philadelphia: Fortress, 2009.

Rascher, A. *Schriftauslegung und Christologie im Hebräerbrief.* BZNW 153. Berlin: de Gruyter, 2007.

Rasimus, T., ed. *The Legacy of John: Second-Century Reception of the Fourth Gospel.* NovTSupp 132. Leiden: Brill, 2010.

Rau, E. 'Weder gefälscht noch authentisch?' and 'Das Geheimnis des Reiches Gottes', in Frey and Schröter, eds., *Jesus in apokryphen Evangelienüberlieferungen*, 139-86, 186-221.
Reed, A. Y. *'Euangelion:* Orality, Textuality, and the Christian Truth in Irenaeus' *Adversus Haereses'*. *VC* 56 (2002): 11-46.
———. '"Jewish Christianity" after the "Parting of the Ways"', in Becker and Reed, eds., *The Ways That Never Parted*, 189-231.
Reitzenstein, R. *The Hellenistic Mystery-Religions*. ³1927. ET Pittsburgh: Pickwick, 1978.
Rhoads, D., J. Dewey, and D. Michie. *Mark as Story: An Introduction to the Narrative of a Gospel*. Minneapolis: Fortress, ²1999.
Richardson, C. C. *Early Christian Fathers*. London: SCM, 1953.
Riches, J. K. *Conflicting Mythologies: Identity Formation in the Gospels of Mark and Matthew*. Edinburgh: T & T Clark, 2000.
Riley, G. J. *Resurrection Reconsidered: Thomas and John in Controversy*. Minneapolis: Fortress, 1995.
Ringe, S. H. *Wisdom's Friends: Community and Christology in the Fourth Gospel*. Louisville: Westminster John Knox, 1999.
Ritschl, A. *Die Entstehung der altkatholischen Kirche*. Bonn, 1850, ²1857.
Rius-Camps, J., and J. Read-Heimerdinger. *The Message of Acts in Codex Bezae: A Comparison with the Alexandrian Tradition*. LNTS, 4 vols. London: T & T Clark, 2004-2009.
Robbins, V. K. *Jesus the Teacher: A Socio-Rhetorical Interpretation of Mark*. Philadelphia: Fortress, 1984.
Robeck, C. M. 'Montanism and Present Day "Prophets"'. *Pneuma: The Journal of the Society for Pentecostal Studies* 32 (2010).
Roberts, C. H., and T. C. Skeat. *The Birth of the Codex*. London: British Academy, 1983.
Robinson, J. A. T. 'The Destination and Purpose of St. John's Gospel', in *Twelve New Testament Studies*, 107-25. London: SCM, 1962.
———. *Redating the New Testament*. London: SCM, 1976.
———. *The Priority of John*. London: SCM, 1985.
Robinson, J. M. 'The Sources of the *Gospel of Judas*', in Scopello, ed., *Gospel of Judas*, 59-67.
Robinson, J. M., et al. *The Critical Edition of Q: Synopsis*. Leuven: Peeters, 2000.
Robinson, J. M., ed. *The Nag Hammadi Library*. Leiden: Brill, ³1988.
Robinson, J. M., and H. Koester. *Trajectories through Early Christianity*. Philadelphia: Fortress, 1971.
Robinson, T. A. *Ignatius of Antioch and the Parting of the Ways: Early Jewish-Christian Relations*. Peabody: Hendrickson, 2009.
Röhl, G. *Die Rezeption des Johannesevangeliums in christlich-gnostischen Schriften aus Nag Hammadi*. Frankfurt: Europäische Hochschulschriften: Reihe 23, 1991.
Roloff, J. *Die Kirche im Neuen Testament*. Göttingen: Vandenhoeck, 1993.
Ropes, J. H. *The Text of Acts* (= vol. III of *BCAA*, 1926), ccxliv-ccxlv.
Rordorf, W. 'Tradition and Composition in the *Acts of Thecla:* The State of the Question', in MacDonald, ed., *The Apocryphal Acts of Apostles*, 44-52.
———. 'Does the Didache Contain Jesus Tradition Independently of the Synoptic Gospels?', in H. Wansbrough, ed., *Jesus and the Oral Gospel Tradition*, 394-423. JSNTS 64. Sheffield: JSOT, 1991.

―――. 'The Relation between the Acts of Peter and the Acts of Paul: State of the Question', in Bremmer, ed., *Apocryphal Acts of Peter,* 178-91.
Rowe, C. K. *Early Narrative Christology: The Lord in the Gospel of Luke.* BZNW 139. Berlin: de Gruyter, 2006.
Rowland, C. 'The Vision of the Risen Christ in Rev. 1.13ff.: The Debt of an Early Christology to an Aspect of Jewish Angelology'. *JTS* 31 (1980): 1-11.
―――. *The Open Heaven: A Study of Apocalyptic in Judaism and Christianity.* London: SPCK, 1982.
Rowley, H. H. *The Relevance of Apocalyptic.* London: Lutterworth, 1944, ³1963.
Rudolph, D., and J. Willitts, eds. *Introduction to Messianic Judaism: Its Ecclesial Context and Biblical Foundations.* Grand Rapids: Zondervan, 2013.
Rudolph, K. *Gnosis: The Nature and History of an Ancient Religion.* Edinburgh: T & T Clark, 1983.
Ruether, R. R. *Faith and Fratricide: The Theological Roots of Anti-Semitism.* New York: Seabury, 1974.
Runia, D. T. *Philo in Early Christian Literature: A Survey.* Assen: Van Gorcum, 1993.
Safrai, S., ed. *The Literature of the Sages.* CRINT II.3.1. Assen: Van Gorcum, 1987.
Saldarini, A. J. 'The Gospel of Matthew and Jewish-Christian Conflict', in Balch, ed., *Social History,* 39-61.
―――. *Matthew's Christian-Jewish Community.* University of Chicago, 1994.
Salvesen, A. 'A Convergence of the Ways?', in Becker and Reed, eds., *The Ways That Never Parted,* 233-58.
Sanday, W. *The Gospels in the Second Century.* London: Macmillan, 1876.
Sanders, J. N. *The Fourth Gospel in the Early Church: Its Origin and Influence on Christian Theology up to Irenaeus.* Cambridge University, 1943.
Sanders, J. T. *The Jews in Luke-Acts.* London: SCM, 1987.
Sandmel, S. *The First Christian Century in Judaism and Christianity.* New York: Oxford University, 1969.
―――. *Anti-Semitism in the New Testament.* Philadelphia: Fortress, 1978.
Satake, A. *Die Gemeindeordnung in der Johannesapokalypse.* Neukirchen: Neukirchener, 1966.
Schaberg, J. *The Father, the Son and the Holy Spirit: The Triadic Phrase in Matthew 28:19b.* SBLDS 61. Chico: Scholars, 1982.
Schäfer, P. 'Die sogenannte Synode von Jabne: Zur Trennung von Juden und Christen im ersten/zweiten Jh. N. Chr.', in *Studien zur Geschichte und Theologie des rabbinischen Judentums,* 45-64. Leiden: Brill, 1978.
―――. *Judeophobia: Attitudes toward the Jews in the Ancient World.* Cambridge: Harvard University, 1997.
―――. *Die Geburt des Judentums aus dem Geist des Christentum.* Tübingen: Mohr Siebeck, 2010.
Schenck, K. 'A Celebration of the Enthroned Son: The Catena of Hebrews 1'. *JBL* 120 (2001): 469-85.
―――. *Understanding the Book of Hebrews.* Louisville: Westminster John Knox, 2003.
―――. *Cosmology and Eschatology in Hebrews: The Settings of the Sacrifice.* SNTSMS 143. Cambridge University, 2007.
Scherbenske, E. W. *Canonizing Paul: Ancient Editorial Practice and the* Corpus Paulinum. Oxford University, 2013.

Scherlitt, F. *Der vorjohanneische Passionsbericht: Eine historisch-kritische und theologische Untersuchung zu Joh 2,13-22; 11,47–14,31 und 18,1-20, 29*. BZNW 154. Berlin: de Gruyter, 2007.

Schiffman, L. H. *Who Was a Jew? Rabbinic and Halakhic Perspectives on Jewish-Christian Schism*. Hoboken: Ktav, 1985.

Schmidt, K. L. *Der Rahmen der Geschichte Jesus: Literarkritische Untersuchungen zur ältesten Jesusüberlieferung*. Berlin: Trowitzsch & Sohn, 1919.

Schmithals, W. *Gnosticism in Corinth*. ³1969. ET Nashville: Abingdon, 1971.

———. *Paul and the Gnostics*. ET Nashville: Abingdon, 1972.

Schneckenburger, M. *Über den Zweck der Apostelgeschichte*. Bern, 1841.

Schnelle, U. *Antidocetic Christology in the Gospel of John*. 1987. ET Minneapolis: Fortress, 1992.

———. *The History and Theology of the New Testament Writings*. 1994. ET London: SCM, 1998.

———. 'Trinitarisches Denken im Johannesevangelium', in Labahn et al., eds., *Israel*, 367-86.

———. *Theology of the New Testament*. ET Grand Rapids: Baker Academic, 2009.

Schoedel, W. R. *Polycarp, Martyrdom of Polycarp, Fragments of Papias*, in R. M. Grant, ed., *The Apostolic Fathers*, vol. 5. London: Nelson, 1967.

———. *Ignatius of Antioch*. Hermeneia. Philadelphia: Fortress, 1985.

———. 'The Apostolic Fathers', in E. J. Epp and G. W. MacRae, eds., *The New Testament and Its Modern Interpreters*, 457-98. Atlanta: Scholars, 1989.

———. 'Ignatius and the Reception of the Gospel of Matthew in Antioch', in Balch, ed., *Social History*, 129-77.

Schoeps, H. J. *Theologie und Geschichte des Judenchristentums*. Tübingen, 1949.

———. *Jewish Christianity*. ET Philadelphia: Fortress, 1969.

Schreiber, J. 'Die Christologie des Markusevangeliums'. *ZTK* 58 (1961).

Schremer, A. *Brothers Estranged: Heresy, Christianity and Jewish Identity in Late Antiquity*. Oxford University, 2010.

Schröter, J. *Erinnerung an Jesu Worte: Studien zur Rezeption der Logienüberlieferung in Markus, Q und Thomas*. WMANT 76. Neukirchen-Vluyn: Neukirchener, 1997.

———. 'Jesus Tradition in Matthew, James, and the Didache: Searching for Characteristic Emphases', in van de Sandt and Zangenberg, eds., *Matthew, James and Didache*, 233-55.

———. *Vom Jesus zum Neuen Testament: Studien zur urchristlichen Theologiegeschichte und zur Entstehung des neutestamentlichen Kanons*. WUNT 204. Tübingen: Mohr Siebeck, 2007.

———. 'Die Herausforderung einer theologischen Interpretation des *Thomasevangeliums*', in Frey, ed., *Das Thomasevangelium*, 435-59.

Schutter, W. L. *Hermeneutic and Composition in First Peter*. WUNT 2.30. Tübingen: Mohr Siebeck, 1989.

Schweizer, E. *Church Order in the New Testament*. 1959. ET London: SCM, 1961.

———. *Matthäus und seine Gemeinde*. SBS 71. Stuttgart: KBW, 1974.

Scopello, M., ed. *The Gospel of Judas in Context*. NHMS 62. Leiden: Brill, 2008.

Scott, J. M. C. *Sophia and the Johannine Jesus*. JSNTS 71. Sheffield: JSOT, 1992.

Segal, A. *Two Powers in Heaven: Early Rabbinic Reports about Christianity and Gnosticism*. Leiden: Brill, 1977.

———. *Rebecca's Children: Judaism and Christianity in the Roman World.* Harvard University, 1986.
———. *The Other Judaisms of Late Antiquity.* Atlanta: Scholars, 1987.
———. 'Matthew's Jewish Voice', in Balch, ed., *Social History,* 3-37.
Sellew, P. H. 'Jesus and the Voice from Beyond the Grave: *Gospel of Thomas* 42 in the Context of Funerary Epigraphy', in Asgeirsson et al., eds., *Thomasine Traditions in Antiquity,* 39-73.
Sellner, H. J. *Das Heil Gottes: Studien zur Soteriologie des lukanischen Doppelwerks.* BZNW 152. Berlin: de Gruyter, 2007.
Siegert, F. 'Unbeachtete Papiaszitate bei armenischen Schriftstellern'. *NTS* 27 (1981): 605-14.
Shanks, H., ed. *Christianity and Rabbinic Judaism: A Parallel History of Their Origins and Early Development.* Washington: Biblical Archaeology Society, ²2011.
———. *Partings: How Judaism and Christianity Became Two.* Washington: Biblical Archaeology Society, 2013.
Shiner, W. *Proclaiming the Gospel: First-Century Performance of Mark.* Harrisburg: TPI, 2003.
Shiner, W. T. *Follow Me!: Disciples in Markan Rhetoric.* SBLDS 145. Atlanta: Scholars Press, 1995.
Shotwell, W. A. *The Biblical Exegesis of Justin Martyr.* London: SPCK, 1965.
Shukster, M. B., and P. Richardson. 'Barnabas, Nerva and the Yavnean Rabbis'. *JTS* 33 (1983): 31-55.
Sibinga, J. S. 'Ignatius and Matthew'. *NovT* 8 (1966): 262-83.
Sim, D. C. *The Gospel of Matthew and Christian Judaism: The History and Social Setting of the Matthean Community.* Edinburgh: T & T Clark, 1998.
Simon, M. *Verus Israel: A Study of the Relations between Christians and Jews in the Roman Empire (AD 135-425).* 1964. Oxford: Oxford University, 1986.
Simonetti, M. *Biblical Interpretation in the Early Church: A Historical Introduction to Patristic Exegesis.* Edinburgh: T & T Clark, 1994.
Skarsaune, O. *The Proof from Prophecy: A Study in Justin Martyr's Proof-Text Tradition.* NovTSupp 66. Leiden: Brill, 1987.
———. 'Jewish Believers in Jesus in Antiquity — Problems of Definition, Method and Sources', in Skarsaune and Hvalvik, eds., *Jewish Believers in Jesus,* 3-21.
———. 'The Ebionites', in Skarsaune and Hvalvik, eds., *Jewish Believers in Jesus,* 419-62.
Skarsaune, O., and R. Hvalvik, eds. *Jewish Believers in Jesus.* Peabody: Hendrickson, 2007.
Skinner, C. W., and K. R. Iverson, eds. *Unity and Diversity in the Gospels and Paul*; F. J. Matera FS. Atlanta: SBL, 2012.
Smallwood, E. M. *The Jews under Roman Rule from Pompey to Diocletian.* Leiden: Brill, 1981.
Smith, C. B. *No Longer Jews: The Search for Gnostic Origins.* Peabody: Hendrickson, 2004.
———. 'Ministry, Martyrdom and Other Mysteries: Pauline Influence on Ignatius of Antioch', in Bird and Dodson, eds., *Paul and the Second Century,* 37-56.
Smith, D. M. *The Composition and Order of the Fourth Gospel.* Yale University, 1953.
———. *Johannine Christianity.* Columbia: University of South Carolina, 1984.

———. *John Among the Gospels: The Relationship in Twentieth-Century Research.* Minneapolis: Fortress, 1992.
———. *The Fourth Gospel in Four Dimensions.* University of South Carolina, 2008.
———. 'Jesus Tradition in the Gospel of John', in *The Fourth Gospel in Four Dimensions* 81-111.
———. 'John and the Apocryphal Gospels: Was John the First Apocryphal Gospel?', in *The Fourth Gospel in Four Dimensions,* 156-65.
Smith, M. *Clement of Alexandria and a Secret Gospel of Mark.* Cambridge, MA: Harvard University, 1973.
———. *The Secret Gospel: The Discovery and Interpretation of the Secret Gospel according to Mark.* Clearlake, CA: Dawn Horse, 1972, 1980.
Snyder, G. F. *The Shepherd of Hermas,* in R. M. Grant, ed., *The Apostolic Fathers,* vol. 6. London: Nelson, 1968.
Soards, M. L. 'The Question of a PreMarcan Passion Narrative', in R. E. Brown, *The Death of the Messiah,* 2 vols., 1492-1524. New York: Doubleday, 1994.
Söding, T. *Glaube bei Markus.* SBB 12. Stuttgart: KBW, ²1987.
Sohm, R. *Kirchenrecht.* Leipzig: Duncker & Humblot, 1892.
Spaulding, M. B. *Commemorative Identities: Jewish Social Memory and the Johannine Feast of Booths.* LNTS 396. London: T & T Clark, 2009.
Spence, S. *The Parting of the Ways: The Roman Church as a Case Study.* Leuven: Peeters, 2004.
Speyer, W. 'Religiöse Pseudepigraphie und Literarische Fälschung im Altertum'. *Jahrbuch für Antike und Christentum* 8/9 (1965-66).
Stanton, G. N. '5 Ezra and Matthean Christianity in the Second Century'. *JTS* 28 (1977): 67-83.
———. 'The Origin and Purpose of Matthew's Gospel: Matthean Scholarship from 1945 to 1980'. *ANRW* II.25.3 (1985): 1889-1951.
———. *A Gospel for a New People: Studies in Matthew.* Edinburgh: T & T Clark, 1992.
———. 'Justin Martyr's Dialogue with Trypho: Group Boundaries, "Proselytes" and "God-fearers"', in Stanton and Stroumsa, *Tolerance and Intolerance,* 263-78.
———. *Jesus and Gospel.* Cambridge University, 2004.
———. 'Jesus of Nazareth: A Magician and a False Prophet Who Deceived God's People', in *Jesus and Gospel,* 127-47.
———. 'Jewish Christian Elements in the Pseudo-Clementine Writings', in Skarsaune and Hvalvik, eds., *Jewish Believers in Jesus,* 305-24.
Stanton, G. N., and G. G. Stroumsa, eds. *Tolerance and Intolerance in Early Judaism and Christianity.* Cambridge University, 1998.
Stein, R. H. 'The Proper Methodology for Ascertaining Markan Redaction'. *NovT* 13 (1971): 181-98.
Stendahl, K. *The School of St. Matthew and Its Use of the Old Testament.* Philadelphia: Fortress, ²1968.
Sterling, G. E. '"Where Two or Three Are Gathered": The Tradition History of the Parable of the Banquet (Matt 22:1-14/Luke 14:16-24/*GThom* 64)', in J. Frey, ed., *Das Thomasevangelium,* 95-121.
Stern, D. H. *Jewish New Testament: A Translation of the New Testament That Expresses Its Jewishness.* Jerusalem: Jewish New Testament Publications, 1989.

Bibliography

Still, T. D. 'Shadow and Light: Marcion's (Mis)construal of the Apostle Paul', in Bird and Dodson, eds., *Paul and the Second Century,* 91-107.

Stoops, R. F. 'Patronage in the Acts of Peter', in D. R. MacDonald, ed., *The Apocryphal Acts of Apostles,* 91-100.

———. 'The *Acts of Peter* in Intertextual Context', in Stoops, ed., *The Apocryphal Acts of the Apostles in Intertextual Prespectives,* 57-86.

Stoops, R. F., ed. *The Apocryphal Acts of the Apostles in Intertextual Perspectives.* Semeia 80. Atlanta: Scholars, 1997.

Strecker, G. 'On the Problem of Jewish Christianity', in ET of Bauer, *Orthodoxy and Heresy,* 241-85.

———. *Das Judenchristentum in den Pseudoklementinen.* Berlin: Akademie, 1981.

———. *Theology of the New Testament.* 1996. Berlin: de Gruyter, 2000.

Streeter, B. H. *The Four Gospels: A Study of Origins.* London: Macmillan, 1924.

Street, D. R. *"They Went Out from Us": The Identity of the Opponents in First John.* BZNW 177. Berlin: de Gruyter, 2011.

Stroker, W. D. *Extracanonical Sayings of Jesus.* Atlanta: Scholars, 1989.

Strotmann, A. 'Relative oder absolute Präexistenz? Zur Diskussion über die Präexistenz der frühjüdischen Weisheitsgestalt im Kontext von Joh 1,1-18', in Labahn et al., eds, *Israel,* 91-106.

Stuckenbruck, L. T. *Angel Veneration and Christology.* WUNT 2.70. Tübingen: Mohr Siebeck, 1995.

Stuhlmacher, P. *Das paulinische Evangelium.* Göttingen: Vandenhoeck, 1968.

———. *Biblische Theologie des Neuen Testaments.* 2 vols. Göttingen: Vandenhoeck, 1992, 1999.

———. 'Matt 28:16 and the Course of Mission in the Apostolic and Postapostolic Age', in Ådna and Kvalbein, eds., *The Mission of the Early Church to Jews and Gentiles,* 17-43.

Suggs, M. J. *Wisdom, Christology and Law in Matthew's Gospel.* Harvard University, 1970.

Swete, H. B. *The Akhmim Fragment of the Apocryphal Gospel of St. Peter.* London: Macmillan, 1893.

Tabbernee, W. *Montanist Inscriptions and Testimonia: Epigraphic Sources Illustrating the History of Montanism.* Macon: Mercer University, 1997.

———. *Prophets and Gravestones: An Imaginative History of Montanists and Other Early Christians.* Peabody, MA: Hendrickson, 2009.

Tabor, J. D. *Paul and Jesus: How the Apostle Transformed Christianity.* New York: Simon & Schuster, 2012.

Tannehill, R. C. 'The Gospel of Mark as Narrative Christology', in Petersen, ed., *Perspectives,* 57-95.

Taylor, J. E. 'The Phenomenon of Early Jewish Christianity: Reality or Scholarly Invention'. *VC* 44 (1990): 313-34.

Taylor, M. S. *Anti-Judaism and Early Christian Identity: A Critique of the Scholarly Consensus.* Leiden: Brill, 1995.

Taylor, V. *Behind the Third Gospel: A Study of the Proto-Luke Hypothesis.* Oxford: Oxford University, 1926.

———. *The Formation of the Gospel Tradition.* London: Macmillan, ²1935.

———. *The Passion Narrative of St Luke. A Critical and Historical Investigation.* SNTSMS 19. Cambridge University, 1972.
Telford, W. R. *Writing on the Gospel of Mark.* Blandford Forum: Deo, 2009.
Thatcher, T. 'The Riddles of Jesus in the Johannine Dialogues', in Fortna and Thatcher, eds., *Jesus in the Johannine Tradition,* 263-77.
———. 'Why John Wrote a Gospel: Memory and History in an Early Christian Community', in A. Kirk and T. Thatcher, eds., *Memory, Tradition, and Text: Uses of the Past in Early Christianity,* 79-97. Semeia Studies 52. Atlanta: SBL, 2005.
———. *Why John Wrote a Gospel: Jesus — Memory — History.* Louisville: Westminster John Knox, 2006.
Theisohn, J. *Der auserwählte Richter: Untersuchungen zum traditionsgeschichtlichen Ort der Menschensohn der Bilderreden des äthipischen Henoch.* Göttingen: Vandenhoeck, 1969.
Theissen, G. *The Gospels in Context: Social and Political History in the Synoptic Tradition.* 1989. ET Minneapolis: Fortress, 1991.
Theobald, M. *Die Fleischwerdung des Logos.* Münster: Aschendorff, 1988.
———. *Studien zum Corpus Iohanneum.* WUNT 267. Tübingen: Mohr Siebeck, 2010.
———. 'Das Johannesevangelium — Zeugnis eines synagogalen "Judenchristentums"?', in *Studien,* 204-53.
———. 'Futurische versus präsentisches Eschatologie', in *Studien,* ch. 22.
Theophilos, M. *The Abomination of Desolation in Matthew 25.15.* LNTS 437. London: T & T Clark, 2012.
Thomas, J. C. *Footwashing in John 13 and the Johannnine Community.* JSNTS 61. Sheffield: JSOT Press, 1991.
Thomassen, E. 'Heracleon', in Rasimus, ed., *The Legacy of John,* 173-210.
Thompson, A. J. *One Lord, One People: The Unity of the Church in Acts in Its Literary Setting.* LNTS 359. London: T & T Clark, 2008.
Thompson, L. L. *The Book of Revelation: Apocalypse and Empire.* New York: Oxford University, 1990.
Thompson, M. M. *The Humanity of Jesus in the Fourth Gospel.* Philadelphia: Fortress, 1988.
———. 'The Historical Jesus and the Johannine Christ', in Culpepper and Black, eds., *Exploring the Gospel of John,* 21-42.
Thompson, W. G. *Matthew's Advice to a Divided Community: Mt 17,22–18,35.* AB 44. Rome Biblical Institute, 1970.
Tomson, P. J., and D. Lambers-Petry, eds. *The Image of the Judaeo-Christians in Ancient Jewish and Christian Literature.* WUNT 158. Tübingen: Mohr Siebeck, 2003.
Trakatellis, D. C. *The Pre-existence of Christ in the Writings of Justin Martyr.* Harvard Dissertations in Religion 6. Missoula: Scholars, 1976.
Trebilco, P. *Jewish Communities in Asia Minor.* SNTSMS 69. Cambridge University, 1991.
———. *The Early Christians in Ephesus from Paul to Ignatius.* WUNT 166. Tübingen: Mohr Siebeck, 2004.
Trevett, C. *A Study of Ignatius of Antioch in Syria and Asia Minor.* Lewiston: Mellen, 1992.
Trilling, W. *Das Wahre Israel: Studien zur Theologie des Matthäusevangeliums.* Leipzig: St. Benno, 1962.

Trobisch, D. *Paul's Letter Collection: Tracing the Origins.* Minneapolis: Fortress, 1994.
Troeltsch, E. *The Social Teaching of the Christian Churches.* ET, vol. 1. London: Allen & Unwin, 1931.
Tuckett, C. M. *The Revival of the Griesbach Hypothesis.* SNTSMS 44. Cambridge: Cambridge University, 1983.
———. *Nag Hammadi and the Gospel Tradition.* Edinburgh: T & T Clark, 1986.
———. 'Mark and Q', in *The Synoptic Gospels: Source Criticism and the New Literary Criticism,* 149-75. BETL 110. Leuven: Leuven University, 1993.
———. 'The Fourth Gospel and Q', in Fortna and Thatcher, eds., *Jesus in the Johannine Tradition,* 280-90.
———. *The Gospel of Mary.* Oxford University, 2007.
———. 'How Early Is "the" "Western" Text of Acts?', in Nicklas and Tilly, eds., *The Book of Acts as Church History,* 69-86.
———. 'The *Didache* and the Writings That Later Formed the New Testament', in Gregory and Tuckett, eds., *Reception,* 83-127.
———. '*2 Clement* and the Writings That Later Formed the New Testament', in Gregory and Tuckett, eds., *Reception,* 251-92.
———. 'The *Gospel of Mary*', in Foster, ed., *Non-Canonical Gospels,* 43-53.
Tuckett, C. M., ed. *The Messianic Secret.* London: SPCK, 1983.
———. *Luke's Literary Achievement: Collected Essays.* JSNTS 116. Sheffield: Sheffield Academic, 1995.
Tugwell, S. *The Apostolic Fathers.* London: Geoffrey Chapman, 1989.
Turner, J. D. *Sethian Gnosticism and the Platonic Tradition.* Quebec: University of Laval, 2001.
———. 'The Place of the *Gospel of Judas* in Sethian Tradition', in Scopello, ed., *The Gospel of Judas in Context,* 187-237.
———. 'The Johannine Legacy: The Gospel and *Apocryphon of John*', in Rasimus, ed., *Legacy of John,* 105-44.
Turner, M. *Power from On High: The Spirit in Israel's Restoration and Witness in Luke-Acts.* Sheffield: Sheffield Academic, 1996.
Turner, M. L. *The Gospel according to Philip: The Sources and Coherence of an Early Christian Collection.* NHMS 38. Leiden: Brill, 1996.
Turner, N. *A Grammar of New Testament Greek.* Edinburgh: T & T Clark, 1976.
Twelftree, G. H. 'Exorcisms in the Fourth Gospel and the Synoptics', in Fortna and Thatcher, eds., *Jesus in the Johannine Tradition,* 135-43.
Uro, R. 'The Social World of the *Gospel of Thomas*', in Asgeirsson et al., eds., *Thomasine Traditions in Antiquity,* 19-38.
———. '*Thomas* and Oral Gospel Tradition', in Uro, ed., *Thomas at the Crossroads,* 8-32.
———. 'Is *Thomas* an Encratite Gospel?', in Uro, ed., *Thomas at the Crossroads,* 140-62.
Uro, R., ed. Thomas *at the Crossroads: Essays on the* Gospel of Thomas. Edinburgh: T & T Clark, 1998.
Valantasis, R. *The Gospel of Thomas.* London: Routledge, 1997.
van de Sandt, H., and D. Flusser, *The Didache: Its Jewish Sources and Its Place in Early Judaism and Christianity.* Assen: Van Gorcum, 2002.

van de Sandt, H., ed. *Matthew and the Didache: Two Documents from the Same Jewish-Christian Milieu.* Assen: Van Gorcum, 2005.
van de Sandt, H., and J. K. Zangenberg, eds. *Matthew, James and Didache: Three Related Documents in Their Jewish and Christian Settings.* Atlanta: SBL, 2008.
van der Horst, P. W. 'The Birkat ha-minim in Recent Research', *Hellenism-Judaism-Christianity: Essays on Their Interaction,* 99-111. Kampen: Pharos, 1994.
van Minnen, P. 'The Akhmim *Gospel of Peter*', in Kraus and Nicklas, eds., *Das Evangelium nach Petrus.*
Van Voorst, R. E. *The Ascents of James: History and Theology of a Jewish-Christian Community.* SBLDS 112. Atlanta: Scholars, 1989.
Verheyden, J. 'Epiphanius on the Ebionites', in Tomson and Lambers-Petry, eds., *The Image of the Judaeo-Christians,* 182-208.
———. 'The De-Johannification of Jesus: The Revisionist Contribution of Some Nineteenth-Century German Scholarship', in Anderson et al., eds., *John, Jesus and History,* vol. 1, 109-20.
———. '*The Shepherd of Hermas* and the Writings That Later Formed the New Testament', in Gregory and Tuckett, eds., *Reception,* 293-329.
———. 'Some Reflections on Determining the Purpose of the "Gospel of Peter"', in Kraus and Nicklas, eds., *Evangelium nach Petrus,* 286-90.
Vermes, G. *Jesus the Jew.* London: Collins, 1973.
———. *Christian Beginnings from Nazareth to Nicaea AD 30-325.* London: Allen Lane, 2012.
Vledder, E.-J. *Conflict in the Miracle Stories: A Socio-Exegetical Study of Matthew 8 and 9.* JSNTS 152. Sheffield: Sheffield Academic, 1997.
von Campenhausen, H. *The Formation of the Christian Bible.* London: Black, 1972.
von Wahlde, U. C. 'The Pool of Siloam: The Importance of New Discoveries . . .', in Anderson et al., eds., *John, Jesus and History,* vol. 2, 155-73.
Wagner, J. R. *Heralds of the Good News: Isaiah and Paul in Concert in the Letter to the Romans.* Leiden: Brill, 2002.
Wander, B. *Trennungsprozesse zwischen frühen Christentum und Judentum im 1. Jahrhundert n. Chr.* Tübingen: Mohr Siebeck, 1994.
Wassmuth, O. *Sibyllinische Orakel 1-2: Studien und Kommentar.* AJEC 76. Leiden: Brill, 2011.
van der Watt, J. G., and R. Zimmermann, eds. *Rethinking the Ethics of John: "Implicit Ethics" in the Johannine Writings.* WUNT 291. Tübingen: Mohr Siebeck, 2012.
Webb, R. L., and P. H. Davids, eds. *Reading Jude with New Eyes.* LNTS 383. London: T & T Clark, 2008.
Webb, R. L., and D. F. Watson, eds. *Reading Second Peter with New Eyes.* LNTS 382. London: T & T Clark, 2010.
Wechsler, A. *Geschichtsbild und Apostelstreit: Eine forschungsgeschichtliche und exegetische Studie über den antiochenischen Zwischenfall (Gal 2,11-14).* BZNW 62. Berlin: de Gruyter, 1991.
Weeden, T. J. *Mark: Traditions in Conflict.* Philadelphia: Fortress, 1971.
Weiss, J. *Earliest Christianity.* 1937. New York: Harper Torchbook, 1959.
Wellhausen, J. *Einleitung in die drei ersten Evangelien.* Berlin: Georg Reimer, 1905.
Wengst, K. *Bedrängte Gemeinde und verherrlichter Christus: Der historische Ort des*

Johannesevangeliums als Schlüssel zu seiner Interpretation. Neukirchen-Vluyn: Neukirchener, 1981.
Wenham, D., ed. *Gospel Perspectives,* vol. 5: *The Jesus Tradition outside the Gospels.* Sheffield: JSOT, 1984.
White, L. M. *From Jesus to Christianity.* HarperSanFrancisco, 2004.
Whitfield, B. *Joshua Traditions and the Argument of Hebrews 3 and 4.* BZNW 194. Berlin: de Gruyter, 2013.
Wiefel, W. 'The Jewish Community in Ancient Rome and the Origins of Roman Christianity'. *Judaica* 26 (1970): 65-88, reprinted in K. P. Donfried, ed., *The Romans Debate,* 85-101. Peabody, MA: Hendrickson, 1991.
Wiles, M. F. *The Divine Apostle: The Interpretation of St Paul's Epistles in the Early Church.* Cambridge University, 1967.
Wilken, R. L. *The Myth of Christian Beginnings.* London: SCM, 1979.
―――. *The Christians as the Romans Saw Them.* New Haven: Yale University Press, 2003.
Willett, M. E. *Wisdom Christology in the Fourth Gospel.* San Francisco: Mellen, 1992.
Williams, A. L. *Justin Martyr: The Dialogue with Trypho.* London: SPCK, 1930.
Williams, C. H. '"I Am" or "I Am He"? Self-Declaratory Pronouncements in the Fourth Gospel and Rabbinic Tradition', in Fortna and Thatcher, eds., *Jesus in the Johannine Tradition,* 343-52.
Williams, J. A. *Biblical Interpretation in the Gnostic Gospel of Truth from Nag Hammadi.* SBLDS 79. Atlanta: Scholars, 1988.
Williams, M. A. *Rethinking "Gnosticism": An Argument for Dismantling a Dubious Category.* Princeton University, 1996.
Williams, M. H. *The Jews among the Greeks and Romans: A Diasporan Sourcebook.* London: Duckworth, 1998.
Williamson, R. *Philo and the Epistle to the Hebrews.* Leiden: Brill, 1970.
Willitts, J. *Matthew's Messianic Shepherd-King: In Search of 'the Lost Sheep of the House of Israel'.* BZNW 147. Berlin: de Gruyter, 2007.
―――. 'Paul and Jewish Christians in the Second Century', in Bird and Dodson, eds., *Paul and the Second Century,* 140-68.
Wilson, S. G. *The Gentiles and the Gentile Mission in Luke-Acts.* SNTSMS 23. Cambridge: Cambridge University, 1973.
―――. *Luke and the Pastoral Epistles.* London: SPCK, 1979.
―――. *Related Strangers: Jews and Christians 70-170 CE.* Minneapolis: Fortress, 1995.
Wink, W. *John the Baptist in the Gospel Tradition.* SNTSMS 7. Cambridge: Cambridge University, 1968.
Witherington, B. *John's Wisdom.* Louisville: Westminster John Knox, 1995.
Wolter, M. *Die Pastoralbriefe als Paulustradition.* FRLANT 146. Göttingen: Vandenhoeck, 1988.
Wrede, W. *Über Aufgabe und Methode der sogenannten neutestamentlichen Theologie.* Göttingen: Vandenhoeck & Ruprecht, 1897; ET 'The Task and Methods of "New Testament Theology"', in R. Morgan, *The Nature of New Testament Theology,* 68-116. London: SCM, 1973.
―――. *Das Messiasgeheimnis in den Evangelien: Zugleich ein Beitrag zum Verstandnis des Markusevangeliums.* Göttingen, 1901; ET *The Messianic Secret.* Cambridge: James Clarke, 1971.

Wright, D. F. 'Apocryphal Gospels: The "Unknown Gospel" (Pap. Egerton 2) and the Gospel of Peter', in Wenham, ed., *Jesus Tradition*, 207-32.
Wright, N. T. 'When Is a Gospel Not a Gospel?', in *Judas and the Gospel of Jesus*, 63-83. Grand Rapids: Baker, 2006.
Yarbrough, M. M. *Paul's Utilization of Preformed Traditions in 1 Timothy*. LNTS 417. London: T & T Clark, 2009.
Yieh, J. Y.-H. *One Teacher: Jesus' Teaching Role in Matthew's Gospel Report*. BZNW 124. Berlin: de Gruyter, 2004.
Young, S. E. *Jesus Tradition in the Apostolic Fathers: Their Explicit Appeals to the Words of Jesus in Light of Orality Studies*. WUNT 2.311. Tübingen: Mohr Siebeck, 2011.
Zahn, T. *Ignatius von Antiochien*. Gotha: Perthes, 1873.
———. *Geschichte des Neutestamentlichen Kanons*. 2 vols. Erlangen: Deichert, 1888, 1890.
Zelyck, L. R. *John Among the Other Gospels: The Reception of the Fourth Gospel in the Extra-Canonical Gospels*. WUNT 2.347. Tübingen: Mohr Siebeck, 2013.
Zöckler, T. *Jesu Lehren im Thomasevangelium*. NHMS 47. Leiden: Brill, 1999.
Zwierlein, O. *Petrus in Rom: die literarische Zeugnisse*. UALG 96. Berlin: de Gruyter, 2009.

Matthew

Davies, W. D., and D. C. Allison. *The Gospel according to Saint Matthew*. ICC; 3 vols. Edinburgh: T & T Clark, 1988, 1991, 1997.
Gnilka, J. *Das Matthäusevangelium*. HTKNT; 2 vols. Freiburg: Herder, 1986, 1988.
Gundry, R. H. *Matthew: A Commentary on His Literary and Theological Art*. Grand Rapids: Eerdmans, 1982.
Hagner, D. A. *Matthew*. WBC 33; 2 vols. Dallas: Word, 1993, 1995.
Luz, U. *Das Evangelium nach Matthäus*. EKK 1; 4 vols. Düsseldorf: Benziger, 1990, 1997, 2002.

Mark

Boring, M. E. *Mark*. NTL. Louisville: Westminster John Knox, 2006.
Collins, A. Y. *Mark*. Hermeneia. Minneapolis: Fortress, 2007.
Evans, C. A. *Mark 8:27–16:20*. WBC 34B. Nashville: Nelson, 2001.
France, R. T. *The Gospel of Mark*. NIGTC. Grand Rapids: Eerdmans, 2002.
Gnilka, J. *Das Evangelium nach Markus*. EKK 2; 2 vols. Zürich: Benziger, 1978, 1979.
Guelich, R. A. *Mark 1–8:26*. WBC 34A. Dallas: Word, 1989.
Hooker, M. D. *The Gospel according to St Mark*. BNTC. London: A & C Black, 1991.
Lührmann, D. *Das Markusevangelium*. HNT 3. Tübingen: Mohr Siebeck, 1987.
Marcus, J. *Mark 1–8*. AB 27. New York: Doubleday, 2000.
Marxsen, W. *Mark the Evangelist*. 1956, 1959; ET Nashville: Abingdon, 1969.
Pesch, R. *Das Markusevangelium*. HTKNT 2; 2 vols. Freiburg: Herder, 1977.

Bibliography

Luke

Bovon, F. *Das Evangelium nach Lukas*. EKK 3; 4 vols. Zürich: Benziger, 1989, 1996, 2001, 2009.
Evans, C. F. *Saint Luke*. London: SCM, 1990.
Fitzmyer, J. A. *The Gospel according to Luke*. AB 28; 2 vols. New York: Doubleday, 1981, 1985.
Klein, H. *Das Lukasevangelium*. KEK. Göttingen: Vandenhoeck, 2006.
Nolland, J. *Luke*. WBC 35; 2 vols. Dallas: Word, 1989, 1993.

John

Barrett, C. K. *The Gospel according to St John*. London: SPCK, 1955, ²1978.
Brown, R. E. *The Gospel according to John*. AB 29; 2 vols. New York: Doubleday, 1966.
Bultmann, R. *The Gospel of John: A Commentary*. 1941; ET Oxford: Blackwell, 1971.
Lincoln, A. T. *The Gospel according to Saint John*. BNTC. London: Continuum, 2005.
Lindars, B. *The Gospel of John*. NCB. London: Oliphants, 1972.
McHugh, J. F. *John 1-4*. ICC. London: T & T Clark, 2009.
Schnackenburg, R. *The Gospel according to St John*, vol. 1. 1965; ET New York: Herder & Herder, 1968.
———. *Das Johannesevangelium*, part 3. HTKNT. Freiburg: Herder, ³1979.
Thyen, H. *Das Johannesevangelium*. HNT 6. Tübingen: Mohr Siebeck, 2005.
von Wahlde, U. C. *The Gospel and Letters of John*. 3 vols. Grand Rapids: Eerdmans, 2010.

Pastoral Epistles

Barrett, C. K. *The Pastoral Epistles*. Oxford: Clarendon, 1963.
Johnson, L. T. *The First and Second Letters to Timothy*. AB 35A. New York: Doubleday, 2001.
Marshall, I. H. *The Pastoral Epistles*. ICC. Edinburgh: T & T Clark, 1999.
Mounce, W. D. *Pastoral Epistles*. WBC 46. Nashville: Nelson, 2000.
Oberlinner, L. *Die Pastoralbriefe: Erste Timotheusbrief*. HTKNT 11/2/1. Freiburg: Herder, 1994.
———. *Die Pastoralbriefe: Zweiter Timotheusbrief*. HTKNT 11/2/2. Freiburg: Herder, 1995.
Quinn, J. D. *The Letter to Titus*. AB 35. New York: Doubleday, 1990.
Roloff, J. *Der erste Brief an Timotheus*. EKK 15. Zürich: Benziger, 1988.

Hebrews

Attridge, H. W. *Hebrews*. Hermeneia. Philadelphia: Fortress, 1989.
Grässer, E. *An die Hebräer*. EKK 16. Zürich: Benziger, 1990, 1993, 1997.
Koester, C. R. *Hebrews*. AB 36. New York: Doubleday, 2001.

Lane, W. L. *Hebrews*. WBC 47; 2 vols. Dallas: Word Books, 1991.
Moffatt, J. *Hebrews*. ICC. Edinburgh: T & T Clark, 1924.
Spicq, C. *Hébreux*. EB. Vol. 1. Paris: Gabalda, 1952.
Weiss, H. F. *Der Brief an die Hebräer.* KEK. Göttingen: Vandenhoeck, 1991.

1 and 2 Peter and Jude

Achtemeier, P. J. *1 Peter.* Hermeneia. Minneapolis: Fortress, 1996.
Bauckham, R. J. *Jude, 2 Peter.* WBC 50. Waco: Word, 1983.
Elliott, J. H. *1 Peter.* AB 37B. New York: Doubleday, 2000.
Goppelt, L. *Der erste Petrusbrief.* KEK. Göttingen: Vandenhoeck, 1978.
Mayor, J. B. *The Epistle of St. Jude and the Second Epistle of St. Peter.* London: Macmillan, 1907.
Neyrey, J. H. *2 Peter, Jude.* AB 37C. New York: Doubleday, 1993.
Schelkle, K. H. *Die Petrusbriefe; Der Judabrief.* HTKNT 13.2. Freiburg: Herder, 1976.
Watson, D. F., and T. Callan. *First and Second Peter.* Paideia. Grand Rapids: Baker Academic, 2012.

1-3 John

Brown, R. E. *The Epistles of John.* AB. New York: Doubleday, 1982.
Klauck, H.-J. *Der erste Johannesbrief.* KEK 23/1. Zürich: Benziger, 1991.
———. *Der zweite und dritte Johannesbriefe.* KEK 23/2. Zürich: Benziger, 1992.
Strecker, G. *Die Johannesbriefe.* KEK 14. Göttingen: Vandenhoeck, 1989.

Revelation

Aune, D. E. *Revelation.* WBC 52; 3 vols. Dallas: Word, 1997-98.
Beale, G. K. *The Book of Revelation.* NIGTC. Grand Rapids: Eerdmans, 1999.
Charles, R. H. *Revelation.* ICC; 2 vols. Edinburgh: T & T Clark, 1920.
Satake, A. *Die Offenbarung des Johannes.* KEK. Göttingen: Vandenhoeck, 2008.
Smalley, S. S. *The Revelation to John.* London: SPCK, 2005.

Index of Authors

Aasgaard, R., 492n.314
Abramowski, L., 452n.168, 453n.171
Achtemeier, P. J., 544n.124
Adams, E., 92n.242
Ådna, J., 603n.24
Aland, B., 79n.167, 501n.338
Aland, K., 50n.20, 51nn.21,23, 55n.44, 61nn.79,82, 79n.167, 83, 86n.201, 147n.191, 369, 469n.228, 501n.338
Alexander, L. C. A., 59n.69, 215n.19, 276n.301, 447n.151
Alexander, P. S., 17n.51, 574n.241, 627n.144,145,147, 628n.149,150, 630n.163
Allison, D. C., 62n.85, 63n.88, 65nn.97,98, 67nn.105,107,109,111, 68n.117, 69n.118, 70-71n.126, 249n.193, 256nn.221,223,224, 257nn.232,233, 258n.238,239, 264n.262, 265n.266, 268n.277, 269n.280, 274n.295, 418n.38, 420nn45,50, 431n.86, 639n.210, 676n.7, 734n.38
Alon, G., 611n.59, 612n.64, 621n.117, 622nn.121,123, 623nn.125,127
Altaner, B., 111n.1
Anderson, C. P., 160n.258
Anderson, P. N., 202n.67, 316n.14,16,17, 319n.21, 321n.41, 325n.55, 331n.82, 334n.92, 335n.96, 336n.101
Appold, M. L., 353n.170
Ashton, J., 327n.66, 359n.188, 361n.196, 367n.218, 369n.229, 630n.166, 641n.217, 760n.9, 761n.15, 768n.39
Attridge, H. W., 92n.239, 93nn.245,247,248, 95n.256, 482n.271, 482n.271, 539n.112, 646nn.241,243, 647, 648n.250, 712n.151
Audet, J.-P., 120n.49
Aune, D. E., 103n.294, 107nn.316,317, 109n.325, 110n.330, 129n.109, 548nn.139,140, 783nn.118,121, 784nn.122,126,127, 786nn.134,135, 788n.144, 789nn.148,150, 790nn.151,158

Bacon, B. W., 256n.227
Bal, M., 212n.11
Baldensperger, W., 339n.115
Barclay, J. M. G., 598n.3, 606n.40
Barnard, L. W., 113n.12, 553n.156, 701n.113
Barnett, A. E., 691n.67
Barr, A., 251n.197
Barrett, C. K., 73n.138, 76nn.152,154, 79n.163, 86n.202, 105n.301, 359n.185, 360n.192, 363n.202, 364n.209, 365n.213, 367n.222, 368n.224, 483n.273, 483n.276, 500n.221, 533n.83, 568n.212, 634n.185, 653n.268, 766n.34, 770n.52, 779n.99, 792n.162, 814n.23
Barth, G., 249n.187
Bartlet, J. V., 695n.88, 696n.90, 697n.93

873

INDEX OF AUTHORS

Barton, S. C., 211n.7, 236n.135
Bauckham, R. J., 15n.45,
  47n.11, 52, 72n.134, 74n.142,
  76n.152, 77n.155, 84n.195,
  97nn.264,266,268, 98nn.273,276,
  99nn.277,278, 100n.281, 101n.283,
  102nn.289,290,292, 103n.294,
  109n.325, 163n.277, 179n.353,
  179n.355, 180n.359, 216n.23, 222n.53,
  353n.168, 355n.172, 365n.213,
  366n.217, 418n.37, 445n.140,
  446nn.145,146,147, 447nn.150,152,
  448n.153, 517n.27, 524n.53, 525n.54,
  526nn.58,60,61,62, 541n.118,
  542n.119, 544nn.125,126,127,
  545nn.129,130, 575n.244, 578n.249,
  579n.253, 590n.313, 619n.106,
  646n.242, 686nn.45,46, 704n.122,
  732n.30,31, 736n.47, 742n.67,
  750n.97, 751n.98, 785n.131
Bauer, J. B., 415n.26
Bauer, W., 6n.11, 10, 11, 21, 31n.122,
  36n.144, 114n.13, 175n.339, 407, 527,
  593, 712n.155, 713n.160
Baum, A., 85n.197
Baur, F. C., 6n.9, 13, 175n.338, 335n.96,
  685, 737
Beale, G. K., 108n.320, 109n.325,
  547n.135, 548n.140, 549n.141,
  789n.150, 790n.151,158
Beasley-Murray, G. R., 238n.144
Beck, N. A., 25
Becker, A. H., 14n.41, 15nn.43,46,
  19n.61, 20n.67, 23nn.79,80
Bell, H. I., 155n.235
Bellinzoni, A. J., 452n.169,
  453nn.171,172, 455n.179
Ben Ezra, D. S., 19n.61
Ben Zeev, M. P., 616nn.82,84
Berding, K., 693n.80, 695n.87
Bernhard, A. E., 148n.192, 155n.237,
  156n.239, 469n.228
Bernheim, P. A., 523n.51, 525n.54,
  554n.160
Bernier, J., 641n.219
Best, E., 233n.116, 236n.134, 237n.139,
  238n.146
Bethge, H.-G., 153n.227, 375n.239
Betz, H. D., 251n.200, 268nn.273,276

Beutler, J., 104n.298, 326n.60,
  335n.351n.162, 358n.182
Beyschlag, K., 552n.150
Bianchi, U., 34n.136, 522n.47
Bieringer, R., 639n.212, 641n.218,
  649n.256, 823n.44
Bird, M. F., 163n.273, 662n.307,
  691n.70, 698n.99, 699n.100
Black, C. C., 225n.70, 235n.126,
  354n.170, 356n.176, 364n.208,
  499n.328, 771n.54, 819n.37
Blackwell, B. C., 720n.200, 722n.205
Blass, F., 55n.45
Blatz, B., 147n.192, 150n.207, 152n.220,
  395n.291, 475n.247, 479n.263
Blomberg, C. L., 316n.14
Blunt, A., 32n.125
Bockmuehl, M., xii, 188n.4, 216n.23,
  542n.119, 724n.2, 727n.12, 731n.27,
  732n.30, 734n.38, 755nn.42,46,
  738n.55, 739n.57, 740nn.60,62,
  741n.63, 743nn.68,71, 745-46n.83,
  749n.92, 753n.103
Bollok, J., 164n.279
Bolt, P. G., 243n.170
Bolyki, J., 166n.288
Borgen, P., 27nn.101,102, 345n.139
Boring, M. E., 48n.11, 54n.40, 56n.48
Bornkamm, G., 249n.187, 262,
  263n.257, 639n.209
Bousset, W., 28n.107, 32n.124
Bovon, F., 59nn.64,65,68,69, 60n.72,
  61nn.78,81, 276n.301, 277n.304,
  278n.306, 282n.320, 283n.322,
  284n.330, 285n.336, 288n.352,
  289n.357, 292n.373, 294n.379,
  296n.384, 302n.406, 304n.410,
  305n.414
Boyarin, D., 14n.40, 16n.50, 20, 21,
  625n.137, 630, 631
Brashler, J., 167n.297, 180n.360,
  181n.362
Bremmer, J. N., 163n.276, 164n.279,
  165n.286, 166n.288, 166n.290,
  167n.292, 179n.353, 179n.355,
  181n.363, 706n.128
Breytenbach, C., 239n.150, 354n.170
Broadhead, E. K., 144n.176, 167n.293,
  167n.298, 226n.71, 230n.95, 324n.54,
  509n.1, 510nn.4,5, 575nn.242,245,

Index of Authors

579n.256, 584nn.279,284, 587nn.295,296, 590n.307,313, 602n.21, 619n.106, 624n.132, 626n.139, 670n.337
Brooks, S. H., 249n.186
Brown, D., 407n.7
Brown, R. E., 52n.29, 54n.40, 56n.52, 59n.65, 61n.78, 62n.83, 63n.88, 64n.91, 65n.95, 69n.118, 70n.126, 72n.132, 76nn.152,153, 78n.159, 80n.170, 82n.182, 92n.238, 95nn.255,258, 98n.276, 102n.290, 103n.296, 104nn.296,297,298, 105nn.300,302, 106nn.306,308,310, 110n.333, 113n.8, 157n.243, 168n.302, 216n.21, 223n.60, 225n.70, 229n.93, 230n.95, 237n.137, 239n.151, 240n.152, 255n.219, 256n.221, 351n.163, 360n.193, 363nn.202,204, 367n.222, 368n.226, 368n.228, 386n.265, 388n.270, 489n.302, 490n.305,306, 509n.2, 510n.2, 534n.90, 542n.120, 553nn.148,149, 592n.321, 643n.231, 676n.6, 680n.22, 687n.52, 731n.27, 733n.36, 734nn.38,40, 735nn.43,44, 738n.54, 739nn.56,57, 740n.62, 744n.75, 753nn.103,104, 760nn.9,11, 763nn.21,22,23, 764n.24,25, 770n.52, 771n.55, 772n.65, 775n.75, 776n.83, 777n.88, 778nn.90,91,92, 781n.108, 782n.115, 786n.137
Brown, S. K., 148n.192, 249n.196
Brox, N., 83
Bryan, C., 214n.15
Bühner, J. A., 345n.139, 643n.229, 767n.37
Bullard, R. A., 180n.360
Bultmann, R., 32n.124, 34, 58n.58, 129n.104, 315n.7, 328n.67, 329n.75, 350n.161, 351n.161, 357n.178, 760n.10, 768, 769, 770, 773n.71
Burchard, C., 162n.270
Burge, G. M., 360n.189, 368n.228
Burke, T., 159n.256
Burkitt, F. C., 246n.174, 294n.332
Burridge, R. A., xii, 194n.36, 366n.215
Burrus, V., 165n.284, 705n.126
Burtchaell, J. T., 813nn.15,17, 814n.26

Byrskog, S., 266n.270, 278n.307, 609n.53

Cameron, R., 11n.28, 147n.188, 149n.202, 150n.209, 151n.214, 158nn.251,254, 161n.265, 382n.251, 384n.262, 397n.297, 448n.154, 463n.209, 468n.224, 469n.229, 471n.34, 472n.242, 475n.249, 476n.251, 477n.254,255, 478n.257, 479n.259,260, 487n.294,296, 491nn.308,310, 492n.313, 499n.328
Cancik, H., 52n.26
Caragounis, C. C., 264n.262, 325n.55
Carey, H. J., 242n.159
Carlson, S. C., 159n.256, 465n.220
Carter, W., 71n.126
Casey, M., 51n.26, 194n.33
Catchpole, D., 57n.55, 270n.281
Chae, Y. S., 254n.217
Charles, R. H., 108nn.319,321
Charlesworth, J. H., 17n.54, 75n.144, 79n.166, 81n.174, 128n.95, 128nn.96,97,100, 129nn.102,109, 571n.225, 572nn.227,228,231, 573n.234, 660nn.292,293, 771n.52, 792n.162
Chartrand-Burke, T., 158nn.253,254
Chestnut, G. F., 141n.160, 143n.172
Chestnutt, R. D., 162n270
Chilton, B., 383n.259, 386n.264 512n.7, 537n.105, 838
Clabeaux, J. J., 39n.159, 40n.161
Clark-Soles, J., 365n.213, 834
Clarke, W. K., 552n.147, 554n.159
Clines, D. J. A., 215n.19
Cockerill, G. L., 541n.118
Cohen, S., 604n.28, 646n.244
Cohn, N., 181n.365
Cohn-Sherbok, D., 23n.82
Collins, A. Y., 47n.7, 48nn.11,13, 49n.14, 51n.24, 54n.36, 55nn.44,45,46, 195n.39, 196n.40, 198n.48, 213n.12, 245n.171, 226nn.71,72, 227nn.78,79, 230n.98, 238n.146, 241n.155, 243n.167
Colpe, C., 34n.137
Conzelmann, H., 102n.294, 279n.310, 294n.380

875

Cook, J. G., 56n.48, 608n.47, 615nn.76,80
Corwin, V., 129n.103
Cotelier, J. B., 111n.2
Cousland, J. R. C., 453n.172
Crewe, J., 212n.11
Crossan, J. D., 11n.28, 35n.141, 372nn.236,237, 379n.244, 463n.209, 468n.224, 487n.296, 489n.300,302,303,304, 839
Crossley, J. G., 53n.31, 531n.73, 641n.218
Crown, A. D., 22n.73, 527n.65
Cullmann, O., 158nn.251,252, 340n.118, 368n.227, 624n.2, 733n.38, 738n.54, 740n.62, 839
Culpepper, R. A., 72n.134, 73n.139, 74n.142, 103n.296, 104n.298, 354n.170, 356n.176, 364n.208, 367n.223, 499n.330, 639n.212, 772nn.52,55, 782n.114, 792n.162, 796n.180, 819n.37
Czachesz, I., 179n.353, 181n.363

Daniélou, J., 22n.75, 509n.2, 529n.71, 559n.178, 840
Das, A. A., 607n.44
Dassmann, E., 688n.54, 690nn.64,65, 693n.80, 702n.120, 707n.131, 711n.148, 840
Davids, P. H., 98n.271
Davies, S. L., 150n.210, 249n.193, 252n.208, 389n.272, 391n.280, 392n.284, 396n.296, 418n.38, 635n.189, 838n.206, 708n..135
Davies, W. D., 62nn.85,88, 63n.88, 65nn.97,98, 67nn.105,107,109,111, 68n.117, 69n.118, 70-71n.126, 150n.210, 246n.177, 249n.193, 252n.208, 256nn.221,224,227, 257nn.232,233, 258nn.238,239, 261n.248, 264n.262, 265nn.265,266, 268n.277, 269n.280, 274n.295, 420nn.45, 50, 424n.66, 431n.86, 639n.210, 734n.38
Davis, S. J., 708n.135
de Boer, E. A., 153n.223
de Boer, M., 582n.276
de Boer, M. C., 641n.218
Debrunner, A., 55n.45

DeConick, A. D., 147n.192, 149n.200, 150n.205, 153n.226, 155nn.231,233, 349n.157, 372n.237, 375n.239, 385n.263, 389n.271, 391nn.279,281, 394n.286 400n.309, 381n.248, 389n.271, 391nn.279,281, 394n.286, 395n.292, 396n.295, 397n.297, 398nn.299,300, 400nn..303,304, 420n.45, 401n.309, 420nn.45, 486n.289,291,292, 487n.293, 594
Deines, R., 268n.276, 400nn.303, 304, 486n.289,291,292, 487n.293
de Jonge, M., 572n.227, 641n.218
de Labriolle, 796n.181
de Lange, N., 18n.57, 212n.11
Delling, G., 681n.23
Del Verne, M., 553n.151, 555n.166
Denaux, A., 329n.72
Deutsch, C., 258n.237
Dewey, J., 214n.15, 224n.62, 329n.76, 336n.102
Dines, J., 579n.218
Dodd, C. H., 192n.25, 213n.12, 300n.396, 319n.32, 320n.33, 321n.37, 324n.54, 326nn.61,62 329n.78, 330nn.78,79, 332, 334nn.91,93,95, 641n.217, 770n.53, 771n,57, 803n.2
Dodson, J. R., 163n.273
Doering, L., 96n.261, 543n,122
Donahue, P. J., 653n.255
Donaldson, T. L., 604n.29
Donelson, L. R., 84n.191
Donfried, K. P., 438n.118. 439nn.119,120, 441nn.129,130, 443n.34, 607n.45, 697n.93, 733n.36, 734n.40, 735nn.43,44, 738n.54, 739nn56,57
Donovan, M. A., 6nn.5,6, 141n.162
Draper, J. A., 118nn.36,42, 120n.49, 429n.79, 430n.84, 432n.92, 433n.94, 553n.154, 554nn.157,159
Drijvers, H. J. W., 149n.204, 172n.320, 173n.326, 173n.329, 174n.330, 174n.331, 400n.306
Dschulnigg, P., 223n.59, 545n.131
Duensing, H., 178n.350
Dunderberg, I., 30nn.116,117,118, 31n.118, 73n.139, 75n.144, 149n.201, 152nn.216,217, 386n.265, 387nn.266,267, 388nn.268,269,270,

Index of Authors

389n.271, 461n.205, 490n.304, 772n.64
Dunn, J. D. G., xxi, 4, 6n.8, 8n.16, 10, 12n.30, 13nn.33,35,37, 18n.56, 21, 25n.96, 26nn.99,100, 31n.123, 32n.124, 35n.141, 41, 43, 47n.8,10, 48n.12, 50n.19, 51nn.25,26, 52n.29, 53nn,32,33,35, 55n.43 57n.55, 58n.58,60,62,63, 59nn.65,66, 61n.76,77,81, 64n.90,92,93, 70n.125, 80n.171, 84n.192, 87nn.206,209,88n.213, 88n.214, 89n.226, 93n.246, 96, 109.327,129n.107, 146n.186, 187, 188n.3 189nn.8,9, 190n.18, 191nn.19,20,23,24, 193n.31,32, 197nn.44,46, 199, 201n.59, 209, 210, 211, 212nn9,10, 212n.10, 213n.12, 215n.20, 216nn.22,23, 217n.27,30, 219n.35, 220n.40, 222n.54,55, 223nn.58,60, 226n.75, 224n.64, 229n.93, 230nn.94,97, 231n.105, 232n.107, 235n.129, 237n.137, 238n.145, 240n.154, 241n.156,157, 242, 246n.177, 248n.185, 247n.181, 247n.182, 248n.183, 245n.177, 253n.210, 256n.222, 257n.229,230, 260n.244, 262n.252,253, 263n.259, 265, 269, 272n.289, 277, 279nn.309,312, 283, 284n.332, 285n.336, 286n.340,341,342,344, 287n.349, 288n.352, 292n.372, 294n.377, 298, 299nn392,394, 301n.339, 302nn.402,403,404,405, 303n.407, 305n.412, 306n.417, 310, 313n.2, 316nn.14,15, 317n.19, 319nn.31,32, 320n.33, 321n.39, 322n.44, 326n.59, 332nn43,46,48, 334n.91,93, 335n.96, 338n.109,111, 341n.120, 342n.125, 344n.133, 346nn.143,145, 355n.172, 359n.185, 360n.192, 366n.215, 368n.226, 371n.233, 379, 380n.246, 383n.253, 384n.261, 386n.264, 387nn.266,267, 388nn.268,269,270, 389n.271, 405n.1, 402n.311, 405n.1, 407n.11, 411n.16, 413n.20, 428n.76, 435n.105, 451n.166, 463n.208, 464n.212, 471n.236, 490n.304, 499n.328, 512nn.8,10, 513nn.12,13,14, 516nn.22,25, 517n.27, 522n.48, 524, 530n.72, 531n.74, 532n.77, 534n.85, 538n.109, 535n.96, 540n.114, 543n.121, 553n.155, 559n.4, 570nn.217,221, 582n.275, 585n.286, 592nn.317,318, 600, 602n.20, 603, 604, 605nn.30, 32,33,34,607nn.41,42,45, 606n.39, 608nn.46,50, 609, 612n.64, 615n.79, 627n.143, 629n.160, 631nn.169.170, 633nn.179,181, 637n.196,200,202, 642n.223, 643nn.226,227, 646n.241, 649nn.255,256, 652n.264, 653n.265, 675n.1, 676nn.2,3,6,7, 678n.11, 682, 683n.33,35,36, 684n.39,40 688n.53, 692nn.73,75,76, 693n.79, 707nn.129,130,134, 709n.141, 711n.145, 715n.168, 721n.203, 725nn.5,7,8, 726n.11, 727nn.13,14, 728nn.18,20, 729n.21, 731n.27,29, 732n.33, 734n.39, 736n.51, 737n.53, 739n.58, 753n.103, 759n.6, 762n.18, 767n.35, 784n.124, 801n.1, 801n.1, 803n.3, 816n.32, 819n.37, 823n.44
Dwyer, T., 243n.169

Edwards, J. R., 228n.88, 280n.315
Edwards, O. C., 135nn.137,139, 136n.144
Ehrman, B. D., 11n.28, 12n.28, 28n.110, 112n.8, 113n.12, 114n.13, 115n.19, 116n.29, 117n.322, 118nn.39,40, 119n.48, 120nn.50,51, 124n.72, 125n.82, 126n.83, 127n.90, 129n.130, 132n.121, 132n.122, 143n.174, 144n.175, 152n.218, 156n.241, 159n.256, 766n160n.257, 218n.32, 397n.297, 407, 480n.264, 482n.271, 484n.278, 485n.283, 487n.294, 491n.310, 491n.313, 553n.154, 560n.187, 561n.190, 651n.260, 718n.184, 766n.34, 777n,88, 778n.90, 571n.225, 572nn.227,228,230
Eisle, W, 93n.247, 148n.192
Elliott, J. H., 743n.74, 744n.75,81
Elliott, J. K., 131n.118, 144nn.176,178, 147n.192, 149n.204, 155n.236, 157nn.243,244,247,249, 158nn.250,251,252,253, 160nn.257,258,261, 161n.265, 162n.267, 163.nn273,274, 165n.283,

166n.290, 167nn.294,297,298,
168n.299, 170n.313, 171n.316,
172nn.319,320, 173n.329, 178n.350,
179nn.351,353,355, 180n.359,
181n.364, 372n.237, 412n.20,
463n.210, 464nn.213,214,215,
466n.221, 479n.260, 469n.228,
473n.242, 479n.260, 481n.268,
485n.282, 487n.294, 488n.299,
488n.299, 491n.310, 492n.313,
497n.321, 522n.42, 543n.124,
544n.124, 661n.299, 723n.208,
796n.178
Elliott, M. W., 723n.208
Ellis, E. E., 546n.132
Emerton, J. A., 128n.95, 129n.103
Epp, E. J., 217n.31, 634n.184
Eubank, N., 533n.81
Evans, C. A., 47n.9, 144n.176, 226n.74,
229n.93, 241n.158, 243n.164,
280n.314, 281n.319, 282n.320,
285nn.333,334, 287n.347, 294n.379,
298n.288, 299n.394, 304n.409,
305n.410, 350n.159, 469n.230, 512n.7,
590n.310, 602n.22
Evans, C. S., 316n.14

Fee, G. D., 681n.29
Feldman, L. H., 18n.58, 19n.66,
570n.222, 598n.3
Feldmeier, R., 543n.122
Fentress, J., 212n.11
Fiorenza, E. S., 108n.322, 549n.143,
788n.144
Fitzmyer, J. A., 57n.56, 58n.61,
59nn.65,66,69, 60nn.70,73,75,
61nn.78,82, 62n.82, 193n.30, 220n.43,
276n.301, 277n.302, 280n.314,
281nn.317,319, 285nn.334,338,
286n.342, 287n.344, 288n.352,
289n.357, 292n.370, 294nn.378,380,
295n.382, 304n.409, 306n.415,
308n.419, 735n.44
Foerster, W., 28, 29n.112, 30n.115,
31n.120, 32n.125, 37nn.150,151,
38nn.152,153,154, 109n.326,
146n.187, 193n.30, 497n.321,
535n.94, 681n.27, 714n.166, 771n.54,
772n.60,61,63
Foley, J. M., 190n.19

Fornberg, T., 99n.278, 102n.293
Fortna, R. T., 328n.68
Foster, P., 79n.163, 156n.238, 157n.243,
158n.252, 159n.256, 418n.38,
419nn.40,42, 420nn.46, 47, 51,
421nn.55, 57, 422n.61, 450n.160,
469n.230, 482n.269, 488n.297,
489n.302, 492n.312, 690n.65, 691n.67,
700nn.102,105, 701nn.112,114,
744n.76
France, R. T., 67n.107, 222n.49,
225n.68, 229n.93, 235n.126, 740n.60
Frankfurter, D., 17n.55, 549n.142
Franklin, E., 57n.54
Frey, J., 84n.189, 144n.175, 146n.182,
354n.170, 368n.223, 379n.244,
380n.245, 388n.269, 400n.309,
390n.276
Freyne, S., 322n.48, 515n.20
Friedlander, G., 267n.272
Friesen, S., 110n.334
Fuller, M. E., 298n.389
Funk, R. W., 35n.141, 210n.2, 312n.1
Funk, W.-P., 179n.352, 479n.262

Gager, J. G., 23n.79
Gamble, H. Y., 125n.80, 817n.34
Gardner-Smith, P., 329n.78
Garrett, S. R., 239n.150
Garrow, A. J. P., 434n.97
Garroway, J. D., 26n.99
Gärtner, B., 604n.27
Gasque, W. W., 685n.43
Gathercole, S., 147n.191, 149n.204,
155nn.232,233, 257n.231, 259n.240,
283n.323, 380n.246,247, 381n.247,
382n.251, 384n.262, 390n.276,
396n.296, 486nn.287,290
Gerdmar, A., 545n.128
Gerhardsson, B., 256n.225
Gnilka, J., 63n.88, 64n.89, 65n.98,
66n.102, 68n.115, 69n.118, 70n.126,
199n.508 227n.78, 233n.114,
247n.182, 249n.193, 253n.213,
255n.218, 256n.228, 267n.271,
734n.38
Goodacre, M., 57n.54, 380n.246,
381n.248, 382n.252, 383n.254
Goodenough, E. R., 27n.101
Goodman, M., 16n.48, 17nn.51,53,

601n.16, 611n.61, 612n.65, 613nn.69,70, 614n.75, 615n.76, 616nn.85,87, 617n.89, 618n.96,100, 619n.103, 620n.111, 621n.117, 622n.121, 623nn.126,128,129
Goppelt, L., 727n.15
Goulder, M. D., 57nn.54,56
Graham, H. H., 113n.11
Grant, R. M., 28n.106, 34n.140, 113n.11, 130n.110, 130n.110,112, 131nn.113,114,118, 132n.123, 133nn.125,129, 135n.139, 136n.141, 137nn.147,148,149, 138nn.151,152,155, 440n.128, 455n.180, 550n.144, 558nn.174, 560n.189, 562n.192, 566n.202, 651n.262, 653n.267, 702n.119, 796n.181, 797nn.184, 798n.193,198,199
Grässer, E., 96n.260
Green, G. L., 100n.281
Green, H. B., 261n.247
Gregory, A. F., 46n.6, 59nn.67,68, 68n.115, 79n.163, 144nn.176,179, 329n.75, 406n.3, 408n.12, 409n.14, 413n.22, 415n.25, 416n.29, 419n.40, 423n.64, 424n.69, 433n.96, 498n.326,237, 688n.54, 696, 744n.75
Griffith-Jones, R., 484n.278
Groh, D. E., 142n.169
Gruen, E., 598n.3
Gruenwald, I., 629nn.154,155, 765n.32
Guelich, R. A., 50n.18, 51n.24, 54n.36, 194n.36, 226n.72, 227n.79, 233n.114, 234n.118, 235n.130, 271n.288
Gundry, R. H., 67n.107, 207n.86

Haenchen, E., 25, 633n.178
Hagner, D. A., 54n.91, 61n.76, 64n.91, 65n.99, 67n.107, 70n.126, 72b.133, 76n.152, 77n.156, 85n.195, 88n.222, 90n.227, 94n.252, 95n.257, 98n.273, 101n.284, 103n.294, 106n.309, 181n.365, 216n.23, 256n.228, 408n.12, 409nn.13,14, 413nn.21, 22, 414n.24, 415n.26, 27, 416nn.29, 30, 417n.33, 420n.46, 424n.66, 428n.76, 433n.95, 435n.106, 442n.131, 452n.168, 453n.172, 603n.22, 603n.209, 687n.52, 688n.55

Häkkinen, S., 578n.249, 581n.268
Halbwachs, M., 212n.11
Hall, S. G., 139n.156, 140n.159, 460n.201, 667n.327
Hällström, G., 586n.291
Hanfmann, G. M. A., 139n.157
Hannah, D. D., 470n.232, 502n.341
Harnack, A., xi-xii, 6n.10, 25, 27, 28n.107, 39n.160, 40n.161, 119n.44, 123n.69, 126n.84, 127n.88, 127n.90, 602n.21, 716n.173, 817n.34
Harris, J. R., 128n.128
Harrison, P. N., 86nn.201,202
Hartog, P., 116n.28, 117nn.31,32, 118n.34, 559n.181, 651n.259, 693n.80, 694n.83
Hasler, 681n.29
Hatina, T. R., 233n.111
Haverly, T. P., 214n.15
Hawkins, J. C., 220n.43, 249n.192, 252n.208
Hays, R. B., 410n.15, 646n.242, 647nn.247,248,249
Head, P. M., 136n.140, 156n.242, 502n.342
Healey, J. F., 149n.204
Heckel, T. K., 499n.331, 502n.341
Hedrick, C. W., 154n.230, 178n.349, 485n.284, 523n.49
Heemstra, M., 615nn.76,78
Held, H. J., 249n.187
Hemer, C. J., 109n.323, 788nn.143,144
Henaut, B. W., 210n.5
Hengel, M., 18n.56, 48nn.11,13, 49nn.14,15,16, 50n.17, 52nn.26,28, 54nn.36,42, 55n.45, 57nn.55,57, 59nn.68,69, 60n.70, 63nn.86,88, 69n.118, 74n.142, 76n.154.156, 81n.178, 156n.242, 188n.3, 192n.26, 194n.35, 194n.36, 195n.39m 237n.137, 247n.179, 248n.184, 352n.167, 415n.24, 445n.142, 452n.168, 460n.201, 494n.318, 495n.319, 213n.14, 214n.14, 499n.328,329,330,331, 501n.335,340, 503n.342, 518n.30, 570n.218, 628n.152, 644n.233, 725n.4, 734n.38, 739n.59, 743n.73, 785n.132
Henry, J. K., 172n.321
Herczeg, P., 706n.128

Herford, R. T., 574n.241, 575nn.243,244,245, 582n.276, 584n.283, 625n.134, 627n.146, 628n.148, 630n.164
Hermer, C. J., 109n.323
Herron, T. J., 113n.12
Herzer, J., 86n.199
Heschel, S., 236n.137
Higgins, 320n.35
Hilhorst, A., 163n.276, 167n.295
Hill, C. E., 45n.5, 156n.240, 161n.265, 407nn.5,6, 421n.57, 422nn.59, 60, 423n.62, 425nn.70,71,437n.115, 449n.158, 450n.160, 451, 455n.180, 456nn.182,183,185, 457nn.188,191, 459nn.194,198, 460nn.199,200,201, 461n.203, 468n.224, 478n.258, 479n.259, 483n.277, 492n.314, 498, 499nn.329,331, 500, 501nn,336,337, 503n.344, 764n.26, 805n.5
Hill, J. H., 136n.146
Hoffman, R. J., 39n.158, 160n.260, 716n.177, 717n.180, 718nn.183,185,189
Hoffmann, P., 57n.56
Hofius, O., 286n.340, 463n.210, 464nn.212,213, 785n.132
Hogan, P. N., 708n135
Holmes, M. W., 111n.2, 117n.31, 125n.82, 127n.90, 127n.1, 130n.111, 132n.123, 415n.27, 423n.64, 424nn.68,69, 425nn.71,72, 449n.157, 693nn.79,80, 694n.81,82, 695nn.85,86, 743n.74
Hooker, M. D., 54nn.40,41
Hoover, R. W., 35n.141, 210n.2
Horbury, W., 12n.29, 23n.78, 122n.65, 188n.4, 189n.13, 558n.173, 562n.192, 616n.87, 619n.105, 626nn.139,140, 656n.276, 658nn.286,288, 659n.288, 663n,310
Horn, C. B., 158n.254
Horner, T. J., 133n.128, 134n.134, 135n.135, 565n.197, 664n.315
Horrell, D. G., 112n.5, 113nn.10,12, 543n.121
Horton, C., 407n.10, 541n.118
Hübner, H., 352n.166
Hübner, R. M., 116n.26
Huizenga, L. A., 254n.214

Hummel, R., 251n.197, 268n.275, 270n.284, 636n.193
Hurst, L. D., 93n.247
Hurtado, L. W., 287n.349, 500n.334, 501n.336, 629n.156, 631n.168
Hvalvik, R., 121nn.53,56, 122nn.61,62,63, 123n.69, 434n.98, 509n.1, 510n.3, 556nn.168,170,171, 558n.172, 559n.181, 571n.225, 574n.241, 578n.249, 586n.291, 656nn.271,277, 567nn.280,281, 658n,287

Incigneri, B., 56n.48
Inge, W. R., 417n.34, 420n.47
Irmscher, J., 175n.339
Isenberg, W. W., 152n.217
Isser, S. J., 527n.65
Iverson, K. R., 237n.138, 268n.276

Jakab, A., 179n.355
James, M. R., 147n.188
Jansen, M., 149n.199
Jarvis, P, 133n.127
Jefford, C. N., 112n.7, 113n.12, 116nn.26,29, 119n.48, 120n.50, 122n.65, 124n.72, 127n.90, 130n.111, 132n.119, 157nn.243,245, 429nn.78,82, 431n.87, 433n.95, 451n.162, 561n.190, 691n.67, 694n.83
Jeremias, J., 253n.211, 344n.134, 463n.210, 554n.162, 604n.29
Jervell, J., 296n.383, 684n.41, 701n.108
Johnson, B. D., 322n.48
Johnson, L. T., 86nn.198,202, 87n.206, 88nn.214,215, 89n.224, 312n.1, 637n.201
Johnston, J. J., 156n.242
Jonas, H., 37n.148
Jones, B. W., 110n.333
Jones, F. S., 175n.338, 176n.340, 176nn.340, 341,342,343, 519nn.32.33. 586n.289, 588nn.300,302, 589n.305
Jossa, G., 608nn.47,50, 609n.52
Judge, E. A., 608n.47
Judge, P. J., 334n.91

Kähler, M., 196
Kaiser, U. U., 158n.254
Karrer, M., 107n.312

Käsemann, E., 92n.240, 354n.172, 368n.229, 541n.116, 768n.39, 770n.51, 773, 774, 777, 781n.112, 816
Kazmierski, C. R., 227n.79
Keck, L. E., 194n.36, 701n.108
Kee, H. C., 56n.49, 236n.136, 572n.222
Keener, C. S., 4n.2, 58n.62, 532n.78, 633n.181, 736n.51
Kelber, W. H., 213.n.13
Kelhoffer, J. A., 155n.234, 207n.88, 208n.92, 438n.119, 439n.121, 499n.331
Kelly, J. N. D., 9n.21, 570n.219, 829n.40, 821n.42
Kenyon, F. G., 501n.335
Kermode, F., 231n.103
Kerr, A. R., 331n.80
Kilpatrick, G. D., 70n.124, 248n.186, 639n.209
King, K. L., xii, 27n.105, 28n.107, 32nn.124,127, 33nn.129,131,132,133,134, 34n.137, 35n.143, 36nn.143,146, 38n.156, 153n.221, 154n.228, 484n.280, 486n.291, 659n.288, 711n.147, 716n.174, 723n.208
Kingsbury, J. D., 69n.118, 70n.126, 226n.71, 252n.209, 253n.209, 254n.213, 259n.242, 639n.209
Kinzig, W., 582n.276, 584n.282, 590n.313, 626n.141
Kirk, A., 212n.11, 489n.303
Klassen, W., 483n.273
Klauck, H. J., 28n.110, 104n.298, 105n.302, 106n.310, 148n.197, 149n.204, 162nn.268,269, 163nn.273,274,275,277, 167n.298, 168nn.299,300,303, 170n.313, 171n.316, 172nn.319,320, 174n.331, 174n.332, 175nn.335,336, 400n.306, 705nn.123,126, 708n.135, 745n.83, 747n.66, 750n.96, 780nn.103,104, 781n.111, 782n.115, 794n.174, 795n.176, 796n.179, 815n.30
Klein, H., 58nn.61,63, 59n.69, 61n.81, 62n.83, 280n.313, 290n.363, 299n.394, 308n.418, 347nn.147,150, 352n.167
Kleinknecht, H., 138n.153
Klijn, A. F. J., 144nn.176,177, 146n.183, 173nn.323,325, 174n.330, 465n.218, 578n.248, 579n.255, 580n.263, 581n.265, 586n.288, 590n.312
Klinzing, G., 604n.27
Kloppenborg, J. S., 57n.56, 201nn.60,61, 371n.233, 426n.75
Knibb, M. A., 571n.224, 572n.226
Knowles, M., 255n.220
Knox, J., 716n.173, 718n.188
Koester, C. R., 93nn.247,248, 94n.252, 95n.255, 136n.145, 142n.167, 357n.178, 362n.198
Koester, H., 6n.11, 11n.28, 16n.49, 35n.142, 43, 44n.3. 52n.28,30, 53n.30, 58n.63, 59n.66, 61n.76, 64n.91, 74n.143, 78n.159, 79n.167, 89n.226, 91n.235, 92n.240, 98n.275, 102n.291, 103n.295, 106nn.305,308, 108n.322, 109n.327, 110n.354, 113n.8, 125n.82, 126n.85, 129n.106, 131n.115, 134n.130, 147n.190, 148n.192, 150nn.205,210, 151n.214, 157n.243, 161n.265, 167n.293, 173n.324, 188n.2, 194nn.36,39, 195n.39, 200n.56, 201n.63, 206n.82, 207n.84,85, 208n.91, 217n.28, 218n.34, 229n.93, 245n.171, 303n.408, 322n.47, 325n.55, 328n.72, 330n.78, 335n.98, 351n.161, 364n.207, 381n.248, 400n.307, 381n.248, 382n.251, 383nn.254,257, 386n.265, 389n.271, 390n.276, 391n.277, 395n.288, 396n.295, 400n.307, 408n.12, 409, 413n.21, 415n.26, 416n.30, 418nn.38, 39, 419n.42, 420n.46,47,48, 421n.56, 424nn.65,68,69, 428n.76, 429nn.77,79, 431nn.86,87, 433n.95, 434n.101, 435nn.104,106, 437nn.113,116, 438n.119, 439n.121, 441nn.129,130, 452n.169, 455n.177, 456n.180, 457n.189, 463n.209, 468nn.224,226, 472, 473, 474n.244, 475nn.248,249,251, 476n.252, 477nn.253,254, 479n.259, 480n.264, 487n.296, 488n.296, 489nn.302,303,304, 500n.334, 539n.112, 540n.113, 556n.169, 558n.177, 559n.184, 562n.192, 593n.331, 632n, 171n.653n.265, 692n.69, 694n.83, 716n.177, 740n.62, 770n.52, 795n.178

Köhler, W.-D., 68n.115, 150n.210, 415nn.24, 26, 27, 416n.29, 417n.31, 418nn.36, 37,38, 420nn.47,49, 421n.56, 423nn.62,64, 424nn.69, 431nn.86,87, 433nn.93,95, 434nn.98,101, 435n.104, 438n.117, 439n.120, 442n.130, 451n.166, 452n.168, 453n.172, 456n.185, 457n.188, 458n.193, 459n.195, 469n.228, 471n.237, 475n.250, 480nn.264,267, 489nn.301,302,303,304, 497n.22, 497n.322
Konradt, M., 255n.219
Kraabel, A. T., 139n.157
Kraft, R. A., 15n.43, 119nn.45,48, 120n.52, 121n.53, 122n.58, 553n.152, 556nn.168,170, 617n.92, 658n.284, 663n.314
Kramer, W., 820n.39
Kraus, T. J., 156n.238, 466n.221, 489nn.300,301,303, 490n.306, 748n.90
Krosney, H., 155n.233
Kruger, M. J., 45n.5, 450n.160, 466n.221, 469n.230
Kuhn, H. W., 223
Kuhn, K. G., 535n.95
Kümmel, W. G., 47n.9, 51n.23, 52nn.28,29, 54n.40, 55n.45, 58n.63, 59n.65, 60nn.71,75, 61n.78, 62n.83, 64n.91, 65n.99, 70n.126, 71n.130, 72n.135, 73nn.137,139, 74nn.140,144; 75nn.148,150, 76n.154, 78n.159, 79n.167, 86n.202, 87n.205, 91n.235, 92n.237, 93n.248, 94n.251, 98n.275, 100n.281, 101n.288, 102n.291, 103n.296, 107n.311, 108n.320, 110nn.329,330,333, 129n.104, 222n.51, 230n.95, 231n.105, 248n.186, 249n.193, 256nn.221,223,227, 270n.281, 274n.296, 276n.300, 281nn.317,319, 282n.320, 295n.381, 314n., 316n.14, 327nn.62,66, 328n.72, 329nn.74,75, 337n.105, 512n.11, 360n.192, 537n.104, 639n.209, 770n.52, 816n.33
Kupp, D. D., 257n.235
Kürzinger, J., 63n.88
Kvalbein, H., 275n.298, 637n.200, Kysar, R., 203n.67

Labahn, M. 320n.34, 333n.90, 341n.124, 350n.158
Lake, K., 113n.10, 127n.88, 143n.172, 559n.183
Lallemann, P. J., 167n.292, 170n.314
Lambers-Petry, D., 22n.76
Lampe, P., 124nn.73,77, 224n.64, 560n.185, 607n.44, 650n.258
Lane, T. J., 299n.395
Lane, W. L., 92n.240, 95nn.255,257, 539n.112, 648n.252
Langer, R., 625n.137
Lapham, F., 101n.286
Lawlor, H. J., 143n.172
Lawson, J., 6n.5
Lehne, S., 647n.249
Lentz, J. C., 682n.31
Levine, L. I. A.,, 611nn.59,61, 617n.88, 618nn.95,97, 622n.122, 623n.125, 647n.247
Lewis, N. D., 32n.125
Lichtenberger, H., 18n.56
Lietzmann, H., 118n.42, 554n.159
Lieu, J., 15n.46, 16n.47, 21n.70, 104n.297, 105n.299, 601n.16, 719n.194, 780n.104, 781n.113, 782n.114
Lightfoot, J. B., 8, 111n.2, 113n.8,9,11,12, 115, 116n.26, 115n.85, 126nn.85,87, 127n.88, 408n.13, 415n.26, 422nn.59, 60, 449n.158, 662n.306
Lincoln, A. T., 73n.139, 74n.142, 75n.144, 127n.88,89, 320n.36, 322n.47, 69n.328, 329n.74, 330n.79, 331n.81, 334nn.94,95, 349n.157, 356n.176, 535n.97,98, 640n.216, 762n.18
Lindars, B., 95nn.254,257, 203n.67, 326nn.59,61, 328nn.68,69, 329n.78
Lindemann, A., 687n.50, 688n.54, 689n.63, 690n.65, 691n.69, 692n.77, 693n.80, 694n.81, 695nn.86,87,88, 696n.92, 697n.93, 698n.98, 700nn.102,105,107, 701nn.109,112,113,114, 712n.149, 713n.161, 716n.177, 720n.198
Lona, H. E., 113nn.11,12, 415n.24, 416n.29, 550n.144, 689nn.56,57
Longenecker, B., xiii, 510n.5

Index of Authors

Lord, A. B., 223n.60
Lüdemann, G., 12n.28, 175n.340, 702n.116
Lührmann, D., 54n.40, 144n.176, 147n.192, 153n.220, 155n.237, 156n.239, 159n.256, 207n.90, 219n.36, 472n.238, 484n.280
Luomanen, P., 28n.108, 29nn.111,113, 30n.116, 33n.134, 39n.157, 135n.137, 578n.250, 582n.270, 583nn.277,278, 584n.280, 585n.285, 586n.290, 594n.334, 796n.181
Luther, M., 93n.248
Luttikhuizen, G. P., 165n.286, 169n.304, 181n.363, 586n.290
Luz, U., xiii, 65nn.97,99, 67nn.105,109, 69n.118, 70n.126, 195n.39, 200n.62, 202n.66, 224n.64, 247n.180, 248n.183, 249n.192, 252n.209, 254n.214, 255n.219, 256n.224, 257n.233, 258n.239, 261nn.248,249,250, 264n.262, 265n.266, 268nn.273,275, 274nn.295,297, 281n.318, 608n.49, 637n.203, 638n.206, 639n.209, 647n.248, 649n.256, 734nn.38,39

Maccoby, H., 24n.86
MacDonald, D. R., 163n.276, 164n.280, 167n.292, 169n.307, 70n.126, 708n.136
MacDonald, J., 340n.117
MacDonald, M. Y., 88n.214, 678n.10
MacLennan, R. S., 123n.66, 139n.158, 665n.320, 667n.329
MacRae, G. W., 34n.138, 179n.352, 351n.161, 482n.270,271, 484n.278
Malherbe, A. J., 164n.279
Malbon, E. S., 214n.15, 219n.38
Marcus, J., 48n.11, 50n.18, 51nn.22,24, 53n.34, 55n.47, 56, 198n.49, 219n.36, 220n.43, 222n.49, 223n.60, 226n.72, 230n.95, 231n.103, 232n.111, 235n.129, 239n.149, 245n.172, 487n.296
Marguerat, D., 163n.277, 223n.60
Marjanen, A., 28n.108, 29nn.111,113, 30n.116, 33n.134, 39n.157, 135n.137, 390n.275, 394n.287, 397n.297, 395n.289, 397n.297, 578n.250, 582n.270, 586n.290,

594n.334, 796n.181, 797nn.189,190, 798nn.192,199
Markschies, C., 30nn.116,118, 36n.147, 154n.230, 156nn.238,241
Marshall, C. D., 237n.141
Marshall, I. H., 85n.197, 86nn.198,202, 87n.206, 88n.214, 89nn.224,225,226, 90n.228, 288n.352, 537n.104, 679n.15, 681n.30
Martyn, J. L., 345n.140, 603n.23, 633n.178, 642n.220, 760n.9, 761n.13,
Marxsen, W., 194n.34, 225, 239n.150
Mason, S. 570n.222
Massaux, E., 68n.115, 413n.22, 414n.24, 415n.27, 416n.28, 417n.33, 422n.59, 424n.67, 429n.77, 431n.86, 433n.94, 434nn.100,102, 436n.110, 442n.131, 451, 453n.172, 457n.188, 458n.193, 459n.195, 463n.210, 468n.225, 469n.228, 489n.301, 492n.311, 497n.322, 700nn.102,105,106, 701nn.108,112, 702nn.117,118,119, 743n.74, 744nn.76,77,78,79,80
Matera, F. J., 268n.276
Matson, M. A., 322n.47, 331n.82
Maurer, C., 157n.243
Mayo, P. L., 632n.171
Mayor, J. B., 99n.278, 100n.281
McCowen, A., 222n.49
McCrum, R., 411n.17
McCullough, W. S., 594n.332
McDonald, J. I. H., 191n.21
McDonald, L. M., 125n.80, 129n.109, 816n.33
McGowan, A., xii
McGrath, J. F., 322n.43, 328n.70, 345n.139, 350n.159, 352nn.164,166, 356n.174, 643n.231
McHugh, J. F., 765n.30, 766n.34
McKnight, E. V., 214n.15
Meade, D. G., 84, 85, 90n.227
Meeks, W. A., 19nn.61,62,66, 364n.208, 369n.229, 592n.321, 606n.40, 643n.229, 649n.257, 654b,270, 701n.108
Meier, J. P., 70n.126, 95n.258, 113n.8, 384n.262, 417n.35, 418n.38, 510n.2, 542n.120, 552nn.148,149, 592n.321, 676n.6, 687n.52, 731n.27, 734n.38, 740n.62, 744n.75, 753n.104

883

Menken, J. J., 341n.124
Merkel, H., 487n.96
Merz, A., 89n.224
Metzger, B. M., 45n.5, 47n.9, 82,
    147n.191, 160n.260, 235n.124,
    337n.105, 349n.154, 432n.89
Meyer, M., 152n.219, 153nn.224,227,
    372n.237, 472n.242, 479n.261,
    480n.264, 282n.271, 486n.286
Meyer, P. W., 354n.170
Michie, D., 224n.62
Miller, J. D., 89n.225
Miller, M. P., 11n.28
Miller, S., 242n.162, 324b.53
Mimouni, C., 509n.1, 510nn.3,5,
    529n.71, 574n.239, 581n.266,
    590n.313, 591n.315, 626n.139,
    654n.269
Minns, D., 133n.127, 452n.168,
    456n.180, 630n.165
Mirecki, P. A., 154n.230, 485n.284,
    489n.302
Moessner, D. P., 276n.301, 282n.320,
    299n.394
Moffatt, J., 62n.84, 648n.250
Moll, S., 39nn.157,158,160, 40n.161,
    717nn.178,179,182, 719n.190
Moloney, F. J., 235n.126, 271n.288
Montefiore, S. S., 611n.58
Moreland, M., 389n.273
Morgan, R., 10n.25
Moses, A. D. A., 257n.228
Moss, C. M., 255n.220
Moss, C. R., 651n.259
Motyer, S., 639n.212
Moule, C. F. D., 286n.339, 366n.217
Mounce, W. D., 85n.197, 86n.198,
    88n.223, 89n.225
Müller, D. G., 179n.353, 180n.358,
    180n.359
Murdock, W. R., 179n.352, 535n.95,
Murphy, J., 600n.6
Murphy-O'Connor, J., 89n.226
Murray, M., 788n.140
Murray, R., 509n.2
Musurillo, H., 166n.289
Mutschler, B., 500n.333
Myllykoski, M., 29n.111, 490n.306

Nagel, P., 464n.210

Nagel, T., 499n.329
Nardoni, E., 813n.19
Neale, D. A., 290n.367
Neusner, J., 70n.121, 512n.7, 600n.6,
    621n.117, 629n.155, 647n.246
Newport, K. G. C., 270n.283
Newsom, C., 646n.245
Neyrey, J. H., 98nn.269,271, 102n.293,
    544n.125
Nicklas, T., 155n.237, 156n.238,
    466n.221, 489nn.300,301,303,
    490n.304,306,307, 521n.37,
    634nn.183,184, 676n.7, 710n.143,
    712n.149, 748n.90
Niebuhr, K.-W., xiii, 8n.15, 9n.20,
    13n.34, 17n.53, 85n.197, 101n.287,
    107n.312, 109n.324, 513n.12,
    543n.122, 600n.7
Niederwimmer, K., 51n.24,
    118nn.37,38,40, 119nn.46,48, 120n.50,
    426n.74, 431nn.85,88, 433n.95,
    553n..152, 554n.158, 512nn.7,11,
    817n.33
Nolland, J., 59n.68, 60n.71
North, W. E. S., 641n.218
Norovitch, N., 492n.315
Novakovic, L., 254n.214

Oberlinner, L., 86n.200, 90n.226
O'Brien, K., 530n.72
O'Day, G. R., 352n.167
Odeberg, H., 345n.141, 359n.185,
    643n.228
O'Leary, A. M., 245n.173, 249n.194
Orton, D. E., 224n.64
Osborn, C. D., 97n.268
Osborn, E., 6n.5, 142n.167,
    460n.202, 461n.203, 567n.209,
    568nn.210,211, 669n.336, 720n.199,
    722nn.205,206,207
Osiek, C., 124nn.71,72 124n.72,
    125n.82, 437n.116, 560n.186, 687n.50
Otero, A. de Santos, 161nn.262,263,264,
    162n.271, 177n.350, 181n.366
Oulton, J. E. L., 143n.172
Overbeck, F., 514n.17
Overman, J. A., 69n.120, 262n.255,
    268n.273, 271nn.286,288, 635n.189,
    637n.200, 638n.206, 639n.209

Index of Authors

Oxford Society of Historical Theology, 46n.6, 408n.12

Packer, J. I., 81n.176
Paffenroth, K., 280n.314
Pagels, E. H., 486n.291, 499n.328, 711n.148, 712n.153, 713n.156,159, 714n.167, 771n.53,56, 772n.63
Paget, J. C., 22n.74, 120n.52, 121n.53, 121n.56, 122n.61, 122n.65, 434n.100, 435n.106, 509n.1, 510n.6, 577n.247, 582n.269, 584n.284, 585n.285, 588n.297, 656nn.276,277, 657n.278,280, 658nn.285,286, 695n.88, 696nn.89,91, 744n.78
Painter, J., 331n.82, 336n.101, 512n.7, 514n.16, 515n.20, 516n.22, 518n.30, 521n.41, 522nn.45,47, 523n.51
Pamment, M., 359n.185
Parker, D. C., 217n.31
Parkes, J., 18, 19n.66
Parrott, D. M., 167n.297, 174n.332, 174n.334, 178n.349, 479n.262
Patterson, S. J., 147n.189, 151n.215, 372n.235, 373n.238, 375n.239, 381nn.247,248
Pearson, B. A., 19n.66, 29n.113, 30n.114, 36n.147, 714n.165, 752n.101
Perkins, P., 475n.250, 724n.2, 726n.10, 727n.15 731n.27, 735n.46, 739n.57
Perrin, N., 150n.206, 179n.352, 224n.61, 499n.330, 713n.161
Pervo, R., 162n269, 167n.292
Pesch, R., 196n.42
Pesthy, M., 165n.285
Petersen, W. L., 135nn.137,138, 136nn.140,142, 150n.206, 213n.13, 407n.10, 594n.333
Peterson, P. M., 172n.319
Peterson, W. L., 136n.145, 457n.189, 753-54n.108
Pétrement, S., 36n.145
Phenix, R. R., 158n.254
Plese, Z., 143n.174, 144n.175
Plisch, U.-K., 486n.288
Poirier, P.-H., 500n.322
Pokorny, P., 49n.16, 189nn.9m12, 191n.19, 194n.36, 195nn.37,39
Popkes, E. E., 151n.213, 393n.285, 397n.297

Porter, S. E., 402n.311, 602n.22, 685n.43, 824n.44
Potter, C. F., 492n.316
Poupon, G., 168n.302
Powell, M. A., 224n.62
Pratscher, W., 126n.85, 127n.90, 439n.121, 440n.124, 441n.129, 442n.130, 444n.126, 512nn.7,9, 515nn.18,19, 516n.24, 517n.27, 521nn.38,40, 523nn.49,50, 696n.92
Prieur, J.-M., 172n.319
Pritz, R. A., 576n.246, 582nn.269,273,276, 583nn.277,278, 584n.282, 585n.286, 586n.288, 590n.313, 624n.132, 670n.338
Prostmeier, F. R., 121nn.53,56, 122nn.59,61,63, 123n.69, 434nn.99,101
Pryke, E. H., 225n.70
Przybilski, B., 271n.288
Puech, H.-C., 152n.220, 479n.263

Quast, K., 738n.54
Quasten, J., 111n.1
Quinn, J. D., 85n.195, 91n.235

Räisänen, H., 10n.25, 39nn.157,160, 40n.162, 231n.104, 236n.133, 717nn.178,179, 720n.196
Rascher, A., 539n.112
Rasimus, T., 499nn.329,330
Rau, E., 159n.256
Reed, A. Y., 14n.41, 15nn.43,46, 19n.61, 20n.67, 23n.79, 207n.90, 588n.298
Reinhartz, A., 26n.99
Reitzenstein, R., 32n.124, 711n,146
Rhoads, D., 224n.62
Richardson, C. C., 112n.8, 119n.47, 122n.65, 126nn.84,85 132n.121, 451n.162
Richardson, P., 122n.6, 126n.85
Riches, J. K., 271n.288
Riley, G. J., 149n.200
Ringe, S. H., 352n.165
Ritschl, A., 6n.7, 10, 236n.137
Rius-Camps, J., 634n.186
Robbins, V. K., 234n.122
Robeck, C. M., 797n.188
Roberts, C. H., 501n.335
Robinson, J. A. T., 67n.107, 76n.152,

95n.257, 322n.48, 326n.61, 329n.78, 330n.78, 349n.156, 362n.200, 366n.215
Robinson, J. M., 11n.28, 16n.49; 32n.125, 57n.56, 64n.91, 147nn.189,190, 150n.210, 201n.63, 217n.25, 364n.207, 375n.239, 396n.295, 463n.209, 472n.242, 479nn.261,262, 486n.288
Robinson, T. A., 654n.270
Rogerson, J. W., 351n.163
Röhl, G., 480n.267
Roloff, J., 366n.217, 679n.13, 681n.24
Römer, C., 160n.261
Ropes, J. H., 634n.183
Rordorf, W., 167n.293, 168n.302, 429n.79, 433n.95, 705n.126
Rowe, C. K., 286nn.338,342
Rowland, C., 548n.137, 629n.154, 643n.232
Rowley, H. H., 783n.117
Rudolph, D., 591n.314
Rudolph, K., 30n.118, 32nn.125,126; 33n.135, 34nn.136,139, 37nn.148,151, 38n.153; 39n.157, 129n.104, 173n.328, 713n.159, 715n.172, 813n.19
Ruether, R. R., 25nn.88,97
Rüger, H. P., 52n.26
Runia, D. T., 27n.102
Russell, D. S., 83n.186

Safrai, S., 601n.11
Saldarini, A. J., 70n.122, 267n.271, 268n.273, 622n.119, 623n.128, 637nn.199,200, 639nn.209,211
Salvesen, A., 15n.43
Sanday, W., 452n.169, 452n.172
Sanders, E. P., 17n.54, 58n.58, 322n.45, 379n.244
Sanders, J. A., 125n.80, 285n.224, 379n.244
Sanders, J. N., 498n.328, 499n.329, 500, 632n.172, 633n.178
Sanders, J. T., 25
Sandmel, S., 24n.85, 25n.89, 600n.6
Satake, A., 108n.321, 110n.334, 632n.171, 783nn.119,121, 784n.123, 785n.132, 788n.144, 789n.150, 790nn.151,159
Schaberg, J., 258n.236

Schäfer, P., 17n.53, 616n.87, 621n.199, 627n.144
Schäferdiek, K., 170n.313, 171n.314, 171n.315
Scheidweiler, F., 157n.246, 158n.250
Schelkle, K. H., 97n.264, 100n.281
Schenck, K., 93nn.244,247, 95n.254, 540n.115
Schenke, H.-M., 174n.332, 174n.333, 174n.335, 479n.261, 480n.264, 482n.269,270
Scherbenske, E. W., 717n.182, 718n.186
Scherlitt, F., 320n.33
Schiffman, L. H., 576n.246, 604n.28
Schilling, O., 188n.6
Schmidt, K. L., 223
Schmithals, W., 713
Schnackenburg, R., 76n.152, 327n.63, 328nn.68,72, 337n.104, 339n.116, 483n.273, 760n.10, 770n.52, 792n.162
Schneckenburger, M., 684n.38, 736n.51
Schneemelcher, W., 131n.118, 155n.236, 157n.243, 158n.250, 160nn.258,259, 163n.273, 163n.274, 163n.276, 164n.280, 166n.290, 167n.291, 167n.293, 479n.262, 480n.221, 490n.306, 491n.308,310, 492n.313
Schnelle, U., 47n.9, 50n.18, 54n.41, 55n.45, 58n.63, 59n.63, 60n.72, 61nn.79,82, 62n.83, 68n.113, 69n.118, 71n.126, 72n.132; 73n.139, 75n.147, 78n.161, 79n.168, 86nn.199,201, 87n.206, 88n.218, 91n.235, 92n.240, 95n.255, 98nn.270,274,276, 100n.281, 103n.296, 106nn.305,309, 108n.321, 216n.24, 220n.43, 224n.63, 231n.99, 235n.131, 237n.137,138, 258n.236, 261n.250, 273n.292, 274n.296, 295n.380, 299n.394, 303n.408, 319n.29, 320n.33, 324n.54, 327n.66, 328n.72, 329n.75, 333n.89, 345n.139, 347n.147, 351n,162, 355n.172, 359n.185, 360n.192, 361n.195, 362n.197, 539n.112, 544n.125, 545nn.130,131, 546n.132, 549n.141, 584n.282, 607n.43, 639n.209, 644n.233, 766n.33, 770n.52, 775n.75
Schoedel, W. R., 68n.113, 75n.149, 112n.4, 114n.13, 115nn.19,21, 116n.28, 117nn.30,31, 118nn.34,35,

123n.69, 124n.78, 125n.82, 128nn.93,94, 177n.347, 417nn.33, 418n.38, 419nn.40,42,44, 420nn.45,48, 422nn.58,60, 479n.262, 552n.150, 553n.154, 559nn.178,181, 560n.188, 651n.259, 691n.67
Schoeps, H. J. 176n.343, 518n.30, 521n.38, 579n.252, 587n.294, 596nn.337,338
Schoon, S., 15n.45
Schreiber, J., 224n.64
Schremer, A., 574nn.240,241, 627nn.142,144, 628n.147, 630nn.161,162
Schröter, J., xiii, 144n.175, 354n.170, 381n.249, 388n.269, 392n.283.405n.1, 429n.79, 464n.210
Schürer, E., 54n.38, 70n.123, 123n.67, 123n.68
Schutter, W. L., 544n.124
Schwartz, D. R., 157n.248
Schweitzer, A., 67n.108
Schweizer, E., 37n.149, 262n.255, 366n.217, 368n.229, 764n.24, 790n.152, 813n.19, 814n.22, 815n.27
Scott, J. M. C., 351n.163, 643n.231
Segal, A., 14n.40, 287n.349, 600n.6, 629n.153,158, 630n.161, 638n.207
Sellew, P. H., 163n.273, 396n.293
Sellner, H. J., 287nn.344,348, 288n.352, 296n.383, 299n.394
Shanks, H., 526n.61, 537n.105, 578n.250, 579n.252, 588n.298, 611n.59, 616n.81, 617n.92, 632n.172
Shiner, W. T., 214n.15, 234n.122
Shotwell, W., A., 195n.39, 456n.186, 561n.191, 562n.192, 664n.315
Shusker, M. B., 122n.65
Sibinga, J. S., 420n.48
Siegert, F., 449n.156
Sim, D. C., 69n.118, 70n.126, 124nn.75,76, 264n.261, 268nn.273, 269n.279, 272n.291, 274n.294, 532n.79, 637n.197, 639n.209, 653n.265
Simon, M., 18, 19
Skarsaune, O., 510n.3, 559n.181, 562n.192, 571n.225, 574n.241, 578n.249, 579nn.254,257, 581n.265, 586nn.288,291, 587n.295, 590n.313,
656n.277, 672n.340, 700nn.102,106, 701n.113
Skeat, T. C., 155n.235
Smalley, S. S, 108n.318
Smallwood, M., 123n.67, 525n.55, 608n.49, 610n.56, 611n.62, 612n.65, 613nn.68,69,70, 614n.74, 615nn.76,79, 616n.87, 617nn.88,89,90, 618nn.94,95,99,101, 619n.102, 620nn.110,111,113,114, 622n.120
Smith, C. B., 28n.108, 36n.146
Smith, M., 356n.176
Smith, M., 158
Snyder, G. F., 124n.72, 125n.79, 436n.110, 483n.273, 559n.183
Soards, M. L., 239n.151
Söding, T., 237n.141, 355n.172
Sohm, R., 813n.19
Spaulding, M. B., 342n.128
Spence, S., 607n.43, 608n.47
Speyer, W., 81, 83n.186
Spicq, C., 93n.244, 94n.250
Stanton, G. N., 21n.70, 57n.56, 67n.107, 71n.126, 176n.341, 188n.4, 195n.40, 216n.23, 246n.174, 248n.187, 249nn.188,189, 250n.195, 252n.200, 254n.217, 255n.219, 258n.237, 262n.251, 271n.285, 274n.293, 450n.161, 452n.168, 455n.177, 456nn.181,184,185, 457n.190, 461n.203, 501nn.335,336, 502n.342, 520n.34, 572n.230, 582n.276, 586n.292, 588nn.296,297,298, 589nn.303,304, 619n.106, 635n.188, 637n.199, 638n.208, 659n.291, 655n.320
Stein, R. H., 224n.64, 225n.79
Stendahl, K., 19n.66, 66n.100
Sterling, G. E., 379n.244, 570n.220
Stern, D. H., 26n.99, 608n.51
Stevenson, J., 51n.20
Still, T. D., 716n.174
Stoops, R. F., 163n.277, 166n.290, 169n.307, 170n.312, 519n.33, 704n.122, 750n.96
Strecker, G., 76n.154, 79n.168, 144nn.176,177,178, 146nn.183,184,185, 175nn.337,339, 366n.215, 465n.218, 513n.15, 589n.306, 591n.315, 777n.87

Street, D. R., 777n.87, 778n.90
Streeter, B. H., 218n.33, 281n.316
Stroker, W. D., 372n.237, 464n.210, 465nn.218,219
Strotmann, A., 350n.158
Stroumsa, G. G., 21n.70
Stuckenbruck, L. T., 785n.131, 786n.136
Stuhlmacher, P., 61n.82, 188nn.3,4, 189n.13, 275n.298, 316n.14, 353n.169, 358n.183, 359n.185, 452n.168, 643n.226, 759n.6
Suggs, M. J., 258n.238
Swete, H. B., 156n.241, 490n.304

Tabbernee, W., 796n.181
Tabor, J. D., 677
Tannehill, R. C., 236n.134, 299n.394
Taylor, J. E., 509n.2
Taylor, M. S., 20n.68
Taylor V., 201n.58, 212n.8, 281n.316,526n.61
Telford, W. R., 221n.47
Thatcher, T., 74n.142, 212n.11, 316n.14, 320n.33, 324n.54, 325n.55, 326nn.59,60,62, 328n.68, 329n.76, 331n.83, 333n.88, 335n.100, 336n.101,102, 355n.173, 641n.217, 642n.225, 762n.20
Theisohn, J., 571n.223
Theissen, G., 60n.75
Theobald, M., 73n.139, 328n.71, 336n.101, 340n.118, 353n.170, 355n.172
Theophilos, M., 67n.110
Thomas, C. M., 109n.327
Thomas, J. C., 365n.213
Thomason, D. A., 160n.257
Thomassen, E., 499n.329
Thompson, A. J., 685n.42
Thompson, L. L., 110n.331
Thompson, M. M., 355n.172, 356n.176, 774n.73
Thompson, W. G., 265n.268
Thyen, H., 73n.139, 79n.167, 329n.74, 359n.185, 367n.222, 368n.229, 368n.229
Tomson, P. J., 15n.45, 22n.76
Tóth, F., 109n.324
Trakatellis, D. C., 565n.196
Trebilco, P., xiii, 77n.155, 78n.159, 112n.6, 305n.414, 338n.109, 598n.3, 651n.259, 668n.332, 788n.140
Trevett, C., 654n.270
Trilling. W., 262n.255, 267n.272
Trobisch, D., 817n.34
Troeltsch, E., 6n.8
Tuckett, C. M., 46n.6, 68n.115, 79n.163, 153nn.220,221,222, 224n.63, 219n.36, 231n.105, 246n.178, 408n.12, 409n.14, 426n.75, 428n.76, 429n.82, 431n.86, 432n.91, 433nn.94,95,96, 475n.428, 477n.254, 479n.261, 480n.267, 482n.272, 482n.272, 484n.278, 497n.321, 634n.183, 686n.49, 696, 697n.93, 744n.77,80
Tugwell, S., 111n.2
Turner, J. D., 33n.131, 153n.226, 479n.261, 486n.286, 500n.332, 794
Turner, M., 292n.370
Turner, M. L., 480n.265, 482n.269, 486n.286
Turner, N., 52n.26, 91n.236, 225n.68
Twelftree, G. H., 333n.88

Uro, R., 210n.3, 380n.247, 381n.247, 395nn.288,290, 396n.296, 397n.297, 474n.246

Valantasis, R., 392n.282, 395n.290, 400n.302
van de Sandt, H., 426n.73, 553n.152, 555n.163
van der Horst, P. W., 625n.137
van der Watt, J. G., 364n.208
van Minnen, P., 156n.238, 180n.356
Van Voorst, R. E., 176n.343, 519n.32, 589n.303
Verheyden, 316n.16, 435-36n.107, 437n.111, 489n.301, 490n.307, 521n.37, 581n.265, 582n.270, 687n.50, 744n.79, 748n.90
Vermes, G., 227n.81, 555n.167, 651n.261, 659n.288
Vielhauer, P., 144nn.176,177,178, 146nn.183,184,185
Vledder, E.-J., 71n.126
von Campenhausen, H., 9n.19, 207n.86, 648n.254, 694n.83
von Wahlde, U. C., 78n.160, 104n.298, 317n.18, 641n.218, 776n.82, 777n.86

Index of Authors

Wagner, J. R., 189n.11, 312n.1
Wander, B., 14n.41, 603n.25, 625n.133
Wassmuth, O., 573n.236
Watson, D. F., 98n.271
Watson, P., 579n.252
Webb, R. L., 98n.271, 100n.281
Wechsler, A., 514n.17
Weeden, T. J., 229n.93
Weiss, H. E., 93n.247, 95n.255, 96n.260, 552n.151, 648n.251
Welborn, L. L., 112n.5, 113n.12
Wellhausen, J., 223, 224
Wengst, K., 78n.158 642n.220
Wenham, D., 408n.12
Werner, 181n.362
White, L. M, 10n.24, 69n.120, 636n.193
Whitfield, B., 541n.117
Wickham, C., 212n.11
Wiefel, W., 607n.45
Wiles, M. F., 694n.81, 702n.117, 712n.155, 714n.167, 715n.170, 718n.189, 719n.195, 723n.208
Wilken, R. L., 5n.4, 19nn.61,62,66, 592n.321, 649n.257, 654n.270
Willett, M. E., 351n.163
Williams, A. L., 134n.133, 135n.136, 664n.315
Williams, C. H., 352n.166
Williams, J. A., 483n.273
Williams, M. A., 33n.134, 35n.143, 38n.152
Williams, M. H., 598n.3, 616n.81
Williamson, R., 93n.244
Willitts, J., 254n.217, 502n.342, 581n.267, 588n.298, 591n.314, 686n.48
Wilson, J. C., 117n.33
Wilson, R. M., 174n.332, 484n.278
Wilson, S. C., 75n.149
Wilson, S. G., 15n.45, 22n.76, 23n.78, 40n.161, 75n.149, 86n.199, 121n.56, 122n.65, 135n.135, 157nn.243,248, 158n.252, 175n.339, 177n.345, 299n.395, 480n.265, 521n.37, 555n.163, 558n.172, 562n.192, 565n.198, 569n.213, 571nn.225,226, 572nn.227,228,231, 573n.235, 575n.245, 578nn.248,249, 579n.252, 580n.259, 586n.288, 610n.54, 616n.81, 619n.106, 620n.112, 621n.116, 624n.130, 625n.137, 626n.141, 627n.147, 632nn.171,172,173, 640n.213, 464n.240, 653n.265, 657n.282, 661n.297, 667n.325, 716, 718n.189, 719n.194
Wingren, G., 6n.5
Wink, W., 338n.112
Wisse, F., 37n.151, 153nn.225,227
Witherington, B., 74n.144, 330n.78, 351n.163, 359n.185
Witulski, T., 109n.324
Wolter, M., xiii, 89n.224, 90n.228, 299n.394
Wrede, W., 10, 197n.44, 224, 231, 232, 233n.115
Wright, D. F., 468nn.224,226
Wright, N. T., 208n.92

Yarbrough, M. M., 89n.224
Yieh, J. Y.-H., 261n.246
Young, L., 588n.298
Young, S. E., 210n4, 211n.6, 214n.15, 408n.12, 413n.21, 415n.27, 416n.31, 417n.33, 419n.40, 423n.64m 424n.65, 431n.86, 439n.119, 442n.130

Zahn, T., 9n.19, 115, 144n.178, 417n.34, 417n.34, 518n.30, 712n.155, 713n.160, 716n.176
Zangenberg, J. K., 120n.48
Zelyck, L. R., 770n.52
Zetterholm, M., 15-16n.46
Zöckler, T., 383n.254
Zwierlein, O., 55n.43, 170n.309

Index of Subjects

Acts
 of *Andrew*, 171-72
  of *John*, 167, 170-71, 794-96
  of *Paul*, §40.6a, 167
  of *Peter*, §40.6b
  of *Peter and the Twelve Apostles*, 174
  of *Philip*, 162n.271
  of *Thomas*, §40.6c
Adversus Judaeos, 648
Agrapha, 412-13, 463-66
Agrippa II, 611
Alexandria, 92-93
Alogoi, 771
Amidah, 625-26
Anabathmoi Jacobou, 176
Andrew, 753n.108
Angel, 784-85
Angel of the Lord, 785
Antichrist, 775-76, 780
Anti-Judaism, §38.3c, 634, 648, 649, 659n.288, 695-96, 806
Antioch, 6
Anti-semitism, 24-25
Aphrahat, 18
Apocalypse, 176-77, 546, 549
 First *Apocalypse of James*, 177-78
 Second *Apocalypse of James*, 178
 Apocalypse of Paul, 178-79
 Coptic *Apocalypse of Paul*, 179
 Apocalypse of Peter, 179-80
 Coptic *Apocalypse of Peter*, 180-81
 Apocalypse of Thomas, 181

Apocalyptic, 180
Apocryphon of John, 792-94,
Apollinarus, §40.2g
Apostle, 789, 812
Apostolic Fathers, §40.1
Apostolic succession, 7, 814
Apostolicity, 9, §50.2c
Aristides, §40.2b
Astonishment, 235
Athenagoras, §40.2h

Baptism, 358-59
 baptismal formula, 429-30
Bar Kochba revolt, 617-20
Barbelo, 486
Barnabas, epistle of, §40.1f
Basilides, 29-30, 527-28
Believe, 356-359
Birkat-ha-minim, 21n.71, 24, 624-26, 641-42
Bishop, 7-8, 790, 813-15
Brother, 775, 778

Canon, 816-20
Carpocrates, 27
Catholic church, 7n.12
Cerdo, 716-17
Cerinthus, 29, 71n.130
Chaldean Christians, 23n.81
Charisma, 679
Chiliasm, 177
Choics, 31, 713

Index of Subjects

Christian, 606-10
Christianity, 4, 7n.12, 12-13, 407, 599-602, 610, 651-54
  Jewishness, 823-24
  and Judaism, §38.3
  Third race, 661
Christology, 681-82
Church, 733-34
Circumcision, 389, 620, 655-57, 664, 697-98, 700
Claudius, 607
Clement, 7, 9, §40.1a, 746-47
  Pseudo-Clementine literature, 175-76, 586-89
2 Clement, §40.1h
Codex, 501-2
Collegia, 609
Constantine, 7n.14
3 Corinthians, 160, 165
Council of Antioch (341), 18
Council of Elvira (c. 300), 19n.66
Council of Laodicea (363), 18
Covenant, 645-47, 655-58, 661, 669, 695
Creedal confession, 9

Day of atonement, 644-45
Deacon, 813
Diatessaron, 136
Didache, §40.1e
Dionysus, bishop of Corinth, 126
Diotrephes, 781-82
Disciples, 234-35
Diversity, 824-25
Dositheus, 527-28

Early Catholicism, 6
Ebionites, 145-46, 576, 578-82, 585, 590n.313, 596
  Christology, 580
  and Paul, 579-80
Ecclesiology, 790-91
Edessa, 148-49, 592-95
Elder, 678-79, 779-82, 789, 812-13
Elkesaites, 585-86
Encratite, 136 and n.142, 173-74
Enlightenment, 10
Enoch, 544-45
Ephesus, 6
Epinoia, 793
Epiphanius, §40.3f

Episcopy, 6
Epistle of Titus, 161
Epistle to Diognetus, §40.2d
Epistle to the Alexandrians, 160n.260
Epistle to the Laodiceans, 160
Epistula Apostolorum, 161-62
Eschatology, 782
Euangelion
  in Mark, 193-94, 219-21
  as Gospel, 194-196, 203, 206-8, 309
Eucharist, 8-9
Eusebius, 4, 7-8, 11, §40.3e

Faith, 290, 679-80
Fiscus Judaicus, 614-616
Flesh, 776-79, 822
Forgiveness, 289-90, 295, 297
Form criticism, 223-24

Gamaliel II, 622, 623n.125, 625
Gentiles, 272-75, 295-96, 299-304, 362-63, 531-32, 535-36, 604-6
Gnosis, 129, 168n.300, 170, 172, 360
Gnosticism, 4-5, §38.4c, 41, 87, 145, 146, 181
  Gnostics, 87, 98, 102, 136n.140, 364, 396-97, 400n.307, 401-2, 473-74, 478, 521-23, 527-28, 537, 594-95, 603n.312, 751, 760, 769-74, §49.7, 804, 818, 821
  Libertine Gnostics, 98
  Pre-Christian Gnosticism, 13, §38.4b
  Redeemer myth, 173-74, 178, 769-74
  Sethian Gnosis, 485-87
Gnostic Christianity, 6, 152-54
Gospel, §41.1, 401-2, 439, 451n.164, 452, 459, 494, 504-5, 802-3, 817
  of Bartholomew, 157-58
  canonical Gospels, §44.8
  of Gamaliel, 157
  Gnostic Gospel, §44.5-6, 504
  Hebrew, 145-46
  Infancy Gospels, 491-92,
  Israel focus, 296-99, 303-4
  Jewish Christian, §40.4a, 471-72
  Narrative Gospels, §44.7
  of Judas, 154-55, 177
  of Mary, 152-53
  of Nicodemus, 157
  of Peter, 155-57

INDEX OF SUBJECTS

of Philip, 152
of the Egyptians, 152
of Truth, 151-52
Great church, 10-11

Hadrian, 123
Halakhah, 600-601
Hebrews, §39.3c
  author, §39.3c(i)
  recipients, §39.3c(ii)
  date, §39.3c(iii)
Hegesippus, §40.3a, 524-26
Hellenization, 26-27, 31
Hermas, *Shepherd* of, §40.1g
Hippolytus, §40.3d
Holy Spirit, 284, 291-92, 295, 359-60, 367-68, 422, 776-79, 797-800, 809, 819
Humility, 305
Hypocrites, 651

Ignatius, 9, 11, 18, §40.1b
Incarnation, 765-66, 822
Irenaeus, 5-6, 11, 44, §40.3b, 460-62, 504
Israel, 655-60, 662, 666-68

James, 390, 507, 511, §45.2, 581, 596, 605, 675-76, 683-85, 687, 726-27, 735, 745-46, 754, 757-58, 764, §50.1b
  brother of Jesus, 7
  Gnostic James, §45.2d
  Jewish-Christian James, §45.2c
  Patristic James, §45.2b
  Protevangelium of, 158
Jerusalem, destruction of, 3, 610-14, 620
Jesus
  death of, 286-87, 288
  embodying divine presence, 257-58, 260
  embodying divine wisdom, 258-60
  fulfillment of scripture, 255, 260, 284
  healer, 228-30, 244
  historical, 823
  impact of, 187, 309
  in Judea, 322-24
  as king, 284
  king of Israel, 341
  as *kyrios*, 285-86
  Messiah, 229-30, 232, 253, 260, 284, 288, 337-44, 355, 391, 529-34, 595, 761
  Moses prophet, 256-57, 260, 284-85
  as prophet, 345, 352
  remembered, §42.5
  resurrection of, 288
  Saviour, 287-88n.350, 288-89, 295
  Son of David, 254, 260, 284
  Son of God, 226-28, 244, 252-53, 260, 283, 288, 344-46, 352-55, 391, 761, 766-67
  Son of Man, 232-33, 244, 253, 285, 345-46, 767
  teacher, 234-39, 244, 260-61
  teaching of, in John, 324-27,
  theios anēr, 229-30
  as truth, 360-62
  as Wisdom, 349-53
  as Word/Logos, 346-55, 761, 768, 766-67,
Jesus tradition, §50.1a
Jewish Christianity, §38.3b, 145-146, Part Twelve, §50.1b
'the Jews' in John, 24-25, 106, 640-42
Jewish revolt, 115-17, 616-17
Jews, 778
  for Jesus, 672
John the Baptist, 317-19, 320-21, 323, 337-40, 420-21, 456
John, Gospel of, §39.2d, §41.4, §43.1, 5, §49, 808-10
  author, §39.2d(i)
  christology, §49.3, 794
  distinctives, 314-16
  discourses, 335-37
  healings, 332-35
  historical value, 316-24
  individualism, 366-68, 809
  place, §39.2d(ii)
1-3 John, §39.3g
  author, §39.3g(i)
  date, §39.3g(iii)
  place of writing, §39.3g(ii)
John Mark, 50-51
Judaeo-Christian sects, 6
Judah the Prince, 623-24
Jude, §39.3e
  date, §39.3e(iii)
  author, §39.3e(i)
  recipients, §39.3e(ii)

Index of Subjects

Judaism, 12-13, 14, 598-600, 610-14, 652-54, 662, 801
Judaizer, 19n.64
Justin Martyr, 11, 44, §40.2e, 452-56

Kerygma Petrou, §40.2c
Kerygmata Petrou, 175-76
Kingdom of God, 292-95
Kosmos/world, 363-64

Last supper, 240
Law/gospel, 717
Law/Torah, 267-72, 537, 543, 622, 668-69, 684, 686
  Law and works, 537
Letter of Peter to Philip, 177
Life, 359-60
Light, 361-62
Living voice, 447
Lord's prayer, 423-24, 430-31
Lord's supper, 8 and n.18
Love, 304, 364-66
Luke, Gospel of, §39.2b, §41.3, §42.4, 310
  author, §39.2b(i)
  date, §39.2b(ii)
  place, §39.2b(iii)
  women in, 306

Mandaeans, 23n.81
Manicheism, 161n.263
  Manichean Psalm Book, 170
Marcion, §38.4d, 44, 527-28, 663n.312, 668, 703, 710-11, 716-20, 817-18
Marcosians, 461
Marcus, 30-31
Mark, Gospel of, §41.2, 199-202, 214-15, §42.2, 310
  author, §39.2a(i)
  christology, §42.2b
  date, §39.2a(ii)
  and discipleship, 233-239
  place of writing, §39.2a(iii)
  reception of, 244-45, 310
Mark, Secret Gospel of, 158-59, 487-88
Mary Magdalene, 484-85, 488, 809
Matthew, §39.2c
  author, §39.2c(i)
  composition, 246-52
  date, §39.2c(ii)

ecclesiology, 261-63
  manual of discipleship, §42.3c
  place, §39.2c(iii)
Melito, §40.2j
Menander, 29
Messianic Jews, 591, 597, 672
Messianic secret, 224, 230-33, 284, 288n.351
Minim, §45.7, 626-31
Minut, 627-30
Mishnah, 623
Monotheism, 680-82, 821-22
Montanism, 137, 142, §49.8, 809
Muratorian Canon, 160
Mystery, 536

Naasenes, 523
Nag Hammadi, 11, 32-35, 39, 147
Nazarenes, 576, 625
Nazoraeans, 582-85, 590n.313, 591, 596, 641n.218
Nero, 166, 608
New Testament canon, 6
Nicaea, 9
Nicodemus, 491

Odes of Solomon, §40.1j
Ophites, 165n.287
Oral tradition, 191, 209-17, 329, 371, 380-81, 383-84, 388-89, 433, §44.2-3, 489, 803-4
  oral to written, 213-17
Origen, 18
Orthodoxy/heresy, 20-21

Papias, 50-51, 63-64, 75, §40.1i, 444-49
Papyri, 466-70, 500-501
Partings of the ways, §38.3a, §46
Passion narrative, 196-98, 199-200, 203, 239-44
Passover, 240
Pastoral Epistles, §39.3b
  author, §39.3b(i)
  date, §39.3b(iii)
  why and to whom, §39.3b(ii)
Paul, 580-81, 584, 587-88, 590, §47, 726, 735, 745-46, 754, 764, 807, 817-18
  execution of, 166
  Gnostic Paul, 711-15
  letters of, 688

and Seneca, 160-61
and Thecla, 163-65
Peace, 290
Pella, 524, 589
Periodoi Petrou, 176
Peter, 7, 675, 683, 685, 700n.101, 708, §48, 758, 763, 764, 804, 808
  authority of, 222
  and Corinth, 725-26
  in John, 738-39
  in Luke-Acts, 735-38
  in Mark, 732
  in Matthew, 263-66, 733-35
2 Peter, §39.3f
  author, §39.3f(i)
  date, §39.3f(iii)
  recipients, §39.3f(ii)
Pharisee, 24, 68, 266-72, 532, 560, 636-39
Philo, 27, 596
Pilate, 157
Polycarp, 75-76, §40.1c, d
Poor, 301-2, 306
Prayer, 306-7
Priest, 8, 814-16
  high priest, 644-45
Priscillianism, 161n.263
Prophecy, false, 789
Prophet, 790, 813
Pseudepigraphy, §39.3a, 694n.84
Psychics/pneumatics/choics, 31, 33
Ptolomaeus, 30-31

Q, 191, 200-202, 216-20, 371-72, 381n.248, 383
Quadratus, §40.2a
Qumran, 760
Quotation/allusion, 409-11

Rabbinic Judaism, 69, 570, 621-24
Redaction criticism, 224-25
Reformation, 10
Repentance, 289-90, 358
Resurrection
  of body, 714-15
  of flesh, 706-7, 714-15
  of Jesus, 386
Revelation (Apocalypse of John), §39.3h
  author, §39.3h(i)
  christology, §49.5a
  churches of, §49.5b
  date, §39.3h(iii)
  place of writing, §39.3h(ii)
Rome, 6, 607-8
Rule of faith, 9 and n.21, 820-23

Sabbath, 389-90, 579-80
Sacraments in John, 368
Salome, 485n.282
Samaria, 340-41
Same yet different, 310, 313, 320, 340, 803-4
Scripture, 438, 561, 566, 568, 596, 694, 806
Sect, 604
Seneca, 709-10
Sepphoris, 611n.60,
Serapion, 155-56, 490
Sermon on the Mount, 428
Seth, 153
Shemoneh 'esreh, 625
Sign, 332-33
Simon of Cyrene, 30
Simon Magus, 28-29, 168-70, 668, 708, 745, 750
Simonians, 527-28
Sinner, 290-291, 295, 301
Social memory, 336n.101
Spätjudentum, 667n.326
Sub-apostolic age, 5
Supersessionism, 303n.408, 646, 658, 69-670
Symeon, son of Clopas, 525-27

Tatian, §40.2f, 594n.333
Temple (Jerusalem), 95-96, 238, 610-614, 618, 622, 644-48
  cleansing of, 321-22, 330-32
Tertullian, §40.3c
Thaddaeus, 593
Thebouthis, 527
Theophilus, §40.2i
Thomas, 593-95, 752, 753, 810-11
Thomas, Gospel of, §40.4b, §43.2-5, 312, 505
  alternative gospel, 392-97
  christology of, 391-92
  distinctive tradition, §43.2b
  and Q, 371-72

Index of Subjects

and Synoptic tradition, 372-84
Thomas, Infancy Gospel of, 158
Timothy, 91
Titus, 91, 164 2.278
Trimorphic Protennoia, 794
Two powers heresy, 629-31, 762
Two ways, 426
Type, 665-66

Valentinus, 30, 40, 141, 152, 527-28
    Valentinians, 461, 481, 483, 817-18, 821-22
Virgin birth, 580, 584, 821
Virginity, 715

Way, 600-601
Wealth, 305-6
Wisdom, 540, 543, 643, 761, 764-65, 768-69
Wisdom christology, 288n.351
Word/Logos, 795-96, 809, 821-22
Worship of Jesus, 259-60, 785

Yahoel, 548n.136
Yaltabaoth, 792-93, 794
Yavneh/Jamnia, 68-70, 621-22, 638n.206
Yohanan ben Zakkai, 69-70, 621-22, 623n.125, 624, 629, 647n.246

Index of Scripture and Other Ancient Writings

OLD TESTAMENT

Genesis
1–3	538
1.3	347
1.6-7	347
1.26	551, 557, 793
1.26-27	394
1.26-28	564, 565
1.27	438n.188, 530
1.28	551, 557
1.31	538
2–3	793
2.2	540
2.2-3	557
2.4	256
2.7	360n.189, 394, 793
2.16	568
2.22	397
2.23	550
3.5	579
3.22	564
4.3-8	550
4.8	540
5.1	256
5.21-22	544
5.24	562
6.1-6	793n.170
7	793n.169
9.3	538
12.1-3	550
12.3	298, 302, 532
13.14-16	550
14.17-20	540, 644
14.17-24	542n.118
14.18-20	540
14.20	540
15.1	347n.148
15.5-6	550
15.6	513, 557
16.7-12	785n.129
16.7-13	547n.136
17.4	557
17.14	562, 695
17.23	557
18.1-3	563
18.14	563
18.18	532n.76
18.27	550
18.31	564n.195
19.4-25	54
19.23-25	564
21.12	540
21.17-18	785
21.2	226n.74
21.9-12	563
22.17	540, 551
25.21-23	557, 696n.90
26.4	551
28.10-19	564
29–30	664
31.11-13	785
31.10-13	564
32.22-30	564
35.6-10	564
47.31	540
48.14	557
48.19	557
49.8-12	563
49.9	598
49.11	564

Exodus
1–2	256
2.14	550
2.23	564
3.2-4	564
3.2-6	547
3.2-14	785n.129
3.11	550
3.14	352, 567
3.16	564, 138n.153
4.22	344n.138
7.1	138n.153
7.11	538
7.22	538
8.19	285
12–17	566n.204
12.6	568
12.10	568
12.46	18n.57, 568
17.8-13	557

896

17.14	557	19.18	269, 304n.409,	7.6-8	534n.88
17.16	563		428n.76, 530, 554	8	256
19.5	534n.91,	20–22	557	9.3	540
	539n.110	20.24-26	627	9.5	539n.111
19.6	536, 728n.17, 814	23.5	141n.165	10.16	557, 605n.31
20.3-4	566n.204	23.29	557	10.16-17	562
20.5	637, 793n.166	26.1	557	10.17	681n.25
20.13-16	429n.81	26.11-12	536	14.1	344n.138
20.13-17	554	26.40-41	562	14.2	534nn.88,91,
20.14-17	566n.203				539n.110, 551
22.21	566n.204	**Numbers**		14.6	557
23.6-8	566n.204	11.26	436n.108	14.8-14	557
23.20	317n.22, 529	12.6-8	520	17.6	540
23.20-21	547, 629, 785	12.7	540	18.15	256, 342n.125
23.21	392	13–14	541	18.18	256, 342n.125
24.8	540	14.18	637n.200	19.15	538
24.18	557	14.29-37	544	21.22-23	287
25.4	644	16	544	21.23	700
25.40	92, 93, 540	16.5	538	24.1	270
31.18	557, 655	18.27	551	24.1-4	270
32.6	562	19	556	24.3	270
32.7	655	21.6-9	342, 533	25.4	538
32.7-19	557	21.8	557	26	534n.89
32.19	655, 657n.279	22	749	26.18	534n.91
33.1	557	22–24	544	28.66	567n.207
33.3	557	24.17	618	30.3-5	555
33.20	349n.153,	27.18	563	30.19	553
	681n.25			31.6	540
33.20-23	561	**Deuteronomy**		32.4	546n.132
34	657n.279	2.24	540	32.8-9	551
34.7	637	4.2	554, 790n.158	32.11	258n.238
34.28	557	4.10	557, 655	32.15	534n.89, 550,
34.29-35	256	4.12	349n.153		562, 681n.27
40.3	529	4.13	655	32.20	562, 563
		4.19	566n.203	32.35-36	540
Leviticus		4:24	540	32.43	540
11.3	557	5.1	557	33.2	544
11.6	557	5.5	347n.148	33.5	534n.89
11.7-15	557	5.9	637n.200,		
11.13-16	557		793n.166	**Joshua**	
11.44-45	543n.123	5.12	557	2	550
14.52	784	5.15	562	5.13–6.2	564
16	557, 644	5.17-20	429n.81	8.27	347n.148
16.7-10	557	6	256		
19	269	6.4	642, 681n.24	**Ruth**	
19.2	543n.123	6.4-5	530	2.12	258n.238, 546
19.15	544	6.5	554		
		7.6	539n.110		

1 Samuel

2.1-10	296
13.14	550
26.9	637n.200

2 Samuel

1.16	637n.200
4.10	188n.4
7.4	347n.148
7.11-13	254n.214
7.14	344n.133, 540
18.20	188n.4
18.22	188n.4
18.25	188n.4
18.27	188n.4
18.31	188n.5

1 Kings

8.15	534n.87
9.3	257n.234
13	555n.166
13.20	347n.148
16.31	789n.146
17.17-24	285n.334
19	700n.107
19.10	563
19.14	563
19.18	563
19.19-21	285n.334
22	555n.166

2 Kings

4.32-37	285n.334
7.9	188n.4

1 Chronicles

25.9-31	789n.150
28.19	644n.234
29.11-13	431n.89

Job

1–2	767
1.1	550
1.21	538
5.17-26	551
9.9	566n.201
14.4-5	550
11.2-3	551
19.26	551
28	351
28.12-28	352
38.11	550

Psalms

1.1	557
1.3-6	557
1.6	553
2.1-2	567
2.7	226n.72, 344n.133, 540
2.7-8	551
3.5	551
4.4	694
8	540
8.4-6	540, 721n.203, 540
8.6	535, 721n.203
11.4	257n.234
12.4-6	550
14.1	566n.203
17.8	258n.238
18.25-26	551
18.44	557
19.1-3	551
19.1-6	564
19.4	563
19.7	563
21.19	435
22	242, 565
22.1	198n.47, 242n.159
22.6-8	550
22.7	242n.159
22.8	198n.47, 242n.161
22.14	543
22.16	557
22.18	198n.47, 242n.159, 435, 557
22.20	557
22.21	539
22.22	540, 557
22.25	557
24	563
24.1	551
24.5	551
28.7	551
31.5	242n.161
31.18	550
31.21	539n.112
32.1-2	551
33.6	347, 566n.201
33.9	543, 559
34.10	550
34.11-17	550
34.12	557
34.13-17	543
34.19	358, 550
35.4	567
35.12	567
36.7	258n.238
37.11	429, 554, 578n.249
37.35-37	550
40.6-8	540
40.9	188n.5
42.4	557
45	563
45.6-7	540, 564
45.6-11	564
47.5-9	563
50	562, 564n.194
50.14-15	551
50.16-23	551
51.1-17	550
51.17	551, 557
57.1	258n.238
61.4	258n.238, 550
62.12	539
63.7	258n.238
68.11	188n.5
68.18	535, 563, 701
69.21	242n.159
69.30-32	551
72	563
72.1-19	564
76.1-2	257n.234
78.2	255
78.36-37	550
80.1	257n.234
80.8-16	343n.130
90.4	557, 258n.238
95.7-8	540

24.5	681n.27

Index of Scripture and Other Ancient Writings

95.7-11	540	3.34	417n.32, 543, 551, 559n.178	6	629
95.11	540			6.3	93n.245, 551
96	564	4.18-19	553n.153	6.9-10	529, 633
96.2	188n.5	4.25	566nn.202,204	6.10	563
99.1-7	564, 563	5.8	575	6.20	301n.400
102.25-27	540	6.1	559n.181	7.10	564
104.4	540, 551	6.27-29	566	7.10-16	563
107.20	347n.149	7.26	575	7.14	255, 257, 564, 565, 570n.218, 668
110	563	8	352, 643		
110.1	286n.342, 435, 535, 540, 551, 557, 564, 629, 721n.203, 783	8.7	352n.165		
		8.22	352, 350	7.21	785n.130
		8.22-36	564, 565	8.4-5	785
		8.27	350	8.12-13	543n.123
110.3-4	564	8.30	350	8.14	543n.123
110.4	540, 541, 644	8.32	352n.165	8.17	540
117.22	543	8.34-35	352n.165	8.18	540
118.6	540	8.35	350, 352	9.1-2	255
118.19-20	551	9.5	352	10.3	543n.123
118.22	384n.262, 557	10.12	543	11.1	548
118.22-23	197, 198n.47, 530	11.31	543	11.1-3	254
		14.12	553n.153	11.2	145, 471, 535n.92, 543n.123
118.24	557	15.9-10	553n.153		
118.25	530	18.17	417n.32, 559n.178	11.10	548
119.29-30	553n.153	20.27	550	11.12	664n.318
119.98	538	21.1	566	12	352
128.4-5	562	24.12	539	12.2	540
130.8	539n.110	25.14	544	13.22	550
135.7	566n.201			22.22	734
137.8-9	26n.98	**Isaiah**		26.2-3	562
139.7-8	551	1.2	557	26.13	538
139.24	553n.153	1.8	563	26.20	551, 557
141.5	551	1.9	701	27.2-6	343
146.6	561	1.10	557	28.16	538, 543n.123, 557
147.15	347n.149	1.11-13	557, 655, 656		
147.18	347n.149	1.13	557	29.13	438n.117, 529, 550, 558n.175, 563, 663n.313
		1.16-17	566n.204		
Proverbs		1.16-20	550		
1.17	557	2.2-4	604n.29	29.14	563
1.23-33	551	2.5-6	562	29.18	563
2.6	538	3–10	557	31.5	258
2.21-22	550	3.4	544	31.6	566n.204
3.11-12	540	3.9-10	557	33.13	557
3.12	551	3.10	567n.207	33.13-19	564
3.17	352n.165	4.3	534n.86	33.16-18	557
3.18	352n.165	5.1-7	343, 530	34.4	558n.175
3.19	350	5.18-20	562	35.1-7	564
3.28	559n.181	5.21	557, 563	40.1-17	563

899

40.2	557		558n.175,	65.16-18	557
40.3	300, 317, 529		559nn.178,181	66.1	557, 562
40.3-5	317n.22	52.6	352	66.2	550
40.4-5	300	52.7	188, 189	66.5	566n.204
40.6-8	543n.123	52.12	198n.47	66.18	438n.117,
40.9	188n.6	53	563		558n.175, 652
40.12	557	53.1-12	550	66.19-20	604n.29
40.26	535n.95	53.4	255, 749	66.23	604n.29
40.28	566n.203	53.4-5	546n.132	66.23-24	563
41.4	352	53.4-6	543n.123	66.24	438n.117,
41.27	188n.6	53.5	557		558n.175,
42.1	226n.72	53.7	557, 567n.207		558n.175
42.1-4	255, 273	53.8	563, 564		
42.5-6	566n.203	53.9	543n.123	**Jeremiah**	
42.5-13	564	53.12	198n.47	2.12-13	557
42.6	299, 656, 657	54.1	438, 558	2.13	562
42.6-7	557	54.9	546n.132	2.21	343n.130
43.5	664n.318	54.11-12	546n.132	3.17	562, 604n.29
43.6	344n.138,	55.3-5	562	4.3-4	563, 605n.31
	664n.318	55.3-13	562	4.4	557
43.10	352	55.6-7	566n.204	4.22	563
43.10-11	565n.200	55.11	347	6.9	566n.204
43.17	664n.318	56.6-8	604n.29	6.16	566n.204
43.20-21	728	56.7	530	7.11	530, 558n.175
43.25	352	57.1-4	562	7.21-22	562
44.2	534n.89	57.19	298	7.22	557
45.1	557	57.20	544	9.23-24	550
45.2-3	557	58.1-11	562	9.25-26	563
45.5	771n.57	58.1-12	270	9.26	557
45.7	716n.177	58.3-10	656	10.10	681n.23
45.12	566n.203	58.6-8	566n.204	10.12-13	566n.203
45.18-19	352	58.9	438n.117,	11.19	564, 567n.207
45.20-23	604n.29		558n.175	12.10-13	343n.130
45.21-22	792n.165	60.6	188n.6	17.24-25	540
46.4	352	60.17	551	18–19	255n.220
46.13	300	61.1	188n.6, 189, 291,	20.7	555n.166
49.6	300		301n.400	21.8	553
49.6-7	557	61.1-2	189, 190, 297,	23.2-3	363n.201
49.17	557		190, 297, 531,	23.5-6	254n.214
50.6-7	557		557	29.7	538n.107
50.7	557	61.1-3	189	31.9	344n.138
50.8-9	557	61.2	189	31.31-32	562
50.10	557	62.10–63.6	563	31.31-34	540, 647
51	352	62.11	255	31.33-34	540
51.4-5	562	63.15–64.12	563	32	255n.220
51.12	352n.166	64.11	664n.318	51.17-18	566n.203
52.5	417n.32,	65.1-3	562		
	438n.117, 440,	65.2	557		

Index of Scripture and Other Ancient Writings

Ezekiel
1   93n.245, 629
1.5-11   549
1.24   547
1.24-27   547, 548
1.26   643
3.1-3   549
8.2   547, 548
9.3-6   549
11.19   557
14.20   563
15.1-8   343n.130
17.5-10   343n.130
18.21-23   566n.204
19.10-14   343n.130
20.12   562
20.19-26   562, 564
20.20   562
23   549
27   549
33.11   550
34   343, 637, 643n.232
34.11-16   298
34.12   363n.201
34.23   363
37.9   360n.189
37.12   551
37.21   363n.201
37.23   539
37.24   363
37.27   536
38–39   549
40–42   549
43.6-9   257n.234
44.9   605n.31
47.12   557

Daniel
4.37   786n.134
7   629
7.7-8   122, 548, 557
7.9   547, 548, 629, 784
7.9-28   563
7.10   551
7.11-12   548
7.13   126, 179, 547, 784;
7.13-14   643, 76
7.14   198n.47
7.18   534
7.21-22   534
7.24   557
7.25   563
10.5-6   547, 548, 629
10.13   544
10.21   544
11.36   544
12.7   294n.379

Hosea
1.6   543n.123
1.9   543n.123
1.10   344n.138
2.25   543n.123
6.6   250, 270, 530, 647n.246
11.1   253, 255, 256, 344n.138
12.6   566n.204

Amos
1.11   582n.274
4.11   544
5.18   562
5.18–6.7   564n.194
5.21-24   270n.282
9.7-8   637
9.11-12   302

Micah
6.6-8   270n.282

Nahum
1.15   188n.6

Zechariah
2.6   664n.318
2.10-11   257n.234
2.11   604n.29
3   541n.117
3.1   544
3.4   544
4.10   548

7.9-10   566
8.17   557
9.9   255, 563
11.13   255
13.7   198n.47, 435, 557, 563
14.8   342

NEW TESTAMENT

Matthew
1–2   248n.186, 318n.26, 454
1.1   254, 272
1.1-2   433n.93
1.2   300
1.3-6   273
1.6   254
1.7-32   68n.115
1.16   253
1.17   254
1.20   254
1.21   266, 288n.350, 454n.175
1.22   255n.219
1.22-23   255
1.23   257
2   228n.82
2.1   273
2.2   255n.218, 259, 420n.47
2.3   254n.217
2.5-6   255n.219
2.6   262, 266
2.8   259
2.11   259, 273, 461, 500n.332
2.13   469
2.15   253, 255, 256, 471
2.16   273
2.16-18   256
2.17   255n.219
2.17-18   255n.219
2.19   516n.26
2.23   255
3–7   256n.227

3	234n.118		252n.206,	5.38-48	248n.185
3.1	317n.19		271n.288, 421,	5.39	427
3.3	255n.219,		423	5.39-40	453, 455
	317n.22	5.10-11	374	5.39-42	248n.185
3.5	317n.21, 398	5.11	285n.335	5.40	427
3.5-6	317n.20	5.11-12	201n.60	5.41	427
3.7	251n.196; 420	5.13	220n.41,	5.42	427, 458
3.7-10	339n.115		248n.185	5.43-44	269
3.8	358n.184	5.14	148n.193,	5.44	424, 426, 455,
3.9	273		248n.185, 373,		459, 469,
3.10	481		382		566n.204
3.11	317n.23, 318n.24	5.15	248n.185, 373	5.44-45	458
3.12	339	5.15-16	220n.41	5.45	252n.203, 454
3.13	317n.20	5.16	68n.115,	5.46	458, 459,
3.13-14	471		248n.185,		566n.204
3.13-15	339n.114, 418		252n.203, 412,	5.46-47	426
3.14	472		453	5.47	262n.255
3.14-15	249, 321n.38	5.17	19-20; 250	5.48	252n.203, 427,
3.15	252n.206, 480	5.17-18	220n.41		429n.82
3.16	318n.25	5.17-19	256, 267	6	271n.288, 431
4.1-10	256	5.17-20	638	6.1	252n.206,
4.3	253	5.18	248n.185,		252n.203, 267,
4.6	253		461n.205		271n.288, 453
4.9-10	259	5.19-20	250	6.1-6	248n.186,
4.14	255n.219	5.20	251n.196,		390n.275
4.14-16	255		252n.206, 267,	6.1-8	430
4.17	193		271, 454	6.1-18	261, 430
4.18-22	735n.41	5.21-22	261n.250, 268	6.2	430
4.19	735n.43	5.21-42	268n.273	6.3	374, 459,
4.21	757n.2	5.21-48	268n.273		566n.204
4.21-25	220	5.22-24	262n.255	6.5	430, 554, 651
4.23	193, 228n.84,	5.24-26	220n.41	6.6	480
	636n.191	5.25-26	29, 248n.185,	6.7-8	251n.199
4.23–5.2	251n.199		428	6.9	252n.203
4.24	71n.126	5.27-28	268	6.9-13	248n.185,
5–7	57n.56, 251, 261	5.28	453, 458, 459,		271n.288,
5	648, 669		566n.204		400n.306, 430
5.3	315n.11, 421, 423	5.29	453	6.10	268n.274
5.3-5	578n.249	5.31	220n.41	6.12	290n.360, 414,
5.3-12	248n.185, 261	5.32	248n.185,		424
5.3–7.27	256n.226		250, 436, 459,	6.13	421, 423, 476
5.5	429, 554		566n.204	6.14-15	290n.360, 424
5.5-8	400n.306	5.33	554	6.16	430
5.6	252n.206, 267,	5.33-37	248n.186	6.16-18	248n.186
	271n.288, 374	5.33-48	268	6.19	457n.187, 497
5.7	414	5.34	454	6.19-20	374, 378, 453
5.10	68n.115,	5.34-37	412	6.20-21	248n.185
	247n.182,	5.37	454	6.22-23	373, 473

6.24	374, 382, 441, 457n.187, 461	7.22-23	454	9.32	251n.199
		7.23	248n.185, 252n.204	9.33-37	247n.182
6.25-30	148n.193, 373, 400n.306			9.34	251n.196
		7.24-27	248n.185, 261, 276n.252, 476.252	9.35	193
6.25-33	305			9.35–12.9	
6.26	252n.203, 400n.306				636n.191
		7.24-39	247n.182	9.36	262n.254
6.30	264n.263, 400n.306	7.28	256n.226	9.37-38	374
		7.28-29	251n.199	9.41	247n.182
6.31-33	453	7.29	636	10	256, 261
6.33	252n.206, 267	8–10	256.227	10.2	263, 265n.265, 757n.2
6.34	400n.306	8	434n.97		
7	228n.82, 487n.296	8.2	259nn.242,243, 432n.91	10.3	65, 593, 810n.8
				10.5	301, 303, 324
7.1	414	8.5-13	248n.185	10.5-6	248n.186, 250, 261, 637, 638
7.1-2	267n.272	8.6	259n.242		
7.2	414, 454	8.8	259n.242	10.5-42	256n.226
7.3-5	148n.193, 262n.255, 373, 376	8.11-12	454, 636	10.6	262, 266, 325n.57
		8.11-13	247n.182	10.7-16	248n.185, 251
		8.12	67, 252n.204, 473	10.8	248n.185, 271n.288
7.6	248n.186, 272n.290, 374, 378, 432	8.17	255, 420n.47		
		8.18-22	262	10.10	432, 473
		8.19	636	10.15	256, 261n.250, 545n.131
7.7	326, 398, 400n.306, 484n.279, 471, 473, 484, 497	8.20	374, 378		
		8.23-27	262, 247n.182	10.16	262n.254, 373, 377, 420, 440, 443n.134, 489n.301
		8.25	234n.119, 259n.242		
		8.26	264n.263		
7.7-8	373, 374, 382	8.28-34	228n.87, 249n.191	10.17	636
7.11	252n.203			10.17-18	326
7.12	248n.185, 268, 426, 428n.76	8.34-38	220	10.21-22	326
		9.2	290n.360	10.23	248n.186, 254n.213
7.13-14	426n.75, 553	9.5	432n.92, 433n.93		
7.15	262n.254, 400n.306, 420n.47, 454, 555nn.163,165	9.5-6	290n.360	10.24	326
		9.9	65	10.24-25	248n.185, 259n.242, 271n.288
		9.10-13	290		
		9.11	251n.196, 261n.246	10.26	373
7.15-20	248n.185	9.13	250, 270, 455	10.26-33	248n.185
7.16	248n.185, 374, 377	9.14	251n.196	10.27	373
		9.14-29	247n.182	10.28	437, 443
7.17	469	9.17	639n.209	10.32	201n.61, 252n.203, 285n.335
7.18-20	248n.186	9.18	259n.243		
7.21	248n.185, 252n.203, 261n.250, 440, 454	9.18-26	228n.87, 249n.191		
				10.33	252n.203
7.21-23	268n.274, 443n.133	9.27	254n.216	10.34	290n.366, 373, 376
		9.27-28	254n.217		
7.22	443	9.27-31	247n.182	10.34-36	248n.185

10.35-36	373	12.9-14	471	13.45-46	374		
10.37	440	12.11-12	248n.186,	13.47-48	373		
10.37-38	248n.185, 374,		262n.254	13.49	271n.288		
	378, 400n.305	12.14	251n.196	13:50	252n.204		
10.38	201n.60	12.17	250n.195,	13.52	65, 636		
10.39	248n.185		255n.219	13.53–18.35			
10.40	248n.185, 326	12.17-21	255		256n.227		
10.40-41	432	12.21	432	13.53	256n.226,		
10.41	248n.185, 263	12.22-23	251n.199		636n.191		
10.42	247n.182	12.23	254, 254n.217	13.55	97n.262, 805		
11.1–13.52		12.24	251n.196	13.58	228n.89, 250		
	256n.227	12.28	291n.369,	14	234n.118, 414		
11	228n.82		332n.88	14.25-33	750		
11.1	251n.199,	12.29	373, 461	14.28-31	248n.186, 250,		
	256n.226	12.31	432		263, 733n.36		
11.2	258, 765	12.31-32	290n.360, 374	14.28	259n.242		
11.3	431, 432n.92	12.33	421	14.29-31	729n.25		
11.5	189, 315n.11,	12.34-35	374, 377	14.30	259n.242		
	334n.95,	12:34-37	248n.186	14.31	264n.263, 250,		
	400n.306	12.36	261n.250		253, 260		
11.7-8	374	12.38	251n.196,	15.1	251n.196		
11.7	433n.93		261n.246	15.1-20	269		
11.8	400n.306	12.41-42	261n.250	15.3	432n.91		
11.10	255n.219	12.43	436n.109	15.3-4	431, 433n.93		
11.11	374	12.43-45	436n.109	15.4	432n.91		
11.11-12	317n.19	12.49-50	262n.256	15.7-9	467		
11.12-13	248n.185	12.50	252n.203,	15.11	373		
11.12-15	454, 455		268n.274, 441,	15.12	251n.196		
11.16	248n.185		442n.130	15.13	252n.203, 420,		
11.19	258, 315n.11, 765	13	261		374, 481		
11.20	251n.199	13.1	251n.199	15.14	373		
11.22	261n.250	13.2	432n.92	15.15	263		
11.24	261n.250	13.3-52	256n.226	15.17	250		
11.25-27	355	13.14-15	255n.219	15.17-20	269		
11.27	253, 258, 473	13.17	373	15.21-28	247n.182		
11.27-24	489	13.24-30	248n.186, 262,	15.22	254		
11.28	400n.306		374	15.24	250, 254, 262,		
11.28-30	248n.186, 258,	13.33	375, 378, 461		266, 346n.144,		
	374, 378	13.35	255		580, 637		
11.29	260	13.36	261n.250	15.25	259n.243		
12	234n.118	13.36-43	262	15.26	272n.290		
12.1	269	13:36-52	248n.186	15.29-31	251n.199		
12.1-13	271	13.41	252n.204,	15.43	250n.195		
12.2	251n.196, 580		268n.276	16	651		
12.3	254n.216, 269	13.41-42	254n.213	16.1	251n.196		
12.5-6	248n.186	13.42	252n.204	16.1-3	374		
12.7	250, 270	13.43	271n.288	16.1-4	247n.182		
12.9-13	482	13.44	375, 451, 457	16.1-8	247n.182		

16.4	454	18.10-14	165, 248n.185	19.28	248n.185, 254n.213, 262m 266, 400n.306, 638
16.6	251n.196	18.12	262n.254, 482		
16.8	164n.263	18.12-13	325n.57, 375		
16.11	251n.196	18.12-14	499n.332		
16.12	251n.196, 580	18.14	248n.185, 265, 252n.203	20.1-15	476n.252
16.13	199			20.1-16	248n.186, 461n.205
16.13-17	520	18.15	248n.185, 262n.255		
16.16	253, 750			20.2	424
16.16-17	454, 742	18.15-17	431n.87	20.17	231n.103
16.16-19	733, 734	18.15-18	265, 470	20.18	199n.53
16.17	252n.203, 263, 753	18.15-20	165n.168, 248n.186, 290n.360	20.20	259n.243
				20.20-21	758n.3
				20.24	758n.3
16.17-18	248n.186, 250, 751, 754	18.17	262, 272n.290, 638	20.28	413n.20, 424
				20.30-31	254n.216
16.17-19	747			21.4	255n.219
16.18	262, 266, 638, 733n.38, 734	18.17-18	264	21.4-5	255
		18.18	264n.264, 269, 734	21.5	255n.218
16.18-19	264, 808			21.9	254, 254n.217
16.19	269, 746n.84	18.18-20	265n.268	21.14-17	248n.186
16.21	199n.52, 253n.213	18.19	252n.203, 265n.269	21.15	254, 254n.217
16.26	441	18.19-20	265, 417	21.15-16	331n.84
16.28	254n.213	18.20	257, 265n.269, 373	21.16	255n.219
17.1	757nn.1,2			21.28-32	248n.186
17.1-8	751	18.21	262n.255, 263	21.31	268n.274
17.1-9	101, 729n.23	18.21-22	248n.185, 265, 290n.360, 471	21.32	252n.206, 545n.131
17.4	259n.242				
17.5	68n.115, 545	18.23-35	265, 248n.186, 290n.360	21.33-34	461
17.10-13	454			21.37	226n.74
17.13	250	18.26	259n.243	21.41	250n.195
17.14-21	249n.191	18.33	414	21.42	255n.219
17.15	234n.119, 256, 259n.242	18.35	252n.203, 262n.255, 414	21.43	267n.271, 450n.161, 636n.193, 637
17.20	264n.263, 411	19–25	256.227		
17.22-23	199n.53	19.1	251n.199, 256n.226	21.43-45	250
17.24	248n.185, 261n.246, 263			21.45	251n.196, 267n.271, 637
		19.3	250, 251n.196, 268n.273, 269		
17.24-27	248n.186, 460, 470			22	253
		19.9	250, 436, 458	22.1-14	66, 248n.185, 330n.79, 380n.245
18	261	19.11	453		
18.1-5	265	19.12	136n.142, 419, 453		
18.3	324, 398, 437			22.2-10	374, 613
18.6	265, 416	19.16-24	471	22.7	66, 636n.193
18.6-9	265	19.18	554	22.7-8	637
18.7	416	19.18-19	429n.81	22.10	262
18.9	420n.47	19.19	459	22.11-14	262
18.10	248n.185, 265, 252n.203	19.23	400n.306	22.13	252n.204
		19.26	455	22.14	434

22.19	420n.47	23.37-39	201nn.60,61	26.1	251n.199, 256n.226
22.21	461	23.38	258		
22.24	251n.196	24–25	261	26.13	193, 194, 195n.40
22.25	251n.196	24	67, 750	26.31	262n.254, 435, 469
22.30	455	24.2	67		
22.37-40	269	24.2-3	67	26.33-34	469
22.40	250	24.2–25.46		26.37	757n.1
22.41	251n.196		256n.226	26.41	421, 423
22.42-45	254n.216	24.3	67	26.42	268n.274
22.43-44	255n.219	24.10	433	26.52-53	400n.306
22.43-45	259n.242	24.10-12	250n.195, 433	26.52-54	250n.195
23	24, 68, 69, 121n.57, 270, 471, 636	24.12	252n.204	26.56	255
		24.13	433	26.61	321
		24.14	193, 195n.40, 272n.291, 484	26.64	241n.157
23.1-2	734n.38			27.3-10	248n.186
23.1-36	248n.186	24.20	270	27.9	255
23.2	251n.196, 270	24.27	254n.213	27.11	241n.157, 255n.218
23.3	270	24.28	248n.186		
23.7	454	24.30	254n.213, 433	27.17	248n.186, 253
23.7-8	68	24.30-33	294	27.24-25	248n.186
23.8	261, 262n.255, 420n.47	24.31	433	27.25	24, 491
		24.37	254n.213	27.29	255n.218
23.8-10	265	24.37-41	248n.185	27.34	435
23.9	252n.203, 457n.187, 818n.35	24.39	254n.213	27.37	255n.218
		24.40-41	374	27.40	253
		24.42	433	27.42	255n.218
23.13	251n.196, 269, 373, 377	24.43	373, 376, 412	27.43	242n.161, 253
		24.51	252n.204	27.45	497
23.15	251n.196	25.1-12	476n.252	27.51	460
23.23	251n.196, 270, 454	25.1-13	248n.186, 330n.79, 470	27.52	420n.47
				27.52-53	248n.186
23.24	258	25.1-15	276n.252	27.54	227n.77, 345
23.25	251n.196, 469	25.14-30	248n.185, 436n.109	27.56	242n.163
23.25-26	269, 374, 390n.275			27.61	242n.163
		25.18	454	27.62	251n.196
23.26	251n.196	25.30	252n.204	27.62-66	489
23.27	251n.196, 454	25.31	261n.250	28.1	242n.163
23.27-29	636n.193, 637	25.31-46	248n.186, 254n.213	28.9	259
23.28	248n.185, 252n.204			28.9-20	248n.186, 271
		25.32	450n.161	28.10	262n.258, 264
23.29	251n.196	25.32-33	262n.254	28.11-15	489
23.32-34	248n.185	25.34	255n.218	28.13	454
23.33	261n.250	25.37	271n.288	28.15	638
23.34	68, 636	25.40	255n.218, 262n.256	28.16-20	258n.236
23.34-36	201n.60			28.17	259, 752
23.37	420n.47	25.41	454	28.18	253, 257
23.37-38	67n.106, 258, 323, 450n.161	25.46	271n.288, 315n.9	28.19	68, 272n.291,
		26	250n.195		

	430, 588, 638, 748	2.10	232, 235n.130, 253n.213	4 4.1	210n.5, 235 225n.65, 234n.121
28.19-20	47n.11, 154, 590n.310	2.12	231n.105, 235n.127	4.2	234n.121
28.20	257	2.13	234n.121	4.10-12	251n.196
		2.13-17	250	4.11	159n.256, 235, 239
Mark		2.14	65		
1.1	49n.16, 193n.28, 194, 195, 207, 225, 227, 230, 252	2.15-17	290	4.11-12	529
		2.15-20	234	4.12	236
		2.16	235n.129, 251n.196	4.13	233
				4.21	220n.42
1.2-3	529	2.17	434	4.21-22	236
1.4	289	2.18	251n.196	4.21-25	220n.45
1.5	529	2.20	197, 200	4.22	382
1.7-8	219	2.21-22	236	4.24	220n.42, 238n.147
1.8	292	2.23–3.5	236		
1.11	226 227	2.24	251n.196	4.26-29	496, 477
1.14	193n.28, 529	2.25	254n.215	4.33-34	225n.65
1.15	193, 239, 293	2.27	529	4.34	231, 252
1.16	732, 736	2.28	232, 253n.213	4.35-41	228, 247n.182
1.16-20	234	3.1	529	4.38	234
1.17	234	3.1-5	228, 460	4.38-40	230n.96
1.21	234n.121, 529	3.4	529	4.39	228n.86
1.21-22	225n.66	3.5	230n.96	4.40	237
1.22	235, 235n.127	3.6	197, 200, 251n.196	4.40-41	233n.112
1.23-25	231			5.1-20	228
1.23-28	228	3.7	231	5.6	259n.243
1.24	226	3.7-12	225n.66	5.6-7	231
1.25	228n.86	3.9	231	5.6-13	230n.96
1.27	234n.121, 235	3.10-12	228	5.7	173n.323, 226
1.28	231n.105, 529	3.11	226, 252	5.19-20	231n.105
1.29-31	228	3.11-12	231	5.20	235n.127
1.32-34	225n.66, 228	3.13-19	234	5.21-24	228n.88
1.34	231	3.14	234, 235	5.21-43	228
1.35	231	3.14-19	529	5.22-24	230n.96
1.39	228, 529	3.15	235nn.129,130	5.25-34	228n.88
1.40-45	228	3.17	51n.21	5.28-34	230n.96
1.41	230n.96	3.18	810n.8	5.35-43	228n.88, 529
1.43	230n.96	3.20	231n.105	5.36	230n.96, 237
1.43-45	231	3.20-21	236	5.37	231
1.44	529	3.22	235n.129, 251n.196	5.40	231
1.45	231n.105			5.40-41	230n.96
2.1-12	228	3.22-27	228	5.42	235n.127, 243n.169
2.1–3.5	197	3.22-29	220n.44		
2.1–3.6	192, 223	3.22-30	228n.88	5.43	231
2.5	230n.96	3.23-27	236	6.2	234n.121, 235, 529
2.6	235n.129	3.28	235n.129		
		3.31-35	236	6.2-3	231n.105

907

6.3	96, 228	7.32-33	230n.96	9.10	233n.112
6.4	148n.193, 226n.71, 529	7.33	231	9.11-13	250
		7.36	231	9.12	232n.109
6.5	228, 250	7.36-37	231n.105	9.15	235n.127
6.6	234n.121	7.37	235n.127	9.17	234n.119
6.7	235n.130	8.2-3	230n.96	9.19	230n.96
6.7-13	235	8.4	233n.112	9.22-23	230n.96
6.12-13	228	8.6-7	240	9.23-24	230n.96, 237
6.14-29	228n.88	8.11	251n.196	9.28-29	237
6.15	226n.71, 529	8.11-12	230	9.31	196, 198n.47, 231, 232n.109, 234n.121
6.17-29	197, 200	8.12	235n.129		
6.18	219	8.15	238n.147, 251n.196		
6.30	234n.121, 235			9.32	233n.112
6.31	231n.105	8.17	233n.112	9.33	231
6.31-32	231	8.18	233n.114	9.33-37	237, 265
6.32-44	228	8.21	233n.112	9.38	234nn.119,120
6.34	230n.96, 234n.121	8.22-23	230n.97	9.38-41	237
		8.22-26	233	9.41	235n.129
6.37	233n.112	8.23	231	9.42-48	237, 265
6.41	240	8.26	231	9.43	220n.42, 247n.182
6.45-52	263	8.27	196n.42		
6.46	231	8.27-29	391	9.49-50	220n.42
6.49-50	230n.96	8.27-30	196, 233, 250, 397	10.1	234n.121
6.51	235n.127			10.1-9	269
6.51-52	260	8.27-33	230n.96	10.2	251n.196
6.52	233n.112, 250, 496	8.28	226n.71, 529	10.2-9	237
		8.29	230, 232, 733, 529	10.2-12	250
6.53-56	225n.66			10.6-8	530
6.56	230n.96	8.29-31	253	10.10	231
7	269n.279	8.29-33	52n.27	10.11	458
7.1	235n.129, 251n.196	8.30	231	10.12	237n.140
		8.31	196, 230, 232, 234n.121	10.13-16	237
7.1-13	236			10.14-15	239
7.1-23	469	8.31-33	233	10.15	235n.129
7.3	277n.304	8.32-33	230, 232, 233n.112	10.17	496
7.3-4	55			10.17-31	237
7.5	235n.129	8.34	56n.48	10.19	530
7.14-23	236	8.34-35	54	10.20	234n.120
7.15	236n.137, 269	8.34-38	220n.45, 237	10.23-25	239
7.17	231	8.35	193	10.24	235n.127
7.18	233n.112	8.38	232n.109	10.24-26	233n.112
7.18-19	250	9.1	235n.129, 239, 293	10.26	235n.127
7.19	53n.31, 236, 238, 269			10.29	193, 235n.129
		9.2-8	205	10.29-30	54, 237
7.24	231	9.5-6	52n.27, 233n.112	10.32	235n.127
7.24-30	237	9.7	226	10.32-34	159 231, 487
7.26-29	230n.96	9.9	231, 232n.110, 233	10.33	232n.109
7.31–8.10	237			10.33-34	196, 198n.47

10.35	234n.120	12.35	230n.98,	14.16-62	230		
10.35-37	233n.112, 758		234n.121,	14.18	235n.129		
10.35-45	286		251n.196	14.18-20	200		
10.38-39	197, 200, 237	12.35-37	254n.215	14.18-21	240		
10.41-45	237	12.38	234n.121,	14.21	232n.109, 416		
10.45	198n.47, 232n.109, 286		235n.129, 238n.147	14.22-24	200		
				14.22-25	240		
10.46	487	12.38-44	238	14.24	530		
10.46-52	231n.105, 247n.182	12.42	55	14.25	235n.129		
		12.43	235n.129	14.26-31	240		
10.47-48	230n.98, 231, 254n.215	13	53, 54, 67, 193, 239, 433	14.27	198n.47, 200, 435		
				14.29-31	52n.27		
10.49-52	230n.96	13.1	234n.120	14.32-42	240		
11.1–16:8	196	13.1-37	238	14.33-36	200		
11.9	530	13.2	53, 204	14.37	52n.27		
11.9-10	254	13.5	238n.147	14.41	232n.109		
11.11-21	238	13.7	53, 238, 239	14.43	235n.129		
11.15-19	228n.88	13.9	238n.147	14.43-50	240		
11.17	56, 234n.121	13.9-12	197	14.49	234n.121		
11.18	234n.121, 235nn.127,129	13.9-13	200	14.51-52	65n.96, 241, 243		
		13.9-20	54, 238				
11.22-24	237	13.10	193, 194, 195, 238, 239, 275	14.53	235n.129		
11.23	235n.129			14.53-54	241		
11.23-24	265n.269	13.14	53, 54, 56, 67, 238	14.55-65	241		
11.25	220n.42, 237			14.56-59	241		
11.27	235n.129	13.18	270	14.58	204, 241, 491		
11.28-33	235n.130	13.22	56, 238	14.61	241		
12.1-9	197	13.23	238, 238n.147	14.61-62	227, 530		
12.6	226	13.26	232n.110	14.61-64	241		
12.6-12	200	13.30	235n.129	14.62	232n.110, 241		
12.7-9	238	13.32	226	14.65	226n.71, 241		
12.9	238	13.32-37	238	14.66-72	52n.27, 241, 729		
12.10-11	197, 198n.47, 530	13.33	238n.147				
		14	194	14.72	243		
12.12	197	14.1	235n.129, 240	15.1	235n.129		
12.13	251n.196	14.1-2	240	15.2	241		
12.13-27	238	14.3-9	240	15.7	242		
12.14	234n.121	14.7	240	15.9-15	242		
12.17	235n.127	14.8	200, 240	15.16	55		
12.28	238n.142, 251n.196	14.9	189, 193, 194, 195, 235n.129, 240	15.19	259		
				15.21	242		
12.28-31	250			15.22-38	242		
12.28-34	238	14.10-11	240	15.24	198n.47, 242n.159		
12.29-31	554	14.12	240				
12.31	365, 530	14.12-15	530	15.26	530		
12.32	234n.120	14.12-16	240	15.29	198n.47, 242		
12.32-34	238n.142	14.14	240	15.29-32	230n.97		
12.33	530	14.16-17	240	15.31	235n.129		

15.34	198n.47,	1.67	291			301n.400,
	242n.159, 496	1.68-75	534n.87			346.144
15.38	242, 530	1.68-79	297	4.23-24		373, 377
15.39	227, 228, 242,	1.69	289	4.25-27		300
	252	1.71	289	4.28-29		300
15.40	242n.163	1.72	297, 531	4.33-37		228n.83
15.40-41	242, 306	1.76	469	4.41-42		148n.193
15.41	242	1.76-77	297	4.42-43		297
15.47	242	1.77	289	4.43		293n.376
16.1-8	242, 243	1.79	290	4.44		228n.84
16.5	243	2.7	470	5.1-11		320, 739
16.5-6	235n.127	2.11	287n.350, 288	5.8		290, 301n.398,
16.7	52n.27, 243, 264,	2.14	290			736, 749
	732, 736, 748	2.21-24	531	5.10		735n.43
16.8	42n.9, 243	2.25	296	5.11		305
16.9-20	42n.9, 499n.331	2.25-27	291	5.12-14		467
16.15	193n.28	2.25-50	296	5.14		468n.226
16.15-18	491	2.29	290n.366	5.16		307
		2.29-32	299, 531	5.17		286n.342
Luke		2.32	302	5.20		290n.362
1–2	306, 318n.26, 531	2.37	296	5.20-21		290n.360
1.1	308	2.41-51	491	5.23-24		290n.360
1.1-3	61	2.47	288	5.28		305
1.1-4	62	3.3	289, 317n.20	5.30		301n.398
1.2	58n.61, 355	3.4	317n.22	5.32		289n.358,
1.3	59, 61, 132, 308	3.4-6	300, 317n.22			301n.398,
1.4	308, 337n.105	3.7	420			435n.103, 455
1.5-6	296	3.7-9	339n.115	5.33-35		375
1.5-23	296	3.8	300, 358n.184	5.39		297
1.10	307	3.10-14	305	6		228n.82
1.15	291	3.16	291n.368,	6.4		413, 464n.211
1.16	296		317n.23, 318n.24	6.9		289n.354
1.17	291	3.17	339n.115	6.12-13		307
1.26	454	3.19-20	318	6.15		810n.8
1.26-38	470	3.21	317n.21, 318n.25	6.17-49		57n.56
1.30	296	3.21-22	307	6.20		301n.400, 306,
1.32	454	3.22	291n.368, 292,			315n.11, 374, 423
1.33	296		318n.25	6.20-49		304
1.35	58n.61, 291, 454	3.23	461	6.21		306, 374
1.36	469	3.38	300	6.22		285n.335, 374
1.41-42	59n.65	4.1	291, 292	6.24		305
1.44	59n.65	4.7-8	259	6.25		306
1.46-55	296, 531	4.9-12	296n.384	6.27		427
1.47-51	59n.63	4.14	291, 292	6.27-28		411, 424, 455,
1.48	305n.411	4.16-21	189, 297			469
1.52	305n.411	4.16-30	330	6.28		458n.192
1.53	305, 306	4.17-21	531	6.29		427, 455
1.54-55	297	4.18	291, 292,	6.29-30		433n.96

6.30	305n.414, 427, 428	8.24	234n.119	10.19	454
		8.25	290n.362	10.21	291
6.31	414, 426	8.28-33	470	10.21-22	258, 355
6.32	419, 458	8.36	289n.355	10.22	473
6.32-35	439, 440	8.43-48	470	10.24	373
6.33	427	8.48	289n.354, 290nn.362,366	10.27	304n.409
6.34	375, 458			10.29	308
6.35	305n.414	8.50	289n.355, 290n.363	10.29-37	291, 304n.409
6.36-38	414			10.30-35	301
6.37	289, 414	8.51	757	10.34	481
6.38	414	9.1-6	300	10.38-42	306, 323
6.39	373	9.11	293n.376	10.39-42	323n.49
6.40	326, 473	9.12-17	297n.386	11.1	307
6.41-42	373, 376	9.18-20	307	11.2-4	431
6.43	421, 469	9.18-21	199	11.4	290n.360, 424
6.44-45	374, 377	9.19	317n.19	11.5-8	307
6.46	440, 467n.467	9.20	733	11.9	326, 398, 471, 473, 484n.279
6.47-49	476n.252	9.22	199n.53		
7.1-10	319	9.23-37	307	11.9-10	373, 374, 382
7.4	305	9.24	289n.354	11.9-13	307
7.6	305	9.26	258n.236	11.13	292
7.9	290n.362, 300	9.27	293, 294	11.20	285, 291n.369, 294, 297n.386, 332n.88
7.11-15	334n.95	9.28	757		
7.13	306	9.28-29	307		
7.20	317n.19	9.31	285, 297n.386	11.21-22	373
7.22	189, 301n.400, 315n.11, 334n.95	9.32	292n.372	11.24	431, 436n.109
		9.44	199n.53	11.24-26	436n.109
7.24-25	374	9.46-48	265, 305n.412	11.27	306
7.28	305n.413, 374	9.48	305n.413	11.27-28	374, 378, 380n.246
7.33	317n.19	9.49	234n.119, 758		
7.34	290, 301n.398, 315n.11	9.51	301	11.33	373
		9.52	340	11.37	297n.387
7.35	258, 355	9.52-54	324n.53	11.39	469
7.36	297n.387	9.52-55	301	11.39-40	374, 390n.275
7.36-50	306	9.58	374, 378	11.41	305n.414
7.37	291, 301n.398	9.59-62	307	11.49	258
7.39	291, 301n.398	9.60	293n.376	11.52	373, 377
7.39-50	301	9.62	293n.376, 295	12.3	373
7.47-49	289	10.1-16	300, 593n.325	12.4-5	443
7.50	289n.356, 290nn.363,366	10.2	374	12.8	57n.56, 285n.335, 440
		10.3	440, 443n.135		
8.2-3	306	10.5-6	290	12.10	290n.360, 291n.368, 374
8.12	289n.355	10.7	412n.20		
8.12-13	290n.363	10.8-9	373	12.12	291n.368
8.14	305	10.9	293, 294	12.13-14	374
8.16	373	10.11	293, 294	12.15	305
8.17	373	10.16	326, 346n.144	12.16-21	305, 374
8.19-21	375, 378	10.18	449	12.22	373

12.22-31	305	15.1-2	291, 301	18.9	305
12.27-28	148n.193	15.1-7	499n.332	18.10-14	307
12.27-30	373	15.3-7	265	18.13-14	291, 301n.398
12.28	264n.263	15.4-6	482	18.14	305n.411
12.32	293n.376, 305n.413, 325n.57	15.4-7	325n.57, 375	18.16-17	305n.412
		15.7	289n.358, 291, 301n.398	18.18	285n.335
				18.22	301n.400, 305, 306
12.33	305, 374, 378	15.10	289n.358, 291, 301n.398		
12.33-34	305n.414			18.24	293n.376
12.35-36	330n.79	15.11-32	174n.330, 302n.406	18.25	306
12.35-38	305n.414			18.26	289n.354
12.39	373, 376, 412	16.4-6	476n.252	18.27	455, 459n.198
12.48	454	16.8-9	476n.252	18.29	293n.376
12.49	373, 382	16.10	439	18.32-33	199n.53
12.51	290n.366, 373, 376	16.13	374, 382, 439, 441	18.42	289n.354, 290n.362
12.52-53	373	16.14	305	19.1-10	305n.413
12.54-56	374	16.16	293, 294, 455	19.7	291, 301n.398
12.57-59	428	16.18	436	19.8	301n.400
13.1-9	291	16.19-31	306	19.8-9	306
13.3	289n.358	16.20	301n.400	19.10	285n.335, 289, 297, 301
13.5	289n.358	16.20-25	332n.85		
13.10-17	306, 344n.132	16.22	301n.400	19.11	103n.294, 293n.376, 294, 436n.109
13.13	285	17	234n.118		
13.20-21	375, 378	17.1-2	265, 416		
13.23	289	17.2	305n.413	19.11-27	436n.109
13.26-27	443	17.3-4	265, 290n.360	19.12-27	293
13.28	293n.376	17.5	290n.363	19.38	290n.366
13.28-29	300	17.6	290n.362	19.42	290n.366
13.31	297n.387	17.11-19	301	19.43-44	60
13.33	297n.386	17.14	468n.226	19.47-48	331n.84
13.34-35	323	17.19	289n.356, 290n.363	20.9-17	384n.262
14.1	297n.387			20.9-18	384n.262
14.1-6	291, 344n.132	17.20	293n.376	20.35-36	455
14.8-10	413n.20	17.20-21	293, 294, 295, 373, 375, 381n.250, 399n.301	21.3	301n.400
14.11	305n.411			21.8	293
14.12-14	305n.414			21.9	294
14.13	301			21.19	289n.354
14.15	293n.376	17.21	293n.376, 484n.279	21.20-24	294
14.15-24	66			21.24	60, 294
14.16-24	374, 380n.245	17.22-30	285	21.25-28	294
14.20	457n.187	17.34-35	374	21.31	293n.376, 294
14.21	301	18.1	307, 346n.109, 436n.109	21.36	285n.335
14.21-23	300			22.8	758n.4
14.25-33	307	18.1-8	291	22.16	294
14.26	400n.306	18.2-5	306	22.18	294
14.26-27	374, 378	18.2-8	476n.252	22.19	453n.170
14.33	305	18.8	290n.363	22.19-20	286

22.20	298	1.1-3	459	1.30	338, 339
22.24-47	286, 305n.412	1.1-5	347	1.31	318, 339
22.27	286, 365n.213	1.1-18	328, 500, 643	1.31-32	318
22.29	293n.376	1.3	350, 457, 458,	1.32	338n.112
22.30	293n.376		459, 772, 791	1.32-34	368
22.31-32	735	1.3-4	772	1.33	318nn.24,25,
22.32	290n.363	1.3-5	388		359n.285
22.40-41	306	1.4	350, 361	1.34	318, 337n.107,
22.45-46	306	1.4-5	333, 769n.45		338n.112, 339,
22.48	285n.335	1.5	315n.13, 350,		344
22.61-62	736		361, 363, 457,	1.35-39	324
22.67	290n.363		791	1.35-40	76n.152
22.70	241n.157	1.6	345	1.35-42	321
23.3	241n.157	1.6-8	339	1.36	339
23.7	454	1.7	357	1.38-39	351
23.27-29	306	1.7-8	338n.112, 361	1.40	738
23.29	380n.246	1.7-9	333	1.40-42	754n.108
23.35	289n.354	1.9	343, 361, 363,	1.41	338, 533
23.37	289n.355		388, 456n.182	1.42	738
23.39	289n.356	1.11	350, 363, 791	1.49	341, 344, 469
23.40-41	489	1.12	357, 363	1.51	326n.58,
23.42	293n.376	1.13	333		345n.141
23.43	287n.344	1.13-14	470	2.19-22	640
23.46	242n.161, 454	1.14	344, 348, 349,	2.1	317, 323n.50, 333
23.47	227n.77, 516n.26		350, 361, 387,	2.1-11	330, 333
23.51	298		444, 456, 643,	2.1-12	470
24.7	285n.335, 454		765, 769n.44,	2.2	477
24.10	242n.163		772, 773, 774,	2.6-10	342, 351
24.12	739, 748		777, 778, 791	2.11	332n.88, 333,
24.18	524	1.15	338, 339		357, 358
24.19	285, 297n.386	1.17	342, 351, 361,	2.12	323n.50,
24.21	285, 297n.386		769n.44		471n.235,
24.25	290n.363	1.18	344, 348, 349,		481n.268
24.27	465n.216		352, 354, 451,	2.13	323n.50
24.34	286, 736		456, 483, 643,	2.13–3.36	322
24.36	290		786n.137, 822	2.13-20	772
24.37-43	292n.372	1.19	338n.112, 533	2.14-22	319, 330
24.39	418, 714	1.19-25	317n.21	2.19	321, 374
24.42-43	418	1.20	339	2.19-21	342
24.47	299	1.20-21	339	2.21	331
24.47-49	289	1.23	317n.22	2.22	335n.99,
24.52	259	1.26	318n.24		357n.179
		1.27	317n.23, 338	2.23	332n.88, 357
John		1.28	317	2.23-25	333, 358
1.1	350, 354,	1.29	322n.47, 339,	3–12	332
	456n.182,		342, 363,	3	487
	457, 459, 765,		365n.214, 469,	3.1-9	324n.52
	786n.137		783	3.1-21	333

3.2	332n.88, 467	3.28	338n.112, 339, 345	4.42	361, 363n.206, 365n.214
3.3	292n.375, 315n.13, 326n.58, 359, 455, 456, 476n.251	3.29	325, 326n.61	4.46	317
		3.30	339	4.46-54	319, 323, 333
		3.31	315n.13, 339	4.48	332n.88, 333, 358
3.3-4	335n.99	3.34	344n.135	4.50-53	333
3.3-5	79, 315n.8, 437	3.35	325, 345, 354, 364n.211	4.53	357, 358
3.3-8	333			4.54	332n.88, 333
3.3-15	325	3.36	315n.10, 357, 359, 360n.191	5	328n.72
3.5	292n.375, 324, 326n.58, 358, 359n.285, 360n.192, 368, 437n. 115, 455, 456, 476n.251			5.1	323n.50
		4	340	5.1-9	333
		4.1-2	358	5.1-11	739
		4.1-3	323n.50, 789	5.1-47	322
		4.2	320	5.2	317
		4.4-6	317	5.9-10	344n.132
3.5-8	359, 480	4.7-26	333	5.10	640n.214, 642n.223
3.6	359, 368, 457n.187	4.10	79n.163, 333, 342n.127, 352, 359, 368n.228, 421, 469, 791	5.10-47	333
				5.15	640n.214
3.7	315n.13			5.16	344n.132, 640n.214, 642n.223
3.7-8	359				
3.8	79n.163, 368	4.10-11	335n.99		
3.11	326n.58, 345, 351, 643	4.10-14	342, 533		
3.13		4.12-14	331	5.17-19	354
3.14	345n.142	4.14	79n.163, 315n.10, 421, 333, 342n.127, 352, 359, 360n.190, 368n.228, 386, 469, 791	5.18	344n.132, 353, 388, 392, 576, 640n.214, 642
3.14-15	342, 533				
3.15	357, 358n.180, 359, 360n.191				
				5.19	326n.58, 345
3.15-16	315n.10, 333, 358n.181			5.19-21	326n.61
				5.19-30	325
3.16	344, 357, 359, 360n.191, 363, 365	4.20-24	367	5.22	345
		4.22	533	5.23	344n.135
		4.23	480	5.24	315n.10, 326n.58, 344n.135, 357, 360n.191
3.16-17	352	4.23-24	763		
3.17	344n.135, 363n.206, 365n.214	4.24	457		
		4.25	338, 360n.193	5.24-26	333
		4.25-26	533	5.25	326n.58
3.18	344, 357	4.26	338	5.25-29	360n.192
3.19	363	4.29	340	5.26	345, 354
3.19-21	315n.13, 333, 362, 388, 398, 769n.45	4.29-30	333	5.27	345
		4.31-38	326n.62	5.30	344n.135, 354
		4.34	344n.135	5.33	361
3.21	325	4.34-46	323n.50	5.33-34	338n.112
3.22-36	320	4.35-36	333	5.36	338n.112, 344n.135
3.23	317	4.36	315n.10, 360n.190		
3.24	318, 320			5.37	344n.135
3.25	317n.21	4.39	367n.220	5.38	344n.135
3.26	338n.112	4.39-43	333	5.39	315n.10, 466
3.27-36	338	4.41	357, 358	5.39-47	342

Index of Scripture and Other Ancient Writings

5.40	333, 360n.191		357, 359,	7.30	467
5.45	466		360n.191	7.31	332n.88,
5.46	357n.179, 466,	6.48	315, 333, 359		341, 357,
	533	6.49	342		640nn.215,216
5.47	357n.179	6.50	342	7.33	344n.135, 485
6.1	323n.50, 328n.72	6.50-51	342, 345n.141	7.33-34	387
6.1-14	322, 333	6.51	315, 333, 357,	7.34	387
6.1-21	229n.90, 319, 323		363, 365n.214	7.35	362,
6.2	332n.88	6.51-56	368n.226		640nn.215,216
6.14	332n.88, 342	6.52	640nn.215,216	7.37-38	342, 367, 791
6.15	322, 343	6.53	357, 359,	7.37-39	368n.228
6.16-21	322, 333		360n.191, 480	7.39	336, 360
6.20	325, 355	6.53-54	333, 367, 368	7.41-42	341
6.25-65	333	6.53-58	766	7.50	324n.52
6.26	332n.88	6.54	315n.10, 359,	7.53–8.11	
6.26-27	335n.99		360n.191, 425		328n.72, 449
6.26-58	325	6.57	344n.135, 354	8–19	398
6.27	315n.10, 333,	6.57-58	333	8	640
	359, 360n.190,	6.58	342, 345n.141	8.12	315, 333,
	457n.187	6.59	323n.50		360n.190, 362,
6.29	344n.135, 357	6.62	345n.141		363, 365n.214,
6.30	332n.88,	6.63	333, 360, 368		388, 398, 769n.45
	357n.179, 358	6.64	358	8.12-30	352
6.30-35	331	6.66	358	8.12-58	327n.62
6.30-58	352	6.67	397	8.14	422
6.32	343, 361, 533	6.67-71	367	8.16	344n.135, 354
6.32-35	342	6.68	315n.10, 333, 738	8.19	349
6.33	333, 345n.141,	6.68-69	319, 397	8.21	387
	359, 363,	6.69	335, 357,	8.22	640n.215
	365n.214		360n.193	8.23	315n.13
6.35	315, 333, 357,	7	340	8.24	315, 357
	359	7.1	323n.50,	8.25	387
6.37	357, 388		640n.214,	8.26	344n.135
6.38	344n.135, 354		642n.223	8.28	315, 335n.100,
6.38-42	345n.141	7.9	323n.50		345n.142,
6.39	344n.135	7.10	322, 323n.50		421n.57
6.40	315n.10, 333,	7.11-12	640nn.215,216	8.28-29	354
	357, 359,	7.13	640n.214	8.29	344n.135,
	360n.191, 425	7.15	640n.215		421n.57
6.40-44	640n.216	7.16	344n.135, 354	8.30	357
6.41	315,	7.18	344n.135	8.31	640n.215
	640nn.215,216	7.20	315n.12	8.31-32	361
6.41-58	422	7.25-36	352	8.31-58	325
6.44	344n.135, 425	7.26	340	8.32	335n.100,
6.44-45	357	7.27	341		360n.193, 481,
6.45	367	7.28	344n.135		769nn.44,46
6.47	315n.10, 333,	7.28-29	360n.193	8.33-35	335n.99
		7.29	344n.135	8.34	480

8.35	326n.61	10.24	341, 640n.215	11.48-52	362
8.42	344n.135, 354	10.26	357	11.49-52	343
8.44	24, 425, 649, 788	10.28	315n.10, 459	11.50-51	363
8.48	640n.214	10.29	354	11.51-52	332
8.48-49	315n.12	10.29-30	388	11.52	363
8.51	386	10.30	353, 387m 392, 458, 772	11.54	317, 640n.215
8.51-52	359, 360			11.57	331
8.52	315n.12, 640n.214	10.30-31	642	12.1-2	323n.49, 332n.85
		10.31	467, 640n.214	12.1-8	319, 323
8.56-58	342	10.33	576, 640n.214	12.3	421
8.57	640n.214	10.33-36	354	12.5-8	315n.11
8.58	315, 352, 643	10.36	344n.135, 353	12.9	640n.215
9	546	10.38	335n.100, 354, 357, 360n.193, 470	12.9-10	332n.85
9.1-7	333			12.9-11	331
9.4	344n.135			12.10	332
9.5	362, 363, 365n.214, 388	10.39	467	12.11	332, 357, 640nn.215,216
		10.41	332n.88, 361		
9.7	317	10.41-42	357	12.13	341
9.8-41	333	11–12	323n.49	12.16	335n.99
9.14	344n.132	11	252n.208, 362, 460, 487	12.17	332n.85
9.16	315n.11, 332n.88, 344n.132			12.17-19	331
		11.1	323	12.18	332n.88
9.18	640n.214	11.1-44	332, 333	12.20	362
9.22	78, 341, 364, 625, 626, 640n.214, 641n.220, 642, 774	11.4	332n.86, 333, 345, 364n.211	12.20-26	326n.62
				12.21-23	362
		11.4-5	332	12.23	345n.142
		11.8	640n.214	12.24	326n.61
9.24-25	315n.11	11.9-10	326n.61	12.24-26	325
9.29	466	11.10	315n.13	12.25	315n.10, 360n.190
9.31	315n.11	11.11-13	335n.99		
9.35-38	345	11.17-44	352	12.27-36	332n.86
10.1-5	326n.61	11.18	323	12.31	363n.205
10.1-18	325, 343, 352	11.19	640n.215	12.32	360n.192
10.3-4	366	11.23-26	333	12.34	341, 640n.216
10.4-5	360n.193	11.23-27	332	12.35	315n.13
10.6	335n.100	11.25	315, 359	12.35-36	362, 363
10.7	315, 437n.115	11.25-26	332n.86, 357	12.36	357, 769n.45
10.9	315, 360n.192	11.25-27	358n.181	12.37	332n.88
10.10	359, 360n.191	11.27	341, 344, 357n.179	12.37-39	357
10.11	315, 485			12.41	349
10.11-39	333	11.33	640n.215	12.42	78, 332, 357, 364
10.14	315, 360n.193	11.36	640n.215	12.44	344n.135, 357
10.16	363, 366	11.42	344n.135, 640n.215	12.44-50	332n.86, 352
10.17	364n.211			12.45	344n.135, 349, 353
10.17-18	354	11.45	357, 640n.215		
10.19	640n.215, 216	11.47	332n.88	12.46	315n.13, 322n.47, 357, 362, 769n.45
10.20-21	315n.12	11.47-53	331		
10.22	343	11.48	78	12.46-47	365n.214

Index of Scripture and Other Ancient Writings

12.47	363n.206	14.11	357n.179	16.9	252n.208, 357
12.49	344n.135	14.11-12	357	16.10	252n.208
12.49-50	354	14.15	365, 366n.216	16.11	363n.205
12.50	315n.10	14.16-17	325, 355n.172	16.12-13	336, 779n.101
13–16	326	14.17	360n.193, 361	16.12-15	356n.175
13.1	365n.212	14.20	335n.99, 360n.193	16.13	361
13.1-11	325, 365n.213			16.16-19	485
13.1-20	326n.62	14.21	365	16.21	326n.61
13.4-10	738	14.21-24	366n.216	16.23-24	265n.269, 326, 398
13.7	335n.99	14.22	738		
13.12-17	365n.213	14.22-23	149	16.26	477n.253
13.13-16	325	14.23	365	16.27	357
13.16	326, 367n.219	14.24	344n.135, 365	16.30	357n.179
13.19	315, 357	14.26	336, 355n.172, 367, 779n.101, 791	16.30-31	357
13.20	326, 344n.135			16.32	354
13.23	73, 74, 324, 365n.212, 444, 738			17–19	640n.216
		14.28	353	17	477
		14.29	357	17.2-3	315n.10
13.23-25	72n.136	14.30	363n.205	17.3	344n.135, 359, 360n.193, 769n.46
13.25	75n.145, 738	14.31	328n.72, 354, 364n.211		
13.28	335n.100				
13.29	315n.11	15–16	328n.72	17.7-8	335
13.31	345n.142	15.1	315, 343, 361, 533	17.8	344n.135, 357
13.33	387, 485			17.11	367, 392
13.34	345n.142, 365, 470	15.4-7	367	17.18	344n.135, 367n.221
		15.5	315		
13.34-35	326, 387	15.9	364n.211, 365n.212	17.20	367n.221
13.35	365			17.20-21	358n.181
13.36-37	387, 738	15.9-10	367	17.21	344n.135, 357
14–16	398	15.10	365, 366n.216	17.21-23	367
14	473	15.12	365, 387	17.23	344n.135, 364n.211, 365n.212
14.1	357	15.13	365, 366		
14.2	449, 772n.66	15.14-16	326		
14.2-12	473	15.16	326	17.24	360n.192, 364n.211
14.3	360n.192	15.17	365		
14.3-5	387	15.18-21	326	17.25	344n.135
14.5	360n.193, 738	15.19	485	17.26	364n.211, 365
14.5-7	149	15.21	344n.135	18.1	317
14.6	315, 359, 361, 437n.115, 482, 769n.44	15.26	355n.172, 361	18.10-11	738
		15.26-27	325, 776	18.15-16	72n.126, 324
		15.27	367	18.15-18	739
14.7	769n.46	16.1-4	326	18.25-27	739
14.8	738	16.2	78, 364	18.28	314n.6
14.9	335n.100, 349, 387, 392, 477	16.4	335n.99	18.30-38	491
		16.4-5	388	18.31-33	79n.167
14.10	459	16.4-15	325	18.33-37	341n.122
14.10-11	354, 357	16.5	344n.135	18.35	362
14.10-12	358n.181	16.7-11	355n.172		

18.36	292n.375, 315n.8, 341	20.30	332n.88	2.22-40	684n.38
18.37	361	20.31	73, 337, 341, 344, 356, 357, 360n.191, 766	2.23	287n.345
18.37-38	79n.167			2.24-32	286n.343
18.39	341n.122	21	72, 73, 74n.143, 327, 367, 739	2.28	736n.48
19–21	78			2.36	286, 287n.345, 632n.174
19.3	341n.122	21.1-2	748	2.38	289n.359, 292, 430n.83
19.11	315n.13	21.1-14	320		
19.13	317	21.1-23	72	2.39	298
19.14	314n.6, 568	21.2	74	2.40	289n.353
19.14-15	341n.122	21.2-3	74n.140	2.41	355
19.19-22	341n.122	21.5-8	739	2.42	307
19.26	324, 365n.212	21.7	72n.136, 324, 365n.212	2.44-45	304
19.26-27	72n.136, 73			3–5	736
19.31	314n.6, 651n.259	21.15-17	367, 735, 739	3.1	74n.141
19.33	322n.47	21.15-19	320	3.1-10	736
19.33-36	342, 533	21.18-19	101, 739	3.3	74n.141, 758n.4
19.34	368n.228, 772, 779n.101	21.19	739	3.4	74n.141, 736n.49
		21.20	72, 365n.212	3.6	736n.49
19.35	72, 73, 77, 361, 370	21.20-23	74, 77	3.11	74n.141, 758n.4
		21.23	72, 79	3.12	736n.49
19.37	452	21.24	72, 77, 79, 327, 361, 370	3.13	287n.345
19.38	324n.52			3.13-15	287n.345
19.39	324n.52	21.24-25	72	3.14	546
20	487	21.25	329n.77, 370, 457	3.16	290n.364
20.1-8	484			3.19	289nn.358,359
20.1-10	735n.45	**Acts**		3.20	294
20.1-18	484, 738	1–5	725, 742n.70	3.20-21	298
20.2-7	739	1.1	296	3.22-23	257
20.2-8	72n.136	1.1-11	712n.153	3.25	298, 302, 531, 532n.76
20.2-10	74, 77	1.3	292n.372, 293		
20.3-10	748n.89	1.4	741	3.26	287n.345
20.8	357	1.5	292	4.1-2	286n.343
20.17	169, 485	1.6	294, 298	4.4	355, 736
20.19	484n.279, 748	1.6-8	295	4.10	287n.345, 632n.174
20.19-23	367	1.7	294		
20.20	786n.137	1.8	292, 299	4.12	289
20.21	344n.135, 484n.279	1.13	757n.1, 810n.8	4.13	74n.141, 758n.4
		1.14	307	4.19	74n.141
20.22	360	1.15	736n.48	4.27	287n.345
20.23	264n.264, 290, 359, 367, 746n.84	1.15-26	298	4.29	355
		1.20-26	532	4.30	287n.345
20.24-29	149	2	292n.370	4.31	355
20.25	357	2.2-4	292n.371	4.32-37	304
20.26	484n.279	2.4	292, 758n.4	4.33	286n.343, 291n.368
20.27	470	2.14	736n.48		
20.28	354, 387	2.21	289n.353	4.36	121
20.29	357, 477	2.22-39	736	5.1-11	736

5.3	736n.49	9.32-34	736	13.9	736
5.15	736	9.36-41	736	13.13	50
5.17	600n.8	9.36-42	306n.416	13.16-41	299
5.30	287, 632n.174	9.51–18.14		13.23	287n.350, 289n.353
5.31	287n.350, 288n.350, 289nn.353,359, 465n.216		285n.333	13.24	289n.359, 358n.184
		10–11	302, 725		
		10	742		
		10.9-15	742n.72	13.26	289n.353
5.33-39	297n.387, 519, 588	10.25	736	13.26-41	736
		10.28	302	13.27-28	287n.345, 632n.174
6–7	603	10.36	191, 290		
6.1	590n.309, 603n.25	10.36-40	191	13.29	287
		10.37-38	319	13.30-37	286n.343
6.5	290n.364	10.38	318	13.33	318n.26
6.7	94n.250, 290n.364, 814	10.39	287, 632n.174	13.38	289n.359
		10.40-41	286n.343	13.43	291n.368, 632n.176
6.8	291n.368	10.41	292n.372		
6.14	241n.156, 322	10.43	289n.359	13.46-47	25n.94, 299n.393, 633
7.11-17	285n.334	10.43-48	292		
7.16	285n.334	10.44-46	292n.371	13.47	289, 302n.404
7.37	257	10.48	430n.83	13.50	306n.416
7.52	287n.345, 546	11.1-18	299n.392	13.52	304
7.56	285	11.13	289	14.1	632n.176
8–9	736n.49	11.14-18	292	14.2	632n.175
8	28, 168, 301, 340, 736	11.15-16	292	14.3	291n.368
		11.18	289nn.358,359	14.8-11	736
8.3	519	11.19-26	70n.124, 753n.105	14.9	290n.364
8.10	28, 168			14.11-13	736
8.12	293	11.22-24	299n.392	14.17	294n.379
8.14	74n.141, 758n.4	11.23	291n.368, 304	14.19-20	705
8.14-17	292	11.24	290n.364	14.19	632n.175
8.14-25	299n.392	11.26	600, 606, 652n.264	14.22	290n.364, 294, 295
8.16	430n.83				
8.17	736	11.27-30	304	14.23	87n.213, 91n.234, 678, 683, 689, 780
8.18	292n.371	11.30	812n.10		
8.18-24	736	12.2	757n.2, 758		
8.20	736n.49	12.9	292n.372	14.26	291n.368
8.22	289n.359	12.12	50, 306n.416	14.27	290n.364
8.30-35	287n.345	12.25	50	15	514; 519, 589n.305, 605, 633, 725, 758
9	676	13–28	676		
9.1-2	519, 588	13–14	705		
9.2	129n.107, 533, 600n.9	13	632n.175	15.1-29	299n.392
		13.1	62n.82, 753n.105, 812	15.1-35	302n.406
9.15	302n.404, 737n.52			15.2	812n.11
		13.4-12	617	15.5	600n.8
9.23-27	683	13.5	50, 676n.5	15.6	812nn.10,11
9.26-30	299n.392	13.6-12	736	15.6-11	683
9.31	290n.366	13.8	290n.364	15.9	290n.364

919

15.11	289n.353, 291n.368	19.6	292n.371, 736	24.25-26	705
		19.8	293	25.21	109n.326
15.13-21	512	19.9	600n.9	25.25	109n.326
15.16-17	302	19.12	736	26.5	600n.8
15.20	302	19.13-20	736	26.6-7	298
15.22	812n.10, 812nn.10,11	19.23-41	705	26.8	746
		20	87	26.17-18	302n.404, 737n.52
15.23	592, 812nn.10,11	20.5-6	61		
15.33	290n.366	20.5-15	61n.80	26.18	289n.359, 290n.364
15.36-39	683	20.7	555n.165		
15.37-39	50	20.7-12	705	26.19	520n.36
15.39	617	20.9-12	736	26.20	289nn.358,359, 302n.404
15.40	291n.368	20.17	87n.206, 91n.234, 780		
16.3	684			27.1–28.16	
16.4	812n.10	20.19	632n.175		61n.80
16.5	290n.364	20.21	289n.359, 290n.364	28	607, 633
16.10-17	61, 61n.80			28.6	736
16.13-15	705n.124	20.22-24	87	28.8	736
16.14-15	306n.416	20.24	291n.368	28.19	632n.175
16.17	289n.353	20.25	293	28.20	298, 531
16.30-31	289	20.28	8n.15, 91n.234, 287	28.23	293
17	709			28.24	632n.176
17.4	306n.416, 705n.124	20.28-30	780	28.25-28	299n.393
		20.29	31	28.26-28	25
17.5	632n.175	20.32	291n.368	28.28	25n.94, 633
17.12	306n.416, 705n.124	20.33-35	304	28.30	89n.223
		20.35	413, 415n.24, 464n.211	28.30-31	87, 293, 299, 633n.180
17.18	286n.343				
17.26	294n.379	20.37-38	304		
17.30	289nn.358,359	20.38	87	**Romans**	
17.30-31	286n.343	21.5	306n.416	1.1	189nn.12,14
17.34	82, 306n.416, 705n.124	21.8-18	61n.80	1.1-3	190
		21.15–23.31		1.3-4	189n.12, 690, 820
18.1-18	753n.104		299n.392	1.4	190n.16
18.2	306n.416, 607	21.18	812n.10	1.9	189n.15
18.6	25n.94, 299n.393, 632n.175, 633	21.20	581, 590, 632n.176	1.16	190n.17
				1.25	698
18.12-17	609	21.20-21	512, 524	1.29-32	689
18.18	306n.416	21.21	605n.35	2–3	380n.246
18.25-26	600n.9	22	600n.9	2.4	290n.361
18.26	306n.416	22.4	600n.9	2.5	421n.53
18.27	291n.368	22.14	546	2.7-9	702n.119
19	795n.175	22.21	302n.404, 737n.52	2.8	421n.53
19.1-6	292			2.12-16	537
19.1-7	339n.116, 760	23.6	297n.387	2.24	697
19.4	289n.359, 358n.184	24.5	582, 604	2.25-32	390n.276
		24.14	600n.9, 604	2.28-29	390n.275, 604, 605n.31, 700, 788
19.5	430n.83	24.24	290n.364		

2.29	698n.96	9.21	697	16.25	699
3.3	12n.31, 600n.7	9.22	421n.53		
3.13-17	700	9.24	605	**1 Corinthians**	
3.20	717n.181	9.29	701	1–4	688
3.27-31	606n.36	10.7	380n.246	1.12	264n.261, 688,
3.29-30	595	10.14-18	748		728, 733n.37,
4	272, 701, 721	10.14-21	662		736n.50
4.3	690, 741,	10.15	189	1.13	430n.83
	753n.103	11	692, 701n.107	1.14-16	679n.12
4.7	290n.361	11.11-12	294n.379	1.15	430n.83
4.7-9	689	11.25	294n.379,	1.18-25	719
4.9-17	695		536n.101,	1.18	690
4.10-11	700		714n.164	1.20	690
4.11	696	12	679	1.22-23	661n.300
4.17	697	12.3-8	819n.38	1.23	190n.16, 690
5.1	690	12.4-8	88	1.31	688
5.2	536n.100	12.6-8	812	2.3	243n.169
5.5	698	12.14	411, 426, 429,	2.6–3.1	713
5.8	291n.368		458n.192	2.9	380n.246,
5.12-21	722	12.14–13.7	609		390n.276, 474,
5.14	721	12.15-21	538		688, 702n.119,
5.21–6.2	689	13.7-8	702n.119		712n.150
6.4	690	13.9	250	2.10	690
6.17	191	14.1–15.6		2.12	512
7.2-3	499		606n.39	2.13	713n.155
7.4-6	717n.181	14.6	537	2.13-14	712, 713
7.9	714n.165	14.10	693	3.1-3	690
7.12-13	537	14.12	693	3.2	166n.288
7.14	714	14.14	53n.31, 707n.133	3.6	753
7.14-19	712n.150	14.17	292n.374	3.11	734
7.18	715n.169	14.23	680n.16	3.16	690
8.3	719, 767	15.3	191	3.22	264n.261,
8.5	690	15.16	189n.14, 190n.17		733n.37
8.7	715n.169	15.19	189n.15	4.4	690
8.9	706	15.20	752n.102	4.15	192, 753
8.12-13	699	15.23-28	87	4.20	292n.374
8.15	706	15.25-28	684	5–10	788
8.17	712n.150	15.26	578n.249	5	678
8.27	712n.150	15.30-31	518n.31	5.7	240, 269n.214,
8.28	363n.203	15.31	512		719
9–11	669	16.1	813	5.7-8	690
9.1	744n.76	16.4	690n.64	5.9-10	712n.150
9.2	691n.66	16.5	690n.64	6.2	694
9.4-5	667	16.7	753	6.5	678
9.5	688	16.14	124n.74	6.9-10	690
9.6-12	605	16.19	420n.45	7	136n.142, 537,
9.7-13	696n.90	16.21	62n82		707n.130
9.10-13	721	16.22	86n.199	7.3-5	706

7.5	702n.117	15.3	287, 706, 713, 822	11.13	718
7.9	706			11.22	590n.309
7.10	412.20	15.3-4	198	11.23-27	687
7.12-16	436-437	15.3-5	189n.12, 243	11.24	286, 626n.140, 636
7.17	690n.64	15.5	731, 733n.37, 736, 746		
7.19	606			11.28	690n.64
7.28-38	707n.132	15.5-6	514	12.1-5	178
7.29	706	15.5-7	484n.281	12.4	713
7.29-31	680n.21	15.7	514, 812	12.13	690n.64
7.36-38	706	15.8	712n.153	12.21	290n.361
7.39-40	687n.50	15.8-9	690		
8	606n.38	15.12-14	690	**Galatians**	
8.1	480, 712n.150	15.12-19	719	1.6	190n.17
9.5	97, 731n.28, 733n.37	15.20	688	1.6-9	683n.36
		15.22	702n.117	1.7	189n.15, 190n.17
9.12	189n.15	15.23	688	1.11	190n.17, 819
9.14	412n.20	15.24	292n.374	1.11-12	712
9.15	690	15.32	690, 705	1.12	713
9.19-23	605	15.36-37	688	1.13	702.121
9.21	684	15.37	715	1.13-14	569n.216, 598, 652
9.22	719	15.42-54	715n.168		
9.27	690	15.44	702n.118, 707	1.15	101n.287, 179
10	606n.38	15.45	719	1.15-16	713
10.4	264n.261	15.50	480, 712n.150	1.16	702n.121
10.25	537	15.53	702n.118	1.17-20	683
10.25-30	788	16.15	812n.14	1.18	725, 731, 733n.37
10.26-27	707n.133	16.15-16	683	1.23	603, 702n.121
10.32	661n.301	16.15-18	678	2	268n.276, 514n.17
11.1	712	16.19	690n.64		
11.16	690n.64	16.22	555	2.1-9	683
11.25	8n.18, 298, 555n.165			2.1-10	725, 737
		2 Corinthians		2.2	190n.17, 714, 819
12	678, 679	1.8	690n.64	2.5	190n.17
12.3	83n.185	2.12	189n.15	2.6	512, 518n.31
12.4-11	88	3	718, 719, 721	2.6-9	718
12.20-26	688	4.4	190, 713, 721	2.7	803
12.28	82nn.11.12, 819n.39	4.6	101n.287	2.7-9	300, 605, 731n.28, 819
		7.9-10	290n.361		
13.2	411	7.15	243n.169	2.8-9	725
13.47	688	8.18-19	690n.64	2.9	512, 725, 733n.37, 758, 763
14	678	8.23-24	690n.64		
14.6	798	9.8	537n.103, 697n.92	2.11	654n.270, 733n.37
14.33-34	690n.64				
14.34-36	707.134	9.9-10	697n.92	2.11-14	514n.17, 518n.31, 592, 605n.35, 683, 736n.50, 752
15	165, 702, 706	9.13	189n.15		
15.1	189n.12	10.13-16	752n.102		
15.1-5	190n.16	10.14	189n.15		
15.1-7	820	11.7	189n.14	2.11-17	753; 105

2.12	725, 728, 742n.72	2.14-16	661n.301	3.3	390n.275, 605n.31, 698n.96, 788n.142
2.12-13	121	2.19	363n.203		
2.12-16	731	2.20	98, 734		
2.13-14	514, 718, 719	3.1-10	675	3.5	590n.309, 702n.121
2.14	190n.17	3.3-6	536n.101		
2.14-17	435	3.3-10	714n.164	3.8	706
2.15	291n.368, 604	3.5	699	3.10	101n.287
2.17	291n.368	3.6	190n.17	3.11	706
2.19	717n.181	4.2	691	3.15	692
2.20	680n.16	4.4-6	820	3.18	693
3	272, 669n.335, 701	4.8	535n.98, 701	3.20	699
		4.11	812nn.11,12	4.3	113n.9
3.1	190n.16	4.23-24	699	4.5	680n.21
3.5-9	721	4.26	693, 694		
3.6-7	700	5.1	699	**Colossians**	
3.8	302n.403, 532n.76, 605, 706	5.2	417n.33, 420n.47	1.1	86n.199
		5.3	417n.32, 559n.178, 744n.76	1.2	534n.86
				1.10	537n.103, 697n.199
3.10-13	700				
3.11	706			1.12	363n.203
3.13	475, 642n.224	5.4	464, 546n.212	1.13	292n.374, 712n.150
3.13-14	582	5.6	421n.53		
3.19	657n.283, 721	5.23	697	1.14	290n.361
3.23-35	667	5.25	691	1.15	349, 701, 822n.43
3.28	442, 606	5.29	691	1.18	734
4.4	767	5.32	480, 714n.162	1.26	536n.101, 714n.164
4.26	693	6.1	420n.47		
4.27	697	6.5	243n.169	2.2	714n.164
5.1-12	683n.36	6.12	712n.150	2.6	191, 699
5.6	606n.36	6.14-17	691	2.9	765
5.14	250	6.19	714n.164	2.11	700
5.16-17	715			2.15	701
5.17	699	**Philippians**		2.16-23	606
5.22	698	1.1	534n.86, 813	2.20-23	171n.181
6.2	268	1.3	743	3.6	41n.53
6.7	693	1.6	537n.103	3.13	424
6.8	702n.117, 715	1.11	697n.92	4.3	714n.164
6.14	690	1.12-18	608n.48	4.10	50, 676n.5, 732n.35
6.17	706	1.27	189n.15		
		2.1	743n.74	4.11	59n.65, 292n.374
Ephesians		2.2	743n.74	4.14	59
1.1	690n.64	2.6-7	767	4.16	48, 160, 688, 694
1.7	290n.361	2.10-11	576	4.18	86n.199
1.9	714n.164	2.12	243n.169		
1.20-22	535n.97	2.16	693	**1 Thessalonians**	
2.5	693	2.19-30	693n.79	1.5	189n.12
2.6	712n.150	2.25	814n.25	1.9-10	189n.12
2.8-9	537, 559, 693	3	121n.57	1.10	421n.53
2.10	537n.103	3.2	683n.36		

2.2	82, 189n.14	3.9	88n.218, 680n.17	1.13-14	88n.222
2.8	189n.14	3.12	707n.132	1.14	88n.220
2.9	189n.14	3.14	87n.206	1.15	690n.64
2.12	292n.374	4.1	88n.218, 680n.17	1.18	87n.204, 95,
2.14-16	25	4.1-3	98n.274, 678n.9		690n.64
3.2	189n.15	4.3	87n.208	2.2	88n.222
4.15	412n.20	4.3-4	707n.133	2.8	190
4.15-17	680n.21	4.4-5	537	2.11	88n.221
5.2	412	4.6	88, 680n.17	2.14	537
5.17	690	4.7	87n.208, 537,	2.16	537
5.19	555n.166		680, 708n.136	2.18	87n.208, 537
		4.9	88n.221	2.23	537
2 Thessalonians		4.9-11	680n.20	2.25	290n.361
1.4	690n.64	4.10	681n.26	3.8	88n.218
1.5	292n.374	4.13	87n.206, 680n.20	3.10	88n.216
1.8	189n.15	4.14	88, 679	3.16	537
2.17	537n.103	4.16	88n.216, 680n.20	4.3	88n.217
2.2	182	5.1	87n.211, 679n.14	4.3-4	98n.274
2.8	721	5.1-16	678n.9	4.6-7	90
		5.8	88n.218, 680n.17	4.6-17	89-90
1 Timothy		5.9	88	4.6-18	89
1.1	681n.26	5.11	88	4.7	88nn.218,222
1.3	87nn.204,206, 95,	5.17	87n.211, 679n.14,	4.9-18	86n.203
	690n.64		680n.20, 689n.58,	4.11	50, 59, 732n.35
1.4	87n.208, 537		813	4.12	690n.63
1.7	87n.207	5.17-22	780n.103	4.17	536
1.7-9	537	5.19	87n.211, 88,	4.20	87n.204
1.10	88n.217, 680n.20		679n.14, 813	4.21	7
1.11	680n.19	5.22	87, 679		
1.12-17	678	6.1	88nn.216,222,	**Titus**	
1.13	698		680	1.2	689n.62
1.15	88n.221, 435	6.3	88, 680n.20	1.3	681n.26
1.19	88n.218, 680n.17	6.7	85n.198, 91n.235	1.5	87, 679, 683n.3
1.19-20	678n.9	6.10	85n.198, 88n.218,	1.5-6	813
1.20	537		91n.235, 680n.17	1.5-11	780n.103
2	681n.30, 690n.64	6.12	88n.218, 680n.17	1.6	707n.132
2.2	85n.198,	6.14	88n.222, 681n.30	1.7	8n.15, 813
	702n.119	6.20	87n.208,	1.7-9	87n.212, 679n.14
2.3	681n.26, 689n.61		88nn.220,222,	1.9	88nn.217,221,
2.7	689n.60		537, 680n.18		222, 680n.20
2.11-12	707n.134	6.20-21	678n.9	1.10	87n.207
3.1	87n.212, 88n.221	6.21	88n.218, 680n.17	1.10-11	537
3.1-7	87n.212, 679n.14,			1.10-16	678
	780n.103	**2 Timothy**		1.13	88n.218,
3.2	8n.15, 707n.132,	1.6	88		680nn.17,20
	813	1.9	537	1.14	87n.208, 537
3.8	813n.20	1.12	88n.220	1.15	87n.208,
3.8-13	87n.212, 679n.14	1.13	88n.219		707n.134

2.1	88n.217	5.6	540	11.37	95n.256
2.2	88n.218, 680	6.14	540	11.37	572
2.4-5	689n.58	7.1-2	540	12.2	288n.350, 645n.239
2.7	88n.216	7.3	8n.17, 644, 814		
2.10	681n.26	7.4	540	12.5-6	540
2.13	681	7.17	540	12.6	95n.256
3.1	689n.59	7.21	540	12.22	645n.237
3.4	681	7.22	645n.239	12.26	540
3.5	537	7.25	645n.237	12.29	540
3.8	88n.221	8.5	92n.242, 540, 644n.235, 648	13.5	540
3.9	87nn.207,208			13.6	540
3.12	87n.204	8.6-13	93n.246	13.18	95n.253
		8.7-12	645n.239	13.22	91
Philemon		8.8-12	540	13.23	90n.232, 92, 96
24	50, 59	8.13	25, 646	13.24	95
		9–10	8		
Hebrews		9	94	**James**	
1.1-3	540	9.6-14	644	1.1	513, 631
1.3	92n.241	9.8-12	93n.246	1.5-6	265n.269
1.3-4	95n.256	9.9	94n.253	1.8	436n.109
1.3-13	95n.256	9.14	94n.253, 784n.124	2.18-26	513
1.5	95n.256, 318n.26, 540			2.2	635n.192
		9.15	93n.246, 645n.239	4.12	437
1.5-14	540	9.20	540	5.6	546n.133
1.6	540	9.23-24	92n.242, 644n.235	5.12	412, 454
1.7	95n.256, 540			5.14	780n.103
1.8-9	540	9.24	92n.242		
1.10-12	540	9.26	93n.246	**1 Peter**	
1.13	95n.256, 540	10	94	1.1	543, 812n.12
2	541	10.1	92n.242, 93n.246, 644	1.2	744n.78
2.5-18	540			1.3	101n.287
2.6-8	540	10.1-2	94n.253	1.7	744n.79
2.10	288n.350	10.1-4	25, 94	1.8	744n.82
2.12	540	10.5-9	540	1.10	744n.76
2.13	540	10.9	93n.246	1.10-11	744n.78
2.18	95n.256	10.11	94	1.12	744n.82
3–4	541	10.12-18	94	1.15-16	744n.75
3.1	95n.256	10.16	93n.246	1.17	744n.78
3.2	95n.256	10.16-17	540	1.18-19	744n.75
3.5	95n.256, 540	10.19-22	645n.237	1.20	744nn.80,81
3.7-11	540	10.22	95n.253	1.21	744n.76
3.15	540	10.28	540	2.1	744n.75
4.3	540	10.30	540	2.1-2	744n.80
4.4	540	10.37-38	540	2.5	728n.17, 744nn.76,78
4.5	540	11.6	645n.237		
4.7	540	11.18	540	2.6-8	744n.78
4.16	645n.237	11.21	540	2.9	728, 744n.75
5.5	318n.26, 540				

2.11	427, 428, 429, 744n.77	2.5	100n.279	2.10	387
		2.6	99, 100	2.12	105n.303
2.12	68n.115, 412	2.9	100	2.12-17	778n.96
2.16	744n.82	2.10	66, 100, 102	2.13-14	775n.77
2.17	744n.75	2.11	100	2.14	778n.94
2.18	419n.44, 744n.77	2.12	100	2.18	98n.274, 104n.297, 546n.132
2.21	744n.75	2.13	9n.18, 100, 102		
2.23	744n.82	2.15-16	100		
2.25	744nn.75,76	2.17	99, 100n.280	2.19	106, 775, 796
3.1-4	744n.75	2.17-18	99	2.20	367, 800
3.1-5	744n.75	2.18	99, 100n.280	2.22	546
3.14	68n.115	2.18-19	102	2.23	104n.297, 778n.94
3.16	728n.19	2.21	545n.131		
3.19	744n.76	2.22	131n.545, 482	2.24	104n.297, 425, 775n.77, 778n.95
3.20	744n.82	3	101n.286, 686		
3.20-21	744n.79	3.1	100, 101	2.27	359n.285, 367, 778n.95, 800
4.3	543	3.1-3	99		
4.6	744n.76	3.3	100n.280	2.28	105n.303, 546n.132, 778n.95
4.8	481, 744nn.75,81	3.3-5	102		
4.11	744n.76	3.4	102		
4.13-16	744n.80	3.5-7	545n.130	2.29	546n.133, 778n.93
4.14	744n.82	3.7	100		
4.17	189n.14	3.8	103	3.2	105n.304
4.19	744n.75	3.9	103	3.5	546n.132
5.1	780n.103, 812	3.10-12	103	3.6	104n.297, 778nn.94,95
5.2	744n.76	3.15	101		
5.5	744n.75, 812	3.15-16	103	3.7	104n.297, 105n.303, 546n.133
5.7	744n.79	3.16	434, 690, 701		
5.9	744n.75				
5.10	728n.19	**1 John**		3.8	425
5.12	50	1.1	425, 775n.77	3.9	778nn.93,95
5.13	50, 51n.23, 54, 55	1.2	367n.221	3.10	104n.297, 387, 778n.96
5.14	728n.19	1.3	778		
		1.3-7	775	3.11	425, 775n.77
2 Peter		1.4	104n.297	3.12	546n.132
1-2	101n.286	1.6	778	3.14-16	387
1.1	101	1.9	546n.132	3.18	104n.297, 105n.303
1.14	101	2.1	105n.303, 546n.133		
1.16	102			3.19-22	778n.93
1.16-18	101, 751	2.2	477n.253	3.21	105n.304
1.17	68n.115, 545n.131	2.3-5	778n.94	3.24	359n.285, 778nn.94,95
		2.4	104n.297		
2	686	2.6	778n.95	4.1	105n.304, 555n.166
2.1	100, 103	2.7	104n.297, 105n.304, 425, 775n.77		
2.1-2	102			4.1-3	83n.185, 98n.274, 359n.285, 789n.147
2.2	100, 600n.9				
2.4	99, 100	2.9-10	363		
2.4-10	99	2.9-11	778n.96	4.2	104n.297

Index of Scripture and Other Ancient Writings

4.2-3	106n.310, 424, 777n.88	9	780	2.9	25, 631		
		9-10	780	2.9-10	110		
4.3	777n.88	11	104n.297	2.13	110		
4.4	105n.303	12	780	2.14	110		
4.6-8	778n.94	13-14	104n.297	2.14-15	98		
4.7	105n.304, 778n.93			2.20	110		
		Jude		2.20-22	98		
4.11	105n.304	3	98, 820n.41	2.27	548n.141		
4.12	778n.95	4	98, 100, 545	3.9	631		
4.13	359n.285, 778nn.94,95	5	100n.279, 544	3.10	110n.332		
		6	99, 100, 544, 545	4	548n.141		
4.14	363n.206, 365n.214, 367n.221	6-8	99	4–10	107n.313, 485		
		7	98, 99, 100, 544	5–8	181		
		8	99, 100	5.5	548		
4.15-16	778n.95	9	100, 544	6.9	107		
4.20-21	387, 778n.96	10	100	6.16-17	421n.53		
5.1	778n.93	11	98, 100, 544	7.16	548n.141		
5.3	104n.297	11-12	98	10.1	548		
5.4	778n.93	12	9n.18, 99, 100, 544, 555	10.7	107n.314		
5.6	778			10.11	107n.315		
5.11	367n.221	12-16	99	11.11	548n.141		
5.12	778n.94	13	99, 100n.280, 545	11.18	107n.314, 421n.53		
5.16	778n.96	14	544, 545				
5.18	778n.93	14-15	97n.268, 545	13–21	107n.313		
5.20	546n.132, 778n.94	15	98, 100	13.1-8	110		
		16	99, 100n.280, 544, 545	13.11-18	110n.329		
5.21	105n.303			13.18	109n.325		
		17	98, 100	14.5	548n.141		
2 John		17-18	99	14.10	421n.53		
1	104, 780	18	100, 544	15.3	548n.141		
2	104n.297	18-19	98	16	181		
4	104n.297	23	544	16.1	107n.314		
4-5	780			16.19	421n.53		
5	425	**Revelation**		18	110		
5-6	104n.297	1.1	107, 72, 106	18.20	107n.314		
7	104n.297, 106n.310, 424	1.1-3	107n.312	18.24	107n.314		
		1.3	107n.315	19.10	107n.315		
8	546n.132	1.4	72, 107	19.15	421n.53, 548n.141		
9	104n.297, 546	1.4-5	107n.312, 258n.236				
10	781			20	177		
12	104n.297	1.7	548n.141	20.4	107		
13	105	1.9	72, 107, 109	20.4-6	177		
		1.10	580n.259	20.9	548n.141		
3 John		1.12-16	547	21.4	548n.141		
1	104, 780	1.13	548n.137	21.7	548n.141		
2	780	2–3	107, 109, 159	22.6	107n.314		
3-4	104n.297, 780	2.1	107	22.7	107n.315		
5-8	780	2.1-7	109, 112n.6	22.8	72, 106, 107		

22.9	107	4.41-46	342	42	34, 769
22.10	107n.315			42.2	350
22.16	548	**2 Maccabees**		45.3	572n.224
22.18	82, 107n.315	2.23	82	48.10	545
22.19	107n.315	4.7-50	343	55.4	572n.224
		6.16	659	60.8	545
		7	572	61.8	572n.224
APOCRYPHA				62.3	572n.224
		Sirach		62.5	572n.224
Wisdom of Solomon		1.5	258n.238	69.29	572n.224
2.12-24	352	1.16	351	71.14	572n.629
6.12-16	351	6.26	352n.165	83.3-5	545n.130
6.22	352n.165	15.3	352	94.1-4	553n.153
7.8-14	351	24	352, 645,	104.11	790n.158
7.26	92n.241,		771n.55, 794		
	352n.165	24.8	350	***Epistle of Aristeas***	
7.29-30	350	24.9	352	145-48	122
8.13	352	24.17	352n.165	166	122
9.1-2	350	24.19-21	351, 352		
9.9	350	24.21	352	***4 Ezra***	
9.10	350, 352	24.23	272, 351, 765	1.25	659
9.16-17	351	24.30-31	352	1.30-31	659
9.17-18	352	27.6	421n.54	2.10	659
10–11	765n.27	36.18-19	257n.234	2.43-47	572n.232
10	352	43.31	349n.153	3.1-3	612n.63
11.9	659n.290	46.13	534	3:28-36	612 n.63
12.12	551	51.25-27	258	8.3	434
12.22	659n.290			8.20-21	643n.232
16.9-10	659n.290			13	643
18.9	534	**OTHER JEWISH**			
18.14-16	347n.149	**LITERATURE**		***Odes of Solomon***	
				3.10	791
Baruch		**OLD TESTAMENT**		4	797n.190
1.11	538n.107	**PSEUDEPIGRAPHA**		4.6	698n.95
3–4	643			5.3	698n.95
3.12	352	***2 Baruch***		5.5-6	128n.99
3.14-15	352	29.5-6	560	6.6	698n.95
3.29	351	29.5-8	177	6.7	797n.190
3.37	350, 769	35.2-4	612	7.1	128
4.1	272, 765n.31	68.5-6	612	7.6	128, 791
4.1-4	351			7.10	698n.95
4.2	350	***1 Enoch***		7.12	791
4.14	434	1.9	97n.268, 545	7.15	128
4.2	350	5.4	545	8	128
		10.4-6	545	8.5	128
1 Maccabees		12.4	545	8.21	128
2.60	539	14.10-20	93n.245	9.3	128
4.3	681	18.15-16	545	9.5	698n.95

10.5	573	41.11-14	791n.161	**1QM**	
11.1-3	697	41.12	128	3.5	534n86
11.2	797n.190	41.13	128	7.4-6	301n.401
11.3	129n.107	41.15	128	10.10	534n.86
11.6-7	421n.58	42.1-2	128		
11.7	791	42.15	128	**4QFlor (4Q174)**	
11.19	128n.99	42.18	128	1.1-7	604n.27
11.67	421n.58			1.10-18	344n.133
12	128	**Psalms of Solomon**			
12.12	128, 791	3.4-12	659n.290	**4QMMT**	
13.2	797n.190	7.1-10	659n.290	C7	661
15.2	128n.99	8.23-34	659n.290		
16.15-16	128n.99	11.1	188	**11QMelchizedek**	
16.19	791	13.5-12	659n.290	2.15-24	188, 189
17.14-15	129n.106	17.21-24	230		
17.17	128	17.21-25	254n.214	**11QTemple**	
18.6	128n.99, 791			45.12-14	301n.401
19.1-4	129n.108	**Testament of Levi**		46.12	257n.234
19.2	128, 797n.190	3.2-4	93n.245		
19.6-9	128	17	572	**CD**	
21	128			1.13	601n.11
21.3	128n.99, 129n.106	**DEAD SEA SCROLLS**		3.12–4.12	604n.27
22	698n.95			5.18-19	538
22.7	129n.107	**1QS**		6.18-19	647n.248
23.18	128	2.3	535n.93	8.20-21	647n.248
23.22	128n.98, 797n.190	3.20-21	553	10.14–11.18	622n.124
24.1	128	4.22	601n.13	19.33-34	647n.248
25.8	797n.190	4.3-5	535n.93	20.11-13	647n.248
26	698n.95	8–9	536, 601n.12		
26.8	129n.106	8.10	601n.13	**PHILO**	
27.1-3	128	8.18	601n.13		
28.1	797n.190	8.21	601n.13	*Det. (Quod deterius potiori insidiari solet)*	
28.8	797n.190	9.5	601n.13	39-40	138n.153
29.6	128	9.17-18	601n.12	124	765n.28
29.8	573	9.21	601n.12	126-32	138n.153
30.1-2	791	10.21	601n.12		
31.8-13	129n.109	11.7-8	535n.94	*Leg. (Legum allegoriae)*	
31.9	128	11.13-15	536	1.46	347n.150
32	128	11.15	534n.87	1.93	347n.150
32.2	129n.106, 791			2.82	765n.28
36	128	**1QSa (1Q28a)**		3.1	347n.150
36.1	797n.190	2.3-10	301n.401	3.80	347n.150
36.3	128, 797n.190	2.11-12	344n.133	3.102-3	93n.243
39.7	129n.107			3.106	347n.150
39.11	128	**1QSb**		3.148	347n.150
41	128	3.2	534n.86		

3.150	347n.150	*Against Apion*		**CHURCH FATHERS**	
		2.77	95n.258		
Migr. (De migratione Abrahami)		2.147	130	**Athenagoras**	
		2.193-98	95n.258	*Legatio pro Christianis*	
70-85	348n.151			4	630
76-84	138n.153	*War of the Jews*		5–9	137
		2.119-66	600n.8	6	630
Mos. (De vita Mosis)		2.433-34	56n.50	9	565
2.74	93n.243	2.444	56n.50	10	137, 630
		2.652	56n.50	10.2-3	499
Mut. (De mutatione nominum)		4.450-51	54n.39	11.1	458, 497
		6.300	258n.239	11.2	424n.69
79-80	765n.28	6.313	56n.50	12	137, 630
151-53	765n.28	7.3	610n.55	12.3	458
208	138n.153	7.29-31	56n.50	17–30	137
		7.41-62	613	18	566, 630
Opif. (De opificio mundi)		7.43	70	21	566
16-44	348n.152	7.45	70	24	137, 630
36	93	7.46-62	70	30	630
143	347n.150	7.218	614	31	702
		7.346	349n.153	31–35	137
Plant. (De plantatione)		7.409-19	613	33.2	458, 495, 496
18	92n.241	7.421	613n.69		
		7.433-36	613n.69	**Augustine**	
Post. (De posteritate Caini)		7.437-41	613	*Epistulae*	
				153.14	161
168-69	349n.153	**MISHNAH, TALMUD, AND RELATED LITERATURE**		*De haeresibus*	
				9-10	583
Qu. Gen. (Quaestiones et solutiones in Genesin)				10	585
		m. 'Abot		32	585
2.62	349n.154	1.6	267n.272		
		3.2	257	*Epistle of Barnabas*	
Qu. Ex. (Quaestiones et solutiones in Exodum)		3.3	257	1.5	120n.52
		3.6	257	1.5-6	121
2.52	93n.243			1.8	121
		b. Berakot		2.4-6	654, 656
Spec. Leg. (De specialibus legibus)		48a	421n.54	2.5	557
				2.7	557
1.209	354n.171	*b. Shabbat*		2.8	557
		31a	268n.277	2.9	656
JOSEPHUS		116a	628n.149	2.10	557
				3.1-3	656
Antiquities of the Jews		*Canticles Rabbah*		3.1-5	557
3.224-57	95n.258	2.14	420n.45	3.6	121, 656, 657
8.100	342n.126			4.3	434n.101
18.11-15	600n.8			4.3-5	122
18.63-64	570			4.4	557
18.85-89	340n.117				

Index of Scripture and Other Ancient Writings

4.5	557	9.8	557	16.5	434n.101, 557
4.6	656	10	121, 122	16.7	120n.52, 121
4.6-7	657	10.1	557	16.10	744n.78
4.6-8	695	10.2	557	18–20	119
4.7	557	10.4	557	18.1–20.2	
4.8	557	10.5	557		553n.156
4.9	121	10.6	557	19.2	426
4.11	120n.52, 557	10.7	557	19.5	426
4.11-12	695	10.10	557		
4.12	744n.78	10.11	557	**1 Clement**	
4.14	494, 656	10.12	656	1.1	551nn.145, 146
5.1	744n.78	11.2-3	557	1.3	112, 689n.58, 744
5.2	557	11.4	557	2.2	744
5.4	557	11.6-7	557	2.4	551n.146, 733
5.5	557, 744n.78	11.10	557	2.6	112
5.5-7	129n.109	12.1	557	2.7	689n.59
5.6	744n.78	12.2	557	3.3	112
5.7	656	12.4	557	4.1	114
5.8	656	12.6	557	5	113, 740n.62
5.9	435, 495n.318	12.7	557	5.1-5	740
5.12	435, 557	12.9	557	5.3	114
5.13	557	12.10	435, 557	5.5-7	687
5.14	557	12.11	435, 557	5.6	689n.60
6.1-2	557	13.1	696	5.7	87n.205, 744, 746
6.2-3	557	13.2	557	6.1	551n.146
6.2-4	744n.78	13.2-3	696n.90	7.1	551n.145
6.3	557	13.4	557	7.2	744
6.4	557	13.5	557	7.3	689n.61
6.6	435, 557	13.7	557, 695	7.4	744
6.7	557	14	695	7.7	744
6.8	557	14.1	696	12.8	551n.145
6.12	557	14.2	557	13.1	688
6.13	557	14.3	557	13.2	408, 413, 414,
6.14	557	14.4-5	656, 696		415, 423,
6.16	557, 656	14.5	121		478n.257, 495
6.18	557	14.7	557	15.2	68n.115, 413n.22
7–8	122	14.8	557	17.1	95n.256
7	121	14.9	557	17.5	95n.256
7.3	435, 557	15.1	557	21.6	112
7.4	557	15.2	557	21.7	744
7.6-8	557	15.3	557	23	103n.294
8.7	56	15.4	557	24.1	688
9.1	557	15.8	557	24.4-5	688
9.2	557	15.8-9	656	24.5	413n.22
9.3	557	16.1-4	618	26.2	551
9.4	121	16.2	557	26.3	551
9.5	557	16.3-4	122	27.2	689n.62
9.6	121, 696	16.4	122	27.5	68n.115, 551

27.7	551	50.4	551	15.2	558n.175, 696n.92
28.3	551	50.6	551	16.3	558n.175
29.2	551	50.6-7	689	16.4	744n.80
29.3	551	52.2	551	17.4	558n.175
30.1	744	52.3	551	17.6	558n.175
30.2	551, 744	52.4	551	19.1	125
30.4	551	54.2	112, 780, 813n.16		
32.2	688	56.3-4	551	**Clement of Alexandria**	
32.4–33.1	689	56.4	95n.256	*Stromata*	
33.5	551	56.5	551	1.1	136n.144
33.6	551	56.5-15	551	1.29	131n.117
34.8	688	57.1	744, 780, 813n.16	2.6.1	120n.52
35.5-6	689	57.3-7	551	2.6.31	120n.52
35.7	551	58.2	112, 551n.146	2.7.35	120n.52
36.1	95n.256, 815	59.2	744	2.9.45	465
36.2	95n.256, 744	61.3	744	2.20.116	120n.52
36.2-6	95n.256	63.2-4	112	3.2	29
36.3	95n.256, 511	65.1	112	3.9.1	465
36.4	95n.256, 511			3.12.81	702n.117
36.5	95n.256, 511	*2 Clement*		3.13	127n.89
37.5–38.2	688	1.3	696n.92	3.13.92	443n.133
40–41	95n.258, 689	1.5	696n.92	3.13.288	395n.288
40.1-5	552n.148	1.8	697	5.14.96	465
41.2	552n.148	1.20	744n.80	6.5	131n.117
42.1-2	114	2	558	6.5.39-41	661
42.1-5	689	2.1	697	6.5.43	464, 662n.302, 748
42.4	812n.14	2.1-3	558n.175	6.6	131n.117
42.4-5	112, 813n.20	2.4	494	6.6.48	465, 748
42.5	551	3.2	442n.130	6.15	131n.117
43.1	95n.256	3.5	558n.175	6.15.128	560n.189, 561
44	113	4.2	442n.130	7	743
44.1	112	5.2	441	7.17	712, 752
44.1-4	689	5.2-4	31n.121, 156n.239	11.2	136n.144
44.4	112	6.2	442n.130		
44.4-5	112n.8	7.1	697	*Excerpta ad Theodoto*	
44.5	780, 813n.16	7.5	558n.175	1.1	777n.89
46.2	551	8.2	697	1.6	772nn.60,61,65
46.5	112	8.5	195n.39, 494n.317	23.2	712
46.7-8	68n.115	9.3	697	43.2	713
46.8	413, 416, 495	9.7	696n.92	54.1-2	33n.134
46.9	112	11.6	696n.92	55.3	31n.119
47.1	112	11.7	697	78.2	37n.152
47.1-3	688, 690	12.2	465		
47.1-4	114	13.2	558n.175, 697	**Cyril of Jerusalem**	
47.6	780, 813n.16	14.1	558n.175	*Catechetical Lectures*	
48.2-3	551	14.2	558, 697, 744n.80	4.36	147n.187
49.5	551n.146, 688, 744				

Index of Scripture and Other Ancient Writings

Didache		13.2	432, 433	30.16.5	145, 464	
1–5	433n.95	14.1	580	30.16.6	176	
1–6	118, 119, 426, 429, 556	15	119	30.16.9	580n.261	
1.1	601n.14	15.1	119n.43	30.17.1	578	
1.2	428n.76	15.3	433n.95	30.17.3	578	
1.2-5	426, 427	15.3-4	431n.87, 434n.97, 494n.318	30.18.1	578, 579n.254	
1.2-6	429n.79, 496	16	119, 433n.95	30.18.2	579n.258	
1.3	419n.44, 424n.69	16.1	433	30.22.4-5	472	
1.3-5	433n.96	16.3	31n.121, 98n.274	31.7.6	715	
1.4	428, 429n.82, 744n.77	16.4	433	31.9.1-27	771n.54	
		16.5	433	38.1.2-5	155	
1.5	427, 428, 497n.323	16.6	433	38.2.5	713	
		16.8	433	38.3.1-5	155	
1.5-6	428			47.1	173n.327	
2.2-3	429n.81	**Epiphanius**		48.1.3-4	798n.191	
3.7	429	*Anacephalaiosis*		48.1.4-13.8	796	
4.11	744n.77	30.1	528	48.2.4	798	
4.13	790n.158			48.4	797n.184	
6.2	429n.82	*Ancoratus*		48.9	798	
6.2-3	553n.152	13.5	585n.287	49.1	798	
7–10	118, 429			49.2.5	799	
7.1	118n.41, 430n.84, 433n.95	*Panarion*		51.2-3	798	
		19.1.2	585	51.3-4	771	
7.2-3	430, 433	19.1.4	585, 586	51.3-5	771	
7.2-4	496	19.1.5	586	53.1.1	585	
8	430	19.2.2	585n.287	53.1.3	586	
8.1	651	19.5.1	582	53.1.4	585	
8.1-2	68n.115, 430, 431n.86, 434, 496, 651n.259	19.5.4	582	61.1	173n.327	
		19.5.7	582	78.14.1-6	516n.22	
		19.15.2	586			
		20	582n.270	**Epistle to Diognetus**		
8.2	120, 192n.26, 433n.95, 434n.97	29.1.3	582n.272	1	561	
		29.6.1	582	1–10	132, 451	
9–10	555n.165	29.6.2	582n.272	2	561	
9.2-4	432n.90	29.6.5	582n.272	2.1	699	
9.5	430n.84, 432, 433n.95, 434, 496n.320	29.7.7	146	3	95n.258	
		29.7.7-8	524, 584	3.1	662	
		29.9.2	582nn.270,271	3.4	561	
10.1	120, 555n.165	29.9.4	145	4.1	699	
10.5	433n.94	30.1.1	578	4.3	451n.162	
11–12	780	30.2.1	579	4.5	699	
11–13	119, 120	30.2.2	580n.262	4.14-15	699	
11.1-4	432, 434	30.2.7	578	5–6	699	
11.3	431n.87, 434n.97, 494n.318	30.3.3-5	580, 585	5.8-9	699	
		30.13.2-3	471	6.4	699	
11.3-6	789	30.13.4-5	471	6.5	699	
11.7	432	30.13.7-8	472	7.2	699	
11.7-12	789n.147	30.14.5	472	7.4	699	

8.1	699	3.22	115	4.16.7-9	133n.126
8.5	451n.162, 561	3.23.3	75n.146, 77	4.18	133
8.10-11	699	3.23.4	77	4.20	137
9	132	3.23.5-19	77	4.22.1	113, 143
9.2-5	699	3.24.6	63n.88	4.22.3-6	143
10.4	699	3.25.3	105n.299	4.22.4	141n.160
10.7	699	3.25.4	120n.52, 179	4.22.8	143
11–12	132, 451n.162	3.25.5	145	4.23.9	126
11.1	132, 699	3.25.6	147n.187, 170	4.23.9-13	126
11.2	699	3.27.1	578n.250	4.23.11	113, 126
11.3	699	3.27.2	579n.257	4.24	138
11.6	561	3.27.4	145	4.26.1	137
12.3-8	561	3.27.6	578n.251	4.26.2	138
12.5	699	3.28.2-5	177	4.27.1	137, 651
12.9	561	3.28.6	75n.147	4.28.2-3	136n.143
17.7	699	3.30.2	743	5.3.4	797n.187
		3.31.3	78	5.5.1-4	137
Eusebius		3.32.7	141n.160	5.8.2	63n.88
Historia ecclesiastica		3.36	114n.14	5.8.3	51n.20, 63
1.11.7-8	570n.222	3.36.2	115, 127, 753	5.8.4	75n.145, 77
1.13.4	148n.196	3.36.12	75n.147	5.10.3	63n.88
1.13.11	148n.196	3.37.9	127n.93	5.16.1	137, 796n.182
2.1.2	7	3.38.4	126	5.16.1-19.2	
2.1.3	52n.43	3.39.1	75, 75n.147, 126,		796n.181
2.1.6	148n.196		742n.66	5.16.7	797n.184
2.13.5-6	28n.109	3.39.2	128n.93	5.16.9	797n.186
2.15.1	51n.20	3.39.3-4	75n.148	5.16.18	798
2.15.2	127	3.39.4	51n.20, 72n.131,	5.17	580n.262
2.16.1	54n.41		77, 741	5.17.4	798n.197
2.22.2	86n.203, 89n.223	3.39.5-7	72n.131	5.19.1-2	137
2.23.3	141	3.39.6	78	5.20.2	790n.158
2.25.8	753	3.39.12	177	5.20.2-8	116
3.1.1	78n.157, 148n.196	3.39.15	331n.83	5.20.5-6	75n.147
		3.39.15-16	50, 63n.87, 145, 741	5.20.6	446n.144
3.3.1	102n.288			5.23	141n.165
3.3.2	166, 179	3.39.17	106n.310	5.23.1	568
3.3.6	124nn.74,77	4.3.1	130	5.24.3	78n.157
3.4.5	91	4.3.2	130	5.24.5	139
3.4.6	61	4.3.3	134	5.24.11-18	
3.4.7	60n.74	4.6.3	619		141n.165
3.4.8-10	7	4.6.4	123n.67, 528n.70, 620	5.24.14	753
3.4.21	113n.9			5.28.4	136n.140
3.11.1-12.1	255n.218	4.11.2	716; 741	6.12	156
		4.13.8	138	6.12.2-6	156
3.15	113n.9	4.14	118n.34	6.12.3	81, 749
3.16	126	4.14.1-9	75n.147	6.12.6	83
3.19-20	255n.218	4.14.6	78	6.14.1	105n.299
3.19.1-3.20.6	97	4.15	117n.32	6.14.2-4	94n.249

6.14.5-7	55n.44	8.3	113, 436n.108	**Hippolytus**	
6.14.6-7	51n.20	14.5	436n.109	*Refutatio omnium*	
6.25.4	63n.88	17.7	437	*haeresium*	
6.25.5	51n.20	23.3	436n.107	5.2	523
6.25.10	105n.299	23.6	416n.30	5.3	712
6.38	586	25.5-7	436n.108	5.7.20	146n.187
7.7-8	108n.319			5.14-17	33
7.22-26	108n.319	*Mandates*		6.25	37n.151
7.25	108n.319	4.4.1-2	687	6.29	713n.160
7.25.3	177	11	83n.185, 124n.75, 555n.166, 789, 813	6.30.6-34.1	33n.135
Praeparatio evangelica				7.7-9	528
13.12.10	350	11.7	555	7.26.3	712n.155, 713
		11.11	555	7.34.1	528, 579
Theophania		11.16	555	8.12	796n.182, 797, 798
4.12	145	12.4.7	124n.76		
		12.6.1	124n.76	9.4	586
Hermas		16	555n.166	9.13.1	586n.289
Visions		26	436n.109	10.22.2	528
1.1.1	124	28.2	436n.109	10.29.1	586n.289
1.1.2	125	29.6	436, 496		
1.1.4	124	30.1	437, 496	**Ignatius**	
1.2.2-4	124n.74	33	436n.109	*Ephesians*	
1.4.3	124n.74	34.7	436n.109	inscr.	116n.25
2.1.4	124n.77	35	436n.109	1	114n.17
2.2.2	124n.74	38.3-5	436n.109	1.1	116n.25
2.3.1	124n.74	39	436n.109	1.2	114
2.3.4	559n.182	43	437	1.3	814n.22
2.4.2	753n.103	43.12	437, 496	1.3–2.1	115n.21
2.4.2-3	125	49.3	437	2	114n.17
2.4.3	125n.82			2.1	813n.20
3–4	436n.108	*Similitudes*		2.2	692n.72
3	744n.79	5.5-6	124n.75	3	114n.17
3.1.6	124n.74	9.1.1	124n.76	3.2	814n.22
3.1.8	125	9.12.2-3	744n.79	4	114n.17
3.1.9	124n.74	9.14.6	744n.79	4.1	814n.22
3.3.5	744n.79	9.22.2-3	124n.75	4.2	692n.72
3.5.1	125	9.27.2	125, 753n.103	5–6	114n.17
3.8.11	124n.74	9.29.1	744n.79	5.2	417, 420;n.47, 496n.320, 815n.28
3.11.3	744n.79	9.29.3	744n.79		
3.22	744n.79	9.33.1	124n.76		
4.1.2	125	54	436n.109	5.3	417n.32, 559n.178, 692n.72, 744n.76
4.1.4	124n.74	55	436n.109		
4.1.7	124n.74	56	436n.109		
4.3.4	744n.79	81.3	436n.107	5.4	464
5.3-4	436n.108	93.4	436n.107	5.6	421n.53
5.7	124	97.1-2	436n.109	6.1	114, 420n.47, 692n.72, 814n.22
7.4	436n.108	97.2-3	436n.110, 496		
8.1	426n.108				

7.2	116n.25, 692n.71	10.2	690	6.1	690
8.2	690	10.3	13n.32, 592, 598, 652	6.3	116n.25
9.1	744n.76	12	559	7.2	79n.163, 690
9.3	744n.76	13	114n.17	7.2-3	421, 499
10.1	690	13.2	692n.74	7.3	422n.59
11.1	420	14.1	114n.15	9.1	114n.15, 744n.75
12.2	689	15	115n.20	9.2	690, 691n.66
14.2	417n.33, 421			9.3	115n.21, 420n.47
15.1	420n.47	*Philadelphians*		10.1	115nn.20,21
15.3	116n.25, 690	inscr.	114n.17		
16.1	690	1	114n.17	*Smyrneans*	
17.1	421, 495	1.2	559n.178	inscr.	691
18.1	690, 691n.66	2.2	31n.121, 420n.47	1.1	67, 116n.25, 417n.33, 418, 496
18.2	116n.25, 690, 692n.71	3–4	114n.17	1.1-2	421n.57
19	420n.47, 559n.178	3.1	417n.33, 420	1.2	654
		3.2	692n.74	2	692n.72
19.2-3	417n.35, 418n.38, 653n.267, 690, 692n.71	3.3	690	2.1	777n.88
		4	422n.59, 814n.22, 815n.28	3.1	692, 707, 714
				3.2	417n.33
19.3	116n.25, 653n.267	5.1	422n.59	3.2-3	418, 497n.323, 741
		5.2	744		
20.2	690	6.1	420n.47, 592, 652, 653	4.2	692n.72, 777n.88
21.1	115n.20			5.1	559
21.2	114n.15	7–8	114n.17	5.2	692n.72, 777n.88
		7	779	6.1	419, 496n.320, 496n.320
Magnesians		7.1	79n.163, 422, 690		
2–4	114n.17	7.1-2	692n.74	7.1	422n.59, 777n.88
2	115n.21	7.2	814n.22	7.2	559
3	814n.22	8.1-2	653	8–9	114n.17
5.2	420n.47	8.2	191n.21, 195n.39, 417n.33	8.1-2	692, 814n.22
6–7	114n.17			8.2	9n.18
6.1	779n.99, 812n.13, 813n.20, 814n.22	9.1	653, 815	9.1	692n.72
		9.1-2	421n.57	10.1	116n.25
6.1-2	692n.74	9.2	192n.26, 195n.39, 417n.33	10.2	691
7.1	421n.57, 692n.74, 814n.22			11.1	114n.16
		10.1	114n.16	11.3	691
7.2	815n.28	11.1-2	115n.23	12.1	115nn.22,23
8–10	18	11.2	115n.22		
8.1	592, 598, 652, 653	*Romans*		*Trallians*	
		inscr.	116n.25, 692n.71	1	115n.21
8.1-2	510, 652	1–2	114	1.11	417n.33
8.2	421n.57, 744n.76	2.2	114	2–3	114n.17
9.1	580, 652, 653	3.3	12n.31, 116n.25, 600n.7	2.1-2	692n.74, 814n.22
9.2	744n.76			3.1	692n.74, 779n.99, 814n.22
9.3	420n.47	4–7	114		
10.1-3	12n.31, 510, 600n.7, 652	4.3	690, 753n.103	3.2	692n.74
		5.1	114, 690	7	114n.17
				7.1	116n.25

7.1-2	692n.74, 815n.28	1.23.5	29	3.19.1	773n.69
7.2	195n.39, 692n.74	1.24.3-5	30	3.21	721n.202
8.1	422n.59	1.25.2	742n.70	3.21.1-8	668n.334
8.2	417n.32, 559n.178	1.25.4	29	3.21.8	742n.69
9–10	690	1.26	668n.334	3.21.10-23.8	721n.202
9.2	744n.76	1.26.1	29	3.23.8	136n.143, 702n.117
10	692n.72	1.26.1-2	528n.68		
10.1	592	1.26.2	145, 579	4.6.2	716n.176
11.1	420	1.27.1	716	4.6.6	568n.210
12.1	115n.20	1.27.2	717	4.8.3	728n.17
12.3	690	1.27.4	28n.109, 718	4.9.2	744n.82
13.1	114n.15	1.28.1	135, 722n.204	4.16.5	744n.82
13.2	114n.17, 692n.74, 814n.22	1.29.1-4	37n.151	4.20.2	744n.82
		1.30	33	4.24.1	721n.202
		1.30.13	714n.166	4.26.2	814n.24
Polycarp		1.31.1	155	4.33.4	668n.334
1.2-3	420n.47	2.6.2	668	4.33.9	744n.82
		2.17.9	744n.82	4.34.1	744n.82
		2.22.5	75n.146	4.35.2	742n.70
Irenaeus		2.27-28	567	4.37.4	744n.82
Adversus haereses		3.1.1	55n.44, 66n.103, 75n.145	5–8	773n.69
1.1-5	30			5.1-3	668n.334
1.1-8	30n.116	3.3	814n.24	5.1.3	580n.262
1.1.1-3	772n.60	3.3.1	113n.9	5.6.1	798n.197
1.1.1-8	771n.54	3.3.2	742n.70, 752	5.7.2	744n.82
1.2.2	772n.58	3.3.4	528n.68, 758n.5	5.7.20	146n.187
1.3.1-4	497n.321	3.6	567	5.8.1	798n.197
1.3.4	713n.160	3.7.1-2	721	5.9-14	714n.167
1.4.1	772n.58	3.9.11	483n.277	5.18.2-3	773n.69
1.5.1	772n.62	3.11.2-3	773n.69	5.20.2	568
1.5.1-6	772n.58	3.11.7	145, 499n.329, 771	5.30.3	109n.324
1.5.4	771n.57			5.33.3	177, 560
1.6.1	497n.321, 772nn.59,62	3.11.8	406n.4	5.33.4	127n.93, 742n.66, 758n.5
		3.11.9	152, 798		
1.6.2	31n.119	3.12.1-7	742n.70	5.36.3	744n.82
1.6.4	31n.119	3.12.7	742		
1.7.4	497n.321	3.12.12	498n.325	**Jerome**	
1.7.5	31n.119	3.12.14-15	514	*Commentariorum in epistulam ad Ephesios*	
1.8.2-4	773n.67	3.13.1	721n.201		
1.8.3	713	3.13.1-3	742n.70	5.4	145, 464
1.9.2-3	499n.329	3.13.2	742n.69		
1.9.3	773n.69	3.15.1	579n.256, 668n.334	*Commentariorum in Ezechielem*	
1.10.1	9n.21, 820			18.7	145
1.13.6	31, 742n.70	3.16.2	773n.69		
1.18.3	744n.82	3.16.8	778	*Commentariorum in Isaiam*	
1.21.4	31	3.16.9	744n.82		
1.23.2	28n.109	3.17.4	773n.69		
1.23.2-4	29	3.18.1	773n.69	11.2	145, 471

Commentariorum in Matthaeum		26.8	133	16.4	663nn.309, 310	
		31–42	561	16.5	562	
Prol.	144n.178	32	630n.165	17.2	562	
12.13	471	32–42	561	18–19	700	
		32–53	133	18.2	700n.104	
Epistulae		35.9	157	19.2	562	
67.4	19n.61	36	630n.165	19.3	562	
112.13	22n.74, 528n.68, 577, 578, 579n.254, 581, 582n.274	46	630n.165	19.6	562	
		47	620n.165	20.1	562	
		48–53	561	20.6	562	
		48.3	157	21–22	564n.194	
112.15	19n.61	52.10-12	664n.318	21.2-4	562	
112.16	579	54–58	133	22.2-5	562	
125.12	578n.248	56	169n.307	22.6	562	
		56.1	132n.124	22.7-10	562	
Adversus Pelagianos		58.1-2	40n.161	22.11	562	
3.2	144n.178	58.2	40n.161	23.4	562, 700n.103	
		59–60	134	24.2	562	
De viris illustribus		62	133	24.3-4	562	
2	145, 471, 512n.9, 513	63	630n.165, 799	25.1-5	563	
		64	133	26.2-4	563	
12	161	65–67	134	27.2-3	563	
18	741n.65	66.3	51, 494	27.3	700	
		67.3	494	27.4	563	
John Chrysostom		68	134	28.2	563	
Adversus Judaeos				28.4	700n.103	
1	19n.62	*2 Apologia*		28.5	563	
2.2	16n.61	1–2	134n.131	29.1	133	
6	649n.257	8	133	31.2-7	563	
		8.1-3	134	32.3	563	
Justin Martyr		13.3-4	134	32.5	563	
1 Apologia				32.6	563	
1.1	132	*Dialogus cum Tryphone*		33.1	563	
1.61.4-5	79	1.1	134	33.1-2	563	
4	133	1.1-2	133	34.1	563	
5	630n.165	2	133	34.2-6	563	
7	133	3.1	133	35.1	701n.110	
12	630n.165	7	133	35.3	31n.121	
14.3	424n.69	8.1-2	133	35.6	578n.250	
15–16	429	10.2	494	36.3-6	563	
15.4	419n.41	11.1	562, 565	37.1	563	
15.8	435, 495n.319	11.3	562	37.2-4	563	
15.9	424n.69	12.1	562	38.3-5	563	
20–29	133	12.3	700n.104	39.1	563, 700n.107	
21–23	630n.165	13.2-9	562	39.2	565	
26	169n.307	14.4-7	562	39.4	563	
26.2	28n.110, 170	15.2-6	562	39.5	563	
26.2-4	132n.124	16	700			
26.5	40n.161	16.1	562			

41.1	665n.322, 701n.111	63	565n.196	110.5	663n.310
		64.1	133	111.1	665n.322
41.2	563	64.4	563	111.2	665n.322, 701n.111
41.4	665n.322, 700n.104	64.6	563		
		64.8	563	113.6-7	700n.104
42.1	563	65.2	561	114.1	665n.322
42.2	563	65.4-6	563	114.4	700n.104
42.4	665n.322	66.2-3	563	116.3	701n.110
43.2	700n.104	66.16	135	119.5-6	700
43.3	563	67.1	565	120.5	665n.322
43.5-6	563	67.2	578n.250, 581	120.6	132, 134
44.2	563	68.1	561, 570n.218	121.1	133
44.3	563	68.6	563	121.3	701n.111
45.4	565	69.5	563	123.6	663n.309
47.1-2	577	69.7	520	125.3	701n.110
47.1-4	590	70.2-3	563	125.5	565n.196
47.3-4	577	71.1-3	570n.218	126–129	565n.196
47.4	663n.309	71.3	563, 565	129	565
48.4	581	72.2	563	131.4	665n.322
49.1	581	73.1–74.2	563	131.5	701n.111
49.6	563	73.6	561	131.6	663n.310
49.8	563, 701n.111	74.3	135	133.6	424n.69, 663n.309
50.3-5	563	78.6	135		
52.2	563	80.1	561, 565	134.3	665n.322
52.4	563	80.3-4	663n.313	137.1	700n.103
53.3	563	81.4	108n.318, 177	137.2	663n.309
53.6	563	84.1-4	565, 570n.218	138.2	701n.110
55.3	563, 701n.110	84.2	701n.110	140.1	665n.322
56	565n.196	85.4	135		
56.2	563	89.2	700	*Martyrdom of Polycarp*	
56.6	563	90.2	665n.322	1.2	417n.33, 691
56.7	563	91.2	665n.322	1.2-3	420n.47
56.12	564	91.3	665n.322	2.1	419, 497n.323
56.14	563	91.4	665n.322	2.2	417n.33, 418n.38, 420
56.16	561	92.4	700n.104		
56.17-18	563	93.4	663n.309, 663n.310	4	117, 191n.21
56.19-21	563			5–6	114n.17
58	565n.196	95.1	700	5.1	691
58.1	561	96.1	700	5.2	744n.76
58.4-5	563	96.2	663n.309	6.1	692n.74
58.8-9	563	96.3	424n.69	6.2	691
58.11-13	563	97.3–106.4	565	7.1	114n.16
59.2	563	100.2	494, 701n.110	8–10	117
60.4	563	100.3	700n.101	8.1	115, 117
61	565	101.2	496	8.3	116n.25
61.3-5	563	106.3	51, 700n.101	9.3	116, 117
62.1-3	565	108.3	663n.309	10.1	12n.31, 117, 600n.7
62.4-5	565n.196	110.2	565		

10.2	743	*Commentarii in*		13–14	117n.30
13.1	650	*evangelium Joannis*		13.2	115n.19, 117,
15–16	117	2.12	471n.235,		126n.86
16.2	7n.12		480n.268,		
17.2	650		481n.268	**Pseudo-Clement**	
18.1	650	13.17	131	*Homilies*	
20.1	117			1.9	121
21	118	**Polycarp**		1.14	121
22.2	116n.28	*Philippians*		2.24	527n.65
		1–12	117n.30	3.20	587n.294
Melito		1.2	559	3.49	587n.294
Peri pascha		1.3	559, 743	17.18-19	712n.154
1-58	665n.323	2	559n.180	18.1	521n.39
7.3-8.1	665	2.1	743n.74		
8	139	2.2	559n.179,	*Recognitions*	
11-15	567		743n.74	1	587n.296
16-19	567	2.3	414, 415, 423,	1.7	121
47-48	567		478n.257,	1.11	121
49-56	567		559n.180	1.16	587n.294
59	567	3	559n.180	1.27-71	176, 586
65	702	3.1	559n.180	1.43	518n.29
69	567	3.2	692	1.65.2-3	588
73-81	667n.326	3.3	559n.179	1.69.8–71.4	746
82-85	140n.159	4.1	85n.198, 91n.235,	1.71.3-4	588
86	667n.326		559nn.179,180	2.8	527
92-93	667n.326	5.1	559n.179	3.74	518
96	667n.326	5.2	424, 425, 495,	5.10	587n.294
99	667n.326		559n.180	8.5	587n.294
		5.3	743n.74	10.51	587n.294
		6.1	12n.31, 13n.32,	55.4	588n.299
Origen			425, 598, 600n.7		
Contra Celsum		6.2	424	**Pseudo-Tertullian**	
1	749	6.3	559n.179	*Adversus omnes haereses*	
2	749	7.1	106n.310,	1	527n.65
2.1-2	743		777n.88	2	165n.287
5.59	7n.12	7.1-2	425, 499	3	528n.68
5.61	22	7.2	423, 495, 743n.74	6	39, 716n.176, 717
6	749	8.1	559n.180, 743	23-24	710n.144
7.9	83n.183	9.1	115n.24,		
			559n.180	**Tatian**	
De Principiis		9.1-2	117	*Address*	
praef. 8	747n.87	10.2	743	2-3	135
1.2.3	163n.276	10.96	9n.18	4.1	499
		11.2	694	5	136
Homiliae in Leviticum		11.3	110n.333,	7	136
5.8	18n.57		693n.79	8-10	135
		12.1	559, 694	13	136
Selecta in Exodum		12.3	425	13.1	499
12.46	18n.57				

18	135	5.14	719	46	710
19	133n.126	5.19	40n.161, 719	48-51	710
21-28	135				
21.1	136n.140	*De baptismo*		*Apocalypse of Peter*	
29	135	1.17	163n.276	3-13	180
33-34	137			6.4	180
34	135	**Theophilus**		13.1	180
36-38	651	*ad Autolycus*		14.1-3	180
36-41	136	1.9-10	138	72.10-13	180
42	135	1.14	566, 702n.1.14	73.12-14	180
		2.2-4	138	74.19	181
Diatessaron		2.10	138, 630n.165	79.22-26	181
51.15	651	2.10-32	138	81.15-23	181
		2.12	138	82.21-83.6	181
Tertullian		2.15	138		
Apologia		2.22	138, 499, 630n.165	*Apocryphon of James*	
5	157			1.10-12	751
21	157	3.8	138	1.8-10	488
39	9n.18	3.9-14	138	1.10-12	488
		3.14	85n.198, 424n.69, 702n.119	2.8-15	478n.257
De praescriptione haereticorum				2.8-21	488
		3.24-25	138	2.10-15	488
13	9n.21, 820	3.27	138n.150	2.19.21	712n.153
21-22	9n.21	3.29	138	2.30.33	475
27	9n.21			3	475
30	39			3.9-10	488
38	718	**NAG HAMMADI CODICES**		3.30-34	476
Ad Marcionem				4.23-30	476
1.2	716n.177			4.26-29	477
1.18	717n.182	*First Apocalypse of James*		5.33	477n.256
1.21	719	8.16-23	496	6-9	475
3.1	9n.21	28.7-19	178	6.2-4	475
3.25	177, 719	32.2-4	522	6.5-7	476
3.5	710n.144	32.38-36.1	178	7.22-23	476
3.8	719			8-10	477
4.1	717n.182	*Second Apocalypse of James*		8.6-10	476
4.2	9n.21, 717			8.11-15	475
4.2-5	718	49.5-6	178	8.16-23	477
4.2.4	498n.325	56.7-13	178	8.23-27	476
4.3	514, 719			8.35-9.4	488
4.5	9n.21	*Apocalypse of Paul*		9.4-6	477n.253
4.8	852n.271	18.15-16	179	9.32-35	476
4.13-43	719	20-30	178	12-14	475
5.1	39, 717	34-36	178	12.12-12.13	488
5.5	719	37	178	12.14-15	476
5.10	719	39	178	12.35-4	477n.253
5.11	713n.161, 719	41	178	12.41-13.1	477
5.13	719	44	710	13-15	477

13.23-25	475	53	152	4.1	146n.187, 385n.263
13.26-36	476	55b	481	4.2-4	395
13.27-19	476	56.31-34	712n.150	4.2-3	373, 380n.246
14.14-19	476	59	480	4.4	385n.263
14.30-31	475	60	480	5	380n.246, 400n.302
14.35-36	488	61	482	5.1-2	373, 382
22-30	476	66	482	5.2	380n.246
		68	482	6.1	385n.263, 390n.275

Apocryphon of John

9.28-31	154n.229	69d	480	6.2-3	385n.263
20.17-19	793	70	480	6.4-5	373
22.4-5	793	72a	480, 481, 496	7.1-2	385
23.1-3	793	73.8	152	8.1-3	373, 383n.256
23.28-29	793	74	480	8.4	373, 382, 384
23.30-31	793	76	480, 482	9	375, 383n.255
23.34-35	793	77.25-26	712n.150	9.1-5	373
24.7	793	78	481	10-12	400n.302
31.5-6	793	79	482	10	373, 382, 383n.257
32.1-5	793	81a	480		
		83.25-29	712n.150	11.1-4	385
		83	480	11.3-4	394

Dialogue of the Saviour

1	474	89	480	12	390, 521
2	474	90a	481	12.1-5	127n.89
34	474	95	480, 481	13	148, 149, 173, 380n.246, 390n.274, 391, 397, 753
37	474	98	482		
50	474	110a	480		
55	474	111b	481, 497n.324		
57	474	122a-d	482		
65	474	123b	481	13.5	386
68	474	123c	481	14.1-3	385n.263, 390n.275
84-85	474	125a	482		
92	474	126a	481	14.4	373, 383n.257
95	474	127	482	14.5	373, 380n.246
				15	387, 392

Gospel of Philip / *Gospel of Thomas*

9a	480	1-7	147n.192	16	383n.254, 384
17a	481	1-6	397n.297	16.1-2	373, 376
17c	481	1	386	16.3	373
19	152, 480	2	383n.254, 398	16.4	395
23b	480, 714n.166	2.1-4	373	17	390n.276
26a	481	3	399n.301, 400n.302	18	393
31	481			18.1-3	385
33	481	3.1-3	373, 380n.246, 381n.250, 383n.257	19-20	380n.247
39	482			19.1	393
42	481			20	383n.255
44	481	3.3-4	392	20.1-4	373, 376
47	480	3.4	385n.263	21	178, 380n.247, 382
49	480	3.5	385n.263, 393		

Index of Scripture and Other Ancient Writings

21.1-4	395	39.1-2	373, 383	63.1-3	374, 378, 383n.257
21.5	373, 376, 383n.254	39.1-3	377	63.4	373
		39.3	373, 380n.246, 383n.256, 420	64	380n.245
21.10	373			64.1-11	374, 378, 383n.254
21.11	373	40.1-2	374, 383n.256		
22	168n.300, 398	41	383n.255	64.12	385
22.1-3	373	41.1-2	374	65-66	384
22.4-7	394	42	385, 396n.293	65	380n.246
23.2	396	43.1-3	387	65.1-7	374
24.1	387	43.2	389	65.8	373
24.2	373	44	380n.246, 383n.254	66	374, 380n.246
24.3	147n.192, 373			67	393
25.1-2	387	44.1-3	374	68-69	384
26-30	147n.192	45.1-4	374, 377, 383n.254	68	382
26	148n.193, 380n.246			68.1	374, 383n.254
26.1-2	373, 376, 383n.254	46.1-2	374, 383n.254	68.2	385n.263
		47	380n.246, 384	69.1	385, 386
27	396n.293	47.1-2	374, 382	69.2	374, 383n.254
27.1	385, 390n.275	47.2	383n.254	70	394
27.2	389	47.3-4	374	71	374
28	393	47.3-5	377	72	380n.246
28.1	387	47.5	374	72.1-3	374, 383n.257
29	394	48	374	73	374, 380n.246, 383n.254
30.1-2	373	49	393		
30.3-4	392	50	393, 396n.293	74	385
31-33.1	147n.192	51.1-2	385, 386	75	396
31	148n.193, 380n.246	52	392	76.1-2	374, 383n.256
		52.1	391n.278	76.3	374, 378, 383n.254
31.1-2	373, 377	52.1-2	389		
32	148n.193, 373, 382, 383n.256	53	389, 400n.306	77	388, 392, 398
		53.3	390n.276	77.2	147n.192
33-34	384	54	374, 383n.254	78.1-3	374, 383n.254
33	380n.246	55	400n.305	79.1-3	374, 378, 383n.257
33.1	373, 383n.254	55.1-2	374, 378, 383n.254		
33.2-3	373, 383n.254			80	394
34	373, 383n.254	56	394	82	392
35.1-2	373	57.1-4	374, 378, 383n.256	83	393
36	148n.193, 400n.306			84	393
		59	392	85	395
36-39	147n.192	60	389	86	380n.246, 391, 396n.293, 400nn.302,306
36.1-3	373, 378, 383n.254	61	382, 391n.280		
		61.1	374, 383n.254		
37	178, 391, 392, 396, 398	61.2-5	388, 392	86.1-2	374, 378, 383n.254
		61.3	588n.299		
38.1	373	62.1	374	87	394
38.2	387	62.2	374, 383n.256	89.1-2	374, 383n.254, 390n.275
39	390, 400n.302	63	380n.246		

90.1-2	374, 378, 383, 384n.260	17.30-31	483n.274	**NEW TESTAMENT**	
		18.4-22	483n.274	**APOCRYPHA**	
91.1-2	374, 383n.254	18.16-21	482		
92-94	384	20.11-14	482	*Acts of Andrew*	
92	400n.302	20.25	33; 482	21	172
92.1-2	382, 383n.254, 388	21.11-18	483	23	172
93.1-2	374, 378, 383	22.9-12	483n.275	349	485
94	400n.306	22.13-20	37n.152; 482, 483	*Acts of John*	
94.1-2	374, 383n.254	22.16-20	483n.274	22	497n.321
95.1-2	375, 383n.257	24-28	500n.332	34	497n.321
96.1-2	375, 378, 383n.254	24.14-20	483n.275	37-44	171
		24.32-25.3		42	795n.175
96.3	373		483n.275	43	795n.177
97	386	27.7-8	483	60-61	171
97.1-4	385	31.28-29	482	62-86	171
98	386	31.35-32.4	482	63	171
99	380n.246, 391n.280	32.18-25	482	88-91	794
		33.15-16	482	90	497n.321
99.1-3	375, 378	38.7-24	483	94	668n.333
100.1-4	375, 378	42.21-25	483n.275	97	497n.321
101.1	374, 383n.257	43.1	483n.275	98	500n.332
101.1-2	378n.242			100	500n.332
102	386, 390			106-15	794
103	373, 376n.241			109	500n.332
104	380n.246	*Letter of Peter to Philip*		112	794
104.1-2	375, 390n.275	134.17-18	154	113	171n.317
105	396	134.20-24	154		
106.1	395	135.10-15	154	*Acts of Paul*	
106.1-2	374	136.16-18	154	2	705
107.1-3	375, 378, 383n.254	137.6-8	154	2.264	97n.265
		139.15-23	154	2.480	97n.265
108-113	396n.294			3.1	705, 706n.127
108	392			3.2-3	164n.278
109.1-3	375, 383n.256	*Second Treatise of the Great Seth*		3.3	164
110	386			3.5	706
111	392	56	153	3.5-7	164n.281
111.2-3	393	65	153	3.12	164n.281
112	394			3.14	163
113.1-4	375, 383n.257, 386	*Teaching of Silvanus*		3.16	164n.282
		1-2	750	3.21-22	164
114	395, 400n.306	14.4-6	750	3.25	163
		95.7-11	420n.45	3.26-36	164
Gospel of Truth				3.34	163n.276, 165
1.38.7	500n.332	*Tripartite Tractate*		3.37-38	165
1.39.19-20		57.8-59.38	33	3.39	165
	500n.332	118.14-122.12	33	3.41	163n.276
17.10-13	483n.274			3.43-45	165

4	163, 705	36-39	169	55-57	180		
5	164	37-38	170	60	174n.331		
6	163 707	38	168n.300	72	174n.331		
8	163, 749n.93	40	169	78	173		
8.1.12-15	165	41	169	80	174n.331		
8.3.4	706			88	173		
8.3.6	165	*Acts of Philip*		96-103	173		
8.3.8	706	140	168n.300	98	174n.331		
8.3.9-10	707			108-13	173		
8.3.10	706	*Acts of Pilate*		117	173		
8.3.20	165	1.5	49	121	173		
8.3.24	165	1.6	49	131	173		
8.3.27	165, 707	2.2	496	132-33	173		
9	705	2.3-5	49	143	174n.331		
10	167, 749	3	49, 491	150	173		
11.1	164n.278, 705	4.1	49, 491	157-58	173		
11.3.2	166	4.3	49	158	174n.331		
11.3.3	166	7.2	496	170	173n.326		
11.3.4-5	166	9.4	49				
11.3	164	10.2	49	*Apostolic Constitutions*			
11.3.6	166	12.3	496	1.2.2	424n.69		
11.5	164n.278	14.1	496	2.61	19n.60		
11.7	163, 164n.278	16.7	49	5.17	19n.60		
12	175n.335, 705			6.27	19n.60		
14	705	*Acts of Thomas*		7.1-32	118		
16	705	1	148n.195	7.23	19n.60		
		1-2	173	7	553n.156		
Acts of Peter		1-3	148n.197	8.33	19n.60		
1-3	168, 708	10	173	30	19n.60		
4	168	11	148n.195, 172	47	19n.60		
5	168, 170n.311	12-15	173				
6	170n.311, 708	17-38	173	*Epistle of the Apostles*			
7	168, 750	17	148n.197	1	161		
8-15	158	20	400n.306	2	752		
10	170n.308	25-27	173	3	470		
16-18	168	29	173	4	470n.321		
19-21	168	31	173	5	470, 496		
20	168n.300	33	174n.331	11	470, 752		
21	170n.310	33-35	174n.331	12	752		
23	169, 170	34	173	14	470		
24	169, 170	39	148n.195, 173, 174n.331	17	470		
25	169			18	161, 470		
26-27	169	43	173	20	161		
28-29	169	43-44	174n.331	24	161		
31	169	47	173, 174n.331	26	161		
32	169	49	173	31	702n.121		
33-34	169	51	173	33	702n.121		
35	167	53-56	174n.331	41	470		

48	470	8.29-11.49	489	**Suetonius**	
150-75	12n.711	9.39	485	*Augustus* 79.2	
		14.60	156		164n.279
Epistle to the Laodiceans		26	748		
20	160	60	748	**Tacitus**	
63-65	160			*Annals*	
64-65	160	*Gospel of the Saviour*		15.4.4	608n.50
		17-19	485	15.44.2	608n.48, 615
Gospel of Judas		48	485	16	609n.51
33.1-6	486	70	485	*Historiae*	
34.11-13	486	75	485	5.5.1	608n.50
34.14-18	486			5.13	258n.239
34.21-22	486	*Passion of St. Perpetua*			
35.17-20	486	*and St. Felicity*			
47-57	486	203	166	**PAPYRI AND**	
51.8-17	487			**FRAGMENTS**	
52.14-21	487	*Protoevangelium of James*			
		4-5	158	*Fayyum*	469, 496
Gospel of Mary		19-20	158	*PCair* 10759	156.239
7.8-9	484n.278			*PEgerton* 2	155,
8.10-11	484n.278	**EARLY GREEK AND**			407n.10, 466-69,
8.13-22	484	**ROMAN WRITERS**			496, 497n.324,
8.14-15	484n.278				499, 500, 501
8.15-17	484n.278	**Philostratus**			
8.18-19	484n.278	*Lives of the Sophists*		*PKöln* 255	155n.237
8.20-21	484n.278	2.552	164n.279	*POxy*	
8.21-22	484n.278			1	147n.192
9.5-12	484	**Plato**		1.1-4	148n.193
9.19-20	484n.278	*Gorgias*		1.30-35	148n.193
15.1-17.7	484	493a	37n.149	1.36-41	148n.193
17.7-18.21	738			654	147n.192
17.10-18.21	484	*Phaedrus*		655	147n.192
19.1-3	484	250c	37n.149	655.1.1-17	
					148n.193
Gospel of Peter		**Pliny**		1224	424n.69
1.1	489	*Epistulae*		2949	156n.239
4.10	490	10.96	9n.18, 615		
4.13	489, 497n.324	10.96-97	616n.81	*PRylands* 463	152
7.26	156				

www.ingramcontent.com/pod-product-compliance
Lightning Source LLC
Chambersburg PA
CBHW032125010526
44111CB00033B/72